W9-BXP-555

Criminal Justice

A Brief Introduction

Ninth Edition

Frank Schmalleger, Ph.D.
Distinguished Professor Emeritus
The University of North Carolina at Pembroke

Prentice Hall
Boston Columbus Indianapolis New York San Francisco Upper Saddle River
Amsterdam Cape Town Dubai London Madrid Milan Munich Paris
Montreal Toronto Delhi Mexico City Sao Paulo Sydney Hong Kong
Seoul Singapore Taipei Tokyo

NOTICE:
This work is protected by U.S. copyright laws and is provided solely for the use of college instructors in reviewing course materials for classroom use. Dissemination or sale of this work, or anypart (including on the World Wide Web), will destroy the integrity of the work and is not permitted.The work and materi-als from it shouldnever be made available to students except by instructors using the accompanying text in their classes. All recipients of this work are expected to abide by these restrictions and to honor the intended pedagogical purposes and the needs of other instructors who relyon these materials.

Editorial Director: Vernon R. Anthony
Senior Acquisitions Editor: Eric Krassow
Assistant Editor: Megan Heintz
Editorial Assistant: Lynda Cramer
Director of Marketing: David Gesell
Senior Marketing Manager: Adam Kloza
Senior Marketing Coordinator: Alicia Wozniak
Marketing Assistant: Les Roberts
Senior Managing Editor: JoEllen Gohr
Project Manager: Steve Robb
Senior Operations Supervisor: Pat Tonneman
Creative Director: Design Development Services, John Christiana
Text and Cover Designer: Mary Siener
Cover Photos: Vadim Telesh/Alamy (Lady Liberty), Michael Matthews—Police Images/Alamy (police officer), Martin Thomas Photography/Alamy (prison), and Exactostock/Superstock (graffiti)
Media Editor: Michelle Churma
Media Project Manager: Karen Bretz
Full-Service Project Management: Janet Bolton, Milford Publishing Services
Composition: S4Carlisle Publishing Services
Printer/Binder: R.R. Donnelley/Willard
Cover Printer: Lehigh-Phoenix Color/Hagerstown
Text Font: ITC Century Light

Chapter opening photo credits:
Ted S. Warren/Associated Press, p. 1; Monika Graff/The Image Works, p. 19; JG Photography/Alamy, p. 58; B. O'Kane/Alamy, p. 87; Mikael Karlsson/Alamy, p. 114; Chris Polydoroff/Associated Press, p. 155; IndexStock/SuperStock, p. 194; Stan Rohrer/Alamy, p. 215; Nelvin C. Cepeda/Associated Press, p. 249; Mikael Karlsson/Alamy, p. 287; Martin Thomas Photography/Alamy, p. 311; Michelle Shephard/Associated Press, 332; ExactoStock/SuperStock, p. 366

Other credits and acknowledgments for material borrowed from other sources and reproduced, with permission, in this textbook appear on the appropriate page within the text.

Copyright © 2012, 2010, 2008, 2006, 2004 Pearson Education, Inc., publishing as Prentice Hall, 1 Lake St., Upper Saddle River, NJ 07458. All rights reserved. Manufactured in the United States of America. This publication is protected by copyright, and permission should be obtained from the publisher prior to any prohibited reproduction, storage in a retrieval system, or transmission in any form or by any means, electronic, mechanical, photocopying, recording, or likewise. To obtain permission(s) to use material from this work, please submit a written request to Pearson Education, Inc., Permissions Department, 1 Lake St., Upper Saddle River, NJ 07458.

Library of Congress Cataloging-in-Publication Data
Schmalleger, Frank.
Criminal justice: a brief introduction / Frank Schmalleger.—9th ed.
p. cm.
Includes bibliographical references and index.
ISBN-13: 978-0-13-706983-5 (alk. paper)
ISBN-10: 0-13-706983-9 (alk. paper)
1. Criminal justice, Administration of—United States. I. Title.
HV9950.S35 2012
364.973—dc22
2010039731

10 9 8 7 6 5 4 3 2 1

Prentice Hall
is an imprint of

www.pearsonhighered.com

ISBN 10: 0-13-802025-6
ISBN 13: 978-0-13-802025-5

For Nicole, Malia, and Ava

Prof. M. Lorenzo

Tel.: 237-1543

Rm. 9113

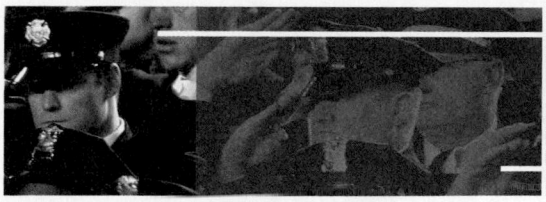

New to the Ninth Edition

- Greater emphasis on presenting concepts *visually*.
- More concise learning objectives.
- All new "CJ Careers" features and many new "CJ News" features.
- New photos, and new or updated charts, graphs, and tables.
- Adjustments in topic coverage to suit current needs.
- Reorganization of content for more logical presentation.
- Updated statistics.

General Changes

Since its first edition, *Criminal Justice: A Brief Introduction* has made use of colorful photographs, charts, graphs, and other visual aids help keep students' attention and to add variety to the text. In the ninth edition, however, we have taken that approach one step further by incorporating many highly visual illustrations that make the field of criminal justice both understandable and interesting. In recognition of the visual orientation of today's learners, this is the first edition of this book in which we have worked to achieve a comprehensive integration of graphic art with the concepts and ideas of criminal justice. Consequently, *Criminal Justice: A Brief Introduction* is now intensely visual. Its layout and design invite readers to explore its pages while powerfully illustrating the critical concepts that are central to the field of criminal justice.

The chapter openers have been reduced to one page in length, and concisely worded learning objectives can be found at the start of each chapter. Each objective is closely integrated with the chapter headings and with the summaries and discussion questions found at the end of each chapter. The last edition's "CJ Careers" boxes have all been replaced with updated boxes featuring new personnel and new agencies. Many new photographs throughout the book, along with updated charts and graphs, round out the general changes that can be found in this new edition of *Criminal Justice: A Brief Introduction*.

Changes in Each Chapter

CHAPTER 1 **What Is Criminal Justice?**

- The section describing the history of crime in America has been shortened.
- The discussion of white-collar crime has been expanded slightly, and coverage of Bernard Madoff has been added.
- The section headed "Social Justice" has been reframed and is now called "Criminal Justice and Basic Fairness."
- The discussion of evidence-based practice in criminal justice has been substantially expanded.
- A new "CJ News" box describing surveillance and security cameras in Atlanta has been included.
- The previous edition's lengthy overview of criminal justice processing has been substantially curtailed and is depicted in a highly visual illustration. Much of the previous text coverage has been integrated into later chapters within the book.
- The discussion of self-defense has been updated.
- The discussion of Andrea Pia Yates has been largely removed from the chapter, as have the discussions of John DeLorean and John Demjanjuk.

CHAPTER 2 The Crime Picture

- This chapter begins with a new story.
- A new figure showing historical trends in American crime rates has been added.
- Other new figures, titled "Murder by Relationship" and "Larceny-Theft Distribution," are included.
- One "CJ News" box has been updated, and a second has been replaced.
- The section on identity theft has been updated.
- A description of the crimes perpetrated by Bernard Madoff has been added.
- A discussion of the crime of mortgage fraud has been added.

CHAPTER 3 Criminal Law

- This chapter has been significantly shortened.
- The types of law are now presented in an illustration, and their discussion has been abbreviated.
- The same changes have been made to the discussion of the categories of law.
- The general features of crime are now illustrated.

CHAPTER 4 Policing: Purpose and Organization

- The section on the FBI has been shortened.
- A link to the NYPD's "Inside the Department" podcasts has been added.
- The discussion of police fusion centers has been substantially enhanced with a new "CJ News" box.
- The section on historical eras in American policing has been revised.
- The discussion of evidence-based policing has been enhanced.

CHAPTER 5 Policing: Legal Aspects

- This chapter has been shortened by reducing the amount of detail discussed in a number of U.S. Supreme Court cases.
- Included now is the 2009 U.S. Supreme Court case of *Herring* v. *U.S.*, in which the Court held that "when police mistakes leading to an unlawful search are the result of isolated negligence . . . rather than systemic error or reckless disregard of constitutional requirements, the exclusionary rule does not apply."
- Similarly, the cases of *Arizona* v. *Johnson* (2009) and *Montejo* v. *Louisiana* (2009) have been added to the chapter.
- The 2010 U.S. Supreme Court case of *Florida* v. *Powell* has also been added. In *Powell*, the justices found that although *Miranda* warnings are generally required prior to police interrogation, the wording of those warnings is not set in stone.

CHAPTER 6 Policing: Issues and Challenges

- This chapter has been shortened, especially in its discussion of private security.
- A new figure, illustrating stress and fatigue among police officers, has been added.
- New line art illustrates (1) perceptions of racial profiling by the police and (2) states with racial profiling bans.
- The statistics on the number of hours required for police training in various states have been updated, as has the discussion of the requirement of a college education for new law enforcement hires.

CHAPTER 7 The Courts

- The chapter begins with a new story.
- Statistics on the workload of U.S. courts have been updated.

- The discussion of the International Criminal Court has been shortened.
- A number of key terms have been moved to this chapter, including *arraignment*, *bail*, *grand jury*, *indictment*, *information*, and *preliminary hearing*.

CHAPTER 8 **The Courtroom Work Group and the Criminal Trial**

- The chapter begins with a new story.
- The "CJ News" box has been replaced with one that describes the plight of public defenders facing budget cuts.
- A new figure illustrates the role of professional and nonprofessional courtroom participants.
- A new "CJ News" box about social networking among jurors has been added, along with a Library Extra link to a set of suggested federal jury instructions designed to alleviate this problem.

CHAPTER 9 **Sentencing**

- The chapter begins with a new story.
- The goals and purposes of sentencing are now shown in a new illustration.
- A new figure has been added that shows the distribution of federal offenders by primary offense category.
- Two new U.S. Supreme Court cases, *U.S.* v. *O'Brien* (2010) and *Oregon* v. *Ice* (2009), have been added.
- New examples of alternative sentencing are provided.
- California's Proposition 9—the Victims' Rights and Protection Act of 2008 (also known as Marsy's Law), the most comprehensive victims' bill of rights of any state in the nation—has been incorporated into the chapter's discussions.
- In the section on the death penalty, retentionist and abolitionist rationales appear within an illustrated table.
- The new North Carolina Innocence Inquiry Commission is now described.
- Two new "CJ News" boxes have been added.
- U.S. Supreme Court cases pertaining to capital punishment appear within an illustrated table.
- Statistics have been updated throughout the chapter.

CHAPTER 10 **Probation, Parole, and Community Corrections**

- The chapter begins with a new story.
- The legal environment of probation and parole supervision is diagrammed in a new illustrated table.
- The parole conditions pertaining to the release from confinement of former National Football League star Michael Vick are discussed.
- A number of new Web Extras, including one leading to the National Reentry Resource Center, are included.
- The chapter now describes the 13 strategies outlined by the Public Safety Performance Project of the Pew Center on the States in its report *Putting Public Safety First*.
- A new figure is included that shows the degree of emphasis that parole officers place on evidence-based practices.

CHAPTER 11 **Prisons and Jails**

- The chapter begins with a new story.
- Statistics have been updated throughout the chapter.
- A new figure provides a breakdown of the annual costs to incarcerate an inmate in California.

- The 2009 release of prison inmates ordered by California's Governor Arnold Schwarzenegger is discussed, and a new "CJ News" box outlines the risks associated with such a release.

CHAPTER 12 **Prison Life**

- The BJS's third annual Prison Rape Elimination Act national survey is discussed.
- Information about incarcerated mothers and their minor children has been updated.
- A new illustration is included that describes adult women in state prisons.
- The section on prison riots has been abbreviated.
- A new illustrated table highlights important U.S. Supreme Court cases involving prisoners' rights.
- The discussion on terrorism in American prisons has been expanded to include the group known as *Jam'iyyat Ul-Islam Is-Saheeh* (the Assembly of Authentic Islam, or JIS), which operates throughout prisons in California.

CHAPTER 13 **Juvenile Justice**

- The chapter begins with a new story.
- The discussion of the history of juvenile justice in America has been shortened.
- A new "CJ News" box has been added.
- The discussion of important cases in juvenile justice has been shortened, and a new figure illustrating those cases has been added.

Brief Contents

PART 1 *Crime in America*

CHAPTER 1 **What Is Criminal Justice?** 1 8/26 - 9/2 1

CHAPTER 2 **The Crime Picture** 19 DIS. #2 9/3 - 9/9

CHAPTER 3 **Criminal Law** 58 DIS. #3 9/10 - 9/16

PART 2 *Policing*

9/17 - 9/23 Discussion #4 - No QUIZ

CHAPTER 4 **Policing: Purpose and Organization** 87

CHAPTER 5 **Policing: Legal Aspects** 114 Discuss. #5 9/24 - 9/30

CHAPTER 6 **Policing: Issues and Challenges** 155 DIS. #6 Oct. 1, - 10/7/12

PART 3 *Adjudication*

Midterm 10/8 - 10/14

CHAPTER 7 **The Courts** 194 10/15

CHAPTER 8 **The Courtroom Work Group and the Criminal Trial** 215 10/22

CHAPTER 9 **Sentencing** 249 10/29

PART 4 *Corrections*

CHAPTER 10 **Probation, Parole, and Community Corrections** 287 11/5

CHAPTER 11 **Prisons and Jails** 311 11/12

CHAPTER 12 **Prison Life** 332 11/19

PART 5 *The Juvenile Justice System*

CHAPTER 13 **Juvenile Justice** 366

Contents

Preface xxiii
Acknowledgments xxv
About the Author xxvii

PART 1 *Crime in America*

CHAPTER 1 **What Is Criminal Justice?** 1

Introduction 2
A Brief History of Crime in America 3
The Theme of This Book 5
Freedom or Safety? You Decide. Giuliani Says: "Freedom Is about Authority" 6
Criminal Justice and Basic Fairness 7
American Criminal Justice: System and Functions 8
The Consensus Model 8
CJ News Atlanta Seeks to Add 500 Surveillance Cameras 9
The Conflict Model 9
American Criminal Justice: The Process 11
Due Process and Individual Rights 11
The Role of the Courts in Defining Rights 12
The Ultimate Goal: Crime Control through Due Process 13
Evidence-Based Practice in Criminal Justice 14
The Start of Academic Criminal Justice 14
Multiculturalism and Diversity in Criminal Justice 15
Summary 17
Questions for Review 18

CHAPTER 2 **The Crime Picture** 19

Introduction 20
Crime Data and Social Policy 20
The Collection of Crime Data 21
The UCR/NIBRS Program 21
Development of the UCR Program 21
The National Incident-Based Reporting System 23
Historical Trends 24
UCR/NIBRS in Transition 27
Freedom or Safety? You Decide. A Dress Code for Bank Customers? 28
Part I Offenses 29
Multiculturalism and Diversity Race and the Criminal Justice System, Part I 35
CJ Exhibit 2–1 Identity Theft: A New Kind of Larceny 36
Career Profile Instructor of Criminal Justice 39
Part II Offenses 39

6 PART I Crime in America

Freedom or Safety? You Decide.
Giuliani Says: "Freedom Is about Authority"

In 2009, U.S. Supreme Court Justice Clarence Thomas spoke to a group of high school essay contest winners in a Washington, D.C., hotel ballroom. Thomas used the occasion, which was dedicated to our nation's Bill of Rights, to point out the importance of obligations as well as rights. "Today there is much focus on our rights," said Thomas. "Indeed, I think there is a proliferation of rights." But then he went on to say, "I am often surprised by the virtual nobility that seems to be accorded those with grievances. Shouldn't there at least be equal time for our Bill of Obligations and our Bill of Responsibilities?"

The challenge for the criminal justice system today, it seems, is to balance individual rights and personal freedoms with social control and respect for legitimate authority. Years ago, during the height of what was then a powerful movement to win back control of our nation's cities and to rein in skyrocketing crime rates, the *New York Post* sponsored a conference on crime and civil rights. The keynote speaker at that conference was the mayor of New York, Rudolph W. Giuliani. In his speech, Giuliani, who sought the Republican nomination as a presidential candidate in 2008, identified the tension between personal freedoms and individual responsibilities as the crux of the crime problem then facing his city and the nation. We mistakenly look to government and elected officials, Giuliani said, to assume responsibility for solving the problem of crime when, instead, each individual citizen must become accountable for fixing what is wrong with our society. "We only see the oppressive side of authority. . . . What we don't see is that freedom is not a concept in which people can do anything they want, be anything they can be. Freedom is about authority. Freedom is about the willingness of every single human being to cede to lawful authority a great deal of discretion about what you do."

YOU DECIDE

How can we, as suggested by Justice Thomas, achieve a balance of rights and obligations in American society? What did Giuliani mean when he said, "What we don't see is that freedom is not a concept in which people can do anything they want, be anything they can be"? Is it possible to balance individual rights and personal freedoms with social control and respect for legitimate authority?

References: Adam Liptak, "Reticent Justice Opens Up to a Group of Students," *New York Times*, April 13, 2009, http://www.nytimes.com/2009/04/14/us/14bar.html (accessed June 2, 2010); and Philip Taylor, "Civil Libertarians: Giuliani's Efforts Threaten First Amendment," Freedom Forum Online, http://www.freedomforum.org.

Those who fight for individual rights continue to carry the banner of civil and criminal rights for the accused and the convicted, while public-order activists proclaim the rights of the victimized and call for an increased emphasis on social responsibility and criminal punishment for convicted criminals. In keeping with these realizations, the theme of this book can be stated as follows:

> There is widespread recognition in contemporary society of the need to balance (1) the freedoms and privileges of our nation's citizens and the respect accorded the rights of individuals faced with criminal prosecution against (2) the valid interests that society has in preventing future crimes, in maintaining public safety, and in reducing the harm caused by criminal activity. While the personal freedoms guaranteed to law-abiding citizens as well as to criminal suspects by the Constitution, as interpreted by the U.S. Supreme Court, must be closely guarded, the urgent social needs of communities for controlling unacceptable behavior and protecting law-abiding citizens from harm must be recognized. Still to be adequately addressed are the needs and interests of victims and the fear of crime and personal victimization often prevalent in the minds of many law-abiding citizens.

Individual Rights
Public Order

FIGURE 1–2
The Theme of This Book
Balancing the concern for individual rights with the need for public order through the administration of criminal justice is the theme of this book.

Figure 1–2 represents our theme and shows that most people today who intelligently consider the criminal justice system assume one of two viewpoints. We will refer to those who seek to protect personal freedoms and civil rights within society, and especially within the criminal justice process, as **individual-rights advocates**. Those who suggest that, under certain circumstances involving criminal threats to public safety, the interests of society (especially crime control and social order) should take precedence over individual rights will be called **public-order advocates**. Recently, retired U.S. Supreme Court Justice Sandra Day O'Connor summed up the differences between these two perspectives by asking, "At what point does the cost to civil liberties from legislation designed to prevent terrorism [and crime] outweigh the added security that that legislation provides?"[30] In this book, we seek to look at ways in which the individual-rights and public-order perspectives can be balanced to serve both sets of needs. Hence you will find our theme discussed throughout this text and within "Freedom or Safety?" boxes.

individual-rights advocate
One who seeks to protect personal freedoms within the process of criminal justice.

public-order advocate
One who believes that under certain circumstances involving a criminal threat to public safety, the interests of society should take precedence over individual rights.

"Freedom or Safety? You Decide" Boxes
Critical-thinking exercises ask students to consider how the criminal justice system balances individual rights and public safety

The National Crime Victimization Survey 40
Comparisons of the UCR and the NCVS 41
Multiculturalism and Diversity Race and the Criminal Justice System, Part II 42
Special Categories of Crime 43
Crime against Women 43
Multiculturalism and Diversity Gender Issues in Criminal Justice 45
Crime against the Elderly 45
Hate Crime 46
Corporate and White-Collar Crime 47
Organized Crime 48
Gun Crime 49
Drug Crime 50
High-Technology and Computer Crime 52
CJ Exhibit 2–2 What Is Terrorist Activity? 54
Terrorism 54
CJ News FBI Warns of Growing Threat from Islamic Extremists "Next Door" 56
Summary 57
Questions for Review 57

CHAPTER 3 **Criminal Law** 58
Introduction 59
The Nature and Purpose of Law 59
The Rule of Law 60
Types of Law 60
General Categories of Crime 63
Freedom or Safety? You Decide. Should Violent Speech Be Free Speech? 64
General Features of Crime 65
The Criminal Act (*Actus Reus*) 65
A Guilty Mind (*Mens Rea*) 67
Concurrence 68
Other Features of Crime 68
Elements of a Specific Criminal Offense 70
The Example of Murder 70
The *Corpus Delicti* of a Crime 71
Types of Defenses to a Criminal Charge 72
Multiculturalism and Diversity Islamic Law 73
Alibi 74
Justifications 74
Excuses 77
Procedural Defenses 83
Summary 85
Questions for Review 86

PART 2 ***Policing***

CHAPTER 4 **Policing: Purpose and Organization** 87
Introduction 88
The Police Mission 88
Enforcing the Law 88

Apprehending Offenders 89
Preventing Crime 89
Preserving the Peace 90
Providing Services 91
American Policing Today: From the Federal to the Local Level 91
Federal Agencies 91
CJ News FBI Retools Most Wanted List 93
State Agencies 95
Local Agencies 95
Fusion Centers 96
Police Administration 97
Police Organization and Structure 97
CJ News Fusion Centers 98
Chain of Command 100
Policing Epochs and Styles 100
Policing Epochs 100
The Watchman Style of Policing 101
Freedom or Safety? You Decide. Liberty Is a Double-Edged Sword 102
The Legalistic Style of Policing 102
The Service Style of Policing 102
Police–Community Relations 102
Team Policing 103
Community Policing 103
Evidence-Based Policing 108
The Kansas City Experiment 108
Evidence-Based Policing Today 109
Discretion and the Individual Officer 111
Summary 112
Questions for Review 113

CHAPTER 5 **Policing: Legal Aspects** 114
Introduction 115
The Abuse of Police Power 116
The Rodney King Incident 116
A Changing Legal Climate 116
Individual Rights 118
Checks and Balances 118
Due Process Requirements 118
Search and Seizure 118
The Warren Court (1953–1969) 121
The Burger Court (1969–1986) and the Rehnquist Court (1986–2005) 122
CJ Exhibit 5–1 Plain-View Requirements 126
Career Profile Patrol Officer 128
Arrest 128
CJ News Legal Issues Being Raised in Subway Searches 130
Searches Incident to Arrest 131
Emergency Searches of Persons 133
Vehicle Searches 134
Freedom or Safety? You Decide. Religion and Public Safety 135

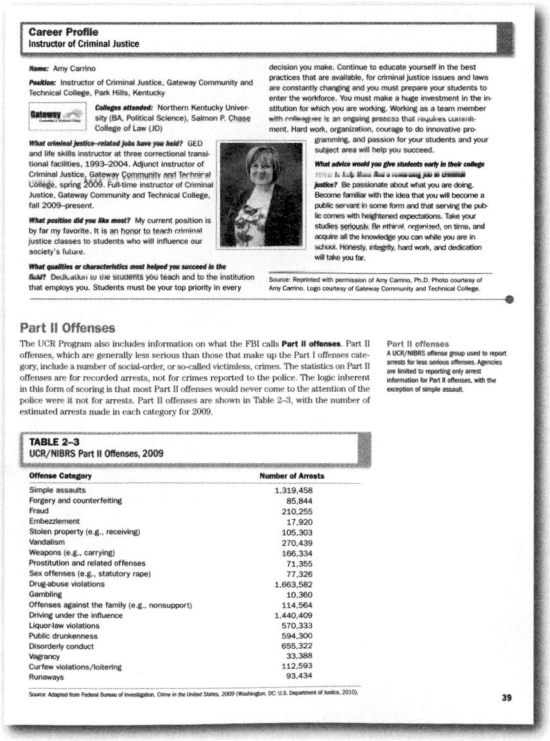

Career Profile
Instructor of Criminal Justice

Name: Amy Carrino

Position: Instructor of Criminal Justice, Gateway Community and Technical College, Park Hills, Kentucky

Colleges attended: Northern Kentucky University (BA, Political Science), Salmon P. Chase College of Law (JD)

What criminal justice–related jobs have you held? GED and life skills instructor at three correctional transitional facilities, 1993–2004. Adjunct instructor of Criminal Justice, Gateway Community and Technical College, spring 2009. Full-time instructor of Criminal Justice, Gateway Community and Technical College, fall 2009–present.

What position did you like most? My current position is by far my favorite. It is an honor to teach criminal justice classes to students who will influence our society's future.

What qualities or characteristics most helped you succeed in the field? Dedication to the students you teach and to the institution that employs you. Students must be your top priority in every decision you make. Continue to educate yourself in the best practices that are available, for criminal justice issues and laws are constantly changing and you must prepare your students to enter the workforce. You must make a huge investment in the institution for which you are working. Working as a team member with colleagues is an ongoing process that requires commitment. Hard work, organization, courage to do innovative programming, and passion for your students and your subject area will help you succeed.

What advice would you give students early in their college career to help them find a rewarding job in criminal justice? Be passionate about what you are doing. Become familiar with the idea that you will become a public servant in some form and that serving the public comes with heightened expectations. Take your studies seriously. Be ethical, organized, on time, and acquire all the knowledge you can while you are in school. Honesty, integrity, hard work, and dedication will take you far.

Source: Reprinted with permission of Amy Carrino, Ph.D. Photo courtesy of Amy Carrino. Logo courtesy of Gateway Community and Technical College.

Part II Offenses

The UCR Program also includes information on what the FBI calls **Part II offenses**. Part II offenses, which are generally less serious than those that make up the Part I offenses category, include a number of social-order, or so-called victimless, crimes. The statistics on Part II offenses are for recorded arrests, not for crimes reported to the police. The logic inherent in this form of scoring is that most Part II offenses would never come to the attention of the police were it not for arrests. Part II offenses are shown in Table 2–3, with the number of estimated arrests made in each category for 2009.

Part II offenses
A UCR/NIBRS offense group used to report arrests for less serious offenses. Agencies are limited to reporting only arrest information for Part II offenses, with the exception of simple assault.

TABLE 2–3
UCR/NIBRS Part II Offenses, 2009

Offense Category	Number of Arrests
Simple assaults	1,319,458
Forgery and counterfeiting	85,844
Fraud	210,255
Embezzlement	17,920
Stolen property (e.g., receiving)	105,303
Vandalism	270,439
Weapons (e.g., carrying)	166,334
Prostitution and related offenses	71,355
Sex offenses (e.g., statutory rape)	77,326
Drug-abuse violations	1,663,582
Gambling	10,360
Offenses against the family (e.g., nonsupport)	114,564
Driving under the influence	1,440,409
Liquor-law violations	570,333
Public drunkenness	594,300
Disorderly conduct	655,322
Vagrancy	33,388
Curfew violations/loitering	112,593
Runaways	93,434

Source: Adapted from Federal Bureau of Investigation, *Crime in the United States, 2009* (Washington, DC: U.S. Department of Justice, 2010).

39

Career Profile Boxes
Criminal justice professionals offer real-world insights into their careers

Suspicionless Searches 137
High-Technology Searches 138
The Intelligence Function 139
Informants 139
Police Interrogation 140
The Right to a Lawyer at Interrogation 142
Suspect Rights: The *Miranda* Decision 143
CJ Exhibit 5–2 The *Miranda* Warnings 144
Gathering of Special Kinds of Nontestimonial Evidence 147
Electronic Eavesdropping 148
CJ Exhibit 5–3 The USA PATRIOT Act of 2001 and the USA PATRIOT Improvement and Reauthorization Act of 2005 151
Summary 153
Questions for Review 154

CHAPTER 6 **Policing: Issues and Challenges** 155
Introduction 156
Police Personality and Culture 156
Corruption and Integrity 157
Multiculturalism and Diversity Policing a Multicultural Society 158
Money—The Root of Police Evil? 161
Building Police Integrity 161
Ethics and Professionalism The Law Enforcement Oath of Honor 162
Drug Testing of Police Employees 163
The Dangers of Police Work 163
CJ News Police DNA Collection Sparks Questions 164
Violence in the Line of Duty 164
Risk of Disease and Infected Evidence 165
Stress and Fatigue among Police Officers 167
Career Profile Police Officer 168
Terrorism's Impact on Policing 169
The FBI's Joint Terrorism Task Forces 170
Intelligence-Led Policing and Antiterrorism 171
Information Sharing and Antiterrorism 171
Police Civil Liability 172
Common Sources of Civil Suits 173
Federal Lawsuits 174
Racial Profiling and Biased Policing 176
Racial Profiling 176
Freedom or Safety? You Decide. Was the LAPD's Community Mapping Project a Form of Religious Profiling? 177
Racially Biased Policing 178
Police Use of Force 179
Deadly Force 180
Less-Lethal Weapons 182
Professionalism and Ethics 183
Ethics and Professionalism The Law Enforcement Code of Ethics 184
Education and Training 184
Recruitment and Selection 186

Ethnic and Gender Diversity in Policing 186
Multiculturalism and Diversity Investigating Crime in a Multicultural Setting 187
Women as Effective Police Officers 188
Private Protective Services 189
Growth of Private Protective Services 189
Freedom or Safety? You Decide. Do Sex-Offender Websites Spur Vigilantism? 189
Integration of Public and Private Security 191
Summary 191
Questions for Review 192

PART 3 *Adjudication*

CHAPTER 7 The Courts 194

Introduction 195
History and Structure of the American Court System 195
The State Court System 196
The Development of State Courts 196
State Court Systems Today 197
The Federal Court System 200
U.S. District Courts 200
U.S. Courts of Appeal 201
The U.S. Supreme Court 203
Pretrial Activities 205
The First Appearance 206
Multiculturalism and Diversity The International Criminal Court 207
CJ Exhibit 7-1 Nonjudicial Pretrial Release Decisions 210
The Grand Jury 211
The Preliminary Hearing 212
Arraignment and the Plea 212
Summary 214
Questions for Review 214

CHAPTER 8 The Courtroom Work Group and the Criminal Trial 215

Introduction 216
The Courtroom Work Group: Professional Courtroom Actors 216
The Judge 218
The Prosecuting Attorney 219
The Defense Counsel 222
Career Profile Attorney and Instructor of Criminal Justice 224
CJ News Public Defenders Reject New Cases 226
Ethics and Professionalism The American Bar Association's *Model Rules of Professional Conduct* 227
The Bailiff 228
The Trial Court Administrator 228
The Court Reporter 228
The Clerk of Court 229
Expert Witnesses 229

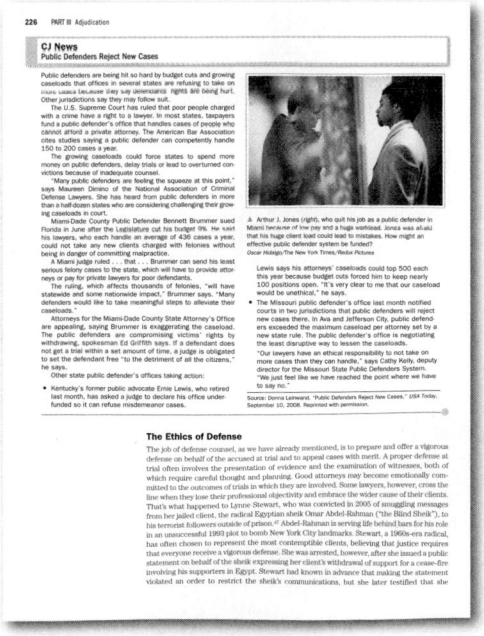

226 PART III Adjudication

CJ News
Public Defenders Reject New Cases

Public defenders are being hit so hard by budget cuts and growing caseloads that offices in several states are refusing to take on more cases because they say defendants' rights are being hurt. Other jurisdictions say they may follow suit.

The U.S. Supreme Court has ruled that poor people charged with a crime have a right to a lawyer. In most states, taxpayers fund a public defender's office that handles cases of people who cannot afford a private attorney. The American Bar Association cites studies saying a public defender can competently handle 150 to 200 cases a year.

The growing caseloads could force states to spend more money on public defenders, delay trials or lead to overturned convictions because of inadequate counsel.

"Many public defenders are feeling the squeeze at this point," says Maureen Dimino of the National Association of Criminal Defense Lawyers. She has heard from public defenders in more than a half-dozen states who are considering challenging their growing caseloads in court.

Miami-Dade County Public Defender Bennett Brummer sued Florida in June after the Legislature cut his budget 9%. He said his lawyers, who each handle an average of 436 cases a year, could not take any new clients charged with felonies without being in danger of committing malpractice.

A Miami judge ruled . . . that . . . Brummer can send his least serious felony cases to the state, which will have to provide attorneys or pay for private lawyers for poor defendants.

The ruling, which affects thousands of felonies, "will have statewide and some nationwide impact," Brummer says. "Many defenders would like to take meaningful steps to alleviate their caseloads."

Attorneys for the Miami-Dade County State Attorney's Office are appealing, saying Brummer is exaggerating the caseload. The public defenders are compromising victims' rights by withdrawing, spokesman Ed Griffith says. If a defendant does not get a trial within a set amount of time, a judge is obligated to set the defendant free "to the detriment of all the citizens," he says.

Other state public defender's offices taking action:

- Kentucky's former public advocate Ernie Lewis, who retired last month, has asked a judge to declare his office underfunded so it can refuse misdemeanor cases.

Arthur J. Jones (right), who quit his job as a public defender in Miami because of low pay and a huge workload. Jones was afraid that his huge client load could lead to mistakes. How might an effective public defender system be funded?
Oscar Hidalgo/The New York Times/Redux Pictures

Lewis says his attorneys' caseloads could top 500 each this year because budget cuts forced him to keep nearly 100 positions open. "It's very clear to me that our caseload would be unethical," he says.

- The Missouri public defender's office last month notified courts in two jurisdictions that public defenders will reject new cases there. In Ava and Jefferson City, public defenders exceeded the maximum caseload per attorney set by a new state rule. The public defender's office is negotiating the least disruptive way to lessen the caseloads.

"Our lawyers have an ethical responsibility to not take on more cases than they can handle," says Cathy Kelly, deputy director for the Missouri State Public Defenders System.

"We just feel like we have reached the point where we have to say no."

Source: Donna Leinwand, "Public Defenders Reject New Cases," *USA Today*, September 10, 2008. Reprinted with permission.

The Ethics of Defense

The job of defense counsel, as we have already mentioned, is to prepare and offer a vigorous defense on behalf of the accused at trial and to appeal cases with merit. A proper defense at trial often involves the presentation of evidence and the examination of witnesses, both of which require careful thought and planning. Good attorneys may become emotionally committed to the outcomes of trials in which they are involved. Some lawyers, however, cross the line when they lose their professional objectivity and embrace the wider cause of their clients. That's what happened to Lynne Stewart, who was convicted in 2005 of smuggling messages from her jailed client, the radical Egyptian sheik Omar Abdel-Rahman ("the Blind Sheik"), to his terrorist followers outside of prison.[47] Abdel-Rahman is serving life behind bars for his role in an unsuccessful 1993 plot to bomb New York City landmarks. Stewart, a 1960s-era radical, has often chosen to represent the most contemptible clients, believing that justice requires that everyone receive a vigorous defense. She was arrested, however, after she issued a public statement on behalf of the sheik expressing her client's withdrawal of support for a cease-fire involving his supporters in Egypt. Stewart had known in advance that making the statement violated an order to restrict the sheik's communications, but she later testified that she

"CJ News" Boxes
News articles present case examples that relate to the chapter topics

Outsiders: Nonprofessional Courtroom Participants 229
Lay Witnesses 229
Jurors 230
The Victim 231
The Defendant 232
Spectators and the Press 232
The Criminal Trial 234
Procedure 234
Nature and Purpose 234
Stages in a Criminal Trial 235
Trial Initiation 236
Jury Selection 237
Opening Statements 239
Presentation of Evidence 239
CJ Exhibit 8-1 Pretrial and Post-trial Motions 241
Closing Arguments 244
Judge's Charge to the Jury 244
Jury Deliberations and the Verdict 244
CJ News Social Networking among Jurors Is Trying Judges' Patience 245
Multiculturalism and Diversity The Bilingual Courtroom 247
Summary 247
Questions for Review 248

CHAPTER 9 **Sentencing** 249
Introduction 250
The Philosophy and Goals of Criminal Sentencing 250
Retribution 251
Incapacitation 252
Deterrence 252
Rehabilitation 252
Restoration 252
Indeterminate Sentencing 254
Explanation of Indeterminate Sentencing 254
Critiques of Indeterminate Sentencing 254
Structured Sentencing 255
CJ Exhibit 9-1 Aggravating and Mitigating Circumstances 257
Federal Sentencing Guidelines 257
The Legal Environment of Structured Sentencing 260
Three-Strikes Laws 261
Mandatory Sentencing 263
Innovations in Sentencing 264
Alternative Sentencing Options 264
Questions about Alternative Sanctions 264
The Presentence Investigation 264
Career Profile Instructor of Criminal Justice 265
The Victim—Forgotten No Longer 266
Victims' Rights 266
CJ Exhibit 9-2 Victims' Rights in California 267

Freedom or Safety? You Decide. To What Degree Should the Personal Values of Workers in the Criminal Justice System Influence Job Performance? 269
Victim-Impact Statements 269
Modern Sentencing Options 270
Sentencing Rationales 270
Sentencing Practices 270
Fines 271
Death: The Ultimate Sanction 272
Habeas Corpus Review 273
Opposition to Capital Punishment 275
CJ News Florida Man Exonerated after 35 Years behind Bars 278
Justifications for Capital Punishment 280
The Courts and the Death Penalty 280
CJ News To Execute or Not: A Question of Cost? 281
The Future of the Death Penalty 284
Freedom or Safety? You Decide. What Are the Limits of Genetic Privacy? 285
Summary 285
Questions for Review 286

PART 4 ***Corrections***

CHAPTER 10 **Probation, Parole, and Community Corrections** 287
Introduction 288
What Is Probation? 288
The Extent of Probation 288
Probation Conditions 289
Multiculturalism and Diversity Culturally Skilled Probation Officers 290
The Federal Probation System 290
What Is Parole? 291
The Extent of Parole 292
Parole Conditions 292
Federal Parole 293
Probation and Parole: The Pluses and Minuses 293
Advantages of Probation and Parole 293
Disadvantages of Probation and Parole 294
The Legal Environment 294
Freedom or Safety? You Decide. Should DNA Links to Unsolved Cases Be Used to Deny Parole? 295
The Job of Probation and Parole Officers 296
Job Descriptions 296
The Challenges of the Job 297
Career Profile Probation Officer 298
Intermediate Sanctions 299
Split Sentencing 300
Shock Probation and Shock Parole 300
Shock Incarceration 300
Mixed Sentencing and Community Service 301
Intensive Probation Supervision 301

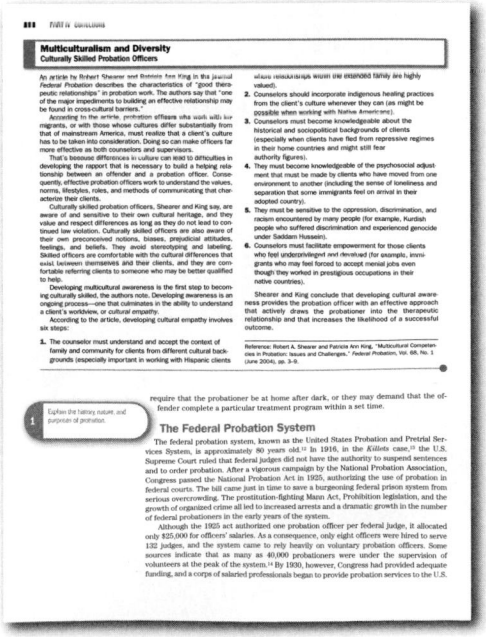

Multiculturalism and Diversity
Culturally Skilled Probation Officers

An article by Robert Shearer and Patricia Ann King in the journal *Federal Probation* describes the characteristics of "good therapeutic relationships" in probation work. The authors say that "one of the major impediments to building an effective relationship may be found in cross-cultural barriers."

According to the article, probation officers who work with immigrants, or with those whose cultures differ substantially from that of mainstream America, must realize that a client's culture has to be taken into consideration. Doing so can make officers far more effective as both counselors and supervisors.

That's because differences in culture can lead to difficulties in developing the rapport that is necessary to build a helping relationship between an offender and a probation officer. Consequently, effective probation officers work to understand the values, norms, lifestyles, roles, and methods of communicating that characterize their clients.

Culturally skilled probation officers, Shearer and King say, are aware of and sensitive to their own cultural heritage, and they value and respect differences as long as they do not lead to continued law violation. Culturally skilled officers are also aware of their own preconceived notions, biases, prejudicial attitudes, feelings, and beliefs. They avoid stereotyping and labeling. Skilled officers are comfortable with the cultural differences that exist between themselves and their clients, and they are comfortable referring clients to someone who may be better qualified to help.

Developing multicultural awareness is the first step to becoming culturally skilled, the authors note. Developing awareness is an ongoing process—one that culminates in the ability to understand a client's worldview, or cultural empathy.

According to the article, developing cultural empathy involves six steps:

1. The counselor must understand and accept the context of family and community for clients from different cultural backgrounds (especially important in working with Hispanic clients where relationships within the extended family are highly valued).
2. Counselors should incorporate indigenous healing practices from the client's culture whenever they can (as might be possible when working with Native Americans).
3. Counselors must become knowledgeable about the historical and sociopolitical backgrounds of clients (especially when clients have fled from repressive regimes in their home countries and might still fear authority figures).
4. They must become knowledgeable of the psychosocial adjustment that must be made by clients who have moved from one environment to another (including the sense of loneliness and separation that some immigrants feel on arrival in their adopted country).
5. They must be sensitive to the oppression, discrimination, and racism encountered by many people (for example, Kurdish people who suffered discrimination and experienced genocide under Saddam Hussein).
6. Counselors must facilitate empowerment for those clients who feel underprivileged and deprived (for example, immigrants who may feel forced to accept menial jobs even though they worked in prestigious occupations in their native countries).

Shearer and King conclude that developing cultural awareness provides the probation officer with an effective approach that actively draws the probationer into the therapeutic relationship and that increases the likelihood of a successful outcome.

Reference: Robert A. Shearer and Patricia Ann King, "Multicultural Competencies in Probation: Issues and Challenges," *Federal Probation*, Vol. 68, No. 1 (June 2004), pp. 3–9.

1 Explain the history, nature, and purposes of probation.

require that the probationer be at home after dark, or they may demand that the offender complete a particular treatment program within a set time.

The Federal Probation System

The federal probation system, known as the United States Probation and Pretrial Services System, is approximately 80 years old.[12] In 1916, in the *Killits* case,[13] the U.S. Supreme Court ruled that federal judges did not have the authority to suspend sentences and to order probation. After a vigorous campaign by the National Probation Association, Congress passed the National Probation Act in 1925, authorizing the use of probation in federal courts. The bill came just in time to save a burgeoning federal prison system from serious overcrowding. The prostitution-fighting Mann Act, Prohibition legislation, and the growth of organized crime all led to increased arrests and a dramatic growth in the number of federal probationers in the early years of the system.

Although the 1925 act authorized one probation officer per federal judge, it allocated only $25,000 for officers' salaries. As a consequence, only eight officers were hired to serve 132 judges, and the system came to rely heavily on voluntary probation officers. Some sources indicate that as many as 40,000 probationers were under the supervision of volunteers at the peak of the system.[14] By 1930, however, Congress had provided adequate funding, and a corps of salaried professionals began to provide probation services to the U.S.

"Multiculturalism and Diversity" Boxes
These boxes showcase selected issues surrounding the multicultural nature of our society and its impact on the justice system

Ethics and Professionalism American Probation and Parole Association Code of Ethics 302
Home Confinement and Remote Location Monitoring 302
The Future of Probation and Parole 304
CJ News More Sex Offenders Tracked by Satellite 305
Changes in Reentry Policies 306
The Reinvention of Probation 308
Summary 309
Questions for Review 310

CHAPTER 11 **Prisons and Jails** 311
Introduction 312
Prisons 312
The Philosophy of Imprisonment 315
Overcrowding 317
Security Levels 319
CJ News California Inmate Release Prompts Public Safety Debate 320
Prison Classification Systems 321
The Federal Prison System 322
Recent Improvements 323
Jails 324
Women and Jail 325
The Growth of Jails 325
Direct-Supervision Jails 326
Jails and the Future 327
Ethics and Professionalism American Jail Association Code of Ethics for Jail Officers 328
Private Prisons 329
CJ Exhibit 11-1 Arguments for and against the Privatization of Prisons 330
Summary 331
Questions for Review 331

CHAPTER 12 **Prison Life** 332
Introduction 333
Research on Prison Life: Total Institutions 333
The Male Inmate's World 334
The Evolution of Prison Subcultures 334
CJ Exhibit 12-1 Prison Argot: The Language of Confinement 335
The Functions of Prison Subcultures 335
Prison Lifestyles and Inmate Types 336
Homosexuality and Sexual Victimization in Prison 337
The Female Inmate's World 339
Gender Responsiveness 341
Institutions for Women 342
Social Structure in Women's Prisons 342
Types of Female Inmates 343
Violence in Women's Prisons 344
The Staff World 344
Facts and Figures 344
The Professionalization of Corrections Officers 345

CJ Exhibit 12–2 The Commission on Safety and Abuse in America's Prisons 346
Ethics and Professionalism American Correctional Association Code of Ethics 347
Prison Riots 347
Causes of Riots 348
Prisoners' Rights 349
The Legal Basis of Prisoners' Rights 350
Freedom or Safety? You Decide. Censoring Prison Communications 351
Grievance Procedures 352
A Return to the Hands-Off Doctrine? 356
Freedom or Safety? You Decide. Should Prison Libraries Limit Access to Potentially Inflammatory Literature? 357
Issues Facing Prisons Today 359
AIDS 359
Geriatric Offenders 360
Mentally Ill and Mentally Deficient Inmates 361
Terrorism 362
CJ News Feds Target Terrorist Recruiting in Prisons 364
Summary 364
Questions for Review 365

PART 5 *The Juvenile Justice System*

CHAPTER 13 **Juvenile Justice** 366
Introduction 367
Juvenile Justice throughout History 368
Earliest Times 368
The Juvenile Court Era 369
The Legal Environment 370
CJ News No Clear-Cut Way to Handle Eight-Year-Old's Case 372
Legislation Concerning Children and Justice 373
The Legal Rights of Juveniles 374
The Juvenile Justice Process Today 374
Adult and Juvenile Justice Compared 375
CJ Exhibit 13–1 Adult Criminal Case Processing versus the Juvenile Justice System 376
The Way the System Works 376
CJ Exhibit 13–2 Juvenile Courts versus Adult Courts 380
The Post–Juvenile Court Era 382
Summary 385
Questions for Review 386

Appendix A: Bill of Rights 387
Appendix B: List of Acronyms 389
Glossary 391
Notes 401
Name Index 433
Case Index 435
Subject Index 439

Preface

Criminal justice is a dynamic field of study. The ever-evolving nature of crime, newsworthy law enforcement initiatives, ongoing threats to our nation's security, newly enacted statutes, innovations in enforcement and justice system technology, precedent-setting U.S. Supreme Court decisions, a changing American society, and rapidly emerging innovations in correctional practice all challenge instructors and students alike to keep pace with a field that is undergoing continual modification.

As accelerated change engulfs the American criminal justice system today, it is appropriate that a streamlined and up-to-date book like this should be in the hands of students. Quick and easy access to accurate and current information has become a vital part of contemporary life. *Criminal Justice: A Brief Introduction* provides such access through its printed pages and interactive website with videos.

The first edition of *Criminal Justice: A Brief Introduction*, which was published before the Internet had become the ubiquitous tool that it is today, resulted from the realization that justice students need to have current information presented in a concise and affordable source. The paperback format of this book makes it possible to quickly translate the latest happenings in the justice field into a pragmatic textbook that is both inexpensive and easy to read. With each new edition, the availability of up-to-date crime- and justice-related information has increased. Like many of its predecessors, the ninth edition draws upon the wealth of Internet resources that serve the needs of criminal justice students and practitioners. It ties those important resources to central ideas in the text, expanding learning opportunities far beyond what was possible in the mere 400 pages of the first edition. In particular, Web Extras point the way to criminal justice agencies and organizations on the Internet, and Library Extras place full-text documentation of many critical contemporary issues at students' fingertips.

True to its origins, the ninth edition focuses on the crime picture in America and the three traditional elements of the criminal justice system: police, courts, and corrections. As in previous editions, the text has been enhanced by the addition of "CJ Careers" boxes that can assist today's pragmatic students in making appropriate career choices. "CJ News" boxes, found throughout the book, use stories from the media to bring a true-to-life dimension to the study of criminal justice and allow insight into the everyday workings of the justice system. "Multiculturalism and Diversity" boxes underscore the diverse nature of American society and highlight the need for justice system personnel capable of working with culturally diverse groups. "Freedom or Safety?" boxes, which build on the text's theme, illustrate some of the personal rights issues that challenge policymakers today. Finally, "Ethics and Professionalism" boxes draw attention to the vital role of moral and ethical standards and behavior in the daily lives of criminal justice practitioners and to the high social expectations inherent in justice-related careers.

As the author of numerous books on criminal justice, I have often been amazed at how the end result of the justice process is sometimes barely recognizable as "justice" in any practical sense of the word. It is my sincere hope that the technological and publishing revolutions that have contributed to the creation and development of this book will combine with a growing social awareness to facilitate needed changes in our system and will help replace self-serving, system-perpetuated injustices with new standards of equity, compassion, understanding, fairness, and heartfelt justice for all. If you use this book, I'd like to hear from you. Please write to me at the e-mail address below.

Supplements

Instructor Supplements

The following supplementary materials are available to support instructors' use of the main text:

- Online Instructor's Manual with Test Bank
- PowerPoint presentations
- Classroom Response System PowerPoints
- MyTest computerized test bank
- Test Item File for Blackboard/Course Compass
- Test Item File for WebCT

To access these supplementary materials online, instructors need to request an instructor access code at **www.pearsonhighered.com/irc**. Within 48 hours after registering, you will receive a confirmation e-mail that includes an instructor access code. When you receive your code, go to the site and log on for full instructions on downloading materials you wish to use.

Alternative Book Versions

Alternatives to traditional printed textbooks, such as our "Student Value Editions" and e-book versions of the text in the "CourseSmart" platform, are available. CourseSmart is an exciting new choice for students looking to save money. As an alternative to purchasing the printed textbook, students can purchase an electronic version of the same content. With a CourseSmart eTextbook, students can search the text, make notes online, print out reading assignments that incorporate lecture notes, and bookmark important passages for later review. For more information, or to purchase access to the CourseSmart eTextbook, visit **www.coursesmart.com**

Frank Schmalleger, Ph.D.
Distinguished Professor Emeritus
The University of North Carolina at Pembroke
schmall@cjtoday.net

Acknowledgments

Many thanks go to all who assisted in many different ways in the development of this textbook. I am grateful to manuscript reviewers Jeanette Areia, Sierra College; Les Boggess, Fairmont State University; Robert Boyer, Luzerne County Community College; Jonathan Brook, Houston Community College; Carolyn S. D'Argenio, Mohawk Valley Community College; Carly Hilinski, Grand Valley State University; Robert Kettlitz, Hastings College; David J. MacDonald, Eastfield College; Kathy Oborn, Pierce College; Victor Ortloff, Troy University; Gregory Osowski, Henry Ford Community College; Morgan Peterson, Palomar College; Michael Pittaro, Council on Alcohol and Drug Abuse, Allentown, PA; Cathy Schuh, Bismarck State College; and Amy Thistlethwaite, Northern Kentucky University, for their helpful comments and valuable insights. I also appreciate the many valuable comments made by Kevin Barret, E. Elaine Bartgis, Bruce Bayley, John M. Boal, Michelle Brown, Jeffrey B. Bumgarner, Joan Luxenburg, Rick Michaelson, Carl E. Russell, Jim Smith, Kevin M. Thompson, and Richard A. Wilson. I thank Eric Krassow, Megan Heintz, Adam Kloza, JoEllen Gohr, Steve Robb, and Pat Tonneman at Prentice Hall, and project manager Janet Bolton. Thank you also to my daughter, Nicole, and her family, to whom this book is dedicated.

Frank Schmalleger, Ph.D.
Distinguished Professor Emeritus
The University of North Carolina at Pembroke

About the Author

Frank Schmalleger, Ph.D., is Distinguished Professor Emeritus at the University of North Carolina at Pembroke, where he taught criminal justice courses for 20 years and chaired the university's Department of Sociology, Social Work, and Criminal Justice for 16 of those years. In 1991 the university awarded him the title of Distinguished Professor, and the university named him Professor Emeritus in 2001.

Dr. Schmalleger holds degrees from the University of Notre Dame and Ohio State University, having earned both a master's (1970) and a doctorate in sociology (1974) with a special emphasis in criminology from Ohio State University.

As an adjunct professor with Webster University in St. Louis, Missouri, Schmalleger helped develop the university's graduate program in security administration and loss prevention. He taught courses in that curriculum for more than a decade. Schmalleger has also taught in the online graduate program of the New School for Social Research, helping to build the world's first electronic classrooms in support of distance learning through computer telecommunications. An avid Web user, Schmalleger is the creator of a number of award-winning websites including one that supports this textbook.

Frank Schmalleger is the author of numerous articles and many books, including the widely used *Criminal Justice Today* (Prentice Hall, 2011); *Criminology Today* (Prentice Hall, 2012); *Criminal Law Today* (Prentice Hall, 2011); and *The Definitive Guide to Criminal Justice and Criminology on the World Wide Web* (Prentice Hall, 2009).

Schmalleger is also founding editor of the journal *Criminal Justice Studies*. He has served as editor for the Prentice Hall series *Criminal Justice in the Twenty-first Century* and as imprint adviser for Greenwood Publishing Group's criminal justice reference series.

Schmalleger's philosophy of both teaching and writing can be summed up in these words: "In order to communicate knowledge, we must first catch, then hold, a person's interest—be it student, colleague, or policymaker. Our writing, our speaking, and our teaching must be relevant to the problems facing people today, and they must in some way help solve those problems."

"Justice is truth in action!"

—Benjamin Disraeli

"Injustice anywhere is a threat to justice everywhere."

—Martin Luther King, Jr.

Criminal Justice

What Is Criminal Justice?

CHAPTER 1

Learning Objectives

After reading this chapter, you should be able to:

1. Provide a brief history of crime in America. 3
2. Identify the theme on which this textbook builds, and highlight the differences between the individual-rights and public-order perspectives. 5
3. Explain the relationship of criminal justice to fundamental notions of fairness and to other wider notions of equity and morality. 7
4. Explain the structure of the American criminal justice system in terms of its major components and the functions they serve. 8
5. Describe the stages typical of American criminal justice case processing. 11
6. Explain the meaning of due process of law, and identify where due process guarantees can be found in the American legal system. 11
7. Explain evidence-based practice, and describe the role of evidence-based research in contemporary criminal justice. 14
8. Explain how multiculturalism and diversity present special challenges to, and opportunities for, the American system of criminal justice. 15

"The rights guaranteed to criminal suspects . . . are fundamental political rights that protect all Americans from governmental abuse of power."

—American Civil Liberties Union[1]

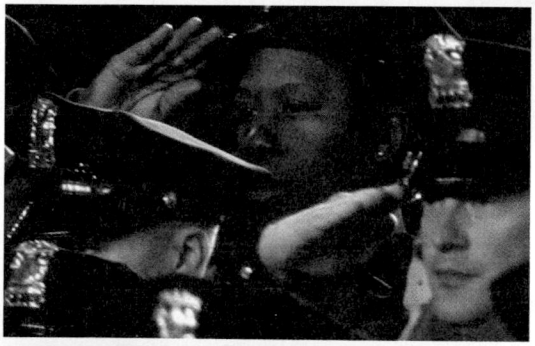

"The Constitution is not a suicide pact."

—Former Secretary of State Warren Christopher, after terrorists destroyed the World Trade Center in New York City in 2001[2]

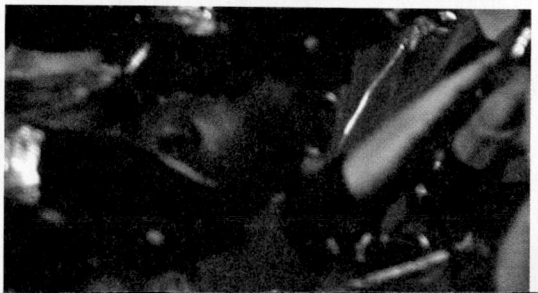

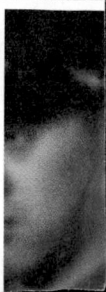

Introduction

Five days after Hurricane Katrina made landfall near New Orleans in 2005, the *Washington Post* described the devastated metropolitan area as "a city of despair and lawlessness."[3] The *Wall Street Journal* ran headlines proclaiming that the city had "plunged into anarchy."[4] As the winds relented, looters ravaged stores, gunshots rang out, and armed gangs could be seen roaming the streets that hadn't been flooded. Some looters used forklifts and construction equipment to bust through storm shutters and steel doors protecting gun shops, liquor stores, and pharmacies.[5] The New Orleans Police Department, hamstrung by the absence of one-third of its 1,600 officers and the loss of critical communications channels and emergency equipment, struggled to keep control over its facilities. In one unflooded precinct, officers used an armored personnel carrier to survey the chaos.[6] Officers from another precinct were forced to barricade themselves in their three-story administrative center, renaming it Fort Apache after a film in which a police station is attacked. "You have to understand," said Juan Lopez, one of the officers who took refuge in the precinct house, "New Orleans was a violent place before the hurricane. After the hurricane, the city just let loose."[7]

> You're looking now not only at a rescue operation but [at] a gigantic crime scene.
>
> —ABC newscaster, on the World Trade Center site a few days after the 9/11 attacks[1]

The storm set into motion a number of events that are still sending shock waves throughout American society. The physical damage done by the hurricane, estimated at billions of dollars, was made worse by the massive social disorder that followed. Thousands of displaced people left their homes—with many never expected to return. Law enforcement and assistance agencies throughout the region suffered serious disruptions in their ability to provide services. Some officers walked off the job, and citizens were left to fend for themselves until thousands of National Guard troops armed with automatic weapons arrived to restore order in the wind- and flood-ravaged area.

The Katrina disaster, which created opportunities for those bent on criminal activity, illustrated the tenuous nature of social order. The social disorganization that followed Katrina continued long after the storm and involved a myriad of criminal offenses—including thousands of people arrested for defrauding the Federal Emergency Management Agency (FEMA), the government agency responsible for helping out after a disaster. FEMA fraud was so widespread that reports showed the number of households receiving FEMA emergency checks in four Louisiana parishes exceeded the number of households that existed there before the storm hit.[8] Almost 360,000 households applied for FEMA's Expedited Assistance payments in Orleans Parish alone—although the area had only 182,000 homes before Katrina. In one case that drew the attention of federal prosecutors, 33-year-old Kenneth McClain was charged with 14 counts of fraud in an elaborate conspiracy that allegedly scammed more than $10,000 in federal relief checks. McClain, who had 27 aliases and a number of open arrest warrants when caught, lived in Texas, far from the storm's wrath. He is accused of using stolen identities, some belonging to dead people, to file for assistance and then waiting in a Texas motel room for the aid checks to arrive.[9]

▲ New Orleans business owner Bob Rue standing in front of his rug store in the aftermath of Hurricane Katrina. His hastily created sign warns potential looters to stay away. Some say that the central purpose of the criminal justice system is the maintenance of social order. Others say that the justice system must respect the rights of those it processes. Are the two perspectives mutually exclusive?
Charlie Riedel/AP Wide World Photos

A very different kind of criminal event thrust itself on American society and our justice system with the September 11, 2001, terrorist attacks that targeted New York City's World Trade Center and the Pentagon. Those attacks, including one on an airliner that crashed in the Pennsylvania countryside, left nearly 3,000 people dead and caused billions of dollars in property damage. They have since been classified as the most destructive criminal activity ever perpetrated on U.S. soil. The resulting "war on terrorism" changed the face of world politics and ushered in a new era in American society. Before the attacks, most Americans lived relatively secure lives, largely unfettered by fear of random personal attack. Following September 11, however, a heated debate has taken place between those wanting to enforce powerful crime-prevention and security measures and others seeking to preserve the individual rights and freedoms that have long been characteristic of American life. This issue, which has continued to feed TV talk shows and newspaper editorials nationwide, asks Americans to determine which rights, freedoms, and conveniences (if any) they are willing to sacrifice to increase personal and

◀ An artist's rendition of the New York City skyline as it will look once buildings envisioned by renowned architect Daniel Libeskind are constructed on the 16-acre World Trade Center site. The plan includes a soaring Freedom Tower that will stand 1,776 feet tall, several other towers, and a memorial to the nearly 3,000 people who were killed in the terrorist attacks that demolished the twin towers in 2001. How did those attacks change the American justice system?
Skidmore, Owings & Merrill LLP/Getty Images—GINS/Entertainment News & Sports

crime
Conduct in violation of the criminal laws of a state, the federal government, or a local jurisdiction, for which there is no legally acceptable justification or excuse.[ii]

individual rights
The rights guaranteed to all members of American society by the U.S. Constitution (especially those rights found in the first ten amendments to the Constitution, known as the *Bill of Rights*). These rights are particularly important to criminal defendants facing formal processing by the criminal justice system.

public safety. It also anticipates the theme on which this book is based—and which is discussed at length later in this chapter.

Regardless of your personal position in the ongoing debate between freedom and safety, it is important to recognize that terrorism is a potentially horrendous **crime**. Many states and the federal government have statutes outlawing terrorism, although terrorism itself can involve many other kinds of crimes. In the case of the September 11 attacks, for example, the crimes committed included murder, kidnapping, hijacking, grand theft, felonious assault, battery, conspiracy, and arson.

A Brief History of Crime in America

What we call *criminal activity* has undoubtedly been with us since the dawn of history, and crime control has long been a primary concern of politicians and government leaders worldwide. Still, the American experience with crime during the last half century has been especially influential in shaping the criminal justice system of today (Figure 1–1). In this country, crime waves have come and gone, including an 1850–1880 crime epidemic that was apparently related to social upheaval caused by large-scale immigration and the Civil War.[10] A spurt of widespread organized criminal activity was associated with the Prohibition years of the early twentieth century. Following World War II, however, American crime rates remained relatively stable until the 1960s.

1 Provide a brief history of crime in America.

The 1960s and 1970s saw a burgeoning concern for the rights of ethnic and racial minorities, women, people with physical and mental challenges, and many other groups. The civil rights movement of the period emphasized equality of opportunity and respect for individuals, regardless of race, color, creed, gender, or personal attributes. As new laws were passed and suits filed, court involvement in the movement grew. Soon a plethora of hard-won individual rights and prerogatives, based on the U.S. Constitution, the Bill of Rights, and new federal and state legislation, were recognized and guaranteed. By the 1980s, the civil rights movement had profoundly affected all areas of social life—from education and employment to the activities of the criminal justice system.

This emphasis on **individual rights** was accompanied by a dramatic increase in reported criminal activity. While some researchers doubted the accuracy of official accounts, reports by the Federal Bureau of Investigation (FBI) of "traditional" crimes like murder, rape, and assault increased considerably during the 1970s and into the 1980s. Many theories were advanced to explain this leap in observed criminality. Some analysts of American culture, for example, suggested that the combination of newfound freedoms and long-pent-up hostilities

FIGURE 1–1
Milestones in Crime History

1850–1880 A crime epidemic spurred by social upheaval brought on by large-scale immigration and the Civil War.

1920–1933 Prohibition spurs the growth of organized crime.

Following World War II, American crime rates remained relatively stable until the 1960s.

1960–1970 The civil rights movement of the period emphasized equality of opportunity and respect for individuals regardless of race, color, creed, gender, or personal attributes. This period also saw a dramatic increase in reported criminal activity.

1970s Reports of crimes such as murder, rape, and assault increased considerably.

1980s By the mid-1980s the dramatic increase in sale and use of illicit drugs led to increased crime. Large cities became havens for drug gangs and cities experienced dramatic declines in property values and quality of life. President Reagan declared a "war on drugs."

1992 The videotaped beating of Rodney King, an African American, by Los Angeles-area police officers was seen as an example of the abuse of police power.

By the late **1990s** the public perception was that crime rates were growing and that many offenders went unpunished. This led to a growing emphasis on responsibility and punishment and the development of a "get tough on crime" era.

2001 A series of terrorist attacks on New York City, Washington, D.C., and elsewhere changed the focus of law enforcement to a proactive and more global approach.

2001 **USA PATRIOT Act** dramatically increases the investigatory authority of federal, state, and local police agencies.

The incidence of personal crime declined throughout the 1990s.

2009 Bernard Madoff plead guilty to the largest Ponzi scheme in history. The crimes of Madoff, and widespread suspicions about the activities of Wall Street financiers, led to a number of white-collar crime investigations. White-collar crime came into focus as a serious threat to the American way of life.

Photo sources (from top): Courtesy of the Library of Congress; Everett Collection/Sarryl Jacobson/ Superstock; SuperStock Inc.; and Steven Hirsch/Splash News/ NewsCom

Thematic Question Do you identify more with what the book calls the individual-rights perspective or the public-order perspective? What experiences have you had that might explain your affinity for that perspective?

Class Activity Have students collect clippings and stories from newspapers, magazines, and the Web and do a short report or presentation noting which criminal justice–related topics (such as individual rights, social control, policing, terrorism, and violent crime) receive the most coverage. A useful website for criminal justice–specific current events is http://thecrimereport.org.

Thematic Question What are the relative merits of the individual-rights perspective, and what are the merits of the public-order point of view? How can the goals of both perspectives be balanced in contemporary society?

of the socially and economically deprived worked to produce social disorganization, which in turn increased criminality.

By the mid-1980s, the dramatic increase in the sale and use of illicit drugs threatened the foundation of American society. Cocaine, and later laboratory-processed "crack," spread to every corner of America. Large cities became havens for drug gangs, and many inner-city areas were all but abandoned to highly armed and well-financed drug racketeers. Cities experienced dramatic declines in property values, and residents wrestled with an eroding quality of life.

A decade later, a few spectacular crimes that received widespread coverage in the news media fostered a sense among the American public that crime in the United States was out of hand and that strict new measures were needed to combat it. One such crime was the 1995 bombing of the Alfred P. Murrah Federal Building in Oklahoma City by antigovernment extremists. Another was the 1999 Columbine High School massacre in Colorado that left 12 students and one teacher dead.[11]

The public's perception that crime rates were growing, coupled with a belief that offenders frequently went unpunished or received only a judicial slap on the wrist, led to a burgeoning emphasis on responsibility and punishment. By the late 1990s, a newfound emphasis on individual accountability began to blossom among an American public fed up with crime and fearful of its own victimization. Growing calls for enhanced responsibility quickly began to replace the previous emphasis on individual rights. As a juggernaut of conservative opinion made itself felt on the political scene, Senator Phil Gramm of Texas observed that the public wants to "grab violent criminals by the throat, put them in prison [and] stop building prisons like Holiday Inns."[12]

Then, in an event that changed the course of our society, public tragedy became forever joined with private victimization in our collective consciousness after a series of highly destructive and well-coordinated terrorist attacks on New York City and Washington, D.C., on September 11, 2001. Those attacks resulted in the collapse and total destruction of the twin 110-story towers of the World Trade Center and a devastating explosion at the Pentagon. Thousands of people perished, and many were injured. Although law enforcement and security agencies were unable to prevent the September 11 attacks, many have since moved from a reactive to a proactive posture in the fight against terrorism—a change that is discussed in more detail in Chapter 6.

The September 11 attacks also made clear that adequate law enforcement involves a global effort at controlling crime and reducing the risk of injury and loss to law-abiding people both at home and abroad. The attacks showed that criminal incidents that take place on the other side of the globe can impact those of us living in the United States, and they illustrated how the acquisition of skills needed to understand diverse cultures can help in the fight against crime and terrorism. As Chapter 2 points out, terrorism is a criminal act, and preventing terrorism and investigating terrorist incidents after they occur are highly important roles for local, state, and federal law enforcement agencies.

A different kind of offending, corporate and white-collar crime, took center stage in 2002 and 2003 as Congress stiffened penalties for unscrupulous business executives who knowingly falsify their company's financial reports.[13] The changes came amidst declining stock market values, shaken investor confidence, and threats to the viability of employee pension plans in the wake of a corporate crime wave involving criminal activities that had been planned and undertaken by executives at a number of leading corporations. In an effort to restore order to American financial markets, President George W. Bush signed the Sarbanes-Oxley Act on July 30, 2002.[14] The law, which has been called "the single most important piece of legislation affecting corporate governance, financial disclosure and the practice of public accounting since the US securities laws of the early 1930s,"[15] is intended to deter corporate fraud and to hold business executives accountable for their actions.

Today, white-collar crime continues to be a focus of federal prosecutors, and in 2009 investment fund manager Bernard Madoff pleaded guilty to operating a Ponzi scheme that defrauded investors out of as much as $50 billion.[16] Madoff pleaded guilty to 11 felony counts, including securities fraud, mail fraud, wire fraud, money laundering, and perjury. On June 29, 2009, Madoff was sentenced to serve 150 years in federal prison—three times as long as federal probation officers had recommended.[17] White-collar crime is discussed in more detail in Chapter 2.

For a detailed look at crimes that have shaped the past hundred years, see **Web Extra 1–1**. **Library Extra 1–1** also describes the changing nature of crime in America.

The Theme of This Book

This book examines the American system of criminal justice and the agencies and processes that constitute it. It builds on a theme that is especially valuable for studying criminal justice today: *individual rights versus public order.* This theme draws on historical developments that have shaped our legal system and our understandings of crime and justice. It is one of the primary determinants of the nature of contemporary criminal justice—including criminal law, police practice, sentencing, and corrections.

2 Identify the theme on which this textbook builds, and highlight the differences between the individual-rights and public-order perspectives.

▲ Ponzi schemer Bernard Madoff being escorted by police and photographed by the media as he leaves U.S. Federal Court in New York after a hearing. Madoff, whose financial crimes may have cost investors as much as $50 billion, was sentenced to 150 years in prison in 2009. Should corporate criminals be treated differently from other offenders?
Lucas Jackson/Reuters/Landov Media

A strong emphasis on individual rights rose to the forefront of American social thought during the 1960s and 1970s, a period known as the *civil rights era.* The civil rights era led to the recognition of fundamental personal rights that had previously been denied illegally to many people on the basis of race, ethnicity, gender, sexual preference, or disability. The civil rights movement soon expanded to include the rights of many other groups, including criminal suspects, parolees and probationers, trial participants, prison and jail inmates, and victims. As the emphasis on civil rights grew, new laws and court decisions broadened the rights available to many.

The treatment of criminal suspects was afforded special attention by those who argued that the purpose of any civilized society should be to secure rights and freedoms for each of its citizens—including those suspected and convicted of crimes. Rights advocates feared unnecessarily restrictive government action and viewed it as an assault on basic human dignity and individual liberty. They believed that at times it was necessary to sacrifice some degree of public safety and predictability to guarantee basic freedoms. Hence criminal rights activists demanded a justice system that limits police powers and that holds justice agencies accountable to the highest procedural standards.

During the 1960s and 1970s, the dominant philosophy in American criminal justice focused on guaranteeing the rights of criminal defendants while seeking to understand the root causes of crime and violence. The past 25 years, however, have witnessed increased interest in an ordered society, in public safety, and in the rights of crime victims. This change in attitudes was likely brought about by national frustration with the perceived inability of our society and its justice system to prevent crimes and to consistently hold offenders to heartfelt standards of right and wrong. Increased conservatism in the public-policy arena was given new life by the September 11, 2001, terrorist attacks and by widely publicized instances of sexual offenses targeting children. It continues to be sustained by the many stories of violent victimization that seem to be the current mainstay of the American media.

> We must not defeat our liberties in trying to defend them.
> —Anthony Lake, former national security adviser[ii]

Today, public perspectives have largely shifted away from seeing the criminal as an unfortunate victim of poor social and personal circumstances who is inherently protected by fundamental human and constitutional rights to seeing him or her as a dangerous social predator who usurps the rights and privileges of law-abiding citizens. Reflecting the "get tough on crime" attitudes of today, many Americans demand to know how offenders can better be held accountable for violating the criminal law. In late 2010, for example, California state senators unanimously passed Chelsea's Law, a bill intended to increase prison sentences and extend parole terms for offenders who commit sex crimes against minors. The bill is named after 17-year-old Chelsea King who was raped and murdered by a convicted sex offender earlier in 2010.[18] The legislation is expected to be signed into law shortly after this book goes to press. Even in an era of difficult budgetary challenges, a number of states, like California, are continuing to extend prison sentences for sex offenders, restrict where released sex offenders can live, and improve public notification of their whereabouts.[19]

As state budgets constrict, the tension between individual rights and social responsibility still forms the basis for most policy-making activity in the criminal justice arena.

Class Activity Poll students to determine their identification with either the individual-rights perspective or the public-order perspective. After polling is complete, assign students to presentation groups by asking those who more closely identify with the public-order perspective to defend individual rights, and vice versa. Such role reversal can be interesting in its own right, but it may also serve to broaden students' appreciation for the values of others.

Thematic Question Do you see a trend in our society in favor of individual rights or public-order interests? What recent examples support your opinion?

Freedom or Safety? You Decide.

Giuliani Says: "Freedom Is about Authority"

In 2009, U.S. Supreme Court Justice Clarence Thomas spoke to a group of high school essay contest winners in a Washington, D.C., hotel ballroom. Thomas used the occasion, which was dedicated to our nation's Bill of Rights, to point out the importance of obligations as well as rights. "Today there is much focus on our rights," said Thomas. "Indeed, I think there is a proliferation of rights." But then he went on to say, "I am often surprised by the virtual nobility that seems to be accorded those with grievances. Shouldn't there at least be equal time for our Bill of Obligations and our Bill of Responsibilities?"

The challenge for the criminal justice system today, it seems, is to balance individual rights and personal freedoms with social control and respect for legitimate authority. Years ago, during the height of what was then a powerful movement to win back control of our nation's cities and to rein in skyrocketing crime rates, the *New York Post* sponsored a conference on crime and civil rights. The keynote speaker at that conference was the mayor of New York, Rudolph W. Giuliani. In his speech, Giuliani, who sought the Republican nomination as a presidential candidate in 2008, identified the tension between personal freedoms and individual responsibilities as the crux of the crime problem then facing his city and the nation. We mistakenly look to government and elected officials, Giuliani said, to assume responsibility for solving the problem of crime when, instead, each individual citizen must become accountable for fixing what is wrong with our society. "We only see the oppressive side of authority. . . . What we don't see is that freedom is not a concept in which people can do anything they want, be anything they can be. Freedom is about authority. Freedom is about the willingness of every single human being to cede to lawful authority a great deal of discretion about what you do."

YOU DECIDE

How can we, as suggested by Justice Thomas, achieve a balance of rights and obligations in American society? What did Giuliani mean when he said, "What we don't see is that freedom is not a concept in which people can do anything they want, be anything they can be"? Is it possible to balance individual rights and personal freedoms with social control and respect for legitimate authority?

References: Adam Liptak, "Reticent Justice Opens Up to a Group of Students," *New York Times*, April 13, 2009, http://www.nytimes.com/2009/04/14/us/14bar.html (accessed June 2, 2010); and Philip Taylor, "Civil Libertarians: Giuliani's Efforts Threaten First Amendment," Freedom Forum Online, http://www.freedomforum.org.

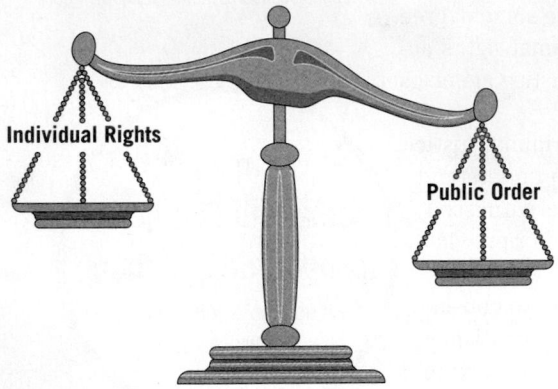

FIGURE 1–2
The Theme of This Book
Balancing the concern for individual rights with the need for public order through the administration of criminal justice is the theme of this book.

Those who fight for individual rights continue to carry the banner of civil and criminal rights for the accused and the convicted, while public-order activists proclaim the rights of the victimized and call for an increased emphasis on social responsibility and criminal punishment for convicted criminals. In keeping with these realizations, the theme of this book can be stated as follows:

> There is widespread recognition in contemporary society of the need to balance (1) the freedoms and privileges of our nation's citizens and the respect accorded the rights of individuals faced with criminal prosecution against (2) the valid interests that society has in preventing future crimes, in maintaining public safety, and in reducing the harm caused by criminal activity. While the personal freedoms guaranteed to law-abiding citizens as well as to criminal suspects by the Constitution, as interpreted by the U.S. Supreme Court, must be closely guarded, the urgent social needs of communities for controlling unacceptable behavior and protecting law-abiding citizens from harm must be recognized. Still to be adequately addressed are the needs and interests of victims and the fear of crime and personal victimization often prevalent in the minds of many law-abiding citizens.

individual-rights advocate
One who seeks to protect personal freedoms within the process of criminal justice.

public-order advocate
One who believes that under certain circumstances involving a criminal threat to public safety, the interests of society should take precedence over individual rights.

Figure 1–2 represents our theme and shows that most people today who intelligently consider the criminal justice system assume one of two viewpoints. We will refer to those who seek to protect personal freedoms and civil rights within society, and especially within the criminal justice process, as **individual-rights advocates**. Those who suggest that, under certain circumstances involving criminal threats to public safety, the interests of society (especially crime control and social order) should take precedence over individual rights will be called **public-order advocates**. Recently, retired U.S. Supreme Court Justice Sandra Day O'Connor summed up the differences between these two perspectives by asking, "At what point does the cost to civil liberties from legislation designed to prevent terrorism [and crime] outweigh the added security that that legislation provides?"[20] In this book, we seek to look at ways in which the individual-rights and public-order perspectives can be balanced to serve both sets of needs. Hence you will find our theme discussed throughout this text and within "Freedom or Safety?" boxes.

◀ Michael Jackson fans gathering outside the courthouse where Jackson's physician, Conrad Murray, appeared on February 8, 2010. What does the word *justice* mean to you?
AP Photo/Jason Redmond

Criminal Justice and Basic Fairness

On Election Day in November 2008, as the final votes were being counted, President-Elect Barack H. Obama gave an inspiring victory speech addressed to the nation and the world. He said, "To all those who have wondered if America's beacon still burns as bright—tonight we proved once more that the true strength of our nation comes not from the might of our arms or the scale of our wealth, but from the enduring power of our ideals: democracy, liberty, opportunity, and unyielding hope." The president-elect concluded that night's remarks with an enduring phrase, telling listeners that "the arc of the moral universe is long, but it bends toward justice." The phrase, a favorite of Obama's, was adapted from remarks that Martin Luther King, Jr., made before the Southern Christian Leadership Conference in 1967.[21]

3 Explain the relationship of criminal justice to fundamental notions of fairness and to other wider notions of equity and morality.

There is no denying that the word *justice* is powerful, and—at the time—the president's choice of words spoke to all Americans. The reality, however, is that *justice* is an elusive term. Although most listeners came away inspired that night, few who heard the president's speech knew exactly what justice might mean and what form it might eventually take. Even to those living within the same society, *justice* means different things. And just as *justice* can be an ambiguous term for politicians, it is not always clear how justice can be achieved in the criminal justice system. For example, is "justice for all" a reasonable expectation of today's—or tomorrow's—system of criminal justice? The answer is unclear because individual interests and social needs often diverge. From the perspective of a society or an entire nation, justice can look very different than it does from the perspective of an individual or a small group of people. Because of this dilemma, we now turn our attention to the nature of justice.

British philosopher and statesman Benjamin Disraeli (1804–1881) defined **justice** as "truth in action." A popular dictionary defines it as "the principle of moral rightness, or conformity to truth."[22] **Social justice** is a concept that embraces all aspects of civilized life. It is linked to notions of fairness and to cultural beliefs about right and wrong. Questions of social justice can arise about relationships between individuals, between parties (such as corporations and agencies of government), between the rich and the poor, between the sexes, between ethnic groups and minorities—between social connections of all sorts. In the abstract, the concept of social justice embodies the highest personal and cultural ideals.

Civil justice, one component of social justice, concerns itself with fairness in relationships between citizens, government agencies, and businesses in private matters, such as those involving contractual obligations, business dealings, hiring, and equality of treatment. **Criminal justice**, on the other hand, refers to the aspects of social justice that concern violations of the criminal law. As mentioned earlier, community interests in the criminal justice sphere demand the apprehension and punishment of law violators. At the same time, criminal justice ideals extend to the protection of the innocent, the fair treatment of offenders, and fair play by the agencies of law enforcement, including courts and correctional institutions.

Lecture Note Explain that criminal justice is the study of how social justice is achieved in criminal courts. Contrast formal criminal justice case processing with alternatives, such as vigilante justice and kangaroo courts. Consider other ways of achieving justice, and examine the meaning of *justice* itself.

> The arc of the moral universe is long, but it bends towards justice.
>
> —Martin Luther King, Jr. (1929–1968)

justice
The principle of fairness; the ideal of moral equity.

social justice
An ideal that embraces all aspects of civilized life and that is linked to fundamental notions of fairness and to cultural beliefs about right and wrong.

civil justice
The civil law, the law of civil procedure, and the array of procedures and activities having to do with private rights and remedies sought by civil action. Civil justice cannot be separated from social justice because the justice enacted in our nation's civil courts reflects basic American understandings of right and wrong.

criminal justice
In the strictest sense, the criminal (penal) law, the law of criminal procedure, and the array of procedures and activities having to do with the enforcement of this body of law. Criminal justice cannot be separated from social justice because the justice enacted in our nation's criminal courts reflects basic American understandings of right and wrong.

administration of justice
The performance of any of the following activities: detection, apprehension, detention, pretrial release, post-trial release, prosecution, adjudication, correctional supervision, or rehabilitation of accused persons or criminal offenders.[iv]

Class Activity Ask representatives from community criminal justice agencies to visit your class, either in person or virtually through computer conferencing. Create a master schedule for speakers, linking it to the topics covered in the class syllabus and in the textbook.

Lecture Note Describe the two models applicable to the study of criminal justice: the consensus model and the conflict model.

Lecture Note Explain that the consensus model of criminal justice envisions the components of the criminal justice system as functioning together to achieve the goal of justice.

Lecture Note Explain that the conflict model of criminal justice envisions the components of the criminal justice system as serving their own interests and competing with one another over scarce resources, public recognition, and various other forms of accomplishment.

Thematic Question Which model, to your mind, best describes the American system of criminal justice: the consensus model or the conflict model? Why?

Criminal justice, ideally speaking, is "truth in action" within the process that we call the **administration of justice**. It is therefore vital to remember that justice, in the truest and most satisfying sense of the word, is the ultimate goal of criminal justice—and of the day-to-day practices and challenges that characterize the American criminal justice system. Reality, unfortunately, typically falls short of the ideal and is severely complicated by the fact that justice seems to wear different guises when viewed from diverse vantage points. To some people, the criminal justice system and criminal justice agencies often seem biased in favor of the powerful. The laws they enforce seem to emanate more from well-financed, organized, and vocal interest groups than they do from any idealized sense of social justice. As a consequence, disenfranchised groups, those who do not feel as though they share in the political and economic power of society, are often wary of the agencies of justice, seeing them more as enemies than as benefactors.

On the other hand, justice practitioners, including police officers, prosecutors, judges, and corrections officials, frequently complain that their efforts to uphold the law garner unfair public criticism. The realities of law enforcement and of "doing justice," they say, are often overlooked by critics of the system who have little experience in dealing with offenders and victims. We must recognize, practitioners often tell us, that those accused of violating the criminal law face an elaborate process built around numerous legislative, administrative, and organizational concerns. Viewed realistically, although the criminal justice process can be fine-tuned to take into consideration the interests of ever-larger numbers of people, it rarely pleases everyone. The outcome of the criminal justice process in any particular case is a social product, and like any product that is the result of group effort, it must inevitably be a patchwork quilt of human emotions, reasoning, and concerns.

Whichever side we choose in the ongoing debate over the nature and quality of criminal justice in America, it is vital that we recognize the plethora of pragmatic issues involved in the administration of justice while also keeping a clear focus on the justice ideal.[23] Was justice done, for example, in the 2005 criminal trial of pop music superstar Michael Jackson on charges of child molestation or in the 1995 murder trial of former football great O. J. Simpson? After Jackson's death, was the investigation of his personal physician, Conrad Murray, just? Has justice been served in the case of Casey Anthony, whom authorities say killed her young daughter (the case is discussed in more detail in Chapter 8)? Similarly, we might ask whether justice was done in the arrest and lengthy detention of hundreds of Muslims after September 11, 2001—even though most were later released when no evidence could be found linking them to any crime?[24] While answers to such questions may reveal a great deal about the American criminal justice system, they also have much to say about the perspectives of those who provide them.

criminal justice system
The aggregate of all operating and administrative or technical support agencies that perform criminal justice functions. The basic divisions of the operational aspects of criminal justice are law enforcement, courts, and corrections.

consensus model
A criminal justice perspective that assumes that the system's components work together harmoniously to achieve the social product we call *justice*.

If we do not maintain Justice, Justice will not maintain us.

—Francis Bacon (1561-1626)

American Criminal Justice: System and Functions

The Consensus Model

4 Explain the structure of the American criminal justice system in terms of its major components and the functions they serve.

We have been discussing a **criminal justice system**[25] consisting of the component agencies of police, courts, and corrections. Each of these components can, in turn, be described in terms of its functions and purpose (Figure 1–3).

The systems perspective on criminal justice is characterized primarily by its assumption that the various parts of the justice system work together by design to achieve the wider purpose we have been calling *justice*. Hence the systems perspective on criminal justice generally encompasses a point of view called the **consensus model**. The consensus model assumes that each of the component parts of the criminal justice system strives toward a common goal and that the movement of cases and people through the system is smooth due to cooperation between the various components of the system.

The systems model of criminal justice is more an analytic tool than a reality, however. An analytic model, whether in the hard sciences or in the social sciences, is simply a convention chosen for its explanatory power. By explaining the actions of criminal justice officials—such as arrest, prosecution, and sentencing—as though they were systematically related, we are able to envision a fairly smooth and predictable process.

The systems model has been criticized for implying a greater level of organization and cooperation among the various agencies of justice than actually exists. The word *system*

CJ News
Atlanta Seeks to Add 500 Surveillance Cameras

Atlanta's other reality show is taping today outside CNN Center, at Woodruff Park and in Midtown.

What you might call Real Pedestrians of Atlanta is a rather modest video surveillance: a few dozen cameras monitoring select locations in the city every second. But the city has applied for millions in federal stimulus funds so it can train about 500 more cameras on city streets. . . .

City officials are seeking $13.7 million in federal cash amid a series of high-profile crimes in recent months: a champion boxer shot dead in the street, a City Council member carjacked at gunpoint, a rash of armed robberies near Georgia Tech.

The system Atlanta plans to use could store images for up to 30 days and support software that reads license plate numbers and detects gunshots. Critics say the system conjures up images from George Orwell's "1984," a novel about a totalitarian state presided over by an all-seeing Big Brother. . . .

"It's kind of creepy," said Marc Rotenberg, executive director of the Washington-based Electronic Privacy Information Center. "Mass surveillance is essentially directed toward everyone, so it doesn't matter if you are someone planning a crime or if you are a resident or tourist or someone who is walking into an office building to go to work. Everyone gets swept into these big databases."

City police, however, point to the spread of such cameras across the country and around the world. Community improvement districts already operate dozens across downtown and Midtown Atlanta. . . .

"Times have changed," said Maj. Khirus Williams, commander [of] the city's downtown police zone. "We are no longer in the 1950s. The good of a camera certainly outweighs 'Is Big Brother watching me?' . . ."

POPULAR ELSEWHERE

Other cities have already installed thousands of these cameras. Baltimore has 480 and Chicago has 2,000, according to the Washington-based Urban Institute, which is studying their impact on crime.

Preliminary results from the study show crime has fallen in parts of both cities where the cameras are located. For example, violent crime and larcenies fell by 25 percent — or 30 incidents per month — in downtown Baltimore. . . .

The Urban Institute's study, meanwhile, has found the cameras are not without their problems. When they automatically pan areas, they may capture only portions of a sequence of events. At night and during bad weather, they might not capture images strong enough for evidence. They are sometimes targeted by vandals. And their maintenance costs can be high. Atlanta has estimated its annual personnel and maintenance cost at $3.2 million for its proposed network. . . .

▲ A Chicago police department surveillance camera system and microphone unit positioned high above the street. This surveillance system includes a camera, high-bandwidth wireless communication, a strobe light, and a gunshot-recognition system, all in a bulletproof enclosure. The city is installing the surveillance system to spot crimes or terrorist activity. Do such units infringe on the personal freedoms of city residents?
Safety Dynamics

"IT DOESN'T BOTHER ME"

. . . Just across the street from the CNN Center in downtown, where a sign declares "Area Under 24 Hours Video Surveillance," Cheryl Semands . . . wasn't troubled by the cameras perched around downtown.

"They do it in London all day long," she said of video surveillance. "It might bother the criminals. It doesn't bother me in the least bit to have security cameras. Of course, I'm not doing anything wrong."

A block away, Davis Petterson and his Zentropy band mates were packing up their instruments . . . in Centennial Olympic Park. Petterson said he would rather see the city hire more police officers instead of putting up cameras like the one that sat above him at Marietta Street and Andrew Young International Boulevard.

"It would get too Orwellian for me," the Little Five Points resident said of the city's plans to install hundreds of the cameras. "Cameras are weird."

Source: J. Redmon, "Atlanta Seeks to Add 500 Surveillance Cameras," *Atlanta Journal-Constitution*, www.ajc.com, © October 24, 2009 Cox Newspapers. All rights reserved. Used by permission and protected by the Copyright Laws of the United States. The printing, copying, redistribution, or retransmission of the Material without express written permission is prohibited.

calls to mind a near-perfect form of social organization. The modern mind associates the idea of a system with machine-like precision in which the problems of wasted effort, redundancy, and conflicting actions are quickly corrected. In practice, the justice system has nowhere near this level of perfection, and the systems model is admittedly an oversimplification. Conflicts among and within agencies are rife; individual actors within the system often do not share immediate goals; and the system may move in different directions depending on political currents, informal arrangements, and personal discretion.

conflict model
A criminal justice perspective that assumes that the system's components function primarily to serve their own interests. According to this theoretical framework, justice is more a product of conflicts among agencies within the system than it is the result of cooperation among component agencies.

The Conflict Model

The **conflict model** provides another approach to the study of American criminal justice. The conflict model says that the interests of criminal justice agencies tend to make actors within the system self-serving. According to this model, the goals of individual agencies

FIGURE 1–3
The Core Components of the American Criminal Justice System and Their Functions

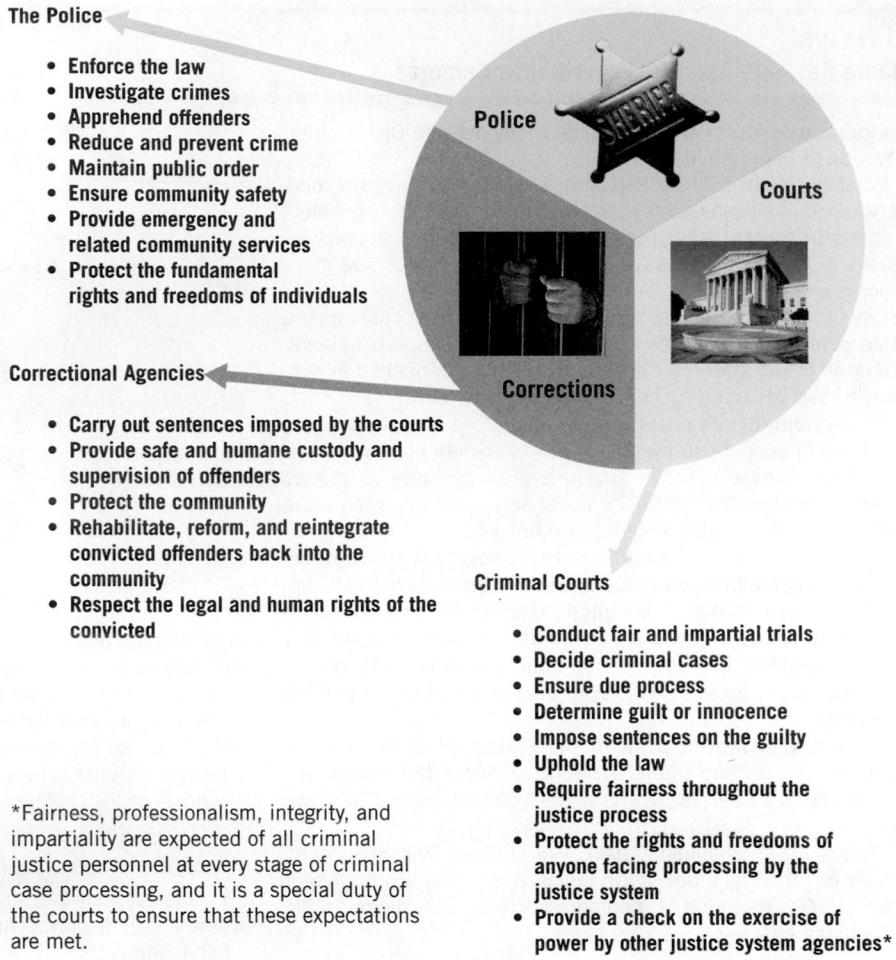

Lecture Note Explain the criminal justice system in terms of its components: the police, the courts, and corrections.

often conflict, and pressures for success, promotion, pay increases, and general accountability fragment the efforts of the system as a whole, leading to a criminal justice *non*system.[26]

A classic study of clearance rates by criminologist Jerome H. Skolnick provides support for the idea of a criminal justice nonsystem.[27] Clearance rates are a measure of crimes solved by the police. The more crimes the police can show they have solved, the better they look to the public they serve. Skolnick discovered an instance in which a burglar was caught red-handed during the commission of a burglary. After his arrest, the police suggested that he confess to many unsolved burglaries that they knew he had not committed. In effect they said, "Help us out, and we will try to help you out." The burglar did confess—to more than 400 other burglaries. Following the confession, the police were satisfied because they could say they had "solved" many burglaries, and the suspect was pleased as well because the police and the prosecutor agreed to speak on his behalf before the judge.

> Justice cannot be for one side alone, but must be for both.
>
> —Eleanor Roosevelt (1884–1962)

Both models have something to tell us. Agencies of justice with a diversity of functions (police, courts, and corrections) and at all levels (federal, state, and local) are linked closely enough for the term *system* to be meaningfully applied to them. On the other hand, the very size of the criminal justice undertaking makes effective cooperation between component agencies difficult. The police, for example, have an interest in seeing offenders put behind bars. Prison officials, on the other hand, are often working with extremely overcrowded facilities. They may favor early-release programs for certain categories of offenders, such as those judged to be nonviolent. Who wins out in the long run might just be a matter of internal politics and quasi-official wrangling. Everyone should be concerned,

FIGURE 1–4 The American Criminal Justice Process

Investigation ▶
After a crime has been discovered, evidence is gathered and follow-up investigations attempt to reconstruct the sequence of activities leading up to and including the criminal event. Efforts to identify suspects are initiated.

Warrant ▶
An arrest warrant issued by a judge provides the legal basis for an apprehension of suspects by police.

Arrest ▶
In an arrest, a person is taken into custody, limiting the arrestee's freedom. Arrest is a serious step in the process of justice. During arrest and before questioning, defendants are usually advised of their constitutional rights, or *Miranda* rights.

Booking ▶
Following arrest, suspects are booked. Booking is an administrative procedure where pictures, fingerprints, and personal information are obtained. A record of the events leading up to and including the arrest is created. In some jurisdictions, DNA evidence may be collected from arrestees.

however, when the goal of justice is affected, and sometimes even sacrificed, because of conflicts within the system.

American Criminal Justice: The Process

Whether part of a system or a nonsystem, the agencies of criminal justice must process the cases that come before them. An analysis of criminal justice case processing provides both a useful guide to this book and a "road map" to the criminal justice system itself. Figure 1–4 illustrates the processing of a criminal case through the federal justice system, beginning with the investigation of reported crimes. The process in most state systems is similar. See **Web Extra 1–2** for an expanded discussion of the process shown in the figure.

The stages illustrated in Figure 1–4 are discussed in detail at various places throughout this book. Chapter 5, "Policing: Legal Aspects," discusses investigation and arrest. All aspects of the first appearance and arraignment, including bail bonds and possible pretrial release, are discussed in Chapter 7, "The Courts." The criminal trial and its participants are described fully in Chapter 8, "The Courtroom Work Group and the Criminal Trial." Chapter 9, "Sentencing," outlines modern sentencing practices and describes the many modern alternatives to imprisonment. Chapter 10, "Probation, Parole, and Community Corrections," deals with the practice of probation and parole and with the issues surrounding it. Chapter 11, "Prisons and Jails," discusses the philosophy behind imprisonment, while Chapter 12, "Prison Life," portrays life on the inside and delineates the social structures that develop in response to the pains of imprisonment. Learn more about the criminal justice process at **Library Extra 1–2**. For a critical look at the justice system, visit **Web Extra 1–3**.

5 Describe the stages typical of American criminal justice case processing.

Due Process and Individual Rights

The U.S. Constitution requires that criminal justice case processing be conducted with fairness and equity; this requirement is referred to as **due process**, which, simply put, means procedural fairness.[28] It recognizes the individual rights of criminal defendants facing prosecution by a state or the federal government. Under the due process standard, rights violations may become the basis for the dismissal of evidence or of criminal charges, especially at the appellate level. Table 1–1 outlines the basic rights to which defendants in criminal proceedings are generally entitled.

6 Explain the meaning of due process of law, and identify where due process guarantees can be found in the American legal system.

Due process underlies the first ten amendments to the Constitution, which are collectively known as the *Bill of Rights*. It is specifically guaranteed by the Fifth, Sixth, and Fourteenth Amendments and is succinctly stated in the Fifth, which reads, "No person shall be . . . deprived of life, liberty, or property, without due process of law." The Fourteenth Amendment makes due process binding on the states, that is, it requires individual states to respect the due process rights of U.S. citizens who come under their jurisdiction.

due process
A right guaranteed by the Fifth, Sixth, and Fourteenth Amendments of the U.S. Constitution and generally understood, in legal contexts, to mean the due course of legal proceedings according to the rules and forms established for the protection of individual rights. In criminal proceedings, due process of law is generally understood to include the following basic elements: a law creating and defining the offense, an impartial tribunal having jurisdictional authority over the case, accusation in proper form, notice and opportunity to defend, trial according to established procedure, and discharge from all restraints or obligations unless convicted.

First Appearance ▶
Within hours of arrest suspects must be brought before a magistrate (a judicial officer) for an initial appearance. The judge will tell them of the charges against them, advise them of their rights, and may provide the opportunity for bail.

Preliminary Hearing ▶
The purpose of a preliminary hearing is to establish whether sufficient evidence exists against a person to continue the justice process. At the preliminary hearing, the hearing judge will seek to determine whether there is probable cause. The process provides the prosecutor with an opportunity to test the strength of the evidence.

Information or Indictment ▶
In some states the prosecutor may seek to continue the case against a defendant by filing an information with the court. Other states require an indictment be returned by a grand jury. The grand jury hears evidence presented by the prosecutor and decides whether the case should go to trial.

Arraignment ▶
At arraignment the accused stands before a judge and hears the information or indictment against him. Defendants are again notified of their rights and asked to enter a plea. Pleas include not guilty, guilty, and no contest. No contest may result in a conviction but cannot be used in trial as an admission of guilt.

TABLE 1–1
Individual Rights Guaranteed by the Bill of Rights[a]

A right to be assumed innocent until proven guilty
A right against unreasonable searches of person and place of residence
A right against arrest without probable cause
A right against unreasonable seizure of personal property
A right against self-incrimination
A right to fair questioning by the police
A right to protection from physical harm throughout the justice process
A right to an attorney
A right to trial by jury
A right to know the charges
A right to cross-examine prosecution witnesses
A right to speak and present witnesses
A right not to be tried twice for the same crime
A right against cruel or unusual punishment
A right to due process
A right to a speedy trial
A right against excessive bail
A right against excessive fines
A right to be treated the same as others, regardless of race, sex, religious preference, and other personal attributes

[a]As interpreted by the U.S. Supreme Court.

The courts, and specifically the U.S. Supreme Court, have interpreted and clarified the guarantees of the Bill of Rights. The due process standard was set in the 1960s by the Warren Court (1953–1969), following a number of far-reaching Supreme Court decisions that affected criminal procedure. Led by Chief Justice Earl Warren, the Warren Court is remembered for its concern with protecting the innocent against the massive power of the state in criminal proceedings.[29] As a result of its tireless efforts to institutionalize the Bill of Rights, the daily practice of modern American criminal justice is now set squarely upon the due process standard.

The Role of the Courts in Defining Rights

Although the Constitution deals with many issues, what we have been calling *rights* are open to interpretation. Many modern rights, although written into the Constitution, would not exist in practice were it not for the fact that the U.S. Supreme Court decided, at some point in history, to recognize them in cases brought before it. In the well-known case of *Gideon* v. *Wainwright* (1963),[30] for example, the Supreme Court embraced the Sixth Amendment guarantee of a right to a lawyer for all criminal defendants and mandated that states provide lawyers for defendants who are unable to pay for them. Before *Gideon*, court-appointed attorneys for defendants unable to afford their own counsel were practically unknown, except in capital cases and in some federal courts. After the *Gideon* decision, court-appointed counsel became commonplace, and measures were instituted in jurisdictions across the nation to select attorneys fairly for indigent defendants. It is important to note, however, that while the Sixth Amendment specifically says, among other things, that "in all criminal prosecutions, the accused shall enjoy the right . . . to have the Assistance of Counsel for his defence," it does not say, in so many words, that the state is *required* to provide counsel. It is the U.S. Supreme Court interpreting the Constitution that has said that.

Thematic Question What is due process? Why is due process such a central notion in American criminal justice? What would our justice system be like without due process? Would you want to live in a society that did not guarantee due process rights?

The U.S. Supreme Court is very powerful, and its decisions often have far-reaching consequences. The decisions rendered by the justices in cases like *Gideon* become, in effect,

Adjudication ▶

A criminal trial may be held, or the defendant may decide to enter a guilty plea. A criminal trial involves an adversarial process that pits the prosecution against the defense. In most trials, a jury hears the evidence and decides issues of guilt or innocence, while the judge ensures the fairness of the proceedings.

Sentencing ▶

After the person has been convicted it is up to the judge to determine the punishment. Prior to sentencing, a sentencing hearing is sometimes held in which attorneys for both sides can present information to influence the judge's decision.

Corrections ▶

The corrections period begins following sentencing. Corrections involves a variety of sentences that can be imposed on a defendant.

Probation and Parole

Not everyone who has been convicted of a crime goes to prison. Probation imposes requirements or restrictions upon offenders. Offenders are required to check in with a probation officer on a regular basis.

After the defendant has served a portion of his prison term he may be freed on parole. Like probation, parole may come with obligations and requires the offender to check in with a parole officer.

Photo sources (from left): Dave King © Dorling Kindersley; Gibson/Shutterstock; and Marc Dietrich/Shutterstock

the law of the land. For all practical purposes, such decisions often carry as much weight as legislative action. For this reason, we speak of "judge-made law" (rather than legislated law) in describing judicial precedents that affect the process of justice.

Rights that have been recognized by court decisions are subject to continual refinement, and although the process of change is usually very slow, new interpretations may broaden or narrow the scope of applicability accorded to constitutional guarantees.

▲ A criminal defendant at a preliminary hearing. Everyone facing criminal prosecution in the United States is guaranteed a constitutional right to due process, meaning that defendants must be afforded a fair opportunity to participate in every stage of criminal proceedings. Should due process rights extend to all offenders—even accused terrorists? *AP Wide World Photos*

The Ultimate Goal: Crime Control through Due Process

Two primary goals were identified in our discussion of this book's theme: (1) the need to enforce the law and to maintain public order and (2) the need to protect individuals from injustice, especially at the hands of the criminal justice system. The first of these principles values the efficient arrest and conviction of criminal offenders. It is often referred to as the **crime-control model** of justice. The crime-control model was first brought to the attention of the academic community in Stanford University law professor Herbert Packer's cogent analysis of the state of criminal justice in the late 1960s.[31] For that reason, it is sometimes referred to as *Packer's crime-control model*.

> Liberty is the perfection of civil society, but still authority must be acknowledged essential to its very existence.
>
> —David Hume (1711–1776)

The second principle is called the **due process model** because of its emphasis on individual rights. Due process is intended to ensure that innocent people are not convicted of crimes; it is a fundamental part of American criminal justice. It requires a careful and informed consideration of the facts of each individual case. Under the due process model, police are required to recognize the rights of suspects during arrest, questioning, and handling. Similarly, prosecutors and judges must recognize constitutional and other guarantees during trial and the presentation of evidence.

The dual goals of crime control and due process are often assumed to be opposing goals. Indeed, some critics of American criminal justice argue that the practice of justice is too often concerned with crime control at the expense of due process. Other analysts of the American scene maintain that our type of justice coddles offenders and does too little to protect the innocent. While it is impossible to avoid ideological conflicts like these, we can think of the American system of justice as representative of *crime control through due process*—that is, as a system of **social control** that is fair to those whom it processes. This model of *law enforcement infused with the recognition of individual rights* provides a workable conceptual framework for understanding the American system of criminal justice.

crime-control model
A criminal justice perspective that emphasizes the efficient arrest and conviction of criminal offenders.

due process model
A criminal justice perspective that emphasizes individual rights at all stages of justice system processing.

social control
The use of sanctions and rewards within a group to influence and shape the behavior of individual members of that group. Social control is a primary concern of social groups and communities, and it is their interest in the exercise of social control that leads to the creation of both criminal and civil statutes.

Evidence-Based Practice in Criminal Justice

In June 2010, Assistant Attorney General Laurie O. Robinson announced a new initiative at the Office of Justice Programs (OJP), an arm of the U.S. Department of Justice that funds implementation of state-of-the-art practices in criminal justice agencies across the country.[32] The initiative, which Robinson said was intended to help "criminal and juvenile justice professionals expand their base of scientific knowledge and transform research into practice," is known as the Evidence Integration Initiative (E2I). E2I is an ongoing OJP-wide effort to integrate science and research throughout the agency and the work it sponsors. "Most importantly," Robinson said, "we are working to move evidence into practice by funding evidence-based programs."

7 Explain evidence-based practice, and describe the role of evidence-based research in contemporary criminal justice.

evidence-based practice
Crime-fighting strategies that have been scientifically tested and are based on social science research.

As the word is used here, *evidence* does not refer to evidence of a crime but means, instead, findings that are supported by studies. Hence, **evidence-based practice** refers to crime-fighting strategies that have been scientifically tested and are based on social science research. Scientific research has become a major element in the increasing professionalization of criminal justice, both as a career field and as a field of study. As Robinson recognized, there is a strong call today within criminal justice policy-making circles for the application of evidence-based practices throughout the justice field.

▲ U.S. Senator Jim Webb, cosponsor of the National Criminal Justice Commission Act of 2010. What is the goal of the proposed legislation?
© Stefan Zaklin/zefa/CORBIS. All Rights Reserved.

In an initiative that strongly supports evidence-based practice, the National Criminal Justice Commission Act of 2010[33] passed the House of Representatives in July 2010 on a voice vote, and legislators were working to reconcile it with a Senate version of the bill. The goal of the proposed legislation is to create a blue-ribbon commission charged with conducting an 18-month top-to-bottom review of the nation's entire criminal justice system. In the words of the proposed legislation, the commission would "institute the use of policies and practices proven effective throughout the spectrum of criminal behavior." As Chapter 4 of this text points out, evidence-based practices can be expected to play an expanded role in policy making and in the administration of criminal justice in the years to come.

The Start of Academic Criminal Justice

The study of criminal justice as an academic discipline began in this country in the late 1920s, when August Vollmer (1876–1955), the former police chief of the Los Angeles Police Department (LAPD), persuaded the University of California to offer courses on the subject.[34] Vollmer was joined by his former student Orlando W. Wilson (1900–1972) and by William H. Parker (who later served as chief of the LAPD from 1950 to 1966) in calling for increased professionalism in police work through better training.[35] Largely as a result of Vollmer's influence, early criminal justice education was practice oriented; it was a kind of extension of on-the-job training for working practitioners. Hence, in the early days of the discipline, criminal justice students were primarily focused on the application of general management principles to the administration of police agencies. Criminal justice came to be seen as a practical field of study concerned largely with issues of organizational effectiveness.

criminology
The scientific study of the causes and prevention of crime and the rehabilitation and punishment of offenders.

By the 1960s, however, police training came to be augmented by criminal justice education[36] as students of criminal justice began to apply the techniques of social scientific research—many of them borrowed from sister disciplines like **criminology**, sociology, psychology, and political science—to the study of all aspects of the justice system. Scientific research into the operation of the criminal justice system was encouraged by the 1967 President's Commission on Law Enforcement and Administration of Justice, which influenced passage of the Safe Streets and Crime Control Act of 1968. The Safe Streets Act led to the creation of the National Institute of Law Enforcement and Criminal Justice, which later became the National Institute of Justice (NIJ). As a central part of its mission, NIJ continues to support research in the criminal justice field through substantial funding for scientific explorations into all aspects of the discipline, and it funnels much of the

$3 billion spent annually by the U.S. Department of Justice to local communities to help fight crime. Now, almost 100 years after its beginnings as a field of study, criminal justice is being revitalized by an evidence-based approach to its subject matter. Assistant Attorney General Robinson puts it this way: "Justice professionals have been collecting, analyzing, and using evidence for centuries—in laboratories and courtrooms. As financial realities demand more innovative approaches, social science research is forming the basis for new programs in areas ranging from reentry to victim services. Evidence has found a new home: in the field."[37]

Multiculturalism and Diversity in Criminal Justice

In 2007, polygamist Warren Steed Jeffs, a leader of the Fundamentalist Church of Jesus Christ of Latter Day Saints (FLDS), an offshoot of the mainstream Mormon church, was convicted of conspiring to rape a child and of being an accessory to child rape for performing a marriage involving a 14-year-old girl and her 19-year-old cousin. Jeffs, who was on the FBI's Ten Most Wanted list, was sentenced on November 20, 2007, to two consecutive sentences of five years to life in prison.[38]

8 Explain how multiculturalism and diversity present special challenges to, and opportunities for, the American system of criminal justice.

The Church of Jesus Christ of Latter-day Saints brought plural marriage to Utah in the early nineteenth century, but the state legislature banned the practice more than 100 years ago. Today, the church officially excommunicates polygamists, although the FLDS practices polygamy as a central tenet. Some estimate the number of polygamists living in Utah and Arizona today at over 30,000.[39] The existence of such alternative family lifestyles is just one indicator that the United States is a multicultural and diverse society.

Class Activity Create a class CJ blog to which members of the class can contribute throughout the term. Students could post their thoughts on topics under class discussion, showcase their opinions about critical criminal justice matters, and let others know what the study of criminal justice entails.

> Without security, government cannot deliver, nor can the people enjoy, the prosperity and opportunities that flow from freedom and democracy.
>
> —Alberto Gonzales, former U.S. attorney general[v]

Multiculturalism describes a society that is home to a multitude of different cultures, each with its own set of norms, values, and routine behaviors. While American society today is truly a multicultural society, composed of a wide variety of racial and ethnic heritages, diverse religions, incongruous values, disparate traditions, and distinct languages, multiculturalism in America is not new. For thousands of years before Europeans arrived in the Western Hemisphere, tribal nations of Native Americans each spoke their own language, were bound to customs that differed significantly from one another, and practiced a wide range of religions. European immigration, which began in earnest in the seventeenth century, led to greater diversity still. Successive waves of immigrants, along with the slave trade of the early and mid-nineteenth century,[40] brought a diversity of values, beliefs, and patterns of behavior to American shores that frequently conflicted with prevailing cultures. Differences in languages and traditions fed the American melting pot of the late nineteenth and early twentieth centuries and made effective communication between groups difficult.

multiculturalism
The existence within one society of diverse groups that maintain unique cultural identities while frequently accepting and participating in the larger society's legal and political systems.[vi] *Multiculturalism* is often used in conjunction with the term *diversity* to identify many distinctions of social significance.

The face of multiculturalism in America today is quite different than it was in the past, due largely to relatively high birthrates among some minority populations and the huge but relatively recent immigration of Spanish-speaking people from Mexico, Cuba, Central America, and South America. Part of that influx consists of substantial numbers of undocumented immigrants who have entered the country illegally and who, because of experiences in their home countries, may have a special fear of police authority and a general distrust for the law. Such fears make members of this group hesitant to report being victimized, and their undocumented status makes them easy prey for illegal scams like extortion, blackmail, and documentation crimes. Learn more about immigration and crime via **Library Extra 1–3**.

Diversity characterizes both immigrant and U.S.-born individuals. Census Bureau statistics show that people identifying themselves as white account for 71% of the U.S.

▶ A group of immigrants taking the pledge of allegiance during a naturalization ceremony at the Miami Beach Convention Center in Florida. American society is multicultural, composed of a wide variety of racial and ethnic heritages, diverse religions, incongruous values, disparate traditions, and distinct languages. What impact does the multicultural nature of our society have on the justice system?
Jeff Greenberg/PhotoEdit Inc.

Lecture Note Explain that multiculturalism is often linked to the concept of social diversity and that multiculturalism and diversity emphasize the importance of the impact of multigroup differences on the criminal justice system.

Class Activity Create a website for your class. Post news of student activities in the criminal justice area, build a discussion area for current criminal justice topics, list links to other criminal justice websites, and perhaps post a brief biography of each student in the class.

population—a percentage that has been dropping steadily for at least the past 40 years. People of Hispanic origin constitute approximately 12% of the population and are the fastest-growing group in the country. Individuals identifying themselves as African American make up another 12% of the population, and people of Asian and Pacific Island origin make up almost 4% of the total. Native Americans, including American Indians, Eskimos, and Aleuts, account for slightly less than 1% of all Americans.[41] Statistics like these, however, are only estimates, and their interpretation is complicated by the fact that surveyed individuals may be of mixed race. Nonetheless, it is clear that American society today is ethnically and racially quite diverse.

Race and *ethnicity* are only buzzwords that people use when they talk about multiculturalism. After all, neither race nor ethnicity determines a person's values, attitudes, or behavior. Just as there is no uniquely identifiable "white culture" in American society, it is a mistake to think that all African Americans share the same values or that everyone of Hispanic descent honors the same traditions or even speaks Spanish.

Multiculturalism, as the term is used today, is but one form of diversity. Taken together, these two concepts—multiculturalism and diversity—encompass many distinctions of social significance. The broad brush of contemporary multiculturalism and social diversity draws attention to variety along racial, ethnic, subcultural, generational, faith, economic, and gender lines. Lifestyle diversity is also important. The fact that influential elements of the wider society are less accepting of some lifestyles than others doesn't mean that such lifestyles aren't recognized from the viewpoint of multiculturalism. It simply means that, at least for now, some lifestyles are accorded less official acceptability than others. As a result, certain lifestyle choices, even within a multicultural society that generally respects and encourages diversity, may still be criminalized, as in the case of polygamy.

Multiculturalism and diversity will be discussed in various chapters throughout this textbook. For now, it is sufficient to recognize that the diverse values, perspectives, and behaviors characteristic of various groups within our society have a significant impact on the justice system. Whether it is the confusion that arises from a police officer's commands to a non-English-speaking suspect, the need for interpreters in the courtroom, a deep-seated distrust of the police in some minority communities, a lack of willingness among some immigrants to report crime, the underrepresentation of women in criminal justice agencies, or some people's irrational suspicions of Arab Americans following the September 11 terrorist attacks, diversity and multiculturalism present special challenges to the everyday practice of criminal justice in America. Finally, as we shall see, the demands and expectations placed on justice agencies in multicultural societies involve a dilemma that is closely associated with the theme of this text: how to protect the rights of individuals to self-expression while ensuring social control and the safety and security of the public.

A PowerPoint presentation that supports this chapter is available from your Prentice Hall representative.

Summary

WHAT IS CRIMINAL JUSTICE?

- The American experience with crime during the last half century has been especially influential in shaping the criminal justice system of today. Although crime waves have come and gone, some events during the past century stand out as especially significant, including a spurt of widespread organized criminal activity associated with the Prohibition years of the early twentieth century, the substantial increase in "traditional" crimes during the 1960s and 1970s, the threat to the American way of life represented by illicit drugs around the same time, and the terrorist attacks of September 11, 2001.
- The theme of this book is one of individual rights versus public order. As this chapter points out, the personal freedoms guaranteed to law-abiding citizens as well as to criminal suspects by the Constitution must be closely guarded. At the same time, the urgent social needs of communities for controlling unacceptable behavior and protecting law-abiding citizens from harm must be recognized. This theme is represented by two opposing groups: individual-rights advocates and public-order advocates. The fundamental challenge facing the practice of American criminal justice is in efficiently enforcing the laws while simultaneously recognizing and supporting the legal rights of suspects and the legitimate personal differences and prerogatives of individuals.
- Although justice may be an elusive concept, it is important to recognize that criminal justice is tied closely to notions of social justice, including personal and cultural beliefs about equity and fairness. As a goal to be achieved, criminal justice refers to those aspects of social justice that concern violations of the criminal law. While community interests in the administration of criminal justice demand the apprehension and punishment of law violators, criminal justice ideals extend to the protection of the innocent, the fair treatment of offenders, and fair play by justice administration agencies.
- In this chapter, we described the process of American criminal justice as a system with three major components—police, courts, and corrections—all of which can be described as working together toward a common goal. We warned, however, that a systems viewpoint is useful primarily for the simplification that it provides. A more realistic approach to understanding criminal justice may be the nonsystem approach. As a nonsystem, the criminal justice process is depicted as a fragmented activity in which individuals and agencies within the process have interests and goals that at times coincide but often conflict.
- The stages of criminal case processing include investigation, the issuance of a warrant, arrest, booking, first appearance in court, defendant's preliminary hearing, return of an indictment by the grand jury or filing of an information by the prosecutor, arraignment of the defendant before the court, adjudication or trial, sentencing, and corrections. As a field of study, corrections includes jails, probation, imprisonment, and parole.
- The principle of due process, which underlies the first ten amendments to the U.S. Constitution, is central to American criminal justice. Due process (also called *due process of law*) means procedural fairness and requires that criminal case processing be conducted with fairness and equity. The ultimate goal of the criminal justice system in America is achieving crime control through due process.
- The study of criminal justice as an academic discipline began in this country in the late 1920s and is well established today. Scientific research has become a major element in the increasing professionalization of criminal justice, and there is a strong call today for the application of evidence-based practices in the justice field. Evidence-based practices are crime-fighting strategies that have been scientifically tested and that are based on social science research.
- America today is a multicultural society, composed of a wide variety of racial and ethnic heritages, diverse religions, incongruous values, disparate traditions, and distinct languages. Multiculturalism complicates the practice of American criminal justice since there is rarely universal agreement in our society about what is right or wrong or about what constitutes justice. As such, multiculturalism presents both challenges and opportunities for today's justice practitioners.

QUESTIONS FOR REVIEW

1. Describe the American experience with crime during the last half century. What noteworthy criminal incidents or activities occurred during that time, and what social and economic conditions might have produced them?
2. What is the theme of this book? According to that theme, what are the differences between the individual-rights perspective and the public-order perspective?
3. What is justice? What aspects of justice does this chapter discuss? How does criminal justice relate to wider notions of equity and fairness?
4. What are the main components of the criminal justice system? How do they interrelate? How might they conflict?
5. List the stages of case processing that characterize the American system of criminal justice.
6. What is meant by the term *due process of law*? Where in the American legal system are guarantees of due process found?
7. What is meant by the term *evidence-based practice*, and what is the role of research in criminal justice? How can research influence crime-control policy?
8. What is multiculturalism? What is social diversity? What impact do multiculturalism and diversity have on the practice of criminal justice in contemporary American society?

The Crime Picture

CHAPTER 2

Learning Objectives

After reading this chapter, you should be able to:

1. Describe the history and nature of the FBI's UCR/NIBRS Program, and explain what it can tell us about crime in the United States today. 21
2. Describe the history and nature of the National Crime Victimization Survey Program, and explain what it can tell us about crime in the United States today. 40
3. Point out significant differences between the UCR and the NCVS. 41
4. Identify the special categories of crime discussed in this chapter, and explain why they are of contemporary significance. 43

"No one way of describing crime describes it well enough."

—President's Commission on Law Enforcement and Administration of Justice

"It may turn out that a free society cannot really prevent crime. Perhaps . . . coping is the best that we can hope for."

—James Q. Wilson, Pepperdine University[1]

Introduction

In 2010, the CBS-TV megahit series *NCIS: Naval Criminal Investigative Service* was recognized by the Paley Center for Media in Los Angeles as the most popular scripted TV show in the world.[2] With more than 20 million dedicated viewers in the United States alone, the show has achieved heights that most other shows can't even dream of. Another immensely popular series on the same network, *CSI: Miami*, has more than 50 million regular viewers in 55 countries. The *CSI* franchise, which follows teams of crime-scene investigators, now includes shows featuring New York City and other locales, and it is available to a global audience of nearly 2 billion viewers in 200 countries.[3]

▲ A scene from the CBS-TV show *NCIS*. The American public has long been enthralled with crime shows, and since the terrorist attacks of 2001, the public's concern with personal safety has surged. Why do so many people like to watch crime shows? *CBS/Cliff Lipson/Landov*

The popularity of prime-time television crime shows is not limited to *NCIS* and *CSI*, as other widely followed series demonstrate: *Body of Proof, Castle*, and *Rookie Blue* on ABC; *Criminal Minds* on CBS; *The Good Guys* on Fox; *Law and Order* and its spin-offs on NBC; and *White Collar* on USA. Social commentators note that the plethora of crime shows bombarding the airwaves today reveals a penchant among American TV viewers for crime-related entertainment and a fascination with police work and the criminal justice system.

The public's interest in real-life stories of criminal victimization, revenge, and reformation has given birth to reality TV crime shows, including *America's Most Wanted* (which premiered on Fox in 1988) and *Cops* (also on Fox). Similarly, video magazine shows like *60 Minutes* (CBS), *20/20* (ABC), and *Nightline* (ABC) frequently focus on justice issues, and any number of movies play off the public's fascination with crime and the personal drama it fosters. Like this textbook, many of today's television shows deliver content across a variety of media. View the *CSI* show's website at **Web Extra 2–1**, or become a fan of *NCIS* on Facebook via **Web Extra 2–2**.

> We can have as much or as little crime as we please, depending on what we choose to count as criminal.
>
> —Herbert L. Packer (1925–1972)

This chapter has a dual purpose. First, it provides a statistical overview of crime in contemporary America by examining information on reported and discovered crimes. Second, it identifies special categories of crime that are of particular interest today, including crime against women, crime against the elderly, hate crime, corporate and white-collar crime, organized crime, gun crime, drug crime, cybercrime, and terrorism.

Lecture Note Explain how unsolicited reports from crime victims to law enforcement agencies (found in the crime reports produced by the UCR/NIBRS Program) can lead to a far different picture of crime in America than a random survey of self-reporters (as in the NCVS).

Although we will look at many crime statistics in this chapter, it is important to remember that statistical aggregates of reported crime, whatever their source, do not reveal the lost lives, human suffering, lessened productivity, and reduced quality of life that crime causes. Unlike the fictional characters on TV crime shows, real-life crime victims as well as real-life offenders lead intricate lives—they have families, hold jobs, and dream dreams. As we examine the crime statistics, we must not lose sight of the people behind the numbers.

Crime Data and Social Policy

Crime statistics provide an overview of criminal activity. If used properly, a statistical picture of crime can serve as a powerful tool for creating social policy. Decision makers at all levels, including legislators, other elected officials, and administrators throughout the criminal justice system, rely on crime data to analyze and evaluate existing programs, to fashion and design new crime-control initiatives, to develop funding requests, and to plan new laws and crime-control legislation. Many "get tough" policies, such as the three-strikes movement that swept the country during the 1990s, have been based in large part on the measured ineffectiveness of existing programs to reduce the incidence of repeat offending.

However, some people question just how objective—and therefore how useful—crime statistics are. Social events, including crime, are complex and difficult to quantify. Even the decision of which crimes should be included and which excluded in statistical reports is itself a judgment reflecting the interests and biases of policymakers. Moreover, public opinion about crime is not always realistic. As well-known criminologist Norval Morris points out, the news media do more to influence public perceptions of crime than any official data do.[4] During the four-year period (in the mid-1990s) covered by Morris's study, for example, the frequency of crime stories reported in the national media increased fourfold. During the same time period, crime was at the top of the list in subject matter covered in news stories at both the local and national levels. The irony, says Morris, is that "the grossly increasing preoccupation with crime stories came at a time of steadily declining crime and violence." However, as Morris adds, "aided and abetted by this flood of misinformation, the politicians, federal and state and local, fostered the view that the public demands our present 'get tough' policies."[5]

The Collection of Crime Data

Nationally, crime statistics come from two major sources: (1) the FBI's **Uniform Crime Reporting (UCR) Program** (also known today as the UCR/NIBRS Program), which produces an annual overview of major crime titled *Crime in the United States*; and (2) the **National Crime Victimization Survey (NCVS)** of the **Bureau of Justice Statistics (BJS)**. The most widely quoted numbers purporting to describe crime in America today probably come from the UCR/NIBRS Program, although the statistics it produces are based largely on *reports* to the police by victims of crime.

Uniform Crime Reporting (UCR) Program
A statistical reporting program run by the FBI's Criminal Justice Information Services (CJIS) division. The UCR Program publishes *Crime in the United States*, which provides an annual summation of the incidence and rate of reported crimes throughout the United States.

National Crime Victimization Survey (NCVS)
An annual survey of selected American households conducted by the Bureau of Justice Statistics to determine the extent of criminal victimization—especially unreported victimization—in the United States.

Bureau of Justice Statistics (BJS)
A U.S. Department of Justice agency responsible for the collection of criminal justice data, including the annual National Crime Victimization Survey.

Another important source of crime data is offender self-reports based on surveys that ask respondents to reveal any illegal activity in which they have been involved. Offender self-reports are not discussed in detail in this chapter because surveys utilizing them are not national in scope and are not undertaken regularly. Moreover, offenders are often reluctant to accurately report ongoing or recent criminal involvement, making information derived from these surveys somewhat unreliable and less than current. However, the available information from offender self-reports reveals that serious criminal activity is considerably more widespread than most "official" surveys show (Figure 2–1).

Other regular publications also contribute to our knowledge of crime patterns throughout the nation. One such publication is the *Sourcebook of Criminal Justice Statistics*—an annual compilation of national information on crime and on the criminal justice system. The *Sourcebook* is produced by the BJS, and a Web-based version of the *Sourcebook* is continually updated as data become available. The National Institute of Justice (NIJ), the primary research arm of the U.S. Department of Justice; the Office of Juvenile Justice and Delinquency Prevention (OJJDP); the Federal Justice Statistics Resource Center; and the National Victims Resource Center provide still more information on crime patterns. Visit **Web Extra 2–3** for an overview of the many sources of crime data. The *Sourcebook* is available directly at **Library Extra 2–1**.

The UCR/NIBRS Program

Development of the UCR Program

1 Describe the history and nature of the FBI's UCR/NIBRS Program, and explain what it can tell us about crime in the United States today.

In 1930, Congress authorized the U.S. attorney general to survey crime in America, and the Federal Bureau of Investigation (FBI) was designated to implement the program. In short order, the bureau built on earlier efforts by the International Association of Chiefs of Police (IACP) to create a national system of uniform crime statistics. As a practical measure, IACP had recommended the use of readily available information, and so it was that citizens' crime reports to the police became the basis of the FBI's plan.[6]

During its first year of operation, the FBI's UCR Program received reports from 400 cities in 43 states; 20 million people were covered by that first comprehensive survey. Today, approximately 18,000 law enforcement agencies provide crime information for the program, with data coming from city, county, university and college, tribal, and state departments. To ensure uniformity in reporting, the FBI has developed standardized definitions of offenses and terminologies used in the program. A number of publications, including the *Uniform Crime Reporting Handbook* and the *Manual of Law Enforcement Records*, are supplied to participating agencies, and training for effective reporting is available through FBI-sponsored seminars and instructional literature.

FIGURE 2–1
The Criminal Justice Funnel

Source: Derived from Thomas H. Cohen and Tracey Kyckelhahn, *Felony Defendants in Large Urban Counties, 2006* (Washington, DC: Bureau of Justice Statistics, 2010).

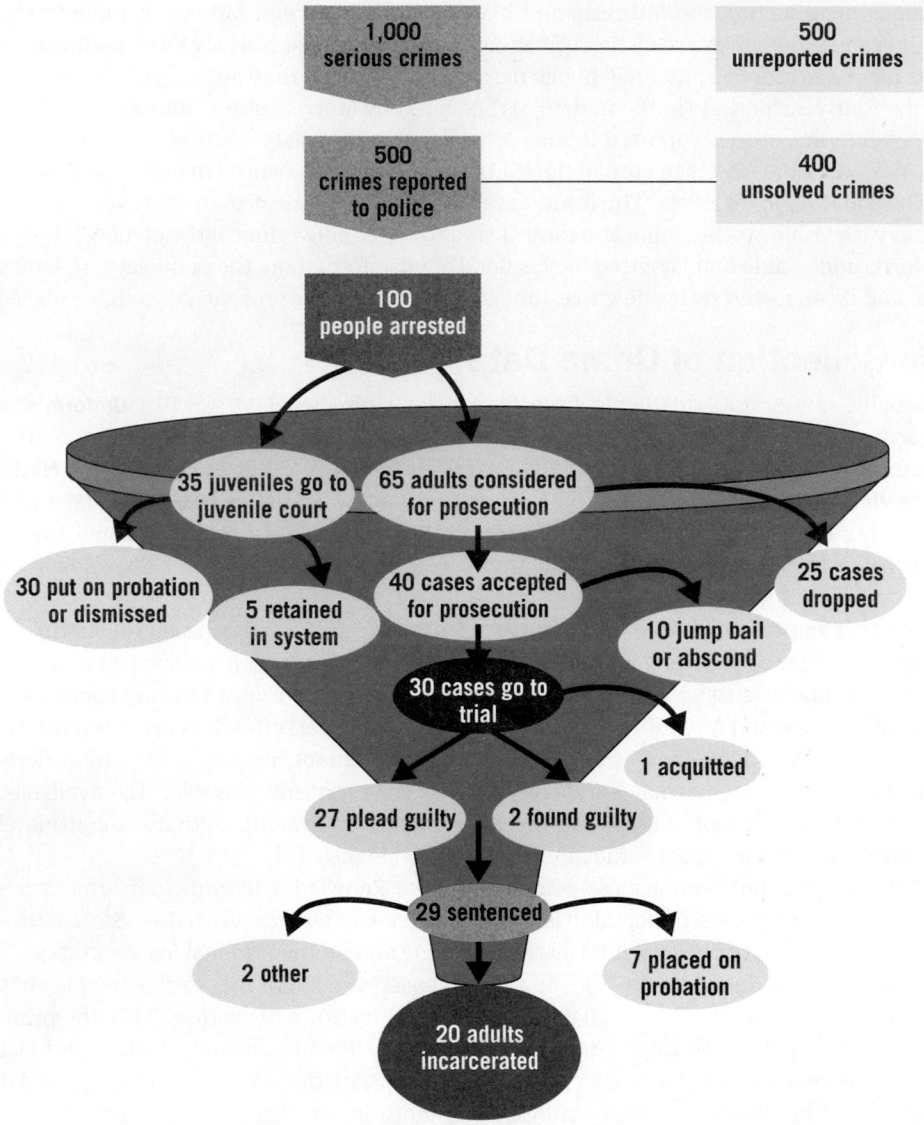

Crime Index
A now-defunct but once-inclusive measure of the UCR Program's violent and property crime categories, or what are called *Part I offenses*. The Crime Index, long featured in the FBI's publication *Crime in the United States*, was discontinued in 2004. The index had been intended as a tool for geographic (state-to-state) and historical (year-to-year) comparisons via the use of crime rates (the number of crimes per unit of population). However, criticism that the index was misleading arose after researchers found that the largest of the index's crime categories, larceny-theft, carried undue weight and led to an underappreciation of changes in the rates of more violent and serious crimes.

Following IACP recommendations, the original UCR Program was designed to permit comparisons over time through construction of a **Crime Index**, which was first published in *Crime in the United States* in 1960. The index summed the occurrences of seven major offenses—murder, forcible rape, robbery, aggravated assault, burglary, larceny-theft, and motor vehicle theft—and expressed the result as a crime rate based on population. In 1979, by congressional mandate, an eighth offense—arson—was added to the index. *Crime Index* was the title used for a simple aggregation of the seven main offense classifications (called Part I offenses).

Over the years, however, concern grew that the Crime Index did not provide a clear picture of criminality because it was skewed by the offense with the highest number of reports—typically larceny-theft. The sheer volume of larceny-theft offenses overshadowed more serious but less frequently committed offenses, skewing perceptions of crime rates for jurisdictions with high numbers of larceny-thefts but low numbers of serious crimes like murder and forcible rape. In June 2004, the FBI's Criminal Justice Information Services (CJIS) Advisory Policy Board officially discontinued the use of the Crime Index in the UCR/NIBRS Program and in its publications and directed the FBI to instead publish simple violent crime totals and property crime totals until a more viable index could be developed.[7]

Although work to develop such an index is still ongoing, UCR/NIBRS Program crime categories continue to provide useful comparisons of specific reported crimes over time and between jurisdictions. It is important to recognize, as you read through the next few pages, that today's UCR/NIBRS Program categories tend to parallel statutory definitions of criminal behavior, but they are not legal classifications—only conveniences created for statistical-reporting purposes. Because many of the definitions of crime used in this textbook are derived from official UCR/NIBRS Program terminology, these definitions may differ from statutory definitions of crime.

The National Incident-Based Reporting System

Beginning in 1988, the FBI's UCR Program initiated development of a new national crime-collection effort called the **National Incident-Based Reporting System (NIBRS)**. NIBRS represents a significant redesign of the original UCR Program. Whereas the original UCR system was summary based, the newly enhanced NIBRS is incident driven (Table 2–1). Under NIBRS, city, county, state, and federal law enforcement agencies throughout the country furnish detailed data on crime and arrest activities at the incident level either to the individual state incident-based reporting programs or directly to the federal NIBRS Program.

National Incident-Based Reporting System (NIBRS)
An incident-based reporting system that collects detailed data on every single crime occurrence. NIBRS data are replacing the kinds of summary data that have traditionally been provided by the FBI's Uniform Crime Reporting Program.

NIBRS is not a separate report; rather it is the new methodology underlying the contemporary UCR system—hence our use of the term *UCR/NIBRS* in describing today's Uniform Crime Reporting Program. Whereas the old UCR system depended on statistical tabulations of crime data, which were often little more than frequency counts, the new UCR/NIBRS system gathers many details about each criminal incident. Included among them is information on place of occurrence, weapon used, type and value of property damaged or stolen, personal characteristics of the offender and the victim, nature of any relationship between the two, and disposition of the complaint.

Under UCR/NIBRS, the traditional distinctions between Part I and Part II offenses are being replaced with 22 general offenses: arson, assault, bribery, burglary, counterfeiting, embezzlement, extortion, forcible sex offenses, fraud, gambling, homicide, kidnapping, larceny, motor vehicle theft, narcotics offenses, nonforcible sex offenses, pornography, prostitution, receiving stolen property, robbery, vandalism, and weapons violations. Other offenses on which UCR/NIBRS data are being gathered include bad checks, vagrancy, disorderly conduct, driving under the influence, drunkenness, nonviolent family offenses, liquor-law violations, Peeping Tom activity, runaways, trespassing, and a general category of all "other" criminal law violations. UCR/NIBRS also collects data on an expanded array of attributes involved in the commission of offenses, including whether the offender is suspected of using alcohol, drugs, or narcotics or may have used a computer in the commission of the offense.

Class Activity Find the latest national summary of campus crime. (*USA Today* periodically publishes a detailed report of such statistics, and data are also available on the Internet.) Have students compare crime on your campus with reports of campus crime elsewhere. What might account for the difference observed?

TABLE 2–1
Differences between Traditional UCR and Enhanced UCR/NIBRS Reporting

Traditional UCR	Enhanced UCR/NIBRS
Consists of monthly aggregate crime counts	Consists of individual incident records for the eight major crimes and 38 other offenses, with details on offense, victim, offender, and property involved
Records one offense per incident, as determined by the hierarchy rule, which suppresses counts of lesser offenses in multiple-offense incidents	Records each offense occurring in an incident
Does not distinguish between attempted and completed crimes	Distinguishes between attempted and completed crimes
Records rape of females only	Records rape of males and females
Collects assault information in five categories	Restructures definition of *assault*
Collects weapon information for murder, robbery, and aggravated assault	Collects weapon information for all violent offenses
Provides counts on arrests for the eight major crimes and 21 other offenses	Provides details on arrests for the eight major crimes and 49 other offenses

Source: Adapted from *Effects of NIBRS on Crime Statistics*, BJS Special Report (Washington, DC: Bureau of Justice Statistics, 2000), p. 1.

The FBI began accepting crime data in NIBRS format in January 1989. Although the bureau intended to have NIBRS fully in place by 1999, delays have been routine, and the NIBRS format has not yet been fully adopted.[8] Because it is a flexible system, changes continue to be made in the data gathered under UCR/NIBRS. In 2003, for example, three new data elements were added to the survey to collect information on law enforcement officers killed and assaulted. Another new data element has been added to indicate the involvement of gang members in reported offenses.

The goals of the innovations introduced under NIBRS are to enhance the quantity, quality, and timeliness of crime-data collection by law enforcement agencies and to improve the methodology used for compiling, analyzing, auditing, and publishing the collected data. A major advantage of UCR/NIBRS, beyond the sheer increase in the volume of data collected, is the ability that NIBRS provides to break down and combine crime offense data into specific information.[9]

In keeping with the FBI's interest in technological improvements and in order to make reports of crime data more widely available, in 2006 the FBI moved all UCR/NIBRS data reporting to the Internet and stopped paper production of its annual publication, *Crime in the United States*. Efforts to improve the usefulness of electronic versions continue. The latest edition of *Crime in the United States* can be viewed at **Library Extra 2–2**. To learn more about the effects of NIBRS innovations on crime statistics, including comparisons of traditional UCR summary data with the newer, more detailed UCR/NIBRS data, see **Web Extra 2–4**. Finally, the BJS provides an NIBRS information website, which can be accessed via **Web Extra 2–5**.

Other changes in crime reporting were brought about by the 1990 Crime Awareness and Campus Security Act, which requires colleges to publish annual security reports.[10] Most campuses share crime data with the FBI, increasing the reported national incidence of a variety of offenses. The U.S. Department of Education reported that 55 murders and 3,287 forcible sex offenses occurred on and around college campuses in 2008. Also reported were 4,562 robberies, 5,026 aggravated assaults, 31,851 burglaries, and 7,465 motor vehicle thefts.[11] Although these numbers may seem high, it is important to realize that except for the crimes of rape and sexual assault, college students experience violence at average annual rates that are lower than those for nonstudents in the same age group.[12] Rates of rape and sexual assault do not differ statistically between students and nonstudents. For the latest campus crime statistics, see **Web Extra 2–6**. **Library Extra 2–3** provides statistical information on the sexual victimization of college women.

Historical Trends

Most UCR/NIBRS information is reported as a rate of crime. Rates are computed as the number of crimes per some unit of population. National reports generally make use of large units of population, such as 100,000 people. Hence, the rate of rape reported by the UCR/NIBRS Program for 2009 was 28.3 forcible rapes per every 100,000 inhabitants of the United States.[13] Rates allow for a meaningful comparison over areas and across time. The rate of reported rape for 1960, for example, was only about 10 per 100,000. We expect the number of crimes to increase as population grows, but rate increases are cause for concern because they indicate that reports of crime are increasing faster than the population is growing. Rates, however, require interpretation. Since the definition of rape that the FBI uses in reporting statistics on that crime includes only female victims, the rate of victimization might be more meaningfully expressed in terms of every 100,000 female inhabitants (56.6 in 2009). Similarly, although there is a tendency to judge an individual's risk of victimization based on rates, such judgments tend to be inaccurate since they are based purely on averages and do not take into consideration individual life circumstances, such as place of residence, wealth, and educational level. While rates may tell us about aggregate conditions and trends, we must be very careful when applying them to individual cases.

Since the FBI's UCR Program began, there have been three major shifts in crime rates—and we now seem to be witnessing the beginning of a fourth. The first occurred during the early 1940s, when crime decreased sharply due to the large number of young men who entered military service during World War II. Young males make up the most crime-prone segment of the population, and their deployment overseas did much to lower crime rates at home. From 1933 to 1941, the Crime Index declined from 770 to 508 offenses per every 100,000 members of the American population.[14]

The second noteworthy shift in offense statistics was a dramatic increase in most forms of crime between 1960 and the early 1990s. Several factors contributed to the increase in reported crime during this period. One was also linked to World War II. With the end of the war and the return of millions of young men to civilian life, birthrates skyrocketed between 1945 and 1955, creating a postwar baby boom. By 1960, the first baby boomers were teenagers—and had entered a crime-prone age. This disproportionate number of young people produced a dramatic increase in most major crimes.

Other factors contributed to the increase in reported crime during the same period. Modified reporting requirements made it less stressful for victims to file police reports, and the publicity associated with the rise in crime sensitized victims to the importance of reporting. Crimes that might have gone undetected in the past began to figure more prominently in official statistics. Similarly, the growing professionalization of some police departments resulted in greater and more accurate data collection, making some of the most progressive departments appear to be associated with the largest crime increases.[15]

The 1960s were tumultuous years. The Vietnam War, a vibrant civil rights struggle, the heady growth of secularism, a dramatic increase in the divorce rate, diverse forms of "liberation," and the influx of psychedelic and other drugs all combined to fragment existing institutions. Social norms were blurred, and group control over individual behavior declined substantially. The "normless" quality of American society in the 1960s contributed greatly to the rise in crime.

From 1960 to 1980, crime rates rose from 1,887 to 5,950 offenses per every 100,000 U.S. residents. In the early 1980s, when postwar boomers began to age out of the crime-prone years and American society emerged from the cultural drift that had characterized the previous 20 years, crime rates leveled out briefly. Soon, however, an increase in drug-related criminal activity led crime rates—especially violent crime rates—to soar once again. Crime rates peaked during the early 1990s (Figure 2–2).

A third major shift came with a significant decline in the rates of most major crimes being reported between 1991 and 2009. During these years, the crime rate dropped from 5,897 to 3,466 offenses per every 100,000 residents—sending it down to levels not seen since 1975. The U.S. Department of Justice suggests various reasons for the decline:[16]

> Crime is like cutting grass. Just because you cut it down doesn't mean it's going to stay there.
>
> —Joseph R. Biden, Jr., vice president of the United States[i]

- A coordinated, collaborative, and well-funded national effort to combat crime, beginning with the Safe Streets Act of 1968 and continuing through the USA PATRIOT Act of 2001
- Stronger, better-prepared criminal justice agencies, resulting from increased spending by federal and state governments on crime-control programs
- The growth in popularity of innovative police programs, such as community policing (see Chapter 4)
- A strong victims' movement and enactment of the 1984 federal Victims of Crime Act (see Chapter 9) and the 1994 Violence against Women Act (discussed later in this chapter), which established the Office for Victims of Crime in the U.S. Department of Justice
- Sentencing reform, including various "get tough on crime" initiatives (see Chapter 9)
- A substantial growth in the use of incarceration (see Chapter 11) due to changes in sentencing law practice (see Chapter 9)
- The "war on drugs," begun in the 1970s,[17] which resulted in stiff penalties for drug dealers and repeat drug offenders
- Advances in forensic science and enforcement technology, including the increased use of real-time communications, the growth of the Internet, and the advent of DNA evidence (see Chapter 9)

More important than new strict laws, an expanded justice system and police funding, or changes in crime-fighting technologies, however, may have been influential economic and demographic factors that were largely beyond the control of policymakers but that combined to produce substantial decreases in rates of crime—including economic expansion

FIGURE 2–2
American Crime Rates: Historical Trends

1933–1959

From 1933 to 1941, the crime rate declined from 770 to 508 offenses per every 100,000 Americans.

In 1941 crime decreased sharply based on the large numbers of young men entering the military during WWII.
Young men make up the most crime-prone segment of the population, and their removal to European and Pacific theaters of war reduced the incidence of offending throughout the country.

1960–1989

From 1960 to 1980, crime rates rose from 1,887 to 5,950 offenses per every 100,000 Americans.

Starting around 1960, crime rates began to increase based on several factors.
The end of the war brought many young men home to the U.S., and birthrates skyrocketed in the years between 1945 and 1955. By 1960 these baby boomers had become teenagers and had entered a crime-prone age.
Also, reporting procedures were simplified and publicity surrounding crime increased the number of reports. Police agencies were becoming more professional, resulting in increased data and more accurate data collection.
Moreover, the 1960s were tumultuous years. The Vietnam War, civil rights struggles, and an influx of drugs combined to create an imbalance in society that led to an increase in crime.

1933 1937 1941 1945 1949 1963 1967 1960 1963 1967 1975 1979 1983 1987

and a significant shift in demographics caused by the aging of the population. During the 1990s, unemployment decreased by 36% in the United States while the number of people ages 20 to 34 declined by 18%. Hence, it may have been the ready availability of jobs combined with demographic shifts in the population—not the official efforts of policymakers—that produced a noteworthy decrease in crime during the 1990s. Read noted criminologist Alfred Blumstein's analysis of crime's decline in **Library Extra 2–4** to learn more about why crime rates fell during the 1990s.

A fourth shift in crime trends seems to be starting now. Some think that recent economic uncertainty, an increased jobless rate among unskilled workers, the growing number of ex-convicts who are back on the streets, the recent growth in the teenage population in this country, the increasing influence of gangs, copycat crimes, and the lingering social disorganization brought on by natural disasters like Hurricane Katrina in 2005 may lead to sustained increases in crime.[18] "We're probably done seeing declines in crime rates for some time to come," says Jack Riley, director of the Public Safety and Justice Program at RAND Corporation in Santa Monica, California. "The question," says Riley, "is how strong and how fast will those rates [rise], and what tools do we have at our disposal to get ahead of the curve."[19]

▲ Los Angeles emergency personnel working at the scene of an apparent gang-related shooting at Sunset Boulevard and Pacific Coast Highway. Some experts fear that violent crime may be starting to rise in big cities after two decades of decline. What would be the consequences for American cities if crime were to increase?
AP Photo/Andrew McKenzie

In 2006, in an effort to draw attention to spiking rates of violent crime in a number of major cities, the Police Executive Research Forum (PERF) released a report titled *A Gathering Storm: Violent Crime in America.*[20] PERF was concerned that official FBI data would take too long to gather and might be released too late to effectively combat the growing trend in violence that PERF felt it had identified. The information used as the basis for the 2006 PERF report had been compiled from law enforcement executives at a "violent crime summit" held at the Mayflower Hotel in Washington, D.C. PERF said that its data show that there are a number of cities across the country reporting large changes in the extent and nature of violent crime.

A second PERF report, this one titled *Violent Crime in America: 24 Months of Alarming Trends*, was released in 2007 and found even more reason for concern.[21] The report noted that urban violent crime increased significantly in 2006 and that "many cities experienced double-digit or even triple-digit percentage increases in homicides and other violence."

1990–2009 ▶ **2010–present**

From 1991 to 2009, crime rates dropped from 5,897 to 3,466 offenses per every 100,000 Americans.

Strict laws, an expanded justice system, and increased police funding for personnel and for crime-fighting technologies are cited as reasons for the drop in crime. Other changes beyond the control of the police may have played a role as well and include economic expansion and an aging population. During the 1990s, unemployment decreased by 36% and likely contributed to the decline in crime rates.

In recent years, some cities have experienced double-digit and sometimes triple-digit increases in homicides and other violent crimes.

A fourth shift in crime trends may be about to begin. Economic uncertainty, increased jobless rates, a growing number of ex-convicts back on the streets as well as an increase in teen populations and gang activity may soon lead to sustained increases in crime.

1990 1994 1997 2001 2005 2009 2010 2011 2012

Photo sources (from left): Everett Collection/SuperStock, Inc.; Everett Collecti

PERF authors said that the most recent crime statistics showed a worsening of a trend first identified by PERF in mid-2005, "when PERF began to hear rumblings from its members that 'violent crime is making a comeback.'"[22]

Finally, in 2008, the Third Way Culture Program, a Washington, D.C.–based nonpartisan strategy center, released a report with conclusions similar to those reached by PERF. Titled *The Impending Crime Wave*,[23] the Third Way report identified what it called "four dangerous new trends" that it sees leading to heightened rates of serious crime in the near future. Those four trends are described as follows: (1) "the reentry explosion" (seen as "a massive and unprecedented population of prisoners reentering society and returning to their often troubled neighborhoods"); (2) "the lengthening shadow of illegal immigration" (said to attract a new kind of opportunistic criminal who serves members of a shadow economy); (3) "the sprawling parentless neighborhood of the Internet" (which puts children at risk of sexual predation and other crimes); and (4) "the surging youth population" (seen as "a demographic surge that is responsible for a million new teenagers and young adults, who are statistically far more prone to commit crimes than the general population"). The entire Third Way report is available online as **Library Extra 2–5**.

Class Activity Ask students to research FBI crime statistics for their home states, counties, or cities for the past few years. Have students compare crime rates for each geographic area and discuss possible reasons for the variations in rates.

UCR/NIBRS in Transition

Reports of crime data available through the UCR/NIBRS Program are now going through a transitional phase as the FBI integrates more NIBRS-based data into its official summaries. The transition to NIBRS reporting is complicated by the fact that not only does NIBRS gather more kinds of data than the older summary UCR Program did but the definitions used for certain kinds of criminal activity under NIBRS are different than they were under the traditional UCR Program. The standard reference publication that the FBI designates for use by police departments in scoring and reporting crimes that occur within their jurisdiction is the *Uniform Crime Reporting Handbook*, and it is the most recent edition of that handbook that guides and informs the discussion of crime statistics that you will find in the next few pages. You can access the entire 164-page *Uniform Crime Reporting Handbook* at **Library Extra 2–6**. A thorough review of that document shows that much of the traditional UCR summary data-reporting terminology and structure remains in place. Learn more about the kinds of information recorded under NIBRS at **Library Extra 2–7**.

Lecture Note Research your state's crime-reporting program, and develop a PowerPoint presentation or other teaching materials showing the incidence of reported Part I offenses in your state during the past year.

Figure 2–3 shows the FBI crime clock, which has long been calculated annually as a shorthand way of diagramming crime frequency in the United States. Note that crime clock data

Freedom or Safety? You Decide.
A Dress Code for Bank Customers?

Dark glasses, a hooded sweatshirt, and a hat have been called the "uniform of choice" for bank robbers. In an effort to thwart an increase in robberies, some banks have begun posting requests for customers to remove hats, hoods, and sunglasses before entering financial establishments. In 2009, for example, Houston-area banks began putting up signs requiring that customers remove even their cowboy hats—a request that some saw as going too far. Since Sterling Bank, with 60 branches across Texas, asked customers to follow such rules, none of its branches has been robbed. Graham Painter, a Sterling Bank spokesman, said, "We don't want our regular customers thinking that we're telling them how they ought to dress. But . . . it seems reasonable and not too much to ask to give us an advantage over the robber."

Not all banks, however, are following the trend. "I think what you have to weigh is convenience to customers versus the added benefits in terms of identifying suspects with a measure like this," said Melodie Jackson, spokeswoman for Citizens Bank of Massachusetts. "We're taking a very close look at things."

Nonetheless, dress code signs are becoming commonplace at banks throughout the country, and it is likely that this request will soon become the *de facto* standard at banking and other financial venues.

YOU DECIDE

Are bank "dress codes" asking too much of customers? How would you feel about doing business with a bank that posts requests like those described here?

References: Cindy Horswell, "Some Banks Strike Hats, Sunglasses from Dress Code," *Houston Chronicle*, April 23, 2009; Michael S. Rosenwald and Emily Ramshaw, "Banks Post Dress Code to Deter Robbers," *Boston Globe*, July 13, 2002; and "Missouri Banks Attempt Unmasking Robbers," *Police Magazine* Online, http://www.policemag.com/t_newspick.cfm?rank571952 (accessed October 25, 2009).

FIGURE 2–3
The FBI Crime Clock

Source: Adapted from Federal Bureau of Investigation, *Crime in the United States, 2009* (Washington, DC: U.S. Department of Justice, 2010).

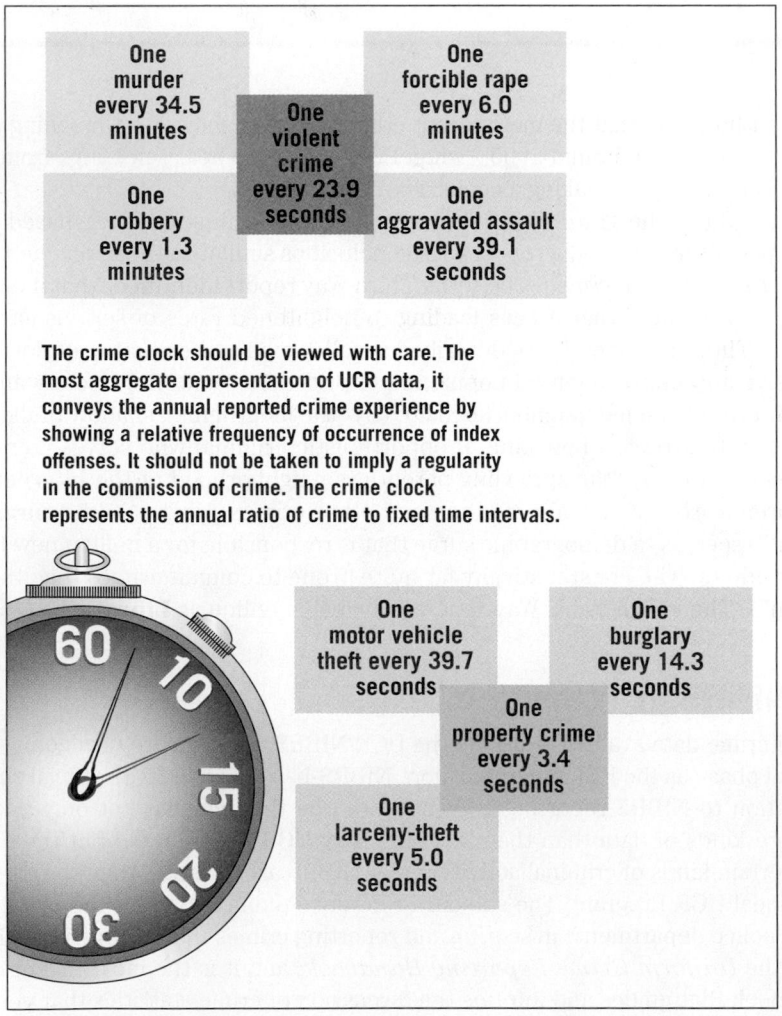

Thematic Question Certain crimes, like rape, assault, and robbery, seem to show seasonal variations. Why do you think this is so?

imply a regularity to crime that, in reality, does not exist.[24] Also, although the crime clock is a useful diagrammatic tool, it is not a rate-based measure of criminal activity and does not allow easy comparisons over time. Seven major crimes are included in the figure: murder, forcible rape, robbery, aggravated assault, motor vehicle theft, burglary, and larceny-theft.

The crime clock distinguishes between two categories of offenses: violent crimes and property crimes. The **violent crimes** (also called *personal crimes*) are murder, forcible rape, robbery, and aggravated assault. The **property crimes** are motor vehicle theft, burglary, and larceny-theft. Other than the use of this simple dichotomy, UCR/NIBRS data do not provide a clear measure of the severity of the crimes they cover.

violent crime
A UCR/NIBRS summary offense category that includes murder, rape, robbery, and aggravated assault.

property crime
A UCR/NIBRS summary offense category that includes burglary, larceny-theft, motor vehicle theft, and arson.

Like most UCR/NIBRS statistics, crime clock data are based on crimes reported to (or discovered by) the police. For a few offenses, the numbers reported are probably close to the numbers that actually occur. Murder, for example, is a crime that is difficult to conceal because of its seriousness. Even when the crime is not immediately discovered, the victim is often quickly missed by family members, friends, and associates, and someone files a "missing persons" report with the police. Auto theft is another crime that is reported in numbers similar to its actual rate of occurrence, probably because insurance companies require that the victim file a police report before they will pay the claim.

A commonly used term in today's UCR/NIBRS reports is **clearance rate**, which refers to the proportion of reported crimes that have been "solved." Clearances are judged primarily on the basis of arrests and do not involve judicial disposition. Once an arrest has been made, a crime is regarded as having been "cleared" for reporting purposes. Exceptional clearances (sometimes called *clearances by exceptional means*) can result when law enforcement authorities believe they know who committed a crime but cannot make an arrest. The perpetrator may, for example, have fled the country or died.

clearance rate
A traditional measure of investigative effectiveness that compares the number of crimes reported or discovered to the number of crimes solved through arrest or other means (such as the death of the suspect).

Table 2–2 summarizes UCR/NIBRS program statistics for 2009.

Part I Offenses

Murder

Murder is the unlawful killing of one human being by another.[25] UCR/NIBRS statistics on murder describe the yearly incidence of all willful and unlawful homicides within the United States. Included in the count are all cases of nonnegligent manslaughter that have been reported to or discovered by the police. Not included in the count are suicides, justifiable homicides (that is, those committed in self-defense), deaths caused by negligence or accident, and murder attempts. In 2009, some 15,241 murders came to the attention of police departments across the United States. First-degree murder is a criminal homicide that is planned; second-degree murder is an intentional and unlawful killing but one that is generally unplanned and that happens "in the heat of the moment."

murder
The unlawful killing of a human being. *Murder* is a generic term that in common usage may include first- and second-degree murder, manslaughter, involuntary manslaughter, and other similar offenses.

TABLE 2–2
Major Crimes Known to the Police, 2009 (UCR/NIBRS Part I Offenses)

Offense	Number	Rate per 100,000	Clearance Rate
Personal/Violent Crimes			
Murder	15,241	5.0	66.6%
Forcible rape[a]	88,097	56.6	41.2
Robbery	408,217	133.0	28.2
Aggravated assault	806,843	262.8	56.8
Property Crimes			
Burglary	2,199,125	727.2	12.5
Larceny-theft	6,327,230	2,060.9	21.5
Motor vehicle theft	794,616	258.8	12.4
Arson[b]	58,871	21.3	34.7
U.S. Total	**10,698,240**	**3,465.5**	

[a]Rates of rape are shown per 100,000 females, but approximately half of that rate figures into the table's totals.
[b]Arson can be classified as either a property crime or a violent crime, depending on whether personal injury or loss of life results from its commission. It is generally classified as a property crime, however. Arson statistics are incomplete for 2009.

Source: Adapted from Federal Bureau of Investigation, *Crime in the United States, 2009* (Washington, DC: U.S. Department of Justice, 2010).

The typical mass murderer is extraordinarily ordinary.
—James Alan Fox, Northeastern University

Lecture Note Remind the class that official definitions (including UCR/NIBRS terminology) for each of the Part I offenses are provided in the glossary.

Lecture Note Review the eight major crimes (and their definitions) that make up the Part I offenses of the Uniform Crime Reports.

Part I offenses
A UCR/NIBRS offense group used to report murder, rape, robbery, aggravated assault, burglary, larceny-theft, motor vehicle theft, and arson, as defined under the FBI's UCR/NIBRS Program.

Murder is the smallest numerical category in the **Part I offenses**. The 2009 murder rate was 5 homicides for every 100,000 residents of the United States. Generally, murder rates peak in the warmest months; in 2009, the greatest number of murders occurred in August. Geographically, murder is most common in the southern states. However, because those states are also the most populous, a meaningful comparison across regions of the country is difficult.

Age is no barrier to murder. Statistics for 2009 reveal that 193 infants (children under the age of one) were victims of homicide, as were 296 people age 75 and over.[26] Young adults between ages 20 and 24 were the most likely to be murdered. Murder perpetrators were also most common in this age group.

> The public is properly obsessed with safety. Of industrialized countries, the U.S. has the highest rate of violent crime.
>
> —Bob Moffitt, Heritage Foundation

Firearms are the weapon used most often to commit murder. In 2009, guns were used in 67.1% of all killings. Handguns outnumbered shotguns almost 15 to one in the murder statistics, with rifles used almost as often as shotguns. Knives were used in approximately 13% of all murders. Other weapons included explosives, poison, narcotics overdose, blunt objects like clubs, and hands, feet, and fists.

Only 12.3% of all murders in 2009 were perpetrated by offenders classified as "strangers." In 43.9% of all killings, the relationship between the parties had not yet been determined. The largest category of killers was officially listed as "acquaintances," which probably includes a large number of former friends. Arguments cause most murders (41.2%), but murders also occur during the commission of other crimes, such as robbery, rape, and burglary. Homicides that follow from other crimes are more likely to be impulsive rather than planned.

Murders may occur in sprees, which "involve killings at two or more locations with almost no time break between murders."[27] One spree killer, John Allen Muhammad, 41, part of the "sniper team" that terrorized the Washington, D.C., area in 2002, was arrested along with 17-year-old Jamaican immigrant Lee Boyd Malvo in the random shootings of 13 people in Maryland, Virginia, and Washington, D.C., over a three-week period. Ten of the victims died.[28] In 2003, Muhammad and Malvo were convicted of capital murder; Muhammad was sentenced to die, and Malvo was given a second sentence of life without the possibility of parole in 2006 after he struck a deal with prosecutors in an effort to avoid the death penalty.[29]

▲ Self-confessed serial killer Gary L. Ridgway. The 54-year-old Ridgway, known as the Green River Strangler, is said to be the nation's worst captured serial killer. In 2003, Ridgway admitted to killing 48 women over a 20-year period in the Pacific Northwest. He is now serving life in prison without possibility of parole. What's the difference between serial killers and mass murderers?
Elaine Thompson/Reuters/Landov Media

In contrast to spree killing, mass murder entails "the killing of four or more victims at one location, within one event."[30] Recent mass murderers have included Seung-Hui Cho, who killed 33 people and wounded 20 on the campus of Virginia Polytechnic Institute and State University in Blacksburg, Virginia, in 2007; Timothy McVeigh, who was the antigovernment Oklahoma City bomber; Mohammed Atta and the terrorists he led, who carried out the September 11, 2001, attacks against American targets; and George Hennard, who killed 24 and wounded 20 at a Luby's Cafeteria in Killeen, Texas, in 1991.

Yet another kind of murder, serial murder, happens over time and officially "involves the killing of several victims in three or more separate events."[31] In cases of serial murder, days, months, or even years may elapse between killings.[32] Some of the more infamous serial killers of recent years are the confessed Wichita BTK murderer, Dennis Rader;[33] Jeffrey Dahmer, who received 936 years in prison for the murders of 15 young men (and who was himself later murdered in prison); Ted Bundy, who killed many college-age women; Henry Lee Lucas, now in a Texas prison, who confessed to 600 murders but later recanted (yet was convicted of 11 murders and linked to at least 140 others);[34] Ottis Toole, who was Lucas's partner in crime; cult leader Charles Manson, who is still serving time for ordering followers to kill seven Californians, including famed actress Sharon Tate; Andrei Chikatilo, the Russian "Hannibal Lecter," who killed 52 people, mostly schoolchildren;[35] David Berkowitz, also known as the "Son of Sam," who killed six people on lovers' lanes around New York City; Theodore Kaczynski, the Unabomber, who perpetrated a series of bomb attacks on "establishment" figures; and Seattle's Green River killer, Gary Leon Ridgway, a 54-year-old painter who in 2003 confessed to killing 48 women in the 1980s.

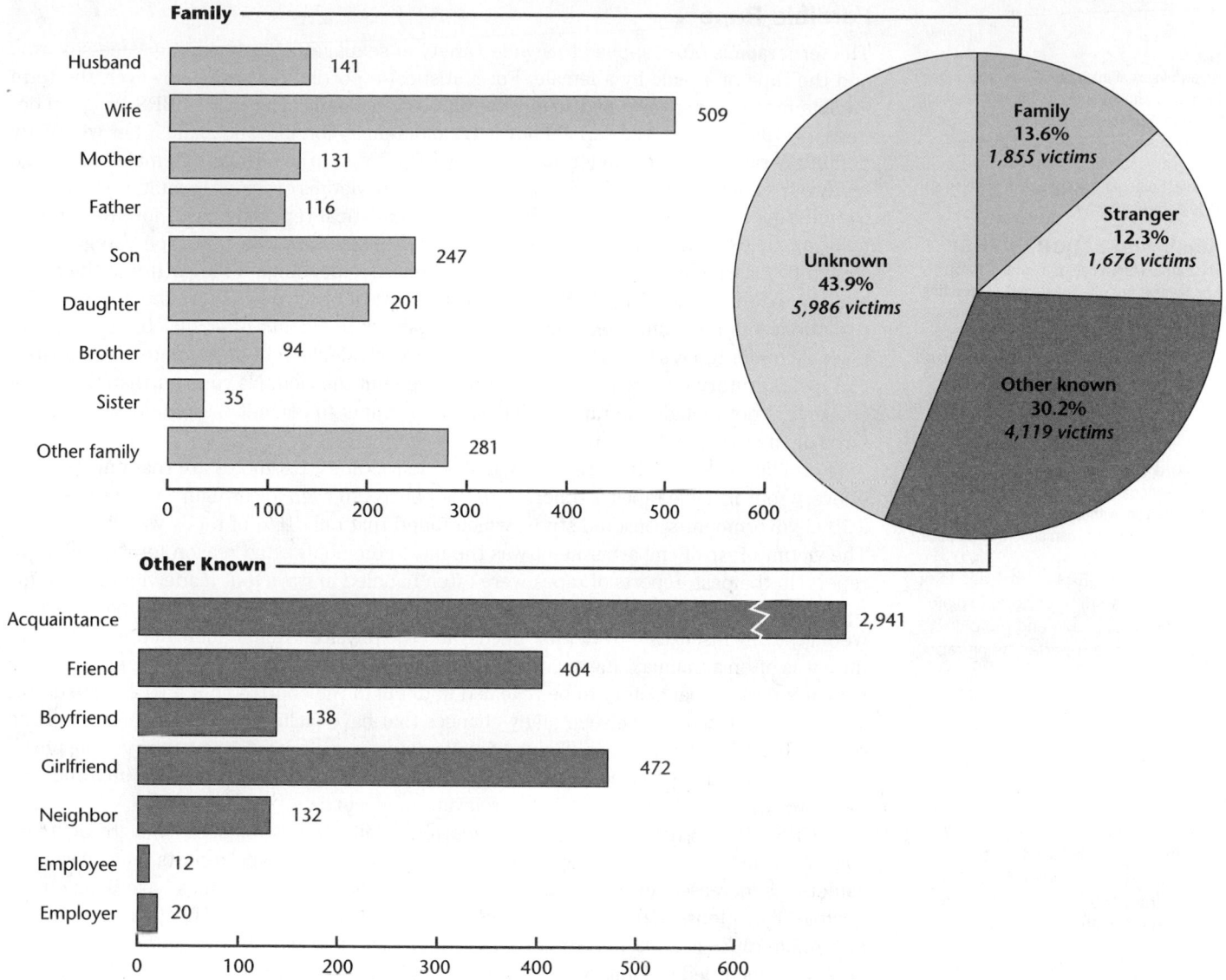

NOTE: Relationship is that of victim to offender. Percentages may not total 100 due to rounding.

FIGURE 2–4
Murder by Relationship, 2009

Source: Federal Bureau of Investigation, *Crime in the United States, 2009* (Washington, DC: U.S. Department of Justice, 2010).

Federal homicide laws changed in 2004 when President George Bush signed the Unborn Victims of Violence Act.[36] The act, which passed the Senate by only one vote, made it a separate federal crime to "kill or attempt to kill" a fetus "at any stage of development" during an assault on a pregnant woman. The fetal homicide statute, better known as Laci and Conner's Law, after homicide victims Laci Peterson and her unborn son (whom she had planned to name Conner), specifically prohibits the prosecution of "any person for conduct relating to an abortion for which the consent of the pregnant woman, or a person authorized by law to act on her behalf, has been obtained."

Because murder is such a serious crime, it consumes substantial police resources. Consequently, over the years the offense has shown the highest clearance rate of any major crime. Over 66.6% of all homicides were cleared in 2009. Figure 2–4 shows expanded homicide data from the FBI. Learn more about homicide trends in the United States at **Library Extra 2–8**.

Lecture Note Discuss the differences between first- and second-degree murder. Explain that although all murders are felonies, the category of felony murder in some jurisdictions refers to the (often unintentional) death of a person during the commission of another crime, such as the bank patron who dies of a heart attack during a bank robbery.

Forcible Rape

rape
Unlawful sexual intercourse achieved through force and without consent. Broadly speaking, the term *rape* has been applied to a wide variety of sexual attacks and may include same-sex rape and the rape of a male by a female. Some jurisdictions refer to same-sex rape as *sexual battery*.

forcible rape (UCR/NIBRS)
The carnal knowledge of a female, forcibly and against her will. For statistical-reporting purposes, the FBI defines *forcible rape* as "unlawful sexual intercourse with a female, by force and against her will, or without legal or factual consent." Statutory rape differs from forcible rape in that it generally involves nonforcible sexual intercourse with a minor.

sexual battery
The intentional and wrongful physical contact with a person, without his or her consent, that entails a sexual component or purpose.

The term **rape** is often applied to a wide variety of sexual attacks, including same-sex rape and the rape of a male by a female. For statistical-reporting purposes, however, the term **forcible rape** has a specific and somewhat different meaning. The UCR/NIBRS Program defines *forcible rape* as "the carnal knowledge of a female forcibly and against her will."[37] By definition, rapes reported under the summary UCR Program are always of females. Although today our society acknowledges that males can be the victims of sexual assault, the *Uniform Crime Reporting Handbook*, which serves as a statistical-reporting guide for law enforcement agencies, says, "Sexual attacks on males are excluded from the rape category and should be classified as assaults or other sex offenses depending on the nature of the crime and the extent of the injury."[38] While it was not part of original UCR terminology, some jurisdictions refer to same-sex rape as **sexual battery**. Incidents of sexual battery are reportable under today's UCR/NIBRS Program as sexual offenses but do not enter the statistics on rape. Statutory rape, where no force is involved but the victim is younger than the age of consent, is not included in rape statistics, but attempts to commit the rape of a female by force or the threat of force are.

Lecture Note Explain that age is no barrier to the crime of rape. Explain that very young girls and the oldest of women have reported being raped.

Forcible rape is the least reported of all violent crimes. Estimates are that only one out of every four forcible rapes is reported to the police. An even lower figure was reported by a 1992 government-sponsored study, which found that only 16% of rapes were reported.[39] The victim's fear of embarrassment was the most commonly cited reason for the failure to report. In the past, reports of rapes were often handled in ways that made victims feel further victimized. Information was usually taken by desk sergeants or male detectives who were typically insensitive to victims' needs, and the physical examination victims had to endure was often a traumatizing experience in itself. Also, many states routinely permitted the woman's past sexual history to be revealed in detail in the courtroom if a trial ensued. But the past few decades have seen many changes that have facilitated the accurate reporting of rape and other sex offenses. Trained female detectives often interview the victims, physicians have become better educated in handling the psychological needs of victims, and sexual histories are no longer regarded as relevant in most trials.

Lecture Note Explain that some people see rape as a crime of power rather than one of sex. Discuss how many rapists seek to humiliate their victims and that they enjoy the sense of power that comes from the abuse. Mention, however, that other researchers have found that imprisoned rapists identify "lust," rather than "power," as their primary criminal motivation.

UCR/NIBRS statistics show 88,097 reported forcible rapes for 2009, a slight decrease over the number of offenses reported for the previous year. Rape reports, however, have sometimes increased, even in years when reports of other violent crimes have been on the decline. The offense of rape follows homicide in its seasonal variation. The greatest numbers of forcible rapes in 2009 were reported in the hot summer months, while the lowest numbers were recorded in January, February, November, and December.

date rape
The unlawful forced sexual intercourse with a female against her will that occurs within the context of a dating relationship. Date rape, or acquaintance rape, is a subcategory of rape that is of special concern today.

Rape is frequently committed by a man known to the victim, as in the case of **date rape**. Victims may be held captive and subjected to repeated assaults.[40] In the crime of heterosexual rape, any female—regardless of age, appearance, or occupation—is a potential victim. Through personal violation, humiliation, and physical battering, rapists seek a sense of personal aggrandizement and dominance. Victims of rape often experience a lessened sense of personal worth; feelings of despair, helplessness, and vulnerability; a misplaced sense of guilt; and a lack of control over their personal lives.

Contemporary wisdom holds that forcible rape is often a planned violent crime that serves the offender's need for power rather than sexual gratification.[41] The "power thesis" has its origins in the writings of feminist Susan Brownmiller, who argued in 1975 that the primary motivation leading to rape is the male desire to "keep women in their place" and to preserve gender inequality through violence.[42] Although many writers on the subject of forcible rape have generally accepted the power thesis, at least one study has caused some to rethink it. In a 1995 survey of imprisoned serial rapists, Dennis Stevens found that "lust" was reported most often (41%) as "the primary motive for predatory rape."[43]

Lecture Note Explain that criminologists believe that far more rapes occur than are reported. Suggest that reasons for underreporting include embarrassment, fear of insensitive handling by the justice system, and fear of the offender.

Statistically speaking, most rapes are committed by acquaintances of the victims and often betray a trust or friendship. Date rape, which falls into this category, appears to be far more common than previously believed. Recently, the growing number of rapes perpetrated with the use of the "date rape drug" Rohypnol has alarmed law enforcement personnel. Rohypnol is an illegal pharmaceutical substance that is virtually tasteless. Available on the black market, it dissolves easily in drinks and can leave anyone who consumes it unconscious for hours, making them vulnerable to sexual assault.

Lecture Note Discuss date rape. Ask whether the phenomenon is of recent origin or has existed for generations. Why has it received so much media attention recently?

Rape within marriage, which has not always been recognized as a crime, is a growing area of concern in American criminal justice, and many laws have been enacted during the past few decades to deter it. Similarly, even though UCR/NIBRS Program statistics officially report only the rape or attempted rape of females, some state statutes criminalize the rape of a male by a female. When it occurs, this offense is typically statutory rape. In 2009, for example, sixth-grade science teacher Rachel L. Holt, a 34-year-old divorcée from Wilmington, Delaware, was sentenced to ten years in prison after pleading guilty to second-degree rape. She had initially been charged with 28 counts of first-degree rape—which prosecutors said was based on the number of times she had had sex with a 13-year-old male student whom she had plied with alcohol and let drive her car. The intense affair took place over a one-week period.

Learn more about the crime of rape and what people can do to protect themselves at **Web Extra 2–7**. Read about statistical measures relating to the sexual victimization of women at **Library Extra 2–9**.

Lecture Note Define *highway robbery* as any robbery that occurs outdoors in a public place. Explain that highway robbery does not necessarily occur on the road or in a vehicle.

Robbery

Robbery is a personal crime involving a face-to-face confrontation between victim and perpetrator. It is often confused with burglary, which is primarily a property crime. (We'll examine burglary later.) Weapons may be used in robbery, or strong-arm robbery may occur through intimidation. Purse snatching and pocket picking are not classified as robbery by the UCR/NIBRS Program but are included under the category of larceny-theft.

In 2009, individuals were the most common target of robbers. Banks, gas stations, convenience stores, and other businesses were the second most common target, with residential robberies accounting for only 15.2% of the total. In 2009, 408,217 robberies were reported to the police. Of that number, 42.8% were highway robberies, meaning that the crime occurred outdoors, most commonly as the victim was walking. Strong-arm robberies, in which the victim was intimidated but no weapon was used, accounted for 41.1% of the total robberies reported. Guns were used in 42.6% of all robberies, and knives were used in 7.7%. Armed robbers are dangerous; guns are actually discharged in 20% of all robberies.[44]

When a robbery occurs, the UCR/NIBRS Program scores the event as one robbery, even when a number of victims were robbed during the event. With the move toward incident-driven reporting, however, the revised UCR/NIBRS Program will soon make data available on the number of individuals robbed in each incident. Because statistics on crime follow what's known as the *hierarchy rule*, they show only the most serious offense that occurred during a particular episode. Hence, robberies are often hidden when they occur in conjunction with more serious crimes. For example, 3% of robbery victims are also raped, and a large number of homicide victims are robbed.[45]

Robbery is primarily an urban offense, and most arrestees are young male minorities. The robbery rate in cities in 2009 was 179 per every 100,000 inhabitants, whereas it was only 17.2 in rural areas. Eighty-eight percent of those arrested for robbery in 2009 were male, 65.2% were under the age of 25, and 56% were minorities.[46]

robbery (UCR/NIBRS)
The unlawful taking or attempted taking of property that is in the immediate possession of another by force or violence and/or by putting the victim in fear. Armed robbery differs from unarmed, or strong-arm, robbery in that it involves a weapon. Contrary to popular conceptions, highway robbery does not necessarily occur on a street—and rarely in a vehicle. The term *highway robbery* applies to any form of robbery that occurs outdoors in a public place.

Aggravated Assault

In April 2006, Arthur J. McClure, 22, of Fort Myers, Florida, was arrested when he allegedly took the head off of an Easter Bunny costume that he was wearing and punched Erin Johansson of Cape Coral, Florida, after the young mother apparently became upset that a mall photo set was closing ten minutes early.[47] The incident was witnessed by dozens of people, including many children who had gathered to have their pictures taken with the rabbit. McClure, who denied he struck Johansson, was fired after the incident.

Assaults are of two types: simple (misdemeanor) and aggravated (felonious). For statistical-reporting purposes, simple assaults typically involve pushing and shoving. While simple assault may also at times include fistfights, the correct legal term to describe such incidents is *battery*. **Aggravated assaults** are distinguished from simple assaults in that either a weapon is used or the assault victim requires medical assistance. When a deadly weapon is employed, an aggravated assault may be charged as attempted murder even if no injury results.[48] In some cases, the UCR/NIBRS Program scores these attempted assaults as aggravated assault because of the potential for serious consequences.

assault (UCR/NIBRS)
An unlawful attack by one person upon another. Historically, *assault* meant only the attempt to inflict injury on another person; a completed act constituted the separate offense of *battery*. Under modern statistical usage, however, attempted and completed acts are grouped together under the generic term *assault*.

aggravated assault
The unlawful, intentional inflicting, or attempted or threatened inflicting, of serious injury upon the person of another. While *aggravated assault* and *simple assault* are standard terms for reporting purposes, most state penal codes use labels like *first-degree* and *second-degree* to make such distinctions.

▲ A man threatening a police officer with a beer bottle in Sydney, Australia, in December 2005, after ethnic tensions erupted into running battles between police and a mob of thousands of youths. An assault is an unlawful attack upon one person by another. What is the difference between assault and aggravated assault?
Rob Griffith/AP Wide World Photos

Lecture Note Most people tend to confuse the terms *robbery* and *burglary*, using them interchangeably. Explain the differences between the two terms, and show why they are not the same.

Lecture Note Discuss the three categories of burglary: forcible entry, unlawful entry where no force is used, and attempted forcible entry.

burglary (UCR/NIBRS)
The unlawful entry of a structure to commit a felony or a theft (excludes tents, trailers, and other mobile units used for recreational purposes). Under the UCR/NIBRS Program, the crime of burglary can be reported if (1) an unlawful entry of an unlocked structure has occurred, (2) a breaking and entering (of a secured structure) has taken place, or (3) a burglary has been attempted.

identity theft
A crime in which an imposter obtains key pieces of information, such as Social Security and driver's license numbers, to obtain credit, merchandise, and services in the name of the victim. The victim is often left with a ruined credit history and the time-consuming and complicated task of repairing the financial damage.[iii]

larceny-theft (UCR/NIBRS)
The unlawful taking or attempted taking, carrying, leading, or riding away of property from the possession or constructive possession of another. Motor vehicles are excluded. Larceny is the most common of the eight major offenses, although probably only a small percentage of all larcenies is actually reported to the police because of the small dollar amounts involved.

In 2009, 806,843 cases of aggravated assault were reported to law enforcement agencies in the United States. Like reports of rape, assault reports were most frequent in the summer months and least frequent in January, February, November, and December. Most aggravated assaults were committed with blunt objects or objects near at hand (34%), while hands, feet, and fists were also commonly used (27%). Less frequently used were knives (19%) and firearms (21%). Because those who commit assaults are often known to their victims, aggravated assaults are relatively easy to solve. About 57% of all aggravated assaults reported to the police in 2009 were cleared by arrest.

Burglary

Although it may involve personal and even violent confrontation, **burglary** is primarily a property crime. Burglars are interested in financial gain and usually fence (that is, illegally sell) stolen items, recovering a fraction of their cash value. About 2.2 million burglaries were reported to the police in 2009. Dollar losses to burglary victims totaled $4.6 billion, with an average loss per offense of $2,096.

The UCR/NIBRS Program employs three classifications of burglary: (1) forcible entry, (2) unlawful entry where no force is used, and (3) attempted forcible entry. In most jurisdictions, force need not be employed for a crime to be classified as burglary. Unlocked doors and open windows are invitations to burglars, and the legal essence of burglary consists not so much of a forcible entry as it does of the intent to trespass and steal. In 2009, 61% of all burglaries were forcible entries, 32.6% were unlawful entries, and 6.5% were attempted forcible entries.[49] The most dangerous burglaries were those in which a household member was home (about 10% of all burglaries).[50] Residents who were home during a burglary suffered a greater than 30% chance of becoming the victim of a violent crime.[51] However, while burglary may evoke images of dark-clothed strangers breaking into houses in which families lie sleeping, burglaries more often are of unoccupied homes and take place during daylight hours.

The clearance rate for burglary, as for other property crimes that we'll look at later, is generally low. In 2009, the clearance rate for burglary was only 12.5%. Burglars usually do not know their victims, and in cases where they do, burglars conceal their identity by committing their crime when the victim is not present.

> Those who insist that crime never pays have never met an identity thief. Identity theft not only pays, it pays extremely well.
> —Jonathan Turley[ii]

Larceny-Theft

In 2002, 25-year-old Thad Roberts and 22-year-old Tiffany Fowler were arrested in Orlando, Florida, and charged with stealing moon rocks from the Johnson Space Center in Houston, Texas. Roberts had been working as a student intern at the center, and Fowler was a Space Center employee.[52] Officials realized that the lunar samples, along with a number of meteorites, were missing when they discovered that a 600-pound safe had disappeared from the Houston facility. They had been alerted to the loss by messages placed on a website run by a mineralogy club in Antwerp, Belgium, offering "priceless moon rocks collected by Apollo astronauts" for sale for up to $5,000 per gram. Roberts and Fowler were arrested by federal agents pretending to be potential purchasers.

Identity theft is a newer type of crime. See Exhibit 2–1 for more information on identity theft.

Larceny is another name for theft, and the UCR/NIBRS Program uses the term **larceny-theft** to describe theft offenses. Some states distinguish between simple larceny and grand larceny, categorizing the crime based on the dollar value of what is stolen. Larceny-theft, as defined by the UCR/NIBRS Program, includes the theft of valuables of any dollar amount.

Multiculturalism and Diversity
Race and the Criminal Justice System, Part I

Several years ago, Professor Lani Guinier of the University of Pennsylvania School of Law was interviewed on *Think Tank*, a public television show. Guinier was asked by Ben Wattenberg, the program's moderator, "When we talk about crime, crime, crime, are we really using a code for black, black, black?" Guinier responded this way: "To a great extent, yes, and I think that's a problem, not because we shouldn't deal with the disproportionate number of crimes that young black men may be committing, but because if we can't talk about race, then when we talk about crime, we're really talking about other things, and it means that we're not being honest in terms of acknowledging what the problem is and then trying to deal with it."[1]

Crimes, of course, are committed by individuals of all races. The link between crimes—especially violent, street, and predatory crimes—and race, however, shows a striking pattern. In most crime categories, arrests of black offenders equal or exceed arrests of whites. In any given year, arrests of blacks account for more than 50% of all arrests for violent crimes. Blacks, however, comprise only 12% of the U.S. population. When *rates* (which are based on the relative proportion of racial groups) are examined, the statistics are even more striking. The murder rate among blacks, for example, is ten times that of whites. Similar rate comparisons, when calculated for other violent crimes, show that far more blacks than whites are involved in other street crimes, such as assault, burglary, and robbery. Related studies show that 30% of all young black men in America are under correctional supervision on any given *day*—a far greater percentage than for members of any other ethnic group in the country.[2]

The real question for anyone interested in the justice system is how to explain such huge race-based disparities. Some authors maintain that racial differences in arrests and in rates of imprisonment are due to the differential treatment of African-Americans at the hands of a discriminatory criminal justice system. University of Wisconsin-Whitewater criminologist Marvin D. Free, Jr., for example, says that the fact that African Americans are underrepresented as criminal justice professionals results in their being overrepresented in arrest and confinement statistics.[3] Some police officers, says Free, are more prone to arrest blacks than whites, frequently arrest blacks without sufficient evidence to support criminal charges, and overcharge in criminal cases involving black defendants—resulting in misleading statistical tabulations that depict blacks as being responsible for a greater proportion of crime than is, in fact, the case.

Even if blacks do engage in more criminal activity than whites, says noted criminologist Thomas J. Bernard, higher rates of offending may be due, at least in part, to their perception that members of their group have historically been treated unfairly by agents of social control—resulting in anger and defiance, which express themselves in criminal activity.[4] Hence, says Bernard, crime—at least crime committed by minority group members—becomes a kind of protest against a system that is perceived as fundamentally unfair.

The question of *actual* fairness of the justice system can be quite different from one of *perceived* fairness. As Katheryn K. Russell of the University of Maryland points out, "Study after study has shown that blacks and whites hold contrary views on the fairness of the criminal justice system's operation; blacks tend to be more cautious in their praise and frequently view the system as unfair and racially biased; by contrast whites have a favorable impression of the justice system. . . . The point is not that whites are completely satisfied with the justice system, but rather that, relative to blacks, they have faith in the system."[5] One reason for such differences may be that blacks are more likely to be victims of police harassment and brutality or may know someone who has been.

▲ NAACP members protesting the police use of Tasers. Some claim that the justice system puts members of underrepresented groups at risk for unfair treatment. Others say the system is equitable. What do you think?
Rick Wood/Milwaukee Journal Sentinel/*NewsCom*

According to Russell, inequities in the existing system may propel African Americans into crime and combine with stereotypical images in the popular media to perpetuate what she calls the *criminalblackman myth*. The criminalblackman myth, says Russell, is a stereotypical portrayal of black men as *inherently* more sinister, evil, and dangerous than their white counterparts. The myth of the criminalblackman, adds Russell, is self-perpetuating, resulting in continued frustration, more crime, and growing alienation among African Americans.

[1]Quoted in "For the Record," *Washington Post* wire service, March 3, 1994.
[2]Marvin D. Free, Jr., *African-Americans and the Criminal Justice System* (New York: Garland, 1996).
[3]Ibid.
[4]Thomas J. Bernard, "Angry Aggression among the 'Truly Disadvantaged,'" *Criminology*, Vol. 28, No. 1 (1990), pp. 73–96.
[5]Katheryn K. Russell, "The Racial Hoax as Crime: The Law as Affirmation," *Indiana Law Journal*, Vol. 71 (1996), pp. 593–621.

CJ Exhibit 2–1
Identity Theft: A New Kind of Larceny

In May 2010, 26-year-old Facebook founder and billionaire Mark Zuckerberg announced that his company would provide users with the ability to significantly upgrade personal security settings.[1] Facebook, said Zuckerberg, would enhance privacy choices in order to reduce the amount of personal information that is publicly available by default. Online settings, which Zuckerberg pledged would become easier to find and to change, would also allow users to opt out of third-party applications associated with Facebook.[2] The announcement came after users, privacy advocates, and lawmakers voiced their concerns over lax security features on the highly popular site. Many were concerned that criminals could use Facebook to acquire information about its users and steal their identities.[3]

Identity theft, which involves obtaining credit, merchandise, or services by fraudulent personal representation, is a special kind of larceny. According to a recent federal survey, 9.9 million Americans were victims of identity theft in 2007, although most did not report the crime.[4] Information from the Bureau of Justice Statistics shows that 6.6% of all households in the United States had at least one member who had been a victim of one or more types of identity theft in 2007.[5] BJS also says that identity theft is the fastest-growing type of crime in America.[6]

Identity theft became a federal crime in 1998 with the passage of the Identity Theft and Assumption Deterrence Act.[7] The law makes it a crime whenever anyone "knowingly transfers or uses, without lawful authority, a means of identification of another person with the intent to commit, or to aid or abet, any unlawful activity that constitutes a violation of federal law, or that constitutes a felony under any applicable state or local law."

The 2004 Identity Theft Penalty Enhancement Act[8] added two years to federal prison sentences for criminals convicted of using stolen credit card numbers and other personal data to commit crimes. It also prescribed prison sentences for those who use identity theft to commit other crimes, including terrorism, and it increased penalties for defendants who exceed or abuse the authority of their position in unlawfully obtaining or misusing means of personal identification.

According to the National White Collar Crime Center, identity thieves use several common techniques. Some engage in "Dumpster diving," going through trash bags, cans, or Dumpsters to get copies of checks, credit card and bank statements, credit card applications, or other records that typically bear identifying information. Others use a technique called "shoulder surfing," which involves looking over the victim's shoulder as he or she enters personal information into a computer or on a written form. Eavesdropping is another simple, yet effective, technique that identity thieves often use. Eavesdropping can occur when the victim is using an ATM machine, giving credit card or other personal information over the phone, or dialing the number for a telephone calling card. Criminals can also obtain personal identifying information from potential victims through the Internet. Some Internet users, for example, reply to "spam" (unsolicited e-mail) that promises them all sorts of attractive benefits while requesting identifying data, such as checking account or credit card numbers and expiration dates, along with their name and address.[9] Identity theft perpetrated through the use of high technology depends on the fact that a person's legal and economic identity in contemporary society is largely "virtual" and supported by technology.

▲ World-renowned film director, producer, and screenwriter Steven Spielberg arriving at the Los Angeles premiere of HBO's *The Pacific* in 2010. Spielberg has been a victim of identity theft at least twice. Why is identity theft so prevalent today? How can it be stopped?
AP Photo/Tammie Arroyo

Learn more about identity theft via **Library Extra 2–10**, and read the National Strategy to Combat Identity Theft at **Library Extra 2–11**. You can take the ID Theft Safety Quiz online at **Library Extra 2–12**.

[1]Jon Swartz, "Facebook Simplifies Its Privacy Controls," *USA Today*, May 27, 2010, p. 1B.

[2]David Gelles and Richard Waters, "Facebook Backtracks on Privacy Controls," *Financial Times*, May 27, 2010, 1A.

[3]"Facebook Warns of Gift Card Scam," *MSN Money*, April 13, 2010, http://articles.moneycentral.msn.com/Banking/FinancialPrivacy/facebook-warns-of-gift-card-scam.aspx (accessed May 27, 2010).

[4]United States Postal Service, Postal Inspectors, "Identity Theft Is America's Fastest-Growing Crime," http://www.usps.com/postalinspectors/idthft_ncpw.htm (accessed May 21, 2008).

[5]Lynn Langton and Katrina Baum, *Identity Theft Reported by Households, 2007—Statistical Tables* (Washington, DC: Bureau of Justice Statistics, 2010).

[6]Katrina Baum, *Identity Theft, 2005* (Washington, DC: Bureau of Justice Statistics, 2007).

[7]U.S. Code, Title 18, Section 1028.

[8]Public Law 108–275.

[9]Much of the information in this paragraph is adapted from National White Collar Crime Center, "WCC Issue: Identity Theft," http://www.nw3c.org/papers/Identity_Theft.pdf (accessed May 18, 2010).

The reports specifically list the following offenses as types of larceny (listed here in order of declining frequency):

- Thefts from motor vehicles
- Shoplifting
- Thefts from buildings
- Thefts of motor vehicle parts and accessories
- Thefts of bicycles
- Thefts from coin-operated machines
- Purse snatching
- Pocket picking

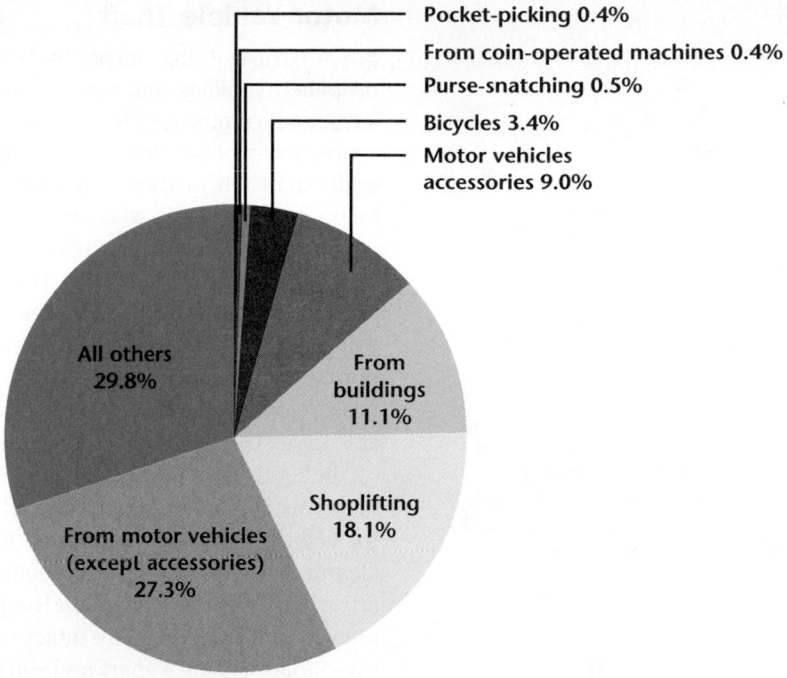

Due to rounding, the percentages may not total 100.

FIGURE 2–5
Larceny-Theft Distribution, 2009

Source: Federal Bureau of Investigation, *Crime in the United States, 2009* (Washington, DC: U.S. Department of Justice, 2010).

From a statistical standpoint, the most common form of larceny in recent years has been theft of motor vehicle parts, accessories, and contents. Tires, wheels, hubcaps, radar detectors, satellite radios, CD players, compact discs, and cellular phones account for many of the items reported stolen (Figure 2–5).

Thefts of farm animals (known as *rustling*) and thefts of most types of farm machinery also fall into the larceny category. In fact, larceny is such a broad category that it serves as a kind of catchall in the UCR/NIBRS Program. In 1995, for example, Yale University officials filed larceny charges against 25-year-old student Lon Grammer, claiming that he had fraudulently obtained university funds.[53] The university maintained that Grammer had stolen his education by forging college and high school transcripts and concocting letters of recommendation prior to admission. Grammer's alleged misdeeds, which Yale University officials said misled them into thinking that Grammer, a poor student before attending Yale, had an exceptional scholastic record, permitted him to receive $61,475 in grants and loans during the time he attended the school. Grammer was expelled.

Reported thefts vary widely, in terms of both the objects stolen and their value. Stolen items range from pocket change to a $100 million aircraft. For reporting purposes, crimes entailing embezzlement, con games, forgery, and worthless checks are specifically excluded from the count of larceny. Because larceny has traditionally been considered a crime that requires physical possession of the item appropriated, some computer crimes, including thefts engineered through online access or thefts of software and information, have not been scored as larcenies unless computer equipment, electronic circuitry, or computer media were actually stolen. In 2004, however, the FBI confirmed that it was working with Cisco Systems, Inc., to investigate the possible theft of some of the company's intellectual property.[54] The theft involved approximately 800 megabytes of proprietary software code used to control the company's Internet routers. Since hardware manufactured by Cisco Systems accounts for more than 60% of all routers used on the Internet,[55] officials feared that the lost software could represent a major security threat for the entire Internet.

> In a field like criminal justice, where sensitive issues abound, none is more sensitive than the issue of race and gender bias.
>
> —Gary LaFree, University of New Mexico

Reports to the police in 2009 showed 6,327,230 larcenies nationwide, with the total value of property stolen placed at $5.5 billion. Larceny-theft is the most frequently reported major crime, according to the UCR/NIBRS Program. It may also be the program's most underreported crime category because small thefts rarely come to the attention of the police. The average value of items reported stolen in 2009 was about $864.

Lecture Note Explain that larceny-theft is the most common of all offenses and that it is often not reported because the value of the property taken is very small.

Lecture Note Describe motor vehicles as self-propelled vehicles that run on the ground and not on rails. Explain that the theft of trains, planes, boats, construction equipment, and most farm machinery falls under the category of larceny-theft for UCR/NIBRS reporting purposes.

Motor Vehicle Theft

For record-keeping purposes, the UCR/NIBRS Program defines *motor vehicles* as self-propelled vehicles that run on the ground and not on rails. Included in the definition are automobiles, motorcycles, motor scooters, trucks, buses, and snowmobiles. Excluded are trains, airplanes, bulldozers, most farm and construction machinery, ships, boats, and spacecraft; the theft of these would be scored as larceny-theft.[56] Vehicles that are temporarily taken by individuals who have lawful access to them are not thefts. Hence, spouses who jointly own all property may drive the family car, even though one spouse may think of the vehicle as his or her exclusive personal property.

motor vehicle theft (UCR/NIBRS)
The theft or attempted theft of a motor vehicle. *Motor vehicle* is defined as a self-propelled road vehicle that runs on land surface and not on rails. The stealing of trains, planes, boats, construction equipment, and most farm machinery is classified as larceny under the UCR/NIBRS Program, not as motor vehicle theft.

As we said earlier, because most insurance companies require police reports before they will reimburse car owners for their losses, most occurrences of **motor vehicle theft** are reported to law enforcement agencies. Some reports of motor vehicle thefts, however, may be false. People who have damaged their own vehicles in solitary crashes or who have been unable to sell them may try to force insurance companies to "buy" them through reports of theft.

In 2009, 794,616 motor vehicles were reported stolen. The average value per stolen vehicle was $6,505, making motor vehicle theft a $5.2 billion crime. The clearance rate for motor vehicle theft was only 12.9% in 2009. Large city agencies reported the lowest rates of clearance (8.6%), while rural counties had the highest rate (23.6%). Many stolen vehicles are quickly disassembled and the parts resold, since auto parts are much more difficult to identify and trace than are intact vehicles. In some parts of the country, chop shops—which take stolen vehicles apart and sell their components—operate like big businesses, and one shop may strip a dozen or more cars per day.

Motor vehicle theft can turn violent, as in cases of carjacking—a crime in which offenders usually force the car's occupants onto the street before stealing the vehicle. For example, in February 2000, Christy Robel watched helplessly as her six-year-old son, Jake, was dragged to his death after a man jumped behind the wheel of her car and sped off.[57] Robel had left the car running with the boy inside as she made a brief stop at a Kansas City sandwich shop. The carjacker, 35-year-old Kim L. Davis, tried to push Jake from the car as he made his escape, but the boy became entangled in his seat belt and was dragged for five miles at speeds of more than 80 mph. In October 2001, Davis was convicted of murder and was sentenced to spend the rest of his life in prison without possibility of parole.[58] The BJS estimates that around 34,000 carjackings occur annually and account for slightly more than 1% of all motor vehicle thefts.[59] Arrest reports for motor vehicle theft show that the typical offender is a young male: 56% of all arrestees in 2009 were under the age of 25, and 82.2% were male.

Lecture Note Explain that the category of arson was added after the UCR/NIBRS Program had been established and that, as a consequence, arson data are not complete.

Arson

The UCR/NIBRS Program received crime reports from nearly 18,000 law enforcement agencies in 2009.[60] Of these, only 14,957 submitted data on **arson** (the intentional burning of property). Even fewer agencies provided complete data as to the type of property burned, the estimated monetary value of the property, the ownership, and so on. Arson data include only the fires that are determined through investigation to have been willfully or maliciously set. Fires of unknown or suspicious origin are excluded from arson statistics.[61]

arson (UCR/NIBRS)
Any willful or malicious burning or attempt to burn, with or without intent to defraud, a dwelling house, public building, motor vehicle or aircraft, personal property of another, and so on. Some instances of arson result from malicious mischief, some involve attempts to claim insurance money, and some are committed in an effort to disguise other crimes, such as murder, burglary, or larceny.

Lecture Note Discuss possible reasons for the incidence of each Part II offense.

The intentional and unlawful burning of structures (houses, storage buildings, manufacturing facilities, and so on) was the type of arson reported most often in 2009 (22,867 instances). The arson of vehicles was the second most common category, with 14,577 such burnings reported. The average dollar loss per instance of arson in 2009 was $17,411, and total nationwide property damage was placed at close to $1 billion.[62] As with most property crimes, the clearance rate for arson was relatively low—34.7% nationally. The crime of arson exists in a kind of statistical limbo. In 1979, Congress ordered that it be added as an eighth Part I offense. Today, however, many law enforcement agencies still have not begun making regular reports to the FBI on arson offenses in their jurisdictions.

Some of these difficulties have been resolved through the Special Arson Program, authorized by Congress in 1982. In conjunction with the National Fire Data Center, the FBI now operates a Special Arson Reporting System, which focuses on fire departments across the nation. The reporting system is designed to provide data to supplement yearly UCR arson tabulations.[63]

Career Profile
Instructor of Criminal Justice

Name: Amy Carrino

Position: Instructor of Criminal Justice, Gateway Community and Technical College, Park Hills, Kentucky

Colleges attended: Northern Kentucky University (BA, Political Science), Salmon P. Chase College of Law (JD)

What criminal justice-related jobs have you held? GED and life skills instructor at three correctional transitional facilities, 1993–2004. Adjunct instructor of Criminal Justice, Gateway Community and Technical College, spring 2009. Full-time instructor of Criminal Justice, Gateway Community and Technical College, fall 2009–present.

What position did you like most? My current position is by far my favorite. It is an honor to teach criminal justice classes to students who will influence our society's future.

What qualities or characteristics most helped you succeed in the field? Dedication to the students you teach and to the institution that employs you. Students must be your top priority in every decision you make. Continue to educate yourself in the best practices that are available, for criminal justice issues and laws are constantly changing and you must prepare your students to enter the workforce. You must make a huge investment in the institution for which you are working. Working as a team member with colleagues is an ongoing process that requires commitment. Hard work, organization, courage to do innovative programming, and passion for your students and your subject area will help you succeed.

What advice would you give students early in their college career to help them find a rewarding job in criminal justice? Be passionate about what you are doing. Become familiar with the idea that you will become a public servant in some form and that serving the public comes with heightened expectations. Take your studies seriously. Be ethical, organized, on time, and acquire all the knowledge you can while you are in school. Honesty, integrity, hard work, and dedication will take you far.

Source: Reprinted with permission of Amy Carrino, Ph.D. Photo courtesy of Amy Carrino. Logo courtesy of Gateway Community and Technical College.

Part II Offenses

The UCR Program also includes information on what the FBI calls **Part II offenses**. Part II offenses, which are generally less serious than those that make up the Part I offenses category, include a number of social-order, or so-called victimless, crimes. The statistics on Part II offenses are for recorded arrests, not for crimes reported to the police. The logic inherent in this form of scoring is that most Part II offenses would never come to the attention of the police were it not for arrests. Part II offenses are shown in Table 2–3, with the number of estimated arrests made in each category for 2009.

Part II offenses
A UCR/NIBRS offense group used to report arrests for less serious offenses. Agencies are limited to reporting only arrest information for Part II offenses, with the exception of simple assault.

Lecture Note Use Table 2–3 to initiate a discussion of the data-gathering activities of law enforcement agencies relative to Part II offenses.

Lecture Note Describe the FBI's Part II offenses, and highlight the fact that drug-law violation is the largest substantive category under this division.

TABLE 2–3
UCR/NIBRS Part II Offenses, 2009

Offense Category	Number of Arrests
Simple assaults	1,319,458
Forgery and counterfeiting	85,844
Fraud	210,255
Embezzlement	17,920
Stolen property (e.g., receiving)	105,303
Vandalism	270,439
Weapons (e.g., carrying)	166,334
Prostitution and related offenses	71,355
Sex offenses (e.g., statutory rape)	77,326
Drug-abuse violations	1,663,582
Gambling	10,360
Offenses against the family (e.g., nonsupport)	114,564
Driving under the influence	1,440,409
Liquor-law violations	570,333
Public drunkenness	594,300
Disorderly conduct	655,322
Vagrancy	33,388
Curfew violations/loitering	112,593
Runaways	93,434

Source: Adapted from Federal Bureau of Investigation, *Crime in the United States, 2009* (Washington, DC: U.S. Department of Justice, 2010).

A Part II offense arrest is counted each time a person is taken into custody. As a result, the statistics in Table 2–3 do not report the number of suspects arrested but rather the number of arrests made. Some suspects were arrested more than once.

The National Crime Victimization Survey

2 Describe the history and nature of the National Crime Victimization Survey Program, and explain what it can tell us about crime in the United States today.

A second major source of statistical data about crime in the United States is the NCVS, which is based on victim self-reports rather than on police reports. The NCVS is designed to estimate the occurrence of all crimes, whether reported or not.[64] The NCVS was first conducted in 1972. It built on efforts in the late 1960s by both the National Opinion Research Center and the President's Commission on Law Enforcement and the Administration of Justice to uncover what some had been calling the **dark figure of crime**. This term refers to those crimes that are not reported to the police and that remain unknown to officials. Before the development of the NCVS, little was known about such unreported and undiscovered offenses.

dark figure of crime
Crime that is not reported to the police and that remains unknown to officials.

Class Activity Have students construct and conduct a local community or campus survey of crime. For example, a random sampling of resident and off-campus students to determine victimization rates with regard to the theft of textbooks, computers, and personal items from dorm rooms and classrooms can provide a picture of crime on campus. (Because of the sensitive personal nature of certain kinds of crimes, such as rape and the use of controlled substances, it may be advisable to limit the survey to property crimes.) The survey could be extended to include professors and administrative staff. If yours is a distance-learning school, invite students to participate in the survey via e-mail or an online questionnaire.

Early data from the NCVS changed the way criminologists thought about crime in the United States. The use of victim self-reports led to the discovery that crimes of all types were more prevalent than UCR statistics indicated. Many cities were shown to have victimization rates that were more than twice the rate of reported offenses. Others, like Saint Louis, Missouri, and Newark, New Jersey, were found to have rates of victimization that very nearly approximated reported crime. New York, often thought of as a high-crime city, was discovered to have one of the lowest rates of self-reported victimization.

Lecture Note Discuss the origins of the NCVS, and explain why the NCVS was needed (to give a more complete picture of crime than the UCR system did at the time). Explain how the NCVS can help uncover the "dark figure of crime."

NCVS data are gathered by the BJS through a cooperative arrangement with the U.S. Census Bureau.[65] Twice each year, Census Bureau personnel interview household members in a nationally representative sample of approximately 43,000 households (about 76,000 people). Approximately 150,000 interviews of individuals age 12 or older are conducted annually. Households stay in the sample for three years, and new households rotate into the sample regularly.

The NCVS collects information on crimes suffered by individuals and households, whether or not those crimes were reported to law enforcement. It estimates the proportion of each crime type reported to law enforcement, and it summarizes the reasons that victims give for reporting or not reporting. BJS statistics are published in annual reports titled *Criminal Victimization* and *Crime and the Nation's Households.*

Thematic Question Which form of data gathering—that represented by the UCR/NIBRS or the NCVS—would individual-rights advocates be more likely to support? Which form would public-order advocates likely support? Why? In a broader sense, how can the form in which data are gathered serve political ends?

Using definitions similar to those employed by the UCR/NIBRS Program, the NCVS includes data on the national incidence of rape, sexual assault, robbery, assault, burglary, personal and household larceny, and motor vehicle theft. Not included are murder, kidnapping, and victimless crimes (crimes that, by their nature, tend to involve willing participants). Commercial robbery and the burglary of businesses were dropped from NCVS reports in 1977. The NCVS employs a hierarchical counting system similar to that of the pre-NIBRS system: It counts only the most "serious" incident in any series of criminal events perpetrated against the same individual. Both completed and attempted offenses are counted, although only people 12 years of age and older are included in household surveys.

NCVS statistics for recent years reveal the following:

- Approximately 15% of American households are touched by crime every year.
- About 20 million victimizations occur each year.
- City residents are almost twice as likely as rural residents to be victims of crime.
- About half of all violent crimes, and slightly more than one-third of all property crimes, are reported to police.[66]
- Victims of crime are more often men than women.
- Younger people are more likely than the elderly to be victims of crime.
- Blacks are more likely than members of other racial groups to be victims of violent crimes.
- Violent victimization rates are highest among people in lower-income families.

Lecture Note Discuss the highlights of the NCVS, which are listed in this chapter. Ask the class what these findings may indicate about the underlying causes of crime in America.

A report by the BJS found that in 2009, NCVS crime rates had reached their lowest level since the survey began.[67] Declines began in the mid-1990s, with violent crime rates dropping

TABLE 2–4
Comparison of UCR/NIBRS and NCVS Data, 2009

Offense	UCR/NIBRS	NCVS[a]
Personal/Violent Crimes		
Homicide	15,241	—
Forcible rape[b]	88,097	125,910
Robbery	408,217	533,790
Aggravated assault	806,843	823,340
Property Crimes		
Burglary[c]	2,199,125	3,134,920
Larceny	6,327,230	11,709,830
Motor vehicle theft	794,616	735,770
Arson[d]	58,871	—
Total Crimes	**10,698,240**	**20,057,180**

[a] NCVS data cover "households touched by crime," not absolute numbers of crime occurrences. More than one victimization may occur per household, but only the number of households in which victimizations occur enters the tabulations.
[b] NCVS statistics include both rape and sexual assault.
[c] NCVS statistics include only household burglary and attempts.
[d] Arson data are incomplete in the UCR/NIBRS and are not reported by the NCVS.

Source: Compiled from Federal Bureau of Investigation, *Crime in the United States, 2009* (Washington, DC: U.S. Department of Justice, 2010); and Jennifer L. Truman and Michael R. Rand, *Criminal Victimization, 2009* (Washington, DC: Bureau of Justice Statistics, 2010).

Lecture Note Describe the differences between the UCR/NIBRS and the NCVS. Ask students which they think would report a higher number of crimes.

Thematic Question From your perspective, which form of data gathering—that represented by the UCR/NIBRS or the NCVS—provides more useful information about crime in America? Why? How can we combine data provided by the two in order to get a more complete picture of crime?

60% between 1993 and 2009.[68] While these statistics indicate that in recent years crime rates have declined, UCR statistics, which go back almost another 40 years, show that today's crime rate is still many times what it was in the early and middle years of the twentieth century.[69] A comparison of UCR/NIBRS and NCVS data can be found in Table 2–4. Explore the latest NCVS data at **Web Extra 2–8**. Like the UCR/NIBRS, the NCVS is also undergoing change. The Bureau of Justice Statistics says that an impending redesign of the NCVS will "improve its methodology, assure its sustainability, increase its value to national and local stakeholders, and better meet the challenges of measuring the extent, characteristics, and consequences of criminal victimization."[70] Learn more about the redesign of the NCVS at **Web Extra 2–9**.

Many researchers trust NCVS data more than UCR/NIBRS data because they believe that self-reports provide a more accurate gauge of criminal incidents than do police reports. Learn more about the use of self-report surveys in the measurement of crime and delinquency via **Library Extras 2–13** and **2–14**.

Comparisons of the UCR and the NCVS

As mentioned earlier in this chapter, crime statistics from the UCR/NIBRS and the NCVS reveal crime patterns that are often the bases for social policies created to deter or reduce crime. These policies also build on explanations for criminal behavior found in more elaborate interpretations of the statistical information. Unfortunately, however, researchers too often forget that statistics, which are merely descriptive, can be weak in explanatory power. For example, NCVS data show that "household crime rates" are highest for households (1) headed by blacks, (2) headed by younger people, (3) with six or more members, (4) headed by renters, and (5) located in central cities.[71] Such findings, combined with statistics that show that most crime occurs among members of the same race, have led some researchers to conclude that values among certain black subcultural group members both propel them into crime and make them targets of criminal victimization. The truth may be, however, that crime is more a function of inner-city location than of culture. From simple descriptive statistics, it is difficult to know which is the case. Learn more about the UCR/NIBRS Program and the NCVS, and see how they compare, by viewing **Web Extra 2–10**.

3 Point out significant differences between the UCR and the NCVS.

Like most statistical data-gathering programs in the social sciences, the UCR/NIBRS and the NCVS programs are not without problems. Because UCR/NIBRS data are based primarily on citizens' crime reports to the police, there are several inherent difficulties.

Multiculturalism and Diversity
Race and the Criminal Justice System, Part II

In *The Myth of a Racist Criminal Justice System*, William Wilbanks claims that while the practice of American criminal justice may have been significantly racist in the past and while some vestiges of racism may indeed remain, the system today is by and large objective in its processing of criminal defendants.[1] Using statistical data, Wilbanks shows that "at every point from arrest to parole there is little or no evidence of an overall racial effect, in that the percentage outcomes for blacks and whites are not very different."[2] Wilbanks claims to have reviewed "all the available studies that have examined the possible existence of racial discrimination from arrest to parole." In essence, he says, "this examination of the available evidence indicates that support for the 'discrimination thesis' is sparse, inconsistent, and frequently contradictory."

Wilbanks is careful to counter arguments advanced by those who continue to suggest that the system is racist. He writes, for example, "Perhaps the black/white gap at arrest is a product of racial bias by the police in that the police are more likely to select and arrest black than white offenders. The best evidence on this question comes from the National Crime Survey [that] interviews 130,000 Americans each year about crime victimization. . . . The percent of offenders described by victims as being black is generally consistent with the percent of offenders who are black according to arrest figures."

Other contemporary research also appears to discount claims that today's American justice system is racist. In 2006, for example, Pauline K. Brennan, a criminologist at the University of Nebraska at Omaha, examined the effects of race and ethnicity on the sentencing of female misdemeanants and found that "race/ethnicity did not directly affect sentencing."[3] Brennan discovered, however, that black and Hispanic females "were more likely to receive jail sentences than their White counterparts due to differences in things like prior record and charge severity."

Similarly, in 2008, a review of the impact of race on parole decision making found that "race did not have a significant impact on decisions at the preliminary screening stage or the parole release stage."[4]

A fundamental critique of statistical studies such as these, however, was offered by Coramae Richey Mann (1931–2002), professor emeritus of criminal justice at the University of Illinois at Chicago, who said that overreliance on quantitative or statistical data fails to capture the reality of racial discrimination within the justice system.[5] White victims, said Mann, tend to overreport being victimized by black offenders because they often misperceive Hispanic and other minority offenders as black. Similarly, she said, black victims are sometimes reluctant to report victimization—especially at the hands of whites.

Mann's arguments are discounted by those who point out that the statistics appear to be overwhelming. *If* they are accurate, then another question emerges: Why do blacks commit more crimes? Wilbanks says, "The assertion that the criminal justice system is not racist does not address the reasons why blacks appear to offend at higher rates than whites before coming into contact with the criminal justice system. . . . It may be that racial discrimination in American society has been responsible for conditions (for example, discrimination in employment, housing, and education) that lead to higher rates of offending by blacks."

Marvin Free, Jr., suggests that African Americans are still systematically denied equal access to societal resources that would allow for full participation in American society—resulting in a higher rate of law violation. In a work that considers such issues in great detail, John Hagan and Ruth D. Peterson acknowledge the reality of higher crime rates among some ethnic minorities and attribute them to (1) concentrated poverty, (2) joblessness, (3) family disruption, and (4) racial segregation.[6]

[1] William Wilbanks, *The Myth of a Racist Criminal Justice System* (Monterey, CA: Brooks/Cole, 1987).
[2] William Wilbanks, "The Myth of a Racist Criminal Justice System," *Criminal Justice Research Bulletin*, Vol. 3, No. 5 (Huntsville, TX: Sam Houston State University, 1987), p. 2.
[3] Pauline K. Brennan, "Sentencing Female Misdemeanants: An Examination of the Direct and Indirect Effects of Race/Ethnicity," *Justice Quarterly*, Vol. 23, No. 1 (March 2006), pp. 60–95.
[4] Kathryn D. Morgan and Brent Smith, "The Impact of Race on Parole Decision-Making," *Justice Quarterly*, Vol. 25, No. 2 (June 2008), pp. 411–412.
[5] Coramae Richey Mann, "The Reality of a Racist Criminal Justice System," in Barry W. Hancock and Paul M. Sharp, eds., *Criminal Justice in America: Theory, Practice, and Policy* (Upper Saddle River, NJ: Prentice Hall, 1996), pp. 51–59.
[6] John Hagan and Ruth D. Peterson, *Crime and Inequality* (Stanford, CA: Stanford University Press, 1995).

First, not all people report when they are victimized. Some victims are afraid to contact the police, while others may not believe that the police can do anything about the offense. Second, certain kinds of crimes are reported rarely, if at all. These include victimless crimes, also known as *social-order offenses*, such as drug use, prostitution, and gambling. Similarly, white-collar and high-technology offenses, such as embezzlement and computer crime—because they often go undiscovered—probably enter the official statistics only rarely. Third, victims' reports may not be entirely accurate. Victims' memories may be faulty, victims may feel the need to impress or please the police, or they may be under pressure from others to misrepresent the facts. Finally, all reports are filtered through a number of bureaucratic levels, which increases the likelihood that inaccuracies will enter the data. As noted methodologist Frank Hagan points out, "The government is very keen on amassing statistics. They collect them, add to them, raise them to the nth power, take the cube root, and prepare wonderful diagrams. But what you must never forget is that every one of these figures comes in the first instance from the *chowty dar* [village watchman], who puts down what he damn pleases."[72]

Thematic Question What was our understanding of crime like before the creation of the UCR/NIBRS and the NCVS? What insights have the UCR/NIBRS and the NCVS provided policymakers?

In contrast to the UCR/NIBRS dependence on crimes reported by victims who seek out the police, the NCVS relies on door-to-door surveys and personal interviews for its data. Survey results, however, may be skewed for several reasons. First, no matter how objective survey questions may appear to be, survey respondents inevitably provide their personal interpretations and descriptions of what may or may not have been a criminal event. Second, by its very nature, the survey includes information from those people who are most willing to talk to surveyors; more reclusive people are less likely to respond regardless of the level of victimization they may have suffered. Also, some victims are afraid to report crimes even to nonpolice interviewers, while others may invent victimizations for an interviewer's sake. As the first page of the NCVS report admits, "Details about the crimes come directly from the victims, and no attempt is made to validate the information against police records or any other source."[73]

Finally, because both the UCR/NIBRS and the NCVS are human artifacts, they contain only data that their creators think appropriate. UCR/NIBRS statistics for 2001, for example, do not include a tally of those who perished in the September 11, 2001, terrorist attacks because FBI officials concluded that the events were too "unusual" to count. Although the FBI's 2001 *Crime in the United States* acknowledges "the 2,830 homicides reported as a result of the events of September 11, 2001," it goes on to say that "these figures have been removed" from the reported data.[74] Crimes resulting from an anomalous event but excluded from reported data highlight the arbitrary nature of the data-collection process itself.

Special Categories of Crime

A **crime typology** is a classification scheme used in the study and description of criminal behavior. There are many typologies, all of which have an underlying logic. The system of classification that derives from any particular typology may be based on legal criteria, offender motivation, victim behavior, characteristics of individual offenders, or the like. Criminologists Terance D. Miethe and Richard C. McCorkle note that crime typologies "are designed primarily to simplify social reality by identifying homogeneous groups of crime behaviors that are different from other clusters of crime behaviors."[75] Hence one common but simple typology contains only two categories of crime: violent and property. In fact, many crime typologies contain overlapping or nonexclusive categories—just as violent crimes may involve property offenses, and property offenses may lead to violent crimes. Thus no one typology is likely to capture all of the nuances of criminal offending.

crime typology
A classification of crimes along a particular dimension, such as legal category, offender motivation, victim behavior, or characteristics of individual offenders.

Social relevance is a central distinguishing feature of any meaningful typology, and it is with that in mind that the remaining sections of this chapter briefly highlight crimes of special importance today. They are crime against women, crime against the elderly, hate crime, corporate and white-collar crime, organized crime, gun crime, drug crime, high-technology and computer crime, and terrorism.

4 Identify the special categories of crime discussed in this chapter, and explain why they are of contemporary significance.

Crime against Women

The victimization of women is a special area of concern, and both the UCR/NIBRS and the NCVS contain data on gender as it relates to victimization. Statistics show that women are victimized less frequently than men in every major personal crime category other than rape.[76] The overall U.S. rate of violent victimization is about 25 per 1,000 males age 12 or older, and 18 per 1,000 females.[77] When women become victims of violent crime, however, they are more likely than men to be injured (29% versus 22%, respectively).[78] Moreover, a larger proportion of women than men make modifications in the way they live because of the threat of crime.[79] Women, especially those living in cities, have become increasingly careful about where they travel and the time of day they leave their homes—particularly if they are unaccompanied—and in many settings are often wary of unfamiliar males.

Date rape, familial incest, spousal abuse, **stalking**, and the exploitation of women through social-order offenses like prostitution and pornography are major issues facing American society today. Testimony before Congress tagged domestic violence as the largest cause of injury to American women.[80] Former Surgeon General C. Everett Koop once identified

stalking
Repeated harassing and threatening behavior by one individual against another, aspects of which may be planned or carried out in secret. Stalking might involve following a person, appearing at a person's home or place of business, making harassing phone calls, leaving written messages or objects, or vandalizing a person's property. Most stalking laws require that the perpetrator make a credible threat of violence against the victim or members of the victim's immediate family.

Cyberspace has become a fertile field for illegal activity.
—Linda Fairstein, chief of the Sex Crimes Prosecution Unit, Manhattan District Attorney's Office[iv]

violence against women by their partners as the number one health problem facing women in America.[81] Findings from the National Violence against Women Survey (NVAWS) reveal the following:[82]

- Physical assault is widespread among American women. Fifty-two percent of surveyed women said that they had been physically assaulted as a child or as an adult.
- Approximately 1.9 million women are physically assaulted in the United States each year.
- Eighteen percent of women experienced a completed or attempted rape at some time in their lives.
- Of those reporting rape, 22% were under 12 years old, and 32% were between 12 and 17 years old, when they were first raped.
- Native American and Alaska Native women were most likely to report rape and physical assault, while Asian/Pacific Islander women were least likely to report such victimization. Hispanic women were less likely to report rape than non-Hispanic women.
- Women report significantly more partner violence than men. Twenty-five percent of surveyed women and only 8% of surveyed men said they had been raped or physically assaulted by a current or former spouse, cohabiting partner, or date.
- Violence against women is primarily partner violence. Seventy-six percent of the women who had been raped or physically assaulted since age 18 were assaulted by a current or former husband, cohabiting partner, or date, compared with 18% of the men.
- Women are significantly more likely than men to be injured during an assault. Thirty-two percent of the women and 16% of the men who had been raped since age 18 were injured during their most recent rape; 39% of the women and 25% of the men who were physically assaulted since age 18 were injured during their most recent physical assault.
- Eight percent of surveyed women and 2% of surveyed men said they had been stalked at some time in their lives. According to survey estimates, approximately 1 million women and 371,000 men are stalked annually in the United States.

Learn more about violence against women via **Library Extra 2–15**.

Survey findings like these show that more must be done to alleviate the social conditions that result in the victimization of women. Suggestions already under consideration call for expansion in the number of federal and state laws designed to control domestic violence, broadening of the federal Family Violence Prevention and Services Act, federal help in setting up state advocacy offices for battered women, increased funding for battered women's shelters, and additional funds for prosecutors and courts to develop spousal abuse units. The federal Violent Crime Control and Law Enforcement Act of 1994 was designed to meet many of these needs through a subsection titled the Violence against Women Act (VAWA). That act signified a major shift in our national response to domestic violence, stalking (which is often part of the domestic-violence continuum), and sexual assault crimes. For the first time in our nation's history, violent crimes against women were addressed in relation to the more general problem of gender inequality.

The VAWA seeks to eradicate violence against women at all levels, and the act allocated $1.6 billion to fight violence against women. Included are funds to (1) educate police, prosecutors, and judges about the special needs of female victims; (2) encourage pro-arrest policies in cases of domestic abuse; (3) provide specialized services for female victims of crime; (4) fund battered women's shelters across the country; and (5) support rape education in a variety of settings nationwide. The law also extends "rape shield law" protections to civil cases and to all criminal cases in order to bar irrelevant inquiries into a victim's sexual history. VAWA was reauthorized by Congress in 2000. Read the text of the original VAWA legislation at **Web Extra 2–11**.

Multiculturalism and Diversity
Gender Issues in Criminal Justice

The Violent Crime Control and Law Enforcement Act of 1994 included significant provisions intended to enhance gender equality throughout the criminal justice system. Title IV of the Violent Crime Control and Law Enforcement Act, known as the Violence against Women Act (VAWA) of 1994, contains the Safe Streets for Women Act. This act increased federal penalties for repeat sex offenders and requires mandatory restitution for sex crimes, including costs related to medical services (including physical, psychiatric, and psychological care); physical and occupational therapy or rehabilitation; necessary transportation, temporary housing, and child-care expenses; lost income; attorneys' fees, including any costs incurred in obtaining a civil protection order; and any other losses suffered by the victim as a result of the offense. The act also requires that compliance with a restitution order be made a condition of probation or supervised release (if such a sentence is imposed by the court) and provides that violation of the order will result in the offender's imprisonment.

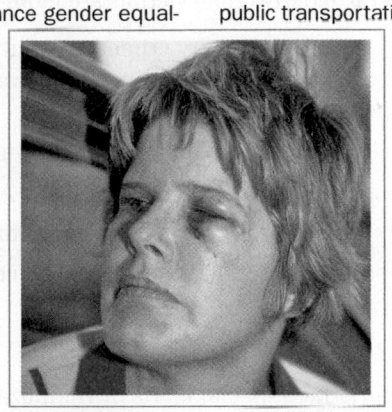

A battered woman posing for police photographers who are documenting her injuries. Intimate partner violence is a problem of special concern to the criminal justice system, and violence against women is an area that is receiving legislative attention, as evidenced by the federal Violence against Women Act. How might laws designed to protect women be improved?
Michael Newman/PhotoEdit Inc.

Chapter 2 of VAWA provided funds for grants to combat violent crimes against women. The purpose of funding was to assist states and local governments to "develop and strengthen effective law enforcement and prosecution strategies to combat violent crimes against women, and to develop and strengthen victim services in cases involving violent crimes against women."

The act also created the crime of crossing state lines in violation of a protection order and the crime of crossing state lines to commit assault on a domestic partner. It established federal penalties for the latter offense of up to life in prison in cases where death results.

Chapter 3 of the act provided funds to increase the "safety for women in public transit and public parks." It authorized up to $10 million in grants through the Department of Transportation to enhance lighting, camera surveillance, and security telephones in public transportation systems used by women.

Chapter 5 of VAWA funded the creation of hot lines, educational seminars, informational materials, and training programs for professionals who provide assistance to victims of sexual assault. Another portion of the law, titled the Safe Homes for Women Act, increased grants for battered women's shelters, encouraged arrest in cases of domestic violence, and provided for the creation of a national domestic-violence hot line to provide counseling, information, and assistance to victims of domestic-violence. The act also mandates that any protection order issued by a state court must be recognized by the other states and by the federal government and must be enforced "as if it were the order of the enforcing state."

VAWA was reauthorized by Congress in 2000 and again in 2005.[1] The 2000 reauthorization provided $3.3 billion in continuation funding and earmarked a portion of the money for programs that coordinate the work of victims' advocates, police, and prosecutors in the fight against domestic violence. The second reauthorization provided continuation monies for critical programs and funded the development of new services to respond to evolving community needs. In recognition of the fact that domestic violence sometimes leaves victims without homes, the 2006 legislation made funds available to expand services to the homeless, including the development of transitional housing options. VAWA will again be up for reauthorization in 2011, about the time that this book goes to press. Reauthorization is expected to pass Congress without difficulty.

[1] VAWA 2005 was signed into law by President George W. Bush on January 5, 2006. It is officially known as the Violence against Women and Department of Justice Reauthorization Act of 2005 (Public Law 109–162).

Finally, the passage of antistalking legislation by all 50 states and the District of Columbia provides some measure of additional protection to women, who comprise 80% of all stalking victims.[83] On the federal level, the seriousness of stalking was addressed when Congress passed the interstate stalking law in 1996.[84] The law[85] also addresses **cyberstalking**, or the use of the Internet by perpetrators seeking to exercise power and control over their victims by threatening them directly or by posting misleading and harassing information about them. Cyberstalking can be especially insidious because it does not require that the perpetrator and the victim be in the same geographic area. Similarly, electronic communication technologies lower the barriers to harassment and threats; a cyberstalker does not need to confront the victim physically.[86] Learn more about stalking and cyberstalking at **Library Extra 2–16**.

cyberstalking
The use of the Internet, e-mail, and other electronic communication technologies to stalk another person.[v]

Crime against the Elderly

Relative to other age groups, older victims rarely appear in the crime statistics. Criminal victimization seems to decline with age, suggesting that older people are only infrequently targeted by violent and property criminals. Moreover, older people are more likely than younger individuals to live in secure areas and to have the financial means to provide for their own personal security.

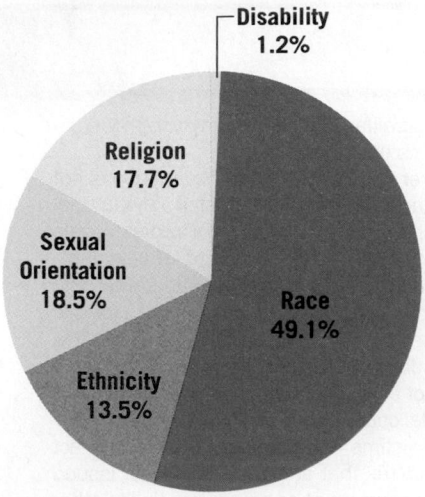

FIGURE 2–6
Motivation of Hate-Crime Offenders, 2009

Source: Total does not equal 100% due to rounding.
Federal Bureau of Investigation, *Crime in the United States, 2009* (Washington, DC: U.S. Department of Justice, 2010).

Victimization data pertaining to older people come mostly from the NCVS, which, for such purposes, looks at people age 65 and older. The elderly generally experience the lowest rate of victimization of any age group in both violent and property crime categories.[87] Some aspects of crime against older people are worth noting, however. In general, elderly crime victims are more likely than younger victims to

- Be victims of property crime (nine out of ten crimes committed against the elderly are property crimes, compared to fewer than four in ten crimes against people between ages 12 and 24)
- Face offenders who are armed with guns
- Be victimized by strangers
- Be victimized in or near their homes during daylight hours
- Report their victimization to the police, especially when they fall victim to violent crime
- Be physically injured

The elderly face special kinds of victimization that only rarely affect younger adults, such as physical abuse at the hands of caregivers. Criminal physical abuse of the elderly falls into two categories: domestic and institutional. Domestic abuse often occurs at the hands of caregivers who are related to their victims; institutional abuse occurs in residential settings like retirement centers, nursing homes, and hospitals. Both forms of elder abuse may also involve criminal sexual victimization. To learn more about domestic and institutional elder abuse, visit the National Center on Elder Abuse (NCEA) via **Web Extra 2–12**.

The elderly are also more often targeted by con artists. Confidence schemes center on commercial and financial fraud (including telemarketing fraud), charitable donation fraud, funeral and cemetery fraud, real estate fraud, caretaker fraud, automobile and home repair fraud, living trust fraud, health-care fraud (e.g., promises of "miracle cures"), and health-care-provider fraud (overbilling and unjustified repeat billing by otherwise legitimate health-care providers). False "friends" may intentionally isolate elderly targets from others in the hopes of misappropriating money through short-term secret loans or outright theft. Similarly, a younger person may feign romantic involvement with an elderly victim or pretend to be devoted to the senior in order to solicit money or receive an inappropriate gift or inheritance. The U.S. Senate's Special Committee on Aging provides additional information on such crimes at its Elder Justice Center website, which can be accessed via **Web Extra 2–13**.

Finally, crime against the elderly will likely undergo a significant increase as baby boomers enter their retirement years. Not only will the elderly comprise an increasingly larger segment of the population as boomers age, but it is anticipated that they will be wealthier than any preceding generation of retirees, making them attractive targets for scam artists and property criminals.[88]

Thematic Question How do hate crimes and the existence of survivalist organizations highlight the dichotomy between individual rights and the need for public order?

Hate Crime

hate crime (UCR/NIBRS)
A criminal offense committed against a person, property, or society that is motivated, in whole or in part, by the offender's bias against a race, religion, disability, sexual orientation, or ethnicity/national origin.

A significant change in crime-reporting practices resulted from the Hate Crime Statistics Act,[89] signed into law by President George H. W. Bush in 1990. The act mandates a statistical tally of **hate crimes**; data collection under the law began in 1991. Congress defined *hate crime* as an offense "in which the defendant's conduct was motivated by hatred, bias, or prejudice, based on the actual or perceived race, color, religion, national origin, ethnicity, gender, or sexual orientation of another individual or group of individuals."[90] In 2009, police agencies reported a total of 6,604 hate-crime incidents, including three murders, across the country. As Figure 2–6 shows, 17.7% of the incidents were motivated by religious bias, 49.1% were caused by racial hatred, and 13.5% were driven by prejudice against ethnicity or national origin. Another 18.5% of all hate crimes were based on sexual orientation, most committed against males believed by their victimizers to be homosexuals.[91] A relatively small number of hate crimes targeted people with physical or mental disabilities.

Following the terrorist attacks of September 11, 2001, authorities in some jurisdictions reported a dramatic shift in the nature of hate crime, with race-motivated crimes declining and crimes motivated by religion or ethnicity increasing sharply.[92] Islamic individuals, in particular, became the target of many such crimes.

Most hate crimes consist of intimidation, although vandalism, simple assault, and aggravated assault also account for a number of hate-crime offenses. A few robberies and rapes were also classified as hate crimes in 2009.

Although hate crimes are popularly conceived of as crimes motivated by racial enmity, the Violent Crime Control and Law Enforcement Act of 1994 created a new category of "crimes of violence motivated by gender." Congress defined this crime as "a crime of violence committed because of gender or on the basis of gender, and due, at least in part, to an animus based on the victim's gender." The 1994 act did not establish separate penalties for gender-motivated crimes, anticipating that they would be prosecuted as felonies under existing laws. The 1994 act also mandated that crimes motivated by biases against people with disabilities be considered hate crimes.

▲ Evidence of a hate crime: Nazi symbols spray-painted on Arab graves. Why are hate crimes given special attention under the law? *Reuters/Vincent Kessler/Landov Media*

Hate crimes are sometimes called *bias crimes.* One form of bias crime that bears special mention is *homophobic homicide*, a term that refers to the murder of a homosexual by those opposed to that lifestyle. The Southern Poverty Law Center, which tracks hate groups, identified 888 such groups operating in the United States in 2007.[93] The center, which is based in Montgomery, Alabama, says that the number of hate groups has jumped 48% since 2000, mostly because of the formation of new anti-immigrant organizations. Learn more about hate crime and what can be done to address it at **Library Extras 2–17** and **2–18**.

Corporate and White-Collar Crime

In 2009, investment fund manager Bernard ("Bernie") Madoff plead guilty to operating a Ponzi scheme that defrauded investors out of as much as $50 billion.[94] Called "Wall Street's biggest fraud" by some, Madoff's shenanigans purportedly cost investors $50 billion in money that seemed to simply disappear.[95] Madoff, a former chairman of the NASDAQ stock market, pleaded guilty to 11 felony counts, including securities fraud, mail fraud, wire fraud, money laundering, and perjury. He was sentenced to 150 years in prison.[96]

> With each arrest, indictment and prosecution, we sent this clear, unmistakable message: corrupt corporate executives are no better than common thieves.
>
> —John Ashcroft, former U.S. attorney general[vi]

The recent economic downturn, combined with the collapse of the housing market and the loss of jobs in many sectors of the economy, sparked a rapid growth in mortgage fraud scams. There are three types of mortgage fraud, which is a federal crime. The first, fraud for profit, involves a scheme by "ghost buyers" to collect cash; these buyers have no interest in owning the property against which money is being borrowed. The second type is fraud for housing, or application fraud, in which otherwise legitimate home buyers fake documents to make them appear eligible for a loan that they would not otherwise get. According to one report, 61% of all reported mortgage frauds in 2008 involved misrepresentations made on applications for a mortgage. The third type of mortgage fraud involves overestimating a property's valuation or submitting a false appraisal to defraud purchasers and lenders.

A study by the Mortgage Asset Research Institute concluded that mortgage fraud was more prevalent in 2009 than it had been at the height of the nation's building boom just a few years earlier.[97] Federal agencies say they're inundated with mortgage fraud cases but are also starting to look into a new breed of scams perpetrated by those who offer to refinance homes or save them from foreclosure. In one of the new scams, criminals offer to help people who are about to lose their homes, collecting several thousand dollars up front before disappearing.[98] In early 2009, the Federal Trade Commission announced a wave of law enforcement actions against businesses using deceptive tactics to market mortgage modification and home foreclosure relief services, including firms that gave the false impression they were affiliated with the federal government.[99]

Under the American system of criminal justice, corporations can be treated as separate legal entities and can be convicted of violations of the criminal law under a legal principle

Lecture Note Describe hate crimes as those in which there is evidence of prejudice based on race, religion, sexual orientation, or ethnicity. Use assaults on Arab Americans following the 2001 terrorist attacks as an example. Ask students whether they think the number and intensity of hate crimes will increase or decrease throughout the twenty-first century and why.

corporate crime
A violation of a criminal statute by a corporate entity or by its executives, employees, or agents acting on behalf of and for the benefit of the corporation, partnership, or other form of business entity.[vii]

white-collar crime
Violations of the criminal law committed by a person of respectability and high social status in the course of his or her occupation. Also, nonviolent crime for financial gain utilizing deception and committed by anyone who has special technical or professional knowledge of business or government, irrespective of the person's occupation.

organized crime
The unlawful activities of the members of a highly organized, disciplined association engaged in supplying illegal goods or services, including gambling, prostitution, loan-sharking, narcotics, and labor racketeering, and in other unlawful activities.[viii]

transnational organized crime
Unlawful activity undertaken and supported by organized criminal groups operating across national boundaries.

known as the *identification doctrine.* In 2002, for example, a federal jury convicted global accounting firm Arthur Andersen of obstruction of justice after its employees shredded documents related to Enron's bankruptcy in an effort to impede an investigation by securities regulators. The conviction, which was overturned by a unanimous U.S. Supreme Court in 2005,[100] capped the firm's demise, and it ended U.S. operations in August 2002.[101]

Although corporations may be convicted of a crime, the human perpetrators of **corporate crime** are business executives known as *white-collar criminals.* **White-collar crime** was first defined in 1939 by Edwin H. Sutherland in his presidential address to the American Sociological Society.[102] Sutherland proposed that "crime in the suites" (a reference to corporate offices) rivaled the importance of street crime in its potential impact on American society.

In July 2002, President George W. Bush unveiled plans to create a new Corporate Fraud Task Force within the federal government and proposed a new law providing criminal penalties for corporate fraud. He told corporate leaders on Wall Street, "At this moment, America's greatest economic need is higher ethical standards—standards enforced by strict laws and upheld by responsible business leaders."[103] A few months later, the president signed into law the Sarbanes-Oxley Act.[104] The new law created tough provisions designed to deter and punish corporate and accounting fraud and corruption and to protect the interests of workers and shareholders. Under the Sarbanes-Oxley Act, corporate officials (chief executive officers and chief financial officers) must personally vouch for the truth and accuracy of their companies' financial statements, and federal penalties for obstructing justice and, specifically, for shredding or destroying documents that might aid in a criminal investigation of business practices are substantially increased. Learn more about corporate and white-collar crime at the National White Collar Crime Center (NW3C) via **Web Extra 2–14**. Established in 1992, the NW3C provides a national support system for the prevention, investigation, and prosecution of multijurisdictional economic crimes. Learn more about how corporations can be held accountable from CorpWatch via **Web Extra 2–15**.

Organized Crime

▲ Actor James Gandolfini (Tony Soprano) from HBO's hit series *The Sopranos*, on right. The popular show explored the life of fictionalized organized crime figures in New Jersey. Why was the show such a hit with viewers?
Globe Photos, Inc.

For many people, the term **organized crime** conjures up images of the Mafia (also called the *Cosa Nostra*) or the hit HBO TV series *The Sopranos.* Although organized criminal activity is decidedly a group phenomenon, the groups involved in such activity in the United States today display a great deal of variation. During the past few decades in the United States, the preeminence of traditional Sicilian American criminal organizations has fallen to such diverse criminal associations as the Black Mafia, the Cuban Mafia, the Haitian Mafia, the Colombian cartels, and Asian criminal groups like the Chinese Tongs and street gangs, Japanese yakuza, and Vietnamese gangs. Included here as well might be inner-city gangs, the best known of which are probably the Los Angeles Crips and Bloods and the Chicago Vice Lords, international drug rings, outlaw motorcycle gangs like the Hell's Angels and the Pagans, and other looser associations of small-time thugs, prison gangs, and drug dealers. Noteworthy among these groups—especially for their involvement in the lucrative drug trade—are the Latino organized bands, including the Dominican, Colombian, Mexican, and Cuban importers of cocaine, heroin, marijuana, and other controlled substances.

The unlawful activities of organized groups that operate across national boundaries are especially significant. Such activity is referred to as **transnational organized crime**. Transnational criminal associations worthy of special mention are the Hong Kong–based Triads, the South American cocaine cartels, the Italian Mafia, the Japanese yakuza, the Russian *Mafiya*, and the West African crime groups—each of which extends its reach well beyond its home country. In some parts of the world, close links between organized crime and terrorist groups involve money laundering, which provides cash to finance the activities of terrorist cells and to finance paramilitary efforts to overthrow established governments.

Former CIA Director R. James Woolsey points out that "while organized crime is not a new phenomenon today, some governments find their authority besieged at home and their foreign policy interests imperiled abroad. Drug trafficking, links between drug traffickers and terrorists, smuggling of illegal aliens, massive financial and bank fraud, arms smuggling, potential involvement in the theft and sale of nuclear material, political intimidation, and corruption all constitute a poisonous brew—a mixture potentially as deadly as what we faced during the cold war."[105] The challenge for today's criminal justice student is to recognize that crime does not respect national boundaries. Crime is global, and what happens in one part of the world could affect us all.[106]

Gun Crime

Guns and gun crime seem to pervade American culture. Constitutional guarantees of the right to bear arms have combined with historical circumstances to make ours a well-armed society. Guns are used in many types of crimes. Each year, approximately 1 million serious crimes—including homicide, rape, robbery, and assault—involve the use of a handgun. In a typical year, approximately 10,000 murders are committed in the United States with firearms. A recent report by the BJS found that 18% of state prison inmates and 15% of federal inmates were armed at the time they committed the crime for which they were imprisoned,[107] and 9% of those in state prisons said they fired a gun while committing the offense for which they were serving time.[108]

Both federal and state governments have responded to public concern over the ready availability of handguns with regulatory statutes. In 1994, Congress passed the Brady Handgun Violence Prevention Act,[109] which President Bill Clinton signed into law. The law was named for former Press Secretary James Brady, who was shot and severely wounded in an attempt on President Ronald Reagan's life on March 30, 1981. The law mandates a five-day waiting period before the purchase of a handgun, and it established a national instant criminal background check system that firearms dealers must use before selling a handgun.[110]

While the Brady law may limit retail purchases of handguns by felons, a BJS study found that most offenders obtain weapons from friends or family members or "on the street" rather than attempt to purchase them at retail establishments.[111] In 2001, undercover congressional investigators were able to show that applicants using fake forms of identification, such as counterfeit driver's licenses with fictitious names, could easily circumvent Brady law provisions.[112] Moreover, according to these studies, an ever-growing number of violent criminals are now carrying handguns. A 2006 study found no evidence that stringent gun-control laws have an impact on crime.[113] The study, which used data from all 50 states, found that gun-control laws do not have an impact on the crime rate or on the occurrence of any specific type of serious crime. Such laws are ineffective in reducing crime, the study authors said, because they do not substantially reduce the availability of firearms to criminal offenders.

Among other legislation, the Violent Crime Control and Law Enforcement Act of 1994[114] regulated the sale of firearms within the United States and banned the manufacture of 19 military-style assault weapons, including those with specific combat features such as high-capacity ammunition clips capable of holding more than ten rounds. The federal ban on assault weapons ended in 2004, however, when it was not renewed by Congress.

The 1996 Domestic Violence Offender Gun Ban[115] prohibited individuals convicted of misdemeanor domestic-violence offenses from owning or using firearms. Soon after the law was passed, however, it became embroiled in controversy when hundreds of police officers across the country who had been convicted of domestic-violence offenses were found to be in violation of the ban. A number of officers lost their jobs, while others were placed in positions that did not require them to carry firearms.[116]

Following the 1999 Columbine High School shooting, many states moved to tighten controls over handguns and assault weapons. The California legislature, for example, restricted gun purchases to one per month and tightened a ten-year-old ban on assault weapons. Similarly, Illinois passed a law requiring that gun owners lock their weapons away from anyone under age 14.

In 2005, in a move that some saw as promoting handgun sales, the federal Protection of Lawful Commerce in Firearms Act granted gunmakers and most gun dealers immunity from

▲ Los Angeles County Deputy Sheriff Jason Molina with a cache of guns turned in by citizens in South Central Los Angeles in exchange for $100 gift cards. The "Gun for Gift Card" exchange event is held twice yearly, on Mother's Day and Christmas. Do you think such programs help reduce gun violence in our society?
AFP Photo/Mark Ralston/NewsCom.com

lawsuits brought by victims of gun crimes and their survivors. The law removed negligence as viable grounds for a civil suit against a gun dealer who carelessly sells a gun to someone who is at risk for using it in a crime. The law states that the dealer can be sued only if he or she knew of the gun buyer's criminal intent before the purchase. Gunmakers were also made immune from suits alleging product liability for having manufactured potentially lethal items.

In 2008, in the case of *District of Columbia* v. *Heller*,[117] the U.S. Supreme Court came down firmly in support of private gun ownership when it ruled that the Constitution's Second Amendment protects an individual's right to possess a firearm and to use that firearm for traditionally lawful purposes, such as self-defense within the home. The *Heller* case addressed three strict gun-control ordinances that the District of Columbia City Council had enacted in 1976 and that entirely banned anyone from carrying a handgun or other deadly or dangerous weapon without a license. The ordinances also required that any firearms, such as rifles and shotguns, be kept either disassembled or with a trigger lock in place. Prior to *Heller*, the Supreme Court had not squarely addressed a Second Amendment case since 1939 and had never previously decided whether the Second Amendment confers a right to bear arms upon individuals or only upon the militias it refers to in its opening clause. In the intervening 69 years, however, many federal and state governments had passed laws regulating and restricting the ownership and use of guns, making the *Heller* decision especially significant.

Because *Heller* concerned a District of Columbia law, gun-control advocates interpreted it as applicable only to federal enclaves and soon questioned the applicability of the Court's ruling to jurisdictions not under direct federal control. In 2010, in the important case of *McDonald* v. *City of Chicago*,[118] the Court established an individual's right to keep a gun for self-defense in the home as a "fundamental" constitutional right. Any right that the Court declares to be fundamental cannot be contravened by laws at any level unless the government can demonstrate a compelling need to do so and only if limits imposed take the narrowest possible approach to addressing the issue. Consequently, in the wake of *McDonald,* states and local jurisdictions may still place restrictions on gun ownership, such as registration requirements or prohibiting the possession of handguns by convicted felons, but those restrictions must be reasonable and cannot be extreme.

In Congress, debate continues about whether to require gun manufacturers to create and retain "ballistic fingerprints" (the marks left on a bullet by the barrel of the gun from which it was fired) of each weapon they produce. Although a national ballistics fingerprinting requirement may still be years away, three states—California, Maryland, and New York—and the District of Columbia already require that a record be kept of the "fingerprint" characteristics of each new handgun sold.[119] Microstamping uses laser engraving to encode a weapon's serial number on each cartridge that it fires, and California authorities believe that the technology will allow handguns to be traced to their manufacturer and then the first purchaser using only spent cartridges left at crime scenes.

For more about issues related to guns and crime, read the 2007 Report to the President on the Virginia Tech campus shooting at **Library Extra 2–19**, and learn more about promising strategies to reduce gun violence at **Library Extra 2–20**. For the latest information on gun violence and gun laws, visit the Brady Center to Prevent Gun Violence via **Web Extra 2–16**. The National Rifle Association (NRA) site at **Web Extra 2–17** provides arguments in support of responsible access to firearms.

Drug Crime

In 2008, 96 young men—including 75 San Diego State University (SDSU) students—were arrested on a variety of drug and weapons charges as a result of a joint Drug Enforcement Agency (DEA)/local police operation called Sudden Fall. During the operation, undercover officers infiltrated seven of the university's fraternity houses and seized four pounds of cocaine, 50 pounds of marijuana, 48 hydroponic marijuana plants, 350 Ecstasy pills, 30 vials of hash oil, methamphetamine, psilocybin (mushrooms), various illicit prescription drugs, a shotgun, three semiautomatic pistols, various sets of brass knuckles, and $60,000 in cash. The agents said that they also found evidence of widespread drug dealing at SDSU's fraternity houses. The investigation had begun a year earlier after a cocaine overdose caused the death of a

19-year-old female student on the SDSU campus. "This operation shows how accessible and pervasive illegal drugs continue to be on our college campuses and how common it is for students to be selling to other students," said San Diego County District Attorney Bonnie Dumanis.[120]

The White House Office of National Drug Control Policy (ONDCP) estimates annual illicit drug sales in the United States of around $65 billion, while the United Nations says that illegal drug revenue in the United States, Canada, and Mexico totals around $142 billion yearly.[121] Unlike most major crimes, drug-law violations continue to increase, lending support to those who feel that this country is experiencing more overall crime than traditional tabulations show. The relentless increase in drug violations largely accounts for the fact that America's prison populations have continued to grow, even when official crime rates are declining. Figure 2–7 shows the number of suspects arrested for drug-law violations in the United States between 1975 and 2009.

▲ San Diego County Deputy District Attorney Damon Mosler (at podium) pointing to drugs and firearms seized during the arrest of 96 people, including 75 students at San Diego State University, in 2008 after an extensive undercover investigation called Operation Sudden Fall. How common are illegal drugs on the nation's campuses?
Dennis Poroy/AP Wide World Photos

Alone, drug-law violations are themselves criminal, but more and more studies are linking drug abuse to other serious crimes. An early study by the RAND Corporation found that most of the "violent predators" among prisoners had extensive histories of heroin abuse, often in combination with alcohol and other drugs.[122] Some cities reported that a large percentage of their homicides were drug related.[123] More recent studies also link drug abuse to other serious crimes. Community leaders perceive, and data analyses confirm, that crack cocaine profoundly impacts violent crime, with homicide rates closely tracking cocaine-use levels among adult male arrestees.[124] Prisoner survey data show that 19% of state inmates and 16% of federal prisoners reported committing their most recent offense to obtain money for drugs.[125] A 2000 study found that 13.3% of convicted jail inmates said that they had committed their offense to get money for drugs.[126]

Criminal justice system costs associated with the handling of drug offenders have increased substantially in recent years. Between 1984 and 2002, for example, the annual number of defendants charged with a drug offense in federal courts increased from 11,854 to more than 30,000.[127] Similarly, between 1984 and 2002, drug offenses accounted for an increased proportion of the federal criminal caseload, even when charges weren't brought. During 1984, 18% of referrals to U.S. attorneys were drug related, compared to 31% during 2002.[128] Some of the increase stems from changes in federal drug laws. Whatever the cause, the drug–crime link is costly to society and shows few signs of abating. Learn more about drug crime and efforts being made to combat it at **Library Extra 2–21**.

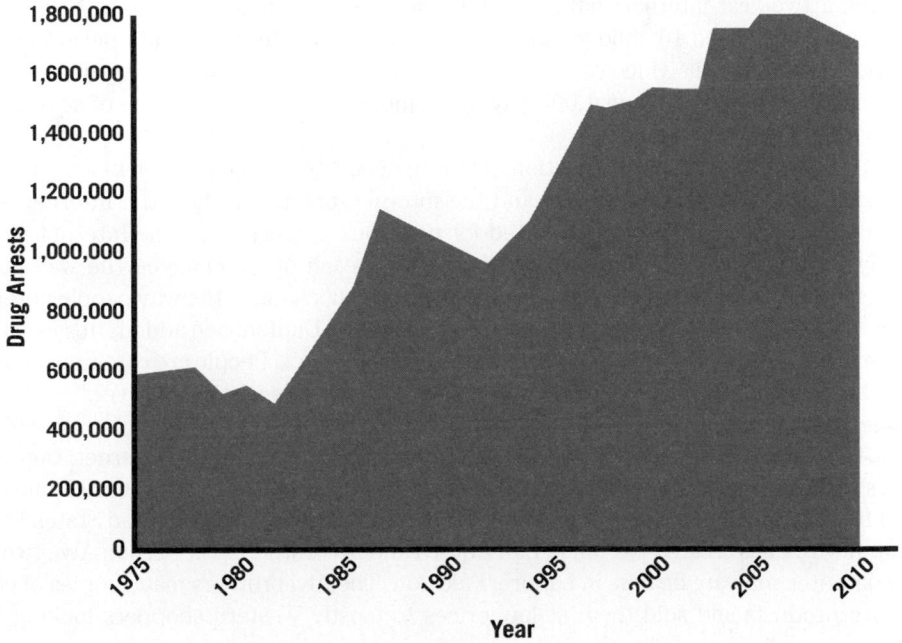

FIGURE 2–7
Drug Arrests in the United States, 1975–2009

Source: Federal Bureau of Investigation, *Crime in the United States* (Washington, DC: U.S. Department of Justice, various years).

malware
Malicious computer programs such as viruses, worms, and Trojan horses.

computer crime
Any crime perpetrated through the use of computer technology. Also, any violation of a federal or state computer-crime statute. Also called *cybercrime*.

High-Technology and Computer Crime

A few years ago, the Ziff Davis digital publication *eWeek* reported the release on the Internet of a **malware** software program that encrypts files on an infected computer and then demands a $300 ransom for e-mail delivery of a decryption password.[129] The malware, identified as Cryzip, makes data files on infected computers unavailable to legitimate users and displays step-by-step instructions on how to pay a ransom with a credit card for file retrieval. Cryzip is a type of software known as *ransomware*, and its release points to an increasing level of sophistication among online thieves practicing computer crime.

▲ Albert Gonzalez, a 28-year-old American believed to be one of the nation's cybercrime kingpins. Gonzales was indicted in 2009 along with two Russian accomplices on charges that they carried out the largest hacking and identity-theft caper in U.S. history. What is cybercrime, and why is it a threat? *Reuters/US Law Enforcement via Wired.com/Landov*

Computer crimes, also called *cybercrimes* or *information technology crimes*, use computers and computer technology as tools in crime commission. Thefts of computer equipment, although sometimes spectacular, are not computer crimes but are instead classified as larcenies. "True" computer criminals go beyond the theft of hardware, focusing instead on the information stored in computer systems and manipulating it in a way that violates the law.

While a generally accepted typology of computer-based crime has yet to be developed,[130] Peter Grabosky of the Australian Institute of Criminology suggests that most such crimes fall into one of the following broad categories:[131] (1) theft of services, such as telephone or long-distance access; (2) communications in furtherance of criminal conspiracies—for example, the e-mail communications said to have taken place between members of Osama bin Laden's al-Qaeda terrorist network;[132] (3) information piracy and forgery—that is, the stealing of trade secrets or copyrighted information; (4) dissemination of offensive materials, such as child pornography, and extortion threats, such as those made against financial institutions by hackers claiming the ability to destroy the institutions' electronic records; (5) electronic money laundering and tax evasion through electronic funds transfers that conceal the origin of financial proceeds; (6) electronic vandalism and terrorism, including computer viruses, worms, Trojan horses, and cyberterrorism—that is, cyberattacks on critical components of a nation's infrastructure, such as its banking system; (7) telemarketing fraud, including investment frauds and illegitimate electronic auctions; (8) illegal interception of telecommunications—that is, illegal eavesdropping; and (9) electronic funds transfer fraud—specifically, the illegal interception and diversion of legitimate transactions.

Many of the crimes committed via the Internet—like prostitution, drug sales, theft, and fraud—are not new forms of offending. They are, rather, traditional forms of offending that use new technology in their commission. In 2010, for example, more than 50 people were arrested in the United States and charged with distributing pornographic images of children following a two-year international law enforcement effort dubbed Operation Nest Egg.[133] The investigation freed 16 child victims, some of whom had been forced to perform sexual activities on adults while video cameras rolled. At one point, according to investigators, the group encompassed more than 1,000 paying members who traded millions of sexually explicit images of children.

U.S. Customs and Border Protection Senior Special Agent Donald Daufenbach, an international expert in child pornography and the Internet, points out that "the Internet is like anything else: It can be bent or perverted for nefarious purposes. . . . The Internet has absolutely changed the way people communicate with each other, changed the way people conduct commerce, changed the way people do research, changed the way people entertain themselves and changed the way people break the law."[134] Daufenbach added, "It's just a new version of what the mails or what the telephones used to be. . . . People are catching on pretty quick, but law enforcement is lagging behind miserably in this whole endeavor."

computer virus
A computer program designed to secretly invade systems and either modify the way in which they operate or alter the information they store. Viruses are destructive software programs that may effectively vandalize computers of all types and sizes.

Computer viruses have become a special concern of the general computer user during the past several years, especially as more people have connected to the Internet. Computer viruses were brought to public attention in 1988 when the Pakistani virus (or Pakistani brain virus) became widespread in personal and office computers across the United States.[135] The Pakistani virus was created by Amjad Farooq Alvi and his brother Basit Farooq Alvi, two cut-rate computer software dealers in Lahore, Pakistan. The Alvi brothers made copies of costly software products and sold them at low prices to mostly Western shoppers looking for a bargain. Motivated by convoluted logic, the brothers hid a virus on each disk they sold to punish buyers for seeking to evade copyright laws. Since then, many other virus attacks have made headlines, including the infamous Michelangelo virus in 1992; the intentional distribution of infected software on an AIDS-related research CD-ROM distributed about the same time; the Kournikova virus in 2000; and the Sircam, Nimda, W32, NastyBrew, Berbew, Mydoom, and Code Red worms, all of which made their appearance or were substantially modified by their creators between 2001 and 2006.

In 2003, federal legislators acted to criminalize the sending of unsolicited commercial e-mail, or **spam**. The federal CAN-SPAM Act (Controlling the Assault of Nonsolicited Pornography and Marketing), which took effect on January 1, 2004, regulates the sending of "commercial electronic mail messages."[136] The law, which applies equally to mass mailings and to individual e-mail messages, defines commercial electronic mail messages as electronic mail whose *primary purpose* is the "commercial advertisement or promotion of a commercial product or service." The CAN-SPAM law requires that a commercial e-mail message include the following three features: (1) a clear and conspicuous identification that the message is an advertisement or solicitation, (2) an opt-out feature allowing recipients to opt out of future mailings, and (3) a valid physical address identifying the sender. Some experts estimate that 80% of all e mail today is spam,[137] and a number of states have enacted their own antispam laws.

spam
Unsolicited commercial bulk e-mail whose primary purpose is the advertisement or promotion of a commercial product or service.

Computer-related crimes can also involve copyright infringement. In 2005, for example, the U.S. Supreme Court agreed to hear an appeal from the music industry, and in the landmark case of *MGM* v. *Grokster*,[138] the Court found that online file-sharing services may be held liable for copyright infringement if they promote their services explicitly as a way for users to download copyrighted music and other content.

One form of cybercrime that relies primarily on social engineering to succeed is *phishing* (pronounced *fishing*). Phishing is a relatively new form of high-technology fraud that uses official-looking e-mail messages to elicit responses from victims, directing them to phony websites. Microsoft Corporation says that phishing is "the fastest-growing form of online fraud in the world today."[139] Phishing e-mails typically instruct recipients to validate or update account information before their accounts are canceled. Phishing schemes, which have targeted most major banks, the Federal Deposit Insurance Corporation, IBM, eBay, PayPal, and some major health-care providers, are designed to steal valuable information such as credit card numbers, Social Security numbers, user IDs, and passwords. Gartner Inc., a leading provider of research and analysis on the global information technology industry, released a report estimating that some 57 million adult Americans received phishing e-mails during the spring of 2004 and that 11 million recipients clicked on the link contained in the messages.[140] Gartner estimated that 1.78 million recipients actually provided personal information to the thieves behind the phishing schemes.

Symantec Corporation's 2010 Information Protection Survey determined that 73% of small and medium-sized businesses experienced cyberattacks in the previous 12 months.[141] Of those, 30% were said to be somewhat or extremely effective, and all attacks resulted in losses ranging from downtime to theft of corporate data. The average annual cost of cyberattacks to small and medium-sized businesses in the year preceding the Symantec survey was $188,242.

Other researchers have determined that some of the most serious corporate computer security threats come from employees, including 70% of all incidents involving unauthorized access to information systems and 95% of all network intrusions that result in significant financial loss.[142]

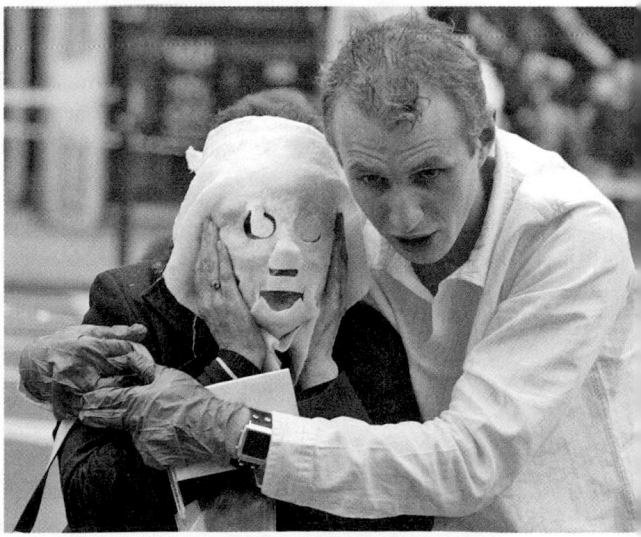

▲ A commuter being helped away from the Edgware Road Station following terrorist bombings in London's subway system in 2005. How might future acts of terrorism be prevented?
Jane Mingay/AP Wide World Photos

In 2004, the BJS released initial results from its 2001 National Computer Security Survey (NCSS), which was conducted in collaboration with the U.S. Census Bureau.[143] The 2004 report summarized findings from a pilot survey of 500 companies nationwide. Nearly three-fourths of businesses surveyed reported detecting at least one computer security incident during the previous 12-month period. Computer viruses were the most common type of incident reported (65%), followed by denial-of-service attacks (25%) and vandalism or

CJ Exhibit 2–2
What Is Terrorist Activity?

Federal law enforcement efforts directed against agents of foreign terrorist organizations derive their primary authority from the Immigration and Nationality Act, found in Chapter 12 of the U.S. Code. The act defines *terrorist activity* as follows:

(ii) "Terrorist activity" defined

As used in this chapter, the term "terrorist activity" means any activity which is unlawful under the laws of the place where it is committed (or which, if committed in the United States, would be unlawful under the laws of the United States or any State) and which involves any of the following:

I. The hijacking or sabotage of any conveyance (including an aircraft, vessel, or vehicle).

II. The seizing or detaining, and threatening to kill, injure, or continue to detain, another individual in order to compel a third person (including a governmental organization) to do or abstain from doing any act as an explicit or implicit condition for the release of the individual seized or detained.

III. A violent attack upon an internationally protected person (as defined in section 1116(b)(4) of title 18) or upon the liberty of such a person.

IV. An assassination.

V. The use of any—

a. biological agent, chemical agent, or nuclear weapon or device, or

b. explosive or firearm (other than for mere personal monetary gain), with intent to endanger, directly or indirectly, the safety of one or more individuals or to cause substantial damage to property.

VI. A threat, attempt, or conspiracy to do any of the foregoing.

(iii) "Engage in terrorist activity" defined

As used in this chapter, the term "engage in terrorist activity" means to commit, in an individual capacity or as a member of an organization, an act of terrorist activity or an act which the actor knows, or reasonably should know, affords material support to any individual, organization, or government in conducting a terrorist activity at any time, including any of the following acts:

I. The preparation or planning of a terrorist activity.

II. The gathering of information on potential targets for terrorist activity.

III. The providing of any type of material support, including a safe house, transportation, communications, funds, false documentation or identification, weapons, explosives, or training, to any individual the actor knows or has reason to believe has committed or plans to commit a terrorist activity.

IV. The soliciting of funds or other things of value for terrorist activity or for any terrorist organization.

V. The solicitation of any individual for membership in a terrorist organization, terrorist government, or to engage in a terrorist activity.

sabotage of computer equipment or computer networks (19%). Other crimes, such as fraud, theft of proprietary information, and embezzlement, were also reported. Not surprisingly, the largest companies experienced the greatest number of incidents. The NCSS was sponsored by the U.S. Department of Justice, Bureau of Justice Statistics and the U.S. Department of Homeland Security, National Cyber Security Division. This data-collection effort was part of the President's 2003 National Strategy to Secure Cyberspace. You may access the NCSS at **Library Extra 2–22**. The CSI/FBI Computer Crime and Security Survey can be found online at **Library Extra 2–23**.

Terrorism

Terrorism as a criminal activity and the prevention of further acts of terrorism became primary concerns of American justice system officials following the September 11, 2001, attacks on the World Trade Center and the Pentagon. Long before the September 11 attacks, however, terrorism was a concern of law enforcement and other government officials. In 2001, for example, international terrorist attacks totaled 864 worldwide—down from the 1,106 reported a year earlier.[144]

There is no single definition of terrorism that is applicable to all places and all circumstances. Some definitions are statutory in nature, while others were created for such practical purposes as gauging success in the fight against terrorism. The FBI, for example, defines **terrorism** as "a violent act or an act dangerous to human life in violation of the criminal laws of the United States or of any state to intimidate or coerce a government, the civilian population, or any segment thereof, in furtherance of political or social objectives."[145] One of the most comprehensive and widely used definitions of terrorist activity can be found in the federal Immigration and Nationality Act, an excerpt of which appears in CJ Exhibit 2–2.

terrorism
A violent act or an act dangerous to human life in violation of the criminal laws of the United States or of any state, committed to intimidate or coerce a government, the civilian population, or any segment thereof in furtherance of political or social objectives.[ix]

Types of Terrorism

It is important to distinguish between two major forms of terrorism: domestic and international. Such distinctions are generally made in terms of the origin, base of operations, and objectives of a terrorist organization. **Domestic terrorism** refers to the unlawful use of force or violence by a group or an individual who is based and operates entirely within the United States and its territories without foreign direction and whose acts are directed against elements of the U.S. government or population.[146] **International terrorism**, in contrast, is the unlawful use of force or violence by a group or an individual who has some connection to a foreign power or whose activities transcend national boundaries against people or property to intimidate or coerce a government, the civilian population, or any segment thereof in furtherance of political or social objectives.[147] International terrorism is sometimes mistakenly called *foreign terrorism*, a term that, strictly speaking, refers only to acts of terrorism that occur outside the United States.

Another new kind of terrorism, called **cyberterrorism**, is lurking on the horizon. Cyberterrorism makes use of high technology, especially computers and the Internet, in the planning and carrying out of terrorist attacks. The term was coined in the 1980s by Barry Collin, a senior research fellow at the Institute for Security and Intelligence in California, who used it to refer to the convergence of cyberspace and terrorism.[148] It was later popularized by a 1996 RAND report that warned of an emerging "new terrorism" distinguished by how terrorist groups organize and by how they use technology. The report warned of a coming "netwar" or "infowar" consisting of coordinated cyberattacks on our nation's economic, business, and military infrastructure.[149] A year later, FBI Agent Mark M. Pollitt offered a working definition of *cyberterrorism*, saying that it is "the premeditated, politically motivated attack against information, computer systems, computer programs, and data which results in violence against noncombatant targets by subnational groups or clandestine agents."[150]

Scenarios describing cyberterrorism possibilities are imaginative and diverse. Some have suggested that a successful cyberterrorist attack on the nation's air traffic control system might cause airplanes to collide in midair or that an attack on food- and cereal-processing plants that drastically altered the levels of certain nutritional supplements might sicken or kill a large number of our nation's young children. Other such attacks might cause the country's power grid to collapse or might muddle the records and transactions of banks and stock exchanges. Possible targets in such attacks are almost endless. A 2005 national survey of computer security experts found that almost half were expecting a "digital Pearl Harbor," in which American society would be plunged into chaos by malicious hackers, to occur within the next few years.[151]

domestic terrorism
The unlawful use of force or violence by a group or an individual who is based and operates entirely within the United States and its territories without foreign direction and whose acts are directed at elements of the U.S. government or population.[x]

international terrorism
The unlawful use of force or violence by a group or an individual who has some connection to a foreign power or whose activities transcend national boundaries against people or property in order to intimidate or coerce a government, the civilian population, or any segment thereof in furtherance of political or social objectives.[xi]

cyberterrorism
A form of terrorism that makes use of high technology, especially computers and the Internet, in the planning and carrying out of terrorist attacks.

Organization and Scope of Terrorist Groups

In 2008, FBI Director Robert S. Mueller III identified three organizational levels that characterize violent extremists seeking to damage the United States and its interests.[152] The top tier, Mueller said, "is the core al-Qaeda organization, which has established new sanctuaries in the ungoverned spaces, tribal areas, and frontier provinces of Pakistan." The middle tier Mueller called the most complex. "We are finding," he said, "small groups who have some ties to an established terrorist organization but are largely self-directed. Think of them as al-Qaeda franchises—hybrids of homegrown radicals and more sophisticated operatives." The bottom tier, Mueller noted, "is made up of homegrown extremists. They are self-radicalizing, self-financing, and self-executing. They meet up on the Internet instead of in foreign training camps. They have no formal affiliation with al-Qaeda, but they are inspired by its message of violence."

Terrorist groups are active throughout the world, and the United States is not their only target. Terrorist organizations operate in South America, Africa, the Middle East, Latin America, the Philippines, Japan, India, Ireland, England, Nepal, and some of the now independent states of the former Soviet Union. The Central Intelligence Agency (CIA) reports that "between now and 2015 terrorist tactics will become increasingly sophisticated and designed to achieve mass casualties."[153] The CIA also notes that nations "with poor governance; ethnic, cultural, or religious tensions; weak economies; and porous borders will be prime breeding grounds for terrorism."[154] Read the entire CIA report on global trends that may increase the risk of terrorism at **Library Extra 2–24**. The U.S. Department of State's annual report, *Patterns of Global Terrorism*, can be found at **Library Extra 2–25**, and the 2004 final report of the National Commission on Terrorist Attacks upon the United States (the 911 Commission) can be read at **Library Extra 2–26**.

CJ News

FBI Warns of Growing Threat from Islamic Extremists "Next Door"

Plots by American-based Islamic terrorists with no direct ties to international terror networks form a large and growing threat to the American homeland, FBI and other security officials say.

"The trend we're seeing is that we are uncovering more instances of people here who have been radicalized . . . where there is not a direct thumbprint of al-Qaeda," says John Miller, the FBI's assistant director for public affairs.

Justice Department records show that the FBI and other federal and local agencies have led prosecutions of a dozen such alleged plots since the Sept. 11 attacks on New York City and Washington. One such prosecution began in May 2007, when five New Jersey Muslim men were charged with plotting to kill soldiers at the Army's Fort Dix, N.J., compound. A sixth man was charged with helping the group obtain illegal firearms.

The government has won terrorism convictions in seven cases. Others are ongoing.

The focus on American-based terror cells is a shift from post 9/11 thinking, when intelligence and security officials expected attacks to come from "sleeper cells" of al-Qaeda agents who, like the Washington and New York City attackers, had filtered into the USA from abroad.

"That was my intuition at the time," says George Tenet in an interview. Tenet was CIA director from 1997 to 2004 and just released a book, *At the Center of the Storm*, about his tenure. Tenet says the lesson is "don't get fixed on a particular face [because] there may be multiple kinds of faces."

Pasquale D'Amuro, the FBI's counterterrorism chief in 2002 and 2003, says the alleged New Jersey plot appears to be such a case. The six men arrested, he notes, were born in the former Yugoslavia, Jordan and Turkey and had lived in the USA without incident. One was a citizen, two were legal residents and three were here illegally. They had lived here at least six years, neighbors told the Associated Press.

"If they look like the neighbors next door, it's because that's what they are," says D'Amuro, CEO of Giuliani Security and Safety in New York.

"That they would come here, be welcomed and then want to attack us—that's what people have a hard time understanding."

In some cases, such as that of six Yemeni-Americans in Lackawanna, N.Y., the accused plotters had undergone training at terrorist camps overseas but had not focused on an American target. In others, such as the New Jersey plot, the government alleges that plotters had identified targets and were trying to purchase arms.

▲ A mosque in Dearborn, Michigan. The greater Detroit area is thought to have about 200,000 Arab Americans—said to be the densest Arab population of any community outside the Middle East. While most American Muslims are peaceful, law-abiding citizens, the FBI has warned about a threat from homegrown radical Islamic fundamentalists. Do you think such a threat should be taken seriously?
Getty Images, Inc.

In six cases, accused plotters sought out undercover agents or informers posing as al-Qaeda representatives. In two cases, alleged plotters are accused of swearing allegiance to al-Qaeda in ceremonies staged by the phony Islamists. In eight cases, the accused plotters were native-born Americans, including about a dozen who were converts to Islam.

Intelligence analysts say the lack of an al-Qaeda-led terror strike here may signal that the group is waiting until it can mount an attack that will equal the 9/11 strikes in casualties and publicity value.

Source: Richard Willing, "FBI, Security Officials Warn of Growing Threat from Islamic Extremists 'Next Door,'" *USA Today*, May 13, 2007. Reprinted with permission.

A PowerPoint presentation that supports this chapter is available from your Prentice Hall representative.

Initial efforts to develop a comprehensive plan of protection for the nation's critical infrastructure began in 2001 when President George W. Bush created the Office of Homeland Security, making its director a cabinet member. It became a department of the federal government in 2002. Visit the Department of Homeland Security via **Web Extra 2–18**, and view **Library Extra 2–27** to learn more about ways of protecting the nation's critical information infrastructure from attacks by terrorists, criminals, and vandals. You can track national and international terror incidents as they occur through the National Counterterrorism Center's Worldwide Incidents Tracking Center, which is available via **Web Extra 2–19**.

Summary

THE CRIME PICTURE

- The FBI's Uniform Crime Reporting (UCR) Program began in the 1930s when Congress authorized the U.S. attorney general to survey crime in America. Today's UCR/NIBRS Program provides annual data on the number of reported Part I offenses, or major crimes, as well as information about arrests that have been made for less serious Part II offenses. The Part I offenses are murder, forcible rape, robbery, aggravated assault, burglary, larceny-theft, motor vehicle theft, and arson. The Part II offenses category covers many more crimes, including drug offenses, driving under the influence, and simple assault. Modifications to the UCR Program, which has traditionally provided only summary crime data, are occurring with the implementation of the National Incident-Based Reporting System (NIBRS). It represents a significant redesign of the original UCR Program and gathers many details about each criminal incident, such as place of occurrence, weapon used, type and value of property damaged or stolen, personal characteristics of the offender and the victim, nature of any relationship between the two, and disposition of the complaint.
- The National Crime Victimization Survey (NCVS) is the second major source of statistical data about crime in the United States. The NCVS, which was first conducted in 1972, is based on victim self-reports rather than on police reports. The NCVS originally built on efforts by both the National Opinion Research Center and the 1967 President's Commission on Law Enforcement and the Administration of Justice to uncover what some had been calling the *dark figure of crime*—that is, those crimes that are not reported to the police and that are relatively hidden from justice system officials. An analysis of victim self-report data led to the realization that crimes of all types were more prevalent than UCR statistics had previously indicated.
- The UCR/NIBRS and NCVS differ in a number of significant ways. First, while the UCR/NIBRS Program makes use of data gleaned from citizens' reports of crime made to enforcement agencies, the NCVS utilizes survey data in compiling its reports. Second, because both the UCR/NIBRS and the NCVS are human creations, they contain only data that their creators think appropriate, and the reports they generate are structured differently.
- This chapter discusses a number of special categories of crime, including crime against women, crime against the elderly, hate crime, corporate and white-collar crime, organized crime, gun crime, drug crime, high-technology and computer crime, and terrorism. Each of these categories is of special concern in contemporary society.

QUESTIONS FOR REVIEW

1. Describe the historical development of the FBI's Uniform Crime Reporting Program, and list the crimes on which it reports. How is the ongoing implementation of the National Incident-Based Reporting System changing the UCR Program? How will data reported under the new UCR/NIBRS differ from the crime statistics reported under the traditional UCR Program?
2. Describe the history of the National Crime Victimization Survey. What do data from the NCVS tell us about crime in the United States today?
3. What are the special categories of crime discussed in this chapter? Why are they important?

CHAPTER 3 Criminal Law

Learning Objectives

After reading this chapter, you should be able to:

1. Explain the nature and purpose of law. 59
2. Discuss the nature of the rule of law, and describe its importance in Western democratic societies. 60
3. Identify the various categories or types of law, and explain the purpose of each. 60
4. List and describe the five categories of crime. 63
5. List and describe the eight general features of crime. 68
6. Explain what is meant by the elements of a specific criminal offense. 70
7. Discuss the four broad categories of criminal defenses that our legal system recognizes. 72

"Law is the art of the good and the fair."

—Ulpian, Roman judge (circa A.D. 200)

"Law should be like death, which spares no one."

—Montesquieu (1689–1755)

"Every law is an infraction of liberty."

—Jeremy Bentham (1748–1832)

Introduction

In 2003, after the American military had toppled the regime of Iraqi dictator Saddam Hussein but before the establishment of a new Iraqi government, soldiers of the U.S. Third Infantry Division had to release a man who had taken his beaten and bloodied wife to a Baghdad hospital for treatment and had continued to beat her while waiting for doctors to arrive.[1] When soldiers restrained the man, he exclaimed that he was exercising his marital rights under Islamic tradition and was beating his wife because she had interfered with his attempts to have intercourse with the couple's 14-year-old daughter. "The sad thing is there was nothing we could do," said Sergeant First Class Michael Shirley of Hinesville, Georgia, "apart from separate them and send her to her mother's house in a taxi, because there are no laws against domestic violence here. The women have to respect their husband's decisions. We can't get involved with religious or cultural beliefs."[2]

In contrast to prewar Iraq, modern postindustrial societies like the United States have developed highly formalized secular legal systems. Laws govern many aspects of our lives, and we are expected to know what the law *says* as it applies to our daily lives and to *follow* it. But do we really know what law is? The job of this chapter is to discuss the law both as a product of rule creation and as a guide for behavior. We will also examine criminal law in some detail, and we will discuss defenses commonly used by defendants charged with violations of the criminal law.

Thematic Question This chapter describes the various purposes of the law. With which of these purposes would individual-rights advocates most likely agree? What about public-order advocates? Why?

Lecture Note Explain what law is by referring to both statutory law and the law of precedent (case law).

Lecture Note Show that statutory law is the result of powerful interest groups that have succeeded in having their values formally endorsed.

Lecture Note When discussing the purposes of law, question students about their preconceptions about what the law is supposed to be and what it is supposed to do.

Lecture Note Describe the purposes of the law. Ask whether laws that enforce moral beliefs serve any significant purpose today and whether they are even enforceable given society's increasing diversity.

The Nature and Purpose of Law

Imagine a society without laws. A **law** mandates or proscribes a certain behavior and can be a product of rule creation, a guide for people's behavior, or both. Without civil law, people would not know what to expect from one another, nor would they be able to plan for the future with any degree of certainty. Without criminal law, people wouldn't feel safe because the more powerful could take what they wanted from the less powerful. Without constitutional law, people could not exercise the basic rights that are available to them as citizens of a free nation. A society needs laws to uphold fairness and to prevent the victimization of innocents.

1 Explain the nature and purpose of law.

law
A rule of conduct, generally found enacted in the form of a statute, that proscribes or mandates certain forms of behavior.

statutory law
The written or codified law; "the law on the books," as enacted by a government body or agency having the power to make laws.

penal code
The written, organized, and compiled form of the criminal laws of a jurisdiction.

case law
The body of judicial precedent, historically built on legal reasoning and past interpretations of statutory laws, that serves as a guide to decision making, especially in the courts.

Practically speaking, laws regulate relationships between people and also between parties, such as government agencies and individuals. They channel and simultaneously constrain human behavior, and they empower individuals while contributing to public order. Laws also serve other purposes. They ensure that the philosophical, moral, and economic perspectives of their creators are protected and made credible. They maintain values and uphold established patterns of social privilege. They sustain existing power relationships; finally, they support a system for the punishment and rehabilitation of offenders (Table 3–1). Modifications of the law, when gradually induced, promote orderly change in the rest of society.

Our laws are found in statutory provisions and constitutional enactments,[3] as well as in hundreds of years of rulings by courts at all levels. According to the authoritative *Black's Law Dictionary*, the word *law* "generally contemplates both statutory and case law."[4] **Statutory law** is "the law on the books." It results from legislative action and is often thought of as "the law of the land." Written laws exist in both criminal and civil areas and are called *codes*. Once laws have been written down in organized fashion, they are said to be *codified*. Federal statutes are compiled in the United States Code (U.S.C.), which is available online in its entirety at **Library Extra 3–1**. State codes and municipal ordinances are also readily available in written, or statutory, form. The written form of the criminal law is called the **penal code**. **Case law**, which we will discuss in detail a bit later, is the law that results from judicial decisions.

TABLE 3–1
What Do Laws Do?

- Laws maintain order in society.
- Laws regulate human interaction.
- Laws enforce moral beliefs.
- Laws define the economic environment.
- Laws enhance predictability.
- Laws support the powerful.
- Laws promote orderly social change.
- Laws sustain individual rights.
- Laws redress wrongs.
- Laws identify wrongdoers.
- Laws mandate punishment and retribution.

common law
The body of law originating from usage and custom rather than from written statutes. The term refers to an unwritten body of judicial opinion, originally developed by English courts, that is based on nonstatutory customs, traditions, and precedents that help guide judicial decision making.

rule of law
The maxim that an orderly society must be governed by established principles and known codes that are applied uniformly and fairly to all of its members.

But the laws of our country are not unambiguous. If all of "the law" could be found in written legal codes, it would be plain to nearly everyone, and we would need far fewer lawyers than are practicing today. But some laws—the precedents established by courts—do not exist "on the books," and even those that do are open to interpretation. This is where common law comes into play. **Common law** is the traditional body of unwritten historical precedents created from everyday social customs, rules, and practices, many of which were supported by judicial decisions during early times. Common law principles are still used to interpret many legal issues in quite a few states. Hence it is not uncommon to hear of jurisdictions within the United States referred to as "common law jurisdictions" or "common law states."

The Rule of Law

The social, economic, and political stability of any society depends largely on the development and institutionalization of a predictable system of laws. Western democratic societies adhere to the **rule of law**, which is sometimes also referred to as the *supremacy of law*. The rule of law centers on the belief that an orderly society must be governed by established principles and known codes that are applied uniformly and fairly to all of its members. Under this tenet, no one is above the law, and those who make or enforce the law must also abide by it. The principle was well illustrated when, in 2007, former Ohio Republican Congressman Robert W. Ney was sentenced to 30 months in prison for corrupt dealings with convicted congressional lobbyist Jack Abramoff.[5]

2 Discuss the nature of the rule of law, and describe its importance in Western democratic societies.

> The law isn't justice. It's a very imperfect mechanism. If you press exactly the right buttons and are also lucky, justice may show up in the answer.
>
> —Raymond Chandler (1888–1959)[i]

The rule of law has been called the greatest political achievement of our culture. Without it, few other human achievements—especially those that require the coordinated efforts of a large number of people—would be possible. President John F. Kennedy eloquently explained the rule of law, saying, "Americans are free to disagree with the law, but not to disobey it; for [in] a government of laws and not of men, no man, however prominent and powerful, no mob, however unruly or boisterous, is entitled to defy a court of law."[6]

The rule of law has also been called "the foundation of liberties in the Western world,"[7] for it means that due process (which was discussed in Chapter 1) has to be followed in any criminal prosecution, and it is due process that serves as a check on arbitrary state power.

The American Bar Association notes that the rule of law includes these elements:[8]

- Freedom from private lawlessness provided by the legal system of a politically organized society
- A relatively high degree of objectivity in the formulation of legal norms and a like degree of evenhandedness in their application
- Legal ideas and juristic devices for the attainment of individual and group objectives within the bounds of ordered liberty
- Substantive and procedural limitations on governmental power in the interest of the individual for the enforcement of which there are appropriate legal institutions and machinery

jurisprudence
The philosophy of law. Also, the science and study of the law.

criminal law
The body of rules and regulations that define and specify the nature of and punishments for offenses of a public nature or for wrongs committed against the state or society. Also called *penal law*.

Jurisprudence is the philosophy of law or the science and study of the law, including the rule of law. To learn more about the rule of law, including its historical development, visit **Web Extra 3–1**.

Types of Law

3 Identify the various categories or types of law, and explain the purpose of each.

Criminal and civil law are the best-known types of modern law. However, scholars and philosophers have drawn numerous distinctions between categories of law that rest on the source, intent, and application of the law (Figure 3–1).

Criminal law, also called *penal law*, refers to the body of rules and regulations that define and specify the nature of and punishments for offenses of a public nature or for

▲ Former Detroit Mayor Kwame Kilpatrick, former Illinois Governors George Ryan and Rod Blagojevich, and former U.S. Representative William Jefferson. As their cases demonstrate, the rule of law means that no one is above the law—not even those who make it. Kilpatrick (*top left*), charged with ten felony counts, pleaded guilty to reduced charges and served 99 days in jail before being released in February 2009; he reentered prison in 2010 for violating probation. Ryan (*bottom right*) was sentenced to six and a half years in federal prison for racketeering and fraud. He entered prison in November 2007. Blagojevich (*top right*) was tried in 2010 on federal criminal conspiracy charges and convicted on one count of making false statements to investigators. Jefferson (*bottom left*) served nine terms in the U.S. House of Representatives prior to being sentenced in 2009 to 13 years in prison for using his office to solicit bribes. How would you explain the rule of law to someone who is unfamiliar with it?

From left to right: Getty Images, Inc./Bill Pugliano; AP Photo/Seth Perlman; AP Photo/Kevin Wolf; and © Tanen Maury/epa/CORBIS All Rights Reserved

Lecture Note Demonstrate the significance of the law of precedent (case law) by pointing to past Senate hearings over Supreme Court nominees (such as Judges Robert Bork and Clarence Thomas), wherein senators readily realized that the philosophical leanings of judicial nominees could create a new social order in the country

Lecture Note Point out the difference between laws intended to prevent harm and laws designed to promote social good. Ask students to identify instances of both in the criminal code of their home state.

Thematic Question Why are clichés like "Ignorance of the law is no excuse" and "No one is above the law" important to our concept of law?

Lecture Note Distinguish among criminal, civil, and administrative law, and give reasons for the distinctions that we draw among these various categories of law.

Lecture Note Discuss "frivolous" litigation and the consequences of such lawsuits for the American system of civil law.

wrongs committed against the state or society. Public order is compromised whenever a criminal act occurs, and those found guilty of violating the criminal law are punished. Punishment for crime is philosophically justified by the fact that the offender *intended* the harm and is responsible for it. Criminal law, which is built on constitutional principles and which operates within an established set of procedures applicable to the criminal justice system, is composed of both statutory (written law) and case law.

Written law is of two types: substantive and procedural. **Substantive criminal law** describes what constitutes particular crimes, such as murder, rape, robbery, and assault, and specifies the appropriate punishment for each particular offense. **Procedural law** is a body of rules that determines the proceedings by which legal rights are enforced. The law of criminal procedure, for example, regulates the gathering of evidence and the processing of offenders by the criminal justice system. General rules of evidence, search and seizure, procedures to be followed in an arrest, trial procedures, and other specified processes by which

substantive criminal law
The part of the law that defines crimes and specifies punishments.

procedural law
The part of the law that specifies the methods to be used in enforcing substantive law.

FIGURE 3–1
Types of Law

CRIMINAL LAW
Criminal law is defined as the body of rules and regulations that define and specify the nature of and punishments for offenses of a public nature or for wrongs committed against the state or society. Fundamental to the concept of criminal law is the assumption that crimanal acts injure not just individuals but society as a whole. Criminal law is also called *penal law.*

These crimes not only offend their victims but also disrupt the peaceful order of society. It is for this reason that the state begins the official process of bringing the offender to justice. The state will be the plaintiff in the criminal proceeding. Those found guilty of violating a criminal law are punished.

EXAMPLES: Murder, rape, robbery, and assault are examples of criminal offenses against which there are laws.

ADMINISTRATIVE LAW
Administrative law is the body of regulations that governments create to control the activities of industries, businesses, and individuals. For the most part, a breach of administrative law is not a crime.

Administrative agencies will sometimes arrange settlements that fall short of court action but that are considered binding on individuals or groups that have not followed the rules of administrative law.

EXAMPLES: Tax laws, health codes, restrictions on pollution and waste disposal, vehicle regulation laws, and building codes are examples of administrative laws.

STATUTORY LAW
Refers to the law on the books; written, codified laws.

EXAMPLE: The acts of legislatures.

Substantive criminal law is a form of statutory law that describes what constitutes particular crimes and specifies the appropriate punishment for the offense.

Procedural law is a type of statutory law. It is a body of rules that determines the proceedings by which legal rights are enforced. These laws regulate the gathering of evidence and the processing of offenders by the criminal justice system.

CIVIL LAW
Civil law governs relationships between and among people, businesses and other organizations, and agencies of government. In contrast to the criminal law, whose violation is against the state or the nation, civil law governs relationships between parties.

Typically civil suits seek compensation (usually in the form of property or money). A violation of the civil law is not a crime. It may be a contract violation or a tort. A tort is a wrongful act, damage, or injury not involving a breach of contract. Because a tort is a personal wrong and not a crime, it is left to the aggrieved individual to bring the case to court. Civil law is more concerned with assessing liability than it is with intent. Civil suits can also be brought against a crime where the intent is clear. His or her victim may decide to seek monetary compensation.

EXAMPLES: Includes things such as rules for contracts, divorces, child support and custody, the creation of wills, property transfers, libel, and many other contractual and social obligations.

CASE LAW
Case law comes from judicial decisions and is also referred to as the law of precedent. It represents the accumulated wisdom of trial and appellate courts. Once a court decision is rendered, it is written down. At the appellate level, the reasoning behind the decision is recorded as well.

The Supreme Court is the highest-level appellete court. *Stare decisis* refers to the principle of recognizing previous decisions as precedents for guiding future deliberations.

A vertical rule requires that decisions made by a higher court be taken into consideration by lower courts.

The horizontal dimension refers to cases handled by the same court that should be decided in a similar way.

EXAMPLES: Under the law of precedent, the reasonings of previous courts should be taken into consideration by other courts in settling similar future cases.

COMMON LAW
Common law is that body of law originating from usage and custom rather than from written statutes.

EXAMPLE: English common law is the basis for much Armerican criminal law, although most states have codified common law principles in their written statutes.

the justice system operates are all contained in procedural law. Each state has its own set of criminal procedure laws, as does the federal government. Laws of criminal procedure balance a suspect's rights against the state's interests in the speedy and efficient processing of criminal defendants. View the Federal Rules of Criminal Procedure and the Federal Rules of Evidence at **Library Extras 3–2** and **3–3**.

civil law
The branch of modern law that governs relationships between parties.

Civil law, in contrast to criminal law, governs relationships between and among people, businesses and other organizations, and agencies of government. It contains rules for contracts, divorces, child support and custody, the creation of wills, property transfers, negligence, libel, unfair practices in hiring, the manufacture and sale of consumer goods with hidden hazards for the user, and many other contractual and social obligations. When the civil law is violated, a civil suit may follow. Typically, civil suits seek compensation (usually in the form of property or monetary damages), not punishment. A violation of the civil law is not a crime. It may be a contract violation or a **tort**—which is a wrongful act, damage, or injury not involving a breach of contract. Because a tort is a personal wrong and not a crime, it is left to the aggrieved individual to set the machinery of the court in motion—that is, to bring a suit. The parties to a civil suit are referred to as the *plaintiff*, who seeks relief, and the *defendant*, against whom relief is sought. Civil suits are also sometimes brought by crime victims against those whose criminal intent is clear. Once the perpetrator of a crime has been convicted, the victim may decide to seek monetary compensation from him or her through our system of civil laws.

tort
A wrongful act, damage, or injury not involving a breach of contract. Also, a private or civil wrong or injury.

Still another kind of law, *administrative law,* is the body of regulations that governments create to control the activities of industries, businesses, and individuals. Tax laws, health codes, restrictions on pollution and waste disposal, vehicle registration laws, and building codes are examples of administrative laws. Other administrative laws cover practices in the areas of customs (imports and exports), immigration, agriculture, product safety, and most areas of manufacturing. For the most part, a breach of administrative law is not a crime. However, criminal law and administrative regulations may overlap. For instance, organized criminal activity is prevelant in the area of toxic waste disposal—an area covered by many administrative regulations—which has led to criminal prosecutions in several states.

Legal experts also talk about case law, or the law of **precedent**. Case law comes from judicial decisions and represents the accumulated wisdom of trial and appellate courts (those that hear appeals) in criminal, civil, and administrative law cases over the years. Once a court decision is rendered, it is written down. At the appellate level, the reasoning behind the decision is recorded as well. Under the law of precedent, this reasoning is then taken into consideration by other courts in settling similar future cases. The principle of recognizing previous decisions as precedents to guide future deliberations, called ***stare decisis***, forms the basis for our modern law of precedent. *Stare decisis* makes for predictability in the law. The court with the greatest influence, of course, is the U.S. Supreme Court, and the precedents it establishes are used as guidelines in the process of legal reasoning by which lower courts reach conclusions.

precedent
A legal principle that ensures that previous judicial decisions are authoritatively considered and incorporated into future cases.

stare decisis
A legal principle that requires that in subsequent cases on similar issues of law and fact, courts are bound by their own earlier decisions and by those of higher courts having jurisdiction over them. The term literally means "standing by decided matters."

> The greatest happiness of the greatest number is the foundation of morals and legislation.
>
> —Jeremy Bentham (1748-1832)

Learn more about the evolution of American criminal law at **Library Extra 3–4**. Online criminal law journals may be accessed at **Library Extras 3–5** and **3–6**.

General Categories of Crime

Violations of the *criminal* law can be of many different types and can vary in severity. Five general categories of criminal law violations can be identified: (1) felonies, (2) misdemeanors, (3) offenses, (4) treason and espionage, and (5) inchoate offenses (Figure 3–2).

4 List and describe the five categories of crime.

Felonies are serious crimes; they include murder, rape, aggravated assault, robbery, burglary, and arson. Today, many felons receive prison sentences, although the range of potential penalties includes everything from probation and a fine to capital punishment. Under common law (which was discussed earlier in this chapter), felons could be sentenced to death, could have their property confiscated, or both. Following common law tradition, people who are convicted of felonies today usually lose certain privileges. Some states, for example, make a felony conviction and incarceration grounds for uncontested divorce. Others prohibit offenders from voting, running for public office, or owning a firearm and exclude them from some professions, such as medicine, law, and police work.

felony
A criminal offense punishable by death or by incarceration in a prison facility for at least one year.

Lecture Note Explain how felonies, misdemeanors, and offenses differ. Suggest that the distinction between these categories is an artificial one and that all offenses are crimes with greater or lesser punishments specified for them by the criminal law.

Misdemeanors are relatively minor crimes, consisting of offenses such as petty theft, which is stealing items of little worth; simple assault, in which the victim suffers no serious injury and in which none was intended; breaking and entering; possessing burglary tools; being disorderly

misdemeanor
An offense punishable by incarceration, usually in a local confinement facility, for a period whose upper limit is prescribed by statute in a given jurisdiction, typically one year or less.

Freedom or Safety? You Decide.
Should Violent Speech Be Free Speech?

In 2005, a Virginia jury convicted 42-year-old Muslim scholar Ali al-Timimi of a number of offenses, including the crime of incitement, conspiring to carry firearms and explosives, and soliciting others to make war against the United States. The U.S.-born Islamic spiritual adviser had spoken frequently at the Center for Islamic Information and Education—also known as the Dar al Arqam Islamic Center—in Falls Church, Virginia. Prosecutors told jurors that al-Timimi had verbally encouraged his followers to train with terrorist organizations and to engage in violent Jihad, or holy war, against America and its allies. Al-Timimi lived much of his life in the Washington, D.C., area and had earned a doctorate in computational biology from George Mason University. As a teenager he spent two years in Saudi Arabia with his family, where he became interested in Islam.

Following conviction, al-Timimi was sentenced to life in prison without the possibility of parole, plus 70 years—a sentence meant to guarantee that he would never leave prison.

The al-Timimi case raises a number of interesting issues, among them the question of when violent speech crosses the line from free expression into criminal advocacy. The First Amendment to the U.S. Constitution guarantees the right to free speech. It is a fundamental guarantee of our democratic way of life. So, for example, the speech of those who advocate a new form of government in the United States is protected, even though their ideas may appear anti-American and ill considered. In the 1957 case of *Roth* v. *United States*, the U.S. Supreme Court held that "the protection given speech and press was fashioned to assure unfettered interchange of ideas for the bringing about of political and social changes desired by the people."

It is important to remember, however, that constitutional rights are not without limit—that is, they have varying applicability under differing conditions. Some forms of speech are too dangerous to be allowed, even under our liberal rules.

Freedom of speech does not mean, for example, that you have a protected right to stand up in a crowded theater and yell "Fire!" That's because the panic that would follow such an exclamation would likely cause injuries and would put members of the public at risk of harm. Hence the courts have held that although freedom of speech is guaranteed by the Constitution, there are limits to it. (Shouting "Fire!" in a public park would likely not be considered an actionable offense.)

Similarly, saying, "The president deserves to die," horrific as it may sound, may be merely a matter of personal opinion. Anyone who says "I'm going to kill the president," however, can wind up in jail because threatening the life of the president is a crime—as is the act of communicating threats of imminent violence in most jurisdictions.

Al-Timimi's mistake may have been the timing of his remarks, which were made to a public gathering in Virginia five days after the September 11, 2001, attacks. In his speech, al-Timimi called for a "holy war" and "violent Jihad" against the West. He was later quoted by converts with whom he met as referring to American forces in Afghanistan as "legitimate targets."

Critics of al-Timimi's conviction point to a seeming double standard under which people can be arrested for unpopular speech, but not for popular speech—regardless of the degree of violence it implies. They note, for example, that conservative columnist Ann Coulter has suggested in writing that "we should invade (Muslim) countries, kill their leaders and convert them to Christianity," but she was never arrested for what she wrote.

YOU DECIDE

Should al-Timimi's advocacy of violence be unlawful? Why or why not? Might we have more to fear from the suppression of speech (even speech like al-Timimi's) than from its free expression? If so, how?

References: "Virginia Man Convicted of Urging War on U.S.," *USA Today*, April 27, 2005; Jonathan Turley, "When Is Violent Speech Still Free Speech?" *USA Today*, May 3, 2005; and Eric Lichtblau, "Administration Continues Eavesdropping Defense," *New York Times*, January 24, 2006, http://www.nytimes.com/2006/01/24/politics/24cnd-wiretap.html (accessed August 28, 2008).

FIGURE 3–2
General Categories of Crime

FELONY
A criminal offense punishable by death or by incarceration in a prison facility for at least one year.

OFFENSE
A violation of the criminal law. Also, in some jurisdictions, a minor crime, such as jaywalking, that is sometimes described as *ticketable*. Such minor offenses are also known as *infractions*.

TREASON
A U.S. citizen's actions to help a foreign government overthrow, make war against, or seriously injure the United States. Also, the attempt to overthrow the government of the society of which one is a member.

INCHOATE OFFENSE
An offense not yet completed. Also, an offense that consists of an action or conduct that is a step toward the intended commission of another offense.

MISDEMEANOR
An offense punishable by incarceration, usually in a local confinement facility, for a period whose upper limit is prescribed by statute in a given jurisdiction, typically one year or less.

ESPIONAGE
The "gathering, transmitting, or losing" of information related to the national defense in such a manner that the information becomes available to enemies of the United States and may be used to their advantage.

in public; disturbing the peace; filing a false crime report; and writing bad checks, although the amount for which the check is written may determine the classification of this offense. In general, misdemeanors are any crime punishable by a year or less in prison. In fact, most misdemeanants receive suspended sentences involving a fine and supervised probation.

A third category of crime is the **offense**. Although, strictly speaking, all violations of the criminal law can be called *criminal offenses*, the term *offense* is used specifically to refer to minor violations of the law that are less serious than misdemeanors. When the term is used in that sense, it refers to such things as jaywalking, spitting on the sidewalk, littering, and committing certain traffic violations, including the failure to wear a seat belt. Another word used to describe such minor law violations is **infractions**. People committing infractions are typically ticketed and released, usually on a promise to appear later in court. Court appearances may often be waived through payment of a small fine that can be mailed to the court.

Felonies, misdemeanors, offenses, and the people who commit them constitute the daily work of the justice system. However, special categories of crime do exist and should be recognized. They include treason and espionage, two crimes that are often regarded as the most serious of felonies. **Treason** can be defined as "a U.S. citizen's actions to help a foreign government overthrow, make war against, or seriously injure the United States."[9] **Espionage**, an offense akin to treason but which can be committed by noncitizens, is the "gathering, transmitting, or losing" of information related to the national defense in such a manner that the information becomes available to enemies of the United States and may be used to their advantage.[10]

> Justice is incidental to law and order.
> —J. Edgar Hoover (1895-1972)[ii]

Another special category of crime is called *inchoate*. The word *inchoate* means "incomplete or partial," and **inchoate offenses** are those that have not been fully carried out. Conspiracies are an example. When a person conspires to commit a crime, any action undertaken in furtherance of the conspiracy is generally regarded as a sufficient basis for arrest and prosecution. For instance, a woman who intends to kill her husband may make a phone call or conduct an Internet search to find a hit man to carry out her plan. The call and search are themselves evidence of her intent and can result in her imprisonment for conspiracy to commit murder. Another type of inchoate offense is the attempt to commit a crime, which occurs when an offender is unable to complete the intended crime. For example, homeowners may arrive just as a burglar is beginning to enter their residence, causing the burglar to drop his tools and run. In most jurisdictions, this frustrated burglar can be arrested and charged with attempted burglary.

▲ An artist's drawing of Chi Mak, a Chinese-born and naturalized U.S. citizen, listening to testimony from his 2007 trial in federal court in Santa Ana, California. Mak was convicted of espionage—specifically, conspiracy to export U.S. defense technology to China—and was sentenced in 2008 to 24 and a half years in federal prison. What's the difference between espionage and treason?
Bill Robles/AP Wide World Photos

offense
A violation of the criminal law. Also, in some jurisdictions, a minor crime, such as jaywalking, that is sometimes described as *ticketable*.

infraction
A minor violation of state statute or local ordinance punishable by a fine or other penalty or by a specified, usually limited, term of incarceration.

treason
A U.S. citizen's actions to help a foreign government overthrow, make war against, or seriously injure the United States.[iii] Also, the attempt to overthrow the government of the society of which one is a member.

espionage
The "gathering, transmitting, or losing"[iv] of information related to the national defense in such a manner that the information becomes available to enemies of the United States and may be used to their advantage.

inchoate offense
An offense not yet completed. Also, an offense that consists of an action or conduct that is a step toward the intended commission of another offense.

actus reus
An act in violation of the law. Also, a guilty act.

Lecture Note Discuss the various features of a crime. Explain that there can be no crime unless all the features are present.

General Features of Crime

From the perspective of Western jurisprudence, all crimes can be said to share certain features (Figure 3–3), and the notion of crime itself can be said to rest on such general principles. Taken together, these features, which are described in this section, make up the legal essence of the concept of crime. Conventional legal wisdom holds that the essence of crime consists of three conjoined elements: (1) the criminal act, which in legal parlance is termed the *actus reus*; (2) a culpable mental state, or *mens rea*; and (3) a concurrence of the two. Hence, as we shall see in the following paragraphs, the essence of criminal conduct consists of a concurrence of a criminal act with a culpable mental state.

The Criminal Act (*Actus Reus*)

A necessary first feature of any crime is some act in violation of the law. Such an act is termed the ***actus reus*** of a crime. The term means "guilty act." Generally, a person must commit some voluntary act before he or she is subject to criminal sanctions. To *be something* is not a crime; to *do something* may be. For example, someone who is caught using drugs can be arrested, while someone who simply admits that he or she is a drug user (perhaps on a TV talk show or on a website) cannot be arrested on that basis. Police who hear the drug user's admission might begin gathering evidence to prove some specific law violation in that

FIGURE 3–3 The Features of a Crime

By definition, a crime requires *actus reus*, *mens rea*, and the concurrence of the two:

Actus Reus

A necessary feature of any crime is some act in violation of the law. This violation is called the *actus reus* (guilty act). Generally a person must commit the act voluntarily for it to be considered a crime.

Mens Rea

A second component of crime is *mens rea*, or guilty mind. This refers to the person's state of mind when they commit the act. There are four types of *mens rea*:

- **Purposeful** (intentional) is an act that is undertaken to achieve some goal.
- **Knowing** behavior is undertaken with awareness. A person who acts purposefully always acts knowingly, but a person may act in a knowing way, but without criminal intent.
- **Reckless** behavior is activity that increases the risk of harm. In this activity, the person may not have intended harm but should know that his behavior could endanger others.
- **Negligent** behavior refers to a situation where the person should have known better and her act, or failure to act, endangers others.

Motive is not the same as *mens rea*. A motive refers to a person's reason for committing a crime. Motive is not an essential feature of a crime.

Concurrence

Concurrence requires that the act and the mental state occur together in order for a crime to have taken place.

Special Categories of Crime

Strict liability (or absolute liability) is a special category of crime that requires no culpable mental state and presents a significant exception to the principle that all crimes require *actus reus* and *mens rea*. These offenses make it a crime to simply do something without the intention of violating the law. Routine traffic offenses are considered an example of strict liability.

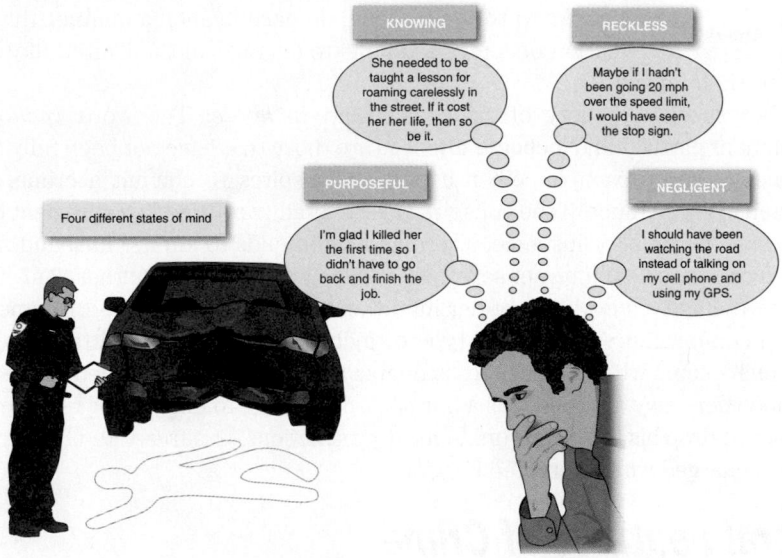

Source: Illlustration from Frank J. Schmalleger, Daniel E. Hall, and John J. Dolatowski, *Criminal Law Today*, 4th Ed. (Upper Saddle River: NJ 2010), pg. 46. Reprinted by permission of Pearson Education, Inc., Upper Saddle River, NJ.

Class Activity Ask the class to create a list of public-order offenses in your state. Suggest that students research the state criminal code while they are working on the list. Have them identify the potential indirect victims in each "victimless crime" they discover. Criminal codes for other states are available on the Internet. Ask students to compare the criminal code of their home state with the laws of other states to determine which jurisdictions have enacted the largest number of "victimless crime" statutes. Ask the class to discuss why some states have criminalized more of these kinds of offenses than other states have.

person's past, or perhaps they might watch that individual for future behavior in violation of the law. A subsequent arrest would then be based on a specific action in violation of the law pertaining to controlled substances.

Vagrancy laws, popular in the early part of the twentieth century, have generally been invalidated by the courts because they did not specify what act violated the law. In fact, the less a person did, the more vagrant he or she was. An omission to act, however, may be criminal where the person in question is required by law to do something. Child-neglect laws, for example, focus on parents and guardians who do not live up to their responsibility to care for their children.

Threatening to act can be a criminal offense. For example, threatening to kill someone can result in an arrest for the offense of communicating threats. Such threats against the president of the United States are taken seriously by the Secret Service, and individuals are arrested for boasting about planned violence directed at the president. Attempted criminal activity is also illegal. An attempt to murder or rape, for example, is a serious crime, even when the planned act is not accomplished.

Conspiracies (mentioned earlier in this chapter) are another criminal act. When a conspiracy unfolds, the ultimate act that it aims to bring about does not have to occur for the parties to the conspiracy to be arrested. When people plan to bomb a public building, for example, they can be legally stopped before the bombing. As soon as they take steps to "further" their plan, they have met the requirement for an act. Buying explosives, telephoning one another, and drawing plans of the building may all be actions in "furtherance of the conspiracy." But not all conspiracy statutes require actions in furtherance of the "target crime" before an arrest can be made. Technically speaking, crimes of conspiracy can be seen as entirely distinct from the target crimes that the conspirators are contemplating. For example, in 1994 the U.S. Supreme Court upheld the drug-related conviction of Reshat Shabani when it ruled that in the case of certain antidrug laws,[11] "it is presumed that Congress intended to adopt the common law definition of conspiracy, which does not make the doing of any act other than the act of conspiring a condition of liability."[12] Hence, according to the Court, "the criminal agreement itself," even in the absence of actions directed toward realizing the target crime, can be grounds for arrest and prosecution.

A Guilty Mind (*Mens Rea*)

Mens rea, the second general component of crime, is a term that literally means "guilty mind," referring to the defendant's specific mental state at the time the behavior in question occurred. The importance of *mens rea* as a component of crime cannot be overemphasized. It can be seen in the fact that some courts have held that "[a]ll crime exists primarily in the mind."[13] The extent to which a person can be held criminally responsible for his or her actions generally depends on the nature of the mental state under which he or she was laboring at the time of the offense.

mens rea
The state of mind that accompanies a criminal act. Also, a guilty mind.

Four levels, or types, of *mens rea* can be distinguished: (1) purposeful (or intentional), (2) knowing, (3) reckless, and (4) negligent. Purposeful or intentional action is that which is undertaken to achieve some goal. Sometimes the harm that results from intentional action may be unintended; however, this does not reduce criminal liability. The doctrine of *transferred intent*, for example, which operates in all U.S. jurisdictions, holds a person guilty of murder if he or she took aim and shot at an intended victim but missed, killing another person instead. The philosophical notion behind the concept of transferred intent is that the killer's intent to kill, which existed at the time of the crime, transferred from the intended victim to the person who was struck by the bullet and died.

Knowing behavior is action undertaken with awareness. A person who acts purposefully always acts knowingly, but a person may act in a knowingly criminal way but for a purpose other than criminal intent. For example, an airline captain who allows a flight attendant to transport cocaine aboard an airplane may do so to gain sexual favors from the attendant, but without the purpose of drug smuggling. Knowing behavior involves near certainty. In this scenario, if the airline captain allows the flight attendant to carry cocaine aboard the plane, it *will* be transported, and the pilot knows it. In another example, if an HIV-infected individual knowingly has unprotected sexual intercourse with another person, the partner *will* be exposed to the virus.

Reckless Behavior and Criminal Negligence

Reckless behavior is activity that increases the risk of harm. In contrast to knowing behavior, knowledge may be part of recklessness, but it exists more in the form of probability than certainty. As a practical example, reckless driving is a frequent charge in many jurisdictions; it is generally brought when a driver engages in risky activity that endangers others.

reckless behavior
An activity that increases the risk of harm.

Nevertheless, *mens rea* is said to be present when a person should have known better, even if the person did not directly intend the consequences of his or her action. A person who acts negligently and thereby endangers others may be found guilty of **criminal negligence** when harm occurs, even though no negative consequences were intended. For example, a parent who leaves a 12-month-old child alone in the tub can be prosecuted for negligent homicide if the child drowns.[14] It should be emphasized, however, that

criminal negligence
A behavior in which a person fails to reasonably perceive substantial and unjustifiable risks of dangerous consequences.

negligence in and of itself is not a crime. Negligent conduct can be evidence of crime only when it falls below some acceptable standard of care. That standard is applied today in criminal courts through the fictional creation of a *reasonable person.* The question to be asked in a given case is whether a reasonable person, in the same situation, would have known better and acted differently from the defendant. The reasonable person criterion provides a yardstick for juries faced with thorny issues of guilt or innocence.

motive
A person's reason for committing a crime.

It is important to note that *mens rea*, even in the sense of intent, is not the same thing as motive. A **motive** refers to a person's reason for committing a crime. While evidence of motive may be admissible during a criminal trial to help prove a crime, motive itself is not an essential element of a crime. As a result, we cannot say that a bad or immoral motive makes an act a crime.

Mens rea is a tricky concept. Not only is it philosophically and legally complex, but a person's state of mind during the commission of an offense can rarely be known directly unless the person confesses. Hence *mens rea* must generally be inferred from a person's actions and from all the circumstances surrounding those actions. Pure accident, however, which involves no recklessness or negligence, cannot serve as the basis for either criminal or civil liability. "Even a dog," the famous Supreme Court Justice Oliver Wendell Holmes once wrote, "distinguishes between being stumbled over and being kicked."[15]

Strict Liability

strict liability
A liability without fault or intention. Strict liability offenses do not require *mens rea*.

A special category of crimes called **strict liability** requires no culpable mental state and presents a significant exception to the principle that all crimes require a concurrence of *actus reus* and *mens rea.* Strict liability offenses, also called *absolute liability offenses*, make it a crime simply to *do* something, even if the offender has no intention of violating the law. Strict liability is philosophically based on the presumption that causing harm is in itself blameworthy, regardless of the actor's intent.

Routine traffic offenses are generally considered strict liability offenses. Driving 65 mph in a 55-mph zone is a violation of the law, even though the driver may be listening to music, thinking, or simply going with the flow of traffic, entirely unaware that his or her vehicle is exceeding the posted speed limit. Statutory rape is another example of strict liability.[16] This crime generally occurs between two consenting individuals; it requires only that the offender have sexual intercourse with a person under the age of legal consent. Statutes describing the crime routinely avoid any mention of a culpable mental state. In many jurisdictions, it matters little whether the "perpetrator" knew the exact age of the "victim" or whether the "victim" lied about his or her age or had given consent, since statutory rape laws are "an attempt to prevent the sexual exploitation of persons deemed legally incapable of giving consent."[17]

Concurrence

concurrence
The coexistence of (1) an act in violation of the law and (2) a culpable mental state.

The concurrence of an unlawful act and a culpable mental state provides the third basic component of crime. **Concurrence** requires that the act and the mental state occur together in order for a crime to take place. If one precedes the other, the requirements of the criminal law have not been met. A person may intend to kill a rival, for example. He drives to the intended victim's house with his gun, fantasizing about how he will commit the murder. Just as he nears the victim's home, the victim crosses the street on the way to the grocery store. If the two accidentally collide and the intended victim dies, there has been no concurrence of act and intent.

Other Features of Crime

5 List and describe the eight general features of crime.

Some scholars contend that the three features of crime that we have just outlined—*actus reus, mens rea*, and concurrence—are sufficient to constitute the essence of the legal concept of *crime*. Other scholars, however, see modern Western law as more complex. They argue that recognition of five additional principles is necessary to fully appreciate contemporary understandings of crime: (1) causation, (2) resulting harm, (3) the principle of legality, (4) the principle of punishment, and (5) necessary attendant circumstances. We will now discuss each of these additional features in turn.

Causation

Causation refers to the fact that the concurrence of a guilty mind and a criminal act may cause harm. While some statutes criminalize only conduct, others require that the offender *cause* a particular result before criminal liability can be incurred. Sometimes, however, a causal link is unclear. For example, let's consider a case of assault with a deadly weapon with intent to kill. A person shoots another, and the victim is seriously injured but is not immediately killed. The victim, who remains in the hospital, survives for more than a year. The victim's death occurs due to a blood clot that forms from lack of activity. In such a case, it is likely that defense attorneys will argue that the defendant did not cause the death; rather, the death occurred because of disease. If a jury agrees with the defense's claim, the shooter may go free or be found guilty of a lesser charge, such as assault.

To clarify the issue of causation, the American Law Institute suggests use of the term **legal cause** to emphasize the notion of a legally recognizable cause and to preclude any assumption that such a cause must be close in time and space to the result it produces. Legal causes can be distinguished from those causes that may have produced the result in question but do not provide the basis for a criminal prosecution because they are too complex, too indistinguishable from other causes, not knowable, or not provable in a court of law.

legal cause
A legally recognizable cause. A legal cause must be demonstrated in court in order to hold an individual criminally liable for causing harm.

Harm

A harm occurs in any crime, although not all harms are crimes. When a person is murdered or raped, harm can be clearly identified. Some crimes, however, can be said to be *victimless*. Perpetrators (and their attorneys) maintain that in committing such crimes, they harm no one but themselves; rather, they say, the crime may actually be pleasurable for those involved. Prostitution, illegal gambling, and drug use are commonly classified as "victimless." What these offenders fail to recognize, say legal theorists, is the social harm caused by their behavior. In areas afflicted with chronic prostitution, illegal gambling, and drug use, property values fall; family life disintegrates; other, more traditional crimes increase as money is sought to support the "victimless" activities; and law-abiding citizens abandon the area.

In a criminal prosecution, however, it is rarely necessary to prove harm as a separate element of a crime since it is subsumed under the notion of a guilty act. In the crime of murder, for example, the "killing of a human being" brings about a harm but is, properly speaking, an act. When committed with the requisite *mens rea*, it becomes a crime. A similar type of reasoning applies to the criminalization of *attempts* that cause no harm. A scenario commonly raised to illustrate this dilemma is one in which attackers throw rocks at a blind man, but because of bad aim, the rocks hit no one and the intended target remains unaware that anyone is trying to harm him. In such a case, should throwing rocks provide a basis for criminal liability? As one authority on the subject observes, "Criticism of the principle of harm has . . . been based on the view that the harm actually caused may be a matter of sheer accident and that the rational thing to do is to base the punishment on the *mens rea*, and the action, disregarding any actual harm or lack of harm or its degree."[18] This observation also shows why we have said that the essence of crime consists only of three things: (1) *actus reus*, (2) *mens rea*, and (3) concurrence of an illegal act and a culpable mental state.

Legality

The principle of legality highlights the fact that a behavior cannot be criminal if no law exists that defines it as such. For example, as long as you are of drinking age, it is all right to drink beer because there is no statute on the books prohibiting it. During Prohibition, of course, the situation was quite different. (In fact, some parts of the United States are still "dry," and the purchase or public consumption of alcohol can be a law violation regardless of age.) The principle of legality also includes the notion that ***ex post facto*** laws are not binding, which means that a law cannot be created tomorrow that will hold a person legally responsible for something he or she does today—laws are binding only from the date of their creation or from some future date at which they are specified as taking effect.[19]

ex post facto
Latin for "after the fact." The Constitution prohibits the enactment of *ex post facto* laws, which make acts committed before the laws in question were passed punishable as crimes.

Punishment

The principle of punishment holds that no crime can be said to occur where punishment has not been specified in the law. Larceny, for example, would not be a crime if the law simply said, "It is illegal to steal." Punishment for the crime must be specified so that if a person is found guilty of violating the law, sanctions can be lawfully imposed.

Necessary Attendant Circumstances

attendant circumstances
The facts surrounding an event.

Finally, statutes defining some crimes specify that certain additional elements must be present for a conviction to be obtained. Generally speaking, these **attendant circumstances** are the "facts surrounding an event";[20] they include such things as time and place. Attendant circumstances that are specified by law as necessary elements of an offense are sometimes called *necessary attendant circumstances*, indicating that the existence of such circumstances is necessary, along with the other elements included in the relevant statute, for a crime to have been committed. Florida law, for example, makes it a crime to "[k]nowingly commit any lewd or lascivious act in the presence of any child under the age of 16 years."[21] In this case, the behavior in question might not be a crime if committed in the presence of someone who is older than 16 years. Sometimes attendant circumstances increase the degree, or level of seriousness, of an offense.

Circumstances surrounding a crime can also be classified as aggravating or mitigating and may, by law, increase or lessen the penalty that can be imposed on a convicted offender. Aggravating and mitigating circumstances are not elements of an offense, however, since they are primarily relevant at the sentencing stage of a criminal prosecution. They are discussed in Chapter 9.

Elements of a Specific Criminal Offense

element (of a crime)
In a specific crime, one of the essential features of that crime, as specified by law or statute.

Now that we have identified the principles that constitute the *general* notion of crime, we can examine individual statutes to see what particular statutory **elements (of a crime)** constitute a *specific* crime. Written laws specify exactly what conditions are necessary for a person to be charged in a given instance of criminal activity, and they do so for every offense. Hence elements of a crime are specific legal aspects of a criminal offense that the prosecution must prove to obtain a conviction. In almost every jurisdiction in the United States, for example, the crime of first-degree murder involves four quite distinct elements:

1. An unlawful killing
2. Of a human being
3. Intentionally
4. With planning (or "malice aforethought")

6 Explain what is meant by the elements of a specific criminal offense.

The elements of any specific crime are the statutory minimum without which that crime cannot be said to have occurred. Since statutes differ between jurisdictions, the specific elements of a particular crime may vary. To convict a defendant of a particular crime, prosecutors must prove to a judge or jury that all of the required statutory elements are present[22] and that the accused was responsible for producing them. If even one element of an offense cannot be established beyond a reasonable doubt, criminal liability will not have been demonstrated, and the defendant will be found not guilty.

The Example of Murder

Every statutory element of a crime serves a purpose. As mentioned, the crime of first-degree murder includes an *unlawful killing* as one of its required elements. Not all killings are unlawful. In war, for instance, human beings are killed. These killings are committed with planning and sometimes with "malice" and are certainly intentional, yet killing in war is not unlawful as long as the belligerents wage war according to international conventions.

The second element of first-degree murder specifies that the killing must be *of a human being.* People kill all the time. They kill animals for meat, they hunt, and they practice euthanasia on aged and injured pets. Even if the killing of an animal is planned and involves malice (perhaps a vendetta against a neighborhood dog that overturns trash cans), it does not constitute first-degree murder. Such a killing, however, may violate statutes pertaining to cruelty to animals.

The third element of first-degree murder, *intentionality*, is the basis for the defense of accident. An unintentional or nonpurposeful killing is not first-degree murder, although it may violate some other statute.

Finally, murder has not been committed unless *malice* is involved. There are different kinds of malice. Second-degree murder involves malice in the sense of hatred or spite. A more extreme form of malice is necessary for a finding of first-degree murder; sometimes the phrase used to describe this requirement is *malice aforethought.* This extreme kind of malice can be demonstrated by showing that planning was involved in the commission of the murder. Often, first-degree murder is described as "lying in wait," a practice that shows that thought and planning went into the illegal killing.

A charge of second-degree murder in most jurisdictions would necessitate proving that a voluntary (or intentional) killing of a human being had taken place—although without the degree of malice necessary for it to be classified as first-degree murder. A crime of passion is an example of second-degree murder. In a crime of passion, the malice felt by the perpetrator is hatred or spite, which is considered less severe than malice aforethought. Manslaughter, or third-degree murder, another type of homicide, can be defined simply as the unlawful killing of a human being. Not only is malice lacking in third-degree murder cases, but so is intention; in fact, the killer may not have intended that *any* harm come to the victim.

Manslaughter charges are often brought when a defendant acted in a negligent or reckless manner. The 2001 sentencing of 21-year-old Nathan Hall to 90 days in jail on charges of criminally negligent homicide following a fatal collision with another ski racer on Vail Mountain near Eagle, Colorado, provides such an example.[23] Hall had been tried on a more serious charge of reckless manslaughter, which carries a sentence of up to 16 years under Colorado law, but the jury convicted him of the lesser charge.

Manslaughter statutes, however, frequently necessitate some degree of negligence on the part of the killer. When a wanton disregard for human life is present—legally defined as "gross negligence"—some jurisdictions permit the offender to be charged with a more serious count of murder.

Lecture Note Distinguish between the ideational "body of the crime" (the *corpus delicti* of an offense) and the physical body of a murder victim. Show that the two are not the same by demonstrating that it is possible to convict a person of murder even though the body of the victim is never recovered. In a case from the 1990s, for example, a military officer whose wife disappeared was convicted of her murder based on the discovery of a computer disk in his office titled "Murder." On it he described in detail how he planned to kill his wife and dispose of her body.

Lecture Note Explain the difference between the *corpus delicti* of crime (which demonstrates that, in fact, a crime has taken place) and the statutory elements necessary to convict a particular person of having committed a specific crime.

The *Corpus Delicti* of a Crime

The term ***corpus delicti*** literally means "the body of the crime." One way to understand the concept of *corpus delicti* is to realize that a person cannot be tried for a crime unless it can first be shown that the offense has, in fact, occurred. In other words, to establish the *corpus delicti* of a crime, the state has to demonstrate that a criminal law has been violated and that someone violated it (Figure 3–4). This term is often confused with the statutory elements of a crime, and sometimes it is mistakenly thought to refer to the body of a murder victim or some other physical result of criminal activity. It actually means something quite different.

corpus delicti
The facts that show that a crime has occurred. The term literally means "the body of the crime."

There are two aspects to the *corpus delicti* of an offense: (1) that a certain result has been produced and (2) that a person is criminally responsible for its production. For example, the crime of larceny requires proof that the property of another has been stolen—that is, unlawfully taken by someone whose intent it was to permanently deprive the owner of its possession.[24] Hence evidence offered to prove the *corpus delicti* in a trial for larceny is insufficient if it fails to prove that any property was stolen or if property found in a defendant's possession cannot be identified as having been stolen. "In an arson case, the *corpus delicti* consists of (1) a burned building or other property, and (2) some criminal agency which caused the burning. . . . In other words, the *corpus delicti* includes not only the fact of burning, but it must also appear that the burning was by the willful act of some person, and not as a result of a natural or accidental cause."[25]

We should note that the identity of the perpetrator is not an element of the *corpus delicti* of an offense. Hence the fact that a crime has occurred can be established without having any idea who committed it or even why it was committed. This principle was clearly enunciated in a Montana case when that state's supreme court held that "the identity of the

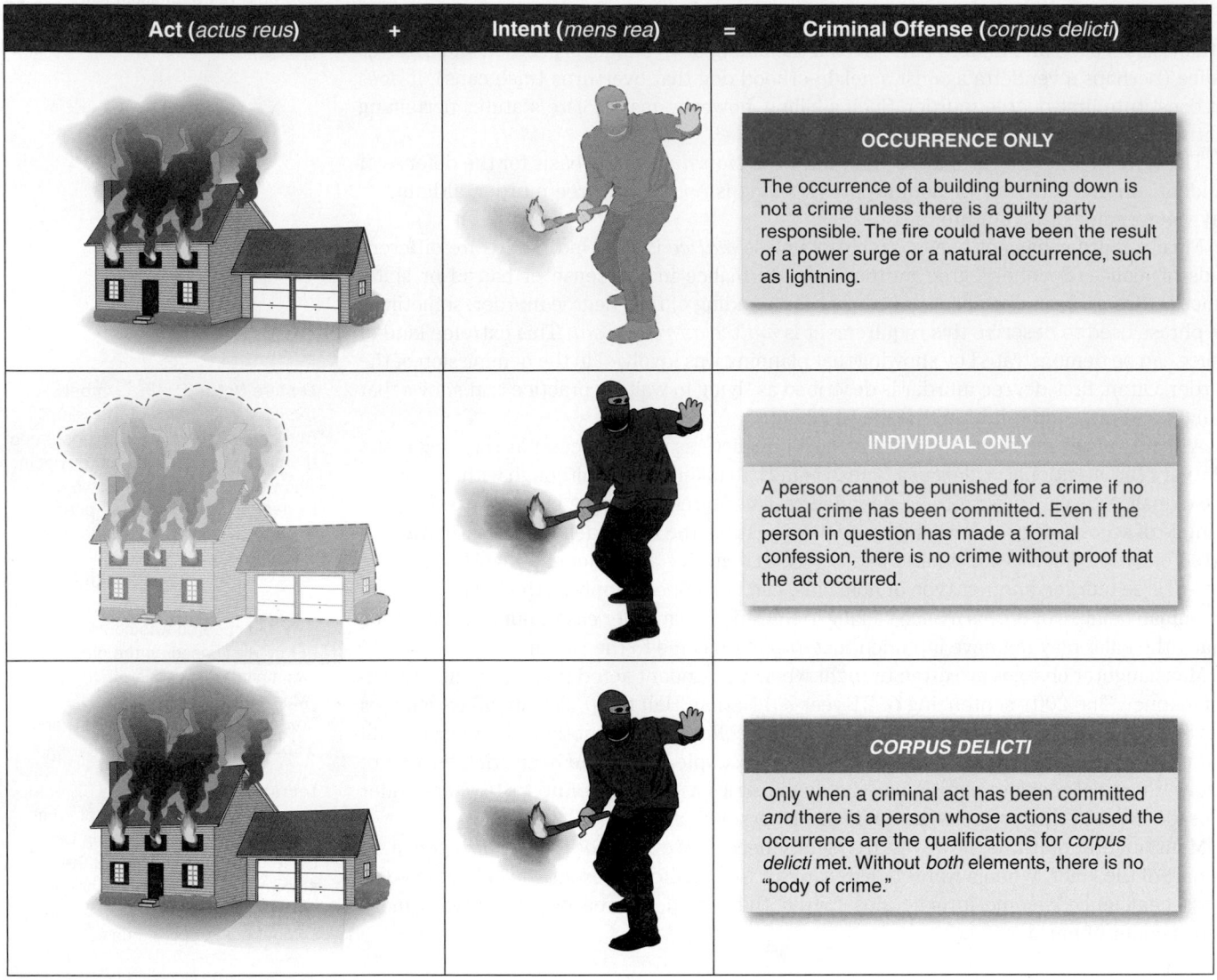

FIGURE 3–4
The Body of Crime

Source: Frank J. Schmalleger, Daniel E. Hall, and John J. Dolatowski, *Criminal Law Today,* 4th Ed. (Upper Saddle River: NJ 2010), pg. 61. Reprinted by permission of Pearson Education, Inc., Upper Saddle River, NJ.

defense (to a criminal charge)
The evidence and arguments offered by a defendant and his or her attorney to show why the defendant should not be held liable for a criminal charge.

alibi
A statement or contention by an individual charged with a crime that he or she was so distant when the crime was committed, or so engaged in other provable activities, that his or her participation in the commission of that crime was impossible.

justification
A legal defense in which the defendant admits to committing the act in question but claims it was necessary in order to avoid some greater evil.

perpetrator is not an element of the *corpus delicti*." In *State* v. *Kindle* (1924),[26] the court said, "We stated that '[i]n a prosecution for murder, proof of the *corpus delicti* does not necessarily carry with it the identity of the slain nor of the slayer.' . . . The essential elements of the *corpus delicti* are . . . establishing the death and the fact that the death was caused by a criminal agency, nothing more." *Black's Law Dictionary* puts it another way: "The *corpus delicti* [of a crime] is the fact of its having been actually committed."[27]

Types of Defenses to a Criminal Charge

When a person is charged with a crime, he or she typically offers some defense. A **defense (to a criminal charge)** consists of evidence and arguments offered by the defendant to show why he or she should not be held liable for a criminal charge. Our legal system generally recognizes four broad categories of defenses: (1) alibi, (2) justifications, (3) excuses, and (4) procedural defenses (Figure 3–5). An **alibi**, if shown to be valid, means that the defendant could not have committed the crime in question because he or she was somewhere else (and generally with someone else) at the time of the crime. When a defendant offers a **justification** as a defense, he or she admits committing the act in

7 Discuss the four broad categories of criminal defenses that our legal system recognizes.

Multiculturalism and Diversity
Islamic Law

Islamic law (or *Shari'ah* in Arabic, which means "path of God") has been of much interest in the United States since the September 11, 2001, terrorist attacks on the United States, the resulting destruction of the Taliban regime in Afghanistan, and the war in Iraq. It is important for American students of criminal justice to recognize that Islamic law refers to legal ideas based on the teachings of Islam and that it bears no intrinsic relationship to acts of terrorism committed by misguided zealots with Islamic backgrounds. Similarly, Islamic law is by no means the same thing as Jihad (Muslim holy war) or Islamic fundamentalism.

Various interpretations of Islam form the basis of laws in many countries, and the entire legal systems of some nations are based on Islamic principles. For example, Article 2 of Chapter 1 (titled "Basic Principles") of the Iraqi Constitution declares that "Islam is the official religion of the state and is a basic source of legislation." Subsection (a) reads: "No law can be passed that contradicts the undisputed rules of Islam." The Iraqi Constitution was approved by a wide margin in a 2005 national referendum. Islamic law also holds considerable sway in many other countries, including Syria, Iran, Pakistan, Saudi Arabia, Kuwait, the United Arab Emirates, Bahrain, Algeria, Jordan, Lebanon, Libya, Ethiopia, Tajikistan, Uzbekistan, and Turkey (which practices official separation of church and state).

Islamic law is based on four historical sources. In order of importance, these sources are (1) the Koran (also spelled *Quran* and *Qur'an*), or Holy Book of Islam, which Muslims believe is the word of God, or Allah; (2) the teachings of the prophet Muhammad; (3) a consensus of the clergy in cases where neither the Koran nor the prophet directly addresses an issue; and (4) reason or logic, which should be used when no solution can be found in the other three sources.[1]

The prophet Muhammad, whom the *Cambridge Encyclopedia of Islam* describes as a "prophet-lawyer,"[2] rose to fame in the city of Mecca (in what is now Saudi Arabia) as a religious reformer. Later, however, he traveled to Medina, where he became the ruler and lawgiver of a newly formed religious society. In his role as lawgiver, Muhammad enacted legislation whose aim was to teach people what to do and how to behave to achieve salvation. As a consequence, Islamic law today is a system of duties and rituals founded on legal and moral obligations, all of which are ultimately sanctioned by the authority of a religious leader (or leaders) who may issue commands (known as fatwas) that the faithful are bound to obey.

Contemporary Islamic law recognizes seven ***Hudud* crimes**—or crimes based on religious strictures. *Hudud* (sometimes spelled *Hodood* or *Huddud*) crimes are essentially violations of "natural law" as interpreted by Arab culture. These crimes are often described as crimes against God. Four *Hudud* crimes for which punishments are specified in the Koran are (1) war against Allah and His messengers, (2) theft, (3) adultery or fornication, and (4) false accusation of fornication or adultery. Three other *Hudud* offenses are mentioned by the Koran for which no punishment is specified: (1) "corruption on earth," (2) drinking of alcohol, and (3) highway robbery. The punishments for these crimes are determined by tradition.[3] "Corruption on earth" is a general category of religious offense, not well understood in the West, which includes activities such as embezzlement, revolution against lawful authority, fraud, and "weakening the society of God."

▲ Iraqi Shiite Muslims flagellating themselves during a procession in Karbala, Iraq, in 2006. Islamic law, which is based on the teachings of Islam, underpins the legal systems of many nations in the Middle East and elsewhere. How does Islamic law differ from the laws of most Western nations?
Hadi Mizban/AP Wide World Photos

All crimes other than *Hudud* crimes fall into an offense category called *tazirat*. ***Tazir* crimes** are regarded as any actions not considered acceptable in a spiritual society. They include crimes against society and against individuals, but not against God. *Tazir* crimes may call for *quesas* (retribution) or *diya* (compensation or fines). Crimes requiring *quesas* are based on the Arabic principle of "an eye for an eye, a nose for a nose, a tooth for a tooth" and generally require physical punishments up to and including death. *Quesas* offenses may include murder, manslaughter, assault, and maiming. Learn more about Islamic law via **Web Extra 3–2**.

[1]Parviz Saney, "Iran," in Elmer H. Johnson, ed., *International Handbook of Contemporary Developments in Criminology* (Westport, CT: Greenwood, 1983), p. 359.

[2]J. Schact, "Law and Justice," *Cambridge Encyclopedia of Islam*, Vol. 2, p. 539, from which most of the information in this paragraph comes.

[3]This paragraph owes much to Matthew Lippman, "Iran: A Question of Justice?" *Criminal Justice International* (1987), pp. 6–7.

question but claims that it was necessary to avoid some greater evil. A defendant who offers an **excuse** as a defense, on the other hand, claims that some personal condition or circumstance at the time of the act was such that he or she should not be held accountable under the criminal law. **Procedural defenses** make the claim that the defendant was in some significant way discriminated against in the justice process or that some important aspect of official procedure was not properly followed in the investigation or prosecution of the crime charged.

excuse
A legal defense in which the defendant claims that some personal condition or circumstance at the time of the act was such that he or she should not be held accountable under the criminal law.

FIGURE 3–5
Types of Defenses to a Criminal Charge

ALIBI: The defendant could not have committed the offense because he or she was somewhere else at the time of the crime.

EXCUSE: Some personal condition or circumstance at the time of the act was such that the actor should not be held accountable under the criminal law.

EXAMPLES: Duress, age, mistake, involuntary intoxication, unconsciousness, provocation, insanity, diminished capacity, and mental incompetence are examples of excuse defenses.

JUSTIFICATION: The defendant admits committing the act in question but claims that it was necessary to avoid some greater evil.

EXAMPLES: Self-defense, necessity, defense of others, consent, defense of home and property, and resisting unlawful arrest are examples of justification defenses.

PROCEDURAL DEFENSE: The defendant was in some significant way discriminated against in the justice process, or some important aspect of official procedure was not properly followed in the investigation or prosecution of the crime charged.

EXAMPLES: Entrapment, denial of a speedy trial, double jeopardy, prosecutorial misconduct, *collateral estoppel*, police fraud, and selective prosecution are examples of procedural defenses.

procedural defense
A defense that claims that the defendant was in some significant way discriminated against in the justice process or that some important aspect of official procedure was not properly followed in the investigation or prosecution of the crime charged.

Islamic law
A system of laws, operative in some Arab countries, based on the Muslim religion and especially the holy book of Islam, the Koran.

***Hudud* crime**
A serious violation of Islamic law that is regarded as an offense against God.

***Tazir* crime**
A minor violation of Islamic law that is regarded as an offense against society, not God.

Alibi

A reference book for criminal trial lawyers says, "Alibi is different from all of the other defenses . . . because . . . it is based upon the premise that the defendant is truly innocent."[28] The defense of alibi denies that the defendant committed the act in question. All of the other defenses we are about to discuss grant that the defendant committed the act but deny that he or she should be held criminally responsible. While justifications and excuses may produce findings of "not guilty," the defense of alibi claims outright innocence.

Alibi is best supported by witnesses and documentation. A person charged with a crime can use the defense of alibi to show that he or she was not present at the scene when the crime was alleged to have occurred. Hotel receipts, eyewitness identifications, and participation in social events have all been used to prove alibis.

Justifications

As defenses, justifications claim a kind of moral high ground. Justifications may be offered by people who find themselves forced to choose between "two evils." Generally speaking, conduct that a person believes is necessary to avoid harm to him- or herself or to another is justifiable if the harm he or she is trying to avoid is greater than the harm the offense seeks to avoid. For example, a firefighter might set a controlled fire to create a firebreak to head off a conflagration threatening a community; while intentionally setting a fire might constitute arson, destroying property to save a town by creating a firebreak may be justifiable behavior in the eyes of the community and in the eyes of the law. Included under the broad category of justifications are (1) self-defense, (2) defense of others, (3) defense of home and property, (4) necessity, (5) consent, and (6) resisting unlawful arrest.

Self-Defense

In May 2009, when Oklahoma City pharmacist Jerome Ersland was confronted by two holdup men, he allegedly pulled a gun and shot one of them in the head.[29] The second man ran away. Then, prosecutors say, Ersland went behind the counter, got another gun, and pumped five more bullets into the wounded robber as he lay on the floor, killing him. The scene was recorded by a security camera in the drugstore, which had been robbed before and is located in a crime-ridden part of the city. Following the incident, Ersland was charged with first-degree murder in a case that has stirred a furious debate over vigilante justice and self-defense. As this book goes to press, Ersland, 57, is free on $100,000 bail, posted by an anonymous donor. Not everyone thinks that Ersland is a hero, however. Anthony Douglas, president of the Oklahoma chapter of the NAACP, calls Ersland's actions "an execution-style murder" and praises the district attorney for bringing charges. Complicating the situation is the fact that Ersland is white, while the two robbery suspects were black. If convicted, Ersland could receive the death penalty.

Self-defense is probably the best known of the justifications. This defense strategy makes the claim that it was necessary for someone to inflict harm on another to ensure his or her own safety in the face of near-certain injury or death. A person who harms an attacker can generally use this defense. However, the courts have held that where a "path of retreat" exists for a person being attacked, it should be taken. In other words, the safest use of self-defense, legally speaking, is only when cornered, with no path of escape.

The amount of defensive force used must be proportional to the amount of force or the perceived degree of threat that one is seeking to defend against. **Reasonable force** is the degree of force that is appropriate in a given situation and that is not excessive. Reasonable force can also be thought of as the minimum degree of force necessary to protect oneself, one's property, a third party, or the property of another in the face of a substantial threat. Deadly force, the highest degree of force, is considered reasonable only when used to counter an immediate threat of great bodily harm or death. Deadly force cannot be used against nondeadly force.

Force, as the term is used within the context of self-defense, means physical force and does not extend to emotional, psychological, economic, psychic, or other forms of coercion. A person who turns the tables on a robber and assaults him during a robbery attempt, for example, may be able to claim self-defense, but a businessperson who physically assaults a financial rival to prevent a hostile takeover of her company will have no such recourse.

Self-defense has sometimes been claimed in killings of abusive spouses. A jury is likely to accept as justified a killing that occurs while the physical abuse is in progress, especially where a history of such abuse can be shown. On the other hand, wives who suffer repeated abuse but coldly plan the killing of their husbands have not fared well in court.

▲ Pharmacist Jerome Ersland being escorted out of a courtroom at the Oklahoma County Courthouse in Oklahoma City in 2009, following a bond hearing. Ersland was charged with first-degree murder, but his case stirred vigorous debate over vigilante justice and self-defense. Was Ersland justified in what he allegedly did?
*Paul B. Southerland/*The Oklahoman*/AP Wide World Photos*

self-defense
The protection of oneself or of one's property from unlawful injury or from the immediate risk of unlawful injury. Also, the justification that the person who committed an act that would otherwise constitute an offense reasonably believed that the act was necessary to protect self or property from immediate danger.

reasonable force
A degree of force that is appropriate in a given situation and is not excessive. Also, the minimum degree of force necessary to protect oneself, one's property, a third party, or the property of another in the face of a substantial threat.

alter ego rule
In some jurisdictions, a rule of law that holds that a person can only defend a third party under circumstances and only to the degree that the third party could legally act on his or her own behalf.

Defense of Others

The use of force to defend oneself has generally been extended to permit the use of reasonable force to defend others who are or who appear to be in imminent danger. The defense of others, sometimes called *defense of a third person*, is circumscribed in some jurisdictions by the **alter ego rule**. This rule holds that a person can only defend a third party under circumstances and only to the degree that the third party could act. In other words, a person who aids another whom he sees being attacked may become criminally liable if that person initiated the attack or if the assault is a lawful one—for example, an assault made by a law enforcement officer conducting a lawful arrest of a person who is resisting. A few jurisdictions, however, do not recognize the alter ego rule and allow a person to act in defense of another if the actor reasonably believes that his or her intervention is immediately necessary to protect the third person.

Defense of others cannot be claimed by an individual who joins an illegal fight merely to assist a friend or family member. Likewise, one who intentionally aids an offender in an assault, even though the tables have turned and the offender is losing the battle, cannot claim defense of others. Under the law, defense of a third person always requires that the defender be free from fault and that he or she act to aid an innocent person who is in the process of being victimized. The same restrictions that apply to self-defense also apply to the defense of a third party. Hence a defender may act only in the face of an immediate threat to another person, cannot use deadly force against nondeadly force, and must act only to the extent and use only the degree of force needed to repel the attack.

Lecture Note Describe the various defenses to a criminal charge that are discussed in this chapter. Explain that a defense to a criminal charge does not necessarily mean that a person denies committing the act in question. Use self-defense as an example of how a person can admit killing another and still be found "not guilty" of murder (by reason of self-defense).

Defense of Home and Property

In most jurisdictions, the owner of property can justifiably use reasonable *nondeadly* force to prevent others from unlawfully taking or damaging it. As a general rule, the preservation of human life outweighs the protection of property, and the use of deadly force to protect property is not justified unless the perpetrator of the illegal act may intend to commit, or is in the act of committing, a violent act against another human being. A person who shoots and kills an unarmed trespasser, for example, could not claim "defense of property" to avoid criminal liability.[30] However, a person who shoots and kills an armed robber while being robbed can make such a claim.

The use of mechanical devices to protect property is a special area of law. Because deadly force is usually not permitted in defense of property, the setting of booby traps, such as spring-loaded shotguns, electrified gates, and explosive devices, is generally not permitted to protect property that is unattended and unoccupied. If an individual is injured as a result of a mechanical device intended to cause injury or death in the protection of property, criminal charges may be brought against the person who set the device.

On the other hand, acts that would otherwise be criminal may carry no criminal liability if undertaken to protect one's home. For purposes of the law, one's "home" is one's dwelling, whether owned, rented, or merely borrowed. Hotel rooms, rooms aboard vessels, and rented rooms in houses belonging to others are all considered, for purposes of the law, one's home. The retreat rule referred to earlier, which requires a person under attack to retreat when possible before resorting to deadly force, is subject to what some call the *castle exception.* The castle exception can be traced to the writings of the sixteenth-century English jurist Sir Edward Coke, who said, "A man's house is his castle—for where shall a man be safe if it be not in his house?"[31] The castle exception generally recognizes that a person has a fundamental right to be in his or her home and that the home is a final and inviolable place of retreat. That is, the home offers a place of retreat from which a person can be expected to retreat no farther. Hence it is not necessary for one to retreat from one's home in the face of an immediate threat, even where such retreat is possible, before resorting to deadly force in protection of the home. A number of court decisions have extended the castle exception to include one's place of business, such as a store or an office.

Necessity

Necessity, or the claim that some illegal action was needed to prevent an even greater harm, is a useful defense in cases that do not involve serious bodily harm. A famous but unsuccessful use of this defense occurred in *The Crown* v. *Dudly & Stephens* in the late nineteenth century.[32] This British case involved a shipwreck in which three sailors and a cabin boy were set adrift in a lifeboat. After a number of days at sea without food, two of the sailors decided to kill and eat the cabin boy. At their trial, they argued that it was necessary to do so, or none of them would have survived. The court, however, reasoned that the cabin boy was not a direct threat to the survival of the men and rejected this defense. Convicted of murder, they were sentenced to death, although they were spared the gallows by royal intervention. Although cannibalism is usually against the law, courts have sometimes recognized the necessity of consuming human flesh where survival was at issue. Those cases, however, involved only "victims" who had already died of natural causes.

No State shall . . . deprive any person of life, liberty, or property, without due process of law.

—Fourteenth Amendment to the U.S. Constitution

Consent

The defense of consent claims that whatever harm was done occurred only after the injured person gave his or her permission for the behavior in question. In the "Condom Rapist Case," for example, Joel Valdez was found guilty of rape in 1993 after a jury in Austin, Texas, rejected his claim that the act became consensual once he complied with his victim's request to use a condom. Valdez, who was drunk and armed with a knife at the time of the offense, claimed that his victim's request was a consent to sex. After that, he said, "we were making love."[33]

Resisting Unlawful Arrest

All jurisdictions make resisting arrest a crime. Resistance, however, may be justifiable, especially if the arresting officer uses excessive force. Some states have statutory provisions detailing the limits imposed on such resistance and the conditions under which it can be used. Such laws generally say that a person may use a reasonable amount of force, other than deadly force, to resist arrest or an unlawful search by a law enforcement officer if the officer uses or attempts to use greater force than necessary to make the arrest or search. Such laws are inapplicable in cases where the defendant is the first to resort to force. Deadly force to resist arrest is not justified unless the law enforcement officer resorts to deadly force when it is not called for.

Excuses

In contrast to a justification, an excuse does not claim that the conduct in question is justified by the situation or that it is moral. An excuse claims, rather, that the actor who engaged in the unlawful behavior was, at the time, not legally responsible for his or her actions and should not be held accountable under the law. For example, a person who assaults a police officer, thinking that the officer is really a disguised space alien who has come to abduct him, may be found "not guilty" of the charge of assault and battery by reason of insanity. Actions for which excuses are offered do not morally outweigh the wrong committed, but criminal liability may still be negated on the basis of some personal disability that the actor has or because of some special circumstances that characterize the situation. Excuses recognized by the law include (1) duress, (2) age, (3) mistake, (4) involuntary intoxication, (5) unconsciousness, (6) provocation, (7) insanity, (8) diminished capacity, and (9) mental incompetence.

Duress

The defense of duress depends on an understanding of the situation. *Duress* has been defined as "any unlawful threat or coercion used by a person to induce another to act (or to refrain from acting) in a manner he or she otherwise would not (or would)."[34] A person may act under duress if, for example, he or she steals an employer's payroll to meet a ransom demand for kidnappers holding the person's children. Should the person later be arrested for larceny or embezzlement, the person can claim that he or she felt compelled to commit the crime to help ensure the safety of the children. Duress is generally not a useful defense when the crime committed involves serious physical harm, since the harm committed may outweigh the coercive influence in the minds of jurors and judges. Duress is sometimes also called *coercion.*

Age

Age offers another kind of excuse to a criminal charge. The defense of "infancy"—as it is sometimes known in legal jargon—has its roots in the ancient belief that children cannot reason logically until around the age of seven. Early doctrine in the Christian church sanctioned that belief by declaring that rationality develops around that age. As a consequence, only older children could be held responsible for their crimes.

The defense of infancy today has been expanded to include young people well beyond the age of seven. Many states set 16 as the age at which a person becomes an adult for purposes of criminal prosecution; others use the age of 17, and still others 18. When a person younger than the age required for adult prosecution commits a "crime," it is termed a *juvenile offense* (see Chapter 13). He or she is not guilty of a criminal violation of the law by virtue of youth. In most jurisdictions, children below the age of seven cannot be charged even with juvenile offenses, no matter how serious their actions may appear to others.

Mistake

Two types of mistakes can serve as a defense. One is mistake of law, and the other is mistake of fact. Rarely is mistake of law held to be an acceptable defense. Most people realize that it is their responsibility to know the law as it applies to them. "Ignorance of the law is no excuse" is an old dictum still heard today. On occasion, however, cases do arise in which such a defense is accepted by authorities. For example, an elderly woman raised marijuana plants because they could be used to make a tea that relieved her arthritis pain. When her garden was discovered, she was not arrested but was advised as to how the law applied to her.

Mistake of fact is a much more useful form of the mistake defense. In 2000, for example, the statutory rape conviction of 39-year-old Charles Ballinger of Bradley County, Tennessee, was reversed by Tennessee's Court of Criminal Appeals at Knoxville on a mistake-of-fact claim.[35] Ballinger admitted that he had had sex with his 15-year-old neighbor, who was under the age of legal consent at the time of the act. In his defense, however, Ballinger claimed that he had had good reason to mistake the girl's age.

Involuntary Intoxication

The claim of involuntary intoxication may form the basis for another excuse defense. Both drugs and alcohol may produce intoxication. Voluntary intoxication is rarely a defense to a criminal charge because it is a self-induced condition. It is widely recognized in our legal tradition that an altered mental condition that is the product of voluntary activity cannot be used to exonerate guilty actions that follow from it. Some state statutes formalize this general principle of law and specifically state that voluntary intoxication cannot be offered as a defense against a charge of criminal behavior.[36]

Lecture Note Explain and differentiate among the different rules and tests for insanity. Ask students which ones make the most sense, and ask them to explain their reasoning.

Involuntary intoxication, however, is another matter. A person might be tricked into consuming an intoxicating substance. Secretly "spiked" punch, popular aphrodisiacs, or drug-laced desserts might be ingested unknowingly. Because the effects and taste of alcohol are so widely known in our society, the defense of involuntary intoxication due to alcohol consumption can be difficult to demonstrate.

▲ Andrea Pia Yates, the Texas mother who admitted to drowning her five young children in a bathtub in 2001, conferring with attorney George Parnham at her retrial in 2006. Convicted of capital murder in 2002, she was found not guilty by reason of insanity in a retrial ordered by a three-judge panel of the First Texas Court of Appeals. In a civil action that followed her acquittal, Yates was ordered committed to the maximum-security North Texas State Hospital in Vernon, Texas. What does *insanity* mean for purposes of the criminal law?
Brett Coomer-Pool/Getty Images–GINS/ Entertainment News & Sports

Unconsciousness

A very rarely used excuse is that of unconsciousness. An individual cannot be held responsible for anything he or she does while unconscious. Because unconscious people rarely do anything at all, this defense is almost never seen in the courts. However, cases of sleepwalking, epileptic seizure, and neurological dysfunction may result in injurious, although unintentional, actions by people so afflicted. Under such circumstances, a defense of unconsciousness might be argued with success.

Provocation

Provocation recognizes that a person can be emotionally enraged by another who intends to elicit just such a reaction. Should the person then strike out at the tormentor, some courts have held, he or she may not be guilty of criminality or may be guilty of a lesser degree of criminality than might otherwise be the case. The defense of provocation is commonly used in cases arising from barroom brawls in which a person's parentage was called into question, although most states don't look favorably on verbal provocation alone. This defense has also been used in some spectacular cases where wives have killed their husbands, or children their fathers, citing years of verbal and physical abuse. In these latter instances, perhaps because the degree of physical harm inflicted—the death of the husband or father—appears to be out of proportion to the abuse suffered by the wife or child, the courts have not readily accepted the defense of provocation. As a rule, the defense of provocation is generally more acceptable in minor offenses than in serious violations of the law.

Insanity

From the point of view of the criminal law, *insanity* is a legal concept, not a medical one. The legal definition of insanity often has very little to do with psychological or psychiatric understandings of mental illness; rather, it is a concept developed to enable the judicial system to assign guilt or innocence to particular defendants. As a consequence, medical conceptions of mental illness do not always fit well into the legal categories of mental illness created by courts and legislatures. The differences between psychiatric and legal conceptualizations of insanity often lead to disagreements among expert witnesses who, in criminal court, may provide conflicting testimony as to the sanity of a defendant.

The **insanity defense** is given a lot of play in the entertainment industry; movies and television shows regularly employ it because it makes for good drama. In practice, however, the defense of insanity is rarely raised. According to an eight-state study funded by the National Institute of Mental Health, the insanity defense was used in less than 1% of the cases that came before county-level courts.[37] The study showed that only 26% of all insanity pleas were argued successfully and that 90% of those who employed the defense had been previously diagnosed with a mental illness. As the American Bar Association says, "The best evidence suggests that the mental nonresponsibility defense is raised in less than one percent of all felony cases in the United States and is successful in about a fourth of these."[38] Even so, there are several rules that guide the legal definition of insanity.

insanity defense
A legal defense based on claims of mental illness or mental incapacity.

Thematic Question In what ways do changes and developments in the insanity defense reflect shifting conceptions of how to balance individual rights with the need to punish wrongdoers?

The M'Naghten Rule

The insanity defense, as we know it today, was nonexistent prior to the nineteenth century. Until then, insane people who committed crimes were punished in the same way as other law violators. It was Daniel M'Naghten (sometimes spelled McNaughten or M'Naughten), a woodworker from Glasgow, Scotland, who became the first person to be found not guilty of a crime by reason of insanity in 1844. M'Naghten had tried to assassinate Sir Robert Peel, the British prime minister. He mistook Edward Drummond, Peel's secretary, for Peel himself and killed Drummond instead. At his trial, defense attorneys argued that M'Naghten suffered from vague delusions centered on the idea that the Tories, a British political party, were persecuting him. Medical testimony at the trial supported the defense's assertion that he didn't know what he was doing at the time of the shooting. The jury accepted M'Naghten's claim, and the insanity defense was born. Later, the House of Lords defined the criteria necessary for a finding of insanity. The **M'Naghten rule**, as it is called today, holds that a person is not guilty of a crime if, at the time of the crime, the person either didn't know what he or she was doing or didn't know that it was wrong. The inability to distinguish right from wrong must be the result of some mental defect or disability.

M'Naghten rule
A rule for determining insanity that asks whether the defendant knew what he or she was doing or whether the defendant knew that what he or she was doing was wrong.

The M'Naghten rule is followed in many U.S. jurisdictions (Figure 3–6) today. In those states, the burden of proving insanity falls on the defendant. Just as defendants are assumed to be innocent, they are also assumed to be sane at the outset of any criminal trial. Learn more about the M'Naghten rule at **Web Extra 3–3**.

Irresistible Impulse

The M'Naghten rule worked well for a time. Eventually, however, some cases arose in which defendants clearly knew what they were doing, and they knew it was wrong. Even so, they argued in their defense that they couldn't stop doing what they knew was wrong. Such people are said to suffer from an *irresistible impulse*, and in a number of states today, they may be found not guilty by reason of that particular brand of insanity. Some states that do not use the irresistible-impulse test in determining insanity may still allow the successful demonstration of such an impulse to be considered in sentencing decisions.

The irresistible-impulse test has been criticized on a number of grounds. Primary among them is the belief that all of us suffer from compulsions. Most of us, however, learn to control them. If we give in to a compulsion, the critique goes, then why not just say it was unavoidable so as to escape any legal consequences?

The Durham Rule

Another rule for gauging insanity is called the *Durham rule*. Originally created in 1871 by a New Hampshire court, it was later adopted by Judge David Bazelon in 1954 as he decided the case of *Durham* v. *U.S.* for the court of appeals in the District of Columbia.[39] The Durham rule states that a person is not criminally responsible for his or her behavior if the person's illegal actions were the result of some mental disease or defect.

Courts that follow the Durham rule typically hear from an array of psychiatric specialists as to the mental state of the defendant. Their testimony is inevitably clouded by the need to

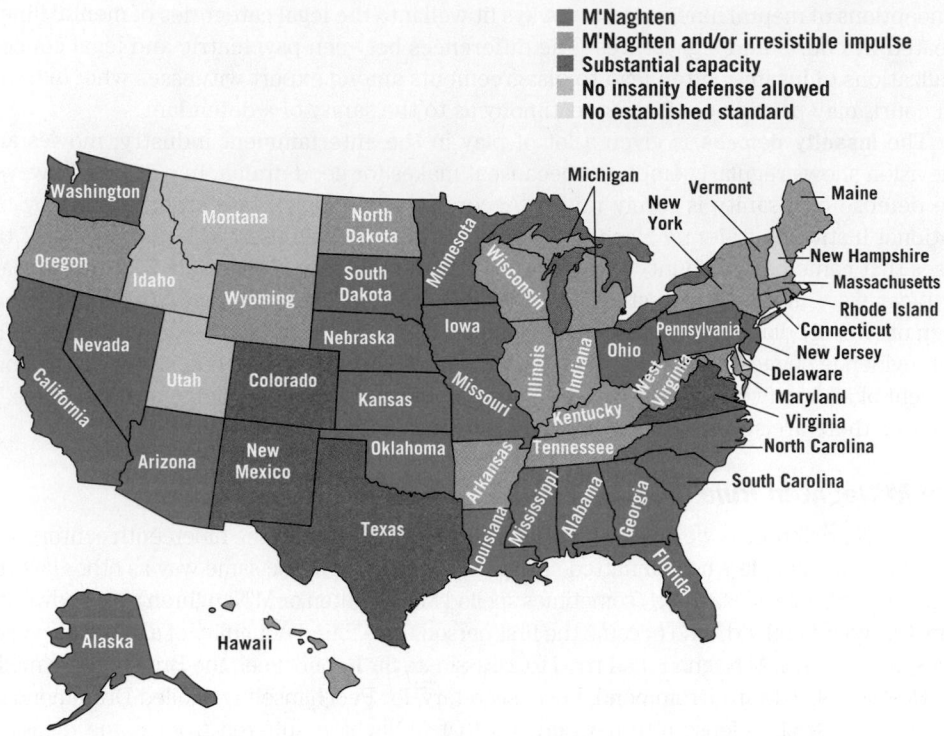

FIGURE 3–6
Standards for Insanity Determinations by Jurisdiction

Source: Adapted from David B. Rottman and Shauna M. Strickland, *State Court Organization, 2004* (Washington, DC: Bureau of Justice Statistics, 2006), pp. 199–202.

Class Activity Ask class members to research the form that the insanity defense takes in their home state. Have them closely examine the laws of criminal procedure or precedent that they discover to determine whether the historical roots of their state's practice lie in the M'Naghten rule or in some other precedent. Ask students to decide which forms of the insanity defense described in the text are closest to their state's understanding of insanity as a criminal defense. Through library or Web-based research, have students determine whether their state makes possible some form of the "guilty but mentally ill" finding. Ask them to tell the class whether they agree or disagree with their state's position on the insanity defense and to explain why.

address the question of cause. A successful defense under the Durham rule necessitates that jurors be able to see the criminal activity in question as the *product* of the defendant's mental deficiencies. And yet many people who suffer from mental diseases or defects never commit crimes. In fact, low IQ, mental retardation, and lack of general mental capacity are not allowable excuses for criminal behavior. Because the Durham rule is especially vague, it provides fertile ground for conflicting claims.

The Substantial-Capacity Test

Nineteen states follow another guideline—the substantial-capacity test—as found in the Model Penal Code (MPC) of the American Law Institute (ALI).[40] Also called the *ALI rule* or the *MPC rule*, it suggests that insanity should be defined as the lack of a substantial capacity to control one's behavior. This test requires a judgment to the effect that the defendant either had or lacked "the mental capacity needed to understand the wrongfulness of his act or to conform his behavior to the requirements of the law."[41] The substantial-capacity test is a blending of the M'Naghten rule and the irresistible-impulse standard. "Substantial capacity" does not require total mental incompetence, nor does the rule require the behavior in question to live up to the criterion of total irresistibility. However, the problem of establishing just what constitutes "substantial mental capacity" has plagued this rule from its conception.

Equal Justice under Law

—Inscription above U.S. Supreme Court building entrance

The Brawner Rule

Judge Bazelon, apparently dissatisfied with the application of the Durham rule, created a new criterion for gauging insanity in the 1972 case of *U.S.* v. *Brawner*.[42] The Brawner rule, as it has come to be called, places responsibility for deciding insanity squarely with the jury. Bazelon suggested that the jury should be concerned with whether the defendant could justly be held responsible for the criminal act in the face of any claims of insanity. Under this proposal, juries are left with few rules to guide them other than their own sense of fairness.

The Insanity Defense and Social Reaction

The insanity defense originated as a way to recognize the social reality of mental disease. However, the history of this defense has been rife with difficulty and contradiction. First, psychiatric testimony is expensive, and expert witnesses are often at odds with one another. Another difficulty with this defense is society's acceptance of it. When "not guilty due to insanity" findings have been made, the public has not always been satisfied that justice has been served. Dissatisfaction with the jumble of rules defining legal insanity peaked in 1982 when John Hinckley was acquitted of trying to assassinate then-President Ronald Reagan. At his trial, Hinckley's lawyers claimed that a series of delusions brought about by a history of schizophrenia left him unable to control his behavior. Government prosecutors were unable to counter defense contentions of insanity. The resulting acquittal shocked the nation and resulted in calls for a review of the insanity defense.

One response has been to ban the insanity defense from use at trial. A ruling by the U.S. Supreme Court in support of a Montana law allows states to prohibit defendants from claiming that they were insane at the time they committed their crimes. In 1994, without comment, the high court let stand a Montana Supreme Court ruling that held that eliminating the insanity defense does not violate the U.S. Constitution. Currently, only three states—Montana, Idaho, and Utah—bar use of the insanity defense.[43]

The Guilty But Mentally Ill Verdict

Another response to public frustration with the insanity and responsibility issue is the **guilty but mentally ill (GBMI)** verdict, now possible in at least 11 states. (In a few states, the finding is "guilty but insane.") A GBMI verdict means that a person can be held responsible for a specific criminal act even though a degree of mental incompetence may be present in his or her personality. In most GBMI jurisdictions, a jury must return a finding of "guilty but mentally ill" if (1) every element necessary for a conviction has been proved beyond a reasonable doubt, (2) the defendant is found to have been *mentally ill* at the time the crime was committed, and (3) the defendant was *not* found to have been *legally insane* at the time the crime was committed. The difference between mental illness and legal insanity is a crucial one, since a defendant can be mentally ill by standards of the medical profession but sane for purposes of the law.

guilty but mentally ill (GBMI)
A verdict, equivalent to a finding of "guilty," that establishes that the defendant, although mentally ill, was in sufficient possession of his or her faculties to be morally blameworthy for his or her acts.

Upon return of a GBMI verdict, a judge may impose any sentence possible under the law for the crime in question. Mandated psychiatric treatment, however, is often part of the commitment order. Once cured, the offender is usually placed in the general prison population to serve any remaining sentence.

As some authors have observed, the GBMI finding has three purposes: "first, to protect society; second, to hold some offenders who were mentally ill accountable for their criminal acts; [and] third, to make treatment available to convicted offenders suffering from some form of mental illness."[44] The U.S. Supreme Court case of *Ford* v. *Wainwright* recognized an issue of a different sort.[45] The 1986 decision specified that prisoners who become insane while incarcerated cannot be executed. Hence, although insanity may not always be a successful defense to criminal prosecution, it can later become a block to the ultimate punishment.

The Defense of Temporary Insanity

Temporary insanity is another possible defense against a criminal charge. Widely used in the 1940s and 1950s, temporary insanity means that the offender claims to have been insane only at the time of the commission of the offense. If a jury agrees, the defendant goes free. The defendant is not guilty of the criminal action by virtue of having been insane at the time, yet he or she cannot be ordered to undergo psychiatric counseling or treatment because the insanity is no longer present. This type of plea has become less popular as legislatures have regulated the circumstances under which it can be made.

The Insanity Defense under Federal Law

Yet another response to the public's concern with the insanity defense and responsibility issue is the federal Insanity Defense Reform Act (IDRA). In 1984, Congress passed this act, which created major revisions in the federal insanity defense. Insanity under the law is now defined as a condition in which the defendant can be shown to have been suffering under a "severe mental disease or defect" and, as a result, "was unable to appreciate the nature and quality or the wrongfulness of his acts."[46] This definition of insanity comes close to that set forth in the old M'Naghten rule.

The act also places the burden of proving the insanity defense squarely on the defendant—a provision that has been challenged a number of times since the act was passed. The Supreme Court supported a similar requirement prior to the act's passage. In 1983, in the case of *Jones v. U.S.*,[47] the Court ruled that defendants can be required to prove their insanity when it becomes an issue in their defense. Shortly after the act became law, the Court held in *Ake v. Oklahoma* (1985)[48] that the government must ensure access to a competent psychiatrist whenever a defendant indicates that insanity will be an issue at trial.

The Consequences of an Insanity Ruling

The insanity defense today is not an easy way out of criminal prosecution, as some people assume. Once a verdict of "not guilty by reason of insanity" is returned, the judge may order the defendant to undergo psychiatric treatment until cured. Because psychiatrists are reluctant to declare any potential criminal "cured," such a sentence may result in more time spent in an institution than would have been spent in a prison. In *Foucha v. Louisiana* (1992),[49] however, the U.S. Supreme Court held that a defendant found not guilty by reason of insanity in a criminal trial could not thereafter be institutionalized indefinitely without a showing that he or she was either dangerous or mentally ill.

Diminished Capacity

diminished capacity
A defense based on claims of a mental condition that may be insufficient to exonerate the defendant of guilt but that may be relevant to specific mental elements of certain crimes or degrees of crime.

Diminished capacity, or *diminished responsibility*, is a defense available in some jurisdictions. In 2003, the U.S. Sentencing Commission issued a policy statement saying that diminished capacity may mean that "the defendant, although convicted, *has a significantly impaired ability* to (A) understand the wrongfulness of the behavior comprising the offense or to exercise the power of reason; or (B) control behavior that the defendant knows is wrongful."[50] Still, "the terms 'diminished responsibility' and 'diminished capacity' do not have a clearly accepted meaning in [many] courts."[51] Some defendants who offer diminished-capacity defenses do so in recognition of the fact that such claims may be based on a mental condition that would not qualify as mental disease or mental defect or be sufficient to support the defense of insanity but that might still lower criminal culpability. According to Peter Arenella, professor of law at UCLA, "the defense [of diminished capacity] was first recognized by Scottish common law courts to reduce the punishment of the 'partially insane' from murder to culpable homicide, a non-capital offense."[52]

The diminished-capacity defense is similar to the defense of insanity in that it depends on a showing that the defendant's mental state was impaired at the time of the crime. As a defense, diminished capacity is most useful when it can be shown that because of some defect of reason or mental shortcoming, the defendant's capacity to form the *mens rea* required by a specific crime was impaired. Unlike an insanity defense, however, which can result in a finding of "not guilty," a diminished-capacity defense is built on the recognition that "[m]ental condition, though insufficient to exonerate, may be relevant to specific mental elements of certain crimes or degrees of crime."[53] For example, a defendant might present evidence of mental abnormality in an effort to reduce first-degree murder to second-degree murder, or second-degree murder to manslaughter, when a killing occurs under extreme emotional disturbance. Similarly, in some jurisdictions, very low intelligence will, if proved, serve to reduce first-degree murder to manslaughter.[54]

As is the case with the insanity defense, some jurisdictions have entirely eliminated the diminished-capacity defense. The California Penal Code, for example, abolished the defense,[55] stating that "[a]s a matter of public policy there shall be no defense of diminished capacity, diminished responsibility, or irresistible impulse in a criminal action or juvenile adjudication hearing."[56]

Mental Incompetence

incompetent to stand trial
In criminal proceedings, a finding by a court that as a result of mental illness, defect, or disability, a defendant is incapable of understanding the nature of the charges and proceedings against him or her, of consulting with an attorney, and of aiding in his or her own defense.

In most states, the defendant must be capable of understanding the nature of the proceedings and must be able to assist in his or her own legal defense before being deemed competent to stand trial. Whereas insanity refers to an assessment of the offender's mental condition at the time the crime was committed, mental incompetence refers to his or her condition immediately before prosecution. Mental illness short of being found **incompetent to stand trial** can bar a defendant from self-representation. In 2008, in the case of *Indiana* v. *Edwards*, the U.S. Supreme Court held that even defendants found competent to stand trial can be prohibited from representing themselves before the court if they are too mentally disturbed to conduct trial proceedings by themselves.[57]

Thematic Question The entrapment defense has been used by a number of well-known individuals (John DeLorean, Mayor Marion Barry of Washington, D.C., and members of Congress accused of taking bribes, for example). What one consideration determines the crucial distinction between guilt and innocence when the entrapment defense is used?

Procedural Defenses

Procedural defenses make the claim that the defendant was in some manner discriminated against in the justice process or that some important aspect of official procedure was not properly followed. As a result, those offering this defense say, the defendant should be released from any criminal liability. The procedural defenses we will discuss here are (1) entrapment, (2) double jeopardy, (3) *collateral estoppel*, (4) selective prosecution, (5) denial of a speedy trial, (6) prosecutorial misconduct, and (7) police fraud.

Entrapment

Entrapment is an improper or illegal inducement to crime by enforcement agents. Entrapment defenses argue that enforcement agents effectively created a crime where there would otherwise have been none. For entrapment to occur, the idea for the criminal activity must originate with official agents of the criminal justice system. Entrapment can also result when overzealous undercover police officers convince a defendant that the contemplated law-violating behavior is not a crime. To avoid claims of entrapment, officers must not engage in activity that would cause a person to commit a crime that he or she would not otherwise commit. Merely providing an opportunity for a willing offender to commit a crime, however, is not entrapment.

No person shall be . . . twice put in jeopardy of life or limb.
—Fifth Amendment to the U.S. Constitution

entrapment
An improper or illegal inducement to crime by agents of law enforcement. Also, a defense that may be raised when such inducements have occurred.

double jeopardy
A common law and constitutional prohibition against a second trial for the same offense.

Double Jeopardy

The Fifth Amendment to the U.S. Constitution makes it clear that no person may be tried twice for the same offense, which is known as **double jeopardy**. In other words, people who have been acquitted or found innocent may not again be "put in jeopardy of life or limb" for the same crime. The same is true of those who have been convicted: They cannot be tried again for the same offense. Cases that are dismissed for a lack of evidence also come under the double jeopardy rule and cannot result in a new trial. The U.S. Supreme Court has ruled that "the Double Jeopardy Clause protects against three distinct abuses: a second prosecution for the same offense after acquittal; a second prosecution for the same offense after conviction; and multiple punishments for the same offense."[58]

Double jeopardy does not apply in cases of trial error. A defendant whose conviction was set aside because of some error in proceedings at a lower court level (for example, inappropriate instructions to the jury by the trial court judge) can be retried on the same charges. Similarly, when a defendant's motion for a mistrial is successful or when members of the jury cannot agree on a verdict (resulting in a hung jury), a second trial may be held. Defendants, however, may be tried in both federal and state courts without necessarily violating the principle of double jeopardy.

Generally, because civil and criminal laws differ as to purpose, it is possible to try someone in civil court to collect damages for a possible violation of civil law, even if they were found "not guilty" in criminal court, without violating the principle of double jeopardy. For example, the 2005 civil trial of actor Robert Blake, following his acquittal at a criminal trial for murdering his wife, resulted in Blake's being ordered to pay $30 million to his wife's children.[59] In cases where civil penalties are "so punitive in form and effect as to render them criminal,"[60] however, a person sanctioned by a court in a civil case may not be tried in criminal court.

▲ Members of the New York City Police Department's Street Crimes Unit preparing for a day's work. Entrapment will likely not be an effective defense for muggers who attack these decoys. Why not?
Courtesy of the New York City Police Department

Collateral Estoppel

Collateral estoppel is similar to double jeopardy, but it applies to facts that have been determined by a "valid and final judgment."[61] Such facts cannot become the object of new litigation. For example, if a defendant has been acquitted of a murder charge by virtue of an alibi, it would not be permissible to try that person again for the murder of a second person killed along with the first.

In all criminal prosecutions, the accused shall enjoy the right to a speedy and public trial, by an impartial jury.
—Sixth Amendment to the U.S. Constitution

Selective Prosecution

The procedural defense of selective prosecution is based on the Fourteenth Amendment's guarantee of "equal protection of the laws." This defense may be available where two or more individuals are suspected of criminal involvement but not all are actively prosecuted. Selective prosecution based fairly on the strength of available evidence is not the object of this defense. However, when prosecution proceeds unfairly on the basis of some arbitrary and discriminatory attribute, such as race, sex, friendship, age, or religious preference, this defense may offer protection. In 1996, in a case that reaffirmed reasonable limits on claims of selective prosecution, the U.S. Supreme Court ruled that for a defendant to successfully "claim that he was singled out for prosecution on the basis of his race, he must make a . . . showing that the Government declined to prosecute similarly situated suspects of other races."[62]

Denial of a Speedy Trial

The Sixth Amendment to the Constitution guarantees a right to a speedy trial. The purpose of the guarantee is to prevent unconvicted and potentially innocent people from languishing in jail. The federal government[63] and most states have laws (generally referred to as *speedy trial acts*) that define the time limit necessary for a trial to be "speedy." They generally set a reasonable period, such as 90 or 120 days following arrest. Excluded from the total number of days are delays that result from requests by the defense to prepare the defendant's case. If the limit set by law is exceeded, the defendant must be set free, and no trial can occur.

Speedy trial claims became an issue in New Orleans after it was ravaged by Hurricane Katrina in August 2005. Nine months after the storm battered the city, Chief District Judge Calvin Johnson told reporters that his staff was continuing to find people who shouldn't be in jail and who were doing "Katrina time."[64] Most pre-Katrina arrestees discovered by Johnson's staff had been taken into custody for misdemeanors before the storm hit. The judge said that he released them when they were found. "We can't have people in jail indeterminately," he said. Speedy trial laws are discussed in more detail in Chapter 8.

Prosecutorial Misconduct

Another procedural defense is prosecutorial misconduct. Generally speaking, legal scholars use the term *prosecutorial misconduct* to describe actions undertaken by prosecutors that give the government an unfair advantage or that prejudice the rights of a defendant or a witness. Prosecutors are expected to uphold the highest ethical standards in the performance of their roles. When they knowingly permit false testimony, when they hide information that would clearly help the defense, or when they make unduly biased statements to the jury in closing arguments, the defense of prosecutorial misconduct may be available to the defendant.

Police Fraud

During the 1995 double-murder trial of O. J. Simpson, defense attorneys suggested that evidence against Simpson had been concocted and planted by police officers with a personal dislike of the defendant. In particular, defense attorneys pointed a finger at Los Angeles Police Detective Mark Fuhrman, suggesting that he had planted a bloody glove at the Simpson estate and had tampered with bloodstain evidence taken from Simpson's white

Ford Bronco. To support allegations that Fuhrman was motivated by racist leanings, defense attorneys subpoenaed tapes Fuhrman had made over a ten-year period with a North Carolina screenwriter who had been documenting life within the Los Angeles Police Department.

As one observer put it, however, the defense of police fraud builds on extreme paranoia about the government and police agencies. This type of defense, says political economist Francis Fukuyama, carries "to extremes a distrust of government and the belief that public authorities are in a vast conspiracy to violate the rights of individuals."[65] It can also be extremely unfair to innocent people, for a strategy of this sort subjects otherwise well-meaning public servants to intense public scrutiny, effectively shifting attention away from criminal defendants and onto the police officers—sometimes with disastrous personal results. The 43-year-old Fuhrman retired from police work before the Simpson trial concluded and has since written two books.

A PowerPoint presentation that supports this chapter is available from your Prentice Hall representative.

Summary

CRIMINAL LAW

- Laws are rules of conduct, usually found enacted in the form of statutes, that regulate relationships between people and also between parties. One of the primary functions of the law is to maintain public order. Laws also serve to regulate human interaction, enforce moral beliefs, define the economic environment of a society, enhance predictability, promote orderly social change, sustain individual rights, identify wrongdoers and redress wrongs, and mandate punishment and retribution. Because laws are made by those in power and are influenced by those with access to power brokers, they tend to reflect and support the interests of society's most powerful members.
- The rule of law, which is sometimes referred to as the *supremacy of law*, encompasses the principle that an orderly society must be governed by established principles and known codes that are applied uniformly and fairly to all of its members. It means that no one is above the law, and it mandates that even those who make or enforce the law must also abide by it. The rule of law is regarded as a vital underpinning in Western democracies, for without it disorder and chaos might prevail.
- This chapter identified various types of law, including criminal law, civil law, administrative law, case law, and procedural law. This chapter is concerned primarily with criminal law, which is that form of the law that defines and specifies punishments for offenses of a public nature or for wrongs committed against the state or against society.
- Violations of the criminal law can be of many different types and can vary in severity. Five categories of violations were discussed in this chapter: (1) felonies, (2) misdemeanors, (3) offenses, (4) treason and espionage, and (5) inchoate offenses.
- From the perspective of Western jurisprudence, all crimes can be said to share certain features. Taken together, these features make up the legal essence of the concept of crime. The essence of crime consists of three conjoined elements: (1) the criminal act, which in legal parlance is termed the *actus reus;* (2) a culpable mental state, or *mens rea;* and (3) a concurrence of the two. Hence the essence of criminal conduct consists of a concurrence of a criminal act with a culpable mental state. Five additional principles, added to these three, allow us to fully appreciate contemporary understandings of crime: (1) causation, (2) resulting harm, (3) legality, (4) punishment, and (5) necessary attendant circumstances.
- Written laws specify exactly what conditions are required for a person to be charged in a given instance of criminal activity. The elements of a crime are specific legal aspects of the criminal offense that the prosecution must prove in order to obtain a conviction. Guilt can be demonstrated, and criminal offenders convicted, only if all of the statutory elements of the particular crime can be proved in court.
- Our legal system recognizes four broad categories of defenses to a criminal charge: (1) alibi, (2) justifications, (3) excuses, and (4) procedural defenses. An alibi, if shown to be valid, means that the defendant could not have committed the crime in question because he or she was not present at the time of the crime. When a defendant offers a justification as a defense,

he or she admits committing the act in question but claims that it was necessary to avoid some greater evil. A defendant who offers an excuse as a defense claims that some personal condition or circumstance at the time of the act was such that he or she should not be held accountable under the criminal law. Procedural defenses make the claim that the defendant was in some significant way discriminated against in the justice process or that some important aspect of official procedure was not properly followed in the investigation or prosecution of the crime charged.

QUESTIONS FOR REVIEW

1. What is the purpose of law? What would a society without laws be like?
2. What is the rule of law? What is its importance in Western democracies? What does it mean to say that "nobody is above the law"?
3. What types of law does this chapter discuss? What purpose does each serve?
4. What are the five categories of criminal law violations? Describe each, and rank the categories in terms of seriousness.
5. List and describe the eight general features of crime. What are the "three conjoined elements" that comprise the legal essence of the concept of crime?
6. What is meant by the *corpus delicti* of a crime? How does the *corpus delicti* of a crime differ from the statutory elements that must be proved to convict a particular defendant of committing that crime?
7. What four broad categories of criminal defenses does our legal system recognize? Under what circumstances might each be employed?

Policing: Purpose and Organization

CHAPTER 4

Learning Objectives

After reading this chapter, you should be able to:

1. Explain the police mission in democratic societies. 88
2. List and describe the three major levels of public law enforcement in the United States today. 91
3. Discuss the various components of police administration, including management, chain of command, organization, and department structure. 97
4. Identify the various historical stages of development in American policing, and describe the characteristics of each stage. 100
5. Describe community policing, and explain how it differs from traditional forms of policing. 102
6. Explain evidence-based policing, and demonstrate the potential that it holds in the area of police management. 108
7. Explain police discretion, and identify some of the factors that influence a police officer's use of discretion. 111

e police in the United States are not separate from the people. They draw their authority from the will and nsent of the people, and they ruit their officers from them. e police are the instrument f the people to achieve and intain order; their efforts are founded on principles of public service and ultimate responsibility to the public."

–National Advisory Commission on Criminal Justice Standards and Goals

"The tragedies of September 11, 2001, have forever changed the roles of traditional law enforcement in this country."

—Major Cities Chiefs Association[1]

▲ Miami riot police advancing through burning trash to control demonstrators protesting a meeting of foreign delegates who were attempting to negotiate an international free-trade agreement in 2003. Order maintenance is an important part of the police mission. What other aspects of the police mission can you identify?
David Adame/AP Wide World Photos

Introduction

In mid-November 2003, thousands of demonstrators protesting the proposed creation of the Free Trade Area of the Americas (FTAA) clashed with hundreds of Miami police officers equipped with riot gear. The protesters—concerned that the creation of the 34-nation FTAA would send thousands of U.S. jobs overseas, exploit cheap labor, and waste natural resources—were targeting a meeting by foreign trade ministers.[2]

Although most demonstrators paraded peacefully and avoided confrontations, some pulled down crowd-control barriers with grappling hooks and scuffled with officers who were trying to maintain order. Before the melee ended, officers had to use batons, plastic shields, concussion grenades, pepper spray, and stun guns to regain control over the unruly protesters. Armored personnel carriers stood ready to move into "hot spots." "We're basically trying to maintain the peace downtown," said police spokesperson Jorge Pino, as demonstrators advanced on police lines.[3] By the time the event ended, 74 people had been arrested and 42 protesters were injured, including ten who had to be hospitalized. Three police officers were also hurt. As the Miami riots demonstrate, the maintenance of social order is an important part of police work today.

The Police Mission

The basic purposes of policing in democratic societies are to (1) enforce the laws of the society of which the police are a part, (2) apprehend offenders who participate in crime, (3) prevent crime, (4) preserve domestic peace and tranquillity, and (5) provide the community with needed enforcement-related services. Simply put, as Sir Robert Peel, founder of the British system of policing, explained in 1822, "The basic mission for which the police exist is to reduce crime and disorder."[4] In the paragraphs that follow, we turn our attention to these five basic elements of the police mission.

1 Explain the police mission in democratic societies.

Enforcing the Law

The police operate under an official public mandate that requires them to enforce the law. Collectively speaking, police agencies are the primary enforcers of federal, state, and local criminal laws. Not surprisingly, police officers see themselves as crime fighters, a view shared by the public and promoted by the popular media.

Although it is the job of the police to enforce the law, it is not their *only* job. Practically speaking, most officers spend the majority of their time answering nonemergency public service calls,[5] controlling traffic, or writing tickets. Most are not involved in intensive, ongoing crime-fighting activities. Research shows that only about 10% to 20% of all calls to the police involve situations that actually require a law enforcement response (that is, situations that might lead to arrest and eventual prosecution), a fact that is described in more detail later in this chapter.[6]

Even when the police are busy enforcing laws, they can't enforce them all. Police resources, including labor, vehicles, and investigative assets, are limited, causing officers to focus more on certain types of law violation than on others. Old laws prohibiting minor offenses that today hold little social significance, like spitting on the sidewalk or scaring horses with a noisy automobile, are typically relegated to the dustbin of statutory history. Even though they are still "on the books," few (if any) officers even think about enforcing such laws. A number of writers have observed that the police tend to tailor their enforcement efforts to meet the contemporary concerns of the populace they serve.[7] For example, if the local community is upset about "massage parlors" operating in certain neighborhoods, it is likely that the local police department will bring enforcement efforts to bear that might eventually lead to the relocation or closing of such businesses. Although the enforcement practices of police agencies are significantly influenced by community interests, individual officers take their cue on enforcement priorities from their departments, their peers, and their supervisors. Learn more about how police supervisory styles influence patrol officer behavior at **Library Extra 4–1**.

The police are expected not only to enforce the law but also to support it. This means that the personal actions of law enforcement personnel should be exemplary and should inspire others to respect and obey the law. Off-duty officers who are seen speeding down the highway or smoking marijuana at a party, for example, do a disservice to the police profession and engender disrespect for all agents of enforcement and for the law itself. Hence, in an important sense, we can say that respect for the law begins with the personal and public behavior of law enforcement officers.

Apprehending Offenders

Some offenders are apprehended during the investigation of a crime or even during its commission or immediately afterward. Fleeing Oklahoma City bomber Timothy McVeigh, for example, was stopped by an Oklahoma Highway Patrol officer on routine patrol only 90 minutes after the destruction of the Alfred P. Murrah Federal Building[8] for driving a car with no license plate. When the officer questioned McVeigh about a bulge in his jacket, McVeigh admitted that it was a gun. The officer then took McVeigh into custody for carrying a concealed weapon. Typically, McVeigh would then have made an immediate appearance before a judge and have been released on bail. As fate would have it, however, the judge assigned to see McVeigh was involved in a protracted divorce case. The longer jail stay proved to be McVeigh's undoing. As the investigation into the bombing progressed, profiler Clinton R. Van Zandt of the Federal Bureau of Investigation (FBI) Behavioral Science Unit concluded that the bomber was likely a native-born white male in his twenties who had been in the military and was probably a member of a fringe militia group—all of which were true of McVeigh.[9] Working together, the FBI and the Oklahoma State Police realized that McVeigh was a likely suspect and questioned him. While McVeigh's capture was the result of a bit of good luck, many offenders are only caught as the result of extensive police work involving a painstaking investigation.

crime prevention
The anticipation, recognition, and appraisal of a crime risk and the initiation of action to eliminate or reduce it.

Preventing Crime

Crime prevention is a proactive approach to the problem of crime; it is "the anticipation, recognition and appraisal of a crime risk and initiation of action to remove or reduce it."[10] In preventing crime, police agencies act before a crime happens, thus preventing victimization from occurring. Although the term *crime prevention* is relatively new, the idea is probably as old as human society. Securing valuables, limiting access to sensitive areas, and monitoring the activities of suspicious people are techniques that were in use long before the establishment of Western police forces in the 1800s.

▲ Chief Deputy Paula Townsend of the Watauga County (North Carolina) Sheriff's Department carrying 11-month-old Breanna Chambers to safety in 2005 after the capture of the child's parents. The parents, who were already wanted on charges related to methamphetamine manufacture, were charged with additional counts of child abduction, felonious restraint, and assault with a gun after they abducted Breanna and her two-year-old brother, James Paul Chambers, from a foster home. Today's police officers are expected to enforce the law while meeting the needs of the community. Do those goals conflict? If so, how?
Watauga Democrat/Marie Freeman/AP Wide World Photos

Techniques and Programs

Modern crime-prevention efforts aim not only to reduce crime and criminal opportunities and lower the potential rewards of criminal activity but also to lessen the public's fear of crime.[11] Law enforcement–led crime-prevention efforts include both techniques and programs. Crime-prevention *techniques* include access control (including barriers to entry and exit), surveillance (such as video surveillance), theft-deterrence devices (that is, locks, alarms, and tethers), security lighting, and visibility landscaping. Crime prevention through environmental design (CPTED) is a tool that can be used by crime-prevention specialists, including architects and public-safety consultants.

In contrast to techniques, crime-prevention *programs* are organized efforts that focus resources on reducing a specific form of criminal threat. The Philadelphia Police Department's Operation Identification, for example, is designed to discourage theft and to help recover stolen property.[12] The program seeks to educate citizens on the importance of identifying, marking, and listing their valuables to deter theft and to aid in their recovery. Through Operation Identification, the police department provides engraving pens, suggests ways of photographing and engraving valuables, and provides window decals and car bumper stickers that identify citizens as participants in the program. Other crime-prevention programs typically target school-based crime, gang activity, drug abuse, violence, domestic abuse, identity theft, vehicle theft, or neighborhood crimes such as burglary.

Today's crime-prevention programs depend on community involvement, an open flow of information, and public education about risks and possible preventive measures. For example,

Neighborhood Watch programs build on active observation by home owners and businesspeople on the lookout for anything unusual. Crime Stoppers International and Crime Stoppers USA are examples of privately sponsored programs that accept tips about criminal activity that they pass on to the appropriate law enforcement organization. Crime Stoppers International can be accessed at **Web Extra 4–1**, and the National Crime Prevention Council can be found at **Web Extra 4–2**.

Predicting Crime

Law enforcement's ability to prevent crimes relies in part on the ability of police planners to predict when and where crimes will occur. Effective prediction means that limited police resources can be correctly assigned to the areas with the greatest need. One technique for predicting criminal activity is **CompStat**.[13] While CompStat may sound like a software program, it is actually a process of crime analysis and police management developed by the New York City Police Department in the mid-1990s to help police managers better assess their performance and foresee the potential for crime.[14] The CompStat process involves first collecting and analyzing the information received from 9-1-1 calls and officer reports.[15] This detailed and timely information is then mapped using special software developed for the purpose. The resulting map sequences, generated over time, reveal the time and place of crime patterns and identify hot spots of ongoing criminal activity. The maps also show the number of patrol officers active in an area, ongoing investigations, arrests made, and so on, thus helping commanders see which anticrime strategies are working.

CompStat
A crime-analysis and police-management process built on crime mapping that was developed by the New York City Police Department in the mid-1990s.

CrimeStat, a Windows-based spatial statistics analysis software program for analyzing crime-incident locations, is a second technique for predicting criminal activity. It produces results similar to CompStat's.[16] Developed by Ned Levine and Associates with grants from the National Institute of Justice (NIJ), CrimeStat provides statistical tools for crime mapping and analysis—including identification of crime hot spots, spatial distribution of incidents, and distance analysis—that help crime analysts target offenses that might be related to one another. CrimeStat software is available online via **Web Extra 4–3**; **Web Extra 4–4** provides a link to chicagocrime.org, which overlays crime statistics on maps of the city.

Preserving the Peace

Enforcing the law, investigating crime and apprehending offenders, and preventing crime are all daunting tasks requiring the full attention of police departments. There are, after all, many laws and numerous offenders. Still, crimes are clearly defined by statute and are therefore limited in number. Peacekeeping, however, is a virtually limitless police activity involving not only activities that violate the law (and hence the community's peace) but many other activities as well. Law enforcement officers who supervise parades, public demonstrations, and picketing strikers, for example, typically attempt to ensure that the behavior of everyone involved remains civil so that it does not disrupt community life.

Robert H. Langworthy, who has written extensively about the police, says that keeping the peace is often left to individual officers.[17] Basically, he says, departments depend on patrol officers "to define the peace and decide how to support it." An officer is doing a good job when his or her beat is quiet, "meaning there are no complaints about loiterers or traffic flow, and commerce is supported."

Many police departments focus on quality-of-life offenses as a crime-reduction and peacekeeping strategy. **Quality-of-life offenses** are minor law violations (sometimes called *petty crimes*) that demoralize residents and businesspeople by creating disorder (for example, excessive noise, graffiti, abandoned cars, and vandalism) or by reflecting social decay (panhandling and aggressive begging, public urination, prostitution, roaming youth gangs, public consumption of alcohol, and street-level substance abuse).[18] Homelessness, while not necessarily a violation of the law (unless it involves some form of trespass),[19] is also typically addressed under quality-of-life programs through police interviews with the homeless, many of whom are relocated to shelters or hospitals or are arrested for some other offense. Many claim that reducing the number of quality-of-life offenses in a community can restore a sense of order, reduce the fear of crime, and lessen the number of serious crimes that occur. However, quality-of-life programs have been criticized by those who say that the police should not be taking a law enforcement approach to social and economic problems.[20]

quality-of-life offense
A minor violation of the law (sometimes called a *petty crime*) that demoralizes community residents and businesspeople. Quality-of-life offenses involve acts that create physical disorder (for example, excessive noise and vandalism) or that reflect social decay (for example, panhandling and prostitution).

A similar approach to keeping the peace can be found in the broken windows model of policing.[21] This thesis is based on the notion that physical decay, such as litter and abandoned buildings, can breed disorder in a community and can lead to crime by signaling that laws are not being enforced.[22] Such decay, the theory postulates, pushes law-abiding citizens to withdraw from the streets, which sends a signal that lawbreakers can operate freely.[23] The broken windows thesis suggests that by encouraging the repair of rundown buildings and controlling disorderly behavior in public spaces, police agencies can create an environment in which serious crime cannot easily flourish.[24]

Fidelity, bravery, and integrity.
—FBI motto

While desirable, public order has its own costs. Noted police author Charles R. Swanson says, "The degree to which any society achieves some amount of public order through police action depends in part upon the price that society is willing to pay to obtain it."[25] Swanson goes on to describe the price to be paid in terms of (1) police resources paid for by tax dollars and (2) "a reduction in the number, kinds, and extent of liberties" that are available to members of the public.

Providing Services

Writers for the NIJ observe that "any citizen from any city, suburb, or town across the United States can mobilize police resources by simply picking up the phone and placing a direct call to the police."[26] "Calling the cops" has been described as the cornerstone of policing in a democratic society. About 70% of the millions of daily calls to 9-1-1 systems across the country are directed to the police, although callers can also request emergency medical and fire services.

Calls received by 9-1-1 operators are prioritized and then relayed to patrol officers, specialized field units, or other emergency personnel. In 2001, for example, the Hastings (Minnesota) Police Department handled a total of 12,895 calls for service.[27] A breakdown of those calls shows that there were 1,837 calls related to serious crimes such as arson, assault, auto theft, burglary, larceny, rape, and robbery. The remaining 11,058 calls were nonemergency calls involving lost and found articles, minor motor vehicle accidents, barking dogs, suspicious persons, and parking and traffic violation reports. Numbers like these have led some cities to adopt nonemergency "Citizen Service System" call numbers in addition to 9-1-1. More than a dozen metropolitan areas, including Baltimore, Dallas, Detroit, Las Vegas, New York, and San Jose, now staff 3-1-1 nonemergency systems around the clock. Plans are afoot in some states to adopt the 3-1-1 system statewide.

American Policing Today: From the Federal to the Local Level

The organization of American law enforcement has been called the most complex in the world. Three major legislative and judicial jurisdictions exist in the United States—federal, state, and local—and each has created a variety of police agencies to enforce its laws. Unfortunately, little uniformity is seen among jurisdictions regarding the naming, function, or authority of enforcement agencies. The matter is complicated still more by the rapid growth of private security firms, which operate on a for-profit basis and provide services that have traditionally been regarded as law enforcement activities.

2 List and describe the three major levels of public law enforcement in the United States today.

Federal Agencies

Dozens of federal law enforcement agencies are distributed among 14 U.S. government departments and 28 nondepartmental entities (Table 4–1). In addition to the enforcement agencies listed in the table, many other federal government offices are involved in enforcement through inspection, regulation, and control activities. The Government Accounting Office (GAO) reports that nonmilitary federal agencies employ a total of 139,929 law enforcement officers, which it defines as individuals authorized to perform any of four specific functions: (1) conduct criminal investigations, (2) execute search warrants, (3) make arrests, or (4) carry firearms.[28] The Federal Bureau of Investigation, one of the best-known federal law enforcement agencies, is described in the paragraphs that follow.

Visit the home pages of many federal law enforcement agencies at **Web Extra 4–5**. Learn more about staffing levels of federal criminal justice agencies at **Library Extra 4–2**.

TABLE 4–1
American Policing: Federal Law Enforcement Agencies

Department of Agriculture
U.S. Forest Service

Department of Commerce
Bureau of Export Enforcement
National Marine Fisheries Administration

Department of Defense
Air Force Office of Special Investigations
Army Criminal Investigation Division
Defense Criminal Investigative Service
Naval Investigative Service

Department of Energy
National Nuclear Safety Administration
Office of Mission Operations
Office of Secure Transportation

Department of Health and Human Services
Food and Drug Administration (FDA), Office of Criminal Investigations

Department of Homeland Security (DHS)
Federal Law Enforcement Training Center (FLETC)
Federal Protective Service
Transportation Security Administration
U.S. Coast Guard
U.S. Customs and Border Protection (CBP), including U.S. Border Patrol
U.S. Immigration and Customs Enforcement (ICE)
U.S. Secret Service (SS)

Department of the Interior
Bureau of Indian Affairs
Bureau of Land Management
Fish and Wildlife Service
National Park Service
U.S. Park Police

Department of Justice
Bureau of Alcohol, Tobacco, Firearms and Explosives (ATF)
Bureau of Prisons (BOP)
Drug Enforcement Administration (DEA)
Federal Bureau of Investigation (FBI)
U.S. Marshals Service

Department of Labor
Office of Labor Racketeering

Department of State
Diplomatic Security Service

Department of Transportation
Federal Air Marshals Program

Department of the Treasury
Internal Revenue Service (IRS), Criminal Investigation Division
Treasury Inspector General for Tax Enforcement

Department of Veterans Affairs (VA)
Office of Security and Law Enforcement

U.S. Postal Service
Postal Inspection Service

Other Offices with Enforcement Personnel
Administrative Office of the U.S. Courts
Amtrak Police
Bureau of Engraving and Printing Police
Environmental Protection Agency (EPA), Criminal Investigations Division
Federal Reserve Board
Tennessee Valley Authority (TVA)
U.S. Capitol Police
U.S. Mint
U.S. Supreme Court Police
Washington, D.C., Metropolitan Police Department

Note: Virtually every cabinet-level federal agency has its own Office of Inspector General, which has enforcement authority.

What we need to do better is be predictive. We have to be proactive. We have to develop the capability to anticipate attacks.

—Robert S. Mueller, director of the FBI[1]

Background of the FBI

The FBI may be the most famous law enforcement agency in the country and in the world. The FBI has traditionally been held in high regard by many Americans, who think of it as an example of what a law enforcement organization should be and who believe that FBI agents are exemplary police officers. William Webster, former director of the FBI, reflected this sentiment when he said, "Over the years the American people have come to expect the most professional law enforcement from the FBI. Although we use the most modern forms of management and technology in the fight against crime, our strength is in our people—in the character of the men and women of the FBI. For that reason we seek only those who have demonstrated that they can perform as professional people who can, and will, carry on our tradition of fidelity, bravery, and integrity."[29]

The history of the FBI spans more than 100 years. It began in 1908 as the Bureau of Investigation. It was designed to serve as the investigative arm of the U.S. Department of Justice. The creation of the bureau was motivated, at least in part, by the inability of other

CJ News
FBI Retools Most Wanted List

Those grainy mug shots, once confined to post office lobbies, are coming to a billboard near you.

The FBI is retooling its Ten Most Wanted list into an increasingly multimedia international appeal for help as it tries to keep its signature program relevant in a crowded media landscape.

"We're trying to exploit every opportunity," FBI spokesman Chris Allen says. The strategy is "probably pretty surprising for a government agency."

Among the changes:

- Launching a billboard campaign. Earlier this month, the FBI began featuring top fugitives on billboards in 20 cities.
- Expanding the list's international reach. The FBI is building on its broadcast alliance with the popular *America's Most Wanted* TV show to solicit tips on similar programs in Hungary, Israel, the Netherlands, Great Britain, and Germany.
- Posting video. The FBI has video of the most recent sightings of some fugitives on its Top 10 website.

In the billboard deal with Clear Channel Outdoor Holdings Inc., which is donating the space, the FBI will get access to about 150 electronic billboards, Allen says.

In Los Angeles, images of Most Wanted suspect Emigdio Preciado, Jr., accused in the attempted murders of two sheriff's deputies, are on display throughout the city.

Marine Cpl. Cesar Laurean, a suspect in the murder of pregnant Lance Cpl. Maria Lauterbach, is not on the Top 10 list, but his image appears on some billboards.

As of December [2007], 489 fugitives had appeared on the list since it began in 1950. Of those, 458 have been located, at least 150 with citizen help, the FBI says. Agents hunt for an estimated 12,000 fugitives at a time.

Rex Tomb, a former chief of the FBI's investigative publicity unit, says the list reflects the evolving nature of crime. The bureau added Osama bin Laden after the 1998 U.S. embassy bombings in Africa. "In the 1950s, it was bank robbery," Tomb says. "Now, you see bin Laden up there."

The bureau . . . quietly removed accused cop killer Donald Eugene Webb from the Top 10, marking only the sixth time a fugitive was taken off before capture.

"That's pretty valuable real estate, and you have to make sure . . . there is going to be a benefit," Tomb says. "Sometimes it works. Sometimes it doesn't."

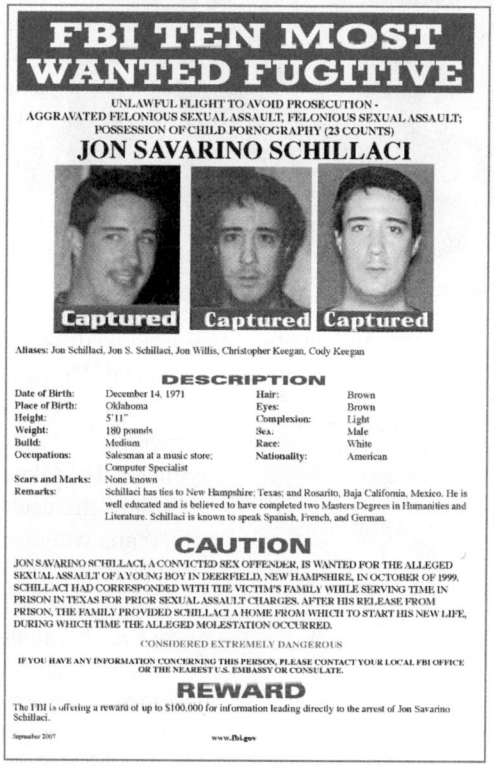
FBI TEN MOST WANTED FUGITIVE

UNLAWFUL FLIGHT TO AVOID PROSECUTION - AGGRAVATED FELONIOUS SEXUAL ASSAULT, FELONIOUS SEXUAL ASSAULT; POSSESSION OF CHILD PORNOGRAPHY (23 COUNTS)

JON SAVARINO SCHILLACI

Captured Captured Captured

Aliases: Jon Schillaci, Jon S. Schillaci, Jon Willis, Christopher Keegan, Cody Keegan

DESCRIPTION

Date of Birth:	December 14, 1971	Hair:	Brown
Place of Birth:	Oklahoma	Eyes:	Brown
Height:	5'11"	Complexion:	Light
Weight:	180 pounds	Sex:	Male
Build:	Medium	Race:	White
Occupations:	Salesman at a music store; Computer Specialist	Nationality:	American
Scars and Marks:	None known		
Remarks:	Schillaci has ties to New Hampshire; Texas; and Rosarito, Baja California, Mexico. He is well educated and is believed to have completed two Masters Degrees in Humanities and Literature. Schillaci is known to speak Spanish, French, and German.		

CAUTION

JON SAVARINO SCHILLACI, A CONVICTED SEX OFFENDER, IS WANTED FOR THE ALLEGED SEXUAL ASSAULT OF A YOUNG BOY IN DEERFIELD, NEW HAMPSHIRE, IN OCTOBER OF 1999. SCHILLACI HAD CORRESPONDED WITH THE VICTIM'S FAMILY WHILE SERVING TIME IN PRISON IN TEXAS FOR PRIOR SEXUAL ASSAULT CHARGES. AFTER HIS RELEASE FROM PRISON, THE FAMILY PROVIDED SCHILLACI A HOME FROM WHICH TO START HIS NEW LIFE, DURING WHICH TIME THE ALLEGED MOLESTATION OCCURRED.

CONSIDERED EXTREMELY DANGEROUS

IF YOU HAVE ANY INFORMATION CONCERNING THIS PERSON, PLEASE CONTACT YOUR LOCAL FBI OFFICE OR THE NEAREST U.S. EMBASSY OR CONSULATE.

REWARD

The FBI is offering a reward of up to $100,000 for information leading directly to the arrest of Jon Savarino Schillaci.

September 2007 www.fbi.gov

▲ An electronic Ten Most Wanted poster. How is the FBI changing the way it uses new types of media and other news outlets to publicize information about fugitives who are on the list?
Federal Bureau of Investigation

See the FBI's ten most wanted fugitives at http://www.fbi.gov/wanted.htm.

Source: Kevin Johnson, "FBI Retools Most Wanted List," *USA Today*, January 16, 2008. Reprinted with permission.

agencies to stem the rising tide of American political and business corruption.[30] Learn about the history of the FBI at **Web Extra 4–6**.

The official purpose of today's FBI is succinctly stated in the agency's mission statement: "The Mission of the FBI is to protect and defend the United States against terrorist and foreign intelligence threats, to uphold and enforce the criminal laws of the United States, and to provide leadership and criminal justice services to federal, state, municipal, and international agencies and partners."[31]

FBI headquarters are located in the J. Edgar Hoover Building on Pennsylvania Avenue in Washington, D.C. Special agents and support personnel who work at the agency's headquarters organize and coordinate FBI activities throughout the country and around the world. Headquarters staffers determine investigative priorities, oversee major cases, and manage the organization's resources, technology, and personnel.

The daily work of the FBI is done by nearly 13,000 special agents assigned to 56 field offices and 400 satellite offices (known as *resident agencies*). A special agent in charge oversees each field office, except for the three largest field offices in Washington, D.C., Los Angeles, and New York City, each of which is headed by an assistant director.

▲ FBI Director Robert S. Mueller III explaining his agency's shift in priorities following the 2001 terrorist attacks on the World Trade Center and the Pentagon. How did the agency's priorities change?
AP Wide World Photos

The FBI also operates legal attaché offices (called *Legats*) in a number of major cities around the world, including London and Paris. Such offices permit the international coordination of enforcement activities and facilitate the flow of law enforcement–related information between the FBI and police agencies in host countries. In 1995, a few years after the end of the cold war, the FBI opened a legal attaché office in Moscow. The Moscow office assists Russian police agencies in the growing battle against organized crime in that country and helps American officials track suspected Russian criminals operating in the United States. Also in 1995, an Eastern European version of the FBI Academy, known as the International Law Enforcement Academy (ILEA), opened in Budapest, Hungary. Its purpose is to train police administrators from all of Eastern Europe in the latest crime-fighting techniques.[32]

The FBI also operates the Combined DNA Index System (CODIS), a computerized forensic database of DNA profiles of offenders convicted of serious crimes (such as rape, other sexual assaults, murder, and certain crimes against children), as well as DNA profiles from unknown offenders.[33] CODIS, now a part of the National DNA Index System (NDIS), was formally authorized by the federal DNA Identification Act of 1994.[34] It is being enhanced daily through the work of federal, state, and local law enforcement agencies that take DNA samples from biological evidence gathered at crime scenes and from offenders themselves. CODIS can rapidly identify a perpetrator when it finds a match between an evidence sample and a stored profile. By 1998, every state had enacted legislation establishing a CODIS database and requiring that DNA from offenders convicted of certain serious crimes be entered into the system. By April 2010, the CODIS database contained more than 8.5 million DNA profiles.[35] Learn more about CODIS at **Web Extra 4–7**.

The FBI Laboratory Division, located in Quantico, Virginia, operates one of the largest and most comprehensive crime laboratories in the world. It provides services related to the scientific solution and prosecution of crimes throughout the country. It is also the only full-service federal forensic laboratory in the United States. Laboratory activities include crime-scene searches, special surveillance photography, latent-fingerprint examinations, forensic examinations of evidence (including DNA testing), court testimony by laboratory personnel, and other scientific and technical services. The FBI offers laboratory services, free of charge, to all law enforcement agencies in the United States. Learn more about the FBI's administrative divisions, including the activities of each, via **Web Extra 4–8**.

The FBI also runs a National Academy Program, which is part of its Training Division. The program offered its first class in 1935 and had 23 students. It was then known as the FBI National Police Training School. In 1940, the school moved from Washington, D.C., to the U.S. Marine Amphibious Base at Quantico, Virginia. In 1972, the facility expanded to 334 acres, and the FBI Academy, as we know it today, officially opened.[36] According to the most recent statistics available, the academy program has produced 37,990 graduates since it began operations. This includes 2,475 graduates from 151 foreign countries and 328 graduates from U.S. territories and possessions. More than 200 sessions have been offered since inception of the training program. Visit the FBI Academy on the Web at **Web Extra 4–9**.

Much of what is wrong with the police is the result of the absurd, fragmented, unworkable nonsystem of more than 17,000 local [police] departments.

—Patrick V. Murphy, former New York City police commissioner

The FBI and Counterterrorism

Soon after the attacks of September 11, 2001, the FBI reshaped its priorities to focus on preventing future terrorist attacks. To combat terrorism, the FBI's Counterterrorism Division collects, analyzes, and shares information and critical intelligence with various federal agencies and departments—including the Central Intelligence Agency (CIA), the National Security Agency (NSA), and the Department of Homeland Security (DHS)—and with law enforcement agencies throughout the country. An essential weapon in the FBI's battle against terrorism is the Joint Terrorism Task Force (JTTF). JTTFs are discussed in more detail in Chapter 6.

In testimony before Congress in 2005, FBI Director Robert S. Mueller III identified three areas of special concern relative to the bureau's ongoing antiterrorism efforts. First, said Mueller, "is the threat from covert operatives who may be inside the U.S. who have the intention to facilitate or conduct an attack."[37] The very nature of trained covert operatives, said the director, is that they are difficult to detect. "I remain very concerned about what we are *not* seeing," said Mueller. Second, Mueller identified a concern "with the growing body of sensitive reporting that continues to show al-Qaeda's clear intention to obtain and ultimately use some form of chemical, biological, radiological, nuclear, or high-energy explosives (CBRNE) material in its attacks against America." Finally, said Mueller, "We remain concerned about the potential for al-Qaeda to . . . exploit radical American converts and other indigenous extremists."

TABLE 4–2
American Policing: State Law Enforcement Agencies

Alcohol law enforcement agencies	Port authorities	State police
Fish and wildlife agencies	State bureaus of investigation	State university police
Highway patrol	State park services	Weigh station operations

State Agencies

Most state police agencies were created in the late nineteenth or early twentieth century to meet specific needs. The Texas Rangers, created in 1835 before Texas attained statehood, functioned as a military organization responsible for patrolling the republic's borders. The apprehension of Mexican cattle rustlers was one of its main concerns.[38] Massachusetts, targeting vice control, was the second state to create a law enforcement agency. Today, a wide diversity of state policing agencies exists. Table 4–2 provides a list of typical state-sponsored law enforcement agencies.

State law enforcement agencies are usually organized after one of two models. In the first, a centralized model, the tasks of major criminal investigations are combined with the patrol of state highways. Centralized state police agencies generally do the following:

- Assist local law enforcement departments in criminal investigations when asked to do so
- Operate a centralized identification bureau
- Maintain a centralized criminal records repository
- Patrol the state's highways
- Provide select training for municipal and county officers

▲ The new LAPD's $437 million headquarters building which opened in 2009. The 500,000-square-foot headquarters building is home to 2,300 LAPD officers and civilian employees. How do the roles of federal, state, and municipal law enforcement agencies differ?
Hans Gutknecht/Los Angeles Daily News/ZUMApress.com/Newscom

The Pennsylvania Constabulary, known today as the Pennsylvania State Police, was the first modern force to combine these duties and has been called the "first modern state police agency."[39] Michigan, New Jersey, New York, Vermont, and Delaware are a few of the states that patterned their state-level enforcement activities after the Pennsylvania model.

The second state model, the decentralized model of police organization, characterizes operations in the southern United States but is found as well in the Midwest and in some western states. The model draws a clear distinction between traffic enforcement on state highways and other state-level law enforcement functions by creating at least two separate agencies. North Carolina, South Carolina, and Georgia are a few of the many states that employ both a highway patrol and a state bureau of investigation. The names of the respective agencies may vary, however, even though their functions are largely the same. In North Carolina, for example, the two major state-level law enforcement agencies are the North Carolina Highway Patrol and the State Bureau of Investigation. Georgia fields a highway patrol and the Georgia Bureau of Investigation, and South Carolina operates a highway patrol and the South Carolina Law Enforcement Division.

States that use the decentralized model usually have a number of other adjunct state-level law enforcement agencies. North Carolina, for example, has created a State Wildlife Commission with enforcement powers, a Board of Alcohol Beverage Control with additional agents, and a separate Enforcement and Theft Bureau for enforcement of certain motor vehicle and theft laws. Learn more about state-level law enforcement agencies by visiting **Web Extra 4–10**.

Local Agencies

Local police agencies, including city and county agencies, represent a third level of law enforcement activity in the United States. The term *local police* encompasses a wide variety of agencies. Municipal departments, rural sheriff's departments, and specialized groups like campus police and transit police can all be grouped under the "local" rubric. Large municipal departments are highly visible because of their vast size, huge budgets, and innovative programs. The nation's largest law enforcement agency, the New York City Police Department (NYPD), for example, has about 45,000 full-time employees, including about 37,800 full-time sworn officers.[40] Learn more about the NYPD via "Inside the Department" podcasts available at **Web Extra 4–11**.

Far greater in number, however, are small-town and county sheriff's departments. There are approximately 12,760 municipal police departments and 3,100 sheriff's departments in the United States.[41] Every incorporated municipality in the country has the authority to create its own police force. Some very small communities hire only one officer, who fills the roles of chief, investigator, and night watch—as well as everything in between. The majority of local agencies employ fewer than ten full-time officers, and about three in eight agencies (more than 7,000 in all) employ fewer than five full-time officers. These smaller agencies include 2,245 (or 12%) with just one full-time officer and 1,164 (or 6%) with only part-time officers.[42] A few communities contract with private security firms for police services, and still others have no active police force at all, depending instead on local sheriff's departments to deal with law violators.

City police chiefs are typically appointed by the mayor or selected by the city council. Their departments' jurisdictions are limited by convention to the geographic boundaries of their communities. **Sheriffs**, on the other hand, are elected public officials whose agencies are responsible for law enforcement throughout the counties in which they function. Sheriff's deputies mostly patrol the unincorporated areas of the county, or those that lie between municipalities. They do, however, have jurisdiction throughout the county, and in some areas they routinely work alongside municipal police to enforce laws within towns and cities.

sheriff
The elected chief officer of a county law enforcement agency. The sheriff is usually responsible for law enforcement in unincorporated areas and for the operation of the county jail.

Sheriff's departments are generally responsible for serving court papers, including civil summonses, and for maintaining security within state courtrooms. Sheriffs also run county jails and are responsible for more detainees awaiting trial than any other type of law enforcement department in the country. For example, the Los Angeles County Jail System, operated by the Custody Operations Division of the L.A. County Sheriff's Department (LASD), is the largest in the world.[43] In 2003, with eight separate facilities, the Custody Operations Division of the LASD had an average daily population of 18,423 inmates—considerably larger than the number of inmates held in many state prison systems.[44] More than 2,200 uniformed officers and 1,265 civilian employees work in the Custody Division of the LASD. That division alone operates with a yearly budget in excess of $200 million.[45]

Sheriff's departments remain strong across most of the country, although in parts of New England, deputies mostly function as court agents with limited law enforcement duties. One report found that most sheriff's departments are small, with more than half of them employing fewer than 25 sworn officers.[46] Only 12 departments employ more than 1,000 officers. Even so, southern and western sheriffs are still considered the chief law enforcement officers in their counties.

A list of conventional police agencies found at the local level is shown in Table 4–3. For information on selected local law enforcement agencies, view **Web Extra 4–12**. Visit **Library Extras 4–3** and **4–4** to learn more about staffing levels at local and state police agencies.

Fusion Centers

In March 2008, more than 900 federal, state, and local law enforcement and homeland security officials attended the National Fusion Center Conference in Washington, D.C.[47] **Fusion centers**, a new concept in policing, pool and analyze information from law enforcement

fusion center
A multiagency law enforcement facility designed to enhance cooperative efforts through a coordinated process for collecting, sharing, and analyzing information in order to develop actionable intelligence.

TABLE 4–3
American Policing: Local Law Enforcement Agencies

Campus police	Housing authority agencies	Sheriff's departments
City/county agencies	Marine patrol agencies	Transit police
Constables	Municipal police departments	Tribal police
Coroners or medical examiners		

agencies at all levels, looking for meaningful patterns and actionable intelligence. More than 70 fusion centers currently operate in 37 states, and they have received $380 million in federal funding over the last five years.[48] These centers are largely an outgrowth of one of the 9/11 Commission's criticisms that law enforcement agencies do not communicate with one another as they should.

Fusion centers vary greatly in size and in the equipment and personnel available to them. Some are small, consisting of little more than limited conference facilities, and have only a few participants. Others are large, high-technology offices that make use of the latest information and computer technologies and that house representatives from many different organizations. Some fusion centers are physically located within the offices of other agencies. The Kentucky Fusion Center, for example, is housed within the state's Department of Transportation building in the state's capitol. Others operate out of stand-alone facilities that are physically separated from parent agencies.

Similarly, although information sharing is their central purpose, the activities of fusion centers are not uniform. Some centers perform investigations, some make arrests, and some exist only to share information. A number of fusion centers, like the National Counterterrorism Center and the National Gang Intelligence Center, focus on clearly defined issues. Most of today's fusion centers do more than target terrorists, however. They work to collect information on a wide variety of offenders, gangs, immigrant smuggling operations, and other threats. Michael Mines, the FBI's deputy assistant director of intelligence, recognizes that actionable intelligence can come from seemingly unrelated areas. He notes that the nation's network of fusion centers is intended to "maximize the ability to detect, prevent, investigate, and respond to criminal and terrorist activity."[49]

Many fusion centers are still developing, and a number of problems remain. Obtaining security clearances for employees of local law enforcement agencies, for example, has sometimes been difficult or time-consuming. Even representatives of federal agencies like the DHS and the FBI sometimes refuse to accept one another's clearances. Nonetheless, a recent hearing before a House intelligence subcommittee shows that federal lawmakers are hopeful about the success of fusion centers and are willing to find the federal dollars needed to support them. As Representative Jane Harman, chairwoman of the Subcommittee on Intelligence, Information Sharing and Terrorism Risk Assessment, said recently, "Everyone recognizes that fusion centers hold tremendous promise."[50]

▲ Texas Governor Rick Perry speaking to a group of Texas Rangers in Austin, Texas, in 2009. The Texas Rangers have long been held in high regard among state police agencies. How do police agencies in the United States relate to one another?
AP Photo/Harry Cabluck

police management
The administrative activities of controlling, directing, and coordinating police personnel, resources, and activities in the service of crime prevention, the apprehension of criminals, the recovery of stolen property, and the performance of a variety of regulatory and helping services.

Police Administration

Police management entails administrative activities that control, direct, and coordinate police personnel, resources, and activities in the service of crime prevention, the apprehension of criminals, the recovery of stolen property, and the performance of a variety of regulatory and helping services.[51] Police managers include sworn law enforcement personnel with administrative authority, from the rank of sergeant to captain, chief, or sheriff, and civilian personnel, such as police commissioners, attorneys general, state secretaries of crime control, and public-safety directors.

3 Discuss the various components of police administration, including management, chain of command, organization, and department structure.

Police Organization and Structure

Almost all American law enforcement organizations are formally structured among divisions and along lines of authority. Roles within police agencies generally fall into one of two categories: line and staff. **Line operations** are field or supervisory activities directly related to daily police work; **staff operations** include support roles such as administration. In organizations that have line operations only, authority flows from the top down in a clear, unbroken line,[52] and no supporting elements (media relations, training, fiscal management divisions, and so on) exist. All line operations are directly involved in providing field services. Because almost all police agencies need support, only the smallest departments have only line operations.

Most police organizations include both line and staff operations. In such organizations, line managers are largely unencumbered with staff operations, such as budgets, training, scientific analysis of evidence, legal advice, shift assignments, and personnel management. Support personnel handle these activities, freeing line personnel to focus on the day-to-day requirements of providing field services.

line operations
In police organizations, the field activities or supervisory activities directly related to day-to-day police work.

staff operations
In police organizations, activities (such as administration and training) that provide support for line operations.

CJ News
Fusion Centers

In Arizona, after determining that the subjects of an international terrorism case were involved in local criminal activity, the FBI referred the case to local law enforcement. In New Mexico, several individuals linked to FBI investigations, including an MS-13 gang member, were identified. In Tennessee, the FBI and its partners developed a formal process for collecting, sharing, and analyzing suspicious activity reports, looking for trends and patterns.

These cooperative efforts—and many more like them—have been made possible through the work of intelligence fusion centers around the country. These centers, usually set up by states or major urban areas and run by state or local authorities, are often supported by federal law enforcement, including the FBI.

Fusion center personnel "fuse" intelligence from participating agencies to create a more comprehensive threat picture, locally and nationally. They don't just collect information. They integrate new data into existing information, evaluate it to determine its worth, analyze it for links and trends, and disseminate their findings to the agency in the best position to do something about it.

In March 2009, nearly 2,000 local, state, tribal, and federal representatives working in fusion centers across the country gathered in Kansas City, Missouri, to continue the process of standardizing fusion center operations. Their goal was to create a network of centers presenting a unified front against terrorism and other national security and criminal threats that put Americans at risk.

Speaking at the Kansas City conference, FBI Chief Intelligence Officer Don Van Duyn said that although the information process could be made "more seamless," the FBI is committed to expanding its "interconnectedness" to help combat threats from terrorist and criminal networks. He also said that during the past year the FBI has rolled out—to all of its 56 field offices—standardized intelligence operations structures, roles, and procedures in an effort to enhance its collaboration with its partners.

Although a few fusion centers were already in existence before 9/11, they really began to crop up after the attacks when local and federal officials recognized the need to quickly coordinate the sharing of information related to terrorism. Their number has been growing ever since. Today, there are some 50 state and 20 regional centers around the country. And some have expanded their focus to include public-safety matters and major criminal threats.

The FBI currently has 114 employees working in 38 fusion centers. About 36% are agents, 61% are intelligence analysts, and the rest are in positions such as language and financial analysts. Fourteen of these centers share space with an FBI Field Intelligence Group or Joint Terrorism Task Force.

▲ Inside the Miami-Dade Police Department's Fusion Center, which serves much of South Florida. The center's combined technologies enhance the power of instant collaboration and information sharing among analysts and investigators from various law enforcement agencies. Why did fusion centers develop?
Reprinted with permission from Microsoft Corporation

Elaine Cummins, the FBI's Chief Information Sharing Officer, says, "Participating in a national network of fusion centers definitely helps us share timely, relevant, and actionable intelligence with our partners—an increasingly important component to our unique national security and law enforcement mission."

Through fusion centers, state and local law enforcement agencies gain access to certain federal databases. They also get the benefit of big-picture terrorism and crime perspectives from their federal partners, along with grant funding, technical assistance, and training. Federal agencies like the FBI gain intelligence from the local level that may fuel terrorism or national security investigations elsewhere in the country or even overseas.

Source: Adapted from FBI, "Fusion Centers: Unifying Intelligence to Protect Americans," March 12, 2009, http://www.fbi.gov/page2/march04/fusion_031209.html (accessed September 3, 2010).

Fusion Centers versus Joint Terrorist Task Forces (JTTFs)

Fusion Centers	Joint Terrorism Task Forces
Run by state and local authorities	Sponsored by the FBI
Are state and locally focused	Are regionally and nationally focused
Deal with terrorism, criminal, and public-safety matters	Deal exclusively with terrorism matters
Produce actionable intelligence for dissemination to appropriate law enforcement agencies but do not generally conduct investigations	Conduct investigations

In a line and staff agency, divisions are likely to exist within both line operations and staff operations. For example, field services, a line operation, may be broken down into enforcement and investigation. Administrative services, a staff operation, may be divided into human resources management, training and education, materials supply, financial management, and facilities management. The line and staff structure easily accommodates functional areas of responsibility within line and staff divisions. The organizational chart detailing the line and staff structure of the Los Angeles County Sheriff's Department—the largest sheriff's department in the world[53]—is shown in Figure 4–1.

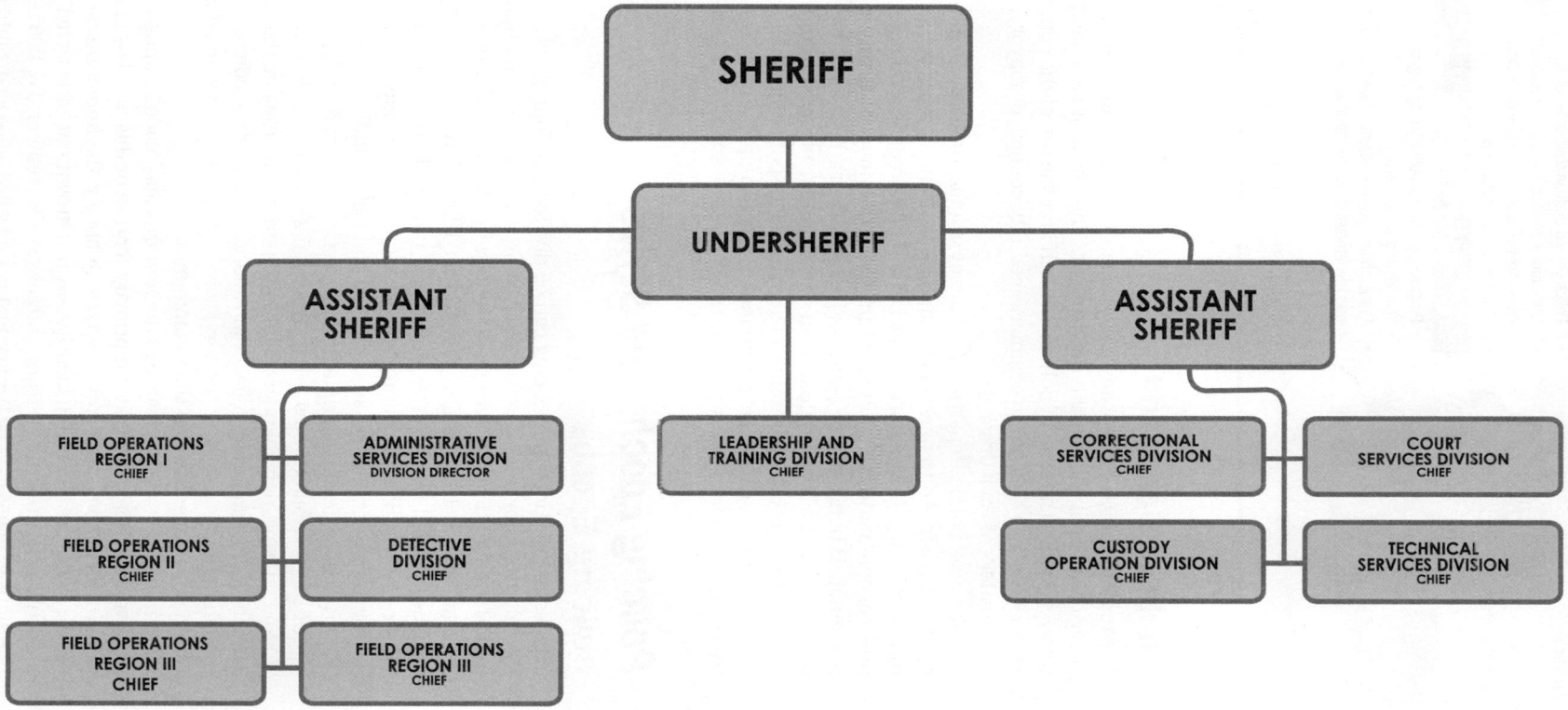

FIGURE 4–1
Organizational Chart of the Los Angeles County Sheriff's Department
Source: Courtesy of Los Angeles County Sheriff's Department.

FIGURE 4–2
Historical Eras in American Policing

POLITICAL ERA

- Close ties between the police and political officials
- Police were organized in paramilitary style, focused on serving the politically powerful
- Politicians appointed/hired the police

1840s–1930

- Came about because of a need for social order and security in a dynamic and rapidly changing society

REFORM ERA

- Police gained pride in their profession
- Law enforcement focused on "traditional" crime-fighting and the capture of criminals
- Crackdown on organized crime

1930–1970s

- Progressive policing policy led by August Vollmer and O. W. Wilson
- Came about because citizens called for reform and the removal of politics from policing

Chain of Command

chain of command
The unbroken line of authority that extends through all levels of an organization, from the highest to the lowest.

The organizational chart of any police agency shows a hierarchical **chain of command**, or the order of authority within the department. The chain of command clarifies who reports to whom. Usually, the chief of police or sheriff is at the top of the command chain (although his or her boss may be a police commissioner, city council, or mayor), followed by the subordinate leaders of each division.

Because police departments employ a quasi-military chain-of-command structure, the titles assigned to personnel (captain, lieutenant, sergeant) are similar to those used by the military. It is important for individual personnel to know who is in charge; hence unity of command is an important principle that must be firmly established within the department. When unity of command exists, every individual has only one supervisor to whom he or she answers and from whom, under normal circumstances, he or she takes orders. **Span of control** refers to the number of police personnel or the number of units supervised by a particular commander. For example, one sergeant may be in charge of five or six officers; they represent the sergeant's span of control.

span of control
The number of police personnel or the number of units supervised by a particular officer.

Policing Epochs and Styles

Policing Epochs

The history of American policing can be divided into four epochs,[54] each distinguishable by the relative dominance of a particular approach to police operations (Figure 4–2). The first period, the political era, was characterized by close ties between police and public officials. It began in the 1840s and ended around 1930. Throughout the period, American police agencies tended to serve the interests of powerful politicians and their cronies, providing public-order and order-maintenance services almost as an afterthought. The second period, the reform era, began around 1930 and lasted until the 1970s. It was characterized by pride in professional crime fighting. Police departments during this period focused most of their resources on solving "traditional" crimes, such as murder, rape, and burglary, and on capturing offenders. The third period, and the one that continues to characterize much of contemporary policing in America today, is the community policing era. This approach to policing stresses the service role of police officers and envisions a partnership between police agencies and their communities.

4 Identify the various historical stages of development in American policing, and describe the characteristics of each stage.

A fourth period, which we call the *new era*, has made its appearance only recently and is still evolving. Some say that the primary feature of this new law enforcement era is policing to secure the homeland, and they have dubbed it the *homeland security era*.[55] From their perspective, the homeland security era has grown out of national concerns with terrorism prevention born of the terrorist attacks of September 11, 2001. As police scholar Gene Stephens explains it, "The twenty-first century has put policing into a whole new milieu—one in which the causes of crime and disorder often lie outside the immediate community, demanding new and innovative approaches."[56] A decline in street crime, says Stephens, has

Thematic Question What happens when police administrators try to combine an order-maintenance orientation with a service mandate? What are the difficulties? How can differences be resolved?

COMMUNITY ERA

- Police departments work to identify and serve the needs of their communities
- Envisions a partnership between the police and the community

1970s–Today

- Police focus on quality-of-life offenses
- Broken windows model of policing
- Came about because of a realization that effective community partnerships can help prevent and solve crimes

THE NEW ERA

- Policing to secure the homeland; emphasis on terrorism prevention and intelligence-led policing
- Builds on partnership with the community to gather intelligence

2001–Today

- Creation of counterterrorism divisions and offices within police departments and the development of actionable intelligence
- Came about because of the terrorist attacks of September 11, 2001, and ongoing threats to the safety and security of Americans

Photo sources (from left): Image Asset Management Ltd./SuperStock, Inc.; SuperStock, Inc.; UpperCut Images/Superstock Royalty Free; and P-59 Photos/Alamy Images

been replaced by concern with new and more insidious types of offending, including terrorism and Internet-assisted crimes. These new kinds of crimes, while they threaten the integrity of local communities, often involve offenders thousands of miles away.

Others, however, see the new era as underpinned by an emphasis on intelligence-led policing (ILP), and they refer to it as the *ILP era*. (ILP is discussed in detail in Chapter 6.) Michael Downing, commander of the Counterterrorism/Criminal Intelligence Bureau of the Los Angeles Police Department, says that ILP represents the next evolutionary stage in how police and sheriff's officers should approach their work. "The necessity to successfully shift into a [new] era, the intelligence-led policing era, with seamless precision has never been more important considering the great threat we face as a nation," says Downing.[57] The good news, some say, "is that ILP is not only an important strategic tool to thwart al-Qaeda and other groups but also a practical one geared toward crime control and quality of life issues."[58] The new era, whatever we choose to call it, is still emerging, but it clearly involves efforts to deal with threats to the homeland and to inform those efforts with situational awareness and shared intelligence.

> Crime is a community problem and stands today as one of the most serious challenges of our generation. Our citizens must . . . recognize their responsibilities in its suppression.
>
> —O. W. Wilson (1900–1972)

The influence of the first three historical phases survives today in what noted social commentator and Presidential Medal of Freedom recipient James Q. Wilson[59] calls "policing styles."[60] A style of policing describes how a particular agency sees its purpose and chooses the methods it uses to fulfill that purpose. Wilson's three policing styles—which he does not link to any particular historical era—are (1) the watchman (which is characteristic of the political era), (2) the legalistic (which is akin to the professional crime fighting of the reform era), and (3) the service (which is common today). These three styles characterize nearly all municipal law enforcement agencies now operating in the United States, although some departments are a mixture of two or more styles.

Lecture Note Describe the watchman style of policing as one in which officers are concerned primarily with maintaining order in the communities they police. Ask students what the watchman style would mean in their home communities.

The Watchman Style of Policing

Police departments marked by the **watchman style** of policing are primarily concerned with achieving a goal that Wilson called "order maintenance." They see their job as controlling illegal and disruptive behaviors. The watchman style makes considerable use of discretion compared to the legalistic style. Order in watchman-style communities may be arrived at by using informal police intervention, including persuasion and threats, or even by "roughing up" a few disruptive people from time to time. Some authors have condemned this style of policing, suggesting that it is unfairly found in lower-class or lower-middle-class communities, especially where interpersonal relations include a fair amount of violence or physical abuse.

watchman style
A style of policing marked by a concern for order maintenance. Watchman policing is characteristic of lower-class communities where informal police intervention into the lives of residents is employed in the service of keeping the peace.

The watchman style was typified by the Los Angeles police officers who took part in the infamous beating of Rodney King in 1992. After the ensuing riots, the Independent Commission on the Los Angeles Police Department (the Christopher Commission) determined that the Los Angeles police "placed greater emphasis on crime control over crime prevention, a policy that distanced cops from the people they serve."[61]

Lecture Note Describe the legalistic style of policing as one in which officers adhere to the letter of the law in making enforcement decisions. Ask students what the legalistic style would mean in their home communities.

Freedom or Safety? You Decide.
Liberty Is a Double-Edged Sword

This chapter builds on the following theme: For police action to be "just," it must recognize the rights of individuals while holding them accountable to the social obligations defined by law. It is important to realize that many democratically inspired legal restraints on the police stem from the Bill of Rights, which comprises the first ten amendments to the U.S. Constitution. Such restraints help ensure individual freedoms in our society and prevent the development of a "police state" in America.

In police work and elsewhere, the principles of individual liberty and social justice are cornerstones on which the American way of life rests. Ideally, the work of police agencies, as well as the American system of criminal justice, is to ensure justice while guarding liberty. The liberty-justice issue is the dual thread that holds together the tapestry of the justice system, from the simplest daily activities of police officers on the beat to the often complex and lengthy renderings of the U.S. Supreme Court.

For the criminal justice system as a whole, the question becomes this: How can individual liberties be maintained in the face of the need for official action, including arrest, interrogation, incarceration, and the like? The answer is far from simple, but it begins with the recognition that liberty is a double-edged sword, entailing obligations as well as rights.

YOU DECIDE

What does it mean to say "For police action to be 'just,' it must recognize the rights of individuals while holding them accountable to the social obligations defined by law"? How can police agencies accomplish this? What can individual officers do to help their agencies in this regard?

The Legalistic Style of Policing

legalistic style
A style of policing marked by a strict concern with enforcing the precise letter of the law. Legalistic departments may take a hands-off approach to disruptive or problematic behavior that does not violate the criminal law.

Departments operating under the **legalistic style** of policing enforce the letter of the law. For example, an officer who tickets a person going 71 mph in a 70-mph zone is likely a member of a department that adheres to the legalistic style of policing. Conversely, legalistic departments routinely avoid community disputes arising from violations of social norms that do not break the law. Police expert Gary Sykes calls this enforcement style "laissez-faire policing" in recognition of its hands-off approach to behaviors that are simply bothersome or inconsiderate of community principles.[62]

The Service Style of Policing

service style
A style of policing marked by a concern with helping rather than strict enforcement. Service-oriented police agencies are more likely to refer citizens to community resources, such as drug-treatment programs, than are other types of agencies.

Lecture Note Describe the service style of policing as one in which officers strive to meet the needs of the citizens they serve. Ask students what the service style would mean in their home communities.

Thematic Question Ask the class to describe the police department that serves your school's community or—if yours is an online-learning class—the department in each student's home community. Is that department characterized by the watchman, legalistic, or service style of policing? Explore the basis for this decision.

Thematic Question Invite the local chief of police to speak to the class. Have students prepare questions to ask that will allow the class to discuss later the style of policing that is most characteristic of the local police department. Ask the chief how policing styles have changed, if at all, in recent years.

In police departments using the **service style**, which strives to meet the needs of the community and serve its members, the police see themselves more as helpers than as soldiers in a "war on crime," and they work with social services and other agencies to provide counseling for minor offenders and to assist community groups in preventing crimes and solving problems. Prosecutors may support the service style of policing by agreeing not to prosecute law violators who seek psychiatric help or who voluntarily participate in programs like Alcoholics Anonymous, family counseling, or drug treatment. The service style is supported in part by citizens who seek to avoid the embarrassment that might result from a public airing of personal problems, thereby reducing the number of criminal complaints filed, especially in minor disputes. While the service style of policing may seem more appropriate to wealthy communities or small towns, it can also exist in cities whose police departments actively seek citizen involvement in identifying issues that the police can help address.

Police-Community Relations

The 1960s were fraught with riots, unrest, and student activism as the war in Vietnam, civil rights concerns, and other social movements produced large demonstrations and marches. The police, generally inexperienced in crowd control, were all too often embroiled in tumultuous encounters—even pitched battles—with citizen groups that viewed the police as agents of "the establishment." To manage these new challenges, the legalistic style of policing, so common in America until then, began to yield to the newer service-oriented style of policing.

5 Describe community policing, and explain how it differs from traditional forms of policing.

As social disorganization increased, police departments across the nation, seeking to understand and better cope with the problems they faced, created **police-community relations (PCR)** programs. PCR programs represented a movement away from an exclusive police emphasis on the apprehension of law violators and meant increasing the level of positive police-citizen interaction. At the height of the PCR movement, city police departments across the country opened storefront centers where citizens could air complaints and interact easily with police representatives. As police scholar Egon Bittner recognized in 1976, PCR programs need to reach to "the grassroots of discontent," where citizen dissatisfaction with the police exists,[63] if they are to be truly effective.

police-community relations (PCR)
An area of police activity that recognizes the need for the community and the police to work together effectively and is based on the notion that the police derive their legitimacy from the community they serve. Many police agencies began to explore PCR in the 1960s and 1970s.

In many contemporary PCR programs, public-relations officers are appointed to provide an array of services, such as Neighborhood Watch programs, drug-awareness workshops, identification projects (using police equipment and expertise to mark valuables for identification in the event of theft), and victims' assistance programs. Modern PCR programs, however, often fail to achieve their goal of increased community satisfaction with police services because they focus on servicing groups already well satisfied with the police. PCR initiatives that do reach disaffected community groups are difficult to manage and may even alienate participating officers from the communities they are assigned to serve. Thus, as Bittner noted, "while the first approach fails because it leaves out those groups to which the program is primarily directed, the second fails because it leaves out the police department."

Every society gets the kind of criminal it deserves. What is equally true is that every community gets the kind of law enforcement it insists on.

—Robert Kennedy, former U.S. attorney general[ii]

Team Policing

During the 1960s and 1970s, a number of communities experimented with the concept of **team policing**, which rapidly became an extension of the PCR movement. With team policing, officers were assigned semipermanently to particular neighborhoods, where they were expected to become familiar with the inhabitants and with their problems and concerns. Patrol officers were given considerable authority in processing complaints, from receipt through resolution. Crimes were investigated and solved at the local level, with specialists called in only if the resources needed to continue an investigation were not available locally. Some authors called team policing a "technique to deliver total police services to a neighborhood."[64] Others, however, dismissed it as "little more than an attempt to return to the style of policing that was prevalent in the United States over a century ago."[65]

team policing
The reorganization of conventional patrol strategies into "an integrated and versatile police team assigned to a fixed district."[iii]

Community Policing

Over the past quarter century, the role of the police in police-community relations has changed considerably. Originally, the PCR model was based on the fact that many police administrators saw police officers as enforcers of the law who were isolated from, and often in opposition to, the communities they policed. As a result, PCR programs were often a shallowly disguised effort to overcome public suspicion and community hostility.

Today, increasing numbers of law enforcement administrators embrace the role of service provider. Modern departments frequently help citizens solve a vast array of personal problems, many of which involve no law-breaking activity. For example, officers regularly aid sick or distraught people, organize community crime-prevention efforts, resolve minor domestic disputes, regulate traffic, and educate children and teens about drug abuse. Because service calls far exceed calls directly related to law violations, most officers more often make referrals for interpersonal problems to agencies such as Alcoholics Anonymous, domestic-violence centers, and drug-rehabilitation programs rather than make arrests.

▲ Los Angeles bike patrol officers conferring with a supervisor. The community policing concept requires that officers become an integral part of the communities they serve. How can community policing help to both prevent and solve crimes?
Michael Newman/PhotoEdit Inc.

In contemporary America, some say, police departments function a lot like business corporations. According to Harvard University's Executive Session on Policing, three generic kinds of "corporate strategies" guide American policing: (1) strategic policing, (2) problem-solving policing, and (3) community policing.[66]

strategic policing
A type of policing that retains the traditional police goal of professional crime fighting but enlarges the enforcement target to include nontraditional kinds of criminals, such as serial offenders, gangs and criminal associations, drug-distribution networks, and sophisticated white-collar and computer criminals. Strategic policing generally makes use of innovative enforcement techniques, including intelligence operations, undercover stings, electronic surveillance, and sophisticated forensic methods.

problem-solving policing
A type of policing that assumes that many crimes are caused by existing social conditions within the community and that crimes can be controlled by uncovering and effectively addressing underlying social problems. Problem-solving policing makes use of community resources, such as counseling centers, welfare programs, and job-training facilities. It also attempts to involve citizens in crime prevention through education, negotiation, and conflict management.

community policing
"A philosophy that promotes organizational strategies, which support the systematic use of partnerships and problem-solving techniques, to proactively address the immediate conditions that give rise to public safety issues such as crime, social disorder, and fear of crime."[iv]

Strategic policing, something of a holdover from the reform era, "emphasizes an increased capacity to deal with crimes that are not well controlled by traditional methods."[67] Strategic policing retains the traditional police goal of professional crime fighting but enlarges the enforcement target to include nontraditional kinds of criminals, such as serial offenders, gangs and criminal associations, drug-distribution networks, and sophisticated white-collar and computer criminals. To meet its goals, strategic policing generally makes use of innovative enforcement techniques, including intelligence operations, undercover sting operations, electronic surveillance, and sophisticated forensic methods.

The other two strategies give greater recognition to Wilson's service style. **Problem-solving policing** (or problem-oriented policing) takes the view that many crimes are caused by existing social conditions in the communities. To control crime, problem-oriented police managers attempt to uncover and effectively address these underlying social problems. Problem-solving policing makes thorough use of community resources, such as counseling centers, welfare programs, and job-training facilities. It also attempts to involve citizens in crime prevention through education, negotiation, and conflict management. For example, police may ask residents of poorly maintained housing areas to clean up litter, install better lighting, and provide security devices for their houses and apartments in the belief that clean, well-lighted, secure areas are a deterrent to criminal activity.

The third and newest strategy, **community policing** (sometimes called community-oriented policing), goes a step beyond the other two. It has been described as a partnership between the police and the community, so that they can work together on solving problems of crime and disorder.[68] A more formal definition, offered by the Office of Community Oriented Policing Services (COPS) office says that community policing "is a philosophy that promotes organizational strategies, which support the systematic use of partnerships and problem-solving techniques, to proactively address the immediate conditions that give rise to public safety issues such as crime, social disorder, and fear of crime."[69]

The community policing concept evolved from the early works of police researchers George Kelling and Robert Trojanowicz. Their studies of foot-patrol programs in Newark, New Jersey,[70] and Flint, Michigan,[71] showed that "police could develop more positive attitudes toward community members and could promote positive attitudes toward police if they spent time on foot in their neighborhoods."[72] Trojanowicz's *Community Policing*, published in 1990,[73] may be the definitive work on this topic.

Community policing seeks to actively involve the community in the task of crime control by creating an effective working partnership between the community and the police.[74] Under the community policing ideal, community members and the police are expected to share responsibility for establishing and maintaining peaceful neighborhoods.[75] As a result, community policing permits members of the community to participate more fully than ever before in defining the police role. Police expert Jerome H. Skolnick says community policing is "grounded on the notion that, together, police and public are more effective and more humane coproducers of safety and public order than are the police alone."[76] According to Skolnick, community policing involves at least one of four elements: (1) community-based crime prevention, (2) reorientation of patrol activities to emphasize the importance of nonemergency services, (3) increased police accountability to the public, and (4) decentralization of command, including a greater use of civilians at all levels of police decision making.[77] As one writer explains it, "Community policing seeks to integrate what was traditionally seen as the different law enforcement, order maintenance and social service roles of the police. Central to the integration of these roles is a working partnership with the community in determining what neighborhood problems are to be addressed, and how."[78]

A successful community policing program . . . requires officers to be well versed in cultural diversity and competent to perform tasks needed to accomplish their duties.

—Samuel D. Pratcher, chief of police, Wilmington, Delaware

Thematic Question What are the differences between the original concept of police-community relations and the contemporary notion of community policing? Which of these ideas do you think would appeal more to individual-rights advocates? To public-order advocates? Why?

Community policing is a two-way street. It requires not only police awareness of community needs but also both involvement and crime-fighting action on the part of citizens themselves. As Detective Tracie Harrison of the Denver Police Department explains, "When the neighborhood takes stock in their community and they're serious they don't want crime, then you start to see crime go down. . . . They're basically fed up and know the police can't do it alone."[79]

Police departments throughout the country continue to join the community policing bandwagon. A recent report by the Bureau of Justice Statistics (BJS) showed that state and local law enforcement agencies across the United States had nearly 113,000 full-time sworn personnel regularly engaged in community policing activities.[80] BJS noted that only about 21,000 officers would have been so categorized in 1997. At the time of the report, 64% of local police departments serving 86% of all residents had full-time officers engaged in some form of community policing activity, compared to 34% of departments serving 62% of all residents in 1997.

The Chicago Police Department launched its comprehensive community policing program, called Chicago's Alternative Policing Strategy (CAPS), in 1993. The development of a strategic plan for "reinventing the Chicago Police Department," from which CAPS evolved, included significant contributions by Mayor Richard M. Daley, who noted that community policing "means doing more than responding to calls for service and solving crimes. It means transforming the Department to support a new, proactive approach to preventing crimes before they occur. It means forging new partnerships among residents, business owners, community leaders, the police, and City services to solve long-range community problems."[81] Read the mayor's original report, written in conjunction with the Chicago Police Department, at **Library Extra 4–5**. Today, CAPS functions on a department-wide basis throughout the city. Learn more about CAPS at **Web Extra 4–13**. A review of Chicago's experience with community policing is available at **Library Extra 4–6**.

Although community policing efforts began in metropolitan areas, the community engagement and problem-solving spirit of these programs has spread to rural regions. Sheriff's departments operating community policing programs sometimes refer to them as *neighborhood-oriented policing* in recognition of the decentralized nature of rural communities. A Bureau of Justice Assistance (BJA) report on neighborhood-oriented policing notes that "the stereotypical view is that police officers in rural areas naturally work more closely with the public than do officers in metropolitan areas."[82] This view, warns the BJA, may not be entirely accurate, and rural departments would do well "to recognize that considerable diversity exists among rural communities and rural law enforcement agencies." As in metropolitan areas, effective community policing requires the involvement of all members of the community in identifying and solving problems.

Lecture Note Describe community policing as an effort to involve the community in solving the problems faced by the police, and vice versa. Explain community policing as an ideational approach to policing that envisions the police and members of the community as sharing responsibility for the solution of problems within the community.

The emphasis on community policing continues to grow. Title I of the Violent Crime Control and Law Enforcement Act of 1994, known as the Public Safety Partnership and Community Policing Act of 1994, highlighted community policing's role in combating crime and funded (among other things) "increas[ing] the number of law enforcement officers involved in activities that are focused on interaction with members of the community on proactive crime control and prevention." The avowed purposes of the Community Policing Act were to (1) substantially increase the number of law enforcement officers interacting directly with the public (through a program known as Cops on the Beat); (2) provide additional and more effective training to law enforcement officers to enhance their problem solving, service, and other skills needed in interacting with community members; (3) encourage development and implementation of innovative programs to permit community members to assist local law enforcement agencies in the prevention of crime; and (4) encourage development of new technologies to assist local law enforcement agencies in reorienting their emphasis from reacting to crime to preventing crime.

Thematic Question How might community policing help combat police corruption as well as crime?

In response to the 1994 law, the U.S. Department of Justice created the Office of Community Oriented Policing Services (COPS). The COPS Office administered the funds necessary to add 100,000 community policing officers to our nation's streets—the number originally targeted by law. In 1999, the U.S. Department of Justice and COPS reached an important milestone by funding the last of the 100,000 officers ahead of schedule and under budget. Although the Community Policing Act originally provided COPS funding only through 2000, Congress has continued to fund COPS, making another $500 million available for the hiring of an additional 50,000 officers.[83] In 2002, the COPS Office adopted the theme "Homeland Security through Community Policing," which emphasizes the local police officer's crucial role in gathering information on terrorist suspects—a topic that is discussed later in this chapter. The federal COPS Office can be found at **Web Extra 4–14**.

About the same time that the Violent Crime Control and Law Enforcement Act was passed, the Community Policing Consortium, based in Washington, D.C., began operations. Administered and funded by the BJA, the consortium provides a forum for training and information exchange in the area of community policing. Members of the consortium include the International Association of Chiefs of Police, the National Sheriff's Association, the Police Executive Research Forum, the Police Foundation, and the National Organization of Black Law Enforcement Executives. Visit the Community Policing Consortium via **Web Extra 4–15**.

Community Policing and Antiterrorism

Noted police scholar David L. Carter says that "a common concern expressed by police executives is that the shift toward increased counterterrorism responsibilities may require a shift of resources away from community policing."[84] That concern, he says, is misdirected because community policing provides a natural conduit for information gathering and the development of counterterrorism intelligence. Information gathered by state and local police departments can be funneled to federal agencies, especially the FBI, that have been charged with developing national security intelligence. Carter notes that the "increased social tension" resulting from the current concern with terrorism has led to a greater need "to maintain a close, interactive dialogue between law enforcement and the community."

Thematic Question Ask students to imagine being a police chief. Have the class identify and discuss the difficulties facing police chiefs today. What are the rewards of the job?

The importance of community policing in the fight against terrorism was reflected in comments made by FBI Director Robert Mueller during the summer of 2004. While pointing to photographs of seven terrorist suspects believed to be in the United States, Mueller said: "We need the support of the American people . . . to cooperate when called upon, as agents will be reaching out to many across the nation to help gather information and intelligence . . . to be aware of your surroundings and report anything suspicious . . . to 'BOLO' [be on the lookout] for those pictured above. . . . Have you seen them in your communities? Have you heard that someone might be helping them to hide? Do you have any idea where they might be? If so, we need you to come forward."[85]

Members of the U.S. Department of Justice's Global Intelligence Working Group (GIWG) also recognized the importance of community-oriented policing efforts when developing the national intelligence sharing plan (described in Chapter 6). "Over the past decade," members noted, "thousands of community policing officers have been building close and productive relationships with the citizens they serve."[86] Community policing officers, they observed, "have immediate and unfettered access to local, neighborhood information as it develops. Citizens are aware of and seek out [community policing] officers to provide them with new information that may be useful to criminal interdiction or long-term problem solving. The positive nature of police/citizen relationships promotes a continuous and reliable transfer of information from one to the other. It is time to maximize the potential for community policing efforts to serve as a gateway of locally based information to prevent terrorism, and all other crimes."[87]

The Office for Domestic Preparedness (ODP) of the DHS notes that community policing can play the following roles in the intelligence process:[88]

- Provide materials to community policing contacts that may aid in the recognition of terrorism-related activities in order to make members of the community aware of suspicious actions, behaviors, and events
- Organize community meetings to emphasize prevention strategies, vigilance, and public awareness
- Ensure that members of the community are aware of the means of and processes for relaying information to police officers and police organizations
- Encourage crime prevention, proactive policing, and close working relationships between the police and the community

In any successful police-community interaction, information flows both ways. While community policing efforts seek information from the public about offenders, police departments can also communicate critical information to the public to aid in preventing crime and reducing fear.

Critique of Community Policing

As some authors have noted, "Community policing has become the dominant theme of contemporary police reform in America."[89] Yet problems have plagued the movement since its inception.[90] For one thing, the range, complexity, and evolving nature of community policing programs make their effectiveness difficult to measure.[91] Moreover, citizen satisfaction with police performance can be difficult to conceptualize and quantify. Most early studies examined citizens' attitudes developed through face-to-face interaction with individual police officers. They generally found a far higher level of dissatisfaction with the police among African Americans than among most other groups. Recent findings continue to show that the attitudes of African Americans toward the police remain poor. The wider reach of these studies, however, led evaluators to discover that this dissatisfaction may be rooted in overall quality of life and type of neighborhood.[92] On average, African Americans continue to experience a lower quality of life than most other U.S. citizens, and they often live in neighborhoods characterized by economic problems, drug trafficking, and street crime. Recent studies conclude that it is these conditions of life, rather than race, that are most predictive of citizen dissatisfaction with the police.

Those who study community policing have often been stymied by ambiguity surrounding the concept of community.[93] Sociologists, who sometimes define the word *community* as "any area in which members of a common culture share common interests,"[94] tend to deny that a community needs to be limited geographically. Police departments, on the other hand, tend to define communities "within jurisdictional, district or precinct lines, or within the confines of public or private housing developments."[95] Robert Trojanowicz cautioned police planners that "the impact of mass transit, mass communications and mass media [has] widened the rift between a sense of community based on geography and one [based] on interest."[96]

Researchers who follow the police definition of *community* recognize that there may be little consensus within and between members of a local community about community problems and appropriate solutions. Robert Bohm and colleagues at the University of Central Florida have found, for example, that while there may be some "consensus about social problems and their solutions . . . the consensus may not be community-wide." It may, in fact, exist only among "a relatively small group of 'active' stakeholders who differ significantly about the seriousness of most of the problems and the utility of some solutions."[97]

Finally, there is continuing evidence that not all police officers or managers are willing to accept nontraditional images of police work. One reason is that the goals of community policing often conflict with standard police performance criteria (such as arrests), leading to a perception among officers that community policing is inefficient at best and, at worst, a waste of time.[98] Similarly, many officers are loathe to take on new responsibilities as service providers whose role is more defined by community needs and less by strict interpretation of the law.

Thematic Question How might community policing alter the police subculture and the types of personalities that characterize it?

Some authors have warned that police subculture is so committed to a traditional view of police work, which is focused almost exclusively on crime fighting, that efforts to promote community policing can demoralize an entire department, rendering it ineffective at its basic tasks.[99] As the Christopher Commission found following the 1992 Rodney King riots, "Too many . . . patrol officers view citizens with resentment and hostility; too many treat the public with rudeness and disrespect."[100] Some analysts warn that only when the formal values espoused by today's innovative police administrators begin to match those of rank-and-file officers can any police agency begin to perform well in terms of the goals espoused by community policing reformers.[101]

Some public officials, too, are unwilling to accept community policing. Fifteen years ago, for example, New York City Mayor Rudolph W. Giuliani criticized the police department's Community Police Officer Program (CPOP), saying that it "has resulted in officers doing too much social work and making too few arrests."[102] Similarly, many citizens are not ready to accept a greater involvement of the police in their personal lives. Although the turbulent, protest-prone years of the 1960s and early 1970s are long gone, some groups remain suspicious of the police. No matter how inclusive community policing programs become, it is doubtful that the gap between the police and the public will ever be entirely bridged. The police role of restraining behavior that violates the law will always produce friction between police departments and some segments of the community. Learn more about measures of police effectiveness, including those related to community policing, at **Library Extra 4–7**, and read a COPS Office perspective on the future of community policing at **Library Extra 4–8**.

Evidence-Based Policing

Law Enforcement Assistance Administration (LEAA)
A now-defunct federal agency established under Title I of the Omnibus Crime Control and Safe Streets Act of 1969 to funnel federal funding to state and local law enforcement agencies.

Lecture Note Describe police agencies as businesses to which general management principles can apply. Highlight the fact that reduced federal funding for scientific studies of the police has resulted in dramatically fewer studies today than in the heyday of public funding.

scientific police management
The application of social sciences techniques to the study of police administration for the purpose of increasing effectiveness, reducing the frequency of citizen complaints, and enhancing the efficient use of available resources.

In 1968, with the passage of the Omnibus Crime Control and Safe Streets Act, the U.S. Congress created the **Law Enforcement Assistance Administration (LEAA)**. LEAA was charged with combating crime through the expenditure of huge amounts of money in support of crime-prevention and crime-reduction programs. Some have compared the philosophy establishing LEAA to that which supported the American space program's goal of landing people on the moon: Put enough money into any problem, and it will be solved! Unfortunately, the crime problem was more difficult to address than the challenge of a moon landing; even after the expenditure of nearly $8 billion, LEAA had not come close to its goal. In 1982, LEAA expired when Congress refused it further funding.

6 Explain evidence-based policing, and demonstrate the potential that it holds in the area of police management.

The legacy of LEAA is an important one for police managers, however. The research-rich years of 1969 to 1982, supported largely through LEAA funding, have left a plethora of scientific findings relevant to police administration and, more important, have established a tradition of program evaluation within police-management circles. This tradition, which is known as **scientific police management**, is a natural outgrowth of LEAA's insistence that every funded program contain a plan for its evaluation. *Scientific police management* refers to the application of social science techniques to the study of police administration for the purpose of increasing effectiveness, reducing the frequency of citizen complaints, and enhancing the efficient use of available resources. The heyday of scientific police management occurred in the 1970s, when federal monies were far more readily available to support such studies than they are today.

LEAA was not alone in funding police research during the 1970s. On July 1, 1970, the Ford Foundation announced the establishment of a Police Development Fund totaling $30 million, to be spent over the next five years to support major crime-fighting strategies of police departments. This funding led to the establishment of the Police Foundation, which continues to exist today with the mission of "foster[ing] improvement and innovation in American policing."[103] Police Foundation–sponsored studies during the past 20 years have added to the growing body of scientific knowledge about policing.

Today, federal support for criminal justice research and evaluation continues under the NIJ and the BJS, both part of the Office of Justice Programs (OJP). OJP, created by Congress in 1984, provides federal leadership in developing the nation's capacity to prevent and control crime. The National Criminal Justice Reference Service (NCJRS), a part of NIJ, assists researchers nationwide in locating information applicable to their research projects. "Custom searches" of the NCJRS computer database can be done online and can yield abundant information in most criminal justice subject areas. NIJ also publishes a series of informative periodic reports, such as the *NIJ Journal* and *NIJ Research in Review*, which serve to keep criminal justice practitioners and researchers informed about recent findings. View the NIJ online publication list at **Web Extra 4–16**.

The Kansas City Experiment

History

Kansas City experiment
The first large-scale scientific study of law enforcement practices. Sponsored by the Police Foundation, it focused on the practice of preventive patrol.

By far the most famous application of social research principles to police management was the **Kansas City experiment** regarding preventive patrol.[104] The results of the yearlong experiment were published in 1974. The study, sponsored by the Police Foundation, divided the southern part of Kansas City, Missouri, into 15 areas. Five of these "beats" were patrolled in the usual fashion. In another group of five beats, patrol activities were doubled. The final third of the beats received a novel treatment indeed: No patrols were assigned to them, and no uniformed officers entered that part of the city unless they were called. The program was kept secret, and citizens were unaware of the difference between the patrolled and unpatrolled parts of the city.

The results of the Kansas City experiment were surprising. Records of "preventable crimes" (those toward which the activities of patrol were oriented), such as burglary, robbery, auto theft, larceny, and vandalism, showed no significant differences in rate of occurrence among the three experimental beats. Similarly, citizens didn't seem to notice the change in patrol patterns in the two areas where patrol frequency was changed. Surveys conducted at the conclusion of the experiment showed no difference in citizens' fear of crime before and after the study. The 1974 study can be summed up in the words of the author of the final report: "The whole idea of riding around in cars to create a feeling of omnipresence just hasn't worked. . . . Good people with good intentions tried something that logically should have worked, but didn't."[105] This study has been credited with beginning the now-established tradition of scientific studies of policing.

A second Kansas City study focused on "response time."[106] It found that even consistently fast police response to citizen reports of crime had little effect either on citizen satisfaction with the police or on the arrest of suspects. The study uncovered the fact that most reports made to the police came only after a considerable amount of time had passed. Hence the police were initially handicapped by the timing of the report, and even the fastest police response was not especially effective.

▲ Members of the Kansas City (Missouri) Police Department being briefed on security measures for a planned city tour by President George W. Bush. Scientific police management was given early credence by studies of preventive patrol undertaken in Kansas City in 1974. What have scientific studies of the police since that time demonstrated?
Courtesy of the Media Office of the Kansas City Missouri Police Department

Effects

The Kansas City studies greatly affected managerial assumptions about the role of preventive patrol and traditional strategies for responding to citizen calls for assistance. As Joseph Lewis, then director of evaluation at the Police Foundation, said, "I think that now almost everyone would agree that almost anything you do is better than random patrol."[107]

While the Kansas City studies called into question some basic assumptions about patrol, it remains the backbone of police work. New patrol strategies for the effective utilization of human resources have led to various activities of **directed patrol**. One form of directed patrol varies the number of officers involved in patrolling according to the time of day or the frequency of reported crimes within an area. The idea is to put the most officers on the street where and when crime is most prevalent. Wilmington, Delaware, was one of the first cities to make use of split-force patrol, in which only a part of the patrol force performs routine patrol.[108] The remaining officers respond to calls for service, take reports, and conduct investigations.

directed patrol
A police-management strategy designed to increase the productivity of patrol officers through the scientific analysis and evaluation of patrol techniques.

In response to the Kansas City study on response time, some cities have prioritized calls for service,[109] ordering a quick police response only when crimes are in progress or when serious crimes have occurred. Less significant offenses, such as minor larcenies and certain citizen complaints, are handled by using the mail or by having citizens come to the police station to make a report.

Early policing studies, such as the Kansas City patrol experiment, were designed to identify and probe some of the basic assumptions that guided police work. The initial response to many such studies was "Why should we study that? Everybody knows the answer already!" As in the case of the Kansas City experiment, however, it soon became obvious that conventional wisdom was not always correct. Scientific studies of special significance to law enforcement are summarized in Table 4–4.

> You can't measure what a patrolman standing on a corner has prevented. There is no product at the end of a policeman's day.
> —Charles McCarthy[v]

Evidence-Based Policing Today

At the close of the twentieth century, noted police researcher Lawrence W. Sherman addressed an audience of criminal justice policymakers, scholars, and practitioners at the Police Foundation in Washington, D.C., and called for a new approach to American policing that would use research to guide and evaluate practice. "Police practices should be based on scientific evidence about what works best," Sherman told his audience. Sherman's lecture, titled "Evidence-Based Policing: Policing Based on Science, Not Anecdote,"[110]

TABLE 4–4
Selected Scientific Studies in Law Enforcement

Year	Study Name	Focus
2009	Evaluation of the Prince William County (Virginia) Police Department's Illegal Immigration Enforcement Policy (Interim Report)	The department's new policy of requiring immigration status checks under certain circumstances[a]
2007	Minneapolis Neighborhood Gunfire Detection System Evaluation	Police response time to gunfire within the city
2005	Effectiveness of Designated Driver Programs	Designated driver campaigns to reduce highway accidents
2002	Reducing Gun Violence (Indianapolis)	Targeted police patrols to reduce gun crime and violence
2001	Boston's Operation Ceasefire Evaluation	Citywide effort to reduce gun violence, especially gang-related homicides
1999	National Evaluation of Weed-and-Seed Programs	Weed-and-seed programs in eight states
1998	Community Policing in Action (Indianapolis)	Police and citizen cooperation and neighborhood security
1994	Kansas City Gun Experiment	Supplemental police patrol to reduce gun crime
1992	New York City Police Department's Cadet Corps Study	Level of education among officers, and hiring of minority officers
1992	Metro-Dade Spouse Abuse Experiment Replication (Florida)	Replication of a 1984 Minneapolis study
1990	Minneapolis "Hot Spot" Patrolling	Intensive patrol of problem areas
1987	Newport News (Virginia) Problem-Oriented Policing	Police solutions to community crime problems
1986	Crime Stoppers: A National Evaluation	Media crime-reduction programs
1986	Reducing Fear of Crime in Houston and Newark	Strategies for fear reduction among urban populations
1984	Minneapolis Domestic Violence Experiment	Effective police action in domestic-violence situations
1981	Newark Foot Patrol Experiment	Costs versus benefits of foot patrol
1977	Cincinnati Team Policing Experiment	Team versus traditional policing
1977	Patrol Staffing in San Diego	One- versus two-officer units
1976	Police Response Time (Kansas City)	Citizen satisfaction with police response
1976	Kansas City Peer Review Panel	Improvement in police behavior
1974	Kansas City Preventive Patrol Experiment	Effectiveness of police patrol

[a] A final report is scheduled for release after this book goes to press.

evidence-based policing (EBP)
The use of the best available research on the outcomes of police work to implement guidelines and evaluate agencies, units, and officers.[vi]

popularized the term **evidence-based policing (EBP)**. EBP, says Sherman, "is the use of best available research on the outcomes of police work to implement guidelines and evaluate agencies, units, and officers."[111] In other words, EBP uses research into everyday police procedures to evaluate current practices and to guide officers and police executives in future decision making. In any discussion of EBP, it is important to remember that the word *evidence* refers to scientific evidence, not criminal evidence.

"The basic premise of evidence-based practice," says Sherman, "is that we are all entitled to our own opinions, but not to our own facts."[112] Our own facts, or our beliefs about the way things should be done, says Sherman, often turn out to be wrong. During the civil rights movement of the 1960s and 1970s, for example, police executives in many areas took a heavy-handed approach in their attempts to control demonstrators. Images of tear gas filling the streets, high-pressure fire hoses being aimed at marchers, and police dogs biting fleeing demonstrators symbolize that era for many people. This heavy-handed approach had unintended consequences and served to inflame protesters. Situations that might have otherwise been contained with simple crowd-control tactics and the use of physical barriers became largely uncontrollable. Sherman reminds us that "the mythic power of subjective and unstructured wisdom holds back every field and keeps it from systematically discovering and implementing what works best in repeated tasks."

In 2008, the EBP movement gained additional traction when Sherman taught a course on the topic to police leaders from a number of countries at Cambridge University's Institute of Criminology. "There is a need for much more scientific guidance behind the way police are used," Sherman told representatives at Cambridge. "In Britain, the government has invested heavily in police resources, but we have not established how to obtain best value for money in deploying those resources. This is an opportunity for us to do that, working in a collaborative way with the police and tying together the education of police officers and the research base of criminology."[113]

The Institute of Criminology at Cambridge University identified the following questions as goals to be answered by evidence-based studies:[114]

- How can policing produce greater public safety without eroding civil liberties?
- How can more value for money be returned from investments in policing to cut the costs of crime?
- Can crime be better forecast for preventive policing by time and place?
- Can unsuccessful police methods be distinguished from cost-effective ones?
- Can better policing reduce the high costs of a growing prison population?
- Can evaluation tools used in evidence-based medicine be adopted by police?
- What are the possibilities for a police service based on cost-effectiveness?
- What are the prospects for developing the knowledge base for such evidence?

Today's EBP model has been called the single "most powerful force for change" in policing today.[115] Leading the movement toward EBP are organizations like the FBI's Futures Working Group, the Campbell Crime and Justice Group, and the Center for Evidence-Based Crime Policy at George Mason University. FBI Supervisory Special Agent Carl J. Jensen III, a member of the Futures Working Group, notes that in the future "successful law enforcement executives will have to be consumers and appliers of research." They won't need to be researchers themselves, Jensen notes, "but they must use research in their everyday work."[116] The Campbell Crime and Justice Group, which emphasizes the use of experimental studies in crime and justice policy making, can be accessed at **Web Extra 4–17**. The Center for Evidence-Based Crime Policy can be accessed at **Web Extra 4–18**. The center's Evidence-Based Policing Hall of Fame recognizes innovative law enforcement practitioners who have been central to the implementation of high-quality research programs. Visit the Hall of Fame at **Web Extra 4–19**.

▲ An officer writing a traffic ticket. Police officers wield a wide degree of discretion, and an individual officer's decision to enforce a particular law or to effect an arrest varies not just with the law's applicability to a particular set of circumstances but with the officer's subjective judgments about the nature of appropriate enforcement activity. What other factors influence police discretion? *David Young-Wolff/PhotoEdit Inc.*

Discretion and the Individual Officer

Even as law enforcement agencies struggle to adapt to the threats posed by international terrorism, individual officers continue to retain considerable discretion in terms of their actions. **Police discretion** refers to the exercise of choice by law enforcement officers in the decision to investigate or apprehend, the disposition of suspects, the carrying out of official duties, and the application of sanctions. As one author has observed, "Police authority can be, at once, highly specific and exceedingly vague."[117] Decisions to stop and question someone, arrest a suspect, and perform many other police tasks are made solely by individual officers and must often be made quickly and in the absence of any close supervision. Kenneth Culp Davis, who pioneered the study

7 Explain police discretion, and identify some of the factors that influence a police officer's use of discretion.

police discretion
The opportunity of law enforcement officers to exercise choice in their daily activities.

Lecture Note Describe police discretion as the exercise of choice by individual officers in the performance of their official duties.

Lecture Note Connect the use of discretion to policing styles and to traditional versus community policing.

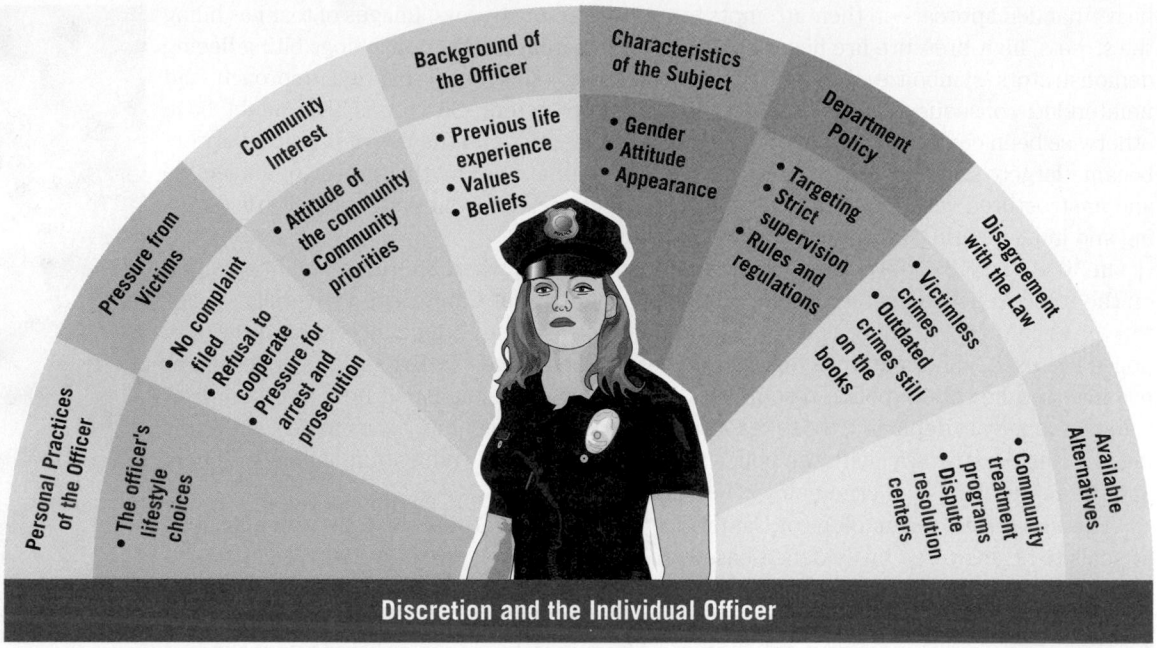

FIGURE 4–3
Discretion and the Individual Officer

of police discretion, says, "The police make policy about what law to enforce, how much to enforce it, against whom, and on what occasions."[118] To those who have contact with the police, the discretionary authority exercised by individual officers is of greater significance than all the department manuals and official policy statements combined.

Thematic Question What is police discretion? How does discretion characterize various aspects of the law enforcement role? Where is it most prevalent?

Lecture Note Explain the importance of personal initiative to professional policing, and relate it to discretion.

A PowerPoint presentation that supports this chapter is available from your Prentice Hall representative.

Patrolling officers often decide against a strict enforcement of the law, preferring instead to handle situations informally. Infractions where minor law violations are committed, crimes committed out of the officer's presence where the victim refuses to file a complaint, and certain violations of the criminal law where the officer suspects that sufficient evidence to guarantee a conviction is lacking may all lead to discretionary action short of arrest. Although the widest exercise of discretion is more likely in routine situations involving relatively less serious violations of the law, serious and clear-cut criminal behavior may occasionally result in discretionary decisions not to make an arrest. Drunk driving, possession of controlled substances, and assault are but a few examples of crimes in which on-the-scene officers may decide warnings or referrals are more appropriate than arrest. Figure 4–3 illustrates a number of factors that studies of police discretion have found to influence the discretionary decisions of individual officers.

Summary

POLICING: PURPOSE AND ORGANIZATION

- The fundamental police mission in democratic societies includes five components: (1) enforcing the law (especially the criminal law), (2) apprehending offenders, (3) preventing crime, (4) preserving the peace, and (5) providing the community with needed enforcement-related services.
- Contemporary American policing presents a complex picture that is structured along federal, state, and local lines. Each federal agency empowered by Congress to enforce specific statutes has its own enforcement arm. In addition, tasks deemed especially significant by state legislatures, such as patrol of the highways, have resulted in the creation of specialized law enforcement agencies under state jurisdiction. For many of today's local law enforcement agencies,

created under county and municipal authority, patrol retains a central role—with investigation, interrogation, and numerous support roles rounding out an increasingly specialized profession.

- Police administration involves the activities of managing, controlling, directing, and coordinating police personnel, resources, and activities in the service of preventing crime, apprehending criminals, recovering stolen property, and performing regulatory and helping services. Virtually all American law enforcement organizations are formally structured among divisions and along lines of authority. Roles within police agencies usually fall into one of two categories: line and staff. Line operations are field or supervisory activities directly related to daily police work; staff operations include support roles such as administration.
- Four historical policing epochs are identified in this chapter: (1) the political era, (2) the reform era, (3) the community policing era, and (4) the new era. Some say that the primary feature of the new law enforcement era is policing to secure the homeland. Others see the new era as being underpinned by an emphasis on intelligence-led policing.
- Police-community relations programs represent a movement away from an exclusive police emphasis on the apprehension of law violators and signify an increasing level of positive police-citizen interaction. Community policing is built on the principle that police departments and the communities they serve should work together as partners in the fight against crime.
- Evidence-based policing consists of the use of best available research on the outcomes of police work to implement guidelines and evaluate agencies, units, and officers. EBP uses research into everyday police procedures to evaluate current practices and to guide officers and police executives in future decision making.
- *Police discretion* refers to the opportunity for police officers to exercise choice in their enforcement activities. Put another way, discretion is the exercise of choice by law enforcement officers in the decision to investigate or apprehend, the disposition of suspects, the carrying out of official duties, and the application of sanctions. The widest exercise of discretion can be found in routine situations involving relatively less serious violations of the law, but serious criminal behavior may also result in discretionary decisions not to make an arrest.

QUESTIONS FOR REVIEW

1. What are the basic purposes of policing in democratic societies? How are they consistent with one another? In what ways might they be inconsistent?
2. What are the three major levels of public law enforcement described in this chapter? Why do we have so many different types of enforcement agencies in the United States? What problems, if any, do you think are created by such a diversity of agencies?
3. What are the various features of police administration described in this chapter? What is a chain of command?
4. What were the stages of historical development in American policing? How did policing styles differ by historical era?
5. What is community policing? How does it differ from traditional policing? Does community policing offer a real opportunity to improve policing services in the United States? Why or why not?
6. What is evidence-based policing? What potential does it hold for managing police organizations in the future?
7. What is police discretion? How does the practice of discretion by today's officers affect their departments and the policing profession as a whole?

CHAPTER 5

Policing: Legal Aspects

Learning Objectives

After reading this chapter, you should be able to:

1. Identify legal restraints on police action, and list instances of the abuse of police power. **116**
2. Explain how the Bill of Rights and democratically inspired legal restraints help protect personal freedoms in our society. **118**
3. Describe the circumstances under which police officers may properly conduct searches or seize property. **118**
4. Define *arrest*, and describe how popular depictions of the arrest process may not be consistent with legal understandings of the term. **128**
5. Describe the intelligence function, including police interrogations, and explain the role of *Miranda* warnings. **139**

"No one is compelled to choose the profession of a police officer, but having chosen it, everyone is obliged to live up to the standard of its requirements."

—Calvin Coolidge[1]

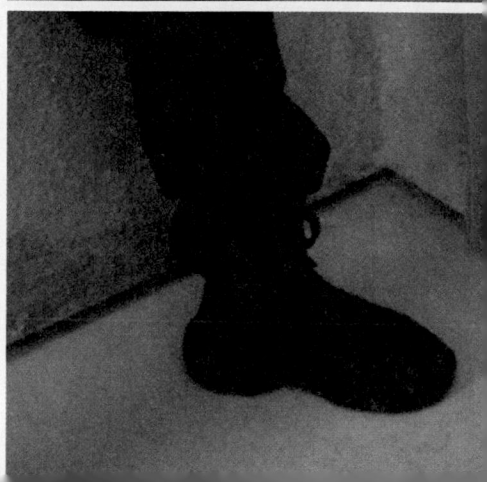

Introduction

Early on a cold November morning in 2006, 23-year-old Sean Bell left a bachelor party at New York City's Kalua Cabaret strip club with two of his friends and climbed into his gray Nissan Altima. Although Bell, who was to be married later that day, didn't know it, undercover New York City Police Department (NYPD) officers had been staking out the club in an investigation into suspected drug and gun dealing there. What happened next remains unclear, but after a chaotic confrontation between Bell's group and the police, followed by a crash involving a van carrying some of the NYPD officers and Bell's car, officers opened fire on the vehicle, firing 50 rounds before the shooting ended. Bell died at the scene, and his friends were seriously injured. The officers later said that they thought Bell and his companions were armed and that they might have been drug dealers. It was not clear if Bell ever knew that the men, dressed in plain clothes, were police officers; he may have thought that he was being robbed or carjacked. On March 17, 2007, a Queens, New York, grand jury indicted three of the detectives involved in the case, charging two with first- and second-degree manslaughter and a third with reckless endangerment.

▲ Protesters at a rally in Queens, New York, demanding answers for the fatal police shooting of Sean Bell as he left a bachelor's party on the night before his wedding in 2006. Bell, who was unarmed, was killed by NYPD officers who fired 50 rounds at him and two friends after they drove Bell's car into a minivan carrying plainclothes officers who were investigating the club where the party took place. The officers were found "not guilty" in a 2008 trial. Might "contagious shooting" explain what happened that night?
Reuters/Mike Segar/Landov Media

Shortly after the indictments were handed down, demonstrators paraded through Queens demanding justice for Bell, who was African American, as were two of the three officers indicted in the shooting. New York City Mayor Michael R. Bloomberg urged residents to "respect the result of our justice system." He added, "It also needs to be said that being a police officer . . . is a very dangerous job. And although a trial will decide whether crimes were committed in this case, day in and day out the N.Y.P.D. does an incredible job under very difficult circumstances."[2] The mayor's words seemed prophetic when, on April 25, 2008, Judge Arthur J. Cooperman found the defendants not guilty of any crime. Describing the evidence, Judge Cooperman said that it was reasonable for the detectives to fear that someone in the crowd had been carrying a gun on the night that the shooting took place. He added that many of the prosecution's witnesses, including Bell's friends and the two wounded victims, were simply not believable.[3]

The Bell shooting was reminiscent of the death of West African immigrant Amadou Diallo, who was killed in a hail of 41 bullets in 1999 as he stood in a New York City doorway and apparently reached for his identification after being told to raise his hands. Diallo reportedly had a poor command of the English language and may not have understood police commands to stay still. Officers had apparently mistaken him for a suspect they were pursuing. Although the officers who shot Diallo were charged with second-degree murder, they were later acquitted.[4] Law enforcement experts said that what happened in both cases might be explained by "contagious shooting"—gunfire that spreads "in the adrenaline-pumping, split-second heat of the moment"[5] among officers who believe that they, or their colleagues, are facing a deadly threat.[6]

Not all questionable cases of police use of force involve shootings. Two months after Hurricane Katrina devastated New Orleans, members of the city's overworked police department became embroiled in a public relations nightmare when an Associated Press Television News (APTN) crew working in the French Quarter filmed two white officers beating an apparently dazed and unresisting 64-year-old African American retired elementary school teacher named Robert Davis. A third officer could be seen grabbing and shoving an APTN producer working with the news team. As the incident ended, Davis, whose family had property in the city, was arrested and charged with public intoxication, resisting arrest, battery on a police officer, and public intimidation. He later told reporters that he hadn't had an alcoholic drink in 25 years but that trouble began when he asked a mounted officer for directions.[7] New Orleans Police Superintendent Warren Riley was quick to condemn the officers' behavior. "The actions that were observed on this video are certainly unacceptable [to] this department," Riley said as he announced the firings of officers Lance Schilling and Robert Evangelist, as well as the suspension without pay of another officer, S. M. Smith. Soon afterward, the U.S. Department of Justice announced that it was opening a civil rights investigation into the incident.[8]

The Abuse of Police Power

The Rodney King Incident

1 Identify legal restraints on police action, and list instances of the abuse of police power.

National publicity surrounding the Davis beating was considerably less intense than that which centered on the 1991 videotaped beating of motorist Rodney King by Los Angeles Police Department (LAPD) officers. King, an unemployed 25-year-old African American, was stopped by LAPD officers for an alleged violation of motor vehicle laws. Police said King had been speeding and had refused to stop for a pursuing patrol car. Officers claimed to have clocked his 1988 Hyundai at 115 mph on the suburban Los Angeles Foothill Freeway—even though the car's manufacturer later said the vehicle was not capable of speeds over 100 mph.

Lecture Note Discuss the Rodney King case, which drew the spotlight of public attention to the abuse of police power. Ask students if they remember learning about the case and, if so, what they learned. How did the media portray this event? Discuss the possibility that the Los Angeles officers were tried by the media, rather than by the courts, and that these officers, too, may have had a story to tell.

Eventually King did stop, but then officers of the LAPD appeared to attack him, shocking him twice with electronic stun guns and striking him with nightsticks and fists. Kicked in the stomach, face, and back, he was left with 11 skull fractures, missing teeth, a crushed cheekbone, and a broken ankle. A witness told reporters that she heard King begging officers to stop the beating but that they "were all laughing, like they just had a party."[9] King eventually underwent surgery for brain injuries. Officers involved in the beating claimed that King, at 6 feet 3 inches and 225 pounds, appeared strung out on phencyclidine (PCP) and that he and his two companions made the officers feel threatened.[10]

The entire incident was captured on videotape by an amateur photographer with a night-sensitive video camera. The two-minute videotape was repeatedly broadcast over national television and was picked up by hundreds of local TV stations. The furor that erupted over the tape led to the ouster of LAPD Chief Daryl Gates and initiated a Justice Department review of law enforcement practices across the country.[11]

Lecture Note Explain how the potential for police abuse of power is anticipated by the Bill of Rights and how restraints on the police must constantly be balanced against the need for the police to be able to do their jobs.

In 1992, a California jury found four police defendants not guilty—a verdict that resulted in days of rioting across Los Angeles. A year later, however, in the spring of 1993, two of the officers, Sergeant Stacey Koon and Officer Laurence Powell, were found guilty in federal court of denying King his constitutional right "not to be deprived of liberty without due process of law, including the right to be . . . free from the intentional use of unreasonable force."[12] Later that year, both were sentenced to two and a half years in prison, far less than might have been expected under federal sentencing guidelines. They were released from prison in December 1995, and a three-year court battle over whether federal sentencing guidelines were violated was resolved in the officers' favor in 1996. Officers Theodore Briseno and Timothy Wind were exonerated at the federal level.

In 1994, King settled a civil suit against the city of Los Angeles for a reported $3.8 million. Observers later concluded that King himself was not a model citizen. At the time of the beating, he was on parole after having served time in prison for robbery. Since then he has been arrested on a variety of other charges, including battery, assault, drug use, and indecent exposure.[13] Learn more about the Rodney King incident and its ramifications at **Web Extra 5–1**.

This chapter shows how no one is above the law—even the police. It describes the legal environment surrounding police activities, from search and seizure through arrest and the interrogation of suspects. As we shall see throughout, democratically inspired legal restraints on the police help ensure individual freedoms in our society and prevent the development of a police state in America. Like anything else, however, the rules by which the police are expected to operate are in constant flux, and their continuing development forms the meat of this chapter. For a police perspective on these issues, visit **Web Extra 5–2**.

A Changing Legal Climate

Bill of Rights
The popular name given to the first ten amendments to the U.S. Constitution, which are considered especially important in the processing of criminal defendants.

The Constitution of the United States is designed—especially in the **Bill of Rights**—to protect citizens against abuses of police power (Table 5–1). However, the legal environment surrounding the police in modern America is much more complex than it was just 45 years ago. Up until that time, the Bill of Rights was largely given only lip service in criminal justice proceedings around the country. In practice, law enforcement, especially on the state and local levels, revolved around tried-and-true methods of

TABLE 5–1
Constitutional Amendments of Special Significance to the American System of Justice

This Right Is Guaranteed	By This Amendment
The right against unreasonable searches and seizures	Fourth
The right against arrest without probable cause	Fourth
The right against self-incrimination	Fifth
The right against "double jeopardy"	Fifth
The right to due process of law	Fifth, Sixth, Fourteenth
The right to a speedy trial	Sixth
The right to a jury trial	Sixth
The right to know the charges	Sixth
The right to cross-examine witnesses	Sixth
The right to a lawyer	Sixth
The right to compel witnesses on one's behalf	Sixth
The right to reasonable bail	Eighth
The right against excessive fines	Eighth
The right against cruel and unusual punishments	Eighth
The applicability of constitutional rights to all citizens, regardless of state law or procedure	Fourteenth

Lecture Note Explain that the due process environment surrounding police action extends to three important areas: search and seizure of evidence, arrest, and interrogation. Refer to Table 5–1 to highlight the rights of criminal defendants.

Lecture Note Describe the growing conservatism of the U.S. Supreme Court. Begin with the liberal Warren Court era of the 1960s, and discuss the Burger, Rehnquist, and Roberts eras. Giving specific examples, describe how confirmation battles are a reflection of the ideological stances of members of Congress and of the nominees themselves.

Lecture Note Describe checks on police action by the courts. Tell how police agencies in foreign countries are often not constrained by "the rule of law," and explain why citizens of such countries often live in fear of unbridled police action.

Lecture Note Explain that the U.S. Constitution (through the Bill of Rights) requires law enforcement personnel to seek a warrant before making an arrest or executing a search. Tell the class that warrants are generally issued by magistrates who check to see that the police have probable cause to believe that the person to be arrested is likely to be the person who committed the crime or that the place to be searched is the place where sought-after evidence is likely to be found.

search, arrest, and interrogation that sometimes left little room for recognition of individual rights. Police operations during that period were often far more informal than they are today, and investigating officers frequently assumed that they could come and go as they pleased, even to the extent of invading someone's home without a search warrant. Interrogations could quickly turn violent, and the infamous "rubber hose," which was reputed to leave few marks on the body, was probably more widely used during the questioning of suspects than many would like to believe. Similarly, "doing things by the book" could mean the use of thick telephone books for beating suspects, since the books spread out the force of blows and left few visible bruises. Although such abuses were not necessarily day-to-day practices in all police agencies and although they probably did not characterize more than a relatively small proportion of all officers, such conduct pointed to the need for greater control over police activities so that even the potential for abuse might be curtailed.

In the 1960s the U.S. Supreme Court, under the direction of Chief Justice Earl Warren (1891–1974), accelerated the process of guaranteeing individual rights in the face of criminal prosecution. Warren Court rulings bound the police to strict procedural requirements in the areas of investigation, arrest, and interrogation. Later rulings scrutinized trial court procedures and enforced humanitarian standards in sentencing and punishment. The Warren Court also seized on the Fourteenth Amendment and made it a basis for judicial mandates requiring that both state and federal criminal justice agencies adhere to the Court's interpretation of the Constitution. The apex of the individual-rights emphasis in Supreme Court decisions was reached in the 1966 case of *Miranda* v. *Arizona*,[14] which established the famous requirement of a police "rights advisement" of suspects. In wielding its brand of idealism, the Warren Court (which held sway from 1953 until 1969) accepted the fact that a few guilty people would go free so that the rights of the majority of Americans would be protected.

In the decades since the Warren Court, a new conservative Court philosophy has resulted in Supreme Court decisions that have brought about what some call a reversal of Warren-era advances in the area of individual rights. By creating exceptions to some of the Warren Court's rules and restraints and by allowing for the emergency questioning of suspects before they are read their rights, a changed Supreme Court has recognized the realities attending day-to-day police work and the need to ensure public safety.

There is more law at the end of the policeman's nightstick than in all the decisions of the Supreme Court.

—Alexander "Clubber" Williams, late-nineteenth-century New York police officer

Individual Rights

Checks and Balances

2 Explain how the Bill of Rights and democratically inspired legal restraints help protect personal freedoms in our society.

The Constitution of the United States provides for a system of checks and balances among the legislative, judicial, and executive (presidential) branches of government. One branch of government is always held accountable to the other branches. The system is designed to ensure that no one individual or agency can become powerful enough to usurp the rights and freedoms guaranteed under the Constitution. Without accountability, it is possible to imagine a police state in which the power of law enforcement is absolute and is related more to political considerations and personal vendettas than to objective considerations of guilt or innocence.

Under our system of government, courts become the arena for dispute resolution, not just between individuals but between citizens and the agencies of government. After handling by the justice system, people who feel they have not received the respect and dignity due them under the law can appeal to the courts for redress. Such appeals are usually based on procedural issues and are independent of more narrow considerations of guilt or innocence.

In this chapter, we focus on cases that are important for having clarified constitutional guarantees concerning individual liberties within the criminal justice arena. They involve issues that most of us have come to call *rights.* Rights are concerned with procedure, that is, with how police and other actors in the criminal justice system handle each part of the process of dealing with suspects. Rights violations have often become the basis for the dismissal of charges, the acquittal of defendants, or the release of convicted offenders after an appeal to a higher court.

Due Process Requirements

As you may recall from Chapter 1, due process is a requirement of the Fifth, Sixth, and Fourteenth Amendments to the U.S. Constitution. It mandates that justice system officials respect the rights of accused individuals throughout the criminal justice process. Most due process requirements of relevance to the police pertain to three major areas: (1) evidence and investigation (often called *search* and *seizure*), (2) arrest, and (3) interrogation. Each of these areas has been addressed by a plethora of landmark U.S. Supreme Court decisions. **Landmark cases** produce substantial changes both in the understanding of the requirements of due process and in the practical day-to-day operations of the justice system. Another way to think of landmark cases is that they help significantly in clarifying the "rules of the game"—the procedural guidelines that the police and the rest of the justice system must follow.

landmark case
A precedent-setting court decision that produces substantial changes both in the understanding of the requirements of due process and in the practical day-to-day operations of the justice system.

> [The police] are not perfect; we don't sign them up on some far-off planet and bring them into police service. They are products of society.
>
> —Daryl Gates, former Los Angeles police chief

The three areas we will discuss have been well defined by decades of court precedent. Keep in mind, however, that judicial interpretations of the constitutional requirement of due process are constantly evolving. As new decisions are rendered and as the composition of the Court itself changes, major changes and additional refinements may occur.

Search And Seizure

3 Describe the circumstances under which police officers may properly conduct searches or seize property.

The Fourth Amendment to the U.S. Constitution declares that people must be secure in their homes and in their persons against unreasonable searches and seizures. This amendment reads, "The right of the people to be secure in their persons, houses, papers, and effects, against unreasonable searches and seizures, shall not be violated, and no

Warrants shall issue, but upon probable cause, supported by Oath or affirmation, and particularly describing the place to be searched, and the persons or things to be seized." The Fourth Amendment, a part of the Bill of Rights, was adopted by Congress and became effective on December 15, 1791.

The language of the Fourth Amendment is familiar to all of us. "**Warrant**," "probable cause," and other phrases from the amendment are frequently cited in editorials, TV news shows, and daily conversations about **illegally seized evidence**. It is the interpretation of these phrases over time by the U.S. Supreme Court, however, that has given them the impact they have on the justice system today.

warrant
In criminal proceedings, a writ issued by a judicial officer directing a law enforcement officer to perform a specified act and affording the officer protection from damages if he or she performs it.

illegally seized evidence
Any evidence seized without regard to the principles of due process as described by the Bill of Rights. Most illegally seized evidence is the result of police searches conducted without a proper warrant or of improperly conducted interrogations.

The Exclusionary Rule

The first landmark case concerning search and seizure was that of *Weeks* v. *U.S.* (1914).[15] Freemont Weeks was suspected of using the U.S. mail to sell lottery tickets, a federal crime. Weeks was arrested, and federal agents went to his home to conduct a search. They had no search warrant, because at the time investigators did not routinely use warrants. They confiscated many incriminating items of evidence, as well as some of the suspect's personal possessions, including clothes, papers, books, and even candy.

Lecture Note Describe the exclusionary rule as a doctrine, created by the U.S. Supreme Court in the 1914 case of *Weeks* v. *U.S.*, that excludes illegally seized evidence from use at trial. Explain that illegally seized evidence is often evidence gathered without a warrant.

Prior to trial, Weeks's attorney asked that the personal items be returned, claiming that they had been illegally seized under Fourth Amendment guarantees. A judge agreed and ordered the materials returned. On the basis of the evidence that was retained, however, Weeks was convicted in federal court and was sentenced to prison. He appealed his conviction through other courts, and his case eventually reached the U.S. Supreme Court. There, his lawyer reasoned that if some of his client's belongings had been illegally seized, then the remainder of them were also taken improperly. The Court agreed and overturned Weeks's earlier conviction.

Thematic Question What is the exclusionary rule? What is the fruit of the poisonous tree doctrine? What would American criminal justice be like without these rules?

The *Weeks* case forms the basis of what is now called the **exclusionary rule**, which holds that evidence illegally seized by the police cannot be used in a trial. The rule acts as a control over police behavior and specifically focuses on the failure of officers to obtain warrants authorizing them either to conduct searches or to effect arrests (especially where arrest may lead to the acquisition of incriminating statements or to the seizure of physical evidence).

exclusionary rule
The understanding, based on U.S. Supreme Court precedent, that incriminating information must be seized according to constitutional specifications of due process or it will not be allowed as evidence in a criminal trial.

The decision of the Supreme Court in the *Weeks* case was binding, at the time, only on federal officers because only federal agents were involved in the illegal seizure. Learn more about *Weeks* v. *U.S.* at **Library Extra 5–1**. See Figure 5–1 for more about the exclusionary rule and its development since *Weeks*.

Problems with Precedent

The *Weeks* case demonstrates the Supreme Court's power in enforcing what we have called the "rules of the game." It also lays bare the much more significant role that the Court plays in rule creation. Until the *Weeks* case was decided, federal law enforcement officers had little reason to think they were acting in violation of due process. Common practice had not required that they obtain a warrant before conducting searches. The rule that resulted from *Weeks* was new, and it would forever alter the enforcement activities of federal officers.

Lecture Note Discuss the fruit of the poisonous tree doctrine. Use the example of an illegally seized document that details the structure of an illegal drug operation. Tell the class that although enforcement agents may set up complex investigative strategies based on the document and may make hundreds of arrests over a period of months or years, the arrests themselves will be illegal—and the defendants will be set free—if it can be shown that the investigation was based solely on information from the illegally seized document.

The *Weeks* case reveals that the present appeals system, focusing as it does on the "rules of the game," presents a ready-made channel for the guilty to go free. There is little doubt that Freemont Weeks had violated federal law; a jury had convicted him. Yet he escaped punishment because of the illegal behavior of the police—behavior that, until the Court ruled, had been widely regarded as legitimate. Even if the police knowingly violate the principles of due process, which they sometimes do, our sense of justice is compromised when the guilty go free. Famed Supreme Court Justice Benjamin Cardozo (1870–1938) once complained, "The criminal is to go free because the constable has blundered."

Thematic Question When police officers violate the "rules of fair play" that apply to criminal investigations, is it unusual for guilty people to go free? Can you think of another way of enticing officers to obey the law, without necessarily letting the guilty go free? Explain your idea.

One solution to the problem would be to allow the Supreme Court to address theoretical questions involving issues of due process. Concerned supervisors and officials could ask how the Court would rule "if. . . ." As things now work, however, the Court can only address

FIGURE 5–1
The Exclusionary Rule

THE FOURTH AMENDMENT TO THE U.S. CONSTITUTION

The right of the people to be secure in their persons, houses, papers, and effects, against unreasonable searches and seizures, shall not be violated, and no Warrants shall issue, but upon probable cause, supported by Oath or affirmation, and particularly describing the place to be searched, and the persons or things to be seized.

Based upon the Fourth Amendment, **the Exclusionary Rule** holds that evidence of an offense that is collected or obtained by law enforcement officers in violation of a defendant's constitutional rights is inadmissible for use in a criminal prosecution in a court of law.

SIGNIFICANT CASES

***Weeks* v. *U.S.* (1914)**

Established the exclusionary rule at the federal level, holding that evidence that is illegally obtained cannot be used in a criminal trial; and that federal officers must have a valid warrant before conducting searches or seizing evidence. Prior to *Weeks,* common practice generally allowed all relevant evidence, no matter how it was obtained, to be used in court.

***Silverthorne Lumber Co.* v. *U.S.* (1920)**

Set forth the **Fruit of the Poisonous Tree Doctrine**, which says that just as illegally seized evidence cannot be used in a trial, neither can evidence that *derives* from an illegal search or seizure. Under this doctrine, complex cases developed after years of police investigative effort may be ruined if defense attorneys are able to demonstrate that the prosecution's case was originally based on a search or seizure that, at the time it occurred, violated due process.

***Mapp* v. *Ohio* (1961)**

Applied the exclusionary rule to criminal prosecutions at the state level. The Court held that the due process clause of the Fourteenth Amendment to the U.S. Constitution makes Fourth Amendment provisions applicable to state proceedings.

SUBSTANTIAL SOCIAL COSTS

***United States* v. *Leon* (1984)** and ***Hudson* v. *Michigan* (2006)**
Recognized that the exclusionary rule generates "substantial social costs," which may include letting the guilty go free and setting the dangerous at large.

EXCEPTIONS TO THE EXCLUSIONARY RULE

THE GOOD-FAITH EXCEPTION

***U.S.* v. *Leon* (1984)**
Allowed evidence that officers had seized in "reasonable good faith" to be used in court, even though the search was later ruled illegal.

***Illinois* v. *Krull* (1987)**
The good-faith exception applied to a warrantless search supported by state law even though the state statute was later found to violate the Fourth Amendment.

***Maryland* v. *Garrison* (1987)**
The use of evidence obtained by officers with a search warrant that was inaccurate in its specifics was allowed.

THE PLAIN-VIEW DOCTRINE

***Harris* v. *U.S.* (1968)**

Police officers have the opportunity to begin investigations or to confiscate evidence, without a warrant, based on what they find in plain view and open to public inspection.

CLERICAL ERRORS EXCEPTION

***Arizona* v. *Evans* (1995)**
A traffic stop that led to the seizure of marijuana was legal even though officers conducted the stop based on an arrest warrant that should have been deleted from the computer database to which they had access.

***Herring* v. *U.S.* (2009)**
When police mistakes leading to an unlawful search are the result of isolated negligence rather than systemic error or reckless disregard of constitutional requirements, the exclusionary rule does not apply.

EMERGENCY SEARCHES OF PROPERTY/EMERGENCY ENTRY

***Brigham City* v. *Stuart* (2006)**
Certain emergencies may justify a police officer's decision to search or enter premises without a warrant.

writ of *certiorari*
A writ issued from an appellate court for the purpose of obtaining from a lower court the record of its proceedings in a particular case. In some states, this writ is the mechanism for discretionary review. A request for review is made by petitioning for a writ of *certiorari*, and the granting of review is indicated by the issuance of the writ.

real cases and does so on a **writ of *certiorari***, in which the Court orders the record of a lower court case to be prepared for review.

The Fruit of the Poisonous Tree Doctrine

The Court continued to build on the rules concerning evidence with its decision in *Silverthorne Lumber Co.* v. *U.S.* (1920).[16] The case against the Silverthornes, owners of a lumberyard, was built on evidence that was illegally seized. Although the tainted evidence was itself not

> The public safety exception [to the exclusionary rule] was intended to protect the police, as well as the public, from danger.
>
> —*U.S.* v. *Brady* (1987)

used in court, its "fruits" (later evidence that derived from the illegal seizure) were and the Silverthornes were convicted. The Supreme Court overturned the decision, holding that any evidence that derives from a seizure that was in itself illegal cannot be used at trial. The *Silverthorne* case articulated a new principle of due process that today we call the **fruit of the poisonous tree doctrine**. This doctrine is potentially far reaching. Complex cases developed after years of police investigative effort may be ruined if defense attorneys are able to demonstrate that the prosecution's case was originally based on a search or seizure that violated due process. In such cases, it is likely that all evidence will be declared "tainted" and will become useless.

▲ An officer patting down a suspect. The legal environment surrounding the police helps ensure proper official conduct. In a stop like this, inappropriate behavior on the part of the officer can later become the basis for civil or criminal action against the officer and the police department. What might constitute inappropriate behavior?
John Boykin/PhotoEdit Inc

The Warren Court (1953–1969)

Before the 1960s, the U.S. Supreme Court intruded only infrequently on the overall operation of the criminal justice system at the state and local levels. As one author has observed, however, the 1960s were a time of youthful idealism, and "without the distraction of a depression or world war, individual liberties were examined at all levels of society."[17] While the exclusionary rule became an overriding consideration in federal law enforcement from the time that it was first defined by the Supreme Court in the *Weeks* case in 1914, it was not until 1961 that the Court, under Chief Justice Earl Warren, decided a case that was to change the face of American law enforcement forever. That case, *Mapp* v. *Ohio* (1961),[18] made the exclusionary rule applicable to criminal prosecutions at the state level. Beginning with the now-famous *Mapp* case, the Warren Court charted a course that would guarantee nationwide recognition of individual rights, as it understood them, by agencies at all levels of the criminal justice system. Learn more about the case of *Mapp* v. *Ohio* at **Library Extra 5–2**.

Searches Incident to Arrest

Another important Warren-era case, that of *Chimel* v. *California* (1969),[19] involved both arrest and search activities by local law enforcement officers. Ted Chimel was convicted of the burglary of a coin shop based on evidence gathered at his home, where he was arrested. Officers, armed with an arrest warrant but not a search warrant, took Chimel into custody when they arrived at his residence and then searched his entire three-bedroom house, including the attic, a small workshop, and the garage. Although officers realized that the search might be challenged in court, they justified it by claiming that it was conducted not so much to uncover evidence but as part of the arrest process. Searches that are conducted incident to arrest, they argued, are necessary for the officers' protection and should not require a search warrant. Coins taken from the burglarized coin shop were found in various places in Chimel's residence, including the garage, and were presented as evidence against him at trial.

Chimel's appeal eventually reached the U.S. Supreme Court, which ruled that the search of Chimel's residence, although incident to arrest, became invalid when it went beyond the person arrested and the area subject to that person's "immediate control." The thrust of the Court's decision was that searches during arrest can be made to protect arresting officers but that without a search warrant, their scope must be strongly circumscribed. The legal implications of *Chimel* v. *California* are summarized in Table 5–2.

Since the early days of the exclusionary rule, other court decisions have highlighted the fact that "the Fourth Amendment protects people, not places."[20] In other words, although the commonly heard claim that "a person's home is his or her castle" has a great deal of validity within the context of constitutional law, people can have a reasonable expectation to privacy in "homes" of many descriptions. Apartments, duplex dwellings, motel rooms—even the cardboard boxes or makeshift tents of the homeless—can all become protected places under the Fourth Amendment. In *Minnesota* v. *Olson* (1990),[21] for example, the U.S. Supreme Court extended the protection against warrantless searches to overnight guests residing in the home of another. The capacity to claim the protection of the Fourth Amendment, said the Court, depends on whether the *person* who makes that claim has a legitimate expectation of privacy in the place searched.

fruit of the poisonous tree doctrine
A legal principle that excludes from introduction at trial any evidence later developed as a result of an illegal search or seizure.

Lecture Note Discuss the way in which *Chimel* v. *California* (1969) defined *what* officers may search, *when* they may search, and *why* they may search. Ask students why such directives are necessary and how they help individual suspects but may hinder police activity. How else might search parameters be defined?

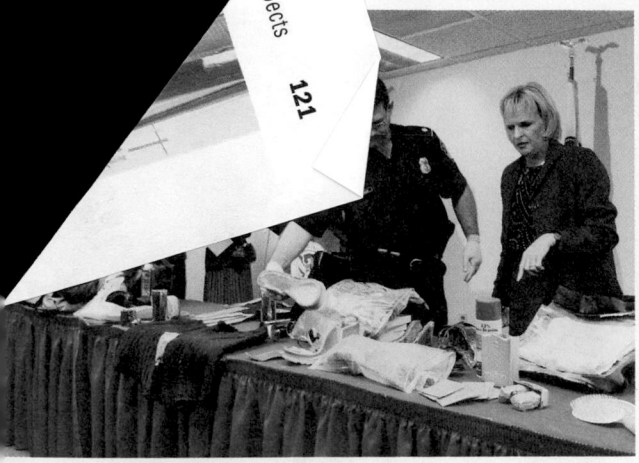

▲ Police officers examining suspected controlled substances after a raid. The exclusionary rule means that illegally gathered evidence cannot be used later in court, requiring that police officers pay close attention to how they gather and handle evidence. How did the exclusionary rule come into being?
Chris O'Meara/AP Wide World Photos

TABLE 5–2
Implications of *Chimel* v. *California* (1969)

What Arresting Officers May Search
The defendant
The physical area within easy reach of the defendant
Valid Reasons for Conducting a Search
To protect the arresting officers
To prevent evidence from being destroyed
To keep the defendant from escaping
When a Search Becomes Illegal
When it goes beyond the defendant and the area within the defendant's immediate control
When it is conducted for other than a valid reason

Lecture Note Ask the class to list each of the Supreme Court decisions discussed in this chapter. Have students group the decisions according to the Court that rendered them (the Warren Court, the Rehnquist Court, etc.). Have class members score each decision from 0 to 10, indicating whether it would likely appeal more to individual-rights advocates (0) or public-order advocates (10). Where does each Court fall along the rights-order continuum?

Lecture Note Describe the notion of good faith and good-faith exceptions to the exclusionary rule. Ask students what they think the ultimate impact of good-faith exceptions will be on American criminal justice and whether they think the Court should ever have created the good-faith exception.

In 1998, in the case of *Minnesota* v. *Carter*,[22] the Court held that for a defendant to be entitled to Fourth Amendment protection, "he must demonstrate that he personally has an expectation of privacy in the place searched, and that his expectation is reasonable." The Court noted that "the extent to which the Amendment protects people may depend upon where those people are. While an overnight guest may have a legitimate expectation of privacy in someone else's home . . . one who is merely present with the consent of the householder may not." Hence an appliance repair person visiting a residence is unlikely to be accorded privacy protection while on the job.

In 2006, in the case of *Georgia* v. *Randolph*,[23] the Court ruled that police officers may not enter a home to conduct a warrrantless search if one resident gives permission but the other says no. The *Randolph* ruling was a narrow one and centered on the stated refusal by a physically present co-occupant to permit warrantless entry in the absence of evidence of physical abuse or other circumstances that might otherwise justify an immediate police entry.[24]

The Burger Court (1969–1986) and the Rehnquist Court (1986–2005)

During the 1980s and 1990s, the United States experienced a swing toward conservatism, giving rise to a renewed concern with protecting the interests—financial and otherwise—of those who live within the law. The Reagan–Bush years, and the popularity of the two presidents who many thought embodied "old-fashioned" values, reflected the tenor of a nation seeking a return to "simpler," less volatile times.

Throughout the late 1980s, the U.S. Supreme Court mirrored the nation's conservative tenor by distancing itself from some earlier decisions of the Warren Court. While the Warren Court embodied the individual-rights heyday in Court jurisprudence, Court decisions beginning in the 1970s were generally supportive of a "greater good era"—one in which the justices increasingly acknowledged the importance of social order and communal safety. Under Chief Justice Warren E. Burger, the new Court adhered to the principle that criminal defendants who claimed violations of their due process rights needed to bear most of the responsibility of showing that police went beyond the law in the performance of their duties. This tenet is still held by the Court today.

Good-Faith Exceptions to the Exclusionary Rule

good-faith exception
An exception to the exclusionary rule. Law enforcement officers who conduct a search or who seize evidence on the basis of good faith (that is, when they believe they are operating according to the dictates of the law) and who later discover that a mistake was made (perhaps in the format of the application for a search warrant) may still use the seized evidence in court.

The Burger Court, which held sway from 1969 until 1986, "chipped away" at the strict application of the exclusionary rule originally set forth in the *Weeks* and *Silverthorne* cases. In the 1984 case of *U.S.* v. *Leon*,[25] the Court recognized what has come to be called the **good-faith exception** to the exclusionary rule. In this case, the Court modified the exclusionary rule to allow evidence that officers had seized in "reasonable good faith" to be used in court, even though the search was later ruled illegal. The suspect, Alberto Leon, was placed under surveillance for drug trafficking following a tip from a confidential informant. Burbank (California) Police Department investigators applied for a search warrant based on information gleaned from the surveillance, believing they were in compliance with the Fourth Amendment requirement that "no Warrants shall issue, but upon probable cause."

Probable cause is a tricky but important concept. Its legal criteria are based on facts and circumstances that would cause a reasonable person to believe that a particular other person has committed a specific crime. Before a warrant can be issued, police officers must satisfactorily demonstrate probable cause in a written affidavit to a magistrate[26]—a low-level judge who ensures that the police establish the probable cause needed for warrants to be obtained. Upon a demonstration of probable cause, the magistrate will issue a warrant authorizing law enforcement officers to effect an arrest or conduct a search.

probable cause
A set of facts and circumstances that would induce a reasonably intelligent and prudent person to believe that a particular other person has committed a specific crime. Also, reasonable grounds to make or believe an accusation. Probable cause refers to the necessary level of belief that would allow for police seizures (arrests) of individuals and full searches of dwellings, vehicles, and possessions.

In *U.S.* v. *Leon*, a warrant was issued, and a search of Leon's three residences yielded a large amount of drugs and other evidence. Although Leon was convicted of drug trafficking, a later ruling in a federal district court resulted in the suppression of evidence against him on the basis that the original affidavit prepared by the police had not, in the opinion of the reviewing court, been sufficient to establish probable cause.

The federal government petitioned the U.S. Supreme Court to consider whether evidence gathered by officers acting in good faith as to the validity of a warrant should fairly be excluded at trial. The impending modification of the exclusionary rule was presaged in the first paragraph of the Court's written decision: "When law enforcement officers have acted in objective good faith or their transgressions have been minor, the magnitude of the benefit conferred on . . . guilty defendants offends basic concepts of the criminal justice system." Reflecting the renewed conservatism of the Burger Court, the justices found for the government and reinstated Leon's conviction.

Thematic Question Given the advent of good-faith exceptions to the exclusionary rule, the plain-view doctrine, and the U.S. Supreme Court's recognition of the need for emergency searches, can we realistically argue that the exclusionary rule is still effective in contemporary American criminal justice? Has the exclusionary rule been so watered down by more recent decisions as to be little more than a paper tiger? Defend your position.

In that same year, the Supreme Court case of *Massachusetts* v. *Sheppard* (1984)[27] further reinforced the concept of good faith. In the *Sheppard* case, officers executed a search warrant that failed to describe accurately the property to be seized. Although they were aware of the error, a magistrate had assured them that the warrant was valid. After the seizure was complete and a conviction had been obtained, the Massachusetts Supreme Judicial Court reversed the finding of the trial court. Upon appeal, the U.S. Supreme Court reiterated the good-faith exception and reinstated the original conviction.

Thematic Question In your opinion, should the U.S. Supreme Court have created exceptions to the exclusionary rule? To *Miranda*? Why or why not?

The cases of *Leon* and *Sheppard* represented a clear reversal of the Warren Court's philosophy, and the trend continued with the 1987 case of *Illinois* v. *Krull*.[28] In *Krull*, the Court, now under the leadership of Chief Justice William H. Rehnquist, held that the good-faith exception applied to a warrantless search supported by state law even though the state statute was later found to violate the Fourth Amendment. Similarly, another 1987 Supreme Court case, *Maryland* v. *Garrison*,[29] supported the use of evidence obtained with a search warrant that was inaccurate in its specifics. In *Garrison*, officers had procured a warrant to search an apartment, believing it was the only dwelling on the building's third floor. After searching the entire floor, they discovered that it housed more than one apartment. Even so, evidence acquired in the search was held to be admissible based on the reasonable mistake of the officers.

The 1990 case of *Illinois* v. *Rodriguez*[30] further diminished the scope of the exclusionary rule. In *Rodriguez*, a badly beaten woman named Gail Fischer complained to police that she had been assaulted in a Chicago apartment. Fischer led police to the apartment—which she indicated she shared with the defendant—produced a key, and opened the door to the dwelling. Inside, investigators found the defendant, Edward Rodriguez, asleep on a bed, with drug paraphernalia and cocaine spread around him. Rodriguez was arrested and charged with assault and possession of a controlled substance.

Before a warrant can be issued, police officers must demonstrate probable cause.

Upon appeal, Rodriguez demonstrated that Fischer had not lived with him for at least a month and argued that she could no longer be said to have legal control over the apartment. Hence, the defense claimed, Fischer had no authority to provide investigators with access to the dwelling. According to arguments made by the defense, the evidence, which had been obtained without a warrant, had not been properly seized. The Supreme Court disagreed, ruling that "even if Fischer did not possess common authority over the premises, there was no Fourth Amendment violation if the police *reasonably believed* at the time of their entry that Fischer possessed the authority to consent."

> The touchstone of the Fourth Amendment is reasonableness. The Fourth Amendment does not proscribe all state-initiated searches and seizures. It merely proscribes those which are unreasonable.
>
> —*Florida* v. *Jimeno* (1991)

In 1995, in the case of *Arizona* v. *Evans*,[31] the U.S. Supreme Court created a "computer errors exception" to the exclusionary rule, holding that a traffic stop that led to the seizure of marijuana was legal even though officers conducted the stop based on an arrest warrant that should have been deleted from the computer database to which they had access. The arrest warrant reported to the officers by their computer had actually been quashed a few weeks earlier but, through the oversight of a court employee, had never been removed from the database.

In reaching its decision, the high court reasoned that police officers could not be held responsible for a clerical error made by a court worker and concluded that the arresting officers had acted in good faith based on the information available to them at the time of the arrest. In addition, the majority opinion said that "the rule excluding evidence obtained without a warrant was intended to deter police misconduct, not mistakes by court employees." In 2009, in the case of *Herring* v. *U.S.*,[32] the Court reinforced its ruling in *Evans*, holding that "when police mistakes leading to an unlawful search are the result of isolated negligence . . . rather than systemic error or reckless disregard of constitutional requirements, the exclusionary rule does not apply." A general listing of established exceptions to the exclusionary rule, along with other investigative powers created by court precedent, is provided in Table 5–3.

Lecture Note Describe the plain-view doctrine. Ask students what they think the ultimate impact of the plain-view doctrine will be on American criminal justice and whether they think the Court should ever have created the plain-view doctrine. Ask how hard this doctrine might be for police officers to keep in mind in their daily work.

During Rehnquist's tenure as chief justice, the Court invoked a characteristically conservative approach to many important criminal justice issues—from limiting the exclusionary rule[33] and generally broadening police powers to sharply limiting the opportunities for state prisoners to bring appeals in federal courts.[34] Preventive detention, "no knock" police searches,[35] the death penalty,[36] and habitual offender statutes[37] (often known as *three-strikes laws*) all found decisive support under Chief Justice Rehnquist.[38] The particular cases in which the Court addressed these issues are discussed elsewhere in this text.

Following Rehnquist's death in 2005, John G. Roberts, Jr., became the nation's seventeenth chief justice. Roberts had previously served as a judge on the U.S. Court of Appeals for the District of Columbia Circuit.

The Plain-View Doctrine

plain view
A legal term describing the ready visibility of objects that might be seized as evidence during a search by police in the absence of a search warrant specifying the seizure of those objects. To lawfully seize evidence in plain view, officers must have a legal right to be in the viewing area and must have cause to believe that the evidence is somehow associated with criminal activity.

Police officers have the opportunity to begin investigations or to confiscate evidence, without a warrant, based on what they find in **plain view** and open to public inspection. The plain-view doctrine was succinctly stated in the U.S. Supreme Court case of *Harris* v. *U.S.* (1968),[39] in which a police officer inventorying an impounded vehicle discovered evidence of a robbery.[40] In the *Harris* case, the Court ruled that "objects falling in the plain view of an officer who has a right to be in the position to have that view are subject to seizure and may be introduced in evidence."[41]

The plain-view doctrine is applicable in common situations such as crimes in progress, fires, accidents, and other emergencies. A police officer responding to a call for assistance, for example, might enter a residence intending to provide aid to an injured person and find drugs or other contraband in plain view. If so, the officer would be within his or her legitimate authority to confiscate the materials and to effect an arrest if the owner can be identified.

The plain-view doctrine applies only to sightings by the police under legal circumstances—that is, in places where the police have a legitimate right to be and, typically, only if the sighting was coincidental. Similarly, the incriminating nature of the evidence seized must have been "immediately apparent" to the officers making the seizure.[42] If officers conspired to avoid the necessity for a search warrant by helping to create a plain-view situation through surveillance, duplicity, or other means, the doctrine likely would not apply.

The plain-view doctrine was restricted by later federal court decisions. In the 1982 case of *U.S.* v. *Irizarry*,[43] the First Circuit Court of Appeals held that officers could not move objects to gain a view of evidence otherwise hidden from view. In the Supreme Court case of *Arizona* v. *Hicks* (1987),[44] the requirement that evidence be in plain view, without requiring officers (who did not have a warrant but who had been invited into a residence) to move or dislodge objects, was reiterated.

TABLE 5–3
Selected Investigative Activities Supported by Court Precedent

This Police Power	Is Supported By
Arrest based on isolated clerical error or negligence	*Herring* v. *U.S.* (2009) *Arizona* v. *Evans* (1995)
Authority to enter and/or search an "open field" without a warrant	*U.S.* v. *Dunn* (1987) *Oliver* v. *U.S.* (1984) *Hester* v. *U.S.* (1924)
Authority to search incident to arrest and/or to conduct a protective sweep in conjunction with an in-home arrest	*Maryland* v. *Buie* (1990) *U.S.* v. *Edwards* (1974) *Chimel* v. *California* (1969)
Gathering of incriminating evidence during interrogation in noncustodial circumstances	*Yarborough* v. *Alvarado* (2004) *Thompson* v. *Keohane* (1996) *Stansbury* v. *California* (1994) *U.S.* v. *Mendenhall* (1980) *Beckwith* v. *U.S.* (1976)
Gathering of incriminating evidence during *Miranda*-less custodial interrogation	*Montejo* v. *Louisiana* (2009) *U.S.* v. *Patane* (2004)
Inevitable discovery of evidence	*Nix* v. *Williams* (1984)
"No knock" searches or quick entry	*Brigham City* v. *Stuart* (2006) *Hudson* v. *Michigan* (2006) *U.S.* v. *Barnes* (2003) *Richards* v. *Wisconsin* (1997) *Wilson* v. *Arkansas* (1995)
Prompt action in the face of threat to public or personal safety or destruction of evidence	*U.S.* v. *Banks* (2003) *Borchardt* v. *U.S.* (1987) *New York* v. *Quarles* (1984) *Warden* v. *Hayden* (1967)
Seizure of evidence in good faith, even in the face of some exclusionary rule violations	*Illinois* v. *Krull* (1987) *U.S.* v. *Leon* (1984)
Seizure of evidence in plain view	*Horton* v. *California* (1990) *Coolidge* v. *New Hampshire* (1971) *Harris* v. *U.S.* (1968)
Stop and frisk/request personal identification	*Arizona* v. *Johnson* (2009) *Hiibel* v. *Sixth Judicial District Court of Nevada* (2004) *Terry* v. *Ohio* (1968)
Use of police informants in jail cells	*Arizona* v. *Fulminante* (1991) *Illinois* v. *Perkins* (1990) *Kuhlmann* v. *Wilson* (1986)
Warrantless naked-eye aerial observation of open areas and/or greenhouses	*Florida* v. *Riley* (1989) *California* v. *Ciraolo* (1986)
Warrantless search incident to a lawful arrest	*U.S.* v. *Rabinowitz* (1950)
Warrantless seizure of abandoned materials and refuse	*California* v. *Greenwood* (1988)
Warrantless vehicle search where probable cause exists to believe that the vehicle contains contraband and/or that the occupants have been lawfully arrested	*Thornton* v. *U.S.* (2004) *Ornelas* v. *U.S.* (1996) *California* v. *Acevedo* (1991) *California* v. *Carney* (1985) *U.S.* v. *Ross* (1982) *New York* v. *Belton* (1981) *Carroll* v. *U.S.* (1925)

CJ Exhibit 5–1
Plain-View Requirements

Following the opinion of the U.S. Supreme Court in the case of *Horton* v. *California* (1990), items seized under the plain-view doctrine may be admissible as evidence in a court of law if *both* of the following conditions are met:

1. The officer who seized the evidence was in the viewing area lawfully.
2. The officer had probable cause to believe that the evidence was somehow associated with criminal activity.

Emergencies may justify a police officer's decision to search or enter premises without a warrant.

Most evidence seized under the plain-view doctrine is discovered "inadvertently"—that is, by accident.[45] However, in 1990, the U.S. Supreme Court ruled in the case of *Horton* v. *California*[46] that "even though inadvertence *is* a characteristic of most legitimate 'plain view' seizures, it is not a necessary condition."[47] In the *Horton* case, a warrant was issued authorizing the search of Terry Brice Horton's home for stolen jewelry. The affidavit, completed by the officer who requested the warrant, alluded to an Uzi submachine gun and a stun gun—weapons purportedly used in the jewelry robbery. It did not request that those weapons be listed on the search warrant. Officers searched the defendant's home but did not find the stolen jewelry. They did, however, seize a number of weapons, among them an Uzi, two stun guns, and a .38-caliber revolver. Horton was convicted of robbery in a trial in which the seized weapons were introduced into evidence. He appealed his conviction, claiming that officers had reason to believe that the weapons were in his home at the time of the search, so they were not seized inadvertently. His appeal was rejected by the Court. As a result of the *Horton* case, inadvertence is no longer considered a condition necessary to ensure the legitimacy of a seizure that results when evidence other than that listed in a search warrant is discovered. See CJ Exhibit 5–1 for more on evidence and the plain-view doctrine.

Emergency Searches of Property and Emergency Entry

Certain emergencies may justify a police officer's decision to search or enter premises without a warrant. In 2006, for example, in the case of *Brigham City* v. *Stuart*,[48] the Court recognized the need for emergency warrantless entries under certain circumstances when it ruled that police officers "may enter a home without a warrant when they have an objectively reasonable basis for believing that an occupant is seriously injured or imminently threatened with such injury." The case involved police entry into a private home to break up a fight.

According to the Legal Counsel Division of the Federal Bureau of Investigation (FBI), there are three threats that "provide justification for emergency warrantless action."[49] They are clear dangers (1) to life, (2) of escape, and (3) of the removal or destruction of evidence. Any one of these situations may create an exception to the Fourth Amendment's requirement of a search warrant.

emergency search
A search conducted by the police without a warrant, which is justified on the basis of some immediate and overriding need, such as public safety, the likely escape of a dangerous suspect, or the removal or destruction of evidence.

Emergency searches, or those conducted without a warrant when special needs arise, are legally termed *exigent circumstances searches*. When emergencies necessitate a quick search of premises, however, law enforcement officers are responsible for demonstrating that a dire situation existed that justified their actions. Failure to do so successfully in court will, of course, taint any seized evidence and make it unusable.

The U.S. Supreme Court first recognized the need for emergency searches in 1967 in the case of *Warden* v. *Hayden*.[50] In that case, the Court approved the warrantless search of a residence following reports that an armed robber had fled into the building. In *Mincey* v. *Arizona* (1978),[51] the Supreme Court held that "the Fourth Amendment does not require police officers to delay in the course of an investigation if to do so would gravely endanger their lives or the lives of others."[52]

A 1990 decision, rendered in the case of *Maryland* v. *Buie*,[53] extended the authority of police to search locations in a house where a potentially dangerous person could hide while an arrest warrant is being served. The *Buie* decision was meant primarily to protect investigators from potential danger and can apply even when officers lack a warrant, probable cause, or even reasonable suspicion.

In 1995, in the case of *Wilson* v. *Arkansas*,[54] the U.S. Supreme Court ruled that police officers generally must knock and announce their identity before entering a dwelling or other premises, even when armed with a search warrant. Under certain emergency circumstances, however, exceptions may be made, and officers may not need to knock or to identify themselves before entering.[55] In *Wilson*, the Court added that the Fourth Amendment requirement that searches be reasonable "should not be read to mandate a rigid rule of announcement that ignores countervailing law enforcement interests." Officers need not announce themselves, the Court said, when suspects may be in the process of destroying evidence, officers are pursuing a recently escaped arrestee, or officers' lives may be endangered by such an announcement. Because the *Wilson* case involved an appeal from a drug dealer who was apprehended by police officers who entered her unlocked house while she was flushing marijuana down a toilet, some said that it establishes a "drug-law exception" to the knock-and-announce requirement.

In 1997, in *Richards* v. *Wisconsin*,[56] the Supreme Court clarified its position on "no knock" exceptions, saying that individual courts have the duty in each case to "determine whether the facts and circumstances of the particular entry justified dispensing with the requirement." The Court went on to say that "[a] 'no knock' entry is justified when the police have a reasonable suspicion that knocking and announcing their presence, under the particular circumstances, would be dangerous or futile, or that it would inhibit the effective investigation of the crime." The Court noted, "This standard strikes the appropriate balance between the legitimate law enforcement concerns at issue in the execution of search warrants and the individual privacy interests affected by no knock entries."

▲ Latasha Smith, who was arrested for failing to appear in court for a previous misdemeanor violation. Although the concept of plain view is difficult to define, Smith provides a personal example of the concept. After Dallas narcotics officers searched the house behind her for crack cocaine, they turned their attention to Smith and discovered the outstanding charges. How would you explain the concept of plain view? *AP Wide World Photos*

In 2001, in the case of *Illinois* v. *McArthur*,[57] the U.S. Supreme Court ruled that police officers with probable cause to believe that a home contains contraband or evidence of criminal activity may reasonably prevent a suspect found outside the home from reentering it while they apply for a search warrant. In 2003, in a case involving drug possession, the Court held that a 15- to 20-second wait after officers knocked, announced themselves, and requested entry was sufficient to satisfy Fourth Amendment requirements.[58]

In the 2006 case of *Hudson* v. *Michigan*,[59] the Court surprised many when it ruled that evidence found by police officers who enter a home to execute a warrant without first following the knock-and-announce requirement can be used at trial despite that constitutional violation. In the words of the Court, "The interests protected by the knock-and-announce rule include human life and limb (because an unannounced entry may provoke violence from a surprised resident), property (because citizens presumably would open the door upon an announcement, whereas a forcible entry may destroy it), and privacy and dignity of the sort that can be offended by a sudden entrance." But, said the Court, "the rule has never protected one's interest in preventing the government from seeing or taking evidence described in a warrant." The justices reasoned that the social costs of strictly adhering to the knock-and-announce rule are considerable and may include "the grave adverse consequence that excluding relevant incriminating evidence always entails—the risk of releasing dangerous criminals." In a ruling that some said signaled a new era of lessened restraints on the police, the Court's majority opinion said that since the interests violated by ignoring the knock-and-announce rule "have nothing to do with the seizure of the evidence, the exclusionary rule is inapplicable."

Anticipatory Warrants

Anticipatory warrants are search warrants issued on the basis of probable cause to believe that evidence of a crime, while not currently at the place described, will likely be there when the warrant is executed. Such warrants anticipate the presence of contraband or other evidence of criminal culpability but do not claim that the evidence is present at the time that the warrant is requested or issued.

anticipatory warrant
A search warrant issued on the basis of probable cause to believe that evidence of a crime, while not currently at the place described, will likely be there when the warrant is executed.

Anticipatory warrants are no different in principle from ordinary search warrants. They require an issuing magistrate to determine that it is probable that contraband, evidence of a crime, or a fugitive will be on the described premises when the warrant is executed.

Career Profile
Patrol Officer

Name: Timothy D. Radtke

Position: Patrol Officer, San Diego, California

Colleges attended: Winona State University (BS); University of Nevada, Las Vegas (MA)

Major: Criminal justice

Year hired: 2008

Please give a brief description of your job. Within a specified area of the city, I respond to radio calls for police service and perform self-initiated activities such as traffic stops and citizen contacts.

What appealed to you most about the position when you applied for it? While pursuing my degrees, I worked closely with two police departments. The officers there inspired me to commit my life to a cause greater than myself—protecting communities. I was eager to put the knowledge I obtained through my education to practical use, to work closely with the community and apply the community-oriented policing and problem-oriented policing strategies I learned during my academic studies.

How would you describe the interview process? The testing process was strenuous. There were eight different tests: written test, preinvestigation questionnaire, physical ability test, comprehensive background investigation, polygraph, appointing authority interview, psychological screening, and medical exam. The most challenging was the appointing authority interview, which was conducted by a lieutenant and a sergeant. They asked questions about my background and what I had done to prepare to serve as a police officer. I was asked to respond to a series of scenarios that police officers often encounter in the field. This process helped them determine whether I could quickly find a logical and appropriate response when presented with an unexpected or stressful situation.

What is a typical day like? Patrol officers begin with "lineup," in which they are briefed about recent crimes and events and assigned to the specific patrol beat they will work throughout their shift. Patrol officers must be prepared to handle the unexpected. One day they may respond to a domestic disturbance, the next help to establish a DUI checkpoint to deter drunk drivers, and the next be asked to locate warrant suspects.

What qualities/characteristics are most helpful for this job? A successful officer must know how to speak with people. The people they interact with daily often need immediate help or have difficulty controlling their emotions. An officer may be faced with an individual who is attempting suicide or an individual who is angry and showing signs of assaultive behavior, or [the officer may be] called upon to interview a child who has suffered abuse. The ability to speak tactfully and quickly build rapport with others is crucial.

What is a typical starting salary? Between $40,000 and $50,000.

What is the salary potential as you move up into higher-level jobs? An officer's salary will increase after graduating from the academy and when promoted within the department. Those with a BA or MA will also receive percentage increases in pay.

What career advice would you give someone in college beginning studies in criminal justice? Classroom instruction in college will help students understand the basics of police work and give them the skills to interpret and appropriately apply laws. It will also increase students' problem-solving and critical thinking skills, which are necessary for finding solutions to the complex problems officers encounter daily.

Source: Reprinted with permission of Timothy D. Radtke. Photo courtesy of Timothy D. Radtke. Logo courtesy University of Nevada at Las Vegas.

The constitutionality of anticipatory warrants was affirmed in 2006, in the U.S. Supreme Court case of *U.S.* v. *Grubbs*. In *Grubbs*,[60] an anticipatory search warrant had been issued for Grubbs's house based on a federal officer's affidavit stating that the warrant would not be executed until a parcel containing a videotape of child pornography—which Grubbs had ordered from an undercover postal inspector—was received at and physically taken into Grubbs's residence. After the package was delivered, the anticipatory search warrant was executed, the videotape seized, and Grubbs arrested.

Arrest

arrest
The act of taking an adult or juvenile into physical custody by authority of law for the purpose of charging the person with a criminal offense, a delinquent act, or a status offense, terminating with the recording of a specific offense. Technically, an arrest occurs whenever a law enforcement officer curtails a person's freedom to leave.

4 Define *arrest*, and describe how popular depictions of the arrest process may not be consistent with legal understandings of the term.

Officers seize not only property but people as well, a process referred to as *arrest*. Most people think of arrest in terms of what they see on popular TV crime shows: The suspect is chased, subdued, and "cuffed" after committing some loathsome act in view of the camera. Some arrests do occur that way. In reality, however, most arrests are far more mundane.

In technical terms, an **arrest** occurs whenever a law enforcement officer restricts a person's freedom to leave. The officer may not yell, "You're under arrest!" No *Miranda* warnings may be offered, and in fact, the suspect may not even consider himself or herself to be in custody. Arrests, and the decisions to enforce them, evolve as the situations between officers and suspects develop. A situation usually begins with polite conversation and a request by the officer for information. Only when the suspect tries to leave and tests the limits of the police response may the suspect discover that he or she is really in custody. In the 1980 case of *U.S.* v. *Mendenhall*,[61] Justice Potter Stewart set forth the "free to leave" test for determining whether a person has been arrested. Stewart wrote, "A person has been 'seized' within the meaning of the Fourth Amendment only if in view of all the circumstances surrounding the incident, a reasonable person would have believed that he was not free to leave." The "free to leave" test has been repeatedly adopted by the Court as the test for a seizure. In 1994, in the case of *Stansbury* v. *California*,[62] the Court once again used such a test in determining the point at which an arrest had been made. In *Stansbury*, where the focus was on the interrogation of a suspected child molester and murderer, the Court ruled, "In determining whether an individual was in custody, a court must examine all of the circumstances surrounding the interrogation, but the ultimate inquiry is simply whether there [was] a formal arrest or restraint on freedom of movement of the degree associated with a formal arrest."

Youth and inexperience do not automatically undermine a reasonable person's ability to assess when someone is free to leave. In the 2004 case of *Yarborough* v. *Alvarado*,[63] the U.S. Supreme Court found that a 17-year-old boy's two-hour interrogation in a police station without a *Miranda* advisement was not custodial, even though the boy confessed to his involvement in a murder and was later arrested. The boy, said the Court, had not actually been in police custody even though he was in a building used by the police for questioning, because actions taken by the interviewing officer indicated that the juvenile had been free to leave. Whether a person is actually free to leave, said the Court, can only be determined by examining the totality of the circumstances surrounding the interrogation.[64]

The 2005 U.S. Supreme Court case of *Muehler* v. *Mena*[65] made clear that an officer's authority to detain occupants of a dwelling incident to the execution of a valid search warrant is absolute and unqualified and does not require any justification beyond the warrant itself—even when the occupants are not suspected of any wrongdoing. In other words, officers who are conducting a lawful search under the authority of a warrant may detain individuals found occupying the premises being searched in order to prevent flights in the event incriminating evidence is found, to minimize the risk of harm to the officers, and simply to facilitate the search itself.[66]

You can only protect your liberties in this world by protecting the other man's freedom.

—Clarence Darrow (1857–1938)

Arrests that follow the questioning of a suspect are probably the most common type of arrest. When the decision to arrest is reached, the officer has come to the conclusion that a crime has been committed and that the suspect is probably the one who committed it. The presence of these elements constitutes the probable cause needed for an arrest. Probable cause is the minimum standard necessary for an arrest under any circumstances.

Arrests may also occur when an officer comes upon a crime in progress. Such situations often require apprehension of the offender to ensure the safety of the public. Most arrests made during crimes in progress, however, are for misdemeanors rather than felonies. In fact, many states do not allow arrest for a misdemeanor unless it is committed in the presence of an officer, since visible crimes in progress clearly provide the probable cause necessary for an arrest. In 2001, in a case that made headlines nationwide,[67] the U.S. Supreme Court upheld a warrantless arrest made by Lago Vista (Texas) Patrolman Bart Turek for a seat belt violation. In what many saw as an unreasonable exercise of discretion, Turek stopped and then arrested Gail Atwater, a young local woman whom he observed driving a pickup truck in which she and her two small children (ages three and five) were unbelted. Facts in the case showed that Turek verbally berated the woman after stopping her vehicle and that he handcuffed her, placed her in his squad car, and drove her to the local police station, where she was made to remove her shoes, jewelry, and eyeglasses and empty her pockets. Officers took her "mug shot" and placed her alone in a jail cell for about an hour, after which she was taken before a magistrate and released on $310 bond. Atwater was charged with a misdemeanor violation of Texas seat belt law. She later pleaded no contest and paid a $50 fine. Soon afterward, she and her husband filed a Section 1983 lawsuit against the officer, his department, and the police chief, alleging that the actions of the officer violated Atwater's Fourth Amendment right to be free from unreasonable seizures. The Court, however, concluded that "the Fourth Amendment does not forbid a warrantless arrest for a minor criminal offense, such as a misdemeanor seatbelt violation punishable only by a fine."

CJ News
Legal Issues Being Raised in Subway Searches

Even more than security experts and intelligence analysts, one group of employees has become central to the new program of bag searches in the transit networks of the New York region: lawyers.

The decision in July 2005 to have police officers inspect the belongings of thousands of subway riders has opened a thicket of legal and constitutional issues, involving criminal procedure, transit security and concerns about potential misuse of the new tactic.

Donna Lieberman, the executive director of the New York Civil Liberties Union, said the organization had begun work on a federal lawsuit, which could be filed soon. Such a challenge will most likely claim that the policy violates the Fourth Amendment's prohibition against "unreasonable searches and seizures.". . .

"It is by no means a foregone conclusion that these searches will be found reasonable under the Fourth Amendment," said Tracey Maclin, a law professor at Boston University. "The number of people involved, the nature and severity of the intrusions, and the uncertain duration of the searches all make this fundamentally very different from anything we have seen before."

At least three United States Supreme Court cases will probably influence any judge assessing the searches.

In 1979, in *Delaware* v. *Prouse*, the court held that random traffic stops, left to the discretion of police officers, were unconstitutional. In 1990, in *Michigan* v. *Sitz*, the court upheld the legality of sobriety checkpoints in which a consistent proportion of drivers was stopped. The court ruled that such roadblocks were permitted as a way to prevent drunken driving. . . .

In 2000, in *Indianapolis* v. *Edmond*, it struck down the use of traffic checkpoints to stop drivers so that trained dogs could sniff the vehicles for narcotics. Unlike checkpoints to make sure that drivers were sober or had valid licenses and registrations, the court said, roadblocks for general law enforcement were unconstitutional.

David D. Cole, a law professor at Georgetown University, said the government was likely to succeed in demonstrating a special need for the current searches in New York.

A judge evaluating a legal challenge, he said, would probably look at three factors: whether the searches are truly random or use standardized criteria; whether riders were given advance notice or provided their consent to the searches; and the degree of intrusiveness. . . .

According to a two-page directive sent to all police commanders . . . the searches were begun "to increase deterrence and detection of potential terrorist activity and to give greater protection to the mass transit-riding public.". . .

The degree of intrusiveness could become a thorny issue. The directive provides that officers may open a package and "physically inspect and manipulate the contents to ensure it does not contain an explosive device." Leaving aside the issue of illegal drugs or weapons, some riders have already voiced misgivings about having the police examine sensitive possessions, like medications and personal hygiene products. . . .

▲ A police officer checking the bag of a subway rider at New York City's 42nd Street/Bryant Park station. Should random bag checks be permitted, or do they unfairly impinge on the rights of people wanting to ride the subway?
John Marshall Mantel/AP Wide World Photos

"For a split second, I thought that because of my skin complexion, they picked me," said James Hamilton, 38, whose attaché case was searched at Herald Square. "I'm not sure if I had brown hair and blue eyes, that that would have happened.". . .

Charles Wilson, 35, a schoolteacher whose bag was searched at Fulton Street in Lower Manhattan, said, "This is not going to make things better between the police and people of color.". . .

A police spokesman, Paul J. Browne, said he strongly disagreed. "These inspections are being conducted in a constitutional manner and have been met with enthusiastic cooperation by the overwhelming majority of riders we've come into contact with," he said.

Source: Sewell Chan and Kareem Fahim, "Legal Issues Being Raised on Searches in Subways," *New York Times*, www.nytimes.com, © July 24, 2005, The New York Times. All rights reserved. Used by permission and protected by the Copyright Laws of the United States. The printing, copying, redistribution, or retransmission of the material without express written permission is prohibited.

Most jurisdictions allow arrest for a felony without a warrant when a crime is not in progress, as long as probable cause can be established; some, however, require a warrant. In those jurisdictions, arrest warrants are issued by magistrates when police officers can demonstrate probable cause. Magistrates will usually require that the officers seeking an arrest warrant submit a written affidavit outlining their reason for the arrest. In the case of *Payton* v. *New York* (1980),[68] the U.S. Supreme Court ruled that unless the suspect gives consent or an emergency exists, an arrest warrant is necessary if an arrest requires entry into a suspect's private residence.[69] In *Payton*, the justices held that "[a]bsent exigent circumstances," the "firm line at the entrance to the house . . . may not reasonably be crossed without a warrant." The Court reiterated its *Payton* holding in the 2002 case of *Kirk* v. *Louisiana*.[70] In *Kirk*, which involved an anonymous complaint about drug sales said to be taking place in the apartment of Kennedy Kirk, the justices reaffirmed their belief that "[t]he Fourth Amendment to the United States Constitution has drawn a firm line at the entrance to the home, and thus, the police need both probable cause to either arrest or search and exigent circumstances to justify a nonconsensual warrantless intrusion into private premises."

Searches Incident to Arrest

The U.S. Supreme Court has established a clear rule that police officers have the right to conduct a search of a person being arrested and to search the area under the arrestee's immediate control to protect themselves from attack. This is true even if the officer and the arrestee are of different sexes.

This "rule of the game" regarding **search incident to an arrest** became firmly established in cases involving personal searches, such as the 1973 case of *U.S.* v. *Robinson*.[71] In *Robinson*, the Court upheld an officer's right to conduct a search without a warrant for purposes of personal protection and to use the fruits of the search when it turns up contraband. In the words of the Court, "A custodial arrest of a suspect based upon probable cause is a reasonable intrusion under the Fourth Amendment; that intrusion being lawful, a search incident to the arrest requires no additional jurisdiction."[72]

search incident to an arrest
A warrantless search of an arrested individual conducted to ensure the safety of the arresting officer. Because individuals placed under arrest may be in possession of weapons, courts have recognized the need for arresting officers to protect themselves by conducting an immediate search of arrestees without obtaining a warrant.

The Court's decision in *Robinson* reinforced an earlier ruling in *Terry* v. *Ohio* (1968)[73] involving a seasoned officer who conducted a pat-down search of two men whom he suspected were casing a store, about to commit a robbery. The arresting officer was a 39-year veteran of police work who testified that the men "did not look right." When he approached them, he suspected they might be armed. Fearing for his life, he quickly spun the men around, put them up against a wall, patted down their clothing, and found a gun on one of the men. The man, Terry, was later convicted in Ohio courts of carrying a concealed weapon.

Terry's appeal was based on the argument that the suspicious officer had no probable cause to arrest him and therefore no cause to search him. The search, he argued, was illegal, and the evidence obtained should not have been used against him. The Supreme Court disagreed, saying, "In view of these facts, we cannot blind ourselves to the need for law enforcement officers to protect themselves and other prospective victims of violence in situations where they may lack probable cause for an arrest."

The *Terry* case set the standard for a brief stop and frisk based on reasonable suspicion. Attorneys refer to such brief encounters as *Terry-type stops*. **Reasonable suspicion** can be defined as a belief, based on a consideration of the facts at hand and on reasonable inferences drawn from those facts, that would induce an ordinarily prudent and cautious person under the same circumstances to conclude that criminal activity is taking place or that criminal activity has recently occurred. It is the level of suspicion needed to justify an officer in making further inquiry or in conducting further investigation. Reasonable suspicion, which is a *general* and reasonable belief that a crime is in progress or has occurred, should be differentiated from probable cause. Probable cause, as noted earlier, is a reasonable belief that a *particular* person has committed a *specific* crime. It is important to note that the *Terry* case, for all the authority it conferred on officers, also made it clear that officers must have reasonable grounds for any stop and frisk that they conduct. Read more about the case of *Terry* v. *Ohio* at **Library Extra 5–3**.

reasonable suspicion
The level of suspicion that would justify an officer in making further inquiry or in conducting further investigation. Reasonable suspicion may permit stopping a person for questioning or for a simple pat-down search. Also, a belief, based on a consideration of the facts at hand and on reasonable inferences drawn from those facts, that would induce an ordinarily prudent and cautious person under the same circumstances to conclude that criminal activity is taking place or that criminal activity has recently occurred. Reasonable suspicion is a *general* and reasonable belief that a crime is in progress or has occurred, whereas probable cause is a reasonable belief that a *particular* person has committed a *specific* crime.

In 1989, in the case of *U.S.* v. *Sokolow*,[74] the Supreme Court clarified the basis on which law enforcement officers, lacking probable cause to believe that a crime has occurred, may stop and briefly detain a person for investigative purposes. In *Sokolow*, the Court ruled that the legitimacy of such a stop must be evaluated according to a "totality of circumstances" criterion in which all aspects of the defendant's behavior, taken in concert, may provide the basis for a legitimate stop based on reasonable suspicion. In this case, the defendant, Andrew Sokolow, appeared suspicious to police because while traveling under an alias from Honolulu, he had paid $2,100 in $20 bills (from a large roll of money) for two airplane tickets after spending a surprisingly small amount of time in Miami. In addition, the defendant was

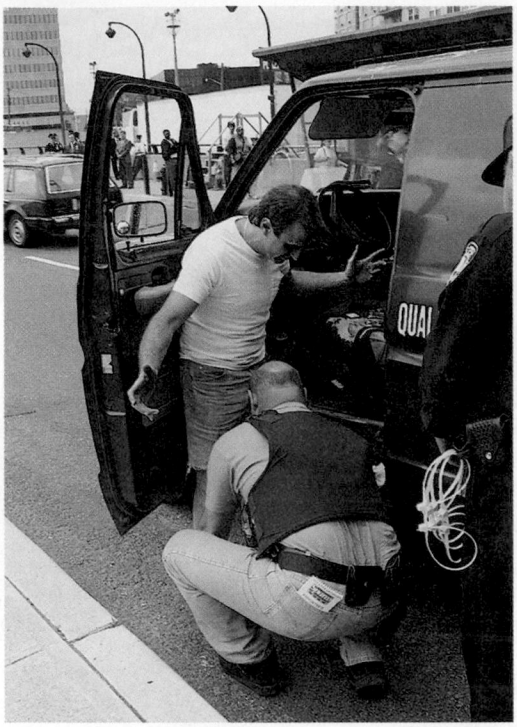

▲ Arresting officers patting down a drug suspect. The courts have generally held that to protect themselves and the public, officers have the authority to search suspects being arrested. What are the limits of such searches?
Craig Filipacchi

obviously nervous and checked no luggage. A warrantless airport investigation by Drug Enforcement Administration (DEA) agents uncovered more than 1,000 grams of cocaine in the defendant's belongings. In upholding Sokolow's conviction, the Court ruled that although no single type of behavior was proof of illegal activity, all his actions together created circumstances under which suspicion of illegal activity was justified.

In 2002, the Court reinforced the *Sokolow* decision in *U.S.* v. *Arvizu* when it ruled that the "balance between the public interest and the individual's right to personal security"[75] "tilts in favor of a standard less than probable cause in brief investigatory stops of persons or vehicles . . . if the officer's action is supported by reasonable suspicion to believe that criminal activity may be afoot."[76] In the words of the Court, "This process allows officers to draw on their own experiences and specialized training to make inferences from and deductions about the cumulative information available."[77]

In 1993, in the case of *Minnesota* v. *Dickerson*,[78] the U.S. Supreme Court placed new limits on an officer's ability to seize evidence discovered during a pat-down search conducted for protective reasons when the search itself was based merely on suspicion and failed to immediately reveal the presence of a weapon. In this case, the high court ruled that "if an officer lawfully pats down a suspect's outer clothing and feels an object whose contour or mass makes its identity immediately apparent, there has been no invasion of the suspect's privacy beyond that already authorized by the officer's search for weapons." However, in *Dickerson*, the justices ruled that "the officer never thought that the lump was a weapon, but did not immediately recognize it as cocaine." The lump was determined to be cocaine only after the officer "squeezed, slid, and otherwise manipulated the pocket's contents." Hence, the Court held, the officer's actions in this case did not qualify under what might be called a "plain feel" exception. In any case, said the Court, the search in *Dickerson* went far beyond what is permissible under *Terry*, where officer safety was the crucial issue. The Court summed up its ruling in *Dickerson* this way: "While *Terry* entitled [the officer] to place his hands on respondent's jacket and to feel the lump in the pocket, his continued exploration of the pocket after he concluded that it contained no weapon was unrelated to the sole justification for the search under *Terry*" and was therefore illegal.

Lecture Note Explain how probable cause, suspicion, and general police procedure are all important in day-to-day police decisions of whom to stop and how to proceed with search and interrogation.

Just as arrest must be based on probable cause, officers may not stop and question an unwilling citizen whom they have no reason to suspect of a crime. In the case of *Brown* v. *Texas* (1979),[79] two Texas law enforcement officers stopped the defendant and asked for identification. Ed Brown, they later testified, had not been acting suspiciously, nor did they think he might have a weapon. The stop was made simply because officers wanted to know who he was. Brown was arrested under a Texas statute that required a person to identify himself properly and accurately when asked to do so by peace officers. Eventually, his appeal reached the U.S. Supreme Court, which ruled that under the circumstances of the *Brown* case, a person "may not be punished for refusing to identify himself."

In the 2004 case of *Hiibel* v. *Sixth Judicial District Court of Nevada*,[80] however, the Court upheld Nevada's "stop and identify" law that requires a person to identify himself or herself to police if they encounter the person under circumstances that reasonably indicate that he or she "has committed, is committing or is about to commit a crime." The *Hiibel* case was an extension of the reasonable suspicion doctrine set forth earlier in *Terry*.

In *Smith* v. *Ohio* (1990),[81] the Court held that an individual has the right to protect his or her belongings from unwarranted police inspection. In *Smith*, the defendant was approached by two officers in plain clothes who observed that he was carrying a brown paper bag. The officers asked him to "come here a minute" and, when he kept walking, identified themselves as police officers. The defendant threw the bag onto the hood of his car and attempted to protect it from the officers' intrusion. Marijuana was found inside the bag, and the defendant was arrested. Since there was little reason to stop the suspect in this case and because control over the bag was not thought necessary for the officers' protection, the Court found that the Fourth Amendment protects both "the traveler who carries a toothbrush and a few articles of clothing in a paper bag" and "the sophisticated executive with the locked attaché case."

The following year, however, in what some Court observers saw as a turnabout, the Court ruled in *California* v. *Hodari D.* (1991)[82] that suspects who flee from the police and throw away evidence as they retreat may later be arrested based on the incriminating nature of the abandoned evidence. The significance of *Hodari* for future police action was highlighted by California prosecutors who pointed out that cases like *Hodari* occur "almost every day in this nation's urban areas."[83]

Police work is the only profession that gives you the test first, then the lesson.
—Anonymous

In 2000, the Court decided the case of William Wardlow.[84] Wardlow had fled upon seeing a caravan of police vehicles converge on an area of Chicago known for narcotics trafficking. Officers caught him, however, and conducted a pat-down search of his clothing for weapons, revealing a handgun. The officers arrested Wardlow on weapons charges, but his lawyer argued that police had acted illegally in stopping him since they did not have reasonable suspicion that he had committed an offense. The Illinois Supreme Court agreed with Wardlow's attorney, holding that "sudden flight in a high crime area does not create a reasonable suspicion justifying a *Terry* stop because flight may simply be an exercise of the right to 'go on one's way.'"[85] The case eventually reached the U.S. Supreme Court, which overturned the Illinois court, finding instead that the officers' actions did not violate the Fourth Amendment. In the words of the Court, "This case, involving a brief encounter between a citizen and a police officer on a public street, is governed by *Terry*, under which an officer who has a reasonable, articulable suspicion that criminal activity is afoot may conduct a brief, investigatory stop. While 'reasonable suspicion' is a less demanding standard than probable cause, there must be at least a minimal level of objective justification for the stop. An individual's presence in a 'high crime area,' standing alone, is not enough to support a reasonable, particularized suspicion of criminal activity, but a location's characteristics are relevant in determining whether the circumstances are sufficiently suspicious to warrant further investigation. . . . In this case, moreover, it was also Wardlow's unprovoked flight that aroused the officers' suspicions. Nervous, evasive behavior is another pertinent factor in determining reasonable suspicion . . . and headlong flight is the consummate act of evasion."[86]

Emergency Searches of Persons

It is easy to imagine emergency situations in which officers may have to search people based on quick decisions: a person who matches the description of an armed robber, a woman who is found unconscious on the floor, a man who has what appears to be blood on his shoes. Such searches can save lives by disarming fleeing felons or by uncovering a medical reason for an emergency situation. They may also prevent criminals from escaping or destroying evidence.

Emergency searches of persons, like those of premises, fall under the exigent circumstances exception to the warrant requirement of the Fourth Amendment. In the 1979 case of *Arkansas* v. *Sanders*,[87] the Supreme Court recognized the need for such searches "where the societal costs of obtaining a warrant, such as danger to law officers or the risk of loss or destruction of evidence, outweigh the reasons for prior recourse to a neutral magistrate."[88]

The 1987 case of *U.S.* v. *Borchardt*,[89] decided by the Fifth Circuit Court of Appeals, held that Ira Eugene Borchardt could be prosecuted for heroin uncovered during medical treatment, even though the defendant had objected to the treatment.

The Legal Counsel Division of the FBI provides the following guidelines for conducting emergency warrantless searches of individuals where the possible destruction of evidence is at issue.[90] (Keep in mind that there may be no probable cause to *arrest* the individual being searched.) All four conditions must apply:

1. There was probable cause at the time of the search to believe that there was evidence concealed on the person searched.
2. There was probable cause to believe an emergency threat of destruction of evidence existed at the time of the search.
3. The officer had no prior opportunity to obtain a warrant authorizing the search.
4. The action was no greater than necessary to eliminate the threat of destruction of evidence.

Lecture Note Discuss the U.S. Supreme Court's rationale for allowing warrantless vehicle searches in cases in which the vehicle might quickly leave the jurisdiction of the investigating officers. Tell the class that because motor vehicles are highly mobile, officers may have the authority to search vehicles they have stopped without a warrant if they have reason to believe that the vehicles may harbor contraband or other evidence.

Vehicle Searches

Vehicles present a special law enforcement problem. They are highly mobile, and when a driver or an occupant is arrested, the need to search the vehicle may be immediate.

The first significant Supreme Court case involving an automobile was that of *Carroll* v. *U.S.*[91] in 1925. In the *Carroll* case, a divided Court ruled that a warrantless search of an automobile or other vehicle is valid if it is based on a reasonable belief that contraband is present. In 1964, however, in the case of *Preston* v. *U.S.*,[92] the limits of warrantless vehicle searches were defined. Preston was arrested for vagrancy and taken to jail. His vehicle was impounded, towed to the police garage, and later searched. Two revolvers were uncovered in the glove compartment, and more incriminating evidence was found in the trunk. Preston was convicted on weapons possession and other charges and eventually appealed to the U.S. Supreme Court. The Court held that the warrantless search of Preston's vehicle had occurred while the automobile was in secure custody and had therefore been illegal. Time and circumstances would have permitted acquisition of a warrant to conduct the search, the Court reasoned. Similarly, in 2009, the Court, in the case of *Arizona* v. *Gant*,[93] found that vehicle searches "incident to a recent occupant's arrest" cannot be authorized without a warrant if there is no possibility the arrestee could gain access to the vehicle at the time of the search."

When the search of a vehicle occurs after it has been impounded, however, that search may be legitimate if it is undertaken for routine and reasonable purposes. In the case of *South Dakota* v. *Opperman* (1976),[94] for example, the Court held that a warrantless search undertaken for purposes of inventorying and safekeeping the personal possessions of the car's owner was not illegal. The intent of the search, which had turned up marijuana, had not been to discover contraband but to secure the owner's belongings from possible theft. Again, in *Colorado* v. *Bertine* (1987),[95] the Court reinforced the idea that officers may open closed containers found in a vehicle while conducting a routine search for inventorying purposes. In the words of the Court, such searches are "now a well-defined exception in the warrant requirement." In 1990, however, in the precedent-setting case of *Florida* v. *Wells*,[96] the Court agreed with a lower court's suppression of marijuana evidence discovered in a locked suitcase in the trunk of a defendant's impounded vehicle. In *Wells*, the Court held that standardized criteria authorizing the search of a vehicle for inventorying purposes were necessary before such a discovery could be legitimate. Standardized criteria, said the Court, might take the form of department policies, written general orders, or established routines.

Generally speaking, where vehicles are concerned, an investigatory stop is permissible under the Fourth Amendment if supported by reasonable suspicion,[97] and a warrantless search of a stopped car is valid if it is based on probable cause.[98] Reasonable suspicion can expand into probable cause when the facts in a given situation so warrant. In the 1996 case of *Ornelas* v. *U.S.*,[99] for example, two experienced Milwaukee police officers stopped a car with California license plates that had been spotted in a motel parking lot known for drug trafficking after the Narcotics and Dangerous Drugs Information System (NADDIS) identified the car's owner as a known or suspected drug trafficker. One of the officers noticed a loose panel above an armrest in the vehicle's backseat and then searched the car. A package of cocaine was found beneath the panel, and the driver and a passenger were arrested. Following conviction, the defendants appealed to the U.S. Supreme Court, claiming that no probable cause to search the car existed at the time of the stop. The majority opinion, however, noted that in the view of the court that originally heard the case, "the model, age, and source-State origin of the car, and the fact that two men traveling together checked into a motel at 4 o'clock in the morning without reservations, formed a drug-courier profile and . . . this profile together with the [computer] reports gave rise to a reasonable suspicion of drug-trafficking activity. . . . [I]n the court's view, reasonable suspicion became probable cause when [the deputy] found the loose panel."[100] Probable cause permits a warrantless search of a vehicle because it is able to quickly leave a jurisdiction. This exception to the exclusionary rule is called the **fleeting-targets exception**.[101]

fleeting-targets exception
An exception to the exclusionary rule that permits law enforcement officers to search a motor vehicle based on probable cause but without a warrant. The fleeting-targets exception is predicated on the fact that vehicles can quickly leave the jurisdiction of a law enforcement agency.

Warrantless vehicle searches can extend to any area of the vehicle and may include sealed containers, the trunk, and the glove compartment if officers have probable cause to conduct a purposeful search or if officers have been given permission to search the vehicle. In the 1991

Freedom or Safety? You Decide.
Religion and Public Safety

In 2003, Florida Judge Janet Thorpe ruled that a Muslim woman could not wear a veil while being photographed for a state driver's license. The woman, Sultaana Freeman, claimed that her religious rights were violated when the state department of motor vehicles required that she reveal her face for the photograph. She offered to show her eyes, but not the rest of her face, to the camera.

Judge Thorpe said, however, that a "compelling interest in protecting the public from criminal activities and security threats" did not place an undue burden on Freeman's ability to practice her religion.

After the hearing, Freeman's husband, Abdul-Maalik Freeman, told reporters, "This is a religious principle; this is a principle that's imbedded in us as believers. So, she's not going to do that. We'll take the next step, and this is what we call the American way." Howard Marks, the Freemans' attorney, said that he would file an appeal in a higher court.

YOU DECIDE

Do the demands of public safety justify the kind of restriction on religious practice described here? Should photo IDs, such as driver's licenses, be replaced with other forms of identification (such as an individual's stored DNA profile) in order to accommodate the beliefs of individuals like the Freemans?

Reference: "Judge: No Veil in Driver's License Photo," Associated Press, June 6, 2003.

case of *Florida* v. *Jimeno*,[102] arresting officers stopped a motorist, who gave them permission to search his car. The defendant was later convicted on a drug charge when a bag on the floor of the car was found to contain cocaine. Upon appeal to the U.S. Supreme Court, however, he argued that the permission given to search his car did not extend to bags and other items within the car. In a decision that may have implications beyond vehicle searches, the Court held that "[a] criminal suspect's Fourth Amendment right to be free from unreasonable searches is not violated when, after he gives police permission to search his car, they open a closed container found within the car that might reasonably hold the object of the search. The amendment is satisfied when, under the circumstances, it is objectively reasonable for the police to believe that the scope of the suspect's consent permitted them to open the particular container."[103]

In *U.S.* v. *Ross* (1982),[104] the Court found that officers had not exceeded their authority in opening a bag in the defendant's trunk that was found to contain heroin. The search was held to be justifiable on the basis of information developed from a search of the passenger compartment. The Court said, "If probable cause justifies the search of a lawfully stopped vehicle, it justifies the search of every part of the vehicle and its contents that may conceal the object of the search."[105] Moreover, according to the 1996 U.S. Supreme Court decision in *Whren* v. *U.S.*,[106] officers may stop a vehicle being driven suspiciously and then search it once probable cause has developed, even if their primary assignment centers on duties other than traffic enforcement or "if a reasonable officer would not have stopped the motorist absent some additional law enforcement objective" (which in the case of *Whren* was drug enforcement).

Motorists[107] and their passengers may be ordered out of stopped vehicles in the interest of officer safety, and any evidence developed as a result of such a procedure may be used in court. In 1997, for example, in the case of *Maryland* v. *Wilson*,[108] the U.S. Supreme Court overturned a decision by a Maryland court that held that crack cocaine found during a traffic stop was seized illegally when it fell from the lap of a passenger ordered out of a stopped vehicle by a Maryland state trooper. The Maryland court reasoned that the police should not have authority to order seemingly innocent passengers out of vehicles—even vehicles that have been stopped for legitimate reasons. The Supreme Court cited concerns for officer safety in overturning the Maryland court's ruling and held that the activities of passengers are subject to police control. Similarly, in 2007, in the case of *Brendlin* v. *California*,[109] the Court ruled that passengers in stopped vehicles are necessarily detained as a result of the stop and that they should expect that, for safety reasons, officers will exercise "unquestioned police command" over them for the duration of the stop. However, any passenger in a stopped automobile may use his or her Fourth Amendment rights to challenge the stop's legality.

In 1998, however, the U.S. Supreme Court placed clear limits on warrantless vehicle searches. In the case of *Knowles* v. *Iowa*,[110] an Iowa policeman stopped Patrick Knowles for speeding, issued him a citation, but did not make a custodial arrest. The officer then conducted a full search of his car without Knowles's consent and without probable cause. Marijuana was found, and Knowles was arrested. At the time, Iowa state law gave officers authority to conduct full-blown automobile searches when issuing only a citation. The Supreme Court found, however, that while concern for officer safety during a routine traffic stop may justify the minimal intrusion of ordering a driver and passengers out of a car, it does not by itself justify what it called "the considerably greater intrusion attending a full field-type search." Hence while a search incident to arrest may be justifiable in the eyes of the Court, a search incident to citation clearly is not.

In the 1999 case of *Wyoming* v. *Houghton*,[111] the Court ruled that police officers with probable cause to search a car may inspect passengers' belongings found in the car that are capable of concealing the object of the search. *Thornton* v. *U.S.* (2004) established the authority of arresting officers to search a car without a warrant even if the driver had previously exited the vehicle.[112]

In 2005, in the case of *Illinois* v. *Caballes*,[113] the Court held that the use of a drug-sniffing dog during a routine and lawful traffic stop is permissible and may not even be a search within the meaning of the Fourth Amendment. In writing for the majority, Justice John Paul Stevens said that "the use of a well-trained narcotics-detection dog—one that does not expose noncontraband items that otherwise would remain hidden from public view—during a lawful traffic stop generally does not implicate legitimate privacy interests." Learn more about motor vehicle searches at **Library Extra 5–4**.

Roadblocks and Motor Vehicle Checkpoints

The Fourth and Fourteenth Amendments to the U.S. Constitution guarantee liberty and personal security to all people residing within the United States. Courts have generally held that police officers have no legitimate authority to detain or arrest people who are going about their business in a peaceful manner, unless there is probable cause to believe that a crime has been committed. In a number of instances, however, the U.S. Supreme Court has decided that community interests may necessitate a temporary suspension of personal liberty, even when probable cause is lacking. One such case is that of *Michigan Dept. of State Police* v. *Sitz* (1990),[114] which involved the legality of highway sobriety checkpoints, including those at which nonsuspicious drivers are subjected to scrutiny. In *Sitz*, the Court ruled that such stops are reasonable insofar as they are essential to the welfare of the community as a whole.

In a second case, *U.S.* v. *Martinez-Fuerte* (1976),[115] the Court upheld brief suspicionless seizures at a fixed international checkpoint designed to intercept illegal aliens. The Court noted that "to require that such stops always be based on reasonable suspicion would be impractical because the flow of traffic tends to be too heavy to allow the particularized study of a given car necessary to identify it as a possible carrier of illegal aliens. Such a requirement also would largely eliminate any deterrent to the conduct of well-disguised smuggling operations, even though smugglers are known to use these highways regularly."[116]

In fact, in 2004, in the case of *Illinois* v. *Lidster*,[117] the Court held that information-seeking highway roadblocks are permissible. The stop in *Lidster*, said the Court, was permissible because its intent was merely to solicit motorists' help in solving a crime. "The law," said the Court, "ordinarily permits police to seek the public's voluntary cooperation in a criminal investigation."

▲ A law enforcement officer searching a vehicle in San Diego, California. Warrantless vehicle searches, where the driver is suspected of a crime, have generally been justified by the fact that vehicles are highly mobile and can quickly leave police jurisdiction. Can passengers in the vehicle also be searched?
Mike Karlsson/Arresting Images Royalty Free

Watercraft and Motor Homes

The 1983 case of *U.S.* v. *Villamonte-Marquez*[118] widened the *Carroll* decision (discussed earlier) to include watercraft. In this case, the Court reasoned that a vehicle on the water can easily leave the jurisdiction of enforcement officials, just as a car or truck can.

In *California* v. *Carney* (1985),[119] the Court extended police authority to conduct warrantless searches of vehicles to include motor homes. Earlier arguments had been advanced that a motor home, because it is more like a permanent residence, should not be considered a vehicle for purposes of search and seizure. In a 6–3 decision, the Court rejected those arguments, reasoning that a vehicle's appointments and size do not alter its basic function of providing transportation.

Houseboats were brought under the automobile exception to the Fourth Amendment warrant requirement in the 1988 Tenth Circuit Court case of *U.S.* v. *Hill.*[120]

Lecture Note Explain the U.S. Supreme Court's rationale in allowing suspicionless searches in cases in which the need to maintain public safety may provide a compelling interest that can negate an individual's right to privacy.

Suspicionless Searches

In two 1989 decisions, the U.S. Supreme Court ruled for the first time in its history that there may be instances when the need to ensure public safety provides a **compelling interest** that negates the rights of any individual to privacy, permitting **suspicionless searches**—those that occur when a person is not suspected of a crime. In the case of *National Treasury Employees Union* v. *Von Raab* (1989),[121] the Court, by a 5–4 vote, upheld a program of the U.S. Customs Service that required mandatory drug testing for all workers seeking promotions or job transfers involving drug interdiction and the carrying of firearms. The Court's majority opinion read, "We think the government's need to conduct the suspicionless searches required by the Customs program outweighs the privacy interest of employees engaged directly in drug interdiction, and of those who otherwise are required to carry firearms."

compelling interest
A legal concept that provides a basis for suspicionless searches when public safety is at issue. In two cases, the U.S. Supreme Court held that public safety may sometimes provide a sufficiently compelling interest to justify limiting an individual's right to privacy.

suspicionless search
A search conducted by law enforcement personnel without a warrant and without suspicion. Suspicionless searches are permissible only if based on an overriding concern for public safety.

The second case, *Skinner* v. *Railway Labor Executives' Association* (1989),[122] was decided on the same day. In *Skinner*, the justices voted 7 to 2 to permit the mandatory testing of railway crews for the presence of drugs or alcohol following serious train accidents. The *Skinner* case involved evidence of drugs in a 1987 train wreck outside of Baltimore, Maryland, in which 16 people were killed and hundreds were injured.

The 1991 Supreme Court case of *Florida* v. *Bostick*,[123] which permitted warrantless "sweeps" of intercity buses, moved the Court deeply into conservative territory. The *Bostick* case came to the attention of the Court as a result of the Broward County (Florida) Sheriff's Department's routine practice of boarding buses at scheduled stops and asking passengers for permission to search their bags. Terrance Bostick, a passenger on one of the buses, gave police permission to search his luggage, which was found to contain cocaine. Bostick was arrested and eventually pleaded guilty to charges of drug trafficking. The Florida Supreme Court, however, found merit in Bostick's appeal, which was based on a Fourth Amendment claim that the search of his luggage had been unreasonable. The Florida court held that "a reasonable passenger in [Bostick's] situation would not have felt free to leave the bus to avoid questioning by the police," and it overturned the conviction.

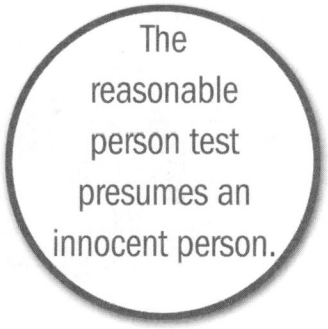

The state appealed to the U.S. Supreme Court, which held that the Florida Supreme Court had erred in interpreting Bostick's *feelings* that he was not free to leave the bus. In the words of the Court, "Bostick was a passenger on a bus that was scheduled to depart. He would not have felt free to leave the bus even if the police had not been present. Bostick's movements were 'confined' in a sense, but this was the natural result of his decision to take the bus." In other words, Bostick was constrained not so much by police action as by his own feelings that he might miss the bus were he to get off. Following this line of reasoning, the Court concluded that warrantless, suspicionless "sweeps" of buses, "trains, planes, and city streets" are permissible as long as officers (1) ask individual passengers for permission before searching their possessions, (2) do not coerce passengers to consent to a search, and (3) do not convey the message that citizen compliance with the search request is mandatory. Passenger compliance with police searches must be voluntary for the searches to be legal.

In contrast to the tone of Court decisions more than two decades earlier, the justices did not require officers to inform passengers that they were free to leave or that they had the right to deny officers the opportunity to search (although Bostick himself was so advised by Florida officers). Any reasonable person, the Court ruled, should feel free to deny the police request. In the words of the Court, "The appropriate test is whether, taking into account all of the circumstances surrounding the encounter, a reasonable passenger would feel free to decline the officers' requests or otherwise terminate the encounter." The Court continued, "Rejected, however, is Bostick's argument that he must have been seized because no reasonable person would freely consent to a search of luggage containing drugs, since the 'reasonable person' test presumes an innocent person."

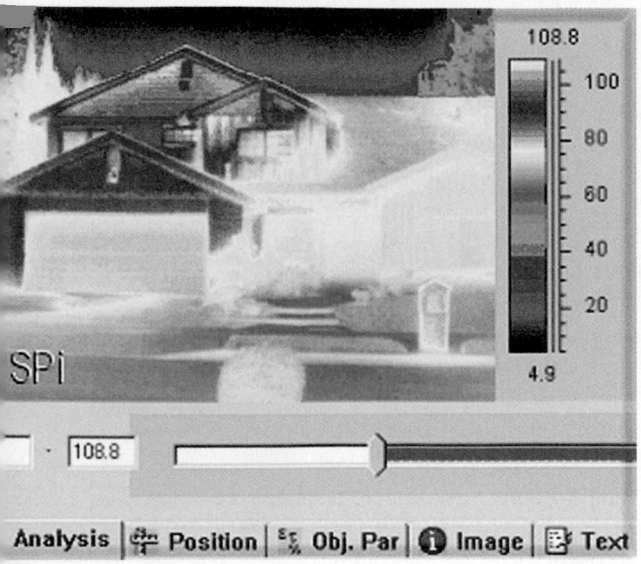

▲ A photo created by a thermal-imaging device. The photo shows "hot spots" in a suspected marijuana grower's home that might be produced by lights used to grow the plants indoors. In *Kyllo* v. *U.S.* (2001), the U.S. Supreme Court held that the police may not use such devices without a search warrant. What was the Court's rationale?
Image compliments of SPi, www.x20.org

Critics of the decision saw it as creating new "gestapo-like" police powers in the face of which citizens on public transportation will feel compelled to comply with police searches. Dissenting Justices Harry Blackmun, John Paul Stevens, and Thurgood Marshall held that "the bus sweep at issue in this case violates the core values of the Fourth Amendment." The Court's majority, however, defended its ruling by writing, "[T]he Fourth Amendment proscribes unreasonable searches and seizures; it does not proscribe voluntary cooperation." In 2000, however, in the case of *Bond* v. *U.S.*,[124] the Court ruled that physical manipulation of a carry-on bag in the possession of a bus passenger without the owner's consent does violate the Fourth Amendment's proscription against unreasonable searches. In the case of *U.S.* v. *Drayton* (2002),[125] the U.S. Supreme Court reiterated its position that police officers are not required to advise bus passengers of their right to refuse to cooperate with officers conducting searches or to refuse to be searched.

In 2004, the U.S. Supreme Court made it clear that suspicionless searches of vehicles at our nation's borders are permitted, even when the searches are extensive. In the case of *U.S.* v. *Flores-Montano*,[126] customs officials disassembled the gas tank of a car belonging to a man entering the country from Mexico and found that it contained 37 kilograms of marijuana. Although the officers admitted that their actions were not motivated by any particular belief that the search would reveal contraband, the Court held that Congress has always granted "plenary authority to conduct routine searches and seizures at the border without probable cause or a warrant." The Court stated that "the Government's authority to conduct suspicionless inspections at the border includes the authority to remove, disassemble, and reassemble a vehicle's fuel tank."

High-Technology Searches

The burgeoning use of high technology to investigate crime and to uncover violations of the criminal law is forcing courts throughout the nation to evaluate the applicability of constitutional guarantees in light of high-tech searches and seizures. In 1996, the California appellate court decision in *People* v. *Deutsch*[127] presaged the kinds of issues that are being encountered as American law enforcement expands its use of cutting-edge technology. In *Deutsch*, judges faced the question of whether a warrantless scan of a private dwelling with a thermal-imaging device constitutes an unreasonable search within the meaning of the Fourth Amendment. Such devices (also called *forward-looking infrared [FLIR] systems*) measure radiant energy in the radiant heat portion of the electromagnetic spectrum[128] and display their readings as thermographs. The "heat picture" that a thermal imager produces can be used, as it was in the case of Dorian Deutsch, to reveal unusually warm areas or rooms that might be associated with the cultivation of drug-bearing plants, such as marijuana. Two hundred cannabis plants, which were being grown hydroponically under high-wattage lights in two walled-off portions of Deutsch's home, were seized following an exterior thermal scan of her home by a police officer who drove by at 1:30 in the morning. Because no entry of the house was anticipated during the search, the officer had acted without a search warrant. The California court ruled that the scan was an illegal search because "society accepts a reasonable expectation of privacy" surrounding "nondisclosed activities within the home."[129]

In the similar case of *Kyllo* v. *U.S.* (2001),[130] the U.S. Supreme Court reached much the same conclusion. Based on the results of a warrantless search conducted by officers using a thermal-imaging device, investigators applied for a search warrant of Kyllo's home. The subsequent search uncovered more than 100 marijuana plants that were being grown under bright lights. In overturning Kyllo's conviction on drug-manufacturing charges, the Court held (with regard to the original warrantless search with the thermal-imaging device), "Where, as here, the Government uses a device that is not in general public use, to explore details of a private home that would previously have been unknowable without physical intrusion, the surveillance is a Fourth Amendment 'search,' and is presumptively unreasonable without a warrant."[131] Learn more about the issues surrounding search and seizure at **Web Extra 5–3**.

The Intelligence Function

5 Describe the intelligence function, including police interrogations, and explain the role of *Miranda* warnings.

The need for information leads police investigators to question both suspects and informants and, even more often, potentially knowledgeable citizens who may have been witnesses or victims. Data gathering is a crucial form of intelligence; without it, enforcement agencies would be virtually powerless to plan and effect arrests.

The importance of gathering information in police work cannot be overstressed. Studies have found that the one factor most likely to lead to arrest in serious crimes is the presence of a witness who can provide information to the police. Undercover operations, Neighborhood Watch programs, Crime Stoppers groups, and organized detective work all contribute this vital information.

Informants

Information gathering is a complex process, and many ethical questions have been raised about the techniques police use to gather information. The use of paid informants, for example, is an area of concern to ethicists who believe that informants are often paid to get away with crimes. The police practice (endorsed by some prosecutors) of agreeing not to charge one offender out of a group if he or she will talk and testify against others is another concern.

As we have seen, probable cause is an important aspect of both police searches and legal arrests. The Fourth Amendment specifies that "no Warrants shall issue, but upon probable cause." As a consequence, the successful use of informants in supporting requests for a warrant depends on the demonstrable reliability of their information. The case of *Aguilar* v. *Texas* (1964)[132] clarified the use of informants and established a two-pronged test. The U.S. Supreme Court ruled that informant information could establish probable cause if both of the following criteria are met:

1. The source of the informant's information is made clear.
2. The police officer has a reasonable belief that the informant is reliable.

> The right of the people to be secure in their persons, houses, papers, and effects, against unreasonable searches and seizures, shall not be violated, and no Warrants shall issue, but upon probable cause, supported by Oath or affirmation, and particularly describing the place to be searched, and the persons or things to be seized.
>
> —Fourth Amendment to the U.S. Constitution

The two-pronged test of *Aguilar* v. *Texas* was intended to prevent the issuance of warrants on the basis of false or fabricated information. The case of *U.S.* v. *Harris* (1971)[133] provided an exception to the two-pronged *Aguilar* test. The *Harris* Court recognized the fact that when an informant provides information that is damaging to him or her, it is probably true. In *Harris*, an informant told police that he had purchased non-tax-paid whiskey from another person. Since the information also implicated the informant in a crime, it was held to be accurate, even though it could not meet the second prong of the *Aguilar* test. "Admissions of crime," said the Court, "carry their own indicia of credibility—sufficient at least to support a finding of probable cause to search."[134]

In 1983, in the case of *Illinois* v. *Gates*,[135] the Court adopted a totality-of-circumstances approach, which held that sufficient probable cause for issuing a warrant exists where an informant can be reasonably believed on the basis of everything that the police know. The *Gates* case involved an anonymous informant who provided incriminating information about another person through a letter to the police. Although the source of the information was not stated and the police were unable to say whether the informant was reliable, the overall sense of things, given what was already known to police, was that the information supplied was probably valid. In *Gates*, the Court held that probable cause exists when "there is a fair probability that contraband or evidence of a crime will be found in a particular place."

In the 1990 case of *Alabama* v. *White*, [136] the Supreme Court ruled that an anonymous tip, even in the absence of other corroborating information about a suspect, could form the basis for an investigatory stop if the informant accurately predicted the *future* behavior of the suspect. The Court reasoned that the ability to predict a suspect's behavior demonstrates

The mandatory recording of police interrogations offers overwhelming benefits at minimal cost.

a significant degree of familiarity with the suspect's affairs. In the words of the Court, "Because only a small number of people are generally privy to an individual's itinerary, it is reasonable for the police to believe that a person with access to such information is likely to also have access to reliable information about that individual's illegal activities."[137]

In 2000, in the case of *Florida* v. *J.L.*,[138] the Court held that an anonymous tip that a person is carrying a gun does not, without more, justify a police officer's stop and frisk of that person. Ruling that such a search is invalid under the Fourth Amendment, the Court rejected the suggestion of a firearm exception to the general stop-and-frisk rule.

The identity of informants may be kept secret only if sources have been explicitly assured of confidentiality by investigating officers or if a reasonably implied assurance of confidentiality has been made. In *U.S. Dept. of Justice* v. *Landano* (1993),[139] the U.S. Supreme Court required that an informant's identity be revealed through a request made under the federal Freedom of Information Act. In that case, the FBI had not specifically assured the informant of confidentiality, and the Court ruled that "the government is not entitled to a presumption that all sources supplying information to the FBI in the course of a criminal investigation are confidential sources."

Police Interrogation

In 2003, Illinois became the first state in the nation to require the electronic recording of police interrogations and confessions in homicide cases.[140] State lawmakers hoped that the use of recordings would reduce the incidence of false confessions as well as the likelihood of convictions based on such confessions. Under the law, police interrogators must create video- or audiotape recordings of any questioning involving suspects. The law prohibits the introduction in court of statements and confessions that have not been taped. Proponents of the law say that it will prevent police intimidation of murder suspects and will put an end to coerced confessions.

Some argue that the mandatory recording of police interrogations offers overwhelming benefits at minimal cost. "By creating an objective and reviewable record," says University of San Francisco Law School's Richard A. Leo, "electronic recording promotes truth-finding in the criminal process, relegates 'swearing contests' to the past, and saves scarce resources at multiple levels of the criminal justice system."[141] According to Leo, requiring that all interrogations be recorded will benefit police and prosecutors by increasing the accuracy of confessions and convictions and "will also reduce the number of police-induced false confessions and the wrongful convictions they cause."

interrogation
The information-gathering activity of police officers that involves the direct questioning of suspects.

Lecture Note Begin a discussion of police interrogation with the 1936 U.S. Supreme Court case of *Brown* v. *Mississippi*, which outlawed the use of physical force in interrogative settings. Discuss how some forms of coercion are inherent rather than obvious and how psychological manipulation can be a form of unfair interrogation.

The U.S. Supreme Court has defined **interrogation** as any behaviors by the police "that the police should know are reasonably likely to elicit an incriminating response from the suspect."[142] Interrogation may involve activities that go well beyond mere verbal questioning, and the Court has held that interrogation may include "staged lineups, reverse lineups, positing guilt, minimizing the moral seriousness of crime, and casting blame on the victim or society." It is noteworthy that the Court has also held that "police words or actions normally attendant to arrest and custody do not constitute interrogation" unless they involve pointed or directed questions. An arresting officer may instruct a suspect on what to do and may chitchat with him or her without engaging in interrogation within the meaning of the law. Once police officers make inquiries intended to elicit information about the crime in question, however, interrogation has begun. The interrogation of suspects, like other areas of police activity, is subject to constitutional limits as interpreted by the courts. A series of landmark decisions by the U.S. Supreme Court has focused on police interrogation (Figure 5–2).

Physical Abuse

The first in a series of significant cases was that of *Brown* v. *Mississippi*,[143] decided in 1936. The *Brown* case began with the robbery of a white store owner in Mississippi in 1934. During the robbery, the victim was killed. A posse formed and went to the home of a local African American man rumored to have been one of the perpetrators. They dragged the suspect from his home, put a rope around his neck, and hoisted him into a tree. They repeated this process a number of times, hoping to get a confession from the man but failing to do so. The posse was headed by a deputy sheriff who then arrested other suspects in the case and laid

FIGURE 5–2
Police Interrogation

INTERROGATION
The U.S. Supreme Court has defined interrogation as any behaviors by the police "that the police should know are reasonably likely to elicit an incriminating response from the suspect." The Court also noted that "police words or actions normally attendant to arrest and custody do not constitute interrogation" unless they involve pointed or directed questions. The interrogation of suspects, like other areas of police activity, is subject to constitutional limits as interpreted by the courts, and a series of landmark decisions by the U.S Supreme Court has focused on police interrogations.

Physical Abuse:
The first in a series of significant cases was ***Brown* v. *Mississippi***. In 1936 the court determined that physical abuse cannot be used to obtain a confession or elicit information from a suspect.

Inherent Coercion:
In the case of ***Ashcraft* v. *Tennessee*** (1944), the U.S. Supreme Court found that interrogation involving inherent coercion was not acceptable. Inherent coercion refers to any form of nonphysical coercion, hostility, or pressure to try to force a confession from a suspect.

Psychological Manipulation:
Interrogation should not involve sophisticated trickery or manipulation. In the case of ***Arizona* v. *Fulminante*** (1991) the U.S. Supreme Court determined that it was not legal to allow an FBI informat posing as a fellow inmate to trick the suspect into a confession. Interrogators do not have to be scrupulously honest in confronting suspects, but there must be limits to the lengths that can be pursued in questioning a suspect.

Right to Lawyer at Interrogation:
Escobedo* v. *Illinois (1964) and ***Minnick* v. *Mississippi*** (1990).

them over chairs in the local jail and whipped them with belts and buckles until they "confessed." These confessions were used in the trial that followed, and all three defendants were convicted of murder. Their convictions were upheld by the Mississippi Supreme Court. In 1936, however, the case was reviewed by the U.S. Supreme Court, which overturned all of the convictions, saying that it was difficult to imagine techniques of interrogation more "revolting" to the sense of justice than those used in this case.

Inherent Coercion

Interrogation need not involve physical abuse for it to be contrary to constitutional principles. In the case of *Ashcraft* v. *Tennessee* (1944),[144] the U.S. Supreme Court found that interrogation involving **inherent coercion** was not acceptable. Ashcraft had been charged with the murder of his wife, Zelma. He was arrested on a Saturday night and interrogated by relays of skilled interrogators until Monday morning, when he purportedly made a statement implicating himself in the murder. During questioning, he had faced a blinding light but was not physically mistreated. Investigators later testified that when the suspect requested cigarettes, food, or water, they "kindly" provided them. The Court's ruling, which reversed Ashcraft's conviction, made it plain that the Fifth Amendment guarantee against self-incrimination prohibits any form of official coercion or pressure during interrogation.

inherent coercion
The tactics used by police interviewers that fall short of physical abuse but that nonetheless pressure suspects to divulge information.

A similar case, *Chambers* v. *Florida*, was decided in 1940.[145] In that case, four black men were arrested without warrants as suspects in the robbery and murder of an elderly white man. After several days of questioning in a hostile atmosphere, the men confessed to the murder. The confessions were used as the primary evidence against them at their trial, and all four were sentenced to die. Upon appeal, the U.S. Supreme Court held that "the very circumstances surrounding their confinement and their questioning, without any formal charges having been brought, were such as to fill petitioners with terror and frightful misgivings."[146] Learn more about *Chambers* v. *Florida* at **Library Extra 5–5**.

Psychological Manipulation

Not only must interrogation be free of coercion and hostility, but it also cannot involve sophisticated trickery designed to ferret out a confession. Interrogators do not necessarily have to be scrupulously honest in confronting suspects, and the expert opinions of medical and psychiatric practitioners may be sought in investigations. However, the use of professionals skilled in **psychological manipulation** to gain confessions was banned by the Court in the case of *Leyra* v. *Denno*[147] in 1954, during the heyday of psychiatric perspectives on criminal behavior.

psychological manipulation
The manipulative actions by police interviewers, designed to pressure suspects to divulge information, that are based on subtle forms of intimidation and control.

In 1991, in the case of *Arizona* v. *Fulminante*,[148] the U.S. Supreme Court threw an even more dampening blanket of uncertainty over the use of sophisticated techniques to gain a confession. Oreste Fulminante was an inmate in a federal prison when he was approached secretly by a fellow inmate who was an FBI informant. The informant told Fulminante that other inmates were plotting to kill him because of a rumor that he had killed a child. He offered to protect Fulminante if he was told the details of the crime. Fulminante then described his role in the murder of his 11-year-old stepdaughter. Fulminante was arrested for that murder, tried, and convicted.

Lecture Note Discuss the implications of the 1991 case of *Arizona* v. *Fulminante*, in which the U.S. Supreme Court held that, under limited circumstances, the admission of a coerced confession in a criminal trial might be nothing more than a "trial error"—one that does not require the automatic reversal of a lower court's conviction.

On appeal to the U.S. Supreme Court, Fulminante's lawyers argued that his confession had been coerced because of the threat of violence communicated by the informant. The Court agreed that the confession had been coerced and ordered a new trial at which the confession could not be admitted into evidence. Simultaneously, however, the Court found that the admission of a coerced confession should be considered a harmless "trial error" that need not necessarily result in reversal of a conviction if other evidence still proves guilt. The decision was especially significant because it partially reversed the Court's earlier ruling, in *Chapman* v. *California* (1967),[149] where it was held that forced confessions were such a basic form of constitutional error that they automatically invalidated any conviction to which they related. At a second trial, where his confession was not entered into evidence, Fulminante was convicted again and sentenced to die. The Arizona Supreme Court overturned his conviction, however, ruling that testimony describing statements the victim had made about fearing for her life prior to her murder, and which had been entered into evidence, were hearsay and had prejudiced the jury.[150]

Lecture Note Explain that as a result of the 1964 U.S. Supreme Court case of *Escobedo* v. *Illinois*, suspects have the right to have a lawyer present during police interrogations.

The Right to a Lawyer at Interrogation

In 1964, in the case of *Escobedo* v. *Illinois*,[151] the right to have legal counsel present during police interrogation was formally recognized. In 1981, the case of *Edwards* v. *Arizona*[152] established a "bright-line rule" (that is, it specified a criterion that cannot be violated) for investigators to use in interpreting a suspect's right to counsel. In *Edwards*, the U.S. Supreme Court reiterated its *Miranda* concern that once a suspect who is in custody and is being questioned has requested the assistance of counsel, all questioning must cease until an attorney is present. The 1986 case of *Michigan* v. *Jackson*[153] provided further support for *Edwards*. In *Jackson*, the Court forbade police from initiating the interrogation of criminal defendants who had invoked their right to counsel at an arraignment or similar proceeding. In 1990, the Court refined the rule in *Minnick* v. *Mississippi*,[154] when it held that after the suspect has had an opportunity to consult his or her lawyer, interrogation may *not* resume unless the lawyer is present. Similarly, according to *Arizona* v. *Roberson* (1988),[155] the police may not avoid the suspect's request for a lawyer by beginning a new line of questioning, even if it is about an unrelated offense.

In 1994, in the case of *Davis* v. *U.S.*,[156] the Court "put the burden on custodial suspects to make unequivocal invocations of the right to counsel." In the *Davis* case, a man being interrogated in the death of a sailor waived his *Miranda* rights but later said, "Maybe I should talk to a lawyer." Investigators asked the suspect clarifying questions, and he responded, "No, I don't want a lawyer." Upon conviction he appealed, claiming that interrogation should have ceased when he mentioned a lawyer. The Court, in affirming the conviction, stated that "it will often be good police practice for the interviewing officers to clarify whether or not [the suspect] actually wants an attorney."

In 2009, in something of an about-face, the U.S. Supreme Court held that "*Michigan* v. *Jackson* should be and now is overruled." In the case of *Montejo* v. *Louisiana*,[157] the Court found that strict interpretations of *Jackson* could lead to practical problems. Montejo had been charged with first-degree murder, and appointment of counsel was ordered at his arraignment. He did not, however, ask to see his attorney. Later that same day, the police read Montejo his *Miranda* rights, and he agreed to accompany them on a trip to locate the murder weapon. During the trip, he wrote an incriminating letter of apology to the victim's widow. Upon returning, he met with his court-appointed attorney for the first time. At trial, his letter was admitted over defense objection, and he was convicted and sentenced to death. In the words of the Court, "Both *Edwards* and *Jackson* are meant to prevent police from badgering defendants into changing their minds about the right to counsel once they have invoked it, but a defendant who never asked for counsel has not yet made up his mind." In effect, although an attorney had been appointed to represent Montejo, he had never actually invoked his right to counsel.

▲ Ernesto Miranda, shown here after a jury convicted him for a second time. Miranda was convicted on rape and kidnapping charges after arresting officers failed to advise him of his rights. His case led to the now-famous *Miranda* warnings. How do the *Miranda* warnings read?
AP Wide World Photos

Suspect Rights: The *Miranda* Decision

In the area of suspect rights, no case is as famous as that of *Miranda* v. *Arizona* (1966),[158] which established the well-known ***Miranda* warnings**. Many people regard *Miranda* as the centerpiece of the Warren Court due process rulings.

The case involved Ernesto Miranda, who was arrested in Phoenix, Arizona, and was accused of having kidnapped and raped a young woman. At police headquarters, he was identified by the victim. After being interrogated for two hours, Miranda signed a confession that formed the basis of his later conviction on the charges.

On appeal, the U.S. Supreme Court rendered what some regard as the most far-reaching opinion to have affected criminal justice in the last half century. The Court ruled that Miranda's conviction was unconstitutional because "[t]he entire aura and atmosphere of police interrogation without notification of rights and an offer of assistance of counsel [tend] to subjugate the individual to the will of his examiner."

The Court continued, saying that the suspect "must be warned prior to any questioning that he has the right to remain silent, that anything he says can be used against him in a court of law, that he has the right to the presence of an attorney, and that if he cannot afford an attorney one will be appointed for him prior to any questioning if he so desires. Opportunity to exercise these rights must be afforded to him throughout the interrogation. After such warnings have been given, and such opportunity afforded him, the individual may knowingly and intelligently waive these rights and agree to answer the questions or make a statement. But unless and until such warnings and waiver are demonstrated by the prosecution at the trial, no evidence obtained as a result of interrogation can be used against him."

To ensure that proper advice is given to suspects at the time of their arrest, the now-famous *Miranda* rights are read before any questioning begins. These rights, as they appear on a *Miranda* warning card commonly used by police agencies, are shown in CJ Exhibit 5–2.

Once suspects have been advised of their *Miranda* rights, they are commonly asked to sign a paper that lists each right in order to confirm that they were advised of their rights and that they understand each right. Questioning may then begin, but only if suspects waive the right not to talk or to have a lawyer present during interrogation.

In 1992, *Miranda* rights were effectively extended to illegal immigrants living in the United States. In a settlement of a class-action lawsuit reached in Los Angeles with the Immigration and Naturalization Service, U.S. District Court Judge William Byrne, Jr., approved the printing of millions of notices in several languages to be given to arrestees. The approximately 1.5 million illegal aliens arrested each year must be told they may (1) talk with a lawyer, (2) make a phone call, (3) request a list of available legal services, (4) seek a hearing before an immigration judge, (5) possibly obtain release on bond, and (6) contact a diplomatic officer representing their country. Notice of this type was "long overdue," said Roberto Martinez of the American Friends

***Miranda* warnings**
The advisement of rights due criminal suspects by the police before questioning begins. *Miranda* warnings were first set forth by the U.S. Supreme Court in the 1966 case of *Miranda* v. *Arizona*.

Lecture Note Discuss the U.S. Supreme Court case of *Miranda* v. *Arizona* (1966). Explain that this case, the hallmark of the 1960s liberal Court's concern with individual rights, requires that a criminal defendant be offered a rights advisement following arrest and before questioning. Use CJ Exhibit 5–2 to review each of the five warnings that law enforcement officers are required to give to defendants.

Lecture Note Ask the class to consider each of the rights statements that make up the *Miranda* decision. Have students debate the wisdom of having law enforcement officers provide such rights statements to criminal suspects.

Thematic Question Examine the impact of each *Miranda* warning on American criminal justice. How might the justice system have functioned differently before 1966 (the date of the *Miranda* decision) than it does now as a result of this decision?

CJ Exhibit 5–2
The *Miranda* Warnings

ADULT RIGHTS WARNING

Suspects 18 years old or older who are in custody must be advised of the following rights before any questioning begins:

1. You have the right to remain silent.
2. Anything you say can be used against you in a court of law.
3. You have the right to talk to a lawyer and to have a lawyer present while you are being questioned.
4. If you want a lawyer before or during questioning but cannot afford to hire a lawyer, one will be appointed to represent you at no cost before any questioning.
5. If you answer questions now without a lawyer here, you still have the right to stop answering questions at any time.

WAIVER OF RIGHTS

After reading and explaining the rights of a person in custody, an officer must also ask for a waiver of those rights before any questioning. The following waiver questions must be answered affirmatively, either by express answer or by clear implication. Silence alone is not a waiver.

1. Do you understand each of these rights I have explained to you? (Answer must be YES.)
2. Having these rights in mind, do you now wish to answer questions? (Answer must be YES.)
3. Do you now wish to answer questions without a lawyer present? (Answer must be YES.)

The following question must be asked of juveniles ages 14, 15, 16, and 17:

1. Do you now wish to answer questions without your parents, guardians, or custodians present? (Answer must be YES.)

Source: North Carolina Justice Academy. Reprinted with permission.

Thematic Question Are there any "rights" that you would add to, or remove from, the *Miranda* rights listed in CJ Exhibit 5–2? If so, which ones?

Lecture Note Ask the class to use the Web to summarize the arguments made by Dickerson's attorneys in the case of *Dickerson* v. *U.S.* (2000). Might these arguments have any merit? If so, why did the U.S. Supreme Court reject them?

Service Committee's Mexico-U.S. border program. "Up to now, we've had total mistreatment of civil rights of undocumented people."[159]

When the *Miranda* decision was originally handed down, some hailed it as ensuring the protection of individual rights guaranteed under the Constitution. To guarantee those rights, they suggested, no better agency is available than the police themselves, since the police are present at the initial stages of the criminal justice process. Critics of *Miranda*, however, argued that the decision put police agencies in the uncomfortable and contradictory position not only of enforcing the law but also of having to offer defendants advice on how they might circumvent conviction and punishment. Under *Miranda*, the police partially assume the role of legal adviser to the accused.

In 1999, however, in the case of *U.S.* v. *Dickerson*,[160] the Fourth Circuit U.S. Court of Appeals upheld an almost-forgotten law that Congress had passed in 1968 with the intention of overturning *Miranda*. That law, Section 3501 of Chapter 223, Part II of Title 18 of the U.S. Code, says that "a confession . . . shall be admissible in evidence if it is voluntarily given." Upon appeal in 2000, the U.S. Supreme Court upheld its original *Miranda* ruling by a 7–2 vote and found that *Miranda* is a constitutional rule (that is, a fundamental right inherent in the U.S. Constitution) that cannot be dismissed by an act of Congress. "*Miranda* and its progeny," the majority wrote in *Dickerson* v. *U.S.*, will continue to "govern the admissibility of statements made during custodial interrogation in both state and federal courts."[161]

In 2004, in the case of *U.S.* v. *Patane*,[162] the U.S. Supreme Court continued to refine its original 1966 *Miranda* ruling. *Patane* surprised some Court watchers because in it the Court held that "a mere failure to give *Miranda* warnings does not, by itself, violate a suspect's constitutional rights or even the *Miranda* rule." The *Patane* case began with the arrest of a convicted felon after a federal agent told officers that the man owned a handgun illegally. At the time of arrest, the officers tried to advise the defendant of his rights, but he interrupted them, saying that he already knew his rights. The officers then asked him about the pistol, and he told them where it was. After the weapon was recovered, the defendant was charged with illegal possession of a firearm by a convicted felon.

At first glance, *Patane* appears to contradict the fruit of the poisonous tree doctrine that the Court established in the 1920 case of *Silverthorne Lumber Co.* v. *U.S.*[163] and that *Wong Sun* v. *U.S.* (1963)[164] made applicable to verbal evidence derived immediately from an illegal search and seizure. An understanding of *Patane*, however, requires recognition of the fact that the *Miranda* rule is based on the self-incrimination clause of the Fifth Amendment to the U.S. Constitution. According to the Court in *Patane*, "that Clause's core protection is a prohibition on compelling a criminal defendant to testify against himself at trial." It cannot be violated, the Court said, "by the introduction of nontestimonial evidence obtained as a result of voluntary statements." In other words, according to the Court, only (1) coerced statements and (2) those voluntary statements made by a defendant that might directly incriminate him or her at a later trial are precluded by a failure to read a suspect his or her *Miranda* rights. Such voluntary statements would, of course, include such things as an outright confession.

Significantly, however, oral statements must be distinguished, the Court said, from the "physical fruits of the suspect's unwarned but voluntary statements." In other words, if an unwarned suspect is questioned by police officers and tells the officers where they can find an illegal weapon or a weapon that has been used in a crime, the weapon can be recovered and later introduced as evidence at the suspect's trial. If the same unwarned suspect, however, tells police that he committed a murder, then his confession will not be allowed into evidence at trial. The line drawn by the Court is against the admissibility of *oral statements* made by an unwarned defendant, not the *nontestimonial physical evidence* resulting from continued police investigation of such statements. Under *Patane*, the oral statements themselves cannot be admitted, but the physical evidence derived from them can be. "Thus," wrote the justices in *Patane*, "admission of nontestimonial physical fruits (the pistol here) does not run the risk of admitting into trial an accused's coerced incriminating statements against himself."

▲ A suspect being read his *Miranda* rights immediately after arrest. Officers often read *Miranda* rights from a card to preclude the possibility of making a mistake. What might be the consequences of a mistake?
Michael Newman/PhotoEdit Inc.

Waiver of *Miranda* Rights by Suspects

Suspects in police custody may legally waive their *Miranda* rights through a voluntary "knowing and intelligent" waiver. A knowing waiver can only be made if a suspect has been advised of his or her rights and was in a condition to understand the advisement. A rights advisement made in English to a Spanish-speaking suspect, for example, cannot produce a knowing waiver. Likewise, an intelligent waiver of rights requires that the defendant be able to understand the consequences of not invoking the *Miranda* rights. In the case of *Moran* v. *Burbine* (1986),[165] the U.S. Supreme Court defined an intelligent and knowing waiver as one "made with a full awareness both of the nature of the right being abandoned and the consequences of the decision to abandon it." In *Colorado* v. *Spring* (1987),[166] the Court held that an intelligent and knowing waiver can be made even though a suspect has not been informed of all the alleged offenses about which he or she is about to be questioned.

Inevitable-Discovery Exception to *Miranda*

The case of Robert Anthony Williams provides a good example of the change in the U.S. Supreme Court philosophy, alluded to earlier in this chapter, from an individual-rights perspective toward a public-order perspective. The case epitomizes what some have called a "nibbling away" at the advances in defendant rights, which reached their apex in *Miranda*. The case began in 1969, at the close of the Warren Court era, when Williams was convicted of murdering a ten-year-old girl, Pamela Powers, around Christmastime. Although Williams had been advised of his rights, detectives searching for the girl's body were riding in a car with the defendant when one of them made what has since come to be known as the "Christian burial speech." The detective told Williams that since Christmas was almost upon them, it would be "the Christian thing to do" to see to it that Pamela could have a decent burial rather than having to lay in a field somewhere. Williams relented and led detectives to the body. However, because Williams had not been reminded of his right to have a lawyer present during his conversation with the detective, the Supreme Court in *Brewer* v. *Williams* (1977)[167] overturned Williams's conviction, saying that the detective's remarks were "a deliberate eliciting of incriminating evidence from an accused in the absence of his lawyer."

In 1977, Williams was retried for the murder, but his remarks in leading detectives to the body were not entered into evidence. The discovery of the body was itself used, however, prompting another appeal to the Supreme Court based on the argument that the body should not have been used as evidence since it was discovered due to the illegally gathered statements. This time, in *Nix* v. *Williams* (1984),[168] the Supreme Court affirmed Williams's

Suspects may legally waive their *Miranda* rights through a voluntary "knowing and intelligent" waiver.

Thematic Question Examine the various court cases involved in developing the public-safety exception to *Miranda*. Does this exception seem to be a reasonable one? What other exceptions to *Miranda* can you imagine?

Thematic Question Explain why each of the *Miranda* warnings is important. What abuses does each prevent, and what police actions does each hamper?

Lecture Note Point out to students that interrogation can be a subtle and complex process, wherein respect for individual rights and police mandates must be carefully balanced to ensure fairness and ultimately just trials and outcomes.

second conviction, holding that the body would have been found anyway, since detectives were searching in the direction where it lay when Williams revealed its location. That ruling came during the heyday of the Burger Court and clearly demonstrates a tilt by the Court away from suspects' rights and an accommodation with the imperfect world of police procedure. The *Williams* case, as it was finally resolved, is said to have created the *inevitable-discovery exception* to the *Miranda* requirements. The inevitable-discovery exception means that evidence, even if it was otherwise gathered inappropriately, can be used in a court of law if it would have invariably turned up in the normal course of events.

Public-Safety Exception to *Miranda*

Also in 1984, the U.S. Supreme Court established what has come to be known as the *public-safety exception* to the *Miranda* rule. The case of *New York* v. *Quarles*[169] centered on a rape in which the victim told police her assailant had fled, with a gun, into a nearby A&P supermarket. Two police officers entered the store and apprehended the suspect. One officer immediately noticed that the man was wearing an empty shoulder holster and, apparently fearing that a child might find the discarded weapon, quickly asked, "Where's the gun?" Quarles was convicted of rape but appealed his conviction, requesting that the weapon be suppressed as evidence because officers had not advised him of his *Miranda* rights before asking him about it. The Supreme Court disagreed, stating that considerations of public safety were overriding and negated the need for rights advisement before limited questioning that focused on the need to prevent further harm.

The U.S. Supreme Court has also held that in cases when the police issue *Miranda* warnings, a later demonstration that a person may have been suffering from mental problems does not necessarily negate a confession. *Colorado* v. *Connelly* (1986)[170] involved a man who approached a Denver police officer and said he wanted to confess to the murder of a young girl. The officer immediately informed him of his *Miranda* rights, but the man waived them and continued to talk. When a detective arrived, the man was again advised of his rights and again waived them. After being taken to the local jail, the man began to hear "voices" and later claimed that it was these voices that had made him confess. At the trial, the defense moved to have the earlier confession negated on the basis that it was not voluntarily or freely given because of the defendant's mental condition. Upon appeal, the U.S. Supreme Court disagreed, saying that "no coercive government conduct occurred in this case." Hence "self-coercion," be it through the agency of a guilty conscience or faulty thought processes, does not appear to bar prosecution based on information revealed willingly by a suspect.

In another refinement of *Miranda*, the lawful ability of a police informant placed in a jail cell along with a defendant to gather information for later use at trial was upheld in the 1986 case of *Kuhlmann* v. *Wilson*.[171] The passive gathering of information was judged to be acceptable, provided that the informant did not make attempts to elicit information.

In the case of *Illinois* v. *Perkins* (1990),[172] the Court expanded its position to say that under appropriate circumstances, even the active questioning of a suspect by an undercover officer posing as a fellow inmate does not require *Miranda* warnings. In *Perkins*, the Court found that, lacking other forms of coercion, the fact that the suspect was not aware of the questioner's identity as a law enforcement officer ensured that his statements were freely given. In the words of the Court, "The essential ingredients of a 'police-dominated atmosphere' and compulsion are not present when an incarcerated person speaks freely to someone that he believes to be a fellow inmate."

In-court references to a defendant's silence following *Miranda* warnings are unconstitutional.

Miranda and the Meaning of Interrogation

Modern interpretations of the applicability of *Miranda* warnings turn on an understanding of interrogation. The *Miranda* decision, as originally rendered, specifically recognized the need for police investigators to make inquiries at crime scenes to determine facts or to establish identities. As long as the individual questioned is not yet in custody and as long as probable cause is lacking in the investigator's mind, such questioning can proceed without *Miranda* warnings. In such cases, interrogation, within the meaning of *Miranda*, has not yet begun.

The case of *Rock* v. *Zimmerman* (1982)[173] provides a different sort of example—one in which a suspect willingly made statements to the police before interrogation began.

The suspect had burned his own house and shot and killed a neighbor. When the fire department arrived, he began shooting again and killed the fire chief. Cornered later in a field, the defendant, gun in hand, spontaneously shouted at police, "How many people did I kill? How many people are dead?"[174] These spontaneous questions were held to be admissible evidence at the suspect's trial.

It is also important to recognize that the Supreme Court, in the *Miranda* decision, required that officers provide warnings only in those situations involving *both* arrest and custodial interrogation—what some call the ***Miranda* triggers**. In other words, it is generally permissible for officers to take a suspect into custody and listen without asking questions while he or she tells a story. Similarly, they may ask questions without providing a *Miranda* warning, even within the confines of a police station house, as long as the person questioned is not a suspect and is not under arrest.[175] Warnings are required only when officers begin to actively and deliberately elicit responses from a suspect whom they know has been indicted or who is in custody.

***Miranda* triggers**
The dual principles of custody and interrogation, both of which are necessary before an advisement of rights is required.

Thematic Question What are the *Miranda* triggers? Why is it necessary for both to be present before a rights advisement is required? How would the meaning of *Miranda* change if the Court required only the first trigger?

A third-party conversation recorded by the police after a suspect has invoked the *Miranda* right to remain silent may be used as evidence, according to a 1987 ruling in *Arizona* v. *Mauro*.[176] In *Mauro*, a man who willingly conversed with his wife in the presence of a police tape recorder, even after invoking his right to keep silent, was held to have effectively abandoned that right.

When a waiver is not made, however, in-court references to a defendant's silence following the issuing of *Miranda* warnings are unconstitutional. In the 1976 case of *Doyle* v. *Ohio*,[177] the U.S. Supreme Court definitively ruled that "a suspect's [post-*Miranda*] silence will not be used against him." Even so, according to the Court in *Brecht* v. *Abrahamson* (1993),[178] prosecution efforts to use such silence against a defendant may not invalidate a finding of guilt by a jury unless the "error had substantial and injurious effect or influence in determining the jury's verdict."[179]

The 2004 case of *Missouri* v. *Seibert*[180] addressed the legality of a two-step police interrogation technique in which suspects were questioned and—if they made incriminating statements—were then advised of their *Miranda* rights and questioned again. The justices found that such a technique could not meet constitutional muster, writing, "When the [*Miranda*] warnings are inserted in the midst of coordinated and continuing interrogation, they are likely to mislead and deprive a defendant of knowledge essential to his ability to understand the nature of his rights and the consequences of abandoning them. . . . And it would be unrealistic to treat two spates of integrated and proximately conducted questioning as independent interrogations . . . simply because *Miranda* warnings formally punctuate them in the middle."

Finally, in the 2010 case of *Florida* v. *Powell*, the U.S. Supreme Court held that although *Miranda* warnings are generally required prior to police interrogation, the wording of those warnings is not set in stone. The Court ruled that "in determining whether police warnings were satisfactory, reviewing courts are not required to examine them as if construing a will or defining the terms of an easement. The inquiry is simply whether the warnings reasonably convey to a suspect his rights as required by *Miranda*."[181]

Gathering of Special Kinds of Nontestimonial Evidence

The role of law enforcement is complicated by the fact that suspects are often privy to special evidence of a nontestimonial sort. Nontestimonial evidence is generally physical evidence, and most physical evidence is subject to normal procedures of search and seizure. A special category of nontestimonial evidence, however, includes very personal items that may be within or part of a person's body, such as ingested drugs, blood cells, foreign objects, medical implants, and human DNA. Also included in this category might be fingerprints and other kinds of biological residue. The gathering of such special kinds of nontestimonial evidence is a complex area rich in precedent. The Fourth Amendment guarantee that people be secure in their homes and in their persons has generally been interpreted by the courts to mean that the improper seizure of physical evidence of any kind is illegal and will result in exclusion of that evidence at trial. When very personal kinds of nontestimonial evidence are considered, however, the issue becomes more complicated.

The Right to Privacy

Two 1985 cases, *Hayes* v. *Florida*[182] and *Winston* v. *Lee*,[183] are examples of limits the courts have placed on the seizure of very personal forms of nontestimonial evidence. The *Hayes* case established the right of suspects to refuse to be fingerprinted when probable cause necessary to effect an arrest does not exist. *Winston* demonstrated the inviolability of the body against surgical and other substantially invasive techniques that might be ordered by authorities against a suspect's will.

In the *Winston* case, Rudolph Lee, Jr., was found a few blocks from the scene of a robbery with a gunshot wound in his chest. The robbery had involved an exchange of gunshots by a store owner and the robber, with the owner noting that the robber had apparently been hit by a bullet. At the hospital, the store owner identified Lee as the robber. The prosecution sought to have Lee submit to surgery to remove the bullet in his chest, arguing that the bullet would provide physical evidence linking him to the crime. Lee refused the surgery, and in *Winston* v. *Lee*, the U.S. Supreme Court ruled that Lee could not be ordered to undergo surgery because such a magnitude of intrusion into his body was unacceptable under the right to privacy guaranteed by the Fourth Amendment. The *Winston* case was based on precedent established in *Schmerber* v. *California* (1966).[184] The *Schmerber* case turned on the extraction against the defendant's will of a blood sample to be measured for alcohol content. In *Schmerber*, the Court ruled that warrants must be obtained for bodily intrusions unless fast action is necessary to prevent the destruction of evidence by natural physiological processes.

Body-Cavity Searches

Lecture Note Explain that "body packing" involves the swallowing or insertion into body cavities of drug-filled containers for the purpose of drug smuggling.

Thematic Question Read what the text has to say about the case of *U.S.* v. *Montoya de Hernandez* (1985). In your opinion, did investigating officers have sufficient reason to detain the suspect in this case? Explain.

Lecture Note Explain that much information in contemporary society exists in electronic form (such as computer files, fax messages, and telecommunications) and can be the target of both criminal offenders and criminal investigators seeking to build cases.

In early 2005, officers of the Suffolk County (New York) Police Department arrested 36-year-old Terrance Haynes and charged him with marijuana possession.[185] After placing him in the back of a patrol car, Haynes appeared to choke and had difficulty breathing. Soon his breathing stopped, prompting officers to use the Heimlich maneuver, which dislodged a plastic bag from Haynes's windpipe. The bag contained 11 packets of cocaine. Although Haynes survived the ordeal, he faced up to 25 years in prison.

While some suspects might literally "cough up" evidence, some are more successful at hiding it *in* their bodies. Body-cavity searches are among the most problematic types of searches for police today. "Strip" searches of convicts in prison, including the search of body cavities, have generally been held to be permissible.

The 1985 Supreme Court case of *U.S.* v. *Montoya de Hernandez*[186] focused on the issue of "alimentary canal smuggling," in which the offender typically swallows condoms filled with cocaine or heroin and waits for nature to take its course to recover the substance. In the *Montoya* case, a woman known to be a "balloon swallower" arrived in the United States on a flight from Colombia. She was detained by customs officials and given a pat-down search by a female agent. The agent reported that the woman's abdomen was firm and suggested that X-rays be taken. The suspect refused and was given the choice of submitting to further tests or taking the next flight back to Colombia. No flight was immediately available, however, and the suspect was placed in a room for 16 hours, where she refused all food and drink. Finally, a court order for an X-ray was obtained. The procedure revealed "balloons," and the woman was detained another four days, during which time she passed numerous cocaine-filled plastic condoms. The Court ruled that the woman's confinement was not unreasonable, based as it was on the supportable suspicion that she was "body-packing" cocaine. Any discomfort she experienced, the Court ruled, "resulted solely from the method that she chose to smuggle illicit drugs."[187]

Electronic Eavesdropping

Modern technology makes possible increasingly complex forms of communication. One of the first and best known of the U.S. Supreme Court decisions involving electronic communications was the 1928 case of *Olmstead* v. *U.S.*[188] In *Olmstead*, bootleggers used their home telephones to discuss and transact business. Agents tapped the lines and based their investigation and ensuing arrests on conversations they overheard. The defendants were convicted and eventually appealed to the high court, arguing that the agents had in effect seized information illegally without a search warrant in violation of the defendants' Fourth Amendment right to be secure in their homes. The Court ruled, however, that telephone lines were not an extension of the defendants' home and therefore were not protected by the constitutional guarantee of security. Subsequent federal statutes (discussed shortly) have substantially modified the significance of *Olmstead*.

Recording devices carried on the body of an undercover agent or an informant were ruled to produce admissible evidence in *On Lee* v. *U.S.* (1952)[189] and *Lopez* v. *U.S.* (1963).[190] The 1967 case of *Berger* v. *New York*[191] permitted wiretaps and "bugs" in instances where state law provided for the use of such devices and where officers obtained a warrant based on probable cause.

Recording devices carried on the body of an undercover agent produce admissible evidence.

The Court appeared to undertake a significant change of direction in the area of electronic eavesdropping when it decided the case of *Katz* v. *U.S.* in 1967.[192] Federal agents had monitored a number of Katz's telephone calls from a public phone using a device separate from the phone lines and attached to the glass of the phone booth. The Court, in this case, stated that what a person makes an effort to keep private, even in a public place, requires a judicial decision, in the form of a warrant issued upon probable cause, to unveil. In the words of the Court, "The government's activities in electronically listening to and recording the petitioner's words violated the privacy upon which he justifiably relied while using the telephone booth and thus constituted a 'search and seizure' within the meaning of the Fourth Amendment."

In 1968, with the case of *Lee* v. *Florida*,[193] the Court applied the Federal Communications Act[194] to telephone conversations that may be the object of police investigation and held that evidence obtained without a warrant could not be used in state proceedings if it resulted from a wiretap. The only person who has the authority to permit eavesdropping, according to that act, is the sender of the message.

The Federal Communications Act, originally passed in 1934, does not specifically mention the potential interest of law enforcement agencies in monitoring communications. Title III of the Omnibus Crime Control and Safe Streets Act of 1968, however, mostly prohibits wiretaps but does allow officers to listen to electronic communications when (1) an officer is one of the parties involved in the communication, (2) one of the parties is not the officer but willingly decides to share the communication with the officer, or (3) officers obtain a warrant based on probable cause. In the 1971 case of *U.S.* v. *White*,[195] the Court held that law enforcement officers may intercept electronic information when one of the parties involved in the communication gives his or her consent, even without a warrant.

Thematic Question What types of electronic information that the typical person generates in an average day might form the basis for the criminal prosecution of those involved in illegal activities?

In 1984, the Supreme Court decided the case of *U.S.* v. *Karo*,[106] in which DEA agents had arrested James Karo for cocaine importation. Officers had placed a radio transmitter inside a 50-gallon drum of ether purchased by Karo for use in processing the cocaine. The transmitter was placed inside the drum with the consent of the seller of the ether but without a search warrant. The shipment of ether was followed to the Karo house, and Karo was arrested and convicted of cocaine-trafficking charges. Karo appealed to the U.S. Supreme Court, claiming that the radio beeper had violated his reasonable expectation of privacy inside his premises and that, without a warrant, the evidence it produced was tainted. The Court agreed and overturned his conviction.

Minimization Requirement for Electronic Surveillance

The Supreme Court established a minimization requirement pertinent to electronic surveillance in the 1978 case of *U.S.* v. *Scott*.[197] *Minimization* means that officers must make every reasonable effort to monitor only those conversations, through the use of phone taps, body bugs, and the like, that are specifically related to the criminal activity under investigation. As soon as it becomes obvious that a conversation is innocent, then the monitoring personnel are required to cease their invasion of privacy. Problems arise if the conversation occurs in a foreign language, if it is "coded," or if it is ambiguous. It has been suggested that investigators involved in electronic surveillance maintain logbooks of their activities that specifically show monitored conversations, as well as efforts made at minimization.[198]

Lecture Note Assign students the task of keeping a daily log of the kinds of electronic signals and forms of electronic information they generate during one week. Ask them to decide how each item of information (and each type of media involved) might be explored by criminal investigators were the students to be accused of criminal activity.

Lecture Note Describe how the Electronic Communications Privacy Act, passed by Congress in 1986, limits the wiretapping and eavesdropping activities of law enforcement officers.

The Electronic Communications Privacy Act of 1986

Passed by Congress in 1986, the **Electronic Communications Privacy Act (ECPA)**[199] brought major changes in the requirements law enforcement officers must meet to intercept wire communications (those involving the human voice). The ECPA deals specifically with

Electronic Communications Privacy Act (ECPA)
A law passed by Congress in 1986 establishing the due process requirements that law enforcement officers must meet in order to legally intercept wire communications.

The PATRIOT Act has not diminished our liberty. It has defended our liberty and made America more secure.

—George W. Bush, forty-third president of the United States

three areas of communication: (1) wiretaps and bugs, (2) pen registers that record the numbers dialed from a telephone, and (3) tracing devices that determine the number from which a call emanates. The act also addresses the procedures to be followed by officers in obtaining records relating to communications services, and it establishes requirements for gaining access to stored electronic communications and records of those communications. The ECPA basically requires that investigating officers must obtain wiretap-type court orders to eavesdrop on *ongoing communications.* The use of pen registers and recording devices, however, is specifically excluded by the law from court order requirements.[200]

A related measure, the Communications Assistance for Law Enforcement Act of 1994,[201] appropriated $500 million to modify the U.S. phone system to allow for continued wiretapping by law enforcement agencies. The law also specifies a standard-setting process for the redesign of existing equipment that would permit effective wiretapping in the face of coming technological advances. In the words of the FBI's Telecommunications Industry Liaison Unit, "This law requires telecommunications carriers, as defined in the Act, to ensure law enforcement's ability, pursuant to court order or other lawful authorization, to intercept communications notwithstanding advanced telecommunications technologies."[202] In 2009, 2,376 wiretap requests were approved by federal and state judges, and approximately 4.6 million conversations were intercepted by law enforcement agencies throughout the country.[203]

The Telecommunications Act of 1996

Title V of the Telecommunications Act of 1996[204] made it a federal offense for anyone engaged in interstate or international communications to knowingly use a telecommunications device "to create, solicit, or initiate the transmission of any comment, request, suggestion, proposal, image, or other communication which is obscene, lewd, lascivious, filthy, or indecent, with intent to annoy, abuse, threaten, or harass another person." The law also provided special penalties for anyone who "makes a telephone call . . . without disclosing his identity and with intent to annoy, abuse, threaten, or harass any person at the called number or who receives the communication" or who "makes or causes the telephone of another repeatedly or continuously to ring, with intent to harass any person at the called number; or makes repeated telephone calls" for the purpose of harassing a person at the called number.

A section of the law, known as the Communications Decency Act (CDA),[205] criminalized the transmission to minors of "patently offensive" obscene materials over the Internet or other computer telecommunications services. Portions of the CDA, however, were invalidated by the U.S. Supreme Court in the case of *Reno* v. *ACLU* (1997).[206]

The USA PATRIOT Act of 2001

USA PATRIOT Act
A federal law (Public Law 107–56) enacted in response to terrorist attacks on the World Trade Center and the Pentagon on September 11, 2001. The law, officially titled the Uniting and Strengthening America by Providing Appropriate Tools Required to Intercept and Obstruct Terrorism Act, substantially broadened the investigative authority of law enforcement agencies throughout America and is applicable to many crimes other than terrorism. The law was slightly revised and reauthorized by Congress in 2006.

The **USA PATRIOT Act** of 2001, which is also discussed in CJ Exhibit 5–3, made it easier for police investigators to intercept many forms of electronic communications. Under previous federal law, for example, investigators could not obtain a wiretap order to intercept *wire* communications for violations of the Computer Fraud and Abuse Act.[207] In several well-known investigations, however, hackers had stolen teleconferencing services from telephone companies and then used those services to plan and execute hacking attacks.

The act[208] added felony violations of the Computer Fraud and Abuse Act to Section 2516(1) of Title 18 of the U.S. Code—the portion of federal law that lists specific types of crimes for which investigators may obtain a wiretap order for wire communications.

The USA PATRIOT Act of 2001 also modified that portion of the ECPA that governs law enforcement access to stored electronic communications (such as e-mail) to include stored wire communications (such as voice mail). Before the modification, law enforcement officers needed to obtain a wiretap order (rather than a search warrant) to obtain unopened voice communications. Because today's e-mail messages may contain digitized voice "attachments," investigators were sometimes required to obtain both a search warrant and a wiretap order to learn the contents of a specific message. Under the act, the same rules now apply to both stored wire communications and stored electronic communications. Wiretap

CJ Exhibit 5–3
The USA PATRIOT Act of 2001 and the USA PATRIOT Improvement and Reauthorization Act of 2005

On October 26, 2001, President George W. Bush signed into law the USA PATRIOT Act, also known as the Uniting and Strengthening America by Providing Appropriate Tools Required to Intercept and Obstruct Terrorism Act. The law, which was drafted in response to the September 11, 2001, terrorist attacks on American targets, substantially increased the investigatory authority of federal, state, and local police agencies.

The act permits longer jail terms for certain suspects arrested without a warrant, broadens authority for **"sneak and peek" searches** (searches conducted without prior notice and in the absence of the suspect), and enhances the power of prosecutors. The law also increases the ability of federal authorities to tap phones (including wireless devices), share intelligence information, track Internet usage, crack down on money laundering, and protect U.S. borders. Many of the crime-fighting powers created under the legislation are not limited to acts of terrorism but apply to many different kinds of criminal offenses.

The 2001 law led individual-rights advocates to question whether the government unfairly expanded police powers at the expense of civil liberties. While many aspects of the USA PATRIOT Act have been criticized as potentially unconstitutional, Section 213, which authorizes delayed notice of the execution of a warrant, may be most vulnerable to court challenge. The American Civil Liberties Union (ACLU) maintains that under this section, law enforcement agents could enter a house, apartment, or office with a search warrant while the occupant is away, search through his or her property, and take photographs without having to tell the suspect about the search until later.[1] The ACLU also believes that this provision is illegal because the Fourth Amendment to the Constitution protects against unreasonable searches and seizures and requires the government to obtain a warrant and to give notice to the person whose property will be searched before conducting the search. The notice requirement enables the suspect to assert his or her Fourth Amendment rights.

In 2005, the U.S. Congress reauthorized most provisions of the USA PATRIOT Act, and on February 27, 2011, President Obama signed legislation providing for an extension of several terrorist surveillance provisions included in the USA PATRIOT Act and in the Intelligence Reform and Terrorism Prevention Act of 2004.

Read the entire USA PATRIOT Act of 2001 at **Library Extra 5–6**. Title 18 of the U.S. Code is available at **Library Extra 5–7**. The USA PATRIOT Improvement and Reauthorization Act of 2005 is available at **Library Extra 5–8**.

[1]Much of the information in this paragraph is taken from American Civil Liberties Union, "How the Anti-Terrorism Bill Expands Law Enforcement 'Sneak and Peek' Warrants," http://www.aclu.org/congress/1102301b.html (accessed February 12, 2005).

References: USA PATRIOT Improvement and Reauthorization Act of 2005 (Public Law 109–177); U.S. Department of Justice, Field Guidance on Authorities (Redacted) Enacted in the 2001 Anti-Terrorism Legislation (Washington, DC: DOJ, no date), http://www.epic.org/terrorism/DOJguidance.pdf (accessed August 28, 2009); USA PATRIOT Act, 2001 (Public Law 107–56); American Civil Liberties Union, "How the Anti-Terrorism Bill Expands Law Enforcement 'Sneak and Peek' Warrants," http://www.aclu.org/congress/1102301b.html (accessed August 28, 2009); American Civil Liberties Union, "How the Anti-Terrorism Bill Limits Judicial Oversight of Telephone and Internet Surveillance," http://www.aclu.org/congress/1102301g.html (accessed August 28, 2009); and the White House, "Bills Signed into Law by the President," February 27, 2010, http://www.whitehouse.gov/the-press-office/bills-signed-law-president (accessed September 16, 2010).

orders, which are often much more difficult to obtain than search warrants, are now only required to intercept real-time telephone conversations.

Before passage of the USA PATRIOT Act, federal law allowed investigators to use an administrative subpoena (that is, a subpoena authorized by a federal or state statute or by a federal or state grand jury or trial court) to compel Internet service providers to provide a limited class of information, such as a customer's name, address, length of service, and means of payment. Also under previous law, investigators could not subpoena certain records, including credit card numbers or details about other forms of payment for Internet service. Such information, however, can be highly relevant in determining a suspect's true identity because, in many cases, users register with Internet service providers using false names.

Previous federal law[209] was also technology specific, relating primarily to telephone communications. Local and long-distance telephone billing records, for example, could be subpoenaed but not billing information for Internet communications or records of Internet session times and durations. Similarly, previous law allowed the government to use a subpoena to obtain the customer's "telephone number or other subscriber number or identity" but did not define what that phrase meant in the context of Internet communications.

The USA PATRIOT Act amended portions of this federal law[210] to update and expand the types of records that law enforcement authorities may obtain with a subpoena. "Records of session times and durations," as well as "any temporarily assigned network address," may now be gathered. Such changes should make the process of identifying computer criminals and tracing their Internet communications faster and easier.

Finally, the USA PATRIOT Act facilitates the use of roving, or multipoint, wiretaps. Roving wiretaps, issued with court approval, target a specific individual and not a particular telephone number or communications device. Hence law enforcement agents armed with

"sneak and peek" search
A search that occurs in the suspect's absence and without his or her prior knowledge. Also known as a *delayed-notification search.*

Thematic Question What is digital (or electronic) evidence? How does it differ from other types of evidence, if at all? How should police investigators secure and handle digital evidence to protect its integrity?

Lecture Note Explain the concept of digital (or electronic) evidence. Explain that digital evidence is similar in many ways to other forms of evidence and that crime scenes involving digital evidence should be secured as soon as possible to avoid contamination or destruction of the evidence.

an order for a multipoint wiretap can follow the flow of communications engaged in by a person as he or she switches from one cellular phone to another or to a wired telephone.

In 2006, President George W. Bush signed the USA PATRIOT Improvement and Reauthorization Act of 2005[211] into law. The act, also referred to as PATRIOT II, made permanent 14 provisions of the original 2001 legislation that had been slated to expire and extended others for another four years (including the roving wiretap provision and a provision that allows authorities to seize business records). It also addressed some of the concerns of civil libertarians who had criticized the earlier law as too restrictive. Finally, the new law provided additional protections for mass transportation systems and seaports, closed some legal loopholes in laws aimed at preventing terrorist financing, and included a subsection called the Combat Methamphetamine Epidemic Act (CMEA). The CMEA contains significant provisions intended to strengthen federal, state, and local efforts designed at curtailing the spread of methamphetamine use.

On February 27, 2010, President Barack Obama signed into law legislation extending a number of provisions of the PATRIOT Act that would have otherwise expired. The president's signature gave new life to the roving wiretap and business records provisions of the act, as well as some others.[212]

Learn more about electronic surveillance and wiretapping in criminal cases via **Web Extra 5–4**, and read the complete 2006 USA PATRIOT Act reauthorization legislation at **Library Extra 5–9**.

Electronic and Latent Evidence

The Internet, computer networks, and automated data systems present many new opportunities for committing criminal activity.[213] Computers and other electronic devices are increasingly being used to commit, enable, or support crimes perpetrated against people, organizations, and property. Whether the crime involves attacks against computer systems or the information they contain or more traditional offenses such as murder, money laundering, trafficking, or fraud, the proper seizure of **electronic evidence** that is specifically described in a valid search warrant has become increasingly important.

electronic evidence
Information and data of investigative value that are stored in or transmitted by an electronic device.[i]

Electronic evidence is "information and data of investigative value that are stored in or transmitted by an electronic device."[214] Such evidence is often acquired when physical items, such as computers, removable disks, CDs, DVDs, SSDs, flash drives, smart phones, SIM cards, iPads, iPods, Blackberrys, and other electronic devices, are collected from a crime scene or are obtained from a suspect.

Electronic evidence has special characteristics: (1) It is latent; (2) it can be sent across national and state borders quickly and easily; (3) it is fragile and can easily be altered, damaged, compromised, or destroyed by improper handling or improper examination; (4) it may be time sensitive. Like DNA or fingerprints, electronic evidence is **latent evidence** because it is not readily visible to the human eye under normal conditions. Special equipment and software are required to "see" and evaluate electronic evidence. In the courtroom, expert testimony may be needed to explain the acquisition of electronic evidence and the examination process used to interpret it.

latent evidence
Evidence of relevance to a criminal investigation that is not readily seen by the unaided eye.

In 2002, in recognition of the special challenges posed by electronic evidence, the Computer Crime and Intellectual Property Section (CCIPS) of the Criminal Division of the U.S. Department of Justice released a how-to manual for law enforcement officers called *Searching and Seizing Computers and Obtaining Electronic Evidence in Criminal Investigations.*[215] The manual, which is a how-to in **digital criminal forensics**, can be accessed via **Library Extra 5–10**.

digital criminal forensics
The lawful seizure, acquisition, analysis, reporting, and safeguarding of data from digital devices that may contain information of evidentiary value to the trier of fact in criminal events.[ii]

About the same time, the Technical Working Group for Electronic Crime Scene Investigation (TWGECSI) released a much more detailed guide for law enforcement officers to use in gathering electronic evidence. The manual, *Electronic Crime Scene Investigation: A Guide for First Responders*,[216] grew out of a partnership formed in 1998 between the National Cybercrime Training Partnership, the Office of Law Enforcement Standards, and the National Institute of Justice. The working group was asked to identify, define, and establish basic criteria to assist federal and state agencies in handling electronic investigations and related prosecutions.

TWGECSI guidelines say that law enforcement must take special precautions when documenting, collecting, and preserving electronic evidence to maintain its integrity. The guidelines also note that the first law enforcement officer on the scene (commonly called the *first responder*) should take steps to ensure the safety of everyone at the scene and to protect the integrity of all evidence, both traditional and electronic. The entire TWGECSI guide, which includes many practical instructions for investigators working with electronic evidence, is available at **Library Extra 5–11**.

Once digital evidence has been gathered, it must be analyzed. Consequently, in 2004, the government-sponsored Technical Working Group for the Examination of Digital Evidence (TWGEDE) published *Forensic Examination of Digital Evidence: A Guide for Law Enforcement*.[217] Among the guide's recommendations are that digital evidence should be acquired in a manner that protects and preserves the integrity of the original evidence and that examination should only be conducted on a *copy* of the original evidence. The entire guide, which is nearly 100 pages long, can be accessed via **Library Extra 5–12**.

Warrantless searches bear special mention in any discussion of electronic evidence. In the 1999 case of *U.S.* v. *Carey*,[218] a federal appellate court held that the consent a defendant had given to police for his apartment to be searched did not extend to the search of his computer once it was taken to a police station. Similarly, in *U.S.* v. *Turner* (1999),[219] the First Circuit Court of Appeals held that the warrantless police search of a defendant's personal computer while in his apartment exceeded the scope of the defendant's consent.

A PowerPoint presentation that supports this chapter is available from your Prentice Hall representative.

Summary

POLICING: LEGAL ASPECTS

- Legal restraints on police action stem primarily from the U.S. Constitution's Bill of Rights, especially the Fourth, Fifth, and Sixth Amendments, which (along with the Fourteenth Amendment) require due process of law. Most due process requirements of relevance to police work concern three major areas: (1) evidence and investigation (often called *search and seizure*), (2) arrest, and (3) interrogation. Each of these areas has been addressed by a number of important U.S. Supreme Court decisions, and this chapter discusses those decisions and their significance for police work.
- The Bill of Rights was designed to protect citizens against abuses of police power. It does so by guaranteeing due process of law for everyone suspected of having committed a crime and by ensuring the availability of constitutional rights to all citizens, regardless of state or local law or procedure. Within the context of criminal case processing, due process requirements mandate that all justice system officials, not only the police, respect the rights of accused individuals throughout the criminal justice process.
- The Fourth Amendment to the Constitution declares that people must be secure in their homes and in their persons against unreasonable searches and seizures. Consequently, law enforcement officers are generally required to demonstrate probable cause in order to obtain a search warrant if they are to conduct searches and seize the property of criminal suspects legally. The Supreme Court has established that police officers, in order to protect themselves from attack, have the right to search a person being arrested and to search the area under the arrestee's immediate control.
- An arrest takes place whenever a law enforcement officer restricts a person's freedom to leave. Arrests may occur when an officer comes upon a crime in progress, but most jurisdictions also allow warrantless arrests for felonies when a crime is not in progress, as long as probable cause can later be demonstrated.
- Information that is useful for law enforcement purposes is called *intelligence*, and as this chapter has shown, intelligence gathering is vital to police work. The need for useful information often leads police investigators to question suspects, informants, and potentially knowledgeable citizens. When suspects who are in custody become subject to interrogation, they must be advised of their *Miranda* rights before questioning begins. The *Miranda* warnings, which were mandated by the Supreme Court in the 1966 case of *Miranda* v. *Arizona*, are listed in this chapter. They ensure that suspects know their rights—including the right to remain silent—in the face of police interrogation.

QUESTIONS FOR REVIEW

1. Name some of the legal restraints on police action, and list some types of behavior that might be considered abuse of police authority.
2. How do the Bill of Rights and democratically inspired legal restraints on the police help ensure personal freedoms in our society?
3. Describe the legal standards for assessing searches and seizures conducted by law enforcement agents.
4. What is arrest, and when does it occur? How do legal understandings of the term differ from popular depictions of the arrest process?
5. What is the role of interrogation in intelligence gathering? List each of the *Miranda* warnings. Which recent U.S. Supreme Court cases have affected *Miranda* warning requirements?

Policing: Issues and Challenges

CHAPTER 6

Learning Objectives

After reading this chapter, you should be able to:

1. Describe the police working personality, relating it to police subculture. 156
2. List and describe different types of police corruption, and discuss possible methods for building police integrity. 157
3. Explain the dangers of police work, and discuss what can be done to reduce those dangers. 163
4. Describe the changed role of American police in the post-9/11 environment. 169
5. Describe the civil liability issues associated with policing, and identify common sources of civil suits against the police. 172
6. Describe racial profiling and biased policing, and explain why they have become significant issues in policing today. 176
7. Describe the situations in which police officers are most likely to use force, and provide some guidelines for determining when too much force has been used. 179
8. Demonstrate why professionalism and ethics are important in policing today. 183
9. Identify some of the issues related to ethnic and gender diversity in policing, and suggest ways of addressing them. 186
10. Describe the nature and extent of private protective services in the United States today, and discuss what role you think they will play in the future. 189

"The continuous threat of terrorism has thrust domestic preparedness obligations to the very top of the law enforcement agenda."

—Colonel Joel Leson, director, IACP Center for Police Leadership[1]

▲ New York City Police Department officers embrace as the ball drops during a Times Square New Year's Eve party, ushering in a new year. The police working personality has been characterized as authoritarian, suspicious, and conservative. How does the police working personality develop?
Gregory Bull/AP Wide World Photos

Introduction

Today's police officers and administrators face many complex issues. Some concerns, such as corruption, on-the-job dangers, and the use of deadly force, derive from the very nature of police work. Others, like racial profiling and exposure to civil liability, have arisen due to common practices, characteristic police values, public expectations, legislative action, and ongoing societal change. One of the most significant challenges facing American law enforcement today is policing a multicultural society. All of these issues are discussed in the pages that follow. We begin, however, with the police recruit socialization process. It is vital to understand this process because the values and expectations learned through it not only contribute to the nature of many important police issues but also determine how the police view and respond to those issues.

Police Personality and Culture

New police officers learn what is considered appropriate police behavior by working with seasoned veterans. Through conversations with other officers in the locker room, in a squad car, or over a cup of coffee, a new recruit is introduced to the value-laden subculture of police work. **Police subculture** can be understood as "the set of informal values which characterize the police force as a distinct community with a common identity."[2] This process of informal socialization plays a much bigger role than formal police academy training in determining how rookies come to see police work. Through it, new officers gain a shared view of the world that can best be described as "streetwise." Streetwise cops know what official department policy is, but they also know the most efficient way to get a job done. By the time rookie officers become streetwise, they know which of the various informal means of accomplishing the job are acceptable to other officers. The police subculture creates few real mavericks, but it also produces few officers who view their jobs exclusively in terms of public mandates and official dictums.

1 Describe the police working personality, relating it to police subculture.

police subculture
A particular set of values, beliefs, and acceptable forms of behavior characteristic of American police with which the police profession strives to imbue new recruits. Socialization into the police subculture commences with recruit training and continues thereafter.

In the 1960s, renowned criminologist Jerome Skolnick described what he called the **police working personality**.[3] Skolnick's description of the police personality was consistent with William Westley's classic study of the Gary (Indiana) Police Department, in which he found a police subculture with its own "customs, laws, and morality,"[4] and with Arthur Niederhoffer's observation that cynicism was pervasive among officers in New York City.[5] More recent authors have claimed that the "big curtain of secrecy" surrounding much of police work shields knowledge of the nature of the police personality from outsiders.[6] Taken in concert, these writers offer the picture of the police working personality shown in Table 6–1.

police working personality
All aspects of the traditional values and patterns of behavior evidenced by police officers who have been effectively socialized into the police subculture. Characteristics of the police personality often extend to the personal lives of law enforcement personnel.

Thematic Question What elements of the police subculture and personality might lead to problems for female officers, both personally and in their underutilization in a police department?

Some characteristics of the police working personality are essential for survival and effectiveness. For example, because officers are often exposed to highly emotional and potentially threatening confrontations with belligerent people, they must develop efficient authoritarian strategies for gaining control over others. Similarly, a suspicious nature makes for a good police officer, especially during interrogations and investigations.

TABLE 6–1
The Police Personality

Authoritarian	Cynical	Secret	Efficient
Honorable			
Insecure	Loyal	Individualistic	Dogmatic
Suspicious	Hostile	Conservative	Prejudiced

However, other characteristics of the police working personality are not as advantageous. For example, many officers are cynical, and some can be hostile toward members of the public who do not share their conservative values. These traits result from regular interaction with suspects, most of whom deny any wrongdoing even when they are clearly guilty in the eyes of the police. Eventually, personal traits that result from typical police work become firmly ingrained, setting the cornerstone of the police working personality.

There are at least two sources of the police personality. On the one hand, it may be that components of the police personality already exist in some individuals and draw them toward police work.[7] Supporting this view are studies that indicate that police officers who come from conservative backgrounds view themselves as defenders of middle-class morality.[8] On the other hand, some aspects of the police personality can be attributed to the socialization into the police subculture that rookie officers experience when they are inducted into police ranks.

Researchers have reported similar elements in police subculture throughout the United States.[9] They have concluded that like all cultures, police subculture is a relatively stable collection of beliefs and values that is unlikely to change from within. Police subculture may, however, be changed through external pressures, such as new hiring practices, investigations into police corruption or misuse of authority, and commission reports that create pressure for police reform.[10] Learn more about police subculture and police behavior at **Web Extra 6–1**.

Lecture Note Describe the police subculture according to the values that this chapter says characterize it. Explain how the police subculture influences the development of the police personality through socialization, and review the characteristics of the police personality by referring to Table 6–1.

Thematic Question What forces gave rise to the police subculture? Which elements of the subculture do you see as particularly desirable or undesirable? Which aspects of the subculture would you change if you could? How would you effect such changes?

Corruption and Integrity

2 List and describe different types of police corruption, and discuss possible methods for building police integrity.

Although most law enforcement officers perform their duties responsibly and with honor, some do not. In 2006, for example, Border Patrol Agent Oscar Antonio Ortiz pleaded guilty to charges of conspiracy to smuggle aliens into the United States, making a false claim to U.S. citizenship, making a false statement in the acquisition of a firearm, and being an illegal alien in possession of a firearm.[11] Ortiz, a Mexican citizen who was born in Tijuana, secured a job with the Border Patrol in 2001 by using a fake birth certificate that listed Chicago as his place of birth. Court documents show that he conspired with at least one other Border Patrol agent to smuggle more than 100 Mexican nationals into the United States. Officials revealed that intercepted phone calls between Ortiz and another agent spoke of payments of up to $2,000 per person smuggled into the United States. The recorded calls also discussed rates that human traffickers working with the agents should be charged to secure the agents' cooperation.[12] On July 28, 2006, a federal district court judge sentenced Ortiz to serve 60 months in prison. He will likely be deported after his sentence is complete.

> Good cops always seem to be able to identify causes of problems and to come up with the least troublesome ways of solving them.
>
> —Jerome Skolnick

The kind of corruption seen in Ortiz's case pales alongside that of two retired New York City police detectives who were convicted in 2006 of giving confidential information to mob leaders and of misusing their authority as law enforcement officers to kidnap and kill rival gangsters.[13] Federal prosecutors successfully portrayed retired police investigator Louis Eppolito, 56, and his former partner, Stephen Caracappa, 63, as assassins working for the Lucchese crime family. The two are suspected of killing at least eight men in one of the city's most spectacular police corruption scandals ever. Their convictions, on 70 counts of racketeering, came 20 years after their first victim was gunned down in a New York City parking garage. Caracappa, who may have been the trigger man in most of the killings, was known for helping to create the New York Police Department (NYPD) Organized Crime Homicide Unit and was described as "a gatekeeper of information about Mafia killings investigated by police." Although the jurors remained anonymous throughout the trial for protection from possible retaliation, one of them, a building safety official from Long Island, told reporters after the trial that he was shocked at the detectives for having broken their oath to uphold the law. "When you're given an oath, and an oath as precious as being a police officer, and a duty to protect and serve people, that is the highest oath ever," said the juror. "It's like, 'How dare you violate that oath?' . . . When you violate [that] oath, you lose the respect of the people you're sworn to protect."[14] In 2010, in an interesting footnote to the Eppolito case, the NYPD agreed to pay $9.9 million in an out-of-court settlement to 62-year-old Barry Gibbs, whom Eppolito had framed for murder in 1988.[15] Gibbs spent 18 years in prison before the injustice was discovered.

Thematic Question What elements of the police subculture might be changed to help fight police corruption? How could such changes be brought about?

Thematic Question What elements of police subculture and personality cause police officers and administrators to avoid acknowledging the psychological stress of using deadly force?

Multiculturalism and Diversity
Policing a Multicultural Society

Members of some social groups have backgrounds, values, and perspectives that, while not directly supportive of law-breaking, contrast sharply with those of many police officials. Robert M. Shusta, a well-known writer on multicultural law enforcement, says that police officers "need to recognize the fact of poor police–minority relations historically, including *unequal* treatment under the law."[1] Moreover, says Shusta, "many officers and citizens are defensive with each other because their contact is tinged with negative historical 'baggage.'"

In other words, even though discrimination in the enforcement of the criminal law may not be commonplace today, it *was* in the past—and perceptions built on past experience are often difficult to change. Moreover, if the function of law enforcement is to "protect and serve" law-abiding citizens from all backgrounds, then it becomes vital for officers to understand and respect differences in habits, customs, beliefs, patterns of thought, and traditions.[2] As Shusta says, "the acts of approaching, communicating, questioning, assisting, and establishing trust with members of different groups require special knowledge and skills that have nothing to do with the fact that 'the law is the law' and must be enforced equally. Acquiring sensitivity, knowledge, and skills leads to [an increased appreciation for the position of others] that will contribute to improved communications with members of all groups."[3]

How can police officers acquire greater sensitivity to the issues involved in policing a diverse multicultural society? Some researchers suggest that law enforcement officers of *all* backgrounds begin by exploring their own prejudices. Prejudices, which are judgments or opinions formed before facts are known and which usually involve negative or unfavorable thoughts about groups of people, can lead to discrimination. Most people, including police officers, are able to reduce their tendency to discriminate against those who are different by exploring and uprooting their own personal prejudices.

One technique for identifying prejudices is cultural awareness training. As practiced in some police departments today, cultural awareness training explores the impact of culture on human behavior—and especially law-breaking behavior. Cultural awareness training generally involves four stages:[4]

- *Clarifying the relationship between cultural awareness and police professionalism.* As Shusta explains it, "The more professional a police officer is, the more sophisticated he or she is in responding to people of all backgrounds and the more successful he or she is in cross-cultural contact."[5]
- *Recognizing personal prejudices.* In the second stage of cultural awareness training, participating officers are asked to recognize and identify their own personal prejudices and biases. Once prejudices have been identified, trainers strive to show how they can affect daily behavior.
- *Acquiring sensitivity to police-community relations.* In this stage of training, participating officers learn about historical and existing community perceptions of the police. Training can often be enhanced through the use of carefully chosen and well-qualified guest speakers or participants from minority communities.
- *Developing interpersonal relations skills.* The goal of this last stage of training is to assist with the development of the positive verbal and nonverbal communications skills necessary for successful interaction with community members. Many trainers believe that basic skills training will result in the continuing development of such skills because officers will quickly begin to see the benefits (in terms of lessened interpersonal conflict) of effective interpersonal skills.

[1]Robert M. Shusta et al., *Multicultural Law Enforcement: Strategies for Peacekeeping in a Diverse Society*, 2nd ed. (Upper Saddle River, NJ: Prentice Hall, 2002), p. 4.

[2]Ibid., p. 16.

[3]Ibid., p. 4.

[4]Ibid., pp. 104–106.

[5]Ibid., p. 4.

police corruption
The abuse of police authority for personal or organizational gain.[i]

Class Activity Ask students to create a list of potentially corrupt police activities. Discuss the list, deciding on a "final" list of activities that most students agree are forms of corruption. Then have the class rank each of the items in the list from the least serious to the most serious.

Police corruption has been a problem in American society since the early days of policing. It is probably an ancient and natural tendency of human beings to attempt to placate or win over those in positions of authority over them. This tendency is complicated in today's materialistic society by greed and by the personal and financial benefits to be derived from evading the law. The temptations toward illegality offered to police range from a free cup of coffee from a restaurant owner to huge monetary bribes arranged by drug dealers to guarantee that the police will look the other way as an important shipment of contraband arrives. As noted criminologist Carl B. Klockars says, policing, by its very nature, "is an occupation that is rife with opportunities for misconduct. Policing is a highly discretionary, coercive activity that routinely takes place in private settings, out of the sight of supervisors, and in the presence of witnesses who are often regarded as unreliable."[16]

The effects of police corruption can be far-reaching. As Michael Palmiotto of Wichita State University notes, "Not only does misconduct committed by an officer personally affect that officer, it also affects the community, the police department that employs the officer and every police department and police officer in America. Frequently, negative police actions caused by inappropriate police behavior reach every corner of the nation, and at times, the world."[17]

Exactly what constitutes corruption is not always clear. Ethicists say that police corruption ranges from minor offenses to serious violations of the law. In recognition of what some have called corruption's "slippery slope,"[18] most police departments now explicitly prohibit even the acceptance of minor gratuities, like a free cup of coffee. The slippery slope perspective holds that even a small thank-you accepted from a member of the public can lead to a more ready acceptance of larger bribes. An officer who begins to accept, and then expect, gratuities may soon find that his or her practice of policing becomes influenced by such gifts and that larger ones soon follow. At that point, the officer may easily slide to the bottom of the moral slope, which was made slippery by previous small concessions.

Thomas Barker and David Carter, who have studied police corruption in depth, make the distinction between "occupational deviance," which is motivated by the desire for personal benefit, and "abuse of authority, which occurs most often to further the organizational goals of law enforcement, including arrest, ticketing, and the successful conviction of suspects."[19]

FBI Special Agent Frank Perry, former chief of the bureau's ethics unit, distinguishes between police deviance and police corruption. Police deviance, according to Perry, consists of "unprofessional on- and off-duty misconduct, isolated instances of misuse of position, improper relationships with informants or criminals, sexual harassment, disparaging racial or sexual comments, embellished/falsified reporting, time and attendance abuse, insubordination, nepotism, cronyism, and noncriminal unauthorized disclosure of information."[20] Deviance, says Perry, is a precursor to individual and organizational corruption. It may eventually lead to outright corruption unless police supervisors and internal affairs units are alert to the warning signs and actively intervene to prevent corruption from developing.

Nearly all men can stand adversity, but if you want to test a man's character, give him power.

—Abraham Lincoln, sixteenth president of the United States[ii]

Figure 6–1 sorts examples of police corruption by their level of seriousness, though not everyone would agree with this ranking. In fact, a survey of 6,982 New York City police officers found that 65% did not classify excessive force, which we define later in this chapter,

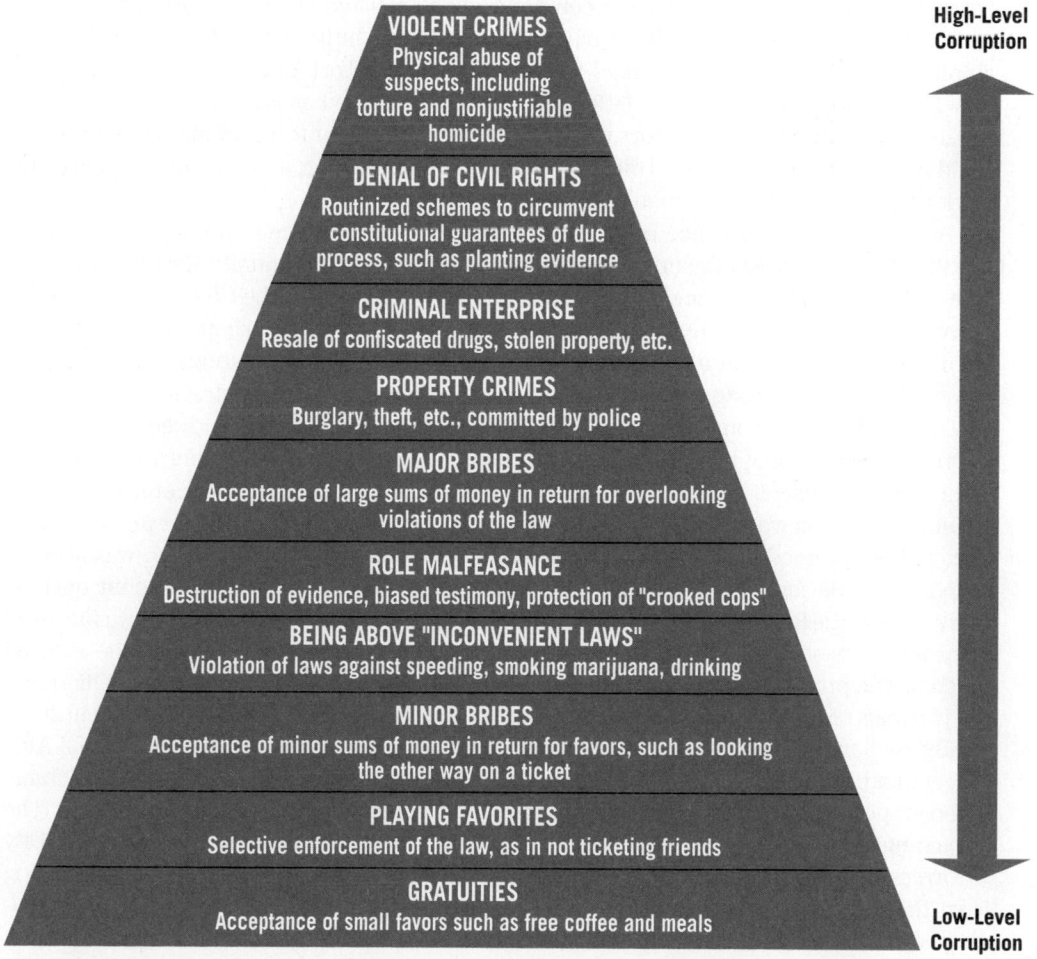

FIGURE 6–1 Types and Examples of Police Corruption

as a corrupt behavior.[21] Likewise, 71% of responding officers said that accepting a free meal is not a corrupt practice, and another 15% said that the personal use of illegal drugs by law enforcement officers should not be considered corruption.

Knapp Commission
A committee that investigated police corruption in New York City in the early 1970s.

In the early 1970s, Frank Serpico made headlines as he testified before the **Knapp Commission** on police corruption in New York City.[22] Serpico, an undercover operative within the police department, revealed a complex web of corruption in which money and services routinely changed hands in "protection rackets" created by unethical officers. The authors of the Knapp Commission report distinguished between two types of corrupt officers, which they termed "grass eaters" and "meat eaters."[23] "Grass eating," the most common form of police corruption, was described as illegitimate activity that occurs from time to time in the normal course of police work. It involves mostly small bribes or relatively minor services offered by citizens seeking to avoid arrest and prosecution. "Meat eating" is a much more serious form of corruption, involving the active seeking of illicit moneymaking opportunities by officers. Meat eaters solicit bribes through threat or intimidation, whereas grass eaters make the simpler mistake of not refusing bribes that are offered.

If you ever get lost, you can go find a policeman. The policeman will help you because he is your friend.
—A second-grade teacher

In 1993, during 11 days of corruption hearings reminiscent of the Knapp Commission era, a parade of crooked New York police officers testified before a commission headed by Milton Mollen, a former judge and deputy mayor of New York. Among the many revelations, officers spoke of dealing drugs, stealing confiscated drug funds, stifling investigations, and beating innocent people. Officer Michael Dowd, for example, told the commission that he had run a cocaine ring out of his station house in Brooklyn and had bought three homes on Long Island and a Corvette with the money he made. Most shocking of all, however, were allegations that high-level police officials attempted to hide embarrassing incidents in a "phantom file" and that many officials may have condoned unprofessional and even criminal practices by the officers under their command. Honest officers, including internal affairs investigators, described how their efforts to end corruption among their fellows had been defused and resisted by higher authorities.

Lecture Note Discuss police corruption, and ask the class to identify pressures that officers are likely to face that might lead to corruption. Focus in particular on the potential of illegal drugs, and the large amounts of money associated with them, for corrupting law enforcement personnel. Refer to Figure 6–1 to outline the various kinds of corrupt police practices.

Repercussions from the Mollen Commission hearings continue to be felt. In 2004, for example, a New York State judge ruled that the city of New York must pay special disability benefits to former police officer Jeffrey W. Baird, who served as an informer for the commission. Baird helped uncover corruption while working as an internal affairs officer but suffered from post-traumatic stress disorder after fellow officers threatened him, vandalized his work area, and sent obscene materials to his home.[24]

Another example of police corruption centered on the Los Angeles Police Department (LAPD) Rampart Division's antigang unit known as CRASH (Community Resources against Street Hoodlums).[25] The scandal began in mid-2000 when many of the CRASH unit's officers became embroiled in accusations claiming that they were operating like members of a criminal organization to threaten and frame hundreds of people through beatings, by planting evidence, and by committing perjury. They and other officers were alleged to be running a drug ring while eliminating competition from civilian dealers by framing them and seeing them sent to prison.[26] Seven shootings and at least two killings were among the illegal activities allegedly committed by officers. The scandal came to light after LAPD Officer Rafael Perez was caught stealing $1 million worth of cocaine from an evidence room. In exchange for an offer of leniency, Perez turned informant and cooperated with prosecutors. Perez, who was also accused of murder by a former girlfriend, provided investigators with details about ongoing corruption in the Rampart area.[27] As events unfolded, LAPD Chief Bernard Parks was accused by prosecutors of withholding critical information needed to build a case against the accused officers. The prosecutors claimed that "on several occasions, the LAPD . . . actually hindered the progress of the investigation."[28] Parks was replaced as chief by William J. Bratton in 2002.

By 2005, more than 100 falsely obtained convictions had been thrown out, and 20 LAPD officers had left active duty.[29] Another seven officers were convicted of conspiring to frame innocent people, but a judge overturned three of the convictions on procedural grounds. The remaining four officers received sentences of up to five years in prison.[30] The Los Angeles City Attorney agreed to pay a total of $70.2 million to settle approximately 214 lawsuits stemming from the corruption scandal. At the time of the settlement, the *Los Angeles Times* complained that much of the money, averaging $400,000 per settlement, went to "drug dealers, gang members and other criminals who said they had been framed, shot, beaten or otherwise mistreated by police."[31] The largest settlement, $15 million, went to former gang member Javier Francisco Ovando, who had been paralyzed by a police shooting. In responding to critics, Cindy Miscikowski, chairwoman of the Los Angeles City Council's Public Safety Committee, pointed out that "regardless of who the plaintiffs were, there was evidence of wrongdoing. That's what we had to recognize. . . . Civil rights are civil rights, and they apply to everyone across the board."[32]

The LAPD is now operating under a consent decree, a legally binding agreement with the U.S. Department of Justice (DOJ) that calls for major reforms. The decree requires the department to install a computer system to track complaints and disciplinary actions against LAPD officers; to collect data on the racial makeup of citizens stopped for traffic violations; and to create a special unit within the department to investigate shootings and beatings by police officers to determine whether excessive force was used.[33] Rafael Perez, sentenced to five years in prison, warned young officers as he was sentenced that "whoever chases monsters must see that he not become a monster himself."[34] Learn more about the Rampart scandal at **Web Extra 6–2**.

▲ The Los Angeles Police Department's Rampart station office, where a corruption scandal occurred in 2000 and 2001. A number of officers assigned to the Rampart Division were investigated on charges ranging from falsifying evidence to the theft and sale of illegal drugs. In what some have called "the biggest police scandal case in Los Angeles history," many criminal cases had to be dismissed. What other forms can police corruption take?
David McNew/Liaison/Getty Images, Inc.

Money—The Root of Police Evil?

Years ago, criminologist Edwin Sutherland applied the concept of *differential association* to the study of deviant behavior.[35] Sutherland suggested that the frequent, continued association of one person with another makes the associates similar. Of course, Sutherland was talking about criminals, not police officers. Consider, however, the dilemma of average officers: Their job entails issuing traffic citations to citizens who try to talk their way out of a ticket, dealing with prostitutes who feel hassled by police, and arresting drug users who think it should be their right to do what they want as long as "it doesn't hurt anyone." Officers regularly encounter personal hostility and experience consistent and often quite vocal rejection of society's formalized norms. And they receive relatively low pay, which indicates to them that their work is not really valued. By looking at the combination of these factors, it is easy to understand how officers often develop a jaded attitude toward the society they are sworn to protect.

Police officers' low pay may be a critical ingredient of the corruption mix. Salaries paid to police officers in this country have been notoriously low when compared to those of other professions involving personal dedication, extensive training, high stress, and risk of bodily harm. As police professionalism increases, many police administrators hope that salaries will rise. No matter how much police pay grows, however, it will never be able to compete with the staggering amounts of money to be made through dealing in contraband.

Working hand in hand with monetary pressures toward corruption is the moral dilemma produced by unenforceable laws that provide the basis for criminal profit. During the Prohibition era, the Wickersham Commission warned of the potential for official corruption inherent in the legislative taboos on alcohol. The immense demand for drink called into question the wisdom of the law while simultaneously providing vast resources designed to circumvent it. Today's drug scene bears some similarities to the Prohibition era. As long as many people are willing to make large financial and other sacrifices to feed the drug trade, the pressures on the police to embrace corruption will remain substantial.

Thematic Question Huge monetary settlements in the LAPD's Rampart scandal went to drug dealers, gang members, and other criminals who claimed that they had been framed, shot, beaten, or otherwise mistreated by police. Do you agree with Los Angeles city councilwoman Cindy Miscikowski who is quoted in this chapter as saying, "Civil rights are civil rights, and they apply to everyone across the board"? Why or why not?

Lecture Note Explain that internal affairs divisions are charged with investigating wrongdoing by police officers, and discuss other methods departments can use to fight corruption.

Building Police Integrity

The difficulties of controlling corruption can be traced to several factors, including the reluctance of police officers to report corrupt activities by their fellow officers, the reluctance of police administrators to acknowledge the existence of corruption in their agencies, the benefits of corrupt transactions to the parties involved, and the lack of victims willing to report corruption. High moral standards, however, embedded in the principles of the police profession and effectively communicated to individual officers through formal training and peer-group socialization can raise the level of integrity in any department. There are, of course, many officers of great personal integrity who hold to the highest of professional ideals. There

Ethics and Professionalism
The Law Enforcement Oath of Honor

On my honor, I will never
Betray my badge, my integrity,
My character or the public trust.
I will always have the courage to hold
Myself and others accountable
for our actions.
I will always uphold the Constitution,
My community, and the agency I serve.

Honor means that one's word is given as a guarantee.
Betray is defined as breaking faith with the public trust.
Badge is the symbol of your office.
Integrity is being the same person in both private and public life.
Character means the qualities that distinguish an individual.
Public trust is a charge of duty imposed in faith toward those you serve.
Courage is having the strength to withstand unethical pressure, fear or danger.
Accountability means that you are answerable and responsible to your oath of office.
Community is the jurisdiction and citizens served.

THINKING ABOUT ETHICS

1. ***How is the Law Enforcement Oath of Honor similar to the Law Enforcement Code of Ethics, which is also found in this chapter? How does it differ?***
2. ***How do the two support one another?***

Source: Adopted at the 107th International Association of Chiefs of Police Annual Conference, November 15, 2000. Reprinted with permission.

is evidence that law enforcement training programs are becoming increasingly concerned with instruction designed to reinforce the high ideals many recruits bring to police work. As one Federal Bureau of Investigation (FBI) article explains it, "Ethics training must become an integral part of academy and in-service training for new and experienced officers alike."[36]

Ethics training is part of a "reframing" strategy that emphasizes integrity to target police corruption. In 2001, the DOJ released a document titled *Principles for Promoting Police Integrity.*[37] The foreword to that document states, "For community policing to be successful, and crime reduction efforts to be effective, citizens must have trust in the police. All of us must work together to address the problems of excessive use of force and racial profiling, and—equally important—the perceptions of many minority residents that law enforcement treats them unfairly, if we are to build the confidence in law enforcement necessary for continued progress. Our goal must be professional law enforcement that gives all citizens of our country the feeling that they are being treated fairly, equally and with respect." The report covered such topics as the use of force; complaints and misconduct investigations; accountability and effective management; training; nondiscriminatory policing; and recruitment, hiring, and retention. Read the full report, which provides examples of promising police practices and policies in support of increased integrity, at **Library Extra 6–1**.

In 2000, the International Association of Chiefs of Police (IACP), in an effort to reinforce the importance of ethical standards in policing, adopted the Law Enforcement Oath of Honor, shown in an "Ethics and Professionalism" box in this chapter. The IACP suggests that the Law Enforcement Oath of Honor should be seen by individual officers as a statement of commitment to ethical behavior. It is meant to reinforce the principles embodied in the Law Enforcement Code of Ethics, which is printed in another "Ethics and Professionalism" box in this chapter.

In December 2005, the National Institute of Justice weighed in on the issue of police integrity with a Research for Practice report titled *Enhancing Police Integrity.*[38] The report noted that "an agency's culture of integrity, as defined by clearly understood and implemented policies and rules, may be more important in shaping the ethics of police officers than hiring the 'right' people."[39] Report authors also noted that officers tend to evaluate the seriousness of various types of misconduct by observing and assessing their department's response in detecting and disciplining it. If unwritten policies conflict with written policies, the authors observed, then the resulting confusion undermines an agency's overall integrity-enhancing efforts. *Enhancing Police Integrity* is available online at **Library Extra 6–2**.

internal affairs
The branch of a police organization tasked with investigating charges of wrongdoing involving members of the department.

Most large law enforcement agencies have their own division of **internal affairs**, which is empowered to investigate charges of wrongdoing made against officers. Where necessary, state police agencies may be called on to examine reported incidents. Federal agencies,

There is more to being a professional than just looking like one.
—Rob Edwards

including the FBI and the Drug Enforcement Administration (DEA), involve themselves when corruption goes far enough to violate federal statutes. The DOJ, through various investigative offices, has the authority to examine possible violations of civil rights that may result from the misuse of police authority. The DOJ is often supported in these endeavors by the American Civil Liberties Union (ACLU), the National Association for the Advancement of Colored People (NAACP), and other watchdog groups.

▲ Federal Way Police Officer G. Castro with flowers given to him by a motorist passing the Lakewood police station. Four Lakewood officers were killed by a gunman at a Parkland coffee shop in November 2009. How might the dangers associated with police work be reduced?
*AP Photo/*The New Tribune, *Dean J. Koepfler*

Drug Testing of Police Employees

The widespread potential for police corruption created by illicit drugs has led to focused efforts to combat drug use by officers. Drug-testing programs in local police departments are an example of such efforts. The IACP has developed a Model Drug Testing Policy for police managers. The policy, designed to meet the needs of local departments, suggests routinely testing all applicants and recruits as well as all employees who are assigned to special "high-risk" areas, such as narcotics and vice.[40]

Today, many police departments require all officers to submit to routine drug testing, and in 2008, the NYPD began randomly testing its officers for anabolic steroid abuse. The department began the testing after several police officers were linked to the investigation of a Brooklyn pharmacy suspected of illegally selling millions of dollars of steroids and human growth hormone.[41]

The courts have supported drug testing based on a reasonable suspicion that drug abuse has been or is occurring,[42] although random testing of officers was banned by a 1986 New York State Supreme Court.[43] Citing overriding public interests, a 1989 decision by the U.S. Supreme Court upheld the testing of U.S. Customs personnel applying for transfer into positions involving drug-law enforcement or requiring a firearm.[44] Many legal issues surrounding employee drug testing remain to be resolved in court, however.

Complicating this issue is the fact that drug and alcohol addictions are "handicaps" protected by the Federal Rehabilitation Act of 1973. As such, federal law enforcement employees, as well as those working for agencies with federal contracts, are entitled to counseling and treatment before action can be taken toward termination.

Employee drug testing in police departments, as in many other agencies, is a sensitive subject. Some claim that existing tests for drug use are inaccurate, yielding a significant number of "false positives." Repeated testing and high threshold levels for narcotic substances in the blood may eliminate many of these concerns. Less easy to address, however, is the belief that drug testing intrudes on the personal rights and professional dignity of individual employees. Learn more about employee drug-testing policies in police departments at **Web Extra 6–3**, and discover more about corruption and the continuing drive toward police integrity with **Library Extras 6–3** and **6–4**.

Lecture Note Explain how the drug testing of police officers is important not just in keeping police departments drug free but also in fighting corruption.

Thematic Question Do you think police officers should be subject to random drug testing? Explain.

Thematic Question Identify some of the dangers of modern police work. What other (perhaps currently unrealized) dangers can you anticipate for the future? How can police officers protect against each of the dangers you've identified?

The Dangers of Police Work

3 Explain the dangers of police work, and discuss what can be done to reduce those dangers.

On October 15, 1991, the National Law Enforcement Officers' Memorial was unveiled in Washington, D.C. The memorial contained the names of 12,561 law enforcement officers killed in the line of duty, including U.S. Marshals Service Officer Robert Forsyth, who in 1794 became the nation's first law enforcement officer to be killed. More than 6,000 names have been added since opening day.[45] At the memorial, an interactive video system provides visitors with brief biographies and photographs of officers who have died. Tour the memorial by visiting **Web Extra 6–4**.

As the memorial suggests, police work is, by its very nature, dangerous. Although many officers never once fire their weapons in the line of duty, we also know that some officers

CJ News
Police DNA Collection Sparks Questions

When a 60-year-old man spat on the sidewalk, his DNA became as public as if he had been advertising it across his chest.

Police officers secretly following Leon Chatt . . . collected the saliva—loaded with Chatt's unique genetic makeup—to compare with DNA evidence from the scene of an old murder they believed he'd committed.

[Later,] Chatt was charged in one of Buffalo's oldest unsolved cases, the 1974 rape and stabbing of . . . Barbara Lloyd.

While secretly collecting a suspect's DNA may be an unorthodox approach to solving crimes, prosecutors say it crosses no legal boundaries—that when someone leaves their DNA in a public place via . . . saliva, for example, they give up any expectation of privacy. . . .

"If we felt it wasn't proper and we didn't have a strong legal foundation, we wouldn't have done it," Erie County [New York] District Attorney Frank Clark said. . . .

DNA, which is unique to every person, has become a cold case squad's best friend. Investigators can re-examine things like hair, blood, semen . . . from decades-old crime scenes and cross-reference the DNA with ever expanding databases kept by law enforcement.

"It's one of the greatest tools that law enforcement has today," said Dennis Richards, the Buffalo Police Department's chief of detectives. . . .

But it is the so-called "abandoned" DNA like that collected from . . . Chatt . . . that concerns people like Elizabeth Joh. The University of California law professor believes it is time legislators consider regulating such collections. . . .

"If we look at this kind of evidence as abandoned, then it really permits the police to collect DNA from anyone—not just cold case issues—from anyone at any time and really for no good reason or any reason at all," Joh said. . . .

Asked whether there should be boundaries on such collections, Richards said, "That's one for the lawyers to argue in a court of law." . . .

Prosecutors tend to view abandoned DNA as akin to trash . . . Joh said.

She pointed to the case of *California* v. *Greenwood*, in which the U.S. Supreme Court ruled in 1988 that police did not need a warrant to search a suspected drug dealer's trash because he should have had no expectation of privacy when he placed it on the curb. . . .

But Joh argued comparing DNA and trash is a poor analogy.

"Obviously, we might want to discard that cigarette, but do we really mean to give up all kinds of privacy claims in the genetic material that might lie therein?" she asked. . . .

Richards, meanwhile, pointed out that while abandoned DNA can confirm a suspect's identity, it also works to the benefit of someone who is innocent.

"DNA rules people in, but it also rules people out," he said.

Barbara Lloyd was killed as her [children] slept. The now-grown children recently persuaded police to take another look at the killing. . . .

▲ Karin Strom, who was strangled in her home almost 30 years ago, allegedly by Utah resident Edward Owens, 56. Owens surrendered to police in 2007 after tests determined that it was his skin that had been scraped from under Strom's fingernails after her murder and had been saved in an evidence locker. Owens was charged with first-degree felony murder in Strom's death. His arrest, like others discussed in this box, has raised questions about how DNA samples can best be collected from criminal suspects. Should "public" DNA be readily available to investigators?
Woods Cross Police Department

"We were very fortunate that at that time there was a detective in the evidence collection unit who was able to secure evidence from the scene which was later used for comparison," Richards said. . . .

Joh suggests proceeding with caution. "My hope is there will be much greater awareness of what this means, not just for these particular cases, but for everyone," she said. "Is DNA sampling going to be ordinary and uncontroversial for the general population, in which case abandoned DNA may not be so alarming, or does it raise a whole host of privacy questions?"

Source: Carolyn Thompson, "Police DNA Collection Sparks Questions," The Associated Press, March 17, 2007. Used with permission of The Associated Press. Copyright © 2009. All rights reserved.

meet death while performing their jobs. On-the-job police deaths occur from stress, training accidents, and auto crashes; however, it is violent death at the hands of criminal offenders that police officers and their families fear most.

Violence in the Line of Duty

When officers are shot and killed, it is most often by a lone suspect armed with a single weapon. In 2009, 127 American law enforcement officers were killed in the line of duty.[46] Figure 6–2 shows the number of officers killed in different types of incidents in 2009. In 2001, the attacks on the World Trade Center resulted in the greatest ever single-incident loss of life of on-duty law enforcement officers when 72 police officers perished.[47]

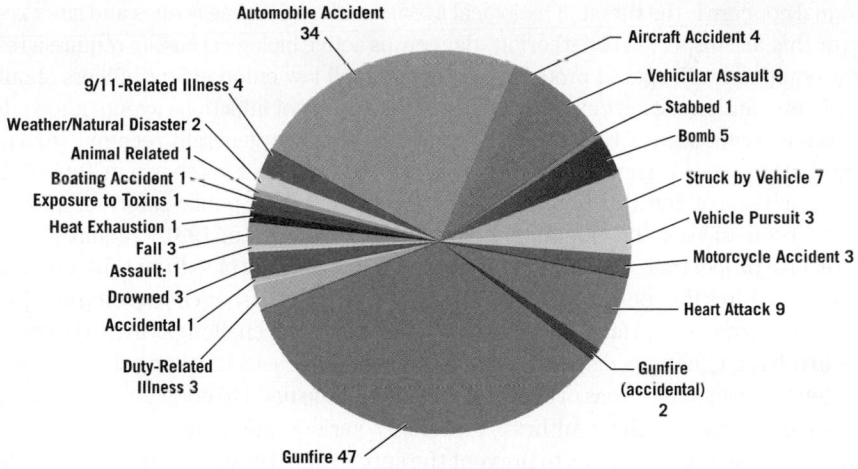

FIGURE 6–2
U.S. Law Enforcement Officers Killed in the Line of Duty, 2009

Source: Based on data from the Officer Down Memorial Page website, http://www.odmp.org.

Lecture Note Explain the dangers of police work by referring to the risk of violence on the job, the danger of infectious diseases (such as AIDS), and terrorism. Use Figure 6–2 to highlight the kinds of situations in which law enforcement officers are most likely to be killed.

A study by the FBI found that slain officers appeared to be good-natured and conservative in the use of physical force, "as compared to other law enforcement officers in similar situations. They were also perceived as being well-liked by the community and the department, friendly to everyone, laid back, and easy going."[48] Finally, the study, which was published before the September 11, 2001, terrorist attacks, also found that most officers who were killed failed to wear protective vests.

For statistics on police killings to have meaning beyond the personal tragedy they entail, it is necessary to place them within a larger framework. There are approximately 730,000 state and local police employees in this country[49] and another 88,000 federal agents.[50] Such numbers demonstrate that the rate of violent death among law enforcement officers in the line of duty is small indeed—and it appears to be declining.

A significant recent decline in police deaths from all causes prompted Craig Floyd, chairman of the National Law Enforcement Officers Memorial Fund, to attribute the drop to an enhanced focus on officer safety by police departments and officers' unions. "Clearly, there is a heightened awareness [of the need for safety] among officers, trainers, union leaders and chiefs," Floyd said.[51] Others attribute the decline in law enforcement deaths to a renewed push for the use of body armor; an increased availability of less-lethal weapons; a broader use of mandatory handcuffing, even at traffic stops; widespread and better analysis of police dashboard videos to critique officer behavior; and better arming of police officers.

> Unlike the soldier fighting a war on foreign soil, police officers, who provide for our safety at home, have never been given the honor that was their due.
>
> —Hubert Williams, president, Police Foundation[iii]

Risk of Disease and Infected Evidence

Dangers other than violence also threaten enforcement officers. The increase in serious diseases that can be transmitted by blood and other body fluids, the possible planned release of active **biological weapons** such as anthrax or smallpox, and the fact that crime and accident scenes are inherently dangerous combine to make *caution* a necessary watchword among investigators and first responders. Routine criminal and accident investigations hold the potential for infection through minor cuts and abrasions resulting from contact with the broken glass and torn metal of a wrecked vehicle, the sharp edges of knives found at the scene of an assault or murder, or drug implements such as razor blades and hypodermic needles secreted in vehicles, homes, and pockets. Such minor injuries, previously shrugged off by many police personnel, have become a focal point for warnings about the dangers of AIDS, hepatitis B, tuberculosis, and other diseases spread through contact with infected blood.

biological weapon
A biological agent used to threaten human life (for example, anthrax, smallpox, or any infectious disease).[iv]

Infection can also occur from the use of breath alcohol instruments on infected persons, the handling of evidence of all types, seemingly innocuous implements such as staples, the emergency delivery of babies in squad cars, and the attack (especially bites) by infected individuals who are being questioned or who are in custody. Understandably, officers are concerned about how to handle the threat of AIDS and other bloodborne diseases. However, as a publication of the NYPD reminds its officers, "Police officers have a professional responsibility to render assistance to those who are in need of our services. We cannot refuse to help. Persons with infectious diseases must be treated with the care and dignity we show all citizens."[52]

Lecture Note Point out that casual contact will not lead to AIDS, that there must be contact with fresh blood or other body fluids, and that breaks in the skin or mucous membranes provide the most likely route for infection to occur. Discuss the roles that accident scenes, rapes, cardiopulmonary resuscitation (CPR), bites, and cuts may play in AIDS transmission.

Of equal concern is the threat of biological agents. Although crime scenes and sites known to harbor (or that are suspected of harboring) dangerous active biological agents require a response by teams equipped with special protective equipment, all law enforcement officers should take reasonable precautions against exposure to the wide variety of infectious agents known to exist at even routine crime scenes. Emergency management agencies generally recommend a number of precautions to defend against exposure to infectious substances, as shown in Table 6–2.

To better combat the threat of infectious diseases among public-safety employees and health-care professionals, the federal Bloodborne Pathogens Act of 1991[53] requires that police officers receive proper training in how to prevent contamination by bloodborne infectious agents. The act also requires that police officers undergo an annual refresher course on the topic.

Police departments will face an increasing number of legal challenges in the years to come in cases involving infectious diseases such as AIDS and in cases involving the release of biological agents. Predictable areas of concern include (1) the need to educate officers and other police employees about AIDS, anthrax, and other serious infectious diseases; (2) the responsibility of police departments to prevent the spread of AIDS and other infectious diseases in police lockups; and (3) the necessity of effective and nondiscriminatory enforcement activities and lifesaving measures by police officers in environments contaminated with active biological agents. With regard to nondiscriminatory activities, the National Institute of Justice (NIJ) has suggested that legal claims in support of an officer's refusal to render assistance to people with AIDS would probably not be effective in court.[54] The reason is twofold: The officer has a basic duty to render assistance to individuals in need of it, and the possibility of AIDS transmission by casual contact has been scientifically established as extremely remote.

A final issue of growing concern involves activities by police officers infected with the AIDS virus. Few statistics are currently available on the number of officers with AIDS, but public reaction to those officers may become a problem that police managers will need to address.

TABLE 6–2
Biological Incident Law Enforcement Concerns

Concern	Precaution and Response
Suspicious material	Responding officers should not handle or come in close physical contact with suspicious material. If it is necessary to handle the material to evaluate it, officers should wear surgical gloves and masks and wash their hands thoroughly with soap and water after handling it.
Human bites	The biter usually receives the victim's blood. Viral transmission through saliva is highly unlikely. If bitten by anyone, milk the wound to make it bleed, wash the area thoroughly, and seek medical attention.
Spitting	Viral transmission through saliva is highly unlikely.
Urine/feces	Virus has been isolated in only very low concentrations in urine and not at all in feces.
	No cases of AIDS or AIDS virus infection associated with either urine or feces have been reported.
Cuts/puncture wounds	Use caution when handling sharp objects and searching areas hidden from view. Needle-stick studies show risk of infection is very low.
CPR/first aid	To eliminate the already minimal risk associated with CPR, use masks/airways.
	Avoid blood-to-blood contact by keeping open wounds covered and wearing gloves when in contact with bleeding wounds.
Body removal	Observe crime-scene rules; do not touch anything. Those who must come in contact with blood or other body fluids should wear gloves.
Casual contact	No cases of AIDS or AIDS virus infection have been attributed to casual contact.
Any contact with blood or body fluids	Wear gloves if contact with blood or body fluids is considered likely. If contact occurs, wash thoroughly with soap and water; clean up spills with one part water to nine parts household bleach.
Contact with dried blood	No cases of infection have been traced to exposure to dried blood. The drying process itself appears to inactivate the virus. Despite low risk, however, caution dictates wearing gloves, a mask, and protective shoe coverings if exposure to dried blood particles is likely (for example, crime-scene investigation).

References: Michigan Department of Community Health, *Anthrax (Bacillus anthracis) Information for Health Care Providers*, http://www.michigan.gov/documents/Healthcare_provider_FAQ-anthrax_08-2004_104327_7.pdf (accessed June 12, 2010); Massachusetts Administrative Office of the Trial Court, *Personnel Policies and Procedures Manual*, Section 24.000 ("Statement of Policy and Procedures on AIDS"), http://www.state.ma.us/courts/admin/hr/section24.html (accessed January 25, 2009); and "Collecting and Handling Evidence Infected with Human Disease-Causing Organisms," *FBI Law Enforcement Bulletin*, July 1987.

Stress and Fatigue among Police Officers

In the week after Hurricane Katrina, two New Orleans police officers used their service weapons to take their own lives. One was Sergeant Paul Accardo, the department's spokesperson; the other was patrolman Lawrence Celestine, an officer described by Deputy Police Chief W. J. Riley as "an outstanding cop."[55] Feelings of powerlessness, personal loss, and an inability to help those in need all seriously heightened the level of stress felt by officers in New Orleans following the 2005 hurricane. "The most stressing part is seeing the citizens we serve every day being treated like refugees," said Riley. "There were cops walking through the crowd at the convention center and people were coming up to beg for food. Not being able to help is a difficult thing. People were calling our names because we knew them and to not be able to help, man, that's stressful."[56]

Lecture Note Discuss police stress as a major occupational hazard for law enforcement personnel, and identify some of the stressors that police officers face.

Traumatic events, like hurricanes, terrorist attacks, and violent confrontations, are instantly stressful, but long-term stress, whose debilitating effects accumulate over years, may be the most insidious and least visible of all threats facing law enforcement personnel today. While some degree of stress can be a positive motivator, serious stress over long periods of time is generally regarded as destructive, even life-threatening.

Long-term stress may be the most insidious of all threats facing law enforcement personnel.

Stress is a natural component of police work (Figure 6–3).[57] The American Institute of Stress, based in Yonkers, New York, ranks policing among the top ten stress-producing jobs in the country.[58] Danger, frustration, paperwork, the daily demands of the job, and a lack of understanding from family members and friends contribute to the negative stress that officers experience. The Bureau of Justice Statistics points out the following:

> [E]xposure to violence, suffering, and death is inherent to the profession of the law enforcement officer. There are other sources of stress as well. Officers who deal with offenders on a daily basis may perceive the public's opinion of police performance to be unfavorable; they often are required to work mandatory, rotating shifts; and they may not have enough time to spend with their families. Police officers also face unusual, often highly disturbing, situations, such as dealing with a child homicide victim or the survivors of vehicle crashes.[59]

Some stressors in police work are particularly destructive. One is frustration brought on by the inability to be effective, regardless of the amount of personal effort expended. The crux of police work involves making arrests based on thorough investigations that lead to convictions and the removal of individuals who are damaging to the social fabric of the community—all under the umbrella of criminal law. Unfortunately, reality is often far from

FIGURE 6–3
Stress and Fatigue among Police Officers

Career Profile
Police Officer

Name: Robert D. Smith, Jr.

Position: Police Officer, Dearborn, Michigan

Colleges attended: Monroe County Community College, University of Michigan-Dearborn, Toledo College of Law, Oakland County Police Academy

Major: Finance, law

Year hired: 2009

Please give a brief description of your job. I am in the police academy, training to be a police officer.

What appealed to you most about the position when you applied for it? My goal is to make a difference in my community. Knowing that each day I go to work I can make a positive difference in people's lives is very rewarding.

How would you describe the interview process? The process lasted over a year, involved many steps, and required patience. The competition for the few available positions was great.

What is a typical day like? Generally I start out with physical training, followed by defensive tactic training and class study. We do a lot of role playing to enact real-life scenarios, which helps us prepare for the streets.

What qualities/characteristics are most helpful for this job? One must desire to help people and be willing to put one's life in dangerous situations. The position requires absolute integrity and courage. Criminals can sense weakness; an officer must show absolute confidence at all times. Officers must have patience and a high tolerance for stress.

What is a typical starting salary? Salaries vary depending on department size and city size. Larger departments *usually* pay better than departments with 10 or fewer officers. Salaries can range from $30,000 to over $65,000, not counting overtime and holiday pay. The benefits are outstanding, and most departments offer a pension.

What is the salary potential as you move up into higher-level jobs? Large departments have more opportunity for growth and offer many different areas, such as the detective bureau, SWAT team, evidence technicians, etc. Education can also help you attain a higher-level job. For example, many large-department police chiefs have a Juris Doctor degree. The higher-rank positions can range from $70,000 up to six figures.

What career advice would you give someone in college beginning their studies in criminal justice? Evaluate your career goals. Early research and networking can help you clarify which field to pursue. Seek out internships or cadet positions with local police departments. Work hard on getting high grades and internship experience, which will be essential in landing prime positions.

Source: Reprinted with permission of Robert D. Smith, Jr. Photo courtesy of Robert D. Smith, Jr. Logo courtesy Monroe County Community College.

the ideal: Arrests may not lead to convictions; evidence available to the officer may not be allowed in court; the sentences imposed may seem too light to the arresting officer. The feelings of powerlessness and frustration that come from seeing repeat offenders back on the streets and from witnessing numerous injustices worked on seemingly innocent victims may greatly stress police officers and cause them to question the purpose of their professional lives. It may also lead to desperate attempts to find relief. As one researcher observes, "The suicide rate of police officers is more than twice that of the general population."[60]

Lecture Note Outline some techniques for stress reduction, such as exercise, meditation, breathing exercises, prayer, music, subliminal conditioning, and diet. Discuss techniques that are most likely to work with law enforcement personnel and those that are least likely to be effective.

Stress is not unique to the police profession, but because of the "macho" attitude that has traditionally been associated with police work, denial of the stress is more prevalent among police officers than in other occupational groups. Certain types of individuals are probably more susceptible to the negative effects of stress than are others. The type A personality, popularized 30 years ago, is more likely to perceive life in terms of pressure and performance, whereas type B people are more laid back and less likely to suffer from the negative effects of stress. Police ranks, drawn as they are from the general population, are filled with both stress-sensitive and stress-resistant personalities.

Stress Reduction

It is natural to want to reduce stress.[61] Humor helps, even if it's somewhat cynical. Health-care professionals, for example, are noted for their ability to joke even though they are caring for patients who are seriously ill or even dying. At times, police officers use humor similarly to defuse their reactions to dark or threatening situations. Keeping an emotional distance from stressful events is another way of coping with them, although such distance is not always easy to maintain. Police officers who have had to deal with serious cases of child abuse often report that they experienced emotional turmoil as a consequence.

Exercise, meditation, deep breathing, biofeedback, self-hypnosis, guided imaging, induced relaxation, subliminal conditioning, music, prayer, and diet have all been cited as useful techniques for stress reduction. Devices to measure stress levels are available in the form of handheld heart-rate monitors, blood pressure devices, "biodots" (which change color according to the amount of blood flow in the extremities), and psychological inventories.

One theory regarding stress among police officers holds that the amount of stress an officer experiences is directly related to his or her reactions to potentially stressful situations.[62] Officers who can filter out extraneous stimuli and who can distinguish between truly threatening situations and those that are benign are much less likely to report job-related stressors than officers lacking these abilities. Because stress-filtering abilities are often closely linked to innate personality characteristics, some researchers suggest careful psychological screening of police applicants to better identify those who have a natural ability to cope with situations that others might perceive as stressful.[63]

▲ A Washington, D.C., Metro Transit police officer searching a train after subway bombings in London prompted increased security in 2005. How has the threat of terrorism altered the police role in America?
Reuters/Larry Downing/Landov Media

A police officer's family members often report feelings of stress that are directly related to the officer's work. As a result, some departments have developed innovative programs to allay family stress. The Collier County (Florida) Spousal Academy, for example, is a family support program that offers training to spouses and other domestic partners of deputies and recruits who are enrolled in the department's training academy. The ten-hour program deals directly with issues that are likely to produce stress and informs participants of department and community resources that are available to help them. Peer-support programs for spouses and life partners and for the adolescent children of officers are also beginning to operate nationwide. **Library Extra 6–5** provides a comprehensive overview of issues related to police officer stress.

Officer Fatigue

Like stress, fatigue can affect a police officer's performance. As criminologist Bryan Vila points out, "Tired, urban street cops are a national icon. Weary from overtime assignments, shift work, night school, endless hours spent waiting to testify, and the emotional and physical demands of the job, not to mention trying to patch together a family and social life during irregular islands of off-duty time, they fend off fatigue with coffee and hard-bitten humor."[64] Vila found levels of police officer fatigue to be six times as high as those of shift workers in industrial and mining jobs.[65] As Vila notes, few departments set work-hour standards, and fatigue associated with the pattern and length of work hours may be expected to contribute to police accidents, injuries, and misconduct.

To address the problem, Vila recommends that police departments "review the policies, procedures, and practices that affect shift scheduling and rotation, overtime moonlighting, the number of consecutive work hours allowed, and the way in which the department deals with overly tired employees."[66] Vila also suggests controlling the work hours of police officers, "just as we control the working hours of many other occupational groups."[67]

Terrorism's Impact on Policing

The terrorist attacks of September 11, 2001, have had a significant impact on policing in the United States. While the core mission of American police departments has not changed, law enforcement agencies at all levels now devote an increased amount of time and other resources to preparing for possible terrorist attacks and to gathering the intelligence necessary to thwart them.

4 Describe the changed role of American police in the post-9/11 environment.

In today's post-9/11 world, local police departments play an especially important role in responding to the challenges of terrorism. They must help prevent attacks and respond when attacks occur—offering critical evacuation, emergency medical, and security functions to help stabilize communities following an incident. A recent survey of 250 police chiefs by the Police Executive Research Forum (PERF) found that the chiefs strongly believe that their departments can make valuable contributions to terrorism prevention by using community policing networks to exchange information with citizens and to gather intelligence.[68] Read the results of the PERF survey online at **Library Extra 6–6**.

The Council on Foreign Relations, headquartered in New York City and Washington, D.C., agrees with PERF that American police departments can no longer assume that federal counterterrorism efforts alone will be sufficient to protect the communities they serve. Consequently, says the council, many police departments have responded to the terrorist threat by strengthening liaisons with federal, state, and local agencies (including fire departments and other police departments); by refining their training and emergency response plans; by creating antiterrorism divisions; and in a number of other ways.[69]

> It is very important that our first line of defense against terrorism—the seven hundred thousand officers on the street—be given adequate training and background information on terrorism, the methods and techniques of the terrorists, and the likelihood of an imminent attack.
>
> —Major Cities Chiefs Association[V]

The extent of local departments' engagement in preventive activities depends substantially on budgetary considerations and is strongly influenced by the assessed likelihood of attack. For example, the NYPD, which has firsthand experience in responding to terrorist attacks (23 of its officers were killed when the World Trade Center towers collapsed), has created a special bureau headed by a deputy police commissioner responsible for counterterrorism training, prevention, and investigation.[70] About 1,000 officers have been reassigned to antiterrorism duties, and the department is training its entire 38,000-member force in how to respond to biological, radiological, and chemical attacks.[71] The NYPD has assigned detectives to work abroad with law enforcement agencies in Canada, Israel, Southeast Asia, and the Middle East to track terrorists who might target New York City,[72] and it now employs officers with a command of the Pashto, Farsi, and Urdu languages of the Middle East to monitor foreign television, radio, and Internet communications. The department has also invested heavily in new hazardous materials protective suits, gas masks, and portable radiation detectors.

In November 2004, in an effort to provide the law enforcement community and policymakers with guidance on critical issues related to antiterrorism planning and critical incident response, the IACP announced its Taking Command Initiative. The IACP described the initiative as "an aggressive project to assess the current state of homeland security efforts in the United States and to develop and implement the actions necessary to protect our communities from the specter of both crime and terrorism."[73] Initial deliberations under the initiative led the IACP to conclude that "the current homeland security strategy is handicapped by a fundamental flaw: It was developed without sufficiently seeking or incorporating the advice, expertise, or consent of public safety organizations at the state, tribal, or local level."[74] Building on that premise, the IACP identified a number of key principles that it says must form the basis of any effective national homeland security strategy.[75] Learn more at **Web Extra 6–5** about the ongoing Taking Command Initiative as its leaders work to "transform the concept of a locally designed, nationally coordinated homeland security strategy into a reality."

Finally, in 2005, the IACP coordinated publication of a Post-9/11 Policing Project resource titled *Assessing and Managing the Terrorism Threat.* The Post-9/11 Policing Project is a collaborative effort of the IACP, the National Sheriffs' Association (NSA), the National Organization of Black Law Enforcement Executives (NOBLE), the Major Cities Chiefs Association (MCCA), and the Police Foundation. Download the publication at **Library Extra 6–7**.

The FBI's Joint Terrorism Task Forces

As the IACP recognizes, workable antiterrorism programs at the local level require effective sharing of critical information between agencies. FBI-sponsored Joint Terrorism Task Forces (JTTFs) facilitate this by bringing together federal and local law enforcement personnel to focus on specific threats. The FBI currently has established or authorized JTTFs in each of its

56 field offices. In addition to the JTTFs, the FBI has created Regional Terrorism Task Forces (RTTFs) to share information with local enforcement agencies. Through the RTTFs, FBI special agents assigned to terrorism prevention and investigation meet twice a year with their federal, state, and local counterparts for common training, discussion of investigations, and intelligence sharing. The FBI says that "the design of this non-traditional terrorism task force provides the necessary mechanism and structure to direct counterterrorism resources toward localized terrorism problems within the United States."[76] Six RTTFs are currently in operation: Inland Northwest, South Central, Southeastern, Northeast Border, Deep South, and Southwest.

Given the changes that have taken place in American law enforcement since the terrorist attacks of September 11, 2001, some say that traditional distinctions between crime, terrorism, and war are fading and that, at least in some instances, military action and civil law enforcement are becoming integrated. The critical question for law enforcement administrators in the near future may be one of discerning the role that law enforcement is to play in the emerging global context.

Intelligence-Led Policing and Antiterrorism

In 2005, the DOJ embraced the concept of **intelligence-led policing (ILP)** as an important technique to be employed by American law enforcement agencies in the battle against terrorism.[77] Intelligence is information that has been analyzed and integrated into a useful perspective. The information used in the development of effective intelligence is typically gathered from many sources, such as newspapers, surveillance, covert operations, financial records, electronic eavesdropping, interviews, the Internet, and interrogations. Law enforcement intelligence, or **criminal intelligence**, is the result of a "process that evaluates information collected from diverse sources, integrates the relevant information into a cohesive package, and produces a conclusion or estimate about a criminal phenomenon by using the scientific approach to problem solving."[78] Although criminal investigation is typically part of the intelligence-gathering process, the intelligence function of a police department is more exploratory and more broadly focused than a single criminal investigation.[79]

intelligence-led policing (ILP)
The collection and analysis of information to produce an intelligence end product designed to inform police decision making at both the tactical and strategic levels.[vi]

criminal intelligence
The information compiled, analyzed, and/or disseminated in an effort to anticipate, prevent, or monitor criminal activity.[vii]

ILP (also known as *intelligence-driven policing*) is the use of criminal intelligence to guide policing. A detailed description of ILP and its applicability to American law enforcement agencies is provided in the FBI publication *The Law Enforcement Intelligence Function* by David L. Carter of Michigan State University's School of Criminal Justice. The document is available at **Library Extra 6–8**.

According to Carter, criminal intelligence "is a synergistic product intended to provide meaningful and trustworthy direction to law enforcement decision makers about complex criminality, criminal enterprises, criminal extremists, and terrorists."[80] Carter goes on to point out that law enforcement intelligence consists of two types: tactical and strategic. Tactical intelligence "includes gaining or developing information related to threats of terrorism or crime and using this information to apprehend offenders, harden targets, and use strategies that will eliminate or mitigate the threat." Strategic intelligence, in contrast, provides information to decision makers about the changing nature of threats for the purpose of "developing response strategies and reallocating resources" to accomplish effective prevention.

Not every agency (especially small ones) has the staff or resources needed to create a dedicated intelligence unit. Even without an intelligence unit, however, a law enforcement organization should have the ability to effectively utilize the information and intelligence products that are developed and disseminated by organizations at all levels of government. In other words, even though a police agency may not have the resources necessary to analyze all of the information it acquires, it should still be able to mount an effective response to credible threat information that it receives. Learn more about the law enforcement intelligence function and ILP at **Library Extra 6–9**.

Information Sharing and Antiterrorism

The need to effectively share criminal intelligence across jurisdictions and between law enforcement agencies nationwide became apparent with the tragic events of September 11, 2001. Consequently, governments at all levels are today working toward the creation of a fully integrated criminal justice information system. According to a recent task force report, a fully

The need for improving homeland security requires a joint effort of all levels of law enforcement, including local, state and federal agencies.

—Major Cities Chiefs Association[viii]

integrated system would be "a network of public safety, justice and homeland security computer systems which provides to each agency the information it needs, at the time it is needed, in the form that it is needed, regardless of the source and regardless of the physical location at which it is stored."[81] The information that is provided would be complete, accurate, and formatted in whatever way is most useful for the agency's tasks. In a fully integrated criminal justice information system, information would be made available at the practitioner's workstation, whether that workstation is a patrol car, desk, laptop, or judge's bench. Within such a system, each agency would share information not only with other agencies in its own jurisdiction but with multiple justice agencies at the federal, state, and local levels. In such an idealized justice information system, accurate information would also be available to nonjustice agencies with statutory authority and a legal obligation to check criminal histories before licensure, employment, weapons purchase, and so on.

One widely used information-sharing system is Law Enforcement Online (LEO). LEO, an intranet intended exclusively for use by the law enforcement community, is a national interactive computer communications system and information service. A user-friendly system, it can be accessed by any approved employee of a duly constituted local, state, or federal law enforcement agency or by an approved member of an authorized law enforcement special-interest group. LEO provides a state-of-the-art communications mechanism to link all levels of law enforcement throughout the United States. The system includes password-accessed e-mail, Internet chat rooms, an electronic library, an online calendar, special-interest topical focus areas, and self-paced distance-learning modules.[82]

NLETS
An acronym referring to the International Justice and Public Safety Information Sharing Network, an important law enforcement information-sharing resource.

Another important law enforcement information-sharing resource is the International Justice and Public Safety Information Sharing Network, which uses the acronym **NLETS**. NLETS members include all 50 states, most federal agencies and territories, and the Royal Canadian Mounted Police (RCMP). NLETS, which has been in operation for nearly 40 years, was formerly called the National Law Enforcement Telecommunications System. It has recently been enhanced to facilitate a variety of encrypted digital communications. It now links 30,000 agencies and more than half a million access devices in the United States and Canada, and it facilitates nearly 41 million transmissions each month. Information available through NLETS includes state criminal histories, homeland alert messages, immigration databases, driver's records and vehicle registrations, aircraft registrations, AMBER Alerts, weather advisories, and hazardous materials (HAZMAT) notifications and regulations. You can reach NLETS on the Web at **Web Extra 6–6**.

The National Criminal Intelligence Sharing Plan

Thematic Question How might discretion lead to civil liability? What can departments do to train officers to use discretion wisely and to avoid major sources of civil liability through the proper exercise of discretion?

Although information-sharing efforts continue to evolve, most experts agree that a fully integrated, nationwide criminal justice information system does not yet exist.[83] Efforts to create one began with the 2003 National Criminal Intelligence Sharing Plan (NCISP). The NCISP was developed under the auspices of the DOJ's Global Justice Information Sharing Initiative and was authored by its Global Intelligence Working Group (GIWG).[84] Federal, local, state, and tribal law enforcement representatives all had a voice in the development of the plan. The NCISP provides specific steps that law enforcement agencies can take to participate in the sharing of critical law enforcement and terrorism prevention information.

Authors of the plan note that not every agency has the staff or resources needed to create a formal intelligence unit. Even without a dedicated intelligence unit, however, the plan says that every law enforcement organization must have the ability to effectively consume the intelligence available from a wide range of organizations at all levels of government.[85] The NCISP is available in its entirety at **Library Extra 6–10**.

Police Civil Liability

5 Describe the civil liability issues associated with policing, and identify common sources of civil suits against the police.

In 1996, 51-year-old Richard Kelley filed suit in federal court against the Massachusetts State Police and the Weymouth (Massachusetts) Police Department.[86] The suit resulted from an incident during which, Kelley alleged, state troopers and Weymouth police officers treated him as a drunk rather than recognizing that he had just suffered a stroke while driving. According to Kelley, following a minor traffic accident caused by the stroke, officers pulled him from his car, handcuffed him, dragged him along the ground, and ignored his pleas for help—forcing him to stay at a state police barracks for seven hours before taking him for medical treatment. Drunk-driving charges against Kelley were dropped after medical tests failed to reveal the presence of any intoxicating substances in his body.

Suits of **civil liability** brought against law enforcement personnel are of two types: state and federal. Suits brought in state courts have generally been the more common form of civil litigation involving police officers. In recent years, however, an increasing number of suits have been brought in federal courts on the claim that the civil rights of the plaintiff, as guaranteed by federal law, were denied.

civil liability
The potential responsibility for payment of damages or other court-ordered enforcement as a result of a ruling in a lawsuit. Civil liability is not the same as criminal liability, which means "open to punishment for a crime."[ix]

Common Sources of Civil Suits

Police officers may become involved in a variety of situations that could result in civil suits against the officers, their superiors, and their departments. Major sources of police civil liability are listed in Table 6–3. Charles R. Swanson, an expert in police procedure, says that the most common sources of lawsuits against the police are "assault, battery, false imprisonment, and malicious prosecution."[87]

Thematic Question What are the major sources of police civil liability? In what way might each of these sources affect individual police departments? Individual officers? Administrators? How can the potential for civil liability be reduced by all concerned?

Of all complaints brought against the police, assault charges are the best known, being subject to high media visibility. Less visible (but not uncommon) are civil suits charging the police with false arrest or false imprisonment. In the 1986 case of *Malley* v. *Briggs*,[88] the U.S. Supreme Court held that a police officer who effects an arrest or conducts a search on the basis of an improperly issued warrant may be liable for monetary damages when a reasonably well-trained officer, under the same circumstances, "would have known that his affidavit failed to establish probable cause and that he should not have applied for the warrant." Significantly, the Court ruled that an officer "cannot excuse his own default by pointing to the greater incompetence of the magistrate."[89] The officer, rather than the judge who issued the warrant, is ultimately responsible for establishing the basis for pursuing the arrest or search.

Lecture Note Explain the importance of department policy in reducing civil liability.

When an officer makes an arrest without just cause or simply impedes an individual's right to leave the scene without good reason, he or she may be liable for the charge of false arrest. Officers who "throw their weight around" are especially subject to this type of suit, grounded as it is in the abuse of police authority. Because employers may be sued for the negligent or malicious actions of their employees, many police departments are being named as codefendants in lawsuits today.

Thematic Question What do you think of the idea of police immunity from prosecution? How far should it extend? Should everyone, even public employees, be responsible for what they do, without shelter of immunity? Explain.

Civil suits are also brought against officers whose actions are deemed negligent. High-speed vehicle pursuits are especially dangerous because of the potential for injury to innocent bystanders. In the case of *Biscoe* v. *Arlington County* (1984),[90] for example, Alvin Biscoe was awarded $5 million after he lost both legs as a consequence of a high-speed chase while he was waiting to cross the street. Biscoe, an innocent bystander, was struck by a police car that went out of control. The officer driving the car had violated department policies prohibiting high-speed chases, and the court found that he had not been properly trained.

Departments may protect themselves to some degree through training combined with regulations limiting the authority of their personnel. One year after the *Biscoe* case was decided, for example, a Louisiana police officer, who had an accident while driving 75 mph in a 40-mph zone, was found to be negligent and was held liable for damages.[91] However, the department was not held liable

TABLE 6–3
Major Sources of Police Civil Liability

Failure to protect property in police custody
Negligence in the care of suspects in police custody
Failure to render proper emergency medical assistance
Failure to prevent a foreseeable crime
Failure to aid private citizens
Lack of due regard for the safety of others
False arrest
False imprisonment
Inappropriate use of deadly force
Unnecessary assault or battery
Malicious prosecution
Violation of constitutional rights
Pattern of unfair and inequitable treatment
Racial profiling

because it had a policy limiting emergency driving to no more than 20 mph over the posted speed limit and because officers were trained in that policy.

The FBI states that "a traffic accident constitutes the most common terminating event in an urban pursuit."[92] Some cities are actively replacing high-speed vehicle pursuits with surveillance technologies employing unmanned aerial vehicles (UAVs). Although helicopters have long been used in this capacity, the advent of UAV technology promises to make the tracking of fleeing suspects much quicker and far safer for all involved.

Law enforcement supervisors may be the object of lawsuits by virtue of the fact that they are responsible for the actions of their officers. If it can be shown that supervisors were negligent in hiring (as when someone with a history of alcoholism, mental problems, sexual deviance, or drug abuse is employed) or if supervisors failed in their responsibility to properly train officers before arming and deploying them, they may be found liable for damages.

In the 1989 case of the *City of Canton, Ohio* v. *Harris*,[93] the U.S. Supreme Court ruled that a "failure to train" can become the basis for legal liability on the part of a municipality where the "failure to train amounts to deliberate indifference to the rights of persons with whom the police come in contact."[94] In that case, Geraldine Harris was arrested and taken to the Canton, Ohio, police station. While at the station, she slumped to the floor several times. Officers left her on the floor and did not call for medical assistance. Upon release, Harris's family took her to a local hospital, where she was found to be suffering from several emotional ailments. Harris was hospitalized for a week and received follow-up outpatient treatment for the next year.

In the 1997 case of *Board of the County Commissioners of Bryan County, Oklahoma* v. *Brown*, however, the Supreme Court ruled that to establish liability, plaintiffs must show that "the municipal action in question was not simply negligent, but was taken with 'deliberate indifference' as to its known or obvious consequences."[95]

Federal Lawsuits

1983 lawsuit
A civil suit brought under Title 42, Section 1983, of the U.S. Code against anyone who denies others their constitutional right to life, liberty, or property without due process of law.

Civil suits alleging police misconduct that are filed in federal courts are often called **1983 lawsuits** because they are based on Section 1983 of Title 42 of the U.S. Code—an act passed by Congress in 1871 to ensure the civil rights of men and women of all races. That act requires due process of law before any person can be deprived of life, liberty, or property and specifically provides redress for the denial of these constitutional rights by officials acting under color of state law. It reads as follows:

> Every person who, under color of any statute, ordinance, regulation, custom, or usage, of any State or Territory, subjects, or causes to be subjected, any citizen of the United States or other person within the jurisdiction thereof to the deprivation of any rights, privileges, or immunities secured by the Constitution and laws, shall be liable to the party injured in an action at law, suit in equity, or other proper proceeding for redress.[96]

A 1983 suit may be brought, for example, against officers who shoot suspects under questionable circumstances, thereby denying them, without due process, their right to life. Similarly, an officer who makes an arrest based on accusations that he or she knows to be untrue may be subject to a 1983 lawsuit.

***Bivens* action**
A civil suit, based on the case of *Bivens* v. *Six Unknown Federal Agents*, brought against federal government officials for denying the constitutional rights of others.

Another type of liability action, this one directed specifically at federal officials or enforcement agents, is called a ***Bivens* action**. The case of *Bivens* v. *Six Unknown Federal Agents* (1971)[97] established a path for legal action against agents enforcing federal laws, which is similar to that found in a 1983 suit. *Bivens* actions may be addressed against individuals but not against the United States or its agencies.[98] Federal officers have generally been granted a court-created qualified immunity and have been protected from suits where they were found to have acted in the belief that their action was consistent with federal law.[99]

Everyone is a prisoner of his own experiences. No one can eliminate prejudices—just recognize them.

—Edward R. Murrow (1908–1965)

In the past, the doctrine of sovereign immunity barred legal actions against state and local governments. Sovereign immunity was a legal theory that held that a governing body could not be sued because it made the law and therefore could not be bound by it. Immunity is a much more complex issue today. Some states have officially abandoned any pretext of immunity through legislative action. New York State, for example, has declared that public agencies are equally as liable as private agencies for violations of constitutional rights. Other states, like California, have enacted statutory provisions that define and limit governmental liability.[100] A number of state immunity statutes have been struck down by court decisions. In general, states are moving in the direction of setting dollar limits on liability and adopting federal immunity principles to protect individual officers, including "good-faith" and "reasonable belief" rules.

▲ Major Juanita Walker-Kirkland of the Miami Police Department, *left*, listening to Manjit Singh, *right*, chairman of Sikh Mediawatch and Task Force during a Building Cultural Competency training program in June 2003. The training program was sponsored by the U.S. Department of Justice in hopes of improving community relations between law enforcement officials and diverse cultural and religious groups. Why are such programs important?
Yesikka Vivancos/AP Wide World Photos

At the federal level, the concept of sovereign immunity is embodied in the Federal Tort Claims Act (FTCA),[101] which grants broad immunity to federal government agencies engaged in discretionary activities. When a federal employee is sued for a wrongful or negligent act, the Federal Employees Liability Reform and Tort Compensation Act of 1988, commonly known as the Westfall Act, empowers the attorney general to certify that the employee was acting within the scope of his or her office or employment at the time of the incident. Upon certification, the employee is dismissed from the action, and the United States is substituted as defendant; the case then falls under the governance of the FTCA.

The U.S. Supreme Court has supported a type of "qualified immunity" for individual officers (as opposed to the agencies for which they work) that "shields law enforcement officers from constitutional lawsuits if reasonable officers believe their actions to be lawful in light of clearly established law and the information the officers possess." The Supreme Court has also described qualified immunity as a defense "which shields public officials from actions for damages unless their conduct was unreasonable in light of clearly established law."[102] The Court said that "the qualified immunity doctrine's central objective is to protect public officials from undue interference with their duties and from potentially disabling threats of liability."[103] In the context of a warrantless arrest, the Court said in *Hunter* v. *Bryant* (1991),[104] "even law enforcement officials who reasonably but mistakenly conclude that probable cause is present are entitled to immunity."[105]

The doctrine of qualified immunity, as it exists today, rests largely on the 2001 U.S. Supreme Court decision of *Saucier* v. *Katz*,[106] in which the Court established a two-pronged test for assessing constitutional violations by government agents.[107] First, the court hearing the case must decide whether the facts, taken in the light most favorable to the party asserting the injury, show that the defendant's conduct violated a constitutional right. Second, the court must then decide whether that right was clearly established. For a right to be clearly established, the Court ruled, "it would be clear to a reasonable [defendant] that his conduct was unlawful in the situation he confronted." In summary, qualified immunity protects law enforcement agents from being sued for damages unless they violate clearly established law that a reasonable official in the agents' position would have known.

The *Saucier* decision has recently faced substantial legal challenges, leading the Court to rule in 2009 that "the rigid *Saucier* procedure" has serious shortcomings. The Court noted that "*stare decisis* does not prevent this Court from determining whether the *Saucier* procedure should be modified or abandoned." The 2009 ruling, *Pearson et al.* v. *Callahan*,[108] is available online at **Library Extra 6–11**.

In 2007, in the case of *Scott* v. *Harris*, the Supreme Court sided with an officer who had rammed a speeding car driven by a teenager, sending it down an embankment and leaving the driver a quadriplegic.[109] The justices reasoned that the driver "intentionally placed himself and the public in danger by unlawfully engaging in reckless, high-speed flight" and noted that those who might have been harmed had the officer not forced him off the road "were entirely innocent." The Court concluded that it was reasonable for the officer, Deputy Timothy Scott, to take the action that he did and rejected the "argument that safety could have been assured if the police simply ceased their pursuit." In essence, the Court found that "a police officer's attempt to terminate a dangerous high-speed car chase that threatens the lives of innocent bystanders does not violate the Fourth Amendment, even when it places the fleeing motorist at risk of serious injury or death."

Criminal charges can be brought against officers who overstep legal boundaries or who act in violation of set standards. In 2001, for example, in the case of *Idaho* v. *Horiuchi*,[110] the Ninth U.S. Circuit Court of Appeals ruled that federal law enforcement officers are not immune from state prosecution where their actions violate state law "either through malice or excessive zeal." The case involved FBI sharpshooter Lon Horiuchi, who was charged with negligent manslaughter by prosecutors in Boundary County, Idaho, following the 1992 incident at Ruby Ridge. Learn more about the Ruby Ridge incident at **Library Extra 6–12**.

Today, most police departments at both state and federal levels carry liability insurance to protect themselves against the severe financial damage that can result from the loss of a large civil suit. Some officers also acquire private policies that provide coverage in the event they are named as individuals in a civil suit. Both types of insurance policies generally cover legal fees up to a certain amount, regardless of the outcome of the case. Police departments that face civil prosecution because of the actions of an officer may find that legal and financial liability extends to supervisors, city managers, and the community itself. Where insurance coverage does not exist or is inadequate, city coffers may be nearly drained to meet the damages awarded.[111]

One study of a large sample of police chiefs throughout Texas found that most believed that lawsuits or the threat of civil litigation against the police makes it harder for individual officers to do their jobs. Most of the chiefs espoused the idea that adequate training, better screening of applicants, close supervision of officers, and "treating people fairly" all reduced the likelihood of lawsuits.[112]

racial profiling
"Any police-initiated action that relies on the race, ethnicity, or national origin rather than [1] on the behavior of an individual, or [2] on information that leads the police to a particular individual who has been identified as being, or having been, engaged in criminal activity."[x]

Racial Profiling and Biased Policing

Racial Profiling

Racial profiling has been defined as any police action initiated on the basis of the race, ethnicity, or national origin of a suspect rather than on the behavior of that individual or on information that identifies the individual as being, or having been, engaged in criminal activity.[113]

6 Describe racial profiling and biased policing, and explain why they have become significant issues in policing today.

Profiling was originally intended to help catch drug couriers attempting to enter the country. The U.S. Customs Service and the DEA developed a number of "personal indicators" that seemed, from the agency's day-to-day enforcement experiences, to be associated with increased likelihood of law violation. Among the indicators were these: speaking Spanish, entering the United States on flights originating in particular Central and South American countries, being an 18- to 32-year-old male, having purchased tickets with cash, and having a short planned stay (often of only a day or two) in the United States. Federal agents frequently used these criteria in deciding which airline passengers to search and which bags to inspect.

▲ An elderly woman showing her displeasure with Transportation Security Administration requirements. Some people fear that the use of profiling techniques could lead to unfair discrimination against members of certain racial and ethnic groups. Others suggest that the careful use of profiling can provide an important advantage in an age of scarce resources. Which perspective appeals to you?
Henry Ray Abrams/AP Wide World Photos

The alleged use by police of racial profiling may take a number of forms. Minority accounts of disparate treatment at the hands of police officers include being stopped for being "in the wrong car" (for example, driving an expensive, late-model BMW); being stopped and questioned for being in the wrong neighborhood (that is, driving through a traditionally white residential neighborhood); and being harassed at the hands of police officers for petty traffic violations (such as having underinflated tires, or having an illegible license plate).[114]

Racial profiling has been derisively referred to as "driving while black" or "driving while brown," although it may also apply to situations other than those involving traffic violations. Racial profiling came to the attention of the public in the late 1990s when police in New Jersey and Maryland were accused of unfair treatment of African American motorists and admitted that race was a factor in traffic stops.

In 2003, in response to widespread public outcry over the use of racial profiling, the DOJ banned its practice in all federal law enforcement agencies except in cases that involve the possible identification of terrorist suspects.[115] According to the DOJ, "The guidance provides that in making routine law enforcement decisions—such as deciding which motorists to stop for traffic infractions—consideration of the driver's race or ethnicity is absolutely forbidden."[116]

Those who defend the use of racial profiling by the police argue that it is not a bigoted practice when based on facts (such as when a police department decides to increase patrols in a particular area because of exceptionally high crime rates) or when significant criminal potential exists among even a few members of a group. An example of the latter is the widespread public suspicions that focused on Arab Americans (and other Arabs living in the United States or traveling through the country) following the terrorist attacks of September 11, 2001. As soon as it was publicly announced that the hijackers had been of Middle Eastern origin, some flight crews demanded that Arab-looking passengers be removed from their airplanes before takeoff, and passengers refused to fly with people who looked like Arabs.[117]

None of this is to say, of course, that race or ethnicity somehow inherently causes crime (or that it somehow causes poverty or increases the risk of victimization). If anything, race and ethnicity may simply display a significant correlation with certain types of crime, as they do with certain kinds of victimization. Although the *real* causes of criminality may be socialization into criminal subcultures, economically deprived neighborhoods, lack of salable job skills, and intergenerational poverty, and not race per se, to some law enforcement agencies race provides one more indicator of the likelihood of criminality. David Cole, a professor at Georgetown University's Law Center, for example, notes that in the minds of many police officials, "racial and ethnic disparities reflect not discrimination [or bigotry] but higher rates of offenses among minorities."[118]

It is practically an article of faith among young, black males that they are more likely than whites to be stopped, frisked, spread-eagled, and arrested by the police, often on the flimsiest of charges.

—Hutchinson Report, July 2001

Class Activity Have students create a questionnaire designed to assess respondents' personal experience (if any) of racial profiling by the police. Have students administer the questionnaire to people on campus, on the Web, or at a local shopping center.

Freedom or Safety? You Decide.

Was the LAPD's Community Mapping Project a Form of Religious Profiling?

In 2007, the Los Angeles Police Department announced that it would terminate plans to have its counterterrorism unit identify isolated social enclaves within the city. Weeks earlier Deputy Chief Michael P. Downing, who heads the department's counterterrorism bureau, issued a press release detailing how the LAPD intended to work with the University of Southern California's Center for Risk and Economic Analysis of Terrorism Events to determine which areas of the city were socially isolated and susceptible to "violent, ideologically based extremism."

The plan had been originally touted as a mapping project "intended to study the language, culture, history, socioeconomic conditions, and country of origin of various communities and neighborhoods" and as an effort to "help groups integrate into broader society by offering access to government and social services."

Although the plan did not specifically target Muslim neighborhoods, Islamic leaders felt that it was a thinly disguised form of racial and religious profiling and that it was aimed squarely at them and at members of their communities. Islamic leaders protested the plan, saying that any mapping based on faith and ethnicity is inappropriate for police departments, which should be concerned instead with crime mapping. "Police should not be in the business of analyzing political views, and religious views," said Hussam Ayloush, a member of the Los Angeles chapter of the Council on American-Islamic Relations.

Estimates hold that about half a million Muslims live in California's Los Angeles, Riverside, and Orange counties.

YOU DECIDE

Is Hussam Ayloush right in saying that police departments should concern themselves with crime mapping and not with other forms of mapping in the cities they serve? Why or why not? Was the LAPD's proposed community mapping project really a form of religious and ethnic profiling? If so, should such profiling be permitted? Why or why not?

References: Peter Prengaman, "LAPD Shelves Muslim Mapping Plan," Associated Press, November 15, 2007 and Mimi Hall, "LAPD Plan Draws Ire from Muslims," *USA Today*, November 9–11, 2007.

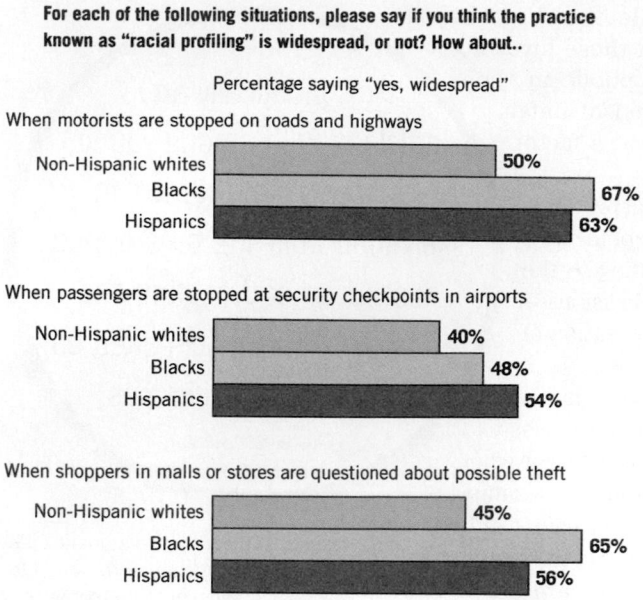

FIGURE 6–4
Racial Profiling and Biased Policing, Perceptions by Race

Source: From The Gallup Poll, http://www.gallup.com. Reprinted with permission of The Gallup Organization.

"Nationwide," says Cole, "blacks are 13 times more likely to be sent to state prisons for drug convictions than are whites, so it would seem rational for police to assume that all other things being equal, a black driver is more likely than a white driver to be carrying drugs." Statistics like this, of course, may further enhance police focus on minorities and may result in even more arrests, thereby reinforcing the beliefs on which racial profiling by enforcement agents is based. Such observations led esteemed sociologist Amitai Etzioni to declare in 2001 that racial profiling is not necessarily racist.[119] Moreover, warned Etzioni, an end to racial profiling "would penalize those African-American communities with high incidences of violent crime" because they would lose the levels of policing that they need to remain relatively secure.

Regardless of arguments offered in support of racial profiling as an enforcement tool, the practice has been widely condemned as being contrary to basic ethical principles. National public opinion polls conducted by the Gallup Poll Organization show that more than 80% of respondents are morally opposed to the practice of racial profiling by the police, although beliefs about the use of racial profiling vary widely by race (Figure 6–4).[120] From a more pragmatic viewpoint, however, racial profiling is unacceptable because it weakens the public's confidence in the police, thereby decreasing police-citizen trust and cooperation.[121] A number of states have enacted legislation banning the use of racial profiling by law enforcement agencies (Figure 6–5). Learn more about racial profiling and police management via **Library Extra 6–13**.

> We must strive to eliminate any racial, ethnic, or cultural bias that may exist among our ranks.
>
> —Sherman Block, former Los Angeles County sheriff

Racially Biased Policing

In 2001, PERF released a detailed report titled *Racially Biased Policing: A Principled Response*.[122] PERF researchers surveyed more than 1,000 police executives, analyzed material from over 250 law enforcement agencies, and sought input from law enforcement agency personnel, community activists, and civil rights leaders about racial bias in policing. Researchers concluded that "the vast majority of law enforcement officers—of all ranks, nationwide—are dedicated men and women committed to serving all citizens

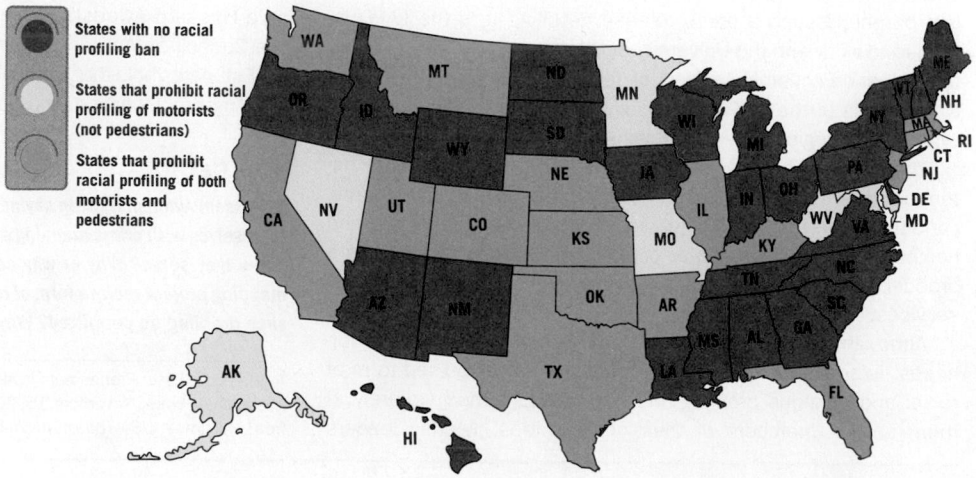

FIGURE 6–5
States That Have Banned Racial Profiling

Source: Amnesty International USA, *Threat and Humiliation: Racial Profiling, Domestic Security, and Human Rights in the United States* (New York: Amnesty International USA Publications, 2004), p. 6. http://www.amnestyusa.org. © Amnesty International USA. Reprinted with permission.

with fairness and dignity." [123] Most police officers, said the report, share an intolerance for racially biased policing. The report's authors noted that some police behaviors may be misinterpreted as biased when, in fact, the officers are just doing their job. "The good officer continually scans the environment for anomalies to normalcy—for conditions, people and behavior that are unusual for that environment," they said. "In learning and practicing their craft, officers quickly develop a sense for what is normal and expected, and conversely, for what is not."[124] Hence for officers of any race to take special notice of unknown young white males who unexpectedly appear in a traditionally African American neighborhood, for example, might be nothing other than routine police procedure. Such an observation, however, is not in itself sufficient for an investigatory stop but might be used in conjunction with other trustworthy and relevant information already in the officers' possession—such as the officers' prior knowledge that young white men have been routinely visiting a particular apartment complex in the neighborhood to purchase drugs—to justify such a stop.

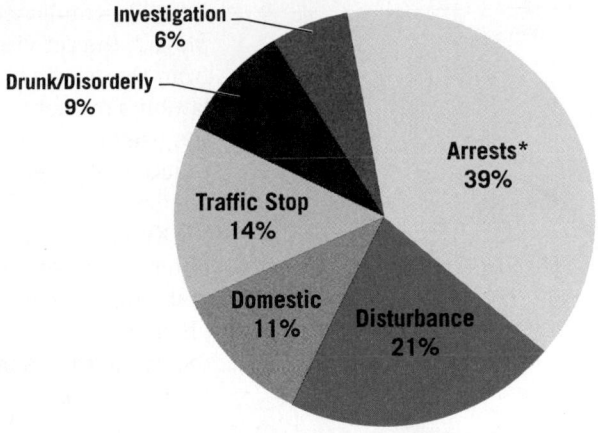

*Includes serving arrest warrants, making field arrests, and effecting other arrests.

FIGURE 6–6
Police Use of Force by Type of Encounter

Source: International Association of Chiefs of Police, *Police Use of Force in America, 2001* (Alexandria, VA: IACP, 2001), p. iii. Reprinted with permission.

The PERF report provides many specific recommendations to help police departments be free of bias. One recommendation, for example, says that "supervisors should monitor activity reports for evidence of improper practices and patterns. They should conduct spot-checks and regular sampling of in-car videotapes, radio transmissions, and in-car computer and central communications records to determine if both formal and informal communications are professional and free from racial bias and other disrespect."[125] Read the entire PERF report at **Library Extra 6–14**.

Police Use Of Force

Police use of force is defined as the use of physical restraint by a police officer when dealing with a member of the public.[126] Law enforcement officers are authorized to use the amount of force that is reasonable and necessary given the circumstances. Most officers are trained in the use of force and typically encounter numerous situations during their careers when the use of force is appropriate—for example, when making some arrests, restraining unruly combatants, or controlling a disruptive demonstration. Force may involve hitting; holding or restraining; pushing; choking; threatening with a flashlight, baton, or chemical or pepper spray; restraining with a police dog; or threatening with a gun. Some definitions of police use of force also include handcuffing.

7 Describe the situations in which police officers are most likely to use force, and provide some guidelines for determining when too much force has been used.

police use of force
The use of physical restraint by a police officer when dealing with a member of the public.[xi]

The NIJ estimates that more than 43.5 million people nationwide have face-to-face contact with the police over a typical 12-month period (nearly 18 million as a result of traffic stops) and that approximately 1.6%, or about 700,000 of these people, become subject to the use of force or the threat of force.[127] When handcuffing is included in the definition of force, the number of people subjected to force increases to 1.2 million, or slightly more than 2.5% of those having contact with the police. Other studies show that police use weaponless tactics in approximately 80% of use-of-force incidents and that half of all use-of-force incidents involve merely grabbing or holding the suspect.[128]

Studies show that police use force in fewer than 20% of adult custodial arrests. Even in instances where force is used, the police primarily use weaponless tactics. Female officers have been found less likely to use physical force and firearms and are more likely to use chemical weapons (mostly pepper spray) than their male counterparts. Figure 6–6 shows the types of encounters in which the use of force is most likely to be employed.

A more complex issue is the use of excessive force. The IACP defines **excessive force** as "the application of an amount and/or frequency of force greater than that required to

excessive force
The application of an amount or frequency of force greater than that required to compel compliance from a willing or unwilling subject.[xii]

compel compliance from a willing or unwilling subject."[129] When excessive force is employed, the activities of the police often come under public scrutiny and receive attention from the media and legislators. Police officers' use of excessive force can also result in lawsuits by members of the public who feel that they have been treated unfairly. Whether the use of excessive force is aberrant behavior on the part of an individual officer or is a practice of an entire law enforcement agency, both the law and public opinion generally condemn it.

Nothing's so sacred as honor.
—Inscription on Wyatt Earp's headstone

Kenneth Adams, an expert in the use of force by police, notes that there is an important difference between the terms *excessive force*, such as shoving or pushing when simply grabbing a suspect would be adequate, and the *excessive use of force*, which refers to the phenomenon of force being used unacceptably, often on a department-wide basis. The second term, says Adams, "deals with relative comparisons among police agencies, and there are no established criteria for judgment."[130] *Use of excessive force* and the *excessive use of force* may be distinguished from the *illegal use of force*, which refers to situations in which the use of force by police violates a law or statute.[131]

In a study reported in 2001, Geoffrey Alpert and Roger Dunham found that the "force factor"—the level of force used by the police relative to the suspect's level of resistance—is a key element to consider in attempting to reduce injuries to both the police and suspects.[132] The force factor is calculated by measuring both the suspect's level of resistance and the officer's level of force on an equivalent scale and by then subtracting the level of resistance from the level of police force used. Results from the study indicate that, on average, the level of force that officers use is closely related to the type of training that their departments emphasize.

problem police officer
A law enforcement officer who exhibits problem behavior, as indicated by high rates of citizen complaints and use-of-force incidents and by other evidence.[xiii]

Excessive force can also be symptomatic of **problem police officers**. Problem police officers are those who exhibit problem behavior, as indicated by high rates of citizen complaints and use-of-force incidents and by other evidence.[133] The Christopher Commission, which studied the structure and operation of the LAPD in the wake of the Rodney King beating, found a number of repeat offenders on the LAPD force.[134] According to the commission, approximately 1,800 LAPD officers were alleged to have used excessive force or improper tactics between 1986 and 1990. Of these officers, more than 1,400 had only one or two allegations against them, another 183 officers had four or more allegations, 44 had six or more, 16 had eight or more, and one had 16 such allegations. The commission also found that, generally speaking, the 44 officers with six complaints or more had received positive performance evaluations that failed to record "sustained" complaints or to discuss their significance.

Recent studies have found that problem police officers do not differ significantly in race or ethnicity from other officers, although they tend to be male and have disciplinary records that are more serious than those of other officers. Some departments are developing early-warning systems to allow police managers to identify potentially problematic officers and to reduce problem police officer behavior. Learn more about the police use of force, as well as force used against the police, from **Library Extras 6–15** and **6–16**.

Deadly Force

deadly force
The force likely to cause death or great bodily harm. Also, "the intentional use of a firearm or other instrument resulting in a high probability of death."[xiv]

Generally speaking, **deadly force** is likely to cause death or great bodily harm. The FBI defines *deadly force* as "the intentional use of a firearm or other instrument resulting in a high probability of death."[135] According to a report released by the Bureau of Justice Statistics in 2001, nearly 400 felons each year die in justifiable homicides by police.[136]

Thematic Question How might a community policing approach alter police views of when deadly force is appropriate?

The use of deadly force by law enforcement officers, especially when it is *not* considered justifiable (as in the *Horiuchi* case mentioned earlier in this chapter), is one area of potential civil liability that has received considerable attention in recent years. Historically, the fleeing-felon rule applied to most U.S. jurisdictions. It held that officers could use deadly force to prevent the escape of a suspected felon even when that person represented no immediate threat to the officer or to the public.

The 1985 U.S. Supreme Court case of *Tennessee* v. *Garner*[137] specified the conditions under which deadly force could be used in the apprehension of suspected felons. Edward Garner, a 15-year-old suspected burglar, was shot to death by Memphis police after he refused their order to halt and attempted to climb over a chain-link fence. In an action initiated by Garner's father, who claimed that his son's constitutional rights had been violated, the Court held that the use of deadly force by the police to prevent the escape of a fleeing felon could be justified only where the suspect could reasonably be thought to represent a significant threat of serious injury or death to the public or to the officer and where deadly force is necessary to effect the arrest. In reaching its decision, the Court declared that "[t]he use of deadly force to prevent the escape of all felony suspects, whatever the circumstances, is constitutionally unreasonable."

In 1989, in the case of *Graham* v. *Connor*,[138] the Court established the standard of "objective reasonableness" under which an officer's use of deadly force could be assessed in terms of "reasonableness at the moment." In other words, whether deadly force has been used appropriately should be judged, the Court said, from the perspective of a reasonable officer on the scene and not with the benefit of "20/20 hindsight." The justices wrote, "The calculus of reasonableness must embody allowance for the fact that police officers are often forced to make split-second judgments—in circumstances that are tense, uncertain, and rapidly evolving—about the amount of force that is necessary in a particular situation."

▲ Cincinnati Police Officer Princess Davis talking with community member Gil Steinberger following a police-sponsored showing of a movie for senior citizens. The event was part of police efforts to improve police-community relations in the city following the November 30, 2003, beating death of 41-year-old Nathaniel Jones. Jones, a 350-pound black man who had ingested PCP and cocaine, lunged at two white officers and knocked one of them down before other officers beat him in an effort to subdue him. His family, charging that excessive force had been used, filed a wrongful death lawsuit against the city in federal court. How can police agencies win the support of the communities they serve?
Al Behrman/AP Wide World Photos

In 1995, following investigations into the actions of federal agents at the deadly siege of the Branch Davidian compound at Waco, Texas, and the tragic deaths associated with a 1992 FBI assault on antigovernment separatists in Ruby Ridge, Idaho, the federal government announced that it was adopting an "imminent danger" standard for the use of deadly force by federal agents. The imminent danger standard restricts the use of deadly force to those situations in which the lives of agents or others are in danger. As the new standard was announced, federal agencies were criticized for having taken so long to adopt it. The federal deadly force policy, as adopted by the FBI, contains the following elements:[139]

- *Defense of life.* Agents may use deadly force only when necessary, that is, only when they have probable cause to believe that the subject poses an imminent danger of serious physical injury or death to the agents or to others.
- *Fleeing subject.* Deadly force may be used to prevent the escape of a fleeing subject if there is probable cause to believe that the subject has committed a felony involving the infliction or threatened infliction of serious physical injury or death and that the subject's escape would pose an imminent danger of serious physical injury or death to the agents or to others.
- *Verbal warning.* If feasible, and if doing so would not increase the danger to the agents or to others, a verbal warning to submit to the authority of the agents should be given before the use of deadly force.
- *Warning shot.* Agents may not fire warning shots.
- *Vehicle.* Agents may not fire weapons solely to disable moving vehicles. Weapons may be fired at the driver or other occupant of a moving motor vehicle only when the agents have probable cause to believe that the subject poses an imminent danger of serious physical injury or death to the agents or to others and when the use of deadly force does not create a danger to the public that outweighs the likely benefits of its use.

Studies of killings by the police have often focused on claims of discrimination—that black and minority suspects are more likely to be shot than whites—but research has not provided solid support for such claims. While individuals shot by police are more likely to be minorities, an early study by James Fyfe found that police officers will generally respond with deadly force when mortally threatened and that minorities are considerably more likely to use weapons in assaults on officers than are whites.[140] Complicating the picture further, Fyfe's study showed that minority officers are involved in the shootings of suspects more often than other officers, a finding that may be due to the assignment of minority officers to inner-city and ghetto areas.

▲ Demonstrators in Harris County, Texas, protesting the police use of Tasers. This less-lethal weapon, manufactured by Taser International, incapacitates potential attackers by delivering an electrical shock to the person's nervous system. The technology is intended to reduce injury rates to both suspects and officers. Why do some people oppose its use?
Ben DeSoto/AP/AP Wide World Photos

However, a later study by Fyfe, which analyzed police shootings in Memphis, Tennessee, found that black property offenders were twice as likely as whites to be shot by police.[141]

Although relatively few police officers ever fire their weapons at suspects during the course of their careers, those who do may find themselves embroiled in a web of social, legal, and personal complications. It is estimated that in an average year, 600 suspects are killed by public police in America, while another 1,200 are shot and wounded, and 1,800 are shot at and missed.[142] The personal side of police shootings is well summarized in the title of an article that appeared in *Police Magazine*. The article, "I've Killed That Man Ten Thousand Times," demonstrates how police officers who have to use their weapons may be haunted by years of depression and despair.[143] Not long ago, according to author Anne Cohen, all departments did to help an officer who had shot someone was to "give him enough bullets to reload his gun." The stress and trauma that result from police shootings are only now being realized, and many departments have yet to develop mechanisms for adequately dealing with them.[144]

Police officers have particular difficulty dealing with instances of "suicide by cop," in which individuals bent on dying engage in behavior that causes responding officers to resort to deadly force. On March 10, 2005, for example, John T. Garczynski, Jr., a father of two preteen boys, died in a hail of 26 police bullets fired by officers who had surrounded his vehicle in a Boca Raton, Florida, condominium parking lot.[145] Garczynski, a Florida Power and Light Company employee, had been separated from his wife months earlier and appeared to have been despondent over financial problems and the breakup of his marriage. The night before his death, Garczynski met his wife at a bowling alley and handed her a packet containing a suicide note, a typed obituary, and a eulogy to be read at his funeral. After he left, Garczynski's wife called police, and officers used the help of a cell phone company to locate Garczynski. As deputies surrounded Garczynski's 2003 Ford Explorer, he attempted to start the vehicle. One of the officers yelled "Freeze!" and then shouted "Let me see your hands!" It was at that point, deputies said, that Garczynski pointed a gun at them and they fired.

Rebecca Stincelli, author of the book *Suicide by Cop: Victims from Both Sides of the Badge*,[146] says an incident like that involving Garczynski can be devastating for police officers. "In the past, people have used rope, a gun, gas, jumped off a building. A police officer is just another method," said Stincelli. "They say it's nothing personal. [But] they are wrong. It's very personal" for the officers involved.[147] The FBI says, "Suicide-by-cop incidents are painful and damaging experiences for the surviving families, the communities, and all law enforcement professionals."[148]

A study of fatal shootings by Los Angeles police officers found that an astonishingly large number—over 10%—could be classified as "suicide by cop."[149] Recently, researchers have identified three main "suicide by cop" categories: direct confrontations, in which suicidal subjects instigate attacks on police officers for the purpose of dying; disturbed interventions, in which potentially suicidal subjects take advantage of police intervention in their suicide attempt in order to die; and criminal interventions, in which criminal suspects prefer death to capture and arrest.[150]

Less-Lethal Weapons

Recent media reports tell of weapons being developed for the military that incapacitate rather than kill. Among them are flash guns (more formally known as optical systems incapacitators), which use powerful strobe lights to trigger "flicker illness"; sonic weapons, which employ intense inaudible sounds to cause pain; and focused microwave beams, which can produce extreme physical pain at close range. Such weapons, which employ less-lethal technologies, are being contemplated for use by military planners seeking to separate enemy fighters from civilian populations.[151] They might also be used by civilian law enforcement agencies in border enforcement or during riots or in other crowd-control situations where physical force is needed but where permanent injury must be avoided.

less-lethal weapon
A weapon that is designed to disable, capture, or immobilize—but not kill—a suspect. Occasional deaths do result from the use of such weapons, however.

Less-lethal weapons also offer what may be a problem-specific solution to potential incidents of "suicide by cop," as well as a generic solution to at least some charges of use of excessive force. **Less-lethal weapons** are those that are designed to disable, capture, or immobilize a suspect rather than kill him or her. Efforts to provide law enforcement officers with less-lethal weapons began in 1987.[152] Stun guns, Tasers (also known as conducted energy devices), rubber bullets, beanbag projectiles, and pepper spray are examples of such weapons that are currently in use. More exotic types of less-lethal weapons, however, are on the horizon. These include snare nets that are fired from shotguns, disabling sticky foam that can be sprayed from a distance, microwave beams that heat the tissue of people exposed to them until they desist in their illegal or threatening behavior or lose consciousness, and high-tech guns that fire bolts of electromagnetic energy at a target, causing painful sensory overload and violent muscle spasms. The NIJ states, "The goal is to give line officers effective and safe alternatives to lethal force."[153]

As their name implies, however, less-lethal weapons are not always safe. On October 21, 2004, for example, 21-year-old Emerson College student Victoria Snelgrove died hours after being hit in the eye with a plastic pepper spray–filled projectile that police officers fired at a rowdy crowd celebrating a Red Sox victory. Witnesses said that officers fired the projectile into the crowd after a reveler near Fenway Park threw a bottle at a mounted Boston police officer.[154]

Thematic Question What are the hallmarks of a profession? In your opinion, is police work a profession in America? Explain.

Professionalism and Ethics

Police administrators have responded in a variety of ways to issues of corruption, danger, and liability. Among the most significant responses have been calls for increased **police professionalism** at all levels of policing. A profession is an organized undertaking characterized by a body of specialized knowledge acquired through extensive education,[155] and by a well-considered set of internal standards and ethical guidelines that hold members of the profession accountable to one another and to society. Associations of like-minded practitioners generally serve to create and disseminate standards for the profession as a whole.

police professionalism
The increasing formalization of police work and the accompanying rise in public acceptance of the police.

> The ability of the police to fulfill their sacred trust will improve as a lucid sense of ethical standards is developed.
>
> —Patrick V. Murphy, former New York City police commissioner

8 Demonstrate why professionalism and ethics are important in policing today.

Contemporary policing has many of the attributes of a profession. Specialized knowledge in policing includes a close familiarity with criminal law, laws of procedure, constitutional guarantees, and relevant Supreme Court decisions; a working knowledge of weapons and hand-to-hand tactics, driving skills, and vehicle maintenance; a knowledge of radio communications; report-writing abilities; interviewing and interrogation techniques; and media and human relations skills. Other specialized knowledge may include equipment operation (such as vehicular radar, the Breathalyzer, and the polygraph), special weapons skills, conflict resolution, and hostage negotiation. Supervisory personnel require an even wider range of skills, including general and personnel administrative skills, management techniques, and strategies for optimum utilization of human and physical resources.

Police work is guided by an ethical code that was originally developed in 1956 by the Peace Officer's Research Association of California (PORAC) in conjunction with Dr. Douglas M. Kelley of Berkeley's School of Criminology.[156] The current version of the Law Enforcement Code of Ethics is reproduced in an "Ethics and Professionalism" box in this chapter. Ethics training has been integrated into most basic law enforcement training programs, and calls for expanded training in **police ethics** are being heard from many corners. A comprehensive resource for enhancing awareness of law enforcement ethics, called the "Ethics Toolkit," is available from the IACP and the federal office of Community Oriented Policing Services (COPS) at **Web Extra 6–7**.

police ethics
The special responsibility to adhere to moral duty and obligation that is inherent in police work.

Many professional associations support police work. One such organization, the Arlington, Virginia–based IACP, has done much to raise professional standards in policing and continually strives for improvements in law enforcement nationwide. In like manner, the Fraternal Order of Police (FOP) is one of the best-known organizations of public-service workers in the United States. The FOP is the world's largest organization of sworn law enforcement officers, with more than 318,000 members in more than 2,100 lodges.

Ethics and Professionalism
The Law Enforcement Code of Ethics

As a Law Enforcement Officer, my fundamental duty is to serve mankind; to safeguard lives and property; to protect the innocent against deception, the weak against oppression or intimidation, and the peaceful against violence or disorder; and to respect the Constitutional rights of all men to liberty, equality, and justice.

I will keep my private life unsullied as an example to all; maintain courageous calm in the face of danger, scorn, or ridicule; develop self-restraint; and be constantly mindful of the welfare of others. Honest in thought and deed in both my personal and official life, I will be exemplary in obeying the laws of the land and the regulations of my department. Whatever I see or hear of a confidential nature or that is confided to me in my official capacity will be kept secret unless revelation is necessary in the performance of my duty.

I will never act officiously or permit personal feelings, prejudices, animosities, or friendships to influence my decisions. With no compromise for crime and with relentless prosecution of criminals, I will enforce the law courteously and appropriately without fear or favor, malice or ill will, never employing unnecessary force or violence, and never accepting gratuities.

I recognize the badge of my office as a symbol of public faith, and I accept it as a public trust to be held so long as I am true to the ethics of the police service. I will constantly strive to achieve these objectives and ideals, dedicating myself before God to my chosen profession . . . law enforcement.

THINKING ABOUT ETHICS

1. ***Why does the Law Enforcement Code of Ethics ask law enforcement officers "to respect the Constitutional rights of all men to liberty, equality, and justice"? Does such respect further the goals of law enforcement? Why or why not?***
2. ***Why is it important for law enforcement officers to keep their private lives "unsullied as an example to all"? What are the potential consequences of not doing so?***

Source: International Association of Chiefs of Police. Reprinted with permission.

Accreditation is another avenue toward police professionalism. The Commission on Accreditation for Law Enforcement Agencies (CALEA) was formed in 1979. Police departments seeking accreditation through the commission must meet hundreds of standards in areas as diverse as day-to-day operations, administration, review of incidents involving the use of a weapon by officers, and evaluation and promotion of personnel. As of September 15, 2010, nearly 600 (3.4%) of the nation's 17,784 law enforcement agencies were accredited,[157] while a number of others were undergoing the accreditation process. However, many accredited agencies are among the nation's largest; as a result, 25% of full-time law enforcement officers in the United States at the state and local levels are members of CALEA-accredited programs.[158] Although accreditation makes possible the identification of high-quality police departments, it is often not valued by agency leaders because it offers few incentives. Accreditation does not guarantee a department any rewards beyond that of peer recognition. Visit CALEA online at **Web Extra 6–8**.

Education and Training

Peace Officer Standards and Training (POST) program
The official program of a state or legislative jurisdiction that sets standards for the training of law enforcement officers. All states set such standards, although not all use the term *POST*.

Basic law enforcement training requirements were begun in the 1950s by the state of New York and through a voluntary **Peace Officer Standards and Training (POST) program** in California. (Additional information on California's POST standards can be accessed via **Web Extra 6–9**.) Today, every jurisdiction mandates POST-like requirements, although they vary considerably from region to region. Modern police education generally involves training in subject areas as diverse as self-defense, human relations, firearms and weapons, communications, legal aspects of policing, patrol, criminal investigations, administration, report writing, ethics, computers and information systems, and cultural diversity. According to a 2009 Bureau of Justice Statistics report, the median number of hours of training required of new officers is 881 in state police agencies, 965 in county departments, 883 in municipal agencies, and 719 in sheriff's departments.[159]

Federal law enforcement agents receive schooling at the Federal Law Enforcement Training Center (FLETC) in Glynco, Georgia. The center provides training for about 60 federal law enforcement agencies, excluding the FBI and the DEA, which have their own training academies in Quantico, Virginia. The center also offers advanced training to state and local police organizations through the National Center for State and Local Law Enforcement Training, located on the FLETC campus. Specialized schools, such as

Northwestern University's Traffic Institute, have also been credited with raising the level of police practice from purely operational concerns to a more professional level.

In 1987, in a move to further professionalize police training, the American Society for Law Enforcement Trainers was formed at the Ohio Peace Officer Training Academy. Today, the organization is known as the American Society for Law Enforcement Training (ASLET). Based in Frederick, Maryland, ASLET works to ensure quality in peace officer training and confers the title Certified Law Enforcement Trainer (CLET) on police training professionals who meet its high standards. ASLET also works with the Police Training Network to provide an ongoing and comprehensive calendar of law enforcement training activities nationwide.

Lecture Note Describe a profession as being characterized by a specialized body of knowledge and some kind of internal control over its members. Explain how the Law Enforcement Code of Ethics and police training provide the rudimentary elements necessary for the professionalization of law enforcement. Ask students to read the Law Enforcement Code of Ethics in an "Ethics and Professionalism" box in this chapter and to comment on whether they think the code is realistic.

A more recent innovation in law enforcement training is the Police Training Officer (PTO) program, whose development was funded by the COPS office starting in 1999.[160] The PTO program was designed by the Reno (Nevada) Police Department, in conjunction with PERF, as an alternative model for police field training. In fact, it represents the first new postacademy field training program for law enforcement agencies in more than 30 years. PTO uses contemporary methods of adult education and a version of problem-based learning specifically adapted to the police environment. It incorporates community policing and problem-solving principles and, according to the COPS office, fosters "the foundation for life-long learning that prepares new officers for the complexities of policing today and in the future."[161] Learn more about PTO at **Library Extra 6–17**.

As the concern for quality policing builds, increasing emphasis is also being placed on the formal education of police officers. As early as 1931, the National Commission on Law Observance and Enforcement (the Wickersham Commission) highlighted the importance of a well-educated police force by calling for "educationally sound" officers.[162] In 1967, the President's Commission on Law Enforcement and Administration of Justice voiced the belief that "the ultimate aim of all police departments should be that all personnel with general enforcement powers have baccalaureate degrees."[163] At the time, the average educational level of police officers in the United States was 12.4 years—slightly beyond a high school degree. In 1973, the National Advisory Commission on Criminal Justice Standards and Goals made the following specific recommendation: "Every police agency should, no later than 1982, require as a condition of initial employment the completion of at least four years of education . . . at an accredited college or university."[164]

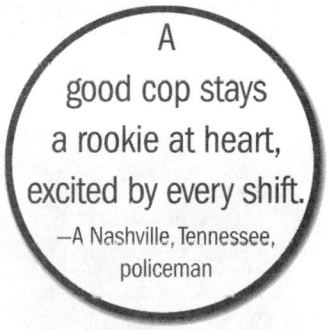

However, recommendations do not always translate into practice. One report found that one in three state agencies have a college requirement for new officers, with 12% requiring a two-year degree and 2%, a four-year degree. About one in four municipal and county police departments have a college requirement, with about one in 10 requiring a degree.[165] One in seven sheriff's offices have a college requirement, including 6% that require a minimum of a two-year degree for new hires.[166] A 2002 report on police departments in large cities found that the percentage of departments requiring new officers to have at least some college rose from 19% in 1990 to 37% in 2000, and the percentage requiring a two-year or four-year degree grew from 6% to 14% over the same period.[167] A Dallas Police Department policy requiring a minimum of 45 semester hours of successful college-level study for new recruits[168] was upheld in 1985 by the Fifth U.S. Circuit Court of Appeals in the case of *Davis v. Dallas*.[169]

Lecture Note Explain the importance of higher education to police officer training, especially in the era of community policing. Ask students how they think education might make a difference in their own approach to policing. Has it already changed their sense of the profession?

An early survey of police departments by PERF stressed the need for educated police officers, citing the following benefits that accrue to police agencies from the hiring of educated officers:[170] (1) better written reports, (2) enhanced communications with the public, (3) more effective job performance, (4) fewer citizen complaints, (5) greater initiative, (6) wiser use of discretion, (7) heightened sensitivity to racial and ethnic issues, and (8) fewer disciplinary problems. However, there are drawbacks to having more educated police forces: Educated officers are more likely to leave police work and to question orders, and they request reassignment more frequently than other officers.

Most federal agencies require college degrees for entry-level positions. Among them are the FBI, the DEA, the Bureau of Alcohol, Tobacco, Firearms and Explosives, the Secret Service, the Bureau of Customs and Border Protection, and the Bureau of Immigration and Customs Enforcement.

Recruitment and Selection

All professions need informed, dedicated, and competent personnel. When the National Advisory Commission on Criminal Justice Standards and Goals issued its 1973 report on the police, it bemoaned the fact that "many college students are unaware of the varied, interesting, and challenging assignments and career opportunities that exist within the police service."[171] Today, police organizations actively recruit new officers from two- and four-year colleges and universities, technical institutions, and professional organizations. The national commission report stressed the setting of high standards for police recruits and recommended a strong emphasis on minority recruitment, an elimination of residence requirements (which required officers to live in the area they were hired to serve) for new officers, a decentralized application and testing procedure, and various recruiting incentives.

A Bureau of Justice Statistics study published in 2006 found that local police departments use a variety of applicant-screening methods.[172] Nearly all use personal interviews, and a large majority use basic skills tests, physical agility measurements, medical exams, drug tests, psychological evaluations, and background investigations into the personal character of applicants. Among departments serving 25,000 or more residents, about eight in ten use physical agility tests and written aptitude tests, more than half check credit records, and about half use personality inventories and polygraph exams. After training, successful applicants are typically placed on probation for one year. The probationary period in police work has been called the "first true job-related test . . . in the selection procedure,"[173] providing the opportunity for supervisors to gauge the new officer's response to real-life situations.

Thematic Question In your opinion, are police departments today doing enough to attract qualified ethnic minorities? Explain. How might hiring police officers from diverse groups help achieve the aims of community policing?

Effective policing, however, may depend more on innate personal qualities than on educational attainment or credit history. One of the first people to attempt to describe the personal attributes necessary in a successful police officer, famed 1930s' police administrator August Vollmer, said that the public expects police officers to have "the wisdom of Solomon, the courage of David, the strength of Samson, the patience of Job, the leadership of Moses, the kindness of the Good Samaritan, the strategic training of Alexander, the faith of Daniel, the diplomacy of Lincoln, the tolerance of the Carpenter of Nazareth, and finally, an intimate knowledge of every branch of the natural, biological, and social sciences."[174] More practically, O. W. Wilson, the well-known police administrator of the 1940s and 1950s, once enumerated some "desirable personal qualities of patrol officers":[175] (1) initiative; (2) responsibility; (3) the ability to deal alone with emergencies; (4) the capacity to communicate effectively with people from diverse social, cultural, and ethnic backgrounds; (5) the ability to learn a variety of tasks quickly; (6) the attitude and ability necessary to adapt to technological changes; (7) the desire to help people in need; (8) an understanding of others; (9) emotional maturity; and (10) sufficient physical strength and endurance.

High-quality police recruits, an emphasis on training with an eye toward ethical aspects of police performance, and higher levels of education are beginning to raise police pay, which has traditionally been low. The acceptance of police work as a true profession should contribute to significantly higher rates of pay in coming years.

▲ Former Birmingham (Alabama) Chief of Police Annetta Nunn. Nunn's tenure as chief from 2003 to 2007 exemplifies expanded opportunities in policing for women and minorities. Nunn, an African American who holds a bachelor's degree in criminal justice from the University of Alabama, was four years old in 1963, when thousands of civil rights demonstrators in Birmingham were beaten and arrested on orders of Police Chief Eugene "Bull" Connor. How do communities benefit from police agencies that are socially and culturally diverse?
Birmingham Police Department

Ethnic and Gender Diversity in Policing

In 2003, Annetta W. Nunn took the reins of the Birmingham (Alabama) Police Department. For many, Nunn, a 44-year-old African American mother and Baptist choir singer, symbolized the changes that had taken place in American policing during the past few decades. The new chief sat in a chair once occupied by Eugene "Bull" Connor, the arch segregationist and a national symbol of the South's fight against integration who jailed thousands of civil rights demonstrators during the 1960s. A 23-year veteran of the department, Nunn headed a force of 838 men and women. She left the department in 2008 to become an advocate for a domestic-violence education program in municipal courts.

9 Identify some of the issues related to ethnic and gender diversity in policing, and suggest ways of addressing them.

A 1968 survey of police supervisors by the National Advisory Commission on Civil Disorders[176] found a marked disparity between the number of black and white officers in leadership positions. One of every 26 black police officers had been promoted to the rank of sergeant, while the ratio among whites was 1 in 12. Only one of every 114 black officers had become a

Multiculturalism and Diversity
Investigating Crime in a Multicultural Setting

In the mid-1990s, the Washington, D.C.–based National Crime Prevention Council (NCPC) published an important guide for American law enforcement officers who work with multicultural groups. The principles it contains can be applied equally to most foreign-born individuals living in the United States and are especially important to patrol officers and criminal investigators.

The NCPC guide points out that it is important for well-intentioned newcomers to this country to learn that the law enforcement system in the United States is not a national police force but a series of local, state, and federal agencies that take seriously their obligation to "serve and protect" law-abiding residents. Newcomers need to know that police officers can teach them how to protect themselves and their families from crime. Many immigrants, especially political refugees, come from countries in which the criminal justice system is based on tyranny, repression, and fear.

The NCPC suggests that law enforcement officers and other members of the criminal justice system can help ease this transition by working not only to communicate with immigrants but also to understand them and the complexities of their native cultures. The mere absence of conflict in a neighborhood does not mean that residents of different cultures have found harmony and a cooperative working relationship, says the NCPC. True multicultural integration occurs when various cultures reach a comfortable day-to-day interaction marked by respect, interest, and caring.

Communities in which immigrants and law enforcement have established close positive ties benefit considerably, according to the NCPC. Immigrants gain greater access to police and other services, such as youth programs, victims' assistance, parenting classes, medical assistance programs, business networking, and neighborhood groups. Crime decreases in communities where law enforcement officers help immigrants learn to protect themselves against crime.

For police officers working in communities in which "language is a serious barrier between cultures," the NCPC suggests the following pointers for communicating more effectively:

- Be patient when speaking with someone who does not clearly understand your language. Speak slowly and distinctly. Be willing to repeat words or phrases if necessary. Remember that shouting never helps a nonnative speaker understand better.
- Be careful with your choice of words, selecting those that are clear, straightforward, and simple to understand. Avoid colloquialisms and slang.
- Allow extra time for investigation when the people involved have not mastered English.

▲ NYPD officers responding to a call for service in New York City's Chinatown. American society is composed of a wide variety of racial and ethnic heritages, diverse religions, incongruous values, disparate traditions, and distinct languages. How does multiculturalism impact American policing?
*Ting-Li Wang/*The New York Times

- Be sure that anyone who serves as an interpreter is fully qualified and has had experience. Interpreting under pressure is a difficult task; lack of training can lead to mistakes.
- Be candid about your ability to speak or understand a language. Trying to "fake it" just leads to confusion, misunderstanding, and misspent time.
- Never assume that someone is less intelligent just because he or she doesn't speak English well.

Visit the NCPC at **Web Extra 6–10**.

Reference: Adapted from National Crime Prevention Council, *Building and Crossing Bridges: Refugees and Law Enforcement Working Together* (Washington, DC: NCPC, 1994).

lieutenant, while among whites the ratio was one in 26. At the level of captain, the disparity was even greater: One out of every 235 black officers had achieved the rank of captain, while one of every 53 whites had climbed to that rank.

Today, many departments, through dedicated recruitment efforts, have dramatically increased their complement of officers from underrepresented groups. The Metropolitan Detroit Police Department, for example, now has a force that is more than 30% black. Nationwide, racial and ethnic minorities comprised 23.6% of full-time sworn police personnel in 2003—up from 17.0% in 1990[177]—and getting closer to the percentage of racial and ethnic minorities in our nation's population, which the U.S. Census Bureau reports is approximately 32%.[178] From 1990 to 2003, the number of African American local police officers increased by 14,800 (or 37%), and the number of Hispanic officers increased by 22,300 (or 98%). Moreover, a 2006 study of 123 African American police executives in the United States found that they were generally well accepted by their peers, well integrated into their leadership roles, and well adjusted socially.[179]

Although ethnic minorities are now employed in policing in significant numbers, women are still significantly underrepresented. The 2001 Status of Women in Policing Survey, conducted

▲ Lieutenant Gail Marsh of the Redmond (Washington) Police Department. Women in uniform are a common sight throughout our nation's cities and towns. What special benefits can women bring to policing?
Therese Frare/Black Star

by the National Center for Women and Policing (NCWP), found that women fill only 12.7% of all sworn law enforcement positions nationwide.[180] On the other hand, the NCWP notes that women account for 46.5% of employed people over the age of 16 nationwide, meaning that they are "strikingly under-represented within the field of sworn law enforcement."[181] A 2010 Bureau of Justice Statistics (BJS) study of women in law enforcement found the following:[182]

- Of 62 federal law enforcement agencies responding to the study, there were about 90,000 sworn officers, of whom approximately 18,200 (20%) were women.
- Women accounted for approximately 18% of total sworn law enforcement officers in large local police departments—those with 2,000 or more personnel. Women, however, held only six percent of full-time sworn positions in small local police departments—those with between one and ten full-time sworn officers.
- Female officers comprised about 13% of total sworn officers in large sheriff's departments; but they held only four percent of sworn positions in small sheriff's offices.

It is unclear just how many women actually *want* to work in policing. Nonetheless, many police departments continue to make substantial efforts to recruit and retain women because they understand the benefits of having more women among the ranks of sworn officers. Benefits stem from the fact that female police officers tend to use less physical force than male officers and are less likely to be accused of using excessive force; female officers are better at defusing and de-escalating potentially violent confrontations with citizens; female officers often possess better communication skills than their male counterparts; and they are better able to facilitate the cooperation and trust required to implement a community policing model. Moreover, the NCWP says that "female officers often respond more effectively to incidents of violence against women—crimes that represent one of the largest categories of calls to police departments. Increasing the representation of women on the force is also likely to address another costly problem for police administrators—the pervasive problem of sex discrimination and sexual harassment—by changing the climate of modern law enforcement agencies."[183] Finally, "because women frequently have different life experiences than men, they approach policing with a different perspective, and the very presence of women in the field will often bring about changes in policies and procedures that benefit both male and female officers."[184] For additional information on how police departments can recruit and retain female officers, see **Library Extra 6–18**.

Women as Effective Police Officers

A 2007 review of the status of women in policing found that "women police officers are no longer viewed as a unique presence in law enforcement and their ability to perform the job is less likely to be measured against traditional standards, though indoctrination in law enforcement continues to stress masculinity over ability."[185] One research report on female police officers in Massachusetts found that female officers (1) are "extremely devoted to their work," (2) "see themselves as women first, and then police officers," and (3) are more satisfied when working in nonuniformed capacities.[186] The researcher identified two groups of female officers: (1) those who felt themselves to be well integrated into their departments and were confident in their jobs and (2) those who experienced strain and on-the-job isolation. The officers' children were cited as a significant influence on what their self-perceptions were and on the way in which they viewed their jobs. The demands that attend child rearing in contemporary society were found to be a major factor contributing to the resignation of female officers. The study also found that the longer female officers stayed on the job, the greater the stress and frustration they tended to experience, primarily as a consequence of the uncooperative attitudes of male officers. Some of the female officers interviewed identified networking as a potential solution to the stresses encountered by female

> Police agencies that understand and value diverse communities create structures and systems that reach outward, enjoining and empowering police officers and citizens to collaborate in problem solving on issues of crime and disorder.
>
> —Police Executive Research Forum[xv]

officers but also said that when women get together to solve problems, they are seen as "crybabies" rather than professionals. Said one of the women in the study, "We've lost a lot of good women who never should have left the job. If we had helped each other, maybe they wouldn't have left."[187] For more information on working in policing, visit **Web Extra 6-11**.

Some studies have found that female officers are often underutilized and that many departments are hesitant to assign women to patrol and to other potentially dangerous field activities.[188] As a consequence, some women in police work experience frustration and a lack of satisfaction with their jobs. An analysis of the genderization of the criminal justice workplace by Susan Ehrlich Martin and Nancy C. Jurik, for example, points out that gender inequality is part of a historical pattern of entrenched forms of gender interaction relating to the division of labor, power, and culture.[189] According to Martin and Jurik, women working in the justice system are viewed in terms of such historically developed filters, causing them to be judged and treated according to normative standards developed for men rather than for women. As a consequence, formal and informal social controls continue to disenfranchise women who wish to work in the system and make it difficult to recognize the specific contributions that they make as women.

Private Protective Services

Growth of Private Protective Services

10 Describe the nature and extent of private protective services in the United States today, and discuss what role you think they will play in the future.

Public police are employed by the government and enforce public laws. Private security personnel work for corporate employers and secure private interests. Private security has been defined as "those self-employed individuals and privately funded business entities and organizations providing security-related services to specific clientele for a fee, for the individual or entity that retains or employs them, or for themselves, in order to protect their

Freedom or Safety? You Decide.
Do Sex-Offender Websites Spur Vigilantism?

In 2006, officials in Maine decided to temporarily shut down the state's sex-offender website after two convicted sex offenders whose identifying information was listed in the online registry were shot and killed. The site provides names, addresses, ages, and offender histories for more than 2,200 nonincarcerated registered sex offenders residing in Maine.

One of the offenders who died, 57-year-old Joseph Gray, was shot five times through a window after being awakened by barking dogs at three o'clock in the morning while sleeping on his living room couch. Gray had been convicted in Massachusetts in 1992 of indecent assault and battery on a child and child rape and had been sentenced to four to six years in prison. Five hours later, William Elliott, age 24, a registered sex offender living in Corinth, Maine, was shot and killed as he answered the door to his ramshackle trailer. In 2002, Elliott had pleaded guilty to two misdemeanor counts of sexual abuse of a minor. The charges stemmed from an intimate relationship he had with a girl two weeks shy of her 16th birthday. He was 19 years old at the time of the offense.

On the night of the killings, Canadian Stephen Marshall, a 20-year-old dishwasher from Nova Scotia and the only suspect in the killings, died when he shot himself in the head with a .45-caliber handgun as police stopped and boarded a bus he was riding to Boston. Marshall had been visiting his father in Houlton, Maine, a town near the Canadian border, where the two had planned to go target shooting. Maine Department of Public Safety officials had quickly zeroed in on Marshall after they determined that he had logged on to the state's sex-offender registry and obtained information on the victims and 32 other men shortly before the killings. Investigators found a small-caliber pistol and a laptop computer in his backpack.

Charles Onley, a research associate at the Center for Sex Offender Management, a U.S. Department of Justice project, told reporters following the Maine killings that critics had previously warned that online offender registries could be used to facilitate vigilante-type killings. The only other known case of vigilantism linked to a sex-offender website occurred in August 2005, when Washington State resident Michael Mullen killed two sex offenders in Bellingham, Washington, after locating them through the city's online sex-offender registry. At the time, Don Pierce, executive director of the Washington Association of Sheriffs and Police Chiefs, said that "the value [of sex-offender registries] to the community far outweighs the risks."

YOU DECIDE

Should society's interest in knowing the identities and residential locations of released sex offenders supersede the concerns for personal safety that those offenders may have? Do you agree with Don Pierce that the value of sex-offender registries far outweighs their risks? Why or why not?

References: Lisa Wangsness and Kathleen Burge, "Police Investigate Alleged Gunman's Motives in Killings," *Boston Globe*, April 18, 2006; and Emily Bazar, "Suspected Shooter Found Sex Offenders' Homes on Website," *USA Today*, April 18, 2006.

Law enforcement can ill afford to continue its traditional policy of isolating and even ignoring the activities of private security.

—National Institute of Justice, *Crime and Protection in America*

private protective services
The independent or proprietary commercial organizations that provide protective services to employers on a contractual basis.

persons, private property, or interests from various hazards."[190] The growth in the size of private security in recent years has been phenomenal. In 2002, for example, $212.7 million was spent for security arrangements at the Olympic winter games in Salt Lake City, Utah—leading to the employment of more than 40,000 private security personnel in association with the event.[191]

A report released by the NIJ in 2001, titled *The New Structure of Policing*,[192] found that "policing is being transformed and restructured in the modern world" in ways that were unanticipated only a few decades ago. Much of the change is due to the development of **private protective services** as an important adjunct to public law enforcement activities in the United States and throughout much of the rest of the world. The NIJ report says that "the key to [understanding] the transformation is that policing, meaning the activity of making societies safe, is no longer carried out exclusively by governments" and that the distinction between private and public police has begun to blur. According to NIJ, "[G]radually, almost imperceptibly, policing has been 'multilateralized,'" meaning that "a host of nongovernmental agencies have undertaken to provide security services." As a result, the NIJ report says that "policing has entered a new era, an era characterized by a transformation in the governance of security." The report concludes:

- In most countries, certainly in the democratic world, private police outnumber public police.
- In these same countries, people spend more time in their daily lives in places where visible crime prevention and control are provided by nongovernmental groups than by governmental police agencies.
- The reconstruction of policing is occurring worldwide despite differences in wealth and economic systems.

View the NIJ report in its entirety at **Library Extra 6–19**.

According to the *Hallcrest Report II*, another widely disseminated document describing the private security industry, more people are employed in private security than in all local, state, and federal police agencies combined.[193] Nearly 2 million people are estimated to be working in private security today, whereas slightly less than half that number are engaged in public law enforcement activities.[194] According to the *Hallcrest Report II*, employment in the field of private security is anticipated to continue to expand by around 4% per year, while public police agencies are expected to grow by only 2.8% per year for the foreseeable future. Still faster growth is predicted in private security industry revenues, which are expected to increase about 7% per year, a growth rate almost three times greater than that projected for the gross national product (GNP). Table 6–4 lists the ten largest private security agencies in business today and some of the services they offer.

TABLE 6–4
Private Security Agencies

Largest Private Security Agencies in the United States		
Advance Security, Inc.	Globe Security	Security Bureau, Inc.
Allied Security, Inc.	Guardsmark, Inc.	Wackenhut Corp.
American Protective Services	Pinkerton's, Inc.	Wells Fargo Guard Services
Burns International Security Services		
Private Security Services		
Airline security	Computer/information security	Nuclear facility security
Automated teller machine (ATM) services	Executive protection	Railroad detectives
Bank guards	Hospital security	School security
Company guards	Loss prevention	Store/mall security

Source: Adapted from William C. Cunningham, John J. Strauchs, and Clifford W. Van Meter, *The Hallcrest Report II: Private Security Trends, 1970–2000* (McLean, VA: Hallcrest Systems, 1990). Reprinted with permission.

Private agencies provide tailored policing funded by the guarded organization rather than through the expenditure of public monies. Experts estimate that the money spent on private security in this country exceeds the combined budgets of all law enforcement agencies—local, state, and federal.[195] Contributing to this vast expenditure is the federal government, which is itself a major employer of private security personnel, contracting for services that range from guards to highly specialized electronic snooping and computerized countermeasures at military installations and embassies throughout the world.

Major reasons for the quick growth of the American proprietary security sector include (1) an increase in crimes in the workplace; (2) an increase in fear (real or perceived) of crime and terrorism; (3) the fiscal crises of the states, which have limited public protection; and (4) an increased public and business awareness and use of more cost-effective private security products and services.[196]

▲ A private security officer conferring with a sworn public law enforcement officer. How can cooperation among private security companies and public law enforcement agencies help solve and prevent crimes?
Michael Newman/PhotoEdit Inc.

A PowerPoint presentation that supports this chapter is available from your Prentice Hall representative.

Integration of Public and Private Security

As the private security field grows, its relationship to public law enforcement continues to evolve. Some people feel that "today, a distinction between public and private policing is increasingly meaningless."[197] As a result, the focus has largely shifted from an analysis of competition between the sectors to the recognition that each form of policing can help the other. One government-sponsored report recommends that the resources of proprietary and contract security should be brought to bear in cooperative, community-based crime-prevention and security-awareness programs. Doing so, says the report, would maximize the cooperative crime-fighting potential of existing private and public security resources.[198]

Summary

POLICING: ISSUES AND CHALLENGES

- The police personality is created through informal pressures on officers by a powerful police subculture that communicates values that support law enforcement interests. This chapter described the police personality as (among other things) authoritarian, conservative, honorable, loyal, cynical, dogmatic, hostile, prejudiced, secret, and suspicious.
- Various types of police corruption were described in this chapter. One type, "grass eating," includes officers who accept small bribes and free services by those wishing to avoid legal problems. "Meat eating" includes much more serious forms of corruption, such as officers who actively seek illegal moneymaking opportunities through the exercise of their law enforcement duties. Ethics training was mentioned as part of a reframing strategy that emphasizes integrity in an effort to target police corruption. Also discussed was an NIJ report that focused on enhancing policing integrity. The report noted that a police department's "culture of integrity" might be more important "in shaping the ethics of police officers than hiring the 'right' people."
- The dangers of police work are many and varied. They consist of violent victimization, disease, exposure to biological or chemical toxins, stressful encounters with suspects and victims, and on-the-job fatigue. Stress-management programs, combined with department policies designed to reduce exposure to dangerous situations and agency practices that support officers' needs, can help combat the dangers and difficulties that police officers face in their day-to-day work.
- Policing in America was forever changed by the events of September 11, 2001. Local law enforcement agencies, many of which previously saw community protection and peacekeeping as their primary roles, are being called upon to protect against potential terrorist threats with international roots. The contemporary emphasis on terrorism prevention, alongside the

need for a rapid response to threats of terrorism, has led to what some see as a new era of policing to secure the homeland. Homeland security policing builds upon the established framework of community policing for the purpose of gathering intelligence to prevent terrorism. Consequently, the notion of intelligence-led policing has become significant and provides a glimpse at one of the features that may characterize American policing in the future.

- Civil liability issues are very important in policing. They arise because officers and their agencies sometimes inappropriately use power to curtail the civil and due process rights of criminal suspects. Both police departments and individual police officers can be targeted by civil lawsuits. Federal suits based on claims that officers acted with disregard for an individual's right to due process are called *1983 lawsuits* because they are based on Section 1983 of Title 42 of the U.S. Code. Another type of civil suit that can be brought specifically against federal agents is a *Bivens* action. Although the doctrine of sovereign immunity barred legal action against state and local governments in the past, recent court cases and legislative activity have restricted the opportunity for law enforcement agencies and their officers to exercise claims of immunity.
- Racial profiling, or racially biased policing, is any police action initiated on the basis of the race, ethnicity, or national origin of a suspect rather than on the behavior of that individual or on information that identifies the individual as being or having been engaged in criminal activity. Racial profiling is a bigoted practice unworthy of the law enforcement professional. It has been widely condemned as being contrary to basic ethical principles, and it weakens the public's confidence in the police, thereby decreasing police-citizen trust and cooperation. This chapter pointed out, however, that racial or ethnic indicators associated with particular suspects or suspect groups may have a place in legitimate law enforcement strategies if they accurately relate to suspects who are being sought for criminal law violations.
- Law enforcement officers are authorized to use the amount of force that is reasonable and necessary in a particular situation. Many officers have encounters where the use of force is appropriate. Nonetheless, studies show that the police use force in fewer than 20% of adult custodial arrests. Even in instances where force is used, police officers primarily use weaponless tactics. Excessive force is the application of an amount or frequency of force greater than that required to compel compliance from a willing or unwilling subject.
- Police professionalism requires that today's law enforcement officers adhere to ethical codes and standards established by the profession. Police professionalism places important limits on the discretionary activities of individual enforcement personnel and helps officers and the departments they work for gain the respect and regard of the public they police.
- This chapter points out that ethnic minorities are now employed in policing in numbers that approach their representation in the general population. Women, however, are still significantly underrepresented. Questions can be raised about the degree of minority participation in the command structure of law enforcement agencies, about the desire of significant numbers of women to work in policing, and about the respect accorded to women and members of other underrepresented groups in law enforcement by their fellow officers.
- Private policing, represented by the recent tremendous growth of for-hire security agencies, adds another important dimension to American policing. While public police are employed by the government and enforce public laws, private security personnel work for corporate or private employers and secure private interests. Private security personnel outnumber public law enforcement officers in the United States by nearly three to one, and private agencies provide tailored protective services funded by the guarded organization rather than by taxpayers. Recognizing the important services that private security personnel provide, many municipal police departments have begun concerted efforts to involve security organizations in their crime-detection and crime-prevention efforts.

QUESTIONS FOR REVIEW

1. What is the police working personality? What are its central features? How does it develop? How does it relate to police subculture?
2. What are the different types of police corruption? What themes run through the findings of the Knapp Commission and the Wickersham Commission? What innovative steps might police departments take to reduce or eliminate corruption among their officers?
3. What are the dangers of police work? What can be done to reduce those dangers?

4. How has the threat of terrorist attack affected American policing today? Are American police agencies prepared to prevent and respond to terrorism? Explain.
5. What are some of the civil liability issues associated with policing? How can civil liability be reduced?
6. What is racial profiling? Why has it become a significant issue in policing today?
7. In what kinds of situations are police officers most likely to use force? When has too much force been used?
8. Is police work a profession? Explain. What are the advantages of viewing policing as a profession? How can police professionalism be enhanced?
9. What ethnic and gender differences characterize policing today? What is the social significance of this diversity?
10. What are the nature and extent of private protective services in the United States today? What role do you think private protective services will play in the future? How can the quality of these services be ensured?

CHAPTER 7

The Courts

Learning Objectives

After reading this chapter, you should be able to:

1. Describe the development of the American court system. **196**
2. Outline the structure of a typical state court system, and describe the jurisdiction of various types of state and local courts. **197**
3. Identify the three levels of the federal judiciary, and enumerate some of the differences between the state and federal court systems. **200**
4. Explain the typical steps taken during pretrial activities, and list the key factors considered by judicial officers in assessing the risks associated with pretrial release. **205**

"The criminal court is the central, crucial institution in the criminal justice system. It is the part of the system that is the most venerable, the most formally organized, and the most elaborately circumscribed by law and tradition. It is the institution around which the rest of the system has developed."

—The President's Commission on Law Enforcement and Administration of Justice[1]

Introduction

On May 4, 2008, a nail-filled pipe bomb exploded at the entrance to the Edward J. Schwartz Federal Courthouse in San Diego, California. The explosion shattered the building's glass door, damaged the lobby, and punched a hole in a window across the street. Although no one was injured, the FBI's Joint Terrorism Task Force in San Diego conducted a vigorous investigation. Three months later, two women and a man were charged with conspiring to bomb the federal courthouse and with another bombing that had taken place 10 days earlier. A 17-count indictment filed against the trio alleges the use of a weapon of mass destruction and shows that at least one of the alleged conspirators had filed over 100 lawsuits in the courthouse that was attacked. He had been sanctioned by a judge for frivolous filings, with the judge noting that "the lawsuits had been a lucrative cottage industry."[2]

▲ FBI and ATF agents investigating damage to the Edward J. Schwartz federal courthouse in San Diego, California, following a bombing that targeted the facility in 2008. What role do the courts play in the American criminal justice system?
Federal Bureau of Investigation/AP Wide World Photos

Incidents like the San Diego bombing highlight the critical role that our nation's courts and the personnel who staff them play in the American system of justice. Without courts to decide guilt or innocence and to impose sentence on those convicted of crimes, the activities of law enforcement officials would become meaningless.

There are many different kinds of courts in the United States, but courts at all levels dispense justice daily and work to ensure that all official actors in the justice system carry out their duties in recognition of the rule of law. At many points in this textbook and in three specific chapters (Chapters 5, 10, and 11), we take a close look at court precedents that have defined the legality of enforcement efforts and correctional action. In Chapter 3, we explored the law-making function of courts. To provide a picture of how courts work, this chapter will describe the American court system at both the state and federal levels. Then in Chapter 8, we will look at the roles of courtroom actors—from attorneys to victims and from jurors to judges—and we will examine each of the steps in a criminal trial.

History and Structure of the American Court System

Two types of courts function within the American criminal justice system: state courts and federal courts. Figure 7–1 outlines the structure of today's **federal court system**, and Figure 7–2 diagrams a typical **state court system**. This dual-court system is the result of

federal court system
The three-tiered structure of federal courts, comprising U.S. district courts, U.S. courts of appeals, and the U.S. Supreme Court.

state court system
A state judicial structure. Most states generally have at least three court levels: trial courts, appellate courts, and a state supreme court.

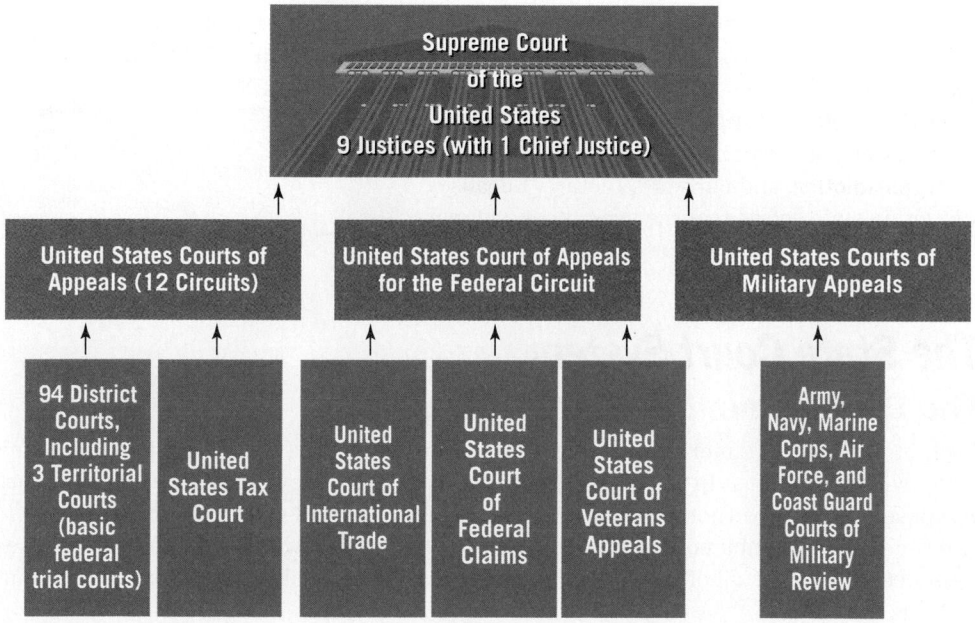

FIGURE 7–1
The Structure of the Federal Courts

FIGURE 7–2
A Typical State Court System

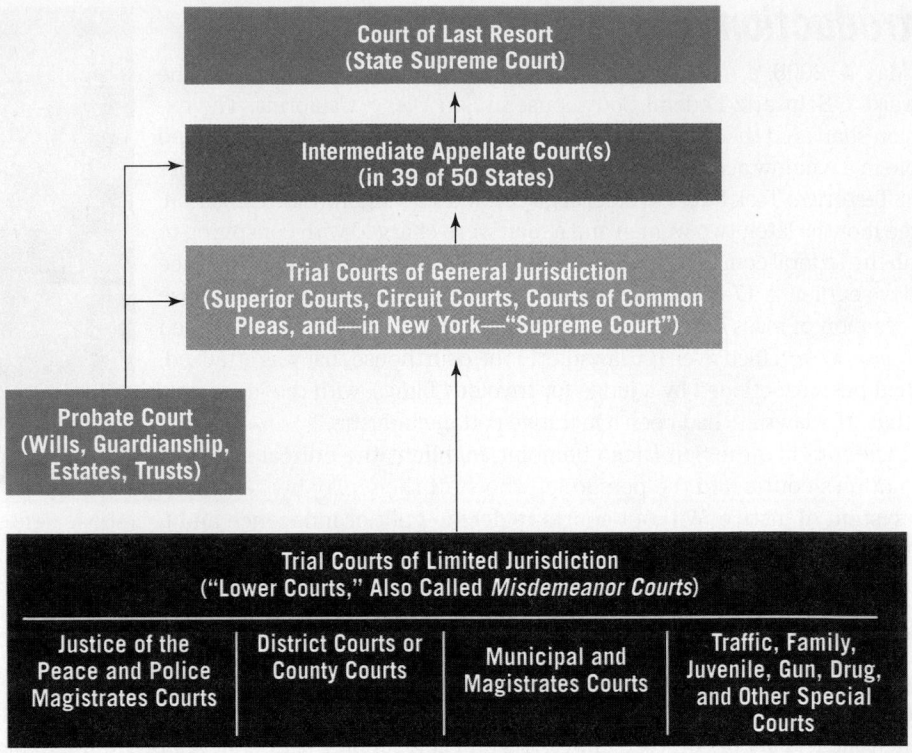

Lecture Note Outline state court development, beginning with the General Court of the Massachusetts Bay Colony and continuing to the present day. Use Figure 7–2 to demonstrate the generic structure of state courts today.

general agreement among the nation's founders about the need for individual states to retain significant legislative authority and judicial autonomy separate from federal control. Under this concept, the United States developed as a relatively loose federation of semi-independent provinces. New states joining the union were assured of limited federal intervention into local affairs. State legislatures were free to create laws, and state court systems were needed to hear cases alleging violations of those laws.

In the last 200 years, states' rights have gradually waned relative to the power of the federal government, but the dual-court system still exists. Even today, state courts do not hear cases involving alleged violations of federal law, nor do federal courts get involved in deciding issues of state law unless there is a conflict between local or state statutes and federal constitutional guarantees. When such conflicts arise, claimed violations of federal due process guarantees—especially those found in the Bill of Rights—can provide the basis for appeals made to federal courts by offenders convicted in state court systems. Learn more about the dual-court system in America at **Library Extra 7–1**.

This chapter describes both state and federal court systems in terms of their historical development, **jurisdiction**, and current structure. Because it is within state courts that the majority of criminal cases originate, we turn our attention first to them.

1 Describe the development of the American court system.

jurisdiction
The territory, subject matter, or people over which a court or other justice agency may exercise lawful authority, as determined by statute or constitution.

Lecture Note Explain original jurisdiction as the lawful authority of a court to hear cases that arise within a specified geographic area or that involve particular kinds of statutory violations.

Lecture Note Explain appellate jurisdiction as the lawful authority of a court to review a decision made by a lower court.

The State Court System

The Development of State Courts

Each of the original American colonies had its own court system for resolving disputes, both civil and criminal. In 1629, the Massachusetts Bay Colony created a General Court, composed of the governor, his deputy, 18 assistants, and 118 elected officials. The General Court was a combined legislature and court that made laws, held trials, and imposed sentences.[3] By 1776, all of the American colonies had established fully functioning court systems.

Following the American Revolution, state court systems were anything but uniform. Initially, most states made no distinction between **original jurisdiction** (the lawful authority of a court to hear cases that arise within a specified geographic area or that involve particular kinds of law violations) and **appellate jurisdiction** (the lawful authority of a court to review a decision made by a lower court). Many, in fact, had no provisions for appeal; Delaware, for example, did not allow appeals in criminal cases until 1897. States that did permit appeals often lacked any established appellate courts and sometimes used state legislatures for that purpose.

original jurisdiction
The lawful authority of a court to hear or to act on a case from its beginning and to pass judgment on the law and the facts. The authority may be over a specific geographic area or over particular types of cases.

appellate jurisdiction
The lawful authority of a court to review a decision made by a lower court.

Lecture Note Explain that most state judicial structures encompass courts at three levels: trial, appellate, and supreme. Mention that a state supreme court is also called a *court of last resort.*

By the late nineteenth century, a dramatic increase in population, growing urbanization, the settlement of the West, and other far-reaching changes in the American way of life led to a tremendous increase in civil litigation and criminal arrests. Legislatures tried to keep pace with the rising tide of cases. They created a multiplicity of courts at the trial, appellate, and supreme court levels, calling them by a diversity of names and assigning them functions that sometimes bore little resemblance to those of similarly named courts in neighboring states. City courts, which were limited in their jurisdiction by community boundaries, arose to handle the special problems of urban life, such as disorderly conduct, property disputes, and enforcement of restrictive and regulatory ordinances. Other tribunals, such as juvenile courts, developed to handle special kinds of problems or special clients. Some, like magistrate's or small-claims courts, handled only minor law violations and petty disputes; still others, like traffic courts, were very narrow in focus. The result was a patchwork quilt of hearing bodies, some only vaguely resembling modern notions of a trial court.

State court systems developed by following one of several models. One was the New York State Field Code of 1848, which was eventually copied by most other states. The Field Code clarified jurisdictional claims and specified matters of court procedure, but it was later amended so extensively that its usefulness as a model dissolved. Another court system model was provided by the federal Judiciary Act of 1789 and later by the federal Reorganization Act of 1801. States that followed the federal model developed a three-tiered structure of (1) trial courts of limited jurisdiction, (2) trial courts of general jurisdiction, and (3) appellate courts.

2 Outline the structure of a typical state court system, and describe the jurisdiction of various types of state and local courts.

State Court Systems Today

The three-tiered federal model was far from perfect, however. Within the structure it provided, many local and specialized courts proliferated. Traffic courts, magistrate's courts, municipal courts, recorder's courts, probate courts, and courts held by justices of the peace were but a few that functioned at the lower levels. A movement toward simplification of state court structures, led primarily by the American Bar Association and the American Judicature Society, began in the early twentieth century. Proponents of state court reform sought to unify redundant courts that held overlapping jurisdictions. Most reformers suggested a uniform model for states everywhere that would build on (1) a centralized court structure composed of a clear hierarchy of trial and appellate courts, (2) the consolidation of numerous lower-level courts with overlapping jurisdictions, and (3) a centralized state court authority that would be responsible for budgeting, financing, and managing all courts within a state.

▲ Junior high school children posing in the pillory in Williamsburg, Virginia. Just as criminal punishments have changed throughout the centuries, so too have criminal courts, which today provide a civilized forum for exploring conflicting claims about guilt and innocence. How might our courts continue to evolve?
Jeff Greenberg/PhotoEdit Inc.

The court reform movement continues today. Although reformers have made substantial progress in many states, there are still many differences between and among state court systems. Reform states, which early on embraced the reform movement, are now characterized by streamlined judicial systems consisting of precisely conceived trial courts of limited and general jurisdiction, supplemented by one or two appellate court levels. Nonreform, or traditional, states retain judicial systems that are a conglomeration of multilevel and sometimes redundant courts with poorly defined jurisdictions. Even in nonreform states, however, most criminal courts can be classified within the three-tiered structure of two trial court echelons and an appellate tier.

▲ A criminal trial in progress. Why are courts sometimes called "the fulcrum of the criminal justice system"?
Ron Chapple/Taxi/Getty Images, Inc.–Taxi

State Trial Courts

Trial courts are where criminal cases begin. The trial court conducts arraignments, sets bail, takes pleas, and conducts trials. (We will discuss these separate functions in more depth later in this chapter and in the next.) If the defendant is found guilty (or pleads guilty), the trial court imposes sentence. Trial courts of limited (or special) jurisdiction are also called *lower courts*. Lower courts are authorized to hear only less serious criminal cases, usually involving misdemeanors, or to hear special types of cases such as traffic violations, family disputes, and small claims. Courts of limited jurisdiction, which are depicted in TV shows like *Judge Judy* and *Joe Brown*, rarely hold jury trials, depending instead on the hearing judge to make determinations of both fact and law. At the lower-court level, a detailed record of the proceedings is not maintained, and case files only include information on the charge, the plea, the finding of the court, and the sentence. All but six of the states make use of trial courts of limited jurisdiction.[4] These lower courts are much less formal than courts of general jurisdiction.

Trial courts of general jurisdiction—variously called *high courts*, *circuit courts*, or *superior courts*—are authorized to hear any criminal case. In many states, they also provide the first appellate level for courts of limited jurisdiction. In most cases, superior courts offer defendants whose cases originated in lower courts the chance for a new trial instead of a review of the record of the earlier hearing. When a new trial is held, it is referred to as a **trial *de novo***.

trial *de novo*
Literally, "new trial." The term is applied to cases that are retried on appeal, as opposed to those that are simply reviewed on the record.

Trial courts of general jurisdiction operate within a fact-finding framework called the *adversarial process.* That process pits the interests of the state, represented by prosecutors, against the professional skills and abilities of defense attorneys. The adversarial process is not a free-for-all; rather, it is constrained by procedural rules specified in law and sustained through tradition. Take a virtual tour of California trial courts at **Web Extra 7–1.**

State Appellate Courts

Most states today have an appellate division, consisting of an intermediate appellate court (often called the *court of appeals*) and a high-level appellate court (generally termed the *state supreme court*). High-level appellate courts are referred to as **courts of last resort**, indicating that no other appellate route remains to a defendant within the state court system once the high court rules on a case. All states have supreme courts, although only 39 have intermediate appellate courts.[5]

court of last resort
The court authorized by law to hear the final appeal on a matter.

An **appeal** by a convicted defendant asks that a higher court review the actions of a lower court. Once they accept an appeal, courts within the appellate division do not conduct a new trial; instead, they review the case on the record. In other words, appellate courts examine the written transcript of lower-court hearings to ensure that those proceedings were carried out in a fair manner and in accordance with proper procedure and state law. They may also allow attorneys for both sides to make brief oral arguments and will generally consider other briefs or information filed by the appellant (the party initiating the appeal) or the appellee (the side opposed to the appeal). State statutes generally require that sentences of life imprisonment or death be automatically reviewed by the state supreme court.

appeal
The request that a court with appellate jurisdiction review the judgment, decision, or order of a lower court and set it aside (reverse it) or modify it.

Lecture Note Explain that the function of appellate courts is to review decisions made by lower courts within their jurisdiction. Tell the class that defendants convicted in a lower court generally have a right to appeal and that most convictions are confirmed upon appeal.

Most convictions are affirmed on appeal. Occasionally, however, an appellate court will determine that the trial court erred in allowing certain kinds of evidence to be heard, that it failed to interpret properly the significance of a relevant statute, or that some other impropriety occurred. When that happens, the verdict of the trial court will be reversed, and the case may be sent back for a new trial, or *remanded.* When a conviction is overturned by an appellate court because of constitutional issues or when a statute is determined to be invalid, the state usually has recourse to the state supreme court; when an issue of federal law is involved, as when a state court has ruled a federal law unconstitutional, it goes to the U.S. Supreme Court.

Defendants who are not satisfied with the resolution of their case within the state court system may attempt an appeal to the U.S. Supreme Court. For such an appeal to have any chance of being heard, it must be based on claimed violations of the defendant's rights, as guaranteed under federal law or the U.S. Constitution. Under certain circumstances, federal district courts may also provide a path of relief for state defendants who can show that their federal constitutional rights were violated. However, in the 1992 case of *Keeney* v. *Tamayo-Reyes*,[6] the U.S. Supreme Court ruled that a "respondent is entitled to a federal evidentiary hearing [only] if he can show cause for his failure to develop the facts in the state-court proceedings and actual prejudice resulting from that failure, or if he can show that a fundamental miscarriage of justice would result from failure to hold such a hearing." Justice Byron White, writing for the Court, said, "It is hardly a good use of scarce judicial resources to duplicate fact-finding in federal court merely because a petitioner has negligently failed to take advantage of opportunities in state court proceedings."

Likewise, in *Herrera* v. *Collins* (1993),[7] the Court ruled that new evidence of innocence is no reason for a federal court to order a new state trial if constitutional grounds are lacking. The *Keeney* and *Herrera* decisions have severely limited access by state defendants to federal courts. See **Library Extra 7–2** for additional information on challenging state court criminal convictions within the federal court system.

State Court Administration

To function efficiently, courts require uninterrupted funding, adequate staffing, trained support personnel, well-managed case flow, and coordination between levels and among jurisdictions. To oversee these and other aspects of judicial management, every state today has its own mechanism for court administration. Most make use of **state court administrators** who manage these operational functions.

state court administrator
A coordinator who assists with case-flow management, operating funds budgeting, and court docket administration.

State court administrators can receive assistance from the National Center for State Courts (NCSC) in Williamsburg, Virginia. The NCSC, founded in 1971 at the behest of Chief Justice Warren E. Burger, is an independent, nonprofit organization dedicated to the improvement of the American court system. You can visit the NCSC at **Web Extra 7–2.**

At the federal level, the court system is administered by the Administrative Office of the United States Courts (AOUSC), located in Washington, D.C. The AOUSC, created by Congress in 1939, prepares the budget and legislative agenda for federal courts. It also performs audits of court accounts, manages funds for the operation of federal courts, compiles and publishes statistics on the volume and type of business conducted by the courts, and recommends plans and strategies to efficiently manage court business. You can visit the AOUSC at **Web Extra 7–3**.

Dispute-Resolution Centers and Community Courts

Often, it is possible to resolve minor disputes (in which minor criminal offenses might otherwise be charged) without a formal court hearing. Some communities have **dispute-resolution centers** that hear victims' claims of minor wrongs they have suffered, such as being subject to the passing of bad checks, trespassing, shoplifting, or petty theft. Such centers function today in more than 200 locations throughout the country.[8] Frequently staffed by volunteer mediators, such programs work to resolve disagreements without assigning blame. Dispute-resolution programs began in the early 1970s, with the earliest being the Community Assistance Project in Chester, Pennsylvania; the Columbus, Ohio, Night Prosecutor Program; and the Arbitration as an Alternative Program in Rochester, New York. Following the lead of these programs, the U.S. Department of Justice helped promote the development of three experimental Neighborhood Justice Centers in Los Angeles, Kansas City, and Atlanta. Each center accepted both minor civil and criminal cases.

dispute-resolution center
An informal hearing place designed to mediate interpersonal disputes without resorting to the more formal arrangements of a criminal trial court.

Lecture Note Describe the relatively recent evolution of dispute-resolution centers as informal mechanisms for the mediation of interpersonal conflicts. Use the example of a dispute over a parking space on a crowded residential street leading to a minor act of vandalism, such as a broken car antenna or a punctured tire, to illustrate the type of disagreement that might benefit more from mediation than from formal intervention by a court of law.

Mediation centers are often closely integrated with the formal criminal justice process and may substantially reduce the caseload of lower-level courts. Some centers are, in fact, run by the courts and work only with court-ordered referrals; others are semiautonomous but may be dependent on courts for endorsement of their decisions; and still others function with complete autonomy. Rarely, however, do dispute-resolution programs entirely supplant the formal criminal justice mechanism, and defendants who appear before a

▲ Graduates of the Oakland County (Michigan) Community Dispute Resolution training program. Staffed largely by volunteers, dispute-resolution programs facilitate cooperative solutions to relatively low-level disputes in which minor criminal offenses might otherwise be charged. How do dispute-resolution programs and centers help relieve some of the pressures facing our criminal courts?
Photo courtesy of Oakland Mediation Center, Bloomfield Hills, Michigan

community court
A low-level court that focuses on quality-of-life crimes that erode a neighborhood's morale, that emphasizes problem solving rather than punishment, and that builds on restorative principles such as community service and restitution.

community mediator may later be charged with a crime. Community mediation programs have become a central feature of today's restorative-justice movement (discussed in more detail in Chapter 9).

Recently, the community justice movement has led to the creation of innovative low-level courts in certain parts of the country. Unlike dispute-resolution centers, **community courts** are always official components of the formal justice system and can hand down sentences, including fines and jail time, without further judicial review. Community courts typically begin as grassroots movements undertaken by community residents and local organizations seeking to build confidence in the way offenders are handled for less serious offenses. Community courts generally sentence convicted offenders to work within the community, "where neighbors can see what they are doing."[9] Like dispute-resolution centers, community courts, which are sometimes called *problem-solving courts*, focus on quality-of-life crimes that erode a neighborhood's morale, emphasize problem solving rather than punishment, and build on restorative principles like community service and restitution.

Both mediation centers and community courts have been criticized because they typically work only with minor offenders, thereby denying the opportunity for mediation to victims and offenders in more serious cases. They have also come under criticism because defendants may see them as just another form of criminal sanction rather than as a true alternative to processing by the criminal justice system.[10] Dispute-resolution centers, in particular, have been criticized for doing little more than providing a forum for shouting matches between the parties involved. Learn more about dispute-resolution centers and community courts at **Library Extra 7–3** and **Web Extras 7–4** and **7–5.**

> The judicial Power of the United States shall be vested in one supreme Court, and in such inferior Courts as the Congress may from time to time ordain and establish.
>
> —Article III of the U.S. Constitution

The Federal Court System

Whereas state courts evolved from early colonial arrangements, federal courts were created by the U.S. Constitution. Article III, Section 1, of the Constitution provides for the establishment of "one supreme Court, and . . . such inferior Courts as the Congress may from time to time ordain and establish." Article III, Section 2, specifies that such courts are to have jurisdiction over cases arising under the Constitution, federal laws, and treaties. Federal courts are also to settle disputes between states and to have jurisdiction in cases where one of the parties is a state.

Lecture Note Discuss the rise of federal courts by referring to Article III, Section I, of the U.S. Constitution, which outlines the specific structure of federal courts.

Today's federal court system represents the culmination of a series of congressional mandates that have expanded the federal judicial infrastructure so that it can continue to carry out the duties envisioned by the Constitution. Notable federal statutes that have contributed to the present structure of the federal court system include the Judiciary Act of 1789, the Judiciary Act of 1925, and the Magistrate's Act of 1968.

3 Identify the three levels of the federal judiciary, and enumerate some of the differences between the state and federal court systems.

As a result of constitutional mandates, congressional action, and other historical developments, today's federal judiciary consists of three levels: (1) U.S. district courts, (2) U.S. courts of appeal, and (3) the U.S. Supreme Court. Each is described in turn in the following sections.

U.S. District Courts

The U.S. district courts are the trial courts of the federal court system.[11] Within limits set by Congress and the Constitution, the district courts have jurisdiction to hear nearly all categories of federal cases, including both civil and criminal matters. There are

94 federal judicial districts, including at least one district in each state (some states, like New York and California, have as many as four), the District of Columbia, and Puerto Rico. Each district includes a U.S. bankruptcy court as a unit of the district court. Three territories of the United States—the Virgin Islands, Guam, and the Northern Mariana Islands—have district courts that hear federal cases, including bankruptcy cases. There are two special trial courts that have nationwide jurisdiction over certain types of cases. The Court of International Trade addresses cases involving international trade and customs issues. The U.S. Court of Federal Claims has jurisdiction over most claims for money damages against the United States, disputes over federal contracts, unlawful "takings" of private property by the federal government, and a variety of other claims against the United States.

Federal district courts have original jurisdiction over all cases involving alleged violations of federal statutes. A district may itself be divided into divisions and may have several places where the court hears cases. District courts were first authorized by Congress through the Judiciary Act of 1789, which allocated one federal court to each state. Because of population increases over the years, new courts have been added in a number of states.

Nearly 650 district court judges staff federal district courts. Because some courts are much busier than others, the number of district court judges varies from a low of two in some jurisdictions to a high of 27 in others. District court judges are appointed by the president and confirmed by the Senate, and they serve for life. An additional 369 full-time and 110 part-time magistrate judges (referred to as *U.S. magistrates* before 1990) serve the district court system and assist the federal judges. Magistrate judges have the power to conduct arraignments and may set bail, issue warrants, and try minor offenders.

U.S. district courts handle tens of thousands of cases per year. During 2008, for example, 70,898 criminal cases[12] and 267,257 civil cases[13] were filed in U.S. district courts. Drug prosecutions, especially in courts located close to the U.S.–Mexico border, have led to considerable growth in the number of cases filed. Federal drug prosecutions in states abutting the Mexican border—California, Arizona, New Mexico, and Texas—more than doubled (from 2,864 to 6,116) between 1994 and 2000, and immigration prosecutions increased more than sevenfold (from 1,056 to 7,613).[14] During the last 20 years, the number of cases handled by the entire federal district court system has grown exponentially. The hiring of new judges and the creation of new courtroom facilities have not kept pace with the increase in caseload, and questions persist as to the quality of justice that overworked judges can deliver.

Lecture Note Refer to Figure 7–3 to describe the federal judicial circuits. Allude to the Judiciary Act of 1789, which created the U.S. Supreme Court and the federal court system.

One of the most pressing issues facing district court judges is the fact that their pay, which at $174,000 in mid-2010[15] placed them in the top 1% of income-earning Americans, is small compared to what most could earn in private practice. Since 1993, the salaries of federal judges have remained relatively stagnant,[16] leading many judges to leave the bench.[17] In 2006, Chief Justice John Roberts called Congress's failure to raise judges' pay "a direct threat to judicial independence."[18] Because of low pay, said Roberts, "judges effectively serve for a term dictated by their financial position rather than for life." Learn more about the federal courts at **Library Extra 7–4.**

U.S. Courts of Appeal

The 94 judicial districts are organized into 12 regional circuits, each of which has a U.S. court of appeals.[19] A court of appeals hears appeals from the district courts located within its circuit, as well as appeals from decisions of federal administrative agencies.

The U.S. Court of Appeals for the Federal Circuit and the 12 regional courts of appeal are often referred to as *circuit courts.* Early in the nation's history, the judges of the first courts of appeal visited each of the courts in one region in a particular sequence, traveling by horseback and riding the "circuit." Today, the regional courts of appeal review matters from the district courts of their geographic regions, from the U.S. Tax Court, and from certain federal administrative agencies. A disappointed party in a district court often has the opportunity to have the case reviewed in the court of appeals for the circuit. Each of the First through Eleventh Circuits includes three or more states, as illustrated in Figure 7–3.

FIGURE 7–3
Geographic Boundaries of the U.S. Courts of Appeal and U.S. District Courts

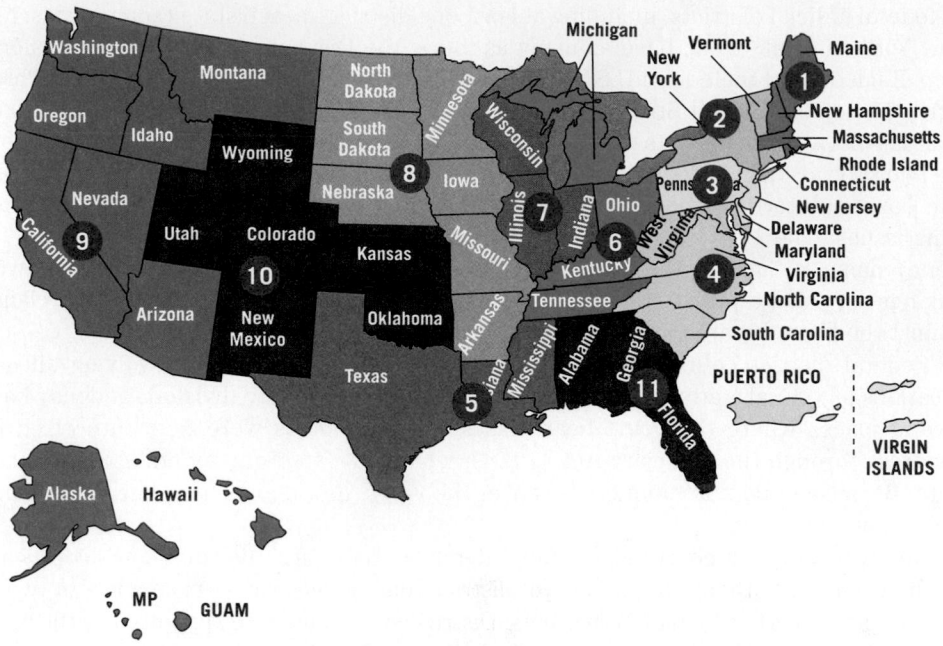

Lecture Note Tell the class that there are 94 federal judicial districts. Explain that federal district courts have original jurisdiction over all cases involving alleged violations of federal statutes.

Lecture Note Highlight the case of *Marbury* v. *Madison* (1803) as significant because it was through this case that the U.S. Supreme Court first asserted its power and laid claim to its continuing role as the ultimate arbitrator of constitutional issues. Have students view http://tinyurl.com/29txrzf for additional insight into this famous case.

Each court of appeals consists of six or more judges, depending on the caseload of the court. Circuit court judges are appointed for life by the president (with the advice and consent of the Senate). The judge who has served on the court the longest and who is under 65 years of age is designated as the chief judge. The chief judge performs administrative duties in addition to hearing cases and serves for a maximum term of seven years. There are 167 judges on the 12 regional courts of appeal.

The U.S. Court of Appeals for the District of Columbia, which is often called the Twelfth Circuit, hears cases arising in the District of Columbia and has appellate jurisdiction assigned by Congress in legislation concerning many departments of the federal government. The U.S. Court of Appeals for the Federal Circuit (in effect, the Thirteenth Circuit) was created in 1982 by the merging of the U.S. Court of Claims and the U.S. Court of Customs and Patent Appeals. The court hears appeals in cases from the U.S. Court of Federal Claims, the U.S. Court of International Trade, the U.S. Court of Veterans Appeals, the International Trade Commission, the Board of Contract Appeals, the Patent and Trademark Office, and the Merit Systems Protection Board. The court also hears appeals from certain decisions involving the secretaries of the Department of Agriculture and the Department of Commerce and cases from district courts involving patents and minor claims against the federal government.

Oyez, oyez, oyez! All persons having business before the honorable, the Supreme Court of the United States, are admonished to draw near and give their attention, for the court is now sitting. God save the United States and this honorable Court.

—Marshal's cry at the opening of public sessions of the U.S. Supreme Court

Almost all appeals from federal district courts go to the court of appeals serving the circuit in which the case was first heard. Federal appellate courts have appellate jurisdiction over the decisions of district courts within their circuits. Criminal appeals from federal district courts are usually heard by panels of three judges sitting on a court of appeals rather than by all the judges of each circuit. A defendant's request for appeal, when granted, has been interpreted to mean the opportunity for one appeal; hence the U.S. Supreme Court need not necessarily hear the appeals of defendants who are dissatisfied with the decision of a federal appeals court.

Federal appellate courts operate under the Federal Rules of Appellate Procedure, although each has also created its own separate Local Rules. Local Rules may mean that one circuit, such as the Second, will depend heavily on oral arguments, while others may prefer written summary depositions. Appeals generally fall into one of three categories: (1) frivolous appeals, which have little substance, raise no significant new issues, and are generally disposed of quickly; (2) ritualistic appeals, which are brought primarily because of the demands of litigants, even though the probability of reversal is negligible; and (3) nonconsensual appeals, which entail major questions of law and policy and on which there is considerable professional disagreement among the courts and within the legal profession.[20] The probability of reversal is, of course, highest in the case of nonconsensual appeals.

In 2007, the Judicial Conference of the United States, the primary policy-making arm of the federal courts, urged Congress to create 67 new federal judgeships in appellate and district courts.[21] The conference cited a need for nine permanent and three temporary court of appeals judgeships as well as 44 permanent and 11 temporary district judgeships. As of late-2010 Congress had yet to act on the recommendation. Learn more about criminal appeals in federal courts at **Library Extra 7–5**.

▲ Protesters in front of the U.S. Supreme Court in 2004. Highlighting its importance as our nation's premier legal institution, the Court became the backdrop for a rally against the USA PATRIOT Act. Protesters claimed that the act unfairly denies foreign terror suspects the right to a quick and impartial hearing. How does the Court serve to balance individual rights and freedoms with the need for public safety and social order?
© William Philpott/Reuters/Corbis

The U.S. Supreme Court

At the apex of the federal court system stands the U.S. Supreme Court. The Supreme Court is located in Washington, D.C., across the street from the U.S. Capitol. The Court consists of nine justices. Eight are associate justices, and the ninth presides over the Court as the chief justice of the United States (Table 7–1). Supreme Court justices are nominated by the president, are confirmed by the Senate, and serve for life. Lengthy terms of service are a tradition among justices. One of the earliest chief justices, John Marshall, served the Court for 34 years, from 1801 to 1835. The same was true of Justice Stephen J. Field, who sat on the bench between 1863 and 1897. Justice Hugo Black passed the 34-year milestone, serving an additional month before retiring in 1971. Justice William O. Douglas set a record for longevity on the bench, retiring in 1975 after 36 years and six months of service. You can view the biographies of today's Supreme Court justices via **Web Extra 7–6**.

The Supreme Court of the United States wields immense power. The Court's greatest authority lies in its capacity for **judicial review** of lower-court decisions and state and federal statutes. By exercising its power of judicial review, the Court decides what laws and lower-court decisions are in keeping with the intent of the U.S. Constitution. The power of judicial review is not explicit in the Constitution but was anticipated by its framers. In the *Federalist Papers*, which urged adoption of the Constitution, Alexander Hamilton wrote that through the practice of judicial review, the Court would ensure that "the will of the whole people," as grounded in the Constitution, would be supreme over the "will of the legislature," which might be subject to temporary whims.[22] It was not

judicial review
The power of a court to review actions and decisions made by other agencies of government.

Lecture Note Explain that the U.S. Supreme Court wields immense judicial power by virtue of its role as interpreter of constitutional mandates.

Thematic Question Throughout the Reagan-Bush era, the U.S. Supreme Court was characterized by an ideological shift toward the right. Many feel that the administration of George W. Bush renewed that shift. The Obama administration, however, has had the opportunity to nominate a new group of justices. How might the daily activities of police officers, lower-court functionaries, and prison administrators be affected by the Court's changing makeup? Which group of individuals would be more supportive of a conservative Supreme Court: individual-rights advocates or public-order advocates? How do you feel about the high court's current ideology?

TABLE 7–1
Justices of the U.S. Supreme Court (as of January 2010)

Justice	Start of Duty	Views
Chief Justice		
John G. Roberts, Jr.	September 2005	Conservative
Associate Justices		
Antonin Scalia	September 1986	Very conservative
Anthony Kennedy	February 1988	Conservative
Clarence Thomas	October 1991	Conservative
Ruth Bader Ginsburg	August 1993	Moderate to liberal
Stephen G. Breyer	August 1994	Moderate
Samuel A. Alito, Jr.	January 2006	Conservative
Sonia M. Sotomayor	August 2009	Moderate to liberal
Elena Kagan	August 2010	Liberal

▲ U.S. Supreme Court Justice Sonia Sotomayor (center) being applauded by President Barack Obama and Vice President Joe Biden at her 2009 nomination to the Court. Do you think that a justice's personal values and beliefs might influence his or her decisions on important matters that come before the court, or do such decisions always result from the impersonal application of relevant law? *Saul Loeb/Agence France Presse/Getty Images*

until 1803, however, that the Court forcefully asserted its power of judicial review. In an opinion written for *Marbury* v. *Madison* (1803),[23] Chief Justice John Marshall established the Court's authority as final interpreter of the U.S. Constitution, declaring, "It is emphatically the province of the judicial department to say what the law is."

The Supreme Court Today

The Supreme Court reviews the decisions of lower courts and may accept cases both from U.S. courts of appeal and from state supreme courts. It has limited original jurisdiction and does not conduct trials except for disputes between states and for some cases of attorney disbarment. For a case to be heard, at least four justices must vote in favor of a hearing. When the Court agrees to hear a case, it will issue a writ of *certiorari* to a lower court, ordering it to send the records of the case forward for review. Once having granted *certiorari*, the justices can revoke the decision. In such cases, a writ is dismissed by ruling it improvidently granted.

The U.S. Supreme Court may review any decision appealed to it that it decides is worthy of review. In fact, however, the Court elects to review only cases that involve a substantial federal question. Of approximately 5,000 requests for review received by the Court yearly, only about 200 are actually heard.

A term of the Supreme Court begins, by statute, on the first Monday in October and lasts until early July. The term is divided among sittings, when cases will be heard, and periods of time for the writing and delivering of opinions. Between 22 and 24 cases are heard at each sitting, with each side allotted 30 minutes for arguments before the justices. Intervening recesses allow justices time to study arguments and supporting documentation and to work on their opinions.

Decisions rendered by the Supreme Court are rarely unanimous. Instead, the opinion that a majority of the Court's justices agree on becomes the judgment of the Court. Justices who agree with the Court's judgment write concurring opinions if they agree for a different

Class Activity Have the class research the congressional confirmation hearings of selected Supreme Court nominees, including Elena Kagan, Sonia Sotomayor, John G. Roberts, Samuel Alito, Robert Bork, David Souter, Clarence Thomas, Ruth Bader Ginsburg, and Stephen Breyer. Ask them to identify the issues raised by both sides in the debates over these candidates. Have the class decide, on the basis of the confirmation hearings, which of these nominees would make the best justice, and have them provide the reasoning behind their decision. Which of these candidates would probably be the favorite of individual-rights advocates? Of public-order advocates? Why?

▲ Justices of the U.S. Supreme Court gather for a group portrait in Washington, DC, on Friday, Oct. 8, 2010. Seated from left are: Associate Justices Clarence Thomas, Antonin Scalia, Chief Justice John Roberts, Associate Justices Anthony M. Kennedy, and Ruth Bader Ginsburg. Standing, from left are: Associate Justices Sonia Sotomayor, Stephen Breyer, Samuel Alito Jr., and Elena Kagan. *Pablo Martinez Monsivais/AP Wide World Photos*

reason than the majority opinion or if they feel that they have some new light to shed on a legal issue involved in the case. Justices who do not agree with the decision of the Court write dissenting opinions, and those dissenting opinions may offer new possibilities for successful appeals at a later date. Visit the U.S. Supreme Court at **Web Extra 7–7**, and learn more about the federal judiciary at **Library Extra 7–6**.

Pretrial Activities

The next chapter discusses the steps in a criminal trial and describes the many roles assumed by courtroom participants, including judges, prosecutors, defense attorneys, victims, and defendants. A number of court-related activities, however, routinely take place *before* trial can begin (Figure 7–4). Although these activities (as well as the names given to them) vary among jurisdictions, they are described generally in the pages that follow.

4 Explain the typical steps taken during pretrial activities, and list the key factors considered by judicial officers in assessing the risks associated with pretrial release.

FIGURE 7–4 Pretrial Activities

First Appearance

An appearance before a magistrate or lower-court judge for the purpose of:

1. hearing the charges against the defendant
2. rights advisement
3. being given the opportunity to retain a lawyer or to have one appointed
4. possibly being given the opportunity for bail

First appearance must be held within 48 hours after arrest (*McNabb* v. *U.S.* [1943]).

Probable Cause first appearance may involve a probable cause hearing; especially when arrests are made without a warrant. A judicial officer will review police documents and reports to ensure that probable cause supports the arrest.

Pretrial Release If the crime is very serious, or if the defendant is a flight risk, he or she will be held in jail until trial. This is called pretrial detention. The majority of defendants, however, are given the opportunity for release.

Early Intervention Programs These programs supervise defendants and monitor their compliance with release conditions and ensure that they appear for future court hearings. They also gather and present information about defendants and potential dispositional options.

Bail is the most common release mechanism. Bail serves two purposes, it helps ensure reapperance of the accused, and it prevents unconvicted persons from suffering imprisonment.

Bail bonds The usual practice is for a defendant to seek bail through a professional bail bondsman. The bondsman will charge a fee (usually 10% to 15% of the bail amount) that the defendant pays up front. The bail bondsman is then responsible for the defendant showing up in court. In many states bail bondsmen are empowered to hunt down and bring back defendants who fail to appear.

Alternatives to bail

Release on Recognizance (ROR)

Property Bonds

Deposit Bail

Conditional Release

Third-Party Custody

Unsecured Bonds

Signature Bonds

The Grand Jury

Involves the hearing of evidence presented by a district attorney or prosecutor to a group of jurors to determine whether there is sufficient evidence to bring the accused person to trial. An indictment by the grand jury is referred to the trial court and forms the basis for further prosecution.

Arraignment and the Plea

An arraignment is the first appearance of the defendant before the trial court. It offers the defendant an opportunity to enter a plea.

The First Appearance

first appearance
An appearance before a magistrate during which the legality of the defendant's arrest is initially assessed and the defendant is informed of the charges on which he or she is being held. At this stage in the criminal justice process, bail may be set or pretrial release arranged. Also called *initial appearance*.

bail
The money or property pledged to the court or actually deposited with the court to effect the release of a person from legal custody.

Following arrest, most defendants do not come into contact with an officer of the court until their **first appearance** before a magistrate or a lower-court judge.[24] A first appearance, sometimes called an *initial appearance* or *magistrate's review*, occurs when defendants are brought before a judge (1) to be given formal notice of the charges against them, (2) to be advised of their rights, (3) to be given the opportunity to retain a lawyer or to have one appointed to represent them, and (4) to possibly be afforded the opportunity for **bail**.

According to the procedural rules of all jurisdictions, defendants who have been taken into custody must be offered an in-court appearance before a magistrate "without unnecessary delay." The 1943 U.S. Supreme Court case of *McNabb* v. *U.S.*[25] established that any unreasonable delay in an initial court appearance would make confessions inadmissible if interrogating officers obtained them during the delay. Based on the *McNabb* decision, 48 hours following arrest became the standard maximum time by which a first appearance should be held.

The first appearance may also involve a probable cause hearing, although such hearings may be held separately because they do not require the defendant's presence. (In some jurisdictions, the probable cause hearing may be combined with the preliminary hearing.) Probable cause hearings are necessary when arrests are made without a warrant because such arrests do not require a prior judicial determination of probable cause. During a probable cause hearing, also called a *probable cause determination*, a judicial officer will review police documents and reports to ensure that probable cause supported the arrest. The review of the arrest proceeds in a relatively informal fashion, with the judge seeking to decide whether, at the time of apprehension, the arresting officer had reason to believe both (1) that a crime had been or was being committed and (2) that the defendant was the person who committed it. Most of the evidence presented to the judge comes either from the arresting officer or from the victim. If probable cause is not found to exist, the suspect is released. As with a first appearance, a probable cause hearing should take place within 48 hours.

Lecture Note Describe the role of the magistrate in terms of deciding whether an arrest was properly made. Discuss what might be a reasonable period of time for a first appearance before a magistrate. Explain the necessity for a quick appearance in terms of the potential for abuse, the detention of political prisoners, and so on.

In 1991, in a class-action suit entitled *County of Riverside* v. *McLaughlin*,[26] the U.S. Supreme Court imposed a promptness requirement on probable cause determinations for in-custody arrestees. The Court held that "a jurisdiction that provides judicial determinations of probable cause within 48 hours of arrest will, as a general matter, comply with the promptness requirement." The Court specified, however, that weekends and holidays could not be excluded from the 48-hour requirement (as they had been in Riverside County, California) and that, depending on the specifics of the case, delays of fewer than two days may still be unreasonable.

During a first appearance, the suspect is not given an opportunity to present evidence, although the U.S. Supreme Court has held that defendants are entitled to representation by counsel at their first appearance,[27] and that an indigent person is entitled to have an attorney appointed for him at his initial appearance.[28] Following a reading of the charges and advisement of rights, counsel may be appointed to represent indigent defendants and proceedings may be adjourned until counsel can be obtained. In cases where a suspect is unruly, intoxicated, or uncooperative, a judicial review may occur without the suspect being present.

Some states waive a first appearance and proceed directly to arraignment (discussed later), especially when the defendant has been arrested on a warrant. In states that move directly to arraignment, the procedures undertaken to obtain a warrant are regarded as sufficient to demonstrate a basis for detention before arraignment.

Pretrial Release

pretrial release
The release of an accused person from custody, for all or part of the time before or during prosecution, upon his or her promise to appear in court when required.

A significant aspect of the first appearance hearing is the consideration of **pretrial release**. Defendants charged with very serious crimes, as well as those thought likely to escape or to injure others, are usually held in jail until trial. Such a practice is called *pretrial detention.* The majority of defendants, however, are afforded the opportunity for release. Many jurisdictions make use of pretrial services programs, which may also be called *early intervention programs.*[29] Such programs, which are typically funded by the states or by individual counties,

Multiculturalism and Diversity
The International Criminal Court

On April 12, 2000, the International Criminal Court (ICC) was created under the auspices of the United Nations. The ICC is a permanent criminal court for trying individuals (not countries) who commit the most serious crimes of concern to the international community, such as genocide, war crimes, and crimes against humanity (including the wholesale murder of civilians, torture, and mass rape). The goal of the ICC is to be a global judicial institution with international jurisdiction complementing national legal systems around the world. Support for the ICC was developed through the United Nations. More than 70 countries approved the court's creation by ratifying the Rome Statute of the International Criminal Court. The ICC's first prosecutor, Luis Moreno Ocampo of Argentina, was elected in April 2003, and was still serving in that capacity in late-2010.[1]

The ICC initiative began after World War II with unsuccessful efforts to establish an international tribunal to try individuals accused of war crimes.[2] In lieu of such a court, military tribunals were held in Nuremberg, Germany, and Tokyo, Japan, to try defendants accused of war crimes. Although the 1948 Genocide Convention called for an international criminal court, efforts to establish a permanent court were delayed for decades by the cold war and by the refusal of some national governments to accept the court's proposed international legal jurisdiction.

In December 1948, the UN General Assembly adopted the Universal Declaration of Human Rights and the Convention on the Prevention and Punishment of the Crime of Genocide. It also called for criminals to be tried "by such international penal tribunals as may have jurisdiction." A number of member states soon asked the United Nations International Law Commission (ILC) to study the possibility of establishing an international criminal court.

Development of the ICC was delayed by the cold war that took place between the world's superpowers, which were not willing to subject their military personnel or commanders to international criminal jurisdiction in the event of a "hot" war. In 1981, however, the UN General Assembly asked the ILC to consider creating an international Code of Crimes.

The 1992 war in Bosnia-Herzegovina, which involved clear violations of the Genocide and Geneva Conventions, heightened world interest in the establishment of a permanent ICC. A few years later, 160 countries participated in a UN conference, held in Rome, to establish a criminal court.[3] At the end of that conference, member states voted overwhelmingly in favor of the Rome Statute calling for the establishment of the ICC.

In 2005, in one of the ICC's first official actions, a panel of judges decided to allow independent Dutch investigators to carry out forensic tests in the Democratic Republic of Congo (DRC) as part of an ongoing investigation into the deaths of thousands of people in genocidal violence throughout central Africa.[4] Learn more about these efforts and other activities of the ICC by visiting the International Criminal Court at **Web Extra 7–8.** You can watch video streams of court hearings when the court is in session at **Web Extra 7–9** (some archived streams are also available).

▲ Former UN Secretary-General Kofi Annan speaking at opening ceremonies that marked the signing of the Treaty on Establishment of the International Criminal Court in Rome, Italy, in 1998. What is the jurisdiction of the ICC?
UN/DPI/E. Schneider

[1]See the Coalition for an International Criminal Court, "Building the Court," http://www.iccnow.org/buildingthecourt.html (accessed July 10, 2010).

[2]Much of the information and some of the wording in this box are adapted from "The International Criminal Court Home Page," http://www.icc-cpi.int/menus/icc (accessed October 1, 2010); and the ICC "Timeline," http://www.iccnow.org/html/timeline.htm (accessed April 12, 2010).

[3]The conference was officially known as the Conference of Plenipotentiaries on the Establishment of an International Criminal Court. *Plenipotentiary* is another word for "diplomat."

[4]"Decision of Pre-Trial Chamber I on the Prosecutor's Request under Article 56 of the Rome Statute," ICC press release, April 26, 2005, http://www.icc-cpi.int/press/pressreleases/105.html (accessed May 20, 2008).

perform two critical functions: (1) They gather and present information about newly arrested defendants and about available release options for use by judicial officers in deciding what (if any) conditions are to be set for defendants' release before trial, and (2) they supervise defendants released from custody during the pretrial period by monitoring their compliance with release conditions and by helping to ensure that they appear for scheduled court events. Learn more about pretrial services at **Library Extra 7–7**.

The initial pretrial release/detention decision is usually made by a judicial officer or by a specially appointed hearing officer after considering the background information provided by the pretrial services program, along with the representations made by the prosecutor and the defense attorney. In making this decision, judicial officers are concerned about two types of risk: (1) the risk of flight or nonappearance for scheduled court appearances and (2) the risk to public safety.

Lecture Note Describe the various alternatives available for the setting of bail: release on recognizance, property bond, deposit bail, conditional release, third-party custody, unsecured bond, and signature bond.

▲ Bounty hunter Duane "Dog" Chapman, owner of Bounty Hunter International and self-proclaimed "greatest bounty hunter in the world." Bounty hunters collect fees from bail bondsmen, who otherwise stand to forfeit the money they posted for clients who do not appear in court. Chapman, an ex-con born-again Christian, makes a living pursuing felons who fail to appear for their court dates after posting bail through a bondsman. He has over 6,000 captures to his credit. Read more about him at http://www.dogthebountyhunter.com. Would you consider work as a bounty hunter? *Jim Ruymen/CORBIS–NY*

bail bond
A document guaranteeing the appearance of a defendant in court as required and recording the pledge of money or property to be paid to the court if he or she does not appear. The bail bond is signed by the person to be released and by anyone else acting in his or her behalf.

Bail

Bail is the most common release/detention decision-making mechanism in American courts. Bail serves two purposes: (1) It helps ensure reappearance of the accused, and (2) it prevents unconvicted persons from suffering imprisonment unnecessarily.

Bail involves the posting of a bond as a pledge that the accused will return for further hearings. **Bail bonds** usually involve cash deposits but may be based on property or other valuables. A fully secured bond requires the defendant to post the full amount of bail set by the court. The usual practice, however, is for a defendant to seek privately secured bail through the services of a professional bail bondsman. The bondsman will assess a percentage (usually 10% to 15%) of the required bond as a fee, which the defendant will have to pay up front. Those who "skip bail" by hiding or fleeing will sometimes find that the court has ordered them to forfeit their bail. Forfeiture hearings must be held before a bond can be taken, and most courts will not order bail forfeited unless it appears that the defendant intends to avoid prosecution permanently. Bail forfeiture will often be reversed if the defendant later appears willingly to stand trial.

In many states, bondsmen are empowered to hunt down and bring back defendants who have fled. In some jurisdictions, bondsmen hold virtually unlimited powers and have been permitted by courts to pursue, arrest, and forcibly extradite their charges from foreign jurisdictions without concern for the due process considerations or statutory limitations that apply to law enforcement officers.[30] Recently, however, a number of states have enacted laws that eliminate for-profit bail bond businesses, replacing them instead with state-operated pretrial services agencies. Visit the Professional Bail Agents of the United States at **Web Extra 7–10** to learn more about the job of bail bondsman and to view the group's code of ethics.

Alternatives to Bail

The Eighth Amendment to the U.S. Constitution does not guarantee the opportunity for bail but does state that "[e]xcessive bail shall not be required." Some studies, however, have found that many defendants who are offered the opportunity for bail are unable to raise the money. Years ago, a report by the National Advisory Commission on Criminal Justice Standards and Goals found that as many as 93% of felony defendants in some jurisdictions were unable to make bail.[31]

To extend the opportunity for pretrial release to a greater proportion of nondangerous arrestees, a number of states and the federal government now make available various alternatives to the cash bond system. Alternatives include (1) release on recognizance, (2) property bond, (3) deposit bail, (4) conditional release, (5) third-party custody, (6) unsecured bond, and (7) signature bond.

Release on Recognizance (ROR)

release on recognizance (ROR)
The pretrial release of a criminal defendant on his or her written promise to appear in court as required. No cash or property bond is required.

Release on recognizance (ROR) involves no cash bond, requiring as a guarantee only that the defendant agree in writing to return for further hearings as specified by the court. As an alternative to a cash bond, ROR was tested during the 1960s in a social experiment called the Manhattan Bail Project.[32] In the experiment, not all defendants were eligible for release on their own recognizance; those arrested for serious crimes, including murder, rape, and robbery, and defendants with extensive prior criminal records were excluded from participating in the project. The rest of the defendants were scored and categorized according to a number of "ideal" criteria used as indicators of both dangerousness and likelihood of pretrial flight. Criteria included (1) no previous convictions, (2) residential stability, and (3) good employment record. Those likely to flee were not released.

Studies of the bail project revealed that it released four times as many defendants before trial as had been freed under the traditional cash bond system.[33] Even more surprising was the finding that only 1% of those released fled from prosecution—the same percentage as for those set free on cash bonds.[34] Later studies, however, were unclear as to the effectiveness of ROR, with some finding a no-show rate as high as 12%.[35]

Property Bonds

Property bonds substitute other items of value in place of cash. Land, houses, automobiles, stocks, and so on may be consigned to the court as collateral against pretrial flight.

property bond
The setting of bail in the form of land, houses, stocks, or other tangible property. In the event that the defendant absconds before trial, the bond becomes the property of the court.

Deposit Bail

Deposit bail, an alternative form of cash bond available in some jurisdictions, places the court in the role of the bondsman, allowing the defendant to post a percentage of the full bail with the court. Unlike private bail bondsmen, court-run deposit bail programs usually return the amount of the deposit except for a small administrative fee (perhaps 1%). If the defendant fails to appear for court, the entire amount of court-ordered bail is forfeited.

Conditional Release

Conditional release imposes a set of requirements on the defendant that might include participation in a drug-treatment program; staying away from specified others, such as potential witnesses; and attendance at a regular job. *Release under supervision* is similar to conditional release but adds the stipulation that defendants report to an officer of the court or to a police officer at designated times.

See CJ Exhibit 7–1 for a discussion of the different people and systems involved in making pretrial release decisions.

> We are under a Constitution, but the Constitution is what the judges say it is, and the judiciary is the safeguard of our liberty and of our property under the Constitution.
>
> —Charles Evans Hughes, eleventh chief justice of the United States

Third-Party Custody

Third-party custody is a bail bond alternative that assigns custody of the defendant to an individual or agency that promises to ensure his or her later appearance in court.[36] Some pretrial release programs allow attorneys to assume responsibility for their clients in this fashion. If a defendant fails to appear, the attorney's privilege to participate in the program may be ended.

Unsecured Bonds

Unsecured bonds are based on a court-determined dollar amount of bail. Like a credit contract, this bail alternative requires no monetary deposit with the court. The defendant agrees in writing that failure to appear will result in forfeiture of the entire amount of the bond, which might then be taken in seizures of land, personal property, bank accounts, and so on.

Signature Bonds

Signature bonds allow release based on the defendant's written promise to appear. Signature bonds involve no particular assessment of the defendant's dangerousness or likelihood of later appearance in court. They are used only in cases of minor offenses, such as traffic-law violations and some petty drug-law violations. Signature bonds may be issued by the arresting officer acting on behalf of the court.

Pretrial Release and Public Safety

Pretrial release is common practice. Approximately 57% of all state-level felony defendants[37] and 66% of all federal felony defendants[38] are released before trial (Figure 7–5). At the state level, 43% of all defendants are detained until the court disposes of their case. Murder defendants (88%) are the most likely to be detained. A majority of defendants charged with motor vehicle theft (61%), robbery (58%), or burglary (54%) are also detained until case disposition. Defendants on parole (83%) were the most likely to be detained.

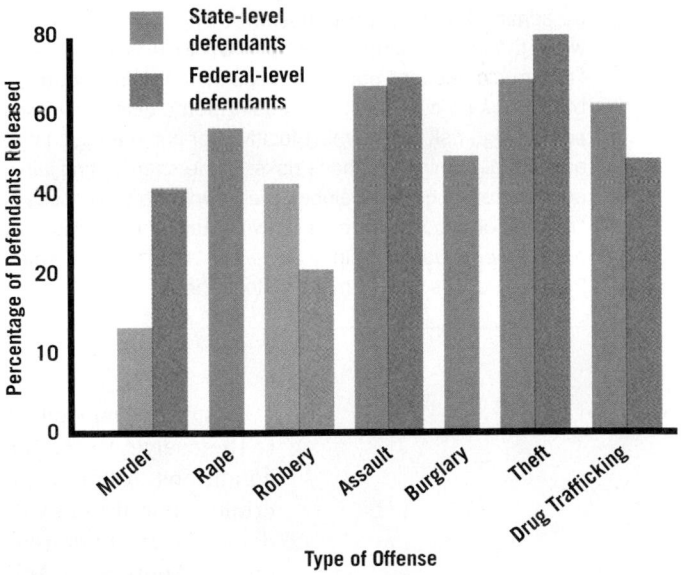

FIGURE 7–5
Proportion of State and Federal Felony Defendants Released before Trial

Note: Federal pretrial release statistics are not available for the crimes of rape and burglary.
Sources: Tracey Kyckelhahn and Thomas H. Cohen, *Felony Defendants in Large Urban Counties, 2004* (Washington, DC: Bureau of Justice Statistics, 2008); and Thomas H. Cohen and Brian A. Reaves, *Pretrial Release of Felony Defendants in State Courts* (Washington, DC: Bureau of Justice Statistics, 2007).

CJ Exhibit 7–1
Nonjudicial Pretrial Release Decisions

In most American jurisdictions, judicial officers decide whether an arrested person will be detained or released. Some jurisdictions, however, allow others to make that decision. Some observers argue that the critical issue is not whether the decision maker is a judge but whether there are clear and appropriate criteria for making the decision, whether the decision maker has adequate information, and whether he or she has been well trained in pretrial release/detention decision making. Nonjudicial decision makers and release/detention mechanisms include the following:

- *Police officers and desk appearance tickets.* Desk appearance tickets, or citations, are summonses given to defendants at the police station, usually for petty offenses or misdemeanor charges. The tickets can greatly reduce the use of pretrial detention and can save the court system a great deal of time by avoiding initial pretrial release or bail hearings in minor cases. However, because they are typically based only on the current charge (and sometimes on a computer search to check for outstanding warrants), high-risk defendants could be released without supervision or monitoring. As computerized access to more criminal history information becomes available, enabling rapid identification of individuals with prior records who pose a risk to the community, desk appearance tickets may be more widely used.
- *Jail administrators.* In many jurisdictions, jail officials have the authority to release (or to refuse to book into jail) arrestees who meet certain criteria. In some localities, jail officials exercise this authority pursuant to a court order that specifies priorities with respect to the categories of defendants who can be admitted to the jail and those who are to be released when the jail population exceeds a court-imposed ceiling. The "automatic release" approach helps minimize jail crowding, but it does so at the risk of releasing some defendants who pose a high risk of becoming fugitives or committing criminal acts. To help minimize these risks, some sheriffs and jail administrators have developed their own pretrial services or "release on recognizance" units with staff who conduct risk assessments based on interviews with arrestees, information from references, and criminal history checks.
- *Bail schedules.* These predetermined schedules set levels of bail (from release on recognizance to amounts of surety bond) based solely on the offense charged. Depending on local practices, release pursuant to a bail schedule may take place at a police station, at the local jail, or at court. This practice saves time for judicial officers and allows the rapid release of defendants who can afford to post the bail amount. However, release determinations based solely on the current charge are of dubious value because there is no proven relationship between a particular charge and the risk of flight or subsequent crime. Release pursuant to a bail schedule depends simply on the defendant's ability to post the amount of the bond; moreover, when a defendant is released by posting bond, there is generally no procedure for supervision to minimize the risks of nonappearance and subsequent crime.
- *Bail bondsmen.* When a judicial officer sets the amount of bond that a defendant must produce to be released or when bond is set mechanically on the basis of a bail schedule, the real decision makers are often the surety bail bondsmen. If no bondsman will offer bond, the defendant without other sources of money remains in jail. The defendant's ability to pay a bondsman the 10% fee (and sometimes to post collateral) bears no relationship to his or her risk of flight or danger to the community.
- *Pretrial services agencies.* In some jurisdictions, pretrial services agencies have authority to release certain categories of defendants. The authority is usually limited to relatively minor cases, although agencies in a few jurisdictions can release some categories of felony defendants. Because the pretrial services agency can obtain information about the defendant's prior record, community ties, and other pending charges, its decision to release or detain is based on more extensive information and criteria than when the decision is based on a bail schedule. However, because these programs lack the independence of judicial officers, they can be targets of political and public pressure.

Source: Adapted from Barry Mahoney et al., *Pretrial Services Programs: Responsibilities and Potential* (Washington, DC: National Institute of Justice, 2001).

A growing movement, arguing that defendants released before trial may be dangerous to themselves or to others, seeks to reduce the number of defendants released under any conditions. Advocates of this conservative policy cite a number of studies documenting crimes committed by defendants released on bond. One study found that 16% of defendants released before trial were rearrested, and of those, 30% were arrested more than once.[39] Another study determined that as many as 41% of those released before trial for serious crimes, such as rape and robbery, were rearrested before their trial date.[40] Not surprisingly, such studies generally find that the longer the time spent out on bail before trial, the greater the likelihood of misconduct.

danger law
A law intended to prevent the pretrial release of criminal defendants judged to represent a danger to others in the community.

In response to findings like these, some states have enacted **danger laws**, which limit the right to bail to certain kinds of offenders.[41] Other states, including Arizona, California, Colorado, Florida, and Illinois, have approved constitutional amendments restricting the use of bail.[42] Most such provisions exclude defendants charged with certain crimes from being eligible for bail and mandate that other defendants being considered for bail meet stringent conditions. Some states combine these strictures with tough release conditions designed to keep close control over defendants before trial.

The 1984 federal Bail Reform Act allows federal judges to assess the danger of an accused to the community and to deny bail to defendants who are thought to be dangerous. In the words of the act, a suspect held in pretrial custody on federal criminal charges must be detained if "after a hearing . . . he is found to pose a risk of flight and a danger to others or the community and if no condition of release can give reasonable assurances against these contingencies."[43] Defendants seeking bail must demonstrate a high likelihood of later court appearance. The act also requires that a defendant have a speedy first appearance and that a detention hearing be held in conjunction with the initial appearance if he or she is to be detained.

In the 1990 case of *U.S.* v. *Montalvo-Murillo*,[44] however, a defendant who was not provided with a detention hearing at the time of his first appearance and was subsequently released by an appeals court was found to have no "right" to freedom because of this "minor" statutory violation. The Supreme Court held that "unless it has a substantial influence on the outcome of the proceedings . . . failure to comply with the Act's prompt hearing provision does not require release of a person who should otherwise be detained" because "[a]utomatic release contravenes the statutory purpose of providing fair bail procedures while protecting the public's safety and assuring a defendant's appearance at trial."[45]

Court challenges to the constitutionality of pretrial detention legislation have not met with much success. The U.S. Supreme Court case of *U.S.* v. *Hazzard* (1984),[46] decided only a few months after enactment of federal bail reform, held that Congress was justified in providing for denial of bail to offenders who represent a danger to the community. Later cases have supported the presumption of flight, which federal law presupposes for certain types of defendants.[47]

> I have tried to minimize what I feel is one of the less desirable aspects of the job . . . that judges can become isolated from the people whose lives their decisions affect.
>
> —Stephen Breyer, U.S. Supreme Court justice

▲ A grand jury in action. Grand jury proceedings are generally very informal, as this picture shows. What is the grand jury's job?
David Young-Wolff/Getty Images, Inc./Riser

Thematic Question What is the proportion of criminal defendants released before trial on the federal level? On the state level? Why is the rate of release so high? How can the community be reasonably protected, given the release of so many criminal suspects? Would you reduce the number of defendants being released? Why or why not?

Lecture Note Explain the role of the grand jury in returning criminal indictments. Comment on the fact that not all states use the grand jury system, although all make use of some form of indictment or information.

The Grand Jury

The federal government and about half of the states use grand juries as part of the pretrial process. **Grand juries** comprise private citizens (often 23 in number) who hear evidence presented by the prosecution. Grand juries serve primarily as filters to eliminate from further processing any cases for which there is not sufficient evidence.

In early times, grand juries served a far different purpose. The grand jury system began in England in 1166 as a way of identifying law violators. Lacking a law enforcement agency with investigative authority, the government looked to the grand jury as a source of information on criminal activity in the community. Even today, grand juries in most jurisdictions may initiate prosecution independently of the prosecutor, although they rarely do.

Grand jury hearings are held in secret, and the defendant is generally not afforded the opportunity to appear before the grand jury.[48] Similarly, the defense has no opportunity to cross-examine prosecution witnesses. Grand juries have the power to subpoena witnesses and to mandate a review of books, records, and other documents crucial to their investigation.

After hearing the evidence, the grand jury votes on the **indictment** (a formal listing of proposed charges) presented to it by the prosecution. If the majority of grand jury members agree to forward the indictment to the trial court, it becomes a "true bill" on which further prosecution will turn.

grand jury
A group of jurors who have been selected according to law and have been sworn to hear the evidence and to determine whether there is sufficient evidence to bring the accused person to trial, to investigate criminal activity generally, or to investigate the conduct of a public agency or official.

indictment
A formal written accusation submitted to the court by a grand jury, alleging that a specified person has committed a specified offense, usually a felony.

The Preliminary Hearing

preliminary hearing
A proceeding before a judicial officer in which three matters must be decided: (1) whether a crime was committed, (2) whether the crime occurred within the territorial jurisdiction of the court, and (3) whether there are reasonable grounds to believe that the defendant committed the crime.

information
A formal written accusation submitted to a court by a prosecutor, alleging that a specified person has committed a specified offense.

States that do not use grand juries rely instead on a **preliminary hearing** "for charging defendants in a fashion that is less cumbersome and arguably more protective of the innocent."[49] In these jurisdictions, the prosecutor files an accusatory document called an **information**, or complaint, against the accused. A preliminary hearing is then held to determine whether there is probable cause to hold the defendant for trial. A few states, notably Georgia and Tennessee, use both the grand jury mechanism and a preliminary hearing as a "double check against the possibility of unwarranted prosecution."[50]

Although the preliminary hearing is not nearly as elaborate as a criminal trial, it has many of the same characteristics. The defendant is taken before a lower-court judge, who summarizes the charges and reviews the rights to which all criminal defendants are entitled. The prosecution may present witnesses and offers evidence in support of the complaint. The defendant is afforded the right to testify and may also call witnesses.

competent to stand trial
A finding by a court, when the defendant's sanity at the time of trial is at issue, that the defendant has sufficient present ability to consult with his or her attorney with a reasonable degree of rational understanding and that the defendant has a rational as well as factual understanding of the proceedings against him or her.

The primary purpose of the preliminary hearing is to give the defendant an opportunity to challenge the legal basis for his or her detention. At this point, defendants who appear to be or claim to be mentally incompetent may be ordered to undergo further evaluation to determine whether they are competent to stand trial. Being **competent to stand trial**, which was briefly discussed in Chapter 3, may become an issue when a defendant appears to be incapable of understanding the proceedings or is unable to assist in his or her own defense due to mental disease or defect.

In 2003, the U.S. Supreme Court placed strict limits on the government's power to forcibly medicate some mentally ill defendants to make them competent to stand trial.[51] In the case of *Sell* v. *U.S.*,[52] the Court ruled that the use of antipsychotic drugs on a nonviolent offender who ,does not represent a danger while institutionalized must be in the defendant's best medical interest and be "substantially unlikely" to cause side effects that might compromise the fairness of the trial.

Barring a finding of mental incompetence, all that is required for the wheels of justice to grind forward is a demonstration "sufficient to justify a prudent man's belief that the suspect has committed or was committing an offense" within the jurisdiction of the court.[53] If the magistrate finds enough evidence to justify a trial, the defendant is bound over to the grand jury. In states that do not require grand jury review, the defendant is sent directly to the trial court. If the complaint against the defendant cannot be substantiated during the preliminary hearing, he or she is released. A release is not a bar to further prosecution, however, and the defendant may be rearrested if further evidence comes to light.

Arraignment and the Plea

Arraignment

arraignment
Strictly, the hearing before a court having jurisdiction in a criminal case in which the identity of the defendant is established, the defendant is informed of the charge and of his or her rights, and the defendant is required to enter a plea. Also, in some usages, any appearance in criminal court before trial.

plea
In criminal proceedings, the defendant's formal answer in court to the charge contained in a complaint, information, or indictment that he or she is guilty of the offense charged, is not guilty of the offense charged, or does not contest the charge.

nolo contendere
A plea of "no contest." A no-contest plea is used when the defendant does not wish to contest conviction. Because the plea does not admit guilt, however, it cannot provide the basis for later civil suits that might follow a criminal conviction.

Once an indictment has been returned or an information has been filed, the accused will be formally arraigned. **Arraignment** is "the first appearance of the defendant before the court that has the authority to conduct a trial."[54] Arraignment is generally a brief process with two purposes: (1) to once again inform the defendant of the specific charges against him or her and (2) to allow the defendant to enter a **plea**. The Federal Rules of Criminal Procedure allow for one of three types of pleas to be entered: guilty, not guilty, and *nolo contendere*. A ***nolo contendere*** (no-contest) plea is much the same as a guilty plea. A defendant who pleads "no contest" is immediately convicted and may be sentenced just as though he or she had pleaded guilty. A no-contest plea, however, is not an admission of guilt and provides one major advantage to defendants: It may not be used later as a basis for civil proceedings that seek monetary or other damages against the defendant.

Some defendants refuse to enter any plea and are said to "stand mute." Standing mute is a defense strategy that is rarely employed. Defendants who choose this alternative simply do not answer the request for a plea; however, for procedural purposes, a defendant who stands mute is considered to have entered a plea of not guilty.

Plea Bargaining

Guilty pleas often are not as straightforward as they might seem and are typically arrived at only after complex negotiations. **Plea bargaining** is a process of negotiation that usually involves the defendant, the prosecutor, and the defense counsel and is founded on the mutual interests of all involved. Defense attorneys and their clients will agree to a plea of guilty when they are unsure of their ability to win acquittal at trial. Prosecutors may be willing to bargain because the evidence they have against the defendant is weaker than they would like it to be. Plea bargaining offers prosecutors the additional advantage of a quick conviction without the need to commit the time and resources necessary for trial. Benefits to the accused include the possibility of reduced or combined charges, reduced defense costs, and a shorter sentence than might otherwise be anticipated.

plea bargaining
The process of negotiating an agreement among the defendant, the prosecutor, and the court as to an appropriate plea and associated sentence in a given case. Plea bargaining circumvents the trial process and dramatically reduces the time required for the resolution of a criminal case.

Lecture Note Describe plea bargaining by highlighting how the process serves the interests of the defendant, the prosecutor, and the court. Ask students to identify those interests, and ask whether plea bargaining might circumvent other community interests.

The U.S. Supreme Court has held that a guilty plea constitutes conviction.[55] To validate the conviction, negotiated pleas require judicial consent. Judges often accept pleas that are the result of a bargaining process because such pleas reduce the court's workload. Although few judges are willing to guarantee a sentence before a plea is entered, most prosecutors and criminal trial lawyers know what sentences to expect from typical pleas.

Bargained pleas are commonplace. Some surveys have found that 90% of all criminal cases prepared for trial are eventually resolved through a negotiated plea.[56] In a study of 37 big-city prosecutors, the Bureau of Justice Statistics found that for every 100 adults arrested on a felony charge, half were eventually convicted of either a felony or a misdemeanor.[57] Of all convictions, fully 94% were the result of a plea; only 6% of convictions were the result of a criminal trial. After a guilty plea has been entered, it may be withdrawn with the consent of the court.

Thematic Question What is the percentage of criminal cases resolved through the use of bargained pleas? Why is plea bargaining so common? How does plea bargaining serve the interests of the various actors in the justice process? Whose interests might be overlooked?

Some Supreme Court decisions, however, have enhanced the prosecutor's authority in the bargaining process by declaring that defendants cannot capriciously withdraw negotiated pleas.[58] Other rulings have supported discretionary actions by prosecutors in which sentencing recommendations were retracted even after bargains had been struck.[59] Some lower-court cases have upheld the government's authority to withdraw from a negotiated plea when the defendant fails to live up to certain conditions.[60] Conditions may include requiring the defendant to provide information on other criminals, on criminal cartels, or on activities of smugglers.

Although it is generally agreed that bargained pleas should relate in some way to the original charges, this is not always the case. Entered pleas may be chosen for the punishments likely to be associated with them rather than for their accuracy in describing the criminal offenses in which the defendants were involved.[61] This is especially true when the defendant wants to minimize the socially stigmatizing impact of the offense. For example, a charge of indecent liberties, in which the defendant is accused of sexual misconduct, may be pleaded out as assault. Such a plea, which takes advantage of the fact that indecent liberties can be considered a form of sexual assault, would effectively disguise the true nature of the offense.

Even though the Supreme Court has endorsed plea bargaining, the public sometimes views it suspiciously. Law-and-order advocates, who generally favor harsh punishments and long jail terms, claim that plea bargaining results in unjustifiably light sentences. As a consequence, prosecutors who regularly engage in the practice rarely advertise it. Plea bargaining can be a powerful prosecutorial tool, but this power carries with it the potential for misuse. Because they circumvent the trial process, plea bargains can be abused by prosecutors and defense attorneys who are more interested in the speedy resolution of cases than they are in seeing justice done. Carried to the extreme, plea bargaining may result in defendants being convicted of crimes they did not commit. Although it is rare, innocent defendants (especially those with prior criminal records) who think a jury will convict them—for whatever reason—may plead guilty to reduced charges to avoid a trial. In an effort to protect defendants against hastily arranged pleas, the Federal Rules of Criminal Procedure require judges to (1) inform the defendant of the various rights he or she is surrendering by pleading guilty, (2) determine that the plea is voluntary, (3) disclose any plea agreements, and (4) make sufficient inquiry to ensure there is a factual basis for the plea.[62]

There is no such thing as justice—in or out of court.
—Clarence Darrow (1857-1938)

Bargained pleas can take many forms and can be quite inventive. The case of Jeffrey Morse illustrates an unusual attempt at a bargained plea. In 1998, Morse, a convicted sex

A PowerPoint presentation that supports this chapter is available from your Prentice Hall representative.

offender, petitioned courts in Illinois for permission to leave jail before sentencing for sexual assaults on two young girls so that he could undergo surgical castration. A judge agreed, and he was surgically castrated in a 45-minute outpatient procedure. Morse's mother noted that the surgery was done in an effort to avoid a long prison sentence. "He will cut whatever bodily part he has to [to] be able to reduce his sentence," she said.[63] Two months later, however, Kane County Judge Donald C. Hudson refused to show leniency for Morse. The judge sentenced Morse to 26 years in prison, saying that he wouldn't "place a seal of approval on trading body parts for a lesser sentence."[64]

Summary

THE COURTS

- In the United States, there are two judicial systems. One consists of state and local courts established under the authority of state and local governments. The other is the federal court system, created by Congress under the authority of the U.S. Constitution. This dual-court system historically results from general agreement among the nation's founders about the need for individual states to retain significant legislative authority and judicial autonomy separate from federal control.
- In most states, criminal courts can be classified within a three-tiered structure of two trial court echelons and an appellate level. There are many differences between and among state court systems, however. So-called reform states are characterized by relatively streamlined judicial systems consisting of trial courts of limited and general jurisdiction, supplemented by one or two appellate court levels. Nonreform, or traditional, states tend to retain judicial systems that are a conglomeration of multilevel and sometimes redundant courts with poorly defined jurisdictions. Regardless of their organizational style, state courts have virtually unlimited power to decide nearly every type of case, subject only to limitations imposed by the U.S. Constitution, their own state constitutions, and state law.
- Today's federal judiciary consists of three levels: (1) U.S. district courts, (2) U.S. courts of appeal, and (3) the U.S. Supreme Court. Federal courts, located principally in larger cities, decide only those cases over which the Constitution gives them authority. The highest federal court, the U.S. Supreme Court, is located in Washington, D.C., and hears cases only on appeal from lower courts.
- Pretrial activities involve the first appearance, the grand jury hearing (in some states), the preliminary hearing, the arraignment, and the plea, all of which are described in this chapter. Before trial, one of the most important decisions facing the courts is that of pretrial release. In considering whether a criminal defendant should be released prior to trial, courts must balance the rights of the unconvicted defendant against the potential for future harm that person may represent.

QUESTIONS FOR REVIEW

1. How did the American court system develop? What are some of the unique features of American court history? What is the dual-court system? Why do we have a dual-court system in America?
2. How is a typical state court system structured? What different types of courts might exist at the state level, and what kinds of jurisdiction might they have?
3. What are the three levels characteristic of the federal judiciary? What are some of the differences between the state and federal court systems in America?
4. What steps are typically taken before the start of a criminal trial?

The Courtroom Work Group and the Criminal Trial

CHAPTER 8

Learning Objectives

After reading this chapter, you should be able to:

1. Identify and explain the roles of professional members of the courtroom work group. **218**
2. Identify and explain the roles of nonprofessional or nonjudicial courtroom participants. **229**
3. Describe the nature and purpose of the criminal trial. **234**
4. Identify the various stages of a criminal trial. **235**

"... in the jury room, ... you learn that justice doesn't merely happen (neatly, reliably, like a crystal taking shape in a distant vacuum); justice is, rather, done, made, manufactured. Made by imperfect, wrangling, venal and virtuous human beings, using whatever means are at their disposal."

—D. Graham Burnett, jury foreman[1]

Introduction

The American criminal justice system is theater to the world.
—Alan Dershowitz, Harvard University

On January 25, 2010, 23-year-old Casey Anthony pleaded guilty in an Orange County (Florida) courtroom to 13 charges involving check fraud, including one count of grand theft, four counts of check forgery, and other charges of fraudulent use of personal identification. The plea cleared the way for Anthony's attorneys to devote more of their efforts to defending her on first-degree murder charges in the death of her two-year-old daughter, Caylee Marie Anthony, who was reported missing on June 15, 2008, by her grandmother—a month after her mother later said she had disappeared.[2] According to prosecutors and law enforcement officials, Casey told a string of lies about her daughter's disappearance, and in October 2008, with Caylee still missing, she was charged with first-degree murder. Prosecutors also charged Casey with aggravated child abuse, aggravated manslaughter, and providing false information to law enforcement officers. Two months after the charges were brought, a utility worker found Caylee's remains among cloth laundry and plastic trash bags near her home. Glittery pink letters that spelled out the phrase "Big Trouble Comes Small" were found with the remains and appear to have been on the shirt that Caylee was wearing at the time of her death. Casey Anthony's trial is set to begin as this book goes to press. Keep up with the latest in the case at **Web Extra 8–1**.

The Courtroom Work Group: Professional Courtroom Actors

To the public eye, criminal trials frequently appear to be well-managed events even though they may entail quite a bit of drama. Like plays on a stage, trials involve many participants, each of whom has a different role to fill. Unlike such plays, however, they are real-life events, and the impact that a trial's outcome has on people's lives can be far-reaching.

trial
In criminal proceedings, the examination in court of the issues of fact and relevant law in a case for the purpose of convicting or acquitting the defendant.

courtroom work group
The professional courtroom actors, including judges, prosecuting attorneys, defense attorneys, public defenders, and others who earn a living serving the court.

Participants in a criminal **trial** can be divided into two categories: professionals and outsiders (Figure 8–1). The professionals are the official courtroom actors. They are well versed in criminal trial practice and set the stage for and conduct the business of the court. Judges, prosecuting attorneys, defense attorneys, public defenders, and others who earn a living serving the court fall into this category. Professional courtroom actors are also called the **courtroom work group**. Some writers have pointed out that aside from statutory requirements and ethical considerations, courtroom interaction among professionals involves an implicit recognition of informal rules of civility, cooperation, and shared goals.[3] Hence even within the adversarial framework of a criminal trial, the courtroom work group is dedicated to bringing the procedure to a successful close.[4]

In contrast, outsiders—those trial participants who are only temporarily involved with the court—are generally unfamiliar with courtroom organization and trial procedure. Jurors and

▶ Two-year-old Caylee Marie Anthony (left), who was reported missing a month after she disappeared. Suspicion soon fell on her mother, Casey (right), who was charged with a number of crimes, including first-degree murder. Caylee's remains were later discovered near her home. Why was the mother charged with such a serious crime even before her daughter's body was found?
Orlando Sentinel/MCT/NewsCom.com and Red Huber/*Orlando Sentinel*/MCT/NewsCom.com

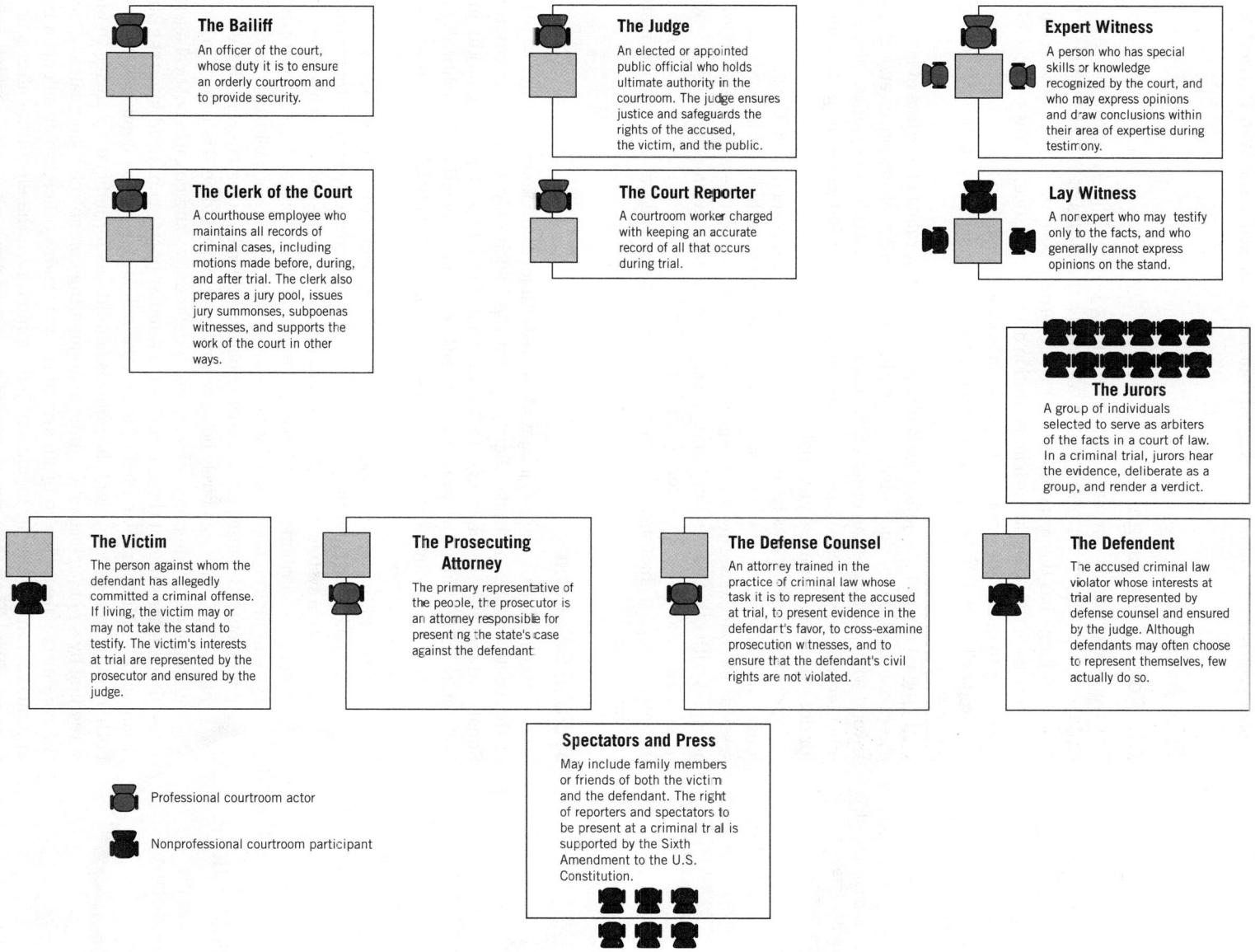

FIGURE 8–1 Participants in a Criminal Trial

1 Identify and explain the roles of professional members of the courtroom work group.

witnesses are outsiders; defendants and victims are also outsiders, even though they may have a greater personal investment in the outcome of the trial than anyone else.

This chapter examines trial court activities, building on the pretrial process described in Chapter 7. To place the trial process within its human context, however, the various roles of the many participants in a criminal trial are discussed first. Learn more about professional and nonprofessional courtroom participants at **Web Extra 8–2**.

The Judge

The Role of the Judge

judge
An elected or appointed public official who presides over a court of law and who is authorized to hear and sometimes to decide cases and to conduct trials.

The trial **judge** has the primary duty of ensuring justice. The American Bar Association (ABA) *Standards for Criminal Justice* describes the duties of the trial judge as follows: "The trial judge has the responsibility for safeguarding both the rights of the accused and the interests of the public in the administration of criminal justice. . . . The purpose of a criminal trial is to determine whether the prosecution has established the guilt of the accused as required by law, and the trial judge should not allow the proceedings to be used for any other purpose."[5]

Class Activity Invite a criminal court judge to speak with the class. Have him or her outline the responsibilities of a judge and discuss the adversarial process. Ask the judge to discuss the greatest challenges he or she faces.

In the courtroom, the judge holds ultimate authority, ruling on matters of law, weighing objections from both sides, deciding on the admissibility of evidence, and disciplining anyone who challenges the order of the court. In most jurisdictions, judges also sentence offenders after a verdict has been returned; in some states, judges decide guilt or innocence for defendants who waive a jury trial.

Lecture Note Explain the general responsibilities of the trial judge by referring to the American Bar Association's *Standards for Criminal Justice*. Stress the judge's role as mediator within an adversarial setting.

Most state jurisdictions have a chief judge who, besides serving on the bench as a trial judge, must also manage the court system. Management includes hiring staff, scheduling sessions of court, ensuring the adequate training of subordinate judges, and coordinating activities with other courtroom actors. Chief judges usually assume their position by virtue of seniority and rarely have any formal training in management. Hence the managerial effectiveness of a chief judge is often a matter of personality and dedication more than anything else.

Judicial Selection

As we discussed in Chapter 7, judges at the federal level are nominated by the president of the United States and take their place on the bench only after confirmation by the Senate. At the state level, things work somewhat differently. Depending on the jurisdiction, state judgeships are won through either popular election or political (usually gubernatorial) appointment. The processes involved in judicial selection at the state level are set by law.

> To hear patiently, to weigh deliberately and dispassionately, and to decide impartially; these are the chief duties of a judge.
>
> –Albert Pike (1809–1891)

Both judicial election and appointment have been criticized because each system allows politics to enter the judicial arena—although in somewhat different ways. Under the election system, judicial candidates must receive the endorsement of their parties, generate contributions, and manage an effective campaign. Under the appointment system, judicial hopefuls must be in favor with incumbent politicians to receive appointments. Because partisan politics plays a role in both systems, critics have claimed that sitting judges can rarely be as neutral as they should be. They carry to the bench with them campaign promises, personal indebtedness, and possible political agendas.

To counter some of these problems, a number of states have adopted the Missouri Plan (or the Missouri Bar Plan) for judicial selection,[6] which combines elements of both election and appointment. It requires candidates for judicial vacancies to undergo screening by a nonpartisan state judicial nominating committee. Candidates selected by the committee are reviewed by an arm of the governor's office, which selects a final list of names for appointment. Incumbent judges must face the electorate after a specified term in office. They then run unopposed in nonpartisan elections in which only their records may be considered. Voters have the choice of allowing a judge to continue in office or asking that another be appointed to take his or her place. Because the Missouri Plan provides for periodic public review of judicial performance, it is also called the *merit plan of judicial selection*.

Judicial Qualifications

A few decades ago, many states did not require any special training, education, or other qualifications for judges. Anyone (even someone without a law degree) who won election or was appointed could assume a judgeship. Today, however, almost all states require that judges in general jurisdiction and appellate courts hold a law degree, be a licensed attorney, and be a member of their state bar association. Many states also require newly elected judges to attend state-sponsored training sessions dealing with such subjects as courtroom procedure, evidence, dispute resolution, judicial writing, administrative record keeping, and ethics.

While most states provide instruction to meet the needs of trial judges, other organizations also provide specialized training. The National Judicial College (NJC), located on the campus of the University of Nevada at Reno, is one such institution. NJC was established in 1963 by the Joint Committee for the Effective Administration of Justice, chaired by Justice Tom C. Clark of the U.S. Supreme Court.[7] More than 3,000 judges enroll annually in courses offered by NJC, and many courses are offered online. NJC, in collaboration with the National Council of Juvenile and Family Court Judges and the University of Nevada at Reno, offers the nation's only advanced judicial degree programs, leading to a master's degree and a doctorate in judicial studies.[8] Visit the NJC at **Web Extra 8–3**.

In some parts of the United States, lower-court judges, such as justices of the peace, local magistrates, and "district" court judges, may still be elected without educational and other professional requirements. Today, in 43 states, some 1,300 nonlawyer judges are serving in mostly rural courts of limited jurisdiction.[9] In New York, for example, of the 3,300 judges in the state's unified court system, approximately 65% are part-time town or village justices, and approximately 80% of town and village justices are not lawyers.[10] The majority of cases that come before New York lay judges involve alleged traffic violations, although the cases may also include misdemeanors, small-claims actions, and some civil cases (of up to $3,000).

Even though some have defended lay judges as being closer to the citizenry in their understanding of justice,[11] in most jurisdictions the number of lay judges is declining. States that continue to use lay judges in lower courts do require that candidates for judgeships not have criminal records, and most states require that they attend special training sessions if elected.

The Prosecuting Attorney

The **prosecutor**—also called the *solicitor, district attorney, state's attorney, county attorney*, or *commonwealth attorney*—is responsible for presenting the state's case against the defendant. Technically speaking, the prosecuting attorney is the primary representative of the people by virtue of the belief that violations of the criminal law are an affront to the public. Except for federal prosecutors (called *U.S. attorneys*) and solicitors in five states, prosecutors are elected and generally serve four-year terms, with the possibility of continuing reelection.[12] Widespread criminal conspiracies, whether they involve government officials or private citizens, may require the services of a special prosecutor whose office can spend the time and resources needed for efficient prosecution.[13]

prosecutor
An attorney whose official duty is to conduct criminal proceedings on behalf of the state or the people against those accused of having committed criminal offenses.

Lecture Note Explain the role of the prosecuting attorney as the primary representative of the state or the people. Stress the fact that within the adversarial context of a criminal trial, the prosecuting attorney is expected to argue the state's case effectively.

Because the job of prosecutor entails too many duties for one person to handle, most prosecutors supervise a staff of assistant district attorneys who do most in-court work. Assistants are trained attorneys, licensed to practice law in the state where they work. They are usually hired directly by the chief prosecutor. Approximately 2,300 chief prosecutors, assisted by 24,000 deputy attorneys, serve the nation's counties and cities.[14]

Lecture Note Discuss the prosecutor's law enforcement role and the need for close cooperation and communication with the police.

Another prosecutorial role has traditionally been that of quasi-legal adviser to local police departments. Because prosecutors are sensitive to the kinds of information needed for conviction, they may help guide police investigations and will exhort detectives to identify credible witnesses, uncover additional evidence, and the like. This role is limited, however. Police departments are independent of the administrative authority of the prosecutor, and cooperation between them, although based on the common goal of conviction, is purely voluntary.

Lecture Note Explain prosecutorial discretion. Demonstrate that the discretionary decision of a prosecutor as to whether a suspect should be charged with a crime makes the prosecutor one of the most powerful actors in the criminal justice system.

Once a trial begins, the job of the prosecutor is to vigorously present the state's case against the defendant. Prosecutors introduce evidence against the accused, steer the testimony of witnesses "for the people," and argue in favor of conviction. Because defendants are presumed innocent until proven guilty, the burden of demonstrating guilt beyond a reasonable doubt rests with the prosecutor.

▲ A reporter shouting questions at Durham County (North Carolina) District Attorney Mike Nifong (right) after a community forum to discuss rape allegations that had been made against three members of the Duke University lacrosse team in 2006. Nifong would not abandon his quest to prosecute the men even when the accuser was discredited and DNA evidence seemed to show definitively that the men were innocent. He was disbarred following a 2007 ethics hearing by the North Carolina State Bar Association. How did Nifong's actions demonstrate the power wielded by local prosecutors throughout the United States?
Gerry Broome/AP Wide World Photos

Prosecutorial Discretion

In May 2007, North Carolina Attorney General Roy A. Cooper dismissed rape charges that had been brought against three former members of the Duke University lacrosse team, saying that the players were innocent of all charges. Those charges had been brought by Durham County Prosecutor Michael B. Nifong after an exotic dancer who had performed at a house party in 2006 told police that she had been raped, sodomized, strangled, and beaten by the partygoers. Contradictions in the accuser's statements, however, along with a lack of DNA and other evidence, convinced Cooper that the attack had never occurred. Cooper told CBS's *60 Minutes* that Nifong should have seen the contradictions himself. Calling Nifong "a rogue prosecutor," Cooper said that "when you have a prosecutor who takes advantage of his enormous power and overreaches like this, then yes, it's offensive."[15] Cooper added that other prosecutors "were offended by a prosecutor who didn't take the time to make sure that he had all of the facts straight before leveling charges." A day later, Nifong apologized to the students, saying "to the extent that I made judgments that ultimately proved to be incorrect, I apologize to the three students that were wrongly accused." He added, "I also understand that when someone has been wrongly accused, the harm caused by the accusations might not be immediately undone merely by dismissing them. It is my sincere desire that the actions of Attorney General Cooper will serve to remedy any remaining injury that has resulted from these cases."[16] Calls for further action against Nifong led to his being disbarred in 2007 following an ethics hearing by the North Carolina Bar Association. He was later found guilty of criminal contempt of court and spent one day in jail.

The "Duke rape case," as it came to be known in the media, highlights the fact that American prosecutors occupy a unique position in the nation's criminal justice system by virtue of the considerable **prosecutorial discretion** they exercise. As U.S. Supreme Court Justice Robert H. Jackson noted in 1940, "The prosecutor has more control over life, liberty, and reputation than any other person in America."[17] Before a case comes to trial, the prosecutor may decide to accept a plea bargain, divert the suspect to a public or private social services agency, ask the suspect to seek counseling, or dismiss the case entirely for lack of evidence or for a variety of other reasons. Studies have found that the prosecution dismisses from one-third to one-half of all felony cases before trial or before a plea bargain is made.[18] Prosecutors also play a significant role before grand juries because states that use the grand jury system depend on prosecutors to bring evidence before the grand jury and to be effective in seeing indictments returned against suspects.

prosecutorial discretion
The decision-making power of prosecutors, based on the wide range of choices available to them, in the handling of criminal defendants, the scheduling of cases for trial, the acceptance of negotiated pleas, and so on. The most important form of prosecutorial discretion lies in the power to charge, or not to charge, a person with an offense.

In preparation for trial, the prosecutor decides what charges are to be brought against the defendant, examines the strength of the incriminating evidence, and decides which witnesses to call. Two important U.S. Supreme Court decisions have held that it is the duty of prosecutors to, in effect, assist the defense in building its case by making available any evidence in their possession. In the first case, *Brady* v. *Maryland* (1963),[19] the Court held that the prosecution is required to disclose to the defense evidence that directly relates to claims of either guilt or innocence. The second and more recent case is that of *U.S.* v. *Bagley*,[20] decided in 1985. In *Bagley*, the Court ruled that the prosecution must disclose any evidence that the defense requests. The Court reasoned that to withhold evidence, even when it does not relate directly to issues of guilt or innocence, may mislead the defense into thinking that such evidence does not exist.

In 2004, in a decision predicated upon *Brady*, the U.S. Supreme Court intervened to stop the execution of 45-year-old Texan Delma Banks ten minutes before it was scheduled to begin. The Court found that prosecutors had withheld vital **exculpatory evidence**, or information that might have cleared Banks of blame, during his trial for the 1980 shooting death of a 16-year-old boy. The Court said that "a rule declaring 'prosecutor may hide, defendant must seek,' is not tenable in a system constitutionally bound to accord defendants due process."[21] Banks had spent 24 years on death row.

exculpatory evidence
Any information having a tendency to clear a person of guilt or blame.

One special decision that the prosecutor makes concerns the filing of separate or multiple charges. The decision to try a defendant simultaneously on multiple charges allows for the presentation of a considerable amount of evidence and permits an in-court demonstration of a complete sequence of criminal events. This strategy has an additional practical advantage: It saves time and money by substituting one trial for what might otherwise be a number of trials if each charge were to be brought separately before the court. From the prosecutor's point of view, however, trying the charges one at a time carries the advantage of allowing for another trial on a new charge if a "not guilty" verdict is returned.

The activities of the prosecutor do not end with a finding of guilt or innocence. Following conviction, prosecutors are usually allowed to make sentencing recommendations to the judge. They can be expected to argue that aggravating factors (discussed in Chapter 9), prior criminal record, or especially heinous qualities of the offense in question call for strict punishment. When a convicted defendant appeals, prosecutors may need to defend their own actions and to argue, in briefs filed with appellate courts, that the conviction was properly obtained. Most jurisdictions also allow prosecutors to make recommendations when defendants they have convicted are being considered for parole or for early release from prison.

Until relatively recently, it had generally been held that prosecutors enjoyed much the same kind of immunity against liability in the exercise of their official duties that judges do. The 1976 U.S. Supreme Court case of *Imbler* v. *Pachtman*[22] provided the basis for such thinking with its ruling that "state prosecutors are absolutely immune from liability . . . for their conduct in initiating a prosecution and in presenting the State's case." However, in the 1991 case of *Burns* v. *Reed*,[23] the Court held that "[a] state prosecuting attorney is absolutely immune from liability for damages . . . for participating in a probable cause hearing, but not for giving legal advice to the police." The *Burns* case involved Cathy Burns of Muncie, Indiana, who allegedly shot her sleeping sons while laboring under a multiple personality disorder. To explore the possibility of multiple personality further, the police asked the prosecuting attorney if it would be appropriate for them to hypnotize the defendant. The prosecutor agreed that hypnosis would be a permissible avenue for investigation, and the suspect confessed to the murders while hypnotized. She later alleged in her complaint to the Supreme Court "that [the prosecuting attorney] knew or should have known that hypnotically induced testimony was inadmissible" at trial.[24]

The Abuse of Discretion

Because prosecutors have so much discretion in their decision making, there is considerable potential for abuse. Many types of discretionary decisions are always inappropriate: accepting guilty pleas to drastically reduced charges in exchange for personal considerations, deciding not to prosecute friends or political cronies, and overzealously prosecuting a case to seek heightened visibility to support political ambitions.

Administrative decisions such as case scheduling, which can wreak havoc with the personal lives of defendants and the professional lives of defense attorneys, can also be used by prosecutors to harass defendants into pleading guilty. Some forms of abuse may be unconscious. At least one study suggests that some prosecutors have an inherent tendency toward leniency where female defendants are concerned and tend to discriminate against minorities when deciding whether to prosecute.[25]

Class Activity Invite a prosecutor and a defense attorney to speak with the class. Ask them to describe their respective roles and to comment on what they believe are the pros and cons of the adversarial process in criminal trials.

Although the electorate is the final authority to which prosecutors must answer, gross misconduct by prosecutors may be addressed by the state supreme court or by the state attorney general's office. Short of addressing *criminal* misconduct, however, most of the options available to the court and to the attorney general are limited.

The Prosecutor's Professional Responsibility

As members of the legal profession, prosecutors are expected to abide by various standards of professional responsibility, such as those found in the ABA *Model Rules of Professional Conduct*. Most state bar associations have adopted their own versions of the ABA rules and expect their members to respect those standards. Serious violations of the rules may result in a prosecutor's being disbarred from the practice of law. Official ABA commentary on Rule 3.8, Special Responsibilities of the Prosecutor, says that "a prosecutor has the responsibility of a minister of justice and not simply that of an advocate; the prosecutor's duty is to seek justice, not merely to convict. This responsibility carries with it specific obligations to see that the defendant is accorded procedural justice and that guilt is decided upon the basis of sufficient evidence."[26] Hence prosecutors are barred by the standards of the legal profession from advocating any fact or position that they know is untrue.

Prosecutors have a voice in influencing public policy affecting the safety of America's communities through the National District Attorneys Association (NDAA). Visit the NDAA at **Web Extra 8–4**.

From the moment you walk into the courtroom, you are the defendant's only friend.

—Michael E. Tigar, Austin defense attorney

The Defense Counsel

defense counsel
A licensed trial lawyer, hired or appointed to conduct the legal defense of a person accused of a crime and to represent him or her before a court of law.

The **defense counsel** is a trained lawyer who may specialize in the practice of criminal law. The defense counsel's task is to represent the accused as soon as possible after arrest and to ensure that the defendant's civil rights are not violated during processing by the criminal justice system. Other duties of the defense counsel include testing the strength of the prosecution's case, taking part in plea negotiations, and preparing an adequate defense to be used at trial. In the preparation of a defense, criminal lawyers may enlist private detectives, experts, witnesses to the crime, and character witnesses. Some lawyers perform aspects of the role of private detective or investigator themselves. Defense attorneys also review relevant court precedents to identify the best defense strategy.

Defense preparation often entails conversations between lawyer and defendant. Such discussions are recognized as privileged communications protected under the umbrella of attorney-client confidentiality; in other words, lawyers cannot be compelled to reveal information that their clients have confided to them.[27]

Lecture Note List the three major categories of criminal defense attorneys: private attorneys, court-appointed counsel, and public defenders.

If the defendant is found guilty, the defense attorney will be involved in arguments at sentencing, may be asked to file an appeal, and will probably counsel the defendant and the defendant's family about any civil matters (payment of debts, release from contractual obligations, and so on) that must be arranged after sentence is imposed. Hence the work of the defense attorney encompasses many roles, including attorney, negotiator, investigator, confidant, family and personal counselor, social worker, and even bill collector.

Three major categories of defense attorneys assist criminal defendants in the United States: (1) private attorneys, usually referred to as *criminal lawyers* or *retained counsel*; (2) court-appointed counsel; and (3) public defenders.

Private Attorneys

Lecture Note Explain that as a result of the Supreme Court decision in *Gideon* v. *Wainwright* (1963), criminal defendants are now entitled to have a lawyer to represent them in court. Ask what impact the *Gideon* decision probably had on the legal profession in this country.

Private attorneys either have their own legal practices or work for law firms in which they are partners or employees. As those who have had to hire a defense attorney know, the fees of private attorneys can be high. Most privately retained criminal lawyers charge in the range of $100 to $200 per hour, and included in their bill is the time it takes to prepare for a case as well as time spent in the courtroom. High-powered criminal defense attorneys who have a reputation for successfully defending their clients can be far more expensive: Fees charged by famous criminal defense attorneys can run into the hundreds of thousands of dollars—and sometimes exceed $1 million—for handling just one case!

Few law students actually choose to specialize in criminal law, even though the job of a criminal lawyer may appear glamorous. Those who do specialize often begin their careers immediately following law school, while others seek to gain experience working as assistant district attorneys or assistant public defenders for a number of years before going into private practice. Visit the National Association of Criminal Defense Lawyers (NACDL) at **Web Extra 8–5** and the Association of Federal Defense Attorneys (AFDA) at **Web Extra 8–6** to learn more about the practice of criminal law.

Court-Appointed Counsel

The Sixth Amendment to the U.S. Constitution guarantees criminal defendants the effective assistance of counsel. A series of U.S. Supreme Court decisions has established that defendants who are unable to pay for private criminal defense attorneys will receive adequate representation at all stages of criminal justice processing. In *Powell* v. *Alabama* (1932),[28] the Court held that the Fourteenth Amendment requires state courts to appoint counsel for defendants in capital cases who are unable to afford their own. In 1938, in *Johnson* v. *Zerbst*,[29] the Court overturned the conviction of an indigent federal inmate, holding that his Sixth Amendment due process right to counsel had been violated. The Court declared, "If the accused . . . is not represented by counsel and has not competently and intelligently waived his constitutional right, the Sixth Amendment stands as a jurisdictional bar to a valid conviction and sentence depriving him of his life or his liberty." The decision established the right of indigent defendants to receive the assistance of appointed counsel in all criminal proceedings in federal courts. The 1963 case of *Gideon* v. *Wainwright*[30] extended the right to appointed counsel to all indigent defendants charged with a felony in state courts. In *Argersinger* v. *Hamlin* (1972),[31] the Court required adequate legal representation for anyone facing a potential sentence of imprisonment. Juveniles charged with delinquent acts were granted the right to appointed counsel in the case of *In re Gault* (1967).[32] In *Alabama* v. *Shelton* (2002),[33] a closely divided Court expanded the Sixth Amendment right to counsel, ruling that defendants in state courts who are facing relatively minor charges must be provided with an attorney at government expense even when they face only the slightest chance of incarceration.

States have responded to the federal mandate for indigent defense in a number of ways. Most now use one of three systems to deliver legal services to criminal defendants who are unable to afford their own: (1) assigned counsel, (2) public defenders, and (3) contractual arrangements. Most such systems are administered at the county level, although funding arrangements may involve state, county, and municipal monies, as well as federal grants and court fees.

Assigned Counsel

Assigned counsel, also known as court-appointed defense attorneys, are usually drawn from a roster of all practicing criminal attorneys within the jurisdiction of the trial court. Their fees are paid at a rate set by the state or local government. These fees are typically low, however, and may affect the amount of effort an assigned attorney puts into a case. In 2010, for example, New York's court-appointed attorneys were paid only $60 per hour for representing misdemeanants and $75 per hour for in-court representation of charged felons. Out-of-court preparation time was reimbursed at around $25 per hour—a rate of pay that is ten to 20 times less than what attorneys normally earn.[34]

Public Defenders

A **public defender** is a state-employed lawyer defending indigent defendants. A public defender program relies on full-time salaried staff, including defense attorneys, defense investigators, and office personnel. Defense investigators gather information in support of the defense effort and may interview friends, family members, and employers of the accused, with an eye toward effective defense.

public defender
An attorney employed by a government agency or subagency, or by a private organization under contract to a government body, for the purpose of providing defense services to indigents, or an attorney who has volunteered such service.

Two 2010 Bureau of Justice Statistics (BJS) reports found that a public defender system is the primary method used to provide indigent counsel for criminal defendants in the United States.[35] According to BJS, approximately 1,000 public defender offices in 49 states and the District of Columbia received nearly 5.6 million cases and employed over 15,000 litigating attorneys in 2007. County-based public defender offices, a system used by 28 states, received more than 4 million indigent defense cases in 2007, accounting for nearly three-quarters of the public defender cases received nationwide. Those offices employed about 10,700 litigating attorneys. Additionally, state-based public defender programs, used in the other 22 states, employed 4,300 litigating attorneys to handle the 1.5 million indigent defense cases that they received in 2007.

The BJS survey found that the majority of both state- and county-based public defender offices employed substantially fewer than the needed number of support staff, such as paralegals, investigators, indigency screeners, and clerical staff. Surveyors determined that the median entry-level salary for assistant public defenders ranged from $42,000 to $45,000 in county-based public defender offices and from $46,000 to $58,000 in state-based programs.

Critics charge that public defenders, because they are government employees, are not sufficiently independent from prosecutors and judges. For the same reason, clients may be suspicious of public defenders, viewing them as state functionaries. Finally, the huge caseloads typical of public defenders' offices create pressure toward an excessive use of plea bargaining.

Career Profile
Attorney and Instructor of Criminal Justice

Name: Maria A. Daniel

Position: Assistant Professor of Justice, Community College of Philadelphia

Community College of Philadelphia

Colleges attended: Spelman College (BS, Computer Science), Rutgers University School of Law (JD)

What criminal justice-related jobs have you held and when? 2000–2005: Assistant defender (public defender) for the Defender Association of Philadelphia, Pennsylvania (criminal defense). 1999–2000: Staff attorney at Mattleman, Weinroth and Miller in Cherry Hill, New Jersey (general practice, family, civil, prepaid legal services). 1998–1999: Law clerk for the Honorable Genece E. Brinkley, Court of Common Pleas in the Commonwealth of Pennsylvania (criminal and civil rotations)

What position did you like most? Assistant defender for the Defender Association of Philadelphia.

What qualities or characteristics most helped you succeed in the field? Passionate advocacy, meticulous preparation, keen knowledge of the law, persuasive writing skills, thinking outside of the box, personal character, determination, and professionalism.

What are the typical salary ranges students can expect entering these fields? $45,000 to $65,000.

What advice would you give students early in their college career to help them find a rewarding job in criminal justice? Discover what area you are passionate about. Locate criminal justice professionals who are in that particular area. Interview them and shadow them for a day. Volunteer your services or otherwise obtain an opportunity to get firsthand experience in this field. Secure a mentor who can guide your educational and career choices. Observe a criminal trial. See how your field of choice affects the criminal trial process.

Source: Reprinted with permission of Maria A. Daniel, Esquire, attorney and professor of criminal justice. Photo courtesy of Maria A. Daniel. Logo courtesy of Community College of Philadelphia.

Contractual Arrangements

Through a third type of indigent defense, contract attorney programs, county and state officials arrange with local criminal lawyers to provide for indigent defense on a contractual basis. Individual attorneys, local bar associations, and multipartner law firms may all be tapped to provide services. Contract defense programs are the least widely used form of indigent defense at present, although their popularity is growing.

Problems with Indigent Defense

Critics of the current system of indigent defense point out that the system is woefully underfunded. Findings from the most recent National Survey of Indigent Defense Systems were published in 2001.[36] In 2000, the report of the National Symposium on Indigent Defense proclaimed, "Indigent defense today, in terms of funding, caseloads, and quality, is in a chronic state of crisis."[37] Some question the quality of services available through public defender systems due to the fact that entry-level public defenders are paid poorly in comparison to what new attorneys entering private law firms might earn.

As a consequence of limited funding, many public defender offices employ what critics call a "plead 'em and speed 'em through" strategy, often involving a heavy use of plea bargaining and initial meetings with clients in courtrooms as trials are about to begin. Mary Broderick of the National Legal Aid and Defender Association says, "We aren't being given the same weapons. . . . It's like trying to deal with smart bombs when all you've got is a couple of cap pistols."[38] Proposed enhancements to indigent defense systems are offered by the National Legal Aid and Defender Association (NLADA). You can visit the NLADA at **Web Extra 8–7**.

The full text of presentations and speeches made at the 2010 National Symposium on Indigent Defense is available at **Library Extra 8–1**; a BJS overview of the National Survey of Indigent Defense Systems can be found at **Library Extra 8–2**. **Library Extra 8–3** provides an overview of state-funded indigent defense services, and **Library Extra 8–4** provides the full text of a recent American Bar Association review of the state of indigent defense in America.

Although state indigent defense services are sometimes woefully underfunded, the same is not true of the federal system. The defense of indigent Oklahoma City bomber Timothy McVeigh, for example, cost taxpayers an estimated $13.8 million—which doesn't include the cost of his appeal or execution. McVeigh's expenses included $6.7 million for attorneys,

$2 million for investigators, $3 million for expert witnesses, and approximately $1.4 million for office rent and secretarial assistance.[39]

In 2000, the BJS reported data on publicly financed counsel nationwide in two research reports that appear to conflict with the conclusions reached by the National Survey of Indigent Defense Systems.[40] BJS statisticians found that court-appointed defense attorneys represent 66% of federal felony defendants, as well as 82% of felony defendants in the nation's 75 most populous counties. The study also found that conviction rates for indigent defendants and those with their own lawyers were about the same in both federal and state courts. About 90% of the federal defendants and 75% of defendants in the most populous counties were found guilty regardless of the type of attorney they had. However, the study showed that those found guilty and represented by publicly financed attorneys were incarcerated at a higher rate than those defendants who paid for their own legal representation—88% compared to 77% in federal courts and 71% compared to 54% in the most populous counties. On average, however, prison sentences for defendants with publicly financed attorneys were shorter than were those with hired counsel. In federal district court, convicted defendants who had publicly financed attorneys were sentenced to less than five years on average and those with private attorneys to just over five years. In large counties, those with publicly financed attorneys were sentenced to an average of two and a half years, while those with private attorneys were sentenced to three years.

Lecture Note Describe the ethical concerns of the defense lawyer by referring to the "Ethics and Professionalism" box in this chapter, which highlights the ABA's *Model Rules of Professional Conduct*. Ask students how the adversarial model (and the win-lose scenario) creates temptations for defense attorneys to violate these standards.

Of course, defendants need not accept any assigned counsel. Defendants may waive their right to an attorney and undertake their own defense—a right held to be inherent in the Sixth Amendment to the U.S. Constitution by the U.S. Supreme Court in the 1975 case of *Faretta* v. *California*.[41] Self-representation is uncommon, however, and only 1% of federal inmates and 3% of state inmates report having represented themselves.[42] Some famous instances of self-representation can be found in the 1995 trial of Long Island Rail Road commuter train shooter Colin Ferguson, the 1999 trial of Dr. Jack Kevorkian, and the 2002 federal competency hearings of Zacarias Moussaoui.

Defendants who are not pleased with the lawyer appointed to defend them are in a somewhat different situation. They may request, through the court, that a new lawyer be assigned to represent them, as Timothy McVeigh did following his conviction and death sentence in the Oklahoma City bombing case. However, unless there is clear reason for reassignment, such as an obvious personality conflict between defendant and attorney, few judges are likely to honor a request of this sort. Short of obvious difficulties, most judges will trust in the professionalism of appointed counsel.

State-supported indigent defense systems may also be called on to provide representation for clients upon appeal. An attorney who is appointed to represent an indigent defendant on appeal, however, may conclude that an appeal would be frivolous. If so, he or she may request that the appellate court allow him or her to withdraw from the case or that the court dispose of the case without requiring the attorney to file a brief arguing the merits of the appeal. In 1967, in the case of *Anders* v. *California*,[43] the U.S. Supreme Court found that to protect a defendant's constitutional right to appellate counsel, appellate courts must safeguard against the risk of accepting an attorney's negative assessment of a case where an appeal is not actually frivolous. The Court also found California's existing procedure for evaluating such requests to be inadequate, and the justices set forth an acceptable procedure. In 1979, in the case of *People* v. *Wende*,[44] the state of California adopted a new standardized procedure that, although not the same as that put forth in *Anders*, was designed to protect the right of a criminal defendant to appeal.

▲ Defense attorney Lynne Stewart, who was sentenced to prison in 2006 for smuggling messages from her jailed client, the radical Egyptian sheik Omar Abdel-Rahman (also known as "the Blind Sheik"), to his terrorist followers outside of prison. Our adversarial system requires that attorneys sometimes defend unpopular clients, but the defense role is carefully prescribed by ethical and procedural standards. How did Stewart's actions violate those standards?
Stephen Chernin/AP Wide World Photos

The *Wende* standard was put to the test in the 2000 case of *Smith* v. *Robbins*.[45] In that case, the U.S. Supreme Court held that the *Anders* procedure is only one method of satisfying the Constitution's requirements for indigent criminal appeals and that the states are free to adopt different procedures as long as those procedures adequately safeguard a defendant's right to appellate counsel.

Finally, in 2001, in the case of *Texas* v. *Cobb*,[46] the Court ruled that the Sixth Amendment right to counsel is "offense specific." It applies only to the offense with which a defendant is charged and not to other offenses, even if they are factually related to the charged offense.

CJ News
Public Defenders Reject New Cases

Public defenders are being hit so hard by budget cuts and growing caseloads that offices in several states are refusing to take on more cases because they say defendants' rights are being hurt. Other jurisdictions say they may follow suit.

The U.S. Supreme Court has ruled that poor people charged with a crime have a right to a lawyer. In most states, taxpayers fund a public defender's office that handles cases of people who cannot afford a private attorney. The American Bar Association cites studies saying a public defender can competently handle 150 to 200 cases a year.

The growing caseloads could force states to spend more money on public defenders, delay trials or lead to overturned convictions because of inadequate counsel.

"Many public defenders are feeling the squeeze at this point," says Maureen Dimino of the National Association of Criminal Defense Lawyers. She has heard from public defenders in more than a half-dozen states who are considering challenging their growing caseloads in court.

Miami-Dade County Public Defender Bennett Brummer sued Florida in June after the Legislature cut his budget 9%. He said his lawyers, who each handle an average of 436 cases a year, could not take any new clients charged with felonies without being in danger of committing malpractice.

A Miami judge ruled . . . that . . . Brummer can send his least serious felony cases to the state, which will have to provide attorneys or pay for private lawyers for poor defendants.

The ruling, which affects thousands of felonies, "will have statewide and some nationwide impact," Brummer says. "Many defenders would like to take meaningful steps to alleviate their caseloads."

Attorneys for the Miami-Dade County State Attorney's Office are appealing, saying Brummer is exaggerating the caseload. The public defenders are compromising victims' rights by withdrawing, spokesman Ed Griffith says. If a defendant does not get a trial within a set amount of time, a judge is obligated to set the defendant free "to the detriment of all the citizens," he says.

Other state public defender's offices taking action:

- Kentucky's former public advocate Ernie Lewis, who retired last month, has asked a judge to declare his office underfunded so it can refuse misdemeanor cases.

▲ Arthur J. Jones (*right*), who quit his job as a public defender in Miami because of low pay and a huge workload. Jones was afraid that his huge client load could lead to mistakes. How might an effective public defender system be funded?
*Oscar Hidalgo/*The New York Times*/Redux Pictures*

Lewis says his attorneys' caseloads could top 500 each this year because budget cuts forced him to keep nearly 100 positions open. "It's very clear to me that our caseload would be unethical," he says.

- The Missouri public defender's office last month notified courts in two jurisdictions that public defenders will reject new cases there. In Ava and Jefferson City, public defenders exceeded the maximum caseload per attorney set by a new state rule. The public defender's office is negotiating the least disruptive way to lessen the caseloads.

"Our lawyers have an ethical responsibility to not take on more cases than they can handle," says Cathy Kelly, deputy director for the Missouri State Public Defenders System. "We just feel like we have reached the point where we have to say no."

Source: Donna Leinwand, "Public Defenders Reject New Cases," *USA Today*, September 10, 2008. Reprinted with permission.

The Ethics of Defense

The job of defense counsel, as we have already mentioned, is to prepare and offer a vigorous defense on behalf of the accused at trial and to appeal cases with merit. A proper defense at trial often involves the presentation of evidence and the examination of witnesses, both of which require careful thought and planning. Good attorneys may become emotionally committed to the outcomes of trials in which they are involved. Some lawyers, however, cross the line when they lose their professional objectivity and embrace the wider cause of their clients. That's what happened to Lynne Stewart, who was convicted in 2005 of smuggling messages from her jailed client, the radical Egyptian sheik Omar Abdel-Rahman ("the Blind Sheik"), to his terrorist followers outside of prison.[47] Abdel-Rahman is serving life behind bars for his role in an unsuccessful 1993 plot to bomb New York City landmarks. Stewart, a 1960s-era radical, has often chosen to represent the most contemptible clients, believing that justice requires that everyone receive a vigorous defense. She was arrested, however, after she issued a public statement on behalf of the sheik expressing her client's withdrawal of support for a cease-fire involving his supporters in Egypt. Stewart had known in advance that making the statement violated an order to restrict the sheik's communications, but she later testified that she

Ethics and Professionalism

The American Bar Association's *Model Rules of Professional Conduct*

To help attorneys understand what is expected of them, the ABA has provided significant guidance in the areas of legal ethics and professional responsibility. The ABA has developed professional standards intended to serve as models for state bar associations and to guide legislative bodies focused on ensuring ethical behavior among attorneys.

The ABA's first major foray into the area of ethical guidelines resulted in the adoption of its original *Canons of Professional Ethics* on August 27, 1908. In 1913, in an effort to keep the association informed about state and local bar activities concerning professional ethics, the ABA established its Standing Committee on Professional Ethics. The name of the group was changed to the Committee on Ethics and Professional Responsibility in 1971, and the committee continues to function under that name today.

In 1969, the ABA formally adopted the committee's *Model Code of Professional Responsibility*. Eventually, the majority of state and federal jurisdictions adopted their own versions of the Model Code.

In 1977, the ABA Commission on Evaluation of Professional Standards was created and charged with rethinking the ethical problems of the legal profession. During the next six years, the commission drafted the *Model Rules of Professional Conduct*, which the ABA adopted on August 2, 1983. The *Model Rules* effectively supplanted the *Model Code of Professional Responsibility*, and today most state and federal jurisdictions have adapted the *Model Rules* to their own particular circumstances.

The *Model Rules* have been periodically amended—most significantly in 2002—but continue to provide the touchstone ethical standards of the American legal profession today. Visit the ABA on the Internet at **Web Extra 8–8**, and learn about its Center for Professional Responsibility at **Web Extra 8–9**.

THINKING ABOUT ETHICS

1. ***Should a defense attorney represent a client whom he or she knows to be guilty?***
2. ***Would it be unethical for an attorney to refuse to represent such a client? Why or why not?***

Reference: American Bar Association, *Model Rules of Professional Conduct—Preface* http://www.abanet.org/cpr/mrpc/preface.html (accessed July 10, 2010).

believed that violence is sometimes necessary to achieve justice. Other evidence showed that she had facilitated forbidden communications between Rahman and a translator by using prearranged cues such as tapping on a table, shaking a water bottle, and uttering key phrases like "chocolate" and "heart attack" during prison visits. In 2006 she was sentenced to serve 28 months in prison. She entered prison in 2009 after exhausting the appeals process.

The nature of the adversarial process, fed by the emotions of the participants combined with the often privileged and extensive knowledge that defense attorneys have about their cases, is enough to tempt the professional ethics of some counselors. Because the defense counsel may often know more about the guilt or innocence of the defendant than anyone else prior to trial, the defense role is carefully prescribed by ethical and procedural considerations. Attorneys violate both law and the standards of their profession if they knowingly misrepresent themselves or their clients. As Michael Ratner, president of the Center for Constitutional Rights, put it when commenting on the Stewart case, "Lawyers need to be advocates, but they don't need to be accomplices."[48]

To help attorneys understand what is expected of them and what the appropriate limits of a vigorous defense might be, the ABA provides significant guidance in the areas of legal ethics and professional responsibility, as the Ethics and Professionalism box in this section explains. Even so, some attorney-client interactions remain especially tricky. Defense attorneys, for example, are under no obligation to reveal information obtained from a client without the client's permission. However, all states permit defense lawyers to violate a client's confidentiality without fear of reprisal if they reasonably believe that doing so could prevent serious injury or death to another person. In 2004, with passage of a new evidence law broadening the state's evidence code, California joined the other 49 states in freeing attorneys to violate client confidentiality in such cases. California law makes disclosure discretionary, not mandatory. Kevin Mohr, a professor at Western State University College of Law in Fullerton, California, noted that the new law provides the first exception to the attorney-client privilege in California in more than 130 years. "A lawyer can now take action and intervene and prevent [a] criminal act from occurring," said Mohr.[49]

> Society asks much of the criminal court. The court is expected to meet society's demand that serious offenders be convicted and punished, and at the same time it is expected to insure that the innocent and unfortunate are not oppressed.
>
> —President's Commission on Law Enforcement and Administration of Justice[i]

Somewhat earlier, the 1986 U.S. Supreme Court case of *Nix* v. *Whiteside*[50] clarified the duty of lawyers to reveal known instances of client perjury. In that case, the Court held that a lawyer's duty to a client "is limited to legitimate, lawful conduct compatible with the very nature of a trial as a search for truth. . . . Counsel is precluded from taking steps or in any way assisting the client in presenting false evidence or otherwise violating the law."[51]

The Bailiff

bailiff
The court officer whose duties are to keep order in the courtroom, to secure witnesses, and to maintain physical custody of the jury.

The **bailiff**, another member of the professional courtroom work group, is usually an armed law enforcement officer. The job of the bailiff, also called a *court officer*, is to ensure order in the courtroom, to announce the judge's entry into the courtroom, to call witnesses, and to prevent the escape of the accused (if the accused has not been released on bond). The bailiff also supervises the jury when it is sequestered and controls public and media access to jury members. Bailiffs in federal courtrooms are deputy U.S. marshals.

The Trial Court Administrator

Many states now employ trial court administrators whose job is to facilitate the smooth functioning of courts in particular judicial districts or areas. A major impetus toward the hiring of local trial court administrators came from the 1967 President's Commission on Law Enforcement and Administration of Justice. Examining state courts, the report found "a system that treats defendants who are charged with minor offenses with less dignity and consideration than it treats those who are charged with serious crimes."[52] A few years later, the National Advisory Commission on Criminal Justice Standards and Goals recommended that all courts with five or more judges create the position of trial court administrator.[53]

Court administrators provide uniform court management, assuming many of the duties previously performed by chief judges, prosecutors, and court clerks. Where trial court administrators operate, the ultimate authority for running the court still rests with the chief judge. Administrators, however, are able to relieve the judge of many routine and repetitive tasks, such as record keeping, scheduling, case-flow analysis, personnel administration, space utilization, facilities planning, and budget management. They may also take the minutes at meetings of judges and their committees.

Juror management is another area in which trial court administrators are becoming increasingly involved. Juror utilization studies can identify problems such as the overselection of citizens for the jury pool and the reasons for excessive requests to be excused from jury service. They can also suggest ways to reduce the time jurors waste waiting to be called or impaneled.

Effective trial court administrators are able to track lengthy cases and identify bottlenecks in court processing. They then suggest strategies to make the administration of justice more efficient for courtroom professionals and more humane for lay participants.

The Court Reporter

The role of the court reporter (also called the *court stenographer* or *court recorder*) is to create a record of all that occurs during a trial. Accurate records are very important in criminal trial courts because appeals may be based entirely on what went on in the courtroom. Especially significant are all verbal comments made in the courtroom, including testimonies, objections, judge's rulings, judge's instructions to the jury, arguments made by lawyers, and results of conferences between the lawyers and the judge. Occasionally, the judge will rule that a statement should be "stricken from the record" because it is inappropriate or unfounded. The official trial record, often taken on a stenotype machine or an audio recorder, may later be transcribed in manuscript form and will become the basis for any appellate review of the trial.

Today's court reporters often employ computer-aided transcription (CAT) software, which translates typed stenographic shorthand into complete and readable transcripts. Court reporters may be members of the National Court Reporters Association, the United States Court Reporters Association, or the Association of Legal Administrators—all of which support the activities of these professionals. You can visit the National Court Reporters Association at **Web Extra 8–10**.

The Clerk of Court

The duties of the clerk of court (sometimes also known as the *county clerk*) extend beyond the courtroom. The clerk maintains all records of criminal cases, including all pleas and motions made both before and after the actual trial. The clerk also prepares a jury pool, issues jury summonses, and subpoenas witnesses for both the prosecution and the defense. During the trial, the clerk (or an assistant) marks physical evidence for identification as instructed by the judge and maintains custody of that evidence. The clerk also swears in witnesses and performs other functions as the judge directs. Some states allow the clerk limited judicial duties, such as the power to issue warrants, to handle certain matters relating to individuals declared mentally incompetent,[54] and to serve as a judge of probate to oversee wills and the administration of estates.

▲ An expert witness testifying in court. Expert witnesses may express opinions and draw conclusions in their area of expertise; they need not limit their testimony to facts alone. Why are expert witnesses permitted such leeway?
Corbis RF

Expert Witnesses

Most of the courtroom "insiders" we've talked about so far either are employees of the state or have ongoing professional relationships with the court (as in the case of defense counsel). Expert witnesses, however, may not have that kind of status, although some do. **Expert witnesses** are recognized as having specialized skills and knowledge in an established profession or technical area. They must demonstrate their expertise through education, work experience, publications, and awards. Their testimony at trial provides an effective way of introducing scientific evidence in such areas as medicine, psychology, ballistics, crime-scene analysis, and photography. Unlike lay witnesses, they are allowed to express opinions and to draw conclusions, but only within their particular area of expertise. Expert witnesses, like the other courtroom actors described in this chapter, are generally paid professionals and (like all other witnesses) are subject to cross-examination.

One difficulty with expert testimony is that it can be confusing to the jury. Sometimes the trouble is due to the nature of the subject matter and sometimes to disagreements between the experts themselves. Often, however, it arises from the strict interpretation given to expert testimony by procedural requirements. The difference between medical and legal definitions of insanity, for example, points to a divergence in both history and purpose between the law and medical science. Courts that attempt to apply criteria like the M'Naghten rule (discussed in Chapter 3) in deciding claims of "insanity" are often faced with the testimony of psychiatric experts who refuse even to recognize the word. Such experts may prefer, instead, to speak in terms of *psychosis* and *neurosis*, words that have no place in legal jargon. Because of the uncertainties they create, legal requirements may pit experts against one another and may confound the jury.

Even so, most authorities agree that expert testimony is usually viewed by jurors as more trustworthy than other forms of evidence. In a study of scientific evidence, one prosecutor commented that if he had to choose between presenting a fingerprint or an eyewitness at trial, he would always go with the fingerprint.[55] As a consequence of the effectiveness of scientific evidence, the National Institute of Justice recommends that "prosecutors consider the potential utility of such information in all cases where such evidence is available."[56]

expert witness
A person who has special knowledge and skills recognized by the court as relevant to the determination of guilt or innocence. Unlike lay witnesses, expert witnesses may express opinions or draw conclusions in their testimony.

Lecture Note Describe an expert witness as someone who is recognized as having special knowledge and skills in an area of concern to the court. Explain that expert witnesses, unlike lay witnesses, may express opinions and draw conclusions in their areas of expertise.

Lecture Note Explain that lay witnesses may testify only about things they know from personal experience to be true.

Outsiders: Nonprofessional Courtroom Participants

Defendants, victims, jurors, and most witnesses are usually unwilling or inadvertent participants in criminal trials. Although they are outsiders who lack the status of paid professional participants, these are precisely the people who provide the grist for the judicial mill. The press, a willing player in many criminal trials, makes up another group of outsiders. Let's look now at each of these courtroom actors.

2 Identify and explain the roles of nonprofessional or nonjudicial courtroom participants.

Lay Witnesses

Nonexpert witnesses, also known as **lay witnesses**, may be called to testify by either the prosecution or the defense. Lay witnesses may be eyewitnesses who saw the crime being committed or who came upon the crime scene shortly after the crime had occurred. Another

lay witness
An eyewitness, character witness, or other person called on to testify who is not considered an expert. Lay witnesses must testify to facts only and may not draw conclusions or express opinions.

▲ A lay witness being sworn in before testifying in a criminal trial. Nonexpert witnesses must generally limit their testimony to facts about which they have direct knowledge. Why are such limits imposed?
© Royalty-Free/CORBIS

type of lay witness is the character witness, who frequently provides information about the personality, family life, business acumen, and so on of the defendant in an effort to show that this is not the kind of person who would commit the crime with which he or she is charged. Of course, the victim may also be a witness, providing detailed and sometimes lengthy testimony about the defendant and the crime.

A written document called a **subpoena** officially notifies witnesses that they are to appear in court to testify. Subpoenas are generally served by an officer of the court or by a police officer, though they are sometimes mailed. Both sides in a criminal case may subpoena witnesses and might ask that individuals called to testify bring with them books, papers, photographs, videotapes, or other forms of physical evidence. Witnesses who fail to appear when summoned may face contempt-of-court charges.

subpoena
A written order issued by a judicial officer or grand jury requiring an individual to appear in court and to give testimony or to bring material to be used as evidence. Some subpoenas mandate that books, papers, and other items be surrendered to the court.

The job of a witness is to provide accurate testimony concerning only those things of which he or she has direct knowledge. Normally, witnesses are not allowed to repeat things that others have told them unless they must do so to account for certain actions of their own. Since few witnesses are familiar with courtroom procedure, the task of testifying is fraught with uncertainty and can be traumatizing.

Everyone who testifies in a criminal trial must do so under oath, in which some reference to God is made, or after affirmation,[57] which is a pledge to tell the truth used by those who find either a reference or swearing to God objectionable.

All witnesses are subject to cross-examination. Lay witnesses may be surprised to find that cross-examination can force them to defend their personal and moral integrity. A cross-examiner may question a witness about past vicious, criminal, or immoral acts, even when such matters have never been the subject of a criminal proceeding.[58] As long as the intent of such questions is to demonstrate to the jury that the witness is not credible, the judge will normally permit them.

Lecture Note Describe some of the hardships endured by witnesses in criminal trials, such as anxiety about the act of testifying, possible fear of the defendant, and lack of knowledge of courtroom procedure, as well as the uncertainty of what is expected of them.

Witnesses have traditionally been shortchanged by the judicial process. Subpoenaed to attend court, they have often suffered from frequent and unannounced changes in trial dates. A witness who promptly responds to a summons to appear may find that legal maneuvering has resulted in unanticipated delays. Strategic changes by either side may make the testimony of some witnesses entirely unnecessary, and people who have prepared themselves for the psychological rigors of testifying often experience an emotional letdown.

To compensate witnesses for their time and to make up for lost income, many states pay witnesses for each day that they spend in court. Payments range from $5 to $30 per day,[59] although some states pay nothing at all (federal courts pay $40 per day). In a 2004 Chicago murder case in which Oprah Winfrey served as a juror, for example, all jurors, including Winfrey (a billionaire), were paid $17.20 a day for their services.[60] The 1991 U.S. Supreme Court case of *Demarest* v. *Manspeaker et al.*[61] held that federal prisoners subpoenaed to testify are entitled to witness fees just as other witnesses would be.

Lecture Note Explain that one of the biggest challenges for jurors is to remain objective and to avoid making up their minds about guilt or innocence until all evidence has been heard.

In an effort to make the job of witnesses less onerous, 39 states and the federal government have laws or guidelines requiring that witnesses be notified of scheduling changes and cancellations in criminal proceedings.[62] In 1982, Congress passed the Victim and Witness Protection Act, which required the U.S. attorney general to develop guidelines to assist victims and witnesses in meeting the demands placed on them by the justice system. A number of **victims' assistance programs** (also called *victim/witness assistance programs*) have also taken up a call for the rights of witnesses and are working to make the courtroom experience more manageable.

victims' assistance program
An organized program that offers services to victims of crime in the areas of crisis intervention and follow-up counseling and that helps victims secure their rights under the law.

Jurors

The Cook County (Chicago) jury on which television diva Oprah Winfrey served convicted a man of first-degree murder in 2004. "It was an eye-opener for all of us," Winfrey said after the three-day trial ended. "It was not an easy decision to make."[63]

Article III of the U.S. Constitution requires that "[t]he trial of all crimes . . . shall be by jury." **Jurors** are citizens selected for jury duty in a court of law. States have the authority to determine the number of jurors in criminal trial juries. Most states use juries composed of 12 people and one or two alternates designated to fill in for jurors who are unable to continue due to accident, illness, or personal emergency. Some states allow for juries smaller than 12 jurors, and juries with as few as six members have survived Supreme Court scrutiny.[64]

juror
A member of a trial or grand jury who has been selected for jury duty and is required to serve as an arbiter of the facts in a court of law. Jurors are expected to render verdicts of "guilty" or "not guilty" as to the charges brought against the accused, although they may sometimes fail to do so (as in the case of a hung jury).

The highest act of citizenship is jury service.
—Abraham Lincoln, sixteenth president of the United States

Jury duty is regarded as a responsibility of citizenship. Other than juveniles and people in certain occupations, such as police personnel, physicians, members of the armed services on active duty, and emergency services workers, those who are called for jury duty must serve unless they can convince a judge that they should be excused for overriding reasons. Noncitizens, convicted felons, and citizens who have served on a jury within the past two years are excluded from jury service in most jurisdictions.

The names of prospective jurors are often gathered from the tax register, motor vehicle records, or voter registration rolls of a county or municipality. Minimum qualifications for jury service include adulthood, basic command of spoken English, citizenship, "ordinary intelligence," and local residency. Jurors are also expected to possess their "natural faculties," meaning that they should be able to hear, speak, see, move, and so forth. Some jurisdictions have recently allowed people with physical disabilities to serve as jurors, although the nature of the evidence to be presented in a case may preclude people with certain kinds of disabilities from serving.

Lecture Note Define a peer jury as a jury composed of a representative cross section of the community.

Thematic Question What constitutes a jury of one's peers? Who are *your* peers? If you were to face trial on a criminal charge, would you want your peers on the jury? Explain.

Ideally, the jury should be a microcosm of society, reflecting the values, rationality, and common sense of the average person. The U.S. Supreme Court has held that criminal defendants have a right to have their cases heard before a jury of their peers.[65] Peer juries are those composed of a representative cross section of the community in which the alleged crime occurred and where the trial is to be held. The idea of a peer jury stems from the Magna Carta's original guarantee of jury trials for "freemen." Freemen in England during the thirteenth century, however, were more likely to be of similar mind than is a cross section of Americans today. Hence, although the duty of the jury is to deliberate on the evidence and, ultimately, to determine guilt or innocence, social dynamics may play just as great a role in jury verdicts as do the facts of a case.

Thematic Question How well does our jury system serve individual-rights and public order needs? Explain.

In a 1945 case, *Thiel* v. *Southern Pacific Co.*,[66] the Supreme Court clarified the concept of a "jury of one's peers" by noting that while it is not necessary for every jury to contain representatives of every conceivable racial, ethnic, religious, gender, and economic group in the community, court officials may not systematically and intentionally exclude any juror solely because of his or her social characteristics. Learn what it's like to serve on a jury in a criminal trial at **Web Extra 8–11**.

The Victim

Not all crimes have clearly identifiable victims. Some, such as murder, do not have victims who survive. Where there is an identifiable surviving victim, however, he or she is often one of the most forgotten people in the courtroom. Although the victim may have been profoundly affected by the crime itself and is often emotionally committed to the proceedings and trial outcome, he or she may not even be permitted to participate directly in the trial process. Although a powerful movement to recognize the interests of victims is in full swing in this country, it is still not unusual for crime victims to be totally unaware of the final outcome of a case that intimately concerns them.[67]

Hundreds of years ago, the situation surrounding victims was far different. During the early Middle Ages in much of Europe, victims or their survivors routinely played a central role in trial proceedings and in sentencing decisions. They testified, examined witnesses, challenged defense contentions, and pleaded with the judge or jury for justice, honor, and often revenge. Sometimes they were even expected to carry out the sentence of the court, by flogging the offender or by releasing the trapdoor used for hangings. This "golden age" of the victim ended with the consolidation of power into the hands of monarchs, who declared that vengeance was theirs alone.

Today, victims (like witnesses) experience many of the following hardships as they participate in the criminal court process:

- Uncertainty as to their role in the criminal justice process
- General lack of knowledge about the criminal justice system, courtroom procedure, and legal issues
- Trial delays resulting in frequent travel, missed work, and wasted time
- Fear of the defendant or of retaliation from the defendant's associates
- Trauma of testifying and of cross-examination

Lecture Note Describe the role of the defendant in the criminal trial. Highlight the choices the defendant makes as the trial proceeds, including the selection of an attorney, the choice of a plea, and the decision of whether to testify.

The trial process itself can make for a bitter experience. If victims take the stand, defense attorneys may test their memory, challenge their veracity, or even suggest that they were somehow responsible for their own victimization. After enduring cross-examination, some victims report feeling as though they—and not the offender—were portrayed as the criminal to the jury. The difficulties encountered by victims have been compared to a second victimization at the hands of the criminal justice system. Additional information on victims and victims' issues, including victims' assistance programs, is provided in Chapter 9.

The Defendant

Generally, defendants must be present at their trials. The Federal Rules of Criminal Procedure, like state rules, require a defendant's presence at every stage of a trial, except that a defendant who is initially present may be voluntarily absent after the trial has commenced.[68] In *Crosby* v. *U.S.* (1993),[69] the U.S. Supreme Court held that a defendant may not be tried in absentia, even if he or she was present at the beginning of a trial, if his or her absence is due to escape or failure to appear. In a related issue in *Zafiro* v. *U.S.* (1993),[70] the justices held that, at least in federal courts, defendants charged with similar or related offenses may be tried together, even when their defenses differ substantially.

The majority of criminal defendants are poor, uneducated, and often alienated from the philosophy that undergirds the American justice system. Many are relatively powerless and are at the mercy of judicial mechanisms. However, experienced defendants, notably those who are career offenders, may be well versed in courtroom demeanor. As we discussed earlier, defendants in criminal trials may even choose to represent themselves, though such a choice may not be in their best interests.

Even without self-representation, every defendant who chooses to do so can substantially influence events in the courtroom. Defendants exercise choice in (1) selecting and retaining counsel, (2) planning a defense strategy with their attorney, (3) deciding what information to provide to (or withhold from) the defense team, (4) deciding what plea to enter, (5) deciding whether to testify personally, and (6) determining whether to file an appeal if convicted.

Nevertheless, even the most active defendants suffer from a number of disadvantages. One is the tendency of others to assume that anyone on trial must be guilty. Although a person is "innocent until proven guilty," the very fact that he or she is accused of an offense casts a shadow of suspicion that may foster biases in the minds of jurors and other courtroom actors. Another disadvantage lies in the often-substantial social and cultural differences that separate the offender from the professional courtroom staff. While lawyers and judges tend to identify with upper-middle-class values and lifestyles, few offenders do. The consequences of such a gap between defendant and courtroom staff may be insidious and far-reaching.

Thematic Question In what ways might pretrial news coverage be damaging to the objective outcome of a criminal trial? Given the emphasis that our society places on freedom of the press and freedom of speech, do you agree that judges should be allowed to issue gag orders restricting the ability of defendants and others to discuss a case outside of court?

Spectators and the Press

Spectators and the press are often overlooked because they do not have an official role in courtroom proceedings. Both spectators and media representatives may be present in large numbers at any trial. Spectators include members of the families of both victim and defendant, friends of either side, and curious onlookers—some of whom are avocational court watchers. Journalists, TV reporters, and other members of the press are apt to be present at spectacular trials (those involving an especially gruesome crime or a famous personality) and at those involving a great deal of community interest. The right of reporters and spectators to be present at a criminal trial is supported by the Sixth Amendment's requirement of a public trial.

Press reports at all stages of a criminal investigation and trial often create problems for the justice system. Significant pretrial publicity about a case may make it difficult to find jurors who have not already formed an opinion as to the guilt or innocence of the defendant. News reports from the courtroom may influence or confuse nonsequestered jurors who hear them, especially when the reports contain information brought to the bench but not heard by the jury.

In the 1976 case of *Nebraska Press Association* v. *Stuart*,[71] the U.S. Supreme Court ruled that trial court judges could not legitimately issue gag orders preventing the pretrial publication of information about a criminal case as long as the defendant's right to a fair trial and an impartial jury could be ensured by traditional means.[72] These means include (1) **change of venue**, whereby the trial is moved to another jurisdiction less likely to have been exposed to the publicity; (2) trial postponement, which would allow for memories to fade and emotions to cool; and (3) jury selection and screening to eliminate biased people from the jury pool. In 1986, the Court extended press access to preliminary hearings, which it said are "sufficiently like a trial to require public access."[73] In 1993, in the case of *Caribbean International News Corporation* v. *Puerto Rico*,[74] the Court effectively applied that requirement to territories under U.S. control. Today, members of the press and their video, television, and still cameras are allowed into most state courtrooms.

change of venue
The movement of a trial or lawsuit from one jurisdiction to another or from one location to another within the same jurisdiction. A change of venue may be made in a criminal case to ensure that the defendant receives a fair trial.

Thematic Question Do you think video cameras should be permitted in criminal courtrooms? Why or why not?

The U.S. Supreme Court has been far less favorably disposed to television coverage than have state courts. In 1981, a Florida defendant appealed his burglary conviction to the Supreme Court,[75] arguing that the presence of television cameras at his trial had turned the court into a circus for attorneys and made the proceedings more a sideshow than a trial. The Supreme Court, recognizing that television cameras have an untoward effect on many people, found in favor of the defendant. In the words of the Court, "Trial courts must be especially vigilant to guard against any impairment of the defendant's right to a verdict based solely upon the evidence and the relevant law."

Cameras of all kinds have been prohibited in all federal district criminal proceedings since 1946 by Rule 53 of the Federal Rules of Criminal Procedure.[76] In 1972, the Judicial Conference of the United States adopted a policy opposing broadcast of civil proceedings in district courts, and that policy was incorporated into the Code of Conduct for United States Judges. Nonetheless, some district courts have local rules that allow photographs and filming during selected proceedings.

A three-year pilot project that allowed television cameras into six U.S. district courts and two appeals courts closed on December 31, 1994, when the Judicial Conference voted to end the project. Conference members expressed concerns that cameras were a distracting influence and were having a "negative impact on jurors [and] witnesses"[77] by exposing them to possible harm by revealing their identities. Still, some federal appellate courts have created their own policy on the use of cameras and broadcast equipment in the courtroom. The official policy of the U.S. Court of Appeals for the Ninth Circuit, for example, permits cameras and media broadcasts that meet certain rules. The policy stipulates, "Three business days advance notice is required from the media of a request to be present to broadcast, televise, record electronically, or take photographs at a particular session. Such requests must be submitted to the Clerk of Court." The policy adds, "The presiding judge of the panel may limit or terminate media coverage, or direct the removal of camera coverage personnel when necessary to protect the rights of the parties or to assure the orderly conduct of the proceedings."[78]

Today's new personal technologies, however, which include cellular telephones with digital camera capabilities, streaming Web-based video, and miniaturized recording devices, all threaten courtroom privacy. For more information on technology trends that might affect the use of cameras in courtrooms, see **Library Extra 8–5**.

The Criminal Trial

From arrest through sentencing, the criminal justice process is carefully choreographed. Arresting officers must follow proper procedure in the gathering of evidence and in the arrest and questioning of suspects. Magistrates, prosecutors, jailers, and prison officials are all subject to their own strictures. Nowhere, however, is the criminal justice process more closely circumscribed than it is at the criminal trial.

Class Activity Have students attend a session of the local criminal court to observe the court in action. Tell them to keep a record of their observations. Have them report back to the class on their impressions.

Procedure

rules of evidence
The court rules that govern the admissibility of evidence at criminal hearings and trials.

The procedure in a modern courtroom is highly formalized. **Rules of evidence**, which govern the admissibility of evidence, and other procedural guidelines determine the course of a criminal hearing and trial. Rules of evidence are partially based on tradition, but all U.S. jurisdictions have formalized rules of evidence in written form. Criminal trials at the federal level generally adhere to the requirements of the Federal Rules of Evidence.

Trials are also circumscribed by informal rules and professional expectations. An important component of law school education is the teaching of rules that structure and define appropriate courtroom demeanor. In addition to statutory rules, law students are thoroughly exposed to the ethical standards of their profession, as found in ABA standards and other writings.

Nature and Purpose

3 Describe the nature and purpose of the criminal trial.

In the remainder of this chapter, we will describe the chronology of a criminal trial and will comment on some of the widely accepted rules of criminal procedure. Before we begin the description, however, it is good to keep two points in mind. One is that the primary purpose of any criminal trial is the determination of the defendant's guilt or innocence. In this regard, it is important to recognize the crucial distinction that scholars make between factual guilt and legal guilt. The term *factual guilt* refers to the issue of whether the defendant is actually responsible for the crime of which he or she stands accused. If the defendant did it, then he or she is, in fact, guilty. *Legal guilt* is not as clear a term and is established only when the prosecutor presents evidence that is sufficient to convince the judge (when a jury trial has been waived and the judge determines the verdict) or the jury that the defendant is guilty as charged. The distinction between factual guilt and legal guilt is crucial because it points to the fact that the burden of proof rests with the prosecution. It indicates the possibility that guilty defendants may, nonetheless, be found "not guilty."

Lecture Note Explain that although the criminal trial depends on an adversarial process, it is not a free-for-all. Explain that the adversarial model relies on well-defined rules of procedure that have evolved through years of common practice and that are often formalized in codified form.

adversarial system
The two-sided structure under which American criminal trial courts operate that pits the prosecution against the defense. In theory, justice is done when the more effective adversary is able to convince the judge or jury that his or her perspective on the case is the correct one.

The second point to remember is that criminal trials under our system of justice are built around an **adversarial system** (prosecution versus defense) and that central to this system is the advocacy model. Participating in the adversarial system are advocates for the state (the prosecutor or the district attorney) and for the defendant (the defense counsel, the public defender, and so on). The philosophy behind the adversarial system is that the greatest number of just resolutions in criminal trials will occur when both sides are allowed to argue their cases effectively and vociferously before a fair and impartial jury. The system requires that advocates for both sides do their utmost, within the boundaries set by law and professional ethics, to protect and advance the interests of their clients (that is, the defendant and the state). The advocacy model makes clear that it is not the job of the defense attorney or the prosecution to determine the guilt of any defendant. Even defense attorneys who are convinced that their client is guilty are still exhorted to offer the best possible defense and to counsel their client as effectively as possible.

The adversarial system has been criticized by some thinkers who point to fundamental differences between law and science in the way the search for truth is conducted.[79] While proponents of traditional legal procedure accept the belief that truth can best be uncovered through an adversarial process, scientists adhere to a painstaking process of research and replication to acquire knowledge. Most of us would agree that scientific advances in recent years may have made factual issues less difficult to ascertain. For example, some of the new scientific techniques in evidence analysis, such as DNA fingerprinting, can now unequivocally link suspects to criminal activity or even show that offenders once thought guilty are actually innocent. Gary Dotson of Illinois became the first person exonerated through the use of such evidence in 1989. Since then, at least 328 convictions have been overturned using DNA evidence. (Read about Dotson's case in "The Rape That Wasn't" at **Library Extra 8–6**.) According to Samuel R. Gross and colleagues at the University of Michigan Law School, who published a comprehensive study of exonerations in 2004, those 328 people "had spent more than 3,400 years in prison for crimes for which they should never have been convicted."[80] Exonerations tend to occur more frequently in cases where DNA evidence is relatively easy to acquire, such as rape and murder. False conviction rates for other crimes, like robbery, are much more difficult to assess using DNA. Hence Gross states that "the clearest and most important lesson from the recent spike in rape exonerations is that false convictions that come to light are the tip of an iceberg."

Whether scientific findings should continue to serve a subservient role to the adversarial process itself is a question now being raised. The ultimate answer will probably be determined by the results that the two processes are able to produce. If the adversarial model results in the acquittal of too many demonstrably guilty people because of legal "technicalities" or if the scientific approach identifies too many suspects inaccurately, either could be restricted.

4 Identify the various stages of a criminal trial.

The beauty of the jury is their morality. Tap into it.

—Tony Serra, San Francisco defense attorney

Stages in a Criminal Trial

We turn now to a discussion of the steps in a criminal trial. As Figure 8–2 shows, trial chronology consists of eight stages:

1. Trial initiation
2. Jury selection
3. Opening statements
4. Presentation of evidence
5. Closing arguments
6. Judge's charge to the jury
7. Jury deliberations
8. Verdict

Jury deliberations and the verdict are discussed jointly. If the defendant is found guilty, a sentence is imposed by the judge at the conclusion of the trial. Sentencing is discussed in the next chapter.

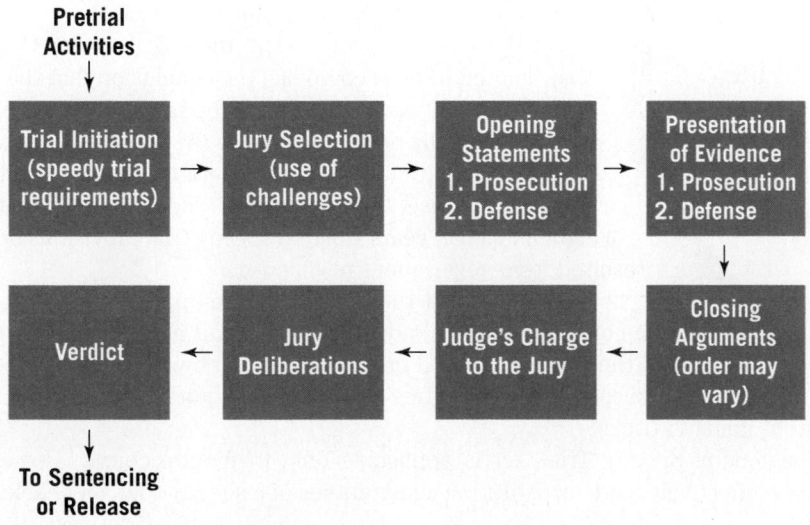

FIGURE 8–2 Stages in a Criminal Trial

▲ James Thomas, who was charged with murder in 1996 and freed in April 2005, after spending eight and a half years in a Louisiana jail waiting for his case to go to trial. A Louisiana state appeals court ruled that the state had taken too long to try him. Why does our system of justice require speedy trials?
Bill Feig/AP Wide World Photos

Trial Initiation

In 2005, a Louisiana state appeals court threw out murder charges against James Thomas and ordered him released. Thomas, an impoverished day laborer, had been arrested in 1996 and spent eight and a half years in jail waiting for a trial that never came. The ruling by the appeals court was widely seen as an indictment of Louisiana's understaffed and underfunded public defender system, members of which had simply been too busy to work on Thomas's case. A private attorney managed to get Thomas set free after his mother scraped together $500 to pay his fee.

The U.S. Constitution contains a speedy trial provision in its Sixth Amendment, which guarantees that "[i]n all criminal prosecutions, the accused shall enjoy the right to a speedy and public trial." Clogged court calendars, limited judicial resources, and general inefficiency, however, often combine to produce what appears to many to be unreasonable delays in trial initiation. The attention of the U.S. Supreme Court was brought to bear on trial delays in three precedent-setting cases: *Klopfer* v. *North Carolina* (1967),[81] *Barker* v. *Wingo* (1972),[82] and *Strunk* v. *U.S.* (1973).[83] The *Klopfer* case involved a Duke University professor and focused on civil disobedience in a protest against segregated facilities. In ruling on Klopfer's long-delayed trial, the Court asserted that the right to a speedy trial is a fundamental guarantee of the Constitution. In the *Barker* case, the Court held that Sixth Amendment guarantees to a quick trial could be illegally violated even in cases where the accused did not explicitly object to delays. In *Strunk*, it found that the denial of a speedy trial should result in the dismissal of all charges.

Speedy Trial Act
A 1974 federal law requiring that proceedings against a defendant in a criminal case begin within a specified period of time, such as 70 working days after indictment. Some states also have speedy trial requirements.

In 1974, against the advice of the Justice Department, the U.S. Congress passed the federal **Speedy Trial Act**.[84] The act allows for the dismissal of federal criminal charges in cases where the prosecution does not seek an indictment or information within 30 days of arrest (a 30-day extension is granted when the grand jury is not in session) or where a trial does not begin within 70 working days after indictment or initial appearance for defendants who plead not guilty. If a defendant is not available for trial or if witnesses cannot be called within the 70-day limit, the period may be extended up to 180 days. Delays brought about by the defendant, through requests for a continuance or because of escape, are not counted in the specified time periods.

In an important 1988 decision, *U.S.* v. *Taylor*,[85] the U.S. Supreme Court applied the requirements of the Speedy Trial Act to the case of a drug defendant who had escaped following arrest. The Court made it clear that trial delays that derive from the willful actions of the defendant do not apply to the 70-day period. The Court also held that trial delays, even when they result from government action, do not necessarily provide grounds for dismissal if they occur "without prejudice." Delays without prejudice are those that are due to circumstances beyond the control of criminal justice agencies.

In *Fex* v. *Michigan* (1993),[86] the U.S. Supreme Court ruled that "common sense compel[s] the conclusion that the 180-day period does not commence until the prisoner's disposition request has actually been delivered to the court and prosecutor of the jurisdiction that lodged the detainer against him." However, in a 1992 case, *Doggett* v. *U.S.*,[87] the Court held that a delay of eight and a half years violated speedy trial provisions because it resulted from government negligence.

In all criminal prosecutions, the accused shall enjoy the right to a speedy and public trial, by an impartial jury . . . , and to be informed of the nature and cause of the accusation; to be confronted with the witnesses against him; to have compulsory process for obtaining witnesses in his favor; and to have the Assistance of Counsel for his defence.
—Sixth Amendment to the U.S. Constitution

In 2006, the Court refused to hear an appeal by suspected dirty bomb conspirator Jose Padilla, letting stand a lower court's decision that said the president could order a U.S. citizen who was arrested in this country for suspected terrorist ties to be held indefinitely without charges and without going to trial.[88]

The federal Speedy Trial Act is applicable only to federal courts. However, the *Klopfer* case effectively made constitutional guarantees of a speedy trial applicable to state courts. In keeping with the trend toward reduced delays, many states have since enacted their own speedy trial legislation. Most state legislation sets a limit of 90 or 120 days as a reasonable period of time for a trial to commence.

Jury Selection

Challenges in Jury Selection

The Sixth Amendment guarantees the right to an impartial jury. An impartial jury is not necessarily an ignorant one. In other words, potential jurors will not always be excused from service on a jury if they have some knowledge of the case before them.[89] However, candidates who have already formed an opinion as to the guilt or innocence of the defendant are likely to be excused.

Some prospective jurors *try* to get excused, whereas others who would like to serve are excused because they are not judged to be suitable. Prosecution and defense attorneys use challenges to ensure the impartiality of the jury being impaneled. Three types of challenges are recognized in criminal courts: (1) challenges to the array, (2) challenges for cause, and (3) **peremptory challenges**.

peremptory challenge
The right to challenge a potential juror without disclosing the reason for the challenge. Prosecutors and defense attorneys routinely use peremptory challenges to eliminate from juries individuals who, although they express no obvious bias, are thought to be capable of swaying the jury in an undesirable direction.

Challenges to the array signify the belief, generally by the defense attorney, that the pool from which potential jurors are to be selected is not representative of the community or is biased in some significant way. A challenge to the array is argued before the hearing judge before jury selection begins.

During **jury selection**, both prosecution and defense attorneys question potential jurors in a process known as *voir dire* examination. Jurors are expected to be unbiased and free of preconceived notions of guilt or innocence. Challenges for cause, which may arise during *voir dire* examination, make the claim that an individual juror cannot be fair or impartial. One special issue of juror objectivity has concerned the U.S. Supreme Court: whether jurors with philosophical opposition to the death penalty should be excluded from juries whose decisions might result in the imposition of capital punishment. In the case of *Witherspoon* v. *Illinois* (1968),[90] the Court ruled that a juror opposed to the death penalty could be excluded from such juries if it were shown that (1) the juror would automatically vote against conviction without regard to the evidence or (2) the juror's philosophical orientation would prevent an objective consideration of the evidence. The *Witherspoon* case left unresolved a number of issues, among them the concern that it is difficult to demonstrate how a juror would automatically vote, a fact that might not even be known to the juror before trial begins.

jury selection
The process whereby, according to law and precedent, members of a particular trial jury are chosen.

Another area of concern that the Supreme Court has addressed involves the possibility that jurors could be influenced by pretrial news stories. In 1991, for example, the Court decided the case of *Mu'Min* v. *Virginia*.[91] Dawud Majud Mu'Min was a Virginia inmate who was serving time for first-degree murder. While accompanying a work detail outside the prison, he committed another murder. At the ensuing trial, eight of the 12 jurors who were seated admitted that they had heard or read something about the case, although none indicated that he or she had formed an opinion in advance as to Mu'Min's guilt or innocence. Following his conviction, Mu'Min appealed to the Supreme Court, claiming that his right to a fair trial had been denied due to pretrial publicity. The Court disagreed and upheld his conviction, citing the jurors' claims that they were not biased.

Lecture Note Explain that peremptory challenges can be used to remove potential jurors without having to cite a reason. Ask whether peremptory challenges based on race should be allowed.

The third kind of challenge, the peremptory challenge, allows attorneys to remove potential jurors without having to give a reason. Peremptory challenges, used by both the prosecution and the defense, are limited in number: Federal courts allow each side up to 20 peremptory challenges in capital cases and as few as three in minor criminal cases.[92] States vary as to the number of peremptory challenges they permit.

Lecture Note Discuss the process of jury selection. Ask why one side in the adversarial process might prefer jurors with certain characteristics, while the other side might not. Ask what characteristics might be relevant in this regard.

A developing field that seeks to take advantage of peremptory challenges is **scientific jury selection**, which uses correlational techniques from the social sciences to gauge the likelihood that a potential juror will vote for conviction or acquittal. It makes predictions based on the economic, ethnic, and other personal and social characteristics of each member of the juror pool. Such techniques generally remove potential jurors who have any knowledge or opinions about the case to be tried. Also removed are people who have been trained in the law or in criminal justice. Anyone working for a criminal justice agency or anyone who has a family member working for such an agency or for a defense attorney will likely be dismissed through

scientific jury selection
The use of correlational techniques from the social sciences to gauge the likelihood that potential jurors will vote for conviction or for acquittal.

peremptory challenges on the chance that they may be biased in favor of one side or the other. Additionally, scientific jury selection techniques may result in the dismissal of highly educated or professionally successful individuals to eliminate the possibility of such individuals exercising undue control over jury deliberations.

Critics of the jury selection process charge that the end result is a jury composed of people who are uneducated, uninformed, and generally inexperienced at making any type of well-considered decision. Some jurors may not understand the charges against the defendant or comprehend what is required for a finding of guilt or innocence. Likewise, some may not even possess the attention span needed to hear all the testimony that will be offered in a case. As a consequence, critics say, decisions rendered by such a jury may be based more on emotion than on findings of fact.

Another emerging technique is the use of what is called a *shadow jury* to assess the impact of a defense attorney's arguments. Shadow jurors are hired court observers who sit in the courtroom and listen to what both sides in a criminal trial have to say. They hear evidence as it is presented and listen as witnesses are examined and cross-examined. Unlike professional legal experts, shadow jurors are laypeople who are expected to give defense attorneys a feel for what the "real" jurors are thinking and feeling as a case progresses, allowing for ongoing modifications in defense strategy.[93]

After the wrangling over jury selection has run its course, the jury is sworn in and alternate jurors are selected (alternates may be called to replace jurors taken ill or dismissed from the jury because they don't conform to the requirements of jury service once trial has begun). At this point, the judge will decide whether the jury is to be sequestered during the trial. Members of **sequestered juries** are not permitted to have contact with the public and are often housed in a motel or hotel until completion of the trial. Anyone who attempts to contact a sequestered jury or to influence members of a nonsequestered jury may be held accountable for jury tampering. Following jury selection, the stage is set for opening arguments[94] to begin.

sequestered jury
A jury that is isolated from the public during the course of a trial and throughout the deliberation process.

Jury Selection and Race

Race alone cannot provide the basis for jury selection, and juries may not be intentionally selected for racial imbalance. As long ago as 1880, the U.S. Supreme Court held that "a statute barring blacks from service on grand or petit juries denied equal protection of the laws to a black man convicted of murder by an all-white jury."[95] Even so, peremptory challenges continued to tend toward racial imbalance. In 1965, for example, a black defendant in Alabama was convicted of rape by an all-white jury (the local prosecutor had used his peremptory challenges to exclude blacks from the jury). The case eventually reached the Supreme Court, where the conviction was upheld.[96] At that time, the Court refused to limit the practice of peremptory challenges, reasoning that to do so would place them under the same judicial scrutiny as challenges for cause.

However, in the 1986 case of *Batson* v. *Kentucky*,[97] following what many claimed was widespread abuse of peremptory challenges by prosecution and defense alike, the Supreme Court was forced to overrule its earlier decision. Batson, an African American man, had been convicted of second-degree burglary and other offenses by an all-white jury. The prosecutor had used his peremptory challenges to remove all African Americans from jury service at the trial. The Court agreed that the use of peremptory challenges for purposeful discrimination constitutes a violation of the defendant's right to an impartial jury.

Lecture Note Tell the class that in the 1991 case of *Powers* v. *Ohio*, the Supreme Court determined that the rights of a white defendant had been infringed when African Americans were excluded from his jury through the use of peremptory challenges. Ask students whether they believe that the exclusion of African Americans from a jury about to try a white defendant is as significant a form of discrimination as their exclusion from a jury about to try an African American defendant.

The *Batson* decision laid out the requirements that defendants must prove when seeking to establish the discriminatory use of peremptory challenges. They include the need to prove that the defendant is a member of a recognized racial group that has been intentionally excluded from the jury and the need to raise a reasonable suspicion that the prosecutor used peremptory challenges in a discriminatory manner. Justice Thurgood Marshall, writing a concurring opinion in *Batson*, presaged what was to come: "The inherent potential of peremptory challenges to destroy the jury process," he wrote, "by permitting the exclusion of jurors on racial grounds should ideally lead the Court to ban them entirely from the criminal justice system."

A few years later, in *Ford* v. *Georgia* (1991),[98] the Court moved much closer to Justice Marshall's position when it remanded a case for a new trial because the prosecutor had misused peremptory challenges. The prosecutor had used nine of the ten peremptory challenges available under Georgia law to eliminate prospective black jurors. In *Ford*, the Court did not find that the right of the defendant to an impartial jury had been breached, but it did determine that the civil rights of the jurors themselves had been violated under the Fourteenth Amendment due to a pattern of discrimination based on race. In another 1991 case, *Powers* v. *Ohio*,[99] the Court found in favor of a white defendant who claimed that his constitutional rights had been violated by the intentional exclusion of blacks from his jury through the use of peremptory challenges.

In the 1992 case of *Georgia* v. *McCollum*,[100] the Court barred defendants and their attorneys from using peremptory challenges to exclude potential jurors on the basis of race. In *McCollum*, Justice Harry Blackmun, writing for the majority, said, "Be it at the hands of the state or defense, if a court allows jurors to be excluded because of group bias, it is a willing participant in a scheme that could only undermine the very foundation of our system of justice—our citizens' confidence in it."

The jury is such a cornerstone of justice and the democratic process, [but] the jury process needs to be brought into the 21st century.

—Robert Grey, president, American Bar Association[ii]

Soon thereafter, peremptory challenges based on gender were similarly restricted (*J.E.B.* v. *Alabama*, 1994[101]), although at the time of this writing the Court has refused to ban peremptory challenges that exclude jurors because of religious or sexual orientation.[102] In the 1998 case of *Campbell* v. *Louisiana*,[103] the Court held that a white criminal defendant can raise equal protection and due process objections to discrimination against blacks in the selection of grand jurors. The Supreme Court reasoned that "regardless of skin color, an accused suffers a significant 'injury in fact' when the grand jury's composition is tainted by racial discrimination." The Court also said, "The integrity of the body's decisions depends on the integrity of the process used to select the grand jurors."

Finally, in the 2003 case of *Miller-El* v. *Cockrell*,[104] the Court found that a convicted capital defendant's constitutional rights had been violated by Dallas County (Texas) prosecutors who engaged in intentional efforts to remove eligible African Americans from the pool of potential jurors. Ten out of 11 eligible African Americans had been excluded through the use of peremptory strikes. The decision was reaffirmed in the 2005 U.S. Supreme Court case of *Miller-El* v. *Dretke*[105] and again in the 2008 case of *Snyder* v. *Louisiana*.[106] The Court's decision in *Snyder* v. *Louisiana*, which provides a good summary of its position on the use of peremptory strikes to eliminate black prospective jurors, is available at **Library Extra 8–7**.

Opening Statements

The presentation of information to the jury begins with **opening statements** made by the prosecution and the defense. The purposes of opening statements are to advise the jury of what the attorneys intend to prove and to describe how such proof will be offered. Evidence is not offered during opening statements. Eventually, however, the jury will have to weigh the evidence presented during the trial and decide which side made the more effective arguments. When a defendant has little evidence to present, the main job of the defense attorney will be to dispute the veracity of the prosecution's version of the facts. Under such circumstances, defense attorneys may choose not to present any evidence or testimony at all, focusing instead on the burden-of-proof requirement facing the prosecution. Such plans will generally be made clear during opening statements. At this time, the defense attorney is also likely to stress the human qualities of the defendant and to remind jurors of the awesome significance of their task.

opening statement
The initial statement of the prosecution or the defense, made in a court of law to a judge, or to a judge and jury, describing the facts that he or she intends to present during trial to prove the case.

Lawyers for both sides are bound by a good-faith ethical requirement in their opening statements. Attorneys may mention only the evidence that they believe actually can and will be presented as the trial progresses. Allusions to evidence that an attorney has no intention of offering are regarded as unprofessional and have been defined by the U.S. Supreme Court as "professional misconduct."[107] When material alluded to in an opening statement cannot, for whatever reason, later be presented in court, opposing counsel gains an opportunity to discredit the other side.

Lecture Note Describe the various kinds of evidence that may be used in court. Explain the difference between direct evidence and circumstantial evidence by underscoring how the latter requires the judge or jury to reach conclusions, while the former needs no interpretation for its significance to be understood.

Presentation of Evidence

The crux of the criminal trial is the presentation of evidence. First, the state is given the opportunity to present evidence intended to prove the defendant's guilt. After prosecutors have rested their case, the defense is afforded the opportunity to provide evidence favorable to the defendant.

Types of Evidence

evidence
Anything useful to a judge or jury in deciding the facts of a case. Evidence may take the form of witness testimony, written documents, videotapes, magnetic media, photographs, physical objects, and so on.

direct evidence
The evidence that, if believed, directly proves a fact. Eyewitness testimony and videotaped documentation account for the majority of all direct evidence heard in the criminal courtroom.

circumstantial evidence
The evidence that requires interpretation or that requires a judge or jury to reach a conclusion based on what the evidence indicates. From the close proximity of the defendant to a smoking gun, for example, the jury might conclude that he or she pulled the trigger.

real evidence
Evidence that consists of physical material or traces of physical activity.

Evidence can be either direct or circumstantial. **Direct evidence**, if believed, proves a fact without requiring the judge or jury to draw inferences. For example, direct evidence may be the information contained in a photograph or videotape. It may be testimonial evidence provided by a witness on the stand. A straightforward statement by a witness—such as "I saw him do it!"—is a form of direct evidence.

Circumstantial evidence is indirect and requires the judge or jury to make inferences and to draw conclusions. At a murder trial, for example, a person who heard gunshots and moments later saw someone run by with a smoking gun in hand might testify to those facts. Even without an eyewitness to the actual homicide, the jury might later conclude that the person seen with the gun was the one who pulled the trigger and committed the crime. Contrary to popular belief, circumstantial evidence is sufficient to produce a verdict and conviction in a criminal trial. In fact, some prosecuting attorneys prefer to work entirely with circumstantial evidence, weaving a tapestry of the criminal act in their arguments to the jury.

Real evidence, which may be either direct or circumstantial, consists of physical material or traces of physical activity. Weapons, tire tracks, ransom notes, and fingerprints all fall into the category of real evidence. Real (or physical) evidence is introduced in the trial by means of *exhibits*, which are objects or displays that may be shown to members of the jury once they are formally accepted as evidence by the judge (see CJ Exhibit 8–1). Documentary evidence, which is one type of real evidence, includes writings such as business records, journals, written confessions, and letters. Documentary evidence can extend beyond paper and ink to include data on magnetic and optical storage devices used in computer operations and video and voice recordings.

Evaluation of Evidence

One of the most significant decisions a trial court judge makes is deciding which evidence can be presented to the jury. In making that decision, judges will examine the relevance of the evidence to the case at hand (relevant evidence has a bearing on the facts at issue). For example, a decade or two ago, it was not unusual for a woman's sexual history to be brought out in rape trials. Under what are called *rape shield statutes*, most states today will not allow this practice, recognizing that these details often have no bearing on the case. Rape shield statutes have been strengthened by U.S. Supreme Court decisions, including the 1991 case of *Michigan* v. *Lucas*.[108]

probative value
The degree to which a particular item of evidence is useful in, and relevant to, proving something important in a trial.

In evaluating evidence, judges must also weigh the **probative value** of an item of evidence (its usefulness and relevance) against its potential inflammatory or prejudicial qualities. Even useful evidence may unduly bias a jury if it is exceptionally gruesome or is presented in such a way as to imply guilt. For example, gory photographs, especially color photographs, may be withheld from the jury's eyes. In one recent case, a new trial was ordered when photos of the crime scene were projected on a wall over the head of the defendant as he sat in the courtroom, and an appellate court found that presentation to have prejudiced the jury.

Sometimes evidence is found to have only limited admissibility, which means that the evidence can be used for a specific purpose but that it might not be accurate in other details. Photographs, for example, may be admitted as evidence for the narrow purpose of showing spatial relationships between objects under discussion, even if the photographs were taken under conditions that did not exist when the offense was committed (such as daylight).

When judges allow the use of evidence that may have been illegally or unconstitutionally gathered, grounds may be created for a later appeal if the trial concludes with a "guilty" verdict. Even when evidence is improperly introduced at trial, however, a number of Supreme Court decisions[109] have held that there may be no grounds for an effective appeal unless such introduction "had substantial and injurious effect or influence in determining the jury's verdict."[110] Called the *harmless error rule*, this standard places the burden on the prosecution to show that the jury's decision would most likely have been the same even in the absence of the inappropriate evidence. The rule is not applicable when a defendant's constitutional guarantees are violated by "structural defects in the constitution of the trial mechanism" itself[111]—such as when a judge gives constitutionally improper instructions to a jury. (We'll discuss those instructions later in this chapter.)

CJ Exhibit 8–1
Pretrial and Post-Trial Motions

A *motion* is "an oral or written request made to a court at any time before, during, or after court proceedings, asking the court to make a specified finding, decision, or order."[1] Written motions are called *petitions*. This exhibit lists the most common motions made by both sides in a criminal case before and after trial.

MOTION FOR DISCOVERY

A motion for discovery, filed by the defense, asks the court to allow the defendant's lawyers to view the evidence that the prosecution intends to present at trial. Physical evidence, lists of witnesses, documents, photographs, and so on, which the prosecution plans to introduce in court, are usually made available to the defense as a result of a motion for discovery.

MOTION TO SUPPRESS EVIDENCE

The defense may file a motion to suppress evidence if it learns, in the preliminary hearing or through pretrial discovery, of evidence that it believes to have been unlawfully acquired.

MOTION TO DISMISS CHARGES

A variety of circumstances may result in the filing of a motion to dismiss charges. They include (1) an opinion, by defense counsel, that the indictment or information is not sound; (2) a violation of speedy trial legislation; (3) a plea bargain with the defendant, which may require testimony against codefendants; (4) the death of an important witness or the destruction or disappearance of necessary evidence; (5) the confession, by a supposed victim, that the facts in the case were fabricated; and (6) the success of a motion to suppress evidence that effectively eliminates the prosecution's case.

MOTION FOR CONTINUANCE

The motion for continuance seeks a delay in the start of the trial. Defense motions of this type are often based on an inability to locate important witnesses, the illness of the defendant, or a change in defense counsel immediately before trial.

MOTION FOR CHANGE OF VENUE

In well-known cases, pretrial publicity may lessen the opportunity for a case to be tried before an unbiased jury. A motion for change of venue asks that the trial be moved to some other area where prejudice against the defendant is less likely to exist.

MOTION FOR SEVERANCE OF OFFENSES

Defendants charged with a number of crimes may ask to be tried separately on all or some of the charges through use of a motion for severance of offenses. Although consolidating charges for trial saves time and money, some defendants believe that it is more likely to make them appear guilty.

MOTION FOR SEVERANCE OF DEFENDANTS

The motion for severance of defendants asks the court to try the accused separately from any codefendants. These motions are likely to be filed when the defendant believes that the jury may be prejudiced against him or her by evidence applicable only to other defendants.

MOTION TO DETERMINE PRESENT SANITY

A lack of "present sanity," even though it may be no defense against the criminal charge, can delay trial because a person cannot be tried, sentenced, or punished while insane. If a defendant is insane at the time a trial is to begin, a motion to determine present sanity may halt the proceedings until treatment can be arranged.

MOTION FOR A BILL OF PARTICULARS

The motion for a bill of particulars asks the court to order the prosecutor to provide detailed information about the charges that the defendant will be facing in court. Defendants charged with a number of offenses, or with a number of counts of the same offense, may make such a motion. They may, for example, seek to learn which alleged instances of an offense will become the basis for prosecution or which specific items of contraband allegedly found in their possession are held to violate the law.

MOTION FOR A MISTRIAL

A mistrial may be declared at any time, and a motion for a mistrial may be made by either side. Mistrials are likely to be declared in cases in which highly prejudicial comments are made by either attorney. Defense motions for a mistrial do not provide grounds for a later claim of double jeopardy.

MOTION FOR ARREST OF JUDGMENT

After the verdict of the jury has been announced but before the sentencing, the defendant may make a motion for arrest of judgment. With this motion, the defendant asserts that some legally acceptable reason exists as to why sentencing should not occur. Defendants who are seriously ill, who are hospitalized, or who have gone insane before judgment has been imposed may file such a motion.

MOTION FOR A NEW TRIAL

After a jury has returned a guilty verdict, the court may entertain a motion for a new trial from the defense. Acceptance of such a motion is usually based on the discovery of new evidence that is of significant benefit to the defense and that will set aside the conviction.

[1]U.S. Department of Justice, *Dictionary of Criminal Justice Data Terminology*, 2nd ed. (Washington, DC: U.S. Government Printing Office, 1982).

Testimony of Witnesses

Testimony given by witnesses is generally the chief means by which evidence is introduced at trial. Witnesses may include victims, police officers, the defendant, specialists in recognized fields, and others with useful information to provide. Some of these witnesses may have been present during the commission of the offense, while most will have had only a later opportunity to investigate the situation or to analyze evidence.

testimony
The oral evidence offered by a sworn witness on the witness stand during a criminal trial.

A jury consists of 12 persons chosen to decide who has the better lawyer.
—Robert Frost (1874–1963)

Before a witness will be allowed to testify to any fact, the questioning attorney must establish the person's competence. Competence to testify requires that witnesses have personal knowledge of the information they will discuss and that they understand their duty to tell the truth.

One of the defense attorney's most critical decisions is whether to put the defendant on the stand. Defendants have a Fifth Amendment right to remain silent and to refuse to testify. In the precedent-setting case of *Griffin* v. *California* (1965),[112] the U.S. Supreme Court declared that if a defendant refuses to testify, prosecutors and judges are enjoined from even commenting on this fact, although a judge should instruct the jury that such a failure cannot be held to indicate guilt. In 2001, in the case of *Ohio* v. *Reiner*,[113] the U.S. Supreme Court extended Fifth Amendment protections to *witnesses* who deny any and all guilt in association with a crime for which another person is being prosecuted.

Lecture Note Refer to the different types of testimony: direct, cross, redirect. Explain that prosecutors and defense attorneys can continue asking questions as long as necessary to get all the information from a witness.

Direct examination of a witness takes place when a witness is first called to the stand. If the prosecutor calls the witness, the witness is referred to as a *witness for the prosecution.* When the direct examiner is a defense attorney, the witness is called a *witness for the defense.*

The direct examiner may ask questions that require a "yes" or "no" answer or may ask narrative questions that allow the witness to tell a story in his or her own words. During direct examination, courts generally prohibit the use of leading questions, that is, those that suggest answers to the witness.[114]

Cross-examination refers to the examination of a witness by someone other than the direct examiner. Anyone who offers testimony in a criminal court has the duty to submit to cross-examination.[115] The purpose of cross-examination is to test the credibility and the memory of the witness.

Most states and the federal government restrict the scope of cross-examination to material covered during direct examination. Questions about other matters, even though they may relate to the case before the court, are not allowed. A small number of states allow the cross-examiner to raise any issue as long as the court deems it relevant. Leading questions, generally disallowed in direct examination, are regarded as the mainstay of cross-examination. Such questions allow for a concise restatement of testimony that has already been offered and serve to focus efficiently on potential problems that the cross-examiner seeks to address.

perjury
The intentional making of a false statement as part of the testimony by a sworn witness in a judicial proceeding on a matter relevant to the case at hand.

Some witnesses commit **perjury**—that is, they make statements that they know to be untrue. Reasons for perjured testimony vary, but most witnesses who lie on the stand probably do so in an effort to help friends accused of crimes. Witnesses who perjure themselves are subject to impeachment, in which either the defense or the prosecution demonstrates that a witness has intentionally offered false testimony. For example, previous statements made by the witness may be shown to be at odds with more recent declarations. When it can be demonstrated that a witness has offered inaccurate or false testimony, the witness has been effectively impeached. Perjury is a serious offense in its own right, and dishonest witnesses may face fines or jail time.

At the conclusion of the cross-examination, the direct examiner may again question the witness. This procedure is called *redirect examination* and may be followed by a recross-examination and so on, until both sides are satisfied that they have exhausted fruitful lines of questioning.

Children as Witnesses

An area of special concern involves the use of children as witnesses in a criminal trial, especially when the children are also victims. Currently, in an effort to avoid what may be traumatizing direct confrontations between child witnesses and the accused, 37 states allow the use of videotaped testimony in criminal courtrooms, and 32 permit the use of closed-circuit television, which allows the child to testify out of the presence of the defendant. In 1988, however, in the case of *Coy* v. *Iowa*,[116] the U.S. Supreme Court ruled that a courtroom screen, used to shield child witnesses from visual confrontation with a defendant in a child sex-abuse case, had violated the Confrontation Clause of the Constitution (found in the Sixth Amendment).

On the other hand, in the 1990 case of *Maryland* v. *Craig*,[117] the Court upheld the use of closed-circuit television to shield children who testify in criminal courts. The Court's decision was partially based on the realization that "a significant majority of States have enacted statutes to protect child witnesses from the trauma of giving testimony in child-abuse cases . . . [which] attests to the widespread belief in the importance of such a policy."

Although a face-to-face confrontation with a child victim may not be necessary in the courtroom, until 1992 the Supreme Court had been reluctant to allow into evidence descriptions of abuse and other statements made by children, even to child-care professionals, when those statements were made outside the courtroom. In *Idaho* v. *Wright* (1990),[118] the Court reasoned that such "statements [are] fraught with the dangers of unreliability which the Confrontation Clause is designed to highlight and obviate."

However, in *White* v. *Illinois* (1992),[119] the Court reversed its stance, ruling that in-court testimony given by a medical provider and the child's babysitter, which repeated what the child had said to them concerning White's sexually abusive behavior, was permissible.

Lecture Note Describe hearsay as anything not based on the personal knowledge of a courtroom witness. Explain the hearsay rule as a constraint against accepting evidence based on hearsay. Observe that some exceptions to the hearsay rule do exist, such as allowing a witness to repeat the final statements of a dying person.

The Hearsay Rule

Hearsay is anything not based on the personal knowledge of a witness. A witness may say, for example, "John told me that Fred did it!" Such a witness becomes a hearsay declarant, and following a likely objection by counsel, the trial judge will have to decide whether the witness's statement will be allowed to stand as evidence. In most cases, the judge will instruct the jury to disregard the witness's comment, thereby enforcing the **hearsay rule**, which prohibits the use of "secondhand evidence." The hearsay rule is based on the Sixth Amendment's Confrontation Clause, which gives a criminal defendant the right to confront his or her accusers. In today's courts, that generally means that the defendant has a right to cross-examine witnesses against him or her.

hearsay
Something that is not based on the personal knowledge of a witness. Witnesses who testify about something they have heard, for example, are offering hearsay by repeating information about a matter of which they have no direct knowledge.

hearsay rule
The long-standing precedent that hearsay cannot be used in American courtrooms. Rather than accepting testimony based on hearsay, the court will ask that the person who was the original source of the hearsay information be brought in to be questioned and cross-examined. Exceptions to the hearsay rule may occur when the person with direct knowledge is dead or is otherwise unable to testify.

Exceptions to the hearsay rule have been established by both precedent and tradition. One exception is the dying declaration, which is a statement made by a person who is about to die. When heard by a second party, it may usually be repeated in court, provided that certain conditions have been met. A dying declaration is generally a valid exception to the hearsay rule when it is made by someone who knows that he or she is about to die and when the statement made relates to the cause and circumstances of the impending death.

Spontaneous statements, also called *excited utterances*, provide another exception to the hearsay rule. A statement is considered spontaneous when it is made in the heat of excitement before the person has had time to make it up. For example, a defendant who is just regaining consciousness following a crime may make an utterance that could later be repeated in court by those who heard it.

Out-of-court statements, especially if they were recorded during a time when a person was experiencing great excitement or while a person was under considerable stress, may also become exceptions to the hearsay rule. Many states, for example, permit juries to hear 9-1-1 tape recordings or to read police transcripts of victim interviews without requiring that the people who made them appear in court. In two cases, however, the U.S. Supreme Court barred admission of tape-recorded 9-1-1 calls when the people making them were alive and in good health but not available for cross-examination. In *Crawford* v. *Washington*,[120] a 2004 case, the Court disallowed a woman's tape-recorded eyewitness account of a fight in which her husband stabbed another man, holding that the Constitution bars admission of testimonial statements of a witness who did not appear at trial unless he or she was unable to testify and the defendant had a prior opportunity for cross-examination. In *Davis* v. *Washington*,[121] decided in 2006, the Court held that a 9-1-1 call made by a woman who said that her former boyfriend was beating her had been improperly introduced as testimonial evidence. The woman had been subpoenaed but failed to appear in court. The key word in both cases is *testimonial*, and the Court indicated that "statements are nontestimonial when made in the course of police interrogation under circumstances objectively indicating that the primary purpose of interrogation is to enable police assistance to meet an ongoing emergency."[122]

The use of other out-of-court statements, such as writings or routine video or audio recordings, usually requires the witness to testify that the statements or depictions were accurate at the time they were made. Witnesses who so testify may be subject to cross-examination by the defendant's attorney. Nonetheless, this "past recollection recorded" exception to the hearsay rule is especially useful in drawn-out court proceedings that occur long after the crime. Under such circumstances, witnesses may no longer remember the details of an event. Their earlier statements to authorities, however, can be introduced into evidence as past recollection recorded.

▲ An attorney making a closing argument to the jury. What other features of the adversarial system can you identify?
Tim Pannell/Corbis RF

Closing Arguments

At the conclusion of a criminal trial, both sides have the opportunity for a final narrative presentation to the jury in the form of a **closing argument**. This summation provides a review and analysis of the evidence. Its purpose is to persuade the jury to draw a conclusion favorable to the presenter. Testimony can be quoted, exhibits referred to, and attention drawn to inconsistencies in the evidence presented by the other side.

States vary as to the order of closing arguments. Nearly all allow the defense attorney to speak to the jury before the prosecution makes its final points. A few permit the prosecutor the first opportunity for summation. Some jurisdictions and the Federal Rules of Criminal Procedure[123] authorize a defense rebuttal (a rebuttal is a response to the closing argument of the other side).

Some specific issues may need to be addressed during summation. If, for example, the defendant has not taken the stand during the trial, the defense attorney's closing argument will inevitably stress that this failure to testify cannot be regarded as indicating guilt. Where the prosecution's case rests entirely on circumstantial evidence, the defense can be expected to stress the lack of any direct proof, and the prosecutor is likely to argue that circumstantial evidence can be stronger than direct evidence, since it is not as easily affected by human error or false testimony.

closing argument
An oral summation of a case presented to a judge, or to a judge and jury, by the prosecution or by the defense in a criminal trial.

Judge's Charge to the Jury

After closing arguments, the judge charges the jury to "retire and select one of your number as a foreman . . . and deliberate upon the evidence which has been presented until you have reached a verdict." The words of the charge vary somewhat between jurisdictions and among judges, but all judges will remind members of the jury of their duty to consider objectively only the evidence that has been presented and of the need for impartiality. Most judges also remind jury members of the statutory elements of the alleged offense, of the burden of proof that rests on the prosecution, and of the need for the prosecution to have proved the defendant's guilt beyond a reasonable doubt before the jury can return a guilty verdict.

In their charge, many judges also provide a summary of the evidence presented, usually from notes they have taken during the trial, as a means of refreshing the jurors' memories of events. About half of all the states allow judges the freedom to express their own views as to the credibility of witnesses and the significance of evidence. The other states only permit judges to summarize the evidence in an objective and impartial manner.

Recently, as the CJ News box in this section shows, the plethora of digital communications devices now available has made it difficult for courts to control jurors' access to out-of-court information. Read a set of jury instructions designed to alleviate this problem at **Library Extra 8–8**.

Following the charge, the jury is removed from the courtroom and is permitted to begin its deliberations. In the absence of the jury, defense attorneys may choose to challenge portions of the judge's charge. If they feel that some oversight has occurred in the original charge, they may ask the judge to provide the jury with additional instructions or information. Such objections, if denied by the judge, often become the basis for an appeal when a conviction is returned.

Jury Deliberations and the Verdict

Deliberations Process

In cases in which the evidence is either very clear or very weak, jury deliberations may be brief, lasting only a matter of hours or even minutes. Some juries, however, deliberate days or sometimes weeks, carefully weighing all the nuances of the evidence they have seen and heard. Many jurisdictions require that juries reach a unanimous **verdict** (decision), although the U.S. Supreme Court has ruled that unanimous verdicts are not required in noncapital cases.[124] Even so, some juries are unable to agree on any verdict. When a jury is deadlocked,

verdict
The decision of the jury in a jury trial or of a judicial officer in a nonjury trial.

CJ News
Social Networking among Jurors Is Trying Judges' Patience

Al Schuler, one of 12 jurors weighing the fate of a 23-year-old charged with killing a homeless man in Maryland, was confused by the word "lividity" and what role it might have played in explaining the circumstances of the victim's beating death.

So, . . . [h]e looked up the definition on Wikipedia, the online encyclopedia. "It was just a definition, like going to the dictionary," Schuler said. "It was very innocent."

A Maryland appeals court didn't think so. In throwing out the defendant's first-degree murder conviction and ordering a new trial, the court ruled that Schuler's inquiry violated [the] judge's order prohibiting jurors from researching the case.

Schuler's query is just the latest example of how modern technology and an information-saturated culture are testing centuries-old notions of how juries and judges mete out justice. . . .

Judges and legal experts are particularly concerned about how technology and culture are affecting jurors and a defendant's right to a fair trial. The Internet has provided easy and instant access to newspaper archives, criminal records, detailed maps, legal opinions and social-networking sites, such as Facebook. . . .

Judges have long instructed jurors to avoid reading newspaper stories about trials and to not discuss the case with one another, aside from their deliberations. They also warn them not to conduct their own investigations. The rules are designed to ensure that jurors contemplate only the evidence admitted at trial and at the appropriate time. . . .

Today, technology has wiped out those barriers, and people have become increasingly reliant on the Internet for information. . . .

In recent years, a half-dozen cases have popped into public view because the misconduct was egregious enough that judges were forced to decide whether to grant new trials.

. . . [F]or example, a federal judge denied requests by defense attorneys to throw out the conviction of a former Pennsylvania state senator because a juror had posted updates to Twitter and Facebook during the trial. . . .

[A] New York appeals court upheld the second-degree murder conviction of a 30-year-old man despite a juror's Internet research into whether the victim's gunshot wound was inflicted at close range. In both instances, the judges found the tweeting and research did not harm the defendants' right to a fair trial.

But that isn't always the case. . . .

A New Jersey appeals court in July overturned the aggravated manslaughter convictions of three cousins because a juror had done Internet research about the victim, the defendants and the amount of prison time they faced and had told her colleagues about it. The men will get a new trial.

In Baltimore, defense attorneys for Baltimore Mayor Sheila Dixon, who was convicted of embezzling about $500 in retail gift cards, accused five jurors of improperly becoming friends and chatting about the case on Facebook. . . .

▲ Jurors listening to testimony in a criminal trial. How might jurors' unauthorized use of modern technology influence their deliberations?
Corbis RF

The counselors wanted Circuit Judge Dennis M. Sweeney to throw out the conviction and hold a new trial.

The issue nearly forced Sweeney to question jurors about their conduct, but Dixon and prosecutors reached a surprise plea deal that ended her appeals.

Jurors would probably have faced a less-than-sympathetic audience with Sweeney, who is considered one of the state's leading authorities on jury issues. . . .

"Modern jurors, so used to instant access, may not fully appreciate the need to divest themselves of the trappings of information-gathering and communication that otherwise dominate their lives," the judge lamented in Baltimore's *Daily Record*.

Sweeney urged judges to order jurors to specifically avoid discussing their cases on Facebook, MySpace and Twitter—a warning he repeated during Dixon's trial.

It appears that such admonishments were not enough for the "Facebook Friends."

Source: Del Quentin Wilber, "Social Networking among Jurors Is Trying Judges' Patience," *The Washington Post*, www.washingtonpost.com, © January 9, 2010 The Washington Post. All rights reserved. Used by permission and protected by the Copyright Laws of the United States. The printing, copying, redistribution, or retransmission of the Material without express written permission is prohibited.

it is said to be a *hung jury*. When a unanimous decision is required, juries may be deadlocked by the strong opposition of only one member to a verdict agreed on by all the others.

In some states, judges are allowed to add a boost to nearly hung juries by recharging them under a set of instructions that the Supreme Court put forth in the 1896 case of *Allen v. U.S.*[125] The *Allen* charge, as it is known in those jurisdictions, urges the jury to vigorous deliberations and suggests to obstinate jurors that their objections may be ill-founded if they make no impression on the other jurors.

Problems with the Jury System

In Suits at common law . . . the right of trial by jury shall be preserved, and no fact tried by a jury, shall be otherwise re-examined in any Court of the United States, than according to the rules of the common law.

—Seventh Amendment to the U.S. Constitution

Judge Harold J. Rothwax, a well-known critic of today's jury system, tells the tale of a rather startling case over which he presided in 1991. The case involved a murder defendant, a handsome young man who had been fired by a New York company that serviced automated teller machines (ATMs). After being fired, the defendant intentionally caused a machine in a remote area to malfunction. When two former colleagues arrived to fix it, he robbed them, stole the money inside the ATM, and shot both men repeatedly. One of the men survived long enough to identify his former coworker as the shooter. The man was arrested, and a trial ensued. After three weeks of hearing the case, the jury deadlocked. Judge Rothwax later learned that the jury had voted 11 to one to convict the defendant, but the one holdout just couldn't believe that "someone so good-looking could . . . commit such a crime."[126]

Many routine cases as well as some highly publicized cases, like the murder trial of O. J. Simpson which the whole world watched, have called into question the ability of the American jury system to do its job—that is, to sort through the evidence and to accurately determine the defendant's guilt or innocence. In a televised 1995 trial, Simpson was acquitted of the charge that he murdered his ex-wife, Nicole Brown, and her friend Ronald Goldman outside Brown's home in 1994. Many people believed that strong evidence tied Simpson to the crimes, and the criminal trial left many people feeling unsatisfied with the criminal justice system and with the criminal trial process. Later, a civil jury ordered Simpson to pay $33.5 million to the Goldman family and to Nicole Brown's estate.

Thematic Question Would you recommend the development of a system of professional jurors in this country? What advantages might such a system offer? What would be the disadvantages?

Because jurors are drawn from all walks of life, many cannot be expected to understand modern legal complexities and to appreciate all the nuances of trial court practice. It is likely that even the best-intentioned jurors cannot understand and rarely observe some jury instructions.[127] In highly charged cases, emotions are often difficult to separate from fact, and during deliberations, some juries are dominated by one or two members with forceful personalities. Jurors may also suffer from inattention or may be unable to understand fully the testimony of expert witnesses or the significance of technical evidence.

Thematic Question How would you improve the adjudication process in criminal cases? What suggestions do you have for streamlining the system, reducing delays, and increasing the quality of justice that results?

Jurors may be less than effective in cases where they fear personal retaliation. In the state-level trial of the police officers accused in the infamous Rodney King beating, for example, jurors reported being afraid for their lives due to the riots in Los Angeles that broke out after their "not guilty" verdict was announced. Some slept with weapons by their side, and others sent their children away to safe locations.[128] Because of the potential for harm that jurors faced in the 1993 federal trial of the same officers, U.S. District Judge John G. Davies ruled that the names of the jurors be forever kept secret. Members of the press called the secrecy order "an unprecedented infringement of the public's right of access to the justice system."[129] Similarly, in the 1993 trial of three black men charged with the beating of white truck driver Reginald Denny during the Los Angeles riots, the judge ordered that the identities of the jurors not be released.

Opponents of the jury system have argued that it should be replaced by a panel of judges who would both render a verdict and impose sentence. Regardless of how well considered such a suggestion may be, such a change could not occur without modification of the Constitution's Sixth Amendment right to trial by jury.

An alternative suggestion for improving the process of trial by jury has been the call for professional jurors. Professional jurors would be paid by the government—like judges, prosecutors, and public defenders—and would be expected to have the expertise to sit on any jury. Professional jurors would be trained to listen objectively and would be taught the kinds of decision-making skills necessary to function effectively within an adversarial context. They would hear one case after another, perhaps moving between jurisdictions in cases of highly publicized crimes.

A PowerPoint presentation that supports this chapter is available from your Prentice Hall representative.

Multiculturalism and Diversity
The Bilingual Courtroom

One of the central multicultural issues facing the criminal justice system today is the need for clear communication with recent immigrants and subcultural groups that have not been fully acculturated. Many such groups hold to traditions and values that differ from those held by the majority of Americans. Such differences influence the interpretation of things seen and heard. Even more basic, however, are language differences that might prevent effective communication with criminal justice system personnel.

Techniques that law enforcement officers can use in overcoming language differences were discussed in Chapter 6. This box focuses on the use of courtroom interpreters to facilitate effective and accurate communication. The role of the courtroom interpreter is to present neutral verbatim, or word-for-word, translations. Interpreters must provide true, accurate, and complete interpretations of the exact statements made by non-English-speaking defendants, victims, and witnesses—whether on the stand, in writing, or in court-related conferences. The Court Interpreters and Translators Association also requires, through its code of professional ethics, that translators remember their "absolute responsibility to keep all oral and written information gained completely confidential."

Although most court interpreters are actually present in the courtroom at the time of trial, telephone interpreting provides an alternative way for courts to reduce problems associated with the lack of access to qualified interpreters. Today, state court administrative offices in Florida, Idaho, New Jersey, and Washington State sponsor programs through which qualified interpreters in metropolitan counties are made available to courts in rural counties by telephone.

The federal Court Interpreters Act of 1978[1] specifically provides for the use of interpreters in federal courts if needed by a witness or defendant who speaks "only or primarily a language other than English" or suffers from a substantial hearing impairment. It applies to both criminal and civil trials and hearings. The act does not require that an interpreter be appointed when a person has a speech impairment that is not accompanied by a hearing impairment. A court is not prohibited, however, from providing assistance to that person if it will aid in the efficient administration of justice.

Because it is a federal law, the Court Interpreters Act does not apply to state courts. Nonetheless, most states have enacted similar legislation. A few states are starting to introduce high-standard testing for court interpreters, although most states currently conduct little or no interpreter screening. The federal government and states with high standards for court interpreters generally require interpreter certification. To become certified, an interpreter must pass an oral examination, such as the federal court interpreter's examination or an examination administered by a state court or by a recognized international agency such as the United Nations.

There is growing recognition among professional court interpreters of the need for standardized interstate testing and certification programs. To meet that need, the National Center for State Courts created the Consortium for State Court Interpreter Certification. The consortium works to pool state resources for developing and administering court interpreter testing and training programs. The consortium's founding states were Minnesota, New Jersey, Oregon, and Washington, although many other states have since joined.

Because certified interpreters are not always available, even by telephone, most states have created a special category of "language-skilled interpreters." To qualify as a language-skilled interpreter, a person must demonstrate to the court's satisfaction his or her ability to interpret court proceedings from English to a designated language and from that language to English. Many states require sign language interpreters to hold a Legal Specialist Certificate, or its equivalent, from the Registry of Interpreters for the Deaf, showing that they are certified in American Sign Language. Learn more about language interpretation in the courts from the National Association of Judiciary Interpreters and Translators via **Web Extra 8–12.**

[1] 28 U.S.C. section 1827.

References: National Association of Judiciary Interpreters and Translators website, http://www.najit.org; Madelynn Herman and Anne Endress Skove, "State Court Rules for Language Interpreters," memorandum number IS 99.1242, National Center for State Courts, Knowledge Management Office, September 8, 1999; Madelynn Herman and Dot Bryant, "Language Interpreting in the Courts," National Center for State Courts, http://www.ncsc.dni.us/KMO/Projects/Trends/99-00/articles/CtInterpreters.htm; and National Crime Prevention Council, *Building and Crossing Bridges: Refugees and Law Enforcement Working Together* (Washington, DC: NCPC, 1994).

Summary

THE COURTROOM WORK GROUP AND THE CRIMINAL TRAIL

- The courtroom work group comprises professional courtroom personnel, including the judge, the prosecuting attorney, the defense counsel, the bailiff, the trial court administrator, the court reporter, the clerk of court, and expert witnesses. The courtroom work group is guided by statutory requirements and ethical considerations, and its members are generally dedicated to bringing the criminal trial and other courtroom procedures to a successful close.
- Also present in the courtroom during a criminal trial are "outsiders"—nonprofessional courtroom participants like lay witnesses, jurors, the victim, the defendant, and spectators and members of the press. Nonprofessional or nonjudicial courtroom personnel may be unwilling or inadvertent participants in a criminal trial.

- The criminal trial involves an adversarial process that pits the prosecution against the defense. Trials are peer-based fact-finding processes intended to protect the rights of the accused while disputed issues of guilt or innocence are resolved. The primary purpose of a criminal trial is to determine whether the defendant violated the criminal law of the jurisdiction in which the court has authority.
- A criminal trial has eight stages: trial initiation, jury selection, opening statements, presentation of evidence, closing arguments, judge's charge to the jury, jury deliberations, and verdict. Each is described in detail in this chapter. At least a few experts have suggested the training and use of a cadre of professional jurors, versed in the law and in trial practice, who could insulate themselves from media portrayals of famous defendants and who would resolve questions of guilt or innocence more on the basis of reason than emotion.

QUESTIONS FOR REVIEW

1. Who are the professional members of the courtroom work group, and what are their roles?
2. Who are the nonprofessional courtroom participants, and what are their roles?
3. What is the purpose of a criminal trial? What is the difference between factual guilt and legal guilt? What do we mean by the term *adversarial system*?
4. What are the various stages of a criminal trial? Describe each one.

Sentencing

CHAPTER 9

Learning Objectives

After reading this chapter, you should be able to:

1. Describe the five goals of contemporary criminal sentencing. **251**
2. Describe the nature of indeterminate sentencing, and explain its purpose. **254**
3. Describe the nature of structured sentencing, and describe the different types of structured sentencing models in use today. **256**
4. Identify alternative sanctions, and assess recent sentencing innovations. **264**
5. Describe the nature and importance of the presentence investigation report. **265**
6. Describe the history of victims' rights and services, and discuss the growing role of the victim in criminal justice proceedings today. **266**
7. List four contemporary sentencing options. **270**
8. Outline the arguments for and against capital punishment. **275**

"In sentencing, we have gone through determinate, indeterminate and back and orth in the last century. But in our time, life moves much aster. It took a hundred years m the peak of indeterminate sentencing, or the full realization of indeterminate sentencing values in the late 1870s to 1900 to wash away by the mid-1970s. . . . Is it possible that, with things happening so much faster, in st twenty or twenty-five years he cycle might once again be changing back in a different direction?"

—Michael Tonry, director, Institute of Criminology, Cambridge University[1]

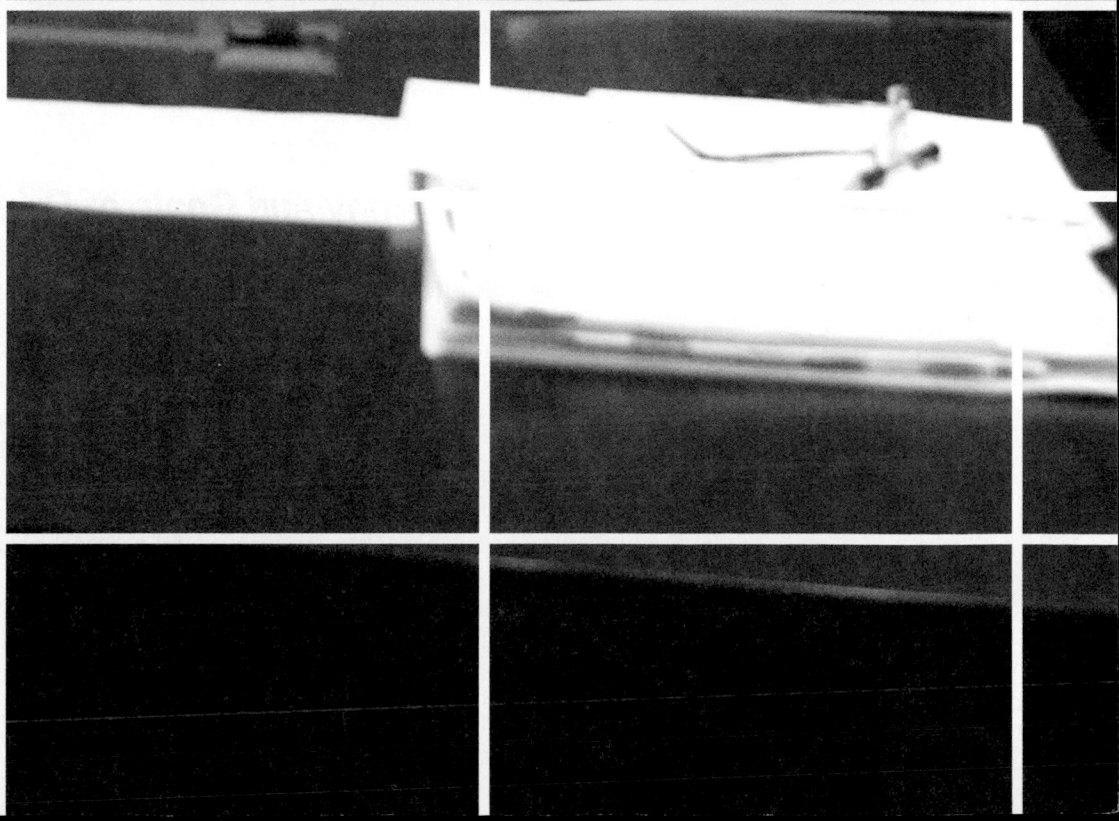

Introduction

In April 2008, Iowa Governor Chet Culver signed the nation's first piece of legislation[2] requiring policymakers to conduct racial-impact studies and to prepare racial-impact statements for any proposed policy changes affecting criminal sentencing, probation, or parole. The action came after research showed that Iowa leads the nation in racial disparity in its prison population. A few months later, a similar piece of legislation[3] was signed into law by Connecticut Governor M. Jodi Rell, and the Illinois General Assembly passed a law[4] creating the state's Commission to Study Disproportionate Justice Impact—a body charged with investigating the extent to which the structure of criminal sentencing in Illinois affects communities of color.

> If you want a small prison population, make punishment certain. If you want a large prison population, make punishment uncertain.
>
> —Newt Gingrich, former Speaker of the House

Marc Mauer, head of the Washington, D.C.–based Sentencing Project, says, "The premise behind racial impact statements is that policies often have unintended consequences that would be best addressed prior to adoption of new initiatives."[5] One example Mauer gives is that of enhanced criminal penalties associated with drug sales near school grounds—a law more likely to be violated by minorities, he says, because they tend to live closer to schools. Studies of the racial impact of sentencing practices force us to examine twin problems in the justice system: (1) the need for policies and practices that can work effectively to promote public safety, and (2) the need to reduce disproportionate rates of minority incarceration when feasible. "These are not competing goals," says Mauer. "If we are successful in addressing crime in a proactive way, we will be able to reduce high imprisonment rates; conversely, by promoting racial justice we will increase confidence in the criminal justice system and thereby aid public safety efforts."

sentencing
The imposition of a criminal sanction by a judicial authority.

Under an organized system of criminal justice, **sentencing** is the imposition of a penalty on a person convicted of a crime. Sentencing follows what is intended to be an impartial judicial proceeding during which criminal responsibility is ascertained. Most sentencing decisions are made by judges, although in some cases, especially where a death sentence is possible, juries may be involved in a special sentencing phase of courtroom proceedings. The sentencing decision is one of the most difficult made by any judge or jury. Not only does it affect the future of the defendant—and at times it is a decision about his or her life or death—but society looks to sentencing to achieve a diversity of goals, some of which are not fully compatible with others.

This chapter examines sentencing in terms of both philosophy and practice. We will describe the goals of sentencing as well as the historical development of various sentencing models in the United States. This chapter also contains a detailed overview of victimization and victims' rights in general, especially as they relate to courtroom procedure and to sentencing practice. Federal sentencing guidelines and the significance of presentence investigations are also described. For an overview of sentencing issues, visit the Sentencing Project at **Web Extra 9–1**. Resources on sentencing and sentencing law are available at **Web Extra 9–2**.

The Philosophy and Goals of Criminal Sentencing

Traditional sentencing options have included imprisonment, fines, probation, and (for very serious offenses) death. Limits on the range of options available to sentencing authorities are generally specified by law. Historically, those limits have shifted as the understanding of crime and the goals of sentencing have changed. Sentencing philosophies, or the justifications on which various sentencing strategies are based, are manifestly intertwined with issues of religion, morals, values, and emotions.[6] Philosophies that gained ascendancy at a particular point in history usually reflected more deeply held social values. Centuries ago, for example, it was thought that crime was due to sin and that suffering was the culprit's due, and judges were expected to be harsh. Capital punishment, torture, and painful physical penalties served this view of criminal behavior.

Lecture Note Describe the various goals of criminal sentencing, including retribution, incapacitation, deterrence, rehabilitation, and restoration.

Thematic Question With which of the goals of criminal sentencing do you most agree? Why?

An emphasis on equitable punishments became prevalent around the time of the American and French Revolutions, brought about (in part) by Enlightenment philosophies. Offenders came to be seen as highly rational beings who intentionally and somewhat carefully chose their course of action. Sentencing philosophies of the period stressed the need for sanctions that outweighed the benefits to be derived from criminal activity. The severity of punishment became less important than quick and certain penalties.

Recent thinking has emphasized the need to limit offenders' potential for future harm by separating them from society. We also still believe that offenders deserve to be punished, and we have not entirely abandoned hope for their rehabilitation. Modern sentencing practices are influenced by five goals, which weave their way through widely disseminated professional and legal models, continued public calls for sentencing reform, and everyday sentencing practices. Each goal represents a quasi-independent sentencing philosophy, since each makes distinctive assumptions about human nature and holds implications for sentencing practice. The five general goals of contemporary sentencing are shown in Table 9–1.

▲ A courtroom drawing showing Rosemary Dillard, whose husband was killed on September 11, 2001, speaking to Zacarias Moussaoui as family members of 9/11 victims listen during the sentencing hearing for the convicted al-Qaeda conspirator. In May 2006, Moussaoui was sentenced to life in prison with no possibility of release. Which of the sentencing goals discussed in this chapter likely played a role in the judge's sentencing decision?
Dana Verkouteren/AP Wide World Photos

Retribution

Retribution, the earliest-known rationale for punishment, is a call for punishment based on a perceived need for vengeance. Most early societies punished all offenders who were caught. Early punishments were immediate—often without the benefit of a hearing—and they were often extreme, with little thought given to whether the punishment fit the crime. Exile and death, for example, were commonly imposed, even for relatively minor offenses. The Old Testament dictum of "an eye for an eye, a tooth for a tooth"—often cited as an ancient justification for retribution—was actually intended to reduce the severity of punishment for relatively minor crimes.

1 Describe the five goals of contemporary criminal sentencing.

Today, retribution corresponds to the model of sentencing called **just deserts**, which holds that offenders are responsible for their crimes. When they are convicted and punished, they are said to have gotten their "just deserts." Retribution sees punishment as deserved, justified, and even required by the offender's behavior.[7] The primary sentencing tool of the just deserts model is imprisonment, but in extreme cases capital punishment (that is, death) becomes the ultimate retribution. Both in the public's view and in political policy making, retribution is still a primary goal of criminal sentencing.

retribution
The act of taking revenge on a criminal perpetrator.

just deserts
A model of criminal sentencing that holds that criminal offenders deserve the punishment they receive at the hands of the law and that punishments should be appropriate to the type and severity of the crime committed.

Thematic Question Which of the goals of criminal sentencing do you think individual-rights advocates would most likely find attractive? Which would public-order advocates favor? Why?

Lecture Note Explain that retribution is similar to the notion of "an eye for an eye, a tooth for a tooth." Add that during Old Testament times, "an eye for an eye" often *reduced* the punishment offenders experienced.

Lecture Note Explain incapacitation as society's interest in making the offender incapable of immediately committing other crimes.

TABLE 9–1
Sentencing Goals and Purposes

Sentencing Goal	Purpose
Retribution	A just deserts perspective that emphasizes taking revenge on a criminal perpetrator or group of offenders.
Incapacitation	The use of imprisonment or other means to reduce the likelihood that a particular offender will commit more crime.
Deterrence	A sentencing rationale that seeks to inhibit criminal behavior through punishment or the fear of punishment.
• General deterrence	Seeks to prevent future crimes like the one for which sentence is being imposed.
• Specific deterrence	Seeks to prevent a particular offender from engaging in repeat criminality.
Rehabilitation	The attempt to reform a criminal offender.
Restoration	A goal of sentencing that seeks to make the victim "whole again."

Incapacitation

incapacitation
The use of imprisonment or other means to reduce the likelihood that an offender will commit future offenses.

Lecture Note Explain deterrence as an attempt to convince others that criminal activity is not worthwhile. Discuss how deterrence might be measured or studied.

Incapacitation, the second goal of criminal sentencing, seeks to protect innocent members of society from offenders who might harm them if not prevented from doing so. In ancient times, mutilation and amputation of the extremities were sometimes used to prevent offenders from repeating their crimes. Modern incapacitation strategies separate offenders from the community to reduce opportunities for further criminality. Incapacitation, sometimes called the *"lock 'em up" approach*, forms the basis for the modern movement toward prison "warehousing." Unlike retribution, incapacitation requires only restraint, not punishment.

Deterrence

deterrence
A goal of criminal sentencing that seeks to inhibit criminal behavior through the fear of punishment.

specific deterrence
A goal of criminal sentencing that seeks to prevent a particular offender from engaging in repeat criminality.

general deterrence
A goal of criminal sentencing that seeks to prevent others from committing crimes similar to the one for which a particular offender is being sentenced by making an example of the person sentenced.

Lecture Note Explain rehabilitation as an attempt to change the offender into a law-abiding citizen. Discuss how rehabilitation might be measured or studied.

Deterrence uses the example or threat of punishment to convince people that criminal activity is not worthwhile; its overall goal is crime prevention. **Specific deterrence** seeks to reduce the likelihood of recidivism (repeat offenses) by convicted offenders, while **general deterrence** strives to influence the future behavior of people who have not yet been arrested and who may be tempted to turn to crime. Deterrence is one of the more rational goals of sentencing because it is an easily articulated goal and because it is possible to investigate objectively the amount of punishment required to deter.

> Nobody gets rehabilitated. Well, I shouldn't say no one; some of them die.
>
> —Daryl Gates, former Los Angeles police chief

Deterrence is compatible with the goal of incapacitation, since at least specific deterrence can be achieved through incapacitating offenders. Tufts University Professor Hugo Adam Bedau, however, points to significant differences between retribution and deterrence.[8] Retribution is oriented toward the past, says Bedau. It seeks to redress wrongs already committed. Deterrence, in contrast, is a strategy for the future and aims to prevent new crimes.

Rehabilitation

rehabilitation
The attempt to reform a criminal offender. Also, the state in which a reformed offender is said to be.

Lecture Note Explain restoration as an attempt to make victims "whole again," insofar as possible. Discuss how restoration might be measured or studied.

Rehabilitation seeks to bring about fundamental changes in offenders and their behavior. As in the case of deterrence, the ultimate goal of rehabilitation is a reduction in the number of criminal offenses. Whereas deterrence depends on a fear of the consequences of violating the law, rehabilitation generally works through education and psychological treatment to reduce the likelihood of future criminality.

The term *rehabilitation*, however, is a misnomer for the kinds of changes that its supporters seek. Rehabilitation literally means to return a person to his or her previous condition. However, it is likely that in most cases restoring criminals to their previous state will result in nothing but a more youthful type of criminality.

In the late 1970s, the rehabilitative goal in sentencing fell victim to the nothing-works doctrine, which was based on studies of recidivism rates that consistently showed that rehabilitation was more an ideal than a reality.[9] With as many as 90% of former convicted offenders returning to lives of crime following release from prison-based treatment programs, public sentiments in favor of incapacitation grew. Although the rehabilitation ideal has clearly suffered in the public arena, emerging evidence has begun to suggest that effective treatment programs do exist and may be growing in number.[10] See **Library Extra 9–1** to read more about treatment programs that work.

Restoration

restoration
A goal of criminal sentencing that attempts to make the victim "whole again."

Victims of crime and their families are frequently traumatized by their experiences. Some victims are killed, and others receive lasting physical or emotional injuries. For many, the world is never the same. The victimized may live in constant fear, be reduced in personal vigor, and be unable to form trusting relationships. **Restoration** is a sentencing goal that seeks to address this damage by making the victim and the community "whole again."

A U.S. Department of Justice report explains restoration this way:

> Crime was once defined as a "violation of the State." This remains the case today, but we now recognize that crime is far more. It is—among other things—a violation of one person by another. While retributive justice may address the first type of violation adequately, restorative justice is required to effectively address the latter. . . . Thus [through restorative justice] we seek to attain a balance between the legitimate needs of the community, the . . . offender, and the victim.[11]

The "healing" of all parties has many aspects, ranging from victims' assistance initiatives to legislation supporting victims' compensation.

Restorative justice (RJ) is also referred to as *balanced and restorative justice*. Conceptually, balance is achieved by giving equal consideration to community safety and offender accountability. Restorative justice focuses on "crime as harm, and justice as repairing the harm."[12] The community safety dimension of the RJ philosophy recognizes that the justice system has a responsibility to protect the public from crime and from offenders.[13] It also recognizes that the community can participate in ensuring its own safety. The accountability element defines criminal conduct in terms of obligations incurred by the offender, both to the victim and to the community.[14] RJ also has what some describe as a competency development element, which holds that offenders who enter the justice system should leave it more capable of participating successfully in the wider society than when they entered. In essence, RJ is community focused; its primary goal is improving the quality of life for all members of the community. See Table 9–2 for a comparison of retributive justice and restorative justice.

Sentencing options that seek to restore the victim have focused primarily on restitution payments that offenders are ordered to make, either to their victims or to a general fund, which may then go to reimburse victims for suffering, lost wages, and medical expenses. In support of these goals, the 1984 Federal Comprehensive Crime Control Act specifically states: "If sentenced to probation, the defendant must also be ordered to pay a fine, make restitution, and/or work in community service."[15]

Some advocates of the restoration philosophy of sentencing point out that restitution payments and work programs that benefit the victim can also have the added benefit of rehabilitating

▲ Inmates in a California prison learning how to repair computer equipment. Skills acquired through prison programs like this might translate into productive noncriminal careers. Rehabilitation is an important, but infrequently voiced, goal of modern sentencing practices. What are some other sentencing goals identified in the text?
Courtesy of Robert W. Winslow

restorative justice (RJ)
A sentencing model that builds on restitution and community participation in an attempt to make the victim "whole again."

TABLE 9–2
Differences between Retributive and Restorative Justice

Retributive Justice	Restorative Justice
Crime is an act against the state, a violation of a law, an abstract idea.	Crime is an act against another person or the community.
The criminal justice system controls crime. Offender accountability is defined as taking punishment.	Crime control lies primarily with the community. Offender accountability is defined as assuming responsibility and taking action to repair harm.
Crime is an individual act with individual responsibility.	Crime has both individual and social dimensions of responsibility.
Victims are peripheral to the process of resolving a crime.	Victims are central to the process of resolving a crime.
The offender is defined by deficits.	The offender is defined by the capacity to make reparation.
The emphasis is on adversarial relationships.	The emphasis is on dialogue and negotiation.
Pain is imposed to punish, deter, and prevent.	Restitution is a means of restoring both parties; the goal is reconciliation.
The community is on the sidelines, represented abstractly by the state.	The community is the facilitator in the restorative process.
The response is focused on the offender's past behavior.	The response is focused on harmful consequences of the offender's behavior; the emphasis is on the future and on reparation.
There is dependence on proxy professionals.	There is direct involvement by both the offender and the victim.

Source: Adapted from Gordon Bazemore and Mark S. Umbreit, *Balanced and Restorative Justice: Program Summary* (Washington, DC: Office of Juvenile Justice and Delinquency Prevention, 1994), p. 7.

the offender. The hope is that such sentences may teach offenders personal responsibility through structured financial obligations, job requirements, and regularly scheduled payments. Learn more about restorative justice by visiting **Library Extra 9–2** and **Web Extra 9–3**.

Lecture Note Explain that the indeterminate sentencing model, the most common model in the United States for most of the twentieth century, assumed that sentenced offenders would take part in their own rehabilitation if offered the chance at early freedom. Ask students what assumptions this model makes about human behavior.

Indeterminate Sentencing

Explanation of Indeterminate Sentencing

While the *philosophy* of criminal sentencing is reflected in the goals of sentencing we have just discussed, different sentencing *practices* have been linked to each goal. During most of the twentieth century, for example, the rehabilitation goal was influential. Since rehabilitation requires that individual offenders' personal characteristics be closely considered in defining effective treatment strategies, judges were generally permitted wide discretion in choosing from among sentencing options. Although incapacitation is increasingly becoming the sentencing strategy of choice today, many state criminal codes still allow judges to impose fines, probation, or widely varying prison terms, all for the same offense. These sentencing practices, characterized primarily by vast judicial choice, constitute a model of **indeterminate sentencing**.

indeterminate sentencing
A model of criminal punishment that encourages rehabilitation through the use of general and relatively unspecific sentences (such as a term of imprisonment of from one to ten years).

Indeterminate sentencing has both a historical and a philosophical basis in the belief that convicted offenders are more likely to participate in their own rehabilitation if participation will reduce the amount of time they have to spend in prison. Inmates exhibiting good behavior will be released early, while recalcitrant inmates will remain in prison until the end of their terms. For that reason, parole generally plays a significant role in states that employ the indeterminate sentencing model.

Lecture Note Describe the differences between indeterminate and structured sentencing, alluding to the fact that the structured approach generally sets a predetermined term in prison, while the indeterminate model sets only minimums and maximums.

Indeterminate sentencing relies heavily on judges' discretion to choose among types of sanctions and to set upper and lower limits on the length of prison stays. Indeterminate sentences are typically imposed with wording like this: "The defendant shall serve not less than five and not more than 25 years in the state's prison, under the supervision of the state department of correction." Judicial discretion under the indeterminate model also extends to the imposition of concurrent or consecutive sentences when the offender is convicted on more than one charge. **Consecutive sentences** are served one after the other, while **concurrent sentences** are served simultaneously.

2 Describe the nature of indeterminate sentencing, and explain its purpose.

consecutive sentence
One of two or more sentences imposed at the same time, after conviction for more than one offense, and served in sequence with the other sentence. Also, a new sentence for a new conviction, imposed upon a person already under sentence for a previous offense, which is added to the previous sentence, thus increasing the maximum time the offender may be confined or under supervision.

concurrent sentence
One of two or more sentences imposed at the same time, after conviction for more than one offense, and served at the same time. Also, a new sentence for a new conviction, imposed upon a person already under sentence for a previous offense, which is served at the same time as the previous sentence.

The indeterminate model was also created to take into consideration differences in degrees of guilt. Under this model, judges can weigh minute differences among cases, situations, and offenders. Under the indeterminate sentencing model, the inmate's behavior (while incarcerated) is the primary determinant of the amount of time served. State parole boards wield great discretion under this model, acting as the final arbiters of the actual sentence served.

A few states employ a partially indeterminate sentencing model. They allow judges to specify only the maximum amount of time to be served; some minimum is generally implied by law but is not under the control of the sentencing authority. General practice is to set one year as a minimum for all felonies, although a few jurisdictions assume no minimum time at all, making offenders eligible for immediate parole.

Critiques of Indeterminate Sentencing

Indeterminate sentencing is still the rule in many jurisdictions, including Georgia, Hawaii, Iowa, Kentucky, Massachusetts, Michigan, Nevada, New York, North Dakota, Oklahoma, Rhode Island, South Carolina, South Dakota, Texas, Utah, Vermont, West Virginia, and Wyoming.[16] Since the 1970s, however, the model has come under fire for contributing to inequality in sentencing. Critics claim that the indeterminate model allows judges' personalities and personal philosophies to produce too wide a range of sentencing practices, from very lenient to very strict. The indeterminate model is also criticized for perpetuating a system under which offenders might be sentenced, at least by some judges, more on the basis of personal and social characteristics, such as race, gender, and social class, than on culpability.

Lecture Note Explain that the indeterminate model failed due to the high rates of recidivism of those sentenced under it. It was replaced in most jurisdictions by the determinate model of sentencing.

Because of the personal nature of judicial decisions under the indeterminate model, offenders often depend on the advice and ploys of their attorneys to appear before a judge who is thought to be a good sentencing risk. Requests for delays are a common defense strategy in indeterminate sentencing states, where they are used to try to manipulate the selection of the judge involved in the sentencing decision.

Another charge leveled against indeterminate sentencing is that it tends to produce "dishonesty" in sentencing. Because of sentence cutbacks for good behavior and involvement in work and study programs, time served in prison is generally far less than sentences would seem to indicate. An inmate sentenced to five to ten years, for example, might actually be released in a couple of years after all **gain time** (time off in recognition of the inmate's project or program participation), **good time** (time off for good behavior), and other special allowances have been calculated. (Some of the same charges can be leveled against determinate sentencing schemes under which corrections officials can administratively reduce the time served by an inmate.) A recent survey by the Bureau of Justice Statistics found that even violent offenders released from state prisons during the study period served, on average, only 51% of the sentences they originally received.[17] Nonviolent offenders served even smaller portions of their sentences. Table 9–3 shows the percentage of an imposed sentence that an offender released from state prison in 2006 had actually served.

To ensure long prison terms in indeterminate jurisdictions, some court officials have gone to extremes. In 1994, for example, Oklahoma Judge Dan Owens sentenced convicted child molester Charles Scott Robinson to 30,000 years in prison.[18] Judge Owens, complying with the jury's efforts to ensure that Robinson would spend the rest of his life behind bars, sentenced him to serve six consecutive 5,000-year sentences (Robinson had 14 previous felony convictions).

▲ Singer Courtney Love being escorted into the Beverly Hills, California, courthouse by a Los Angeles County bailiff. In 2005, Love was sentenced to probation and ordered to undergo anger-management counseling, pay fines, submit to random drug tests, and perform 100 hours of community service after she pleaded no contest to assault charges. The charges were related to an incident at the home of an ex-boyfriend. Love also pleaded guilty to a drug charge stemming from an earlier break-in at the same residence. Should Love have gone to prison?
Nick Ut/AP Wide World Photos

Structured Sentencing

Until the 1970s, all 50 states used some form of indeterminate (or partially indeterminate) sentencing. Eventually, however, calls for equity and proportionality in sentencing, heightened by claims of racial disparity in the sentencing practices of some judges,[19] led many states to move toward greater control over their sentencing systems.

Critics of the indeterminate model called for the recognition of three fundamental sentencing principles: proportionality, equity, and social debt. **Proportionality** refers to the belief that the severity of sanctions should bear a direct relationship to the seriousness of the crime committed. **Equity** means that similar crimes should be punished with the same degree of severity, regardless of the social or personal characteristics of the offenders. According to the principle of equity, for example, two bank robbers in different parts of the country, who use the same techniques and weapons with the same degree of implied threat, should receive roughly the same sentence even though

gain time
The amount of time deducted from time to be served in prison on a given sentence as a consequence of participation in special projects or programs.

good time
The amount of time deducted from time to be served in prison on a given sentence as a consequence of good behavior.

proportionality
A sentencing principle that holds that the severity of sanctions should bear a direct relationship to the seriousness of the crime committed.

equity
A sentencing principle, based on concerns with social equality, that holds that similar crimes should be punished with the same degree of severity, regardless of the social or personal characteristics of the offenders.

TABLE 9–3
Percentage of Sentence to Be Served by New Court Commitments to State Prison

Offense Type	Percentage
Violent	62
Property	47
Drug	40
Public-order	51
Average for all felonies	**52**

Source: National Corrections Reporting Program, "First Releases from State Prison, 2006: Sentence Length and Time Served in Prison, by Offense and Race" (May 25, 2010); http://bjs.ojp.usdoj.gov/content/data/ncrpt06.zip (accessed October 25, 2010).

social debt
A sentencing principle that holds that an offender's criminal history should objectively be taken into account in sentencing decisions.

they are tried under separate circumstances and in different jurisdictions. The equity principle needs to be balanced, however, against the notion of **social debt**, meaning that an offender's criminal history should be considered in his or her sentencing. In the case of the bank robbers, the offender who has a prior criminal record can be said to have a higher level of social debt than the first-time robber, where all else is equal. Greater social debt, of course, suggests a more severe punishment or a greater need for treatment.

structured sentencing
A model of criminal punishment that includes determinate and commission-created presumptive sentencing schemes, as well as voluntary/advisory sentencing guidelines.

determinate sentencing
A model of criminal punishment in which an offender is given a fixed term of imprisonment that may be reduced by good time or gain time. Under the model, for example, all offenders convicted of the same degree of burglary would be sentenced to the same length of time behind bars.

voluntary/advisory sentencing guidelines
Recommended sentencing policies that are not required by law.

presumptive sentencing
A model of criminal punishment that meets the following conditions: (1) The appropriate sentence for an offender convicted of a specific charge is presumed to fall within a range of sentences authorized by sentencing guidelines that are adopted by a legislatively created sentencing body, usually a sentencing commission. (2) Sentencing judges are expected to sentence within the range or to provide written justification for failing to do so. (3) There is a mechanism for review, usually appellate, of any departure from the guidelines.

Lecture Note Explain that the determinate model of criminal sentencing establishes fixed terms of confinement, with dramatically reduced possibilities for parole.

Beginning in the 1970s, a number of states addressed these concerns by developing a different model of sentencing, known as **structured sentencing**, which includes determinate, presumptive, and voluntary/advisory sentencing guidelines. One form of structured sentencing, called **determinate sentencing**, requires that a convicted offender be sentenced to a fixed term that may be reduced by good time or gain time. Determinate sentencing states eliminated the use of parole and created explicit standards to specify the amount of punishment appropriate for a given offense. Determinate sentencing practices also specify an anticipated release date for each sentenced offender.

3 Describe the nature of structured sentencing, and describe the different types of structured sentencing models in use today.

In a 1996 report that traced the historical development of determinate sentencing, the National Council on Crime and Delinquency (NCCD) observed that "the term 'determinate sentencing' is generally used to refer to the sentencing reforms of the late 1970s. At that time, the legislatures of California, Illinois, Indiana, and Maine abolished the parole release decision and replaced indeterminate penalties with fixed (or flat) sentences that could be reduced by good-time provisions."[20]

In response to the then-growing determinate sentencing movement, a few states developed **voluntary/advisory sentencing guidelines** during the 1980s. These guidelines consist of recommended sentencing policies that are not required by law, are usually based on past sentencing practices, and serve as guides to judges. The guidelines may build on either determinate or indeterminate sentencing structures. Florida, Maryland, Massachusetts, Michigan, Rhode Island, Utah, and Wisconsin all experimented with voluntary/advisory guidelines during the 1980s. Voluntary/advisory guidelines constitute a second form of structured sentencing.

A third model of structured sentencing employs what NCCD calls "commission-based presumptive sentencing guidelines."[21] Presumptive sentencing became common in the 1980s as states began to experiment with sentencing guidelines developed by sentencing commissions. Guidelines for the model of **presumptive sentencing** differed from both determinate and voluntary/advisory guidelines in three respects: (1) They were not developed by the state legislature but by a sentencing commission that often represented a diverse array of criminal justice and sometimes private interests. (2) They were explicit and highly structured, typically relying on a quantitative scoring instrument to classify the offense for which a person was to be sentenced. (3) They were not voluntary/advisory in that judges had to adhere to the sentencing system or provide a written rationale for departing from it.

By 2006, the federal government and 16 states had established commission-created sentencing guidelines. Ten of the 16 states used presumptive sentencing guidelines; the remaining six relied on voluntary/advisory guidelines. As a consequence, by 2000, sentencing guidelines authored by legislatively created sentencing commissions had become the most popular form of structured sentencing. Learn more about the history of sentencing reform at **Library Extras 9–3** and **9–4**.

aggravating circumstances
Circumstances relating to the commission of a crime that make it more grave than the average instance of that crime.

mitigating circumstances
Circumstances relating to the commission of a crime that may be considered to reduce the blameworthiness of the offender.

Guideline jurisdictions, which specified a presumptive sentence for a given offense, generally allowed for aggravating or mitigating circumstances—indicating a greater or lesser degree of culpability—which judges could take into consideration when imposing a sentence somewhat at variance from the presumptive term. **Aggravating circumstances** call for a tougher sentence and may include especially heinous behavior, cruelty, injury to more than one person, and so on.

Mitigating circumstances, which indicate that a lesser sentence is called for, are generally similar to legal defenses, although in this case they only reduce criminal responsibility,

CJ Exhibit 9–1
Aggravating and Mitigating Circumstances

Listed here are typical aggravating and mitigating circumstances that judges may consider in arriving at sentencing decisions in presumptive sentencing jurisdictions.

AGGRAVATING CIRCUMSTANCES

- The defendant induced others to participate in the commission of the offense.
- The offense was especially heinous, atrocious, or cruel.
- The defendant was armed with or used a deadly weapon during the crime.
- The defendant committed the offense to avoid or prevent a lawful arrest or to escape from custody.
- The offense was committed for hire.
- The offense was committed against a current or former law enforcement or correctional officer while that person was engaged in the performance of official duties or because of the past exercise of official duties.
- The defendant took advantage of a position of trust or confidence to commit the offense.

MITIGATING CIRCUMSTANCES

- The defendant has no record of criminal convictions punishable by more than 60 days of imprisonment.
- The defendant has made substantial or full restitution.
- The defendant has been a person of good character or has a good reputation in the community.
- The defendant aided in the apprehension of another felon or testified truthfully on behalf of the prosecution.
- The defendant acted under strong provocation, or the victim was a voluntary participant in the criminal activity or otherwise consented to it.
- The offense was committed under duress, coercion, threat, or compulsion that was insufficient to constitute a defense but that significantly reduced the defendant's culpability.
- At the time of the offense, the defendant was suffering from a mental or physical condition that was insufficient to constitute a defense but that significantly reduced the defendant's culpability.

Note: Recent U.S. Supreme Court rulings have held that facts influencing sentencing enhancements, other than prior record or admissions made by a defendant, must be determined by a jury, not by a judge.

not eliminate it. Mitigating circumstances include such things as cooperation with the investigating authority, surrender, and good character. Common aggravating and mitigating circumstances are listed in CJ Exhibit 9–1.

Federal Sentencing Guidelines

In 1984, with the passage of the Comprehensive Crime Control Act, the federal government adopted presumptive sentencing for nearly all federal offenders.[22] The act also addressed the issue of **truth in sentencing**, described as "a close correspondence between the sentence imposed upon those sent to prison and the time actually served prior to prison release."[23] Under the old federal system, on average, good-time credits and parole reduced time served to about one-third of the actual sentence.[24] At the time, the sentencing practices of most states reflected the federal model. While sentence reductions may have benefited offenders, they often outraged victims, who felt betrayed by the sentencing process. The 1984 act nearly eliminated good-time credits[25] and began the process of both phasing out federal parole and eliminating the U.S. Parole Commission (read more about the commission in Chapter 10).[26] The emphasis on truth in sentencing created, in effect, a sentencing environment of "what you get is what you serve." Truth in sentencing has become an important policy focus of many state legislatures and the U.S. Congress. The Violent Crime Control and Law Enforcement Act of 1994 set aside $4 billion in federal prison construction funds (Truth in Sentencing Incentive Funds) for states that adopt truth-in-sentencing laws and are able to guarantee that certain violent offenders will serve 85% of their sentences.

truth in sentencing
A close correspondence between the sentence imposed on an offender and the time actually served in prison.[i]

Thematic Question What aggravating circumstances, if any, would you add to the list in CJ Exhibit 9–1? What mitigating circumstances, if any, would you add? Why?

Lecture Note Discuss the role of aggravating and mitigating circumstances in criminal sentencing. Use CJ Exhibit 9–1 to provide examples of such sentencing considerations.

Title II of the Comprehensive Crime Control Act, called the Sentencing Reform Act of 1984,[27] established the nine-member U.S. Sentencing Commission. The commission, which continues to function today, comprises presidential appointees, including three federal judges. The Sentencing Reform Act limited the discretion of federal judges by mandating the creation of federal sentencing guidelines, which federal judges were required to follow. The Sentencing Commission was given the task of developing structured sentencing guidelines to reduce disparity, promote consistency and uniformity, and increase fairness and equity in sentencing.

The guidelines established by the commission took effect in November 1987 but quickly became embroiled in a series of legal disputes, some of which challenged Congress's authority to form the U.S. Sentencing Commission. In January 1989, in the case of *Mistretta v. U.S.*,[28] the U.S. Supreme Court held that Congress had acted appropriately in establishing the U.S. Sentencing Commission and that the guidelines developed by the commission could be applied in federal cases nationwide. The federal Sentencing Commission continues to meet at least once a year to review the effectiveness of the guidelines it created. Visit the U.S. Sentencing Commission via **Web Extra 9–4**.

Federal Guideline Provisions

Lecture Note Describe the federal government's adoption of determinate sentencing under the 1984 Comprehensive Crime Control Act.

Lecture Note Explain how federal structured sentencing, which has become largely advisory because of recent U.S. Supreme Court decisions, involves two main components: the level of the offense and the criminal history of the offender. Give examples of various levels and history categories to give students a clear sense of how this model works.

As originally established, federal sentencing guidelines specified a sentencing range from which judges had to choose, but if a particular case had atypical features, judges were allowed to depart from the guidelines. Departures were generally expected only in the presence of aggravating or mitigating circumstances, a number of which are specified in the guidelines.[29] Aggravating circumstances may include the possession of a weapon during the commission of a crime, the degree of criminal involvement (whether the defendant was a leader or a follower in the criminal activity), and extreme psychological injury to the victim. Punishments also increase when a defendant violates a position of public or private trust, uses special skills to commit or conceal offenses, or has a criminal history. Defendants who express remorse, cooperate with authorities, or willingly make restitution may have their sentences reduced under the guidelines. Any departure from the guidelines may, however, become the basis for appellate review concerning the reasonableness of the sentence imposed, and judges who deviate from the guidelines were originally required to provide written reasons for doing so.

Federal sentencing guidelines are built around a table containing 43 rows, each corresponding to one offense level. The penalties associated with each level overlap those of the levels above and below to discourage unnecessary litigation. A person convicted of a crime involving $11,000, for example, and sentenced under the guidelines is unlikely to receive a penalty substantially greater than if the amount had been somewhat less than $10,000. A change of six levels roughly doubles the sentence imposed under the guidelines, regardless of the level at which one starts. Because of their matrix-like quality, federal sentencing provisions have been referred to as *structured.* The federal sentencing table is available at **Web Extra 9–5**.

Lecture Note Mention that plea bargains, which account for most of the criminal sentences handed down in federal courts, were relatively unaffected by the structured sentencing guidelines adopted in 1984.

The sentencing table also contains six rows corresponding to the criminal history category into which an offender falls, and these categories are determined on a point basis. Offenders earn points for previous convictions. For example, each prior sentence of imprisonment for more than one year and one month counts as three points, and two points are assigned for each prior prison sentence over six months or if the defendant committed the offense while on probation, parole, or work release. The system also assigns points for other types of previous convictions and for offenses committed less than two years after release from imprisonment. Points are added to determine the criminal history category into which an offender falls. Thirteen points or more are required for the highest category. At each offense level, sentences in the highest criminal history category are generally two to three times as severe as for the lowest category. The types of offenses for which federal offenders are sentenced, and how the proportion of those types have changed over time, can be seen in Figure 9–1.

Defendants may also move into the highest criminal history category by virtue of being designated a career offender. Under the sentencing guidelines, a defendant is a career offender if "(1) the defendant was at least 18 years old at the time of the . . . offense, (2) the . . . offense is a crime of violence or trafficking in a controlled substance, and (3) the defendant has at least two prior felony convictions of either a crime of violence or a controlled substance offense."[30]

According to the U.S. Supreme Court, an offender may be adjudged a career offender in a single hearing, even when previous convictions are lacking.[31]

Plea Bargaining under the Guidelines

Lecture Note Explain that structured sentencing can result in sentences that mislead the public because inmates in some jurisdictions are still released early for good behavior and other reasons.

Plea bargaining plays a major role in the federal judicial system. Approximately 90% of all federal sentences are the result of guilty pleas,[32] and the large majority of those stem from plea negotiations. In the words of former Sentencing Commission Chairman William W. Wilkins, Jr., "With respect to plea bargaining, the Commission has proceeded cautiously. . . . The Commission did not believe it wise to stand the federal criminal justice system on its head by making too drastic and too sudden a change in these practices."[33]

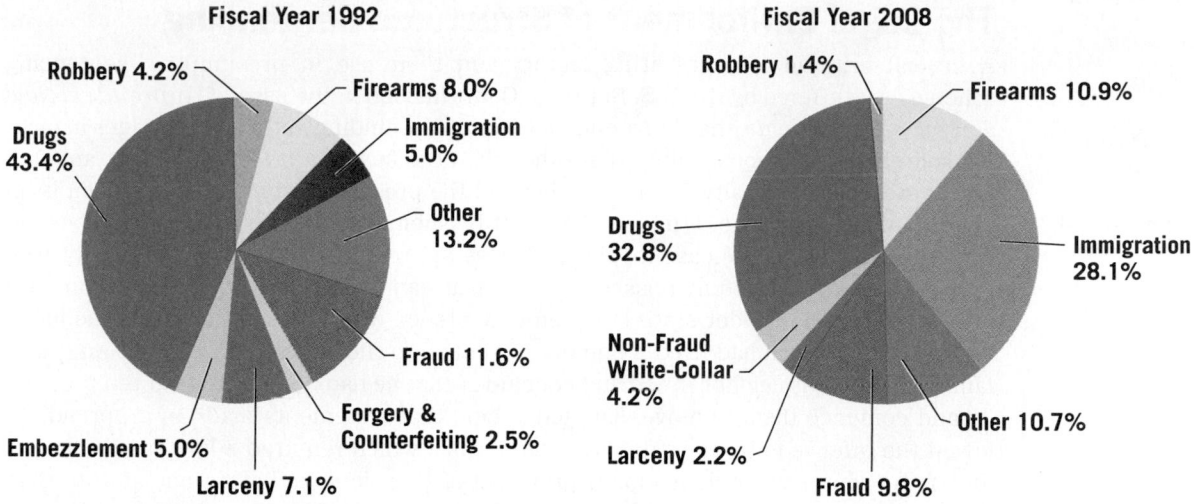

FIGURE 9–1 Distribution of Federal Offenders in Each Primary Offense Category, Fiscal Years 1992 and 2008

Source: U.S. Sentencing Commission, 2008 Datafile, USSC, FY08, and the 1992 Datafile, USSC FY92.

Although the commission allowed plea bargaining to continue, it required that the agreement (1) be fully disclosed in the record of the court (unless there is an overriding and demonstrable reason why it should not be) and (2) detail the actual conduct of the offense. Under these requirements, defendants are unable to hide the actual nature of their offense behind a substitute plea, and information on the decision-making process itself is available to victims, the media, and the public.

In 1996, in the case of *Melendez* v. *U.S.*,[34] the U.S. Supreme Court held that a government motion requesting that a trial judge deviate from the federal sentencing guidelines as part of a cooperative plea agreement does not permit imposition of a sentence below a statutory minimum specified by law. In other words, under *Melendez*, while federal judges could depart from the guidelines, they could not accept plea bargains that would have resulted in sentences lower than the minimum required by law for a particular type of offense. The total number of offenders sentenced under federal sentencing guidelines for the years 1992 to 2008 can be seen in Figure 9–2.

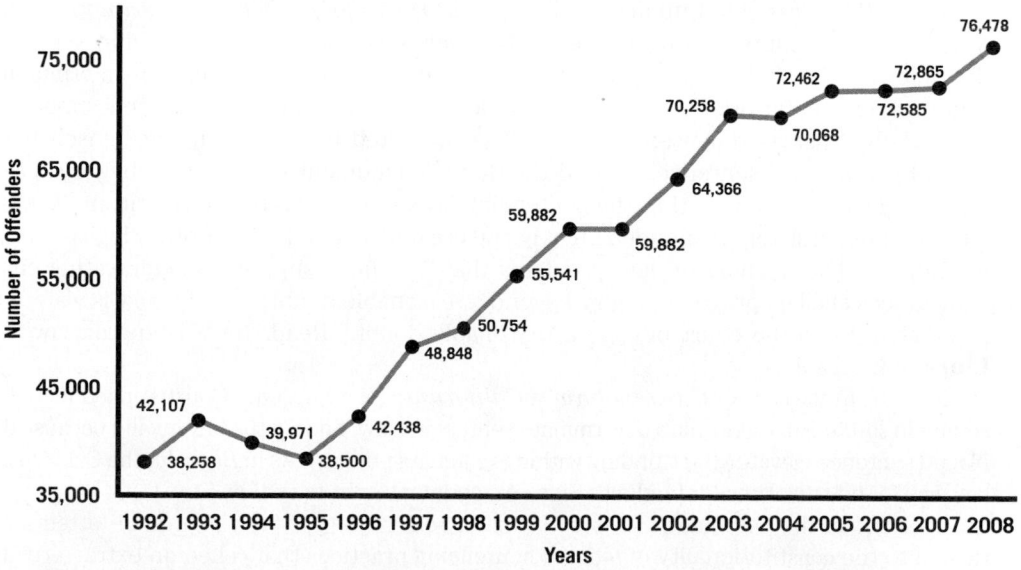

FIGURE 9–2 Total Number of Offenders Sentenced under Federal Sentencing Guidelines, 1992–2008

Source: *U.S. Sentencing Commission Annual Report*, FY1992–FY1995; U.S. Sentencing Commission, *Sourcebook of Federal Sentencing Statistics*, FY 1996–FY2008.

Thematic Question Do you prefer the indeterminate model or the structured model of criminal sentencing? Why?

Lecture Note Discuss the impact that the adoption of structured sentencing has had on federal prison populations and on other aspects of the federal criminal justice system.

The Legal Environment of Structured Sentencing

A crucial critique of aggravating factors and their use in presumptive sentencing schemes was offered by the U.S. Supreme Court in 2000 in the case of *Apprendi* v. *New Jersey*.[35] In *Apprendi*, the Court questioned the fact-finding authority of judges in making sentencing decisions, ruling that other than the fact of a prior conviction, any fact that increases the penalty for a crime beyond the prescribed statutory maximum is, in effect, an element of the crime, which must be submitted to a jury and proved beyond a reasonable doubt. The case involved Charles Apprendi, a New Jersey defendant who pleaded guilty to unlawfully possessing a firearm—an offense that carried a prison term of five to ten years under state law. Before sentence was imposed, however, the judge found that Apprendi had fired a number of shots into the home of an African American family living in his neighborhood and concluded that he had done so to frighten the family and convince them to move. The judge held that statements made by Apprendi allowed the offense to be classified as a hate crime, which required a longer prison term under the sentencing enhancement provision of New Jersey's hate-crime statute than did the weapons offense to which Apprendi had confessed. The Supreme Court, in overturning the judge's finding and sentence, took issue with the fact that after Apprendi pleaded guilty, an enhanced sentence was imposed without the benefit of a jury-based fact-finding process. The high court ruled that "under the Due Process Clause of the Fifth Amendment and the notice and jury trial guarantees of the Sixth Amendment, any fact (other than prior conviction) that increases the maximum penalty for a crime must be charged in an indictment, submitted to a jury, and proven beyond a reasonable doubt."

The *Apprendi* case essentially says that requiring sentencing judges to consider facts not proven to a jury violates the federal Constitution. It raised the question of whether judges anywhere could legitimately deviate from established sentencing guidelines or apply sentence enhancements based solely on judicial determinations of aggravating factors—especially when such determinations involve findings of fact that might otherwise be made by a jury.[36] Since *Apprendi*, the Court has expanded the number and types of facts that must be decided by a jury. In 2010, for example, in the case of *U.S.* v. *O'Brien*,[37] the Court held that a determination that a firearm was a machine gun, as described by relevant law, is an element to be proved to a jury beyond a reasonable doubt, not a sentencing factor to be proved to a sentencing judge. The finding affected a sentencing requirement that a 30-year minimum term of imprisonment be imposed for convictions involving the use of a fully automatic firearm during the commission of a crime.

The *O'Brien* case built upon the important 2004 case of *Blakely* v. *Washington*,[38] in which the U.S. Supreme Court effectively invalidated any state sentencing schema that allows judges rather than juries to determine any factor that increases a criminal sentence, except for prior convictions. The Court found that because the facts supporting Blakely's increased sentence were neither admitted by the defendant himself nor found by a jury, the sentence violated the Sixth Amendment right to trial by jury. The *Blakely* decision required that the sentencing laws of eight states be rewritten. Washington State legislators responded quickly and created a model law for other legislatures to emulate. The Washington law mandates that "the facts supporting aggravating circumstances shall be proved to a jury beyond a reasonable doubt," or "if a jury is waived, proof shall be to the court beyond a reasonable doubt." Read the Washington law at **Library Extra 9–5**.

In 2007, in the case of *Cunningham* v. *California*,[39] the Supreme Court applied its reasoning in *Blakely* to California's determinate sentencing law, finding the law invalid because it placed sentence-elevating fact-finding within the judge's purview. As in *Blakely*, the California law was found to violate a defendant's Sixth Amendment right to trial by jury.

In 2005, in the combined cases of *U.S.* v. *Booker*[40] and *U.S.* v. *Fanfan*,[41] attention turned to the constitutionality of *federal* sentencing practices that relied on extra-verdict determinations of fact in the application of sentencing enhancements. In *Booker*, the U.S. Supreme Court issued what some have called an "extraordinary opinion,"[42] which actually encompasses two separate decisions. The combined cases brought a dual issue before the

Court: (1) whether fact-finding done by judges under federal sentencing guidelines violates the Sixth Amendment right to trial by jury; and (2) if so, whether the guidelines are themselves unconstitutional. As in the preceding cases discussed in this section, the Court found that on the first question, defendant Freddie Booker's drug-trafficking sentence had been improperly enhanced under the guidelines on the basis of facts found solely by a judge. In the view of the Court, the Sixth Amendment right to trial by jury is violated where, under a mandatory guidelines system, a sentence is increased because of an enhancement based on facts found by the judge that were not found by a jury or admitted by the defendant.[43] Consequently, Booker's sentence was ruled unconstitutional and invalidated. On the second question, the Court reached a compromise and did not strike down the federal guidelines as many thought it would. Instead, the Court held that the guidelines could be *considered* by federal judges during sentencing but that they were no longer mandatory.

The *Apprendi* ruling has had a severely destabilizing effect on our criminal justice system.

—Sandra Day O'Connor, former U.S. Supreme Court justice, dissenting in *Ring* v. *Arizona*[ii]

In effect, the decisions in *Booker* and *Fanfan* turned the federal sentencing guidelines on their head, making them merely advisory and giving federal judges wide latitude in imposing punishments. While federal judges *must* still take the guidelines into consideration in reaching sentencing decisions, they do not have to follow them. In the words of the high court, "[T]he federal sentencing statute, as modified by *Booker*, requires a court to give respectful consideration to the Guidelines but permits the court to tailor the sentence in light of other concerns as well."[44] Deviations from the guidelines must still be explained, and in the words of the justices, "a district judge must consider the extent of any departure from the Guidelines and must explain the appropriateness of an unusually lenient or harsh sentence with sufficient justifications."[45]

In 2007, in a continued clarification of *Booker*, the Supreme Court ruled that federal appeals courts that hear challenges from defendants about prison time may presume that federal criminal sentences are reasonable if they fall within federal sentencing guidelines.[46] In that case, *Rita* v. *U.S.*, the Court held that "even if the presumption increases the likelihood that the judge, not the jury, will find 'sentencing facts,' it does not violate the Sixth Amendment." The justices reasoned that "a nonbinding appellate reasonableness presumption for Guidelines sentences does not *require* the sentencing judge to impose a Guidelines sentence."

In 2009, in what appeared to be a loosening of prohibitions on judges' sentencing authority, the U.S. Supreme Court found that the Constitution does not prohibit judges from imposing consecutive sentences based on facts not found by a jury. Writing for a slim 5-4 majority in *Oregon* v. *Ice*, Justice Ruth Bader Ginsburg said, "In light of historical practice and the States' authority over administration of their criminal justice systems, the Sixth Amendment does not inhibit states from assigning to judges, rather than to juries, the finding of facts necessary to the imposition of consecutive, rather than concurrent, sentences for multiple offenses."[47]

In another 2007 case, *Gall* v. *U.S.*,[48] the Court clarified its position on appellate review of sentencing decisions by lower courts when it held that "because the Guidelines are now advisory, appellate review of sentencing decisions is limited to determining whether they are 'reasonable.'"

A recent survey by the U.S. Sentencing Commission found that 61.2% of all federal sentences handed down in the year following *Booker* and *Fanfan* were within ranges specified under federal sentencing guidelines.[49] In comparison, in the year prior to *Blakely*, 72.2% were within guideline ranges.[50] In light of the Court's decisions, it is now up to Congress to reconsider federal sentencing law in light of *Booker*—a process that has been under way for the past few years. In the meantime, some expect the federal courts to be flooded with inmates appealing their sentences.

Three-Strikes Laws

In the spring of 1994, California legislators passed the state's now-famous "three strikes and you're out" bill. Amid much fanfare, Governor Pete Wilson signed the "three-strikes" measure into law, calling it "the toughest and most sweeping crime bill in California history."[51]

California's law, which is retroactive in that it counts offenses committed before the date the legislation was signed, requires a sentence of 25 years to life for three-time felons with convictions for two or more serious or violent prior offenses. Criminal offenders facing a "second strike" can receive up to double the normal sentence for their most recent offense. Parole consideration is not available until at least 80% of the sentence has been served.

Today, about half of the states have passed three-strikes legislation, and other states may be considering it. At the federal level, the Violent Crime Control and Law Enforcement Act of 1994 contains a three-strikes provision that mandates life imprisonment for federal criminals convicted of three violent felonies or drug offenses.

Questions remain, however, about the effectiveness of three-strikes legislation, and many people are concerned about its impact on the justice system. A 2001 study of the original California legislation and its consequences concluded that three-strikes laws are overrated.[52] According to the study, which was conducted by the Washington, D.C.–based Sentencing Project, "California's three-strikes law has increased the number and severity of sentences for nonviolent offenders—and contributed to the aging of the prison population—but has had no significant effect on the state's decline in crime." The study found that declines in California crime rates that are often attributed to the legislation are consistent with nationwide declines in the rate of crime and would mostly have occurred without the law. "Crime had been declining for several years prior to the enactment of the three-strikes law, and what's happening in California is very consistent with what's been happening nationally, including in states with no three-strikes law," said Marc Mauer, an author of the study.

Supporters of three-strikes laws argue that those convicted under them are career criminals who will be denied the opportunity to commit more violent crimes. "The real story here is the girl somewhere that did not get raped," said Mike Reynolds, a Fresno, California, photographer whose 18-year-old daughter was killed by a paroled felon. "The real story is the robbery that did not happen," he added.[53]

Practically speaking, California's three-strikes law has had a dramatic impact on the state's criminal justice system. By 1999, more than 40,000 people had been sentenced under the law. But the law has its critics. "'Three strikes and you're out' sounds great to a lot of people," says Alan Schuman, president of the American Probation and Parole Association. "But no one will cop a plea when it gets to the third time around. We will have more trials, and this whole country works on plea bargaining and pleading guilty, not jury trials," Schuman said at a meeting of the association.[54] According to RAND, full enforcement of the law could cost as much as $5.5 billion annually—or $300 per California taxpayer.

Researchers at RAND conclude that while California's sweeping three-strikes legislation could cut serious adult crime by as much as one-third throughout the state, the high cost of enforcing the law may keep it from ever being fully implemented. In 2003, however, in two separate cases, the U.S. Supreme Court upheld the three-strikes California convictions of Gary Ewing[55] and Leandro Andrade in California. Ewing, who had four prior felony convictions, had received a sentence of 25 years to life following his conviction for felony grand theft of three golf clubs. Andrade, who also had a long record, was sentenced to 50 years in prison for two petty theft convictions.[56] In writing for the Court in the *Ewing* case, Justice Sandra Day O'Connor noted that states should be able to decide when repeat offenders "must be isolated from society . . . to protect the public safety," even when nonserious crimes trigger the lengthy sentence. In deciding these two cases, both of which were based on Eighth Amendment claims, the Court found that it is *not* cruel and unusual punishment to impose a possible life term for a nonviolent felony when the defendant has a history of serious or violent convictions.

In 2004, Californians voted down Proposition 66, a ballot initiative that would have changed the state's three-strikes law so that only specified serious or violent crimes could be counted as third strikes. Passage of the proposition would also have meant that only previous convictions for violent or serious felonies, brought and tried separately, would have qualified for second- and third-strike sentence increases.

California's three-strikes law remains firmly in place. In its current form, it punishes anyone who commits a third felony, regardless of its severity, with a mandatory sentence of 25 years to life if the first two felonies were violent or serious.

Mandatory Sentencing

Mandatory sentencing, another form of structured sentencing, deserves special mention.[57] **Mandatory sentencing** is just what its name implies: a structured sentencing scheme that mandates clearly enumerated punishments for specific offenses or for habitual offenders convicted of a series of crimes. Mandatory sentencing, because it is truly *mandatory*, differs from presumptive sentencing, which allows at least a limited amount of judicial discretion within ranges established by published guidelines. Some mandatory sentencing laws require only modest mandatory prison terms (for example, three years for armed robbery), while others are much more far-reaching.

mandatory sentencing
A structured sentencing scheme that allows no leeway in the nature of the sentence imposed. Under mandatory sentencing, clearly enumerated punishments are mandated for specific offenses or for habitual offenders convicted of a series of crimes.

Typical of far-reaching mandatory sentencing schemes are three-strikes laws. Three-strikes laws (and in some jurisdictions, two-strikes laws) require mandatory sentences (sometimes life in prison without the possibility of parole) for offenders convicted of a third (or second) serious felony. Such mandatory sentencing enhancements are aimed at deterring known and potentially violent offenders and are intended to incapacitate convicted criminals through long-term incarceration.

Lecture Note Explain that some critics of structured sentencing charge that the model does little to promote rehabilitation. Ask students what aspects of the model might lead to such criticism.

Thematic Question Do you think three-strikes laws serve a useful purpose? If so, what is that purpose? What other sentencing arrangements, if any, might meet that purpose?

Thematic Question How might three-strikes laws affect state and federal spending on the criminal justice system? Do you think that such spending can be justified? If so, why?

Three-strikes laws impose longer prison terms than most earlier mandatory minimum sentencing laws. California's three-strikes law, for example, requires that offenders who are convicted of a violent crime and who have had two prior convictions serve a minimum of 25 years in prison. It also doubled prison terms for offenders convicted of a second violent felony.[58] Three-strikes laws also vary in breadth. The laws of some jurisdictions stipulate that both of the prior convictions and the current one be for violent felonies; others require only that the prior convictions be for violent felonies. Some three-strikes laws count only prior adult convictions, while others permit consideration of juvenile offenses.

> Our sentencing system works best when judges have some discretion, but discretion that is bounded by mandatory sentencing guidelines created through the legislative process.
>
> —Alberto Gonzales, former U.S. attorney general[iii]

By passing mandatory sentencing laws, legislators convey the message that certain crimes are deemed especially grave and that people who commit them deserve, and should expect, harsh sanctions. These laws are sometimes passed in response to public outcries following heinous or well-publicized crimes.

diversion
The official suspension of criminal or juvenile proceedings against an alleged offender at any point after a recorded justice system intake, but before the entering of a judgment, and referral of that person to a treatment or care program administered by a nonjustice or private agency. Also, release without referral.

Research findings on the impact of mandatory sentencing laws on the criminal justice system have been summarized by British criminologist Michael Tonry.[59] Tonry found that under mandatory sentencing, officials tend to make earlier and more selective decisions involving arrest, charging, and **diversion** (suspension of criminal proceedings before sentencing and referral to a private agency). They also tend to bargain less and to bring more cases to trial.

In an analysis of federal sentencing guidelines, other researchers found that blacks receive longer sentences than whites, not because they received differential treatment by judges but because they constitute the large majority of those convicted of trafficking in crack cocaine (versus powdered cocaine)[60]—a crime Congress has singled out for especially harsh mandatory penalties. In 2006, for example, 82% of those sentenced under federal crack cocaine laws were black, and only 8.8% were white—even though more than two-thirds of people who use crack cocaine are white.[61] This pattern can be seen as constituting a "disparity in results," and partly for this reason, the U.S. Sentencing Commission has recommended to Congress that it eliminate the legal distinction between crack and regular cocaine for purposes of sentencing (a recommendation that Congress rejected). Recent indications, however, are that the heightened discretion available to federal judges in the wake of *Booker* and *Fanfan* is resulting in sentences that are similar for all types of cocaine trafficking and that vary more by the amount than the type of cocaine involved.[62]

▲ Alternative sentencing in action: Alexandra Espinoso-Amaya, 24, wearing a homemade sign outside the Orlando (Florida) Police Department. Judges sometimes use creative sentences in an attempt to deter offenders from future law violations. How effective a deterrent do you think Espinoso-Amaya's sentence will be?
Orlando Sentinel, *George Skene*/ The Orlando Sentinel

Innovations in Sentencing

Alternative Sentencing Options

4 Identify alternative sanctions, and assess recent sentencing innovations.

In an ever-growing number of cases, innovative judges in certain jurisdictions are using discretionary sentencing to impose truly unique punishments. In 2008, for example, more than two dozen young people who broke into the former home of Pulitzer Prize–winning poet Robert Frost to hold a beer party were required to take classes in Frost's poetry as part of their punishment.[63] Also in 2008, a Florida judge ordered two young men who had thrown 32-ounce cups of soda and ice at a Taco Bell clerk to post a recorded apology on the video-sharing website YouTube.[64]

Lecture Note Describe some of the questions that have been raised about alternative sentencing options by referring to the issues listed here. Ask students how valid they think these objections are. How can these questions best be answered?

Faced with prison overcrowding, high incarceration costs, and public calls for retribution, other judges have used shaming strategies to deter wrongdoers. At least one Florida court ordered those convicted of drunk driving to put a "Convicted DUI" sticker on their license plates. Similarly, a few years ago Boston courts began ordering men convicted of sexual solicitation to spend time sweeping streets in Chinatown, an area known for prostitution, and the public was invited to watch men sentenced to the city's "John Sweep" program clean up streets and alleyways littered with used condoms and sexual paraphernalia. In still other examples, an Arkansas judge made shoplifters walk in front of the stores they stole from, carrying signs describing their crimes, and in California, a purse snatcher was ordered to wear noisy tap dancing shoes whenever he went out in public.[65]

Lecture Note Describe the usefulness of presentence reports in assisting judges in determining the appropriate kind and length of sentence for convicted offenders.

There is considerable support in criminal justice literature for shaming as a crime-reduction strategy. Australian criminologist John Braithwaite, for example, found shaming to be a particularly effective strategy because, he said, it holds the potential to enhance moral awareness among offenders, thereby building conscience and increasing inner control.[66] Dan Kahan, a professor at the University of Chicago Law School, points out that "shame supplies the main motive why people obey the law, not so much because they're afraid of formal sanctions, but because they care what people think about them."[67]

Whether public shaming will grow in popularity as an alternative sentencing strategy is unclear. What is clear, however, is that the American public and an ever-growing number of judicial officials are now looking for workable alternatives to traditional sentencing options.

Questions about Alternative Sanctions

alternative sentencing
The use of court-ordered community service, home detention, day reporting, drug treatment, psychological counseling, victim-offender programming, or intensive supervision in lieu of other, more traditional sanctions, such as imprisonment and fines.

Alternative sentencing includes the use of court-ordered community service, home detention, day reporting, drug treatment, psychological counseling, victim-offender mediation, or intensive supervision in lieu of other, more traditional sanctions, such as imprisonment and fines. Many of these strategies are discussed in more detail in the next chapter.

> Punishment, that is justice for the unjust.
> —Saint Augustine (A.D. 354–430)

As prison populations continue to rise, alternative sentencing strategies are likely to become increasingly attractive. A number of questions must be answered, however, before most alternative sanctions can be employed with confidence, including whether alternative sentencing programs increase the threat to public safety, whether alternative sanctions are cost-effective, and how program outcomes should be judged.[68] Learn more about sentencing in America today by reading the Sentencing Project's report, *The State of Sentencing 2007: Developments in Policy and Practice*, at **Library Extra 9–6**.

The Presentence Investigation

presentence investigation (PSI)
The examination of a convicted offender's background prior to sentencing. Presentence examinations are generally conducted by probation or parole officers and are submitted to sentencing authorities.

Before imposing sentence, a judge may request information on the background of a convicted defendant. This is especially true in indeterminate sentencing jurisdictions, where judges retain considerable discretion in selecting sanctions. Traditional wisdom has held that certain factors increase the likelihood of rehabilitation and reduce the need for lengthy prison terms. These factors include a good job record, satisfactory educational attainment, strong family ties, church attendance, no prior arrests for violent offenses, and psychological stability.

Information about a defendant's background often comes to the judge in the form of a **presentence investigation (PSI)** report. The task of preparing PSI reports usually falls to the

Career Profile
Instructor of Criminal Justice

Name: Carol P. Getty

Position: Associate Professor of Criminal Justice, Park University

Colleges attended: University of Missouri—Kansas City (PhD, Public Administration and Political Science), Arizona State University (MS, Criminal Justice), Wellesley College (BA, Mathematics)

What criminal justice-related jobs have you held? 1978–1983: Member and vice chair of the Arizona Board of Pardons and Parole. I was appointed vice chair following years of volunteer service to the Junior League of Phoenix, City of Phoenix, Maricopa County Board of Supervisors, and the Arizona Governor's Office. 1983–1996: Commissioner of the U.S. Parole Commission, North Central Region.

1991–1992: Chairman of the U.S. Parole Commission in Washington, D.C. I was appointed by President Bush and was the first and only woman to chair the commission in its 75-year history.

1997–2000: Assistant professor; then associate professor of criminal justice.

2001–2008: Chair of the Criminal Justice Department.

What positions did you like most? I've liked all my criminal justice positions for different reasons. I liked being in charge and running a region and a commission because these positions fit my personality. It was confidence-building and personally rewarding to lead both the region and the commission, although certainly frustrating at times.

I also love helping students understand the criminal justice system and enjoy watching them succeed and graduate. It's rewarding to teach and not worry about all the decisions connected with managing and leading.

What qualities or characteristics most helped you succeed in the field? I have a desire to change the current retributive system of criminal justice and return it to a rehabilitative system. I strongly believe in the importance of the positions I have held and have tried to do my best; I have a strong work ethic. Besides caring, I believe I am a good listener and a good decision maker.

What are the typical salary ranges students can expect entering these fields? Salary ranges depend on the times and the level of government, with the federal criminal justice system paying better than the state or local criminal justice agencies.

What advice would you give students early in their college career to help them find a rewarding job in criminal justice? Begin working in institutional or community corrections. Once you are working in criminal justice and have an understanding how systems actually function, consider transferring to a position in courts or law enforcement, if you prefer. Volunteer whenever and wherever you can, even as a high school or college student.

Source: Reprinted by permission of Carol P. Getty, Ph.D. Photo courtesy of Carol P. Getty. Logo courtesy of Park University.

probation or parole office. The report takes one of three forms: (1) a detailed written report on the defendant's personal and criminal history, including an assessment of present conditions in the defendant's life (often called the *long form*); (2) an abbreviated written report summarizing the information most likely to be useful in a sentencing decision (the *short form*); and (3) a verbal report to the court made by the investigating officer based on field notes but structured according to established categories. A PSI report is much like a résumé, except that it focuses on what might be regarded as negative as well as positive life experiences.

The data on which a presentence report is based come from a variety of sources. The FBI's National Crime Information Center (NCIC), begun in 1967, contains computerized information on people wanted for criminal offenses throughout the United States. Individual jurisdictions also maintain criminal records repositories that can provide comprehensive files on the criminal history of those who have been processed by the justice system.

Sometimes the defendant provides much of the information for the PSI. In this case, efforts must be made to corroborate the defendant's information. Unconfirmed data are generally marked on the report as "defendant-supplied data" or simply "unconfirmed."

5 Describe the nature and importance of the presentence investigation report.

In a PSI report, most third-party data are subject to ethical and legal considerations. The official records of almost all agencies and organizations, though often an ideal source of information, are protected by state and federal privacy requirements; in particular, the federal Privacy Act of 1974[69] may limit access to these records. Investigators must first check on the legal availability of all records before requesting them and must receive in writing the defendant's permission to access the records. Other public laws, among them the federal Freedom of Information Act,[70] may make the presentence report available to the defendant, although courts and court officers have generally been held to be exempt from the provision of such statutes.

Thematic Question How do the elements of a presentence report reflect assumptions about the causes of criminal behavior? Are the elements more supportive of an individual-rights approach or a public-order approach to crime control?

▲ U.S. Attorney General Eric H. Holder, Jr., speaking at the 2009 Office for Victims of Crime Candlelight Ceremony. What more can the justice system do for crime victims? What more should it do? *© S. Craig Crawford/U.S. Department of Justice*

The final section of a PSI report is usually devoted to the investigating officer's recommendations. A recommendation may be made in favor of probation, split sentencing, a term of imprisonment, or any other sentencing option available in the jurisdiction. Participation in community service programs or in drug- or substance-abuse programs may be recommended for probationers. Most judges are willing to accept the report writer's recommendation because they recognize the professionalism of the presentence investigator and because they know that the investigator may be assigned to supervise the defendant if he or she is sentenced to a community alternative.

Jurisdictions vary in their use of the information in a PSI. Federal law mandates PSI reports in federal criminal courts and specifies 15 topical areas that each report must cover. The 1984 federal Determinate Sentencing Act directs report writers to include the classification of the offense and of the defendant under the offense-level and criminal history categories established by the statute. Some states require presentence reports only in felony cases. Some require them in cases where the defendant faces the possibility of incarceration for six months or more. Other states have no requirement for PSI reports beyond those ordered by a judge.

Report writing, rarely anyone's favorite task, may seriously tax the limited resources of probation agencies. In September 2004, officers from the New York City Department of Probation wrote 2,414 reports for adult offenders and 461 reports for juvenile offenders, averaging about 10 reports per probation officer per month.[71] Learn more about the sentencing environment at **Library Extra 9–7**.

The Victim—Forgotten No Longer

Victims' Rights

Thanks to a grassroots resurgence of concern for the plight of victims that began in this country in the early 1970s, the sentencing process now frequently includes consideration of the needs of victims and their survivors.[72] In times past, although victims might testify at trial, the criminal justice system frequently downplayed victims' experiences, including the psychological trauma engendered both by having been victims and by having to endure the criminal proceedings that bring a criminal to justice. That changed in 1982 when the President's Task Force on Victims of Crime gave focus to a burgeoning victims' rights movement and urged the widespread expansion of victims' assistance programs during what was then their formative period.[73] Victims' assistance programs today offer services in the areas of crisis intervention and follow-up counseling and help victims secure their rights under the law.[74] Following successful prosecution, some victims' assistance programs also advise victims on the filing of civil suits to recoup financial losses directly from the offender.

6 Describe the history of victims' rights and services, and discuss the growing role of the victim in criminal justice proceedings today.

About the same time, voters in California approved Proposition 8, a resolution that called for changes in the state's constitution to reflect concern for victims. A continuing goal of victims' advocacy groups is an amendment to the U.S. Constitution, which such groups say is needed to provide the same kind of fairness to victims that is routinely accorded to defendants. In the past, for example, the National Victims' Constitutional Amendment Project (NVCAP) has sought to add a phrase to the Sixth Amendment—"likewise, the victim, in every criminal prosecution, shall have the right to be present and to be heard at all critical stages of judicial proceedings." NVCAP now advocates the addition of a new amendment to the U.S. Constitution. Visit NVCAP at **Web Extra 9–6**.

In September 1996, a victims' rights constitutional amendment—Senate Joint Resolution 65—was proposed by a bipartisan committee in the U.S. Congress,[75] but problems of wording and terminology prevented its passage. A revised amendment was proposed in 1998,[76] but its wording was too restrictive for it to gain endorsement from victims' organizations.[77] In 1999, a

Lecture Note Discuss the growing victims' rights movement, and draw students' attention to the now widespread demand for a victims' bill of rights.

Class Activity Invite a victims' rights advocate to speak with the class, either in person or through virtual conferencing. Ask him or her to describe the important issues represented by the victims' rights movement and to discuss how the structure of criminal trials currently overlooks the interests of victims.

Thematic Question Do you support a constitutional amendment setting forth the rights of victims in a criminal proceeding? If so, what provisions should the amendment contain? If not, why not?

CJ Exhibit 9–2
Victims' Rights in California

In order to preserve and protect a victim's rights to justice and due process, a victim shall be entitled to the following rights:

1. To be treated with fairness and respect for his or her privacy and dignity, and to be free from intimidation, harassment, and abuse, throughout the criminal or juvenile justice process.
2. To be reasonably protected from the defendant and persons acting on behalf of the defendant.
3. To have the safety of the victim and the victim's family considered in fixing the amount of bail and release conditions for the defendant.
4. To prevent the disclosure of confidential information or records to the defendant, the defendant's attorney, or any other person acting on behalf of the defendant, which could be used to locate or harass the victim or the victim's family or which disclose confidential communications made in the course of medical or counseling treatment, or which are otherwise privileged or confidential by law.
5. To refuse an interview, deposition, or discovery request by the defendant, the defendant's attorney, or any other person acting on behalf of the defendant, and to set reasonable conditions on the conduct of any such interview to which the victim consents.
6. To reasonable notice of and to reasonably confer with the prosecuting agency, upon request, regarding the arrest of the defendant if known by the prosecutor, the charges filed, the determination whether to extradite the defendant, and, upon request, to be notified of and informed before any pretrial disposition of the case.
7. To reasonable notice of all public proceedings, including delinquency proceedings, upon request, at which the defendant and the prosecutor are entitled to be present and of all parole or other post-conviction release proceedings, and to be present at all such proceedings.
8. To be heard, upon request, at any proceeding, including any delinquency proceeding, involving a post-arrest release decision, plea, sentencing, post-conviction release decision, or any proceeding in which a right of the victim is at issue.
9. To a speedy trial and a prompt and final conclusion of the case and any related post-judgment proceedings.
10. To provide information to a probation department official conducting a pre-sentence investigation concerning the impact of the offense on the victim and the victim's family and any sentencing recommendations before the sentencing of the defendant.
11. To receive, upon request, the pre-sentence report when available to the defendant, except for those portions made confidential by law.
12. To be informed, upon request, of the conviction, sentence, place and time of incarceration, or other disposition of the defendant, the scheduled release date of the defendant, and the release of or the escape by the defendant from custody.
13. To restitution.
14. To the prompt return of property when no longer needed as evidence.
15. To be informed of all parole procedures, to participate in the parole process, to provide information to the parole authority to be considered before the parole of the offender, and to be notified, upon request, of the parole or other release of the offender.
16. To have the safety of the victim, the victim's family, and the general public considered before any parole or other post-judgment release decision is made.
17. To be informed of the rights enumerated in paragraphs (1) through (16).

Source: Section 28(e) of Article I of the California Constitution.

new amendment was proposed by the Senate Judiciary Committee's Subcommittee on the Constitution, Federalism, and Property, but it did not make it to the Senate floor. The U.S. Department of Justice, which had previously supported the measure, reversed its position due to a provision in the proposed amendment that gives crime victims the right to be notified of any state or federal grant of clemency. The U.S. attorney general apparently believed that the provision would impede the power of the president. The legislation also lacked the support of President Bill Clinton and was officially withdrawn by its sponsors in 2000.

Although a victims' rights amendment to the federal Constitution may not yet be a reality, more than 30 states have passed their own victims' rights amendments.[78] According to NVCAP, California Proposition 9, or the Victims' Rights and Protection Act of 2008 (also known as *Marsy's Law*), is the most comprehensive victims' bill of rights of any state in the nation.[79] Proposition 9, which appeared on the November 4, 2008, statewide ballot in California, passed with 53.8% of the vote. It amended the California Constitution by adding new provisions that provide victims in California with a number of specifically enforceable rights (CJ Exhibit 9–2).

> Of all the initiatives that this Congress could undertake, few will touch the heart of Americans as dearly as the measure seeking to ensure that the judicial process is just and fair for the victims of crime.
>
> —Orrin Hatch, U.S. senator from Utah

At the federal level, the 1982 Victim and Witness Protection Act (VWPA)[80] requires judges to consider victim-impact statements at federal sentencing hearings and places responsibility for their creation on federal probation officers. In 1984, the federal Victims of Crime Act (VOCA) was enacted with substantial bipartisan support. VOCA authorized federal

We will not punish a man because he hath offended, but that he may offend no more.
—Seneca (4 B.C.–A.D. 65)

funding to help states establish victims' assistance and victims' compensation programs. Under VOCA, the U.S. Department of Justice's Office for Victims of Crime provides a significant source of both funding and information for victims' assistance programs.

The rights of victims were further strengthened under the Violent Crime Control and Law Enforcement Act of 1994, which created a federal right of allocution, or right to speak, for victims of violent and sex crimes. This gave victims the right to speak at the sentencing of their assailants. The 1994 law also requires sex offenders and child molesters convicted under federal law to pay restitution to their victims and prohibits the diversion of federal victims' funds to other programs. Other provisions of the 1994 law provide civil rights remedies for victims of felonies motivated by gender bias and extend rape shield law protections to civil cases and to all criminal cases, prohibiting inquiries into a victim's sexual history. A significant feature of the 1994 law can be found in a subsection titled the Violence against Women Act (VAWA). VAWA, which provides financial support for police, prosecutors, and victims' services in cases involving sexual violence or domestic abuse, is discussed in greater detail in Chapter 2.

Much of the philosophical basis of today's victims' movement can be found in the restorative justice model, which was discussed briefly earlier in this chapter. Restorative justice emphasizes offender accountability and victim reparation. It also provides the basis for victims' compensation programs, which are another means of recognizing the needs of crime victims. Today, all 50 states have passed legislation providing for monetary payments to victims of crime. Such payments are primarily designed to compensate victims for medical expenses and lost wages. All existing programs require that applicants meet certain eligibility criteria, and most set limits on the maximum amount of compensation that can be received. Generally disallowed are claims from victims who are significantly responsible for their own victimization, such as those who end up being the losers in fights they provoke. In 2002, California's victims' compensation program, the largest in the nation, provided $117 million to more than 50,000 victims for crime-related expenses. A comprehensive California proposal to improve victims' services can be read at **Library Extra 9–8**.

In 2001, the USA PATRIOT Act amended the Victims of Crime Act of 1984 to make victims of terrorism and their families eligible for victims' compensation payments.[81] It also created an antiterrorism emergency reserve fund to help provide compensation to victims of terrorism. A year earlier, in November 2000, the federal Office for Victims of Crime (OVC) created the Terrorism and International Victims Unit (TIVU) to develop and manage programs and initiatives that help victims of domestic and international terrorism, mass violence, and crimes with transnational dimensions.[82]

On October 9, 2004, the U.S. Senate passed the Crime Victims' Rights Act,[83] as part of the Justice for All Act of 2004. Some saw the legislation as at least a partial statutory alternative to a constitutional crime victims' rights amendment. The Crime Victims' Rights Act establishes statutory rights for victims of federal crimes and gives them the necessary legal authority to assert those rights in federal court. The act grants the following rights to victims of federal crimes:[84]

1. The right to be reasonably protected from the accused
2. The right to reasonable, accurate, and timely notice of any public proceeding involving the crime or of any release or escape of the accused
3. The right to be included in any such public proceeding
4. The right to be reasonably heard at any public proceeding involving release, plea, or sentencing
5. The right to confer with the federal prosecutor handling the case
6. The right to full and timely restitution as provided by law
7. The right to proceedings free from unreasonable delay
8. The right to be treated with fairness and with respect for the victim's dignity and privacy

In addition to establishing these rights, the legislation expressly requires federal courts to ensure that they are afforded to victims. In like manner, federal law enforcement officials are required to make their "best efforts to see that crime victims are notified of, and

Lecture Note Discuss the purpose of victim-impact statements and the role they play during a sentencing hearing.

Thematic Question What is a victim-impact statement? Do you think victim-impact statements should be admissible at the sentencing stage of criminal trials? If so, what material should they contain? What material should not be permitted in such reports? How could the information in victim-impact statements best be verified?

Freedom or Safety? You Decide.
To What Degree Should the Personal Values of Workers in the Criminal Justice System Influence Job Performance?

In 2007, a 21-year-old college student who was visiting Tampa, Florida, for the annual Gasparilla festival, a pirate-themed parade, called police to say that she was attacked and raped while walking back to her car. The woman's story took an interesting twist. Investigating officers first took her to a nearby rape crisis center where she was physically examined and given the first dose of an emergency postcoital contraception pill, also known as a *morning-after pill*, to prevent unwanted pregnancy.

Officers then drove the victim through the area where the attack was said to have taken place in an effort to find the rapist and to pinpoint the scene of the crime. As they drove, officers entered the woman's identifying information into their car's computer system and discovered an outstanding juvenile warrant that had been issued against her in 2003 for unpaid restitution in a theft case. Once they discovered the warrant, they promptly arrested the woman. She remained behind bars for two days until her family could hire an attorney who arranged for her release.

While she was jailed, the victim said that a jail health-care worker refused to administer a second—and required—dose of the morning-after medication. The medicine's manufacturer specifies that two doses of the medication, administered 20 hours apart, are needed to prevent pregnancy. Some members of the local media, which accused the police department of insensitivity to the needs of crime victims, reported that the jail worker felt compelled to deny the woman the medication due to personal religious beliefs against use of the pill.

Vic Moore, the jailed woman's attorney, told reporters that he was "[S]hocked. Stunned. Outraged. I don't have words to describe it." He notes, "She is not a victim of any one person. She is a victim of the system. There's just got to be some humanity involved when it's a victim of rape."

The Tampa Police Department, which was stung by media reports in the case, has since initiated a policy telling officers not to arrest a crime victim who has suffered injury or mental trauma whenever reasonably possible.

YOU DECIDE

To what extent (if at all) should the values of workers within the criminal justice system be allowed to influence their performance of job-related tasks? Do you feel that the jail health-care worker was within her "rights" to deny a second dose of the morning-after pill to the victim of an alleged rape? Why or why not?

Reference: Phil Davis, "Rape Victim Is Jailed on Old Warrant," Associated Press, January 31, 2007.

accorded," these rights. To teach citizens about the rights of victims of crime, the federal government created crimevictims.gov, which you can access at **Web Extra 9–7**. This resource includes an online directory of crime victims' services, which can be searched locally, nationally, and internationally.

Victim-Impact Statements

Another consequence of the national victims' rights movement has been a call for the use of a **victim-impact statement**—a written document describing the losses, suffering, and trauma experienced by the crime victim or by the victim's survivors—before sentencing. Judges are expected to consider such a statement in arriving at an appropriate sanction for the offender.

victim-impact statement
An in-court statement made by the victim or by survivors to sentencing authorities seeking to make an informed sentencing decision.

The drive to mandate inclusion of victim impact statements in sentencing decisions, already required in federal courts by the 1982 VWPA, was substantially enhanced by the "right of allocution" provision of the Violent Crime Control and Law Enforcement Act of 1994. Victim-impact statements played a prominent role in the sentencing of Timothy McVeigh, who was convicted of the 1995 bombing of the Murrah Federal Building in Oklahoma City and was executed in 2001. Some states, however, have gone further than the federal government. In 1984, for example, California passed legislation giving victims a right to attend and participate in sentencing and parole hearings.[85] Approximately 20 states now have laws requiring citizen involvement in sentencing. All 50 states and the District of Columbia "allow for some form of submission of a victim impact statement either at the time of sentencing or to be contained in the presentence investigation reports" made by court officers.[86] Where written victim-impact statements are not available, courts may invite the victim to testify directly at sentencing. An alternative to written statements and to the appearance of victims at sentencing hearings is the victim-impact video. Some contemporary victim-impact videos display photo montages of victims' lives and are set to music and narrated. In 2008, for example, the U.S. Supreme Court rejected an appeal from a death-row inmate wanting to exclude just such a digitized narrative set to music by Enya that had played to the jury during the sentencing phase of his trial.[87] The full video is available at **Library Extra 9–9**.

Thematic Question What individual rights might be supported by victim-impact statements? What rights might be harmed?

Lecture Note Tell the class that victim-impact evidence is simply another form of guidance available to sentencing judges. Discuss the possibility that victim-impact statements might result in the imposition of inequitable sentences.

Thematic Question Advocates of victim-impact statements argue that some victims have a greater inherent worth than others when measured in terms of social harm. Do you agree? Explain.

One study of the efficacy of victim-impact statements found that sentencing decisions are rarely affected by them. The authors concluded that victim-impact statements have little effect on courts because judges and other officials "have established ways of making decisions which do not call for explicit information about the impact of crime on victims."[88] Learn more about the rights of crime victims and the history of the victims' movement at **Web Extra 9–8**.

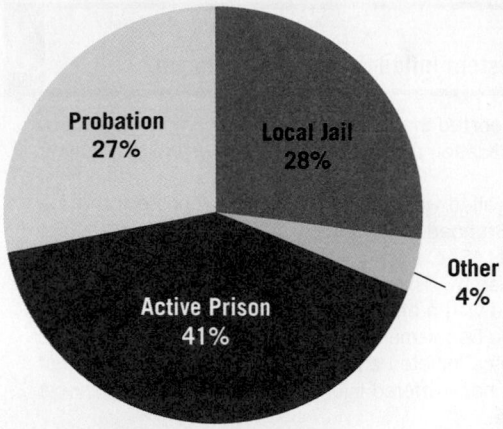

FIGURE 9–3 The Sentencing of Convicted Felons in State Courts, by Type of Sentence

Source: Data from Sean Rosenmerkel, Matthew Durose, and Donald Farole, Jr., *Felony Sentences in State Courts, 2006* (Washington, DC: Bureau of Justice Statistics, December 2009).

Modern Sentencing Options

Sentencing Rationales

7 List four contemporary sentencing options.

Sentencing is fundamentally a risk-management strategy designed to protect the public while serving the ends of retribution, incapacitation, deterrence, rehabilitation, and restoration. Because the goals of sentencing are difficult to agree on, so too are sanctions. Lengthy prison terms do little for rehabilitation, while community release programs can hardly protect the innocent from offenders bent on continuing criminality.

Assorted sentencing philosophies continue to permeate state-level judicial systems. Each state has its own sentencing laws, and frequent revisions of those statutes are not uncommon. Because of huge variations from one state to another in the laws and procedures that control the imposition of criminal sanctions, sentencing has been called "the most diversified part of the Nation's criminal justice process."[89]

There is at least one commonality, however. It can be found in the four traditional sanctions that continue to dominate the thinking of most legislators and judges: fines, probation, imprisonment, and death. Fines and the death penalty are discussed in this chapter; probation is described in Chapter 10, and imprisonment is covered in Chapters 11 and 12.

Thematic Question What are the four traditional sentencing options identified in this chapter? What kinds of crimes, or sets of circumstances, are most appropriate for the imposition of each of these sentences?

In jurisdictions that employ indeterminate sentencing, fines, probation, and imprisonment are widely available to judges. The option selected generally depends on the severity of the offense and the judge's best guess as to the likelihood of the defendant's future criminal involvement. Sometimes two or more options are combined, such as when an offender is fined and sentenced to prison or placed on probation and fined in support of restitution payments.

Jurisdictions that operate under presumptive sentencing guidelines generally limit the judge's choice to only one option and often specify the extent to which that option can be applied. Dollar amounts of fines, for example, are rigidly set, and prison terms are specified for each type of offense. The death penalty remains an option in a fair number of jurisdictions, but only for a highly select group of offenders.

Sentencing Practices

A recent report by the Bureau of Justice Statistics on the sentencing practices of trial courts found that state courts convicted 1,132,000 felons in 2006.[90] Another 66,518 felony convictions occurred in federal courts. As shown in Figure 9–3, the report also found the following for offenders convicted of felonies in state courts:

- About 41% were sentenced to active prison terms; another 28% received jail sentences involving less than one year's confinement.
- The average sentence length for those sent to state prisons has decreased since 1990 (from six years to four years and eleven months).
- Felons sentenced in 2006 were likely to serve more of their sentence before release (50%) than those sentenced in 1990 (33%).
- Of the total, 27% percent were sentenced to probation with no jail or prison time to serve.
- The average probation sentence was 38 months.
- The largest offense category for which state felons were sent to prison was drug offenses.

Although the percentage of felons who receive active sentences may seem low, the number of criminal defendants receiving active prison time has increased dramatically.

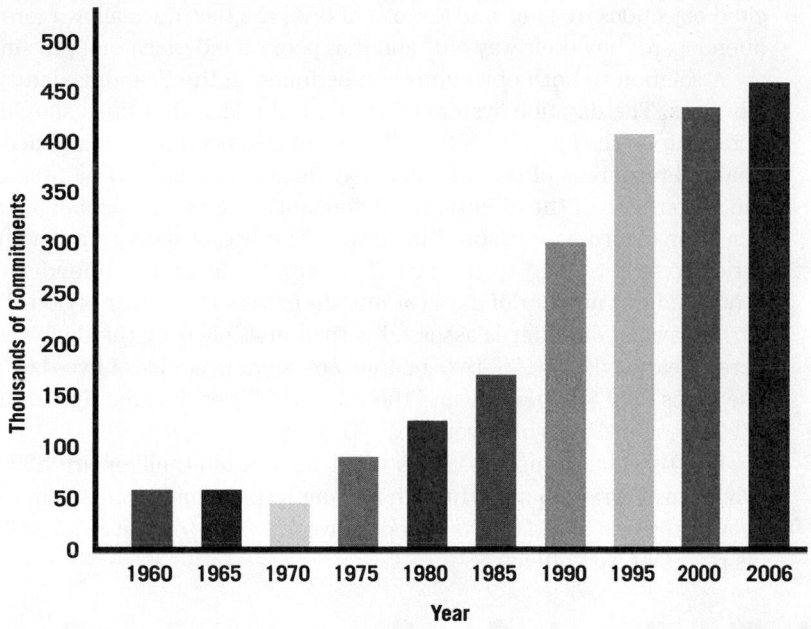

FIGURE 9–4 Court-Ordered Prison Commitments, 1960–2006

Source: Data from Sean Rosenmerkel, Matthew Durose, and Donald Farole, Jr., *Felony Sentences in State Courts, 2006* (Washington, DC: Bureau of Justice Statistics, December 2009), and other years.

Figure 9–4 shows that the number of court-ordered prison commitments has increased nearly eightfold in the past 40 years.

> There is only one basic human right, the right to do as you please unless it causes others harm. With it comes the only basic human duty, the duty to take the consequences.
>
> —P. J. O'Rourke

Fines

While the fine is one of the oldest forms of punishment, the use of fines as a criminal sanction suffers from built-in inequities and a widespread failure to collect them. Inequities arise when offenders with vastly different financial resources are fined similar amounts. A fine of $100, for example, can place a painful economic burden on a poor defendant but is negligible when imposed on a wealthy offender.

Nonetheless, fines are once again receiving attention as a serious sentencing alternative. One reason for the renewed interest is the stress placed on state resources by burgeoning prison populations. The extensive imposition of fines not only results in less crowded prisons but can contribute to state and local coffers and can lower the tax burden of law-abiding citizens. There are other advantages:

- Fines can deprive offenders of the proceeds of criminal activity.
- Fines can promote rehabilitation by enforcing economic responsibility.
- Fines can be collected by existing criminal justice agencies and are relatively inexpensive to administer.
- Fines can be made proportionate to both the severity of the offense and the ability of the offender to pay.

A National Institute of Justice (NIJ) survey found that an average of 86% of convicted defendants in courts of limited jurisdiction receive fines as sentences, some in combination with another penalty.[91] Fines are also widely used in courts of general jurisdiction, where the NIJ study found judges imposing fines in 42% of all cases that came before them for sentencing. Some studies estimate that more than $1 billion in fines are collected nationwide each year.[92]

Fines are often imposed for relatively minor law violations, such as driving while intoxicated, reckless driving, disturbing the peace, disorderly conduct, public drunkenness, and vandalism. Judges in many courts, however, report the use of fines for relatively serious violations of the law, including assault, auto theft, embezzlement, fraud, and sale and possession of various controlled substances. Fines are most likely to be imposed where the offender has both a clean record and the ability to pay.[93]

Studies have found that courts of limited jurisdiction, which are the most likely to impose fines, are also the least likely to have adequate information on offenders' financial status.[94] Perhaps as a consequence, some judges are reluctant to impose fines. Two of the most widely

Lecture Note Discuss Figure 9–4. Ask the class to identify likely reasons for the increase in court-ordered prison commitments between 1960 and 2004.

Lecture Note Review the usefulness of monetary fines as criminal sanctions in terms of the advantages identified in this chapter.

Lecture Note Review the objections to the use of fines. Discuss whether these objections might be more appropriate for certain classes of offenders (drug dealers, for example) than for others.

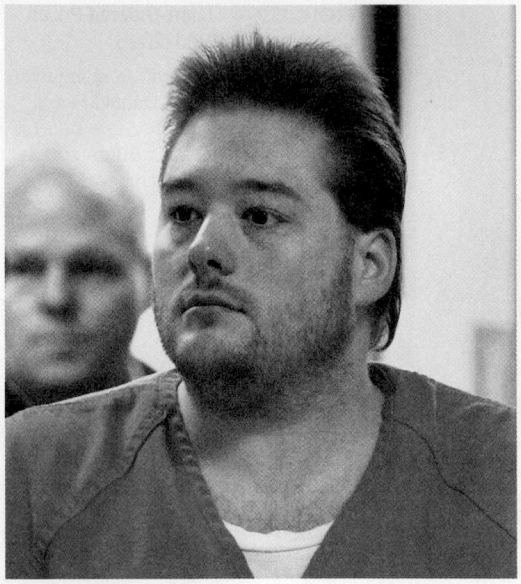

▲ Kevin Ray Underwood, who murdered his ten-year-old neighbor when he was 26. Underwood had planned to cannibalize the girl's body but was arrested before he could carry out his plans. He was sentenced to death in 2008. Was the sentence just?
The Oklahoman/*Steve Sisney/AP Wide World Photos*

cited objections by judges to the use of fines are that fines allow more affluent offenders to "buy their way out" and that poor offenders cannot pay fines.[95]

A solution to both objections can be found in the Scandinavian system of day fines. The day-fine system is based on the idea that fines should be proportionate to the severity of the offense but also need to take into account the financial resources of the offender. Day fines are computed by first assessing the seriousness of the offense, the defendant's degree of culpability, and his or her prior record as measured in "days." The use of days as a benchmark of seriousness is related to the fact that, without fines, the offender could be sentenced to a number of days (or months or years) in jail or prison. The number of days an offender is assessed is then multiplied by the daily wages that person earns. Hence, if two people are sentenced to a five-day fine but one earns only $20 per day and the other $200 per day, the first would pay a $100 fine and the second would pay $1,000.

In 2010, for example, a Swiss court fined a multimillionaire $290,000 for driving his Ferrari 85 mph through a 35-mph speed limit zone.[96] The court calculated the fine based on the speeder's wealth (said to total $22.7 million) and his record of past offenses.

Death: The Ultimate Sanction

Some crimes are especially heinous and seem to cry out for extreme punishment. In 2008, for example, a 28-year-old grocery store stock clerk named Kevin Ray Underwood was sentenced to death in the murder of a 10-year-old girl in what authorities said was an elaborate plan to cannibalize the girl's flesh.[97] Underwood had been the girl's neighbor in Purcell, Oklahoma, and her mutilated body, covered with deep saw marks, was discovered in his apartment. Investigators told reporters that Underwood had sexually assaulted the little girl and had planned to eat her corpse using the meat tenderizer and barbecue skewers that they confiscated from his kitchen. "In my 24 years as a prosecutor, this ranks as one of the most heinous and atrocious cases I've ever been involved with," said McClain County Prosecutor Tim Kuykendalls.

capital punishment
The death penalty. Capital punishment is the most extreme of all sentencing options.

capital offense
A criminal offense punishable by death.

Many states today have statutory provisions that provide for a sentence of **capital punishment** (the death penalty) for especially repugnant crimes (known as **capital offenses**). Estimates are that more than 18,800 legal executions have been carried out in the United States since 1608, when records began to be kept on capital punishment.[98] Although capital punishment was widely used throughout the eighteenth and nineteenth centuries, the mid-twentieth century offered a brief respite in the number of offenders legally executed in this country. Between 1930 and 1967, the year in which the U.S. Supreme Court ordered a nationwide stay of pending executions, nearly 3,800 people were put to death. The peak years were 1935 and 1936, with nearly 200 legal killings each year. Executions declined substantially every year thereafter. Between 1967 and 1977, a *de facto* moratorium existed, with no executions carried out in any U.S. jurisdiction. Following the lifting of the moratorium, executions resumed (Figure 9–5). In 1983, only five offenders were put to death, while 52 were executed nationwide in 2009.[99] A modern record for executions was set in 1999, with 98 executions—35 in Texas alone.

Today, the federal government and 37 of the 50 states[100] permit execution for first-degree murder, while treason, kidnapping, aggravated rape, murder of a police or correctional officer, and murder while under a life sentence are punishable by death in selected jurisdictions. New Jersey, which up until recently was among states with a death penalty, repealed its capital punishment statute in 2007, replacing it with a sentence of life in prison without possibility of parole.

Thematic Question Choose three offenses usually punishable by a fine, and consider other appropriate sanctions that might be applied. In your opinion, are fines the most effective way to deal with the offender in each case?

Lecture Note Review the historical imposition of the death penalty, beginning with the early Greeks.

The list of crimes punishable by death under federal jurisdiction increased dramatically with passage of the Violent Crime Control and Law Enforcement Act of 1994 and was expanded still further by the 2001 USA PATRIOT Act, a federal law that focuses on fighting terrorism. The list now includes a total of about 60 offenses. State legislators have also worked to expand the types of crimes for which a death sentence can be imposed. In 1997, for example, the Louisiana Supreme Court upheld the state's year-old child rape statute, which allows for the imposition of a capital sentence when the victim is younger than

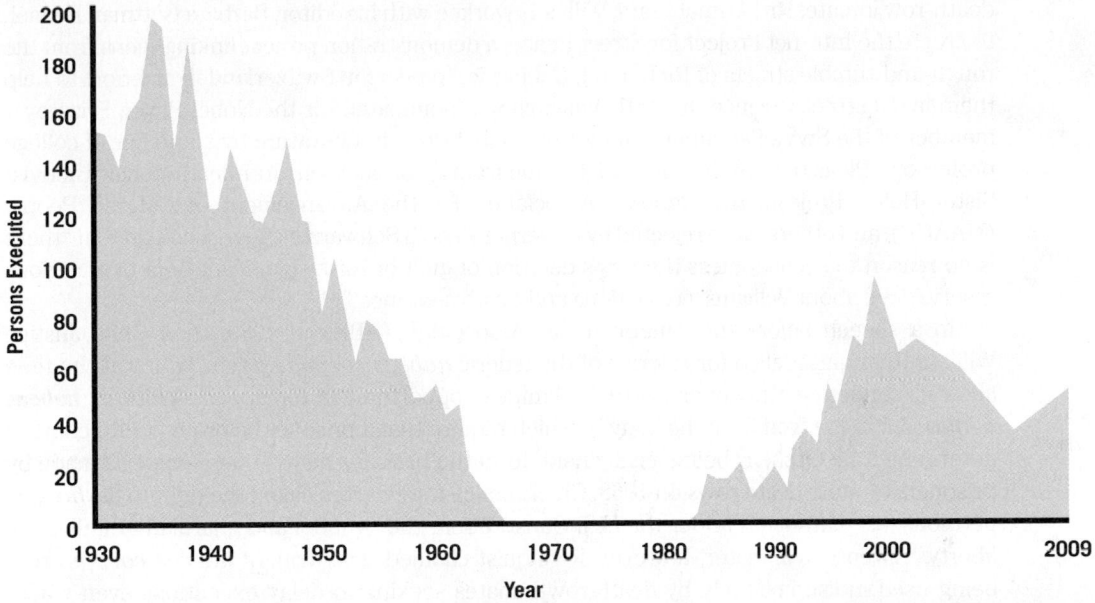

FIGURE 9–5 Court-Ordered Executions Carried Out in the United States, 1976–2009

Source: Reprinted with permission from the Death Penalty Information Center.

12 years of age. The case involved an AIDS-infected father who raped his three daughters, ages five, eight, and nine. In upholding the father's death sentence, the Louisiana court ruled that child rape is "like no other crime."[101] In 2008, however, in the case of *Kennedy* v. *Louisiana*,[102] the U.S. Supreme Court ruled that the Eighth Amendment bars Louisiana (and other states) from imposing the death penalty for the rape of a child where the crime did not result, and was not intended to result, in the victim's death.

A total of 3,261 offenders were under sentence of death throughout the United States on January 1, 2010.[103] The latest statistics show that 98.2% of those on death row are male, approximately 44.4% are white, 11.8% are Hispanic, 41.4% are African American, and a small number are of other races (mostly Native American and Pacific Islander).[104]

Methods of imposing death vary by state. The majority of death-penalty states authorize execution through lethal injection. Electrocution is the second most common means of dispatch, while hanging, the gas chamber, and firing squads have survived, at least as options available to the condemned, in a few states.[105] For the most current statistical information on capital punishment, visit the Death Penalty Information Center (DPIC) at **Web Extra 9–9**. Learn more about the history of capital punishment at **Library Extra 9–10**.

Habeas Corpus Review

The legal process through which a capital sentence is carried to conclusion is fraught with problems. One serious difficulty centers on the fact that automatic review of all death sentences by appellate courts and constant legal maneuvering by defense counsel often lead to a dramatic delay between the time the sentence is handed down and the time it is carried out. Today, an average of ten years and eight months passes between the imposition of a death penalty and execution.[106] Such lengthy delays, compounded by uncertainty over whether an execution will ever occur, directly contravene the generally accepted notion that punishment should be swift and certain.

Thematic Question What factors go into determining whether someone deserves the death penalty? What assumptions about people with mental or physical disabilities might affect the application of the death penalty? What alternatives do we have for such defendants?

Even death-row inmates can undergo life-altering changes. When that happens, long-delayed executions can become highly questionable events. The case of Stanley "Tookie" Williams, who was executed at California's San Quentin Prison in 2005 at age 51, is illustrative.[107] Williams, self-described cofounder of the infamous Crips street gang in the early 1970s, was sentenced to die for the brutal shotgun murders of four people during a robbery 26 years earlier. In 1993, however, he experienced what he called a "reawakening" and began working from prison as an antigang crusader. Williams found a sympathetic publisher and wrote a series of children's books titled *Tookie Speaks Out against Gang Violence.* The series was intended to help urban youth reject the lure of gang membership and embrace traditional values. He also wrote *Life in Prison*, an autobiography describing the isolation and despair experienced by death-row inmates. In his final years, Williams worked with his editor, Barbara Cottman Becnel, to create the Internet Project for Street Peace, a demonstration project linking teens from the rough-and-tumble streets of Richmond, California, to peers in Switzerland in an effort to help them avoid street violence. In 2001, Williams was nominated for the Nobel Peace Prize by a member of the Swiss Parliament and for the Nobel Prize in Literature by a number of college professors. Pleas to spare his life, which came from Jesse Jackson, anti-death-penalty activist Sister Helen Prejean, the National Association for the Advancement of Colored People (NAACP), and others, were rejected by Governor Arnold Schwarzenegger, who said that "there is no reason to second-guess the jury's decision of guilt or raise significant doubts or serious reservations about Williams' convictions and death sentence."[108]

writ of *habeas corpus*
A writ that directs the person detaining a prisoner to bring him or her before a judicial officer to determine the lawfulness of the imprisonment.

In a speech before the American Bar Association (ABA) in 1989, then–Chief Justice William Rehnquist called for reforms of the federal *habeas corpus* system, which at the time allowed condemned prisoners virtually limitless opportunities for appeal. **Writs of *habeas corpus*** (Latin for "you have the body"), which require that a prisoner be brought into court to determine if he or she is being legally held, form the basis for many federal appeals made by prisoners on state death rows. In 1968, Chief Justice Earl Warren called the right to file *habeas* petitions, as guaranteed under the U.S. Constitution, the "symbol and guardian of individual liberty." Twenty years later, however, Rehnquist claimed that writs of *habeas corpus* were being used indiscriminately by death-row inmates seeking to delay executions even where grounds for delay did not exist. "The capital defendant does not need to prevail on the merits in order to accomplish his purpose," said Rehnquist. "He wins temporary victories by postponing a final adjudication."[109]

In a move to reduce delays in the carrying out of executions, the U.S. Supreme Court, in the case of *McCleskey* v. *Zant* (1991),[110] limited the number of appeals a condemned person may lodge with the courts. Saying that repeated filing for the sole purpose of delay promotes "disrespect for the finality of convictions" and "disparages the entire criminal justice system," the Court established a two-pronged criterion for future appeals. According to *McCleskey*, in any petition beyond the first filed with the federal court, a capital defendant must (1) demonstrate good cause why the claim now being made was not included in the first filing and (2) explain how the absence of that claim may have harmed the petitioner's ability to mount an effective defense. Two months later, the Court reinforced *McCleskey* when it ruled, in *Coleman* v. *Thompson* (1991),[111] that state prisoners could not cite "procedural default," such as a defense attorney's failure to meet a state's filing deadline for appeals, as the basis for an appeal to federal court.

In 1995, in the case of *Schlup* v. *Delo*,[112] the Court continued to define standards for further appeals from death-row inmates, ruling that before appeals based on claims of new evidence could be heard, "a petitioner must show that, in light of the new evidence, it is more likely than not that no reasonable juror would have found him guilty beyond a reasonable doubt." A "reasonable juror" was defined as one who "would consider fairly all of the evidence presented and would conscientiously obey the trial court's instructions requiring proof beyond a reasonable doubt."

I think this country would be much better off if we did not have capital punishment. . . . We cannot ignore the fact that in recent years a disturbing number of inmates on death row have been exonerated.

—John Paul Stevens, U.S. Supreme Court justice[iv]

Opportunities for federal appeals by death-row inmates were further limited by the Antiterrorism and Effective Death Penalty Act (AEDPA) of 1996,[113] which sets a one-year postconviction deadline for state inmates filing federal *habeas corpus* appeals. The deadline is six months for state death-row inmates who were provided a lawyer for *habeas* appeals at the state level. The act also requires federal courts to presume that the factual findings of state courts are correct; does not permit the claim of state court misinterpretations of the U.S. Constitution as a basis for *habeas* relief unless those misinterpretations are "unreasonable"; and requires that all petitioners must show, prior to obtaining a hearing, facts sufficient to establish by clear and convincing evidence that but for constitutional error, no reasonable fact finder would have found the petitioner guilty. The act also requires approval by a three-judge panel before an inmate can file a second federal appeal raising newly discovered evidence of innocence. In 1996, in the case of *Felker* v. *Turpin*,[114] the U.S. Supreme Court ruled that limitations on the authority of federal courts to consider successive *habeas corpus* petitions imposed by AEDPA are permissible since they do not deprive the U.S. Supreme Court of its original jurisdiction over such petitions.

Some recent statements by Supreme Court justices have indicated that long delays caused by the government in carrying out executions may render the punishment unconstitutionally cruel and unusual. One example comes from the 1998 case of *Elledge* v. *Florida*,[115] where the execution of William D. Elledge had been delayed for 23 years. Although the full Court refused to hear the case, Justice Stephen Breyer observed, "Twenty-three years under sentence of death is unusual—whether one takes as a measuring rod current practice or the practice in this country and in England at the time our Constitution was written." Moreover, wrote Breyer, execution after such a long delay could be considered cruel because Elledge "has experienced that delay because of the State's own faulty procedures and not because of frivolous appeals on his own part." Elledge died at the Union Correctional Institution in Florida in 2008 while awaiting execution.[116] He had been under sentence of death for 34 years.

▲ Death-penalty opponent Mark Bherand sitting outside San Quentin Prison holding a sign as he awaits the execution of convicted killer Stanley "Tookie" Williams on December 13, 2005. Williams, reputed cofounder of the Crips street gang, had been convicted of four murders that occurred in 1979. He was denied clemency by California Governor Arnold Schwarzenegger. How do you feel about capital punishment?
Justin Sullivan/Getty Images–GINS/ Entertainment News & Sports

Opposition to Capital Punishment

Thirty years ago, David Magris, who was celebrating his twenty-first birthday with a crime spree, shot Dennis Tapp in the back during a holdup, leaving Tapp a paraplegic. Tapp had been working a late-night shift, tending his father's quick-serve gas station. Magris went on to commit more robberies that night, killing 20-year-old Steven Tompkins in a similar crime. Although Margis was sentenced to death by a California court, the U.S. Supreme Court overturned the state's death-penalty law in 1972, opening the door for Magris to be paroled in 1985. Long before Magris was freed from prison, however, Tapp had already forgiven him. A few minutes after the shooting happened, Tapp regained consciousness, dragged himself to a telephone, and called for help. The next thing he did was ask "God to forgive the man who did this to me."[117] Today, the men—both staunch death-penalty opponents—are friends, and Magris is president of the Northern California Coalition to Abolish the Death Penalty. "Don't get me wrong," says Tapp. "What [David] did was wrong. . . . He did something stupid and he paid for it."[118]

Lecture Note Discuss the fact that a period of 11 years typically elapses between the time a sentence of death is imposed and the time it is carried out. Ask whether that is too long. Ask how it might be reduced.

Because the death penalty is such an emotional issue for many, attempts have been made to abolish capital punishment since the founding of the United States. The first recorded effort to eliminate the death penalty occurred at the home of Benjamin Franklin in 1787.[119] At a meeting there on March 9 of that year, Dr. Benjamin Rush, a signer of the Declaration of Independence and a leading medical pioneer, read a paper against capital punishment to a small but influential audience. Although his immediate efforts came to naught, his arguments laid the groundwork for many debates that followed. Michigan, widely regarded as the first abolitionist state, joined the Union in 1837 without a death penalty. A number of other states, including Alaska, Hawaii, Massachusetts, Minnesota, West Virginia, and Wisconsin, have since spurned death as a possible sanction for criminal acts. As noted earlier, it remains a viable sentencing option in 38 of the states and in all federal jurisdictions, so arguments continue to rage over its value.

Lecture Note List the various arguments for and against the death penalty as a form of criminal sentencing. Engage the class in a discussion as to the relative merits of each of these arguments.

8 Outline the arguments for and against capital punishment.

Today, six main rationales for abolishing capital punishment are heard, as shown in Table 9–4.

TABLE 9–4
Capital Punishment: Abolitionist and Retentionist Rationales

Reasons to Abolish

Execution of Innocent People

CLAIM. The death penalty can be and has been inflicted on innocent people.

COUNTERCLAIM. While it has been shown that some innocent people have been condemned to death, and while it can be assumed that a number of innocent people remain on death row, it has not been demonstrated that innocent people have actually been executed.

Lack of Proven Deterrence

CLAIM. The death penalty is not an effective deterrent, as numerous studies have shown.

COUNTERCLAIM. If capital punishment were imposed with both certainty and swiftness, then it would be effective as a deterrent. It is our system of appeals and lengthy delays that makes it ineffective.

Arbitrariness

CLAIM. The imposition of the death penalty is, by the very nature of our legal system, arbitrary. Effective legal representation and access to the courts are not equally available to everyone.

COUNTERCLAIM. Many safeguards exist at all levels of criminal justice processing to protect the innocent and to ensure that only the guilty are actually put to death.

Discrimination

CLAIM. The death penalty discriminates against certain ethnic and racial groups.

COUNTERCLAIM. Any examination of disproportionality must go beyond simple comparisons and must measure both frequency and seriousness of capital crimes between and within racial groups. The Supreme Court, in the 1987 case of *McCleskey* v. *Kemp*, held that a simple showing of racial discrepancies in the application of the death penalty does not constitute a constitutional violation. Members of underrepresented groups were more likely to be sentenced to death but only because they were more likely to be arrested on facts that could support a capital charge, not because the justice system acts in a discriminatory fashion.

Expense

CLAIM. Because of all the appeals involved in death-penalty cases, the cost to a state can run into the millions of dollars for each execution.

COUNTERCLAIM. Although official costs associated with capital punishment are high, no cost is *too* high if it achieves justice.

Sacredness of Human Life

CLAIM. Killing at the hands of the state is not a righteous act but instead lowers all of us to the same moral level as the crimes committed by the condemned.

COUNTERCLAIM. If life is sacred, then the taking of life demands revenge.

For additional perspectives:

The National Coalition to Abolish the Death Penalty, http://www.ncadp.org

Reasons to Keep

Just Deserts

CLAIM. Some people deserve to die for what they have done. Anything less than death cannot suffice as a sanction for the most heinous crimes.

COUNTERCLAIM. Capital punishment is a holdover from primitive times. Contemporary standards of human decency mandate alternatives, such as life imprisonment.

Revenge/Retribution

CLAIM. Capital punishment can be seen as revenge for the pain and suffering that the criminal inflicted on the victim. In *Gregg* v. *Georgia*, the U.S. Supreme Court wrote that "[t]he instinct for retribution is part of the nature of man." Hence sentencing a capital offender to death can provide closure to a victim's family members.

COUNTERCLAIM. Forgiveness and rehabilitation are higher goals than revenge and retribution.

Protection

CLAIM. Executed offenders cannot commit further crimes, and execution serves as an example to other would-be wrongdoers of the fate that awaits them. Moreover, society has a duty to act in defense of others and to protect its innocent members.

COUNTERCLAIM. Societal interests in protection can be met in other ways, such as incarceration.

Note: For additional perspectives visit Pro-Death Penalty.com, http://www.prodeathpenalty.com.

Death Penalty and Innocent People

The DPIC claims that 138 people in 25 states were freed from death row between 1973 and late 2009 after it was determined that they were innocent of the capital crime of which they had been convicted.[120] One study of felony convictions that used analysis of DNA to provide postconviction evidence of guilt or innocence found 28 cases in which defendants had been wrongly convicted and sentenced to lengthy prison terms. The study *Convicted by Juries, Exonerated by Science* effectively demonstrated that the judicial process can be flawed.[121] DNA testing can play a critical role in identifying wrongful convictions because, as Barry Scheck and Peter Neufeld (cofounders of the Innocence Project at the Benjamin N. Cardozo School of Law) point out, "Unlike witnesses who disappear or whose recollections fade over time, DNA in biological samples can be reliably extracted decades after the commission of the crime. The results of such testing have invariably been found to have a scientific certainty that easily outweighs the eyewitness identification testimony or other direct or circumstantial proof that led to the original conviction."[122] They go on to say, "Very simply, . . . DNA testing has demonstrated that far more wrongful convictions occur than even the most cynical and jaded scholars had suspected."[123]

A 2000 study by Columbia Law School professors James S. Liebman, Jeffrey Fagan, and Simon H. Rifkind examined 4,578 death-penalty cases in state and federal courts from 1973 to 1995.[124] The researchers found that appellate courts overturned the conviction or reduced the sentence in 68% of the cases examined. In 82% of the successful appeals, defendants were found to be deserving of a lesser sentence, while convictions were overturned in 7% of such appeals. According to the study's authors, "Our 23 years worth of findings reveal a capital punishment system collapsing under the weight of its own mistakes." You can read their report in its entirety at **Library Extra 9–11**.

Claims of innocence are being partially addressed today by recently passed state laws that mandate DNA testing of all death-row inmates in situations where DNA testing might help establish guilt or innocence (that is, in cases where blood or semen from the perpetrator is available for testing).[125] In 2000, Illinois Governor George Ryan announced that he was suspending all executions in his state indefinitely, a proclamation that came after DNA testing showed that 13 Illinois death-row prisoners could not have committed the capital crimes of which they were convicted.[126] In 2006, the New Jersey legislature voted to suspend use of the death penalty until a state task force made its report on whether capital punishment is fairly imposed.[127]

In 2004, in recognition of the potential of DNA testing to exonerate the innocent, President George W. Bush signed the Innocence Protection Act[128] into law. The act provides federal funds to eliminate the backlog of unanalyzed DNA samples in the nation's crime laboratories.[129] It also sets aside money to improve the capacity of federal, state, and local crime laboratories to conduct DNA analyses.[130] In addition, the act facilitates access to postconviction DNA testing for those serving time in state[131] or federal prisons or on death row, and it sets forth conditions under which a federal prisoner asserting innocence may obtain postconviction DNA testing of specific evidence. Similarly, the legislation requires the preservation of biological evidence by federal law enforcement agencies for any defendant under a sentence of imprisonment or death.

In 2006, in the only state action of its kind to date, the North Carolina General Assembly established the North Carolina Innocence Inquiry Commission and charged it with investigating and evaluating postconviction claims of factual innocence.[132] The commission, which comprises eight members selected by the chief justice of the North Carolina Supreme Court and the chief judge of the North Carolina Court of Appeals, only examines new evidence that was not considered at trial. As of mid-2010, the commission had considered 756 cases, resulting in one exoneration.[133]

Not all claims of innocence are supported by DNA tests or by other forms of inquiry, however. In 2006, for example, DNA test results confirmed the guilt of Roger Keith Coleman, a Virginia coal miner who had steadfastly maintained his innocence until he was executed in 1992. Coleman, executed for the 1981 rape and

There can be no doubt that the taking of the life of the President creates much more societal harm than the taking of the life of a homeless person.

—Charles Burson, Tennessee attorney general, arguing before the U.S. Supreme Court in *Payne* v. *Tennessee*[v]

CJ News
Florida Man Exonerated after 35 Years behind Bars

James Bain used a cell phone for the first time Thursday, calling his elderly mother to tell her he had been freed after 35 years behind bars for a crime he did not commit.

Mobile devices didn't exist in 1974, the year he was sentenced to life in prison for kidnapping a 9-year-old boy and raping him in a nearby field.

Neither did the sophisticated DNA testing that officials more recently used to determine he could not have been the rapist.

"Nothing can replace the years Jamie has lost," said Seth Miller, a lawyer for the Florida Innocence Project, which helped Bain win freedom. "Today is a day of renewal." . . .

As Bain walked out of the Polk County courthouse Thursday, wearing a black T-shirt that said "not guilty," he spoke of his deep faith and said he does not harbor any anger.

"No, I'm not angry," he said. "Because I've got God." . . .

Friends and family surrounded him as he left the courthouse after Judge James Yancey ordered him freed. His 77-year-old mother, who is in poor health, preferred to wait for him at home. With a broad smile, he said he looks forward to spending time with her and the rest of his family.

"That's the most important thing in my life right now, besides God," he said.

Earlier, the courtroom erupted in applause after Yancey ruled.

"Mr. Bain, I'm now signing the order," Yancey said. "You're a free man. Congratulations." . . .

Attorneys from the Innocence Project of Florida got involved in Bain's case earlier this year after he had filed several previous petitions asking for DNA testing, all of which were thrown out. . . .

[Bain] was convicted largely on the strength of the victim's eyewitness identification, though testing available at the time did not definitively link him to the crime. The boy said his attacker had bushy sideburns and a mustache. The boy's uncle, a former assistant principal at a high school, said it sounded like Bain, a former student.

The boy picked Bain out of a photo lineup, although there are lingering questions about whether detectives steered him.

The jury rejected Bain's story that he was home watching TV with his twin sister when the crime was committed, an alibi she repeated at a news conference. . . . He was 19 when he was sentenced.

Ed Threadgill, who prosecuted the case originally, said he didn't recall all the specifics, but the conviction seemed right at the time.

"I wish we had had that evidence back when we were prosecuting cases. I'm ecstatic the man has been released," said Threadgill, now a 77-year-old retired appeals court judge. "The whole system is set up to keep that from happening. It failed."

▲ James Bain (*center*) smiling outside the Polk County Courthouse in Bartow, Florida, in December 2009 after being released from prison after 35 years. DNA evidence cleared Bain and proved his innocence on the charge of kidnapping and raping a nine-year-old boy. Should wider use be made of DNA testing?
AP Photo/Steve Nesius

Eric Ferrero, spokesman for the Innocence Project, said a DNA profile can be extracted from decades-old evidence if it has been preserved properly. That means sealed in a bag and stored in a climate-controlled place, which is how most evidence is handled as a matter of routine.

The project has a bigger problem with lost or destroyed evidence than getting usable DNA profiles from existing evidence, he said.

Florida . . . passed a law that automatically grants former inmates found innocent $50,000 for each year they spent in prison. No legislative approval is needed. That means Bain is entitled to $1.75 million.

Source: Mitch Stacy, "Florida Man Exonerated after 35 Years behind Bars," Associated Press, December 17, 2009. Used with permission of The Associated Press. Copyright © 2010. All rights reserved.

murder of his sister-in-law, Wanda McCoy, died declaring his innocence and proclaiming that he would one day be exonerated. His case became a cause célèbre for death-penalty opponents, who convinced Virginia Governor Mark Warner to order DNA tests on surviving evidence. Coleman's supporters claimed that the tests would provide the first scientific proof that an innocent man had been executed in the United States. Results from the tests, however, conclusively showed that blood and semen found at the crime scene had come from Coleman. After the test results were announced, James McCloskey, director of a New Jersey prison ministry and one of the leaders in the effort to clear Coleman's name, told reporters, "We who seek the truth must live or die by the sword of DNA, [but] this particular truth feels like a kick in the stomach." Learn more about DNA testing and how it can help determine guilt or innocence from the President's DNA Initiative at **Web Extra 9–10**.

278 Innonce Project

Death Penalty and Deterrence

During the 1970s and 1980s, the deterrent effect of the death penalty became a favorite subject for debate in academic circles.[134] Studies of states that had eliminated the death penalty failed to show any increase in homicide rates.[135] Similar studies of neighboring states, in which jurisdictions retaining capital punishment were compared with those that had abandoned it, also failed to demonstrate any significant differences.[136] Although death-penalty advocates remain numerous, few still argue for the penalty based on its deterrent effects. One study that offers support for the deterrent effect of the death penalty was reported in 2001 by Hashem Dezhbakhsh and his colleagues at Emory University.[137] According to the researchers, "Our results suggest that capital punishment has a strong deterrent effect. . . . In particular, each execution results, on average, in 18 fewer murders."[138] They note that most other studies in the area not only have been methodologically flawed but have failed to consider the fact that a number of states sentence select offenders to death but do not carry out executions. They write, "If criminals know that the justice system issues many death sentences but the executions are not carried out, then they may not be deterred by an increase in probability of a death sentence."[139]

> Life is sacred. It's about the only sacred thing on earth—and no one has a right to do away with it.
>
> —Aldona DeVetsco, mother of a murder victim, commenting on the execution of her son's killer

Death Penalty and Discrimination

The claim that the death penalty is discriminatory is hard to investigate. Although past evidence suggests that blacks and other minorities in the United States have been disproportionately sentenced to death,[140] more recent evidence is not as clear. At first glance, disproportionality seems apparent: 45 of the 98 prisoners executed between January 1977 and May 1988 were black or Hispanic, and 84 of the 98 had been convicted of killing whites.[141] A 1996 study found that blacks accused of killing whites in Kentucky between 1976 and 1991 had a higher-than-average probability of being charged with a capital crime and of being sentenced to die than did homicide offenders of other races.[142] For an accurate appraisal to be made, however, any claims of disproportionality must go beyond simple comparisons with racial representation in the larger population and must somehow measure both frequency and seriousness of capital crimes between and within racial groups. Following that line of reasoning, the Supreme Court, in the 1987 case of *McCleskey* v. *Kemp*,[143] held that a simple showing of racial discrepancies in the application of the death penalty does not constitute a constitutional violation. A 2001 study of racial and ethnic fairness in federal capital punishment sentences attempted to go beyond mere percentages in its analysis of the role played by race and ethnicity in capital punishment sentencing decisions.[144] Although the study, which closely reviewed 950 capital punishment cases, found that approximately 80% of federal death-row inmates are African American, researchers found "no intentional racial or ethnic bias in how capital punishment was administered in federal cases."[145] Underrepresented groups were more likely to be sentenced to death, "but only because they are more likely to be arrested on facts that could support a capital charge, not because the justice system acts in a discriminatory fashion," the report said.[146] Read the entire report at **Library Extra 9–12**.

Another 2001 study, this one by New Jersey Supreme Court Special Master David Baime, found no evidence of bias against African American defendants in capital cases in New Jersey between August 1982 and May 2000. The study concluded, "Simply stated, we discern no sound basis from the statistical evidence to conclude that the race or ethnicity of the defendant is a factor in determining which cases advance to a penalty trial and which defendants are ultimately sentenced to death. The statistical evidence abounds the other way—it strongly suggests that there are no racial or ethnic disparities in capital murder prosecution and death sentencing rates."[147]

Evidence of socioeconomic discrimination in the imposition of the death penalty in Nebraska between 1973 and 1999 was found in a 2001 study of more than 700 homicide cases in that state. The study, which had been mandated by the state legislature, found that while race did not appear to influence death-penalty decisions, killers of victims with high socioeconomic status received the death penalty four times as often as would otherwise be expected. According to the study, "The data document significant statewide disparities in charging and sentencing outcomes based on the socio-economic status of the victim."[148]

Thematic Question Former U.S. Supreme Court Justice William Brennan has said that the death penalty will be abolished one day in the United States. Do you agree? Explain.

Thematic Question Discuss Web Extra 9–11, which contains opinions by Justices Harry Blackmun and Antonin Scalia. Which comes closer to your own point of view? Why?

Justifications for Capital Punishment

On February 11, 2004, 47-year-old Edward Lewis Lagrone was executed by lethal injection in Huntsville, Texas, for the murder of three people in their home. Earlier, Lagrone had molested and impregnated one of the victims, a 10-year-old child, whom he shot in the head as she was trying to protect her 19-month-old sister.[149] Lagrone also killed two of the child's great-aunts who were in the house at the time of the attack. One of the women, 76-year-old Caola Lloyd, was deaf, blind, and bedridden with cancer. Prior to the killings, Lagrone had served seven years of a 20-year prison sentence for another murder and was on parole. "He's a poster child to justify the death penalty," said David Montague, the Tarrant County assistant district attorney who prosecuted Lagrone.

Like many others today, Montague feels that "cold-blooded murder" justifies a sentence of death. Justifications for the death penalty are collectively referred to as the *retentionist position*. The three retentionist arguments are (1) just deserts, (2) revenge, and (3) protection.

The just deserts argument makes the simple and straightforward claim that some people deserve to die for what they have done. Death is justly deserved; anything less cannot suffice as a sanction for the most heinous crimes. As U.S. Supreme Court Justice Potter Stewart once wrote, "The decision that capital punishment may be the appropriate sanction in extreme cases is an expression of the community's belief that certain crimes are themselves so grievous an affront to humanity that the only adequate response may be the penalty of death."[150]

closure

Those who justify capital punishment as revenge attempt to appeal to the idea that survivors, victims, and the state are entitled to closure. Only after execution of the criminal perpetrator, they say, can the psychological and social wounds engendered by the offense begin to heal.

The retentionist claim of protection asserts that offenders, once executed, can commit no further crimes. Clearly the least emotional of the retentionist claims, the protectionist argument may also be the weakest, since societal interests in protection can also be met in other ways, such as incarceration. In addition, various studies have shown that there is little likelihood of repeat offenses among people convicted of murder and later released.[151] (The heinous Lagrone case is the exception, not the rule.) One reason for such results, however, may be that murderers generally serve lengthy prison sentences prior to release and may have lost whatever youthful propensity for criminality they previously possessed. For an intriguing dialogue between two U.S. Supreme Court justices over the constitutionality of the death penalty, see **Web Extra 9–11**.

The Courts and the Death Penalty

The U.S. Supreme Court has for some time served as a sounding board for issues surrounding the death penalty. One of the Court's earliest cases in this area was *Wilkerson* v. *Utah* (1878),[152] which questioned shooting as a method of execution and raised Eighth Amendment claims that firing squads constituted a form of cruel and unusual punishment. The Court disagreed, however, contrasting the relatively civilized nature of firing squads with the various forms of torture often associated with capital punishment around the time the Bill of Rights was written.

Similarly, the Court supported electrocution as a permissible form of execution in *In re Kemmler* (1890).[153] In *Kemmler*, the Court defined cruel and unusual methods of execution as follows: "Punishments are cruel when they involve torture or a lingering death; but the punishment of death is not cruel, within the meaning of that word as used in the Constitution. It implies there is something inhuman and barbarous, something more than the mere extinguishing of life."[154] Almost 60 years later, the Court ruled that a second attempt at the electrocution of a convicted person, when the first did not work, did not violate the Eighth Amendment.[155] The Court reasoned that the initial failure was the consequence of accident or unforeseen circumstances and not the result of an effort on the part of executioners to be intentionally cruel.

It was not until 1972, however, in the landmark case of *Furman* v. *Georgia*,[156] that the Court recognized "evolving standards of decency"[157] that might necessitate a reconsideration of Eighth Amendment guarantees. In a 5–4 ruling, the *Furman* decision invalidated Georgia's death-penalty statute on the basis that it allowed a jury unguided discretion in the

CJ News
To Execute or Not: A Question of Cost?

After decades of moral arguments reaching biblical proportions, after long, twisted journeys to the nation's highest court and back, the death penalty may be abandoned by several states for a reason having nothing to do with right or wrong:

Money.

Turns out, it is cheaper to imprison killers for life than to execute them, according to a series of recent surveys. . . .

"It's 10 times more expensive to kill them than to keep them alive," though most Americans believe the opposite, said Donald McCartin, a former California jurist known as "the Hanging Judge of Orange County" for sending nine men to death row. . . .

California's slow appeals system produces an average wait of nearly 20 years from conviction to fatal injection—the longest in the nation. Of the nine convicted killers McCartin sent to death row, only one has died. Not by execution, but from a heart attack in custody. . . .

In 2007, time and money were the reasons New Jersey became the first state to ban executions since the U.S. Supreme Court reinstated the death penalty in 1976. . . .

Out of 36 remaining states with the death penalty, at least eight have considered legislation . . . to end it—Maryland, Nebraska, Colorado, New Mexico, Montana, New Hampshire, Washington and Kansas. . . .

"This is the first time in which cost has been the prevalent issue in discussing the death penalty," said Richard Dieter, director of the Death Penalty Information Center, a data clearinghouse that favors abolition of capital punishment.

Death-penalty trials are more expensive for several reasons: They often require extra lawyers; there are strict experience requirements for attorneys, leading to lengthy appellate waits while capable counsel is sought for the accused; security costs are higher, as well as costs for processing evidence—DNA testing, for example, is far more expensive than simple blood analyses.

After sentencing, prices continue to rise. It costs more to house death row inmates, who are held in segregated sections, in individual cells. . . .

There are many, of course, who refuse to change their minds, believing execution is the ultimate wage of the ultimate sin. They also say that death-penalty cases don't have to be so expensive.

Kent Scheidegger, legal director of the Criminal Justice Legal Foundation, a pro-capital-punishment group, said, "Having an effective appeals process might very well cost less." . . .

But court systems and their costs vary greatly among states, as does the time it takes to exhaust appeals. It's doubtful that change could come quickly enough to generate savings during this roiling recession.

▲ A session of the California legislature. States like California are considering the cost of capital punishment, along with public sentiment and moral aspects of court-ordered executions, in weighing the future of the death penalty in their states. What role, if any, should cost play in capital punishment decisions?
Max Whittaker/Getty Images, Inc.

"It's all about money," said McCartin, the former California judge. . . .

But if convicted killers get life imprisonment instead of death, is that letting them off easy?

Not a chance, says 52-year-old Gordon "Randy" Steidl. He lived on death row and then in the general prison population, after his sentence was commuted to life. He preferred his former accommodations. . . .

The state of Illinois spent $3.5 million trying to execute him, "only to end up giving me a life sentence," Steidl said. "And then 5 1/2 years after that, I was exonerated." . . .

"If you really want to kill someone, give them life without parole," Steidl said in an even voice. . . .

"It's worse than dying."

Source: Deborah Hastings, "To Execute or Not: A Question of Cost?" The Associated Press, March 7, 2009. Used with permission of The Associated Press. Copyright © 2010. All rights reserved.

imposition of a capital sentence. The majority of justices concluded that the Georgia statute, which permitted a jury to decide issues of guilt or innocence while it weighed sentencing options, allowed for an arbitrary and capricious application of the death penalty.

Many other states with statutes similar to Georgia's were affected by the *Furman* ruling but moved quickly to modify their procedures. What evolved was the two-step procedure used today in capital cases. In the first stage, guilt or innocence is decided. If the defendant is convicted of a crime for which execution is possible or if he pleads guilty to such an offense, a second (or penalty) phase ensues. The penalty phase, a kind of mini-trial, generally permits the introduction of new evidence that may have been irrelevant to the question of guilt but that may be relevant to punishment, such as drug use or childhood abuse. In most death-penalty jurisdictions, juries determine the punishment. However, in Arizona, Idaho, Montana, and Nebraska, the trial judge sets the

A punishment is "cruel and unusual" . . . if it does not comport with human dignity.

—William Brennan, former U.S. Supreme Court justice, concurring in *Furman* v. *Georgia*[vi]

sentence in the second phase of capital murder trials. Alabama, Delaware, Florida, and Indiana allow juries only to recommend a sentence to the judge. The Supreme Court formally approved the two-step trial procedure in *Gregg* v. *Georgia* (1976).[158] Post-*Gregg* decisions set limits on the use of death as a penalty for all but the most severe crimes. Other important U.S. Supreme Court decisions of relevance to the death penalty are shown in Table 9–5.

Following *Apprendi* v. *New Jersey* (discussed earlier in this chapter), attorneys for an Arizona death-row inmate successfully challenged that state's practice of allowing judges, sitting without a jury, to make factual determinations necessary for imposition of the death penalty. In *Ring* v. *Arizona* (2002),[159] a jury had found Timothy Stuart Ring guilty of felony murder occurring in the course of an armed robbery for the killing of an armored car driver in 1994 but deadlocked on the charge of premeditated murder. Under Arizona law, Ring could not be sentenced to death, the statutory maximum penalty for first-degree murder, unless a judge made further findings in a separate sentencing hearing. The death penalty could be imposed only if the judge found the existence of at least one aggravating circumstance specified by law that was not offset by mitigating circumstances. During such a hearing, the judge listened to an accomplice who said that Ring planned the robbery and shot the guard. The judge then determined that Ring was the actual killer and found that the killing was committed for financial gain (an aggravating factor). Following the hearing, Ring was sentenced to death. His attorneys appealed, claiming that by the standards set forth in *Apprendi*, Arizona's sentencing scheme violated the Sixth Amendment's guarantee of a jury trial because it entrusted a judge with fact-finding powers that allowed Ring's sentence to be

Class Activity Ask the class to undertake an inquiry into opinions about the death penalty. Have students construct a survey instrument and conduct personal interviews to gauge the degree of opposition to or support for the death penalty. Have students use different offender characteristics (for example, race and gender) as well as different offenses (for example, rape-murder, terrorism, school shooting) in the survey to see how support varies.

TABLE 9–5
U.S. Supreme Court Cases Relating to the Death Penalty

Year	U.S. Supreme Court Case	Ruling
2008	*Baze* v. *Rees*	The capital punishment protocol of lethal injection involving a three-drug "cocktail" used by Kentucky does not violate the Eighth Amendment because it does not create a substantial risk of wanton and unnecessary infliction of pain, torture, or lingering death.
2005	*Deck* v. *Missouri*	The Constitution forbids the use of visible shackles during a capital trial's penalty phase, as it does during the guilt phase, unless that use is "justified by an essential state interest"—such as courtroom security—specific to the defendant on trial.
2005	*Roper* v. *Simmons*	The Eighth and Fourteenth Amendments forbid imposition of the death penalty on offenders who were under the age of 18 when their crimes were committed.
2004	*Schriro* v. *Summerlin*	The rule established in *Apprendi* and *Ring* cannot be applied retroactively to sentences already imposed because it is merely a new procedural rule and not a substantive change.
2002	*Atkins* v. *Virginia*	Executing mentally retarded people violates the Constitution's ban on cruel and unusual punishments.
2002	*Ring* v. *Arizona*	Juries—not judges—must decide the facts, including those relating to aggravating circumstances, that may lead to a death sentence.
1977	*Coker* v. *Georgia*	A Georgia law imposing the death penalty for the rape of an adult woman was struck down. The Court concluded that capital punishment under such circumstances is "grossly disproportionate" to the crime.
1976	*Gregg* v. *Georgia*	A new two-stage (bifurcated) procedural requirement of Georgia's revised capital punishment statute was upheld. The law requires guilt or innocence to be determined in the first stage of a bifurcated trial. Upon a guilty verdict, a presentence hearing is held where the judge or jury hears additional aggravating and mitigating evidence. At least one of ten specified aggravating circumstances must be found to exist beyond a reasonable doubt before a death sentence can be imposed.
1976	*Woodson* v. *North Carolina*	A state law requiring mandatory application of the death penalty for all first-degree murders was found to be unconstitutional.
1972	*Furman* v. *Georgia*	The Court recognized "evolving standards of decency" in invalidating Georgia's death-penalty statute because it allowed a jury unguided discretion in the imposition of a capital sentence. The Georgia statute, which permitted a jury to decide issues of guilt or innocence while simultaneously weighing sentencing options, was found to allow for an arbitrary and capricious application of the death penalty.

raised above what would otherwise have been the statutory maximum. The U.S. Supreme Court agreed and overturned Ring's sentence, finding that "Arizona's enumerated aggravating factors operate as the functional equivalent of an element of a greater offense." *Ring* established that juries—not judges—must decide the facts that lead to a death sentence. The *Ring* ruling called into question at least 150 judge-imposed death sentences[160] in at least five states (Arizona, Colorado, Idaho, Montana, and Nebraska).[161]

▲ Timothy Ring, the Arizona death-row inmate who won a 2002 U.S. Supreme Court case that might invalidate the death sentences of at least 150 other prisoners. In that case, *Ring* v. *Arizona*, the Court held that defendants have a Sixth Amendment right to have a jury, and not just a judge, determine the existence of aggravating factors justifying the death penalty. What other decisions, made by the Court since then, have further refined the *Ring* ruling?
Matt York/AP Wide World Photos

Although questions may arise about sentencing practices, the majority of justices on today's high court seem largely convinced of the fundamental constitutionality of a sentence of death. Open to debate, however, is the constitutionality of *methods* for execution. In a 1993 hearing, *Poyner* v. *Murray*,[162] the U.S. Supreme Court hinted at the possibility of revisiting questions first raised in *Kemmler*. The case challenged Virginia's use of the electric chair, calling it a form of cruel and unusual punishment. Syvasky Lafayette Poyner, who originally brought the case before the Court, lost his bid for a stay of execution and was electrocuted in March 1993. Nonetheless, in *Poyner*, Justices David H. Souter, Harry A. Blackmun, and John Paul Stevens wrote, "The Court has not spoken squarely on the underlying issue since *In re Kemmler* . . . and the holding of that case does not constitute a dispositive response to litigation of the issue in light of modern knowledge about the method of execution in question."

In a still more recent ruling, members of the Court questioned the constitutionality of hanging, suggesting that it too may be a form of cruel and unusual punishment. In that case, *Campbell* v. *Wood* (1994),[163] the defendant, Charles Campbell, raped a woman, was released from prison at the completion of his sentence, and then went back and murdered her. His request for a stay of execution was denied since the law of Washington State, where the murder occurred, offered Campbell a choice of various methods of execution and, therefore, an alternative to hanging. Similarly, in 1996, the Court upheld California's death-penalty statute, which provides for lethal injection as the primary method of capital punishment in that state.[164] The constitutionality of the statute had been challenged by two death-row inmates who claimed that a provision in the law that permitted condemned prisoners the choice of lethal gas in lieu of injection brought the statute within the realm of allowing cruel and unusual punishments.

Questions about the constitutionality of electrocution as a means of execution again came to the fore in 1997, when flames shot from the head and the leather mask covering the face of Pedro Medina during his Florida execution. Similarly, in 1999, blood poured from behind the mask covering Allen Lee "Tiny" Davis's face as he was put to death in Florida's electric chair. State officials claimed that the 344-pound Davis suffered a nosebleed brought on by hypertension and the blood-thinning medication that he had been taking. Photographs of Davis taken during and immediately after the execution showed him grimacing while bleeding profusely onto his neck and chest. In 2001, the Georgia Supreme Court declared electrocution to be unconstitutional, ending its use in that state.[165] The Georgia court cited testimony from lower court records showing that electrocution may not result in a quick death or in an immediate cessation of consciousness. By the time of the court's decision, however, the Georgia legislature had already passed a law establishing lethal injection as the state's sole method of punishment for capital crimes. Today, only one state, Nebraska, still uses electrocution as its sole method of execution.[166]

> When a juvenile commits a heinous crime, the State can exact forfeiture of some of the most basic liberties, but the State cannot extinguish his life and his potential to attain a mature understanding of his own humanity.
>
> —*Roper* v. *Simmons* (2005)

In 2006, questions were raised about whether lethal injections constitute cruel and unusual punishment. Those questions originated with eyewitness accounts, postmortem blood testing, and execution logs that seemed to show that some of those executed remained conscious but paralyzed and experienced excruciating pain before dying.[167] Such claims focused on the composition of the chemical cocktail used in executions, which contains one drug (sodium thiopental, a short-acting barbiturate) to induce sleep, another (pancuronium bromide) to paralyze the muscles without causing unconsciousness, and a third (potassium chloride) to stop the heart. If the first chemical is improperly administered, the condemned person remains conscious, and the procedure can cause discomfort or even severe pain. Complicating matters is the fact that the ethical codes of most professional medical organizations forbid medical practitioners to take life—meaning that although the codes are not legally binding, medical professionals are largely excluded from taking part in executions, other than to verify the fact that death has occurred. To counter fears that lethal injections cause pain, some states have begun using medical monitoring devices that show brain activity and can ensure that sleep is occurring.[168]

So justice, while she winks at crimes, stumbles on innocence sometimes.

—Samuel Butler, *Hudibras* (canto II, pt. II, l. 1177)

In 2008, the U.S. Supreme Court took up this issue in the case of *Baze* v. *Rees*, which had been brought by prisoners on Kentucky's death row.[169] The Court held that the capital punishment protocol used by Kentucky does not violate the Eighth Amendment because it does not create a substantial risk of wanton and unnecessary infliction of pain, torture, or lingering death. "Because some risk of pain is inherent in even the most humane execution method," wrote the justices, "the Constitution does not demand the avoidance of all risk of pain."

The Future of the Death Penalty

Support for the death penalty varies considerably from state to state and from one region of the country to another. Short of renewed Supreme Court intervention, the future of capital punishment may depend more on popular opinion than on arguments pro or con. A Gallup Poll taken in May 2003 found 79% of those polled to be in favor of the death penalty under certain circumstances. A similar poll by the same organization found that although most respondents voiced support for the death penalty, that support dropped to 53% when respondents were offered an alternative sentence of life without parole.[170] Pollsters also learned that the percentage of Americans supporting capital punishment appeared to have increased substantially following the events of September 11, 2001.[171]

Ultimately, public opinion about the death penalty may turn on the issue of whether innocent people have been executed. According to a number of recent studies, Americans from all walks of life are less likely to support capital punishment if they believe that innocent people have been put to death at the hands of the justice system or that the death penalty is being applied unfairly.[172] A 2007 survey by the Death Penalty Information Center, for example, found that "a significant majority of 58% responding in this poll believed it was time for a moratorium on the death penalty while the process undergoes a careful review."[173] The study's authors note that support for the death penalty among Americans varies by race, with African Americans less likely to support capital punishment than whites. They found that much of the difference, however, is explained by differing beliefs between the races about the number of executed innocents and the perceived fairness in application of capital sanctions. Consequently, execution of the innocent is at the center of today's debate concerning the legitimacy of capital punishment, and it is likely to determine the future of the death penalty in individual states as local legislatures move to mandate procedural enhancements meant to guarantee fairness.

In 2002, a special commission appointed by Illinois Governor George Ryan to examine the imposition of capital punishment in Illinois made its report, saying that the system through which capital sentences are imposed should be modified to encompass a number of procedural safeguards. Safeguards that were recommended included (1) tighter controls on how the police investigate cases, including a requirement that investigators "continue to pursue all reasonable lines of inquiry, whether these point toward or away from the suspect"; (2) controls on the potential fallibility of eyewitness testimony, including lineups where the person in charge is not aware of which person in the lineup is the suspect (to preclude him or her from unconsciously identifying the suspect); and (3) statutory reform so that the death penalty cannot be applied based solely on the testimony of any single accomplice or eyewitness without further corroboration.[174] In April 2003, incoming Illinois Governor Rod R. Blagojevich said that because of his concerns over executing innocent people, he would not lift his state's ban on executions even if the state's legislature passed a bill aimed at improving the system.[175] Blagojevich was forced out of office in 2009 over a scandal involving claims that he wanted to profit from his ability as governor to fill the vacant Senate seat that Barack Obama left when he was sworn in as president. Consequently, the future of capital punishment in Illinois remains in doubt.

A PowerPoint presentation that supports this chapter is available from your Prentice Hall representative.

Freedom or Safety? You Decide.
What Are the Limits of Genetic Privacy?

In 2005, police in Truro, Massachusetts, charged Christopher M. McCowen, a garbage man with a long rap sheet, with the murder of 46-year-old Christa Worthington, a fashion writer who had been raped and stabbed to death in the kitchen of her isolated home in 2002. The case, which had baffled authorities for three years, drew national interest when Truro authorities asked the town's 790 male residents to voluntarily submit saliva-swab DNA samples for analysis. Investigators were hoping to use genetic testing to match semen recovered from the murder scene with the killer. "We're trying to find the person who has something to hide," said Sergeant David Perry of the Truro Police Department. Although McCowen voluntarily submitted a DNA sample from a cheek swab in early 2004, it took the state crime lab more than a year to analyze it.

As the Massachusetts case shows, DNA profiling can be a powerful forensic tool, although its use in criminal investigations is barely 20 years old. The first well-known DNA forensic analysis occurred in 1986, when British police sought the help of Alec Jeffreys, a geneticist at the University of Leicester who is widely regarded as the "father of DNA fingerprinting." The police were trying to solve the vicious rape and murder of two young schoolgirls. At the center of their investigation was a young man who worked at a mental institution close to where the girls' bodies had been found. Soon after he was questioned, the man confessed to the crimes and was arrested, but police were uncertain of the suspect's state of mind and wanted to be sure that they had the right person.

Jeffreys compared the suspect's DNA to DNA taken from semen samples found on the victims. The samples did not match, leading to a wider police investigation. Lacking any clear leads, the authorities requested that all males living in the area of the killings voluntarily submit to DNA testing so that they might be excluded as suspects. By the fall of 1987, the number of men tested had exceeded 4,500, but the murderer still hadn't been found. Then, however, investigators received an unexpected tip. They learned that a local baker named Colin Pitchfork had convinced another man to provide a DNA sample in his place. Pitchfork was picked up and questioned. He soon confessed, providing details about the crime that only the perpetrator could know. Pitchfork became the 4,583rd man to undergo DNA testing, and his DNA proved a perfect match with that of the killer.

In the past 20 years, the use of DNA testing by police departments has come a long way. Today, the FBI's CODIS (Combined DNA Index System) database makes use of computerized records to match the DNA of individuals previously convicted of certain crimes with forensic samples gathered at crime scenes across the country.

Advocates of genetic privacy, however, question whether anyone—even those convicted of crimes—should be sampled against their wishes and have their genetic profiles added to government databases. The Truro case, in which the American Civil Liberties Union (ACLU) sent letters to the town's police chief and Cape Code prosecutor calling for an end to the "DNA dragnet," highlights what many fear—especially when local police announced that they would pay close attention to those who refused to cooperate. One commentator noted that it is "a very old trap" to say that "if you have nothing to hide, then why not cooperate?"

YOU DECIDE

What degree of "genetic privacy" should an individual be entitled to? Should the government require routine genetic testing of nonoffenders for identification purposes? How might such information be used in the event of a terrorist attack?

References: "Man Charged with 2002 Murder of Cape Cod Writer," *USA Today*, April 15, 2005, http://www.usatoday.com/news/nation/2005-04-15-cape-cod-murder_x.htm (accessed October 1, 2010); "ACLU Slams Mass DNA Collection," CBSNews.com, January 10, 2005, http://www.cbsnews.com/stories/2005/01/10/national/main665938.shtml (accessed October 1, 2010); and Howard C. Coleman and Eric D. Swenson, *DNA in the Courtroom: A Trial Watcher's Guide* (Seattle, WA: Genelex Corporation, web edition 2000), http://www.genelex.com/paternitytesting/paternitybook.html (accessed October 1, 2010).

Summary

SENTENCING

- The goals of criminal sentencing include retribution, incapacitation, deterrence, rehabilitation, and restoration. Retribution corresponds to the just deserts model of sentencing, which holds that offenders are responsible for their crimes. Incapacitation seeks to protect innocent members of society from offenders who might harm them if not prevented from doing so. The goal of deterrence is to prevent future criminal activity through the example or threat of punishment. Rehabilitation seeks to bring about fundamental changes in offenders and their behavior to reduce the likelihood of future criminality, and restoration seeks to address the damage done by crime by making the victim and the community "whole again."
- The indeterminate sentencing model is characterized primarily by vast judicial choice. It builds on the belief that convicted offenders are more likely to participate in their own rehabilitation if such participation will reduce the amount of time that they have to spend in prison.
- Structured sentencing is largely a child of the just deserts philosophy that grew out of concerns with proportionality, equity, and social debt—all of which this chapter discusses. A number of different types of structured sentencing models have been created, including determinate sentencing, which requires that a convicted offender be sentenced to a fixed term that may be reduced by good time or gain time, and voluntary/advisory sentencing, which consists of recommended sentencing guidelines that are not required by law, are usually based on past sentencing practices, and are meant to guide judges. Mandatory sentencing, another form of structured sentencing, requires clearly enumerated punishments for specific offenses or for

habitual offenders convicted of a series of crimes. The applicability of structured sentencing guidelines has been called into question by recent U.S. Supreme Court decisions.

- Alternative sanctions include the use of court-ordered community service, home detention, day reporting, drug treatment, psychological counseling, victim-offender mediation, or intensive supervision in lieu of other, more traditional sanctions such as imprisonment and fines. A number of questions have been raised about alternative sentences, including questions about their impact on public safety, the cost-effectiveness of such sanctions, and the long-term effects of community sanctions on people assigned to alternative programs.
- Probation and parole officers routinely conduct presentence investigations to provide information that judges may use in deciding on the appropriate kind or length of sentence for convicted offenders.
- Historically, criminal courts have often allowed victims to testify at trial but have otherwise downplayed the experience of victimization and the suffering it causes. A new interest in the experience of victims, beginning in the 1970s in this country, has led to a greater legal recognition of victims' rights, including a right to allocution (the right to be heard during criminal proceedings). Many states have passed victims' rights amendments to their constitutions, although a federal victims' rights amendment has yet to be enacted. The Crime Victims' Rights Act of 2004 established statutory rights for victims of federal crimes and gives them the necessary legal authority to assert those rights in federal court.
- The four traditional sentencing options identified in this chapter are fines, probation, imprisonment, and—in cases of especially horrific offenses—death. Fines and the death penalty were discussed in this chapter, and the pros and cons of each were examined.
- Arguments for capital punishment identified in this chapter include revenge, just deserts, and protection of society. The revenge argument builds upon the need for personal and communal closure, while the just deserts argument makes the straightforward claim that some people deserve to die for what they have done. Societal protection is couched in terms of deterrence, since those who are executed cannot commit future crimes, and execution serves as an example to other would-be wrongdoers. Arguments against capital punishment are based on findings that a death sentence has been imposed on innocent people, that the death penalty has not been found to be an effective deterrent, that it is often arbitrarily imposed, that it tends to discriminate against powerless groups and individuals, and that it is very expensive because of the numerous court appeals involved. Opponents also argue that the state should recognize the sanctity of human life.

QUESTIONS FOR REVIEW

1. Describe the five goals of contemporary criminal sentencing. Which of these goals do you think ought to be the primary goal of sentencing? How might your choice vary with the type of offense? In what circumstances might your choice be less acceptable?
2. Describe the nature of indeterminate sentencing, and explain its positive aspects. What led some states to abandon indeterminate sentencing?
3. What is structured sentencing? What structured sentencing models are in use today? Which model holds the best promise for long-term crime reduction? Why?
4. What are alternative sanctions? Give some examples of alternative sanctions, and offer an assessment of how effective they might be.
5. What is a presentence investigation? How do PSIs contribute to the contents of presentence reports? How are presentence reports used?
6. Describe the history of victims' rights and services in this country. What role does the victim play in criminal justice proceedings today?
7. What are four modern sentencing options? Under what circumstances might each be appropriate?
8. Do you support or oppose the use of capital punishment? Outline the arguments on both sides of the issue.

Probation, Parole, and Community Corrections

CHAPTER 10

Learning Objectives

After reading this chapter, you should be able to:

1. Explain the history, nature, and purposes of probation. 290
2. Explain the history, nature, and purposes of parole. 291
3. Describe the advantages and disadvantages of probation and parole. 293
4. Describe the legal environment surrounding the use of probation and parole, and name the significant court cases. 294
5. Explain the nature of the job of probation and parole officers. 297
6. Explain what intermediate sanctions are, and list the advantages of intermediate sanctions over more traditional forms of sentencing. 299
7. Describe the likely future of probation and parole. 304

ommunity corrections
an integral part of the
riminal justice system
and should be fully
implemented and
promoted in order to
save expensive and
scarce jail and prison
space for violent and
serious offenders."

ional Association of Counties, Justice and Public Safety Steering Committee[1]

"Parole supervision can and should play an important role in facilitating the transition from prison to community, effecting positive behavioral change, and increasing public safety. To achieve these goals, however, parole agencies must systematically adopt the practices and policies that have been demonstrated to work."

—Urban Institute[2]

▲ Friends and neighbors placed flowers and gifts at the Chicago, Illinois, house of singer Jennifer Hudson's mother on October 27, 2008. Hudson's brother-in-law, William Balfour, a parolee who had spent almost seven years in prison for attempted murder, was arrested and charged with three counts of first-degree murder and one count of home invasion in the deaths of three of Hudson's relatives. What do cases like Balfour's say about the proper supervision of parolees?
Tasos Katopodis/Getty Images, Inc.—Liaison

Introduction

In October 2008, the mother, brother, and seven-year-old nephew of Oscar-winning actress Jennifer Hudson were shot to death by a man whom police identified as William Balfour, 27.[3] Balfour, who was married to Hudson's sister, Julia, was a parolee who had spent almost seven years in prison for attempted murder.

Stories like this appear all too frequently in the media and cast a harsh light on the early release and poor supervision of criminal offenders. This chapter takes a close look at the realities behind the practice of **community corrections** (also termed *community-based corrections*), which is a sentencing style that depends less on traditional confinement options and more on correctional resources available in the community. Community corrections includes a wide variety of sentencing options, such as probation, parole, home confinement, remote location monitoring of offenders, and other new and developing programs—all of which are covered in this chapter. Learn more about community corrections by visiting the International Community Corrections Association via **Web Extra 10–1**.

What Is Probation?

Probation, one aspect of community corrections, is "a sentence served while under supervision in the community."[4] Like other sentencing options, probation is a court-ordered sanction. Its goal is to retain some control over criminal offenders while using community programs to help rehabilitate them. Most of the alternative sanctions discussed later in this chapter are, in fact, predicated on probationary sentences in which the offender is ordered to abide by certain conditions—such as participation in a specified program—while remaining free in the community. Although the court in many jurisdictions can impose probation directly, most probationers are sentenced first to confinement but then immediately have their sentences suspended and are remanded into the custody of an officer of the court—the probation officer.

community corrections
The use of a variety of officially ordered program-based sanctions that permit convicted offenders to remain in the community under conditional supervision as an alternative to an active prison sentence.

probation
A sentence of imprisonment that is suspended. Also, the conditional freedom granted by a judicial officer to a convicted offender, as long as the person meets certain conditions of behavior.

Lecture Note Discuss community corrections, including its assumptions, its forms, and its prevalence.

Lecture Note Explain probation as a sentence of imprisonment that is suspended. Tell the class that offenders who violate the conditions of probation may be sent to prison to serve the remainder of their sentences.

Class Activity Visit a local criminal court. Observe the sentencing choices of individual judges. Are some judges more likely to order probation than others? If so, how great is the difference?

Lecture Note Referring to Figure 10–1, describe the percentages of individuals under the various types of correctional supervision in the United States. Ask why probation is such a commonly used alternative.

The Extent of Probation

Today, probation is the most common form of criminal sentencing in the United States. Among persons sentenced for a felony in state courts nationwide in 2006, an estimated 27% received a probation sentence with no jail or prison time.[5] Among misdemeanants, the proportion receiving a probationary sentence is far higher. Figure 10–1 shows that 70% of all offenders under correctional supervision in the United States as of January 1, 2009,

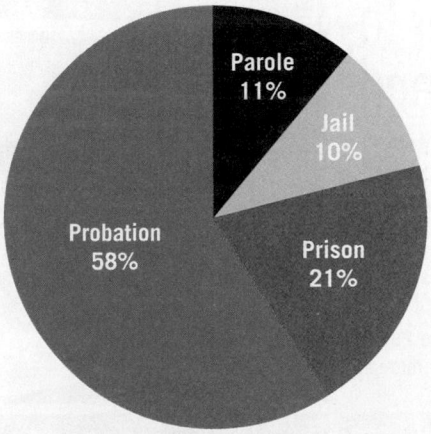

FIGURE 10–1 Offenders under Correctional Supervision in the United States, by Type of Supervision
Source: Bureau of Justice Statistics, Correctional Surveys.

were on probation. Not shown is that the number of offenders supervised yearly on probation has increased from slightly more than 1 million in 1980 to almost 4.3 million today—a 400% increase.[6]

Even violent offenders stand about a one in five chance of receiving a probationary term. A Bureau of Justice Statistics study of felony sentences found that 5% of people convicted of homicide were placed on probation, as were 21% of convicted sex offenders.[7] Twelve percent of convicted robbers and 30% of those committing aggravated assault were similarly sentenced to probation rather than active prison time. In one example, 47-year-old Carrie Mote of Vernon, Connecticut, was sentenced to probation for shooting her fiancé in the chest with a .38-caliber handgun after he called off their wedding.[8] Mote, who faced a maximum of 20 years in prison, claimed to be suffering from diminished psychological capacity at the time of the shooting because of the emotional stress brought on by the canceled wedding. In 2007, the *Dallas Morning News* reported on 56 cases in which murderers received probation in exchange for guilty pleas in the Dallas area between 2000 and 2006. The paper said that prosecutors often offered probation in exchange for guilty pleas in cases with shaky evidence.[9]

At the beginning of 2009 a total of 4,270,917 adults were on probation throughout the nation.[10] Individual states, however, make greater or lesser use of probation. North Dakota authorities, with the smallest probationary population, supervise only 4,496 people, while Texas reports 434,306 offenders on probation. On a per capita basis, New Hampshire has the lowest rate of probation (443 for every 100,000 residents), while Massachusetts has the highest (3,620 for every 100,000 residents). The national average is 1,845 for every 100,000 residents. More than half of the 2.3 million adults discharged from probation in 2008 had successfully met the conditions of their supervision. Approximately 17% of those discharged from supervision, however, were incarcerated because of a rule violation or because they committed a new offense. Another 4% absconded, and 10% had their probation sentence revoked without being ordered to serve time.[11] See more statistics describing community corrections at **Library Extra 10–1**.

▲ Hotel heiress Paris Hilton arriving for a birthday party for namesake celebrity gossip blogger Perez Hilton in West Hollywood, California, on March 23, 2007. Only two months earlier, Paris had pleaded "no contest" to an alcohol-related reckless driving offense in Los Angeles and was sentenced to three years' probation. She was also fined $1,500 plus court costs and ordered to participate in an alcohol-education program. In 2010, she was arrested for possession of a controlled substance after cocaine was found in her purse by Las Vegas police during a vehicle stop. Apparently probation wasn't enough to deter Paris. Why not?
Francis Specker/Landov Media

Probation Conditions

Those sentenced to probation must agree to abide by court-mandated conditions of probation, with a violation of conditions possibly leading to **probation revocation**. Conditions are of two types: general and specific. General conditions apply to all probationers in a given jurisdiction and usually require that the probationer obey all laws, maintain employment, remain within the jurisdiction of the court, possess no firearms, allow the probation officer to visit at home or at work, and so forth. As a general condition of probation, many probationers are also required to pay a fine to the court, usually in a series of installments, that is designed to reimburse victims for damages and to pay lawyers' fees and other court costs.

probation revocation
A court order taking away a convicted offender's probationary status and usually withdrawing the conditional freedom associated with that status in response to a violation of the conditions of probation.

There is ample evidence that well-designed reentry programs reduce recidivism.
—Arlen Specter, former chairman of the Senate Judiciary Committee[i]

Special conditions may be mandated by a judge who feels that the probationer is in need of particular guidance or control. Depending on the nature of the offense, a judge may require that the offender surrender his or her driver's license; submit at reasonable times to warrantless and unannounced searches by a probation officer; supply breath, urine, or blood samples as needed for drug or alcohol testing; complete a specified number of hours of community service; or pass the general equivalency diploma (GED) test within a specified time. The judge may also dictate special conditions tailored to the probationer's situation. Such individualized conditions may prohibit the offender from associating with named others (a codefendant, for example), they may

Lecture Note Ask the class to discuss the merits of granting probation to violent offenders. Explain that probation may result when the prosecutor's evidence is especially weak or when a plea bargain is accepted in lieu of a jury trial.

Multiculturalism and Diversity
Culturally Skilled Probation Officers

An article by Robert Shearer and Patricia Ann King in the journal *Federal Probation* describes the characteristics of "good therapeutic relationships" in probation work. The authors say that "one of the major impediments to building an effective relationship may be found in cross-cultural barriers."

According to the article, probation officers who work with immigrants, or with those whose cultures differ substantially from that of mainstream America, must realize that a client's culture has to be taken into consideration. Doing so can make officers far more effective as both counselors and supervisors.

That's because differences in culture can lead to difficulties in developing the rapport that is necessary to build a helping relationship between an offender and a probation officer. Consequently, effective probation officers work to understand the values, norms, lifestyles, roles, and methods of communicating that characterize their clients.

Culturally skilled probation officers, Shearer and King say, are aware of and sensitive to their own cultural heritage, and they value and respect differences as long as they do not lead to continued law violation. Culturally skilled officers are also aware of their own preconceived notions, biases, prejudicial attitudes, feelings, and beliefs. They avoid stereotyping and labeling. Skilled officers are comfortable with the cultural differences that exist between themselves and their clients, and they are comfortable referring clients to someone who may be better qualified to help.

Developing multicultural awareness is the first step to becoming culturally skilled, the authors note. Developing awareness is an ongoing process—one that culminates in the ability to understand a client's worldview, or *cultural empathy*.

According to the article, developing cultural empathy involves six steps:

1. The counselor must understand and accept the context of family and community for clients from different cultural backgrounds (especially important in working with Hispanic clients where relationships within the extended family are highly valued).
2. Counselors should incorporate indigenous healing practices from the client's culture whenever they can (as might be possible when working with Native Americans).
3. Counselors must become knowledgeable about the historical and sociopolitical backgrounds of clients (especially when clients have fled from repressive regimes in their home countries and might still fear authority figures).
4. They must become knowledgeable of the psychosocial adjustment that must be made by clients who have moved from one environment to another (including the sense of loneliness and separation that some immigrants feel on arrival in their adopted country).
5. They must be sensitive to the oppression, discrimination, and racism encountered by many people (for example, Kurdish people who suffered discrimination and experienced genocide under Saddam Hussein).
6. Counselors must facilitate empowerment for those clients who feel underprivileged and devalued (for example, immigrants who may feel forced to accept menial jobs even though they worked in prestigious occupations in their native countries).

Shearer and King conclude that developing cultural awareness provides the probation officer with an effective approach that actively draws the probationer into the therapeutic relationship and that increases the likelihood of a successful outcome.

Reference: Robert A. Shearer and Patricia Ann King, "Multicultural Competencies in Probation: Issues and Challenges," *Federal Probation*, Vol. 68, No. 1 (June 2004), pp. 3–9.

1 Explain the history, nature, and purposes of probation.

require that the probationer be at home after dark, or they may demand that the offender complete a particular treatment program within a set time.

The Federal Probation System

The federal probation system, known as the United States Probation and Pretrial Services System, is approximately 80 years old.[12] In 1916, in the *Killets* case,[13] the U.S. Supreme Court ruled that federal judges did not have the authority to suspend sentences and to order probation. After a vigorous campaign by the National Probation Association, Congress passed the National Probation Act in 1925, authorizing the use of probation in federal courts. The bill came just in time to save a burgeoning federal prison system from serious overcrowding. The prostitution-fighting Mann Act, Prohibition legislation, and the growth of organized crime all led to increased arrests and a dramatic growth in the number of federal probationers in the early years of the system.

Although the 1925 act authorized one probation officer per federal judge, it allocated only $25,000 for officers' salaries. As a consequence, only eight officers were hired to serve 132 judges, and the system came to rely heavily on voluntary probation officers. Some sources indicate that as many as 40,000 probationers were under the supervision of volunteers at the peak of the system.[14] By 1930, however, Congress had provided adequate funding, and a corps of salaried professionals began to provide probation services to the U.S.

courts. Today, approximately 7,750 federal probation officers (also known as *community corrections officers*), whose services are administered through the Administrative Office of the United States Courts, serve the 94 federal judicial districts in more than 500 locations across the country.[15] At any given time they supervise approximately 151,000 offenders—a number that has increased annually throughout the past decade.

Federal probation and pretrial services officers are federal law enforcement officers who have statutory authority to arrest or detain individuals suspected or convicted of federal offenses and to arrest probationers for violations of the conditions of probation. Under existing policy, however, they are encouraged to obtain an arrest warrant from a court, and the warrant is to be executed by the U.S. Marshals Service. Most federal probation officers may carry a firearm for defensive purposes while on duty. Before doing so, however, they must complete rigorous training and certification requirements, provide objective justification for doing so, and be approved to do so on an individual basis. Some federal districts do not allow any probation officers to carry firearms in the performance of their official duties. These include the eastern and western districts of Wisconsin, eastern Virginia, eastern Virgin Islands, central Tennessee, Massachusetts, Connecticut, and central California.[16]

▲ Angel Coronado, age 20, rushing through the door of the Huntsville (Texas) Prison Unit after being released due to overcrowding. Coronado, who has been in trouble nearly half his life, had spent almost two years in a 6- by 10-foot cell by himself. The U.S. Supreme Court has held that "an inmate who has been released under a program to relieve prison crowding cannot be reincarcerated without getting a chance to show at a hearing that he has met the conditions [of his release] and is entitled to remain free." How likely are people like Coronado to commit new crimes? *Todd Bigelow Photography*

What Is Parole?

Parole is the supervised early release of inmates from correctional confinement. It is a strategy of **prisoner reentry** into the community from prison that differs from probation in both purpose and implementation. Whereas probationers generally avoid serving time in prison, parolees have already been incarcerated. Whereas probation is a sentencing option available to a judge who determines the form probation will take, parole results from an administrative decision by a legally designated paroling authority. Probation is a sentencing strategy; parole is a correctional strategy whose primary purpose is to return offenders gradually to productive lives. By making early release possible, parole can also act as a stimulus for positive behavioral change.

2 Explain the history, nature, and purposes of parole.

States differ as to the type of parole decision-making mechanism they use, as well as the level at which it operates. Two major models prevail: (1) **Parole boards** (state paroling authorities) grant parole based on the board members' judgment and assessment, and their release decisions are termed *discretionary parole*. (2) Statutory decrees produce mandatory release, with release dates usually set near the completion of the inmate's prison sentence, minus time off for good behavior and other special considerations. Fifteen states have entirely abolished **discretionary release** from prison by a parole board for all offenders. Another five states have abolished discretionary release for those who commit certain violent offenses or other crimes against a person. Some states, like Alabama, have abandoned traditional parole but grant their parole boards the authority to revoke the postrelease supervision status of offenders who violate release conditions, ordering them to return to custody. As a result of the movement away from release by parole boards, statutory release, usually involving a brief mandatory period of postrelease supervision, has become the most common method of release from prison.[17]

States that do not utilize discretionary parole can still have substantial reentry populations, and everyone who is released from prison faces the challenges of reentering society. California, for example, is one of the states that no longer use parole boards for release decisions, and it has the largest reentry population in the country.[18] (Although it does not have a parole board, California does have a Board of Prison Terms, which determines when the state's most serious offenders are ready for release from

parole
The status of a convicted offender who has been conditionally released from prison by a paroling authority before the expiration of his or her sentence, is placed under the supervision of a parole agency, and is required to observe the conditions of parole.

prisoner reentry
The managed return to the community of individuals released from prison. Also called *reentry*.

parole board
A state paroling authority. Most states have parole boards that decide when an incarcerated offender is ready for conditional release. Some boards also function as revocation hearing panels.

discretionary release
The release of an inmate from prison to supervision that is decided by a parole board or other authority.

Lecture Note Explain parole as supervised early release from prison. Tell the class that offenders who violate the terms of parole may be returned to prison to complete the remaining portion of their sentence (just as can happen with probationers).

Thematic Question How well do the terms imposed on probationers and parolees serve the rights of individuals? How well do they serve the needs of the community? What issues or needs are not addressed but should be?

prison. These offenders, however, make up only a very small percentage of the state's prison population.)

The Extent of Parole

Parolees make up one of the smallest of the correctional categories shown in Figure 10–1. The growing reluctance to use parole today seems to be due to the realization that correctional routines have generally been ineffective at producing any substantial reformation among many offenders before their release back into the community. The abandonment of the rehabilitation goal, combined with a return to determinate sentencing in many jurisdictions—including the federal judicial system—has substantially reduced the amount of time the average correctional client spends on supervised parole.

Although discretionary parole releases are far less common than they used to be, about 25% of inmates who are freed from prison are still paroled by a paroling authority such as a parole board.[19] States operating under determinate sentencing guidelines, however, often require that inmates serve a short period of time, such as 90 days, on *reentry parole*—a form of supervised **mandatory release**. Mandatory parole releases have increased 91% since 1990,[20] even though they typically involve either a very small amount of time on parole or no time under supervision. As a result, determinate sentencing schemes have changed the face of parole in America, resulting in a dramatic reduction in the average time spent under postprison supervision. They have had little or no impact on the actual number of offenders released from prison, however.

mandatory release
The release of an inmate from prison that is determined by statute or sentencing guidelines and is not decided by a parole board or other authority.[ii]

At the beginning of 2009, the number of people under parole supervision throughout the United States stood at 828,169.[21] As with probation, states vary considerably in the use they make of parole, influenced as they are by the legislative requirements of sentencing schemes. For example, on January 1, 2009, Maine (a state that is phasing out parole) reported only 32 people under parole supervision (the lowest of all the states). North Dakota had only 340, while California (the highest of all) had a parole population in excess of 123,764, and Texas officials were busy supervising more than 101,748 parolees. The per capita rate at which parole is used varies as well: Only three out of every 100,000 Maine residents are on parole, whereas 1,274 out of every 100,000 District of Columbia residents are on parole. The national average is 358 per 100,000.[22]

Nationwide, approximately 49% of parolees successfully complete parole. About 25% are returned to prison for **parole violation** (failure to meet parole conditions), another 9% go back to prison for new offenses during their parole period, and others may be transferred to new jurisdictions, abscond and not be caught, or die—bringing the total to 100%.[23] (Those on probation who do not meet probation conditions commit **probation violations**.) Learn more about trends in parole at **Library Extra 10–2**.

parole (probation) violation
An act or a failure to act by a parolee (or probationer) that does not conform to the conditions of his or her parole (or probation).

conditions of parole (probation)
The general and special limits imposed on an offender who is released on parole (or probation). General conditions tend to be fixed by state statute, whereas special conditions are mandated by the sentencing authority (court or board) and take into consideration the background of the offender and the circumstances of the offense.

parole revocation
The administrative action of a paroling authority removing a person from parole status in response to a violation of lawfully required conditions of parole, including the prohibition against committing a new offense, and usually resulting in a return to prison.

restitution
A court requirement that an alleged or convicted offender pay money or provide services to the victim of the crime or provide services to the community.

Parole Conditions

In those jurisdictions that retain discretionary parole, the **conditions of parole** remain very similar to the **conditions of probation** and usually include agreement not to leave the state as well as to obey extradition requests from other jurisdictions. Parolees must also periodically report to parole officers, and parole officers may visit parolees at their homes and places of business, often arriving unannounced.

The successful continued employment of parolees is one of the major concerns of parole boards and their officers, and studies have found that successful employment is a major factor in reducing the likelihood of repeat offenses.[24] Hence the importance of continued employment is typically stressed on parole agreement forms, with the condition that failure to find employment within 30 days may result in **parole revocation** (loss of parole status and usually a return to prison). As with probationers, parolees who are working can be ordered to pay fines and penalties. A provision for making payments of **restitution** in the form of money or services to the victim or to the community is also frequently included as a condition of parole.

As with probation, special parole conditions may be added by the judge and might require the parolee to pay a "parole supervisory fee" (often around $15 to $20 per month).

A relatively new innovation, the parole supervisory fee shifts some of the expense of community corrections to the offender.

Certain types of offenders can be subject to unique conditions. In 2007, for example, New Jersey's state parole board imposed a supervision condition on 4,400 sex offenders under parole board supervision that prohibits them from using the Internet to socialize.[25] The parole board imposed the restriction after law enforcement officials reported that data received under subpoena from several social-networking websites revealed that sex offenders under parole supervision had created profiles on such sites that could potentially be used to lure new victims.

Lecture Note Describe probation and parole revocation. Explain that, in most cases, revocation orders can be issued only after a hearing in front of a neutral body and that certain procedures must be followed.

Federal Parole

Federal parole decisions are made by the U.S. Parole Commission, which uses hearing examiners to visit federal prisons. Examiners typically ask inmates to describe why, in their opinion, they are ready for parole. The inmate's job readiness, home plans, past record, accomplishments while in prison, good behavior, and previous experiences on probation or parole form the basis for the examiners' report to the commission. The 1984 Comprehensive Crime Control Act, which mandated federal fixed sentencing and abolished parole for offenses committed after November 1, 1978, began a planned phaseout of the U.S. Parole Commission. Under the act, the commission was to be abolished by 1992, but various pieces of federal legislation have since extended the life of the commission. Visit the commission's website at **Web Extra 10–2**. Read a detailed history of the federal parole system at **Library Extra 10–3**.

Probation and Parole: The Pluses and Minuses

Probation is used to meet the needs of offenders who require some correctional supervision short of imprisonment while providing a reasonable degree of security to the community. Parole fulfills a similar purpose for offenders released from prison.

3 Describe the advantages and disadvantages of probation and parole.

Advantages of Probation and Parole

Both probation and parole provide a number of advantages over imprisonment:

- *Lower cost.* Imprisonment is expensive. Incarcerating a single offender in Georgia, for example, costs approximately $39,501 per year, while the cost of intensive probation is as little as $1,321 per probationer.[26] The expense of imprisonment in some other states may be more than three times as high as it is in Georgia.
- *Increased employment.* Few people in prison have the opportunity for productive employment. Work-release programs, correctional industries, and inmate labor programs operate in most states, but they usually provide only low-paying jobs and require few skills. At best, such programs include only a small portion of the inmates in any given facility. Probation and parole, on the other hand, make it possible for offenders under correctional supervision to work full-time at jobs in the "free" economy. Offenders can contribute to their own and their families' support, stimulate the local economy by spending their wages, and support the government by paying taxes.
- *Restitution.* Offenders who are able to work are candidates for court-ordered restitution. Society's interest in restitution may be better served by a probationary sentence or parole than by imprisonment. Restitution payments to victims may help restore the victims' standard of living and personal confidence while teaching the offenders responsibility.
- *Community support.* The decision to sentence a convicted offender to probation is often partially based on considerations of family and other social ties. Such decisions are made in the belief that offenders will be more subject to control in the community if they participate in a web of positive social relationships. An advantage of both probation and parole is that they allow the offender to continue personal and social

Lecture Note List and discuss the advantages of probation and parole, such as lower costs versus imprisonment, the opportunity for restitution, and the reduced risk of criminal socialization.

Lecture Note List and discuss the disadvantages of probation and parole, including the relatively low degree of punishment inherent in both options. Ask students to decide whether the advantages outweigh the disadvantages and how such a decision might be reached in individual circumstances.

Thematic Question Do communities have the right to be informed when convicts are released from prison? Do victims? How can we as a society balance the community's right to self-protection with individuals' right to live where they choose, even in the case of ex-convicts?

Lecture Note Explain that courts have not held probation and parole officers to the same standards as police officers in the gathering of evidence. Discuss the fact that probation and parole officers may turn incriminating statements made by clients over to prosecutors and that officers may enter clients' homes without a warrant.

Thematic Question This textbook emphasizes the divergent orientations represented by individual-rights advocates and public-order advocates. In your opinion, which of the two perspectives would be more likely to favor the use of probation as a sentencing option? Which would favor parole? Why?

relationships. Probation avoids splitting up families, while parole may reunite family members separated from each other by a prison sentence.

- *Reduced risk of criminal socialization.* Criminal values permeate prisons. In fact, prison has been called a "school in crime." Probation insulates adjudicated offenders, at least to some degree, from these kinds of values. Parole, by virtue of the fact that it follows time served in prison, is less successful than probation in reducing the risk of criminal socialization.
- *Increased use of community services.* Probationers and parolees can take advantage of services offered through the community, including psychological therapy, substance abuse counseling, financial services, support groups, church outreach programs, and social services. While a few similar opportunities may be available in prison, the community environment itself can enhance the effectiveness of treatment programs by reducing the stigmatization of the offender and by allowing the offender to participate in a more "normal" environment.
- *Increased opportunity for rehabilitation.* Probation and parole can both be useful behavioral management tools: They reward cooperative offenders with freedom and allow for the opportunity to shape the behavior of offenders who may be difficult to reach through other programs.

Disadvantages of Probation and Parole

Any honest appraisal of probation and parole must recognize that they share a number of strategic drawbacks:

- *Relative lack of punishment.* The just deserts model of criminal sentencing insists that punishment should be a central theme of the justice process. While rehabilitation and treatment are recognized as worthwhile goals, the model suggests that punishment serves both society's need for protection and victims' need for revenge. Probation, which many view as practically no punishment at all, is coming under increasing criticism as a sentencing strategy. Parole is likewise accused of unhinging the scales of justice because (1) it releases some offenders early, even when they have been convicted of serious crimes while some relatively minor offenders remain in prison, and (2) it is dishonest because it does not require completion of the offender's entire sentence behind bars.
- *Increased risk to the community.* Probation and parole are strategies designed to deal with convicted criminal offenders. The release into the community of such offenders increases the risk that they will commit additional offenses. Community supervision can never be so complete as to eliminate such a possibility, and evaluations of parole have pointed out that an accurate assessment of offender dangerousness is beyond our present capability.[27]
- *Increased social costs.* Some offenders placed on probation and parole will effectively and responsibly discharge their obligations; others, however, will become social liabilities. In addition to the increased risk of new crimes, probation and parole increase the chance that added expenses will accrue to the community in the form of child support, welfare costs, housing expenses, legal aid, indigent health care, and the like.

4 Describe the legal environment surrounding the use of probation and parole, and name the significant court cases.

The Legal Environment

Eleven especially significant U.S. Supreme Court decisions provide the legal framework for probation and parole supervision. Among those cases, that of *Griffin* v. *Wisconsin* (1987)[28] may be the most significant. In *Griffin*, the Supreme Court ruled that probation officers may conduct searches of a probationer's residence without either a search warrant or probable cause. According to the Court, "A probationer's home, like anyone else's, is protected by the Fourth Amendment's requirement that searches be 'reasonable.'" However, "[a] State's operation of a probation system . . . presents 'special needs' beyond normal law enforcement that may justify departures from the usual warrant and probable cause requirements."

Thematic Question Consider the diverse sentencing goals identified in Chapter 9. Which of the goals identified there are most likely to be met through the use of probation? Which through parole? Why?

Freedom or Safety? You Decide.

Should DNA Links to Unsolved Cases Be Used to Deny Parole?

DNA testing has been called the "new fingerprinting in criminal investigations." It is a powerful tool that, when used correctly, leaves little doubt about the personal identity of a criminal suspect. The federal government has a huge DNA database, consisting of millions of records gathered from convicted offenders, members of the military, and federal employees in sensitive positions. Starting in 1990, states and the federal government began sharing their DNA records through the nation's Combined DNA Index System (CODIS).

While most of the records in CODIS are those of convicted criminals, a number of states (including California, Kansas, Louisiana, Minnesota, New Mexico, Texas, and Virginia) and the federal government recently enacted legislation to allow the collection of DNA samples from all people who are arrested and charged with felonies. At least six other states are moving in the same direction.[1] In addition, federal authorities are contemplating adding the genetic records of terrorism suspects arrested overseas and of anyone detained for immigration law violations, including those caught illegally crossing the nation's borders (and often quickly returned to their country of origin). If advocates of preconviction genetic testing have their way, the number of records available through CODIS will soar.

Recently, the American Civil Liberties Union (ACLU) filed suit in federal court in San Francisco, challenging California's law that permits the genetic testing of unconvicted arrestees, saying that such testing amounts to an unconstitutional search. Complicating the picture is the fact that some parole authorities have begun hunting for DNA matches in CODIS for inmates who become eligible for early release and then using such matches to hold suspects longer. In Utah, for example, parole-eligible robber Rudy Romero had his release date pushed back 25 years after DNA linked him to five unsolved rapes—even though he has not been charged with any of them.[2] Authorities now think that Romero is the man who came to be known as the "Parkway Rapist" after an unsolved series of brutal attacks and rapes of ten teenage girls and three women near Salt Lake City's Jordan River Parkway between 1990 and 1993.

Although advocates of preconviction testing say that it helps secure justice, some of the matches that turn up involve crimes for which the statute of limitations has expired and that can never be prosecuted. Those opposed to the use of genetic testing to determine parole eligibility say that it is unfair because inmates seeking release do not have the opportunity to defend themselves and that the rules at parole hearings are not like those in criminal trials where defendants are allowed to be represented by attorneys.

YOU DECIDE

Should states inventory the DNA of all suspects who have been arrested for felonies? Of those convicted of felonies? Of those arrested for or convicted of misdemeanors? Should parole authorities be allowed to use apparent DNA links to unsolved crimes in denying the release of parole-eligible inmates?

[1]Although most state laws require the DNA records of anyone found not guilty to be expunged from their databases and for their DNA samples to be destroyed, records may still be available for a long time because there are delays in the justice process and because it takes time for the administrative process to conclude.

[2]It is unlikely that rape charges will ever be brought against Romero because Utah has a four-year statute of limitations that bars prosecution.

References: Kevin Johnson and Richard Willing, "New DNA Links Used to Deny Parole," *USA Today*, February 8–10, 2008; Richard Willing, "Many DNA Matches Aren't Acted On," *USA Today*, November 21, 2006; Richard Willing, "Officials Increase DNA Profiles," *USA Today*, May 1, 2006; Richard Willing, "Detainee DNA May Be Put in Database," *USA Today*, January 19–21, 2007; Jennifer Dobner, "DNA May ID 1990s Rapist," *Desert Morning News* (Salt Lake City), September 3, 2004.

Probation, the Court concluded, is similar to imprisonment because it is a "form of criminal sanction imposed upon an offender after a determination of guilt." Similarly, in the 1998 case of *Pennsylvania Board of Probation and Parole* v. *Scott*,[29] the Court declined to extend the exclusionary rule to apply to searches by parole officers, even where such searches yield evidence. Table 10–1 provides an overview of these and other significant cases in the field of probation and parole.

Other court cases focus on the conduct of probation or parole **revocation hearings**, which may result in an order that a probationer's suspended sentence be made "active" or that a parolee be returned to prison to complete his or her sentence in confinement. Revocation is a common procedure. Annually, about 25% of those on probation and 26% of adults on parole throughout the United States have their **conditional release** (release into the community based on certain conditions) revoked.[30] The supervising officer may request that probation or parole be revoked if a client has violated the conditions of community release or has committed a new crime. The most frequent violations for which revocation occurs are (1) failure to report as required to a probation or parole officer, (2) failure to participate in a stipulated treatment program, and (3) alcohol or drug abuse while under supervision.[31]

Another important legal issue today surrounds the potential liability of probation officers and parole boards for the criminal actions of offenders they supervise or whom they have released. Some courts have held that officers are generally immune from suit because they are performing a judicial function on behalf of the state.[32] Other courts, however, have indicated that parole board members who do not carefully consider mandated criteria for judging parole eligibility could be liable for injurious actions committed by

revocation hearing
A hearing held before a legally constituted hearing body (such as a parole board) to determine whether a parolee or probationer has violated the conditions and requirements of his or her parole or probation.

conditional release
The release of an inmate from prison to community supervision with a set of conditions for remaining on parole. If a condition is violated, the individual can be returned to prison or face another sanction in the community.[iii]

Thematic Question Is it appropriate for an offender to be given certain procedural considerations in probation or parole hearings that must nevertheless stop short of introducing an adversarial element into the proceedings? Explain.

TABLE 10–1
U.S. Supreme Court Decisions of Special Significance for Probation and Parole

In This Case	The Court Held That
Samson v. *California* (2006)	Police officers may conduct a warrantless search of a person who is subject to a parole search condition, even when there is no suspicion of criminal wrongdoing and even when the sole reason for the search is that the person is on parole.
U.S. v. *Knights* (2001)	The warrantless search authority normally reserved for probation and parole officers extends to police officers when supported by reasonable suspicion and authorized by the conditions of probation.
Pennsylvania Board of Probation and Parole v. *Scott* (1998)	The exclusionary rule does not apply to searches by parole officers, even when such searches yield evidence of parole violations.
Griffin v. *Wisconsin* (1987)	Probation officers may conduct searches of a probationer's residence without a search warrant or probable cause.
Minnesota v. *Murphy* (1984)	A probationer's incriminating statements to a probation officer may be used as evidence against him or her if the probationer does not specifically claim a right against self-incrimination.
Bearden v. *Georgia* (1983)	Probation cannot be revoked for failure to pay a fine and make restitution if it can't be shown that the defendant was responsible for the failure. Moreover, if a defendant lacks the capacity to pay a fine or make restitution, then the hearing authority must consider any viable alternatives to incarceration before imposing a prison sentence.
Greenholtz v. *Nebraska Penal Inmates* (1979)	Parole boards do not have to specify the evidence or reasoning used in deciding to deny parole.
Gagnon v. *Scarpelli* (1973)	The safeguards identified in *Morrissey* v. *Brewer* were extended to probationers.
Morrissey v. *Brewer* (1972)	Procedural safeguards are necessary in revocation hearings involving parolees. They include (a) written notice of the claimed violations of parole; (b) disclosure to the parolee of evidence against him or her; (c) opportunity to be heard in person and to present witnesses and documentary evidence; (d) the right to confront and cross-examine adverse witnesses (unless the hearing officer specifically finds good cause for not allowing confrontation); (e) a "neutral and detached" hearing body such as a traditional parole board, members of which need not be judicial officers or lawyers; and (f) a written statement.
Mempa v. *Rhay* (1967)	Both notice and a hearing are required before probation revocation, and the probationer should have the opportunity for representation by counsel before a deferred prison sentence is imposed.
Escoe v. *Zerbst* (1935)	Probation "comes as an act of grace to one convicted of a crime," and the revocation of probation without hearing or notice to the probationer is permissible. This decision has been greatly modified by later decisions.

Thematic Question What competing needs and rights must parole boards weigh? Whose rights or needs should be given the greatest consideration?

Lecture Note Tell the class that members of parole boards have generally been immune to lawsuits arising from "bad" release decisions. Ask students whether they think parole decision makers should be held personally liable for the decisions they make.

parolees.[33] In general, however, most experts agree that parole board members cannot be successfully sued unless release decisions are made in a grossly negligent or wantonly reckless manner.[34] Discretionary decisions made by individual probation and parole officers that result in harm to members of the public, however, may be more actionable under civil law, especially where their decisions were not reviewed by a judicial authority.[35]

The Job of Probation and Parole Officers

Job Descriptions

5 Explain the nature of the job of probation and parole officers.

The tasks performed by probation and parole officers are often quite similar, and some jurisdictions combine the roles of both into one job. This section describes the duties of probation and parole officers, whether performed by the same or different individuals. Probation or parole work consists primarily of four functions: (1) presentence investigations, (2) intake procedures, (3) diagnosis and needs assessment, and (4) client supervision.

Where probation is a possibility, intake procedures may include a presentence investigation, which examines the offender's background to provide the sentencing judge with facts needed to make an informed sentencing decision. Intake procedures may also involve a dispute-settlement process during which the probation officer works with the defendant and the victim to resolve the complaint before sentencing. Intake duties tend to be more common for juvenile offenders than they are for adults, but all

◀ Georgia probation officers preparing to excavate a site at the Tri-State Crematory in Noble, Georgia, in 2002. Officials found the remains of hundreds of corpses on the crematory's 16-acre grounds. The crematory's operator, Ray Brent Marsh, was charged with 787 felony counts including theft by deception, abuse of a corpse, and burial service fraud. He was also charged with 47 counts of making false statements to authorities. Convicted on many of the charges, he was sentenced to 12 years in prison in 2005. As this photo shows, a probation officer's job can involve a wide variety of duties. What are some aspects of a probation officer's job?
Mark Humphrey/AP Wide World Photos

Lecture Note Describe the job of a probation or parole officer in terms of both its difficulties and its rewards. Ask students if they would consider careers in the field of probation and parole. Discuss their choices.

officers may eventually have to recommend to the judge the best sentencing alternative for a particular case.

Diagnosis, the psychological inventorying of the probation or parole client, may be done either formally with written tests administered by certified psychologists or through informal arrangements, which typically depend on the observational skills of the officer. Needs assessment, another area of officer responsibility, extends beyond the psychological needs of the client to a cataloging of the services necessary for a successful experience on probation or parole.

Supervision of sentenced probationers or released parolees is the most active stage of the probation or parole process. It might involve months (and sometimes years) of periodic meetings between the officer and the client and an ongoing assessment of the success of the probation or parole endeavor in each case.

All probation and parole officers must keep confidential the details of the presentence investigation, including psychological tests, needs assessment, and conversations between their clients and themselves. On the other hand, courts have generally held that communications between the officer and the client are not privileged, as they might be between a doctor and a patient or between a social worker and his or her client.[36] Hence officers can share with the appropriate authorities any incriminating evidence that a client relates.

> Probation and parole have essentially shifted from legitimate correctional options in their own right to temporary diversionary strategies that we are using while we are trying to figure out how to get tough on crime, [pay] no new taxes, and not pay for any prisons at all, or to pay as little as we can, or pass it off to another generation.
>
> —Charles M. Friel, Sam Houston State University

The Challenges of the Job

One of the biggest challenges that probation and parole officers face is the need to balance two conflicting sets of duties: to provide quasi–social work services and to handle custodial responsibilities. In effect, two inconsistent models of the officer's role coexist. The social work model stresses an officer's service role and views probationers and parolees as clients. In this model, officers are caregivers whose goals are to accurately assess the needs of their clients and to match clients with community resources, such as job placement, indigent medical care, family therapy, and psychological and substance abuse counseling. The social work model depicts probation or parole as a "helping profession" wherein officers assist their clients in meeting the conditions imposed on them by their sentence. The other model for officers is

Class Activity Invite a probation or parole officer to speak with the class either in person or through virtual conferencing. Have students prepare questions in advance to ask the speaker about the use of alternative sentencing options in the local area and about the rewards and difficulties associated with his or her job.

Career Profile
Probation Officer

Name: Stephanie Drury

Position: Probation Officer, Pontiac, Michigan

College attended: Wayne State University (BS, Criminal Justice; MS, Criminal Justice)

What criminal justice-related jobs have you held? 2005: Probation officer for the State of Michigan.

2009: Probation officer for the Oakland County (Michigan) Adult Treatment Court.

Please give a brief description of your job. I am a probation officer for approximately 110 men. The Adult Treatment Court is a specialty court for offenders with severe substance-abuse problems, and many of them also have a mental health diagnosis. My role there is to provide intensive supervision. I attend court with them every two weeks to inform the judge of their progress. Additionally, I see each of them at least once a week in order to ensure they are complying with all conditions of the program and maintaining their sobriety.

What appealed to you most about this job when you applied for it? I completed an internship with the federal probation department in Detroit and thoroughly enjoyed probation work, so I applied for the state probation job. The Adult Treatment Court position was appealing because I work directly with the judge and am able to provide intensive supervision to my probationers.

How would you describe the interview process? The interview consisted of a panel of three members of the Michigan Department of Corrections followed by a written test. Questions were based on my academic experience, along with any professional experience I had that would make me a perfect candidate. Also, real-life situations and scenarios were discussed in order to show the panel how I might deal with a particular situation.

What is a typical day like for you? I monitor the daily development of the females of the Adult Treatment Court, which includes probation supervision and making sure they are taking their medication, going to therapy, and attending programs such as Narcotics Anonymous. With the men on general supervision, I complete presentence investigations, fieldwork, jail visits, and court appearances.

What qualities or characteristics are most helpful for this job? You have to be strong and in control at all times. If you don't have a backbone, the offenders will walk all over you and not take you seriously. It is a demanding job, and you have to be very organized to successfully supervise so many individuals on your caseload. You can exercise a lot of discretion and be your own boss, yet you also have a supervisor who will assist you in times of need.

What is the typical starting salary for this position? $16.54 per hour with benefits.

What is the salary potential as you move up into higher-level jobs? A probation officer with six years or more of experience will earn approximately $28.00 per hour or more, depending on their classification.

What career advice would you give someone in college beginning studies in criminal justice? Find internships to gain experience in specific areas in the field of criminal justice. Engage yourself in as much real-life experience as possible, and network with as many professionals as possible, as these two methods will set you apart from other job candidates.

Source: Reprinted with permission of Stephanie Drury. Photo courtesy of Stephanie Drury. Logo courtesy of Wayne State University.

correctional. In this model, probation and parole clients are "wards" whom officers are expected to control. This model emphasizes community protection, which officers are supposed to achieve through careful and close supervision. Custodial supervision means that officers will periodically visit their charges at work and at home, often arriving unannounced. It also means that they must be willing to report clients for new offenses and for violations of the conditions of their release.

Most officers, by virtue of their personalities and experiences, probably identify more with one model than with the other. They think of themselves primarily either as caregivers or as correctional officers. Regardless of the emphasis that appeals more to individual officers, however, the demands of the job are bound to generate role conflict at one time or another.

caseload
The number of probation or parole clients assigned to one probation or parole officer for supervision.

A second challenge of probation and parole work is large **caseloads** (the number of clients assigned to probation or parole officers). Back in 1973, the President's Commission on Law Enforcement and Administration of Justice recommended that probation and parole caseloads average around 35 clients per officer.[37] However, caseloads of 250 clients are common in some jurisdictions today. Large caseloads, combined with limited training and the time constraints imposed by administrative demands, culminate in stopgap supervisory measures. "Postcard probation," in which clients mail in a letter or card once a month to report on their whereabouts and circumstances, is an example of one stopgap measure that harried agencies with large caseloads use to keep track of their wards.

Another difficulty with probation and parole work is the frequent lack of opportunity for career mobility within the profession. Probation and parole officers are generally assigned to small agencies serving limited geographic areas, under the leadership of one or two chief probation officers. Unless retirement or death claims a supervisor, there is little chance for other officers to advance.

A 2005 report by the National Institute of Justice (NIJ) found that probation and parole officers experienced a lot of stress.[38] The major sources of stress for probation and parole officers were found to be high caseloads, extensive paperwork, and pressures associated with deadlines. Stress levels have also increased in recent years because offenders who are sentenced to probation and released on parole today have committed more serious crimes than in the past, and more offenders have serious drug-abuse histories and show less hesitation in using violence.[39] The NIJ study found that officers typically cope by requesting transfers, retiring early, or taking "mental health days" off from work. The report says, however, that "physical exercise is the method of choice for coping with the stress."[40]

Learn more about working as a probation or parole officer at the American Probation and Parole Association (APPA) website at **Web Extra 10–3**.

Intermediate Sanctions

As noted in Chapter 9, significant new alternative sentencing options have become available to judges during the past few decades. These options are called **intermediate sanctions** because they employ sentencing alternatives that fall somewhere between outright imprisonment and simple probationary release back into the community. They are also sometimes termed *alternative sentencing strategies*. Michael J. Russell, former director of the NIJ, states:

> [I]ntermediate punishments are intended to provide prosecutors, judges, and corrections officials with sentencing options that permit them to apply appropriate punishments to convicted offenders while not being constrained by the traditional choice between prison and probation. Rather than substituting for prison or probation, however, these sanctions—which include intensive supervision, house arrest with electronic monitoring (also referred to as *remote location monitoring*), and shock incarceration (programs that stress a highly structured and regimented routine, considerable physical work and exercise, and at times intensive substance abuse treatment)—bridge the gap between those options and provide innovative ways to ensure swift and certain punishment.[41]

intermediate sanctions
The use of split sentencing, shock probation or parole, shock incarceration, mixed sentencing, community service, intensive probation supervision, or home confinement in lieu of other, more traditional sanctions, such as imprisonment and fines.

6 Explain what intermediate sanctions are, and list the advantages of intermediate sanctions over more traditional forms of sentencing.

A number of citizen groups and special-interest organizations are working to widen the use of sentencing alternatives. One organization of special note is the Sentencing Project. The Sentencing Project, based in Washington, D.C., is dedicated to promoting a greater use of alternatives to incarceration and provides technical assistance to public defenders, court officials, and other community organizations.

Lecture Note Explain that intermediate sanctions resulted from the desire to improve the effectiveness of rehabilitative efforts.

The Sentencing Project and other groups like it have contributed to the development of more than 100 locally based alternative sentencing programs. Most alternative sentencing programs work in conjunction with defense attorneys to develop written sentencing plans. Such plans are basically well-considered citizen suggestions as to appropriate sentencing in a given instance. They are often quite detailed and may include letters of support from employers, family members, the defendant, and even victims. Sentencing plans may be used in plea bargaining sessions or may be presented to judges following trial and conviction. More than a decade ago, for example, lawyers for country western singer Willie Nelson successfully proposed an alternative option to tax court officials that allowed the singer to pay huge past tax liabilities by performing in concerts for that purpose. Lacking such an alternative, the tax court might have seized Nelson's property or even ordered the singer to be confined to a federal facility. More recently, NBA player DeShawn Stevenson was sentenced to two years of probation and ordered to perform 100 hours of community service for the statutory rape of a 14-year-old girl whom he had plied with brandy.[42] Stevenson, who played for the Utah Jazz at the time of the offense, fulfilled the terms of his sentence by delivering motivational speeches at Boys Clubs in California and New York.

Thematic Question Contrast the intermediate sentencing options described in this chapter with the goals of sentencing identified in Chapter 9. Which option is most likely to achieve each goal? Why?

▲ A New Mexico boot camp staff member conducting a push-up drill with young offenders. Boot camps use military-style discipline in an attempt to reduce the chance for recidivism among young first-time offenders. Are boot camps likely to reduce recidivism?
Vladimir Chaloupka/Las Cruces Sun-News/AP Wide World Photos

The basic philosophy behind intermediate sanctions is this: When judges are offered well-planned alternatives to imprisonment for offenders who appear to represent little or no continuing threat to the community, the likelihood of a prison sentence is reduced. An analysis of alternative sentencing plans like those sponsored by the Sentencing Project shows that judges accept them in up to 80% of the cases in which they are recommended and that as many as two-thirds of offenders who receive intermediate sentences successfully complete them.[43]

Intermediate sanctions have three distinct advantages: (1) They are less expensive to operate per offender than imprisonment; (2) they are socially cost-effective because they keep the offender in the community, thus avoiding both the breakup of the family and the stigmatization of imprisonment; and (3) they provide flexibility in terms of resources, time of involvement, and place of service.[44] Some of these new sentencing options are described in the paragraphs that follow.

Split Sentencing

In jurisdictions where **split sentences** are an option, judges may impose a combination of a brief period of imprisonment and probation. Defendants who are given split sentences are often ordered to serve time in a local jail rather than in a long-term confinement facility. Ninety days in jail, together with two years of supervised probation, is a typical split sentence. Split sentences are frequently given to minor drug offenders. They serve notice that continued law violations may result in imprisonment for much longer periods.

split sentence
A sentence explicitly requiring the convicted offender to serve a period of confinement in a local, state, or federal facility, followed by a period of probation.

Shock Probation and Shock Parole

Shock probation strongly resembles split sentencing because the offender serves a relatively short period of time in custody (usually in a prison rather than a jail) and is released on probation by court order, but the difference is that shock probation clients must *apply* for probationary release from confinement and cannot be certain of the judge's decision. In shock probation, the court in effect makes a resentencing decision. Probation is only a statutory possibility and often little more than a vague hope for the offender as imprisonment begins. If probationary release is ordered, it may well come as a "shock" to the offender, who, facing a sudden reprieve, may forswear future criminal involvement. Shock probation was begun in Ohio in 1965.[45] It is used today in about half of the states.[46] Shock probation lowers the cost of confinement, maintains community and family ties, and may be an effective rehabilitative tool.

shock probation
The practice of sentencing offenders to prison, allowing them to apply for probationary release, and enacting such release in surprise fashion. Offenders who receive shock probation may not be aware that they will be released on probation and may expect to spend a much longer time behind bars.

Similar to shock probation is shock parole. Whereas shock probation is ordered by judicial authority, shock parole is an administrative decision made by a paroling authority. Parole boards or their representatives may order an inmate's early release, hoping that the brief exposure to prison has reoriented the offender's life in a positive direction.

Shock Incarceration

Shock incarceration, which became quite popular during the 1990s, utilizes military-style "boot camp" prison settings to provide highly regimented environments involving strict discipline, physical training, and hard labor.[47] Shock incarceration programs are designed primarily for young first offenders and are of short duration, generally lasting for only 90 to 180 days. Offenders who successfully complete these programs are typically returned to the community under some form of supervision. Program "failures" may be moved into the general prison population for longer terms of confinement.

shock incarceration
A sentencing option that makes use of "boot camp"–type prisons to impress on convicted offenders the realities of prison life.

Lecture Note Discuss the alternative sentencing options described in this chapter. Have the class identify the types of offenders and offenses on which shock incarceration programs might have the most effect.

Georgia established the first shock incarceration program in 1983.[48] Following Georgia's lead, more than 30 other states began their own programs.[49] The federal government and some Canadian provinces also operate shock incarceration programs. About half of the states provide for voluntary entry into the program, and a few states allow inmates to decide when and whether they want to quit. Although most states allow judges to place offenders into these programs, some delegate that authority to corrections officials. Two states,

Louisiana and Texas, give judges and corrections personnel joint authority in the decision-making process.[50] Some states, including Massachusetts, accept female inmates into boot camp settings. The Massachusetts program, which first accepted women in 1993, requires inmates to spend nearly four months undergoing the rigors of training.

One of the most comprehensive studies to date of boot camp prison programs focused on eight states: Florida, Georgia, Illinois, Louisiana, New York, Oklahoma, South Carolina, and Texas. The report found that boot camp programs have been popular because "they are . . . perceived as being tough on crime" and "have been enthusiastically embraced as a viable correctional option." However, the report notes, "the impact of boot camp programs on offender recidivism is at best negligible."[51] More limited studies, such as one that focused on shock incarceration in New York State, have found that boot camp programs can be effective money savers. The research indicates that such programs save money in two ways: "first by reducing expenditures for care and custody" (since the intense programs reduce time spent in custody, and participation in them is the only way New York inmates can be released from prison before their minimum parole eligibility dates), and "second, by avoiding capital costs for new prison construction."[52] A 1995 study of Oregon's Summit boot camp program reached a similar conclusion. Although they did not study **recidivism** (repetition of criminal behavior), the Oregon researchers found that "the Summit boot camp program is a cost-effective means of reducing prison overcrowding by treating and releasing specially selected inmates earlier than their court-determined minimum period of incarceration."[53]

▲ Supermodel Naomi Campbell showing off a safety vest and boots at the Manhattan Sanitation Depot after being ordered by a judge to perform community service following an assault on a domestic worker at her residence. Campbell pleaded guilty to hitting her housekeeper on the head with a cell phone after she couldn't find a pair of Campbell's jeans. Was Campbell's sentence appropriate?
Kevin Mazur/Getty Images–WireImage.com

Mixed Sentencing and Community Service

Some **mixed sentences** require that offenders serve weekends in jail and receive probation supervision during the week. Other types of mixed sentencing require offenders to participate in treatment programs or **community service** (work administered by a community agency) while on probation. Community service programs began in Minnesota in 1972 with the Minnesota Restitution Program, which gave property offenders the opportunity to work and turn over part of their pay as restitution to their victims.[54] Courts throughout the nation quickly adopted the idea and began to build restitution orders into suspended-sentence agreements.

Community service is more an adjunct to rather than a type of correctional sentence and is compatible with most other forms of innovation in probation and parole. Even with home confinement (discussed below), offenders can be sentenced to community service activities that are performed in the home or at a job site during the hours they are permitted to be away from their homes. Washing police cars, cleaning school buses, refurbishing public facilities, and assisting in local government offices are typical forms of community service. Some authors have linked the development of community service sentences to the notion that work and service to others are good for the spirit.[55] Community service participants are usually minor criminals, drunk drivers, and youthful offenders.

One problem with community service sentences is that authorities rarely agree on what they are supposed to accomplish. Most people admit that offenders who work in the community are able to reduce the costs of their own supervision, but there is little agreement on whether such sentences reduce recidivism, act as a deterrent, or serve to rehabilitate offenders.

Intensive Probation Supervision

Intensive probation supervision (IPS)—described as the "strictest form of probation for adults in the United States"[56]—is designed to achieve control in a community setting over offenders who would otherwise go to prison. Some states have extended a type of IPS to parolees, allowing the early release of some who would otherwise serve longer prison terms.

recidivism
The repetition of criminal behavior. In statistical practice, a recidivism rate may be any of a number of possible counts or instances of arrest, conviction, correctional commitment, or correctional status change related to repetitions of these events within a given period of time.

mixed sentence
A sentence that requires that a convicted offender serve weekends (or other specified periods of time) in a confinement facility (usually a jail) while undergoing probationary supervision in the community.

community service
A sentencing alternative that requires offenders to spend at least part of their time working for a community agency.

intensive probation supervision (IPS)
A form of probation supervision involving frequent face-to-face contact between the probationer and the probation officer.

Ethics and Professionalism
American Probation and Parole Association Code of Ethics

- I will render professional service to the justice system and the community at large in effecting the social adjustment of the offender.
- I will uphold the law with dignity, displaying an awareness of my responsibility to offenders while recognizing the right of the public to be safeguarded from criminal activity.
- I will strive to be objective in the performance of my duties, recognizing the inalienable right of all persons, appreciating the inherent worth of the individual, and respecting those confidences which can be reposed in me.
- I will conduct my personal life with decorum, neither accepting nor granting favors in connection with my office.
- I will cooperate with my coworkers and related agencies and will continually strive to improve my professional competence through the seeking and sharing of knowledge and understanding.
- I will distinguish clearly, in public, between my statements and actions as an individual and as a representative of my profession.
- I will encourage policy, procedures, and personnel practices, which will enable others to conduct themselves in accordance with the values, goals, and objectives of the American Probation and Parole Association.
- I recognize my office as a symbol of public faith and I accept it as a public trust to be held as long as I am true to the ethics of the American Probation and Parole Association.
- I will constantly strive to achieve these objectives and ideals, dedicating myself to my chosen profession.

THINKING ABOUT ETHICS

1. ***Which of the ethical principles enumerated here might also apply to correctional officers working in prisons and jails?***
2. ***Which might apply to law enforcement officers?***
3. ***Which might apply to prosecutors and criminal defense attorneys?***

Source: American Probation and Parole Association. Reprinted with permission.

Thematic Question Discuss the value of each of the intermediate sanctions described in this chapter. Which of these options are, in your opinion, the most fair? Why?

Georgia was the first state to implement IPS, beginning its program in 1982. The Georgia program involves a minimum of five face-to-face contacts between the probationer and the supervising officer per week, mandatory curfew, required employment, weekly check of local arrest records, routine and unannounced alcohol and drug testing, 132 hours of community service, and automatic notification of probation officers via the State Crime Information Network when an IPS client is arrested.[57] The caseloads of probation officers involved in IPS are much lower than the national average. Georgia officers work as a team, with one probation officer and two surveillance officers supervising about 40 probationers.[58]

A study published in 2000 shows that IPS programs can be effective at reducing recidivism, especially if the programs are well planned and fully implemented.[59] The study, which examined programs in California's Contra Costa and Ventura Counties, found that the programs worked because, among other things, they used team approaches in their supervision activities and had clear missions and goals.

Home Confinement and Remote Location Monitoring

home confinement
House arrest. Individuals ordered confined to their homes are sometimes monitored electronically to ensure they do not leave during the hours of confinement. Absence from the home during working hours is often permitted.

remote location monitoring
A supervision strategy that uses electronic technology to track offenders who are sentenced to house arrest or those who have been ordered to limit their movements while completing a sentence involving probation or parole.

Home confinement, also referred to as *house arrest*, can be defined as "a sentence imposed by the court in which offenders are legally ordered to remain confined in their own residences."[60] Home confinement usually makes use of a system of **remote location monitoring**, which is typically performed via a computerized system of electronic bracelets. Participants wear a waterproof, shock-resistant transmitting device around the ankle 24 hours a day. The transmitter continuously emits a radio-frequency signal that is detected by a receiving unit connected to the home telephone. Older systems use random telephone calls that require the offender to insert a computer chip worn in a wristband into a specially installed modem in the home, verifying his or her presence. Some use voice recognition technology and require the offender to verify his or her presence in the home by answering computerized

> Probation and parole services are characteristically poorly staffed and often poorly administered.
>
> —President's Commission on Law Enforcement and Administration of Justice

calls. Modern electronic monitoring systems alert the officer when a participant leaves a specific location or tampers with the electronic monitoring equipment. Some systems even make it possible to record the time a supervised person enters or leaves the home.

Much of the electronic monitoring equipment in use today only indicates when participants enter or leave the equipment's range, not where they have gone or how far they have traveled. Newer satellite-supported systems, however, are capable of continuously monitoring and tracking an offender as he or she moves from place to place (Figure 10–2). Satellite-based systems can alert officials when participants venture into geographically excluded locations or when they fail to present themselves at required locations at specific times.[61]

Most remotely monitored offenders on home confinement may leave home only to go to their jobs, attend to medical emergencies, or buy household essentials. Because of the strict limits it imposes on offender movements, house arrest has been cited as offering a valuable alternative to prison for offenders with special needs. Pregnant women, geriatric convicts, offenders with special handicaps, seriously or terminally ill offenders, and the intellectually disabled may all be better supervised through home confinement than traditional incarceration.

One of the best-known people to be placed under house arrest with a remote location monitoring system is former National Football League star Michael Vick. He was released from prison in May 2009 after serving 18 months for taking part in a brutal dog-fighting ring. Vick spent the last two months of his prison sentence under house arrest at his home in Hampton, Virginia. He reportedly had to wear an electronic ankle bracelet that allowed federal officers to track his movements.[62] He was allowed to go to work at a full-time construction job and to leave home another five hours a week for other court-approved activities. Vick was also

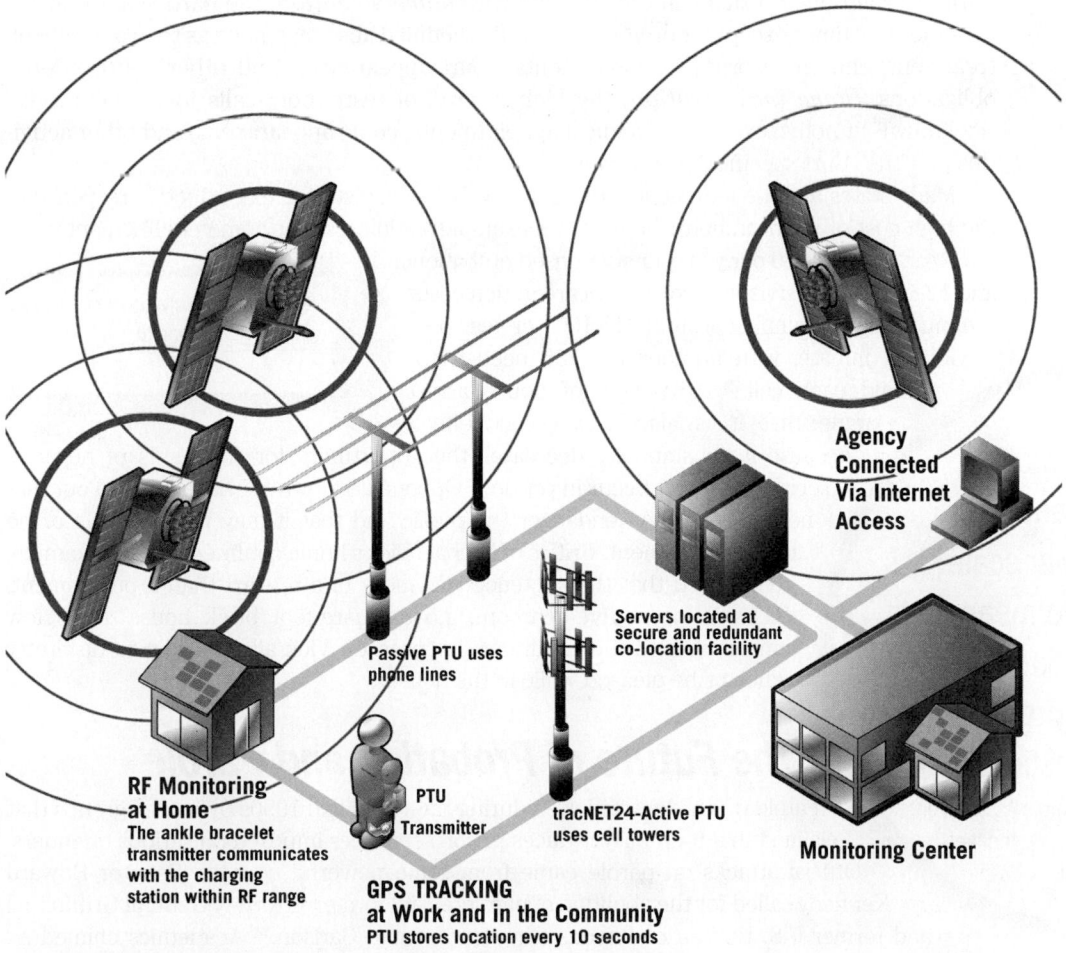

FIGURE 10–2 Remote Location monitoring—How It Works

Source: From iSECUREtrac Corporation, copyright © 2006 iSECUREtrac Corporation. All rights reserved. Used with permission.

▲ National Football League star Michael Vick, who served time in prison for his role in a brutal dog-fighting ring. Vick spent the last two months of his prison sentence under house arrest, wearing an electronic ankle bracelet that allowed federal officers to track his movements. What kinds of offenders are most likely to benefit from remote location monitoring?
UPI Photo/Haraz N. Ghanbari/POOL/ Landov Media

Lecture Note Discuss home confinement as a sentencing option with built-in inequities. Explain how some offenders are better able to afford the court-ordered costs associated with this alternative and how some homes are obviously more comfortable "prisons" than others.

ordered to serve an additional probationary term, scheduled to end in 2012, during which time he is not permitted to own a dog.

The Community Justice Assistance Division of the Texas Department of Criminal Justice runs one of the most ambitious home confinement programs in the country. In 1997, nearly 90,000 adults (3.5% of the state's probationers) were being electronically monitored on probation.[63] By 2006, parole offices throughout the state had adopted electronic monitoring, and 1,056 electronic monitoring units were available for use with parolees.[64]

The electronic monitoring of offenders has steadily increased nationwide. A survey by the NIJ in 1987, as the use of electronic monitoring was just beginning, showed only 826 offenders being monitored electronically in the United States.[65] By 2000, however, more than 16,000 defendants and offenders under the supervision of U.S. pretrial services and probation officers were on home confinement, most under electronic monitoring programs.[66] A 2005 estimate put the number of persons in the United States under electronic monitoring at up to 75,000.[67]

In 1999, South Carolina's Probation and Parole Department began using satellites to track felons recently paroled from state prisons. The satellite-tracking plan, which makes use of 21 satellites in the Global Positioning System (GPS), allows the agency's officers to track every move made by convicts wearing electronic bracelets.[68] The system, which also notifies law enforcement officers when a bracelet-wearing offender leaves his or her assigned area, can electronically alert anyone holding a restraining order whenever the offender comes within two miles of him or her. Statistics available from the Bureau of Justice Statistics showed that 12,096 persons throughout the United States were being monitored by the use of Global Positioning System technology at the start of 2009.[69]

The home confinement program in the federal court system has three components, or levels of restriction.[70] *Curfew* requires program participants to remain at home every day during certain times, usually in the evening. With *home detention*, the participant remains at home at all times except for preapproved and scheduled absences, such as for work, school, treatment, church, attorney's appointments, court appearances, and other court-ordered obligations. *Home incarceration*, the highest level of restriction, calls for 24-hour-a-day "lockdown" at home, except for medical appointments, court appearances, and other activities that the court specifically approves.

Many states and the federal government view house arrest as a cost-effective response to the high cost of imprisonment. Georgia, for example, estimates that home confinement costs approximately $1,130 per year per supervised probationer and $2,190 per supervised parolee.[71] Incarceration costs are much higher, running around $18,100 per year per Georgia inmate, with another $43,756 needed to build each cell.[72] Advocates of house arrest argue that it is also socially cost-effective because it substantially decreases the opportunity for the kinds of negative socialization that occur in prison.[73] Opponents, however, have pointed out that house arrest may endanger the public and that it may provide little or no actual punishment. Critics of Michael Vick's home confinement, for example, complained that the sentence was more of a reward than a punishment. Vick's home, a five-bedroom, 3,538-square-foot brick house, lacks few amenities, and the conditions imposed on Vick allowed him to do pretty much as he pleased while in the house.

7 Describe the likely future of probation and parole.

> The abolition of parole has been tried and has failed on a spectacular scale. . . . The absence of parole means that offenders simply walk out the door of prison at the end of a predetermined period of time, no questions asked.
>
> —American Probation and Parole Association and Association of Paroling Authorities International

The Future of Probation and Parole

Parole was widely criticized during the 1980s and 1990s by citizen groups that claimed that it unfairly reduces prison sentences imposed on serious offenders. Official attacks on parole came from some powerful corners. Senator Edward Kennedy called for the abolition of parole, as did former Attorney General Griffin Bell and former U.S. Bureau of Prisons Director Norman Carlson.[74] Academics chimed in,

CJ News
More Sex Offenders Tracked by Satellite

. . . In May 2006, Wisconsin joined a rapidly rising number of states using GPS to monitor convicted sex offenders. At least 23 states are doing so, according to a survey in February by the Pennsylvania Board of Probation and Parole. Others have since begun or expanded GPS programs.

"In the last several months, it's been exponential growth," says Steve Chapin, president of Pro-Tech, a Florida-based firm that provides GPS services to 27 statewide agencies. . . .

As of January 2006, 13 states had laws requiring or allowing GPS tracking. . . .

Aside from Wisconsin, governors in at least six states (Arkansas, Georgia, Kansas, Virginia, Washington and Michigan) have signed such bills this year [2006]. . . .

"It's the law you can't vote against," says Chapin.

Several of the laws are named after Jessica Lunsford, a 9-year-old Florida girl who was kidnapped, raped and killed in February 2005. The man charged with killing her was a convicted sex offender who hadn't reported that he lived across the street from her family. . . .

Even states without specific GPS laws . . . are testing the technology and expanding its use.

Congress may accelerate such efforts. The House and Senate have each passed sex offender bills this year that approve funding for GPS tracking. . . .

MORE ACCURATE TECHNOLOGY

The surge in GPS use coincides with the technology's dramatic advancements. The devices have become smaller and more accurate, often pinpointing a person's position within 30 feet. They are more precise than older devices that use radio frequencies. . . .

California uses GPS to track 430 sex offenders and has funds to follow 2,500 offenders by 2009, says Elaine Jennings of the California Department of Corrections and Rehabilitation. Since the program began in July 2005, 45 offenders have been arrested for violating parole and no new crimes have been committed, she says. . . .

Massachusetts has issued eight arrest warrants for violations by the 192 high-risk offenders it has tracked since its . . . GPS program began in May 2005, says Paul Lucci, one of the state's deputy probation commissioners. . . .

Michigan finished three pilot programs in 2003 and plans this summer [2006] to begin tracking up to 1,000 sex offenders, says Steve Bock of the Michigan Department of Corrections Electronic Monitoring Center. . . .

OPPOSITION TO GPS TRACKING

Jake Goldenflame, . . . a convicted sex offender released 15 years ago, opposes lifetime GPS tracking. "If a man is so dangerous he needs it, he shouldn't be released," he says. . . . Goldenflame says such monitoring may provide a "false sense of security," because it tells where the offender is, not what he's doing.

▲ A computer screen image demonstrating how Global Positioning System (GPS) technology allows parole officers to track the movements of supervised offenders. What do you see as the advantages and disadvantages of this technology? How would individual-rights and public-safety advocates see this technology? *Courtesy of Pro Tech Monitoring*

"It is not an effective way to prevent sexual assaults," says Richard Wright, a professor of criminal justice at Bridgewater State College. He says many serious sex offenders evade police by failing to register and others may re-offend regardless of tracking. He says no definitive study proves GPS deters crime.

Chapin says GPS reduces recidivism. . . . He says a December 2004 analysis by the Florida Department of Corrections found 3.8% of offenders tracked with GPS committed a new felony within two years compared to 7.7% of those supervised without it.

Offenders tracked by GPS were 90% less likely to abscond or re-offend than those not electronically monitored, says a February [2006] study by Florida State University of 75,661 offenders placed on home confinement. . . . "It's not a cost-free device," says Mark Carey, president of the American Probation and Parole Association. "It's an augmentation of what we do. It's not a replacement."

Source: Wendy Koch, "More Sex Offenders Tracked by Satellite," *USA Today*, June 6, 2006. Reprinted by permission.

alleging that parole programs can provide no assurance that criminals will not commit further crimes. The media joined the fray, condemning parole for its inability to curb recidivism and highlighting the so-called revolving prison door as representative of the failure of parole.

These criticisms are not without warrant. Today, more than 735,000 former prisoners—more than 2,000 per day—are released from state and federal prisons and returned to society each year, most of them on some form of supervised release.[75] If past trends continue, just over half of them will be reincarcerated within three years (although some of them will have successfully completed parole prior to their return to prison).[76] Parole violators account for more than half of prison admissions in California (67%), Utah (55%), and Montana and Louisiana (both 53%). Seventy percent of parole violators in prison were arrested or were convicted of a new offense while on parole.[77] Many of these offenses involve drugs. Critics say that numbers like this are indicative of poor reintegration of prisoners into the community and are associated with wide-ranging social costs, including decreased public safety and weakened family and community ties.[78]

> I understand that people want violent criminals locked up. We all do. But not every inmate is violent. We must look to supervised probation, to education. We must overcome the fear and think this out.
>
> —Edwin Edwards, former governor of Louisiana

Even prisoners have challenged the fairness of parole, saying it is sometimes arbitrarily granted and creates an undue amount of uncertainty and frustration in the lives of inmates. Parolees have complained about the unpredictable nature of the parole experience, citing their powerlessness in the parole contract.

Against the pressure of attacks like these, parole advocates struggled to clarify and communicate the value of supervised release in the correctional process. As more and more states moved toward the elimination of parole, advocates called for moderation. A 1995 report by the APPA, for example, concluded that states that have eliminated parole "have jeopardized public safety and wasted tax dollars." The researchers wrote, "Getting rid of parole dismantles an accountable system of releasing prisoners back into the community and replaces it with a system that bases release decisions solely on whether a prison term has been completed."[79]

Changes in Reentry Policies

By the close of the twentieth century, criticisms of parole had begun to wane, and a number of recent reports have supported well-considered offender reentry and postrelease supervision programs. In 2005, for example, the Reentry Policy Council, a bipartisan assembly of almost 100 leading elected officials, policymakers, corrections leaders, and practitioners from community-based organizations around the country, released a report on offender reentry titled *Charting the Safe and Successful Return of Prisoners to the Community*. The 500-page document pointed out that virtually every person incarcerated in a jail in this country, as well as 97% of those incarcerated in prisons, will eventually be released back into society. This, said the report, results in nearly 650,000 people being released from prisons, and more than 7 million others being released from jails, throughout the United States each year—many of them without any form of postrelease supervision.[80]

As the report pointed out, almost two out of every three people released from prison are rearrested within three years of their release.[81] Report authors noted that while the number of people reentering society has increased fourfold in the past 20 years and spending on corrections has increased nearly sevenfold in the past two decades, the likelihood of a former prisoner succeeding in the community upon release has not improved.

A host of complex issues creates barriers to successful reentry. Three-quarters of those released from prison and jail, for example, have a history of substance abuse. Two-thirds have no high school diploma. Nearly half of those leaving jail earned less than $600 per month immediately prior to their incarceration, and they leave jail with significantly diminished opportunities for employment. Moreover, said the report, more than a third of jail inmates are saddled with a physical or mental disability, and the rate of serious mental illness among released inmates is at least three times higher than the rate of mental illness among the general population.[82]

The report states that "the multi-faceted—and costly—needs of people returning to their families and communities require a re-inventing of reentry akin to the reinvention of welfare in the 90s."[83] It requires, the report continued, "a multi-system, collaborative approach that takes into account all aspects of [the] problem." In other words, "the problems faced by re-entering adults are not merely the problems of corrections or community corrections, but also of public health workers, housing providers, state legislators, workforce development staff, and others."

To guide states and local jurisdictions in the creation of successful offender reentry programs, the report provides 35 policy statements, each of which is supported by a series of research highlights. The report can be read in its entirety at **Library Extra 10–4**. A 24-page summary is available at **Library Extra 10–5**.

In 2003, the U.S. Department of Justice, in conjunction with other federal agencies, initiated funding for 89 reentry sites across the country under the Serious Violent Offender Reentry Initiative (SVORI).[84] SVORI programs are geared toward serious and violent offenders, particularly adults released from prison, and juveniles released from correctional

FIGURE 10–3 The SVORI Program Model

Source: Laura Winterfield and Susan Brumbaugh, *The Multi-Site Evaluation of the Serious and Violent Offender Reentry Initiative* (RTI International and the Urban Institute, 2006). Reprinted with permission of the Urban Institute.

facilities.[85] The goal of the SVORI initiative is to reduce the likelihood of reincarceration by providing tailored supervision and services to improve the odds for a successful transition to the community. SVORI services include employment assistance, education and skills training, substance-abuse counseling, and help with postrelease housing. SVORI programs also try to reduce criminality by closely monitoring participant noncompliance, reoffending, rearrest, reconviction, and reincarceration.[86] The initiative's priorities include providing services both to those adults and juveniles who are most likely to pose a risk to the community upon release and to those who face multiple challenges upon returning to the community. SVORI funding supports the creation of a three-phase continuum of services that begins in prison, moves to a structured reentry phase before and during the early months of release, and continues for several years as released prisoners take on increasingly productive roles in the community. These phases have been described in SVORI-related publications as follows (Figure 10–3):[87]

- *Phase 1—Protect and Prepare: Institution-Based Programs.* These programs are designed to prepare offenders to reenter society. Services provided in this phase include education, mental health and substance-abuse treatment, job training, mentoring, and full diagnostic and risk assessment.
- *Phase 2—Control and Restore: Community-Based Transition Programs.* These programs work with offenders prior to and immediately following their release from correctional institutions. Services provided in this phase include, as appropriate, education, monitoring, mentoring, life skills training, assessment, job skills development, and mental health and substance-abuse treatment.
- *Phase 3—Sustain and Support: Community-Based Long-Term Support Programs.* These programs connect individuals who have left the supervision of the justice system with a network of social services agencies and community-based organizations to provide ongoing services and mentoring relationships.

Although evaluation of SVORI programs is ongoing, a recent review identified several reentry strategies that appear to work. In particular, vocational and work-release programs were found to improve job skills and to reduce recidivism, and some prerelease SVORI-sponsored drug-treatment programs were found to be successful. SVORI evaluators also found that program participants who stayed in halfway houses committed less severe and fewer crimes than those who lived elsewhere, and a number of educational programs were found to be capable of increasing achievement scores among reentry program participants.

One innovative approach to managing former prisoners who are returning to their communities is the use of reentry courts. Reentry courts are based on the drug-court model, begun in Miami in 1989, which functions to rapidly place drug-affected defendants into appropriate treatment programs with close supervision by a single judge familiar with both the treatment and the offenders.[88] Similarly, under the reentry court concept, reentry court judges oversee an offender's supervised release into the community.[89] The Indiana Department of Corrections, for example, operates a SVORI-funded reentry court program.[90] Under the program, when released, participants are brought to Allen County Community Corrections (ACCC) in Fort Wayne, Indiana, and given in-depth risk assessments. A remote location monitoring system keeps track of each offender after release. On the first Friday after release, offenders appear before the reentry court judge for their first reentry court hearing. At the hearing they learn about the program and its goals and are told what's expected of them. Two weeks later, offenders meet with the judge individually, and a reintegration plan is imposed by the court. Successful adherence to the plan is a condition for continued freedom. Participants continue to appear

▲ David Duke, the former Ku Klux Klan leader whose case raised eyebrows when he was released on federal parole in 2004. Duke, who served a year in federal prison on fraud charges, was released to a halfway house in Baton Rouge, Louisiana, and met the work requirements of his release by performing duties for the "white civil rights group" that he heads. Could a more suitable placement have been found for him?
Burt Steel/AP Wide World Photos

before the court every two to five weeks to review progress and to assess any problems that have arisen. The reentry court offers an array of reintegration services to which participants can be referred and provides continual oversight using a preestablished set of graduated sanctions and rewards. The court also has a strong relationship with the faith community, and local pastors attend court hearings and offer mentoring services. Throughout the program, ACCC provides ongoing offender supervision for up to two years, and a reentry case management team makes continual recommendations to the judge.

Faith-based organizations in the SVORI program generally provide services such as emergency aid (clothing and food, for example), mentoring, pastoral counseling, employment, transportation, and housing. They also conduct prerelease and postrelease needs assessments for program participants, coordinate family and community support for individual offenders, provide guidance to the program through participation in the program's steering committee or advisory board, and serve as community advocates for the SVORI program. Learn more about the SVORI initiative and its individual programs at **Library Extra 10–6**. Reports about ongoing SVORI-related research can be read online at **Web Extra 10–4**. **Web Extra 10–5** links to the Prisoner Reentry Initiative at John Jay College, and **Web Extra 10–6** takes readers to the National Reentry Resource Center, a joint effort begun in 2009 by the Urban Institute, the American Probation and Parole Association, the Center of Juvenile Justice Reform at Georgetown University, the Association of State Correctional Administrators, and the Council of State Governments' Justice Center.

In March 2008, in an effort to help the nearly 700,000 people leaving prison each year, the U.S. Congress passed the Second Chance Act.[91] The bill was signed into law by President George W. Bush shortly afterward. The act authorized the expenditure of approximately $400 million in federal funds between 2008 and 2012 to "break the cycle of criminal recidivism [by assisting] offenders reentering the community from incarceration to establish a self-sustaining and law-abiding life."[92] The legislation funds prison-to-community transition services and programs through grants to nonprofit organizations. Such services and programs include the following:

- Education and job training while in prison
- Mentoring programs for adults and juveniles leaving confinement
- Drug treatment (including family-based treatment) for incarcerated parents during and after incarceration
- Alternatives to incarceration for parents convicted of nonviolent drug offenses
- Supportive programming for children of incarcerated parents
- Early release for certain elderly prisoners convicted of nonviolent offenses
- Reentry research through research awards to study parole and postsupervision revocation and related community safety issues

The legislation also allocates funding for federal Bureau of Prisons–specific programs that do the following:

1. Provide prisoners nearing the completion of their sentences with information concerning health care, nutrition, employment opportunities, money management, and availability of government assistance.
2. Allow certain nonviolent prisoners over 60 years of age to be placed in home detention for the duration of their sentences.
3. Educate juvenile offenders on the consequences of drug use and criminal activity.

The legislation also slightly increases the percentage of federal sentences that can be served in home confinement.

The Reinvention of Probation

Although probation has generally fared better than parole, it too has its critics. The primary purpose of probation has always been rehabilitation, and probation is a powerful rehabilitative tool because, at least in theory, it allows the resources of a community to be focused on the offender. Unfortunately for advocates of probation, the rehabilitative ideal is far less popular today than it has been in the past. The contemporary demand for just deserts appears to have reduced society's tolerance for even relatively minor offenders. Also, because it has been too frequently and inappropriately used with repeat or relatively serious offenders, the image of probation has been tarnished. Probation advocates have been forced to admit that it is not a very powerful deterrent because it is far less punishing than a term of imprisonment.

In a series of reports issued in 1999 and 2000, the Reinventing Probation Council, a project of New York's Manhattan Institute, called for the "reinvention of probation."[93] Probation is in the midst of a crisis, said the council, because probationers are not being held to even simple standards of behavior and because the field of probation lacks leadership. The council went on to say that "probation will be reinvented when the probation profession places public safety first and works with and in the community." Read the council's full reports at **Library Extras 10–7** and **10–8**.

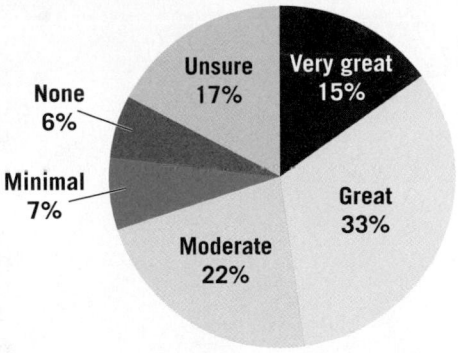

FIGURE 10–4 Degree of Emphasis Parole Offices Place on Evidence-Based Practices

Source: Jesse Jannetta, Brian Elderbroom, Amy Solomon, Megan Cahill, and Barbara Parthasarthy, *An Evolving Field: Findings from the 2008 Parole Practices Survey* (Washington, DC: Urban Institute, 2009), p. 14. Reprinted with permission of the Urban Institute.

In late 2008, the Public Safety Performance Project of the Pew Center on the States released a report outlining strategies for successful probation supervision and parole reentry. The report, titled *Putting Public Safety First*, outlined 13 strategies that the center says "can reduce recidivism and hold offenders accountable for their actions while also cutting substance abuse and unemployment, and restoring family bonds."[94] Primary among the strategies is defining the success of probation and parole in terms of recidivism reduction. The entire report can be accessed at **Library Extra 10–9**.

About a year later, in an effort to assess the degree to which the Pew Center's 13 strategies were being implemented, the Justice Policy Center of the Urban Institute published a lengthy review of parole practices across the country.[95] While the review found that few agencies are using all of the 13 strategies, it did find that most agencies are moving toward implementing many of them. Although 93% of survey respondents reported that their offices have the goal of reducing recidivism, only 75% said that they were tracking the recidivism rates of current parolees. An amazingly low 13% of offices said that they continued to track recidivism rates of parolees who have completed parole. Moreover, definitions of recidivism varied considerably between agencies and included "reincarceration," "reconviction," "new arrest," and "technical violation."[96] One positive finding from the survey is that the awareness and use of evidence-based practices among parole agencies have become relatively widespread (Figure 10–4). This, say the report's authors, "suggests that a consensus on the value of the general concept is emerging." Nonetheless, the review also found that "there is considerable uncertainty on what evidence-based practice means in parole."[97] For a national portrait of contemporary parole practices, see **Library Extra 10–10**.

> There is considerable uncertainty on what evidence-based practice means in parole.
> —Urban Institute

A PowerPoint presentation that supports this chapter is available from your Prentice Hall representative.

Summary

PROBATION, PAROLE, AND COMMUNITY CORRECTIONS

- Probation, simply put, is a sentence of imprisonment that is suspended. Its goal is to retain some control over criminal offenders while using community programs to help rehabilitate them. Probation, a court-ordered sanction, is one form of community corrections, a sentencing style that depends less on traditional confinement options and more on correctional resources available in the community. In 1925, the federal government enacted legislation enabling federal district court judges to appoint paid probation officers and to impose probationary terms.

- Parole, the conditional early release of a convicted offender from prison, is a corrections strategy whose primary purpose is to return offenders gradually to productive lives. Parole differs from probation in that parolees, unlike probationers, have been incarcerated. Parole supports the concept of indeterminate sentencing, which allows a prisoner to earn early release through good behavior and self-improvement.
- Both probation and parole provide opportunities for the reintegration of offenders into the community through the use of resources not readily available in institutional settings. They are far less expensive than imprisonment, lead to increased employment among program participants, make possible restitution payments, and increase opportunities for rehabilitation. Unfortunately, however, increased freedom for criminal offenders also means some degree of increased risk for other members of society and increased social costs. Until the problems of inaccurate risk assessment, increased recidivism, and inadequate supervision are solved, probation and parole will continue to be viewed with suspicion by a public that has become intolerant of crime and criminal offenders.
- Eleven especially significant U.S. Supreme Court decisions provide the legal framework for probation and parole supervision. The 1987 case of *Griffin* v. *Wisconsin* may be the most significant. In *Griffin*, the Supreme Court ruled that probation officers may conduct searches of a probationer's residence without either a search warrant or probable cause. Other important court decisions include the 1998 case of *Pennsylvania Board of Probation and Parole* v. *Scott*, in which the Court declined to extend the exclusionary rule to apply to searches by parole officers, and the 2001 case of *U.S.* v. *Knights*, which expanded the search authority normally reserved for probation and parole officers to police officers under certain circumstances.
- Probation or parole work consists primarily of four functions: (1) presentence investigations, (2) other intake procedures, (3) diagnosis and needs assessment, and (4) client supervision. The tasks performed by probation and parole officers are often quite similar, and some jurisdictions combine the roles of both into one job.
- Intermediate sanctions employ sentencing alternatives that fall somewhere between outright imprisonment and simple probationary release back into the community. These sanctions include shock incarceration, intensive probation supervision, and home confinement with remote location monitoring. Intermediate sanctions have three distinct advantages: (1) They are less expensive than imprisonment, (2) they are socially cost-effective because they keep the offender in the community, and (3) they provide flexibility in terms of resources, time of involvement, and place of service.
- In recent years, parole and sometimes probation have been criticized for increasing the risk of community victimization by known offenders. In response, many states have eliminated or significantly curtailed parole opportunities. The future of parole may lie in an emerging concept of reentry that envisions successfully transitioning released inmates into the community using a variety of resources, including institutional and community programs. The federal Second Chance Act of 2008 provides an example of new initiatives being undertaken in the reentry arena.

QUESTIONS FOR REVIEW

1. What is probation? What purpose does it serve?
2. What is parole? How do probation and parole differ? How are they alike?
3. List and explain the advantages and disadvantages of probation and parole.
4. Name and describe significant court cases that have had an impact on the practices of probation and parole.
5. What do probation and parole officers do? What role do probation officers play in the sentencing of convicted offenders?
6. What are intermediate sanctions? How do they differ from more traditional forms of sentencing? What advantages do they offer?
7. How are probation and parole changing? What does the future hold for each?

Prisons and Jails

CHAPTER 11

Learning Objectives

After reading this chapter, you should be able to:

1. Discuss the major characteristics and purposes of today's prisons. **313**
2. Explain the role that jails play in American corrections, and discuss the issues that jail administrators currently face. **324**
3. Describe the role of private prisons today, and assess their future. **329**

"After a 700-percent increase in the U.S. prison population between 1970 and 2005, you'd think the nation would finally have run out of lawbreakers to put behind bars."

—Public Safety Performance Project of the Pew Charitable Trusts[1]

▲ The maximum-security Thomson Correctional Center in Thomson, Illinois. In late 2009, the Obama administration ordered the federal government to purchase the facility to house up to 100 terror suspects previously detained at Guantanamo Bay, Cuba. The center, which had been virtually unoccupied, comprises 1,600 cells and is part of a 146-acre prison complex. How might the operation of a federal prison help surrounding communities? How might it hurt them?
David Greedy/Liaison/Getty Images

Introduction

The small town of Thomson, Illinois, is set to become the new home of terrorism detainees being held at Guantanamo Bay, Cuba. In December 2009, the federal government said that it would purchase and convert the eight-year-old maximum-security Thomson Correctional Center. The center, which is located about 150 miles west of Chicago, opened eight years ago as a state prison at a cost of $145 million, but a decline in the Illinois prison population left it virtually unused. The conversion plan announced enthusiastically by the Obama administration was seen as an important step toward closing the controversial federal detention center at Guantanamo Bay. Once purchased by the federal government, the new facility at Thomson will house both federal inmates and up to 100 detainees from Guantanamo Bay. It will be run jointly by the U.S. Department of Defense and the federal Bureau of Prisons.

The move has been heralded by state legislators and local business leaders as a welcomed boost to the local economy.[2] Speaking at the White House, Illinois Governor Pat Quinn said, "This will be the most secure prison in America," adding that "more than 3,000 jobs will be created. More than a billion dollars will be brought by having a new federal prison."[3] Once it is fully operational, the converted correctional center is expected to employ around 3,000 officers and support staff—many from the local area. Learn more about how prisons and prison construction impact local economies at **Library Extra 11–1**.

prison
A state or federal confinement facility that has custodial authority over adults sentenced to confinement.

Prisons

While new prisons may provide economic windfalls for struggling communities, this chapter considers the wider impact of imprisonment on American society and describes the characteristics of today's **prisons** (state and federal confinement facilities for incarcerated adults) and prison populations. There are approximately 1,325 state prisons and 84 federal prisons in operation across the country today.[4] More are being built as both the states and the federal government continue to fund and construct new facilities. America's prison population has more than quadrupled since 1980, although the growth rate has been slowing recently. On January 1, 2010, the nation's state and federal prisons held 1,613,656 sentenced inmates.[5] Slightly more than 7% (or 114,852) of those imprisoned were women.[6] Figure 11–1 shows the rise in the U.S. prison population during the past 50 years. A special report released by the Public Safety Performance Project of the Pew Charitable Trusts in 2007 predicts that the nation's prison population will rise significantly in the future.[7] From a comparative perspective, the number of people behind bars in the United States is striking, and a recent report from Pew notes that "the United States incarcerates more people than any country in the world, including the far more populous nation of China."[8]

The incarceration rate for state and federal prisoners sentenced to more than a year has reached a record 504 prisoners for every 100,000 U.S. residents. This rate means that about 1 in every 200 U.S. residents was serving a prison term of more than one year in early 2009.[9] If incarceration rates remain unchanged, 6.6% of U.S. residents born in 2001 will go to prison sometime during their lifetime.[10]

High incarceration rates persist in the United States today even in the face of declining crime rates. As noted in Chapter 2, between 1991 and 2009 the official rate of crime in the United States dropped from 5,897 to 3,466 offenses per every 100,000 residents—a level that had not been seen since 1975.[11] Hence a 42% *decrease* in the national crime rate over an 18-year period was accompanied by a 70% *increase* in the rate of imprisonment. Crime-control advocates, of course, would argue that increased rates of incarceration are at least partially responsible for reduced crime rates, since incarceration removes from the community those who are likely to reoffend.

Class Activity Schedule a tour of a local prison. Ask to see as many facilities as possible, including dormitories, shops, cafeteria, segregation units, and religious and assembly areas.

Lecture Note Refer to Figure 11–1. Ask students what factors have contributed to the huge increase in prison populations during the past few decades.

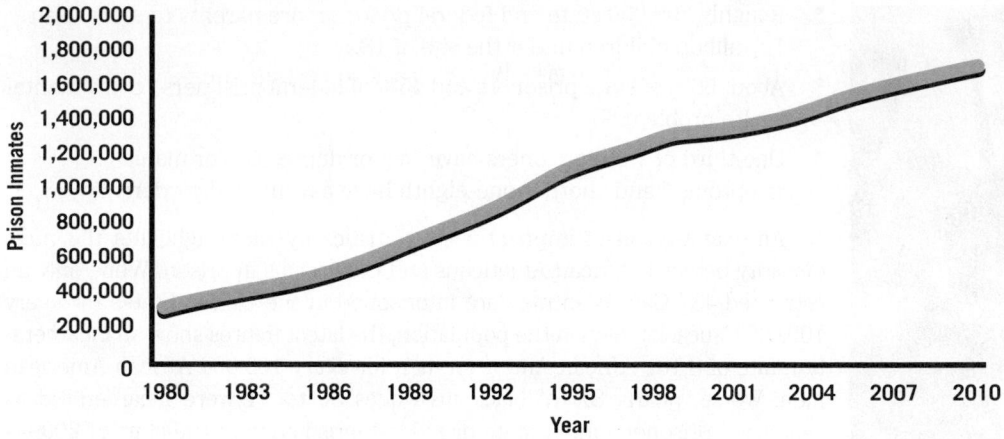

FIGURE 11–1 U.S. Prison Population, 1980–2010

Source: Bureau of Justice Statistics.

Today's high rate of imprisonment can be attributed to a number of historical factors:[12]

1. A staunch "get tough on crime" philosophy that swept America during the mid- to late-twentieth century (and that is still largely with us today)
2. The nation's war on drugs as well as a zero-tolerance policy toward illicit drugs, drug users, and drug sellers
3. The increased use of punishments, including mandated prison terms for drug-related felonies
4. A growing reluctance to release parolees in the face of fears about their likelihood of continued crime commission
5. The new mandates in many jurisdictions requiring probation officers to report technical violations of the conditions of probation committed by those in their charge
6. The elimination of good-time prison credits, resulting in longer prison stays for most offenders
7. The abandonment of discretionary (and therefore often early) parole release decisions and the concomitant elimination of parole boards in many states
8. The truth-in-sentencing legislative provisions requiring offenders to serve ever-longer terms (now typically 85% of their sentences) before release
9. The two- and three-strikes legislation, mandating lengthy or life sentences for repeat offenders

One out of every 100 adults is behind bars because one out of every 100 adults has committed a serious criminal offense.

—Paul Cassell, University of Utah, former federal judge[1]

Statistics tell us quite a bit about those in our prisons. Most people sentenced to state prisons were convicted of violent crimes (50%). Property crimes (21%) and drug crimes (20%) are nearly tied as the second most common type of offenses for which inmates were sentenced.[13] In contrast, prisoners sentenced for drug-law violations were the single largest group of federal inmates (52%), and the increase in the imprisonment of drug offenders accounts for more than three-quarters of the total growth in the number of federal inmates since 1980.[14]

1 Discuss the major characteristics and purposes of today's prisons.

According to a 2008 report, today's prison population "is overwhelmingly uneducated, riddled with drug abuse, often illiterate, with weak and troubled job histories, strained family ties, likely to suffer from mental illness, and lacking the basic skills to succeed."[15] Consider these statistics:

- About 68% of state prisoners lack a high school diploma.
- Roughly half are functionally illiterate.
- About 53% of state prisoners are dependent on drugs.
- The work histories and skills of prisoners are well below those of the general population, and only one in five prisoners has a job lined up at the time of release.

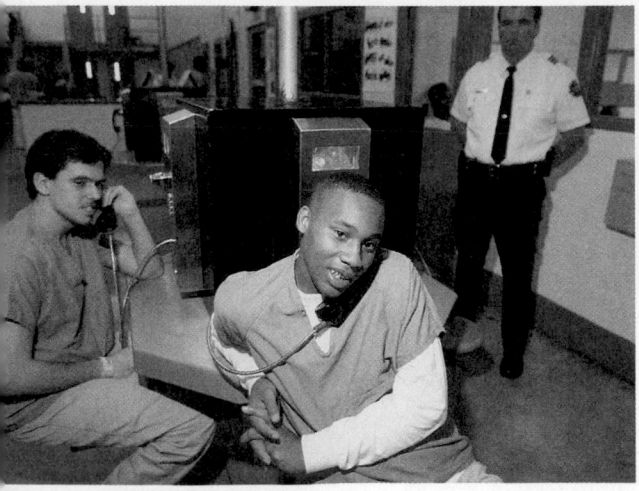

▲ Inmates making collect phone calls at the Davidson County Prison in Tennessee. There are approximately 1,325 state prisons and 84 federal prisons in operation across the country today. Together, they hold more than 1.57 million inmates. The prison shown here is run by the Corrections Corporation of America. Why is the number of inmates growing while the crime rate continues to fall?
A. Ramey/PhotoEdit Inc.

- Roughly 700,000 state and federal prisoners are parents to more than 1.5 million children under the age of 18.
- About 56% of state prisoners and 45% of federal prisoners have a mental health problem.[16]
- One-third of state prisoners have "major depression or mania symptoms," and another one-eighth have psychotic disorders.[17]

An examination of imprisonment statistics by race highlights the huge disparity between African Americans and Caucasians in prison. While only an estimated 487 Caucasian men are imprisoned in the United States for every 100,000 Caucasian men in the population, the latest figures show an incarceration rate of 3,161 African American men for every 100,000 African American men. Worse, nearly 8% of black men ages 30 to 34 were incarcerated as sentenced prisoners under state or federal jurisdiction at the start of 2009—seven times greater than the figure for Caucasians.[18] The imprisonment rate of African Americans has increased dramatically during the past ten years, while the rate of Caucasian imprisonment grew much more slowly. Almost 17% of adult African American men in the United States have served time in prison—a rate over twice as high as that for adult Hispanic males (7.7%) and over six times as high as that for adult Caucasian males (2.6%).[19] According to the Bureau of Justice Statistics (BJS), an African American male living in America today has a 32.3% lifetime chance of going to prison, and an African American female has a 5.6% lifetime chance of imprisonment. These figures contrast sharply with the lifetime chances of imprisonment for Caucasian males (5.9%) and Caucasian females (0.9%).[20]

The use of imprisonment varies considerably between states. While the average rate of imprisonment in the United States at the start of 2009 was 504 per every 100,000 people in the population,[21] some state rates were nearly double that figure.[22] Louisiana, for example, was holding 865 out of every 100,000 of its citizens in prison on January 1, 2009, and Mississippi was close behind with an incarceration rate of 734. Texas, a state with traditionally high rates of imprisonment, held 669 prisoners per every 100,000 people. Maine had the lowest rate of imprisonment of all the states (148), while other states with low rates were Rhode Island (235), New Hampshire (222), and North Dakota (221). More statistics are available at **Library Extra 11–2**.

A study by David F. Greenberg and Valerie West identified factors that contribute to variation in incarceration rates among states.[23] Greenberg and West found that a state's violent crime rate was a significant determinant of its incarceration rate but was not the only factor involved. Also important were the political leanings of the state's population (more politically conservative states made greater use of imprisonment), the amount of money available to build and maintain prisons (more money led to more imprisonment), the employment rate (unemployment contributed to higher rates of imprisonment), the percentage of African American men in the state's population (the higher the percentage, the higher the rate of imprisonment), and the level of welfare support available to the poor (higher welfare payments meant less imprisonment). The authors also found that income inequality was *not* a predictor of imprisonment rates and that the degree of urbanization in a state had no effect on imprisonment.

The size of prison facilities varies greatly. One out of every four state institutions is a large maximum-security prison, with a population approaching 1,000 inmates. A few exceed that figure, but the typical state prison is small, with an inmate population of less than 500. Community-based facilities average around 50 residents. The typical prison system in relatively populous states consists of the following:[24]

- One high-security prison for long-term high-risk offenders
- One or more medium-security institutions for non-high-risk offenders
- One institution for adult women
- One or two institutions for young adults (generally under age 25)

> Prison and jail populations have skyrocketed during the past two decades, spurring new construction and often generating crowded conditions in our institutions and facilities. Substance abuse is directly and indirectly responsible for a large portion of this population increase.
>
> —James A. Gondles, Jr., executive director, American Correctional Association[ii]

FIGURE 11–2 Annual Costs to Incarcerate an Inmate in Prison in California, 2008–09

Source: The California Legislative Analyst's Office, *California's Criminal Justice System: A Primer*, http://www.lao.ca.gov. Reprinted with permission.

California's Annual Costs to Incarcerate an Inmate in Prison

2008–09

Type of Expenditure	Per Inmate Costs
Security	$19,663
Inmate Health Care	**$12,442**
Medical care	$8,768
Psychiatric services	1,928
Pharmaceuticals	998
Dental care	748
Operations	**$7,214**
Facility operations (maintenance, utilities, etc.)	$4,503
Classification services	1,773
Maintenance of inmate records	660
Reception, testing, assignment	261
Transportation	18
Administration	**$3,493**
Inmate Support	**$2,562**
Food	$1,475
Inmate activities	439
Inmate employment and canteen	407
Clothing	171
Religious activities	70
Rehabilitation Programs	**$1,612**
Academic education	$944
Vocational training	354
Substance abuse programs	313
Miscellaneous	**$116**
Total	**$47,102**

- One or two specialized mental hospital–type security prisons for mentally ill prisoners
- One or more open-type institutions for low-risk, nonviolent inmates

Incarceration costs average around $62 per inmate per day at both the state and federal levels when all types of adult correctional facilities are averaged together.[25] Imprisonment is especially costly in some states, like California, where citizens pay almost $130 per day to house each inmate (Figure 11–2). Prison systems across the nation face spiraling costs as the number of inmates grows and as the age of the inmate population increases. The cost of running the nation's correctional programs approached $64 billion in 2003, of which more than half, or $39 billion, went to run state prisons.[26]

The Philosophy of Imprisonment

Prisons in this country were originally built for the purpose of rehabilitation and as an alternative to the corporal punishments of earlier times.[27] Although many of today's correctional administrators continue to avow a philosophy of rehabilitation and although American corrections continues to serve a variety of purposes, the central policy that influences the course of our nation's prisons today is retribution. Today's overcrowded prisons with their depressing conditions are largely the result of "get tough on crime" attitudes that have swept the nation for the past few decades. These attitudes are based on a perspective that is sometimes referred to as the **justice model** or the *just deserts model*. This model, which

justice model
A contemporary model of imprisonment based on the principle of just deserts.

Class Activity Invite a correctional administrator (warden, programs director, shift supervisor, etc.) to speak with the class either in person or via virtual conferencing. Ask him or her to comment on the ideas discussed in this chapter, such as warehousing and rehabilitation. Ask the speaker whether he or she believes that rehabilitation can effectively occur in a prison setting and what elements are necessary for successful rehabilitation. With what kinds of inmates has the speaker seen rehabilitation succeed or fail?

emphasizes individual responsibility and the punishment of offenders, has become the operative principle underlying many of today's correctional initiatives. The philosophy is grounded squarely on a just deserts theme, in which imprisonment is seen as a *fully deserved* consequence of criminal behavior.

While many would probably agree that "get tough" philosophies come and go, the current wave of such feelings is far from exhausted. During the 1990s, in recognition of such national sentiments, state legislatures everywhere scrambled to place limits on inmate privileges and to increase the pains of imprisonment. In 1995, for example, Alabama became the first state in modern times to reinstitute the prison chain gang.[28] Under the Alabama system, shotgun-armed guards oversaw prisoners who were chained together by the ankles while they worked the state's roadsides picking up trash, clearing brush, and filling ditches. The system, intended primarily for parole violators who must reenter prison, was tough and unforgiving. Inmates served up to 90 days on chain gangs, during which they worked 12-hour shifts and remained chained even while using portable toilets. Following Alabama's lead, in 1995 Arizona became the second state to field prison chain gangs, followed shortly thereafter by Florida.[29] Alabama chain gangs, which had expanded to include female prisoners, were discontinued in 1996 following a lawsuit against the state.

The Florida Department of Corrections continues to use restricted labor squads (its name for chain gangs) at seven correctional institutions. Florida chain gang inmates are shackled at the ankles but are not connected to one another in any way.[30]

Nationally, chain gang proponents, though dwindling in number, continue to be adamant about the purpose this punishment serves. "If a person knows they're going to be out on the highway in chains, they are going to think twice about committing a crime," says former Georgia Prison Commissioner Ron Jones.[31] Opponents of the chain gang, however, like American Civil Liberties Union (ACLU) National Prison Project spokeswoman Jenni Gainsborough, call it "a giant step backward" and "a return to the dark ages."[32]

In 1995, in another example of the move toward greater punishments indicative of the just deserts era, Virginia abolished parole, increased sentences for certain violent crimes by as much as 700%, and announced that it would build a dozen new prisons.[33] Changes in state law, initiated by the administration of Governor George Allen, were intended to move the state further in the direction of truth in sentencing and to appease the state's voters, who—reflecting what appears to have been a groundswell of public opinion nationwide—demanded a "get tough" stance toward criminals. William P. Barr, former U.S. attorney general under President George Bush and cochair of the Virginia commission that developed the state's plan, explained why no provisions for rehabilitation and crime prevention had been included: "The most effective method of prevention," he said, "is to take the rapist off the street for 12 years instead of four."[34]

"Get tough" initiatives can be seen in the "three strikes and you're out" laws that swept through state legislatures everywhere in the late 1990s.[35] Three-strikes legislation, which is discussed in more detail in CJ Exhibit 9–2 in Chapter 9, mandates lengthy prison terms for criminal offenders convicted of a third violent crime or felony. While three-strikes laws either have been enacted or are being considered in more than 30 states and by the federal government, critics of such laws say that they will not prevent crime.[36] Jerome Skolnick of the University of California at Berkeley, for example, criticizes three-strikes legislation because although it may satisfy society's desire for retribution to "lock 'em up and throw away the key," such a practice will almost certainly not reduce the risk of victimization—especially the risk of becoming a victim of random violence.[37] That is so, says Skolnick, because most violent crimes are committed by young men between the ages of 13 and 23. "It follows," according to Skolnick, "that if we jail them for life after their third conviction, we will get them in the twilight of their careers, and other young offenders will take their place." Three-strikes programs, says Skolnick, will lead to the creation of "the most expensive, taxpayer-supported middle-age and old-age entitlement program in the history of the world," which will provide housing and medical care to older, burned-out law violators. Another author puts it this way: "The question . . . is whether it makes sense to continue to incarcerate aged prisoners beyond the time they would have served under ordinary sentences. This is unnecessary from the standpoint of public safety, and it is expensive."[38]

The central aim of a true prison system is the protection of society against crime, not the punishment of criminals.

—Zebulon R. Brockway (1827–1920)[iii]

Alan Schuman, past president of the American Probation and Parole Association, feels much the same way. While building more prisons may be a popular quick fix to crime, says Schuman, such a strategy will cost millions of dollars without making streets safer. "The draconian single-level approach of merely building new institutions will cause us problems for decades," Schuman says.[39]

Thematic Question What explains the rapid rise in incarceration rates that has occurred throughout the United States during the last few decades? Do you feel such an increase is justified by the change in crime rates that has taken place? How does the increase in the use of imprisonment as a criminal sanction reflect a renewed emphasis on public order?

Criticisms like these, however, fail to appreciate the sentiments underlying the current correctional era. Proponents of "get tough" policies, while no doubt interested in personal safety, lower crime rates, and balanced state and federal budgets, are keenly focused on retribution. And where retribution fuels a correctional policy, deterrence, reformation, and economic considerations play only secondary roles. The real issue for those advocating retribution-based correctional policies is not whether they deter crime or lower crime rates but rather the overriding conviction that criminals deserve punishment. As more and more states enacted three-strikes and other "get tough" legislation, prison populations across the nation continued to swell. The just deserts philosophy, however, now provides what has become for many an acceptable rationale for continued prison expansion.

Many now claim that the prevailing retribution-based "lock 'em up" philosophy bodes ill for the future of American corrections. "I am worried there is going to be a disaster in our prisons," says J. Michael Quinlan, director of the Federal Bureau of Prisons (BOP) under Presidents Ronald Reagan and George Bush.[40] The combination of burgeoning prison populations and restrictions on inmate privileges could have a catastrophic and disastrous effect—leading to riots, more prison violence, work stoppages, increased numbers of inmate suicides, and other forms of prison disorder—says Quinlan.[41]

Overcrowding

The Dimensions of Overcrowding

The just deserts philosophy led to substantial and continued increases in the American prison population even as crime rates were dropping. In 1990, for example, the U.S. rate of imprisonment stood at 292 prisoners per every 100,000 residents. By 1995, it had reached 399, and on January 1, 2009, it was 504.[42] By 2010 the rate of growth had slowed and may have finally stopped.

Even though many new prisons have been built throughout the nation during the past 20 years to accommodate the growing number of inmates, prison overcrowding is still very much a reality in many jurisdictions (Figure 11–3). Some of the most crowded prisons are those in the federal system: The crowding rate in all federal prisons (which are not included in Figure 11–3) recently stood at 34% over capacity, while crowding at federal

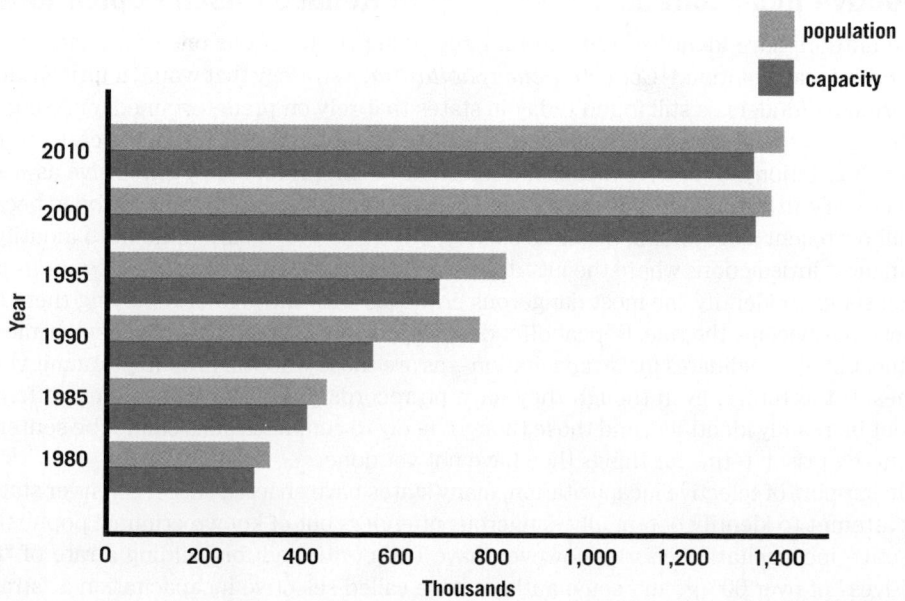

FIGURE 11–3 State Prison Populations, Inmates versus Capacity, 1980–2010

Source: Bureau of Justice Statistics, *Correctional Populations in the United States* (Washington, DC: BJS, various years).

medium-security prisons stood at 62%.[43] Prison overcrowding can be measured along a number of dimensions:

- Space available per inmate (such as square feet of floor space)
- Length of confinement of inmates in cells or housing units (versus time spent on recreation and other activities)
- Living arrangements (for example, single versus double bunks)
- Type of housing (use of segregation facilities, tents, and so on in place of general housing)

Further complicating the picture is the fact that prison officials have developed three definitions of **prison capacity** (the size of a prison population that a facility can hold):[44]

1. **Rated capacity** refers to the size of the inmate population that a facility can handle according to the judgment of experts.
2. **Operational capacity** is the number of inmates that a facility can effectively accommodate based on an appraisal of the institution's staff, programs, and services.
3. **Design capacity** refers to the inmate population that the institution was originally built to handle.

prison capacity
The size of the correctional population an institution can effectively hold.[iv] There are three types of prison capacity: rated, operational, and design.

rated capacity
The number of inmates a prison can handle according to the judgment of experts.

operational capacity
The number of inmates a prison can effectively accommodate based on management considerations.

design capacity
The number of inmates a prison was intended to hold when it was built or modified.

Rated capacity estimates usually yield the largest inmate capacities, while design capacity (on which observations in this chapter are based) typically shows the highest amount of overcrowding.

Overcrowding by itself is not cruel and unusual punishment, according to the U.S. Supreme Court in *Rhodes* v. *Chapman* (1981),[45] which considered the issue of double bunking along with other alleged forms of "deprivation" at the Southern Ohio Correctional Facility. The Court, reasoning that overcrowding is not necessarily dangerous if other prison services are adequate, held that prison housing conditions may be "restrictive and even harsh," for they are part of the penalty that offenders pay for their crimes.

However, overcrowding combined with other negative conditions may lead to a finding against the prison system. The American Correctional Association (ACA) believes that such a totality-of-conditions approach requires courts to assess the overall quality of prison life while viewing overcrowded conditions in combination with other issues:

- The meeting of basic human needs
- The adequacy of the facility's staff
- The program opportunities available to inmates
- The quality and strength of the prison management

Selective Incapacitation: A Strategy to Reduce Prison Populations

Some authors have identified the central issue of imprisonment as one of selective versus collective incapacitation.[46] *Collective incapacitation*, a strategy that would imprison almost all serious offenders, is still found today in states that rely on predetermined, or fixed, sentences for given offenses or for a series of specified kinds of offenses (as in the case of three-strikes legislation). Collective incapacitation is, however, prohibitively expensive as well as unnecessary, in the opinion of many experts. Not all offenders need to be imprisoned because not all represent a continuing threat to society, but those who do are difficult to identify.[47]

In most jurisdictions where the just deserts model holds sway, *selective incapacitation*, which seeks to identify the most dangerous criminals with the goal of removing them from society, has become the rule. Repeat offenders with records of serious and violent crimes are the most likely candidates for incapacitation—as are those who will probably commit violent crimes in the future, even though they have no records. But potentially violent offenders cannot be readily identified, and those thought likely to commit crimes cannot be sentenced to lengthy prison terms for things they have not yet done.

In support of selective incapacitation, many states have enacted career offender statutes that attempt to identify potentially dangerous offenders out of known criminal populations. Selective incapacitation efforts, however, have been criticized for yielding a rate of "false positives" of over 60%,[48] and some authors have called selective incapacitation a "strategy of failure."[49] Nevertheless, in an analysis of recidivism studies, Canadians Paul Gendreau, Tracy Little, and Claire Goggin found that criminal history, a history of preadult antisocial behavior, and "criminogenic needs"—which were defined as measurable antisocial thoughts, values, and behaviors—were all dependable predictors of recidivism.[50]

Some states, however, have had to scramble in an attempt to implement selective incarceration principles. In 2009, for example, a federal judicial panel ordered the release of almost 60,000 California prison inmates due to overcrowding. Governor Arnold Schwarzenegger worked quickly with legislators to establish programs to encourage the diversion or release of nonviolent offenders while assuring the public that murderers, rapists, robbers, and, other violent felons would remain behind bars. The incident, which is described in a CJ News box in this chapter, caused a statewide uproar and media furor.

Recently, the just deserts philosophy has run headlong into funding realities caused by economic contraction and state budget shortfalls. As a consequence, a number of jurisdictions have begun releasing nonviolent offenders sentenced to short terms of confinement in record numbers, hoping to save the money needed to keep more hard-core offenders behind bars. Los Angeles County jail officials, for example, report releasing around 600 minor offenders each day (47,000 per year) before their sentences have been served in a money-saving effort. Los Angeles County Sheriff Lee Baca says he had hoped the practice would be short term but now sees no end in sight. "For misdemeanor offenders our system has come to a grinding halt," says the sheriff. "With thousands being freed after having paid less than 10 percent of their sentence, there simply is no sense of deterrence whatever. This is no way to run a criminal-justice system."[51] Sharp drops in tax income and resulting budget cuts have seriously impacted prisons and jails across the nation. Budget cuts in California over the past three years, for example, have totaled close to $200 million—equal to about 12% of the sheriff's department budget.

> Incarceration is a crash course in extortion and criminal behavior.
>
> —Vincent Schiraldi, executive director, Justice Policy Institute

Security Levels

Maximum-custody prisons tend to be massive old buildings with large inmate populations. However, some—like Central Prison in Raleigh, North Carolina—are much newer and incorporate advances in prison architecture to provide tight security without sacrificing building aesthetics. Such institutions provide a high level of security characterized by high fences, thick walls, secure cells, gun towers, and armed prison guards. Maximum-custody prisons tend to locate cells and other inmate living facilities at the center of the institution and place a variety of barriers between the living area and the institution's outer perimeter. Technological innovations, such as electric perimeters, laser motion detectors, electronic and pneumatic locking systems, metal detectors, X-ray machines, television surveillance, radio communications, and computer information systems, are frequently used today to reinforce the more traditional maximum-security strategies. These technologies have helped to lower the cost of new prison construction. However, some people argue that prisons may rely too heavily on electronic detection devices that have not yet been adequately tested.[52]

Death-row inmates are all maximum-security prisoners, although the level of security on death row exceeds even that experienced by most prisoners held in maximum custody. Prisoners on death row must spend much of the day in single cells. They are often permitted a brief shower only once a week under close supervision.

Most states today have one large, centrally located maximum-security institution. Some of these prisons combine more than one custody level and may be both maximum- and medium-security facilities. Medium security is a custody level that in many ways resembles maximum security. Medium-security prisoners, however, are generally permitted more freedom to associate with one another and can go to the prison yard, exercise room, library, and shower and bathroom facilities under less intense supervision than their maximum-security counterparts.

An important security tool in medium-security prisons is the count, which is literally a head count of inmates taken at regular intervals. Counts may be taken four times a day and usually require inmates to report to designated areas to be counted. Until the count has been "cleared," all other inmate activity must cease.

Medium-security prisons tend to be smaller than maximum-security institutions and often have barbed-wire-topped chain-link fences instead of the more secure stone or

CJ News
California Inmate Release Prompts Public Safety Debate

Without a U.S. Supreme Court reprieve, California will have to free roughly a third of its prison inmates in a few years, and how that can be done safely is still hotly debated.

Corrections officials said . . . they are struggling with their response to a tentative federal court ruling . . . that the state must remove as many as 57,000 inmates over the next two or three years.

The state's 33 adult prisons now hold about 158,000 inmates. But the judges said overcrowding is so severe it unconstitutionally compromises medical care of inmates, and releasing prisoners is the only solution.

"We are just now beginning to have discussions (about) who these types of inmates would be. Then, how do we get to that number?" said Matthew Cate, secretary of the state Department of Corrections and Rehabilitation.

The department has no contingency plan, he said, other than appealing to the U.S. Supreme Court once the ruling becomes final.

The judges said their ruling does not amount to throwing open the cell doors.

"The state has a number of options, including reform of the earned credit and parole systems, that would serve to reduce the population . . . without adversely affecting public safety," the judges wrote. . . .

Gov. Arnold Schwarzenegger already has asked lawmakers to take a number of steps to reduce the inmate population:

- Ending parole for former inmates not convicted of a violent or sex-related crime. That would lead to fewer parolees being sent back to prison because they violated rules.
- Raising the monetary limit for property crimes to be considered felonies. That would send more petty thieves to county jails instead of state prisons.
- Giving inmates more early release credits for completing educational or vocational programs.

Even if all Schwarzenegger's proposals were adopted, they still would fall short of the judges' target, said Cate, the corrections secretary.

Freeing or diverting inmates as the judges suggest is "a dangerous game of Russian roulette," said Stanislaus County Chief Probation Officer Jerry Powers, who heads the statewide chief probation officers association.

He said counties lack the capacity to handle additional offenders.

Law enforcement groups also object that Schwarzenegger's proposal would rule out prison for those convicted of drug offenses, drunken driving, white collar or property crimes such as vehicle theft, grand theft or receiving stolen property, among others.

The state likely could not reach the judges' target without also freeing some serious repeat offenders and inmates serving life sentences, they said.

Republican Assemblyman Jim Nielson, a former chairman of the state parole board, said California should accelerate construction of new prison cells to ease the overcrowding rather than release inmates, although building plans have stalled for nearly two years.

The state already has transferred 6,600 inmates to private prisons in other states, and could try to boost the transfers as an alternative to freeing convicts early.

Source: Don Thompson, "California Inmate Release Prompts Public Safety Debate," The Associated Press, February 10, 2009. Used with permission of The Associated Press. Copyright © 2010. All rights reserved.

concrete block walls found in many of the older maximum-security facilities. Cells and living quarters tend to have more windows and are often located closer to the perimeter of the institution than is the case in maximum-security facilities. Dormitory-style housing, where prisoners live together in wardlike arrangements, may be employed in medium-security facilities, and there are generally more opportunities for inmates to participate in recreational and other prison programs than in maximum-custody facilities.

In minimum-security institutions, inmates are generally housed in dormitory-like settings and are free to walk the yard and to visit most of the prison facilities. Some newer prisons provide minimum-security inmates with private rooms, which they can decorate (within limits) according to their tastes. Inmates usually have free access to a canteen that sells items such as cigarettes, toothpaste, and candy bars. Minimum-security inmates often wear uniforms of a different color from those of inmates in higher custody levels. In some institutions, they may wear civilian clothes. They work under only general supervision and usually have access to recreational, educational, and skills-training programs on the prison grounds. Guards are unarmed, gun towers do not exist, and fences (if they are present at all) are usually low and sometimes even unlocked. Many minimum-security prisoners participate in some sort of work- or study-release program, and some have extensive visitation and furlough privileges. Counts may be taken, although most minimum-security institutions keep track of inmates through daily administrative work schedules. The primary "force" holding inmates in minimum-security institutions is their own restraint. Inmates live with the knowledge that minimum-security institutions are one step removed from close correctional supervision. If they fail to meet the expectations of administrators, they will be transferred into more secure institutions, which will probably delay their release. Inmates returning from assignments in the community may be frisked for contraband, but body-cavity searches are rare in minimum custody, being reserved primarily for inmates suspected of smuggling.

The typical American prison today is medium or minimum custody. Some states have as many as 80 or 90 small institutions, which may originally have been located in every county to serve the needs of public works and highway maintenance. Medium- and minimum-security institutions house the bulk of the country's prison population. They offer a number of programs and services designed to assist with the rehabilitation of offenders and to create the conditions necessary for a successful reentry of the inmates into society. Most prisons offer psychiatric services, academic education, vocational education, substance-abuse treatment, health care, counseling, recreation, library services, religious programs, and industrial and agricultural training.[53] To learn more about all aspects of contemporary prisons, visit the Corrections Connection via **Web Extra 11–1**.

▲ Inmates flashing gang signs for the camera. If you were a warden, what changes might you make to improve the management of a prison like this one?
Damian Dovarganes/AP Wide World Photos

Prison Classification Systems

Most states use a **classification system** to assign new prisoners to initial custody levels based on their type of offense, perceived dangerousness, and escape risk. A prisoner might be assigned to a minimum-, medium-, or maximum-custody institution. Inmates move through custody levels according to the progress they are judged to have made in self-control and demonstrated responsibility. Serious violent criminals who begin their prison careers with lengthy sentences in maximum custody have the opportunity in most states to work their way up to minimum security, although the process usually takes a number of years. Those prisoners who represent continual disciplinary problems are returned to closer custody levels. Minimum-security prisons, as a result, house inmates convicted of all types of criminal offenses.

classification system
A system used by prison administrators to assign inmates to custody levels based on offense history, assessed dangerousness, perceived risk of escape, and other factors.

Once an inmate has been assigned to a custody level, he or she may be reassessed for living and work assignments within the institution. Just as initial (or external) custody classification systems determine security levels, internal classification systems are designed to help determine appropriate housing plans and program interventions within a particular facility for inmates who share a common custody level. In short, initial classification determines the institution in which an inmate is placed, and internal classification determines placement and program assignment within that institution.[54] Learn more about internal prison classification systems at **Library Extra 11–3**.

Objective prison classification systems were adopted by many states in the 1980s, but it wasn't until the late 1990s that such systems were refined and validated. Fueled by litigation and overcrowding, classification systems are now viewed as the principal management tool for allocating scarce prison resources efficiently and for minimizing the potential for violence or escape. Classification systems are also expected to provide greater accountability and to forecast future prison bed-space needs. A properly functioning classification system is the "brain" of prison management, governing and influencing many important decisions, including such fiscal matters as staffing levels, bed space, and programming.[55]

> We spend $60,000 building a prison cell, another $35,000 a year to keep that inmate. . . . At the same time we spend less than $4,000 on each school student. . . . Let's put the money in education. That's the only answer to crime.
>
> —Cleo Fields, former U.S. representative from Louisiana

One of the best-known internal classification systems in use today is the adult internal management system (AIMS). AIMS was developed more than 20 years ago to reduce institutional predatory behavior by identifying potential predators and separating them from vulnerable inmates. AIMS assesses an inmate's predatory potential by quantifying aspects of his or her (1) record of misconduct, (2) ability to follow staff directions, and (3) level of aggression toward other inmates.

Before concluding this discussion of classification, it is important to recognize that the criteria used to classify prisoners must be relevant to the legitimate security needs of the institution. In the 2005 case of *Johnson* v. *California*,[56] for example, the U.S. Supreme Court invalidated the California Department of Corrections and Rehabilitation's (CDCR)

▲ The Federal Bureau of Prisons ADMAX facility in Florence, Colorado, which opened in 1995. It is the only ultra-high-security institution in the federal system. What kinds of inmates are sent there?
Bob Daemmrich/Agence France Presse/Getty Images

ADMAX
An acronym for administrative maximum. This term is used by the federal government to denote ultra-high-security prisons.

Lecture Note Describe prisons as long-term confinement facilities in which convicted criminal offenders serve out their sentences. Differentiate prisons from jails.

unwritten policy of racially segregating prisoners in double cells for up to 60 days each time they entered a new correctional facility. The policy had been based on a claim that it prevented violence caused by racial gangs. The Court, however, held that the California policy was "immediately suspect" as an "express racial classification" and found that the CDCR was unable to demonstrate that the practice served a compelling state interest.

The Federal Prison System

The federal prison system consists of 103 institutions, six regional offices, the Central Office (headquarters), two staff-training centers, and 28 community corrections offices. The regional offices and the Central Office provide administrative oversight and support to the institutions and to the community corrections offices, which oversee community corrections centers and home-confinement programs. The federal correctional workforce is one of the fastest growing in the country, and at mid-2010, the BOP employed 36,800 persons.[57]

The BOP classifies its institutions according to five security levels: (1) administrative maximum (**ADMAX**), (2) high security, (3) medium security, (4) low security, and (5) minimum security. High-security facilities are called *U.S. penitentiaries* (USPs), medium- and low-security institutions are both called *federal correctional institutions* (FCIs), and minimum-security prisons are termed *federal prison camps* (FPCs).[58] Minimum-security facilities (like Eglin Air Force Base in Florida and Maxwell Air Force Base in Alabama) are essentially honor-type camps with barracks-type housing and no fencing. Low-security facilities in the federal prison system are surrounded by double chain-link fencing and employ vehicle patrols around their perimeters to enhance security. Medium-security facilities (like those in Terminal Island, California; Lompoc, California; and Seagoville, Texas) make use of similar fencing and patrols but supplement them with electronic monitoring of the grounds and perimeter areas. High-security facilities (USPs like those in Atlanta, Georgia; Lewisburg, Pennsylvania; Terre Haute, Indiana; and Leavenworth, Kansas) are architecturally designed to prevent escapes and to contain disturbances, and they also make use of armed patrols and intense electronic surveillance.

A separate federal prison category is that of administrative facilities, consisting of institutions with special missions that are designed to house all types of inmates. Most administrative facilities are metropolitan detention centers (MDCs). MDCs, which are generally located in large cities close to federal courthouses, are the jails of the federal correctional system and hold defendants awaiting trial in federal court. Another five administrative facilities, medical centers for federal prisoners (MCFPs), function as hospitals.

Federal correctional facilities exist either as single institutions or as federal correctional complexes, that is, sites consisting of more than one type of correctional institution (Figure 11–4). The federal correctional complex at Allenwood, Pennsylvania, for example, consists of a U.S. penitentiary, a federal prison camp, and two federal correctional institutions (one low and one medium security), each with its own warden. Federal institutions can be classified by type as follows: 55 are FPCs (holding 35% of all federal prisoners), 17 are low-security facilities (28%), 26 are medium-security facilities (23%), eight are high-security prisons (13%), and one is an ADMAX facility (1%).

> With the huge expansion of prisons starting in the 1980s, most prison systems gave up believing they had any responsibility for changing offenders or [for] what happened after offenders were released.
>
> —Todd Clear, John Jay College of Criminal Justice

The federal system's only ADMAX unit, the $60 million ultra-high-security prison at Florence, Colorado, is a relatively recent addition to the federal system. Dubbed "the Alcatraz of the Rockies," the 575-bed facility was designed to be the most secure prison ever built by the government.[59] Opened in 1995, it holds mob bosses, spies, terrorists, murderers, and escape artists. Dangerous inmates are confined to their cells 23 hours per day and are not allowed to see or associate with other inmates. Electronically controlled doors throughout the institution channel inmates to individual exercise sessions. Educational courses, religious services, and administrative matters are conducted via closed-circuit television piped directly into the prisoners' cells. Remote-controlled heavy steel doors within the prison allow corrections staff to section off the institution in

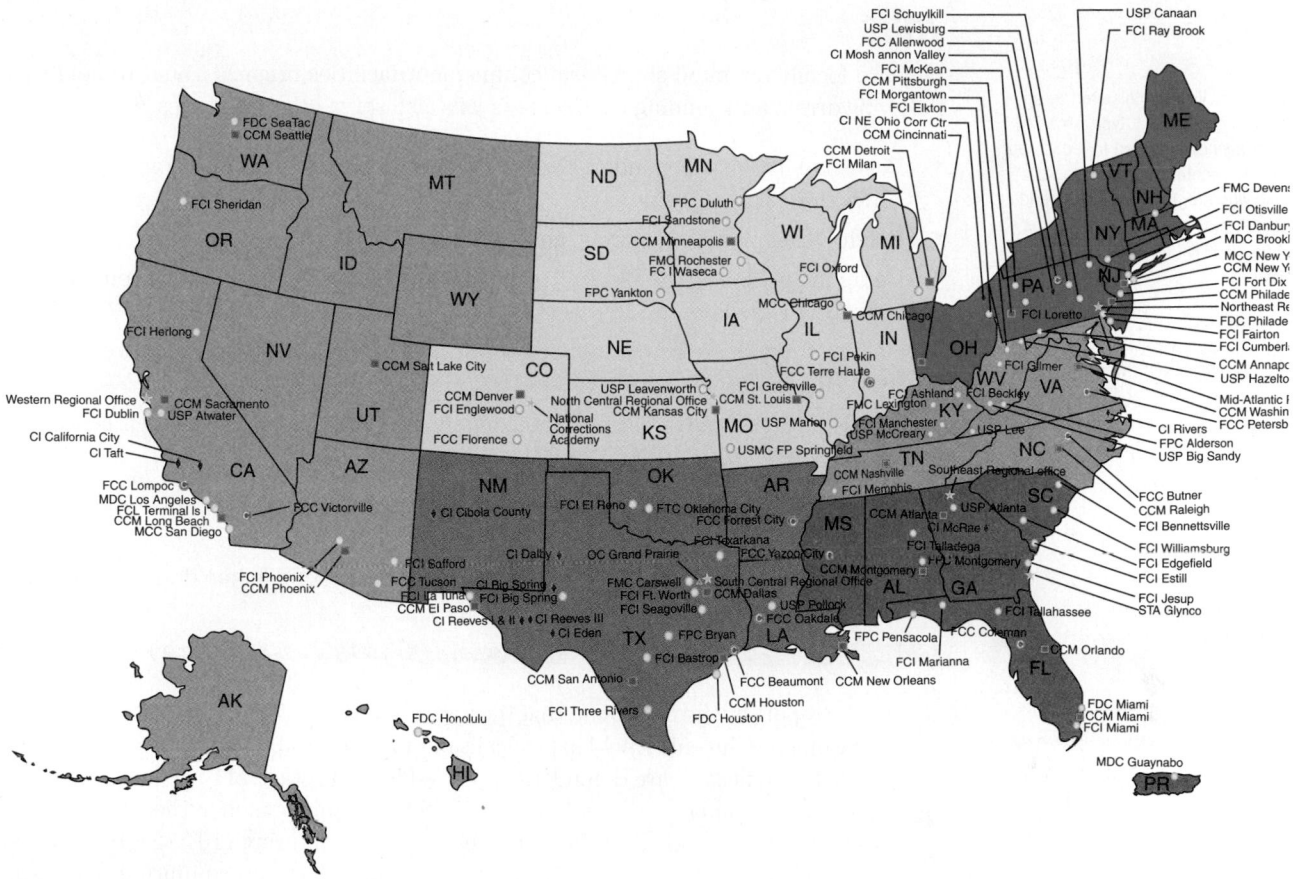

FIGURE 11–4 Federal Bureau of Prisons Facilities by Region

Source: Federal Bureau of Prisons.

the event of rioting, and the system can be controlled from outside if the entire prison is compromised.

In an effort to combat rising expenses associated with a rapidly growing federal prison population, the U.S. Congress passed legislation in 1992 that imposes a "user fee" on federal inmates who are able to pay the costs associated with their incarceration.[60] Under the law, inmates may be assessed a dollar amount up to the cost of a year's incarceration—currently around $22,600.[61] The statute, which was designed so as not to impose hardships on poor offenders or their dependents, directs that collected funds (estimated to total $48 million per year) are to be used to improve alcohol- and drug-abuse programs within federal prisons. To learn more about the BOP, visit **Web Extra 11–2** and read **Library Extras 11–4** and **11–5**.

Recent Improvements

In the midst of frequent lawsuits, court-ordered changes in prison administration, and overcrowded conditions, outstanding prison facilities are being recognized through the ACA accreditation program. The ACA Commission on Accreditation has developed a set of standards that correctional institutions can use for conducting self-evaluations. Institutions that meet the standards can apply for accreditation under the program.

Another avenue toward improvement of the nation's prisons can be found in the National Academy of Corrections, the training arm of the National Institute of Corrections. The academy, located in Boulder, Colorado, offers seminars, videoconferencing, and training sessions for state and local corrections managers, trainers, personnel directors, sheriffs, and state legislators.[62] Issues covered include strategies to control overcrowding, community corrections program management, prison programs, gangs and disturbances, security, and public and media relations.[63]

Lecture Note Describe jails as temporary confinement facilities originally intended to hold defendants awaiting trial or to house convicted offenders awaiting sentencing. Explain that many jurisdictions now use jails in lieu of prisons for offenders sentenced to short terms of imprisonment.

Jails

jail
A confinement facility administered by an agency of local government, typically a law enforcement agency, intended for adults but sometimes also containing juveniles. Jails hold people who are being detained pending adjudication or who were committed after adjudication, usually those sentenced to a year or less.

Class Activity Schedule a tour of a local jail. Ask to see as many areas of the jail as possible, including living quarters, shops, the cafeteria, segregation units, and religious assembly areas. Ask students to compare their observations of the jail with those of the prison. What are the major differences? The similarities?

Jails are locally operated short-term confinement facilities originally built to hold suspects following arrest and pending trial. Today's jails also serve other purposes:[64]

- Receiving individuals pending their arraignment, and holding them for their trial, conviction, or sentencing
- Readmitting probation, parole, and bail-bond violators and absconders
- Detaining juveniles, the mentally ill, and others temporarily, pending their transfer to appropriate facilities
- Holding individuals for the military, for protective custody, for contempt of court, and for the courts as witnesses
- Releasing convicted inmates to the community upon completion of their sentences
- Transferring inmates to federal, state, or other authorities
- Housing inmates for federal, state, or other authorities because of overcrowding in their facilities
- Operating community-based programs with day reporting, home detention, electronic monitoring, or other types of supervision
- Holding inmates sentenced to short terms (generally under one year)

2 Explain the role that jails play in American corrections, and discuss the issues that jail administrators currently face.

A 2010 report by the BJS found that the nation's jails held 767,620 inmates, 12% of whom were women.[65] Juveniles held in local jails numbered 7,220. About 62% of jail inmates are pretrial detainees or are defendants involved in some stage of the trial process. Jail authorities also supervised an additional 65,884 men and women in the community under programs that included the following: electronic monitoring (10,782), home detention without electronic monitoring (332), day reporting (3,969), community service (13,592), and weekender programs (14,523).[66]

A total of 3,360 jails operate throughout the United States today, staffed by approximately 207,600 jail employees—the equivalent of about one employee for every three jail inmates.[67] Overall, the nation's jail budget is huge, and facilities are overflowing. State and local governments spend $10 billion every year to operate the nation's jails,[68] with more than $1 billion in additional monies earmarked for new jail construction and for renovation. On average, the housing of one jail inmate costs more than $14,500.[69]

▲ Los Angeles County's Twin Towers Jail. The $373 million jail, also known as the Twin Towers Correctional Facility, opened in 1997 and is one of the world's largest jails. What are the differences between a prison and a jail?
A. Ramey/PhotoEdit Inc.

Approximately 20 million people are admitted (or readmitted) to the nation's jails each year. Some jail inmates stay for as little as one day, while others serve extended periods of time. Significantly, one of the fastest-growing sectors of today's jail population consists of sentenced offenders serving time in local jails because overcrowded prisons cannot accept them.

Most people processed through the country's jails are members of minority groups (58%), with 39% of jail inmates classifying themselves as African American, 16% as Hispanic, and 2% as other minorities. Less than 1% report being of more than one race, and 42% of jail inmates classify themselves as Caucasian. Slightly less than 88% are male, and 7.8% are noncitizens.[70] The typical jail inmate is an unmarried African American male between 25 and 34 years of age who reports having had some high school education. Typical charges include drug trafficking (12.1%), assault (11.7%), drug possession (10.8%), and larceny (7%).[71]

According to the BJS, about 6% of jail facilities house more than half of all jail inmates in the nation.[72] So although most jails are small—many were built to house 50 or fewer inmates—most people who spend time in jail do so in larger institutions. Across the country, a handful of "megajails" house thousands of inmates each, with the largest such facilities in Los Angeles; New York City; Cook County, Illinois; Harris County, Texas; and Maricopa County, Arizona. Los Angeles County's 4,000-bed Twin Towers Correctional Facility cost $373 million to build and opened in 1997.[73] The largest employer among these huge jails is Cook County Jail, with more than 1,200 personnel on its payroll.[74] In 2009 four states—California, Florida, Georgia, and Texas—incarcerated more than a third of the nation's total jail inmates.[75] The two jurisdictions with the most jail inmates, Los Angeles County and New York City, together held approximately 33,300 inmates, or 5% of the national total. More jail statistics are available at **Library Extra 11–6**.

Women and Jail

Although women comprise only 12% of the country's jail population, they are the largest growth group in jails nationwide.[76] Jailed women face a number of special problems. Only 25.7% of the nation's jails report having a classification system specifically designed to evaluate female inmates.[77] Although many jurisdictions have plans "to build facilities geared to the female offender,"[78] not all jurisdictions today even provide separate housing areas for women. Educational levels are very low among jailed women, with fewer than half being high school graduates.[79] Drug abuse is another significant source of difficulty for jailed women: Over 30% of women who are admitted to jail have a substance abuse problem at the time of admission, and in some parts of the country, that figure may be as high as 70%.[80]

Lecture Note Tell students that the proportion of women in jails across the nation has risen steadily during the past two decades. Ask students to name some of the reasons for that increase.

Pregnancy is another problem. Nationally, 4% of female inmates are pregnant when they enter jail,[81] but in urban areas, as many as 10% of female inmates are reported to be pregnant on any given day.[82] As a consequence, a few hundred children are born in jails each year. However, substantive medical programs for female inmates, such as obstetrics and gynecological care, are often lacking. Some writers have advised jail administrators to expect to see an increasingly common kind of inmate in the future: "an opiate-addicted female who is pregnant with no prior prenatal care having one or more sexually transmitted diseases, and fitting a high-risk category for AIDS (prostitution, IV drug use)."[83]

Not only are jailed mothers separated from their children, but they may have to pay for their support. About 12% of all jails in one study reported requiring employed female inmates to contribute to the support of their dependent children.

When we consider women and jails, female inmates are only half the story. Women who work in corrections are the other half. In one study, Linda Zupan, one of a new generation of outstanding jail scholars, found that women made up 22% of the correctional officer force in jails across the nation.[84] The deployment of female personnel, however, was disproportionately skewed toward jobs in the lower ranks: Although 60% of all support staff (secretaries, cooks, and janitors) were women, only one in every ten chief administrators was female. Zupan explains this pattern by pointing to the "token status" of female staff members in some of the nation's jails.[85] Even so, Zupan did find that female corrections employees were significantly committed to their careers and that the attitudes of male workers toward female coworkers in jails were generally positive. Zupan's study uncovered 626 jails in which over 50% of the corrections officer force consisted of women. On the opposite side of the coin, however, 954 of the nation's 3,316 jails operating at the time of the study had no female officers at all.[86] Zupan noted that "an obvious problem associated with the lack of female officers in jails housing females concerns the potential for abuse and exploitation of women inmates by male staff."[87]

> The first two decades of the [twenty-first] century, at least, will see a major growth in prison populations.
>
> —Alfred Blumstein, dean of the School of Urban and Public Affairs, Carnegie Mellon University

Jails that do hire women generally accord them equal footing with male staffers. Although cross-gender privacy is a potential area of legal liability, few jails limit the supervisory areas that female officers working in male facilities may visit. In three-quarters of the jails studied by Zupan, female officers were assigned to supervise male housing areas, and only one in four jails that employed women restricted their access to unscreened shower and toilet facilities used by men or to other areas, such as sexual offender units.

The Growth of Jails

Jails have been called the "shame of the criminal justice system." Many are old, poorly funded, scantily staffed by underpaid and poorly trained employees, and given low priority in local budgets. By the end of the 1980s, many of our nation's jails had become seriously overcrowded, and court-ordered caps were sometimes placed on jail populations. One of the first such caps was imposed on the Harris County Jail in Houston (Texas) in 1990. In that year, the jail was forced to release 250 inmates after missing a deadline for reducing its resident population of 6,100 people.[88] A nationwide survey by the BJS, undertaken around this time, found that 46% of all jails had been built more than 25 years earlier, and of that percentage, over half were more than 50 years old.[89]

TABLE 11–1
Jail Facts

	1983	1988	1993	2000	2005	2009
Number of jails	3,338	3,316	3,304	3,365	3,360	3,365
Number of jail inmates	223,551	343,569	459,804	621,149	747,529	767,620
Rated capacity of jails	261,556	339,949	475,224	677,787	789,001	849,544
Percentage of capacity occupied	85%	101%	97%	92%	95%	90%

Source: William J. Sabol, Heather C. West, and Matthew Cooper, *Prisoners in 2008* (Washington, DC: Bureau of Justice Statistics, December 2009) and other years; Todd D. Minton, *Jail Inmates at Midyear 2009* (Washington, DC: Bureau of Justice Statistics, 2010) and other years.

A 1983 national census revealed that jails were operating at 85% of their rated capacity (Table 11–1).[90] In 1990, however, the nation's jails were running at 104% of capacity, and new jails could be found on drawing boards and under construction across the country. By 2009, jail capacity had increased substantially, and overall jail occupancy was reported at 90.4% of rated capacity. Some individual facilities, however, were still desperately overcrowded.[91]

Thematic Question What are direct-supervision jails? How do they differ from traditional jails? Advocates of direct-supervision jails make many arguments in support of them. Do you believe, however, that such jails are superior to their predecessors? Why or why not?

Although jail overcrowding is not the issue it was a decade ago, it is still a problem. Overcrowded prisons have taken a toll on jails, with thousands of inmates being held in local jails because of overcrowding in state and federal prisons. Also, the practice of giving jail sentences to offenders who are unable or unwilling to make restitution, alimony, or child-support payments has added to jail occupancy and has made the local lockup at least partially a debtors' prison. Symptomatic of problems brought on by huge jail populations, the BJS reported 314 suicides in jails across the nation during a recent year.[92] Jail deaths from all causes total about 980 annually.

Other factors conspire to keep jail populations high. These include the inability of jail inmates to make bond, delays between arrest and case disposition, an overburdened criminal justice system, and what some have called "unproductive statutes" requiring that specified nonviolent offenders be jailed.[93]

Some innovative jurisdictions have successfully contained the growth of jail populations by diverting arrestees to community-based programs. San Diego, California, for example, uses a privately operated detoxification reception program to divert many inebriates from the "drunk tank."[94] Officials in Galveston County, Texas, routinely divert mentally ill arrestees directly to a mental health facility.[95] Other areas use pretrial services and magistrates' offices, which are open 24 hours a day, for setting bail, making release possible. Learn more about jail overcrowding by reading **Library Extra 11–7**.

▲ Inmates playing cards at the Los Angeles North County Correctional Facility in Saugus, California. The Los Angeles County jail system is the largest in the world, housing more than 20,000 inmates on a given day. What kinds of inmates do jails hold? *Damian Dovarganes/AP Wide World Photos*

Direct-Supervision Jails

Some suggest that the problems found in many jails stem from "mismanagement, lack of fiscal support, heterogeneous inmate populations, overuse and misuse of detention, overemphasis on custodial goals, and political and public apathy."[96] Others propose that environmental and organizational aspects of traditional jail architecture and staffing have led to many difficulties.[97] Traditional jails, say these observers, were built on the assumption that inmates are inherently violent and potentially destructive. They were constructed to give staff maximum control over inmates through the use of thick walls, bars, and other architectural barriers to the free movement of inmates. Such institutions, however, also limit the corrections staff's visibility and their access to confinement areas. As a consequence, they tend to encourage just the kinds of inmate behavior that jails were meant to control. Today, efficient hallway patrols and expensive video technology help in overcoming the limits that old jail architecture places on supervision.

In an effort to solve many of the problems that dogged jails in the past, a new jail management strategy emerged during the 1970s. Called the **direct-supervision jail**, or *podular/direct supervision (PDS) jail*, this approach joined "podular/unit architecture with a participative, proactive management philosophy."[98] Often built in a system of pods, or modular self-contained housing areas linked to one another, direct-supervision jails helped eliminate the old physical barriers that separated staff and inmates. Gone were the bars and the isolated, secure observation areas for officers, and they were replaced by an open environment in which inmates and corrections personnel could mingle with relative freedom. In a number of such "new-generation" jails, large reinforced Plexiglas panels supplanted walls and served to separate activity areas, such as classrooms and dining halls, from one another. Soft furniture is the rule throughout such institutions, and individual rooms take the place of cells, allowing inmates at least a modicum of personal privacy. In today's direct-supervision jails, 16 to 46 inmates typically live in one pod, with corrections staffers present among the inmate population around the clock.

direct-supervision jail
A temporary confinement facility that eliminates many of the traditional barriers between inmates and corrections staff. Physical barriers in direct-supervision jails are far less common than in traditional jails, allowing staff members the opportunity for greater interaction with, and control over, residents.

Direct-supervision jails have been touted for their tendency to reduce inmate dissatisfaction and for their ability to deter rape and violence among the inmate population. By eliminating architectural barriers to staff-inmate interaction, direct-supervision facilities are said to place officers back in control of institutions. A number of studies have demonstrated the success of such jails at reducing the likelihood of inmate victimization. One such study, published in 1994, also found that staff morale in direct-supervision jails was far higher than in traditional institutions, that inmates reported reduced stress levels, and that fewer inmate-on-inmate and inmate-on-staff assaults occurred.[99] Similarly, sexual assault, jail rape, suicide, and escape have all been found to occur far less frequently in direct-supervision facilities than in traditional institutions.[100] Significantly, new-generation jails appear to be substantially less susceptible to lawsuits brought by inmates and to adverse court-ordered judgments against jail administrators.

Some authors have recognized that new-generation jails are too frequently run by old-style managers and that corrections personnel sometimes lack the training needed to make the transition to the direct style of supervision.[101] Other authors have suggested that managers of direct-supervision jails, especially mid-level managers, could benefit from clearer job descriptions and additional training.[102] In the words of one direct-supervision advocate, "Training becomes particularly critical in direct-supervision jails where relationships are more immediate and are more complex."[103] Finally, those tasked with hiring have recommended psychological screening and intensive use of preemployment interviews to determine the suitability of applicants for corrections officer positions in direct-supervision jails.[104]

Thematic Question What unique qualities do jails have (because of inmate profiles, sentences, location, etc.) that prisons do not? How might jail administrators capitalize on those qualities?

Jails and the Future

In contrast to more visible issues confronting the justice system—such as the death penalty, gun control, the war on drugs, terrorism, and big-city gangs—jails have received relatively little attention from the media and have generally escaped close public scrutiny.[105] National efforts are under way, however, to improve the quality of jail life. Some changes involve adding crucial programs for inmates. An American Jail Association (AJA) study of drug-treatment programs in jails, for example, found that "a small fraction (perhaps fewer than 10%) of inmates needing drug treatment actually receive these services."[106]

Thematic Question How does the AJA Code of Ethics seek to balance the individual rights of inmates and guards with public-order concerns?

Jail industries are another growing programmatic area. The best of them serve the community while training inmates in marketable skills.[107] In an exemplary effort to humanize its megajails, for example, the Los Angeles County Sheriff's Department opened an inmate telephone-answering service.[108] Many callers contact the sheriff's department daily, requesting information about the county's 19,869 jail inmates. These requests for information were becoming increasingly difficult to handle due to the growing fiscal constraints facing local government. To handle the huge number of calls effectively without tying up sworn law enforcement personnel, the department began using inmates specially trained to handle incoming calls. Eighty inmates were assigned to the project, with groups of different sizes covering shifts throughout the day. Each inmate staffer went through a training program to learn how to use proper telephone procedures and how to run computer terminals containing routine data on the department's inmates.

Ethics and Professionalism
American Jail Association Code of Ethics for Jail Officers

As an officer employed in a detention/correctional capacity, I swear (or affirm) to be a good citizen and a credit to my community, state, and nation at all times. I will abstain from all questionable behavior which might bring disrepute to the agency for which I work, my family, my community, and my associates. My lifestyle will be above and beyond reproach and I will constantly strive to set an example of a professional who performs his/her duties according to the laws of our country, state, and community and the policies, procedures, written and verbal orders, and regulations of the agency for which I work. On the job I promise to:

Keep the institution secure so as to safeguard my community and the lives of the staff, inmates, and visitors on the premises.

Work with each individual firmly and fairly without regard to rank, status, or condition.

Maintain a positive demeanor when confronted with stressful situations of scorn, ridicule, danger, and/or chaos.

Report either in writing or by word of mouth to the proper authorities those things which should be reported, and keep silent about matters which are to remain confidential according to the laws and rules of the agency and government.

Manage and supervise the inmates in an evenhanded and courteous manner.

Refrain at all times from becoming personally involved in the lives of the inmates and their families.

Treat all visitors to the jail with politeness and respect and do my utmost to ensure that they observe the jail regulations.

Take advantage of all education and training opportunities designed to assist me to become a more competent officer.

Communicate with people in or outside of the jail, whether by phone, written word, or word of mouth, in such a way so as not to reflect in a negative manner upon my agency.

Contribute to a jail environment which will keep the inmate involved in activities designed to improve his/her attitude and character.

Support all activities of a professional nature through membership and participation that will continue to elevate the status of those who operate our nation's jails.

Do my best through word and deed to present an image to the public at large of a jail professional, committed to progress for an improved and enlightened criminal justice system.

THINKING ABOUT ETHICS

1. ***Why does the AJA Code of Ethics require jail officers to "[t]ake advantage of all education and training opportunities designed to assist [them] to become a more competent officer"? What does education have to do with ethics?***
2. ***Is there anything that you might add to this code? Is there anything that you might delete?***

Source: American Jail Association, *Code of Ethics for Jail Officers*, adopted January 10, 1991. Revised May 19, 1993. Reprinted with permission.

The new system now handles 4,000 telephone inquiries a day, and the time needed to answer a call and to provide information has dropped from 30 minutes under the old system to a remarkable ten seconds today.

Jail "boot camps," like the one run by the Harris County (Texas) Probation Department, are also popular. Jail boot camps give offenders who are sentenced to probationary terms a taste of both confinement and the rigors of life behind bars. The Harris County Courts Regimented Intensive Probation Program (CRIPP) facility began operation in 1991 and is located in Humble, Texas. Separate CRIPPs are run for about 400 male and 50 female probationers.[109] The most recent comprehensive study of jail boot camps found only ten such jail-based programs in the country,[110] but current numbers are probably higher.

regional jail
A jail that is built and run using the combined resources of a variety of local jurisdictions.

Capturing much recent attention are **regional jails**, that is, jails that are built and run using the combined resources of a variety of local jurisdictions. Regional jails have begun to replace smaller and often antiquated local jails in at least a few locations. One example of a regional jail is the Western Tidewater Regional Jail, serving the cities of Suffolk and Franklin and the county of Isle of Wright in Virginia.[111] Regional jails, which are just beginning to come into their own, may develop quickly in Virginia, where the state, recognizing the economies of consolidation, offers to reimburse localities up to 50% of the cost of building regional jails.

> Our current justice system imprisons many people who could have been held accountable (and, if necessary, safely supervised) in the community.
> —Justice Policy Institute

One final element in the unfolding saga of jail development should be mentioned: the emergence of state jail standards. Of the 50 states, 32 have set standards for municipal and county jails,[112] and in 25 states, those standards are mandatory. The purpose of jail standards is to identify basic minimum conditions necessary for inmate health and safety. On the national level, the Commission on Accreditation for Corrections, operated jointly by the ACA and the federal government, has developed its own set of jail standards,[113] as has the National Sheriff's Association. Both sets of standards are designed to ensure a minimal level of comfort and safety in local lockups. Increased standards, though, are costly. Local jurisdictions, already hard-pressed to meet other budgetary demands, will probably be slow to upgrade their jails to meet such external guidelines unless forced to do so. In a study of 61 jails that was designed to test compliance with National Sheriff's Association guidelines, Ken Kerle discovered that in many standards areas—especially those of tool control, armory planning, community resources, release preparation, and riot planning—the majority of jails were badly out of compliance.[114] Lack of a written plan was the most commonly cited reason for failing to meet the standards. Learn more about jails by visiting the AJA at **Web Extra 11–3**.

Private Prisons

State-run prison systems have always contracted with private industries for food, psychological testing, training, and recreational and other services, and it is estimated that more than three dozen states today rely on private businesses to serve a variety of correctional needs. It follows, then, that states have now turned to private industry for the provision of prison space. The movement toward **privatization** (use of privately run rather than government-run prisons), which began in the early 1980s, was slow to catch on, but it has since grown at a rapid pace. In 1986, only 2,620 prisoners could be found in privately run confinement facilities,[115] but by 2009, privately operated correctional facilities serving as prisons and jails held over 128,520 state and federal prisoners across 33 states and the District of Columbia.[116] **Private prisons** (prisons operated by private companies) held 6.8% of all state prisoners and 16.5% of federal prisoners at the start of 2009. One source says that the growth rate of the private prison industry has been around 35% annually,[117] which is comparable to the highest growth rates anywhere in the corporate sector.

3 Describe the role of private prisons today, and assess their future.

privatization
The movement toward the wider use of private prisons.

private prison
A correctional institution operated by a private firm on behalf of a local or state government.

Lecture Note Explain the advantages and disadvantages of private prisons.

Privately run prisons are operated by Cornell Corrections, Corrections Corporation of America (CCA), Correctional Services Corporation (CSC), Wackenhut Corrections Corporation, and numerous other smaller companies. Most states that use private firms to supplement their prison resources contract with such companies to provide a full range of custodial and other correctional services. State corrections administrators use private companies to reduce overcrowding, lower operating expenses, and avoid lawsuits targeted at state officials and employees.[118] But some studies have shown that private prisons may not bring the kinds of cost savings that had been anticipated.[119] One 1996 study was done by the U.S. General Accounting Office.[120] It found, for example, "neither cost savings nor substantial differences in the quality of services" between private and publicly run prisons.[121] Similar findings emerged in a 2001 report by the Bureau of Justice Assistance. That report, titled *Emerging Issues on Privatized Prisons*, found that "private prisons offer only modest cost savings, which are basically a result of moderate reductions in staffing patterns, fringe benefits, and other labor-related costs."[122]

▲ The 2,300-bed California City Correctional Center in the Mojave Desert town of California City. The facility, which opened in December 1999, was built by Corrections Corporation of America (CCA) to provide medium-security correctional services under a contract with the Federal Bureau of Prisons. Nashville-based CCA says that it can run prisons as efficiently as the government, and its supporters claim that private prisons are the way of the future. Do you agree?
Reed Saxon/AP Wide World Photos

Many hurdles remain before the privatization movement can effectively provide large-scale custodial supervision. Among the most significant barriers to privatization are old state laws that prohibit private involvement in correctional management. Other practical hurdles exist as well. States that do contract with private firms may face the specter of strikes by correctional officers, who are not subject to state laws restricting the ability of public employees to strike. Moreover, since responsibility for the protection of inmate rights still lies with the states, their liability will not transfer to private corrections.[123] In today's legal climate, it appears that the courts are unlikely to allow states to shield themselves or their employees through private prison contracting. To limit their own liability, states will probably have to oversee private operations as well as set standards for training and custody. In 1997, in the case of *Richardson* v. *McKnight*,[124] the U.S. Supreme Court made it clear that correctional officers employed by a private firm are not entitled to qualified immunity from suits by prisoners charging a violation of Section 1983 of Title 42 of the U.S. Code. (See Chapter 6 for more information on

CJ Exhibit 11–1
Arguments for and against the Privatization of Prisons

REASONS TO PRIVATIZE

1. Private operators can provide construction financing options that allow the government to pay only for capacity as needed in lieu of assuming long-term debt.
2. Private companies offer state-of-the-art correctional facility designs that are efficient to operate and that are based on cost-benefit considerations.
3. Private operators typically design and construct a new correctional facility in half the time it takes to build a comparable government project.
4. Private companies provide government with the convenience and accountability of one entity for all compliance issues.
5. Private companies can mobilize rapidly and specialize in unique facility missions.
6. Private companies provide economic development opportunities by hiring and purchasing locally.
7. Government can reduce or share its liability exposure by contracting with private corrections companies.
8. Government can retain flexibility by limiting the contract's duration and by specifying the facility's mission.
9. The addition of alternative service providers injects competition among both public and private organizations.

REASONS NOT TO PRIVATIZE

1. There are certain responsibilities that only the government should meet, such as public safety. The government has legal, political, and moral obligations to provide incarceration. Constitutional issues underlie both public and private corrections and involve deprivation of liberty, discipline, and preservation of inmate rights. Related issues include use of force, equitable hiring practices, and segregation.
2. Few private companies are available from which to choose.
3. Private operators may be inexperienced with key corrections issues.
4. A private operator may become a monopoly through political ingratiation, favoritism, and so on.
5. Government may, over time, lose the capability to perform the corrections function.
6. The profit motive will inhibit the proper performance of corrections duties. Private companies have financial incentives to cut corners.
7. The procurement process is slow, inefficient, and open to risks.
8. Creating a good, clear contract is a daunting task.
9. The lack of enforcement remedies in contracts leaves only termination or lawsuits as recourse.

Source: Dennis Cunningham, "Public Strategies for Private Prisons," paper presented at the Private Prison Workshop, Institute on Criminal Justice, University of Minnesota Law School, January 29–30, 1999. Reprinted with permission.

Section 1983 lawsuits.) In 2001, however, in the case of *Correctional Services Corporation* v. *Malesko*,[125] the Court found that private corporations acting under color of federal law cannot be held responsible in a *Bivens* action because the purpose of *Bivens* (which was discussed in Chapter 6) "is to deter individual federal officers from committing Constitutional violations."[126]

Perhaps the most serious legal issues confront states that contract to hold inmates outside of their own jurisdiction. In 1996, for example, two inmates escaped from a 240-man sex-offender unit run by Corrections Corporation of America under contract with the state of Oregon. Problems immediately arose because the CCA unit was located near Houston, Texas—not in Oregon, where the men had originally been sentenced to confinement. Following the escape, Texas officials were unsure whether they even had arrest power over the former prisoners because the escapees had not committed any crimes in Texas. While prison escape is a crime under Texas law, the law only applies to state-run facilities, not to private facilities where corrections personnel are not employed by the state or empowered in any official capacity by state law. Harris County (Texas) Prosecutor John Holmes explained the situation this way: "They have not committed the offense of escape under Texas law . . . and the only reason at all that they're subject to being arrested and were arrested was because during their leaving the facility, they assaulted a guard and took his motor vehicle. That we can charge them with and have."[127]

Opponents of the movement toward privatization cite many issues (see CJ Exhibit 11–1). They claim that, aside from legal concerns, cost reductions via the use of private facilities can only be achieved by lowering standards. They fear a return to the inhumane conditions of early jails as private firms seek to turn prisons into profit-making operations. For states that do choose to contract with private firms, the National Institute of Justice (NIJ) recommends a "regular and systematic sampling" of former inmates to appraise prison conditions, as well as annual on-site inspections of each privately run institution. State personnel serving as monitors should be stationed in large facilities, says NIJ, and a "meticulous review" of all services should be conducted before the contract renewal date.[128] You can learn more about prison privatization at **Library Extra 11–8** and at **Web Extra 11–4**.

A PowerPoint presentation that supports this chapter is available from your Prentice Hall representative.

Summary

PRISONS AND JAILS

- Today's prisons are classified according to security level, such as maximum, medium, and minimum security. Most contemporary American correctional facilities are medium or minimum security. Although the goals of recidivism and deterrence are still important in the minds of corrections administrators, today's prisons tend to warehouse inmates awaiting release. Public disappointment with high rates of recidivism has produced a prison system today that is focused largely on the concept of just deserts. Overcrowded facilities are still the norm in many jurisdictions, although a prison building boom over the last decade has alleviated some of the extremely overcrowded conditions that had previously existed.
- In contrast to prisons, which are long-term confinement facilities designed to hold those who have been sentenced to serve time for committing crime, jails are short-term confinement facilities whose traditional purpose has been to hold those awaiting trial or sentencing. Inmates who have been tried and sentenced may also be held at jails until their transfer to a prison facility, and today's jails sometimes hold inmates serving short sentences of confinement. Recently, the emergence of direct-supervision jails seems to have reduced the incidence of jail violence and improved the conditions of jailed inmates in jurisdictions where such facilities operate. In direct-supervision jails, the traditional barriers between inmates and staff have been mostly eliminated.
- Privately run correctional facilities, or private prisons, have grown in number over the past few decades as the movement toward the privatization of correctional facilities has gained steam. Private prisons, operated by for-profit corporations, hold inmates on behalf of state governments or the federal government and provide for inmates' care and security. A number of questions remain as to the role such facilities will play in the future, including whether they can be cost-effective and whether they can somehow reduce the legal liability of state governments and government employees.

QUESTIONS FOR REVIEW

1. What are today's prisons like? What purpose do they serve?
2. What role do jails play in American corrections? What are some of the issues that jail administrators currently face?
3. What is the role of private prisons today? What will be the state of private prisons two or three decades from now?

CHAPTER 12

Prison Life

Learning Objectives

After reading this chapter, you should be able to:

1. Describe the realities of prison life and prison subculture from the inmate's point of view. **333**
2. Illustrate the significant differences between men's prisons and women's prisons. **334**
3. Describe the realities of prison life from the corrections officer's point of view. **345**
4. Describe the causes of prison riots. **348**
5. Discuss the legal aspects of prisoners' rights, and explain the consequences of precedent-setting U.S. Supreme Court cases in the area of prisoners' rights. **350**
6. Describe the major problems and issues that prisons face today. **359**

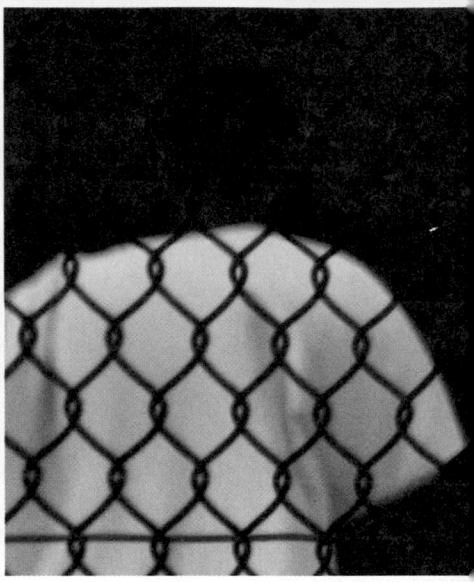

"The number of people under criminal justice supervision in this country has reached a record high."

—Julie E. Samuels, U.S. Department of Justice[1]

"What happens inside ja
and prisons does not st
inside jails and prisons
comes home with prisone
after they are released a
with corrections officers
the end of each day's sh
We must create safe a
productive conditions
confinement not o
because it is the right thi
to do, but because
influences the safety, heal
and prosperity of us a

—Commission on Safety and Abuse in America's Pri

Introduction

On the FOX TV show *Prison Break*, Wentworth Miller played the role of an engineer named Michael Scofield who holds up a bank so that he can join his brother in the fictional Fox River State Penitentiary. Scofield's brother, Lincoln (Dominic Purcell), has been convicted of a sensational murder and is housed on the prison's death row. The show, which centered around Michael's elaborate plan to break Lincoln out and to prove that he's innocent, drew a large weekly audience, demonstrating the fascination that the American public has with prison life.

For many years, prisons and prison life could be described by the phrase "out of sight, out of mind." Very few citizens cared about prison conditions, and those unfortunate enough to be locked away were regarded as lost to the world. By the mid-twentieth century, however, this attitude started to change. Concerned citizens began to offer their services to prison administrations, neighborhoods began accepting work-release prisoners and halfway houses, and social scientists initiated a serious study of prison life. Today, as shows like *Prison Break* make clear, prisons and prison life have entered the American mainstream. Part of the reason for this is that prisons today hold more people than ever before, and incarceration affects not only those imprisoned but also family members, friends, and victims on the outside.

▲ Dominic Purcell (*left*) and Wentworth Miller, stars of the FOX TV show *Prison Break*. The popularity of the show, which was filmed at a former prison that once held serial killer John Wayne Gacy, illustrated a growing awareness of prisons and prison life in American culture today. What do Americans think of prisons and prisoners?
John Zich/CORBIS–NY

This chapter describes the realities of prison life, including prisoner lifestyles, prison subcultures, sexuality in prison, prison violence, and prisoners' rights and grievance procedures. We discuss both the inmate world and the staff world. A separate section on women in prison details the social structure of women's prisons, daily life in those facilities, and the various types of female inmates. We begin with a brief overview of early research on prison life.

Research on Prison Life: Total Institutions

1 Describe the realities of prison life and prison subculture from the inmate's point of view.

In 1935, Hans Reimer, who was then chairman of the Department of Sociology at Indiana University, set the tone for studies of prison life when he voluntarily served three months in prison as an incognito participant-observer.[3] Reimer reported the results of his studies to the American Prison Association, stimulating many other, albeit less spectacular, efforts to examine prison life. Other early studies include Donald Clemmer's *The Prison Community* (1940),[4] Gresham M. Sykes's *The Society of Captives: A Study of a Maximum Security Prison* (1958),[5] Richard A. Cloward and Donald R. Cressey's *Theoretical Studies in Social Organization of the Prison* (1960),[6] and Cressey's edited volume, *The Prison: Studies in Institutional Organization and Change* (1961).[7]

These studies and others focused primarily on maximum-security prisons for men. They treated correctional institutions as formal or complex organizations and employed the analytic techniques of organizational sociology, industrial psychology, and administrative science.[8] As modern writers on prisons have observed, "The prison was compared to a primitive society, isolated from the outside world, functionally integrated by a delicate system of mechanisms, which kept it precariously balanced between anarchy and accommodation."[9]

Another approach to the study of prison life was developed by Erving Goffman, who coined the term **total institutions** in a 1961 study of prisons and mental hospitals.[10] Goffman described total institutions as places where the same people work, recreate, worship, eat, and sleep together daily. Such places include prisons, concentration camps, mental hospitals, seminaries, and other facilities in which residents are cut off from the larger society either forcibly or willingly. Total institutions are small societies. They evolve their own distinctive values and styles of life and pressure residents to fulfill rigidly prescribed behavioral roles.

Generally speaking, the work of prison researchers built on findings of other social scientists who discovered that any group with similar characteristics, confined in the

Lecture Note Describe total institutions as enclosed places where residents share all aspects of their daily lives. Explain that inhabitants of total institutions work, recreate, worship, eat, and sleep together.

Thematic Question What are total institutions? What are the positive and negative qualities of total institutions? Would prisons be better at rehabilitating inmates if they were more open to the outside world?

total institution
An enclosed facility separated from society both socially and physically, where the inhabitants share all aspects of their daily lives.

same place at the same time, develops its own subculture with specific components that govern hierarchy, behavioral patterns, values, and so on. Prison subcultures, described in the next section, also provide the medium through which prison values are communicated and expectations are made known. Learn more about prison research at **Library Extra 12–1**.

The Male Inmate's World

2 Illustrate the significant differences between men's prisons and women's prisons.

Two social realities coexist in prison settings. One is the official structure of rules and procedures put in place by the wider society and enforced by prison staff. The other is the more informal but decidedly more powerful inmate world.[11] The inmate world, best described by how closely it touches the lives of inmates, is controlled by **prison subculture**, consisting of inmate values and behaviors. The realities of prison life—including a large and often densely packed inmate population that must look to the prison environment for all its needs—mean that prison subculture develops independently of the plans of prison administrators and is not easily subjected to the control of prison authorities.

prison subculture
The values and behavioral patterns characteristic of prison inmates. Prison subculture has been found to be surprisingly consistent across the country.

Inmates entering prison discover a whole new social world in which they must participate or face consequences ranging from dangerous ostracism to physical violence and homicide.[12] The socialization of new inmates into the prison subculture has been described as a process of **prisonization**,[13] through which the new prisoner learns the convict values, attitudes, roles, and even language. By the time this process is complete, new inmates have become "cons." Gresham Sykes and Sheldon Messinger recognized five elements of the prison code in 1960:[14]

prisonization
The process whereby newly institutionalized offenders come to accept prison lifestyles and criminal values. Although many inmates begin their prison experience with only a few values that support criminal behavior, the socialization experience they undergo while incarcerated leads to a much wider acceptance of such values.

Lecture Note Define *prisonization* as the socialization of new inmates into prison subculture. Use the five elements of the prison code discussed in the text to describe the realities of that subculture.

1. Don't interfere with the interests of other inmates. Never rat on a con.
2. Don't lose your head. Play it cool and do your own time.
3. Don't exploit inmates. Don't steal. Don't break your word. Be right.
4. Don't whine. Be a man.
5. Don't be a sucker. Don't trust the guards or staff.

Some criminologists have suggested that the prison code is simply a reflection of general criminal values. If so, these values are brought to the institution rather than created there. Either way, the power and pervasiveness of the prison code require convicts to conform to the worldview held by the majority of prisoners.

Stanton Wheeler, Ford Foundation Professor of Law and Social Sciences at the University of Washington, closely examined the concept of prisonization in an early study of the Washington State Reformatory.[15] Wheeler found that the degree of prisonization experienced by inmates tends to vary over time. He described changing levels of inmate commitment to prison norms and values by way of a U-shaped curve. When an inmate first enters prison, Wheeler said, the conventional values of outside society are of paramount importance. As time passes, inmates adopt the lifestyle of the prison. However, within the half year prior to release, most inmates begin to demonstrate a renewed appreciation for conventional values. Learn more about both the positive and negative impacts of imprisonment at **Library Extra 12–2**.

Lecture Note Use CJ Exhibit 12–1 to explain prison argot, the slang used by inmates. Relate it to the slang used by other groups, such as the language used to describe activities on the Internet.

Different prisons share aspects of a common inmate culture.[16] Prison-wise inmates who enter a new facility far from their home will already know the ropes. **Prison argot**, or jargon, provides one example of how widespread prison subculture can be. The terms used to describe inmate roles in one institution are generally understood in others. The word *rat*, for example, is prison slang for an informer. Popularized by crime movies of the 1950s, the term is also understood today by members of the wider society. Other words common to prison argot are shown in CJ Exhibit 12–1. View an online prisoners' dictionary at **Web Extra 12–1**.

prison argot
The slang that is characteristic of prison subculture and prison life.

The Evolution of Prison Subcultures

Thematic Question What similarities do you notice between prison society, as described in this chapter, and free society? What are some differences? What might account for the similarities and differences you observe?

Prison subcultures change constantly. Like any other American subculture, they evolve to reflect the concerns and experiences of the wider culture, reacting to new crime-control strategies and embracing novel opportunities for crime. The AIDS epidemic of the 1970s and 1980s, for example, brought about changes in prison sexual behavior, at least for a segment of the

CJ Exhibit 12–1
Prison Argot: The Language of Confinement

Writers who have studied prison life often comment on prisoners' use of a special language or slang called *prison argot*. This language generally describes the roles assigned by prison culture to types of inmates as well as to prison activities. This box lists a few of the many words and phrases identified in studies by different authors. The first group of words is characteristic of men's prisons; the last few words have been used in women's prisons.

MEN'S PRISON SLANG

Ace duce: Best friend

Badge (bull, hack, the man, or screw): Corrections officer

Banger (burner, shank, or sticker): Knife

Billy: White man

Boneyard: Conjugal visiting area

Cat-J (J-cat): Prisoner in need of psychological or psychiatric therapy or medication

Cellie: Cellmate

Chester: Child molester

Dog: Homeboy or friend

Fag: Male inmate who is believed to be a "natural" or "born" homosexual

Featherwood: White prisoner's woman

Fish: Newly arrived inmate

Gorilla: Inmate who uses force to take what he wants from others

Homeboy: Prisoner from one's hometown or neighborhood

Ink: Tattoos

Lemon squeezer: Inmate who masturbates frequently

Man walking: Phrase used to signal that a guard is coming

Merchant (peddler): One who sells when he should give

Peckerwood (or wood): White prisoner

Punk: Male inmate who is forced into a submissive role during homosexual relations

Rat (snitch): Inmate who squeals (provides information about other inmates to the prison administration)

Schooled: Knowledgeable in the ways of prison life

Shakedown: Search of a cell or of a work area

Tree jumper: Rapist

Turn out: To rape or make into a punk

Wolf: Male inmate who assumes the dominant role during homosexual relations

WOMEN'S PRISON SLANG

Cherry (cherrie): Female inmate who has not yet been introduced to lesbian activities

Fay broad: White female inmate

Femme (mommy): Female inmate who plays the female role during lesbian relations

Safe: Vagina (especially when used for hiding contraband)

Stud broad (daddy): Female inmate who assumes the male role during lesbian relations

References: Gresham Sykes, *The Society of Captives* (Princeton, NJ: Princeton University Press, 1958); Rose Giallombardo, *Society of Women: A Study of a Woman's Prison* (New York: John Wiley, 1966); and Richard A. Cloward et al., *Theoretical Studies in Social Organization of the Prison* (New York: Social Science Research Council, 1960). For a more contemporary listing of prison slang terms, see Reinhold Aman, *Hillary Clinton's Pen Pal: A Guide to Life and Lingo in Federal Prison* (Santa Rosa, CA: Maledicta Press, 1996); Jerome Washington, *Iron House: Stories from the Yard* (Ann Arbor, MI: QED Press, 1994); Morrie Camhi, *The Prison Experience* (Boston: Charles Tuttle, 1989); and Harold Long, *Survival in Prison* (Port Townsend, WA: Loompanics, 1990).

inmate population. The emergence of a high-tech criminal group has further differentiated convict types. Because of such changes, John Irwin, as he was completing his classic study titled *The Felon* (1970), expressed worry that his book was already obsolete.[17] *The Felon*, for all its insights into prison subcultures, follows in the descriptive tradition of works by Clemmer and Reimer. Irwin recognized that by 1970, prison subcultures had begun to reflect the cultural changes sweeping America. A decade later, other investigators of prison subcultures were able to write, "It was no longer meaningful to speak of a single inmate culture or even subculture. By the time we began our field research . . . it was clear that the unified, oppositional convict culture, found in the sociological literature on prisons, no longer existed."[18]

Department Mission: To protect the public safety, to ensure the safety of Department personnel, and to provide proper care and supervision of all offenders under our jurisdiction while assisting, as appropriate, their reentry into society.

—Florida Department of Corrections

The Functions of Prison Subcultures

How do social scientists and criminologists explain the existence of prison subcultures? Although people around the world live in groups and create their own cultures, in few cases does the intensity of human interaction approach the level found in prisons. As we discussed in Chapter 11, many of today's prisons are densely crowded places where inmates can find no retreat from the

Lecture Note Describe prison subculture as a lifestyle that reflects criminal values and behavior patterns characteristic of incarcerated offenders. Note that prison subculture shows amazing consistency among prisons across the United States.

It is better to prevent crimes than to punish them.
—Cesare Bonesana, Marchese di Beccaria (1738–1794)

Lecture Note Describe the evolution of prison subculture as new generations of convicts arrive. Explore some of the differences between traditional and emerging subcultural values.

Lecture Note Describe inmate types as adaptive roles inmates take on to define themselves in prison society. Ask the class what factors, types of crime, or backgrounds might lead a prisoner to adopt a particular style. How might prison staff respond to each of the types described in this chapter?

constant demands of staff and the pressures of fellow prisoners. Prison subcultures, according to some authors, are fundamentally an adaptation to deprivation and confinement. They are a way of addressing the psychological, social, physical, and sexual needs of prisoners living within a highly controlled and regimented institutional setting.

What are some of the deprivations that prisoners experience? In *The Society of Captives*, Sykes called felt deprivations the "pains of imprisonment."[19] The pains of imprisonment—the frustrations induced by the rigors of confinement—form the nexus of a *deprivation model* of prison subculture. Sykes said that prisoners are deprived of (1) liberty, (2) goods and services, (3) heterosexual relationships, (4) autonomy, and (5) personal security. Sykes also stated that these deprivations lead to the development of subcultures intended to ameliorate the personal pains that accompany deprivation.

In contrast to the deprivation model, the *importation model* of prison subculture suggests that inmates bring with them values, roles, and behavior patterns from the outside world. Such external values (second nature to career offenders) depend substantially on the criminal worldview. When offenders are confined, these external elements shape the social world of inmates.

The social structure of the prison, a concept that refers to accepted and relatively permanent social arrangements, is another element that shapes prison subculture. Clemmer's early prison study recognized nine structural dimensions of inmate society:[20]

1. Prisoner-staff dichotomy
2. Three general classes of prisoners
3. Work gangs and cell-house groups
4. Racial groups
5. Type of offense
6. Power of inmate "politicians"
7. Degree of sexual abnormality
8. Record of repeat offenses
9. Personality differences due to preprison socialization

Clemmer's nine structural dimensions are probably still descriptive of prison life today. When applied to individuals, they designate an inmate's position in the prison "pecking order" and create expectations of the appropriate role for that person. Prison roles serve to satisfy the needs of inmates for power, sexual performance, material possessions, individuality, and personal pleasure. They also define the status of one prisoner relative to another. For example, inmate leaders, sometimes referred to as *real men* or *toughs* by prisoners in early studies, offer protection to those who live by the rules. They also provide for a redistribution of wealth inside prison and see to it that the rules of the complex prison-derived economic system—based on barter, gambling, and sexual favors—are observed. For an intimate multimedia portrait of life behind bars, visit **Web Extra 12–2**.

Prison Lifestyles and Inmate Types

Prison society is strict and often unforgiving. Even so, inmates are able to express some individuality through the choice of a prison lifestyle. John Irwin viewed these lifestyles (like the subcultures of which they are a part) as adaptations to the prison environment.[21] Other writers have since elaborated on these coping mechanisms. Listed in the paragraphs that follow are some of the types of prisoners that researchers have described:

- *The mean dude.* Some inmates adjust to prison by being violent, and other inmates know that these prisoners are best left alone. The mean dude is frequently written up and spends much time in solitary confinement. This role is most common in male institutions and in maximum-security prisons. For some prisoners, the role of mean dude in prison is similar to the role they played in their life prior to being incarcerated. Certain personality types, such as the psychopath, may feel a natural attraction to this role. Plus, prison culture supports violence in two ways: (1) by the expectation that inmates should be tough and (2) through the prevalence of the idea that only the strong survive inside prison.

- *The hedonist.* Some inmates build their lives around the limited pleasures available within the confines of prison. The smuggling of contraband, homosexuality, gambling, drug running, and other officially condemned activities provide the center of interest for prison hedonists. Hedonists generally have an abbreviated view of the future, living only for the "now."
- *The opportunist.* The opportunist takes advantage of the positive experiences prison has to offer. Schooling, trade training, counseling, and other self-improvement activities are the focal points of the opportunist's life in prison. Opportunists are generally well liked by prison staff, but other prisoners shun and mistrust them because they come closest to accepting the role that the staff defines as "model prisoner."
- *The retreatist.* Prison life is rigorous and demanding. Badgering by the staff and actual or feared assaults by other inmates may cause some prisoners to attempt psychological retreat from the realities of imprisonment. Such inmates may experience neurotic or psychotic episodes, become heavily involved in drug and alcohol abuse through the illicit prison economy, or even attempt suicide. Depression and mental illness are the hallmarks of the retreatist personality in prison.
- *The legalist.* The legalist is the "jailhouse lawyer." Convicts facing long sentences, with little possibility for early release through the corrections system, are most likely to turn to the courts in their battle against confinement.
- *The radical.* Radical inmates view themselves as political prisoners. They see society and the successful conformists who populate it as oppressors who have forced criminality on many "good people" through the creation of a system that distributes wealth and power inequitably. The inmate who takes on the radical role is unlikely to receive much sympathy from prison staff.
- *The colonizer.* Some inmates think of prison as their home and don't look forward to leaving. They "know the ropes," have many friends inside, and may feel more comfortable institutionalized than on the streets, and they typically hold positions with power or respect among the inmate population. Once released, some colonizers commit new crimes to return to prison.
- *The religious.* Some prisoners profess a strong religious faith. They may be "born-again" Christians, committed Muslims, or even Satanists or witches. Religious inmates frequently attend services, may form prayer groups, and sometimes ask the prison administration to allocate meeting facilities or to create special diets to accommodate their claimed spiritual needs. While it is certainly true that some inmates have a strong religious faith, staff members are apt to be suspicious of the overly religious prisoner.
- *The gangbanger.* Gangbangers are affiliated with prison gangs and depend upon the gang for defense and protection. They display gang signs, sport gang-related tattoos, and use their gang membership as a channel for the procurement of desired goods and services both inside and outside prison.
- *The realist.* The realist sees confinement as a natural consequence of criminal activity and time spent in prison as an unfortunate cost of doing business. This stoic attitude toward incarceration generally leads the realist to "pull his (or her) own time" and to make the best of it. Realists tend to know the inmate code, are able to avoid trouble, and continue in lives of crime once released.

▲ A male inmate dressing as a female in the protective custody wing of the Ferguson Unit in Midway, Texas. Homosexuality is common in both men's and women's prisons. How does it differ between the two?
Andrew Lichtenstein

Lecture Note Discuss homosexuality in prison, and ask why it appears to be so common. Describe the difference between prison homosexuality and homosexual behavior in the free society as the contrast between limited opportunity and free choice. Note that relatively few offenders involved in homosexual activities in prison will continue them upon release. Explain that at least some homosexuality in prison is a form of adaptive behavior.

Homosexuality and Sexual Victimization in Prison

Sexual behavior inside prisons is both constrained and encouraged by prison subculture. Sykes's early study of prison argot found many words describing sexual activity, and quite a few of them related to homosexuality. Included here are the terms *wolf*, *punk*, and *fag*. Wolves are aggressive men who assume the masculine role in homosexual relations, punks are forced into submitting to the female role, and fag describes a special category of men who have a natural proclivity toward homosexual activity and effeminate mannerisms. While both wolves and punks are fiercely committed to their heterosexual identity and participate in homosexuality only because of prison conditions, fags generally engage in homosexual lifestyles before their entry into prison and continue to emulate feminine mannerisms and styles of dress once incarcerated.

Prison homosexuality depends to a considerable degree on the naïveté of young inmates experiencing prison for the first time. Even when newly arrived inmates are protected from fights, older prisoners looking for homosexual liaisons may ingratiate themselves by offering cigarettes, money, drugs, food, or protection. At some future time, these "loans" will be called in, with payoffs demanded in sexual favors. Because the inmate code requires the repayment of favors, the "fish" who tries to resist may quickly find himself face-to-face with the brute force of inmate society.

Prison rape, which is generally considered to involve physical assault, represents a special category of sexual victimization behind bars. In 2003, Congress mandated the collection of statistics on prison rape as part of the Prison Rape Elimination Act (PREA).[22] PREA requires the Bureau of Justice Statistics (BJS), under the direction of the National Prison Rape Elimination Commission, to collect sexual victimization data in federal and state prisons, county and city jails, and juvenile institutions. The U.S. Census Bureau acts as the official repository for collected data.

In 2007, the Bureau of Justice Statistics completed its third annual national survey of administrative records and adult correctional facilities for PREA purposes.[23] The survey found that reports of sexual violence varied significantly between prisons and across states, with every state prison system except Alaska and New Mexico reporting at least one allegation of sexual violence. Among the 344 local jail jurisdictions participating in the survey, 47% reported at least one allegation of sexual violence. About 52% of privately operated prisons and jails similarly reported at least one such allegation. Overall, the survey found 5,605 allegations of sexual violence. Extrapolating from that data, BJS estimated that the total number of prison and jail sexual assaults throughout the nation for that year was around 6,500.

BJS's PREA surveys include only inmates in state and federal prisons and do not take into account the many other settings in which sexual violence occurs, including jails, community corrections, immigration facilities, and youth detention facilities. In 2008, the National Prison Rape Elimination Commission, in conjunction with BJS, published a report on sexual victimization in local jails.[24] The report identified common characteristics of victims and perpetrators of rape in county jails and the characteristics of U.S. jails with the highest and lowest incidence of rape. That report, *Sexual Victimization in Local Jails Reported by Inmates*, is available at **Library Extra 12–3**.

PREA surveys are only a first step in understanding and eliminating rape. As BJS notes, "Due to fear of reprisal from perpetrators, a code of silence among inmates, personal embarrassment, and lack of trust in staff, victims are often reluctant to report incidents to corrections authorities."[25] Provisions of PREA were extended by congressional action in 2008.[26] Learn more about PREA and read new survey results as they become available at **Web Extra 12–3**.

Humbolt State University sociologist Lee H. Bowker, reviewing studies of sexual violence in prison, provides the following summary observations:[27]

- Most sexual aggressors do not consider themselves homosexuals.
- Sexual release is not the primary motivation for sexual attack.
- Many aggressors must continue to participate in gang rapes to avoid becoming victims themselves.
- The aggressors have themselves suffered much damage to their masculinity in the past.

As in cases of heterosexual rape, sexual assaults in prison are likely to leave psychological scars on the victims long after the physical event is over.[28] Victims of prison rape live in fear, may feel constantly threatened, and may turn to self-destructive activities.[29]

Many victims question their masculinity and undergo a personal devaluation. Some victims of prison sexual assault become violent, attacking and sometimes killing the person who raped them. The Human Rights Watch researchers found that prisoners "fitting any part of the following description" are more likely to become rape victims: "young, small in size, physically weak, white, gay, first offender, possessing 'feminine' characteristics such as long hair or a high voice; being unassertive, unaggressive, shy, intellectual, not street-smart, or 'passive'; or having been convicted of a sexual offense against a minor." The researchers also noted that "prisoners with several overlapping characteristics are much more likely than other prisoners to be targeted for abuse." The report concluded that to reduce the incidence of prison rape, "prison officials should take considerably more care in matching cell mates, and that, as a general rule, double-celling should be avoided." Learn more about male rape in U.S. prisons at **Library Extra 12–4**.

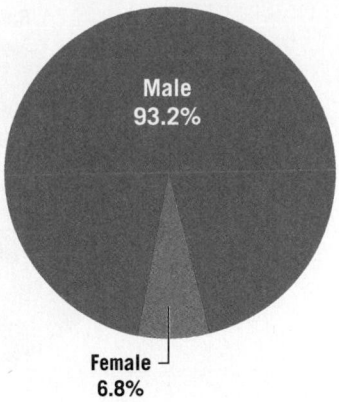

Gender

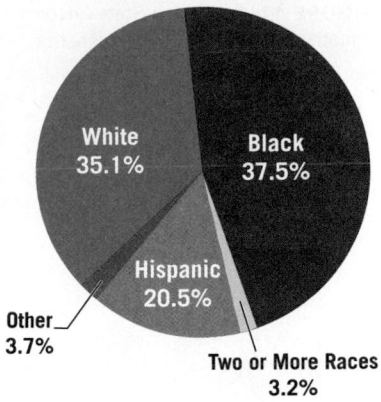

Ethnicity

FIGURE 12–1 Prison Inmates by Gender and Ethnicity in State and Federal Prisons, 2008

Source: William J. Sabol, Heather C. West, and Matthew Cooper, *Prisoners in 2008* (Washington, DC: Bureau of Justice Statistics, revised June 30, 2010).

The Female Inmate's World

As Chapter 11 showed, more than 114,852 women were imprisoned in state and federal correctional institutions throughout the United States at the start of 2009, accounting for 7% of all prison inmates.[30] Texas had the largest number of female prisoners (13,853), exceeding even the federal government.[31] Figure 12–1 provides a breakdown of the total American prison population by gender and ethnicity. While there are still far more men imprisoned across the nation than women (approximately 15 men for every woman), the number of female inmates is rising.[32] In 1981, women made up only 4% of the nation's overall prison population, but the number of female inmates nearly tripled during the 1980s and is continuing to grow at a rate greater than that of male inmates.

In 2003, the National Institute of Corrections (NIC) published the results of its three-year project on female offenders in adult correctional settings.[33] Findings from the study produced a national profile of incarcerated women that is shown in Table 12–1. Figures 12–2 and 12–3 provide additional details.

NIC says that "women involved in the criminal justice system represent a population marginalized by race, class, and gender."[34] African American women, for example, are

Thematic Question Figure 12–1 shows that women account for only 7% of all prisoners and that African Americans make up approximately 38% of our nation's prison population. How do you account for the huge disparity between these figures and the percentages of women (about 52%) and African Americans (about 12%) in American society?

Lecture Note Use Figure 12–1 to discuss the relative proportions of ethnic groups in the nation's prison population. Note that the pie charts shown in the figure do not even approximate the proportions of racial and ethnic groups in the wider society. Do students believe that society should strive to create a more racially "balanced" prison population? Why or why not?

Lecture Note Use Figure 12–1 to discuss the proportion of underrepresented groups in prison. Ask why the proportion of women in prison is so small and why it continues to grow. Should society strive to achieve a more "equitable" representation of women among the inmate population? Why or why not?

TABLE 12–1
National Profile of Female Offenders

A profile based on national data for female offenders reveals the following characteristics:

- Disproportionately women of color
- In their early to middle 30s
- Most likely to have been convicted of a drug-related offense
- From fragmented families that include other family members who also have been involved with the criminal justice system
- Survivors of physical and/or sexual abuse as children and adults
- Individuals with significant substance-abuse problems
- Individuals with multiple physical and mental health problems
- Unmarried mothers of minor children
- Individuals with a high school or general equivalency diploma (GED) but limited vocational training and sporadic work histories

Source: Barbara Bloom, Barbara Owen, and Stephanie Covington, *Gender-Responsive Strategies: Research, Practice, and Guiding Principles for Women Offenders* (Washington, DC: National Institute of Corrections, 2003).

FIGURE 12–2 Women State Prison Inmates: Features and Characteristics

Source: Lawrence A. Greenfeld and Tracy L. Snell, *Women Offenders* (Washington, DC: Bureau of Justice Statistics, October 2000).

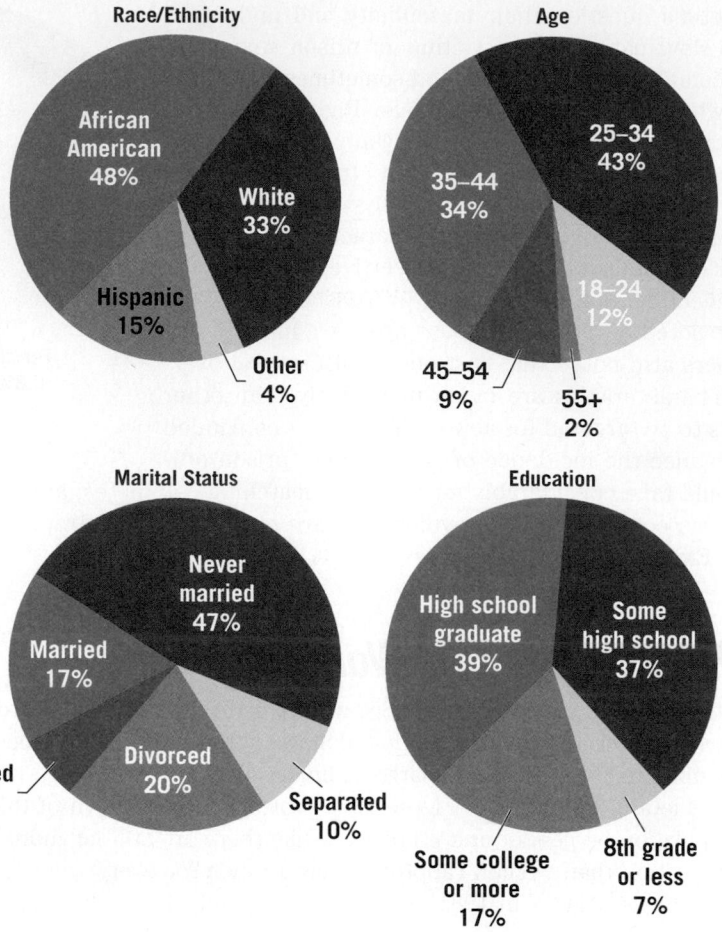

> We must remember always that the doors of prisons swing both ways.
>
> —Mary Belle Harris, first female federal warden

overrepresented in correctional populations. While they constitute only 13% of women in the United States, nearly 50% of women in prison are African American, and African American women are eight times more likely than white women to be incarcerated.

According to NIC, women face life circumstances that tend to be specific to their gender, such as sexual abuse, sexual assault, and domestic violence, as well as the responsibility of being the primary caregiver for dependent children. Research shows that female offenders differ significantly from their male counterparts regarding personal histories and pathways to crime.[35] A female offender, for example, is more likely than a male offender to have been the primary caregiver of young children at the time of her arrest, more likely to have experienced physical and/or sexual abuse, and more likely to have distinctive physical and mental health needs. Women's most common pathways to crime, said NIC, involve survival strategies that result from physical and sexual abuse, poverty, and substance abuse (Figure 12–4).

Children and marital status were identified as another important life circumstance by the NIC study—80% of women entering prison are mothers, and 85% of those women had custody of their children at the time of admission. Approximately 70% of all women under correctional supervision have at least one child younger than age 18. Two-thirds of incarcerated women have minor children; about two-thirds of women in state prisons and half of women in federal prisons had lived with their young children before entering prison. One out of four women entering prison either has recently given birth

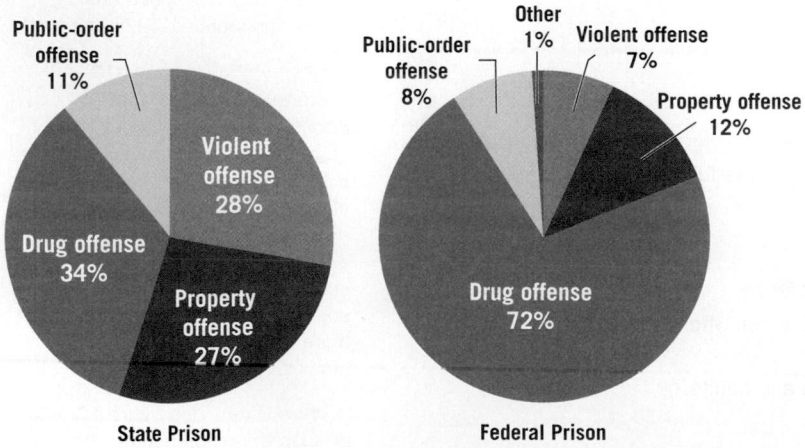

FIGURE 12–3 Most Serious Offenses of Women in State and Federal Prisons

Source: Lawrence A. Greenfeld and Tracy L. Snell, *Women Offenders* (Washington, DC: Bureau of Justice Statistics, October 2000).

or is pregnant. Pregnant inmates, many of whom are drug users, malnourished, or sick, often receive little prenatal care, a situation that risks additional complications.

In 2007, 1.7 million American children had a parent in prison.[36] The number of mothers who are incarcerated has more than doubled in the past 15 years, from 29,500 in 1991 to 65,600 in 2007. Statistically speaking, one out of every 43 American children has a parent in prison today, and ethnic variation in the numbers is striking. While only one out of every 111 white children has experienced the imprisonment of a parent, one out of every 15 black children has had that experience. Moreover, between 1991 and 2007, the number of incarcerated fathers rose 76%, while the number of incarcerated mothers increased 122%.

Separation from their children is a significant deprivation for many women. Although husbands or boyfriends may assume responsibility for the children of their imprisoned partners, this situation is the exception rather than the rule. Eventually, many children of imprisoned mothers are placed into foster care or are put up for adoption.

Some states offer parenting classes for female inmates with children. In a national survey of prisons for women, 36 states responded that they provide parenting programs that deal with caretaking, reduction of violence toward children, visitation problems, and related issues.[37] Some offer play areas furnished with toys, while others attempt to alleviate difficulties attending mother-child visits. The typical program studied meets for two hours per week and lasts from four to nine weeks.

▲ A female inmate being housed in the segregation unit of a Rhode Island correctional facility because of disciplinary problems. The number of women in prison is growing steadily. Why?
Richard Falco/Black Star

Of children whose fathers are incarcerated, approximately 90% live with their mothers; however, only 25% of the children of female offenders live with their fathers. Grandparents are most likely to be the caregivers of the children of female offenders. Approximately 10% of these children are in foster care or group homes. More than half of the children of female prisoners never visit their mothers during the period of incarceration.[38] The lack of visits is due primarily to the remote location of prisons, a lack of transportation, and the inability of caregivers to arrange visitation.

Gender Responsiveness

Critics have long charged that female inmates face a prison system designed for male inmates and run by men. Consequently, meaningful prison programs for women are often lacking. The programs that are in place were originally based on models adapted from men's prisons or were based on traditional views of female roles that leave little room for employment opportunities in the contemporary world. Many trade-training programs still emphasize low-paying jobs, such as cook, beautician, or laundry machine operator, and classes in homemaking are not uncommon.

A central purpose of the NIC report on the female offender was to identify effective gender-responsive approaches for managing female prisoners. The study defined gender responsiveness as "creating an environment . . . that reflects an understanding of the realities of women's lives and addresses the issues of women."[39] The NIC report concluded with a call for recognition of the behavioral and social differences between female and male offenders—especially those differences that have specific implications for gender-responsive policies and practices. Among the report's recommendations are the following:

- The creation of an effective system for female offenders that is structured differently from a system for male offenders
- The development of gender-responsive policies and practices targeting women's pathways to criminality in order to provide effective interventions that address the intersecting issues of substance abuse, trauma, mental health, and economic marginality
- The modification of criminal justice sanctions and interventions to recognize the low risk to public safety represented by the typical female offender
- The consideration of women's relationships, especially those with their children, and women's roles in the community in deciding appropriate correctional sanctions

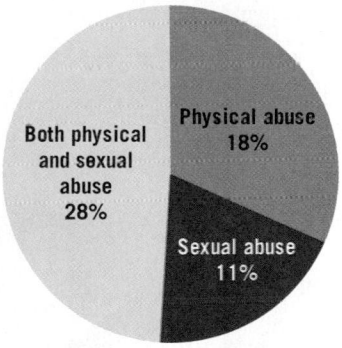

FIGURE 12–4 Women State Prison Inmates: Physical and Sexual Abuse History

Source: Lawrence A. Greenfeld and Tracy L. Snell, *Women Offenders* (Washington, DC: Bureau of Justice Statistics, October 2000).

The NIC study concluded that gender-responsive correctional practices can improve outcomes for female offenders by considering their histories, behaviors, and life circumstances. It also suggested that investments in gender-responsive policies and procedures will likely produce long-term dividends for the criminal justice system and the community as well as for female offenders and their families. Read the entire NIC report at **Library Extra 12–5**.

Institutions for Women

1/3 drug related crimes

Most female inmates are housed in centralized state facilities that are dedicated exclusively to incarcerating female felons. Although there is not a typical women's prison, the American Correctional Association (ACA) 1990 report by the Task Force on the Female Offender found that the institutions that house female inmates could be generally described as follows:[40]

- Most prisons for women are located in towns with fewer than 25,000 inhabitants.
- A significant number of facilities were not designed to house female inmates.
- Some facilities that house female inmates also house men.
- Few facilities for women have programs especially designed for female offenders.
- Few major disturbances or escapes are reported among female inmates.
- * Substance abuse among female inmates is very high.
- Few work assignments are available to female inmates.

Social Structure in Women's Prisons

Lecture Note Explain the "family" structures so frequently found in prisons for women. Note that "families" are found cross-culturally in women's institutions. Ask the class to explain the phenomenon.

"Aside from sharing the experience of being incarcerated," says Professor Marsha Clowers of the John Jay College of Criminal Justice, "female prisoners have much in common. They are likely to be black or Hispanic, poor, uneducated, abuse survivors, single parents, and in poor health."[41] Shared social characteristics may lead to similar values and behaviors. One type of behavior identified by early prison researchers as characteristic of a fair number of incarcerated women concerns the way in which female inmates construct organized pseudofamilies. Typical of such studies are D. Ward and G. Kassebaum's *Women's Prison: Sex and Social Structure* (1966),[42] Esther Heffernan's *Making It in Prison: The Square, the Cool, and the Life* (1972),[43] and Rose Giallombardo's *Society of Women: A Study of Women's Prisons* (1966).[44]

▲ Female inmates in Sheriff Joe Arpaio's "equal opportunity jail" in Maricopa County, Arizona, being inspected by a corrections officer before leaving for chain-gang duty. Not all states make use of chain gangs, and only a few use female inmates on chain gangs. Should jail chain gangs be more widely used? *Jack Kurtz/The Image Works*

Giallombardo, for example, examined the Federal Reformatory for Women at Alderson, West Virginia, spending a year gathering data in the early 1960s. Focusing closely on the social formation of families among female inmates, she titled one of her chapters "The Homosexual Alliance as a Marriage Unit." In it, she described in great detail the sexual identities assumed by women at Alderson and the symbols they chose to communicate those roles. Hairstyle, dress, language, and mannerisms were all used to signify "maleness" or "femaleness." Giallombardo detailed "the anatomy of the marriage relationship from courtship to 'fall out,' that is, from inception to the parting of the ways, or divorce."[45] Romantic love at Alderson was of central importance to any relationship between inmates, and all homosexual relationships were described as voluntary. Through marriage, the "stud broad" became the husband and the "femme" the wife.

Studies attempting to document the extent of inmate involvement in prison "families" have produced varying results. Some have found as many as 71% of female prisoners involved in the phenomenon, while others have found none.[46] The kinship systems described by Giallombardo and others, however, extend beyond simple "family" ties to the formation of large, intricately related groups involving a large number of nonsexual relationships. In these groups, the roles of "children," "in-laws," "grandparents," and so on may be explicitly recognized. Even "birth order" within a family can become an issue for kinship groups.[47]

Kinship groups sometimes occupy a common household, usually a prison cottage or a dormitory area. The descriptions of women's prisons provided by authors like Giallombardo show a closed society in which social interactions—including expectations, normative forms of behavior, and emotional ties—are regulated by an inventive system of artificial relationships that mirror those of the outside world.

Many studies of female prisoners show that incarcerated women suffer intensely from the loss of affectional relationships once they enter prison and that they form homosexual liaisons to compensate for such losses.[48] Those liaisons then become the foundation of prison social organization.

Barbara Owen, professor of Criminology at California State University, Fresno, conducted a study of female inmates at the Central California Women's Facility (the largest prison for women in the world). Her book, *In the Mix: Struggle and Survival in a Women's Prison*,[49] describes the daily life of female inmates, with an emphasis on prison social structure. Owen found that prison culture for women is tied directly to the roles that women normally assume in free society as well as to other factors shaped by the conditions of women's lives in prison and in the free world. *In the Mix* describes the lives of women before prison and suggests that those lifestyles shape women's adaptation to prison culture. Owen found that preexisting economic marginalization, self-destructive behaviors, and personal histories of physical, sexual, and substance abuse may be important defining features of inmates' lives before they enter prison.[50] She also discovered that the sentences that women have to serve, along with their work and housing assignments, effectively pattern their daily lives and relationships. Owen described "the mix" as that aspect of prison culture that supports the rule-breaking behavior that propels women into crime and causes them to enter prison. Owen concluded that prison subcultures for women are very different from the violent and predatory structure of contemporary male prisons.[51] Like men, women experience "pains of imprisonment," but their prison culture offers them other ways to survive and adapt to these deprivations.

> The person of a prisoner sentenced to imprisonment in the State prison is under the protection of the law, and any injury to his person, not authorized by law, is punishable in the same manner as if he were not convicted or sentenced.
>
> —California Penal Code, Section 2650

A 2001 study of a women's correctional facility in the southeastern United States found that female inmates who were asked about their preincarceration sexual orientation gave answers that were quite different than when they were asked about their sexual orientation while incarcerated.[52] In general, 64% of inmates interviewed reported being exclusively heterosexual, 28% said they were bisexual, and 8% said that they were lesbians before being incarcerated. In contrast, these same women reported sexual orientations while incarcerated of 55% heterosexual, 31% bisexual, and 13% lesbian. Researchers found that same-sex sexual behavior within the institution was more likely to occur in the lives of young inmates who had had such experiences before entering prison. The study also found that female inmates tended to become more involved in lesbian behavior the longer they were incarcerated.

Finally, a significant aspect of sexual activity far more commonly found in women's prisons than in prisons for men involves sexual misconduct between staff and inmates. While a fair amount of such behavior is attributed to the exploitation of female inmates by male corrections officers acting from positions of power, some studies suggest that female inmates may sometimes attempt to manipulate unsuspecting male officers into illicit relationships in order to gain favors.[53]

Thematic Question How do the types of female inmates described in this chapter compare to the types of male inmates? In what ways do they reflect or not reflect male and female roles in the larger society?

Types of Female Inmates

As in institutions for men, the subculture of women's prisons is multidimensional. Esther Heffernan, for example, found that three terms used by the female prisoners she studied—the *square*, the *cool*, and the *life*—were indicative of three styles of adaptation to prison life.[54] Square inmates had few early experiences with criminal lifestyles and tended to sympathize with the values and attitudes of conventional society. Cool prisoners were more likely to be career offenders. They tended to keep to themselves and generally supported inmate values. Women who participated in the life subculture were quite familiar with lives of crime. Many had been arrested repeatedly for prostitution, drug use, theft,

▲ Tom Hanks playing the role of a corrections officer in the movie *The Green Mile.* The job of a corrections officer centers largely on the custody and control of inmates, but growing professionalism is enhancing both personal opportunities and job satisfaction among officers. Why is professionalism important to job satisfaction?
Photofest

and so on. They were full participants in the economic, social, and familial arrangements of the prison. Heffernan believed that the life option offered an alternative lifestyle to women who had experienced early and constant rejection by conventional society. With the life characteristics, women could establish relationships, achieve status, and find meaning in their lives. The square, the cool, and the life represented subcultures to Heffernan because individuals with similar adaptive choices tended to relate closely to one another and to support the lifestyle characteristic of that type.

Recently, the social structure of women's prisons has been altered by the arrival of "crack kids," as they are called in prison argot. Crack kids, whose existence highlights generational differences among female offenders, are streetwise young women with little respect for traditional prison values, for their elders, or even for their own children. They are known for frequent fights and for their lack of even simple domestic skills. Many older inmates, some of whom call the younger inmates "animalescents," quickly separate themselves from these young women.

Violence in Women's Prisons

Some authors have suggested that violence in women's prisons is less frequent than it is in institutions for men. Lee Bowker observes that "except for the behavior of a few 'guerrillas,' it appears that violence is only used in women's prisons to settle questions of dominance and subordination when other manipulative strategies fail to achieve the desired effect."[55] It appears that few homosexual liaisons are forced, perhaps representing a general aversion among women to such victimization in wider society. At least one study, however, has shown the use of sexual violence in women's prisons as a form of revenge against inmates who are overly vocal in their condemnation of lesbian practices among other prisoners.[56]

Not all abuse occurs at the hands of inmates. In 1992, 14 corrections officers (ten men and four women) were indicted for the alleged abuse of female inmates at the 900-bed Women's Correctional Institute in Hardwick, Georgia. The charges resulted from affidavits filed by 90 female inmates alleging "rape, sexual abuse, prostitution, coerced abortions, sex for favors, and retaliation for refusal to participate" in such activities.[57] One inmate who was forced to have an abortion after becoming pregnant by a male staff member said, "As an inmate, I simply felt powerless to avoid the sexual advances of staff and to refuse to have an abortion."[58]

Class Activity Invite a corrections administrator (warden, programs director, shift supervisor, etc.) to speak with the class either in person or via virtual conferencing. Ask him or her to comment on the ideas discussed in this chapter, such as inmate typology. Does the speaker believe that these concepts adequately describe prison reality as he or she has experienced it? Inquire into the terminology of local prison argot.

To address the problems of imprisoned women, including violence, the Task Force on the Female Offender recommended a number of changes in the administration of prisons for women:[59]

- Substance-abuse programs should be available to female inmates.
- Female inmates need to acquire greater literacy skills, and literacy programs should form the basis on which other programs are built.
- Female offenders should be housed in buildings without male inmates.
- Institutions for women should develop programs for keeping children in the facility in order to "fortify the bond between mother and child."
- To ensure equal access to assistance, institutions should be built to accommodate programs for female offenders.

Learn more about women in prison and their special needs at **Library Extras 12–6** and **12–7**.

The Staff World

Facts and Figures

Lecture Note Describe the jobs and roles that prison staff members fulfill. Describe how one staffer may wear many different hats.

The flip side of inmate society can be found in the world of the prison staff, which includes many people working in various professions. Staff roles encompass those of warden, psychologist, counselor, area supervisor, program director, instructor, corrections officer, and—in some large prisons—physician and therapist.

According to the federal government, approximately 748,000 people are employed in corrections,[60] with the majority performing direct custodial tasks in state institutions: 62% of corrections employees work for state governments, followed by 33% at the local level and 5% at the federal level.[61] On a per capita basis, the District of Columbia has the most state and local corrections employees (53.3 per every 10,000 residents), followed by Texas (43.8).[62] Across the nation, 70% of corrections officers are Caucasian, 22% are African American, and slightly over 5% are Hispanic.[63] Women account for 20% of all corrections officers, with the proportion of female officers increasing at around 19% per year. The ACA encourages correctional agencies to "ensure that recruitment, selection, and promotion opportunities are open to women."[64]

Class Activity If you did not do so while discussing Chapter 11, now would be a good time to schedule a tour of a local prison. Ask to see as many facilities as possible, including dormitories, workshops, cafeterias, segregation units, and religious assembly areas. If possible, schedule time to hear from inmates about the challenges of prison life. Ask if there are any positive aspects to "being on the inside."

Corrections officers, generally considered to be at the bottom of the staff hierarchy, may be divided into cell-block guards and tower guards. Others are assigned to administrative offices, where they perform clerical tasks. The ratio averages around four inmates for each corrections officer in state prisons.[65]

Like prisoners, corrections officers undergo a socialization process that helps them function by the official and unofficial rules of staff society. In a now-classic study, Lucien X. Lombardo described the process by which officers are socialized into the prison work world.[66] Lombardo interviewed 359 corrections personnel at New York's Auburn Prison and found that rookie officers quickly had to abandon preconceptions of both inmates and other staff members. According to Lombardo, new officers learn that inmates are not the "monsters" much of the public makes them out to be. On the other hand, rookies may be seriously disappointed in their experienced colleagues when they realize that the ideals of professionalism, often emphasized during early training, rarely translate into reality. The pressures of the institutional work environment, however, soon force most corrections personnel to adopt a united front when relating to inmates.

3 Describe the realities of prison life from the corrections officer's point of view.

One of the leading formative influences on staff culture is the potential threat that inmates pose. Inmates far outnumber corrections personnel in every institution, and the hostility they feel for guards is only barely hidden even at the best of times. Corrections personnel know that however friendly inmates may appear, a sudden change in institutional climate—as can happen with anything from simple disturbances in the yard to full-blown riots—can quickly and violently unmask deep-rooted feelings of mistrust and hatred.

As in years past, prison staffers are still most concerned with custody and control. Society, especially under the just deserts philosophy of criminal sentencing, expects corrections staff to keep inmates in custody—the basic prerequisite of successful job performance. Custody is necessary before any other correctional activities, such as instruction or counseling, can be undertaken. Control, the other major staff concern, ensures order, and an orderly prison is thought to be safe and secure. In routine daily activities, control over almost all aspects of inmate behavior becomes paramount in the minds of most corrections officers. It is the twin interests of custody and control that lead to institutionalized procedures for ensuring security in most facilities. The enforcement of strict rules; body and cell searches; counts; unannounced shakedowns; the control of dangerous items, materials, and contraband; and the extensive use of bars, locks, fencing, cameras, and alarms all support the staff's vigilance in maintaining security. See CJ Exhibit 12–2 for a commission's report on safety in prisons.

▲ A notice posted on a prison wall. Custody and control remain the primary concerns of prison staffers throughout the country—a fact reinforced by this notice. Is the emphasis on custody and control justified?
Mike Fiala/Agence Francis Press/Getty Images

The Professionalization of Corrections Officers

Corrections officers have generally been accorded low occupational status. Historically, the role of prison guard required minimal formal education and held few opportunities for professional growth and career advancement. The job was typically low paying, frustrating, and often boring. Growing

CJ Exhibit 12–2
The Commission on Safety and Abuse in America's Prisons

On June 8, 2006, the Commission on Safety and Abuse in America's Prisons released its long-awaited final report.[1] The commission was formed more than a year earlier, with support from the Vera Institute of Justice, following the widely publicized scandals at Abu Ghraib prison in Iraq. The commission's avowed purpose was to explore the most serious problems inside U.S. correctional facilities and to assess their impact on the incarcerated, corrections personnel, and society at large.[2] "As President Bush was calling the abuse at Abu Ghraib 'un-American,'" said the commission's website, "many Americans raised questions about the treatment of prisoners here at home."

The commission's 21-member nonpartisan panel was co-chaired by former U.S. Attorney General Nicholas Katzenbach and the Honorable John J. Gibbons, former chief judge of the U.S. Third Circuit Court of Appeals.

During much of 2005 and into 2006, the commission held public hearings across the country and interviewed corrections professionals, legislators, and interested parties to explore the most serious problems facing correctional facilities today, including violence, sexual abuse, the degradation of prisoners, overcrowding, treatment for the mentally ill, and the working conditions of corrections officers. Interim reports were released following each hearing.

"How we treat correctional officers and inmates is an issue that goes beyond the walls of our prisons, impacting the families and communities of both correctional officers and inmates," said Senator Patrick Leahy, the ranking member of the Senate Judiciary Committee, in commenting on the commission's work.[3]

The commission's final report was built around practical recommendations intended to be useful to local, state, and federal policymakers seeking to improve conditions in the prisons and jails in their jurisdictions. Recommendations were made in the areas of violence reduction, health care, high-security segregation, corrections leadership and professionalism, oversight and accountability, and development, collection, and use of standardized data helpful in the creation of public policy about prison and jails.

A summary of the commission's recommendations in the area of corrections leadership follows:

1. *Promote a culture of mutual respect.* Create a positive culture in jails and prisons grounded in an ethic of respectful behavior and interpersonal communication that benefits prisoners and staff.
2. *Recruit and retain a qualified corps of officers.* Enact changes at the state and local levels to advance the recruitment and retention of a diverse high-quality workforce and otherwise further the professionalism of the workforce.
3. *Support today's leaders and cultivate the next generation.* Governors and local executives must hire the most qualified leaders and support them politically and professionally, and corrections administrators must, in turn, use their positions to promote healthy and safe prisons and jails. Equally important, the skills and capacities of middle-level managers, who play a large role in running safe facilities and are poised to become the next generation of senior leaders, must be developed.

For more information about the commission and to read the commission's final report, visit www.prisoncommission.org.

[1]Commission on Safety and Abuse in America's Prisons, *Confronting Confinement: A Report of the Commission on Safety and Abuse in America's Prisons* (New York: Vera Institute of Justice, 2006).

[2]Vera Institute of Justice, "National Commission to Examine U.S. Prison Conditions: Post–Abu Ghraib, Panel to Study U.S. Prisons and Their Impact on Prisoners, Corrections Officers and Society at Large," press release, March 1, 2005.

[3]Commission on Safety and Abuse in America's Prisons, "Federal Policy Makers Support Commission," press release, March 2, 2005.

Lecture Note Explain that custody and control are still the major concerns of corrections staffers—just as they have been since the inception of imprisonment.

Lecture Note Discuss how the ACA Code of Ethics is designed to uphold both the standards of the profession and the values of society. Ask students what social values the code embodies.

Thematic Question How does the ACA Code of Ethics attempt to balance prisoners' needs and rights with those of prison staff and with the need for security and order?

problems in our nation's prisons, including emerging issues of legal liability, however, increasingly require a well-trained and adequately equipped force of professionals. As corrections personnel have become better trained and more proficient, the old concept of guard has been supplanted by that of corrections officer. The ACA has published a code of ethics for corrections officers that is reproduced in the "Ethics and Professionalism" box in this chapter.

Many states and a growing number of large-city correctional systems try to eliminate individuals with potentially harmful personality characteristics from corrections officer applicant pools. New Jersey, New York, Ohio, Pennsylvania, and Rhode Island, for example, all use some form of psychological screening when assessing candidates for prison jobs.[67]

Although only some states utilize psychological screening, all make use of training programs intended to prepare successful applicants for prison work. New York, for example, requires trainees to complete six weeks of classroom-based instruction, 40 hours of rifle range practice, and six weeks of on-the-job training. Training days begin around 5 A.M. with a mile run and conclude after dark with study halls for students who need extra help. To keep

Ethics and Professionalism
American Correctional Association Code of Ethics

PREAMBLE

The American Correctional Association expects of its members unfailing honesty, respect for the dignity and individuality of human beings and a commitment to professional and compassionate service. To this end, we subscribe to the following principles:

- Members shall respect and protect the civil and legal rights of all individuals.
- Members shall treat every professional situation with concern for the welfare of the individuals involved and with no intent [of] personal gain.
- Members shall maintain relationships with colleagues to promote mutual respect within the profession and improve the quality of service.
- Members shall make public criticisms of their colleagues or their agencies only when warranted, verifiable, and constructive.
- Members shall respect the importance of all disciplines within the criminal justice system and work to improve cooperation with each segment.
- Members shall honor the public's right to information and share information with the public to the extent permitted by law subject to individuals' right to privacy.
- Members shall respect and protect the right of the public to be safeguarded from criminal activity.
- Members shall refrain from using their positions to secure personal privileges or advantages.
- Members shall refrain from allowing personal interest to impair objectivity in the performance of duty while acting in an official capacity.
- Members shall refrain from entering into any formal or informal activity or agreement which presents a conflict of interest or is inconsistent with the conscientious performance of duties.
- Members shall refrain from accepting any gift, service, or favor that is or appears to be improper or implies an obligation inconsistent with the free and objective exercise of professional duties.
- Members shall clearly differentiate between personal views/statements and views/statements/positions made on behalf of the agency or association.
- Members shall report to appropriate authorities any corrupt or unethical behaviors in which there is sufficient evidence to justify review.
- Members shall refrain from discriminating against any individual because of race, gender, creed, national origin, religious affiliation, age, disability, or any other type of prohibited discrimination.
- Members shall preserve the integrity of private information; they shall refrain from seeking information on individuals beyond that which is necessary to implement responsibilities and perform their duties; members shall refrain from revealing nonpublic information unless expressly authorized to do so.
- Members shall make all appointments, promotions, and dismissals in accordance with established civil service rules, applicable contract agreements, and individual merit, and not in furtherance of partisan interests.
- Members shall respect, promote, and contribute to a workplace that is safe, healthy, and free of harassment in any form.

THINKING ABOUT ETHICS

1. ***How does the ACA's Code of Ethics differ from the American Jail Association's Code of Ethics found in Chapter 11? How is it similar?***
2. ***Should one code of ethics cover corrections officers working in both jails and prisons? Why or why not?***

Adopted August 1975 at the 105th Congress of Correction. Revised August 1990 at the 120th Congress of Correction. Revised August 1994 at the 124th Congress of Correction.

Source: Reprinted with permission of the American Correctional Association, Alexandria, Virginia. Visit the American Correctional Association at http://www.aca.org.

pace with rising inmate populations, the state has often had to run a number of simultaneous training academies.[68]

Prison Riots

In 2004, a disturbance took place at the medium- to high-security Arizona State Prison Complex at Lewis. Two corrections officers and a staff member were injured in a ruckus that broke out during breakfast preparations, and two other officers were captured and held hostage for 15 days in a watchtower. The episode, covered by the major news services, may have begun as an escape attempt. Officials were able to keep disorder from spreading to the rest of the facility, and the incident ended when inmates released the officers and surrendered. "It could have been a lot worse," said Joe Masella, president of the Arizona Correctional Peace Officers' Association. "Once these inmates get a taste of blood, so to speak, there's no telling what they can do."[69]

Although today's prisons are relatively calm, the ten years between 1970 and 1980 were called the "explosive decade" of prison riots.[70] The decade began with a massive uprising at

▲ The Arizona State Prison Complex at Lewis, where two inmates held two corrections officers hostage in a watchtower in 2004. One officer, a female, was raped. On April 30, 2004, inmate Steven Coy was sentenced to seven consecutive life sentences for his part in the hostage crisis. How can the safety of corrections workers be improved?
Tom Hood/AP Wide World Photos

Attica Prison in New York State in September 1971, which resulted in 43 deaths and more than 80 wounded men. The "explosive decade" ended in 1980 at Santa Fe, New Mexico. There, in a riot at the New Mexico Penitentiary, 33 inmates died, the victims of vengeful prisoners out to eliminate rats and informants. Many of the deaths involved mutilation and torture, more than 200 other inmates were beaten and sexually assaulted, and the prison was virtually destroyed.

Although the number of prison riots decreased after the 1970s, they did continue. For 11 days in 1987, the Atlanta (Georgia) Federal Penitentiary was under the control of inmates. The institution was heavily damaged, and inmates had to be temporarily relocated while it was rebuilt. The Atlanta riot followed on the heels of a similar, but less intense, disturbance at the federal detention center at Oakdale, Louisiana. Both outbreaks were attributed to the dissatisfaction of Cuban inmates, most of whom had arrived in the mass exodus known as the Mariel boat lift.[71]

Easter Sunday 1993 marked the beginning of an 11-day rebellion at the 1,800-inmate Southern Ohio Correctional Facility in Lucasville, one of the country's toughest maximum-security prisons. When the riot ended, nine inmates and one corrections officer were dead. (The officer had been hung.) The close of the riot—involving a parade of 450 inmates—was televised as prisoners had demanded. Among other demands were (1) no retaliation by officials, (2) review of medical staffing and care, (3) review of mail and visitation rules, (4) review of commissary prices, and (5) better enforcement against what the inmates called "inappropriate supervision."[72]

Riots related to inmate grievances over perceived disparities in federal drug-sentencing policies and the possible loss of weight-lifting equipment occurred throughout the federal prison system in October 1995. Within a few days, the unrest led to a nationwide lockdown of 73 federal prisons. Although fires were set and a number of inmates and guards were injured, no deaths resulted. In February 2000, a riot between 200 black and Hispanic prisoners in California's infamous Pelican Bay State Prison led to the death of one inmate and injuries to 15 other inmates. In November 2000, 32 inmates took a dozen corrections officers hostage at the privately run Torrance County Detention Facility in Estancia, New Mexico. Two of the guards were stabbed and seriously injured, while another eight were beaten. The riot was finally quelled after an emergency response team threw tear-gas canisters into the area where the prisoners had barricaded themselves.[73]

Lecture Note Explore the causes of prison riots. Discuss the importance of informal controls within prison subculture in keeping order and preventing riots.

In 2005, 42 inmates were injured when a fight broke out during breakfast between Hispanic and Caucasian prisoners at California's San Quentin State Prison. The riot occurred in a section of the prison housing about 900 inmates who were under lockdown because of previous fighting between the groups.[74] In 2008, the Federal Correctional Institution in Three Rivers, Texas, was locked down following two gang-related fights that killed one inmate and injured 22. The altercations were broken up by corrections officers with the help of plumbers, electricians, secretaries, and others who were working at the facility when the fights broke out.[75]

Causes of Riots

Researchers have suggested a variety of causes for prison riots:[76]

4 Describe the causes of prison riots.

- *Insensitive prison administration and neglect of inmates' demands.* Calls for fairness in disciplinary hearings, better food, more recreational opportunities, and the like may lead to riots when they are ignored.
- *Previous lifestyles of most inmates.* It should be no surprise that prisoners use organized violence when many of them were violent people when they were out on the streets.
- *Dehumanizing prison conditions.* Overcrowded facilities, lack of opportunity for individual expression, and other aspects of total institutions culminate in riots and other explosive situations.

- *Regulation of inmate society and redistribution of power balances among inmate groups.* Riots provide the opportunity to "cleanse" the prison population of informers and rats and to resolve struggles among power brokers and ethnic groups within the institution.
- *Power vacuums.* Changes in prison administration, the transfer of influential inmates, and court-ordered injunctions significantly alter the power structure and informal social-control mechanisms of the institution.

Although riots are difficult to predict in specific institutions, some state prison systems appear ripe for disorder. The Texas prison system, for example, is home to a number of gangs, referred to by corrections personnel as **security threat groups (STGs)**, among whom turf violations can easily lead to widespread disorder. Gang membership among inmates in the Texas prison system, practically nonexistent in 1983, was estimated at more than 1,200 in 1992.[77] The Texas Syndicate, the Aryan Brotherhood of Texas, and the Mexican Mafia (sometimes known as *La Eme*, Spanish for the letter *M*) are probably the largest gangs functioning in the Texas prison system. Each has around 300 members.[78] Other gangs known to operate in some Texas prisons include the Aryan Warriors, Black Gangster Disciples (mostly in midwestern Texas), Black Guerrilla Family, Confederate Knights of America, and Nuestra Familia (an organization of Hispanic prisoners).

security threat group (STG)
An inmate group, gang, or organization whose members act together to pose a threat to the safety of corrections staff or the public, who prey on other inmates, or who threaten the secure and orderly operation of a correctional institution.

Gangs in Texas grew rapidly in part because of the power vacuum created when a court ruling ended the "building tender" system.[79] Building tenders were tough inmates who were given almost free rein by prison administrators to keep other inmates in line, especially in many of the state's worst prisons. The end of the building tender system dramatically increased demands on the Texas Department of Criminal Justice for increased abilities and professionalism among its guards and other prison staff.

Lecture Note Explain the hands-off doctrine as a nonintervention policy that American courts assumed with regard to prisons before the late 1960s. Explain that widespread abuses of power by corrections staff, combined with an increasingly sensitive Supreme Court, led to many decisions relative to corrections administration during the past two decades.

The real reasons for any riot are probably specific to the institution and may not allow for easy generalization. However, it is no simple coincidence that the explosive decade of prison riots coincided with the growth of a revolutionary prisoner subculture. As the old convict code began to give way to an emerging perception of social victimization among inmates, it was probably only a matter of time until those perceptions turned to militancy.

Prisoners' Rights

In May 1995, Limestone Prison inmate Larry Hope was handcuffed to a hitching post after arguing with another inmate while working on a chain gang near an interstate highway in Alabama.[80] Hope was released two hours later, after a supervising officer determined that Hope had not instigated the altercation. During the two hours that he was coupled to the post, Hope was periodically offered drinking water and bathroom breaks, and his responses to those offers were recorded on an activity log. Because of the height of the hitching post, however, his arms grew tired, and it was later determined that whenever he tried moving his arms to improve his circulation, the handcuffs cut into his wrists, causing pain.

One month later, Hope was punished more severely after he had taken a nap during the morning bus ride to the chain gang's work site. When the bus arrived, he was slow in responding to an order to exit the vehicle. A shouting match soon led to a scuffle with an officer, and four other guards intervened and subdued Hope, handcuffing him and placing him in leg irons for transportation back to the prison. When he arrived at the facility, officers made him take off his shirt and again put him on the hitching post. He stood in the sun for approximately seven hours, sustaining a sunburn; Hope was given water only once or twice during that time and was provided with no bathroom breaks. At one point, an officer taunted him about his thirst. According to Hope: "[The guard] first gave water to some dogs, then brought the water cooler closer to me, removed its lid, and kicked the cooler over, spilling the water onto the ground."

Eventually Hope filed a civil suit against three officers, claiming that he experienced "unnecessary pain" and that the "wanton infliction of pain . . . constitutes cruel and unusual punishment forbidden by the Eighth Amendment." His case eventually reached the U.S. Supreme Court, and on June 27, 2002, the Court found that Hope's treatment was

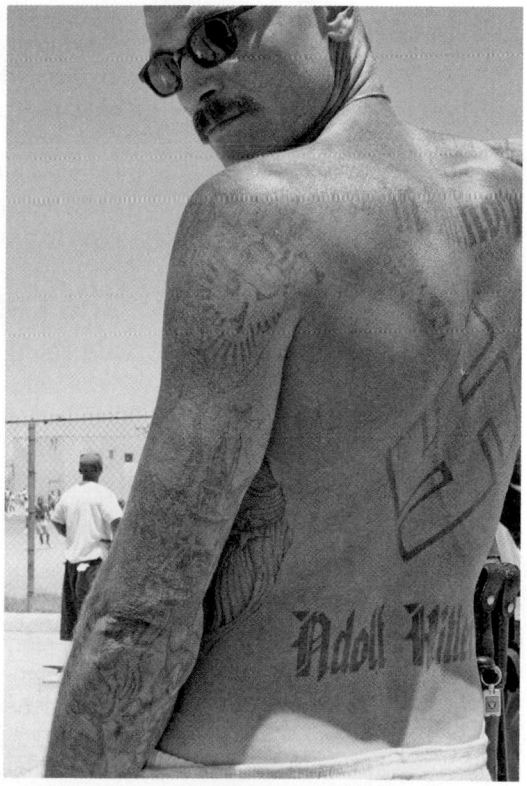

▲ A California inmate with Aryan Brotherhood ties showing off his tattoos in a sensitive-needs housing facility at Calipatria State Prison. What are security threat groups? Can you name some?
© *Mark Allen Johnson/* ZUMA Press

"totally without penological justification" and constituted an Eighth Amendment violation. The Court ruled that "[d]espite the clear lack of emergency, respondents knowingly subjected [Hope] to a substantial risk of physical harm, unnecessary pain, unnecessary exposure to the sun, prolonged thirst and taunting, and a deprivation of bathroom breaks that created a risk of particular discomfort and humiliation."

In deciding the *Hope* case, the Court built on almost 40 years of precedent-setting decisions in the area of prisoners' rights. It may be surprising, but before the 1960s, American courts had taken a neutral approach—commonly called the **hands-off doctrine**—toward the running of prisons. Judges assumed that prison administrators were sufficiently professional in the performance of their duties to balance institutional needs with humane considerations. The hands-off doctrine rested on the belief that defendants lost most of their rights upon conviction, suffering a kind of **civil death**. Many states defined civil death through legislation that denied inmates the right to vote, to hold public office, and even to marry. Some states made incarceration for a felony a basis for uncontested divorce at the request of the noncriminal spouse. Aspects of the old notion of civil death are still a reality in a number of jurisdictions today. The Sentencing Project says that 3.9 million American citizens across the nation are barred from voting because of previous felony convictions.[81]

hands-off doctrine
A policy of nonintervention with regard to prison management that U.S. courts tended to follow until the late 1960s. For 30 years, the doctrine languished as judicial intervention in prison administration dramatically increased, although there is now evidence that a new hands-off era is beginning.

civil death
The legal status of prisoners in some jurisdictions who are denied the opportunity to vote, hold public office, marry, or enter into contracts by virtue of their status as incarcerated felons. While civil death is primarily of historical interest, some jurisdictions still limit the contractual opportunities available to inmates.

Although the concept of civil death has not entirely disappeared, the hands-off doctrine ended in 1970, when a federal court declared the entire Arkansas prison system to be unconstitutional after hearing arguments that it constituted a form of cruel and unusual punishment.[82] The court's decision resulted from what it judged to be pervasive overcrowding and primitive living conditions. Longtime inmates claimed that a number of other inmates had been beaten or shot to death by guards and buried over the years in unmarked graves on prison property. An investigation did unearth some skeletons in old graves, but their origin was never determined.

Detailed media coverage of the Arkansas prison system gave rise to suspicions about correctional institutions everywhere. Within a few years, federal courts intervened in the running of prisons in Florida, Louisiana, Mississippi, New York City, and Virginia.[83] In 1975, in a precedent-setting decision, U.S. District Court Judge Frank M. Johnson issued an order banning the Alabama Board of Corrections from accepting any more inmates. Citing a population that was more than double the capacity of the state's system, Judge Johnson enumerated 44 standards to be met before additional inmates could be admitted to prison. Included in the requirements were specific guidelines on living space, staff-to-inmate ratios, visiting privileges, racial makeup of staff, and food service modifications.

The Legal Basis of Prisoners' Rights

In 1974, the U.S. Supreme Court case of *Pell* v. *Procunier*[84] established a "balancing test" that, although originally addressing only First Amendment rights, eventually served as a general guideline for all prison operations. In *Pell*, the Court ruled that the "prison inmate retains those First Amendment rights that are not inconsistent with his status as a prisoner or with the legitimate penological objectives of the corrections system."[85] In other words, inmates have rights, much the same as people who are not incarcerated, provided that the legitimate needs of the prison for security, custody, and safety are not compromised. Other courts have declared that order maintenance, security, and rehabilitation are all legitimate concerns of prison administration but that financial exigency and convenience are not. As the **balancing test** makes clear, we see reflected in prisoners' rights a microcosm of the individual-rights versus public-order dilemma found in wider society.

5 Discuss the legal aspects of prisoners' rights, and explain the consequences of precedent-setting U.S. Supreme Court cases in the area of prisoners' rights.

balancing test
A principle, developed by the courts and applied to the corrections arena by *Pell* v. *Procunier* (1974), that attempts to weigh the rights of an individual, as guaranteed by the Constitution, against the authority of states to make laws or to otherwise restrict a person's freedom in order to protect the state's interests and its citizens.

Further enforcing the legal rights of prisoners is the Civil Rights of Institutionalized Persons Act (CRIPA) of 1980.[86] The law, which has been amended over time, applies to all adult and juvenile state and local jails, detention centers, prisons, mental hospitals, and other care facilities (such as those operated by a state, county, or city for inmates who are physically challenged or chronically ill).

Significantly, the most recent version of CRIPA states:[87]

> No action shall be brought with respect to prison conditions under section 1983 of this title, or any other Federal law, by a prisoner confined in any jail, prison, or other correctional facility until such administrative remedies as are available are exhausted.

Freedom or Safety? You Decide.
Censoring Prison Communications

On February 28, 2005, NBC News announced that it had learned that Arab terrorists in federal maximum-security prisons had been sending letters to extremists on the outside exhorting them to attack Western interests. The terrorists included Mohammed Salameh, a follower of radical sheik Omar Abdel-Rahman. Salameh had been sentenced to more than 100 years in prison for his part in the 1993 bombing attack on New York's World Trade Center. That attack, which killed six and injured more than 1,000, blew a huge hole in the basement parking garage of one of the towers but failed to topple the buildings.

The men were being held in the federal ADMAX facility in Florence, Colorado, which is the country's most secure federal prison. While there, NBC News revealed, they sent at least 14 letters to a Spanish terror cell, praised Osama bin Laden in Arabic newspapers, and advocated additional terror attacks. In July 2002, Salameh, a Palestinian with a degree in Islamic law from a Jordanian university, sent a letter to the *Al-Quds* Arabic daily newspaper proclaiming that "Osama Bin Laden is my hero of this generation."

Andy McCarthy, a former federal prosecutor who worked to send the terrorists to prison, said that Salameh's letters were "exhorting acts of terrorism and helping recruit would-be terrorists for the *Jihad*." Michael Macko, who lost his father in the Trade Center bombing, posed this question: "If they are encouraging acts of terrorism internationally, how do we know they're not encouraging acts of terrorism right here on U.S. soil?"

Prison officials told reporters that communications involving the imprisoned bombers had not been closely censored because the men hadn't been considered very dangerous. The letters didn't contain any plans for attacks, nor did they name any specific targets. One Justice Department official said that Salameh was "a low level guy" who was not under any special restrictions and that his letters were seen as "generic stuff" and "no cause for concern."

Rights advocates suggested that inmates should have the right to free speech—even those imprisoned for acts of terrorism—and that advocating terrorism is not the same thing as planning it or carrying it out. After all, they said, calls for a holy war, however repugnant they may be in the current international context, are merely political statements—and politics is not against the law.

YOU DECIDE

What kinds of prison communications should be monitored or restricted (letters, telephone calls, e-mail)? Do you believe that communications containing statements like those described here should be confiscated? What kinds of political statements (if any) should be permitted?

References: Lisa Myers, "Imprisoned Terrorists Still Advocating Terror," NBC Nightly News, February 28, 2005, http://www.msnbc.msn.com/id/7046691 (accessed August 28, 2005); and Lisa Myers, "Bureau of Prisons under Fire for Jihad Letters," March 1, 2005, http://www.msnbc.msn.com/id/7053165 (accessed August 28, 2005).

Another federal law, the Religious Land Use and Institutionalized Persons Act (RLUIPA) of 2000, has particular relevance to prison programs and activities that are at least partially supported with federal monies. RLUIPA states:

> No government shall impose a substantial burden on the religious exercise of a person residing in or confined to an institution even if the burden results from a rule of general applicability, unless the government demonstrates that imposition of the burden on that person (1) is in furtherance of a compelling governmental interest; and (2) is the least restrictive means of furthering that compelling governmental interest.

Prisoners' rights, because they are constrained by the legitimate needs of imprisonment, can be thought of as *conditional* rights rather than *absolute* rights. The Second Amendment to the U.S. Constitution, for example, grants citizens the right to bear arms. The right to arms is, however, necessarily compromised by the need for order and security in prison, and we would not expect a court to rule that inmates have a right to weapons. Prisoners' rights must be balanced against the security, order-maintenance, and treatment needs of correctional institutions.

> The Privilege of the Writ of Habeas Corpus shall not be suspended, unless when in Cases of Rebellion or Invasion the public Safety may require it.
>
> —Article I of the U.S. Constitution

Conditional rights, because they are subject to the exigencies of imprisonment, bear a strong resemblance to privileges, which should not be surprising

▲ West Virginia inmates Thomas Casey (*left*) and Robert McCabe reviewing statutes in the Huttonsville Correctional Center's law library. Casey and McCabe are known to others in the institution as jailhouse lawyers. What role do jailhouse lawyers play in today's prisons? *Courtesy Huttonsville Correctional Center*

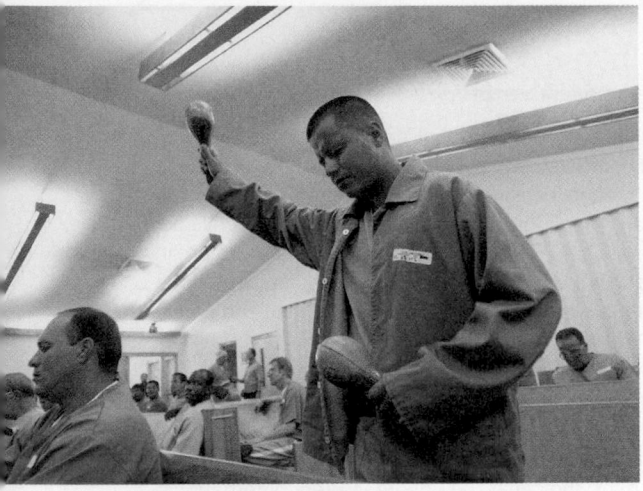

▲ Inmate Antonio Ferreria participating in a Catholic worship service at Florida's Everglades Correctional Institution. Florida has established what are called "faith-based" programs at nine of its correctional facilities. Faith-based programs are sponsored by religious organizations and supplement government-sponsored training and rehabilitation programs. What special roles might such programs play?
*© Deborah Coleman/*Palm Beach Post

since privileges were all that inmates officially had until the modern era. The practical difference between privileges and conditional rights is that privileges exist only at the convenience of granting institutions and can be revoked at any time for any reason. The rights of prisoners, in contrast, have a basis in the Constitution and in law external to the institution. The institution may restrict such rights for legitimate correctional reasons, but those rights may not be infringed without good cause that can be demonstrated in a court of law. Mere institutional convenience does not provide a sufficient legal basis for the denial of rights.

The past few decades have seen many lawsuits brought by prisoners challenging the constitutionality of some aspect of confinement. As mentioned in Chapter 9, suits filed by prisoners with the courts are generally called writs of *habeas corpus* and formally request that the person detaining a prisoner bring him or her before a judicial officer to determine the lawfulness of the imprisonment. The ACA says that most prisoner lawsuits are based on "[1] the Eighth Amendment prohibition against cruel and unusual punishment; [2] the Fourteenth Amendment prohibition against the taking of life, liberty, or property without due process of law; and [3] the Fourteenth Amendment provision requiring equal protection of the laws."[88] Aside from appeals by inmates that question the propriety of their convictions and sentences, such constitutional challenges represent the bulk of legal action initiated by those who are imprisoned. However, state statutes and federal legislation, including Section 1983 of the Civil Rights Act of 1871, provide other bases for challenges to the legality of specific prison conditions and procedures. The U.S. Supreme Court has not yet spoken with finality on a number of prisoners' rights questions. Nonetheless, high court decisions of the last few decades and a number of lower court findings can be interpreted to identify the existing conditional rights of prisoners, as shown in Table 12–2. Table 12–3 shows a number of important U.S. Supreme Court cases involving prisoners' rights claims.

Grievance Procedures

grievance procedure
A formalized arrangement, usually involving a neutral hearing board, whereby institutionalized individuals have the opportunity to register complaints about the conditions of their confinement.

Today, all sizable prisons have established **grievance procedures** through which an inmate can file a complaint with local authorities and receive a mandated response. Grievance procedures range from the use of a hearing board composed of staff members and inmates

Thematic Question Which of the conditional rights of prisoners listed in this chapter do you agree should apply to incarcerated individuals? Why? Which, in your opinion, should not? Why not?

Lecture Note Note that offenders are sentenced to prison *as* punishment, not *for* punishment. Explain that incarcerated individuals may not be physically or mentally abused and that their basic needs, including protection from harm, must be met.

Lecture Note Explain that the Eighth Amendment (against cruel and unusual punishment) and the Fourteenth Amendment (equal protection of the laws) have been used as the basis for most inmate suits against the conditions of confinement.

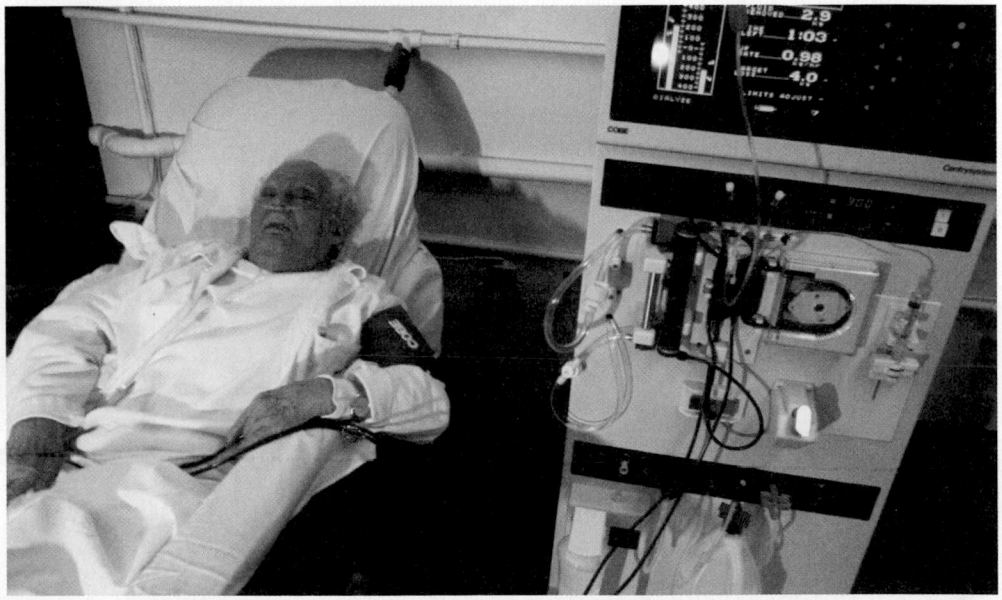

▲ Inmate Santos Pagon undergoing kidney dialysis at Laurel Highlands Prison in Pennsylvania. Court decisions over the years have established a firm set of inmate rights. Among them is the right to necessary health care. What other rights do inmates have?
Mark Peterson/CORBIS–NY

Lecture Note Review Table 12–2, and describe the conditional rights of prisoners as identified by various court decisions.

TABLE 12–2
The Conditional Rights of Inmates[a]

Communications and Visitation

A right to receive publications directly from the publisher

A right to meet with members of the press[b]

A right to communicate with nonprisoners

Religious Freedom

A right of assembly for religious services and groups

A right to attend services of other religious groups

A right to receive visits from ministers

A right to correspond with religious leaders

A right to observe religious dietary laws

A right to wear religious insignia

Access to the Courts and Legal Assistance

A right to have access to the courts[c]

A right to visits from attorneys

A right to have mail communications with lawyers[d]

A right to communicate with legal assistance organizations

A right to consult jailhouse lawyers[e]

A right to assistance in filing legal papers, which should include one of the following:

- Access to an adequate law library
- Paid attorneys
- Paralegal personnel or law students

Medical Care

A right to sanitary and healthy conditions

A right to medical attention for serious physical problems

A right to required medications

A right to treatment in accordance with "doctor's orders"

Protection from Harm

A right to food, water, and shelter

A right to protection from foreseeable attack

A right to protection from predictable sexual abuse

A right to protection against suicide

Institutional Punishment and Discipline

An absolute right against corporal punishments (unless sentenced to such punishments)

A limited right to due process before punishment, including the following:

- A notice of charges
- A fair and impartial hearing
- An opportunity for defense
- A right to present witnesses
- A written decision

[a]All "rights" listed are provisional in that they may be constrained by the legitimate needs of imprisonment.

[b]But this right does not go beyond the opportunities afforded for inmates to meet with members of the general public.

[c]This right is subject to the restrictions in the Prison Litigation Reform Act of 1996.

[d]Mail communications are generally designated as privileged or nonprivileged. Privileged communications include those between inmates and their lawyers or court officials and cannot legitimately be read by prison officials. Nonprivileged communications include most other written communications.

[e]Jailhouse lawyers are inmates with experience in the law, usually gained from filing legal briefs on their own behalf or on the behalf of others. Consultation with jailhouse lawyers was ruled permissible in the Supreme Court case of *Johnson* v. *Avery*, 393 U.S. 483 (1968), unless inmates are provided with paid legal assistance.

TABLE 12–3
Important U.S. Supreme Court Cases Involving Prisoners' Rights Claims, by Year of Decision

Case	Year Decided	Constitutional Basis	Finding
U.S. v. *Georgia*	2006		Under the Americans with Disabilities Act, a state may be liable for rights deprivations suffered by disabled inmates held in its prisons.
Johnson v. *California*	2005		A California Department of Corrections and Rehabilitation's unwritten policy of racially segregating prisoners in double cells each time they enter a new correctional facility was invalidated.
Wilkinson v. *Austin*	2005		The Court upheld an Ohio policy allowing the most dangerous offenders to be held in "supermax" cells following several levels of review prior to transfer.
Overton v. *Bazzetta*	2003		The Court upheld a visitation regulation that denies most visits to prisoners who commit two substance-abuse violations while incarcerated.
Porter v. *Nussle*	2002	Eighth Amendment	The Prison Litigation Reform Act's "exhaustion requirement" applies to all inmate suits about prison life, whether they involve general circumstances or particular events and whether they allege excessive force or some other wrong.
Hope v. *Pelzer*	2002	Eighth Amendment	The Court found a constitutional violation in the case of a prisoner who was subjected to unnecessary pain, humiliation, and risk of physical harm.
Booth v. *Churner*	2001	Eighth Amendment	The Court upheld the Prison Litigation Reform Act's requirement that state inmates must "exhaust such administrative remedies as are available" before filing a suit over prison conditions.
Lewis v. *Casey*	1996		Inmates need not be given the wherewithal to file any and every type of legal claim. All that is required is "that they be provided with the tools to attack their sentences."
Sandin v. *Conner*	1995	Fourteenth Amendment	The Court rejected the argument that disciplining inmates is a deprivation of constitutional due process rights.
Helling v. *McKinney*	1993	Eighth Amendment	Environmental conditions of prison life, including second-hand cigarette smoke, that pose a threat to inmate health have to be corrected.
Wilson v. *Seiter*	1991	Eighth Amendment	The Court clarified the totality of conditions concept by holding that some conditions of confinement, taken "in combination," may violate prisoners' rights when each would not do so alone.
Washington v. *Harper*	1990	Eighth Amendment	A mentally ill inmate who is a danger to self or others may be forcibly treated with psychoactive drugs.
Turner v. *Safley*	1987	First Amendment	A ban on correspondence between Missouri inmates was upheld as "reasonably related to legitimate penological interests."
O'Lone v. *Estate of Shabazz*	1987	First Amendment	An inmate's right to religious practice was not violated by prison officials who refused to alter his work schedule so that he could attend Friday afternoon services.
Whitley v. *Albers*	1986	Eighth Amendment	The shooting and wounding of an inmate was not a violation of that inmate's rights, because "the shooting was part and parcel of a good-faith effort to restore prison security."
Ponte v. *Real*	1985		Inmates are entitled to certain rights in disciplinary hearings.
Hudson v. *Palmer*	1984	Fourth Amendment	A prisoner has no reasonable expectation of privacy in his prison cell and no protections against what would otherwise be "unreasonable searches."

(*continued*)

TABLE 12–3
Important U.S. Supreme Court Cases Involving Prisoners' Rights Claims, by Year of Decision (*continued*)

Case	Year Decided	Constitutional Basis	Finding
Block v. *Rutherford*	1984	First Amendment	State regulations may prohibit meetings of inmate unions as well as the use of the mail to deliver union information within the prison; also, prisoners do not have a right to be present during cell searches.
Rhodes v. *Chapman*	1981	Eighth Amendment	Double-celling of inmates is not in itself cruel and unusual punishment.
Ruiz v. *Estelle*	1980	Eighth Amendment	Unconstitutional conditions were found to exist within the Texas prison system—including overcrowding, understaffing, brutality, and substandard medical care.
Cooper v. *Morin*	1980		Neither inconvenience nor cost is an acceptable excuse for treating female inmates differently from male inmates.
Bell v. Wolfish	1979	Fourth Amendment	Strip searches, including body-cavity searches, may be conducted when the need for such searches outweighs individual rights.
Jones v. *North Carolina Prisoners' Labor Union, Inc.*	1977	First Amendment	Inmates have no inherent right to publish newspapers or newsletters for use by other inmates.
Bounds v. *Smith*	1977		This decision resulted in the creation of law libraries in many prisons.
Estelle v. *Gamble*	1976	Eighth Amendment	Prison officials have a duty to provide proper inmate medical care.
Ruiz v. *Estelle*	1975	Eighth Amendment	Conditions of confinement within the Texas prison system were found to be unconstitutional.
Wolff v. *McDonnell*	1974	Fourteenth Amendment	Sanctions cannot be levied against inmates without appropriate due process.
Procunier v. *Martinez*	1974	First Amendment	Censorship of inmate mail is acceptable only when necessary to protect legitimate governmental interests.
Pell v. *Procunier*	1974	First Amendment	Inmates retain First Amendment rights that are not inconsistent with their status as prisoners or with the legitimate penological objectives of the corrections system.
U.S. v. *Hitchcock*	1972	Fourth Amendment	A warrantless cell search is not unreasonable.
Cruz v. *Beto*	1972	First Amendment	Inmates have to be given a "reasonable opportunity" to pursue their religious faiths; also, visits can be banned if they constitute a threat to security.
Johnson v. *Avery*	1968		Inmates have a right to consult "jailhouse lawyers" when trained legal assistance is not available.
Monroe v. *Pape*	1961		Inmates have a right to bring action in federal court when deprived of their rights by state officers acting under color of state law.

to a single staff appointee charged with the resolution of complaints. Inmates who are dissatisfied with the handling of their grievances can generally appeal beyond the local prison.

Disciplinary actions by prison authorities may also require a formalized hearing process, especially when staff members bring charges of rule violations against inmates that might result in some form of punishment being imposed on them. In a precedent-setting decision in the case of *Wolff* v. *McDonnell* (1974),[89] the Supreme Court decided that sanctions could not be levied against inmates without appropriate due process. The *Wolff* case involved an inmate who had been deprived of previously earned good-time credits because of misbehavior. The Court established that good-time credits were a form of "state-created right(s)," which, once created, could not be "arbitrarily abrogated."[90] *Wolff* was especially significant because it began an era of court scrutiny of what came to be called *state-created liberty interests*, which were said to be based on the language used in published prison regulations and were held, in effect, to confer due process guarantees on prisoners. Hence if a prison regulation said that a disciplinary hearing should be held before a prisoner could be sent to solitary confinement and that the hearing should permit a discussion of the evidence for and against the prisoner, courts interpreted that regulation to mean that the prisoner had a state-created right to a hearing. Sending him or her to solitary confinement in violation of the regulation was seen as a violation of a state-created liberty interest. In later court decisions, state-created rights and privileges were called *protected liberties* and were interpreted to include any significant change in a prisoner's status.

Lecture Note Comment on the observation made in the text that the U.S. Supreme Court may have signaled at least a partial return to the hands-off doctrine. Use the case of *Wilson* v. *Seiter* (1991) as the basis for a discussion of the issue.

Thematic Question What was the hands-off doctrine? Do you believe we should return to a hands-off policy? Explain. Would the hands-off doctrine be more likely to appeal to public-order advocates or to individual-rights advocates? Why?

In the interest of due process, and especially where written prison regulations governing the hearing process exist, courts have generally held that inmates going before disciplinary hearing boards are entitled to (1) a notice of the charges brought against them, (2) the chance to organize a defense, (3) an impartial hearing, and (4) the opportunity to present witnesses and evidence in their behalf. A written statement of the hearing board's conclusions should be provided to the inmate.[91] In the case of *Ponte* v. *Real* (1985),[92] the Supreme Court held that prison officials must provide an explanation to inmates who are denied the opportunity to have a desired witness at their hearing. The case of *Vitek* v. *Jones* (1980)[93] extended the requirement of due process to inmates about to be transferred from prisons to mental hospitals.

So that inmates will know what is expected of them as they enter prison, the ACA recommends that "a rulebook that contains all chargeable offenses, ranges of penalties and disciplinary procedures [be] posted in a conspicuous and accessible area; [and] a copy . . . given to each inmate and staff member."[94]

A Return to the Hands-Off Doctrine?

Many state-created rights and protected liberties may soon be a thing of the past. In June 1991, an increasingly conservative U.S. Supreme Court signaled the beginning of what appears to be at least a partial return to the hands-off doctrine of earlier times. The case, *Wilson* v. *Seiter*,[95] involved a Section 1983 suit brought against Richard P. Seiter, then-director of the Ohio Department of Rehabilitation and Correction, and Carl Humphreys, warden of the Hocking Correctional Facility (HCF) in Nelsonville, Ohio. In the suit, Pearly L. Wilson, a felon incarcerated at HCF, alleged that a number of the conditions of his confinement constituted cruel and unusual punishment in violation of the Eighth and Fourteenth Amendments to the U.S. Constitution. Specifically, Wilson cited overcrowding, excessive noise, insufficient locker storage space, inadequate heating and cooling, improper ventilation, unclean and inadequate restrooms, unsanitary dining facilities and food preparation, and housing with mentally and physically ill inmates. Wilson asked for a change in prison conditions and sought $900,000 from prison officials in compensatory and punitive damages.

Both the federal district court in which Wilson first filed affidavits and the Sixth Circuit Court of Appeals held that no constitutional violations existed because the conditions cited by Wilson were not the result of malicious intent on the part of officials. The U.S. Supreme Court agreed, noting that the **deliberate indifference** standard applied in *Estelle* v. *Gamble* (1976)[96] to claims involving medical care is similarly applicable to other cases in which prisoners challenge the conditions of their confinement. In effect, the Court created a standard that effectively means that all future challenges to prison conditions by inmates, which are brought under the Eighth Amendment, must show deliberate indifference by the officials responsible for the existence of those conditions before the Court will hear the complaint.

deliberate indifference
A wanton disregard by corrections personnel for the well-being of inmates. Deliberate indifference requires both actual knowledge that a harm is occurring and disregard of the risk of harm that is occurring. A prison official may be held liable under the Eighth Amendment for acting with deliberate indifference to inmate health or safety only if he or she knows that inmates face a substantial risk of serious harm and disregards that risk by failing to take reasonable measures to abate it.

The written opinion of the Court in *Wilson* v. *Seiter* is telling. Writing for the majority, Justice Antonin Scalia observed that "if a prison boiler malfunctions accidentally during a cold winter, an inmate would have no basis for an Eighth Amendment claim, even if he suffers objectively significant harm. If a guard accidentally stepped on a prisoner's toe and broke it, this would not be punishment in anything remotely like the accepted meaning of the word." At the time that the *Wilson* decision was handed down, critics voiced concerns that the decision could effectively excuse prison authorities from the need to improve living conditions within institutions on the basis of simple budgetary constraints.

Freedom or Safety? You Decide.

Should Prison Libraries Limit Access to Potentially Inflammatory Literature?

In mid-2007, Federal Bureau of Prisons (BOP) authorities ordered chaplains at BOP facilities nationwide to remove potentially inflammatory literature from the shelves of chapel libraries. The move came in response to a report by the U.S. Justice Department's Office of the Inspector General, which recommended that prisons should take steps to avoid becoming recruiting grounds for militant Islamists and other radical groups.

Thousands of books were soon removed under what the BOP called the Standardized Chapel Library Project (SCLP), which it admitted was an effort to bar inmate access to literature that the BOP felt could "discriminate, disparage, advocate violence or radicalize." In identifying materials for removal, the BOP relied on the advice of experts who were asked to identify up to 150 book titles and 150 multimedia resources for each of 20 religious categories ranging from Bahaism to Yoruba. Prayer books were explicitly excluded from the list of materials targeted for removal.

Soon after the project was made public, however, members of Congress and a number of religious leaders urged the BOP to reverse its stance and return the books to chapel shelves.

In the fall of 2007, the Republican Study Committee, a group of conservative Republicans in the House of Representatives, sent a letter to BOP Director Harley G. Lappin, saying, "We must ensure that in America the federal government is not the undue arbiter of what may or may not be read by our citizens."

Representative Jeb Hensarling, who heads the Republican Study Committee, explained that "anything that impinges upon the religious liberties of American citizens, be they incarcerated or not, is something that's going to cause . . . great concern." For its part, the BOP countered that it has a legitimate interest in screening out and removing items from inside of its facilities that could incite violence.

The controversy appeared to have been partially resolved when, on September 26, 2007, a BOP spokesperson announced that "in response to concerns expressed by members of several religious communities, the Bureau of Prisons has decided to alter its planned course of action with respect to the Chapel Library Project [and] the bureau will begin immediately to return to chapel libraries materials that were removed . . . with the exception of any publications that have been found to be inappropriate, such as materials that could be radicalizing or incite violence."

The controversy appears to have ended in 2008 with passage of the Second Chance Act (Public Law No 110–199). This federal legislation, which funded a number of reentry initiatives for people leaving prison, required the director of the BOP "to discontinue the Standardized Chapel Library project or any other project that limits prisoner access to reading and other educational material." The Second Chance Act is discussed in more detail in Chapter 10.

YOU DECIDE

Should prison libraries be permitted to limit access to library literature that might incite violence or endanger the safety of inmates and staff? Would it matter if that literature is religious in nature? How might the Bureau of Prisons meet the concerns of the Republican Study Committee, religious leaders, and authors of the Second Chance Act while still accomplishing its objective of removing literature that it believes might incite violence?

References: Laurie Goodstein, "Prisons Purging Books on Faith from Libraries," *New York Times*, September 10, 2007; Laurie Goodstein, "Critics Right and Left Protest Book Removals," *New York Times*, September 21, 2007; and Neela Banerjee, "Prisons to Restore Purged Religious Books," *New York Times*, September 27, 2007.

In the 1995 case of *Sandin* v. *Conner*,[97] the U.S. Supreme Court took a much more definitive stance in favor of a new type of hands-off doctrine and voted 5 to 4 to reject the argument that any state action taken for a punitive reason encroaches on a prisoner's constitutional due process right to be free from the deprivation of liberty. In *Sandin*, Demont Conner, an inmate at the Halawa Correctional Facility in Hawaii, was serving an indeterminate sentence of 30 years to life for numerous crimes, including murder, kidnapping, robbery, and burglary. In a lawsuit in federal court, Conner alleged that prison officials had deprived him of procedural due process when a hearing committee refused to allow him to present witnesses during a disciplinary hearing and then sentenced him to segregation for alleged misconduct. An appellate court agreed with Conner, concluding that an existing prison regulation that instructed the hearing committee to find guilt in cases where a misconduct charge is supported by substantial evidence meant that the committee could not impose segregation if it did not look at all the evidence available to it.

The Supreme Court, however, reversed the decision of the appellate court, holding that while "such a conclusion may be entirely sensible in the ordinary task of construing a statute defining rights and remedies available to the general public, [i]t is a good deal less sensible in the case of a prison regulation primarily designed to guide corrections officials in the administration of a prison." The Court concluded that "such regulations [are] not designed to confer rights on inmates" but are meant only to provide guidelines to prison staff members.

In *Sandin*, the Court effectively set aside substantial portions of earlier decisions, such as *Wolff* v. *McDonnell* (1974)[98] and *Hewitt* v. *Helms* (1983),[99] which, wrote the justices, focused more on procedural issues than on those of "real substance." As a consequence, the majority opinion held, past cases like these have "impermissibly shifted the focus" away from

To return to society discharged prisoners unreformed is to poison it with the worst elements possible.

–Zebulon R. Brockway (1827-1920)[i]

the nature of a due process deprivation to one based on the language of a particular state or prison regulation. "The *Hewitt* approach," wrote the majority in *Sandin*, "has run counter to the view expressed in several of our cases that federal courts ought to afford appropriate deference and flexibility to state officials trying to manage a volatile environment. The time has come," said the Court, "to return to those due process principles that were correctly established and applied" in earlier times. In short, *Sandin* made it much more difficult for inmates to effectively challenge the administrative regulations and procedures imposed on them by prison officials, even when stated procedures are not explicitly followed.

A more recent case whose findings support the action of federal corrections officers is that of *Ali* v. *Federal Bureau of Prisons.* The case, decided by the U.S. Supreme Court in 2008,[100] involved a federal prisoner named Abdus-Shahid M. S. Ali, who claimed that some of his personal belongings disappeared when he was transferred from one federal prison to another. The missing items, which were to have been shipped in two duffle bags belonging to Ali, included copies of the Koran, a prayer rug, and a number of religious magazines. Ali filed suit against the Bureau of Prisons (BOP) under the Federal Tort Claims Act (FTCA),[101] which authorizes "claims against the United States for money damages . . . for injury or loss of property . . . caused by the negligent or wrongful act or omission of any employee in the government while acting within the scope of his office or employment." In denying Ali's claim, the Court found that the law specifically provides immunity for federal law enforcement officers and determined that federal corrections personnel are "law enforcement officers" within the meaning of the law.

The Prison Litigation Reform Act of 1996

Only about 2,000 petitions per year concerning inmate problems were filed with the courts in 1961, but by 1975 the number of filings had increased to around 17,000. In 1996, prisoners filed 68,235 civil rights lawsuits in federal courts nationwide.[102] Some inmate-originated suits seemed patently ludicrous and became the subject of much media coverage in the mid-1990s. One such suit involved Robert Procup, a Florida State Prison inmate serving time for the murder of his business partner. Procup repeatedly sued Florida prison officials—once because he got only one roll with his dinner, again because he didn't get a luncheon salad, a third time because prison-provided TV dinners didn't come with a drink, and a fourth time because his cell had no television. Two other well-publicized cases involved an inmate who went to court asking to be allowed to exercise religious freedom by attending prison chapel services in the nude and an inmate who, thinking he could become pregnant via homosexual relations, sued prison doctors who wouldn't provide him with birth-control pills. An infamous example of seemingly frivolous inmate lawsuits was one brought by inmates claiming religious freedom and demanding that members of the Church of the New Song, or CONS, be provided steak and Harvey's Bristol Cream every Friday in order to celebrate communion. The CONS suit stayed in various courts for ten years before finally being thrown out.[103]

The huge number of inmate-originated lawsuits in the mid-1990s created a backlog of cases in many federal courts and was targeted by the media and by some citizens' groups as an unnecessary waste of taxpayers' money. The National Association of Attorneys General, which supports efforts to restrict frivolous inmate lawsuits, estimated that lawsuits filed by prisoners cost states more than $81 million a year in legal fees alone.[104]

In 1996, the federal Prison Litigation Reform Act (PLRA) became law.[105] The PLRA is a clear legislative effort to restrict inmate filings to worthwhile cases and to reduce the number of suits brought by state prisoners in federal courts by the following means:

- Requiring inmates to exhaust any available administrative remedies (generally, their prison's grievance procedures) before filing a federal lawsuit challenging prison conditions
- Requiring judges to screen all inmate complaints against the federal government and to immediately dismiss those deemed frivolous or without merit
- Prohibiting prisoners from filing a lawsuit for mental or emotional injury unless they can also show there has been physical injury

- Requiring inmates to pay court filing fees (prisoners who don't have the needed funds can pay the filing fee over a period of time through deductions to their prison commissary accounts)
- Limiting the award of attorneys' fees in successful lawsuits brought by inmates
- Revoking the credits earned by federal prisoners toward early release if they file a malicious lawsuit
- Mandating that court orders affecting prison administration cannot go any further than necessary to correct a violation of a particular inmate's civil rights
- Making it possible for state officials to have court orders lifted after two years unless there is a new finding of a continuing violation of federally guaranteed civil rights
- Mandating that any court order requiring the release of prisoners due to overcrowding be approved by a three-member court before it can become effective

The U.S. Supreme Court has upheld provisions of the PLRA on a number of occasions.[106] According to one BJS study, the PLRA has been effective in reducing the number of frivolous lawsuits filed by inmates alleging unconstitutional prison conditions.[107] The study found that the filing rate of inmates' civil rights petitions in federal courts had been cut in half four years after passage of the act.

Opponents of the PLRA fear that it is stifling the filing of meritorious suits by inmates facing real deprivations. According to the American Civil Liberties Union (ACLU), for example, "The Prison Litigation Reform Act . . . attempts to slam the courthouse door on society's most vulnerable members. It seeks to strip the federal courts of much of their power to correct even the most egregious prison conditions by altering the basic rules which have always governed prison reform litigation. The PLRA also makes it difficult to settle prison cases by consent decree, and [it] limits the life span of any court judgment."[108] The ACLU has led a nationwide effort to have many provisions of the PLRA overturned, but so far, its effort has borne little fruit.

Issues Facing Prisons Today

Prisons are society's answer to a number of social problems because they house outcasts, misfits, and some highly dangerous people. Although prisons provide a part of the answer to the question of crime control, they also face problems of their own. A few of those special problems are described here.

6 Describe the major problems and issues that prisons face today.

AIDS

Chapter 6 discussed the steps that police agencies are taking to deal with health threats from acquired immunodeficiency syndrome (AIDS). In 2009, the Justice Department reported finding that 21,987 state and federal inmates were infected with the human immunodeficiency virus (HIV).[109] At the time of the survey, 1.9% of all female state prison inmates tested positive for HIV infection, as did 1.5% of male prisoners. Some states have especially high rates of HIV infection among their prisoners. Almost 6% of New York prison inmates, for example, are HIV-positive.

Lecture Note Identify some of the major issues facing prisons today, including AIDS, geriatric offenders, and mentally ill inmates. Ask students whether they can envision any similar kinds of issues that might be on the horizon, waiting to emerge.

The incidence of HIV infection among the general population stands at 140 cases per 100,000, according to a recent report by the Centers for Disease Control and Prevention. Among inmates, however, best estimates place the reported HIV infection rate at 510 cases per 100,000[110]—more than two times as great. A few years ago, AIDS was the leading cause of death among prison inmates.[111] Today, however, the number of inmates who die from AIDS (or, more precisely, from AIDS-related complications such as pneumonia or Kaposi's sarcoma) is much lower than it has been in the past. The introduction of drugs such as protease inhibitors and the useful combinations of antiretroviral therapies have reduced inmate deaths from AIDS by 73% since 1995.[112]

140 cases general pop.

510 prison inmates

Most infected inmates brought HIV into prison with them. One study found that fewer than 10% of HIV-positive inmates acquired the virus while in prison.[113] Nonetheless, the virus can be spread behind bars through homosexual activity (including rape), intravenous drug use, and the sharing of tainted tattoo and hypodermic needles. Inmates who were infected before entering prison are likely to have had histories of high-risk behavior, especially intravenous drug use.

A report by the National Institute of Justice (NIJ) suggests that corrections administrators can use two types of strategies to reduce the transmission of AIDS.[114] One strategy relies on medical technology to identify seropositive inmates and to segregate them from the rest of the prison population. Mass screening and inmate segregation, however, may be prohibitively expensive, and such actions may also be illegal. Some states specifically prohibit HIV testing without the informed consent of the person tested.[115] The related issue of confidentiality may be difficult to manage, especially when the purpose of testing is to segregate infected inmates from others. In addition, civil liability may result if inmates are falsely labeled as infected or if inmates known to be infected are not prevented from spreading the disease. Only Alabama and South Carolina still segregate all known HIV-infected inmates,[116] but more limited forms of separation are practiced elsewhere. Many state prison systems have denied HIV-positive inmates jobs, educational opportunities, visitation privileges, conjugal visits, and home furloughs, causing some researchers to conclude that "inmates with HIV and AIDS are routinely discriminated against and denied equal treatment in ways that have no accepted medical basis."[117] In 1994, for example, a federal appeals court upheld a California prison policy that bars inmates who are HIV-positive from working in food-service jobs.[118] In contrast, in 2001, the Mississippi Department of Correction ended its policy of segregating HIV-positive prisoners from other inmates in educational and vocational programs.

The second strategy is one of prevention through education. Educational programs teach both inmates and staff members about the dangers of high-risk behavior and suggest ways to avoid HIV infection. An NIJ model program recommends the use of simple, straightforward messages presented by knowledgeable and approachable trainers.[119] Alarmism, says NIJ, should be avoided. One survey found that 98% of state and federal prisons provide some form of AIDS/HIV education and that 90% of jails do as well—although most such training is oriented toward corrections staff rather than inmates.[120] Learn more about HIV in prisons and jails at **Library Extra 12–8**. Inmate medical problems in general are discussed at **Library Extra 12–9**.

Geriatric Offenders

In 2003, Eugene Guevara of El Monte, California, allegedly shot a physician at Kaiser Permanente's Baldwin Park Medical Center.[121] Surveillance cameras filmed Guevara, who was in his late 70s, fleeing the scene with the aid of a walker. Crimes committed by the elderly, especially violent crimes, have recently been on the decline. Nonetheless, the significant expansion of America's retiree population has led to an increase in the number of elderly people who are behind bars. In fact, crimes of violence are what bring most older people into the correctional system. According to one early study, 52% of inmates who were over the age of 50 when they entered prison had committed violent crimes, compared with 41% of younger inmates.[122] On January 1, 2009, a total of 77,800 inmates ages 55 or older were housed in state and federal prisons, and the number of prisoners older than age 55 increased more than 450% between 1990 and 2009.[123] Similarly, the per capita rate of incarceration for inmates age 55 and over now stands at 258 per 100,000 residents of like age and continues to increase.

▲ Elderly inmates inside the geriatric unit of Texas's Estelle Prison. Geriatric inmates are becoming an increasingly large part of the inmate population. Why is the proportion of geriatric inmates increasing?
Andrew Lichtenstein/The Image Works

Not all of today's elderly inmates were old when they entered prison. Because of harsh sentencing laws passed throughout the country in the 1990s, a small but growing number of inmates (10%) will serve 20 years or more in prison, and 5% will never be released.[124] This means that many inmates who enter prison when they are young will grow old behind bars. This "graying" of America's prison population has a number of causes:[125]

1. The general aging of the American population, which is reflected inside prisons
2. Some new sentencing policies such as "three strikes," "truth in sentencing," and "mandatory minimum" laws that send more criminals to prison for longer stretches

3. A massive prison building boom that took place in the 1980s and 1990s and [that] has provided space for more inmates, reducing the need to release prisoners to alleviate overcrowding
4. Significant changes in parole philosophies and practices

The last point means that state and federal authorities are phasing out or canceling parole programs, thereby forcing jailers to hold inmates with life sentences until they die.

Long-termers and geriatric inmates have special needs: They tend to suffer from handicaps, physical impairments, and illnesses not generally encountered among their more youthful counterparts. Unfortunately, few prisons are equipped to deal adequately with the medical needs of aging offenders. Some large facilities have begun to set aside special sections to care for elderly inmates with "typical" disorders, such as Alzheimer's disease, cancer, or heart disease. Unfortunately, such efforts have barely kept pace with the problems that geriatric offenders present. The number of inmates requiring around-the-clock care is expected to increase dramatically during the next two decades.[126]

The idea of rehabilitation takes on a new meaning where geriatric offenders are concerned. What kinds of programs are most useful in providing the older inmate with the tools needed for success on the outside? Which counseling strategies hold the greatest promise for introducing socially acceptable behavior patterns into the long-established lifestyles of elderly offenders about to be released? There are few answers to these questions. Learn about some of the oldest prisoners in America at **Web Extra 12–4**.

Lecture Note Discuss the factors leading to a higher incidence of geriatric offenders. How does this situation affect prisoners' rights to medical treatment, which was discussed earlier in this chapter?

Mentally Ill and Mentally Deficient Inmates

Mentally ill inmates make up another group with special needs. Some mentally ill inmates are neurotic or have personality problems, which increase tension in prison. Others have serious psychological disorders that may have escaped diagnosis at trial or that did not provide a legal basis for the reduction of criminal responsibility. A fair number of offenders develop psychiatric symptoms while in prison.

Inmates suffering from significant mental illnesses account for a substantial number of those imprisoned. A 2002 lawsuit brought by a New York advocacy group on behalf of mentally ill prisoners in New York's penal institutions put the number of inmates suffering from psychiatric illnesses at 16,000 (out of a total state prison population of 67,000). The suit alleges that problem inmates with psychiatric illnesses are often isolated, exacerbating their condition and resulting in a "cycle of torment" for inmates unable to conform to prison regimens.[127]

In contrast to the allegations made by the lawsuit, a 2000 BJS survey of public and private state-level adult correctional facilities (excluding jails) found that 51% of such institutions provide 24-hour mental health care, while 71% provide therapy and counseling by trained mental health professionals as needed.[128] A large majority of prisons distribute psychotropic medications (when such medications are ordered by a physician), and 66% have programs to help released inmates obtain community mental health services. According to the BJS, 13% of state prisoners were receiving some type of mental health therapy at the time of the survey, and 10% were receiving psychotropic medications (including antidepressants, stimulants, sedatives, and tranquilizers).

Unfortunately, few state-run correctional institutions have any substantial capacity for the in-depth psychiatric treatment of inmates who have serious mental illnesses. A number of states, however, do operate facilities that specialize in the psychiatric confinement of convicted criminals. The BJS reports that state governments throughout the nation operate 12 facilities devoted exclusively to the care of mentally ill inmates and that another 143 prisons report psychiatric confinement as one specialty among other functions that they perform.

As mentioned previously, the U.S. Supreme Court has ruled that mentally ill inmates can be required to take antipsychotic drugs, even against their wishes.[129] One BJS study found that the nation's prisons and jails hold an estimated 283,800 mentally ill inmates (16% of those confined) and that 547,800 such offenders are on probation.[130] The government study also found that 40% of mentally ill inmates receive no treatment at all. For more details about the report, visit **Web Extra 12–5**.

Mentally deficient inmates constitute still another group with special needs. Some studies estimate the proportion of mentally deficient inmates at about 10%.[131] Inmates with low IQs are less likely than other inmates to complete training and rehabilitative programs successfully, and they also evidence difficulty in adjusting to the routines of prison life. As a consequence, they are likely to exceed the averages in proportion of sentence served.[132] Only seven states report special facilities or programs for the mentally retarded inmate.[133] Other state systems "mainstream" such inmates, making them participate in regular activities with other inmates.

Terrorism

Today's antiterrorism efforts have brought to light the important role that corrections personnel can play in preventing future attacks on American society and in averting crises that could arise in correctional institutions as a result of terrorist action. In 2005, former New York City Police Commissioner Bernard B. Kerik told participants at the ACA's winter conference that corrections officers can help in the fight against terrorism through effective intelligence gathering and intelligence sharing. "Intelligence—that's the key to the success of this battle," Kerik said.[134] "You have to be part of that, because when we take the people off the streets in this country that go to jail, they communicate and they talk, they work with other criminals, organized gangs, organized units. You've got to collect that information, [and] you have to get it back to the authorities that need it."

Jess Maghan, director of the Forum for Comparative Corrections and professor of criminal justice at the University of Illinois at Chicago, points to the critical role that intelligence gathering and analysis by correctional agencies can play in providing critical information to prevent terrorist attacks. Maghan states that "the interaction of all people in a prison (staff, officers, and inmates) can become important intelligence sources."[135] Moreover, says Maghan, the flow of information between inmates and the outside world must be monitored to detect attack plans, especially when prisons house known terrorist leaders or group members. Vital intelligence, according to Maghan, can be passed through legal visits (where people conveying information may have no idea of its significance), sub-rosa communications networks in prisons that can support communications between inmates and the outside world, and prison transportation systems.

The security problems presented by potential information leaks were demonstrated in 2003 at the U.S. Navy's Guantanamo Bay prison in Cuba when a translator working with Arab internees was accused of having unlawful possession of classified information, including diagrams of the prison layout and names of the prisoners. Prison administrators responsible for the incarceration of suspected al-Qaeda and Taliban members, like those at Guantanamo, face especially delicate situations as opponents of the government's policies challenge the propriety of using military assets in what they argue is a "law enforcement" role.

Prison administrators must also be concerned about the potential impact of outside terrorist activity on their facility's inmate and staff populations. Of particular concern to today's prison administrators is the possibility of bioterrorism because a concentrated population like that of a prison or jail is highly susceptible to the rapid transmission of biological agents.[136]

The threat of a terrorist act being undertaken by inmates within a prison or jail can be an important consideration in facility planning and management, especially because inmates may be particularly vulnerable to recruitment by terrorist organizations. According to Chip Ellis, research and program coordinator for the National Memorial Institute for the Prevention of Terrorism, "Prisoners are a captive audience, and they usually have a diminished sense of self or a need for identity and protection. They're usually a disenchanted or disenfranchised group of people, [and] terrorists can sometimes capitalize on that situation."[137] Inmates can be radicalized in many ways, including exposure to other radical inmates, distribution of extremist literature, and anti-U.S. sermons heard during religious services.

Thematic Question What role can corrections personnel play in preventing future attacks of terrorism?

Officials of the Federal Bureau of Investigation (FBI) say al-Qaeda continues to actively recruit members in U.S. prisons and looks especially to the 9,600 Muslims held in the federal prison system. "These terrorists seek to exploit our freedom to exercise religion to their advantage by using radical forms of Islam to recruit operatives," says FBI Counterterrorism

Chief John Pistole. "Unfortunately, U.S. correctional institutions are a viable venue for such radicalization and recruitment."[138] In 2005, the Institute for the Study of Violent Groups, located at Sam Houston State University, charged that the most radical form of Islam, or Wahhabism, was being spread in American prisons by clerics approved by the Islamic Society of North America, one of two organizations chosen by the BOP to select prison chaplains.[139] "Proselytizing in prisons," said an institute spokesperson, "can produce new recruits with American citizenship."

An example of such activity can be found in the story of accused terrorist Kevin James, who, in 2009, was sentenced to 16 years in federal prison. James pleaded guilty in 2007 to conspiracy to wage war against the United States[140] and was accused of plotting terrorist attacks on Jewish and military targets throughout California. Among his targets were Los Angeles International Airport, the Israeli Consulate, and Army recruiting centers. Investigators found that James had formed an Islamic terrorist group in California's Tehachapi Prison in 1997. While serving a ten-year sentence for robbery, James joined the Nation of Islam—a traditional American Islamic faith. Soon, however, he became involved with a fringe group of Sunni Muslims at Tehachapi. Today, the group, known as *Jam'iyyat Ul-Islam Is-Saheeh* (the Assembly of Authentic Islam, or JIS), operates throughout prisons in California. This radical Islamist prison gang advocates attacking enemies of the Islamic faith, the U.S. government, Jews, "infidels," and supporters of Israel. Eventually, James took control of JIS and began distributing a handwritten manifesto in which he justified the killing of infidels. Following transfer to the maximum-security California State Prison in Sacramento, James recruited more inmates to join JIS and used inmates who were about to be paroled to recruit additional members outside of prison. Through smuggled letters and phone calls, James communicated his plans for terrorist attacks to recruits on the outside.

Thematic Question What kinds of terrorist activity might occur in prison? What steps can corrections personnel take to reduce the threat of terrorist activity in their facilities?

In 2004 the Office of the Inspector General of the U.S. Department of Justice released its review of the BOP's practices in selecting Muslim clergy to minister to inmates in BOP facilities. The report concluded that the primary threat of radicalization comes from inmates, not chaplains, contractors, or volunteers. The report goes on to say that "inmates from foreign countries politicize Islam and radicalize inmates, who in turn radicalize more inmates when they transfer to other prisons."[141] The report also identified a form of Islam unique to the prison environment called "prison Islam."[142] Prison Islam, the report said, adapts itself to prison values and is used by gangs and radical inmates to further unlawful goals. It was found to be especially common in institutions where religious services are led by lay *mullahs* (spiritual leaders)—a practice made necessary by a lack of Muslim chaplains. The report concluded with a number of recommendations, including one that the BOP should provide staff training on Islam so that corrections officers can recognize radical Islamist messages.

In response, the BOP implemented a number of new practices, and today it coordinates with other federal agencies to share intelligence information about suspected or known terrorists in its inmate population. The BOP closely tracks inmates with known or suspected terrorist ties and monitors their correspondence and other communications. The bureau also trains staff members to recognize terrorist-related activity and to effectively manage convicted terrorists within a correctional environment. A BOP program to counter radicalization efforts among inmates has been in place for the past several years.[143]

The incarceration of convicted terrorists presents new challenges for corrections administrators at both the state and federal levels. Sheik Omar Abdel-Rahman, a blind Muslim cleric and spiritual leader for many Islamic terrorists (including Osama bin Laden), is currently serving a life sentence in a U.S. federal penitentiary for conspiring to assassinate Egyptian President Hosni Mubarak and to blow up five New York City landmarks in the 1990s. Speculation that the sheik continues to motivate terrorist acts against the United States gained credibility when his attorney and three others were indicted in April 2002 for allegedly passing illegal communications between Abdel-Rahman and an Egyptian-based terrorist organization known as the Islamic Group.[144]

The current world situation, and the environment in which correctional agencies operate, is likely to ensure that the issues identified here will take on ever-increasing significance for prison administrators of the future. Learn more about prison issues of all kinds from the Prison Policy Initiative at **Web Extra 12–6**. Read about concerns about Muslim religious services in correctional institutions at **Library Extra 12–10**.

A PowerPoint presentation that supports this chapter is available from your Prentice Hall representative.

CJ News
Feds Target Terrorist Recruiting in Prisons

The federal government is working with prisons in dozens of states to improve intelligence gathering and monitoring of inmates in a stepped-up campaign to curb homegrown terrorism behind bars.

The FBI and Homeland Security Department are urging prison officials to do more extensive background checks on workers and volunteers who meet with inmates. And members of Congress are looking at possible reforms in prison security as a way to combat the spread of extremist Islamic beliefs.

Chief among the concerns is that radical Muslim clerics could have access to prisoners and coerce them with terrorist literature.

"It's a concern because we know that violent extremist groups will target people in prisons," said Donald Van Duyn, the FBI's counterterrorism director. "We're working to improve monitoring, improve training and increase awareness."

The intensified surveillance follows the recent arrests of people alleged to be homegrown terrorism suspects in London and Canada, which have raised concerns that the United States may be vulnerable to terrorism at the hands of its own citizens. British authorities said in August [2006] that they broke up a conspiracy to blow up U.S.-bound airliners with liquid bombs, and Canadian officials charged 17 people in June [2006] with an al-Qaeda-inspired plot to possess 3 tons of bomb-making materials.

Homeland Security officials, who are sending investigators to prisons around the country to gather intelligence on inmate radicalization, are worried that similar plots could be hatched in U.S. prisons. "Prisons can be a breeding ground," says Charles Allen, Homeland Security's top intelligence officer.

Among the steps that the FBI and Homeland Security are urging prisons to take:

- Develop more informants and set up more intelligence units in state prison systems. The FBI is encouraging prison systems to set up their own intelligence units and to work with local agents to share information. The bureau won't say whether it has undercover agents in the nation's prisons.
- Train more prison staff to recognize signs that prisoners are turning to extremist propaganda, sharing radical views, and attempting to convert other inmates.
- Conduct background checks on volunteers and workers to ensure extremist Muslim clerics don't have access to prisoners.

"Our concern is not with prison inmates converting to Islam," says Sen. Susan Collins, R–Maine, chairwoman of the Senate Homeland Security Committee. "For many converts, this religion brings the direction and purpose their lives previously lacked."

▲ Muslim inmate Christopher McCullon, with his prayer rug draped over his shoulder, talking with Muslim corrections officer Umar Abddullah after weekly worship in a room used as a mosque at Rikers Island Correctional Institution in New York City. How might corrections officers help in the nation's fight against terrorism? *Stephan Savoia/AP Wide World Photos*

A case in California shows how some U.S. prisons have spawned converts to radical forms of Islam.

Members of an extremist group robbed a dozen Los Angeles gas stations in 2005 to raise money to finance terrorist attacks on the United States.

The group's founder, Kevin James, is alleged by the FBI to have recruited members from prison. Four members of the group are awaiting trial on charges including conspiracy to levy war against the U.S. government.

"We have to wonder how many other such conspiracies are taking shape under the radar in other prisons," Collins says.

Source: Mimi Hall, "Feds Target Terrorist Recruiting in Prisons," *USA Today*, November 7, 2006, p. 1A. Reprinted with permission.

Summary

PRISON LIFE

- Prisons are small self-contained societies that are sometimes described as total institutions. Studies of prison life have detailed the existence of prison subcultures, or inmate worlds, replete with inmate values, social roles, and lifestyles. New inmates who are socialized into prison subcultures are said to undergo the process of prisonization. Prison subcultures are very influential, and both inmates and staff must reckon with them. Today's prisons are miniature societies, reflecting the problems and challenges that exist in the larger society of which they are a part.
- Female inmates represent a small but growing proportion of the nation's prison population. Many female inmates have histories of physical and sexual abuse. Although they are likely to

have dependent children, their parenting skills may be limited. Most female inmates are housed in centralized state facilities known as *women's prisons*, which are dedicated exclusively to incarcerating female felons. Some states, however, particularly those with small populations, continue to keep female prisoners in special wings of what are otherwise institutions for men. Few facilities for women have programs especially designed for female offenders.

- Like prisoners, corrections officers undergo a socialization process that helps them function by the official and unofficial rules of staff society. Prison staffers are most concerned with custody and control. The enforcement of strict rules; body and cell searches; counts; unannounced shakedowns; the control of dangerous items, materials, and contraband; and the extensive use of bars, locks, fencing, cameras, and alarms all support the staff's vigilance in maintaining security. Although concerns with security still command center stage, professionalism is playing an increasing role in corrections today, and today's corrections personnel are better trained and more proficient than ever before.
- As this chapter discusses, the causes of prison riots are diverse. They include (1) unmet inmate needs, (2) violent tendencies of some inmates, (3) dehumanizing conditions of imprisonment, (4) desires to regulate inmate society and redistribute power, and (5) power vacuums created by changes in prison administration, the transfer of influential inmates, or court-ordered injunctions.
- For many years, courts throughout the nation assumed a hands-off approach to prisons, rarely intervening in the day-to-day administration of prison facilities. That changed in the late 1960s when the U.S. Supreme Court began to identify inmates' rights mandated by the Constitution. Rights identified by the Court include the right to physical integrity, an absolute right to be free from unwarranted corporal punishments, certain religious rights, and procedural rights, such as those involving access to attorneys and to the courts. The conditional rights of prisoners, which have repeatedly been supported by the Court, mandate professionalism among prison administrators and require vigilance in the provision of correctional services. High court decisions have generally established that prison inmates retain those constitutional rights that are not inconsistent with their status as prisoners or with the legitimate penological objectives of the correctional system. In other words, inmates have rights, much the same as people who are not incarcerated, provided that the legitimate needs of the prison for security, custody, and safety are not compromised. The era of prisoners' rights was sharply curtailed in 1996 with the passage of the Prison Litigation Reform Act, spurred on by a growing recognition of the legal morass resulting from unregulated access to federal courts by inmates across the nation.
- The major problems and issues facing prisons today include (1) the threat from infectious diseases such as AIDS, (2) the need to deal with a growing geriatric offender population (the result of longer sentences and the aging of the American population), (3) a sizable number of mentally ill and mentally deficient inmates, and (4) a concern over inmates with terrorist leanings and those incarcerated for terrorism-related crimes.

QUESTIONS FOR REVIEW

1. What are prison subcultures, and how do they influence prison life? How do they develop, and what purpose do they serve?
2. How do women's prisons differ from men's? Why have women's prisons been studied less often than institutions for men?
3. What are the primary concerns of prison staff? What other goals do staff members focus on?
4. What causes prison riots? How might riots be prevented?
5. What are the commonly accepted rights of prisoners in the United States today? Where do these rights come from? What U.S. Supreme Court cases are especially significant in the area of prisoners' rights?
6. What are some of the major issues that prisons face today? What new issues might the future bring?

CHAPTER 13

Juvenile Justice

Learning Objectives

After reading this chapter, you should be able to:

1. Describe the history and evolution of the juvenile justice system in the Western world. **368**
2. Name the important U.S. Supreme Court decisions of relevance to juvenile
justice, and describe their impact on the handling of juveniles by the system. **370**
3. Explain the similarities and differences between the juvenile and adult justice systems. **374**
4. Identify possible future directions in juvenile justice. **383**

"We fight for our children, that they may enjoy the promise of America. We fight for their innocence and their dreams. It is a fight for our future."

—Alberto R. Gonzales, former U.S. attorney general[1]

"Our society's fearful of our kids. I think we don't know how to set limits on them. They begin to behave in severely outrageous ways, and nobody stops them."

—David York, cofounder, Tough Love International[2]

Introduction

Serious crimes committed by juveniles and preteens seem ever more commonplace. In 2009, for example, five Florida boys ages 13 to 15 were taken into custody after allegedly setting a 15-year-old former friend, Michael Brewer, on fire.[3] Three of the boys were eventually charged with second-degree attempted murder in connection with the attack.[4] Brewer, who tattled on one of them for stealing a bicycle, was surrounded by the boys and covered with rubbing alcohol, which was then ignited—resulting in severe burns to more than 65% of his body. In another sad story, a nine-year-old girl, identified by court records only as Shanice K., admitted that she fatally stabbed her 11-year-old Brooklyn, New York, playmate in the heart in 2005 with a steak knife during an argument over a rubber ball.[5] The killing occurred in the midst of a Memorial Day barbecue that was being held at Shanice's home. In a final example, two 12-year-old St. Lucie County, Florida, girls were charged in 2001 with trying to drown a classmate in a lake near her home. According to police, the victim, 12-year-old Nicole Maines, had refused to surrender her swimming mask and flippers, causing the other girls to jump into the water, grab her gear, and beat her.[6] When the attackers shoved Maines's head underwater, a bystander, 16-year-old Hosea Rivers, jumped into the lake and pulled the girls apart. A police report showed that Maines suffered cuts and bruises all over her body. "People really need to wake up and see what's going on with this generation," Michael Brewer's mother told *Good Morning America*. "They need to take hold of our children and really do something," she said.[7]

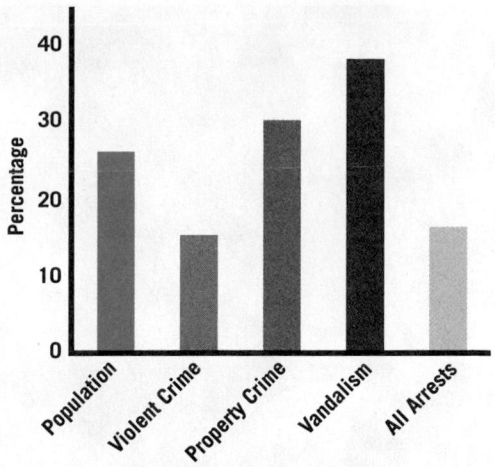

FIGURE 13–1
Juvenile Involvement in Crime versus System Totals, 2009

Note: The term *juvenile* refers to people younger than 18 years of age.
Source: Federal Bureau of Investigation, *Crime in the United States, 2009.*

A key finding of the Study Group on Serious and Violent Juvenile Offenders, convened by the Office of Juvenile Justice and Delinquency Prevention (OJJDP), is that most chronic juvenile offenders begin their delinquency careers before age 12, and some start as early as age ten.[8] The most recent national data show that in 2009 police arrested about 91,000 children ages 12 and younger.[9] These very young offenders (known as *child delinquents*) represent about 6% of the total number of **juveniles** (those up to age 18) who are arrested.

juvenile
A youth at or below the upper age of juvenile court jurisdiction in a particular state.

Although states vary as to the age at which a person legally enters adulthood, statistics on crime make it clear that young people are disproportionately involved in certain offenses. A recent report, for example, found that nearly 15% of all violent crimes and 24% of all property crimes are committed by people younger than age 18, while this age group makes up 26% of the population of the United States.[10] On average, about 14% of all arrests in any year are of juveniles,[11] and people younger than age 18 have a higher likelihood of being arrested for robbery and other property crimes than do people in any other age group. Figure 13–1 shows Uniform Crime Report (UCR)/National Incident-Based Reporting System (NIBRS) statistics on juvenile arrests for selected offense categories.

There was nothing to do.

—Terrance Wade, 15, on why he and his friends allegedly raped, stomped, stabbed, and ultimately murdered a Boston woman

The OJJDP is a primary source of information on juvenile justice in the United States. A sweeping OJJDP overview of juvenile crime and the juvenile justice system in America reveals the following:[12]

- About 1.6 million juveniles (under age 18) are arrested annually in America.
- Violent crime by juveniles is decreasing.
- Younger juveniles account for a substantial proportion of juvenile arrests and of the juvenile court caseload.
- Female delinquency has grown substantially, increasing 76% in the last decade.
- The number of juveniles held in public facilities has increased sharply.
- Minority juveniles are greatly overrepresented in the custody population.
- Crowding is a serious problem in juvenile facilities.

Learn more about OJJDP at **Web Extra 13–1**.

This chapter has four purposes. First, we will briefly look at the history of the **juvenile justice system**, comprising government agencies involved with youth who are offenders or

Lecture Note Discuss the stories that open this chapter. Ask students to speculate about the causes of such acts of violence by young people today.

Lecture Note Discuss Figure 13–1. Explain that although juveniles make up only a relatively small proportion of the entire U.S. population, they account for a seemingly large proportion of all offenses. Ask the class to suggest reasons for this phenomenon.

Lecture Note Explain the historical treatment of juveniles as small adults. Underscore the fact that in past centuries, juveniles who committed crimes were treated much the same as adults. Discuss whether that might happen again.

juvenile justice system
The government agencies that function to investigate, supervise, adjudicate, care for, or confine youthful offenders and other children subject to the jurisdiction of the juvenile court.

▲ Columbine (Colorado) High School shooters Eric Harris (*left*) and Dylan Klebold examining a sawed-off shotgun in a still image taken from a videotape made at a makeshift shooting range in 1999. About six weeks after the video was made, Harris (age 18) and Klebold (age 17) shot and killed 15 people and injured 20 more at the school. How might such disasters be averted in the future?
Jefferson County Sheriff's Department/Getty Images, Inc.–Getty News

subjects of court oversight. The juvenile justice system has its roots in the adult system, but in the juvenile system, we find a more uniform philosophical base and a relatively clear agreement about the system's purpose. These differences may be due to the fact that the system is relatively new and that society generally agrees that young people who have gone wrong are worth salvaging. However, the philosophy that underlies the juvenile justice system in America is increasingly being questioned by "get tough" advocates of law and order, many of whom are fed up with violent juvenile crime.

Our second purpose is to compare the juvenile and adult systems as they currently operate. The reasoning behind the juvenile justice system has led to administrative and other procedures that, in many jurisdictions, are not found in the adult system. The juvenile justice process, for example, is frequently not as open as the adult system: Hearings may be held in secret, names of offenders are not published, and records of juvenile proceedings may later be destroyed.[13]

Our third purpose is to describe the agencies, processes, and problems of the juvenile justice system itself. Although each state may have variations, a common system structure is shared by all.

Near the end of this chapter, we will turn to our fourth focus and will consider some of the issues raised by critics of the current system. Although conservative attitudes began to bring changes in the adult criminal justice system during the last few decades, the juvenile justice system has remained relatively unchanged. Based on premises quite different from those of the adult system, juvenile justice has long been a separate decision-making arena in which the best interests of the child have been accorded great importance. As we will see, substantial changes are now afoot.

Juvenile Justice throughout History

Earliest Times

Thematic Question What is the doctrine of *parens patriae*? Is the concept still applicable today? Do you agree that the primary purpose of the juvenile justice system should be to help children rather than to punish them? Do you think some children need punishment rather than help? Explain.

Before the modern era, children who committed crimes in the Western world received no preferential treatment because of their youth. They were adjudicated and punished alongside adults. In fact, a number of recorded cases have come down through history of children as young as age six being hung or burned at the stake.[14] In like fashion, little distinction was made between criminality and **delinquency** (misbehavior or conduct of juveniles in violation of the law) or other kinds of undesirable behavior.[15]

1 Describe the history and evolution of the juvenile justice system in the Western world.

delinquency
In the broadest usage, juvenile actions or conduct in violation of criminal law, juvenile status offenses, and other juvenile misbehavior.

Early philosophy in dealing with juveniles derived from a Roman principle called *patria potestas*. Under Roman law (circa 753 B.C.), children were members of their family, but the father had absolute control over them, and they in turn had an absolute responsibility to obey his wishes. Roman understanding of the social role of children strongly influenced English culture and eventually led to the development of the legal principle of ***parens patriae*** in Western law, which allowed the king (or the English state) to take the place of parents in dealing with children who broke the law.

parens patriae
A common law principle that allows the state to assume a parental role and to take custody of a child when he or she becomes delinquent, is abandoned, or is in need of care that the natural parents are unable or unwilling to provide.

By the end of the eighteenth century, social conditions in Europe and America had begun to change, and the Enlightenment, a highly significant intellectual and social movement, emphasized human potential. In this new age, children were recognized as the only true heirs to the future, and society became increasingly concerned about their well-being.

By the middle of the nineteenth century, large-scale immigration to America was under way. Some immigrant families fell victims of the cities that drew them, settling in squalor in hastily formed ghettos. Many children, abandoned by families unable to support them, were forced into lives on the streets, where they formed tattered gangs, surviving off the refuse of the glittering cities.

An 1823 report by the Society for the Prevention of Pauperism in the city of New York called for the development of "houses of refuge" to save children from lives of crime and poverty. In 1824, the first house of refuge opened in New York City.[16] It sheltered mostly young thieves, vagrants, and runaways. Other children, especially those with more severe delinquency problems, were placed in adult prisons and jails. Houses of refuge became popular in New York, and other cities quickly copied them. It was not long, however, before overcrowding developed and living conditions deteriorated.

Not long afterward, the American child-savers movement began. Child savers espoused a philosophy of productivity and eschewed idleness and unprincipled behavior.[17] One product of the child-savers movement was the reform school—a place for delinquent juveniles that embodied the atmosphere of a wholesome family environment. By the middle of the nineteenth century, the reform school approach to handling juveniles led to the creation of the Chicago Reform School, which opened in the 1860s. Reform schools focused primarily on predelinquent youth who showed tendencies toward more serious criminal involvement.

▲ A small group of teenagers. American juveniles have many opportunities but also face numerous challenges. What are the six categories of children that state juvenile justice statutes usually describe as subject to juvenile court jurisdiction?
Michael Newman/PhotoEdit Inc.

Lecture Note Describe the Chicago Reform School as one product of the child-savers movement of the mid-nineteenth century.

The Juvenile Court Era

In 1870, an expanding recognition of children's needs led the state of Massachusetts to enact legislation that required separate hearings for juveniles.[18] New York followed with a similar law in 1877,[19] which also prohibited contact between juvenile and adult offenders. Rhode Island enacted juvenile court legislation in 1898, and in 1899 the Colorado School Law became the first comprehensive legislation designed to adjudicate problem children.[20] It was, however, the 1899 codification of Illinois juvenile law that became the model for juvenile court statutes throughout the nation.

The Illinois Juvenile Court Act created a **juvenile court**, separate in form and function from adult criminal courts. To avoid the lasting stigma of criminality, the law applied the term *delinquent* rather than *criminal* to young adjudicated offenders. The act specified that juvenile court judges were to use the best interests of the child as a guide for decision making in their deliberations. In effect, judges were to serve as advocates for juveniles, guiding their development. The determination of guilt or innocence took second place to the betterment of the child. The law abandoned a strict adherence to the due process requirements of adult prosecutions, allowing informal procedures designed to scrutinize the child's situation. By sheltering the juvenile from the punishment philosophy of the adult system, the Illinois Juvenile Court emphasized reformation in place of retribution.[21]

juvenile court
Any court that has jurisdiction over matters involving juveniles.

Lecture Note Discuss the Puritan system for handling problem children, which included a heavy-handed approach to serious offenders. Underscore how this approach influenced early American practices. Ask how it affects policy today.

In 1938, the federal government passed the Juvenile Court Act, which embodied many of the features of the Illinois statute. By 1945, every state had enacted special legislation focusing on the handling of juveniles, and the juvenile court movement became well established.[22]

Lecture Note Explain that rehabilitative goals were developed early in the evolution of the juvenile justice system and continue today. Contrast early reform attempts with today's programs and anticipated future reforms.

The juvenile court movement was based on five philosophical principles that can be summarized as follows:[23]

1. The state is the "higher or ultimate parent" of all the children within its borders.
2. Children are worth saving, and nonpunitive procedures should be used to save them.
3. Children should be nurtured, and while the nurturing process is under way, they should be protected from the stigmatizing impact of formal adjudicatory procedures.
4. To accomplish the goal of reformation, justice needs to be individualized, that is, each child is different, and the needs, aspirations, living conditions, and so on of each child must be known in their individual particulars if the court is to be helpful.
5. Noncriminal procedures are necessary to give primary consideration to the needs of the child. For this reason, the denial of due process can be justified in the face of constitutional challenges because the court acts not to punish but to help.

Lecture Note Explain the juvenile court movement as an effort to give children separate hearings with different goals and protocols than those of the adult system.

Learn more about the history of juvenile justice and the juvenile court at **Library Extra 13–1**.

Lecture Note Discuss the various legal categories most states apply to children within their jurisdiction. Refer to the definitions provided in the text to be sure students understand the differences between the categories.

FIGURE 13–2 The Legal Environment of Juvenile Justice

1966 ▶

Kent v. United States

Courts must provide the "essentials of due process" in juvenile proceedings.
This important case signaled the beginning of systematic U.S. Supreme Court review of lower-court practices in delinquency hearings.

1967 ▶

In re Gault

In hearings that could result in commitment to an institution juveniles have four basic rights:

Notice of charges

Right to counsel

Right to confront and to cross-examine witnesses

Protection against self-incrimination

1970 ▶

In re Winship

In delinquency matters the state must prove its case beyone a reasonable doubt.
Prior to *Winship*, a lower standard of evidence had been required by juvenile courts in some states—a mere preponderance of the evidence.

1971 ▶

Mckeiver v. Pennsylvania

Jury trials are not constitutionally required in juvenile cases. At the same time the Court established that jury trials are not prohibited for juveniles.
Today, 12 states allow for jury trials in serious cases involving juveniles.

Thematic Question What are the different statutory categories of children? Should there be other categories? If so, which categories would you add?

delinquent child
A child who has engaged in activity that would be considered a crime if the child were an adult. The term *delinquent* is used to avoid the stigma associated with the term *criminal*.

undisciplined child
A child who is beyond parental control, as evidenced by his or her refusal to obey legitimate authorities, such as school officials and teachers.

dependent child
A child who has no parents or whose parents are not available or are unable to care for him or her.

neglected child
A child who is not receiving the proper level of physical or psychological care from his or her parents or guardians or who has been placed up for adoption in violation of the law.

abused child
A child who has been physically, emotionally, or sexually abused. Most states also consider a child who is forced into delinquent activity by a parent or guardian to be abused.

status offender
A child who commits an act that is contrary to the law by virtue of the offender's status as a child. Purchasing cigarettes, buying alcohol, and being truant are examples of such behavior.

status offense
An act or conduct that is declared by statute to be an offense, but only when committed by or engaged in by a juvenile, and that can be adjudicated only by a juvenile court.

Categories of Children in the Juvenile Justice System

By the time of the Great Depression, most states had expanded juvenile statutes to include the following six categories of children. These categories are still used today in most jurisdictions to describe the variety of children subject to juvenile court jurisdiction.

1. *Delinquent child.* A **delinquent child** is one who violates the criminal law. If the delinquent child were an adult, the word *criminal* would be applied instead.
2. *Undisciplined child.* An **undisciplined child** is said to be beyond parental control, as evidenced by his or her refusal to obey legitimate authorities, such as school officials and teachers. Such a child needs state protection.
3. *Dependent child.* A **dependent child** typically has no parents or guardians to care for him or her. The child's parents are deceased, the child was placed up for adoption, or the child was abandoned in violation of the law.
4. *Neglected child.* A **neglected child** is one who does not receive proper care from parents or guardians. Such a child may suffer from malnutrition or may not be provided with adequate shelter.
5. *Abused child.* An **abused child** is one who suffers physical abuse at the hands of his or her custodians. This category was later expanded to include emotional and sexual abuse.
6. *Status offender.* The term **status offender** is a special category that embraces children who violate laws written only for them. In some states, status offenders are referred to as persons in need of supervision (PINS).

Status offenses include behavior such as truancy, vagrancy, running away from home, and incorrigibility, and the youthful status of juveniles is a necessary element in such offenses. Adults, for example, may "run away from home" and not violate any law. Runaway children, however, are subject to apprehension and juvenile court processing because state laws require that they be subject to parental control.

Status offenses were a natural outgrowth of juvenile court philosophy. As a consequence, however, juveniles in need of help often faced procedural dispositions that treated them as though they were delinquent. Rather than lowering the rate of juvenile incarceration, the juvenile court movement led to its increase. Critics of the juvenile court movement quickly focused on the abandonment of due process rights, especially in the case of status offenders, as a major source of problems. Detention and incarceration, they argued, were inappropriate options for situations in which children had not committed crimes.

The Legal Environment

Throughout the first half of the twentieth century, the U.S. Supreme Court followed a hands-off approach to juvenile justice, much like its early approach to prisons (see Chapter 12). The adjudication and further processing of juveniles by the system were left mostly to specialized juvenile courts or to local appeals courts. Although one or two early Supreme Court decisions[24] dealt with issues of juvenile justice, it was not until the 1960s that the Court began close legal scrutiny of the principles underlying the system itself. Some of the most important U.S. Supreme Court cases relating to juvenile justice are shown in Figure 13–2.

2 Name the important U.S. Supreme Court decisions of relevance to juvenile justice, and describe their impact on the handling of juveniles by the system.

1975 ▶

Breed v. Jones

Severely restricted the conditions under which transfers from juvenile to adult courts may occur. In this case Jones was adjudicated delinquent in juvenile court and then transferred to adult court resulting in double jeopardy. Today, transfers to adult court, if they are to occur, must be made before an adjudicatory hearing in juvenile court.

1984 ▶

Schall v. Martin

The Court overturned lower court decisions banning the pretrial detention of juveniles, and held that such detention may be necessary for the protection of the child and of others.

2005 ▶

Roper v. Simmons

The U.S. Supreme Court ruled that age is a bar to execution when the offender commits a capital crime when he is younger than age 18. The Court held that "even a heinous crime committed by a juvenile" is not "evidence of irretrievably depraved character." *Roper* invalidated the capital sentences of 72 death-row inmates in 12 states.

2010 ▶

Graham v. Florida

The Eighth Amendment's ban on cruel and unusual punishments prohibits the imprisonment of a juvenile for life without the possibility of parole as punishment for a crime not involving homicide.

In 1966, in the case of *Kent* v. *U.S.*,[25] the U.S. Supreme Court began what would become an ongoing examination of juvenile justice and the processes surrounding it. In *Kent*, the justices held that courts must provide the "essentials of due process" in juvenile proceedings. This important case signaled the beginning of systematic U.S. Supreme Court review of lower-court practices in delinquency hearings.

Lecture Note Describe the hands-off approach to juvenile justice that the U.S. Supreme Court followed until the 1960s. Then discuss the precedent-setting cases that have been decided since then.

It was followed, a year later, by *In re Gault*, in which the U.S. Supreme Court held, in part, as follows:

> [T]he Juvenile Court Judge's exercise of the power of the state as *parens patriae* [is] not unlimited. . . . Notice, to comply with due process requirements, must be given sufficiently in advance of scheduled court proceedings so that reasonable opportunity to prepare will be afforded. . . . The probation officer cannot act as counsel for the child. His role in the adjudicatory hearing, by statute and in fact, is as arresting officer and witness against the child. There is no material difference in this respect between adult and juvenile proceedings of the sort here involved. . . . A proceeding where the issue is whether the child will be found to be "delinquent" and subjected to the loss of his liberty for years is comparable in seriousness to a felony prosecution. The juvenile needs the assistance of counsel to cope with the problems of law, to make skilled inquiry into the facts, to insist upon regularity of the proceedings, and to ascertain whether he has a defense and to prepare and submit it.[26]

Lecture Note Spotlight the 1967 *Gault* decision as the most significant of all the court precedents relating to the handling of juveniles. Explain that the decision extended many of the rights of adult defendants to juveniles.

In this 1967 case, however, the Court did not agree with another contention of Gault's lawyers: that transcripts of juvenile hearings should be maintained. Transcripts are not necessary, the Court said, because (1) there is no constitutional right to a transcript, and (2) no transcripts are produced in the trials of most adult misdemeanants.

Today, the impact of *Gault* is widely felt throughout the juvenile justice system, where juveniles are now guaranteed many of the same procedural rights as adults. Most precedent-setting Supreme Court decisions that followed *Gault* further clarified the rights of juveniles, focusing primarily on those few issues of due process that it had not explicitly addressed. One of these was the 1970 case of *In re Winship*, which centered on the standard of evidence needed in juvenile hearings. Winship's attorney had argued that the guilt of a juvenile facing a hearing should have to be proved beyond a reasonable doubt—the evidentiary standard of adult criminal trials. In its ruling the Court agreed, saying:

> [T]he constitutional safeguard of proof beyond a reasonable doubt is as much required during the adjudicatory stage of a delinquency proceeding as are those constitutional guards applied in *Gault*. . . . We therefore hold . . . that where a 12 year old child is charged with an act of stealing which renders him liable to confinement for as long as six years, then, as a matter of due process . . . the case against him must be proved beyond a reasonable doubt.[27]

As a consequence of *Winship*, allegations of delinquency today must be established beyond a reasonable doubt. The Court allowed, however, the continued use of the lower evidentiary standard in adjudicating juveniles charged with status offenses. Even though both standards continue to exist, most jurisdictions have chosen to use the stricter burden-of-proof requirement for all delinquency proceedings.

Cases like *Gault* and *Winship* have not extended all adult procedural rights to juveniles charged with delinquency. The case of *McKeiver* v. *Pennsylvania* (1971),[28] for example,

CJ News
No Clear-Cut Way to Handle Eight-Year-Old's Case

What do you do with an 8-year-old boy charged with two counts of premeditated murder?

Prosecutors and a defense lawyer in rural eastern Arizona are struggling to come up with an answer in the shocking case of a child accused of shooting his father and his father's friend early last month [November 2008]. . . . Although Arizona law allows 8-year-olds to be found delinquent and to be charged as adults, experts say children at that age are far from fully formed mentally and most don't understand the finality of death and the consequences of murder.

". . . Whatever they do has to be tailored to meet his specific individual needs, and it's not like 'Oh, we've got just the program for this young man.' . . . That's not going to work," said Charles Ewing, a psychologist and law professor at the University at Buffalo Law School.

Prosecutors in the case . . . are conflicted.

It's not their desire, they say, to "persecute" a child who may not fit the description of normal. But . . . a balance must be struck between rehabilitation and justice for the victims while considering the boy's "tender age."

Police say the boy planned and methodically carried out the shootings, using a .22-caliber rifle when his father, Vincent Romero, and Tim Romans returned home from work on Nov. 5.

In a police interview, the boy admitted firing at least two shots at each of the men, but the child's attorney has questioned the admissibility of the confession. . . .

Judge Michael Roca recently ordered all proceedings stayed until competency evaluations of the boy are complete. . . .

Prosecutors also have offered a plea deal. Defense attorney Benjamin Brewer has said he's considering the offer, which would resolve the case without transferring it to adult court. . . .

The case has tugged at the hearts of people across the country, who look at their own children and question how an 8-year-old could possibly have been responsible for such a crime.

"It is not a crime in the traditional way we define a crime," says Marsha Levick, legal director of the Juvenile Law Center in Philadelphia, "because he simply lacks the intent to commit a crime." . . .

"I think there should be great doubt in the public's mind of whether this child is even guilty of the crime," she said. "Even if he in fact pulled the trigger, treating him as an adult, holding him responsible in the same way we hold adults responsible is completely inappropriate."

. . . Only 13 states have set a minimum age at which children can be adjudicated delinquent, according to the National Juvenile Defender Center. In eight of those states, the age is 10; Arizona statute specifies an age of 8; three states set a minimum age of 7; and in North Carolina a 6-year-old can be found delinquent. . . .

▲ Marsha Levick, legal director of the Juvenile Law Center in Philadelphia. Discussing the eight-year-old described in this box, Levick says, "Even if he in fact pulled the trigger, treating him as an adult, holding him responsible in the same way we hold adults responsible is completely inappropriate." Do you agree?
AP Photo/Mark Moran, The Citizen's Voice

If the boy is convicted in juvenile court, he could be locked up until he's 18. Brewer fears the boy could be in prison for life if he were transferred to the adult system.

. . . Currently, there are no 8-year-old children in Arizona's juvenile or adult corrections systems. The average age of children incarcerated in the state juvenile corrections department is 15, and the youngest was 11, said Nancy Molever, spokeswoman for the juvenile department.

"With an 8-year-old, that's going to be really no more a challenge than any other kid," she said. "Every kid who comes to us has their own set of challenges, their own needs."

Source: Felicia Fonseca, "No Clear-Cut Way to Handle Eight-Year-Old's Case," Associated Press, December 13, 2008. Used with permission of The Associated Press. Copyright © 2010. All rights reserved.

reiterated what earlier cases had established—specifically, that juveniles do not have the constitutional right to a trial by a jury of their peers. It is important to note, however, that the *McKeiver* decision did not specifically prohibit jury trials for juveniles. As a consequence, approximately 12 states today allow the option of jury trials for juveniles.

In 1975, in the case of *Breed* v. *Jones* the Court severely restricted the conditions under which transfers from juvenile to adult courts may occur by mandating that such transfers as do occur must be made before any adjudicatory hearing in juvenile court.[29] In 1984, in the case of *Schall* v. *Martin*,[30] the U.S. Supreme Court upheld the constitutionality of a New York state statute, ruling that pretrial detention of juveniles based on "serious risk" does not violate the principle of fundamental fairness required by due process. In so holding, the Court recognized that states have a legitimate interest in preventing future delinquency by juveniles thought to be dangerous. Although the *Schall* decision upheld the practice of preventive detention, the

Court seized on the opportunity provided by the case to impose procedural requirements on the detaining authority. Consequently, preventive detention today cannot be imposed without (1) prior notice, (2) an equitable detention hearing, and (3) a statement by the judge setting forth the reason(s) for detention.

In 1988, in the case of *Thompson* v. *Oklahoma*,[31] the U.S. Supreme Court determined that national standards of decency did not permit the execution of any offender who was under age 16 at the time of the crime. In 2005, in the case of *Roper* v. *Simmons*,[32] the Court set a new standard when it ruled that age *is* a bar to execution when the offender commits a capital crime when he is younger than age 18. In *Roper*, the justices stated, "[The fact] that juveniles still struggle to define their identity means it is less supportable to conclude that even a heinous crime committed by a juvenile is evidence of irretrievably depraved character." The *Roper* ruling invalidated the capital sentences of 72 death-row inmates in 12 states.[33] Finally, in the 2010 case of *Graham* v. *Florida*,[34] the Court interpreted the cruel and unusual punishment clause of the U.S. Constitution to mean that a juvenile offender cannot be sentenced to life in prison without parole for a crime not involving homicide. This ruling, said the Court, "gives the juvenile offender a chance to demonstrate maturity and reform."

Legislation Concerning Children and Justice

In response to the rapidly increasing crime rates of the late 1960s, Congress passed the Omnibus Crime Control and Safe Streets Act of 1968, which provided money and technical assistance for states and municipalities seeking to modernize their justice systems. The Safe Streets Act also provided funding for youth services bureaus, which had been recommended by the 1967 presidential commission report *The Challenge of Crime in a Free Society*.[35] These bureaus were available to police, juvenile courts, and probation departments and acted as a centralized community resource for handling delinquents and status offenders. Youth services bureaus also handled juveniles referred by schools and young people who referred themselves. Unfortunately, within a decade after their establishment, most youth services bureaus succumbed to a lack of continued federal funding.

In 1974, recognizing the special needs of juveniles, Congress passed the Juvenile Justice and Delinquency Prevention (JJDP) Act. Employing much the same strategy as the 1968 bill, the JJDP Act provided federal grants to states and cities seeking to improve their handling and disposition of delinquents and status offenders. Nearly all the states chose to accept federal funds through the JJDP Act. Participating states had to meet two conditions within five years:

1. They had to agree to a "sight and sound separation mandate," under which juveniles would not be held in institutions where they might come into regular contact with adult prisoners.
2. Status offenders had to be deinstitutionalized, with most being released into the community or placed in foster homes.

Within a few years, institutional populations were cut by more than half, and community alternatives to juvenile institutionalization were rapidly being developed. Jailed juveniles were housed in separate wings of adult facilities or were removed from adult jails entirely.

When the JJDP Act was reauthorized for funding in 1980, the separation mandate was expanded to require that separate juvenile jails be constructed by the states. Studies supporting reauthorization of the JJDP Act in 1984 and 1988, however, found that nearly half the states had failed to come into "substantial compliance" with the new jail and lockup removal mandate. As a consequence, Congress modified the requirements of the act, continuing funding for states making "meaningful progress" toward removing juveniles from adult jails.[36] The 1988 reauthorizing legislation added a "disproportionate minority confinement" (DMC) requirement under which states seeking federal monies for their juvenile justice systems had to agree to ameliorate conditions leading to the disproportionate confinement of minority juveniles.[37]

In 1996, in the face of pressures toward punishment and away from treatment for violent juvenile offenders, the OJJDP proposed new rules for jailing juveniles. The new rules allow an adjudicated delinquent to be detained for up to 12 hours in an adult jail before a court appearance and make it easier for states to house juveniles in separate wings of adult jails.[38] The most recent JJDP reauthorization occurred in 2002.[39] It expanded the DMC concept to include all stages of the juvenile justice process. Consequently, *DMC* has come to mean "disproportionate minority contact" under today's law.[40] By 2005, 56 of 57 eligible states and U.S. territories had agreed to all of the act's requirements and were receiving federal funding under the legislation.[41]

In 2003, Congress passed child-protection legislation in what is commonly called the *AMBER Alert law*. Officially known as the PROTECT Act of 2003 (Prosecutorial Remedies and Other Tools to End the Exploitation of Children Today), the law provides federal funding to the states to ensure creation of a national AMBER (America's Missing: Broadcast Emergency Response) network to facilitate rapid law enforcement and community response to kidnapped or abducted children. The law also established the position of federal AMBER Alert coordinator and set uniform standards for the use of AMBER Alerts across our country. Another provision of the law provides for the prosecution of anyone engaged in pandering of child pornography. It also contains an extraterritorial clause that makes possible the federal prosecution of U.S. citizens who travel outside of the country to engage in child sex tourism.[42] The federal government's AMBER Alert website can be accessed at **Web Extra 13–2**.

The Legal Rights of Juveniles

Thematic Question What are the rights of juveniles who appear before a juvenile court? How did these rights come to be recognized?

Class Activity Invite a juvenile court official (judge, intake person, etc.) to speak with the class. (If you are teaching online, you might arrange to use virtual conferencing for this purpose.) Before the speaker's arrival, have students prepare questions about the challenges and rewards of his or her work.

Most jurisdictions today have statutes designed to extend the *Miranda* provisions to juveniles, and many police officers routinely offer *Miranda* warnings to juveniles in their custody before questioning them. It is unclear, however, whether juveniles can legally waive their *Miranda* rights. A 1979 U.S. Supreme Court ruling held that juveniles should be accorded the opportunity for a knowing waiver when they are old enough and sufficiently educated to understand the consequences of a waiver.[43] A later high court ruling upheld the murder conviction of a juvenile who had been advised of his rights and waived them in the presence of his mother.[44]

One important area of juvenile rights centers on investigative procedures. In 1985, for example, the U.S. Supreme Court ruled in *New Jersey* v. *T.L.O.*[45] that schoolchildren have a reasonable expectation of privacy in their personal property. The case involved a 14-year-old girl who was accused of violating school rules by smoking in a high school bathroom. A vice principal searched the girl's purse and found evidence of marijuana use. Juvenile officers were called, and the girl was eventually adjudicated in juvenile court and found delinquent.

On appeal to the New Jersey Supreme Court, the girl's lawyers were successful in having her conviction reversed on the grounds that the search of her purse, as an item of personal property, had been unreasonable. The state's appeal to the U.S. Supreme Court resulted in a ruling that prohibited school officials from engaging in unreasonable searches of students or their property. A reading of the Court's decision leads to the conclusion that a search could be considered reasonable if it (1) is based on a logical suspicion of rule-breaking actions; (2) is required to maintain order, discipline, and safety among students; and (3) does not exceed the scope of the original suspicion.

The Juvenile Justice Process Today

Juvenile court jurisdiction rests on the offender's age and conduct. The majority of states today define a child subject to juvenile court jurisdiction as a person who has not yet turned 18 years of age. A few states set the age at 16, and several use age 17. Figure 13–3 shows the upper ages of children subject to juvenile court jurisdiction in delinquency matters, by state. When they reach their eighteenth birthday, children in most states become subject to the jurisdiction of adult criminal courts.

3 Explain the similarities and differences between the juvenile and adult justice systems.

In 2009, OJJDP reported that U.S. courts with juvenile jurisdiction annually handle slightly more than 1.7 million delinquency cases.[46] Depending on the laws of the state and the behavior involved, the jurisdiction of the juvenile court may be exclusive.

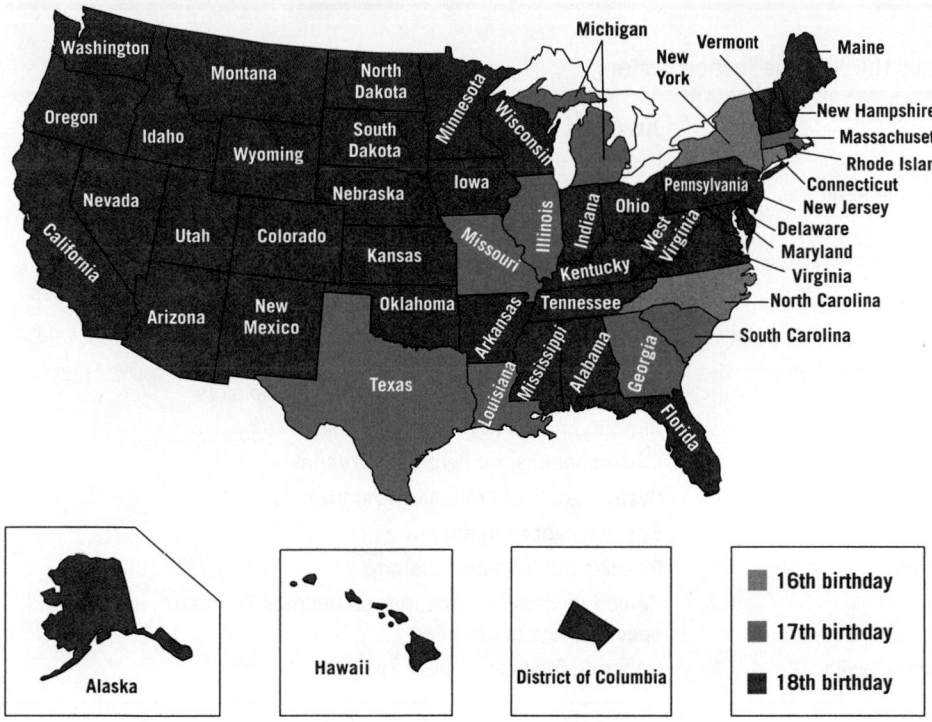

FIGURE 13–3
Limit of Juvenile Court Jurisdiction over Young Offenders, by State

Source: Office of Juvenile Justice and Delinquency Prevention.

Exclusive jurisdiction applies when the juvenile court is the only court that has statutory authority to deal with children for specified infractions. For example, status offenses such as truancy normally fall within the exclusive jurisdiction of juvenile courts. Delinquency, which involves violation of the criminal law, however, is often not within the juvenile court's exclusive jurisdiction. All 50 states, the District of Columbia, and the federal government have provisions that allow juveniles who commit serious crimes to be bound over to criminal court. In 46 states, juvenile court judges have the power to waive jurisdiction over cases involving juveniles so that they can be transferred to criminal court.[47] Fifteen states have "direct file" provisions that authorize the prosecutor to decide where to file certain kinds of serious cases, in either juvenile or criminal court. Juveniles who commit violent crimes or who have prior records are among the most likely to be transferred to adult courts.[48]

Where juvenile court authority is not exclusive, the jurisdiction of the court may be original or concurrent. *Original jurisdiction* means that a particular offense must originate (begin) with juvenile court authorities, and juvenile courts have original jurisdiction over most delinquency petitions and all status offenses. *Concurrent jurisdiction* exists where other courts have equal statutory authority to originate proceedings. For example, if a juvenile has committed a homicide, rape, or another serious crime, an arrest warrant may be issued by the adult court.

Some states specify that juvenile courts have no jurisdiction over certain specified offenses. Delaware, Louisiana, and Nevada, for example, allow no juvenile court jurisdiction over children charged with first-degree murder. Another 29 states have statutes that exclude certain serious, violent, and/or repeat offenders from the juvenile court's jurisdiction.

Adult and Juvenile Justice Compared

The court cases of relevance to the juvenile justice system that we have identified in this chapter have two common characteristics: They all turn on due process guarantees specified by the Bill of Rights, and they all make the claim that adult due process should serve as a model for juvenile proceedings. Due process guarantees, as interpreted by the U.S. Supreme Court, are clearly designed to ensure that juvenile proceedings are fair and that the interests of juveniles are protected. However, the Court's interpretations do not offer any pretense of providing juveniles with the same kinds of protections guaranteed to adult

Under our Constitution, the condition of being a boy does not justify a kangaroo court.
—In re *Gault* (1967)

CJ Exhibit 13–1
Adult Criminal Case Processing versus the Juvenile Justice System

CRIMINAL PROCEEDINGS	JUVENILE PROCEEDINGS
Focus on criminality	Focus on delinquency and a special category of "status offenses"
Comprehensive rights against unreasonable searches of person, home, and possessions	Limited rights against unreasonable searches
Assumption of innocence until proven guilty	Right against self-incrimination (waivers are questionable)
	Guilt and innocence not the primary issues (the system focuses on the interests of the child)
Adversarial setting	Helping context
Most arrests based on arrest warrants	Apprehension based on petitions or complaints
Right to an attorney	Right to an attorney
Public trial	Closed hearing; no right to a jury trial
System goals of punishment and reformation	System goals of protection and treatment
No right to treatment	Specific right to treatment
Possibility of bail or release on recognizance	Release into parental custody
Public record of trial and judgment	Sealed records (records may sometimes be destroyed by specified age of offender)
Possible incarceration in adult correctional facility	Separate facilities at all levels

Lecture Note Summarize the differences between the adult and juvenile justice systems by referring to CJ Exhibit 13–1. Point out that although the U.S. Supreme Court has held that juveniles are entitled to the protection of due process, it has refrained from declaring that juveniles have a right to all aspects of the due process afforded adults.

Thematic Question Which of the differences shown in CJ Exhibit 13–1 between the adult and juvenile justice systems do you think should be maintained or even enhanced? Which differences, if any, do you think might best be eliminated or minimized? Why?

Lecture Note Describe the juvenile justice system as being built around the processes of intake, adjudication, disposition, and postadjudicatory review.

Lecture Note Explain the differences between adult and juvenile intake procedures, and highlight the wide variety of options available in the juvenile justice system.

juvenile petition
A document filed in juvenile court alleging that a juvenile is a delinquent, a status offender, or a dependent and asking that the court assume jurisdiction over the juvenile or that an alleged delinquent be transferred to a criminal court for prosecution as an adult.

defendants. While the high court has tended to agree that juveniles are entitled to due process protection, it has refrained from declaring that juveniles have a right to all aspects of due process afforded adult defendants. See CJ Exhibit 13–1 for a comparison of adult criminal proceedings and juvenile proceedings.

Juvenile court philosophy brings with it other differences from the adult system. Among them are (1) reduced concern with legal issues of guilt or innocence and an emphasis on the child's best interests; (2) emphasis on treatment rather than punishment; (3) privacy and protection from public scrutiny through the use of sealed records, laws against publishing the names of juvenile offenders, and so forth; (4) use of the techniques of social science in dispositional decision making rather than sentences determined by a perceived need for punishment; (5) no long-term confinement, with most juveniles being released from institutions by their twenty-first birthday, regardless of offense; (6) separate facilities for juveniles; and (7) broad discretionary alternatives at all points in the process.[49] This combination of court philosophy and due process requirements has created a unique justice system for juveniles that takes into consideration the special needs of young people while attempting to offer reasonable protection to society. The juvenile justice process is diagrammed in Figure 13–4.

The Way the System Works

The juvenile justice system can be viewed as a process that, when carried to completion, moves through four stages: intake, adjudication, disposition, and postadjudicatory review. Though organizationally similar to the adult criminal justice process, the juvenile system is far more likely to maximize the use of discretion and to employ diversion from further formal processing at every point in the process. Each stage is discussed in the pages that follow.

Intake

Delinquent juveniles may come to the attention of the police or juvenile court authorities either through arrest or through the filing of a **juvenile petition** by an aggrieved party. (A juvenile petition is much like a criminal complaint in that it alleges illegal behavior.) Juvenile petitions are most often filed by teachers, school administrators, neighbors, store managers, or others who have frequent contact with juveniles. Parents who are unable to control the behavior of their teenage children are the source of many other petitions. Crimes

THE JUVENILE JUSTICE SYSTEM

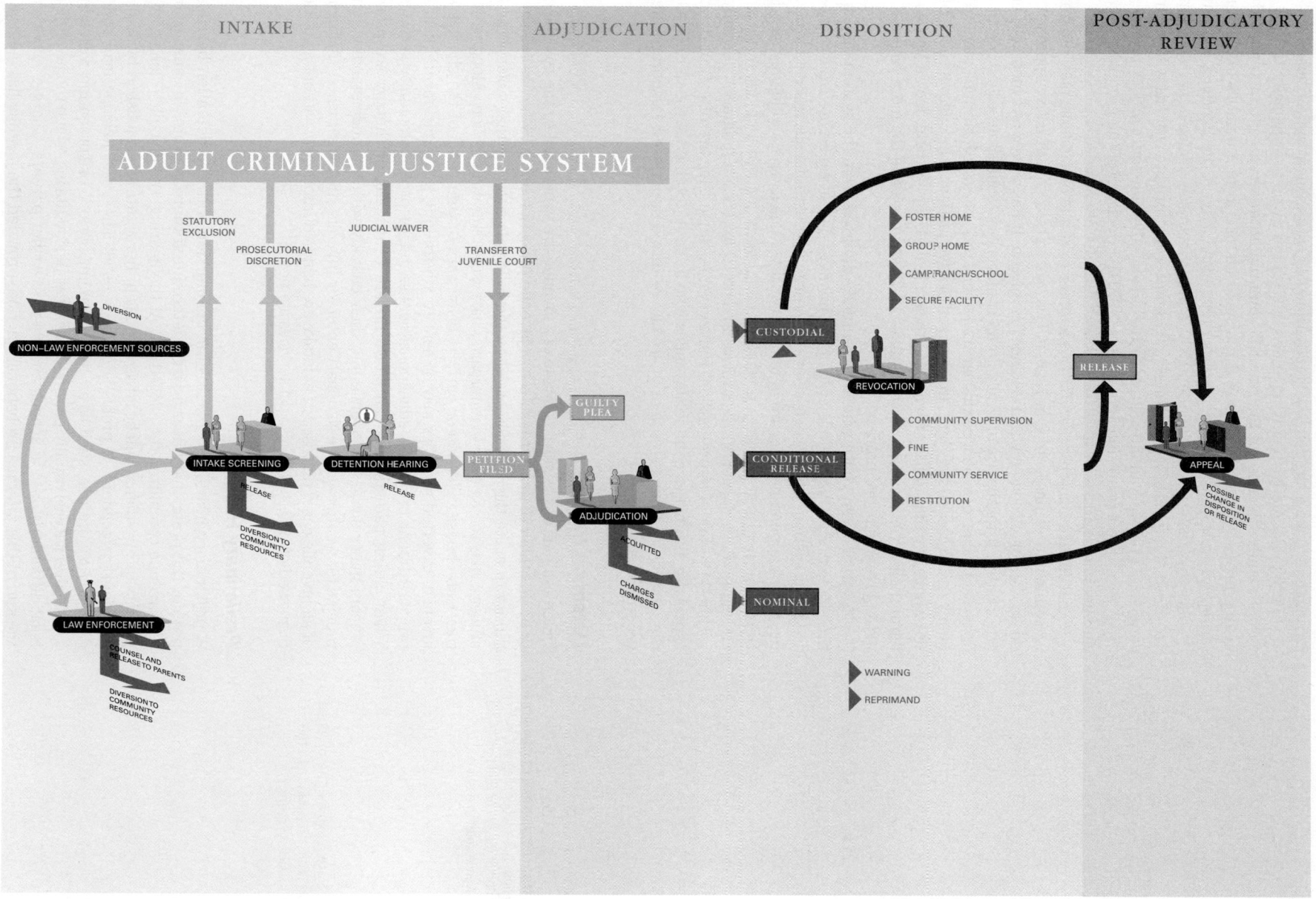

FIGURE 13–4 The Juvenile Justice System

in progress bring other juveniles to the attention of the police, with three-quarters of all referrals to juvenile court coming directly from law enforcement authorities.[50]

Many police departments have juvenile officers who are specially trained in dealing with juveniles. Because of the emphasis on rehabilitation that characterizes the juvenile justice process, juvenile officers can usually choose from a number of discretionary alternatives in the form of special programs, especially in the handling of nonviolent offenders. In Delaware County, Pennsylvania, for example, police departments participate in "youth aid panels." These panels are composed of private citizens who volunteer their services to provide an alternative to the formal juvenile court process. Youngsters who are referred to a panel and agree to abide by the decision of the group are diverted from the juvenile court.

Thematic Question How is the tension between individual rights and public order reflected in the juvenile justice process? How do both sets of concerns influence ideas for revision of the juvenile justice system?

Real Justice Conferencing (RJC) is another example of a diversionary program. Started in Bethlehem, Pennsylvania, in 1995, RJC is said to be a cost-effective approach to juvenile crime, school misconduct, and violence prevention. It has served as a model for programs in other cities. It makes use of family group conferences (sometimes called *community conferences*) in lieu of school disciplinary or judicial processes or as a supplement to them. The family group conference, built around a restorative justice model, allows young offenders to tell what they did, to hear from those they affected, and to help decide how to repair the harm their actions caused. Successful RJC participants avoid the more formal mechanisms of the juvenile justice process.

However, even youth who are eventually diverted from the system may spend some time in custody. One juvenile case in five involves detention before adjudication.[51] Unlike the adult system, where jail is seen as the primary custodial alternative for people awaiting a first appearance, secure detention for juveniles is acceptable only as a last resort. Detention hearings investigate whether candidates for confinement represent a "clear and immediate danger to themselves and/or to others," a judgment normally rendered within 24 hours of apprehension. Runaways, because they are often not dangerous, are especially difficult to confine. Juveniles who are not detained are generally released into the custody of their parents or guardians or into a supervised temporary shelter, like a group home.

Detention Hearing

intake
The first step in decision making regarding a juvenile whose behavior or alleged behavior is in violation of the law or could otherwise cause a juvenile court to assume jurisdiction.

Detention hearings regarding **intake** of a juvenile are conducted by the juvenile court judge or by an officer of the court, such as a juvenile probation officer, who has been given the authority to make this decision based on the (alleged) behavior that violates the law. Intake officers, like their police counterparts, have substantial discretion. Along with detention, they can choose diversion or outright dismissal of some or all of the charges against the juvenile. Diverted juveniles may be sent to job-training programs, mental health facilities, drug-treatment programs, educational counseling, or other community services agencies. When caring parents who can afford private counseling or therapy are present, intake officers may release the juvenile into their custody with the understanding that they will provide for treatment. The National Center for Juvenile Justice estimates that more than half of all juvenile cases disposed of at intake are handled informally, without a petition, and are dismissed or diverted to a social services agency.[52]

Lecture Note Explain the purpose of the preliminary hearing in the juvenile justice system.

Preliminary Hearing

A preliminary hearing may be held in conjunction with the detention hearing. The purpose of the preliminary hearing is to determine if there is probable cause to believe that the juvenile committed the alleged act. At the hearing, the juvenile (along with the child's parents or guardians) will be advised of his or her rights as established by state legislation and court precedent. If probable cause is established, the juvenile may still be offered diversionary options, such as an "improvement period" or "probation with adjudication." These alternatives usually provide a one-year period during which the juvenile must avoid legal difficulties, attend school, and obey his or her parents. Charges may be dropped at the end of this informal probationary period, provided the juvenile has met the conditions specified.

Transfer Hearing

When a serious offense is involved, statutory provisions may allow for transfer of the case to adult court at the prosecuting attorney's request. Transfer hearings are held in juvenile court and focus on (1) whether transfer statutes apply to the case under consideration and (2) whether the juvenile is amenable to treatment through the resources available to the juvenile justice system. Exceptions exist where statutes mandate transfer (which, as mentioned earlier, is sometimes the case with first-degree murder).

Adjudication

Adjudicatory hearings for juveniles are fact-finding processes during which the juvenile court decides whether there is sufficient evidence of a law violation. Adjudicatory hearings are similar to adult trials, with some notable exceptions. Similarities derive from the fact that the due process rights of children and adults are essentially the same. Differences between adjudicatory hearings and adult trials include the following:

adjudicatory hearing
The fact-finding process wherein the juvenile court determines whether there is sufficient evidence to sustain the allegations in a petition.

Lecture Note Explain why juveniles do not have a right to trial by jury.

- *Emphasis on privacy.* An important distinctive characteristic of the juvenile system is its concern with privacy. Juvenile hearings are not open to the public or to the mass media. Witnesses are permitted to be present only to offer testimony and may not stay for the rest of the hearing, and no transcript of the proceedings is created. One purpose of the emphasis on privacy is to prevent juveniles from being negatively labeled by the community.
- *Informality.* Whereas the adult criminal trial is highly structured, the juvenile hearing is more informal and less adversarial. The juvenile court judge takes an active role in the fact-finding process rather than serving as arbitrator between prosecution and defense.
- *Speed.* Informality, the lack of a jury, and the absence of an adversarial environment promote speed. While the adult trial may run into weeks or even months, the juvenile hearing is normally completed in a matter of hours or days.
- *Evidentiary standard.* On completion of the hearing, the juvenile court judge must weigh the evidence. If the charge involves a status offense, the judge may adjudicate the juvenile as a status offender upon finding that a preponderance of the evidence supports this finding. (A preponderance of the evidence exists when evidence of an offense is more convincing than evidence offered to the contrary.) If the charge involves a criminal-type offense, the evidentiary standard rises to the level of reasonable doubt.
- *Philosophy of the court.* Even in the face of strong evidence pointing to the offender's guilt, the judge may decide that it is not in the child's best interests to be adjudicated delinquent. The judge also has the power, even after the evidence is presented, to divert the juvenile from the system. Juvenile court statistics indicate that only about 57% of all cases disposed of by juvenile courts are processed formally.[53] Formal processing involves the filing of a petition requesting an adjudicatory or transfer hearing. Informal cases, on the other hand, are handled without a petition. Among informally handled (nonpetitioned) delinquency cases, almost half were dismissed by the court, whereas 67% of petitioned cases resulted in the child being adjudicated delinquent.[54]
- *No right to trial by jury.* As referred to earlier in the U.S. Supreme Court decision in *McKeiver* v. *Pennsylvania*,[55] juveniles do not have a constitutional right to trial by jury, and most states do not provide juveniles with a statutory opportunity for a jury trial.[56]

Eventually, the justice system may need to adapt to a new environment in which all criminal matters are referred to a single system, regardless of the offender's age.

—Jeffrey Butts and Ojmarrh Mitchell, Urban Institute[i]

Lecture Note Explain the reasons behind the concern for children's privacy. Ask students how this concern fits with the overall juvenile justice philosophy of the last half century.

See CJ Exhibit 13–2 for a comparison of the language used in juvenile and adult courts.

Some jurisdictions, however, allow juveniles to be tried by their peers in **teen courts**. The juvenile court in Columbus County, Georgia, for example, began experimenting with teen courts and peer juries in 1980.[57] In Georgia, peer juries are composed of youth under the age of 17 who receive special training by the court. Jurors are required to be successful in school and may not be under the supervision of the court or have juvenile petitions

teen court
An alternative approach to juvenile justice in which alleged offenders are judged and/or sentenced by a jury of their peers.

CJ Exhibit 13–2
Juvenile Courts versus Adult Courts

The language used in juvenile courts is less harsh than that used in adult courts. For example, juvenile courts do the following:

- Accept "petitions of delinquency" rather than criminal complaints
- Conduct "hearings," not trials
- "Adjudicate" juveniles to be "delinquent" rather than find them guilty of a crime
- Order one of a number of available "dispositions" rather than sentences

pending against them. Training consists of classroom exposure to the philosophy of the juvenile court system, Georgia's juvenile code, and Supreme Court decisions affecting juvenile justice.[58] The county's youthful jurors are used only in the dispositional (or sentencing) stage of the court process and only when adjudicated youth volunteer to go before the jury.

Today, hundreds of teen court programs are in operation across the country. OJJDP notes that teen courts are "an effective intervention in many jurisdictions where enforcement of misdemeanor charges is sometimes given low priority because of heavy caseloads and the need to focus on more serious offenders."[59] Teen courts, says OJJDP, "present communities with opportunities to teach young people valuable life and coping skills and promote positive peer influence for youth who are defendants and for volunteer youth who play a variety of roles in the teen court process." Learn more about teen courts at **Web Extra 13–3**.

Disposition

dispositional hearing
The final stage in the processing of adjudicated juveniles in which a decision is made on the form of treatment or penalty that should be imposed on the child.

Once a juvenile has been found delinquent, the judge will set a **dispositional hearing**, which is similar to an adult sentencing hearing and is used to decide what action the court should take relative to the child. As in adult courts, the judge may order a presentence investigation before making a dispositional decision. This type of investigation is conducted by special court personnel, sometimes called *juvenile court counselors*, who are, in effect, juvenile probation officers. Attorneys on both sides of the issue will also have the opportunity to make recommendations concerning dispositional alternatives.

juvenile disposition
The decision of a juvenile court that concludes a dispositional hearing. The adjudicated juvenile might be committed to a juvenile correctional facility; be placed in a juvenile residence, shelter, or care or treatment program; be required to meet certain standards of conduct; or be released.

The juvenile justice system typically gives the judge a much wider range of sentencing alternatives than does the adult system. Two major classes of **juvenile disposition** exist: to confine or not to confine. Because rehabilitation is still the primary objective of the juvenile court, the judge is likely to select the least restrictive alternative that meets the needs of the juvenile while recognizing the legitimate concerns of society for protection.

Most judges decide not to confine juveniles. Statistics indicate that in 2004 (the latest year for which statistics are available), the court ordered out-of-home placement in 22% of all cases adjudicated delinquent, down from 32% in 1985. Probation was the most restrictive disposition used in 63% (393,100) of the cases adjudicated delinquent in 2004, and it remains the most likely sanction to be imposed by juvenile courts.[60]

Probationary disposition usually means that juveniles will be released into the custody of a parent or guardian and ordered to undergo some form of training, education, or counseling. As in the adult system, juveniles placed on probation may be ordered to pay fines or to make restitution. In 11% of adjudicated delinquency cases, courts order juveniles to pay restitution or a fine, to participate in some form of community service, or to enter a treatment or counseling program—all dispositions that require minimal continuing supervision by probation staff.[61] Because juveniles rarely have financial resources or jobs, most economic sanctions take the form of court-ordered work programs, such as refurbishing schools or cleaning school buses.

Of course, not all juveniles who are adjudicated delinquent receive probation. Nearly one-quarter (24%) of adjudicated cases resulted in the youth being placed outside the home in a residential facility. In a relatively small number of cases (4%), the juvenile was adjudicated delinquent, but the case was then dismissed or the youth was otherwise released.[62]

Secure Institutions for Juveniles

Juveniles who demonstrate the potential for serious new offenses may be ordered to participate in rehabilitative programs within a secure environment, such as a youth center or a training school. As of late 2007, approximately 92,850 young people were being held under custodial supervision in the United States.[63] Of these, 33% were being held for personal crimes like murder, rape, or robbery; 25% were being held for property crimes; 9% were locked up for drug offenses; 11% were being held for public-order offenses (including weapons offenses); and 4% were being held for status offenses. Probation and parole violations accounted for another 16% of those confined.[64]

Most confined juveniles are held in semisecure facilities designed to look less like prisons and more like residential high school campuses. Most states, however, operate at least one secure facility for juveniles that is intended as a home for the most recalcitrant youthful offenders. Halfway houses, "boot camps,"[65] ranches, forestry camps, wilderness programs, group homes, and state-hired private facilities also hold some of the juveniles reported to be under confinement. Children placed in group homes continue to attend school and live in a family-like environment in the company of other adjudicated children, shepherded by "house parents." Learn more about the juvenile justice systems of each state from the National Center for Juvenile Justice's State Juvenile Justice Profiles at **Web Extra 13–4**.

▲ Juvenile court in action. Juvenile courts are expected to act in the best interests of the children who come before them. Should that rule apply to all juveniles who come before the court, regardless of their offense?
Richard Hutchings/PhotoEdit Inc.

The operative philosophy of custodial programs for juveniles focuses squarely on the rehabilitative ideal. Juveniles are usually committed to secure facilities for indeterminate periods of time, with the typical stay being less than one year. Release is often timed to coincide with the beginning or the end of the school year.

Most juvenile facilities are small, with 80% designed to hold 40 residents or fewer.[66] Many institutionalized juveniles are held in the thousand or so homelike facilities across the nation that are limited to ten residents or fewer.[67] At the other end of the scale are the nation's 70 large juvenile institutions, each designed to hold more than 200 hard-core delinquents.[68] Residential facilities for juveniles are intensively staffed. One study found that staff members outnumber residents ten to nine on average in state-run institutions and by an even greater ratio in privately run facilities.[69]

Jurisdictions vary widely in their use of secure detention for juveniles. In 2004, juvenile custody populations ranged from a low of 54 in Vermont to a high of 15,057 in California.[70] This variance reflects population differences as well as economic realities and philosophical beliefs. Some jurisdictions, like California, expect rehabilitative costs to be borne by the state rather than by families or local government agencies. Hence California shows a higher rate of institutionalization than many other states. Similarly, some states have more firmly embraced the reformation ideal and are more likely to use diversionary options for juveniles.

Lecture Note Mention that states vary widely in their use of secure detention for adjudicated juveniles. Whereas some states institutionalize thousands of juveniles, others have almost none in training facilities. Ask the class to suggest reasons why—population differences aside—this variation exists.

Characteristics of Juveniles in Confinement

Institutionalized juveniles are a small but special category of young people with serious problems. A recent report on institutionalized youth by the Bureau of Justice Statistics found five striking characteristics:[71]

1. The majority (85.5%) were male.
2. In terms of ethnicity, 39.4% were Caucasian, 38.9% were African American, and 17.3% were Hispanic.
3. About 6.5% were institutionalized for having committed a status offense, such as being truant, running away, or violating curfew.
4. Less than half (42.4%) were in residential facilities for a serious personal or property offense.
5. Only 1% were charged with homicide.

Class Activity Arrange for a tour of a local training school. Ask to see as many areas of the facility as possible during the tour, including the cafeteria, school, vocational training areas, and dormitories.

Overcrowding in Juvenile Facilities

As in adult prisons, overcrowding exists in many juvenile institutions. In one survey, half of all states reported overcrowding in juvenile facilities, and 22 states were operating facilities at more than 50% over capacity.[72]

A national study of the conditions of confinement in juvenile detention facilities conducted by OJJDP found that "there are several areas in which problems in juvenile facilities are substantial and widespread—most notably living space, health care, security, and control of suicidal behavior."[73] Using a variety of evaluative criteria, the study found that 47% of juveniles were confined in facilities whose populations exceeded their reported design capacity and that 33% of residents had to sleep "in rooms that were smaller than required by nationally recognized standards." To address the problem, the authors of the study recommended the use of alternative placement options so that only juveniles judged to be the most dangerous to their communities would be confined in secure facilities. Similarly, because it found that injuries to residents were most likely to occur within large dormitory-like settings, the OJJDP study recommended that "large dormitories be eliminated from juvenile facilities." Finally, the study recommended that "all juveniles be screened for risk of suicidal behavior immediately upon their admission to confinement" and that initial health screenings be "carried out promptly at admission." Other problems that OJJDP found "important enough to warrant attention" included education and treatment services. Further study of both areas is needed, OJJDP said.

A number of states use private facilities. A survey found that 13 states contract with 328 private facilities—most of which were classified as halfway houses—for the custody of adjudicated juveniles.[74] In the past few years, admissions to private facilities (comprising primarily halfway houses, group homes, shelters, and ranches, camps, or farms) have increased by more than 100%, compared with an increase of only about 10% for public facilities (mostly detention centers and training schools).[75] The fastest-growing category of detained juveniles comprises drug and alcohol offenders. Approximately 12% of all juvenile detainees are being held because of alcohol- and drug-related offenses.[76] Reflecting widespread socioeconomic disparities, an OJJDP report found that "a juvenile held in a public facility . . . was most likely to be black, male, between 14 and 17 years of age, and held for a delinquent offense such as a property crime or a crime against a person. On the other hand, a juvenile held in custody in a private facility . . . was most likely to be white, male, 14 to 17 years of age, and held for a nondelinquent offense such as running away, truancy, or incorrigibility."[77] The report also noted that "juvenile corrections has become increasingly privatized."

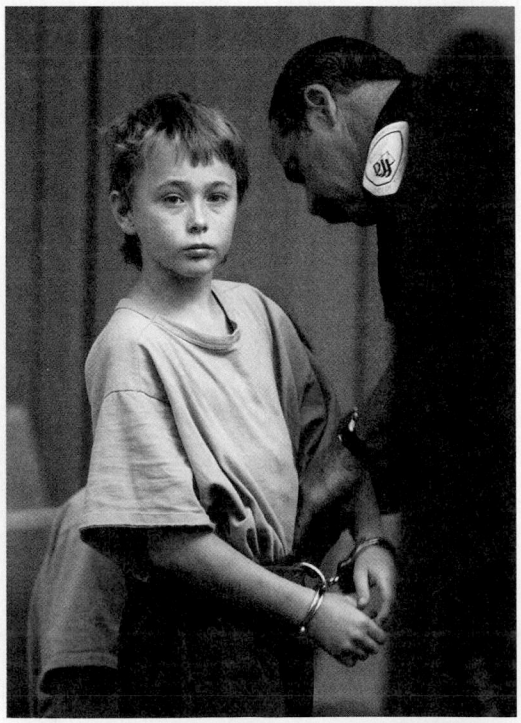

▲ Timothy Becton, 10, having his shackles adjusted by a Department of Juvenile Justice worker at a juvenile court hearing in 1996 in Bartow, Florida. Becton allegedly aimed a 12-gauge shotgun at a deputy who brought a truant officer to his home. What changes have recently occurred in the handling of juvenile offenders?
*Scott Wheeler/*The Ledger*/AP Wide World Photos*

Postadjudicatory Review

The detrimental effects of institutionalization on young offenders may make the opportunity for appellate review more critical for juveniles than it is for adults. However, federal court precedents have yet to establish a clear right to appeal from juvenile court, although most states do have statutory provisions that make such appeals possible.[78]

From a practical point of view, however, juvenile appeals may not be as consequential as are appeals of adult criminal convictions. Most juvenile complaints are handled informally, and only a relatively small proportion of adjudicated delinquents are placed outside the family. Moreover, because sentence lengths are short for most confined juveniles, appellate courts hardly have time to complete the review process before a juvenile is released.

The Post–Juvenile Court Era

In August 2005, Mitchell Johnson was released from a federal facility for youthful offenders.[79] Johnson, whose release was mandated by law on his twenty-first birthday, was 13 years old in 1998 when he and an 11-year-old friend, Andrew Golden, murdered four children and a teacher at Westside Middle School in Jonesboro, Arkansas, with hunting rifles they had taken from Golden's grandfather. At the time of the killings, laws in Arkansas and many other states allowed children to be confined only until they reached their eighteenth birthdays—no matter how serious their offense. It was only Johnson's conviction on federal gun charges that kept him locked up for an additional three years.

Cases like Johnson's, combined with extensive media coverage of violent juvenile crime across the United States, fueled public perceptions that violence committed by teenagers had reached epidemic proportions and that no community was immune to random acts of youth violence. At the same time, the apparent "professionalization" of delinquency, the hallmark of which is the repeated and often violent criminal involvement of juveniles in drug-related gang activity, came to be viewed as a major challenge to the idealism of the juvenile justice system. Consequently, by the turn of the twenty-first century, the issue of youth violence was at or near the top of nearly every state legislature's and governor's agenda. Most states took some form of legislative or executive action to stem what was seen as an escalating level of dangerous crime by juveniles. As OJJDP observed, "This level of [legislative and political] activity has occurred only three other times in our nation's history: at the outset of the juvenile court movement at the turn of the [twentieth] century; following the U.S. Supreme Court's *Gault* decision in 1967; and with the enactment of the Juvenile Justice and Delinquency Prevention Act in 1974."[80] OJJDP has identified five significant developments that have taken place in many states during the past decade:[81]

4 Identify possible future directions in juvenile justice.

1. *Transfer provisions.* New transfer provisions made it easier to move juvenile offenders from the juvenile justice system to the criminal justice system.
2. *Sentencing authority.* New laws on sentencing have given criminal and juvenile courts the authority to use expanded sentencing options such as the **blended sentence** (the combination of a juvenile disposition followed by a suspended adult sentence if the former is carried out successfully) in cases involving juveniles.
3. *Confidentiality changes.* Modifications were made to laws containing court confidentiality provisions in order to make juvenile records and proceedings more open.
4. *Victims' rights.* Laws were passed that increased the role of victims of juvenile crime in the juvenile justice process.
5. *Correctional programming.* New correctional programs in adult and juvenile facilities were developed to handle juveniles sentenced as adults or as violent juvenile offenders.

blended sentence
A juvenile court disposition that imposes both a juvenile sanction and an adult criminal sentence on an adjudicated delinquent. The adult sentence is suspended on the condition that the juvenile offender successfully completes the term of the juvenile disposition and refrains from committing any new offense.[ii]

Juvenile justice experts Jeffrey Butts and Ojmarrh Mitchell say that "[current] policymakers throughout the United States have greatly dissolved the border between juvenile and criminal justice. Young people who violate the law are no longer guaranteed special consideration from the legal system. Some form of juvenile court still exists in every state, but the purposes and procedures of juvenile courts are becoming indistinguishable from those of criminal courts."[82] Butts and Mitchell, who are members of the Program on Law and Behavior at the Urban Institute in Washington, D.C., also claim that "changes in juvenile law and juvenile court procedure are slowly dismantling the jurisdictional border between juvenile and criminal justice."[83] As evidence, Butts and Mitchell note that juvenile courts across the United States are becoming increasingly similar to criminal courts in the methods they use to reach conclusions and to process cases, as well as in the general atmosphere that characterizes them.

As a result of ongoing changes, some say that many states have substantially "criminalized" juvenile courts. In March 2000, for example, California voters endorsed sweeping changes in the state's juvenile justice system by passing Proposition 21, the Gang Violence and Juvenile Crime Prevention Act. The law reduces confidentiality in the juvenile court, limits the use of probation for young offenders, and increases the power of prosecutors to send juveniles to adult court and to put them in adult prisons. Public support for the measure was undiminished by projections that it would increase operational costs in the California juvenile justice system by $500 million annually.[84] Because laws like California's Proposition 21 are being passed at a growing rate throughout the country, a leading expert on juvenile

Children are the living messages we send to a time we will not see.
—John W. Whitehead[iii]

justice notes that "the similarities of juvenile and adult courts are becoming greater than the differences between them."[85]

Cindy Lederman, presiding judge of the Miami-Dade Juvenile Court, refers to the changes as the "adultification" of the juvenile justice system.[86] The juvenile court, says Lederman, has undergone significant change since it was created. In the early twentieth century, the juvenile court focused on social welfare and was primarily concerned with acting in a child's best interest, but by the mid-twentieth century, it had seized on the issue of children's due process rights as an important guiding principle. The court today, says Lederman, has turned its focus to accountability and punishment.

Proposals for further change abound. In 2001, the Task Force on Juvenile Justice Reform (TFJJR) of the American Academy of Child and Adolescent Psychiatry issued a report on juvenile justice reform.[87] The report covered many areas, including competence to stand trial, forensic evaluations of children and adolescents, recommended standards for juvenile detention and confinement facilities, health care in the juvenile justice system, females in the juvenile justice system, disproportionate minority confinement, educational needs of youth in juvenile justice facilities, and transfers of juvenile cases to criminal court. Read the entire report at **Library Extra 13–2**.

The Department of Justice Authorization Act for fiscal year 2003[88] set dramatic new accountability standards for federally funded programs for juveniles who violate the law.[89] The law built on the premise that juvenile offenders should be held accountable for their offenses through the swift and consistent application of sanctions that are proportionate to the offense.[90] Lawmakers made it clear that it was their belief that enhanced accountability and swift sanctions were both a matter of basic justice and a way to combat delinquency and improve the quality of life in our nation's communities.

> The current [juvenile justice] system, a relic from a more innocent time, teaches youthful offenders that crime pays and that they are totally immune and insulated from responsibility.
>
> —National Policy Forum

The Washington, D.C.–based Sentencing Project stated that "the treatment of juveniles, especially those nearing adulthood, is a contentious issue in many states."[91] The decision to prosecute children as adults, say Sentencing Project authors, "has lasting ramifications on their experience within the criminal justice system and their prospects for rehabilitation." True to this understanding, legislators nationwide have worked to distinguish between serious and habitual juvenile offenders and those whose law-breaking behavior is relatively minor and likely to be transitory.

In 2007, for example, California's Senate Bill (SB) 81, also known to some as the Juvenile Justice Realignment Act, passed by state legislators with bipartisan support and quickly enacted into law, mandated that juveniles charged with all but the most serious felonies be adjudicated and supervised within their counties of residence.[92] Touted as a landmark reform to California's juvenile justice system, SB 81 provides money for the development of county-based rehabilitative programs, and it awards counties an average of $130,000 per supervised youth annually. SB 81 shifts nonviolent juvenile offenders out of secure facilities operated by the state Division of Juvenile Justice and into county facilities and programs.

Bill highlights include the following:

- By banning future commitments of nonviolent juvenile offenders to state facilities, SB 81 will cut the population from 2,500 to about 1,500 incarcerated juvenile offenders within two years.
- Counties will now be responsible for the custody and care of juvenile offenders who can no longer be sent to state institutions.
- SB 81 provides counties with block grant funds to pay for local alternatives to state commitment, at an average of $130,000 per ward.
- The bill authorizes up to $100 million statewide in construction bonds for the design and construction of new or renovated county facilities for youthful offenders.
- The bill requires the state Juvenile Justice Commission, a 12-member statewide commission of stakeholders, to produce a Juvenile Operations Master Plan, including standardized risk-needs assessments, standard data-collection elements, and recommended evidence-based programs, for youthful offenders.

A PowerPoint presentation that supports this chapter is available from your Prentice Hall representative.

Summary

JUVENILE JUSTICE

- Under today's laws, children occupy a special status that is tied closely to cultural advances that occurred in the Western world during the past 200 years. Before the modern era, children who committed crimes received no preferential treatment and were adjudicated, punished, and imprisoned alongside adults. Beginning a few hundred years ago, England (from which we derive many of our legal traditions) adapted the principle of *parens patriae*. That principle allowed the government to take the place of parents in dealing with children who broke the law. Around the middle of the nineteenth century, the child-savers movement began in the United States. It espoused a philosophy of productivity and eschewed idleness and unprincipled behavior. Not long afterward, the 1899 codification of Illinois juvenile law became the model for juvenile court statutes throughout the United States. It created a juvenile court separate in form and function from adult criminal courts and based on the principle of *parens patriae*. To avoid the lasting stigma of criminality, the term *delinquent* (rather than *criminal*) began to be applied to young adjudicated offenders. Soon, juvenile courts across the country focused primarily on the best interests of the child as a guide in their deliberations.
- Important U.S. Supreme Court decisions of special relevance to the handling of juveniles by the justice system include (1) *Kent* v. *U.S.* (1966), which established minimal due process standards for juvenile hearings; (2) *In re Gault* (1967), in which the Court found that a child has many of the same due process rights as an adult; (3) *In re Winship* (1970), which held that the constitutional safeguard of proof beyond a reasonable doubt is required during the adjudicatory stage of a delinquency proceeding; (4) *McKeiver* v. *Pennsylvania* (1971), which held that jury trials were not required in delinquency cases; (5) *Breed* v. *Jones* (1975), which restricted the conditions under which transfers from juvenile to adult court may occur; (6) *Schall* v. *Martin* (1984), in which the Court held that pretrial detention of juveniles based on "serious risk" does not violate due process, although prior notice, an equitable detention hearing, and a statement by the juvenile court judge explaining the reasons for detention are required; and (7) *Roper* v. *Simmons* (2005), which held that age *is* a bar to capital punishment when the offender commits a capital crime when he or she is younger than age 18.
- The juvenile justice system of today is infused with due process guarantees designed to ensure that juvenile proceedings are fair and that the interests of juveniles are protected. Although the U.S. Supreme Court has established that juveniles are entitled to fundamental due process protections, it has refrained from declaring that juveniles have a right to all aspects of due process afforded adult defendants. The juvenile justice system differs from the adult system in a number of ways: (1) It is less concerned with legal issues of guilt or innocence and focuses on the child's best interests; (2) it emphasizes treatment rather than punishment; (3) it ensures privacy and protection from public scrutiny through the use of sealed records and laws against publishing the names of juvenile offenders; (4) it uses the techniques of social science in dispositional decision making rather than sentences determined by a perceived need for punishment; (5) it does not order long-term confinement, with most juveniles being released from institutions by their twenty-first birthday; (6) it has separate facilities for juveniles; and (7) it allows broad discretionary alternatives at all points in the process.
- The juvenile justice system's commitment to a philosophy of protection and restoration, expressed in the juvenile court movement of the late nineteenth and early twentieth centuries, has begun to dissipate. The present juvenile system, for the most part, still differs substantially from the adult system in the multitude of opportunities it provides for diversion and in the emphasis it places on rehabilitation rather than punishment. However, the "professionalization" of delinquency, the hallmark of which is the repeated and often violent criminal involvement of juveniles in drug-related gang activity, represents a major challenge to the idealism of the juvenile justice system. Efforts to address that challenge are starting to result in what some have called the "adultification" of the juvenile justice system.

QUESTIONS FOR REVIEW

1. Describe the history and evolution of the juvenile justice system in the Western world, and list the six categories of children recognized by the laws of most states.
2. Name the important U.S. Supreme Court decisions of relevance to juvenile justice. What was the impact of each of these decisions on juvenile justice in America?
3. What are the major similarities and differences between the juvenile and adult justice systems?
4. What directions might juvenile justice take in the future? What might provide the impetus for such changes?

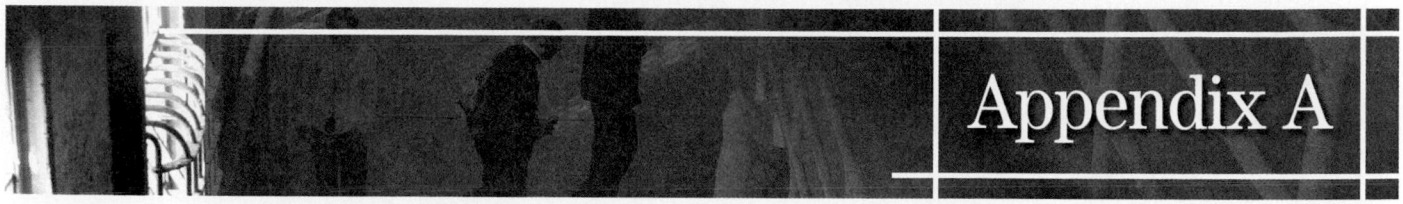

Appendix A

Bill of Rights The first ten amendments to the U.S. Constitution are known as the *Bill of Rights*. These amendments, ratified in 1791, have special relevance to criminal justice and are reproduced here.

Amendment I Congress shall make no law respecting an establishment of religion, or prohibiting the free exercise thereof; or abridging the freedom of speech, or of the press; or the right of the people peaceably to assemble, and to petition the Government for a redress of grievances.

Amendment II A well regulated Militia, being necessary to the security of a free State, the right of the people to keep and bear Arms, shall not be infringed.

Amendment III No Soldier shall, in time of peace be quartered in any house, without the consent of the Owner, nor in time of war, but in a manner to be prescribed by law.

Amendment IV The right of the people to be secure in their persons, houses, papers, and effects, against unreasonable searches and seizures, shall not be violated, and no Warrants shall issue, but upon probable cause, supported by Oath or affirmation, and particularly describing the place to be searched, and the persons or things to be seized.

Amendment V No person shall be held to answer for a capital, or otherwise infamous crime, unless on a presentment or indictment of a Grand Jury, except in cases arising in the land or naval forces, or in the Militia, when in actual service in time of War or public danger; nor shall any person be subject for the same offence to be twice put in jeopardy of life or limb; nor shall be compelled in any criminal case to be a witness against himself, nor be deprived of life, liberty, or property, without due process of law; nor shall private property be taken for public use, without just compensation.

Amendment VI In all criminal prosecutions, the accused shall enjoy the right to a speedy and public trial, by an impartial jury of the State and district wherein the crime shall have been committed, which district shall have been previously ascertained by law, and to be informed of the nature and cause of the accusation; to be confronted with the witnesses against him; to have compulsory process for obtaining witnesses in his favor, and to have the Assistance of Counsel for his defence.

Amendment VII In Suits at common law, where the value in controversy shall exceed twenty dollars, the right of trial by jury shall be preserved, and no fact tried by a jury, shall be otherwise re-examined in any Court of the United States, than according to the rules of the common law.

Amendment VIII Excessive bail shall not be required, nor excessive fines imposed, nor cruel and unusual punishments inflicted.

Amendment IX The enumeration in the Constitution, of certain rights, shall not be construed to deny or disparage others retained by the people.

Amendment X The powers not delegated to the United States by the Constitution, nor prohibited by it to the States, are reserved to the States respectively, or to the people.

Appendix B

List of Acronyms

ABA	American Bar Association
ACA	American Correctional Association
ACJS	Academy of Criminal Justice Sciences
ACLU	American Civil Liberties Union
ADAM	Arrestee Drug Abuse Monitoring
ADMAX	administrative maximum
AEDPA	Antiterrorism and Effective Death Penalty Act (1996)
AFDA	Association of Federal Defense Attorneys
AFIS	automated fingerprint identification system
AIDS	acquired immunodeficiency syndrome
AJA	American Jail Association
ALI	American Law Institute
AMBER	America's Missing: Broadcast Emergency Response
AOUSC	Administrative Office of the United States Courts
APPA	American Probation and Parole Association
ASC	American Society of Criminology
ASIS	American Society for Industrial Security
ASLET	American Society for Law Enforcement Training
ATF	Bureau of Alcohol, Tobacco, Firearms and Explosives
BJA	Bureau of Justice Assistance
BJS	Bureau of Justice Statistics
BOP	Bureau of Prisons
CALEA	Commission on Accreditation for Law Enforcement Agencies
CAPS	Chicago's Alternative Policing Strategy
CAT	computer-aided transcription
CCA	Corrections Corporation of America
CDA	Communications Decency Act (1996)
CFAA	Computer Fraud and Abuse Act (1986)
CIA	Central Intelligence Agency
CID	Criminal Investigative Division
CJIS	Criminal Justice Information Services (FBI)
CLET	Certified Law Enforcement Trainer
CODIS	Combined DNA Index System (FBI)
COPS	Community Oriented Policing Services
CPOP	Community Police Officer Program (New York City)
CPTED	crime prevention through environmental design
CRIPA	Civil Rights of Institutionalized Persons Act (1980)
CRIPP	Courts Regimented Intensive Probation Program
CSA	Controlled Substances Act (1970)
CSC	Correctional Services Corporation
DEA	Drug Enforcement Administration
DHS	Department of Homeland Security
DNA	deoxyribonucleic acid
DOJ	U.S. Department of Justice
DPIC	Death Penalty Information Center
DUI	driving under the influence (of alcohol or drugs)
DWI	driving while intoxicated
ECPA	Electronic Communications Privacy Act (1986)
FBI	Federal Bureau of Investigation
FCC	federal correctional complex
FCI	federal correctional institution
FLETC	Federal Law Enforcement Training Center
FLIR	forward-looking infrared
FOP	Fraternal Order of Police
FPC	federal prison camp
FTCA	Federal Tort Claims Act (1946)
GBMI	guilty but mentally ill
HIV	human immunodeficiency virus
IACP	International Association of Chiefs of Police
ICC	International Criminal Court
ICE	Immigration and Customs Enforcement
IDRA	Insanity Defense Reform Act (1984)
ILC	International Law Commission (United Nations)
ILEA	International Law Enforcement Academy (FBI)
INTERPOL	International Criminal Police Organization
IPS	intensive probation supervision
JJDP	Juvenile Justice and Delinquency Prevention Act (1974)
JTTF	Joint Terrorism Task Force
LAPD	Los Angeles Police Department
LEAA	Law Enforcement Assistance Administration
LEMAS	Law Enforcement Management and Administrative Statistics
MCFP	medical center for federal prisoners
MDC	metropolitan detention center
MPC	Model Penal Code
NAACP	National Association for the Advancement of Colored People
NACDL	National Association of Criminal Defense Lawyers
NCAVC	National Center for the Analysis of Violent Crime
NCCD	National Council on Crime and Delinquency
NCIC	National Crime Information Center (FBI)
NCISP	National Criminal Intelligence Sharing Plan
NCJRS	National Criminal Justice Reference Service
NCPC	National Crime Prevention Council
NCSC	National Center for State Courts
NCVS	National Crime Victimization Survey
NCWP	National Center for Women and Policing

NDAA	National District Attorneys Association
NDIS	National DNA Index System (FBI)
NIBRS	National Incident-Based Reporting System (FBI)
NIJ	National Institute of Justice
NJC	National Judicial College
NLADA	National Legal Aid and Defender Association
NOBLE	National Organization of Black Law Enforcement Executives
NVAWS	National Violence against Women Survey
NVC	National Victims Center
NVCAP	National Victims' Constitutional Amendment Project
NW3C	National White Collar Crime Center
NYGC	National Youth Gang Center
NYPD	New York Police Department
OJJDP	Office of Juvenile Justice and Delinquency Prevention
OJP	Office of Justice Programs
ONDCP	Office of National Drug Control Policy
PCR	police-community relations
PDS	podular/direct supervision
PERF	Police Executive Research Forum
PINS	persons in need of supervision
PLRA	Prison Litigation Reform Act (1996)
POST	Peace Officer Standards and Training
PROTECT Act	Prosecutorial Remedies and Other Tools to End the Exploitation of Children Today Act (2003)
RICO	Racketeer Influenced and Corrupt Organizations (statute)
RISE	Reintegrative Shaming Experiments (Australian Institute of Criminology)
RJC	Real Justice Conferencing (Pennsylvania)
ROR	release on recognizance
RTTF	Regional Terrorism Task Force
SAMHSA	Substance Abuse and Mental Health Services Administration
SBI	State Bureau of Investigation
SCU	Street Crimes Unit (New York City)
SEARCH	National Consortium for Justice Information and Statistics
SIIA	Software and Information Industry Association
STG	security threat group
SVORI	Serious Violent Offender Reentry Initiative
SWAT	special weapons and tactics
TFJJR	Task Force on Juvenile Justice Reform
TIPS	Terrorist Information and Prevention System
TWGEDE	Technical Working Group for the Examination of Digital Evidence
UCR	Uniform Crime Reports (FBI)
USA PATRIOT Act	Uniting and Strengthening America by Providing Appropriate Tools Required to Intercept and Obstruct Terrorism Act (2001)
U.S.C.	United States Code
USP	United States penitentiary
USSC	United States Sentencing Commission
VAWA	Violence against Women Act (1994)
VCAN	Victims' Constitutional Amendment Network
VICAP	Violent Criminal Apprehension Program (FBI)
VOCA	Victims of Crime Act (1984)
VWPA	Victim and Witness Protection Act (1982)

Glossary

abused child[1] A child who has been physically, emotionally, or sexually abused. Most states also consider a child who is forced into delinquent activity by a parent or guardian to be abused.

actus reus An act in violation of the law. Also, a guilty act.

adjudicatory hearing The fact-finding process wherein the juvenile court determines whether there is sufficient evidence to sustain the allegations in a petition.

ADMAX An acronym for administrative maximum. This term is used by the federal government to denote ultra-high-security prisons.

administration of justice The performance of any of the following activities: detection, apprehension, detention, pretrial release, post-trial release, prosecution, adjudication, correctional supervision, or rehabilitation of accused persons or criminal offenders.[2]

adversarial system The two-sided structure under which American criminal trial courts operate that pits the prosecution against the defense. In theory, justice is done when the more effective adversary is able to convince the judge or jury that his or her perspective on the case is the correct one.

aggravated assault The unlawful, intentional inflicting, or attempted or threatened inflicting, of serious injury upon the person of another. While *aggravated assault* and *simple assault* are standard terms for reporting purposes, most state penal codes use labels like *first-degree* and *second-degree* to make such distinctions.

aggravating circumstances Circumstances relating to the commission of a crime that make it more grave than the average instance of that crime.

alibi A statement or contention by an individual charged with a crime that he or she was so distant when the crime was committed, or so engaged in other provable activities, that his or her participation in the commission of that crime was impossible.

alter ego rule In some jurisdictions, a rule of law that holds that a person can only defend a third party under circumstances and only to the degree that the third party could legally act on his or her own behalf.

alternative sentencing The use of court-ordered community service, home detention, day reporting, drug treatment, psychological counseling, victim-offender programming, or intensive supervision in lieu of other, more traditional sanctions, such as imprisonment and fines.

anticipatory warrant A search warrant issued on the basis of probable cause to believe that evidence of a crime, while not currently at the place described, will likely be there when the warrant is executed.

appeal The request that a court with appellate jurisdiction review the judgment, decision, or order of a lower court and set it aside (reverse it) or modify it.

appellate jurisdiction The lawful authority of a court to review a decision made by a lower court.

arraignment Strictly, the hearing before a court having jurisdiction in a criminal case in which the identity of the defendant is established, the defendant is informed of the charge and of his or her rights, and the defendant is required to enter a plea. Also, in some usages, any appearance in criminal court before trial.

arrest The act of taking an adult or juvenile into physical custody by authority of law for the purpose of charging the person with a criminal offense, a delinquent act, or a status offense, terminating with the recording of a specific offense. Technically, an arrest occurs whenever a law enforcement officer curtails a person's freedom to leave.

arson (UCR/NIBRS) Any willful or malicious burning or attempt to burn, with or without intent to defraud, a dwelling house, public building, motor vehicle or aircraft, personal property of another, and so on. Some instances of arson result from malicious mischief, some involve attempts to claim insurance money, and some are committed in an effort to disguise other crimes, such as murder, burglary, or larceny.

assault (UCR/NIBRS) An unlawful attack by one person upon another. Historically, assault meant only the attempt to inflict injury on another person; a completed act constituted the separate offense of battery. Under modern statistical usage, however, attempted and completed acts are grouped together under the generic term *assault.*

attendant circumstances The facts surrounding an event.

bail The money or property pledged to the court or actually deposited with the court to effect the release of a person from legal custody.

bail bond A document guaranteeing the appearance of a defendant in court as required and recording the pledge of money or property to be paid to the court if he or she does not appear. The bail bond is signed by the person to be released and by anyone else acting in his or her behalf.

bailiff The court officer whose duties are to keep order in the courtroom, to secure witnesses, and to maintain physical custody of the jury.

balancing test A principle, developed by the courts and applied to the corrections arena by *Pell* v. *Procunier* (1974), that attempts to weigh the rights of an individual, as guaranteed by the Constitution, against the authority of any state to make laws or to otherwise restrict a person's freedom in order to protect the state's interests and its citizens.

Bill of Rights The popular name given to the first ten amendments to the U.S. Constitution, which are considered especially important in the processing of criminal defendants.

biological weapon A biological agent used to threaten human life (for example, anthrax, smallpox, or any infectious disease).[3]

***Bivens* action** A civil suit, based on the case of *Bivens* v. *Six Unknown Federal Agents,* brought against federal government officials for denying the constitutional rights of others.

blended sentence A juvenile court disposition that imposes both a juvenile sanction and an adult criminal sentence on an adjudicated delinquent. The adult sentence is suspended on the condition that the juvenile offender successfully completes the term of the juvenile disposition and refrains from committing any new offense.[4]

Bureau of Justice Statistics (BJS) A U.S. Department of Justice agency responsible for the collection of criminal justice data, including the annual National Crime Victimization Survey.

burglary (UCR/NIBRS) The unlawful entry of a structure to commit a felony or a theft (excludes tents, trailers, and other mobile units used for recreational purposes). Under the UCR/NIBRS Program, the crime of burglary can be reported if (1) an unlawful entry of an unlocked structure has occurred, (2) a breaking and entering (of a secured structure) has taken place, or (3) a burglary has been attempted.

capital offense A criminal offense punishable by death.

capital punishment The death penalty. Capital punishment is the most extreme of all sentencing options.

case law The body of judicial precedent, historically built on legal reasoning and past interpretations of statutory laws, that serves as a guide to decision making, especially in the courts.

caseload The number of probation or parole clients assigned to one probation or parole officer for supervision.

chain of command The unbroken line of authority that extends through all levels of an organization, from the highest to the lowest.

change of venue The movement of a trial or lawsuit from one jurisdiction to another or from one location to another within the same jurisdiction. A change of venue may be made in a criminal case to ensure that the defendant receives a fair trial.

circumstantial evidence The evidence that requires interpretation or that requires a judge or jury to reach a conclusion based on what the evidence indicates. From the close proximity of the defendant to a smoking gun, for example, the jury might conclude that he or she pulled the trigger.

civil death The legal status of prisoners in some jurisdictions who are denied the opportunity to vote, hold public office, marry, or enter into contracts by virtue of their status as incarcerated felons. While civil death is primarily of historical interest, some jurisdictions still limit the contractual opportunities available to inmates.

civil justice The civil law, the law of civil procedure, and the array of procedures and activities having to do with private rights and remedies sought by civil action. Civil justice cannot be separated from social justice because the justice enacted in our nation's civil courts reflects basic American understandings of right and wrong.

civil law The branch of modern law that governs relationships between parties.

civil liability The potential responsibility for payment of damages or other court-ordered enforcement as a result of a ruling in a lawsuit. Civil liability is not the same as criminal liability, which means "open to punishment for a crime."[5]

classification system A system used by prison administrators to assign inmates to custody levels based on offense history, assessed dangerousness, perceived risk of escape, and other factors.

clearance rate A traditional measure of investigative effectiveness that compares the number of crimes reported or discovered to the number of crimes solved through arrest or other means (such as the death of the suspect).

closing argument An oral summation of a case presented to a judge, or to a judge and jury, by the prosecution or by the defense in a criminal trial.

common law The body of law originating from usage and custom rather than from written statutes. The term refers to an unwritten body of judicial opinion, originally developed by English courts, that is based on nonstatutory customs, traditions, and precedents that help guide judicial decision making.

community corrections The use of a variety of officially ordered program-based sanctions that permit convicted offenders to remain in the community under conditional supervision as an alternative to an active prison sentence.

community court A low-level court that focuses on quality-of-life crimes that erode a neighborhood's morale, that emphasizes problem solving rather than punishment, and that builds on restorative principles such as community service and restitution.

community policing "A philosophy that promotes organizational strategies, which support the systematic use of partnerships and problem-solving techniques, to proactively address the immediate conditions that give rise to public safety issues such as crime, social disorder, and fear of crime."[6]

community service A sentencing alternative that requires offenders to spend at least part of their time working for a community agency.

compelling interest A legal concept that provides a basis for suspicionless searches when public safety is at issue. In two cases, the U.S. Supreme Court held that public safety may sometimes provide a sufficiently compelling interest to justify limiting an individual's right to privacy.

competent to stand trial A finding by a court, when the defendant's sanity at the time of trial is at issue, that the defendant has sufficient present ability to consult with his or her attorney with a reasonable degree of rational understanding and that the defendant has a rational as well as factual understanding of the proceedings against him or her.

CompStat A crime-analysis and police-management process built on crime mapping that was developed by the New York City Police Department in the mid-1990s.

computer crime Any crime perpetrated through the use of computer technology. Also, any violation of a federal or state computer-crime statute. Also called *cybercrime.*

computer virus A computer program designed to secretly invade systems and either modify the way in which they operate or alter the information they store. Viruses are destructive software programs that may effectively vandalize computers of all types and sizes.

concurrence The coexistence of (1) an act in violation of the law and (2) a culpable mental state.

concurrent sentence One of two or more sentences imposed at the same time, after conviction for more than one offense, and served at the same time. Also, a new sentence for a new conviction, imposed upon a person already under sentence for a previous offense, which is served at the same time as the previous sentence.

conditional release The release of an inmate from prison to community supervision with a set of conditions for remaining on parole. If a condition is violated, the individual can be returned to prison or face another sanction in the community.[7]

conditions of parole (probation) The general and special limits imposed on an offender who is released on parole (or probation). General conditions tend to be fixed by state statute, whereas special conditions are mandated by the sentencing authority (court or board) and take into consideration the background of the offender and the circumstances of the offense.

conflict model A criminal justice perspective that assumes that the system's components function primarily to serve their own interests. According to this theoretical framework, justice is more a product of conflicts among agencies within the system than it is the result of cooperation among component agencies.

consecutive sentence One of two or more sentences imposed at the same time, after conviction for more than one offense, and served in sequence with the other sentence. Also, a new sentence for a new conviction, imposed upon a person already under sentence for a previous offense, which is added to the previous sentence, thus increasing the maximum time the offender may be confined or under supervision.

consensus model A criminal justice perspective that assumes that the system's components work together harmoniously to achieve the social product we call *justice.*

corporate crime A violation of a criminal statute by a corporate entity or by its executives, employees, or agents acting on behalf of and for the benefit of the corporation, partnership, or other form of business entity.[8]

corpus delicti The facts that show that a crime has occurred. The term literally means "the body of the crime."

court of last resort The court authorized by law to hear the final appeal on a matter.

courtroom work group The professional courtroom actors, including judges, prosecuting attorneys, defense attorneys, public defenders, and others who earn a living serving the court.

crime Conduct in violation of the criminal laws of a state, the federal government, or a local jurisdiction, for which there is no legally acceptable justification or excuse.

crime-control model A criminal justice perspective that emphasizes the efficient arrest and conviction of criminal offenders.

Crime Index A now-defunct but once-inclusive measure of the UCR Program's violent and property crime categories, or what are called *Part I offenses.* The Crime Index, long featured in the FBI's publication *Crime in the United States,* was discontinued in 2004. The index had been intended as a tool for geographic (state-to-state) and historical (year-to-year) comparisons via the use of crime rates (the number of crimes per unit of population). However, criticism that the index was misleading arose after researchers found that the largest of the index's crime categories, larceny-theft, carried undue weight and led to an underappreciation of changes in the rates of more violent and serious crimes.

crime prevention The anticipation, recognition, and appraisal of a crime risk and the initiation of action to eliminate or reduce it.

crime typology A classification of crimes along a particular dimension, such as legal category, offender motivation, victim behavior, or characteristics of individual offenders.

criminal intelligence The information compiled, analyzed, and/or disseminated in an effort to anticipate, prevent, or monitor criminal activity.[9]

criminal justice In the strictest sense, the criminal (penal) law, the law of criminal procedure, and the array of procedures and activities having to do with the enforcement of this body of law. Criminal justice cannot be separated from social justice because the justice enacted in our nation's criminal courts reflects basic American understandings of right and wrong.

criminal justice system The aggregate of all operating and administrative or technical support agencies that perform criminal justice functions. The basic divisions of the operational aspects of criminal justice are law enforcement, courts, and corrections.

criminal law The body of rules and regulations that define and specify the nature of and punishments for offenses of a public nature or for wrongs committed against the state or society. Also called *penal law.*

criminal negligence A behavior in which a person fails to reasonably perceive substantial and unjustifiable risks of dangerous consequences.

criminology The scientific study of the causes and prevention of crime and the rehabilitation and punishment of offenders.

cybercrime See *computer crime.*

cyberstalking The use of the Internet, e-mail, and other electronic communication technologies to stalk another person.[10]

cyberterrorism A form of terrorism that makes use of high technology, especially computers and the Internet, in the planning and carrying out of terrorist attacks.

danger law A law intended to prevent the pretrial release of criminal defendants judged to represent a danger to others in the community.

dark figure of crime Crime that is not reported to the police and that remains unknown to officials.

date rape The unlawful forced sexual intercourse with a female against her will that occurs within the context of a dating relationship. Date rape, or acquaintance rape, is a subcategory of rape that is of special concern today.

deadly force The force likely to cause death or great bodily harm. Also, "the intentional use of a firearm or other instrument resulting in a high probability of death."[11]

defense (to a criminal charge) The evidence and arguments offered by a defendant and his or her attorney to show why the defendant should not be held liable for a criminal charge.

defense counsel A licensed trial lawyer hired or appointed to conduct the legal defense of a person accused of a crime and to represent him or her before a court of law.

delayed-notification search See *"sneak and peek" search.*

deliberate indifference A wanton disregard by corrections personnel for the well-being of inmates. Deliberate indifference requires both actual knowledge that a harm is occurring and disregard of the risk of harm that is occurring. A prison official may be held liable under the Eighth Amendment for acting with deliberate indifference to inmate health or safety only if he or she knows that inmates face a substantial risk of serious harm and disregards that risk by failing to take reasonable measures to abate it.

delinquency In the broadest usage, juvenile actions or conduct in violation of criminal law, juvenile status offenses, and other juvenile misbehavior.

delinquent child A child who has engaged in activity that would be considered a crime if the child were an adult. The term *delinquent* is used to avoid the stigma associated with the term *criminal.*

dependent child A child who has no parents or whose parents are not available or are unable to care for him or her.

design capacity The number of inmates a prison was intended to hold when it was built or modified.

determinate sentencing A model of criminal punishment in which an offender is given a fixed term of imprisonment that may be reduced by good time or gain time. Under the model, for example, all offenders convicted of the same degree of burglary would be sentenced to the same length of time behind bars.

deterrence A goal of criminal sentencing that seeks to inhibit criminal behavior through the fear of punishment.

digital criminal forensics The lawful seizure, acquisition, analysis, reporting, and safeguarding of data from digital devices that may contain information of evidentiary value to the trier of fact in criminal events.[12]

diminished capacity A defense based on claims of a mental condition that may be insufficient to exonerate the defendant of guilt but that may be relevant to specific mental elements of certain crimes or degrees of crime.

directed patrol A police-management strategy designed to increase the productivity of patrol officers through the scientific analysis and evaluation of patrol techniques.

direct evidence The evidence that, if believed, directly proves a fact. Eyewitness testimony and videotaped documentation account for the majority of all direct evidence heard in the criminal courtroom.

direct-supervision jail A temporary confinement facility that eliminates many of the traditional barriers between inmates and corrections staff. Physical barriers in direct-supervision jails are far less common than in traditional jails, allowing staff members the opportunity for greater interaction with, and control over, residents.

discretionary release The release of an inmate from prison to supervision that is decided by a parole board or other authority.

dispositional hearing The final stage in the processing of adjudicated juveniles in which a decision is made on the form of treatment or penalty that should be imposed on the child.

dispute-resolution center An informal hearing place designed to mediate interpersonal disputes without resorting to the more formal arrangements of a criminal trial court.

diversion The official suspension of criminal or juvenile proceedings against an alleged offender at any point after a recorded justice system intake, but before the entering of a judgment, and referral of that person to a treatment or care program administered by a nonjustice or private agency. Also, a release without referral.

domestic terrorism The unlawful use of force or violence by a group or an individual who is based and operates entirely within the United States and its territories without foreign direction and whose acts are directed at elements of the U.S. government or population.[13]

double jeopardy A common law and constitutional prohibition against a second trial for the same offense.

due process A right guaranteed by the Fifth, Sixth, and Fourteenth Amendments of the U.S. Constitution and generally understood, in legal contexts, to mean the due course of legal proceedings according to the rules and forms established for the protection of individual rights. In criminal proceedings, due process of law is generally understood to include the following basic elements: a law creating and defining the offense, an impartial tribunal having jurisdictional authority over the case, accusation in proper form, notice and opportunity to defend, a trial according to established procedure, and discharge from all restraints or obligations unless convicted.

due process model A criminal justice perspective that emphasizes individual rights at all stages of justice system processing.

Electronic Communications Privacy Act (ECPA) A law passed by Congress in 1986 establishing the due process requirements that law enforcement officers must meet in order to legally intercept wire communications.

electronic evidence Information and data of investigative value that are stored in or transmitted by an electronic device.[14]

element (of a crime) In a specific crime, one of the essential features of that crime, as specified by law or statute.

emergency search A search conducted by the police without a warrant, which is justified on the basis of some immediate and overriding need, such as public safety, the likely escape of a dangerous suspect, or the removal or destruction of evidence.

entrapment An improper or illegal inducement to crime by agents of law enforcement. Also, a defense that may be raised when such inducements have occurred.

equity A sentencing principle, based on concerns with social equality, that holds that similar crimes should be punished with the same degree of severity, regardless of the social or personal characteristics of the offenders.

espionage The "gathering, transmitting, or losing"[15] of information related to the national defense in such a manner that the information becomes available to enemies of the United States and may be used to their advantage.

evidence Anything useful to a judge or jury in deciding the facts of a case. Evidence may take the form of witness testimony, written documents, videotapes, magnetic media, photographs, physical objects, and so on.

evidence-based policing (EBP) The use of the best available research on the outcomes of police work to implement guidelines and evaluate agencies, units, and officers.[16]

evidence-based practice Crime-fighting strategies that have been scientifically tested and are based on social science research.

excessive force The application of an amount or frequency of force greater than that required to compel compliance from a willing or unwilling subject.[17]

exclusionary rule The understanding, based on U.S. Supreme Court precedent, that incriminating information must be seized according to constitutional specifications of due process or it will not be allowed as evidence in a criminal trial.

exculpatory evidence Any information having a tendency to clear a person of guilt or blame.

excuse A legal defense in which the defendant claims that some personal condition or circumstance at the time of the act was such that he or she should not be held accountable under the criminal law.

expert witness A person who has special knowledge and skills recognized by the court as relevant to the determination of guilt or innocence. Unlike lay witnesses, expert witnesses may express opinions or draw conclusions in their testimony.

ex post facto Latin for "after the fact." The Constitution prohibits the enactment of *ex post facto* laws, which make acts committed before the laws in question were passed punishable as crimes.

federal court system The three-tiered structure of federal courts, comprising U.S. district courts, U.S. courts of appeals, and the U.S. Supreme Court.

felony A criminal offense punishable by death or by incarceration in a prison facility for at least one year.

first appearance An appearance before a magistrate during which the legality of the defendant's arrest is initially assessed and the defendant is informed of the charges on which he or she is being held. At this stage in the criminal justice process, bail may be set or pretrial release arranged. Also called *initial appearance.*

fleeting-targets exception An exception to the exclusionary rule that permits law enforcement officers to search a motor vehicle based on probable cause but without a warrant. The fleeting-targets exception is predicated on the fact that vehicles can quickly leave the jurisdiction of a law enforcement agency.

forcible rape (UCR/NIBRS) The carnal knowledge of a female, forcibly and against her will. For statistical-reporting purposes, the FBI defines *forcible rape* as "unlawful sexual intercourse with a female, by force and against her will, or without legal or factual consent." Statutory rape differs from forcible rape in that it generally involves nonforcible sexual intercourse with a minor.

fruit of the poisonous tree doctrine A legal principle that excludes from introduction at trial any evidence later developed as a result of an illegal search or seizure.

fusion center A multiagency law enforcement facility designed to enhance cooperative efforts through a coordinated process for collecting, sharing, and analyzing information in order to develop actionable intelligence.

gain time The amount of time deducted from time to be served in prison on a given sentence as a consequence of participation in special projects or programs.

general deterrence A goal of criminal sentencing that seeks to prevent others from committing crimes similar to the one for which a particular offender is being sentenced by making an example of the person sentenced.

good-faith exception An exception to the exclusionary rule. Law enforcement officers who conduct a search or who seize evidence on the basis of good faith (that is, when they believe they are operating according to the dictates of the law) and who later discover that a mistake was made (perhaps in the format of the application for a search warrant) may still use the seized evidence in court.

good time The amount of time deducted from time to be served in prison on a given sentence as a consequence of good behavior.

grand jury A group of jurors who have been selected according to law and have been sworn to hear the evidence and to determine whether there is sufficient evidence to bring the accused person to trial, to investigate criminal activity generally, or to investigate the conduct of a public agency or official.

grievance procedure A formalized arrangement, usually involving a neutral hearing board, whereby institutionalized individuals have the opportunity to register complaints about the conditions of their confinement.

guilty but mentally ill (GBMI) A verdict, equivalent to a finding of "guilty," that establishes that the defendant, although mentally ill, was in sufficient possession of his or her faculties to be morally blameworthy for his or her acts.

hands-off doctrine A policy of nonintervention with regard to prison management that U.S. courts tended to follow until the late 1960s. For 30 years, the doctrine languished as judicial intervention in prison administration dramatically increased, although there is now evidence that a new hands-off era is beginning.

hate crime (UCR/NIBRS) A criminal offense committed against a person, property, or society that is motivated, in whole or in part, by the offender's bias against a race, religion, disability, sexual orientation, or ethnicity/national origin.

hearsay Something that is not based on the personal knowledge of a witness. Witnesses who testify about something they have heard, for example, are offering hearsay by repeating information about a matter of which they have no direct knowledge.

hearsay rule The long-standing precedent that hearsay cannot be used in American courtrooms. Rather than accepting testimony based on hearsay, the court will ask that the person who was the original source of the hearsay information be brought in to be questioned and cross-examined. Exceptions to the hearsay rule may occur when the person with direct knowledge is dead or is otherwise unable to testify.

home confinement House arrest. Individuals ordered confined to their homes are sometimes monitored electronically to ensure they do not leave during the hours of confinement. Absence from the home during working hours is often permitted.

***Hudud* crime** A serious violation of Islamic law that is regarded as an offense against God.

identity theft A crime in which an imposter obtains key pieces of information, such as Social Security and driver's license numbers, to obtain credit, merchandise, and services in the name of the victim. The victim is often left with a ruined credit history and the time-consuming and complicated task of repairing the financial damage.[18]

illegally seized evidence Any evidence seized without regard to the principles of due process as described by the Bill of Rights. Most illegally seized evidence is the result of police searches conducted without a proper warrant or of improperly conducted interrogations.

incapacitation The use of imprisonment or other means to reduce the likelihood that an offender will commit future offenses.

inchoate offense An offense not yet completed. Also, an offense that consists of an action or conduct that is a step toward the intended commission of another offense.

incompetent to stand trial In criminal proceedings, a finding by a court that as a result of mental illness, defect, or disability, a defendant is incapable of understanding the nature of the charges and proceedings against him or her, of consulting with an attorney, and of aiding in his or her own defense.

indeterminate sentencing A model of criminal punishment that encourages rehabilitation through the use of general and relatively unspecific sentences (such as a term of imprisonment of from one to ten years).

indictment A formal written accusation submitted to the court by a grand jury alleging that a specified person has committed a specified offense, usually a felony.

individual rights The rights guaranteed to all members of American society by the U.S. Constitution (especially those rights found in the first ten amendments to the Constitution, known as the *Bill of Rights*). These rights are particularly important to criminal defendants facing formal processing by the criminal justice system.

individual-rights advocate One who seeks to protect personal freedoms within the process of criminal justice.

information A formal written accusation submitted to a court by a prosecutor alleging that a specified person has committed a specified offense.

infraction A minor violation of state statute or local ordinance punishable by a fine or other penalty or by a specified, usually limited, term of incarceration.

inherent coercion The tactics used by police interviewers that fall short of physical abuse but that nonetheless pressure suspects to divulge information.

initial appearance See *first appearance.*

insanity defense A legal defense based on claims of mental illness or mental incapacity.

intake The first step in decision making regarding a juvenile whose behavior or alleged behavior is in violation of the law or could otherwise cause a juvenile court to assume jurisdiction.

intelligence-led policing (ILP) The collection and analysis of information to produce an intelligence end product designed to inform police decision making at both the tactical and strategic levels.[19]

intensive probation supervision (IPS) A form of probation supervision involving frequent face-to-face contact between the probationer and the probation officer.

intermediate sanctions The use of split sentencing, shock probation or parole, shock incarceration, mixed sentencing, community service, intensive probation supervision, or home confinement in lieu of other, more traditional sanctions, such as imprisonment and fines.

internal affairs The branch of a police organization tasked with investigating charges of wrongdoing involving members of the department.

International Justice and Public Safety Information Sharing Network (NLETS) An important law enforcement information-sharing resource.

international terrorism The unlawful use of force or violence by a group or an individual who has some connection to a foreign power or whose activities transcend national boundaries against people or property in order to intimidate or coerce a government, the civilian population, or any segment thereof in furtherance of political or social objectives.[20]

interrogation The information-gathering activity of police officers that involves the direct questioning of suspects.

Islamic law A system of laws, operative in some Arab countries, based on the Muslim religion and especially the holy book of Islam, the Koran.

jail A confinement facility administered by an agency of local government, typically a law enforcement agency, intended for adults but sometimes also containing juveniles. Jails hold people who are being detained pending adjudication or who were committed after adjudication, usually those sentenced to a year or less.

judge An elected or appointed public official who presides over a court of law and who is authorized to hear and sometimes to decide cases and to conduct trials.

judicial review The power of a court to review actions and decisions made by other agencies of government.

jurisdiction The territory, subject matter, or people over which a court or other justice agency may exercise lawful authority, as determined by statute or constitution.

jurisprudence The philosophy of law. Also, the science and study of the law.

juror A member of a trial or grand jury who has been selected for jury duty and is required to serve as an arbiter of the facts in a court of law. Jurors are expected to render verdicts of "guilty" or "not guilty" as to the charges brought against the accused, although they may sometimes fail to do so (as in the case of a hung jury).

jury selection The process whereby, according to law and precedent, members of a particular trial jury are chosen.

just deserts A model of criminal sentencing that holds that criminal offenders deserve the punishment they receive at the hands of the law and that punishments should be appropriate to the type and severity of the crime committed.

justice The principle of fairness; the ideal of moral equity.

justice model A contemporary model of imprisonment based on the principle of just deserts.

justification A legal defense in which the defendant admits to committing the act in question but claims it was necessary in order to avoid some greater evil.

juvenile A youth at or below the upper age of juvenile court jurisdiction in a particular state.

juvenile court Any court that has jurisdiction over matters involving juveniles.

juvenile disposition The decision of a juvenile court that concludes a dispositional hearing. The adjudicated juvenile might be committed to a juvenile correctional facility; be placed in a juvenile residence, shelter, or care or treatment program; be required to meet certain standards of conduct; or be released.

juvenile justice system The government agencies that function to investigate, supervise, adjudicate, care for, or confine youthful offenders and other children subject to the jurisdiction of the juvenile court.

juvenile petition A document filed in juvenile court alleging that a juvenile is a delinquent, a status offender, or a dependent and asking that the court assume jurisdiction over the juvenile or that an alleged delinquent be transferred to a criminal court for prosecution as an adult.

Kansas City experiment The first large-scale scientific study of law enforcement practices. Sponsored by the Police Foundation, it focused on the practice of preventive patrol.

Knapp Commission A committee that investigated police corruption in New York City in the early 1970s.

landmark case A precedent-setting court decision that produces substantial changes both in the understanding of the requirements of due process and in the practical day-to-day operations of the justice system.

larceny-theft (UCR/NIBRS) The unlawful taking or attempted taking, carrying, leading, or riding away of property, from the possession or constructive possession of another. Motor vehicles are excluded. Larceny is the most common of the eight major offenses, although probably only a small percentage of all larcenies is actually reported to the police because of the small dollar amounts involved.

latent evidence Evidence of relevance to a criminal investigation that is not readily seen by the unaided eye.

law A rule of conduct, generally found enacted in the form of a statute, that proscribes or mandates certain forms of behavior.

Law Enforcement Assistance Administration (LEAA) A now-defunct federal agency established under Title I of the Omnibus Crime Control and Safe Streets Act of 1968 to funnel federal funding to state and local law enforcement agencies.

lay witness An eyewitness, character witness, or other person called on to testify who is not considered an expert. Lay witnesses must testify to facts only and may not draw conclusions or express opinions.

legal cause A legally recognizable cause. A legal cause must be demonstrated in court in order to hold an individual criminally liable for causing harm.

legalistic style A style of policing marked by a strict concern with enforcing the precise letter of the law. Legalistic departments may take a hands-off approach to disruptive or problematic behavior that does not violate the criminal law.

less-lethal weapon A weapon that is designed to disable, capture, or immobilize—but not kill—a suspect. Occasional deaths do result from the use of such weapons, however.

line operations In police organizations, the field activities or supervisory activities directly related to day-to-day police work.

malware Malicious computer programs such as viruses, worms, and Trojan horses.

mandatory release The release of an inmate from prison that is determined by statute or sentencing guidelines and is not decided by a parole board or other authority.[21]

mandatory sentencing A structured sentencing scheme that allows no leeway in the nature of the sentence imposed. Under mandatory sentencing, clearly enumerated punishments are mandated for specific offenses or for habitual offenders convicted of a series of crimes.

mens rea The state of mind that accompanies a criminal act. Also, a guilty mind.

***Miranda* triggers** The dual principles of custody and interrogation, both of which are necessary before an advisement of rights is required.

***Miranda* warnings** The advisement of rights due criminal suspects by the police before questioning begins. *Miranda* warnings were first set forth by the U.S. Supreme Court in the 1966 case of *Miranda* v. *Arizona.*

misdemeanor An offense punishable by incarceration, usually in a local confinement facility, for a period whose upper limit is prescribed by statute in a given jurisdiction, typically one year or less.

mitigating circumstances Circumstances relating to the commission of a crime that may be considered to reduce the blameworthiness of the offender.

mixed sentence A sentence that requires that a convicted offender serve weekends (or other specified periods of time) in a confinement facility (usually a jail) while undergoing probationary supervision in the community.

M'Naghten rule A rule for determining insanity that asks whether the defendant knew what he or she was doing or whether the defendant knew that what he or she was doing was wrong.

motive A person's reason for committing a crime.

motor vehicle theft (UCR/NIBRS) The theft or attempted theft of a motor vehicle. *Motor vehicle* is defined as a self-propelled road vehicle that runs on land surface and not on rails. The stealing of trains, planes, boats, construction equipment, and most farm machinery is classified as larceny under the UCR/NIBRS Program, not as motor vehicle397theft.

multiculturalism The existence within one society of diverse groups that maintain unique cultural identities while frequently accepting and participating in the larger society's legal and political systems.[22] Multiculturalism is often used in conjunction with the term *diversity* to identify many distinctions of social significance.

murder The unlawful killing of a human being. *Murder* is a generic term that in common usage may include first- and second-degree murder, manslaughter, involuntary manslaughter, and other similar offenses.

National Crime Victimization Survey (NCVS) An annual survey of selected American households conducted by the Bureau of Justice Statistics to determine the extent of criminal victimization—especially unreported victimization—in the United States.

National Incident-Based Reporting System (NIBRS) An incident-based reporting system that collects detailed data on every single crime occurrence. NIBRS data are replacing the kinds of summary data that have traditionally been provided by the FBI's Uniform Crime Reporting Program.

neglected child A child who is not receiving the proper level of physical or psychological care from his or her parents or guardians or who has been placed up for adoption in violation of the law.

1983 lawsuit A civil suit brought under Title 42, Section 1983, of the U.S. Code against anyone who denies others their constitutional right to life, liberty, or property without due process of law.

nolo contendere A plea of "no contest." A no-contest plea is used when the defendant does not wish to contest conviction. Because the plea does not admit guilt, however, it cannot provide the basis for later civil suits that might follow a criminal conviction.

offense A violation of the criminal law. Also, in some jurisdictions, a minor crime, such as jaywalking, that is sometimes described as *ticketable.*

opening statement The initial statement of the prosecution or the defense, made in a court of law to a judge, or to a judge and jury, describing the facts that he or she intends to present during trial to prove the case.

operational capacity The number of inmates a prison can effectively accommodate based on management considerations.

organized crime The unlawful activities of the members of a highly organized, disciplined association engaged in supplying illegal goods or services, including gambling, prostitution, loan-sharking, narcotics, and labor racketeering, and in other unlawful activities.[23]

original jurisdiction The lawful authority of a court to hear or to act on a case from its beginning and to pass judgment on the law and the facts. The authority may be over a specific geographic area or over particular types of cases.

parens patriae A common law principle that allows the state to assume a parental role and to take custody of a child when he or she becomes delinquent, is abandoned, or is in need of care that the natural parents are unable or unwilling to provide.

parole The status of a convicted offender who has been conditionally released from prison by a paroling authority before the expiration of his or her sentence and placed under the supervision of a parole agency, and is required to observe the conditions of parole.

parole board A state paroling authority. Most states have parole boards that decide when an incarcerated offender is ready for conditional release. Some boards also function as revocation hearing panels.

parole (probation) violation An act or a failure to act by a parolee (or probationer) that does not conform to the conditions of his or her parole (or probation).

parole revocation The administrative action of a paroling authority removing a person from parole status in response to a violation of lawfully required conditions of parole, including the prohibition against committing a new offense, and usually resulting in a return to prison.

Part I offenses A UCR/NIBRS offense group used to report murder, rape, robbery, aggravated assault, burglary, larceny-theft, motor vehicle theft, and arson, as defined under the FBI's UCR/NIBRS Program.

Part II offenses A UCR/NIBRS offense group used to report arrests for less serious offenses. Agencies are limited to reporting only arrest information for Part II offenses, with the exception of simple assault.

Peace Officer Standards and Training (POST) program The official program of a state or legislative jurisdiction that sets standards for the training of law enforcement officers. All states set such standards, although not all use the term *POST.*

penal code The written, organized, and compiled form of the criminal laws of a jurisdiction.

penal law See *criminal law.*

peremptory challenge The right to challenge a potential juror without disclosing the reason for the challenge. Prosecutors and defense attorneys routinely use peremptory challenges to eliminate from juries individuals who, although they express no obvious bias, are thought to be capable of swaying the jury in an undesirable direction.

perjury The intentional making of a false statement as part of the testimony by a sworn witness in a judicial proceeding on a matter relevant to the case at hand.

petty crime See *quality-of-life offense.*

plain view A legal term describing the ready visibility of objects that might be seized as evidence during a search by police in the absence of a search warrant specifying the seizure of those objects. To lawfully seize evidence in plain view, officers must have a legal right to be in the viewing area and must have cause to believe that the evidence is somehow associated with criminal activity.

plea In criminal proceedings, the defendant's formal answer in court to the charge contained in a complaint, information, or indictment that he or she is guilty of the offense charged, is not guilty of the offense charged, or does not contest the charge.

plea bargaining The process of negotiating an agreement among the defendant, the prosecutor, and the court as to an appropriate plea and associated sentence in a given case. Plea bargaining circumvents the trial process and dramatically reduces the time required for the resolution of a criminal case.

police-community relations (PCR) An area of police activity that recognizes the need for the community and the police to work together effectively and is based on the notion that the police derive their legitimacy from the community they serve. Many police agencies began to explore PCR in the 1960s and 1970s.

police corruption The abuse of police authority for personal or organizational gain.[24]

police discretion The opportunity of law enforcement officers to exercise choice in their daily activities.

police ethics The special responsibility to adhere to moral duty and obligation that is inherent in police work.

police management The administrative activities of controlling, directing, and coordinating police personnel, resources, and activities in the service of crime prevention, the apprehension of criminals, the recovery of stolen property, and the performance of a variety of regulatory and helping services.

police professionalism The increasing formalization of police work and the accompanying rise in public acceptance of the police.

police subculture A particular set of values, beliefs, and acceptable forms of behavior characteristic of American police with which the police profession strives to imbue new recruits. Socialization into the police subculture commences with recruit training and continues thereafter.

police use of force The use of physical restraint by a police officer when dealing with a member of the public.[25]

police working personality All aspects of the traditional values and patterns of behavior evidenced by police officers who have been effectively socialized into the police subculture. Characteristics of the police personality often extend to the personal lives of law enforcement personnel.

precedent A legal principle that ensures that previous judicial decisions are authoritatively considered and incorporated into future cases.

preliminary hearing A proceeding before a judicial officer in which three matters must be decided: (1) whether a crime was committed, (2) whether the crime occurred within the territorial jurisdiction of the court, and (3) whether there are reasonable grounds to believe that the defendant committed the crime.

presentence investigation (PSI) The examination of a convicted offender's background prior to sentencing. Presentence examinations are generally conducted by probation or parole officers and are submitted to sentencing authorities.

presumptive sentencing A model of criminal punishment that meets the following conditions: (1) The appropriate sentence for an offender convicted of a specific charge is presumed to fall within a range of sentences authorized by sentencing guidelines that are adopted by a legislatively created sentencing body, usually a sentencing commission; (2) sentencing judges are expected to sentence within the range or to provide written justification for failing to do so; and (3) There is a mechanism for review, usually appellate, of any departure from the guidelines.

pretrial release The release of an accused person from custody, for all or part of the time before or during prosecution, upon his or her promise to appear in court when required.

prison A state or federal confinement facility that has custodial authority over adults sentenced to confinement.

prison argot The slang that is characteristic of prison subculture and prison life.

prison capacity The size of the correctional population an institution can effectively hold.[26] There are three types of prison capacity: rated, operational, and design.

prisoner reentry The managed return to the community of individuals released from prison. Also called *reentry.*

prisonization The process whereby newly institutionalized offenders come to accept prison lifestyles and criminal values. Although many inmates begin their prison experience with only a few values that support criminal behavior, the socialization experience they undergo while incarcerated leads to a much wider acceptance of such values.

prison subculture The values and behavioral patterns characteristic of prison inmates. Prison subculture has been found to be surprisingly consistent across the country.

private prison A correctional institution operated by a private firm on behalf of a local or state government.

private protective services The independent or proprietary commercial organizations that provide protective services to employers on a contractual basis.

privatization The movement toward the wider use of private prisons.

probable cause A set of facts and circumstances that would induce a reasonably intelligent and prudent person to believe that a particular other person has committed a specific crime. Also, reasonable grounds to make or believe an accusation. Probable cause refers to the necessary level of belief that would allow for police seizures (arrests) of individuals and full searches of dwellings, vehicles, and possessions.

probation A sentence of imprisonment that is suspended. Also, the conditional freedom granted by a judicial officer to a convicted offender, as long as the person meets certain conditions of behavior.

probation revocation A court order taking away a convicted offender's probationary status and usually withdrawing the conditional freedom associated with that status in response to a violation of the conditions of probation.

probative value The degree to which a particular item of evidence is useful in, and relevant to, proving something important in a trial.

problem police officer A law enforcement officer who exhibits problem behavior, as indicated by high rates of citizen complaints and use-of-force incidents and by other evidence.[27]

problem-solving policing A type of policing that assumes that many crimes are caused by existing social conditions within the community and that crimes can be controlled by uncovering and effectively addressing underlying social problems. Problem-solving policing makes use of community resources, such as counseling centers, welfare programs, and job-training facilities. It also attempts to involve citizens in crime prevention through education, negotiation, and conflict management.

procedural defense A defense that claims that the defendant was in some significant way discriminated against in the justice process or that some important aspect of official procedure was not properly followed in the investigation or prosecution of the crime charged.

procedural law The part of the law that specifies the methods to be used in enforcing substantive law.

property bond The setting of bail in the form of land, houses, stocks, or other tangible property. In the event that the defendant absconds before trial, the bond becomes the property of the court.

property crime A UCR/NIBRS summary offense category that includes burglary, larceny-theft, motor vehicle theft, and arson.

proportionality A sentencing principle that holds that the severity of sanctions should bear a direct relationship to the seriousness of the crime committed.

prosecutor An attorney whose official duty is to conduct criminal proceedings on behalf of the state or the people against those accused of having committed criminal offenses.

prosecutorial discretion The decision-making power of prosecutors, based on the wide range of choices available to them, in the handling of criminal defendants, the scheduling of cases for trial, the acceptance of negotiated pleas, and so on. The most important form of prosecutorial discretion lies in the power to charge, or not to charge, a person with an offense.

psychological manipulation The manipulative actions by police interviewers, designed to pressure suspects to divulge information, that are based on subtle forms of intimidation and control.

public defender An attorney employed by a government agency or subagency, or by a private organization under contract to a government body, for the purpose of providing defense services to indigents, or an attorney who has volunteered such service.

public-order advocate One who believes that under certain circumstances involving a criminal threat to public safety, the interests of society should take precedence over individual rights.

quality-of-life offense A minor violation of the law (sometimes called a *petty crime*) that demoralizes community residents and businesspeople. Quality-of-life offenses involve acts that create physical disorder (for example, excessive noise and vandalism) or that reflect social decay (for example, panhandling and prostitution).

racial profiling "Any police-initiated action that relies on the race, ethnicity, or national origin rather than [1] the behavior of an individual, or [2] on information that leads the police to a particular individual who has been identified as being, or having been, engaged in criminal activity."[28]

rape Unlawful sexual intercourse achieved through force and without consent. Broadly speaking, the term *rape* has been applied to a wide variety of sexual attacks and may include same-sex rape and the rape of a male by a female. Some jurisdictions refer to same-sex rape as *sexual battery.*

rated capacity The number of inmates a prison can handle according to the judgment of experts.

real evidence Evidence that consists of physical material or traces of physical activity.

reasonable force A degree of force that is appropriate in a given situation and is not excessive. Also, the minimum degree of force necessary to protect oneself, one's property, a third party, or the property of another in the face of a substantial threat.

reasonable suspicion The level of suspicion that would justify an officer in making further inquiry or in conducting further investigation. Reasonable suspicion may permit stopping a person for questioning or for a simple pat-down search. Also, a belief, based on a consideration of the facts at hand and on reasonable inferences drawn from those facts, that would induce an ordinarily prudent and cautious person under the same circumstances to conclude that criminal activity is taking place or that criminal activity has recently occurred. Reasonable suspicion is a *general* and reasonable belief that a crime is in progress or has occurred, whereas probable cause is a reasonable belief that a *particular* person has committed a *specific* crime.

recidivism The repetition of criminal behavior. In statistical practice, a recidivism rate may be any of a number of possible counts or instances of arrest, conviction, correctional commitment, or correctional status change related to repetitions of these events within a given period of time.

reckless behavior An activity that increases the risk of harm.

reentry See *prisoner rentry.*

regional jail A jail that is built and run using the combined resources of a variety of local jurisdictions.

rehabilitation The attempt to reform a criminal offender. Also, the state in which a reformed offender is said to be.

release on recognizance (ROR) The pretrial release of a criminal defendant on his or her written promise to appear in court as required. No cash or property bond is required.

remote location monitoring A supervision strategy that uses electronic technology to track offenders who are sentenced to house arrest or those who have been ordered to limit their movements while completing a sentence involving probation or parole.

restitution A court requirement that an alleged or convicted offender pay money or provide services to the victim of the crime or provide services to the community.

restoration A goal of criminal sentencing that attempts to make the victim "whole again."

restorative justice (RJ) A sentencing model that builds on restitution and community participation in an attempt to make the victim "whole again."

retribution The act of taking revenge on a criminal perpetrator.

revocation hearing A hearing held before a legally constituted hearing body (such as a parole board) to determine whether a parolee or probationer has violated the conditions and requirements of his or her parole or probation.

robbery (UCR/NIBRS) The unlawful taking or attempted taking of property that is in the immediate possession of another by force or violence and/or by putting the victim in fear. Armed robbery differs from unarmed, or strong-arm, robbery in that it involves a weapon. Contrary to popular conceptions, highway robbery does not necessarily occur on a street—and rarely in a vehicle. The term *highway robbery* applies to any form of robbery that occurs outdoors in a public place.

rule of law The maxim that an orderly society must be governed by established principles and known codes that are applied uniformly and fairly to all of its members.

rules of evidence The court rules that govern the admissibility of evidence at criminal hearings and trials.

scientific jury selection The use of correlational techniques from the social sciences to gauge the likelihood that potential jurors will vote for conviction or for acquittal.

scientific police management The application of social sciences techniques to the study of police administration for the purpose of increasing effectiveness, reducing the frequency of citizen complaints, and enhancing the efficient use of available resources.

search incident to an arrest A warrantless search of an arrested individual conducted to ensure the safety of the arresting officer. Because individuals placed under arrest may be in possession of weapons, courts have recognized the need for arresting officers to protect themselves by conducting an immediate search of arrestees without obtaining a warrant.

security threat group (STG) An inmate group, gang, or organization whose members act together to pose a threat to the safety of corrections staff or the public, who prey on other inmates, or who threaten the secure and orderly operation of a correctional institution.

self-defense The protection of oneself or of one's property from unlawful injury or from the immediate risk of unlawful injury. Also, the justification that the person who committed an act that would otherwise constitute an offense reasonably believed that the act was necessary to protect self or property from immediate danger.

sentencing The imposition of a criminal sanction by a judicial authority.

sequestered jury A jury that is isolated from the public during the course of a trial and throughout the deliberation process.

service style A style of policing marked by a concern with helping rather than strict enforcement. Service-oriented police agencies are more likely to refer citizens to community resources, such as drug-treatment programs, than are other types of agencies.

sexual battery The intentional and wrongful physical contact with a person, without his or her consent, that entails a sexual component or purpose.

sheriff The elected chief officer of a county law enforcement agency. The sheriff is usually responsible for law enforcement in unincorporated areas and for the operation of the county jail.

shock incarceration A sentencing option that makes use of "boot camp"–type prisons to impress on convicted offenders the realities of prison life.

shock probation The practice of sentencing offenders to prison, allowing them to apply for probationary release, and enacting such release in surprise fashion. Offenders who receive shock probation may not be aware that they will be released on probation and may expect to spend a much longer time behind bars.

"sneak and peek" search A search that occurs in the suspect's absence and without his or her prior knowledge. Also known as a *delayed-notification search.*

social control The use of sanctions and rewards within a group to influence and shape the behavior of individual members of that group. Social control is a primary concern of social groups and communities, and it is their interest in the exercise of social control that leads to the creation of both criminal and civil statutes.

social debt A sentencing principle that holds that an offender's criminal history should objectively be taken into account in sentencing decisions.

social justice An ideal that embraces all aspects of civilized life and that is linked to fundamental notions of fairness and to cultural beliefs about right and wrong.

spam Unsolicited commercial bulk e-mail whose primary purpose is the advertisement or promotion of a commercial product or service.

span of control The number of police personnel or the number of units supervised by a particular officer.

specific deterrence A goal of criminal sentencing that seeks to prevent a particular offender from engaging in repeat criminality.

Speedy Trial Act A 1974 federal law requiring that proceedings against a defendant in a criminal case begin within a specified period of time, such as 70 working days after indictment. Some states also have speedy trial requirements.

split sentence A sentence explicitly requiring the convicted offender to serve a period of confinement in a local, state, or federal facility, followed by a period of probation.

staff operations In police organizations, activities (such as administration and training) that provide support for line operations.

stalking Repeated harassing and threatening behavior by one individual against another, aspects of which may be planned or carried out in secret. Stalking might involve following a person, appearing at a person's home or place of business, making harassing phone calls, leaving written messages or objects, or vandalizing a person's property. Most stalking laws require that the perpetrator make a credible threat of violence against the victim or members of the victim's immediate family.

stare decisis A legal principle that requires that in subsequent cases on similar issues of law and fact, courts be bound by their own earlier decisions and by those of higher courts having jurisdiction over them. The term literally means "standing by decided matters."

state court administrator A coordinator who assists with case-flow management, operating funds budgeting, and court docket administration.

state court system A state judicial structure. Most states generally have at least three court levels: trial courts, appellate courts, and a state supreme court.

status offender A child who commits an act that is contrary to the law by virtue of the offender's status as a child. Purchasing cigarettes, buying alcohol, and being truant are examples of such behavior.

status offense An act or conduct that is declared by statute to be an offense, but only when committed by or engaged in by a juvenile, and that can be adjudicated only by a juvenile court.

statutory law The written or codified law; the "law on the books," as enacted by a government body or agency having the power to make laws.

strategic policing A type of policing that retains the traditional police goal of professional crime fighting but enlarges the enforcement target to include nontraditional kinds of criminals, such as serial offenders, gangs and criminal associations, drug-distribution networks, and sophisticated white-collar and computer criminals. Strategic policing generally makes use of innovative enforcement techniques, including intelligence operations, undercover stings, electronic surveillance, and sophisticated forensic methods.

strict liability A liability without fault or intention. Strict liability offenses do not require *mens rea.*

structured sentencing A model of criminal punishment that includes determinate and commission-created presumptive sentencing schemes, as well as voluntary/advisory sentencing guidelines.

subpoena A written order issued by a judicial officer or grand jury requiring an individual to appear in court and to give testimony or to bring material to be used as evidence. Some subpoenas mandate that books, papers, and other items be surrendered to the court.

substantive criminal law The part of the law that defines crimes and specifies punishments.

suspicionless search A search conducted by law enforcement personnel without a warrant and without suspicion. Suspicionless searches are permissible only if based on an overriding concern for public safety.

***Tazir* crime** A minor violation of Islamic law that is regarded as an offense against society, not God.

team policing The reorganization of conventional patrol strategies into "an integrated and versatile police team assigned to a fixed district."[29]

teen court An alternative approach to juvenile justice in which alleged offenders are judged and/or sentenced by a jury of their peers.

terrorism A violent act or an act dangerous to human life in violation of the criminal laws of the United States or of any state, committed to intimidate or coerce a government, the civilian population, or any segment thereof in furtherance of political or social objectives.[30]

testimony The oral evidence offered by a sworn witness on the witness stand during a criminal trial.

tort A wrongful act, damage, or injury not involving a breach of contract. Also, a private or civil wrong or injury.

total institution An enclosed facility separated from society both socially and physically, where the inhabitants share all aspects of their daily lives.

transnational organized crime Unlawful activity undertaken and supported by organized criminal groups operating across national boundaries.

treason A U.S. citizen's actions to help a foreign government overthrow, make war against, or seriously injure the United States.[31] Also, the attempt to overthrow the government of the society of which one is a member.

trial In criminal proceedings, the examination in court of the issues of fact and relevant law in a case for the purpose of convicting or acquitting the defendant.

trial *de novo* Literally, "new trial." The term is applied to cases that are retried on appeal, as opposed to those that are simply reviewed on the record.

truth in sentencing A close correspondence between the sentence imposed on an offender and the time actually served in prison.[32]

undisciplined child A child who is beyond parental control, as evidenced by his or her refusal to obey legitimate authorities, such as school officials and teachers.

Uniform Crime Reporting (UCR) Program A statistical reporting program run by the FBI's Criminal Justice Information Services (CJIS) division. The UCR Program publishes *Crime in the United States*, which provides an annual summation of the incidence and rate of reported crimes throughout the United States.

USA PATRIOT Act A federal law (Public Law 107–56) enacted in response to terrorist attacks on the World Trade Center and the Pentagon on September 11, 2001. The law, officially titled the Uniting and Strengthening America by Providing Appropriate Tools Required to Intercept and Obstruct Terrorism Act, substantially broadened the investigative authority of law enforcement agencies throughout America and is applicable to many crimes other than terrorism. The law was slightly revised and reauthorized by Congress in 2006.

verdict The decision of the jury in a jury trial or of a judicial officer in a nonjury trial.

victim-impact statement An in-court statement made by the victim or by survivors to sentencing authorities seeking to make an informed sentencing decision.

victims' assistance program An organized program that offers services to victims of crime in the areas of crisis intervention and follow-up counseling and that helps victims secure their rights under the law.

violent crime A UCR/NIBRS summary offense category that includes murder, rape, robbery, and aggravated assault.

voluntary/advisory sentencing guidelines Recommended sentencing policies that are not required by law.

warrant In criminal proceedings, a writ issued by a judicial officer directing a law enforcement officer to perform a specified act and affording the officer protection from damages if he or she performs it.

watchman style A style of policing marked by a concern for order maintenance. Watchman policing is characteristic of lower-class communities where informal police intervention in the lives of residents is employed in the service of keeping the peace.

white-collar crime Violation of the criminal law committed by a person of respectability and high social status in the course of his or her occupation. Also, a nonviolent crime for financial gain utilizing deception and committed by anyone who has special technical or professional knowledge of business or government, irrespective of the person's occupation.

writ of *certiorari* A writ issued from an appellate court for the purpose of obtaining from a lower court the record of its proceedings in a particular case. In some states, this writ is the mechanism for discretionary review. A request for review is made by petitioning for a writ of *certiorari*, and the granting of review is indicated by the issuance of the writ.

writ of *habeas corpus* A writ that directs the person detaining a prisoner to bring him or her before a judicial officer to determine the lawfulness of the imprisonment.

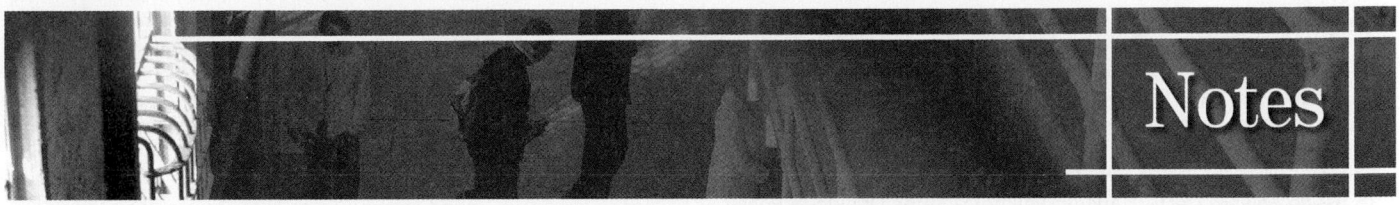

Notes

Chapter 1: What Is Criminal Justice?

i. ABC News, September 16, 2001.
ii. All boldfaced terms are explained whenever possible using definitions provided by the Bureau of Justice Statistics under a mandate of the Justice System Improvement Act of 1979. That mandate found its most complete expression in the *Dictionary of Criminal Justice Data Terminology* (Washington, DC: Bureau of Justice Statistics, 1982), the second edition of which provides the wording for many definitions in this text.
iii. ABC News, September 11, 2001.
iv. Adapted from U.S. Code, Title 28, Section 20.3 (2[d]). Title 28 of the U.S. Code defines the term *administration of criminal justice.*
v. Prepared remarks of U.S. Attorney General Alberto Gonzales, Address to the National Association of Counties Legislative Conference, Washington, DC, March 7, 2005.
vi. Adapted from Robert M. Shusta et al., *Multicultural Law Enforcement*, 2nd ed. (Upper Saddle River, NJ: Prentice Hall, 2002), p. 443.

---

1. American Civil Liberties Union website, http://www.aclu.org/issues/criminal/iscj.html (accessed January 22, 2010).
2. ABC News, September 11, 2001. Christopher was repeating a phrase generally attributed to former U.S. Supreme Court Justice Arthur Goldberg.
3. Sam Coates and Dan Eggen, "A City of Despair and Lawlessness," *Washington Post*, September 2, 2005, p. A1.
4. Mark Gongloff, "Anarchy in New Orleans," *Wall Street Journal*, September 1, 2005.
5. "Looters Ransack Stores in Downtown New Orleans," *Wall Street Journal*, August 31, 2005.
6. Ibid.
7. Kevin Johnson, "Officers at 'Fort Apache' Finally Get Breather," *USA Today*, September 7, 2005, p. 3A.
8. Kevin McCoy, "Fraud Mounts in Katrina Aid Program," *USA Today*, February 13, 2006, p. 1A.
9. Ibid.
10. For a thorough discussion of immigration as it relates to crime, see Ramiro Martinez, Jr., and Matthew T. Lee, "On Immigration and Crime," in National Institute of Justice, *Criminal Justice 2000, Vol. 1: The Nature of Crime—Continuity and Change* (Washington, DC: U.S. Department of Justice, Office of Justice Programs, 2000).
11. "Inside Columbine," *Rocky Mountain News*, http://www.rockymountainnews .com/drmn/columbine (accessed July 4, 2010).
12. "Cries of Relief," *Time*, April 26, 1993, p. 18.
13. Laurence McQuillan, "Bush to Urge Jail for Execs Who Lie," *USA Today*, July 9, 2002, http://www.usatoday.com/news/washdc/2002/07/09/bush-business.htm (accessed July 9, 2006).
14. Sarbanes-Oxley Act of 2002 (officially known as the Public Company Accounting Reform and Investor Protection Act), Public Law 107–204, 116 Stat. 745 (July 30, 2002).
15. PricewaterhouseCoopers, "The Sarbanes-Oxley Act," http://www.pwcglobal.com/Extweb/NewCoAtWork.nsf/docid/D0D7F79003C6D64485256CF30074D66C (accessed July 8, 2007).
16. Richard Esposito, Eloise Harper, and Maddy Sauer, "Bernie Madoff Pleads Guilty to Ponzi Scheme, Goes Straight to Jail, Says He's 'Deeply Sorry,'" ABC News, March 12, 2009, http://abcnews.go.com/Blotter/WallStreet/Story?id=7066715&page=1 (accessed July 4, 2010).
17. Robert Lenzner, "Bernie Madoff's $50 Billion Ponzi Scheme," Forbes.com, December 12, 2008, http://www.forbes.com/2008/12/12/madoff-ponzi-hedge-pf-ii-in_rl_1212croesus_inl .html (accessed September 28, 2010).
18. Emanuella Grinberg, "California Senate Passes Tougher Sentencing Laws for Sex Offenders," CNN Justice, August 24, 2010, http://www.cnn.com/2010/CRIME/08/24/california.chelseas.law/ (accessed September 4, 2010).
19. Wendy Koch, "States Get Tougher with Sex Offenders," *USA Today*, May 24, 2006, p. 1A.
20. Ibid.
21. Martin Luther King, in an address to the Tenth Anniversary Convention of the Southern Christian Leadership Conference in Atlanta, Georgia, on August 16, 1967. It was abolitionist and Unitarian minister Theodore Parker who first used a similar phrase in the mid-1800s, saying, "I do not pretend to understand the moral universe; the arc is a long one. . . . And from what I see I am sure it bends toward justice."
22. *The American Heritage Dictionary on CD-ROM* (Boston: Houghton Mifflin, 1991).
23. For a good overview of the issues involved, see Judge Harold J. Rothwax, *Guilty: The Collapse of Criminal Justice* (New York: Random House, 1996).
24. For one perspective on the detention of Muslims following September 11, 2001, see the plaintiff's motion to stay proceedings on defendant's summary judgment motion pending discovery, in *Center for National Security Studies* v. *U.S. Department of Justice*, U.S. District Court for the District of Columbia (Civil Action No. 01–2500; January 2002), http://www.aclu.org/court/cnssjan22.pdf (accessed September 24, 2007).
25. The systems model of criminal justice is often attributed to the frequent use of the term *system* by the 1967 Presidential Commission in its report *The Challenge of Crime in a Free Society* (Washington, DC: U.S. Government Printing Office, 1967).
26. One of the first published works to use the nonsystem approach to criminal justice was the American Bar Association's *New Perspective on Urban Crime* (Washington, DC: ABA Special Committee on Crime Prevention and Control, 1972).
27. Jerome H. Skolnick, *Justice without Trial* (New York: John Wiley, 1966), p. 179.
28. "The Defendants' Rights at a Criminal Trial," http://www.mycounsel.com/content/arrests/court/rights.html (accessed February 10, 2010).
29. For a complete and now-classic analysis of the impact of decisions made by the Warren Court, see Fred P. Graham, *The Due Process Revolution: The Warren Court's Impact on Criminal Law* (New York: Hayden Press, 1970).
30. *Gideon* v. *Wainwright*, 372 U.S. 353 (1963).
31. Herbert Packer, *The Limits of the Criminal Sanction* (Stanford, CA: Stanford University Press, 1968).

32. "Understanding and Using Evidence-Based Practices," Justice Resource Update, http://www.ojp.gov/justiceresourceupdate/june2010 (accessed June 3, 2010).
33. Senate Bill 714; H.R. 5143.
34. For an excellent history of policing in the United States, see Edward A. Farris, "Five Decades of American Policing, 1932–1982," *Police Chief* (November 1982), pp. 30–36.
35. Gene Edward Carte, "August Vollmer and the Origins of Police Professionalism," *Journal of Police Science and Administration*, Vol. 1, No. 1 (1973), pp. 274–281.
36. Chris Eskridge distinguishes between police *training*, which is "job-specific" and is intended to teach trainees *how* to do something (like fire a weapon), and *justice education*, whose purpose is to "develop a general spirit of inquiry." See C. W. Eskridge, "Criminal Justice Education and Its Potential Impact on the Sociopolitical-Economic Climate of Central European Nations," *Journal of Criminal Justice Education*, Vol. 14, No. 1 (spring 2003), pp. 105–118; and James O. Finckenauer, "The Quest for Quality in Criminal Justice Education," *Justice Quarterly*, Vol. 22, No. 4 (December 2005), pp. 413–426.
37. "Understanding and Using Evidence-Based Practices."
38. KVBC-TV (Las Vegas), "Warren Jeffs Sentenced," http://www.kvbc.com/Global/story.asp?S=7388968 (accessed May 1, 2010).
39. "Polygamist Wins Parole from Utah State Prison," Associated Press, August 27, 2007.
40. On March 22, 1794, the U.S. Congress barred American citizens from transporting slaves from the United States to another nation or between foreign nations. On January 1, 1808, the importation of slaves into the United States became illegal, and Congress charged the U.S. Revenue Cutter Service (now known as the U.S. Coast Guard) with enforcing the law on the high seas. Although some slave ships were seized, the importation of Africans for sale as slaves apparently continued in some southern states until the early 1860s. See U.S. Coast Guard, "U.S. Coast Guard in Illegal Immigration (1794–1971)," http://www.uscg.mil/hq/g-o/g-opl/mle/amiohist.htm (accessed October 13, 2009).
41. U.S. Census Bureau website, http://www.census.gov (accessed March 22, 2010). Population statistics are estimates because race is a difficult concept to define and Census Bureau interviewers allow individuals to choose more than one race when completing census forms.

Chapter 2: The Crime Picture

i. Dan Eggen, "Major Crimes in U.S. Increase: 2001 Rise Follows Nine Years of Decline," *Washington Post*, June 23, 2002, p. A1.
ii. Jonathan Turley, "Arrest Me . . . Before I Strike Again," *USA Today*, February 22, 2005, p. 13A.
iii. Identity Theft Resource Center website, http://www.idtheftcenter.org (accessed April 24, 2010).
iv. Violence against Women Office, *Stalking and Domestic Violence: Report to Congress* (Washington, DC: U.S. Department of Justice, 2001), p. 5.
v. Ibid.
vi. Andrew Backover, "Two Former WorldCom Execs Charged," *USA Today* Online, August 1, 2002, http://www.usatoday.com/money/industries/telecom/2002-08-01-worldcom-execs-surrender_x.htm (accessed August 2, 2006).
vii. Michael L. Benson, Francis T. Cullen, and William J. Maakestad, *Local Prosecutors and Corporate Crime* (Washington, DC: National Institute of Justice, 1992), p. 1.
viii. The Organized Crime Control Act of 1970.
ix. Federal Bureau of Investigation Counterterrorism Section, *Terrorism in the United States, 1987* (Washington, DC: FBI, December 1987).
x. Federal Bureau of Investigation, *FBI Policy and Guidelines: Counterterrorism*, http://www.fbi.gov/contact/fo/jackson/cntrterr.htm (accessed August 26, 2009).
xi. Ibid.

---

1. James Q. Wilson, "Point of View," *Chronicle of Higher Education*, June 10, 1992, p. A40.
2. Chris Balish, "NCIS Honored as Top Scripted TV Series," OnTheRedCarpet.com, March 23, 2010, http://ontheredcarpet.typepad.com/ontheredcarpet/2010/03/crime-drama-ncis-honored-as-top-scripted-tv-series.html (accessed September 1, 2010).
3. Gerard Gilbert, "*CSI*: The Cop Show That Conquered the World," *The (London) Independent*, December 19, 2006, http://www.findarticles.com/p/articles/mi_qn4158/is_20061219/ai_n17081057 (accessed March 10, 2010).
4. Norval Morris, "Crime, the Media, and Our Public Discourse," National Institute of Justice, Perspectives on Crime and Justice video series, recorded May 13, 1997.
5. Ibid.
6. Federal Bureau of Investigation, *Crime in the United States, 1987* (Washington, DC: U.S. Department of Justice, 1988), p. 1.
7. Federal Bureau of Investigation, "About the UCR Program," no date, http://www.fbi.gov/ucr/05cius/about/about_ucr.html (accessed May 29, 2009). The term *crime index* was originally recommended for reevaluation in 2004, but it wasn't until 2006 that use of the term was officially discontinued.
8. Statistics on state agency participation in NIBRS can be seen at Bureau of Justice Statistics, "UCR and NIBRS Participation," http://bjs.ojp.usdoj.gov/content/nibrsstatus.cfm (accessed September 4, 2010).
9. See the FBI's UCR/NIBRS website at http://www.fbi.gov/hq/cjisd/ucr.htm (accessed August 27, 2010).
10. The 1990 Crime Awareness and Campus Security Act (Public Law 101–542) required college campuses to commence publishing annual security reports beginning in September 1992.
11. U.S. Department of Education, *Summary Campus Crime and Security Statistics, 2006–2008: Criminal Offenses* (Washington, DC: U.S. Department of Education, 2010), http://www2.ed.gov/admins/lead/safety/criminal2006-08.xls (accessed September 4, 2010).
12. Katrina Baum and Patsy Klaus, *Violent Victimization of College Students, 1995–2002* (Washington, DC: Bureau of Justice Statistics, 2005).
13. Federal Bureau of Investigation, *Crime in the United States, 2009* (Washington, DC: U.S. Department of Justice, 2010).
14. President's Commission on Law Enforcement and Administration of Justice, *The Challenge of Crime in a Free Society* (Washington, DC: U.S. Government Printing Office, 1967). The commission relied on UCR data. The other crime statistics reported in this section come from Uniform Crime Reports for various years.
15. Frank Hagan, *Research Methods in Criminal Justice and Criminology* (New York: Macmillan, 1982).
16. U.S. Department of Justice, *Fiscal Years 2000–2005 Strategic Plan* (Washington, DC: U.S. Government Printing Office, 2000).
17. The war on drugs, and the use of that term, can be traced back to the Nixon administration. See Dan Baum, *Smoke and Mirrors: The War on Drugs and the Politics of Failure* (reprint, Boston: Little, Brown, 1997).
18. John J. Dilulio, Jr., "The Question of Black Crime," *Public Interest* (fall 1994), pp. 3–12.
19. Quoted in Eggen, "Major Crimes in U.S. Increase," p. A1.

20. Police Executive Research Forum, *A Gathering Storm* (Washington, DC: PERF, 2006).
21. Police Executive Research Forum, *Violent Crime in America: 24 Months of Alarming Trends* (Washington, DC: PERF, 2007).
22. Ibid., p. i.
23. Jim Kessler, Rachel Laser, Michael Earls, and Nikki Yamashiro, *The Impending Crime Wave: Four Dangerous New Trends and How to Stop Them* (Washington, DC: Third Way Foundation, February 2008).
24. For example, while crime clock data may imply that one murder occurs every half hour or so, most murders actually occur during the evening, and only a very few take place around sunrise.
25. Most offense definitions in this chapter are derived from those used by the UCR/NIBRS Program and are taken from the FBI's *Crime in the United States, 2009*, or from the Bureau of Justice Statistics, *Criminal Justice Data Terminology*, 2nd ed. (Washington, DC: BJS, 1981).
26. These and other statistics in this chapter are derived primarily from the FBI's *Crime in the United States, 2009*.
27. Bureau of Justice Statistics, *Report to the Nation on Crime and Justice*, 2nd ed. (Washington, DC: U.S. Government Printing Office, 1988), p. 4.
28. "Feds Deny Thwarting Sniper Suspect's Confession," CNN.com, October 31, 2002, http://www.cnn.com/2002/US/10/30/snipers.interrogation/index.html (accessed October 31, 2002).
29. "Sniper Malvo Given Second Life Sentence," *USA Today*, October 27, 2004, p. 3A.
30. BJS, *Report to the Nation on Crime and Justice*, p. 4.
31. Ibid.
32. For excellent coverage of serial killers, see Steven Egger, *The Killers among Us: An Examination of Serial Murder and Its Investigation* (Upper Saddle River, NJ: Prentice Hall, 1998); Steven A. Egger, *Serial Murder: An Elusive Phenomenon* (Westport, CT: Praeger, 1990); and Stephen J. Giannangelo, *The Psychopathology of Serial Murder: A Theory of Violence* (New York: Praeger, 1996).
33. *BTK* stands for "Bind, Torture, and Kill," an acronym that Rader applied to himself in letters he sent to the media during the 1970s.
34. Several years ago, Lucas recanted all of his confessions, saying that he had never killed anyone—except possibly his mother, a killing he said he didn't remember. See "Condemned Killer Admits Lying, Denies Slayings," *Washington Post*, October 1, 1995.
35. Chikatilo was executed in 1994.
36. Public Law 108–212.
37. FBI, *Crime in the United States, 2009*.
38. Federal Bureau of Investigation, *Uniform Crime Reporting Handbook, 2004* (Washington, DC: FBI, 2005), p. 19.
39. "Study: Rape Vastly Underreported," Associated Press, April 26, 1992.
40. Ronald Barri Flowers, *Women and Criminality: The Woman as Victim, Offender, and Practitioner* (Westport, CT: Greenwood Press, 1987), p. 36.
41. A. Nichols Groth, *Men Who Rape: The Psychology of the Offender* (New York: Plenum Press, 1979).
42. Susan Brownmiller, *Against Our Will: Men, Women, and Rape* (New York: Simon and Schuster, 1975).
43. Dennis J. Stevens, "Motives of Social Rapists," *Free Inquiry in Creative Sociology*, Vol. 23, No. 2 (November 1995), pp. 117–126.
44. BJS, *Report to the Nation on Crime and Justice*, p. 5.
45. Ibid.
46. FBI, *Crime in the United States, 2009*. For UCR Program reporting purposes, *minorities* are defined as African Americans, Native Americans, Asians, Pacific Islanders, and Alaskan Natives.
47. "Easter Bunny Charged with Battery for Mall Attack," Associated Press, April 18, 2006.
48. This offense is sometimes called *assault with a deadly weapon with intent to kill (AWDWWITK)*.
49. FBI, *Crime in the United States, 2009*.
50. BJS, *Report to the Nation on Crime and Justice*, p. 6.
51. Ibid.
52. "Four Arrested for Stealing Moon Rocks," Associated Press, July 23, 2002; and Sheena McFarland, "U. Student Arrested for Moon Rock Theft," *Daily Utah Chronicle*, http://www.dailyutahchronicle.com/main.cfm/include/detail/storyid/259076.html (accessed August 22, 2005).
53. "Yale Says Student Stole His Education," *USA Today*, April 12, 1995.
54. Steven J. Vaughan-Nichols, "Cisco Source Code Reportedly Stolen," *eWeek*, May 18, 2004, http://www.eweek.com/article2/0,1759,1593862,00.asp (accessed May 17, 2009).
55. Ibid.
56. FBI, *Uniform Crime Reporting Handbook, 2004*, p. 28.
57. Matt Stearns and Donald Bradley, "Boy's Last Moments of Life Are Frozen in Mother's Memory," *Kansas City Star*, February 23, 2000.
58. "Jury Recommends Life Term in Dragging Death Wednesday," Associated Press, October 3, 2001.
59. Patsy Klaus, *Carjacking, 1993–2002* (Washington, DC: Bureau of Justice Statistics, July 2004).
60. FBI, *Crime in the United States, 2009*.
61. As indicated in the UCR definition of *arson*. See Federal Bureau of Investigation, *Crime in the United States, 1998* (Washington, DC: U.S. Department of Justice, 1999).
62. FBI, *Crime in the United States, 2009*.
63. Ibid.
64. "Trends in Crime and Victimization," *Criminal Justice Research Reports*, Vol. 2, No. 6 (July/August 2001), p. 83.
65. For additional information, see Michael Rand and Shannan M. Catalano, *Criminal Victimization, 2006* (Washington, DC: Bureau of Justice Statistics, 2007); and Patsy A. Klaus, *Crime and the Nation's Households, 2006* (Washington, DC: Bureau of Justice Statistics, 2007).
66. Klaus, *Crime and the Nation's Households, 2006*.
67. Rand and Catalano, *Criminal Victimization, 2006*.
68. Ibid., p. 1.
69. See, for example, President's Commission on Law Enforcement and Administration of Justice, *The Challenge of Crime in a Free Society*, pp. 22–23.
70. Bureau of Justice Statistics, *NCVS Redesign*, http://bjs.ojp.usdoj.gov/index.cfm?ty=tp&tid=91 (accessed September 13, 2010).
71. BJS, *Report to the Nation on Crime and Justice*, p. 27.
72. Hagan, *Research Methods in Criminal Justice and Criminology*, p. 89.
73. Bureau of Justice Statistics, *Criminal Victimization in the United States, 1985* (Washington, DC: U.S. Government Printing Office, 1987), p. 1.
74. FBI, *Crime in the United States, 2001*, preliminary data, http://www.fbi.gov./ucr/01prelim.pdf (accessed August 27, 2002).
75. Terance D. Miethe and Richard C. McCorkle, *Crime Profiles: The Anatomy of Dangerous Persons, Places, and Situations* (Los Angeles: Roxbury, 1998), p. 19.
76. The definition of *rape* employed by the UCR/NIBRS Program, however, automatically excludes crimes of homosexual rape such as might occur in prisons and jails. As a consequence, the rape of males is excluded from the official count for crimes of rape.
77. Rand and Catalano, *Criminal Victimization, 2006*, p. 4.

78. Thomas Simon et al., *Injuries from Violent Crime, 1992–98* (Washington, DC: Bureau of Justice Statistics, 2001), p. 5.
79. See, for example, Elizabeth Stanko, "When Precaution Is Normal: A Feminist Critique of Crime Prevention," in Loraine Gelsthorpe and Allison Morris, eds., *Feminist Perspectives in Criminology* (Philadelphia: Open University Press, 1990).
80. For more information, see Eve S. Buzawa and Carl G. Buzawa, *Domestic Violence: The Criminal Justice Response* (Thousand Oaks, CA: Sage, 1996).
81. "Battered Women Tell Their Stories to the Senate," *Charlotte (NC) Observer*, July 10, 1991.
82. Patricia Tjaden and Nancy Thoennes, *Full Report of the Prevalence, Incidence, and Consequences of Violence against Women: Findings from the National Violence against Women Survey* (Washington, DC: National Institute of Justice, 2000).
83. Violence against Women Office, *Stalking and Domestic Violence: Report to Congress* (Washington, DC: U.S. Department of Justice, 2001).
84. U.S. Code, Title 18, Section 2261A.
85. As modified through VAWA 2000.
86. Violence against Women Office, *Stalking and Domestic Violence*.
87. Many of the data in this section come from Bureau of Justice Statistics, *Crimes against Persons Age 65 or Older, 1993–2002* (Rockville, MD: BJS, 2005).
88. Lamar Jordan, "Law Enforcement and the Elderly: A Concern for the Twenty-First Century," *FBI Law Enforcement Bulletin*, May 2002, pp. 20–23.
89. Public Law 101–275.
90. H.R. 4797, 102d Cong. 2d Sess. (1992).
91. FBI, *Crime in the United States, 2007* (Washington, DC: U.S. Dept. of Justice, 2008).
92. "Sept. 11 Attacks Cited in Nearly 25 Percent Increase in Florida Hate Crimes," Associated Press, August 30, 2002.
93. "Number of Hate Groups Rises, Poverty Law Center Reports," *Criminal Justice Newsletter*, April 15, 2008, p. 7.
94. Richard Esposito, Eloise Harper, and Maddy Sauer, "Bernie Madoff Pleads Guilty to Ponzi Scheme, Goes Straight to Jail, Says He's 'Deeply Sorry,'" ABC News, March 12, 2009, http://abcnews.go.com/Blotter/WallStreet/Story?id=7066715&page=1 (accessed July 4, 2009).
95. Joanna Chung and Henny Sender, "Investors Fear $50bn Loss in Madoff's 'Big Lie,'" *Financial Times*, December 14, 2008.
96. Diana B. Henriques, "Madoff Is Sentenced to 150 Years for Ponzi Scheme," *New York Times*, June 29, 2009, http://www.nytimes.com/2009/06/30/business/30madoff.html (accessed September 28, 2010).
97. Dina ElBoghdady, "Mortgage Fraud Up as Credit Tightens," *Washington Post*, March 17, 2009, http://www.washingtonpost.com/wp-dyn/content/article/2009/03/16/AR2009031601612.html (accessed May 13, 2009).
98. Jennifer Liberto, "More Muscle Sought in Fraud Fight," CNNMoney.com, May 8, 2009, http://money.cnn.com/2009/05/08/news/economy/mortgage_fraud/index.htm (accessed May 13, 2009).
99. Federal Trade Commission, "Federal and State Agencies Crack Down on Mortgage Modification and Foreclosure Rescue Scams," http://www.ftc.gov/opa/2009/04/hud.shtm (accessed May 13, 2009).
100. *Andersen* v. *U.S.*, 544 U.S. 696 (2005).
101. Public Broadcasting System, "Enron: After the Collapse," http://www.pbs.org/newshour/bb/business/enron/player6.html (accessed August 27, 2005).
102. Edwin H. Sutherland, "White-Collar Criminality," *American Sociological Review* (February 1940), p. 12.
103. Scott Lindlaw, "Bush to Propose Crackdown on Corporate Abuses: President's Own Business Dealings Come under Scrutiny," Associated Press, July 9, 2002, http://www.washingtonpost.com/wp-dyn/articles/A43384-2002Jul9.html (accessed May 17, 2005).
104. Public Law 107–204.
105. Quoted on the Transnational Threats Initiative home page of the Center for Strategic and International Studies (CSIS), http://www.csis.org/tnt/index.htm (accessed August 22, 2007).
106. These ideas were originally expressed by Assistant U.S. Attorney General Laurie Robinson in an address given at the Twelfth International Congress on Criminology, Seoul, Korea, August 28, 1998.
107. Caroline Wolf Harlow, *Firearm Use by Offenders* (Washington, DC: Bureau of Justice Statistics, 2001).
108. Ibid., p. 1.
109. Public Law 103–159.
110. U.S. Code, Title 18, Section 922(q)(1)(A).
111. Harlow, *Firearm Use by Offenders*.
112. *Firearms Purchased from Federal Firearm Licensees Using Bogus Identification* (Washington, DC: General Accounting Office, 2001).
113. John C. Moorhouse and Brent Wanner, "Does Gun Control Reduce Crime or Does Crime Increase Gun Control?" *CATO Journal*, Vol. 103 (2006), pp. 103–124.
114. Public Law 103–322, 108, Stat. 1796 (codified as amended in scattered sections of 18, 21, 28, 42, etc., U.S. Code).
115. Public Law 104–208, an amendment to U.S. Code, Title 18, Section 921(a). Also known as the Lautenberg Amendment.
116. Jacob R. Clark, "Police Careers May Take a Beating from Fed Domestic-Violence Law," *Law Enforcement News*, Vol. 23, No. 461 (February 14, 1997), p. 1.
117. *District of Columbia* v. *Heller*, 554 U.S. ___ (2008).
118. *McDonald* v. *City of Chicago*, U.S. Supreme Court, No. 08-1521 (decided June 28, 2010).
119. Sarah Brady, "Statement on the Sniper Shootings," October 8, 2002, http://www.bradycampaign.org/press/release.asp?Record 5429 (accessed October 16, 2007); and Microstamping of Firearms Required by California Law," *Criminal Justice Newsletter*, October 2, 2007, p. 1.
120. Tony Perry, "96 Arrested in San Diego State Drug Bust," *Los Angeles Times*, May 7, 2008, http://www.latimes.com/news/local/la-me-drugbust7-2008may07,0,3741335.story?page=1 (accessed May 7, 2008).
121. As cited in Donna Leinwand, "Drug, Terror Rings Find New Ways to Launder Money," *USA Today*, January 12, 2006.
122. J. M. Chaiken and M. R. Chaiken, *Varieties of Criminal Behavior* (Santa Monica, CA: RAND Corporation, 1982).
123. D. McBride, "Trends in Drugs and Death," paper presented at the annual meeting of the American Society of Criminology, Denver, 1983.
124. National Criminal Justice Reference Service, *The Micro Domain: Behavior and Homicide*, http://www.ncjrs.org/pdffiles/167262-3.pdf (accessed February 23, 2002).
125. Bureau of Justice Statistics, *Substance Abuse and Treatment: State and Federal Prisoners* (Washington, DC: U.S. Department of Justice, January 1999).
126. Bureau of Justice Statistics, *Drug Use, Testing, and Treatment in Jails* (Washington, DC: U.S. Department of Justice, May 2000).
127. Information in this paragraph comes from John Scalia, *Federal Drug Offenders, 1999, with Trends, 1984–99* (Washington, DC: Bureau of Justice Statistics, 2001); and Bureau of Justice Statistics, *Federal Criminal Case Processing, 2002—With Trends, 1982–2002* (Washington, DC: BJS, 2005).
128. Ibid.
129. Ryan Naraine, "Cryzip Trojan Encrypts Files, Demands Ransom," eWeek.com, March 13, 2006, http://www.eweek.com/article2/0,1895,1937408,00.asp?kc=ewnws031406dtx1k0000599 (accessed January 5, 2007).

130. For suggested computer-crime categories, see Peter Grabosky, "Computer Crime: A Criminological Overview," paper presented at the Workshop on Crimes Related to the Computer Network, Tenth United Nations Congress on the Prevention of Crime and the Treatment of Offenders, Vienna, Austria, April 15, 2000, http://www.aic.gov.au/conferences/other/compcrime/computercrime.pdf (accessed January 12, 2002). Also see David L. Carter, "Computer Crime Categories: How Techno-Criminals Operate," *FBI Law Enforcement Journal* (July 1995), pp. 21–26.
131. Grabosky, "Computer Crime."
132. Kevin Johnson, "Hijackers' E-Mails Sifted for Clues," *USA Today*, October 11, 2001.
133. Wendy Koch, "Dozens Arrested in Online Child Porn Ring," *USA Today*, May 27, 2010.
134. Richard Zitrin, "Woman Charged with Online Prostitution," APB Online, June 10, 1999, http://www.apbonline.com/911/1999/06/10/hooker0610_01.html (accessed June 19, 1999).
135. "Invasion of the Data Snatchers!" *Time*, September 26, 1988, pp. 62–67.
136. Public Law 108–187.
137. Peter Firstbrook, "META Trend Update: The Changing Threat Landscape," Meta Group, March 24, 2005, http://www.metagroup.com/us/displayArticle.do?oid551768 (accessed July 5, 2005).
138. *MGM* v. *Grokster*, 545 U.S. 913 (2005).
139. Gregg Keizer, "Microsoft Says Phishing Bad, Offers Little New for Defense," *TechWeb News*, March 15, 2005, http://www.techweb.com/wire/159900391 (accessed July 7, 2005).
140. Avivah Litan, "Phishing Victims Likely Will Suffer Identity Theft Fraud," Gartner, Inc., May 14, 2004, http://www.gartner.com/Display-Document?ref5g_search&id544811 (accessed July 6, 2005).
141. Symantec Corporation, *2010 SMB Information Protection Survey*, http://www.slideshare.net/symantec/2010-smb-information-protection-survey#text-version (accessed September 8, 2010).
142. "Focus on Physical Security, Too," *eWeek*, January 27, 2003, p. 6a.
143. Ramona R. Rantala, *Cybercrime against Businesses: Pilot Test Results, 2001 Computer Security Survey* (Washington, DC: Bureau of Justice Statistics, 2004).
144. Emergency Response and Research Institute, *Summary of Emergency Response and Research Institute Terrorism Statistics: 2000 and 2001*, http://www.emergency.com/2002/terroris00-01.pdf (accessed August 22, 2002).
145. Federal Bureau of Investigation, Counterterrorism Section, *Terrorism in the United States, 1987* (Washington, DC: FBI, 1987), in which the full version of the definition offered here can be found. See also *FBI Policy and Guidelines: Counterterrorism*, which offers a somewhat less formal definition of the term; http://www.fbi.gov/contact/fo/jackson/cntrterr.htm (accessed January 15, 2002).
146. Adapted from *FBI Policy and Guidelines*.
147. Ibid.
148. See Barry Collin, "The Future of Cyberterrorism," *Crime and Justice International* (March 1997), pp. 15–18.
149. John Arquilla and David Ronfeldt, *The Advent of Netwar* (Santa Monica, CA: RAND Corporation, 1996).
150. Mark M. Pollitt, "Cyberterrorism: Fact or Fancy?" in *Proceedings of the Twentieth National Information Systems Security Conference*, October 1997, pp. 285–289.
151. "Chief Security Officers Remind Citizens of the Dangers of Cyberattacks and Recommend Tips," *CSO Magazine*, http://www2.csoonline.html/info/release.html?CID=9065 (accessed August 28, 2006).
152. Robert S. Mueller III, executive speech at Chatham House, London, England, April 7, 2008, http://www.fbi.gov/pressrel/speeches/mueller040708.htm (accessed May 20, 2008).
153. Central Intelligence Agency, National Foreign Intelligence Council, *Global Trends, 2015: A Dialogue about the Future with Nongovernment Experts* (Washington, DC: U.S. Government Printing Office, 2000).
154. Ibid.

Chapter 3: Criminal Law

i. World of Quotes, http://www.worldofquotes.com/author/Raymond-Chandler/1/index.html (accessed January 10, 2010).
ii. 'Lectric Law Library, http://www.lectlaw.com/ref.html (accessed July 28, 2006).
iii. Daniel Oran, *Oran's Dictionary of the Law* (St. Paul, MN: West, 1983), p. 306.
iv. Henry Campbell Black, Joseph R. Nolan, and Jacqueline M. Nolan-Haley, *Black's Law Dictionary*, 6th ed. (St. Paul, MN: West, 1990), p. 24.

---

1. The details for this story come from Maureen Fan, "Iraqi Legal System in Transition: U.S. Occupiers Trying to Re-establish Order Even without Laws," *San Jose Mercury News*, June 7, 2003, http://www.bayarea.com/mld/mercurynews/news/world/6036097.htm (accessed June 8, 2008).
2. Ibid.
3. Henry Campbell Black, Joseph R. Nolan, and Jacqueline M. Nolan-Haley, *Black's Law Dictionary*, 6th ed. (St. Paul, MN: West, 1990), p. 884.
4. Ibid.
5. Susan Schmidt and James V. Grimaldi, "Ney Sentenced to 30 Months in Prison for Abramoff Deals," *Washington Post*, January 20, 2007.
6. John F. Kennedy, *Profiles in Courage* (New York: Harper and Row, 1956).
7. Fareed Zakaria, "The Enemy Within," *New York Times*, December 17, 2006, http://www.nytimes.com/2006/12/17/books/review/Zakaria.t.html (accessed August 28, 2008).
8. American Bar Association Section of International and Comparative Law, *The Rule of Law in the United States* (Chicago: American Bar Association, 1958).
9. Daniel Oran, *Oran's Dictionary of the Law* (St. Paul, MN: West, 1983), p. 306.
10. Black, Nolan, and Nolan-Haley, *Black's Law Dictionary*, p. 24.
11. Specifically, U.S. Code, Title 21, Section 846.
12. *U.S.* v. *Shabani*, 510 U.S. 1108 (1994).
13. *Gordon* v. *State*, 52 Ala. 3008, 23 Am. Rep. 575 (1875).
14. But not for a more serious degree of homicide, since leaving a young child alone in a tub of water, even if intentional, does not necessarily mean that the person who so acts intends the child to drown.
15. O. W. Holmes, *The Common Law*, Vol. 3 (Boston: Little, Brown, 1881).
16. There is disagreement among some jurists as to whether the crime of statutory rape is a strict liability offense. Some jurisdictions treat it as such and will not accept as a defense a reasonable mistake about the victim's age. Others, however, do accept such a mistake as a defense.
17. *State* v. *Stiffler*, 763 P.2d 308 (Idaho App. 1988).
18. John S. Baker, Jr., et al., *Hall's Criminal Law*, 5th ed. (Charlottesville, VA: Michie, 1993), p. 138.
19. The same is not true for procedures within the criminal justice system, which can be modified even after a person has been sentenced and, hence, become retroactive. See, for example, the U.S. Supreme Court case of *California Department of*

Corrections v. *Morales*, 514 U.S. 499 (1995), in which the Court allowed changes in the length of time between parole hearings, even though those changes applied to offenders who had already been sentenced.
20. Black, Nolan, and Nolan-Haley, *Black's Law Dictionary*, p. 127.
21. The statute also says, "A mother's breastfeeding of her baby does not under any circumstance violate this section."
22. Common law crimes, of course, are not based on statutory elements.
23. *People* v. *Hall—Final Analysis*, SkiSafety.com, http://www.skisafety.com/amicuscases-hall2.html (accessed August 28, 2007).
24. See *Maughs* v. *Commonwealth*, 181 Va. 117, 120, 23 S.E.2d 784, 786 (1943).
25. *State* v. *Stephenson*, Opinion No. 24403 (South Carolina, 1996). See also *State* v. *Blocker*, 205 S.C. 303, 31 S.E.2d 908 (1944).
26. *State* v. *Kindle*, 71 Mont. 58, 64, 227 (1924).
27. Black, Nolan, and Nolan-Haley, *Black's Law Dictionary*, p. 343.
28. Patrick L. McCloskey and Ronald L. Schoenberg, *Criminal Law Deskbook* (New York: Matthew Bender, 1988), Section 20.03[13].
29. Details for this story come from Tim Talley, "Folk Hero or Killer: Druggist Who Killed Robber," Associated Press, May 30, 2009, http://abcnews.go.com/US/wireStory?id=7713776 (accessed May 31, 2009).
30. The exception, of course, is that of a trespasser who trespasses in order to commit a more serious crime.
31. Sir Edward Coke, 3 *Institute*, 162.
32. *The Crown* v. *Dudly & Stephens*, 14 Q.B.D. 273, 286, 15 Cox C. C. 624, 636 (1884).
33. "Jury Convicts Condom Rapist," *USA Today*, May 14, 1993.
34. Black, Nolan, and Nolan-Haley, *Black's Law Dictionary*, p. 504.
35. *State of Tennessee* v. *Charles Arnold Ballinger*, No. E2000-01339-CCA-R3-CD (Tenn. Crim. App. 01/09/2000).
36. See, for example, *Montana* v. *Egelhoff*, 116 S.Ct. 2013, 135 L.Ed.2d 361 (1996).
37. L. A. Callahan et al., "The Volume and Characteristics of Insanity Defense Pleas: An Eight-State Study," *Bulletin of the American Academy of Psychiatry and the Law*, Vol. 19, No. 4 (1991), pp. 331–338.
38. American Bar Association Standing Committee on Association Standards for Criminal Justice, *Proposed Criminal Justice Mental Health Standards* (Chicago: American Bar Association, 1984).
39. *Durham* v. *U.S.*, 214 F.2d 867, 875 (D.C. Cir. 1954).
40. American Law Institute, *Model Penal Code: Official Draft and Explanatory Notes* (Philadelphia: American Law Institute, 1985).
41. Ibid.
42. *U.S.* v. *Brawner*, 471 F.2d 969, 973 (D.C. Cir. 1972).
43. See Joan Biskupic, "Insanity Defense: Not a Right; In Montana Case, Justices Give States Option to Prohibit Claim," *Washington Post* wire service, March 29, 1994.
44. Ibid.
45. *Ford* v. *Wainwright*, 477 U.S. 399, 106 S.Ct. 2595, 91 L.Ed.2d 335 (1986).
46. U.S. Code, Title 18, Section 401.
47. *Jones* v. *U.S.*, U.S. Sup. Ct., 33 CrL. 3233 (1983).
48. *Ake* v. *Oklahoma*, 470 U.S. 68, 105 S.Ct. 1087, 84 L.Ed.2d 53 (1985).
49. *Foucha* v. *Louisiana*, 504 U.S. 71 (1992).
50. U.S. Sentencing Commission, "Supplement to the 2002 Federal Sentencing Guidelines: Section 5K2.13. Diminished Capacity (Policy Statement)," April 30, 2003, http://www.ussc.gov/2002suppb/5K2_13.htm (accessed May 8, 2008). Italics added.
51. *U.S.* v. *Pohlot*, 827 F.2d 889 (1987).
52. Peter Arenella, "The Diminished Capacity and Diminished Responsibility Defenses: Two Children of a Doomed Marriage," *Columbia Law Review*, Vol. 77 (1977), p. 830.
53. *U.S.* v. *Brawner*, 471 F.2d 969 (1972).
54. Black, Nolan, and Nolan-Haley, *Black's Law Dictionary*, p. 458.
55. California Penal Code, Section 25(a).
56. Ibid., Section 28(b).
57. *Indiana* v. *Edwards*, 554 U.S. 164 (2008).
58. *U.S.* v. *Halper*, 490 U.S. 435 (1989).
59. "Robert Blake Found Liable for Wife's Death," Associated Press, November 18, 2005.
60. See, for example, *Hudson* v. *U.S.*, 18 S.Ct. 488 (1997); and *U.S.* v. *Ursery*, 518 U.S. 267 (1996).
61. McCloskey and Schoenberg, *Criminal Law Deskbook*, Section 20.02[4].
62. *U.S.* v. *Armstrong*, 116 S.Ct. 1480, 134 L.Ed.2d 687 (1996).
63. Speedy Trial Act, U.S. Code, Title 18, Section 3161. Significant cases involving the Speedy Trial Act are those of *U.S.* v. *Carter*, 476 U.S. 1138, 106 S.Ct. 2241, 90 L.Ed.2d 688 (1986); and *Henderson* v. *U.S.*, 476 U.S. 321, 106 S.Ct. 1871, 90 L.Ed.2d 299 (1986).
64. Peter Whoriskey, "New Orleans Justice System Besieged," *Boston Globe*, April 17, 2006, http://www.boston.com/news/nation/articles/2006/04/17/new_orleans_justice_system_besieged (accessed May 10, 2007).
65. Francis Fukuyama, "Extreme Paranoia about Government Abounds," *USA Today*, August 24, 1995.

Chapter 4: Policing: Purpose and Organization

i. Quote of the Day, *New York Times*, May 30, 2002.
ii. Robert Kennedy, *The Pursuit of Justice*, part 3, "Eradicating Free Enterprise in Organized Crime" (New York: Harper and Row, 1964).
iii. Sam S. Souryal, *Police Administration and Management* (St. Paul, MN: West, 1977), p. 261.
iv. Office of Community Oriented Policing Services, *Community Policing Defined* (Washington, DC: U.S. Department of Justice, 2009), p. 3.
v. Cited in Anderson's Police Pages at http://andersonspolicepage.tripod.com/
vi. Lawrence W. Sherman, *Evidence-Based Policing* (Washington, DC: Police Foundation, 1998), p. 3.

---

1. Major Cities Chiefs Association, *Terrorism: The Impact on State and Local Law Enforcement*, Intelligence Commanders Conference Report, June 2002, http://www.neiassociates.org/mccintelligencereport.pdf (accessed September 30, 2009).
2. "Police, Protestors Clash Near Miami Trade Talks," CNN.com, November 20, 2003, http://www.cnn.com/2003/US/South/11/20/miami.protests (accessed June 3, 2009).
3. "Demonstrators, Police Clash during Free Trade Talks," *USA Today*, November 20, 2003, http://www.usatoday.com/news/nation/2003-11-20-miami-protests_x.htm (accessed June 3, 2009).
4. Andrew P. Sutor, *Police Operations: Tactical Approaches to Crimes in Progress* (St. Paul, MN: West, 1976), p. 68, citing Peel.
5. C. D. Hale, *Police Patrol: Operations and Management* (Englewood Cliffs, NJ: Prentice Hall, 1994).
6. Victor Kappeler et al., *The Mythology of Crime and Criminal Justice* (Prospect Heights, IL: Waveland Press, 1996).
7. Darl H. Champion and Michael K. Hooper, *Introduction to American Policing* (New York: McGraw-Hill, 2003), p. 133.

8. Details for this story come from Ted Ottley, "Bad Day Dawning," Court TV's Crime Library, http://www.crimelibrary.com/serial_killers/notorious/mcveigh/dawning_1.html (accessed June 22, 2008).
9. Ibid.
10. This definition has been attributed to the National Crime Prevention Institute (see http://www.lvmpd.com/community/crmtip25.htm).
11. See Steven P. Lab, *Crime Prevention at a Crossroads* (Cincinnati, OH: Anderson, 1997).
12. Visit the Philadelphia Police Department online at http://www.phillypolice.com.
13. The term *CompStat* is sometimes interpreted to mean computer statistics, comparative statistics, or computer comparative statistics, although it is generally accorded no specific meaning.
14. Learn more about CompStat from Vincent E. Henry, *The COMPSTAT Paradigm: Management Accountability in Policing, Business, and the Public Sector* (Flushing, NY: Looseleaf Law Publications, 2002).
15. Much of the information in this section comes from the Philadelphia Police Department, "The COMPSTAT Process," http://www.ppdonline.org/ppd_compstat.htm (accessed May 28, 2007).
16. See Ned Levine, *CrimeStat: A Spatial Statistics Program for the Analysis of Crime Incident Locations*, version 2.0 (Washington, DC: National Institute of Justice, May 2002).
17. Robert H. Langworthy and Lawrence P. Travis III, *Policing in America: A Balance of Forces*, 2nd ed. (Upper Saddle River, NJ: Prentice Hall, 1999), p. 194.
18. Adapted from Bronx County (New York) District Attorney's Office, "Quality of Life Offenses," December 24, 2002, http://www.bronxda.net/fighting_crime/quality_of_life_offenses.html (accessed June 20, 2003).
19. Other violations may be involved as well. On December 29, 2000, for example, Judge John S. Martin, Jr., of the Federal District Court in Manhattan, ruled that homeless people in New York City could be arrested for sleeping in cardboard boxes in public. Judge Martin held that a city Sanitation Department regulation barring people from abandoning cars or boxes on city streets could be applied to the homeless who were sleeping in boxes.
20. Norman Siegel, executive director of the New York Civil Liberties Union, as reported in "Quality of Life Offenses Targeted," *Western Queens Gazette*, November 22, 2000, http://www.qgazette.com/News/2000/1122/Editorial_pages/e01.html (accessed June 12, 2007).
21. The broken windows thesis was first suggested by George L. Kelling and James Q. Wilson in "Broken Windows: The Police and Neighborhood Safety," *Atlantic Monthly*, March 1982.
22. For a critique of the broken windows thesis, see Bernard E. Harcourt, *Illusion of Order: The False Promise of Broken Windows Policing* (Cambridge, MA: Harvard University Press, 2001).
23. Peter Schuler, "Law Professor Harcourt Challenges Popular Policing Method, Gun Violence Interventions," *Chicago Chronicle*, Vol. 22, No. 12 (March 20, 2003), http://chronicle.uchicago.edu/030320/harcourt.shtml (accessed August 28, 2008).
24. George L. Kelling, Catherine M. Coles, and James Q. Wilson, *Fixing Broken Windows: Restoring Order and Reducing Crime in Our Communities* (reprint, New York: Touchstone, 1998).
25. Charles R. Swanson, Leonard Territo, and Robert W. Taylor, *Police Administration: Structures, Processes, and Behavior*, 4th ed. (Upper Saddle River, NJ: Prentice Hall, 1998), p. 1.
26. Lorraine Mazerolle et al., *Managing Citizen Calls to the Police: An Assessment of Nonemergency Call Systems* (Washington, DC: National Institute of Justice, 2001), p. 1.
27. The Hastings (Minnesota) Police Department website at http://www.ci.hastings.mn.us/Police/deptnews.htm (accessed May 24, 2009).
28. Government Accounting Office, "Federal Law Enforcement: Survey of Federal Civilian Law Enforcement Functions and Authorities," December 2006 (highlights of GAO-07-121).
29. U.S. Department of Justice, *A Proud History, a Bright Future: Careers with the FBI*, pamphlet (Washington, DC: DOJ, October 1986), p. 1.
30. Much of the information in this section comes from U.S. Department of Justice, *The FBI: The First Seventy-Five Years* (Washington, DC: U.S. Government Printing Office, 1986).
31. Some of the information in this section is adapted from Federal Bureau of Investigation, "Facts and Figures 2003," http://www.fbi.gov/priorities/priorities.htm (accessed March 25, 2006).
32. Telephone conversation with FBI officials, April 21, 1995.
33. Information in this section comes from Christopher H. Asplen, "National Commission Explores Its Future," *NIJ Journal* (January 1999), pp. 17–24.
34. The DNA Identification Act is Section 210301 of the Violent Crime Control and Law Enforcement Act of 1994.
35. Federal Bureau of Investigation, "NDIS Statistics," http://www.fbi.gov/hq/lab/codis/clickmap.htm (accessed May 28, 2010).
36. Much of the information in this paragraph comes from the FBI Academy website at http://www.fbi.gov/hq/td/academy/academy.htm (accessed March 3, 2008).
37. Testimony of Robert S. Mueller III, director of the Federal Bureau of Investigation, before the Senate Committee on Intelligence, February 16, 2005.
38. Henry M. Wrobleski and Karen M. Hess, *Introduction to Law Enforcement and Criminal Justice*, 4th ed. (St. Paul, MN: West, 1993), p. 34.
39. Ibid., p. 35.
40. New York City Police Department website, http://www.nyc.gov/html/nypd (accessed June 21, 2009). *PoliceLink* reported a head count of 34,771 in early 2009 but said that the city had plans to hire an additional 1,600 officers. See "NYPD Cuts 2010 Academy, Affects 1,000 Recruits," *PoliceLink*, February 12, 2009, http://www.policelink.com/news/articles/94792-nypd-cuts-2010-academy-affects-1000-recruits (accessed May 9, 2010).
41. Brian A. Reaves, *Census of State and Local Law Enforcement Agencies, 2004* (Washington, DC: Bureau of Justice Statistics, 2007).
42. Ibid. See also Matthew J. Hickman and Brian A. Reaves, *Local Police Departments, 2003* (Washington, DC: Bureau of Justice Statistics, 2006).
43. Note, however, that New York City jails may have daily populations that, on a given day, exceed those of Los Angeles County.
44. Los Angeles County Sheriff's Department, "About LASD," http://www.lasd.org/aboutlasd/about.html (accessed June 25, 2008).
45. Police Assessment Resource Center, *The Los Angeles County Sheriff's Department—19th Semiannual Report* (Los Angeles: PARC, February 2005); and telephone communication with Deputy Ethan Marquez, L.A. County Sheriff's Department, Custodial Division, January 24, 2002.
46. Reaves, *Census of State and Local Law Enforcement Agencies, 2004.*
47. Office of the Director of National Intelligence, "Second National Fusion Center Conference Held to Foster Greater Collaboration," news release, March 20, 2008.
48. Estimates of the number of centers vary, and classifying a work group as a "fusion center" depends largely on the

perspective assumed. A March 2008 press release by the federal Office of the Director of National Intelligence (see note 47) put the number of operational fusion centers at more than 50 in 46 states.

49. Michael C. Mines, "Statement before the House Committee on Homeland Security, Subcommittee on Intelligence, Information Sharing and Terrorism Risk Assessment," September 27, 2007.
50. "State and Local Fusion Centers Face Challenges as They Grow," *Criminal Justice Newsletter*, September 18, 2007, p. 1.
51. The elements of this definition draw on the now-classic work by O. W. Wilson, *Police Administration* (New York: McGraw-Hill, 1950), pp. 2–3.
52. Charles R. Swanson, Leonard Territo, and Robert W. Taylor, *Police Administration: Structures, Processes, and Behavior* (Upper Saddle River, NJ: Prentice Hall, 1998), p. 167.
53. Los Angeles County Sheriff's Department, "About LASD," http://www.lasd.org/aboutlasd/about.html (accessed June 25, 2010).
54. For more information on the first three categories, see Francis X. Hartmann, "Debating the Evolution of American Policing," *Perspectives on Policing*, No. 5 (Washington, DC: National Institute of Justice, 1988).
55. Willard M. Oliver, "The Homeland Security Juggernaut: TheEnd of the Community Policing Era," *Crime and Justice International*, Vol. 20, No. 79 (2004), pp. 4–10. See also Willard M. Oliver, "The Era of Homeland Security: September 11, 2001 to . . ." *Crime and Justice International*, Vol. 21, No. 85 (2005), pp. 9–17.
56. Gene Stephens, "Policing the Future: Law Enforcement's New Challenges," *The Futurist*, March/April 2005, pp. 51–57.
57. As cited in Bernie G. Thompson, *A Law Enforcement Assistance and Partnership Strategy* (Washington, DC: U.S. Congress, 2008), p. 5. Congressman Thompson is ranking member of the Democratic staff of the Committee on Homeland Security.
58. Ibid., p. 5.
59. To learn more about Wilson, see http://www.nndb.com/people/796/000167295 (accessed January 5, 2011).
60. James Q. Wilson, *Varieties of Police Behavior: The Management of Law and Order in Eight Communities* (Cambridge, MA: Harvard University Press, 1968).
61. Independent Commission on the Los Angeles Police Department, *Report of the Independent Commission on the Los Angeles Police Department* (Los Angeles: The Commission, 1991).
62. Gary W. Sykes, "Street Justice: A Moral Defense of Order Maintenance Policing," *Justice Quarterly*, Vol. 3, No. 4 (December 1986), p. 505.
63. Egon Bittner, "Community Relations," in Alvin W. Cohn and Emilio C. Viano, eds., *Police Community Relations: Images, Roles, Realities* (Philadelphia: J. B. Lippincott, 1976), pp. 77–82.
64. Paul B. Weston, *Police Organization and Management* (Pacific Palisades, CA: Goodyear, 1976), p. 159.
65. Hale, *Police Patrol.*
66. Mark H. Moore and Robert C. Trojanowicz, "Corporate Strategies for Policing," *Perspectives on Policing*, No. 6 (Washington, DC: National Institute of Justice, 1998).
67. Ibid., p. 6.
68. Community Policing Consortium, *Community Policing Is Alive and Well* (Washington, DC: Community Policing Consortium, 1995), p. 1.
69. Office of Community Oriented Policing Services, *Community Policing Defined* (Washington, DC: U.S. Department of Justice, 2009), p. 3.
70. George L. Kelling, *The Newark Foot Patrol Experiment* (Washington, DC: Police Foundation, 1981).
71. Robert C. Trojanowicz, "An Evaluation of a Neighborhood Foot Patrol Program," *Journal of Police Science and Administration*, Vol. 11 (1983), pp. 410–419.
72. Bureau of Justice Assistance, *Understanding Community Policing: A Framework for Action* (Washington, DC: Bureau of Justice Statistics, 1994), p. 10.
73. Robert C. Trojanowicz and Bonnie Bucqueroux, *Community Policing* (Cincinnati, OH: Anderson, 1990).
74. Moore and Trojanowicz, "Corporate Strategies for Policing," p. 8.
75. S. M. Hartnett and W. G. Skogan, "Community Policing: Chicago's Experience," *National Institute of Justice Journal* (April 1999), pp. 2–11.
76. Jerome H. Skolnick and David H. Bayley, *Community Policing: Issues and Practices around the World* (Washington, DC: National Institute of Justice, 1988).
77. Ibid.
78. William L. Goodbody, "What Do We Expect New-Age Cops to Do?" *Law Enforcement News* (April 30, 1995), pp. 14, 18.
79. Sam Vincent Meddis and Desda Moss, "Many 'Fed-Up' Communities Cornering Crime," *USA Today*, May 22, 1995, p. 8A.
80. Matthew J. Hickman and Brian A. Reaves, *Community Policing in Local Police Departments, 1997 and 1999*, Bureau of Justice Statistics Special Report (Washington, DC: U.S. Department of Justice, 2001).
81. Richard M. Daley and Matt L. Rodriguez, *Together We Can: A Strategic Plan for Reinventing the Chicago Police Department* (Chicago: Chicago Police Department, 1993), http://www.ci.chi.il.us/CommunityPolicing/Statistics/Reports/TWC.pdf (accessed March 5, 2007).
82. Bureau of Justice Assistance, *Neighborhood-Oriented Policing in Rural Communities: A Program Planning Guide* (Washington, DC: Bureau of Justice Statistics, 1994), p. 4.
83. See the COPS Office website at http://www.cops.usdoj.gov (accessed September 6, 2010).
84. David L. Carter, *Law Enforcement Intelligence: A Guide for State, Local, and Tribal Law Enforcement Agencies* (Washington, DC: U.S. Department of Justice, 2004), p. 39.
85. Federal Bureau of Investigation, "Protecting America from Terrorist Attacks," Press BOLO for US, May 26, 2004, http://www.fbi.gov/page2/may04/bolo052604.htm (accessed August 28, 2007).
86. Office of Justice Programs, *The National Criminal Intelligence Sharing Plan* (Washington, DC: U.S. Department of Justice, 2005), p. 4.
87. International Association of Chiefs of Police, *Recommendations from the IACP Intelligence Summit, Criminal Intelligence Sharing: A National Plan for Intelligence-Led Policing at the Local, State and Federal Levels* (Alexandria, VA: IACP, 2002), p. 2.
88. Office for Domestic Preparedness, *Guidelines for Homeland Security* (Washington, DC: U.S. Department of Homeland Security, 2003).
89. Jihong Zhao, Nicholas P. Lovrich, and Quint Thurman, "The Status of Community Policing in American Cities: Facilitators and Impediments Revisited," *Policing*, Vol. 22, No. 1 (1999), p. 74.
90. For a good critique and overview of community policing, see Geoffrey P. Alpert et al., *Community Policing: Contemporary Readings* (Prospect Heights, IL: Waveland Press, 1998).
91. Jack R. Greene, "Community Policing in America: Changing the Nature, Structure, and Function of the Police," in U.S. Department of Justice, *Criminal Justice 2000*, Vol. 3 (Washington, DC: DOJ, 2000), pp. 299–370.
92. Michael D. Reisig and Roger B. Parks, "Experience, Quality of Life, and Neighborhood Context: A Hierarchical Analysis of Satisfaction with Police," *Justice Quarterly*, Vol. 17, No. 3 (2000), p. 607.

93. Mark E. Correla, "The Conceptual Ambiguity of Community in Community Policing: Filtering the Muddy Waters," *Policing*, Vol. 23, No. 2 (2000), pp. 218–233.
94. Adapted from Donald R. Fessler, *Facilitating Community Change: A Basic Guide* (San Diego: San Diego State University, 1976), p. 7.
95. Daniel W. Flynn, *Defining the "Community" in Community Policing* (Washington, DC: Police Executive Research Forum, 1998).
96. Robert C. Trojanowicz and Mark H. Moore, *The Meaning of Community in Community Policing* (East Lansing: Michigan State University's National Neighborhood Foot Patrol Center, 1988).
97. Robert M. Bohm, K. Michael Reynolds, and Stephen T. Holms, "Perceptions of Neighborhood Problems and Their Solutions: Implications for Community Policing," *Policing*, Vol. 23, No. 4 (2000), p. 439.
98. Ibid., p. 442.
99. Malcolm K. Sparrow, "Implementing Community Policing," *Perspectives on Policing*, No. 9 (Washington, DC: National Institute of Justice, 1988).
100. "L.A. Police Chief: Treat People Like Customers," *USA Today*, March 29, 1993.
101. Robert Wasserman and Mark H. Moore, "Values in Policing," *Perspectives in Policing*, No. 8 (Washington, DC: National Institute of Justice, 1988), p. 7.
102. "New York City Mayor Sparks Debate on Community Policing," *Criminal Justice Newsletter*, Vol. 25, No. 2 (January 18, 1994), p. 1.
103. Thomas J. Deakin, "The Police Foundation: A Special Report," *FBI Law Enforcement Bulletin* (November 1986), p. 2.
104. George L. Kelling et al., *The Kansas City Patrol Experiment* (Washington, DC: Police Foundation, 1974).
105. George Kelling quoted in Kevin Krajick, "Does Patrol Prevent Crime?" *Police* (September 1978), pp. 11–13.
106. William Bieck and David Kessler, *Response Time Analysis* (Kansas City, MO: Board of Police Commissioners, 1977). See also J. Thomas McEwen et al., *Evaluation of the Differential Police Response Field Test: Executive Summary* (Alexandria, VA: Research Management Associates, 1984); and Lawrence Sherman, "Policing Communities: What Works?" in Michael Tonry and Norval Morris, eds., *Crime and Justice: An Annual Review of Research*, Vol. 8 (Chicago: University of Chicago Press, 1986), pp. 343–386.
107. Kevin Krajick, "Does Patrol Prevent Crime?" *Police Magazine* (September 1978): pp. 11–13.
108. Ibid.
109. Ibid.
110. "Evidence-Based Policing," Police Foundation press release, March 17, 1998, www.policefoundation.org/docs/evidence.html (accessed January 5, 2006).
111. Lawrence W. Sherman, *Evidence-Based Policing* (Washington, DC: Police Foundation, 1998), p. 3.
112. Much of the information in this section comes from Sherman, *Evidence-Based Policing*.
113. "World's Top Police Officers to Study at Cambridge University," University of Cambridge, News and Events, December 3, 2007, http://www.admin.cam.ac.uk/news/dp/2007120301 (accessed July 5, 2008).
114. University of Cambridge, "Evidence-Based Policing: Possibilities and Prospects," revised and final program announcement, June 30 2008.
115. Carl J. Jensen III, "Consuming and Applying Research: Evidence-Based Policing," *Police Chief*, Vol. 73, No. 2 (February 2006), http://policechiefmagazine.org/magazine/index.cfm?fuseaction=display_arch&article_id=815&issue_id=22006 (accessed May 17, 2007).
116. Ibid.
117. Howard Cohen, "Overstepping Police Authority," *Criminal Justice Ethics* (summer/fall 1987), pp. 52–60.
118. Kenneth Culp Davis, *Police Discretion* (St. Paul, MN: West, 1975).

Chapter 5: Policing: Legal Aspects

i. Adapted from Technical Working Group for Electronic Crime Scene Investigation, *Electronic Crime Scene Investigation: A Guide for First Responders* (Washington, DC: National Institute of Justice, 2001), p. 2.
ii. Adapted from Larry R. Leibrock, "Overview and Impact on 21st Century Legal Practice: Digital Forensics and Electronic Discovery," no date, http://www.courtroom21.net/FDIC.pps (accessed July 5, 2008).

---

1. Remarks of Governor Calvin Coolidge at the Worcester Police Outing, Worcester, Massachusetts (October 2, 1920).
2. Ellen Barry and Colin Moynihan, "Three Detectives Plead Not Guilty in 50-Shot Killing," *New York Times*, March 20, 2007, http://www.nytimes.com/2007/03/20/nyregion/20cops.html (accessed August 28, 2008).
3. Michael Wilson, "3 Detectives Acquitted in Bell Shooting," *New York Times*, April 26, 2008, www.nytimes.com/2008/04/26/nyregion/26BELL.html?ref=nyregion (accessed August 28, 2008).
4. Cara Buckley, "Diallo Verdict May Have Made Prosecutors Cautious," *New York Times*, March 20, 2007, http://www.nytimes.com/2007/03/20/nyregion/20charges.html?fta=y (accessed August 28, 2008).
5. Marcus Baram, "How Common Is Contagious Shooting?" ABC News, November 17, 2006, http://abcnews.go.com/Politics/story?id=2681947&page=1 (accessed May 21, 2007).
6. Michael Wilson, "50 Shots Fired, and the Experts Offer a Theory," *New York Times*, November 27, 2006, http://www.nytimes.com/2006/11/27/nyregion/27fire.html (accessed August 28, 2008).
7. "Victim of Police Beating Says He Was Sober," Associated Press, October 10, 2005, http://www.msnbc.msn.com/id/9645260 (accessed July 10, 2007).
8. "New Investigation May Postpone Police Trial in Video-Tape," KATC-TV, http://www.katc.com/Global/story.asp?S=4345819&nav=EyAz (accessed March 19, 2008).
9. "Police Brutality!" *Time*, March 25, 1991, p. 18.
10. "Police Charged in Beating Case Say They Feared for Their Lives," *Boston Globe*, May 22, 1991.
11. "Police Brutality!" pp. 16–19.
12. "Cries of Relief," *Time*, April 26, 1993, p. 18.
13. "Rodney King Slams SUV into House, Breaks Pelvis," CNN.com, April 16, 2003, http://www.cnn.com/2003/US/West/04/15/rodney.king.ap/index.html (accessed April 18, 2006).
14. *Miranda* v. *Arizona*, 384 U.S. 436 (1966).
15. *Weeks* v. *U.S.*, 232 U.S. 383 (1914).
16. *Silverthorne Lumber Co.* v. *U.S.*, 251 U.S. 385 (1920).
17. Clemmens Bartollas, *American Criminal Justice* (New York: Macmillan, 1988), p. 186.
18. *Mapp* v. *Ohio*, 367 U.S. 643 (1961).
19. *Chimel* v. *California*, 395 U.S. 752 (1969).
20. *Katz* v. *U.S.*, 389 U.S. 347, 88 S.Ct. 507 (1967).
21. *Minnesota* v. *Olson*, 110 S.Ct. 1684 (1990).
22. *Minnesota* v. *Carter*, 525 U.S. 83 (1998).
23. *Georgia* v. *Randolph*, 547 U.S. 103 (2006).
24. The ruling left open the possibility that any evidence relating to criminal activity undertaken by the consenting party might be admissible in court. In the words of the Court, refusal by a

co-occupant "renders entry and search unreasonable and invalid as to him."
25. *U.S.* v. *Leon*, 468 U.S. 897, 104 S.Ct. 3405, 82 L.Ed.2d 677, 52 U.S.L.W. 5155 (1984).
26. Judicial titles vary among jurisdictions. Many lower-level state judicial officers are called *magistrates*. Federal magistrates, however, generally have a significantly higher level of judicial authority.
27. *Massachusetts* v. *Sheppard*, 104 S.Ct. 3424 (1984).
28. *Illinois* v. *Krull*, 107 S.Ct. 1160 (1987).
29. *Maryland* v. *Garrison*, 107 S.Ct. 1013 (1987).
30. *Illinois* v. *Rodriguez*, 110 S.Ct. 2793 (1990).
31. *Arizona* v. *Evans*, 115 S.Ct. 1185, 131 L.Ed.2d 34 (1995).
32. *Herring* v. *U.S.*, 555 U.S. ___ (2009).
33. See *California* v. *Acevedo*, 500 U.S. 565 (1991); *Ornelas* v. *U.S.*, 517 U.S. 690 (1996); and others.
34. See *Edwards* v. *Balisok*, 520 U.S. 641 (1997); *Booth* v. *Churner*, 532 U.S. 731 (2001); and *Porter* v. *Nussle*, 534 U.S. 516 (2002).
35. See *Wilson* v. *Arkansas*, 115 S.Ct. 1914 (1995); and *Richards* v. *Wisconsin*, 117 S.Ct. 1416 (1997).
36. See *McCleskey* v. *Kemp*, 481 U.S. 279, 107 S.Ct. 1756, 95 L.Ed.2d 262 (1987); *McCleskey* v. *Zant*, 499 U.S. 467, 493–494 (1991); *Coleman* v. *Thompson*, 501 U.S. 722 (1991); *Schlup* v. *Delo*, 115 S.Ct. 851, 130 L.Ed.2d 808 (1995); *Felker* v. *Turpin, Warden*, 117 S.Ct. 30, 135 L.Ed.2d 1123 (1996); *Boyde* v. *California*, 494 U.S. 370 (1990); and others.
37. See *Ewing* v. *California*, 538 U.S. 11 (2003); and *Lockyer* v. *Andrade*, 538 U.S. 63 (2003).
38. Richard Lacayo and Viveca Novak, "How Rehnquist Changed America," *Time*, June 30, 2003, pp. 20–25.
39. *Harris* v. *U.S.*, 390 U.S. 234 (1968).
40. The legality of plain-view seizures was also confirmed in earlier cases, including *Ker* v. *California*, 374 U.S. 23, 42–43 (1963); *U.S.* v. *Lee*, 274 U.S. 559 (1927); *U.S.* v. *Lefkowitz*, 285 U.S. 452, 465 (1932); and *Hester* v. *U.S.*, 265 U.S. 57 (1924).
41. As cited in Kimberly A. Kingston, "Look But Don't Touch: The Plain View Doctrine," *FBI Law Enforcement Bulletin* (December 1987), p. 18.
42. *Horton* v. *California*, 110 S.Ct. 2301, 47 CrL. 2135 (1990).
43. *U.S.* v. *Irizarry*, 673 F.2d 554, 556–67 (1st Cir. 1982).
44. *Arizona* v. *Hicks*, 107 S.Ct. 1149 (1987).
45. Inadvertence, as a requirement of legitimate plain-view seizures, was first cited in the U.S. Supreme Court case of *Coolidge* v. *New Hampshire*, 403 U.S. 443, 91 S.Ct. 2022 (1971).
46. *Horton* v. *California*, 110 S.Ct. 2301, 47 CrL. 2135 (1990).
47. Ibid.
48. *Brigham City* v. *Stuart*, 547 U.S. 398 (2006).
49. John Gales Sauls, "Emergency Searches of Premises," Part 1, *FBI Law Enforcement Bulletin* (March 1987), p. 23.
50. *Warden* v. *Hayden*, 387 U.S. 294 (1967).
51. *Mincey* v. *Arizona*, 437 U.S. 385, 392 (1978).
52. Sauls, "Emergency Searches of Premises," p. 25.
53. *Maryland* v. *Buie*, 110 S.Ct. 1093 (1990).
54. *Wilson* v. *Arkansas*, 115 S.Ct. 1914 (1995).
55. For additional information, see Michael J. Bulzomi, "Knock and Announce: A Fourth Amendment Standard," *FBI Law Enforcement Bulletin* (May 1997), pp. 27–31.
56. *Richards* v. *Wisconsin*, 117 S.Ct. 1416 (1997), syllabus.
57. *Illinois* v. *McArthur*, 531 U.S. 326 (2001).
58. *U.S.* v. *Banks*, 124 S.Ct. 521 (December 2, 2003).
59. *Hudson* v. *Michigan*, 547 U.S. 586 (2006).
60. *U.S.* v. *Grubbs*, 547 U.S. 90 (2006).
61. *U.S.* v. *Mendenhall*, 446 U.S. 544 (1980).
62. *Stansbury* v. *California*, 114 S.Ct. 1526, 1529, 128 L.Ed.2d 293 (1994).
63. *Yarborough* v. *Alvarado*, 541 U.S. 652 (2004).
64. *Thompson* v. *Keohane*, 516 U.S. 99, 112 (1996).
65. *Muehler* v. *Mena*, 125 S.Ct. 1465 (2005).
66. See *Michigan* v. *Summers*, 452 U.S. 692 (1981).
67. *Atwater* v. *Lago Vista*, 532 U.S. 318 (2001).
68. *Payton* v. *New York*, 445 U.S. 573 (1980).
69. In 1981, in the case of *U.S.* v. *Steagald* (451 U.S. 204), the Court ruled that a search warrant is also necessary when the planned arrest involves entry into a third party's premises.
70. *Kirk* v. *Louisiana*, 536 U.S. 635 (2002).
71. *U.S.* v. *Robinson*, 414 U.S. 218 (1973).
72. Ibid.
73. *Terry* v. *Ohio*, 392 U.S. 1 (1968).
74. *U.S.* v. *Sokolow*, 109 S.Ct. 1581 (1989).
75. The Court was quoting from *U.S.* v. *Brignoni-Ponce*, 422 U.S. 873, 878 (1975).
76. *U.S.* v. *Arvizu*, 534 U.S. 266 (2002).
77. Ibid.
78. *Minnesota* v. *Dickerson*, 113 S.Ct. 2130, 124 L.Ed.2d 334 (1993).
79. *Brown* v. *Texas*, 443 U.S. 47 (1979).
80. *Hiibel* v. *Sixth Judicial District Court of Nevada*, 542 U.S. 177 (2004).
81. *Smith* v. *Ohio*, 110 S.Ct. 1288 (1990).
82. *California* v. *Hodari D.*, 111 S.Ct. 1547 (1991).
83. *Criminal Justice Newsletter*, May 1, 1991, p. 2.
84. *Illinois* v. *Wardlow*, 528 U.S. 119 (2000).
85. Ibid., syllabus, http://supct.law.cornell.edu/supct/html/98-1036.ZS.html (accessed April 1, 2008).
86. Ibid.
87. *Arkansas* v. *Sanders*, 442 U.S. 753 (1979).
88. Ibid.
89. *U.S.* v. *Borchardt*, 809 F.2d 1115 (5th Cir. 1987).
90. *FBI Law Enforcement Bulletin* (January 1988), p. 28.
91. *Carroll* v. *U.S.*, 267 U.S. 132 (1925).
92. *Preston* v. *U.S.*, 376 U.S. 364 (1964).
93. *Arizona* v. *Gant*, U.S. Supreme Court, No. 07-542 (decided April 21, 2009).
94. *South Dakota* v. *Opperman*, 428 U.S. 364 (1976).
95. *Colorado* v. *Bertine*, 479 U.S. 367, 107 S.Ct. 741 (1987).
96. *Florida* v. *Wells*, 110 S.Ct. 1632 (1990).
97. *Terry* v. *Ohio*, 392 U.S. 1 (1968).
98. *California* v. *Acevedo*, 500 U.S. 565 (1991).
99. *Ornelas* v. *U.S.*, 517 U.S. 690, 696 (1996).
100. Ibid.
101. The phrase is usually attributed to the 1991 U.S. Supreme Court case of *California* v. *Acevedo* (500 U.S. 565 [1991]). See Devallis Rutledge, "Taking an Inventory," *Police*, November 1995, pp. 8–9.
102. *Florida* v. *Jimeno*, 111 S.Ct. 1801 (1991).
103. Ibid., syllabus, http://laws.findlaw.com/us/500/248.html (accessed March 2, 2008).
104. *U.S.* v. *Ross*, 456 U.S. 798 (1982).
105. Ibid.
106. *Whren* v. *U.S.*, 517 U.S. 806 (1996).
107. See *Pennsylvania* v. *Mimms*, 434 U.S. 106 (1977).
108. *Maryland* v. *Wilson*, 117 S.Ct. 882 (1997).
109. *Brendlin* v. *California*, 551 U.S. (2007).
110. *Knowles* v. *Iowa*, 525 U.S. 113 (1998).
111. *Wyoming* v. *Houghton*, 526 U.S. 295 (1999).
112. *Thornton* v. *U.S.*, 541 U.S. 615 (2004).
113. *Illinois* v. *Caballes*, 543 U.S. 405 (2005).
114. *Michigan Dept. of State Police* v. *Sitz*, 110 S.Ct. 2481 (1990).
115. *U.S.* v. *Martinez-Fuerte*, 428 U.S. 543 (1976).
116. Ibid., syllabus.
117. *Illinois* v. *Lidster*, 540 U.S. 419 (2004).
118. *U.S.* v. *Villamonte-Marquez*, 462 U.S. 579 (1983).

119. *California* v. *Carney*, 471 U.S. 386, 105 S.Ct. 2066, 85 L.Ed.2d 406, 53 U.S.L.W. 4521 (1985).
120. *U.S.* v. *Hill*, 855 F.2d 664 (10th Cir. 1988).
121. *National Treasury Employees Union* v. *Von Raab*, 489 U.S. 656 (1989).
122. *Skinner* v. *Railway Labor Executives' Association*, 489 U.S. 602 (1989).
123. *Florida* v. *Bostick*, 111 S.Ct. 2382 (1991).
124. *Bond* v. *U.S.*, 529 U.S. 334 (2000).
125. *U.S.* v. *Drayton*, 122 S.Ct. 2105 (2002).
126. *U.S.* v. *Flores-Montano*, 541 U.S. 149 (2004).
127. *People* v. *Deutsch*, 96 C.D.O.S. 2827 (1996).
128. The thermal imager differs from infrared devices (such as night-vision goggles) in that infrared devices amplify the infrared spectrum of light, whereas thermal imagers register solely the portion of the infrared spectrum that we call *heat*.
129. *People* v. *Deutsch*, 96 C.D.O.S. 2827 (1996).
130. *Kyllo* v. *U.S.*, 533 U.S. 27 (2001).
131. Ibid.
132. *Aguilar* v. *Texas*, 378 U.S. 108 (1964).
133. *U.S.* v. *Harris*, 403 U.S. 573 (1971).
134. Ibid., at 584.
135. *Illinois* v. *Gates*, 426 U.S. 213 (1983).
136. *Alabama* v. *White*, 110 S.Ct. 2412 (1990).
137. Ibid., at 2417.
138. *Florida* v. *J.L.*, 529 U.S. 266 (2000).
139. *U.S. Dept. of Justice* v. *Landano*, 113 S.Ct. 2014, 124 L.Ed.2d 84 (1993).
140. Richard Willing, "Third Law First to Order Taping Murder Confessions," *USA Today*, July 18, 2003.
141. Richard A. Leo and Kimberly D. Richman, "Mandate the Electronic Recording of Police Interrogations," *Crime and Public Policy*, Vol. 6 (June 2008), http://ssrn.com/abstract=1141335 (accessed September 8, 2010).
142. *South Dakota* v. *Neville*, 103 S.Ct. 916 (1983).
143. *Brown* v. *Mississippi*, 297 U.S. 278 (1936).
144. *Ashcraft* v. *Tennessee*, 322 U.S. 143 (1944).
145. *Chambers* v. *Florida*, 309 U.S. 227 (1940).
146. Ibid.
147. *Leyra* v. *Denno*, 347 U.S. 556 (1954).
148. *Arizona* v. *Fulminante*, 111 S.Ct. 1246 (1991).
149. *Chapman* v. *California*, 386 U.S. 18 (1967).
150. *State* v. *Fulminante*, No. CR-95-0160-AP (1999).
151. *Escobedo* v. *Illinois*, 378 U.S. 478 (1964).
152. *Edwards* v. *Arizona*, 451 U.S. 477, 101 S.Ct. 1880, 68 L.Ed.2d 378 (1981).
153. *Michigan* v. *Jackson*, 475 U.S. 625 (1986).
154. *Minnick* v. *Mississippi*, 498 U.S. 146 (1990).
155. *Arizona* v. *Roberson*, 486 U.S. 675, 108 S.Ct. 2093 (1988).
156. *Davis* v. *U.S.*, 114 S.Ct. 2350 (1994).
157. *Montejo* v. *Louisiana*, 556 U.S. ___ (2009).
158. *Miranda* v. *Arizona*, 384 U.S. 436 (1966).
159. "Immigrants Get Civil Rights," *USA Today*, June 11, 1992.
160. *U.S.* v. *Dickerson*, 166 F.3d 667 (1999).
161. *Dickerson* v. *U.S.*, 530 U.S. 428 (2000).
162. *U.S.* v. *Patane*, 542 U.S. 630 (2004).
163. *Silverthorne Lumber Co.* v. *U.S.*, 251 U.S. 385 (1920).
164. *Wong Sun* v. *U.S.*, 371 U.S. 471 (1963).
165. *Moran* v. *Burbine*, 475 U.S. 412, 421 (1986).
166. *Colorado* v. *Spring*, 479 U.S. 564, 107 S.Ct. 851 (1987).
167. *Brewer* v. *Williams*, 430 U.S. 387 (1977).
168. *Nix* v. *Williams*, 104 S.Ct. 2501 (1984).
169. *New York* v. *Quarles*, 104 S.Ct. 2626, 81 L.Ed.2d 550 (1984).
170. *Colorado* v. *Connelly*, 107 S.Ct. 515, 93 L.Ed.2d 473 (1986).
171. *Kuhlmann* v. *Wilson*, 477 U.S. 436 (1986).
172. *Illinois* v. *Perkins*, 495 U.S. 292 (1990).
173. *Rock* v. *Zimmerman*, 543 F.Supp. 179 (M.D. Pa. 1982).
174. Ibid.
175. See *Oregon* v. *Mathiason*, 429 U.S. 492, 97 S.Ct. 711 (1977).
176. *Arizona* v. *Mauro*, 107 S.Ct. 1931, 95 L.Ed.2d 458 (1987).
177. *Doyle* v. *Ohio*, 426 U.S. 610 (1976).
178. *Brecht* v. *Abrahamson*, 113 S.Ct. 1710, 123 L.Ed.2d 353 (1993).
179. Citing *Kotteakos* v. *U.S.*, 328 U.S. 750 (1946).
180. *Missouri* v. *Seibert*, 542 U.S. 600 (2004).
181. *Florida* v. *Powell*, U.S. Supreme Court, No. 08-1175 (decided February 23, 2010).
182. *Hayes* v. *Florida*, 470 U.S. 811, 105 S.Ct. 1643 (1985).
183. *Winston* v. *Lee*, 470 U.S. 753, 105 S.Ct. 1611 (1985).
184. *Schmerber* v. *California*, 384 U.S. 757 (1966).
185. "Man Coughs Up Cocaine While in Custody," *Police Magazine*, March 4, 2005, http://www.policemag.com/t_newspick.cfm?rank574703 (accessed January 4, 2007).
186. *U.S.* v. *Montoya de Hernandez*, 473 U.S. 531, 105 S.Ct. 3304 (1985).
187. Ibid.
188. *Olmstead* v. *U.S.*, 277 U.S. 438 (1928).
189. *On Lee* v. *U.S.*, 343 U.S. 747 (1952).
190. *Lopez* v. *U.S.*, 373 U.S. 427 (1963).
191. *Berger* v. *New York*, 388 U.S. 41 (1967).
192. *Katz* v. *U.S.*, 389 U.S. 347 (1967).
193. *Lee* v. *Florida*, 392 U.S. 378 (1968).
194. Federal Communications Act of 1934, 47 U.S.C. Section 151.
195. *U.S.* v. *White*, 401 U.S. 745 (1971).
196. *U.S.* v. *Karo*, 468 U.S. 705 (1984).
197. *U.S.* v. *Scott*, 436 U.S. 128 (1978).
198. For more information, see *FBI Law Enforcement Bulletin* (June 1987), p. 25.
199. Electronic Communications Privacy Act of 1986, Public Law 99–508.
200. For more information on the ECPA, see Robert A. Fiatal, "The Electronic Communications Privacy Act: Addressing Today's Technology," *FBI Law Enforcement Bulletin* (April 1988), pp. 24–30.
201. Communications Assistance for Law Enforcement Act of 1994, Public Law 103–414.
202. Federal Bureau of Investigation, "Notice: Implementation of the Communications Assistance for Law Enforcement Act," February 23, 1995.
203. Administrative Office of the United States Courts, *2009 Wiretap Report*, http://www.uscourts.gov/Statistics/WiretapReports/WiretapReport2009.aspx (accessed July 20, 2010).
204. Telecommunications Act of 1996, Public Law 104, 110 Stat. 56.
205. Title 47, U.S.C.A., Section 223(a)(1)(B)(ii) (Supp. 1997).
206. *Reno* v. *ACLU*, 117 S.Ct. 2329 (1997).
207. 18 U.S.C. Section 1030.
208. Section 202.
209. 18 U.S.C. Section 2703(c).
210. Ibid.
211. Public Law 109–177.
212. Stephanie Woodrow, "Obama Signs Reauthorization of Three Patriot Act Provisions," February 27, 2010, http://www.mainjustice.com/2010/02/27/obama-signs-patriot-act-reauthorization (accessed May 20, 2010).
213. Adapted from Technical Working Group for Electronic Crime Scene Investigation, *Electronic Crime Scene Investigation: A Guide for First Responders* (Washington, DC: National Institute of Justice, 2001), from which much of the information in this section is taken.
214. Ibid., p. 2.
215. Computer Crime and Intellectual Property Section, U.S. Department of Justice, *Searching and Seizing Computers and Obtaining Electronic Evidence in Criminal Investigations*

(Washington, DC: U.S. Department of Justice, 2002), http://www.usdoj.gov/criminal/cybercrime/s&smanual2002.htm (accessed August 4, 2007).

216. Technical Working Group, *Electronic Crime Scene Investigation*, p. 2.
217. Technical Working Group for the Examination of Digital Evidence, *Forensic Examination of Digital Evidence: A Guide for Law Enforcement* (Washington, DC: National Institute of Justice, 2004).
218. *U.S.* v. *Carey*, 172 F.3d 1268 (10th Cir. 1999).
219. *U.S.* v. *Turner*, 169 F.3d 84 (1st Cir. 1999).

Chapter 6: Policing: Issues and Challenges

i. Carl B. Klockars et al., "The Measurement of Police Integrity," National Institute of Justice Research in Brief (Washington, DC: NIJ, 2000), p. 1.
ii. Karyn S. Hunttings, *Quotation World*, http://s-2000.com/quoteworld/character.html (accessed March 20, 2007).
iii. Police Foundation, *Annual Report, 1991* (Washington, DC: Police Foundation, 1992).
iv. Technical Working Group on Crime Scene Investigation, *Crime Scene Investigation: A Guide for Law Enforcement* (Washington, DC: National Institute of Justice, 2000), p. 12.
v. Major Cities Chiefs Association, *Terrorism: The Impact on State and Local Law Enforcement*, Intelligence Commanders Conference Report (June 2002), http://www.neiassociates.org/mccintelligencereport.pdf (accessed September 30, 2008).
vi. Angus Smith, ed., *Intelligence-Led Policing* (Richmond, VA: International Association of Law Enforcement Intelligence Analysts, 1997), p. 1.
vii. Office of Justice Programs, *The National Criminal Intelligence Sharing Plan* (Washington, DC: U.S. Department of Justice, 2005), p. 27.
viii. Major Cities Chiefs Association, *Terrorism*.
ix. Adapted from Gerald Hill and Kathleen Hill, *The Real Life Dictionary of the Law*, http://www.law.com (accessed June 11, 2008)
x. Deborah Ramirez, Jack McDevitt, and Amy Farrell, *A Resource Guide on Racial Profiling Data Collection Systems: Promising Practices and Lessons Learned* (Washington, DC: U.S. Department of Justice, 2000), p. 3.
xi. National Institute of Justice, *Use of Force by Police: Overview of National and Local Data* (Washington, DC: NIJ, 1999).
xii. International Association of Chiefs of Police, *Police Use of Force in America, 2001* (Alexandria, VA: IACP, 2001), p. 1.
xiii. Samuel Walker, Geoffrey P. Albert, and Dennis J. Kenney, *Responding to the Problem Police Officer: A National Study of Early Warning Systems* (Washington, DC: National Institute of Justice, 2000).
xiv. Sam W. Lathrop, "Reviewing Use of Force: A Systematic Approach," *FBI Law Enforcement Bulletin* (October 2000), p. 18.
xv. Lorie Fridell et al., *Racially Biased Policing: A Principled Response* (Washington, DC: Police Executive Research Forum, 2001), p. 41.

---

1. Joel Leson, *Assessing and Managing the Terrorism Threat* (Washington, DC: U.S. Department of Justice, 2005).
2. Janine Rauch and Etienne Marasis, "Contextualizing the Waddington Report," http://www.wits.ac.za/csvr/papers/papwadd.html (accessed January 5, 2009).
3. Jerome H. Skolnick, *Justice without Trial: Law Enforcement in a Democratic Society* (New York: John Wiley, 1966).
4. William A. Westley, *Violence and the Police: A Sociological Study of Law, Custom, and Morality* (Cambridge, MA: MIT Press, 1970); and William A. Westley, "Violence and the Police," *American Journal of Sociology*, Vol. 49 (1953), pp. 34–41.
5. Arthur Niederhoffer, *Behind the Shield: The Police in Urban Society* (Garden City, NY: Anchor, 1967).
6. Thomas Barker and David L. Carter, *Police Deviance* (Cincinnati, OH: Anderson, 1986). See also Christopher P. Wilson, *Cop Knowledge: Police Power and Cultural Narrative in Twentieth-Century America* (Chicago: University of Chicago Press, 2000).
7. Richard Bennett and Theodore Greenstein, "The Police Personality: A Test of the Predispositional Model," *Journal of Police Science and Administration*, Vol. 3 (1975), pp. 439–445.
8. James Teevan and Bernard Dolnick, "The Values of the Police: A Reconsideration and Interpretation," *Journal of Police Science and Administration* (1973), pp. 366–369.
9. Bennett and Greenstein, "The Police Personality," pp. 439–445.
10. Ibid.
11. Office of the U.S. Attorney for the Southern District of California press release, July 28, 2006.
12. NBC News San Diego, "Border Patrol Agent Faces Immigrant-Smuggling Charges," August 5, 2005, http://www.nbcsandiego.com/news/4816916/detail.html (accessed July 4, 2009).
13. Alan Feuer, "2 Ex-Detectives Guilty in Killings," *New York Times*, April 7, 2006, http://www.nytimes.com/2006/04/07/nyregion/07cops.html (accessed April 7, 2009).
14. Andy Newman, "A Juror's Question That Went Unanswered: 'How Dare You Violate That Oath?'" *New York Times*, April 7, 2006, http://www.nytimes.com/2006/04/07/nyregion/07scene.html (accessed April 7, 2009).
15. Jason Fisher, "$10 M for Victim of Mob Cop," *New York Post*, June 4, 2010, http://www.nypost.com/p/news/local/brooklyn/for_victim_of_mob_cop_fb4Ki0Ap3vDubZc41qC6OO (accessed June 5, 2010).
16. Carl B. Klockars et al., "The Measurement of Police Integrity," *National Institute of Justice Research in Brief* (Washington, DC: NIJ, 2000), p. 1.
17. Michael J. Palmiotto, ed., *Police Misconduct: A Reader for the Twenty-First Century* (Upper Saddle River, NJ: Prentice Hall, 2001), preface.
18. Tim Prenzler and Peta Mackay, "Police Gratuities: What the Public Thinks," *Criminal Justice Ethics* (winter/spring 1995), pp. 15–25.
19. Thomas Barker and David L. Carter, *Police Deviance* (Cincinnati, OH: Anderson, 1986). For a detailed overview of the issues involved in police corruption, see Victor E. Kappeler, Richard D. Sluder, and Geoffrey P. Alpert, *Forces of Deviance: Understanding the Dark Side of Policing*, 2nd ed. (Prospect Heights, IL: Waveland Press, 1998); Dean J. Champion, *Police Misconduct in America: A Reference Handbook* (Santa Barbara, CA: ABC-CLIO, 2002); and Kim Michelle Lersch, ed., *Policing and Misconduct* (Upper Saddle River, NJ: Prentice Hall, 2002).
20. Frank L. Perry, "Repairing Broken Windows: Preventing Corruption within Our Ranks," *FBI Law Enforcement Bulletin* (February 2001), pp. 23–26.
21. "Nationline: NYC Cops—Excess Force Not Corruption," *USA Today*, June 16, 1995.
22. *Knapp Commission Report on Police Corruption* (New York: George Braziller, 1973).
23. Ibid.
24. Sabrina Tavernise, "Victory for Officer Who Aided Corruption Inquiry," *New York Times*, April 3, 2004.
25. See Erwin Chemerinsky, *An Independent Analysis of the Los Angeles Police Department's Board of Inquiry Report on the*

Rampart Scandal, September 11, 2000, http://www.usc.edu/dept/law/faculty/chemerinsky/rampartfinalrep.html (accessed January 10, 2002).
26. Linda Deutsch, "Appeals Court Intercedes in LAPD Corruption Trial," Associated Press, October 12, 2000, http://www.newstimes.com/archive2000/oct12/nah.htm (accessed January 20, 2002).
27. "Three LAPD Officers Convicted," *USA Today* Online, November 15, 2000 (accessed July 16, 2001).
28. "Prosecutors: LAPD Hindering Police Corruption Trial," Associated Press, October 6, 2000, http://www.newstimes.com/archive2000/oct06/nac.htm (accessed February 2, 2008).
29. Scott Glover and Matt Lait, "LAPD Settling Abuse Scandal," *Los Angeles Times*, March 31, 2005.
30. "Three LAPD Officers Convicted" and "This Week's Corrupt Cop Story," http://www.stopthedrugwar.org/chronicle/266/copcorruption.shtml (accessed October 2, 2003).
31. Glover and Lait, "LAPD Settling Abuse Scandal."
32. Ibid.
33. Tina Daunt and Jim Newton, "Council OKs Police Reform Pact with Justice Department," *Los Angeles Times* Online, November 3, 2000 (accessed May 20, 2006).
34. Scott Glover and Matt Lait, "A Tearful Perez Gets Five Years," *Los Angeles Times* Online, February 26, 2000 (accessed August 28, 2001).
35. Edwin H. Sutherland and Donald Cressey, *Principles of Criminology*, 8th ed. (Philadelphia: J. B. Lippincott, 1970).
36. Tim R. Jones, Compton Owens, and Melissa A. Smith, "Police Ethics Training: A Three-Tiered Approach," *FBI Law Enforcement Bulletin* (June 1995), pp. 22–26.
37. U.S. Department of Justice, *Principles for Promoting Police Integrity: Examples of Promising Police Practices* (Washington, DC: DOJ, 2001).
38. National Institute of Justice, *Enhancing Police Integrity* (Washington, DC: U.S. Department of Justice, 2005).
39. Ibid., p ii.
40. International Association of Chiefs of Police, *Employee Drug Testing* (St. Paul, MN: IACP, 1999).
41. Tom Hays, "NYPD to Start Random Steroid Testing," Associated Press, April 9, 2008, http://www.wtopnews.com/?sid=1383781&nid=104 (accessed July 24, 2008).
42. *Maurice Turner* v. *Fraternal Order of Police*, 500 A.2d 1005 (D.C. 1985).
43. *Philip Caruso, President of P.B.A.* v. *Benjamin Ward, Police Commissioner*, New York State Supreme Court, Pat. 37, Index no. 12632-86, 1986.
44. *National Treasury Employees Union* v. *Von Raab*, 489 U.S. 656, 659 (1989).
45. National Law Enforcement Officers' Memorial Fund, "Facts and Figures," http://www.nleomf.org/facts (accessed Octdober 1, 2010).
46. Officer Down Memorial Page, http://odmp.org/year.php?year=2009 (accessed June 15, 2010).
47. Officer Down Memorial Page, http://www.odmp.org/yeardisp.php?year52001 (accessed January 16, 2001).
48. Anthony J. Pinizzotto and Edward F. Davis, "Cop Killers and Their Victims," *FBI Law Enforcement Bulletin* (December 1992), p. 10.
49. Bureau of Labor Statistics, *Occupational Outlook Handbook, 2000–01 Edition* (Washington, DC: BLS, 2000); and Brian A. Reaves and Matthew J. Hickman, *Law Enforcement Management and Administrative Statistics, 2000: Data for Individual State and Local Agencies with 100 or More Officers* (Washington, DC: Bureau of Justice Statistics, 2004). Note that the LEMAS report only includes data from approximately 700 state and local law enforcement agencies that employ 100 or more full-time sworn personnel and that assign 50 or more of these officers to respond to calls for service. LEMAS reports finding 402,000 full-time sworn personnel among those departments in its 2000 survey. BLS data are more comprehensive and include part-time personnel.
50. Brian A. Reaves and Timothy C. Hart, *Federal Law Enforcement Officers, 2000* (Washington, DC: Bureau of Justice Statistics, 2001).
51. Kevin Johnson, "Better Defense Tactics Helping to Curb Police Deaths," *USA Today*, April 22, 2008, p. 3A.
52. *AIDS and Our Workplace*, New York City Police Department pamphlet, November 1987.
53. See Occupational Safety and Health Administration, OSHA Bloodborne Pathogens Act of 1991 (29 CFR 1910.1030).
54. *National Institute of Justice Reports*, No. 206 (November/December 1987).
55. "Suicides, Resignations Hit New Orleans' Thin Blue Line," *USA Today*, September 4, 2005, http://www.usatoday.com/news/nation/2005-09-04-neworleanspolicesuicides_x.htm (accessed April 2, 2006).
56. Ibid.
57. See "On-the-Job Stress in Policing: Reducing It, Preventing It," *National Institute of Justice Journal* (January 2000), pp. 18–24.
58. "Stress on the Job," *Newsweek*, April 25, 1988, p. 43.
59. "On-the-Job Stress in Policing," p. 19.
60. Kevin Barrett, "Police Suicide: Is Anyone Listening?" *Journal of Safe Management of Disruptive and Assaultive Behavior* (spring 1997), pp. 6–9.
61. For an excellent review of coping strategies among police officers, see Robin N. Haarr and Merry Morash, "Gender, Race, and Strategies of Coping with Occupational Stress in Policing," *Justice Quarterly*, Vol. 16, No. 2 (June 1999), pp. 303–336.
62. Mark H. Anshel, "A Conceptual Model and Implications for Coping with Stressful Events in Police Work," *Criminal Justice and Behavior*, Vol. 27, No. 3 (2000), p. 375.
63. Ibid.
64. Bryan Vila, "Tired Cops: Probable Connections between Fatigue and the Performance, Health, and Safety of Patrol Officers," *American Journal of Police*, Vol. 15, No. 2 (1996), pp. 51–92.
65. Bryan Vila et al., *Evaluating the Effects of Fatigue on Police Patrol Officers: Final Report* (Washington, DC: National Institute of Justice, 2000).
66. Bryan Vila and Dennis Jay Kenney, "Tired Cops: The Prevalence and Potential Consequences of Police Fatigue," *National Institute of Justice Journal*, No. 248 (2002), p. 19.
67. Bryan Vila and Erik Y. Taiji, "Fatigue and Police Officer Performance," paper presented at the annual meeting of the American Society of Criminology, Chicago, 1996.
68. Police Executive Research Forum, *Local Law Enforcement's Role in Preventing and Responding to Terrorism* (Washington, DC: PERF, October 2, 2001), http://www.policeforum.org/terrorismfinal.doc (accessed June 1, 2003).
69. Council on Foreign Relations, "Terrorism Questions and Answers: Police Departments," http://www.terrorismanswers.com/security/police.html (accessed April 19, 2005).
70. Ibid.
71. Michael Weissenstein, "NYPD Shifts Focus to Terrorism, Long Considered the Turf of Federal Agents," Associated Press, March 21, 2003, http://www.nj.com/newsflash/national/index.ssf?/cgi-free/getstory_ssf.cgi?a0801_BC_NYPD-Counterterror&&news&newsflash-national (accessed May 25, 2003).
72. Ibid.

73. International Association of Chiefs of Police, *From Hometown Security to Homeland Security: IACP's Principles for a Locally Designed and Nationally Coordinated Homeland Security Strategy* (Alexandria, VA: IACP, 2005).
74. Ibid.
75. Joseph G. Estey, "President's Message: Taking Command Initiative—An Update" (Washington, DC: International Association of Chiefs of Police, 2005), http://www.theiacp.org/documents/index.cfm?fuseaction5document&document_id5697 (accessed July 25, 2009).
76. Robert J. Jordan (FBI), Congressional Statement on Information Sharing before the U.S. Senate Committee on the Judiciary, Subcommittee on Administrative Oversight and the Courts, Washington, DC, April 17, 2002, http://www.fbi.gov/congress/congress02/jordan041702.htm (accessed April 19, 2006).
77. The concept of intelligence-led policing appears to have been first fully articulated in Angus Smith, ed., *Intelligence-Led Policing* (Richmond, VA: International Association of Law Enforcement Intelligence Analysts, 1997).
78. David L. Carter, *Law Enforcement Intelligence: A Guide for State, Local, and Tribal Law Enforcement Agencies* (Washington, DC: U.S. Department of Justice, 2004), p. 7.
79. Much of the information and some of the wording in this section are taken from Carter, *Law Enforcement Intelligence*.
80. David L. Carter, "The Law Enforcement Intelligence Function," *FBI Law Enforcement Bulletin*, Vol. 74, No. 6 (June 2005), pp. 1–10.
81. Governor's Commission on Criminal Justice Innovation, *Final Report* (Boston: Governor's Commission, 2004), p. 57, from which much of the wording in the rest of this paragraph is taken.
82. Federal Bureau of Investigation, Law Enforcement online, http://www.fbi.gov/hq/cjisd/leo.htm (accessed September 1, 2006).
83. Bernard H. Levin, "Sharing Information: Some Open Secrets and a Glimpse at the Future," *Police Futurist*, Vol. 14, No. 1 (winter 2006), pp. 8–9.
84. The plan was an outgrowth of the IACP Criminal Intelligence Sharing Summit held in Alexandria, Virginia, in March 2002. Results of the summit are documented in International Association of Chiefs of Police, *Recommendations from the IACP Intelligence Summit, Criminal Intelligence Sharing*.
85. Office of Justice Programs, *The National Criminal Intelligence Sharing Plan* (Washington, DC: U.S. Department of Justice, 2003).
86. "Stroke Victim Sues State over Arrest," Associated Press, April 24, 1996.
87. Charles R. Swanson, Leonard Territo, and Robert W. Taylor, *Police Administration: Structures, Processes, and Behavior*, 2nd ed. (New York: Macmillan, 1988).
88. *Malley* v. *Briggs*, 475 U.S. 335, 106 S.Ct. 1092 (1986).
89. Ibid., at 4246.
90. *Biscoe* v. *Arlington County*, 238 U.S. App. D.C. 206, 738 F.2d 1352, 1362 (1984). See also 738 F.2d 1352 (D.C. Cir. 1984), *cert. denied*; 469 U.S. 1159; and 105 S.Ct. 909, 83 L.E.2d 923 (1985).
91. *Kaplan* v. *Lloyd's Insurance Co.*, 479 So.2d 961 (La. App. 1985).
92. John Hill, "High-Speed Police Pursuits: Dangers, Dynamics, and Risk Reduction," *FBI Law Enforcement Bulletin* (July 2002), pp. 14–18.
93. *City of Canton, Ohio* v. *Harris*, 489 U.S. 378 (1989).
94. Ibid., at 1204.
95. *Board of the County Commissioners of Bryan County, Oklahoma* v. *Brown*, 520 U.S. 397 (1997).
96. U.S. Code, Title 42, Section 1983.
97. *Bivens* v. *Six Unknown Federal Agents*, 403 U.S. 388 (1971).
98. See *F.D.I.C.* v. *Meyer*, 510 U.S. 471 (1994), in which the U.S. Supreme Court reiterated its ruling under *Bivens*, stating that only government employees and not government agencies can be sued.
99. *Wyler* v. *U.S.*, 725 F.2d 157 (2d Cir. 1983).
100. California Government Code, Section 818.
101. Federal Tort Claims Act, 28 U.S.C. 1346(b), 2671–2680.
102. *Elder* v. *Holloway*, 114 S.Ct. 1019, 127 L.Ed.2d 344 (1994).
103. Ibid.
104. *Hunter* v. *Bryant*, 112 S.Ct. 534 (1991).
105. William U. McCormack, "Supreme Court Cases: 1991–1992 Term," *FBI Law Enforcement Bulletin* (November 1992), p. 30.
106. *Saucier* v. *Katz*, 533 U.S. 194 (2001).
107. See also *Brosseau* v. *Haugen*, 543 U.S. 194 (2004).
108. *Pearson et al.* v. *Callahan*, 555 U.S. ___ (2009).
109. *Scott* v. *Harris*, 550 U.S. 372 (2007).
110. *Idaho* v. *Horiuchi*, 253 F.3d 359 (9th Cir. 2001).
111. For more information on police liability, see Daniel L. Schofield, "Legal Issues of Pursuit Driving," *FBI Law Enforcement Bulletin* (May 1988), pp. 23–29.
112. Michael S. Vaughn, Tab W. Cooper, and Rolando V. del Carmen, "Assessing Legal Liabilities in Law Enforcement: Police Chiefs' Views," *Crime and Delinquency*, Vol. 47, No. 1 (2001), p. 3.
113. Adapted from Deborah Ramirez, Jack McDevitt, and Amy Farrell, *A Resource Guide on Racial Profiling Data Collection Systems: Promising Practices and Lessons Learned* (Washington, DC: U.S. Department of Justice, 2000), p. 3.
114. David Harris, *Driving While Black: Racial Profiling on Our Nation's Highways* (Washington, DC: American Civil Liberties Union, 1999).
115. "Justice Department Bars Race Profiling, with Exception for Terrorism," *Criminal Justice Newsletter* (July 15, 2003), pp. 6–7.
116. "Justice Department Issues Policy Guidance to Ban Racial Profiling," U.S. Department of Justice press release (No. 355), June 17, 2003.
117. Blaine Harden and Somini Sengupta, "Some Passengers Singled Out for Exclusion by Flight Crew," *New York Times*, September 22, 2001.
118. David Cole and John Lambreth, "The Fallacy of Racial Profiling," *New York Times* Online, May 13, 2001, http://college1.nytimes.com/buests/articles/2001/05/13/846196.xml (accessed August 28, 2004).
119. Amitai Etzioni, "Another Side of Racial Profiling," *USA Today*, May 21, 2001.
120. Gallup Poll Organization, "Racial Profiling Seen as Pervasive, Unjust," July 20, 2004, http://www.gallup.com/poll/12406/Racial-Profiling-Seen-Pervasive-Unjust.aspx (accessed August 1, 2010).
121. Ramirez, McDevitt, and Farrell, *A Resource Guide on Racial Profiling Data Collection Systems*, p. 3.
122. Police Executive Research Forum, *Racially Biased Policing: A Principled Response* (Washington, DC: PERF, 2001).
123. Ibid., foreword.
124. Ibid., p. 39.
125. Ibid., p. 47.
126. Some of the material in this section is adapted or derived from National Institute of Justice, *Use of Force by Police: Overview of National and Local Data* (Washington, DC: NIJ, 1999).
127. Matthew R. Durose, Erica L. Smith, and Patrick A. Langan, *Contacts between Police and the Public, 2005* (Washington, DC: Bureau of Justice Statistics, 2007).
128. Joel H. Garner and Christopher D. Maxwell, "Measuring the Amount of Force Used by and against the Police in Six

Jurisdictions," in National Institute of Justice, *Use of Force by Police*, p. 41.
129. International Association of Chiefs of Police, *Police Use of Force in America, 2001* (Alexandria, VA: IACP, 2001), p. 1.
130. Kenneth Adams, "What We Know about Police Use of Force," in National Institute of Justice, *Use of Force by Police*, p. 4.
131. International Association of Chiefs of Police, *Police Use of Force in America, 2001*.
132. Geoffrey P. Alpert and Roger G. Dunham, *The Force Factor: Measuring Police Use of Force Relative to Suspect Resistance—A Final Report* (Washington, DC: National Institute of Justice, 2001).
133. Samuel Walker, Geoffrey P. Alpert, and Dennis J. Kenney, *Responding to the Problem Police Officer: A National Study of Early Warning Systems* (Washington, DC: National Institute of Justice, 2000).
134. See Human Rights Watch, "The Christopher Commission Report," from which some of the wording in the paragraph is adapted, http://www.hrw.org/reports98/police/uspo73.htm (accessed March 30, 2002).
135. Sam W. Lathrop, "Reviewing Use of Force: A Systematic Approach," *FBI Law Enforcement Bulletin* (October 2000), p. 18.
136. Jodi M. Brown and Patrick A. Langan, *Policing and Homicide, 1976–98: Justifiable Homicide by Police, Police Officers Murdered by Felons* (Washington, DC: Bureau of Justice Statistics, 2001), p. iii.
137. *Tennessee* v. *Garner*, 471 U.S. 1 (1985).
138. *Graham* v. *Connor*, 490 U.S. 386, 396–397 (1989).
139. John C. Hall, "FBI Training on the New Federal Deadly Force Policy," *FBI Law Enforcement Bulletin* (April 1996), pp. 25–32.
140. James Fyfe, *Shots Fired: An Examination of New York City Police Firearms Discharges* (Ann Arbor, MI: University Microfilms, 1978).
141. James Fyfe, "Blind Justice? Police Shootings in Memphis," paper presented at the annual meeting of the Academy of Criminal Justice Sciences, Philadelphia, March 1981.
142. It is estimated that American police shoot at approximately 3,600 people every year. See William Geller, *Deadly Force* study guide, Crime File Series (Washington, DC: National Institute of Justice, n.d.).
143. Anne Cohen, "I've Killed That Man Ten Thousand Times," *Police Magazine* (July 1980).
144. For more information, see Joe Auten, "When Police Shoot," *North Carolina Criminal Justice Today*, Vol. 4, No. 4 (summer 1986), pp. 9–14.
145. Details for this story come from Stephanie Slater, "Suicidal Man Killed by Police Fusillade," *Palm Beach Post*, March 11, 2005, p. 1A.
146. Rebecca Stincelli, *Suicide by Cop: Victims from Both Sides of the Badge* (Folsom, CA: Interviews and Interrogations Institute, 2004).
147. Slater, "Suicidal Man Killed by Police Fusillade."
148. Anthony J. Pinizzotto, Edward F. Davis, and Charles E. Miller III, "Suicide by Cop: Defining a Devastating Dilemma," *FBI Law Enforcement Bulletin*, Vol. 74, No. 2 (February 2005), p. 15.
149. "Ten Percent of Police Shootings Found to Be 'Suicide by Cop,'" *Criminal Justice Newsletter* (September 1, 1998), pp. 1–2.
150. Robert J. Homant and Daniel B. Kennedy, "Suicide by Police: A Proposed Typology of Law Enforcement Officer–Assisted Suicide," *Policing: An International Journal of Police Strategies and Management*, Vol. 23, No. 3 (2000), pp. 339–355.
151. David Hambling, "Flash Gun," *Science News*, May 10–16, 2008, pp. 38–40.
152. David W. Hayeslip and Alan Preszler, "NIJ Initiative on Less-Than-Lethal Weapons," *NIJ Research in Brief* (Washington, DC: National Institute of Justice, 1993).
153. Ibid.
154. Thomas Farragher and David Abel, "Postgame Police Projectile Kills an Emerson Student," *Boston Globe*, October 22, 2004, http://www.boston.com/sports/baseball/redsox/articles/2004/10/22/postgame_police_projectile_kills_an_emerson_student (accessed July 25, 2005).
155. Michael Siegfried, "Notes on the Professionalization of Private Security," *Justice Professional* (spring 1989).
156. See Edward A. Farris, "Five Decades of American Policing, 1932–1982: The Path to Professionalism," *Police Chief* (November 1982), p. 34.
157. InsideDiscoverPolicing.org, "Inside CALEA Accreditation," http://blog.discoverpolicing.org/uncategorized/inside-calea-accreditation (accessed October 15, 2010). Agency estimates are from Reaves and Hickman, *Census of State and Local Law Enforcement Agencies, 2000*.
158. *CALEA Update*, No. 81 (February 2003), http://www.calea.org/newweb/newsletter/No81/81index.htm (accessed May 21, 2003).
159. Brian A. Reaves, *State and Local Law Enforcement Training Academies, 2006* (Washington, DC: Bureau of Justice Statistics, 2009), p. 6.
160. Information in this paragraph comes from "PTO Program," COPS Office, U.S. Department of Justice (no date), http://www.cops.usdoj.gov/print.asp?Item=461 (accessed June 3, 2007).
161. Ibid.
162. National Commission on Law Observance and Enforcement, *Report on Police* (Washington, DC: U.S. Government Printing Office, 1931).
163. President's Commission on Law Enforcement and Administration of Justice, *The Challenge of Crime in a Free Society* (Washington, DC: U.S. Government Printing Office, 1967).
164. National Advisory Commission on Criminal Justice Standards and Goals, *Report on the Police* (Washington, DC: U.S. Government Printing Office, 1973).
165. Reaves and Hickman, *Law Enforcement Management and Administrative Statistics, 2000*.
166. Ibid.
167. Brian A. Reaves and Matthew J. Hickman, *Police Departments in Large Cities, 1990–2000* (Washington, DC: Bureau of Justice Statistics, 2002), p. 1.
168. "Dallas PD College Rule Gets Final OK," *Law Enforcement News* (July 7, 1986), pp. 1, 13.
169. *Davis* v. *Dallas*, 777 F.2d 205 (5th Cir. 1985).
170. David L. Carter, Allen D. Sapp, and Darrel W. Stephens, *The State of Police Education: Policy Direction for the Twenty-First Century* (Washington, DC: Police Executive Research Forum, 1989), pp. xxii–xxiii.
171. National Advisory Commission on Criminal Justice Standards and Goals, *Report on the Police*, p. 238.
172. Matthew J. Hickman and Brian A. Reaves, *Local Police Departments, 2003* (Washington, DC: Bureau of Justice Statistics, 2006), p. 5.
173. Matthew J. Hickman and Brian A. Reaves, *Local Police Departments, 2000* (Washington, DC: Bureau of Justice Statistics, 2003), p. 270.
174. August Vollmer, *The Police and Modern Society* (Berkeley: University of California Press, 1936), p. 222.
175. O. W. Wilson and Roy Clinton McLaren, *Police Administration*, 4th ed. (New York: McGraw-Hill, 1977), p. 259.
176. *Report of the National Advisory Commission on Civil Disorders* (New York: E. P. Dutton, 1968), p. 332.
177. Hickman and Reaves, *Local Police Departments, 2003*.
178. U.S. Census Bureau, *National Population Estimates: Characteristics*, http://www.census.gov/popest/national/asrh/NC-EST2005-srh.html.

179. R. Alan Thompson, "Black Skin—Brass Shields: Assessing the Presumed Marginalization of Black Law Enforcement Executives," *American Journal of Criminal Justice*, Vol. 30, No. 2 (2006), pp. 163–175.
180. National Center for Women and Policing, *Equality Denied: The Status of Women in Policing, 2001* (Los Angeles: NCWP, 2002), p. 1.
181. Ibid.
182. Lynn Langston, *Women in Law Enforcement, 1987–2008* (Washington, DC: Bureau of Justice Statistics, June 2010).
183. National Center for Women and Policing, *Recruiting and Retaining Women: A Self-Assessment Guide for Law Enforcement* (Los Angeles: NCWP, 2001), p. 22.
184. Ibid.
185. Mary Dodge, "Women in Policing: Time to Forget the Differences and Focus on the Future," *Criminal Justice Research Reports* (July/August 2007), p. 82.
186. C. Lee Bennett, "Interviews with Female Police Officers in Western Massachusetts," paper presented at the annual meeting of the Academy of Criminal Justice Sciences, Nashville, TN, March 1991.
187. Ibid., p. 9.
188. Carole G. Garrison, Nancy K. Grant, and Kenneth L. J. McCormick, "Utilization of Police Women," unpublished manuscript.
189. Susan Ehrlich Martin and Nancy C. Jurik, *Doing Justice, Doing Gender: Women in Law and Criminal Justice Occupations* (Thousand Oaks, CA: Sage, 1996).
190. *Private Security: Report of the Task Force on Private Security* (Washington, DC: U.S. Government Printing Office, 1976), p. 4.
191. "Olympic Committee to Review Salt Lake Security in Wake of Terror Attacks," Associated Press, September 17, 2001.
192. David H. Bayley and Clifford D. Shearing, *The New Structure of Policing: Description, Conceptualization, and Research Agenda* (Washington, DC: National Institute of Justice, 2001).
193. William C. Cunningham, John J. Strauchs, and Clifford W. Van Meter, *The Hallcrest Report II: Private Security Trends, 1970–2000* (McLean, VA: Hallcrest Systems, 1990).
194. Includes full-time employees working for local police, sheriff's departments, special police, and state police. See Brian A. Reaves and Andrew L. Goldberg, *Census of State and Local Law Enforcement Agencies, 1996* (Washington, DC: Bureau of Justice Statistics, 1998); Reaves and Hickman, *Law Enforcement Management and Administrative Statistics, 2000*; Bureau of Labor Statistics, *Occupational Outlook Handbook, 2000–01 Edition*; and Bureau of Labor Statistics Occupational Outlook Handbook, http://www.bls.gov/oco/ocos159.htm#outlook (accessed May 20, 2010).
195. See http://www.spyandsecuritystore.com/conex.html (accessed June 5, 2010).
196. Cunningham, Strauchs, and Van Meter, *The Hallcrest Report II*, p. 236.
197. Bayley and Shearing, *The New Structure of Policing*, p. 15.
198. National Institute of Justice, *Crime and Protection in America: A Study of Private Security and Law Enforcement Resources and Relationships—Executive Summary* (Washington, DC: U.S. Department of Justice, 1985), pp. 59–72.

Chapter 7: The Courts

1. *The Challenge of Crime in a Free Society: Report of The President's Commission on Law Enforcement and the Administration of Justice* (Washington, DC: USGPO, 1967), p. 125.
2. John Mattes, "Motives for Bombing Downtown Federal Courthouse?" August 8, 2008, http://www.sandiego6.com/content/unit6/story/Motives-for-Bombing-Downtown-Federal-Courthouse/ZGo7RgwzaUagS6XDW7cypQ.cspx (accessed July 1, 2010).
3. Law Enforcement Assistance Administration, *Two Hundred Years of American Criminal Justice* (Washington, DC: U.S. Government Printing Office, 1976), p. 31.
4. David B. Rottman, Carol R. Flango, and R. Shedine Lockley, *State Court Organization, 1993* (Washington, DC: Bureau of Justice Statistics, 1995), p. 11.
5. In 1957, only 13 states had permanent intermediate appellate courts. Now, all but 12 states have these courts, and North Dakota is operating one on a temporary basis to assist in handling the rising appellate caseload in that state. See Rottman, Flango, and Lockley, *State Court Organization, 1993*, p. 5.
6. *Keeney* v. *Tamayo-Reyes*, 504 U.S. 1 (1992).
7. *Herrera* v. *Collins*, 113 S.Ct. 853, 122 L.Ed.2d 203 (1993).
8. Martin Wright, *Justice for Victims and Offenders* (Bristol, PA: Open University Press, 1991), p. 56.
9. "Bridging the Gap between Communities and Courts," http://www.communityjustice.org (accessed November 22, 2010).
10. Wright, *Justice for Victims and Offenders*, pp. 104 and 106.
11. Most of the information and some of the wording in this section come from Administrative Office of the U.S. Courts, "Understanding the Federal Courts," http://www.uscourts.gov/UFC99.pdf (accessed April 2, 2010).
12. Administrative Office of the U.S. Courts, "U.S. District Courts: Criminal Cases and Defendants Filed, Terminated, Pending," http://www.uscourts.gov/uscourts/Statistics/JudicialFactsAndFigures/2008/Table501.pdf (accessed August 4, 2010).
13. Administrative Office of the U.S. Courts, "U.S. District Courts: Civil Cases Filed, Terminated, Pending," http://www.uscourts.gov/uscourts/Statistics/JudicialFactsAndFigures/2008/Table401.pdf (accessed August 4, 2010).
14. Administrative Office of the U.S. Courts, "Federal Judicial Pay Increase Fact Sheet," http://www.uscourts.gov/JudgesAndJudgeships/JudicialCompensation/JudicialPayIncreaseFact.aspx (accessed August 4, 2010).
15. Administrative Office of the U.S. Courts, "Comparison of Average Salaries of Deans and Senior Professors of Top Law Schools with U.S. District Court Judges," http://www.uscourts.gov/judicialcompensation/payfactsheet.html, no date (accessed July 30, 2010).
16. See American Bar Association, *Federal Judicial Pay Erosion: A Report on the Need for Reform* (Chicago: ABA, 2001).
17. Although the Ethics Reform Act of 1989 was supposed to allow for a cost-of-living increase in federal judicial salaries, Congress blocked the automatic increases from 1995 to 1999 because they also applied to the salaries of members of Congress and were seen as politically unpalatable.
18. Justice John Roberts, "2005 Year-End Report on the Federal Judiciary," *The Third Branch*, Vol. 38, No. 1 (January 2006), http://www.uscourts.gov/ttb/jan06ttb/yearend/index.html (accessed March 30, 2008).
19. Much of the information and some of the wording in this section come from Administrative Office of the U.S. Courts, "About the Federal Courts," www.uscourts.gov/about.html (accessed October 4, 2010).
20. Stephen L. Wasby, *The Supreme Court in the Federal Judicial System*, 3rd ed. (Chicago: Nelson-Hall, 1988), p. 58.
21. Administrative Office of the U.S. Courts, "Federal Judiciary Says New Judgeships Needed," March 13, 2007, http://www.uscourts.gov/Press_Releases/judconf031307.html (accessed September 5, 2008).
22. *The Supreme Court of the United States* (Washington, DC: U.S. Government Printing Office, n.d.). p. 4.

23. *Marbury* v. *Madison*, 1 Cranch 137 (1803).
24. *Arraignment* is also a term used to describe an initial appearance, although we will reserve use of that word to describe a later court appearance following the defendant's indictment by a grand jury or the filing of an information by the prosecutor.
25. *McNabb* v. *U.S.*, 318 U.S. 332 (1943).
26. *County of Riverside* v. *McLaughlin*, 111 S.Ct. 1661 (1991).
27. *White* v. *Maryland*, 373 U.S. 59 (1963).
28. *Rothgery* v. *Gillespie County, Texas*, 554 U.S. _ (2008).
29. Much of the information in this section comes from Barry Mahoney et al., *Pretrial Services Programs: Responsibilities and Potential* (Washington, DC: National Institute of Justice, 2001).
30. *Taylor* v. *Taintor*, 83 U.S. 66 (1873).
31. National Advisory Commission on Criminal Justice Standards and Goals, *The Courts* (Washington, DC: U.S. Government Printing Office, 1973), p. 37.
32. C. Ares, A. Rankin, and H. Sturz, "The Manhattan Bail Project: An Interim Report on the Use of Pretrial Parole," *New York University Law Review*, Vol. 38 (January 1963), pp. 68–95.
33. H. Zeisel, "Bail Revisited," *American Bar Foundation Research Journal*, Vol. 4 (1979), pp. 769–789.
34. Ibid.
35. "Twelve Percent of Those Freed on Low Bail Fail to Appear," *New York Times*, December 2, 1983.
36. Bureau of Justice Statistics, *Report to the Nation on Crime and Justice*, 2nd ed. (Washington, DC: U.S. Department of Justice, 1988), p. 76.
37. Tracey Kyckelhahn and Thomas H. Cohen, *Felony Defendants in Large Urban Counties, 2004* (Washington, DC: Bureau of Justice Statistics, 2008), p. 2, http://www.ojp.gov/bjs/pub/pdf/fdluc04.pdf (accessed June 4, 2010). See also Thomas H. Cohen and Brian A. Reaves, *Pretrial Release of Felony Defendants in State Courts* (Washington, DC: Bureau of Justice Statistics, 2007).
38. Thomas H. Cohen and Brian A. Reaves, *Pretrial Release of Felony Defendants in State Courts* (Washington, DC: Bureau of Justice Statistics, 2007).
39. Donald E. Pryor and Walter F. Smith, "Significant Research Findings Concerning Pretrial Release," *Pretrial Issues*, Vol. 4, No. 1 (Washington, DC: Pretrial Services Resource Center, February 1982). See also the Pretrial Justice Institute on the Web at http://www.pretrial.org/Pages.
40. BJS, *Report to the Nation on Crime and Justice*, p. 77.
41. According to Joseph B. Vaughn and Victor E. Kappeler, the first such legislation was the 1970 District of Columbia Court Reform and Criminal Procedure Act. See Vaughn and Kappeler, "The Denial of Bail: Pre-trial Preventive Detention," *Criminal Justice Research Bulletin*, Vol. 3, No. 6 (Huntsville, TX: Sam Houston State University, 1987), p. 1.
42. Ibid.
43. Bail Reform Act of 1984, 18 U.S.C. 3142(e).
44. *U.S.* v. *Montalvo-Murillo*, 495 U.S. 711 (1990).
45. Ibid., syllabus.
46. *U.S.* v. *Hazzard*, 35 CrL. 2217 (1984).
47. See, for example, *U.S.* v. *Motamedi*, 37 CrL. 2394, CA 9 (1985).
48. A few states now have laws that permit the defendant to appear before the grand jury.
49. John M. Scheb and John M. Scheb II, *American Criminal Law* (St. Paul, MN: West, 1996), p. 31.
50. Ibid.
51. The information in this paragraph is adapted from Linda Greenhouse, "Supreme Court Limits Forced Medication of Some for Trial," *New York Times*, June 16, 2003, http://www.nytimes.com/2003/06/17/politics/17DRUG.html (accessed June 17, 2003).
52. *Sell* v. *U.S.*, 123 S.Ct. 2174 (2003).
53. Federal Rules of Criminal Procedure, Rule 5.1(a).
54. Scheb and Scheb, *American Criminal Law*, p. 32.
55. *Kercheval* v. *U.S.*, 274 U.S. 220, 223, 47 S.Ct. 582, 583 (1927); *Boykin* v. *Alabama*, 395 U.S. 238 (1969); and *Dickerson* v. *New Banner Institute, Inc.*, 460 U.S. 103 (1983).
56. Bureau of Justice Statistics, *The Prosecution of Felony Arrests* (Washington, DC: U.S. Government Printing Office, 1983).
57. Barbara Boland et al., *The Prosecution of Felony Arrests, 1987* (Washington, DC: U.S. Government Printing Office, May 1990).
58. *Santobello* v. *New York*, 404 U.S. 257 (1971).
59. *Mabry* v. *Johnson*, 467 U.S. 504 (1984).
60. *U.S.* v. *Baldacchino*, 762 F.2d 170 (1st Cir. 1985); *U.S.* v. *Reardon*, 787 F.2d 512 (10th Cir. 1986); and *U.S.* v. *Donahey*, 529 F.2d 831 (11th Cir. 1976).
61. For a classic discussion of such considerations, see David Sudnow, "Normal Crimes: Sociological Features of the Penal Code in a Public Defender Office," *Social Problems*, Vol. 123, No. 3 (winter 1965), p. 255.
62. Federal Rules of Criminal Procedure, No. 11.
63. "A Desperate Act," *Prime Time Live*, ABCNews.com, January 28, 1998, http://archive.abcnews.go.com/onair/PTL/html-files/transcripts/ptl0128c.html (accessed July 21, 2001).
64. Dan Rozek, "Castration Doesn't Gain Leniency for Pedophile," *Chicago Sun-Times*, March 4, 1998.

Chapter 8: The Courtroom Work Group and the Criminal Trial

i. President's Commission on Law Enforcement and Administration of Justice, *The Challenge of Crime in a Free Society* (Washington, DC: U.S. Government Printing Office, 1967), p. 125.
ii. Quoted in Richard Willing, "Courts Try to Make Jury Duty Less of a Choice," *USA Today*, March 17, 2005.

---

1. D. Graham Burnett, "Anatomy of a Verdict: The View from a Juror's Chair," *New York Times Magazine*, August 26, 2001.
2. Many of the details for this story come from CBS News. See, for example, Mike Ballou, "Caylee Anthony Autopsy Reveals Grim Details But Sheds Little Light on Mystery," June 22, 2009, http://www.cbsnews.com/8301-504083_162-5103384-504083.html (accessed May 20, 2010).
3. See, for example, Jeffrey T. Ulmer, *Social Worlds of Sentencing: Court Communities under Sentencing Guidelines* (Ithaca: State University of New York Press, 1997); and Roy B. Flemming, Peter F. Nardulli, and James Eisenstein, *The Craft of Justice: Politics and Work in Criminal Court Communities* (Philadelphia: University of Pennsylvania Press, 1993).
4. See, for example, Edward J. Clynch and David W. Neubauer, "Trial Courts as Organizations," *Law and Policy Quarterly*, Vol. 3 (1981), pp. 69–94.
5. American Bar Association, *ABA Standards for Criminal Justice: Special Functions of the Trial Judge*, 3rd ed. (Chicago: ABA, 2000).
6. In 1940, Missouri became the first state to adopt a plan for the "merit selection" of judges based on periodic public review.
7. National Judicial College, "About the NJC," http://www.judges.org/about (accessed May 2, 2010).
8. See National Judicial College, *National Impact, 2006*, http://www.judges.org/downloads/general_information/national_impact06 (accessed May 22, 2006).
9. "Nonlawyer Judges and the Professionalization of Justice: Should an Endangered Species Be Preserved?" *Journal of*

Contemporary Criminal Justice, No. 17 (February 2001), pp. 19–36; see also Doris Marie Provine, *Judging Credentials: Nonlawyer Judges and the Politics of Professionalism* (Chicago: University of Chicago Press, 1986).

10. Town and village justices in New York State serve part-time and may or may not be lawyers; judges of all other courts must be lawyers, whether or not they serve full-time. From New York State Commission on Judicial Conduct, *2001 Annual Report*, http://www.scjc.state.ny.us/annual.html (accessed March 10, 2006).
11. Ibid.
12. Bureau of Justice Statistics, *Report to the Nation on Crime and Justice: The Data* (Washington, DC: U.S. Department of Justice, 1983).
13. For a discussion of the resource limitations that district attorneys face in combating corporate crime, see Michael L. Benson et al., "District Attorneys and Corporate Crime: Surveying the Prosecutorial Gatekeepers," *Criminology*, Vol. 26, No. 3 (August 1988), pp. 505–517.
14. Carol J. DeFrances and Greg W. Steadman, *Prosecutors in State Courts, 1996* (Washington, DC: Bureau of Justice Statistics, 1998).
15. "Duke Case DA's Apology Not Accepted," USA *Today*, May 13, 2007.
16. Duff Wilson, "Prosecutor Apologizes to Former Duke Players," *New York Times*, April 12, 2007.
17. Kenneth Culp Davis, *Discretionary Justice* (Baton Rouge: Louisiana State University Press, 1969), p. 190.
18. Barbara Borland, *The Prosecution of Felony Arrests* (Washington, DC: Bureau of Justice Statistics, 1983).
19. *Brady* v. *Maryland*, 373 U.S. 83 (1963).
20. *U.S.* v. *Bagley*, 473 U.S. 667 (1985).
21. *Banks* v. *Dretke*, 124 S.Ct. 1256, 1280 (2004).
22. *Imbler* v. *Pachtman*, 424 U.S. 409 (1976).
23. *Burns* v. *Reed*, 500 U.S. 478 (1991).
24. Ibid., complaint, p. 29.
25. Cassia Spohn, John Gruhl, and Susan Welch, "The Impact of the Ethnicity and Gender of Defendants on the Decision to Reject or Dismiss Felony Charges," *Criminology*, Vol. 25, No. 1 (1987), pp. 175–191.
26. American Bar Association Center for Professional Responsibility, *Model Rules of Professional Conduct* (Chicago: ABA, 2003), p. 87.
27. The same is true under federal law, and in almost all of the states, of communications between defendants and members of the clergy, psychiatrists and psychologists, medical doctors, and licensed social workers in the course of psychotherapy. See, for example, *Jaffee* v. *Redmond*, 116 S.Ct. 1923 (1996).
28. *Powell* v. *Alabama*, 287 U.S. 45 (1932).
29. *Johnson* v. *Zerbst*, 304 U.S. 458 (1938).
30. *Gideon* v. *Wainwright*, 372 U.S. 335 (1963).
31. *Argersinger* v. *Hamlin*, 407 U.S. 25 (1972).
32. *In re Gault*, 387 U.S. 1 (1967).
33. *Alabama* v. *Shelton*, 535 U.S. 654 (2002).
34. New York State Supreme Court, Appellate Division, Assigned Counsel Plan (18B), http://www.nycourts.gov/courts/ad1/Committees&Programs/18B/index.shtml (accessed June 5, 2010).
35. Donald Farole, Jr., and Lynn Langton, *State Public Defender Programs, 2007* (Washington, DC: BJS, 2010); and Donald Farole, Jr., and Lynn Langton, *County-Based and Local Public Defender Offices, 2007* (Washington, DC: BJS, 2010).
36. Carol J. DeFrances, *State-Funded Indigent Defense Services, 1999* (Washington, DC: National Institute of Justice, 2001), from which the information in this paragraph is derived.
37. National Symposium on Indigent Defense, *Improving Criminal Justice Systems through Expanded Strategies and Innovative Collaborations* (Washington, DC: Office of Justice Programs, 2000).
38. Ibid.
39. "Nationline: McVeigh's Defense Cost Taxpayers $13.8 Million," *USA Today*, July 3, 2001.
40. Caroline Wolf Harlow, *Defense Counsel in Criminal Cases* (Washington, DC: Bureau of Justice Statistics, 2000); and Carol J. DeFrances and Marika F. X. Litras, *Indigent Defense Service in Large Counties, 1999* (Washington, DC: Bureau of Justice Statistics, 2000).
41. *Faretta* v. *California*, 422 U.S. 806 (1975).
42. S. K. Smith and C. J. DeFrances, *Indigent Defense* (Washington, DC: Bureau of Justice Statistics, 1996), pp. 2–3.
43. *Anders* v. *California*, 386 U.S. 738 (1967).
44. *People* v. *Wende*, 25 Cal.3d 436, 600 P.2d 1071 (1979).
45. *Smith* v. *Robbins*, 528 U.S. 259 (2000).
46. *Texas* v. *Cobb*, 532 U.S. 162 (2001).
47. Details for this story come from Chisun Lee, "Punishing Mmes. Stewart: The Parallel Universes of Martha and Lynne," *Village Voice*, February 15, 2005, http://www.refuseandresist.org/article-print.php?aid51757 (accessed January 5, 2006).
48. "Lawyer Convicted of Terrorist Support," *USA Today*, February 11, 2005.
49. Mike McKee, "California State Bar to Allow Lawyers to Break Confidentiality," *The Recorder*, May 17, 2004, http://www.law.com/jsp/article.jsp?id51084316038367 (accessed August 25, 2005).
50. *Nix* v. *Whiteside*, 475 U.S. 157 (1986).
51. Ibid.
52. President's Commission on Law Enforcement and Administration of Justice, *The Challenge of Crime in a Free Society* (Washington, DC: U.S. Government Printing Office, 1967), p. 129.
53. National Advisory Commission on Criminal Justice Standards and Goals, *Courts* (Washington, DC: U.S. Government Printing Office, 1973), Standard 9.3.
54. See, for example, Joan G. Brannon, *The Judicial System in North Carolina* (Raleigh, NC: Administrative Office of the United States Courts, 1984), p. 14.
55. Joseph L. Peterson, "Use of Forensic Evidence by the Police and Courts," *Research in Brief* (Washington, DC: National Institute of Justice, 1987), p. 3.
56. Ibid., p. 6.
57. *California* v. *Green*, 399 U.S. 149 (1970).
58. Patrick L. McCloskey and Ronald L. Schoenberg, *Criminal Law Deskbook* (New York: Matthew Bender, 1988), Section 17, p. 123.
59. Bureau of Justice Statistics, *Report to the Nation on Crime and Justice*, 2nd ed. (Washington, DC: BJS, 1988), p. 82.
60. Anna Johnson, "Jury with Oprah Winfrey Convicts Man of Murder," Associated Press, August 19, 2004.
61. *Demarest* v. *Manspeaker et al.*, 498 U.S. 184, 111 S.Ct. 599, 112 L.Ed.2d 608 (1991).
62. Bureau of Justice Statistics, *Report to the Nation on Crime and Justice*.
63. Johnson, "Jury with Oprah Winfrey Convicts Man of Murder."
64. *Williams* v. *Florida*, 399 U.S. 78, 90 S.Ct. 1893, 26 L.Ed.2d 446 (1970).
65. *Smith* v. *Texas*, 311 U.S. 128 (1940). That right does not apply when the defendants are facing the possibility of a prison sentence less than six months in length or even when the potential aggregate sentence for multiple petty offenses exceeds six months (see *Lewis* v. *U.S.*, 518 U.S. 322 [1996]).
66. *Thiel* v. *Southern Pacific Co.*, 328 U.S. 217 (1945).
67. The author was himself the victim of a felony some years ago. His car was stolen in Columbus, Ohio, and recovered a year later in Cleveland. He was informed that the person who had

taken it was in custody, but he never heard what happened to him, nor could he learn where or whether a trial was to be held.
68. Federal Rules of Criminal Procedure, Rule 43.
69. *Crosby* v. *U.S.*, 113 S.Ct. 748, 122 L.Ed.2d 25 (1993).
70. *Zafiro* v. *U.S.*, 113 S.Ct. 933, 122 L.Ed.2d 317 (1993).
71. *Nebraska Press Association* v. *Stuart*, 427 U.S. 539 (1976).
72. However, it is generally accepted that trial judges may issue limited gag orders aimed at trial participants.
73. *Press Enterprise Company* v. *Superior Court of California, Riverside County*, 478 U.S. 1 (1986).
74. *Caribbean International News Corporation* v. *Puerto Rico*, 508 U.S. 147 (1993).
75. *Chandler* v. *Florida*, 499 U.S. 560 (1981).
76. Rule 53 of the Federal Rules of Criminal Procedure reads, "The taking of photographs in the court room during the progress of judicial proceedings or radio broadcasting of judicial proceedings from the court room shall not be permitted by the court."
77. Harry F. Rosenthal, "Courts-TV," Associated Press, September 21, 1994. See also "Judicial Conference Rejects Cameras in Federal Courts," *Criminal Justice Newsletter*, September 15, 1994, p. 6.
78. U.S. Court of Appeals for the Ninth Circuit, http://www.ce9.uscourts.gov/web/OCELibra.nsf/504ca249c786e20f85256284006da7ab/ba060a3e537d2866882569760067ac8e?OpenDocument (accessed September 16, 2005).
79. Marc G. Gertz and Edmond J. True, "Social Scientists in the Courtroom: The Frustrations of Two Expert Witnesses," in Susette M. Talarico, ed., *Courts and Criminal Justice: Emerging Issues* (Beverly Hills, CA: Sage, 1985), pp. 81–91.
80. Samuel R. Gross et al., *Exonerations in the United States, 1989 through 2003*, April 4, 2004, http://www.mindfully.org/Reform/2004/Prison-Exonerations-Gross19apr04.htm (accessed May 24, 2007).
81. *Klopfer* v. *North Carolina*, 386 U.S. 213 (1967).
82. *Barker* v. *Wingo*, 407 U.S. 514 (1972).
83. *Strunk* v. *U.S.*, 412 U.S. 434 (1973).
84. Speedy Trial Act, 18 U.S.C. 3161 (1974); Public Law 93–619.
85. *U.S.* v. *Taylor*, 487 U.S. 326, 108 S.Ct. 2413, 101 L.Ed.2d 297 (1988).
86. *Fex* v. *Michigan*, 113 S.Ct. 1085, 122 L.Ed.2d 406 (1993).
87. *Doggett* v. *U.S.*, 112 S.Ct. 2686 (1992).
88. *Padilla* v. *Hanft*, No. 05-533, *cert. denied.*
89. See, for example, the U.S. Supreme Court's decision in the case of *Murphy* v. *Florida*, 410 U.S. 525 (1973).
90. *Witherspoon* v. *Illinois*, 391 U.S. 510 (1968).
91. *Mu'Min* v. *Virginia*, 500 U.S. 415 (1991).
92. Federal Rules of Criminal Procedure, Rule 24(6).
93. Learn more about shadow juries from Molly McDonough, "Me and My Shadow: Shadow Juries Are Helping Litigators Shape Their Cases during Trial," *National Law Journal* (May 17, 2001).
94. Although the words *argument* and *statement* are sometimes used interchangeably to refer to opening remarks, defense attorneys are enjoined from drawing conclusions or "arguing" to the jury at this stage in the trial. Their task, as described in the section that follows, is simply to explain to the jury how the defense will be conducted.
95. Supreme Court majority opinion in *Powers* v. *Ohio*, 499 U.S. 400 (1991), citing *Strauder* v. *West Virginia*, 100 U.S. 303 (1880).
96. *Swain* v. *Alabama*, 380 U.S. 202 (1965).
97. *Batson* v. *Kentucky*, 476 U.S. 79, 106 S.Ct. 1712 (1986).
98. *Ford* v. *Georgia*, 498 U.S. 411 (1991), footnote 2.
99. *Powers* v. *Ohio*, 499 U.S. 400 (1991).
100. *Georgia* v. *McCollum*, 505 U.S. 42 (1992).
101. *J. E. B.* v. *Alabama*, 114 S.Ct. 1419 (1994).
102. See, for example, *Davis* v. *Minnesota*, 511 U.S. 1115 (1994).
103. *Campbell* v. *Louisiana*, 523 U.S. 392 (1998).
104. *Miller-El* v. *Cockrell*, 537 U.S. 322 (2003).
105. *Miller-El* v. *Dretke*, 545 U.S. 231 (2005).
106. *Snyder* v. *Louisiana*, 552 U.S. ___ (2008).
107. *U.S.* v. *Dinitz*, 424 U.S. 600, 612 (1976).
108. *Michigan* v. *Lucas*, 500 U.S. 145 (1991).
109. *Kotteakos* v. *U.S.*, 328 U.S. 750 (1946); *Brecht* v. *Abrahamson*, 113 S.Ct. 1710, 123 L.Ed.2d 353 (1993); and *Arizona* v. *Fulminante*, 111 S.Ct. 1246 (1991).
110. The Court, citing *Kotteakos* v. *U.S.*, 328 U.S. 750 (1946), in *Brecht* v. *Abrahamson*, 113 S.Ct. 1710, 123 L.Ed.2d 353 (1993).
111. *Sullivan* v. *Louisiana*, 113 S.Ct. 2078, 124 L.Ed.2d 182 (1993).
112. *Griffin* v. *California*, 380 U.S. 609 (1965).
113. *Ohio* v. *Reiner*, 123 S.Ct. 1252, 532 U.S. 17 (2001).
114. Leading questions may, in fact, be permitted for certain purposes, including refreshing a witness's memory, impeaching a hostile witness, introducing undisputed material, and helping a witness with impaired faculties.
115. *In re Oliver*, 333 U.S. 257 (1948).
116. *Coy* v. *Iowa*, 487 U.S. 1012, 108 S.Ct. 2798 (1988).
117. *Maryland* v. *Craig*, 497 U.S. 836, 845–847 (1990).
118. *Idaho* v. *Wright*, 497 U.S. 805 (1990).
119. *White* v. *Illinois*, 112 S.Ct. 736 (1992).
120. *Crawford* v. *Washington*, 541 U.S. 36 (2004).
121. *Davis* v. *Washington*, 547 U.S. 813 (2006). See also *Hammon* v. *Indiana*, 547 U.S. 813 (2006).
122. *Davis* v. *Washington*, syllabus.
123. Federal Rules of Criminal Procedure, Rule 29.1.
124. See *Johnson* v. *Louisiana*, 406 U.S. 356 (1972); and *Apodaca* v. *Oregon*, 406 U.S. 404 (1972).
125. *Allen* v. *U.S.*, 164 U.S. 492 (1896).
126. Judge Harold J. Rothwax, *Guilty: The Collapse of Criminal Justice* (New York: Random House, 1996).
127. Amiram Elwork, Bruce D. Sales, and James Alfini, *Making Jury Instructions Understandable* (Charlottesville, VA: Michie, 1982).
128. "King Jury Lives in Fear from Unpopular Verdict," *Fayetteville (N.C.) Observer-Times*, May 10, 1992.
129. "Los Angeles Trials Spark Debate over Anonymous Juries," *Criminal Justice Newsletter* (February 16, 1993), pp. 3–4.

Chapter 9: Sentencing

i. Lawrence A. Greenfeld, *Prison Sentences and Time Served for Violence*, Bureau of Justice Statistics Selected Findings, No. 4 (Washington, DC: BJS, April 1995).
ii. *Ring* v. *Arizona*, 122 S.Ct. 2428, 153 L.Ed.2d 556 (2002); dissent (with Chief Justice William Rehnquist).
iii. "Prepared Remarks of Attorney General Alberto Gonzales," Sentencing Guidelines Speech, Washington, DC, June 21, 2005.
iv. "Fireside chat" with U.S. Supreme Court Justices John Paul Stevens and Stephen Breyer, 53rd annual meeting of the Seventh Circuit Bar Association and Judicial Conference of the Seventh Circuit, Chicago, May 9, 2004.
v. *Payne* v. *Tennessee*, 501 U.S. 808 (1991).
vi. *Furman* v. *Georgia*, 408 U.S. 238 (1972).

---

1. Michael Tonry, "Implementing, Changing, and Maintaining Sentencing Guidelines in the Political Climate of the 1990's," http://students.washington.edu/ths123/state.htm (accessed January 3, 2006).
2. Iowa House File 2393, Minority Impact Statements.
3. Iowa House Bill 5933, Racial Impact Statements.
4. Illinois Public Act 95–0995 (October 3, 2008).

5. Marc Mauer, "Racial Impact Statements: Changing Policies to Address Disparities," *Criminal Justice*, Vol. 23, No. 4 (winter 2009).
6. For a thorough discussion of the philosophy of punishment and sentencing, see David Garland, *Punishment and Modern Society: A Study in Social Theory* (Chicago: University of Chicago Press, 1990). See also Ralph D. Ellis and Carol S. Ellis, *Theories of Criminal Justice: A Critical Reappraisal* (Wolfeboro, NH: Longwood Academic, 1989); and Colin Summer, *Censure, Politics, and Criminal Justice* (Bristol, PA: Open University Press, 1990).
7. Punishment is said to be required because social order (and the laws that represent it) could not exist for long if transgressions went unsanctioned.
8. Hugo Adam Bedau, "Retributivism and the Theory of Punishment," *Journal of Philosophy*, Vol. 75 (November 1978), pp. 601–620.
9. The definitive study during this period was Douglas Lipton, Robert Martinson, and J. Woks, *The Effectiveness of Correctional Treatment: A Survey of Treatment Valuation Studies* (New York: Praeger, 1975).
10. See, for example, Lawrence W. Sherman et al., *Preventing Crime: What Works, What Doesn't, What's Promising* (Washington, DC: National Institute of Justice, 1997).
11. Gordon Bazemore and Mark S. Umbreit, foreword to *Balanced and Restorative Justice: Program Summary* (Washington, DC: Office of Juvenile Justice and Delinquency Prevention, 1994).
12. Shay Bilchik, *Balanced and Restorative Justice for Juveniles: A Framework for Juvenile Justice in the 21st Century* (Washington, DC: Office of Juvenile Justice and Delinquency Prevention, 1997), p. ii.
13. Ibid., p.14.
14. Ibid.
15. 18 U.S.C. 3563 (a)(2).
16. Donna Hunzeker, "State Sentencing Systems and 'Truth in Sentencing,'" *State Legislative Report*, Vol. 20, No. 3 (Denver: National Conference of State Legislatures, 1995).
17. Paula M. Ditton and Doris James Wilson, *Truth in Sentencing in State Prisons* (Washington, DC: Bureau of Justice Statistics, 1999).
18. "Oklahoma Rapist Gets 30,000 Years," United Press International, southwest edition, December 23, 1994.
19. For a historical consideration of alleged disparities, see G. Kleck, "Racial Discrimination in Criminal Sentencing: A Critical Evaluation of the Evidence with Additional Evidence on the Death Penalty," *American Sociological Review*, No. 46 (1981), pp. 783–805; and G. Kleck, "Life Support for Ailing Hypotheses: Modes of Summarizing the Evidence for Racial Discrimination in Sentencing," *Law and Human Behavior*, No. 9 (1985), pp. 271–285.
20. National Council on Crime and Delinquency, *National Assessment of Structured Sentencing* (Washington, DC: Bureau of Justice Administration, 1996).
21. Ibid.
22. As discussed later in this chapter, federal sentencing guidelines did not become effective until 1987 and still had to meet many court challenges.
23. Lawrence A. Greenfeld, *Prison Sentences and Time Served for Violence* (Washington, DC: Bureau of Justice Statistics, April 1995).
24. U.S. Sentencing Commission, *Federal Sentencing Guidelines Manual* (Washington, DC: U.S. Government Printing Office, 1987), p. 2.
25. Inmates can still earn a maximum of 54 days per year of good-time credit.
26. The Parole Commission Phaseout Act of 1996 requires the attorney general to report to Congress yearly as to whether it is cost-effective for the Parole Commission to remain a separate agency or whether its functions (and personnel) should be assigned elsewhere. Under the law, if the attorney general recommends assigning the Parole Commission's functions to another component of the Department of Justice, federal parole will continue as long as necessary.
27. For an excellent review of the act and its implications, see Gregory D. Lee, "U.S. Sentencing Guidelines: Their Impact on Federal Drug Offenders," *FBI Law Enforcement Bulletin*, May 1995, pp. 17–21.
28. *Mistretta* v. *U.S.*, 488 U.S. 361, 371 (1989).
29. For an engaging overview of how mitigating factors might be applied under the guidelines, see *Koon* v. *U.S.*, 116 S.Ct. 2035, 135 L.Ed.2d 392 (1996).
30. U.S. Sentencing Commission, *Federal Sentencing Guidelines Manual*, p. 207.
31. *Deal* v. *U.S.*, 113 S.Ct. 1993, 124 L.Ed.2d 44 (1993).
32. U.S. Sentencing Commission, *Federal Sentencing Guidelines Manual*, p. 8.
33. National Institute of Justice, *Sentencing Commission Chairman Wilkins Answers Questions on the Guidelines*, NIJ Research in Action Series (Washington, DC: NIJ, 1987), p. 7.
34. *Melendez* v. *U.S.*, 117 S.Ct. 383, 136 L.Ed.2d 301 (1996).
35. *Apprendi* v. *New Jersey*, 120 S.Ct. 2348 (2000).
36. See, for example, Alexandra A. E. Shapiro and Jonathan P. Bach, "Applying 'Apprendi' to Federal Sentencing Rules," *New York Law Journal*, March 23, 2001, http://www.lw.com/pubs/articles/pdf/applyingApprendi.pdf (accessed June 30, 2007); and Freya Russell, "Limiting the Use of Acquitted and Uncharged Conduct at Sentencing: *Apprendi* v. *New Jersey* and Its Effect on the Relevant Conduct Provision of the United States Sentencing Guidelines," *California Law Review*, Vol. 89 (July 2001), p. 1199.
37. *U.S.* v. *O'Brien*, U.S. Supreme Court, No. 08-1569 (decided May 24, 2010).
38. *Blakely* v. *Washington*, 542 U.S. 296 (2004). Blakely was convicted in 2005 of plotting to hire hit men to kill his ex-wife and daughter from his jail cell. He was sentenced to 35 years in prison.
39. *Cunningham* v. *California*, 549 U.S. 270 (2007).
40. *U.S.* v. *Booker*, 125 S.Ct. 738 (2005).
41. Combined with *U.S.* v. *Booker* (2005).
42. Stanley E. Adelman, "Supreme Court Invalidates Federal Sentencing Guidelines . . . to an Extent," *On the Line*, newsletter of the American Correctional Association (May 2005), p. 1.
43. See *U.S.* v. *Rodriguez*, 398 F.3d 1291, 1297 (11th Cir. 2005).
44. *Kimbrough* v. *U.S.*, 552 U.S. 85 (2007), syllabus.
45. *Gall* v. *U.S.*, 552 U.S. 38 (2007).
46. *Rita* v. *U.S.*, 551 U.S. 338 (2007).
47. *Oregon* v. *Ice*, U.S. Supreme Court, No. 07-901 (decided January 14, 2009).
48. *Gall* v. *U.S.*, 552 U.S. 38 (2007).
49. "A Year after *Booker*: Most Sentences Still within Guidelines," *Third Branch*, newsletter of the Administrative Office of the U.S. Courts, Vol. 38, No. 2 (February 2006), p. 1.
50. Ibid.
51. Michael Miller, "California Gets 'Three Strikes' Anti-Crime Bill," Reuters, March 7, 1994.
52. Tamar Lewin, "Three-Strikes Law Is Overrated in California, Study Finds," *New York Times*, August 23, 2001, http://query.nytimes.com/gst/fullpage.html?res=9505E7DB1531F930A1575BC0A9679C8B63 (accessed September 2, 2009).
53. Bruce Smith, "Crime Solutions," Associated Press, January 11, 1995.

54. Ryan S. King and Marc Mauer, *Aging behind Bars: "Three Strikes" Seven Years Later* (Washington, DC: Sentencing Project, August 2001).
55. *Ewing* v. *California*, 538 U.S. 11 (2003); and *Lockyer* v. *Andrade*, 538 U.S. 63 (2003).
56. Under California law, a person who commits petty theft can be charged with a felony if he or she has prior felony convictions. The charge is known as "petty theft with prior convictions." Andrade's actual sentence was two 25-year prison terms to be served consecutively.
57. Much of the material in this section is derived from Dale Parent et al., *Mandatory Sentencing*, NIJ Research in Action Series (Washington, DC: NIJ, 1997).
58. In mid-1996, the California Supreme Court ruled the state's three-strikes law an undue intrusion into judges' sentencing discretion, and California judges now use their own discretion in evaluating which offenses "fit" within the meaning of the law.
59. Michael Tonry, *Sentencing Reform Impacts* (Washington, DC: National Institute of Justice, 1987).
60. D. C. McDonald and K. E. Carlson, *Sentencing in the Courts: Does Race Matter? The Transition to Sentencing Guidelines, 1986–90* (Washington, DC: Bureau of Justice Statistics, 1993).
61. U.S. Sentencing Commission, *Special Report to Congress: Cocaine and Federal Sentencing Policy* (Washington, DC: U.S. Sentencing Commission, May 2007).
62. "Court Ruling Found to Reduce Crack Cocaine Prison Terms," *Corrections Journal* (February 7, 2006), p. 1.
63. Michelle Healy, "Frost House Vandals Do Time Studying Poet," *USA Today*, June 3, 2008.
64. Keyonna Summers, "Teens Must Post Apology on YouTube," *USA Today*, June 9, 2008.
65. Richard Willing, "Thief Challenges Dose of Shame as Punishment," *USA Today*, August 18, 2004.
66. John Braithwaite, *Crime, Shame, and Reintegration* (Cambridge, England: Cambridge University Press, 1989).
67. Such evidence does, in fact, exist. See, for example, Harold G. Grasmick, Robert J. Bursik, Jr., and Bruce J. Arneklev, "Reduction in Drunk Driving as a Response to Increased Threats of Shame, Embarrassment, and Legal Sanctions," *Criminology*, Vol. 31, No. 1 (1993), pp. 41–67.
68. Joan Petersilia, *House Arrest*, National Institute of Justice Crime File Study Guide (Washington, DC: NIJ, 1988).
69. Privacy Act of 1974, 5 U.S.C.A. 522a, 88 Statute 1897, Public Law 93–579, December 31, 1974.
70. Freedom of Information Act, 5 U.S.C. 522, and amendments. The status of presentence investigative reports has not yet been clarified under this act to the satisfaction of all legal scholars, although state and federal courts are generally thought to be exempt from the provisions of the act.
71. City of New York, Citywide Accountability Program, S.T.A.R.S. (Statistical Tracking, Analysis, and Reporting System), http://www.nyc.gov/html/prob/pdf/stars_92005.pdf (accessed May 12, 2008).
72. For a good review of the issues involved, see Robert C. Davis, Arthur J. Lurigio, and Wesley G. Skogan, *Victims of Crime*, 2nd ed. (Thousand Oaks, CA: Sage, 1997); and Leslie Sebba, *Third Parties: Victims and the Criminal Justice System* (Columbus: Ohio State University Press, 1996).
73. President's Task Force on Victims of Crime, *Final Report* (Washington, DC: U.S. Government Printing Office, 1982).
74. Peter Finn and Beverly N. W. Lee, *Establishing and Expanding Victim-Witness Assistance Programs* (Washington, DC: National Institute of Justice, 1988).
75. Senate Joint Resolution (SJR) 65 is a major revision of an initial proposal, SJR 52, which Senators Kyl and Feinstein introduced on April 22, 1996. Representative Henry Hyde introduced House Joint Resolution (HJR) 174, a companion to SJR 52, and a similar proposal, HJR 173, on April 22, 1996.
76. Senate Joint Resolution 44, 105th Congress.
77. See the National Center for Victims of Crime's critique of the 1998 amendment at http://www.ncvc.org/law/Ncvca.htm (accessed January 10, 2009).
78. National Victims' Constitutional Amendment Passage, "States Victim Rights Amendments," http://www.nvcap.org/stvras.htm (accessed August 28, 2006).
79. National Victims' Constitutional Amendment Project, http://www.nvcap.org (accessed June 9, 2009).
80. Public Law 97–291.
81. USA PATRIOT Act of 2001, Section 624.
82. Office for Victims of Crime, *Report to the Nation, 2003* (Washington, DC: OVC, 2003).
83. Crime Victims' Rights Act, 18 U.S.C. 3771.
84. U.S. Senate, Republican Policy Committee, Legislative Notice No. 63, April 22, 2004.
85. Proposition 8, California's Victims' Bill of Rights.
86. National Victim Center, Mothers against Drunk Driving, and American Prosecutors Research Institute, *Impact Statements: A Victim's Right to Speak; A Nation's Responsibility to Listen* (Washington, DC: Office for Victims of Crime, July 1994).
87. *Kelly* v. *California*, 555 U.S. _____ (2008).
88. Robert C. Davis and Barbara E. Smith, "The Effects of Victim Impact Statements on Sentencing Decisions: A Test in an Urban Setting," *Justice Quarterly*, Vol. 11, No. 3 (September 1994), pp. 453–469.
89. Bureau of Justice Statistics, *Report to the Nation on Crime and Justice*, 2nd ed. (Washington, DC: U.S. Government Printing Office, 1988), p. 90.
90. Sean Rosenmerkel, Matthew Durose, and Donald Farole, Jr., *Felony Sentences in State Courts, 2006—Statistical Tables* (Washington, DC: Bureau of Justice Statistics, December, 2009). Data for 1990 come from Matthew R. Durose, David J. Levin, and Patrick A. Langan, *Felony Sentences in State Courts, 1998* (Washington, DC: Bureau of Justice Statistics, 2001).
91. Ibid., p. 2.
92. Sally T. Hillsman, Joyce L. Sichel, and Barry Mahoney, *Fines in Sentencing* (New York: Vera Institute of Justice, 1983).
93. Ibid., p. 2.
94. Ibid., p. 4.
95. Ibid.
96. "Swiss Speeder Fined a Record $290,000," *USA Today*, January 7, 2010, http://content.usatoday.com/communities/ondeadline/post/2010/01/swiss-speeder-fined-a-record-290000/1 (accessed July 5, 2010).
97. James S. Tyree and Tony Thornton, "Judge Sentences Underwood to Die," *Oklahoman*, April 3, 2008, http://newsok.com/article/3224954/1207252268 (accessed May 28, 2008).
98. Capital Punishment Research Project, University of Alabama Law School.
99. Death Penalty Information Center, "Executions by Year," http://www.deathpenaltyinfo.org/executions-year (accessed May 20, 2010).
100. Ryan S. King, *The State of Sentencing, 2007: Developments in Policy and Practice* (Washington, DC: Sentencing Project, 2008).
101. Richard Willing, "Expansion of Death Penalty to Nonmurders Faces Challenges," *USA Today*, May 14, 1997.
102. *Kennedy* v. *Louisiana*, 554 U.S. ___ (2008).
103. NAACP Legal Defense & Educational Fund, *Death Row USA*, Winter 2010.
104. Ibid., p. 1.
105. In 2004, Utah repealed the use of a firing squad as a method of execution for all persons sentenced to death on or after May 3, 2004 (Utah Code Ann. section 77-18-5.5). The law allows for use of a firing squad for those sentenced prior to that date or in the event that lethal injection is found to be unconstitutional.

106. Tracy L. Snell, *Capital Punishment, 2005* (Washington, DC: Bureau of Justice Statistics, 2006), p. 1.
107. Details for this story come from Jenifer Warren and Maura Dolan, "Tookie Williams Is Executed," *Los Angeles Times*, December 13, 2005, http://www.latimes.com/news/local/la-me-execution13dec13,0,799154.story?coll=la-home-headlines (accessed May 20, 2006).
108. "Warden: Williams Frustrated at End," CNN.com, December 13, 2005, http://www.cnn.com/2005/LAW/12/13/williams.execution (accessed July 2, 2006).
109. "Chief Justice Calls for Limits on Death Row *Habeas* Appeals," *Criminal Justice Newsletter* (February 15, 1989), pp. 6–7.
110. *McCleskey* v. *Zant*, 499 U.S. 467, 493–494 (1991).
111. *Coleman* v. *Thompson*, 501 U.S. 722 (1991).
112. *Schlup* v. *Delo*, 115 S.Ct. 851, 130 L.Ed.2d 808 (1995).
113. Public Law 104–132.
114. *Felker* v. *Turpin*, 117 S.Ct. 30, 135 L.Ed.2d 1123 (1996).
115. *Elledge* v. *Florida*, No. 98-5410 (1998).
116. See "Profiles on Florida's Death Row," http://floridadeathrow.wordpress.com/category/died-on-death-row (accessed October 2, 2010).
117. Michelle Locke, "Victim Forgives," Associated Press, May 19, 1996.
118. Ibid.
119. Arthur Koestler, *Reflections on Hanging* (New York: Macmillan, 1957), p. xii.
120. Death Penalty Information Center, "Innocence: List of Those Freed from Death Row," http://www.deathpenaltyinfo.org/innocence-list-those-freed-death-row (accessed July 21, 2010).
121. Edward Connors et al., *Convicted by Juries, Exonerated by Science: Case Studies in the Use of DNA Evidence to Establish Innocence after Trial* (Washington, DC: National Institute of Justice, 1996).
122. Barry Scheck and Peter Neufeld, "DNA and Innocence Scholarship," in Saundra D. Westervelt and John A. Humphrey, eds., *Wrongly Convicted: Perspectives on Failed Justice* (New Brunswick, NJ: Rutgers University Press, 2001), pp. 248–249.
123. Ibid., p. 246.
124. James S. Liebman, Jeffrey Fagan, and Simon H. Rifkind, *A Broken System: Error Rates in Capital Cases, 1973–1995* (New York: Columbia University School of Law, 2000), http://justice.policy.net/jpreport/finrep.PDF (accessed March 3, 2004).
125. See, for example, Jim Yardley, "Texas Retooling Criminal Justice in Wake of Furor on Death Penalty," *New York Times*, June 1, 2001.
126. In a sad footnote to the Illinois proclamation, former Governor Ryan, who drew international praise for his stance against the death penalty and who had been nominated for the Nobel Prize, was found guilty in 2006 of racketeering and fraud in a corruption scandal that ended his political career.
127. "New Jersey Suspends Death Penalty Pending a Task Force Review," *Criminal Justice Newsletter* (January 17, 2006), p. 8.
128. Title IV of the Justice for All Act of 2004.
129. At the time the legislation was enacted, Congress estimated that 300,000 rape kits remained unanalyzed in police department evidence lockers across the country.
130. The act also provides funding for the DNA Sexual Assault Justice Act (Title III of the Justice for All Act of 2004) and the Rape Kits and DNA Evidence Backlog Elimination Act of 2000 (42 U.S.C. 14135), authorizing more than $500 million for programs to improve the capacity of crime labs to conduct DNA analysis, reduce non-DNA backlogs, train evidence examiners, support sexual assault forensic examiner programs, and promote the use of DNA to identify missing persons.
131. In those states that accept federal monies under the legislation.
132. See N.C. G.S. section 15A-1460-75.
133. North Carolina Innocence Inquiry Commission, "Case Statistics," http://www.innocencecommission-nc.gov/statistics.htm (accessed June 20, 2010).
134. Studies include S. Decker and C. Kohfeld, "A Deterrence Study of the Death Penalty in Illinois: 1933–1980," *Journal of Criminal Justice*, Vol. 12, No. 4 (1984), pp. 367–379; and S. Decker and C. Kohfeld, "An Empirical Analysis of the Effect of the Death Penalty in Missouri," *Journal of Crime and Justice*, Vol. 10, No. 1 (1987), pp. 23–46.
135. See, especially, W. C. Bailey, "Deterrence and the Death Penalty for Murders in Utah: A Time Series Analysis," *Journal of Contemporary Law*, Vol. 5, No. 1 (1978), pp. 1–20; and W. C. Bailey, "An Analysis of the Deterrent Effect of the Death Penalty for Murder in California," *Southern California Law Review*, Vol. 52, No. 3 (1979), pp. 743–764.
136. B. E. Forst, "The Deterrent Effect of Capital Punishment: A Cross-State Analysis of the 1960's," *Minnesota Law Review*, Vol. 61, No. 5 (1977), pp. 743–767.
137. Hashem Dezhbakhsh, Paul Rubin, and Joanna Mehlhop Shepherd, "Does Capital Punishment Have a Deterrent Effect? New Evidence from Post-Moratorium Panel Data," Emory University, January 2001, http://userwww.service.emory.edu/cozden/Dezhbakhsh_01_01_paper.pdf (accessed November 13, 2006).
138. Ibid., abstract.
139. Ibid., p. 19.
140. As some of the evidence presented before the Supreme Court in *Furman* v. *Georgia*, 408 U.S. 238 (1972), suggested.
141. *USA Today*, April 27, 1989.
142. Thomas J. Keil and Gennaro F. Vito, "Race and the Death Penalty in Kentucky Murder Trials: 1976–1991," *American Journal of Criminal Justice*, Vol. 20, No. 1 (1995), pp. 17–36 (published December 1996).
143. *McCleskey* v. *Kemp*, 481 U.S. 279, 107 S.Ct. 1756, 95 L.Ed.2d 262 (1987).
144. *The Federal Death Penalty System: Supplementary Data, Analysis and Revised Protocols for Capital Case Review* (Washington, DC: Department of Justice, 2001).
145. David Stout, "Attorney General Says Report Shows No Racial Bias in Federal Death Sentences," *New York Times*, June 7, 2001, http://nytimes.com/2001/06/07/politics/07DEAT.html (accessed September 19, 2010).
146. "Expanded Study Shows No Bias in Death Penalty, Ashcroft Says," *Criminal Justice Newsletter*, Vol. 31, No. 13 (June 18, 2001), p. 4.
147. Mary P. Gallagher, "Race Found to Have No Effect on Capital Sentencing in New Jersey," *New Jersey Law Journal* (August 21, 2001), p. 1.
148. "Nebraska Death Penalty System Given Mixed Review in a State Study," *Criminal Justice Newsletter*, Vol. 31, No. 16 (August 2001), pp. 4–5.
149. Details for this story come from Michael Graczyk, "Killer of Pregnant 10-Year-Old Set to Die Tonight," Associated Press, February 10, 2004; and Texas Execution Information Center, "Edward Lagrone," http://www.txexeutions.org/reports/318.asp (accessed May 15, 2004).
150. Justice Potter Stewart, as quoted in *USA Today*, April 27, 1989.
151. Arthur Koestler, *Reflections on Hanging* (New York: Macmillan, 1957), pp. 147–148 and Gennaro F. Vito and Deborah G. Wilson, "Back from the Dead: Tracking the Progress of Kentucky's *Furman*-Commuted Death Row Population," *Justice Quarterly*, Vol. 5, No. 1 (1988), pp. 101–111.
152. *Wilkerson* v. *Utah*, 99 U.S. 130 (1878).
153. *In re Kemmler*, 136 U.S. 436 (1890).

154. Ibid., p. 447.
155. *Louisiana ex rel. Francis* v. *Resweber*, 329 U.S. 459 (1947).
156. *Furman* v. *Georgia*, 408 U.S. 238 (1972).
157. A position first adopted in *Trop* v. *Dulles*, 356 U.S. 86 (1958).
158. *Gregg* v. *Georgia*, 428 U.S. 153 (1976).
159. *Ring* v. *Arizona*, 536 U.S. 584 (2002).
160. "Dozens of Death Sentences Overturned," Associated Press, June 24, 2002.
161. The ruling could also affect Florida, Alabama, Indiana, and Delaware, where juries recommend sentences in capital cases but judges have the final say.
162. *Poyner* v. *Murray*, 113 S.Ct. 1573, 123 L.Ed.2d 142 (1993).
163. *Campbell* v. *Wood*, 114 S.Ct. 1337, 127 L.Ed.2d 685 (1994).
164. *Director Gomez, et al.* v. *Fierro and Ruiz*, 117 S.Ct. 285 (1996).
165. The court issued its decision after reviewing two cases: *Dawson* v. *State* and *Moore* v. *State*.
166. Thomas P. Bonczar and Tracy L. Snell, *Capital Punishment, 2004* (Washington, DC: Bureau of Justice Statistics, 2005), p. 4.
167. Adam Liptak, "Judges Set Hurdles for Lethal Injection," *New York Times*, April 12, 2006.
168. "North Carolina, Using Medical Monitoring Device, Executes Killer," Associated Press, April 22, 2006.
169. *Baze* v. *Rees*, 553 U.S. 35 (2008).
170. Gallup Organization, May 27, 2003, http://www.gallup.com.
171. See Janet L. Conley, "Execution Protests Wane as Opponents Shift Focus," *Fulton County Daily Report*, August 22, 2002. For the latest information on public opinion polls as they relate to capital punishment, visit the Death Penalty Information Center online at http://www.deathpenaltyinfo.org.
172. James D. Unnever and Francis T. Cullen, "Executing the Innocent and Support for Capital Punishment," *Criminology and Public Policy*, Vol. 4, No. 1 (2005), p. 3.
173. Death Penalty Information Center, *Crisis of Confidence: Americans' Doubts about the Death Penalty* (Washington, DC: DPIC, June 9, 2007).
174. "Illinois Commission Calls for Restrictions on Death Penalty," *Criminal Justice Newsletter*, Vol. 32, No. 7 (April 2002), pp. 1–3.
175. "Death Penalty Freeze to Remain in Illinois," *USA Today*, April 25, 2003.

Chapter 10: Probation, Parole, and Community Corrections

i. Quoted in *Criminal Justice Newsletter*, January 3, 2006, p. 1.
ii. Jeremy Travis and Sarah Lawrence, *Beyond the Prison Gates: The State of Parole in America* (Washington, DC: Urban Institute Press, 2002), p. 3.
iii. Ibid.

---

1. Quoted in *Criminal Justice Newsletter*, January 19, 1993, p. 1.
2. Jesse Jannetta et al., *An Evolving Field: Findings from the 2008 Parole Practices Survey* (Washington, DC: Urban Institute Press, 2009), p. 1.
3. Sara Olkon and Margaret Ramirez, "Jennifer Hudson's Nephew Julian King: Sweet, Gentle, Loved," *Chicago Tribune*, October 28, 2008, http://www.chicagotribune.com/news/local/chi-julian-king-jennifer-hudson-oct28,0,7263400.story (accessed June 4, 2009).
4. James M. Byrne, *Probation*, National Institute of Justice Crime File Series Study Guide (Washington, DC: U.S. Department of Justice, 1988), p. 1.
5. Sean Rosenmerkel, Matthew Durose, and Donald Farole, Jr., *Felony Sentences in State Courts, 2006* (Washington, DC: Bureau of Justice Statistics, December 2009), p. 2.
6. Lauren E. Glaze and Thomas P. Bonczar, *Probation and Parole in the United States, 2008* (Washington, DC: Bureau of Justice Statistics, December 2009).
7. Jodi M. Brown and Patrick A. Langan, *Felony Sentences in the United States, 1996* (Washington, DC: Bureau of Justice Statistics, 1999).
8. "Woman Gets Probation for Shooting Fiancé," Associated Press, April 16, 1992.
9. "On Deadline: Getting Away with Murder in Dallas," *USA Today*, November 14, 2007.
10. Glaze and Bonczar, *Probation and Parole in the United States, 2008*, p. 2.
11. Ibid, p. 4.
12. This section owes much to Sanford Bates, "The Establishment and Early Years of the Federal Probation System," *Federal Probation* (June 1987), pp. 4–9.
13. *Ex parte United States*, 242 U.S. 27 (1916).
14. Bates, "The Establishment and Early Years of the Federal Probation System," p. 6.
15. U.S. Probation and Pretrial Services System, *Year-in-Review Report: Fiscal Year 2004* (Washington, DC: U.S. Probation and Pretrial Services System, 2005).
16. See Brian A. Reaves and Timothy C. Hart, *Federal Law Enforcement Officers, 2000* (Washington, DC: Bureau of Justice Statistics, 2002), p. 4, from which some of the wording in this paragraph has been adapted.
17. Adapted from Timothy A. Hughes, Doris James Wilson, and Allen J. Beck, *Trends in State Parole, 1990–2000* (Washington, DC: Bureau of Justice Statistics, 2001), p. 1.
18. Ibid.
19. Ibid.
20. Ibid.
21. Glaze and Bonczar, *Probation and Parole in the United States, 2008*, p. 3.
22. Ibid., p. 37.
23. Ibid., p. 7.
24. "The Effectiveness of Felony Probation: Results from an Eastern State," *Justice Quarterly* (December 1991), pp. 525–543.
25. State of New Jersey, State Parole Board, Media Release, "Parole Board Votes Unanimously to Restrict Sex Offender Internet Socializing," November 29, 2007.
26. State of Georgia, Board of Pardons and Paroles, "Adult Offender Sanction Costs for Fiscal Year 2001," http://www.pap.state.ga.us/otisweb/corrcost.html (accessed March 11, 2007).
27. See Andrew von Hirsch and Kathleen J. Hanrahan, *Abolish Parole?* (Washington, DC: Law Enforcement Assistance Administration, 1978).
28. *Griffin* v. *Wisconsin*, 483 U.S. 868, 107 S.Ct. 3164 (1987).
29. *Pennsylvania Board of Probation and Parole* v. *Scott*, 524 U.S. 357 (1998).
30. Glaze and Bonczar, *Probation and Parole in the United States, 2008*.
31. Robyn. L. Cohen, *Probation and Parole Violators in State Prison, 1991* (Washington, DC: Bureau of Justice Statistics, 1995).
32. *Harlow* v. *Clatterbuick*, 30 CrL. 2364 (Va. S.Ct. 1986); *Santangelo* v. *State*, 426 N.Y.S.2d 931 (1980); *Welch* v. *State*, 424 N.Y.S.2d 774 (1980); and *Thompson* v. *County of Alameda*, 614 P.2d 728 (1980).
33. *Tarter* v. *State of New York*, 38 CrL. 2364 (N.Y. Sup. Ct. 1986); *Grimm* v. *Arizona Board of Pardons and Paroles*, 115 Arizona 260, 564 P.2d 1227 (1977); and *Payton* v. *U.S.*, 636 F.2d 132 (5th Cir. 1981).
34. Rolando V. del Carmen, *Potential Liabilities of Probation and Parole Officers* (Cincinnati, OH: Anderson, 1986), p. 89.

35. See, for example, *Semler* v. *Psychiatric Institute*, 538 F.2d 121 (4th Cir. 1976).
36. *Minnesota* v. *Murphy*, 465 U.S. 420 (1984).
37. National Advisory Commission on Criminal Justice Standards and Goals, *Task Force Report: Corrections* (Washington, DC: U.S. Government Printing Office, 1973).
38. National Institute of Justice, *Stress among Probation and Parole Officers and What Can Be Done about It* (Washington, DC: NIJ, 2005).
39. Ibid., p. 1.
40. Ibid., p. ii.
41. From the introduction to James Austin, Michael Jones, and Melissa Bolyard, *The Growing Use of Jail Boot Camps: The Current State of the Art* (Washington, DC: National Institute of Justice, 1993), p. 1.
42. Michael McCarthy and Jodi Upton, "Athletes Lightly Punished after Their Day in Court," *USA Today*, May 4, 2006.
43. Sentencing Project, *Changing the Terms of Sentencing: Defense Counsel and Alternative Sentencing Services* (Washington, DC: Sentencing Project, n.d.).
44. Joan Petersilia, *Expanding Options for Criminal Sentencing* (Santa Monica, CA: RAND Corporation, 1987).
45. Ohio Revised Code, Section 2946.06.1 (July 1965).
46. Lawrence Greenfield, *Probation and Parole, 1984* (Washington, DC: U.S. Government Printing Office, 1986).
47. For a good overview of such programs, especially as they apply to juvenile corrections, see Doris Layton MacKenzie et al., *A National Study Comparing the Environments of Boot Camps with Traditional Facilities for Juvenile Offenders* (Washington, DC: National Institute of Justice, 2001).
48. Doris Layton MacKenzie and Deanna Bellew Ballow, "Shock Incarceration Programs in State Correctional Jurisdictions—An Update," *NIJ Reports* (May/June 1989), pp. 9–10.
49. "Shock Incarceration Marks a Decade of Expansion," *Corrections Compendium* (September 1996), pp. 10–28.
50. MacKenzie and Ballow, "Shock Incarceration Programs in State Correctional Jurisdictions."
51. National Institute of Justice, *Multisite Evaluation of Shock Incarceration* (Washington, DC: NIJ, 1995).
52. Cherie L. Clark, David W. Aziz, and Doris L. MacKenzie, *Shock Incarceration in New York: Focus on Treatment* (Washington, DC: National Institute of Justice, 1994), p. 8.
53. "Oregon Boot Camp Is Saving the State Money, Study Finds," *Criminal Justice Newsletter*, May 1, 1995, pp. 5–6.
54. Douglas C. McDonald, *Restitution and Community Service*, National Institute of Justice Crime File Series Study Guide (Washington, DC: U.S. Department of Justice, 1988).
55. Richard J. Maher and Henry E. Dufour, "Experimenting with Community Service: A Punitive Alternative to Imprisonment," *Federal Probation* (September 1987), pp. 22–27.
56. James P. Levine, Michael C. Musheno, and Dennis J. Palumbo, *Criminal Justice in America: Law in Action* (New York: John Wiley, 1986), p. 549.
57. Billie S. Erwin and Lawrence A. Bennett, "New Dimensions in Probation: Georgia's Experience with Intensive Probation Supervision," *Research in Brief* (Washington, DC: National Institute of Justice, 1987).
58. Probation Division, State of Georgia, "Intensive and Specialized Probation Supervision," http://www.dcor.state.ga.us/ProbationDivision/html/ProbationDivision.html (accessed March 2, 2008).
59. Crystal A. Garcia, "Using Palmer's Global Approach to Evaluate Intensive Supervision Programs: Implications for Practice," *Corrections Management Quarterly*, Vol. 4, No. 4 (2000), pp. 60–69.
60. Joan Petersilia, *House Arrest*, National Institute of Justice Crime File Series Study Guide (Washington, DC: U.S. Department of Justice, 1988).
61. Darren Gowen, "Remote Location Monitoring: A Supervision Strategy to Enhance Risk Control," *Federal Probation*, Vol. 65, No. 2 (2001), p. 39.
62. "Vick to Be Monitored for 2 Months in Home Confinement," *Sports Illustrated*, May 18, 2009, http://sportsillustrated.cnn.com/2009/football/nfl/05/18/vick.confinement.ap/index.html (accessed May 21, 2009).
63. *Electronic Monitoring*, TDCJ-CJAD Agency Brief (Austin: Texas Department of Criminal Justice, March 1999).
64. Texas Department of Criminal Justice, Parole Division, *Contract Information: Electronic Monitoring*, http://www.tdcj.state.tx.us/parole/parole-contracts/parolecont-em.htm (accessed September 28, 2008).
65. Marc Renzema and David T. Skelton, *The Use of Electronic Monitoring by Criminal Justice Agencies, 1989* (Washington, DC: National Institute of Justice, 1990).
66. U.S. Probation and Pretrial Services, *Court and Community* (Washington, DC: Administrative Office of the U.S. Courts, 2000).
67. *Sourcebook of Criminal Justice Statistics Online* (2005), "Persons under Jail Supervision" (Table 6.14, year 2003), http://www.albany.edu/sourcebook/wk1/t614.wk1 (accessed October 26, 2006).
68. "Satellites Tracking People on Parole," Associated Press, April 13, 1999.
69. Glaze and Bonczar, *Probation and Parole in the United States, 2008*, p. 35.
70. U.S. Probation and Pretrial Services, "Home Confinement," http://www.uscourts.gov/misc/cchome.pdf (accessed March 22, 2008).
71. State of Georgia Board of Pardons and Paroles, "Adult Offender Sanction Costs for Fiscal Year 2001," http://www.pap.state.ga.us/otisweb/corrcost.html (accessed September 20, 2005).
72. Construction costs are for cells classified as "medium security."
73. *BI Home Escort: Electronic Monitoring System*, advertising brochure (Boulder, CO: BI Inc., n.d.).
74. James A. Inciardi, *Criminal Justice*, 2nd ed. (New York: Harcourt Brace Jovanovich, 1987), p. 664.
75. William J. Sabol, Heather C. West, and Mathew Cooper, *Prisoners in 2008* (Washington, DC: BJS, 2009).
76. Patrick A. Langan and David J. Levin, *National Recidivism Study of Released Prisoners: Recidivism of Prisoners Released in 1994* (Washington, DC: Bureau of Justice Statistics, 2002).
77. "Forty-Two Percent of State Parole Discharges Were Successful," Bureau of Justice Statistics press release, October 3, 2001.
78. Urban Institute and RTI International, *National Portrait of SVORI* (Washington, DC: Urban Institute Press, 2004).
79. American Probation and Parole Association and the Association of Paroling Authorities International, *Abolishing Parole: Why the Emperor Has No Clothes* (Lexington, KY: APPA, 1995).
80. Much of this information is taken from Reentry Policy Council, *Report of the Reentry Policy Council: Charting the Safe and Successful Return of Prisoners to the Community—Executive Summary* (New York: Council of State Governments, 2005).
81. Langan and Levin, *National Recidivism Study of Released Prisoners;* and *Does Parole Work? Analyzing the Impact of Postprison Supervision on Rearrest Outcomes* (Washington, DC: Urban Institute Press, 2005).
82. Esther Griswold, Jessica Pearson, and Lanae Davis, *Testing a Modification Process for Incarcerated Parents* (Denver: Center for Policy Research), pp. 11–12.
83. Ibid.

84. See Pamela K. Lattimore, "Reentry, Reintegration, Rehabilitation, Recidivism, and Redemption," *Criminologist*, Vol. 31, No. 3 (May/June 2006), pp. 1, 3–6.
85. Urban Institute and RTI International, *National Portrait of SVORI*, from which some of the wording in this section is taken.
86. See Laura Winterfield and Susan Brumbaugh, *The Multi-site Evaluation of the Serious and Violent Offender Reentry Initiative* (Washington, DC: Urban Institute Press, 2005).
87. U.S. Department of Justice, Office of Justice Programs, "Learn about Reentry," http://www.reentry.gov/learn.html (accessed May 29, 2008).
88. Lane County (Oregon) Circuit Court, "Drug Court," http://www.ojd.state.or.us/lan/drugcrt/index.htm (accessed May 29, 2006).
89. See, for example, Jeremy Travis, *But They All Come Back: Facing the Challenges of Prisoner Reentry* (Washington, DC: Urban Institute Press, 2005).
90. Urban Institute and RTI International, *National Portrait of SVORI*, pp. 21, 23.
91. Public Law 110–199.
92. Congressional Budget Office, "Cost Estimate: S. 1060, Second Chance Act of 2007," p. 4, http://www.cbo.gov/ftpdocs/86xx/doc8620/s1060.pdf (accessed August 28, 2008).
93. Reinventing Probation Council, *"Broken Windows" Probation: The Next Step in Fighting Crime* (New York: Manhattan Institute, 1999); and Reinventing Probation Council, *Transforming Probation through Leadership: The "Broken Windows" Model* (New York: Center for Civic Innovation at the Manhattan Institute, 2000), from which some of the quoted material in these paragraphs comes.
94. Public Safety Performance Project, *Putting Public Safety First: 13 Strategies for Successful Supervision and Reentry* (Washington, DC: Pew Center on the States, 2008).
95. Jannetta et al., *An Evolving Field*.
96. Ibid., p. 22.
97. Ibid., p. 2.

Chapter 11: Prisons and Jails

i. Adam Liptak, "U.S. Imprisons One in 100 Adults, Report Finds," *New York Times*, February 29, 2008, http://www.nytimes.com/2008/02/29/us/29prison.html (accessed September 21, 2010).
ii. James A. Gondles, Jr., "Who Should Be behind Bars?" *Corrections Today* (August 2002), http://www.aca.org/admin/pix/ctmagarticles/200208_whoshouldbebehindbars.pdf (accessed September 12, 2005).
iii. Zebulon R. Brockway, *The Ideal of a True Prison System for a State* (1865), reprinted in *Journal of Correctional Education*, Vol. 46, No. 2 (June 1995), pp. 68–74.
iv. Paige M. Harrison and Allen J. Beck, *Prisoners in 2005* (Washington, DC: Bureau of Justice Statistics, 2006), p. 7.

---

1. Public Safety Performance Project of the Pew Charitable Trusts, *Public Safety, Public Spending: Forecasting America's Prison Population, 2007–2011* (Philadelphia: Pew, February 2007), p. 1.
2. WBBM-TV, "Thomson Prison to Hold Terror Trials," CBS News, December 15, 2009, http://cbs2chicago.com/local/Gitmo.Thomson.White.2.1369991.html (accessed May 22, 2010).
3. Sarah Schulte, "Ill. Prison May Hold Guantanamo Detainees," WLS-TV, November 16, 2009, http://abclocal.go.com/wls/story?section=news/local/illinois&id=7118811 (accessed May 22, 2010).
4. James J. Stephan and Jennifer C. Karberg, *Census of State and Federal Correctional Facilities, 2000* (Washington, DC: Bureau of Justice Statistics, 2003).
5. Heather C. West, *Prisoners at Yearend 2009: Advance Counts* (Washington, DC: Bureau of Justice Statistics, 2010).
6. Ibid.
7. Public Safety Performance Project of the Pew Charitable Trusts, *Public Safety, Public Spending*.
8. Public Safety Performance Project of the Pew Charitable Trusts, *One in 100: Behind Bars in America, 2008* (Philadelphia: Pew, 2008), p. 5.
9. West, *Prisoners at Yearend 2009*.
10. Thomas P. Bonczar, *Prevalence of Imprisonment in the U.S. Population, 1974–2001* (Washington, DC: Bureau of Justice Statistics, 2003), p. 1.
11. Federal Bureau of Investigation, *Crime in the United States, 2009*, and other years.
12. Some of the ideas in this paragraph are taken from Public Safety Performance Project of the Pew Charitable Trusts, *One in 100*.
13. West, *Prisoners at Yearend 2009*.
14. Bureau of Justice Statistics, *National Corrections Reporting Program, 1998* (Ann Arbor, MI: Interuniversity Consortium for Political and Social Research, 2001); and West, *Prisoners at Yearend 2009*.
15. Jim Kessler et al., *The Impending Crime Wave: Four Dangerous New Trends and How to Stop Them* (Washington, DC: Third Way Foundation, February 2008).
16. "Study Finds More Than Half of All Prison and Jail Inmates Have Mental Health Problems," U.S. Department of Justice, Office of Justice Programs, press release, September 6, 2006.
17. Most of the items in this list and some of the wording are taken from Kessler et al., *The Impending Crime Wave*, p. 7.
18. West, *Prisoners at Yearend 2009*.
19. Bonczar, *Prevalence of Imprisonment in the U.S. Population, 1974–2001*, p. 1.
20. Ibid., p. 8.
21. The number includes both state and federal prisoners.
22. Information in this paragraph comes from West, *Prisoners at Yearend 2009*.
23. David F. Greenberg and Valerie West, "State Prison Populations and Their Growth, 1971–1991," *Criminology*, Vol. 39, No. 3 (2001), p. 615.
24. Robert M. Carter, Richard A. McGee, and E. Kim Nelson, *Corrections in America* (Philadelphia: J. B. Lippincott, 1975), pp. 122–123.
25. James J. Stephan, *State Prison Expenditures, 2001* (Washington, DC: Bureau of Justice Statistics, 2004); and e-mail correspondence with Susan Allison, Federal Bureau of Prisons, October 29, 2001.
26. Kristen A. Hughes, *Justice Expenditure and Employment in the United States, 2003* (Washington, DC: Bureau of Justice Statistics, 2006); and Stephan, *State Prison Expenditures, 2001*, p. 3.
27. See, for example, Harry Elmer Barnes and Negley K. Teeters, *New Horizons in Criminology*, 3rd ed. (Englewood Cliffs, NJ: Prentice Hall, 1959).
28. Although many other states require inmates to work on road maintenance and although the inmates are typically supervised by armed guards, Alabama became the first state in modern times to shackle prisoners.
29. See "Back on the Chain Gang: Florida Becomes Third State to Resurrect Forced Labor," Associated Press, November 22, 1995.
30. Florida Department of Corrections, *Corrections in Florida: 1998 Opinion Survey*, http://www.dc.state.fl.us/pub/survey/index.html (accessed January 24, 2008).
31. Lori Sharn and Shannon Tangonan, "Chain Gangs Back in Alabama," *USA Today*, May 4, 1995.
32. Ibid.

33. See Debra L. Dailey, *Summary of the 1998 Annual Conference of the National Association of Sentencing Commissions*, http://www.ussc.gov/states/dailefsr.pdf (accessed October 30, 2005).
34. Peter Baker, "Allen Crime Plan Ends Parole; Expensive Va. Proposal Would Strain Budget, Require More Prisons," *Washington Post* wire service, August 17, 1994.
35. The state of Washington is generally credited with having been the first state to pass a three-strikes law by voter initiative (in 1993).
36. For a good overview of the topic, see David Shichor and Dale K. Sechrest, *Three Strikes and You're Out: Vengeance as Public Policy* (Thousand Oaks, CA: Sage, 1996).
37. David S. Broder, "When Tough Isn't Smart," *Washington Post* wire service, March 24, 1994.
38. "The Klaas Case and the Crime Bill," *Washington Post* wire service, February 21, 1994.
39. Bruce Smith, "Crime Solutions," Associated Press, January 11, 1995.
40. Quinlan is now senior vice president at Corrections Corporation of America.
41. Quoted in David Lawsky, "Prison Wardens Decry Overcrowding, Survey Says," Reuters, December 21, 1994.
42. West, *Prisoners at Yearend 2009.*
43. Federal Bureau of Prisons, *State of the Bureau, 2004* (Washington, DC: BOP, 2005), p. 7.
44. Adapted from Bureau of Justice Statistics, *Report to the Nation on Crime and Justice*, 2nd ed. (Washington, DC: U.S. Government Printing Office, 1988), p. 108.
45. *Rhodes* v. *Chapman*, 452 U.S. 337 (1981).
46. D. Greenberg, "The Incapacitative Effect of Imprisonment, Some Estimates," *Law and Society Review*, Vol. 9 (1975), pp. 541–580. See also Jacqueline Cohen, "Incapacitating Criminals: Recent Research Findings," National Institute of Justice *Research in Brief* (December 1983).
47. For information on identifying dangerous repeat offenders, see M. Chaiken and J. Chaiken, *Selecting Career Criminals for Priority Prosecution*, final report (Cambridge, MA: Abt Associates, 1987).
48. J. Monahan, *Predicting Violent Behavior: An Assessment of Clinical Techniques* (Beverly Hills, CA: Sage, 1981).
49. S. Van Dine, J. P. Conrad, and S. Dinitz, *Restraining the Wicked: The Incapacitation of the Dangerous Offender* (Lexington, MA: Lexington Books, 1979).
50. Paul Gendreau, Tracy Little, and Claire Goggin, "A Meta-Analysis of the Predictors of Adult Offender Recidivism: What Works!" *Criminology*, Vol. 34, No. 4 (November 1996), pp. 575–607.
51. Daniel B. Wood, "Budget Cuts Are Setting Convicts Free," *Christian Science Monitor*, April 21, 2004.
52. George Camp and Camille Camp, "Stopping Escapes: Perimeter Security," *Prison Construction Bulletin* (Washington, DC: National Institute of Justice, 1987).
53. Adapted from G. A. Grizzle and A. D. Witte, "Efficiency in Collections Agencies," in Gordon P. Whitaker and Charles D. Phillips, *Evaluating the Performance of Criminal Justice Agencies* (Washington, DC: NIJ, 1983).
54. Patricia L. Hardyman et al., *Internal Prison Classification Systems: Case Studies in Their Development and Implementation* (Washington, DC: National Institutions of Corrections, 2002), from which some of the wording in this section is taken.
55. Ibid.
56. *Johnson* v. *California*, 543 U.S. 499 (2005).
57. Federal Bureau of Prisons, *Staff Breakdown*, http://www.bop.gov/about/facts.jsp#5 (accessed June 6, 2010).
58. Most of the information in this section comes from telephone conversations with and faxed information from the Federal Bureau of Prisons, August 25, 1995.
59. For additional information, see Dennis Cauchon, "The Alcatraz of the Rockies," *USA Today*, November 16, 1994.
60. "Congress OKs Inmate Fees to Offset Costs of Prison," *Criminal Justice Newsletter*, October 15, 1992, p. 6.
61. Stephan, *State Prison Expenditures, 2001*, p. 3.
62. National Institute of Corrections, http://www.nicic.org (accessed March 2, 2006).
63. Ibid.
64. James J. Stephan, *Census of Jails, 1999* (Washington, DC: Bureau of Justice Statistics, 2001), p. 2.
65. Much of the information in this paragraph comes from Todd D. Minton, *Jail Inmates at Midyear 2009* (Washington, DC: Bureau of Justice Statistics, 2010).
66. Ibid., p. 14.
67. Stephan, *Census of Jails, 1999.*
68. Ibid.
69. Ibid.
70. Minton, *Jail Inmates at Midyear 2009*; and Doris J. James, *Profile of Jail Inmates, 2002* (Washington, DC: Bureau of Justice Statistics), p. 2.
71. James, *Profile of Jail Inmates, 2002.*
72. Stephan, *Census of Jails, 1999.*
73. See Gale Holland, "L.A. Jail Makes Delayed Debut," *USA Today*, January 27, 1997.
74. See Dale Stockton, "Cook County Illinois Sheriff's Office," *Police* (October 1996), pp. 40–43. The Cook County Department of Correction operates ten separate jails, which house approximately 9,000 inmates. The department employs more than 2,800 correctional officers.
75. Minton, *Jail Inmates at Midyear 2009*, p. 4.
76. William Reginald Mills and Heather Barrett, "Meeting the Special Challenge of Providing Health Care to Women Inmates in the '90's," *American Jails*, Vol. 4, No. 3 (September/October 1990), p. 55.
77. Ibid.
78. Ibid., p. 21.
79. Ibid.
80. Ibid., p. 55.
81. American Correctional Association, *Vital Statistics in Corrections* (Laurel, MD: ACA, 2000).
82. Mills and Barrett, "Meeting the Special Challenge," p. 55.
83. Ibid.
84. Linda L. Zupan, "Women Corrections Officers in the Nation's Largest Jails," *American Jails* (January/February 1991), pp. 59–62.
85. Ibid., p. 11.
86. Linda L. Zupan, "Women Corrections Officers in Local Jails," paper presented at the annual meeting of the Academy of Criminal Justice Sciences, Nashville, TN, March 1991.
87. Ibid., p. 6.
88. "Jail Overcrowding in Houston Results in Release of Inmates," *Criminal Justice Newsletter*, October 15, 1990, p. 5.
89. Bureau of Justice Statistics, *Census of Local Jails, 1988* (Washington, DC: BJS, 1991), p. 31.
90. Kathleen Maguire and Ann L. Pastore, *Sourcebook of Criminal Justice Statistics, 1994* (Washington, DC: U.S. Government Printing Office, 1995).
91. Minton, *Jail Inmates at Midyear 2009.*
92. Christopher J. Mumola, *Suicide and Homicide in State Prisons and Local Jails* (Washington, DC: Bureau of Justice Statistics, 2005), p. 1.
93. George P. Wilson and Harvey L. McMurray, "System Assessment of Jail Overcrowding Assumptions," paper presented at the annual meeting of the Academy of Criminal Justice Sciences, Nashville, TN, March 1991.
94. Andy Hall, *Systemwide Strategies to Alleviate Jail Crowding* (Washington, DC: National Institute of Justice, 1987).
95. Ibid.

96. Linda L. Zupan and Ben A. Menke, "The New Generation Jail: An Overview," in Joel A. Thompson and G. Larry Mays, eds., *American Jails: Public Policy Issues* (Chicago: Nelson-Hall, 1991), p. 180.
97. Ibid.
98. Herbert R. Sigurdson, Billy Wayson, and Gail Funke, "Empowering Middle Managers of Direct Supervision Jails," *American Jails* (winter 1990), p. 52.
99. Byron Johnson, "Exploring Direct Supervision: A Research Note," *American Jails* (March/April 1994), pp. 63–64.
100. H. Sigurdson, *The Manhattan House of Detention: A Study of Podular Direct Supervision* (Washington, DC: National Institute of Corrections, 1985). For similar conclusions, see Robert Conroy, Wantland J. Smith, and Linda L. Zupan, "Officer Stress in the Direct Supervision Jail: A Preliminary Case Study," *American Jails* (November/December 1991), p. 36.
101. Jerry W. Fuqua, "New Generation Jails: Old Generation Management," *American Jails* (March/April 1991), pp. 80–83.
102. Sigurdson, Wayson, and Funke, "Empowering Middle Managers."
103. Duncan J. McCulloch and Time Stiles, "Technology and the Direct Supervision Jail," *American Jails* (winter 1990), pp. 97–102.
104. Susan W. McCampbell, "Direct Supervision: Looking for the Right People," *American Jails* (November/December 1990), pp. 68–69.
105. For a good overview of the future of American jails, see Ron Carroll, "Jails and the Criminal Justice System in the Twenty-First Century," *American Jails* (March/April 1997), pp. 26–31.
106. Robert L. May II, Roger H. Peters, and William D. Kearns, "The Extent of Drug Treatment Programs in Jails: A Summary Report," *American Jails* (September/October 1990), pp. 32–34.
107. See, for example, John W. Dietler, "Jail Industries: The Best Thing That Can Happen to a Sheriff," *American Jails* (July/August 1990), pp. 80–83.
108. Robert Osborne, "Los Angeles County Sheriff Opens New Inmate Answering Service," *American Jails* (July/August 1990), pp. 61–62.
109. Robert J. Hunter, "A Locally Operated Boot Camp," *American Jails* (July/August 1994), pp. 13–15.
110. James Austin, Michael Jones, and Melissa Bolyard, *The Growing Use of Jail Boot Camps: The Current State of the Art* (Washington, DC: National Institute of Justice, 1993).
111. See J. R. Dewan, "Regional Jail—The New Kid on the Block," *American Jails* (May/June 1995), pp. 70–72.
112. Tom Rosazza, "Jail Standards: Focus on Change," *American Jails* (November/December 1990), pp. 84–87.
113. American Correctional Association, *Manual of Standards for Adult Local Detention Facilities*, 3rd ed. (College Park, MD: ACA, 1991).
114. Ken Kerle, "National Sheriff's Association Jail Audit Review," *American Jails* (spring 1987), pp. 13–21.
115. Allen J. Beck and Paige M. Harrison, *Prisoners in 2000* (Washington, DC: Bureau of Justice Statistics, 2001), p. 7.
116. West, *Prisoners at Yearend 2009*.
117. Eric Bates, "Private Prisons: Over the Next Five Years Analysts Expect the Private Share of the Prison 'Market' to More Than Double," *The Nation*, Vol. 266, No. 1 (1998), pp. 11–18.
118. Gary Fields, "Privatized Prisons Pose Problems," *USA Today*, November 11, 1996.
119. Dale K. Sechrest and David Shichor, "Private Jails: Locking Down the Issues," *American Jails* (March/April 1997), pp. 9–18.
120. U.S. General Accounting Office, *Private and Public Prisons: Studies Comparing Operational Costs and/or Quality of Service* (Washington, DC: U.S. Government Printing Office, 1996).
121. Sechrest and Shichor, "Private Jails," p. 10.
122. James Austin and Garry Coventry, *Emerging Issues on Privatized Prisons* (Washington, DC: Bureau of Justice Statistics, 2001), p. ix.
123. For a more detailed discussion of this issue, see Austin and Coventry, *Emerging Issues on Privatized Prisons*.
124. *Richardson* v. *McKnight*, 117 S.Ct. 2100, 138 L.Ed.2d 540 (1997).
125. *Correctional Services Corporation* v. *Malesko*, 122 S.Ct. 515 (2001).
126. Ibid.
127. Quoted in Bates, "Private Prisons."
128. Judith C. Hackett et al., "Contracting for the Operation of Prisons and Jails," National Institute of Justice *Research in Brief* (June 1987), p. 6.

Chapter 12: Prison Life

i. Zebulon R. Brockway, *The Ideal of a True Prison System for a State* (1865). Reprinted in the *Journal of Correctional Education*, Vol. 46, No. 2 (1995), pp. 68–74.

---

1. Re-entry Policy Council, *Report of the Re-entry Policy Council: Charting the Safe and Successful Return of Prisoners to the Community—Report Preview* (New York: Council of State Governments, 2005), p. 4.
2. Commission on Safety and Abuse in America's Prisons, *Confronting Confinement: A Report of the Commission on Safety and Abuse in America's Prisons* (New York: Vera Institute of Justice, 2006).
3. Hans Reimer, "Socialization in the Prison Community," *Proceedings of the American Prison Association, 1937* (New York: American Prison Association, 1937), pp. 151–155.
4. Donald Clemmer, *The Prison Community* (Boston: Holt, Rinehart and Winston, 1940).
5. Gresham M. Sykes, *The Society of Captives: A Study of a Maximum Security Prison* (Princeton, NJ: Princeton University Press, 1958).
6. Richard A. Cloward et al., *Theoretical Studies in Social Organization of the Prison* (New York: Social Science Research Council, 1960).
7. Donald R. Cressey, ed., *The Prison: Studies in Institutional Organization and Change* (New York: Holt, Rinehart and Winston, 1961).
8. Lawrence Hazelrigg, ed., *Prison within Society: A Reader in Penology* (Garden City, NY: Anchor, 1969), preface.
9. Charles Stastny and Gabrielle Tyrnauer, *Who Rules the Joint? The Changing Political Culture of Maximum-Security Prisons in America* (Lexington, MA: Lexington Books, 1982), p. 131.
10. Erving Goffman, *Asylums: Essays on the Social Situation of Mental Patients and Other Inmates* (Garden City, NY: Anchor, 1961).
11. For a firsthand account of the prison experience, see Victor Hassine, *Life without Parole: Living in Prison Today* (Los Angeles: Roxbury, 1996); and W. Rideau and R. Wikberg, *Life Sentences: Rage and Survival behind Prison Bars* (New York: Times Books, 1992).
12. Gresham M. Sykes and Sheldon L. Messinger, "The Inmate Social System," in Richard A. Cloward et al., eds., *Theoretical Studies in Social Organization of the Prison* (New York: Social Science Research Council, 1960), pp. 5–19.
13. The concept of prisonization is generally attributed to Clemmer, *The Prison Community*, although Quaker penologists of the late eighteenth century were actively concerned with preventing "contamination" (the spread of criminal values) among prisoners.
14. Sykes and Messinger, "The Inmate Social System," p. 5.

15. Stanton Wheeler, "Socialization in Correctional Communities," *American Sociological Review*, Vol. 26 (October 1961), pp. 697–712.
16. Sykes, *The Society of Captives*, p. xiii.
17. As cited in Stastny and Tyrnauer, *Who Rules the Joint?* p. 135.
18. Ibid.
19. Sykes, *The Society of Captives.*
20. Clemmer, *The Prison Community*, pp. 294–296.
21. John Irwin, *The Felon* (Englewood Cliffs, NJ: Prentice Hall, 1970).
22. Public Law 108–79.
23. Allen J. Beck, *Sexual Violence Reported by Correctional Authorities, 2006* (Washington, DC: Bureau of Justice Statistics, 2007).
24. Bureau of Justice Statistics, *Sexual Victimization in Local Jails Reported by Inmates, 2007* (Washington, DC: BJS, 2008).
25. Dee Halley, "The Prison Rape Elimination Act of 2003: Addressing Sexual Assault in Correctional Settings," *Corrections Today* (June 2005), p. 2.
26. Section 261 of the 2008 Second Chance Act (Public Law No. 110–199) amended the Prison Rape Elimination Act of 2003 to extend the date for the report of the National Prison Rape Elimination Commission on the impact of prison rape, thus extending the commission's termination date.
27. Lee H. Bowker, *Prison Victimization* (New York: Elsevier, 1980), p. 42.
28. Ibid., p. 1.
29. Hans Toch, *Living in Prison: The Ecology of Survival* (New York: Free Press, 1977), p. 151.
30. William J. Sabol, Heather C. West, and Matthew Cooper, *Prisoners in 2008* (Washington, DC: Bureau of Justice Statistics, 2010), p. 3.
31. Ibid.
32. Some of the information in this section comes from the American Correctional Association, Task Force on the Female Offender, *The Female Offender: What Does the Future Hold?* (Washington, DC: St. Mary's Press, 1990); and "The View from behind Bars," *Time* (fall 1990, special issue), pp. 20–22.
33. Much of the information and some of the wording in this section come from Barbara Bloom, Barbara Owen, and Stephanie Covington, *Gender-Responsive Strategies: Research, Practice, and Guiding Principles for Women Offenders* (Washington, DC: National Institute of Corrections, 2003).
34. Barbara Bloom, "Triple Jeopardy: Race, Class and Gender as Factors in Women's Imprisonment," paper presented at the annual meeting of the American Society of Criminology, 1997.
35. Joanne Belknap, *The Invisible Woman: Gender, Crime, and Justice* (Belmont, CA: Wadsworth, 2001).
36. Data in this paragraph come from L. E. Glaze and L. M. Maruschak, *Parents in Prison and Their Minor Children* (Washington, DC: Bureau of Justice Statistics, 2008).
37. Mary Jeanette Clement, "National Survey of Programs for Incarcerated Women," paper presented at the annual meeting of the Academy of Criminal Justice Sciences, Nashville, TN, March 1991, pp. 8–9.
38. B. Bloom and D. Steinhart, *Why Punish the Children? A Reappraisal of the Children of Incarcerated Mothers in America* (San Francisco: National Council on Crime and Delinquency, 1993).
39. Barbara Bloom and Stephanie Covington, "Gendered Justice: Programming for Women in Correctional Settings," paper presented at the annual meeting of the American Society of Criminology, San Francisco, November 2000, p. 11.
40. ACA, *The Female Offender.*
41. Marsha Clowers, "Dykes, Gangs, and Danger: Debunking Popular Myths about Maximum Security Life," *Journal of Criminal Justice and Popular Culture*, Vol. 9, No. 1 (2001), pp. 22–30.
42. D. Ward and G. Kassebaum, *Women's Prison: Sex and Social Structure* (London: Weidenfeld and Nicolson, 1966).
43. Esther Heffernan, *Making It in Prison: The Square, the Cool, and the Life* (London: Wiley-Interscience, 1972).
44. Rose Giallombardo, *Society of Women: A Study of Women's Prisons* (New York: John Wiley, 1966).
45. Ibid., p. 136.
46. For a summary of such studies (including some previously unpublished), see Lee H. Bowker, *Prisoner Subcultures* (Lexington, MA: Lexington Books, 1977), p. 86.
47. Giallombardo, *Society of Women*, p. 162.
48. David Ward and Gene Kassebaum, *Women's Prison: Sex and Social Structure* (Piscataway, NJ: Aldine Transaction, 2008).
49. Barbara Owen, *"In the Mix": Struggle and Survival in a Women's Prison* (Albany: State University of New York Press, 1998).
50. Barbara Owen, "Prisons: Prisons for Women—Prison Subcultures," available online at http://law.jrank.org/pages/1802/Prisons-Prisons-Women-Prison-subcultures.html.
51. See Joanne Belknap, Book Review of Barbara Owen, "'In the Mix': Struggle and Survival in a Women's Prison," in *Western Criminology Review* (1999), http://wcr.sonoma.edu/v1n2/belknap.html (accessed April 11, 2009).
52. Mary Koscheski and Christopher Hensley, "Inmate Homosexual Behavior in a Southern Female Correctional Facility," *American Journal of Criminal Justice*, Vol. 25, No. 2 (2001), pp. 269–277.
53. See, for example, Margie J. Phelps, "Sexual Misconduct between Staff and Inmates," *Corrections Technology and Management*, Vol. 12 (1999).
54. Heffernan, *Making It in Prison.*
55. Bowker, *Prison Victimization*, p. 53.
56. Giallombardo, *Society of Women.*
57. "Georgia Indictments Charge Abuse of Female Inmates," *USA Today*, November 16, 1992.
58. Ibid.
59. ACA, *The Female Offender*, p. 39.
60. Kristen A. Hughes, *Justice Expenditure and Employment in the United States, 2003* (Washington, DC: Bureau of Justice Statistics, 2006), p. 7.
61. Ibid., p. 6.
62. Hughes, *Justice Expenditure and Employment in the United States, 2003*, data table 5: "Justice System Employment and Percent Distribution of Full-Time Equivalent Employment, by State and Types of Government."
63. American Correctional Association, "Correctional Officers in Adult Systems," in *Vital Statistics in Corrections* (Laurel, MD: ACA, 2000). "Other" minorities round out the percentages to a total of 100%.
64. Ibid.
65. Ibid.
66. Lucien X. Lombardo, *Guards Imprisoned: Correctional Officers at Work* (New York: Elsevier, 1981), pp. 22–36.
67. Leonard Morgenbesser, "NY State Law Prescribes Psychological Screening for CO Job Applicants," *Correctional Training* (winter 1983), p. 1.
68. "A Sophisticated Approach to Training Prison Guards," *Newsday*, August 12, 1982.
69. "Two Guards Taken Hostage by Inmates at Arizona Prison," *USA Today*, January 18, 2004, http://www.usatoday.com/news/nation/2004-01-18-prison-hostage_x.htm (accessed July 12, 2004).
70. Stastny and Tyrnauer, *Who Rules the Joint?* p. 1.
71. See Frederick Talbott, "Reporting from behind the Walls: Do It before the Siren Wails," *The Quill* (February 1988), pp. 16–21.
72. "Ohio Prison Rebellion Is Ended," *USA Today*, April 22, 1993.

73. "Guards Hurt in Prison Riot," Associated Press, November 11, 2000.
74. "San Quentin Prison Riot Leaves 42 Injured," *USA Today*, August 9, 2005.
75. Ralph Blumenthal, "Gang Fights in Prison Injure 22 and Kill One," *New York Times*, March 29, 2008.
76. See, for example, American Correctional Association, *Riots and Disturbances in Correctional Institutions* (College Park, MD: ACA, 1981); Michael Braswell et al., *Prison Violence in America* (Cincinnati, OH: Anderson, 1985); and R. Conant, "Rioting, Insurrectional and Civil Disorderliness," *American Scholar*, Vol. 37 (summer 1968), pp. 420–433.
77. Robert S. Fong, Ronald E. Vogel, and S. Buentello, "Prison Gang Dynamics: A Look inside the Texas Department of Corrections," in A. V. Merlo and P. Menekos, eds., *Dilemmas and Directions in Corrections* (Cincinnati, OH: Anderson, 1992).
78. Ibid.
79. *Ruiz* v. *Estelle*, 503 F. Supp. 1265 (S.D. Texas, 1980).
80. The facts in this story are taken from *Hope* v. *Pelzer*, 536 U.S. 730 (2002).
81. "Convictions Bar 3.9 Million from Voting," Associated Press, September 22, 2000.
82. *Holt* v. *Sarver*, 309 F. Supp. 362 (E.D. Ark. 1970).
83. Vergil L. Williams, *Dictionary of American Penology: An Introduction* (Westport, CT: Greenwood Press, 1979), pp. 6–7.
84. *Pell* v. *Procunier*, 417 U.S. 817, 822 (1974).
85. Ibid.
86. Title 42 U.S.C.A. 1997, Public Law 104–150.
87. Civil Rights of Institutionalized Persons Act, Section 1997e.
88. American Correctional Association, *Legal Responsibility and Authority of Correctional Officers: A Handbook on Courts, Judicial Decisions and Constitutional Requirements* (College Park, MD: ACA, 1987), p. 8.
89. *Wolff* v. *McDonnell*, 94 S.Ct. 2963 (1974).
90. Ibid.
91. Ibid.
92. *Ponte* v. *Real*, 471 U.S. 491, 105 S.Ct. 2192, 85 L.Ed.2d 553 (1985).
93. *Vitek* v. *Jones*, 445 U.S. 480 (1980).
94. American Correctional Association, Standard 2–4346. See ACA, *Legal Responsibility and Authority of Correctional Officers*, p. 49.
95. *Wilson* v. *Seiter*, 501 U.S. 294 (1991).
96. *Estelle* v. *Gamble*, 429 U.S. 97, 106 (1976).
97. *Sandin* v. *Conner*, 63 U.S.L.W. 4601 (1995).
98. *Wolff* v. *McDonnell*, 94 S.Ct. 2963 (1974).
99. *Hewitt* v. *Helms*, 459 U.S. 460 (1983).
100. *Ali* v. *Federal Bureau of Prisons*, 552 U.S. ___ (2008).
101. 28 U.S.C. Section 1346(b)(1).
102. Laurie Asseo, "Inmate Lawsuits," Associated Press, May 24, 1996; and Bureau of Justice Statistics, "State and Federal Prisoners Filed 68,235 Petitions in U.S. Courts in 1996," press release, October 29, 1997.
103. Ibid.
104. Asseo, "Inmate Lawsuits."
105. 42 U.S.C. Section 1997e(a). Public Law 104–134. Although the PLRA was signed into law on April 26, 1996, and is frequently referred to as the Prison Litigation Reform Act of 1996, the official name of the act is the Prison Litigation Reform Act of 1995.
106. See *Edwards* v. *Balisok*, 520 U.S. 641 (1997); *Booth* v. *Churner*, 532 U.S. 731 (2001); *Porter* v. *Nussle*, 534 U.S. 516 (2002); and *Woodford* v. *Ngo*, 548 U.S. 81 (2006).
107. John Scalia, *Prisoner Petitions Filed in U.S. District Courts, 2000, with Trends 1980–2000* (Washington, DC: Bureau of Justice Statistics, 2002).
108. American Civil Liberties Union, *Prisoners' Rights*, http://www.aclu.org/prisoners-rights (accessed December 3, 2010).
109. Laura M. Maruschak and Randy Beavers, *HIV in Prisons, 2007–2008* (Washington, DC: Bureau of Justice Statistics, 2009).
110. Ibid., p. 1.
111. Dennis Cauchon, "AIDS in Prison: Locked Up and Locked Out," *USA Today*, March 31, 1995.
112. Laura M. Maruschak, *HIV in Prisons, 2003* (Washington, DC: Bureau of Justice Statistics, 2005).
113. Centers for Disease Control and Prevention, "HIV Transmission among Male Inmates in a State Prison System: Georgia, 1992–2005," *Morbidity and Mortality Weekly Report*, Vol. 55, No. 15 (April 21, 2006), pp. 421–426.
114. Theodore M. Hammett, *AIDS in Correctional Facilities: Issues and Options*, 3rd ed. (Washington, DC: National Institute of Justice, 1988), p. 37.
115. At the time of this writing, California, Massachusetts, New York, Wisconsin, and the District of Columbia were among those jurisdictions.
116. "Mississippi Eases Policy of Separating Inmates with HIV," *Corrections Journal*, Vol. 5, No. 6 (2001), p. 5.
117. Cauchon, "AIDS in Prison."
118. See "Court Allows Restriction on HIV-Positive Inmates," *Criminal Justice Newsletter*, Vol. 25, No. 23 (December 1, 1994), pp. 2–3.
119. Ibid.
120. Darrell Bryan, "Inmates, HIV, and the Constitutional Right to Privacy: AIDS in Prison Facilities," *Corrections Compendium*, Vol. 19, No. 9 (September 1994), pp. 1–3.
121. Alexandria Sage, "Doctor Shot at Los Angeles–Area Hospital," Associated Press, September 20, 2003.
122. Lincoln J. Fry, "The Older Prison Inmate: A Profile," *Justice Professional*, Vol. 2, No. 1 (spring 1987), pp. 1–12.
123. Sabol, West, and Cooper, *Prisoners in 2008*, p. 36.
124. "The Nation's Prison Population Grew by 60,000 Inmates Last Year," Bureau of Justice Statistics press release, August 15, 1999.
125. Jim Krane, "Demographic Revolution Rocks U.S. Prisons," APB Online, April 12, 1999, http://www.apbonline.com/safestreets/oldprisoners/mainpris0412.html (accessed January 5, 2006).
126. Ronald Wikbert and Burk Foster, "The Longtermers: Louisiana's Longest Serving Inmates and Why They've Stayed So Long," paper presented at the annual meeting of the Academy of Criminal Justice Sciences, Washington, DC, 1989, p. 51.
127. *Disability Advocates, Inc.* v. *New York State Office of Mental Health*, filed in Federal District Court (NY 2002).
128. Allen J. Beck and Laura M. Maruschak, *Mental Health Treatment in State Prisons, 2000*, BJS Special Report (Washington, DC: Bureau of Justice Statistics, 2001), p. 1, from which most of the information in this paragraph and the next is derived.
129. *Washington* v. *Harper*, 494 U.S. 210 (1990).
130. Paula M. Ditton, *Mental Health and Treatment of Inmates and Probationers* (Washington, DC: Bureau of Justice Statistics, 1999).
131. Robert O. Lampert, "The Mentally Retarded Offender in Prison," *Justice Professional*, Vol. 2, No. 1 (spring 1987), p. 61.
132. Ibid., p. 64.
133. George C. Denkowski and Kathryn M. Denkowski, "The Mentally Retarded Offender in the State Prison System: Identification, Prevalence, Adjustment, and Rehabilitation," *Criminal Justice and Behavior*, Vol. 12 (1985), pp. 55–75.
134. "Opening Session: Kerik Emphasizes the Importance of Corrections' Protective Role for the Country," http://www.aca.org/conferences/Winter05/updates05.asp (accessed July 20, 2007).

135. Jess Maghan, "Intelligence-Led Penology: Management of Crime Information Obtained from Incarcerated Persons," paper presented at the Investigation of Crime World Conference, 2001, p. 6.
136. Keith Martin, *Corrections Prepares for Terrorism*, Corrections Connection News Network, January 21, 2002, http://www.corrections.com (accessed June 15, 2006).
137. Quoted in Meghan Mandeville, "Information Sharing Becomes Crucial to Battling Terrorism behind Bars," Corrections.com, December 8, 2003, http://database.corrections.com/news/results2.asp?ID_8988 (accessed July 11, 2006).
138. "FBI: Al-Qaida Recruiting in U.S. Prisons," United Press International, January 7, 2004, http://database.corrections.com/news/results2.asp?ID_9148 (accessed July 1, 2006).
139. Institute for the Study of Violent Groups, "Land of Wahhabism," *Crime and Justice International* (March/April 2005), p. 43.
140. *International Herald Tribune*, "Man behind U.S. Terrorism Plot Gets 16 Years," March 6, 2009, http://www.iht.com/articles/ap/2009/03/06/america/NA-US-Terrorism-Probe.php (accessed March 27, 2009).
141. Ibid., p. 8.
142. Ibid.
143. Federal Bureau of Prisons, *State of the Bureau, 2004* (Washington, DC: BOP, 2005).
144. Associated Press, "Attorney, Three Others Indicted for Alleged 'Support of Terrorism,'" *Dallas Morning News*, April 9, 2002, http://www.dallasnews.com/latestnews/stories/040902dnnatterrorindictment.66910.html (accessed July 25, 2003).

Chapter 13: Juvenile Justice

i. Jeffrey A. Butts and Ojmarrh Mitchell, "Brick by Brick: Dismantling the Border between Juvenile and Adult Justice," in Phyllis McDonald and Janice Munsterman, eds., *Boundary Changes in Criminal Justice Organizations*, Vol. 2 of *Criminal Justice 2000* (Washington, DC: National Institute of Justice, 2000), pp. 167–213.
ii. Howard N. Snyder and Melissa Sickmund, *Juvenile Offenders and Victims: 2006 National Report* (Washington, DC: Office of Juvenile Justice and Delinquency Prevention, 2006).
iii. John W. Whitehead, *The Stealing of America* (Wheaton, IL: Crossway Books, 1983).

---

1. Prepared Remarks of Attorney General Alberto R. Gonzales at the Protect Our Children conference, Kansas City, Missouri, September 14, 2006.
2. Elliot Grossman, "Toughlove Parents Scared," *Allentown (PA) Morning Call*, March 7, 1995.
3. Rich Phillips, "Florida Teens Accused of Burning Boy Plead Not Guilty," CNN Justice, November 19, 2009, http://www.cnn.com/2009/CRIME/11/19/florida.burned.boy/index.html (accessed May 22, 2010).
4. Edecio Martinez, "Michael Brewer, Florida Teen Set on Fire, Expected Attack," January 13, 2010, CBS News, http://www.cbsnews.com/8301-504083_162-6087018-504083.html (accessed October 8, 2010).
5. "9-Year-Old Pleads Guilty to Manslaughter," Associated Press, October 8, 2005, http://www.msnbc.com/id/9626361 (accessed May 20, 2006).
6. "Florida Girls Charged with Attempting to Drown Classmate," Associated Press, March 14, 2001.
7. Sarah Netter, Anne Marie Dorning, and Polson Kanneth, "Mother of Severely Burned Florida Boy Pleads for End to Childhood Violence," ABC's *Good Morning America*, October 15, 2009, http://abcnews.go.com/GMA/mother-burned-boy-teens-accused-setting-son-fire/story?id=8831563&page=2 (accessed May 22, 2010).
8. Office of Juvenile Justice and Delinquency Prevention, *OJJDP Research, 2000* (Washington, DC: OJJDP, 2001).
9. Federal Bureau of Investigation, *Crime in the United States, 2009*, http://www.fbi.gov/about-us/cjis/ucr/crime-in-the-u.s/2009 (accessed October 8, 2010), from which many of the statistics are taken.
10. Ibid.; and U.S. Census Bureau, *Age, 2000: A Census 2000 Brief* (Washington, DC: U.S. Census Bureau, 2001), http://www.census.gov/prod/2001pubs/c2kbr01-12.pdf (accessed January 2, 2008).
11. The term *juvenile* refers to people under 18 years of age.
12. H. Snyder, C. Puzzanchera, and W. Kang, *Easy Access to FBI Arrest Statistics, 1994–2002* (Washington, DC: Office of Juvenile Justice and Delinquency Prevention, 2005), http://ojjdp.ncjrs.org/ojstatbb/ezaucr (accessed November 11, 2008).
13. A reform movement, now under way, may soon lead to changes in the way juvenile records are handled.
14. For an excellent review of the handling of juveniles throughout history, see Wiley B. Sanders, ed., *Juvenile Offenders for a Thousand Years* (Chapel Hill: University of North Carolina Press, 1970).
15. Robert M. Mennel, *Thorns and Thistles: Juvenile Delinquents in the United States, 1925–1940* (Hanover, NH: University Press of New England, 1973).
16. See Sanford Fox, "Juvenile Justice Reform: An Historical Perspective," in Sanford Fox, ed., *Modern Juvenile Justice: Cases and Materials* (St. Paul, MN: West, 1972), pp. 15–48.
17. Anthony Platt, *The Child Savers: The Invention of Delinquency*, 2nd ed. (Chicago: University of Chicago Press, 1977).
18. Thomas A. Johnson, *Introduction to the Juvenile Justice System* (St. Paul, MN: West, 1975), p. 3.
19. Ibid.
20. Ibid.
21. Fox, "Juvenile Justice Reform," p. 47.
22. Ibid., p. 5.
23. Principles adapted from Robert G. Caldwell, "The Juvenile Court: Its Development and Some Major Problems," in Rose Giallombardo, ed., *Juvenile Delinquency: A Book of Readings* (New York: John Wiley, 1966), p. 358.
24. See, for example, *Haley* v. *Ohio*, 332 U.S. 596 (1948).
25. *Kent* v. *U.S.*, 383 U.S. 541 (1966).
26. *In re Gault*, 387 U.S. 1 (1967).
27. *In re Winship*, 397 U.S. 358 (1970).
28. *McKeiver* v. *Pennsylvania*, 403 U.S. 528 (1971).
29. *Breed v. Jones*, 421 U.S. 519 (1975).
30. *Schall* v. *Martin*, 467 U.S. 253 (1984).
31. *Thompson* v. *Oklahoma*, 487 U.S. 815, 818–838 (1988).
32. *Roper* v. *Simmons*, 543 U.S. 551 (2005).
33. Death Penalty Information Center, "Juvenile Offenders Currently on Death Row, or Executed, by State," http://www.deathpenaltyinfo.org/article.php?scid527&did5882 (accessed September 10, 2007).
34. *Graham* v. *Florida*, U.S. Supreme Court, No. 08–7412 (decided May 17, 2010).
35. President's Commission on Law Enforcement and Administration of Justice, *The Challenge of Crime in a Free Society* (Washington, DC: U.S. Government Printing Office, 1967).
36. "Drug Bill Includes Extension of OJJDP, with Many Changes," *Criminal Justice Newsletter*, Vol. 19, No. 22 (November 15, 1988), p. 4.
37. The Formula Grants Program supports state and local delinquency prevention and intervention efforts and juvenile justice system improvements. Through this program, OJJDP provides funds directly to states, territories, and the District of Columbia to help them implement comprehensive state juvenile justice plans based on detailed studies of needs in

their jurisdictions. The Formula Grants Program is authorized under the JJDP Act of 2002 (42 U.S.C. 5601 *et seq.*).
38. See "OJJDP Eases Rules on Juvenile Confinement," *Corrections Compendium* (November 1996), p. 25.
39. Juvenile Justice and Delinquency Prevention Act of 2002 (Public Law 107–273).
40. Howard N. Snyder and Melissa Sickmund, *Juvenile Offenders and Victims: 2006 National Report* (Washington, DC: Office of Juvenile Justice and Delinquency Prevention, 2006).
41. Ibid., p. 97.
42. See, for example, *U.S.* v. *Williams*, 553 U.S. 285 (2008), which upheld the law's provision criminalizing the possession and distribution of material pandered as child pornography; and U.S. Department of State, *Trafficking in Persons Report* (Washington, DC: U.S. Department of State, June 2007), p. 72.
43. *Fare* v. *Michael C.*, 442 U.S. 707 (1979).
44. *California* v. *Prysock*, 453 U.S. 355 (1981).
45. *New Jersey* v. *T.L.O.*, 105 S.Ct. 733 (1985).
46. Office of Juvenile Justice and Delinquency Prevention, "Juvenile Court Cases," *Statistical Briefing Book*, http://ojjdp.ncjrs.gov/ojstatbb/court/qa06201.asp (accessed June 1, 2009).
47. National Center for Juvenile Justice, *State Juvenile Justice Profiles*, http://www.ncjj.org/stateprofiles (accessed August 10, 2008).
48. Charles M. Puzzanchera, *Delinquency Cases Waived to Criminal Court, 1990–1999* (Washington, DC: Office of Juvenile Justice and Delinquency Prevention, 2003).
49. Adapted from Peter Greenwood, *Juvenile Offenders: A Crime File Study Guide* (Washington, DC: National Institute of Justice, n.d.).
50. Bureau of Justice Statistics, *Report to the Nation on Crime and Justice*, 2nd ed. (Washington, DC: U.S. Government Printing Office, 1988), p. 78.
51. Ibid.
52. Ibid.
53. Anne L. Stahl et al., *Juvenile Court Statistics, 2003–2004* (Washington, DC: Office of Juvenile Justice and Delinquency Prevention, 2007), various pages.
54. Ibid.
55. *McKeiver* v. *Pennsylvania*, 403 U.S. 528 (1971).
56. Some states, like West Virginia, do provide juveniles with a statutory right to trial.
57. Other early peer juries in juvenile courts began operating in Denver, Colorado; Duluth, Minnesota; Deerfield, Illinois; Thompkins County, New York; and Spanish Fork City, Utah, at about the same time. See Philip Reichel and Carole Seyfrit, "A Peer Jury in the Juvenile Court," *Crime and Delinquency*, Vol. 30, No. 3 (July 1984), pp. 423–438.
58. Ibid.
59. Tracy M. Godwin, *A Guide for Implementing Teen Court Programs* (Washington, DC: Office of Juvenile Justice and Delinquency Prevention, 1996).
60. Stahl et al., *Juvenile Court Statistics, 2003–2004*, p. 56.
61. Ibid.
62. Charles M. Puzzanchera, *Juvenile Delinquency Probation Caseload, 1990–1999* (Washington, DC: Office of Juvenile Justice and Delinquency Prevention, 2003), p. 1.
63. Melissa Sickmund, T. J. Sladky, and Wei Kang, *Census of Juveniles in Residential Placement Databook*, http://www.ojjdp.ncjrs.gov/ojstatbb/cjrp (accessed October 8, 2010).
64. Ibid. Figures do not total 100% due to rounding.
65. See, for example, Blair B. Bourque et al., "Boot Camps for Juvenile Offenders: An Implementation Evaluation of Three Demonstration Programs," *NIJ Research in Brief* (Washington, DC: National Institute of Justice, 1996).
66. Melissa Sickmund, *Juvenile Offenders in Residential Placement, 1997* (Washington, DC: Office of Juvenile Justice and Delinquency Prevention, 2002), p. 110.
67. Ibid.
68. Ibid.
69. Ibid.
70. Sickmund, Sladky, and Kang, *Census of Juveniles in Residential Placement Databook.*
71. Ibid.
72. "Juvenile Offenders in Residential Placement, 1997," in *Office of Juvenile Justice and Delinquency Prevention Fact Sheet* (Washington, DC: OJJDP, 1999).
73. Dale G. Parent et al., *Conditions of Confinement: Juvenile Detention and Corrections Facilities* (Washington, DC: Office of Juvenile Justice and Delinquency Prevention, 1994).
74. *Corrections Compendium* (December 1993), p. 14.
75. Ibid.
76. Ibid., p. 22.
77. Office of Juvenile Justice and Delinquency Prevention, *National Juvenile Custody Trends, 1978–1989* (Washington, DC: U.S. Department of Justice, 1992), p. 2.
78. Section 59 of the Uniform Juvenile Court Act recommends the granting of a right to appeal for juveniles (National Conference of Commissioners on Uniform State Laws, Uniform Juvenile Court Act, 1968).
79. Mark Memmott, "Release of Ark. School Killer Raises Questions of Justice," *USA Today*, August 12, 2005.
80. Patricia Torbet et al., *State Responses to Serious and Violent Juvenile Crime* (Washington, DC: Office of Juvenile Justice and Delinquency Prevention, 1996).
81. Snyder and Sickmund, *Juvenile Offenders and Victims*, pp. 96–97.
82. Jeffrey A. Butts and Ojmarrh Mitchell, "Brick by Brick: Dismantling the Border between Juvenile and Adult Justice," in Phyllis McDonald and Janice Munsterman, eds., *Criminal Justice 2000, Vol. 2: Boundary Changes in Criminal Justice Organizations* (Washington, DC: National Institute of Justice, 2000), p. 207.
83. Ibid., p. 167.
84. Ibid., pp. 167–213.
85. Barry C. Feld, "Abolish the Juvenile Court: Youthfulness, Criminal Responsibility, and Sentencing Policy," *Journal of Criminal Law and Criminology* (winter 1998), pp. 68–136.
86. Cindy S. Lederman, "The Juvenile Court: Putting Research to Work for Prevention," *Juvenile Justice*, Vol. 6, No. 2 (1999), p. 23.
87. American Academy of Child and Adolescent Psychiatry Task Force on Juvenile Justice Reform, *Recommendations for Juvenile Justice Reform* (Washington, DC: AACAP, 2001).
88. Public Law 107–273.
89. Activities funded under the legislation fall under the Juvenile Accountability Block Grants (JABG) program.
90. See Cheryl Andrews and Lynn Marble, "Changes to OJJDP's Juvenile Accountability Program," *Juvenile Justice Bulletin* (Washington, DC: OJJDP, 2003).
91. Ryan S. King, *The State of Sentencing, 2007: Developments in Policy and Practice* (Washington, DC: Sentencing Project, 2008), p. 19.
92. Much of the information and some of the wording in this paragraph are taken from ibid., p. 21.

Glossary

1. All boldfaced terms are explained whenever possible using definitions provided by the Bureau of Justice Statistics under a mandate of the Justice System Improvement Act of 1979. That mandate found its most complete expression in the *Dictionary of Criminal Justice Data Terminology* (Washington, DC: Bureau of Justice Statistics, 1982), the second edition of which provides the wording for many definitions in this text.

2. Adapted from U.S. Code, Title 28, Section 20.3 (2[d]). Title 28 of the U.S. Code defines the term *administration of criminal justice.*
3. Technical Working Group on Crime Scene Investigation, *Crime Scene Investigation: A Guide for Law Enforcement* (Washington, DC: National Institute of Justice, 2000), p. 12.
4. Howard N. Snyder and Melissa Sickmund, *Juvenile Offenders and Victims: 2006 National Report* (Washington, DC: Office of Juvenile Justice and Delinquency Prevention, 2006).
5. Adapted from Gerald Hill and Kathleen Hill, *The Real Life Dictionary of the Law*, http://www.law.com (accessed June 11, 2008).
6. Office of Community Oriented Policing Services,*Community Policing Defined* (Washington, DC: U.S. Department of Justice, 2009), p. 3.
7. Jeremy Travis and Sarah Lawrence, *Beyond the Prison Gates: The State of Parole in America* (Washington, DC: Urban Institute Press, 2002), p. 3.
8. Michael L. Benson, Francis T. Cullen, and William J. Maakestad, *Local Prosecutors and Corporate Crime* (Washington, DC: National Institute of Justice, 1992), p. 1.
9. Office of Justice Programs, *The National Criminal Intelligence Sharing Plan* (Washington, DC: U.S. Department of Justice, 2005), p. 27.
10. Violence against Women Office, *Stalking and Domestic Violence: Report to Congress* (Washington, DC: U.S. Department of Justice, 2001), p. 5.
11. Sam W. Lathrop, "Reviewing Use of Force: A Systematic Approach," *FBI Law Enforcement Bulletin* (October 2000), p. 18.
12. Adapted from Larry R. Leibrock, "Overview and Impact on 21st Century Legal Practice: Digital Forensics and Electronic Discovery," no date, http://www.courtroom21.net/FDIC.pps (accessed July 5, 2008).
13. Federal Bureau of Investigation, *FBI Policy and Guidelines: Counterterrorism*, http://www.fbi.gov/contact/fo/jackson/cntrterr.htm (accessed August 26, 2002).
14. Adapted from Technical Working Group for Electronic Crime Scene Investigation, *Electronic Crime Scene Investigation: A Guide for First Responders* (Washington, DC: National Institute of Justice, 2001), p. 2.
15. Henry Campbell Black, Joseph R. Nolan, and Jacqueline M. Nolan-Haley, *Black's Law Dictionary*, 6th ed. (St. Paul, MN: West, 1990), p. 24.
16. Lawrence W. Sherman, *Evidence-Based Policing* (Washington, DC: Police Foundation, 1998), p. 3.
17. International Association of Chiefs of Police, *Police Use of Force in America, 2001* (Alexandria, VA: IACP, 2001), p. 1.
18. Identity Theft Resource Center website, http://www.idtheftcenter.org (accessed April 24, 2008).
19. Angus Smith, ed., *Intelligence-Led Policing* (Richmond, VA: International Association of Law Enforcement Intelligence Analysts, 1997), p. 1.
20. Ibid.
21. Jeremy Travis and Sarah Lawrence, *Beyond the Prison Gates: The State of Parole in America* (Washington, DC: Urban Institute Press, 2002), p. 3.
22. Adapted from Robert M. Shusta et al., *Multicultural Law Enforcement*, 2nd ed. (Upper Saddle River, NJ: Prentice Hall, 2002), p. 443.
23. The Organized Crime Control Act of 1970.
24. Carl B. Klockars et al., *The Measurement of Police Integrity*, National Institute of Justice Research in Brief (Washington, DC: NIJ, 2000), p. 1.
25. National Institute of Justice, *Use of Force by Police: Overview of National and Local Data* (Washington, DC: NIJ, 1999).
26. Paige M. Harrison and Allen J. Beck, *Prisoners in 2005* (Washington, DC: Bureau of Justice Statistics, 2006), p. 7.
27. Samuel Walker, Geoffrey P. Albert, and Dennis J. Kenney, *Responding to the Problem Police Officer: A National Study of Early Warning Systems* (Washington, DC: National Institute of Justice, 2000).
28. Deborah Ramirez, Jack McDevitt, and Amy Farrell, *A Resource Guide on Racial Profiling Data Collection Systems: Promising Practices and Lessons Learned* (Washington, DC: U.S. Department of Justice, 2000), p. 3.
29. Sam S. Souryal, *Police Administration and Management* (St. Paul, MN: West, 1977), p. 261.
30. Federal Bureau of Investigation Counterterrorism Section, *Terrorism in the United States, 1987* (Washington, DC: FBI, December 1987).
31. Daniel Oran, *Oran's Dictionary of the Law* (St. Paul, MN: West, 1983), p. 306.
32. Lawrence A. Greenfeld, *Prison Sentences and Time Served for Violence*, Bureau of Justice Statistics Selected Findings, No. 4 (Washington, DC: Bureau of Justice Statistics, April 1995).

Name Index

A

Adams, Kenneth, 180
Alpert, Geoffrey, 180
al-Timimi, Ali, 64
Arenella, Peter, 82

B

Baca, Lee, 319
Baime, David, 279
Barker, Thomas, 159
Barr, William P., 316
Bazelon, David, 79
Bell, Sean, 115
Bittner, Egon, 103
Blagojevich, Rod R., 284
Bloomberg, Michael R., 115
Bowker, Lee H., 338, 344
Braithwaite, John, 264
Bratton, William J., 160
Brennan, Pauline K., 42
Breyer, Stephen, 275
Broderick, Mary, 224
Brummer, Bennett, 226
Burger, Warren E., 122–123, 199
Bush, George W., 4
Butts, Jeffrey, 383

C

Cardozo, Benjamin, 119
Carter, David L., 106, 159, 171
Clark, Tom C., 219
Clemmer, Donald, 333, 335, 336
Cloward, Richard A., 333
Clowers, Marsha, 342
Cohen, Anne, 182
Cole, David, 177–178
Cooper, Roy A., 220
Cressey, Donald R., 333
Cummins, Elaine, 98

D

D'Amuro, Pasquale, 56
Daufenbach, Donald, 52
Davies, John G., 246
Davis, Kenneth Culp, 111
Dezhbakhsh, Hashem, 279
Dimino, Maureen, 226
Disraeli, Benjamin, 7
Douglas, Anthony, 74–75
Downing, Michael P., 101, 177
Dunham, Roger, 180

E

Ellis, Chip, 362

F

Fagan, Jeffrey, 277
Fairstein, Linda, 44
Floyd, Craig, 165
Free, Marvin, Jr., 42
Fuhrman, Mark, 84–85
Fukuyama, Francis, 85
Fyfe, James, 181–182

G

Garczynski, John T., Jr., 182
Gendreau, Paul, 319
Giallombardo, Rose, 342
Giuliani, Rudolph W., 6, 107
Goffman, Erving, 333
Goggin, Claire, 319
Grabosky, Peter, 52
Gramm, Phil, 4
Grammer, Lon, 37
Greenberg, David F., 314
Gross, Samuel R., 235
Guinier, Lani, 35

H

Hagan, Frank, 42
Hagan, John, 42
Hamilton, Alexander, 203
Hinckley, John, 81

I

Irwin, John, 335

J

Jeffs, Warren Steed, 15
Jensen, Carl J., III, 111
Johnson, Calvin, 84
Johnson, Frank M., 350

K

Kahan, Dan, 264
Kassebaum, G., 342
Kelley, Douglas M., 183
Kelling, George, 104
Kennedy, John F., 60
Kerik, Bernard B., 362
King, Martin Luther, Jr., 7
King, Rodney, 116, 246
Klockars, Carl B., 158

L

Langworthy, Robert H., 90
Lederman, Cindy, 384
Leo, Richard A., 140
Leon, Alberto, 123
Liebman, James S., 277
Little, Tracy, 319
Lombardo, Lucien X., 345

M

Madoff, Bernard, 47
Maghan, Jess, 362
Marshall, John, 203
Marshall, Thurgood, 238
Masella, Joe, 347
Mauer, Marc, 250
McCarthy, Andy, 351
McCorkle, Richard C., 43
McVeigh, Timothy, 89, 224–225
Messinger, Sheldon, 334
Miethe, Terance D., 43
Mincs, Michael, 97
Mitchell, Ojmarrh, 383
Morris, Norval, 21
Mueller, Robert S., III, 55, 94–95, 106

N

Neufeld, Peter, 277
Nifong, Michael B., 220
Nunn, Annetta W., 186

O

Obama, Barack H., 7
Onley, Charles, 189
Owen, Barbara, 343
Owens, Dan, 255

P

Packer, Herbert, 13
Palmiotto, Michael, 158
Parker, William H., 14

Parks, Bernard, 160
Peel, Sir Robert, 88
Perry, Frank, 159
Peterson, Ruth D., 42
Pierce, Don, 189
Pollitt, Mark M., 55

Q

Quinlan, J. Michael, 317

R

Rehnquist, William, 274
Reimer, Hans, 333
Rifkind, Simon H., 277
Robinson, Laurie O., 14, 15
Rodriguez, Edward, 123
Rothwax, Harold J., 246
Rush, Benjamin, 275
Russell, Katheryn K., 35
Ryan, George, 277, 284

S

Scheck, Barry, 277
Schuman, Alan, 262, 317
Serpico, Frank, 160
Shearer, Robert, 290
Sherman, Lawrence W., 109
Shusta, Robert M., 158
Simpson, O. J., 84–85, 246
Skolnick, Jerome H., 10, 104, 156, 316
Stephens, Gene, 100–101
Stewart, Lynne, 225, 226
Stewart, Potter, 129, 280
Stincelli, Rebecca, 182
Sutherland, Edwin, 161
Swanson, Charles R., 91, 173
Sykes, Gresham, 333, 334, 336

T

Tenet, George, 56
Thomas, Clarence, 6
Thorpe, Janet, 135
Tonry, Michael, 263
Trojanowicz, Robert, 104

V

Van Duyn, Don, 98
Van Zandt, Clinton R., 89
Vick, Michael, 303–304
Vila, Bryan, 169
Vollmer, August, 14, 186

W

Ward, D., 342
Warren, Earl, 117
Webster, William, 92
Westley, William, 156
Wheeler, Stanton, 334
Wilbanks, William, 42
Wilkins, William W., Jr., 258
Wilson, James Q., 101
Wilson, Orlando W., 14, 186
Woolsey, R. James, 48

Z

Zuckerberg, Mark, 36
Zupan, Linda, 325

Case Index

A

Aguilar v. *Texas*, 139
Ake v. *Oklahoma*, 82
Alabama v. *Shelton*, 223
Alabama v. *White*, 139
Ali v. *Federal Bureau of Prisons*, 358
Allen v. *U.S.*, 245
Anders v. *California*, 225
Apprendi v. *New Jersey*, 260, 282
Argersinger v. *Hamlin*, 223
Arizona v. *Evans*, 120, 124, 125
Arizona v. *Fulminante*, 125, 141, 142
Arizona v. *Gant*, 134
Arizona v. *Hicks*, 124
Arizona v. *Johnson*, 125
Arizona v. *Mauro*, 147
Arizona v. *Roberson*, 142
Arkansas v. *Sanders*, 133
Ashcraft v. *Tennessee*, 141
Atkins v. *Virginia*, 282

B

Barker v. *Wingo*, 236
Batson v. *Kentucky*, 238
Baze v. *Rees*, 282, 284
Bearden v. *Georgia*, 296
Beckwith v. *U.S.*, 125
Bell v. *Wolfish*, 355
Berger v. *New York*, 149
Biscoe v. *Arlington County*, 173
Bivens v. *Six Unknown Federal Agents*, 174, 391
Blakely v. *Washington*, 260
Block v. *Rutherford*, 355
Board of the County Commissioners of Bryan County, Oklahoma v. *Brown*, 174
Bond v. *U.S.*, 138
Booth v. *Churner*, 354
Borchardt v. *U.S.*, 125
Bounds v. *Smith*, 355
Brady v. *Maryland*, 220
Brecht v. *Abrahamson*, 147
Breed v. *Jones*, 371, 372, 385
Brendlin v. *California*, 135
Brewer v. *Williams*, 145
Brigham City v. *Stuart*, 120, 125, 126
Brown v. *Mississippi*, 140, 141
Brown v. *Texas*, 132
Burns v. *Reed*, 221

C

California v. *Acevedo*, 125
California v. *Carney*, 125, 136
California v. *Ciraolo*, 125
California v. *Greenwood*, 125, 164
California v. *Hodari D.*, 133
Campbell v. *Louisiana*, 239
Campbell v. *Wood*, 283
Caribbean International News Corporation v. *Puerto Rico*, 233
Carroll v. *U.S.*, 125, 134
Chambers v. *Florida*, 141
Chapman v. *California*, 142
Chimel v. *California*, 121, 122, 125
City of Canton, Ohio v. *Harris*, 174
Coker v. *Georgia*, 282
Coleman v. *Thompson*, 274
Colorado v. *Bertine*, 134
Colorado v. *Connelly*, 146
Colorado v. *Spring*, 145
Coolidge v. *New Hampshire*, 125
Cooper v. *Morin*, 355
Correctional Services Corporation v. *Malesko*, 330
County of Riverside v. *McLaughlin*, 206
Coy v. *Iowa*, 242
Crawford v. *Washington*, 243
Crosby v. *U.S.*, 232
Cruz v. *Beto*, 355
Cunningham v. *California*, 260

D

Davis v. *Dallas*, 185
Davis v. *U.S.*, 142
Davis v. *Washington*, 243
Deck v. *Missouri*, 282
Delaware v. *Prouse*, 130
Demarest v. *Manspeaker et al.*, 230
Dickerson v. *U.S.*, 144
District of Columbia v. *Heller*, 50
Doggett v. *U.S.*, 236
Doyle v. *Ohio*, 147
Durham v. *U.S.*, 79

E

Edwards v. *Arizona*, 142
Elledge v. *Florida*, 275
Escobedo v. *Illinois*, 141, 142
Escoe v. *Zerbst*, 296
Estelle v. *Gamble*, 355, 356

F

Faretta v. *California*, 225
Felker v. *Turpin*, 274
Fex v. *Michigan*, 236
Florida v. *Bostick*, 137
Florida v. *Jimeno*, 124, 135
Florida v. *J. L.*, 140
Florida v. *Powell*, 147
Florida v. *Riley*, 125
Florida v. *Wells*, 134
Ford v. *Georgia*, 238
Ford v. *Wainwright*, 81
Foucha v. *Louisiana*, 82
Furman v. *Georgia*, 280, 281, 282

G

Gagnon v. *Scarpelli*, 296
Gall v. *U.S.*, 261
Georgia v. *McCollum*, 239
Georgia v. *Randolph*, 122
Gideon v. *Wainwright*, 12, 222, 223
Graham v. *Connor*, 181
Graham v. *Florida*, 371, 373
Greenholtz v. *Nebraska Penal Inmates*, 296
Gregg v. *Georgia*, 276, 282
Griffin v. *California*, 242
Griffin v. *Wisconsin*, 294, 296, 310

H

Harris v. *U.S.*, 120, 124, 125
Hayes v. *Florida*, 148
Helling v. *McKinney*, 354
Herrera v. *Collins*, 199
Herring v. *U.S.*, 120, 124, 125
Hester v. *U.S.*, 125
Hewitt v. *Helms*, 357
Hiibel v. *Sixth Judicial District Court of Nevada*, 125, 132
Hope v. *Pelzer*, 354
Horton v. *California*, 125, 126
Hudson v. *Michigan*, 120, 125, 127
Hudson v. *Palmer*, 354
Hunter v. *Bryant*, 175

I

Idaho v. *Horiuchi*, 176
Idaho v. *Wright*, 243
Illinois v. *Caballes*, 136
Illinois v. *Gates*, 139
Illinois v. *Krull*, 120, 123, 125
Illinois v. *Lidster*, 136
Illinois v. *McArthur*, 127
Illinois v. *Perkins*, 125, 146
Illinois v. *Rodriguez*, 123
Imbler v. *Pachtman*, 221
Indiana v. *Edwards*, 83
Indianapolis v. *Edmond*, 130

In re Gault, 223, 370, 371, 375, 385
In re Kemmler, 280, 283
In re Winship, 370, 371, 385

J

J.E.B. v. *Alabama*, 239
Johnson v. *Avery*, 353, 355
Johnson v. *California*, 321, 354
Johnson v. *Zerbst*, 223
Jones v. *North Carolina Prisoners' Labor Union, Inc.*, 355
Jones v. *U.S.*, 82

K

Katz v. *U.S.*, 149
Keeney v. *Tamayo-Reyes*, 199
Kennedy v. *Louisiana*, 273
Kent v. *United States*, 370, 371, 385
Khulmann v. *Wilson*, 125, 146
Kirk v. *Louisiana*, 131
Klopfer v. *North Carolina*, 236
Knowles v. *Iowa*, 135
Kyllo v. *U.S.*, 138

L

Lee v. *Florida*, 149
Lee v. *U.S.*, 149
Lewis v. *Casey*, 354
Leyra v. *Denno*, 142
Lopez v. *U.S.*, 149

M

Malley v. *Briggs*, 173
Mapp v. *Ohio*, 120, 121
Marbury v. *Madison*, 204
Maryland v. *Buie*, 125, 126
Maryland v. *Craig*, 242
Maryland v. *Garrison*, 120, 123
Maryland v. *Wilson*, 135
Massachusetts v. *Sheppard*, 123
McCleskey v. *Kemp*, 276, 279
McCleskey v. *Zant*, 274
McDonald v. *City of Chicago*, 50
McKeiver v. *Pennsylvania*, 370, 371, 379, 385
McNabb v. *U.S.*, 205, 206
Melendez v. *U.S.*, 259
Mempa v. *Rhay*, 296
MGM v. *Grokster*, 53
Michigan v. *Jackson*, 142, 143
Michigan v. *Lucas*, 240
Michigan v. *Sitz*, 130
Michigan Dept. of State Police v. *Sitz*, 136
Miller-El v. *Cockrell*, 239
Miller-El v. *Dretke*, 239
Mincey v. *Arizona*, 126
Minnesota v. *Carter*, 122
Minnesota v. *Dickerson*, 132
Minnesota v. *Murphy*, 296
Minnesota v. *Olson*, 121
Minnick v. *Mississippi*, 141, 142
Miranda v. *Arizona*, 117, 143, 153, 396
Missouri v. *Seibert*, 147
Mistretta v. *U.S.*, 258
Monroe v. *Pape*, 355
Montejo v. *Louisiana*, 125, 143
Moran v. *Burbine*, 145
Morrissey v. *Brewer*, 296
Muehler v. *Mena*, 129
Mu'Min v. *Virginia*, 237

N

National Treasury Employees Union v. *Von Raab*, 137
Nebraska Press Association v. *Stuart*, 233
New Jersey v. *T.L.O.*, 374
New York v. *Belton*, 125
New York v. *Quarles*, 125, 146
Nix v. *Whiteside*, 227
Nix v. *Williams*, 125, 145

O

Ohio v. *Reiner*, 242
Oliver v. *U.S.*, 125
Olmstead v. *U.S.*, 148
O'Lone v. *Estate of Shabazz*, 354
Oregon v. *Ice*, 261
Ornelas v. *U.S.*, 125, 134
Overton v. *Bazzetta*, 354

P

Payne v. *Tennessee*, 277
Payton v. *New York*, 130
Pearson et al. v. *Callahan*, 175
Pell v. *Procunier*, 130, 350, 391
Pennsylvania Board of Probation and Parole v. *Scott*, 295, 296, 310
People v. *Deutsch*, 138
People v. *Wende*, 225
Ponte v. *Real*, 354, 356
Porter v. *Nussle*, 354
Powell v. *Alabama*, 222
Powers v. *Ohio*, 239
Poyner v. *Murray*, 283
Preston v. *U.S.*, 134
Procunier v. *Martinez*, 355

R

Reno v. *ACLU*, 150
Rhodes v. *Chapman*, 318, 355
Richards v. *Wisconsin*, 125, 127
Richardson v. *McKnight*, 329
Ring v. *Arizona*, 261, 282, 283
Rita v. *U.S.*, 261
Rock v. *Zimmerman*, 146
Roper v. *Simmons*, 282, 283, 371, 373, 385
Roth v. *United States*, 64
Ruiz v. *Estelle*, 355

S

Samson v. *California*, 296
Sandin v. *Conner*, 354, 357
Saucier v. *Katz*, 175
Schall v. *Martin*, 371, 372, 385
Schlup v. *Delo*, 274
Schmerber v. *California*, 148
Schriro v. *Summerlin*, 282
Scott v. *Harris*, 175
Sell v. *U.S.*, 212
Silverthorne Lumber Co. v. *U.S.*, 120, 121, 144
Skinner v. *Railway Labor Executives' Association*, 137
Smith v. *Ohio*, 132
Smith v. *Robbins*, 225
Snyder v. *Louisiana*, 239
South Dakota v. *Opperman*, 134
Stansbury v. *California*, 125, 129
State v. *Kindle*, 72
Strunk v. *U.S.*, 236

T

Tennessee v. *Garner*, 180
Terry v. *Ohio*, 125, 131
Texas v. *Cobb*, 225
The Crown v. *Dudly & Stephens*, 76
Thiel v. *Southern Pacific Co.*, 231
Thompson v. *Keohane*, 125
Thompson v. *Oklahoma*, 373
Thornton v. *U.S.*, 125, 136
Turner v. *Safley*, 354

U

U.S. v. *Arvizu*, 132
U.S. v. *Bagley*, 220
U.S. v. *Banks*, 125
U.S. v. *Barnes*, 125
U.S. v. *Booker*, 260
U.S. v. *Borchardt*, 133
U.S. v. *Brady*, 120
U.S. v. *Brawner*, 80
U.S. v. *Carey*, 153
U.S. v. *Dickerson*, 144
U.S. v. *Drayton*, 138
U.S. v. *Dunn*, 125
U.S. v. *Edwards*, 125
U.S. v. *Fanfan*, 260
U.S. v. *Flores-Montano*, 138
U.S. v. *George*, 354
U.S. v. *Grubbs*, 128
U.S. v. *Harris*, 139
U.S. v. *Hazzard*, 211
U.S. v. *Hill*, 137
U.S. v. *Hitchcock*, 355
U.S. v. *Irizarry*, 124
U.S. v. *Karo*, 149
U.S. v. *Knights*, 296, 310
U.S. v. *Leon*, 120, 122, 123, 125
U.S. v. *Martinez-Fuerte*, 136
U.S. v. *Mendenhall*, 125, 129
U.S. v. *Montalvo-Murillo*, 211
U.S. v. *Montoya de Hernandez*, 148
U.S. v. *O'Brien*, 260

U.S. v. *Patane*, 125, 144
U.S. v. *Rabinowitz*, 125
U.S. v. *Robinson*, 131
U.S. v. *Ross*, 125, 135
U.S. v. *Scott*, 149
U.S. v. *Sokolow*, 131
U.S. v. *Taylor*, 236
U.S. v. *Turner*, 153
U.S. v. *Villamonte-Marquez*, 136
U.S. v. *White*, 149
U.S. Dept. of Justice v. *Landano*, 140

V

Vitek v. *Jones*, 356

W

Warden v. *Hayden*, 125, 126
Washington v. *Harper*, 354
Weeks v. *U.S.*, 119, 120
White v. *Illinois*, 243
Whitley v. *Albers*, 354
Whren v. *U.S.*, 135
Wilkerson v. *Utah*, 280
Wilkinson v. *Austin*, 354
Wilson v. *Arkansas*, 125, 127
Wilson v. *Seiter*, 354, 356
Winston v. *Lee*, 148
Witherspoon v. *Illinois*, 237
Wolff v. *McDonnell*, 355, 357
Wong Sun v. *U.S.*, 144
Woodson v. *North Carolina*, 282
Wyoming v. *Houghton*, 136

Y

Yarborough v. *Alvarado*, 125, 129

Z

Zafiro v. *U.S.*, 232
Zipkin v. *Mozon*, 371

Subject Index

A

abused child, 370
abuse of discretion, 221
abuse of police power, 116–117
  police interrogation and, 140–141
actus reus (criminal act), 65–67
adjudication, 13
adjudicatory hearings,
  for juveniles, 379–380
administration of justice, 8
administrative law, 62, 63
Administrative Office of the United States Courts (AOUSC), 199
adversarial process, 198
adversarial system, in criminal trials, 234–235
African Americans, community policing and, 107
age, as excuse to a criminal charge, 77
aggravated assault, 33–34
aggravating circumstances, 70, 256
AIDS (acquired immunodeficiency syndrome), 166, 359–360
alibi, 72, 74
ALI rule, 80
al-Qaeda, 52, 55, 56, 95, 101, 362, 364
alter ego rule, 75
alternative sentencing, 264
al-Timimi case, 64
AMBER Alert law, 371
American Bar Association *Model Rules of Professional Conduct*, 221, 227
American Correctional Association Code of Ethics, 347
American Jail Association Code of Ethics for Jail Officers, 328
American Probation and Parole Association Code of Ethics, 302
American Society for Law Enforcement Training (ASLET), 185
anticipatory warrants, 127–128
antiterrorism. *See also* terrorism
  community policing and, 106
  information sharing and, 171–173
appeals, 198
appellate courts, state, 198–199
appellate jurisdiction, 197
argot, prison, 334, 335
arraignment, 205, 212
arrest, 128–138
arson, 38
assault
  aggravated, 33–34
  against women, 44
assigned counsel, 223
attendant circumstances, 70
attorneys. *See* counsel

B

bail, 205, 206, 208–211
bail bonds, 205, 208
bail bondsmen, 210
bailiff (court officer), 217, 228
Bail Reform Act, 211
bail schedules, 210
balancing test, 350
bias crimes (hate crimes), 46–47
Bill of Rights, 3, 11, 116–117
biological weapons, 165–166
Bivens actions, 174, 192, 330
blended sentence, 383
Bloodborne Pathogens Act, 166
body-cavity searches, 148
Brady Handgun Violence Prevention Act, 49
Brawner rule, 80
Bureau of Justice Statistics (BJS), 21
burglary, 34

C

cameras in the courts, 233
CAN-SPAM Act (Controlling the Assault of Nonsolicited Pornography and Marketing), 53
capital punishment (death penalty), 272–285
  the courts and, 280–284
  deterrence and, 270
  discrimination and, 279
  future of, 284
  innocent people and, 277–278
  justifications for, 280
  opposition to, 275–279
case law, 59–60, 62
castle exception, 76
causation, 69
censoring prison communications, 351
Central Intelligence Agency (CIA), 55
Certified Law Enforcement Trainer (CLET), 185
certiorari, writ of, 204
chain of command, 100
change of venue, 233
checks and balances, system of, 118
Chicago Police Department, 105
Chicago's Alternative Policing Strategy (CAPS), 105
children
  legislation concerning, 373–374
  as witnesses, 242–243
Christopher Commission, 101, 107, 180
Church of Jesus Christ of Latter Day Saints (Mormons), 15
circuit courts, 198
circuit courts (U.S. Courts of Appeal), 201–203
circumstantial evidence, 240
citations, 210
civil death, 350
civil justice, 7
civil law, 62–63
civil liability of police, 172–176
civil rights era, 5
classification systems, 321–322
clearance rate, 29
clerk of court, 229
closing arguments, 244
Code of Ethics
  American Correctional Association, 347
  American Probation and Parole Association, 302
  for Jail Officers, American Jail Association, 328
  Law Enforcement, 183, 184
codes, 59
coercion, inherent, 141
collateral estoppel, 84
collective incapacitation, 318
Combat Methamphetamine Epidemic Act (CMEA), 152
Combined DNA Index System (CODIS), 94, 295
Commission on Accreditation for Law Enforcement Agencies (CALEA), 184
Commission on Safety and Abuse in America's Prisons, 346
common law, 60, 62
Communications Assistance for Law Enforcement Act of 1994, 150
community conferences, 378
community corrections, 288
community courts, 200
Community Oriented Policing Services (COPS), 105
Community Police Officer Program (CPOP), 107
community policing, 103–108
  antiterrorism and, 106
  critique of, 107–108
Community Policing Consortium, 106
community service, 301
compelling interest, 137
competent to stand trial, 212
complaint (information), 212
CompStat, 90
computer crimes, 52–54
Computer Fraud and Abuse Act, 150
computer viruses, 52–53
concurrence, 68
concurrent sentences, 254
conditional release, 209, 295
confessions, psychological manipulation and, 142
conflict model of criminal justice, 9–11
consecutive sentences, 254
consensus model of criminal justice, 8–9
consent, defense of, 76
conspiracy, 67

contractual arrangements (contract attorney programs), 224
corporate crime, 47–48
corpus delicti of a crime, 71–72
corrections, 13, 312. *See also* prisons
community, 288
for juveniles, 381
probation. *See* Probation
corrections officers, professionalization of, 345–348
corruption, 157–163
counsel (attorneys)
assigned, 223
contractual arrangements (contract attorney programs), 224
court-appointed, 222–223
defense, 217, 222–228
indigent defense, 224–225
private, 222
public defenders, 223, 226
right to, at interrogation, 142–143
counterterrorism, the FBI and, 94–95
court officer (bailiff), 228
court reporters, 217, 228
courtroom work group, 216
courts (court system), 195–214
bilingual courtrooms, 247
federal court system, 200–205
history and structure of, 195–196
International Criminal Court (ICC), 207
pretrial activities, 205–214
state court system, 196–200
Courts of Appeal, U.S., 201–203
courts of last resort, 198
CRASH (Community Resources against Street Hoodlums), 160
crime(s)
definition of, 3, 66
general categories of, 63–65
general features of, 65–70
special categories of, 66
typology, 43
crime-control model of justice, 13
crime data (crime statistics), 20–29
collection of, 21
Crime Index, 22
Crime in the United States, 24
crime prevention, 89–90
through environmental design (CPTED), 89
CrimeStat, 90
Crime Victims' Rights Act, 268
criminal act (*actus reus*), 65–67
criminal activity, 3
criminal defendants, 63, 217, 232
criminal intelligence, 171. *See also* information gathering
criminal justice system, 7, 8–11
as an academic discipline, 14
career profile of an instructor of, 39
gender issues in, 45
multiculturalism and diversity in, 15–16
process of, 11
race and, 35, 42
criminal law (penal law), 59–86
substantive, 61
criminal negligence, 67–68
criminal trials, 216, 234–247
stages in, 235–247
criminology, 14
cross-examination, 242
Cryzip, 52
cyberstalking, 45
cyberterrorism, 55

D

danger laws, 210
dangers of police work, 163–169
date rape, 32
deadly force, 180–182
death penalty (capital punishment), 272–285
the courts and, 280–284
deterrence and, 279
discrimination and, 279
future of, 284
innocent people and, 277–278
justifications for, 280
opposition to, 275–279
defendants, 63, 217, 232
defense
of home and property, 75–76
of others, 75
defense counsel, 217, 222–228
ethics of, 226–228
defenses (to criminal charges), 72–77
procedural, 83–85
deliberate indifference standard, 356
deliberations process, 244–245
delinquency, 368. *See also* juvenile justice system
dependent child, 370
deposit bail, 209
deprivation model of prison subculture, 336
desk appearance tickets, 210
detention hearings, 378
determinate sentencing, 256
deterrence
death penalty and, 279
as goal of sentencing, 252
digital criminal forensics, 152
diminished capacity, 82
directed patrol, 109
direct evidence, 240
direct-supervision jails, 327
discretion
police, 111–112
prosecutorial, 220–221
discretionary release, 291
discrimination. *See also* race
death penalty and, 279
disease, risk of, infected evidence and, 165–166
dispositional hearings, 380
dispute-resolution centers, 199–200
diversion, 263
diversity, 15–16
DNA evidence, 164, 277, 285
parole and, 295
domestic terrorism, 55
Domestic Violence Offender Gun Ban, 49
double jeopardy, 83
drug crime, 50–51
drug testing, of police employees, 163
due process, 11–12, 118
crime control through, 13–14
due process model, 13
duress, 77
Durham rule, 79

E

early intervention programs, 205
elderly, the
crime against, 45–46
as offenders, 360–361
Electronic Communications Privacy Act of 1986, 149–150
electronic eavesdropping (electronic surveillance), 148–153
electronic evidence, 152
elements of a crime, 70–72
emergency searches of persons, 133
enforcement of the law, 88–89
entrapment, 83
equity, 255
espionage, 65
ethics, 162, 183, 184. *See also* Code of Ethics
defense counsel, 226–228
ethnic and gender diversity in policing, 186–189
ethnicity, 16
evidence, 14
circumstantial, 240
direct, 240
electronic, 152
evaluation of, 240
exculpatory, 220
infected, 165–166
latent, 152
presentation of, 239–243
real (or physical), 240
rules of, 234
types of, 240
evidence-based policing, 108–111
evidence-based practice, 14
excessive force, 179–180
exclusionary rule, 119–121
good-faith exceptions to, 122–124
exculpatory evidence, 220
excuses, 73, 77
exigent circumstances searches, 126
expert witnesses, 217, 229
ex post facto laws, 69

F

Facebook, 36
factual guilt, 234
family group conferences, 378
fatigue, police officer's, 169
Federal Bureau of Investigation (FBI), 91–95
Joint Terrorism Task Forces (JTTFs), 170–171
federal court system, 195–196, 200–205
Federal Employees Liability Reform and Tort Compensation Act (Westfall Act), 175
Federalist Papers, 203
Federal Law Enforcement Training Center (FLETC), 184
federal lawsuits, 174–176
federal parole, 293
federal sentencing guidelines, 257–259

Federal Tort Claims Act (FTCA), 175
felonies, 63
female prisoners, 339–344
fines, 271–272
first appearance, 12, 205–211
fleeting-targets exception, 134
force
deadly, 180–182
definition of, 75
police use of, 179–183
forcible rape, 32–33
Fourth Amendment, 119
fraud, police, 84–85
free speech, violent speech as, 64
fruit of the poisonous tree doctrine, 120–121
fusion centers, 96–98

G

gain time, 255
gender diversity in policing, 186, 188–189
gender issues, 45
gender-responsive approaches for managing female prisoners, 341–342
general deterrence, 252
geriatric offenders, 360–361
Global Intelligence Working Group (GIWG), 106
good-faith exception to the exclusionary rule, 122–124
good time, 255
grand juries, 211
grievance procedures, 352, 355–356
guilty but mentally ill (GBMI) verdict, 81
guilty mind (*mens rea*), 65, 67–69
gun crime, 49–50

H

habeas corpus, writs of, 273–275, 352
hands off doctrine, 350, 356–359
harm, 69
harmless error rule, 240
hate crimes (bias crimes), 46–47
Hate Crime Statistics Act, 46
hearsay rule, 243
Heller case, 50
high courts, 198
high-technology searches, 138
history of crime, 3–4
HIV infection, 359–360
home confinement (house arrest), 302–304
homophobic homicide, 47
homosexuality, in prison, 337–341
house arrest (home confinement), 302–304
Hudud crimes, 73
hung jury, 245

I

identification doctrine, 48
identity theft, 34, 36
illegal use of force, 180
ILP era, 101
The Impending Crime Wave (Third Way report), 27
importation model of prison subculture, 336
incapacitation, as goal of criminal sentencing, 252
inchoate offenses, 65
incompetent to stand trial, 82–83
indeterminate sentencing, 254–255
indictment, 12, 211
indigent defense, 224–225
individual rights, 3, 5, 6, 118
versus public order, 5, 6
infected evidence, 165–166
information (complaint), 212
information gathering (intelligence function), 139–153, 171
informants, 139–140
police interrogation, 140–143
information sharing, antiterrorism and, 171–173
infractions, 65
inherent coercion, 141
Innocence Protection Act, 277
Insanity Defense Reform Act (IDRA), 81–82
insanity (insanity defense), 78–83
intake of juveniles, 376, 378
intelligence-led policing (ILP), antiterrorism and, 171
intensive probation supervision (IPS), 301–302
intentionality, 71
intermediate sanctions, 299–304
internal affairs divisions, 162–163
International Association of Chiefs of Police (IACP), 162, 170
International Criminal Court (ICC), 207
international terrorism, 55
interrogation, police, 140–143
intoxication, involuntary, 78
irresistible impulse, 79
Islamic law (Shari'ah), 73

J

jails, 324–329
direct-supervision, 326–327
future of, 327–329
growth of, 325–326
private prisons, 329–331
Joint Terrorism Task Forces (JTTFs), 170–171
judges, 217, 218–219
charge to the jury, 244
qualifications for, 219
judicial review, 203
jurisdiction, juvenile court, 374, 375
jurisprudence, 60
jurors, 217, 230–231
jury
deliberations, 244–245
judge's charge to the, 244
problems with the jury system, 246
selection, 237–239
just deserts model, 251
selective incapacitation and, 318, 319
justice, definition of, 7
Justice for All Act, 268
justice model (just deserts model), 315
justification, 72, 74
juvenile court counselors, 380
juvenile court era, 369
Juvenile Justice and Delinquency Prevention (JJDP) Act, 373–374
juvenile justice system, 367–384
adjudication, 379–380
adult and juvenile justice compared, 375
categories of children in, 370
characteristics of juveniles in confinement, 381
detention hearings, 378
disposition, 380
history of, 368–370
intake, 376, 378
jurisdiction, 374, 375
legal environment of, 370–374
legal rights of juveniles, 374
legislation concerning children, 373–374
overcrowding in juvenile facilities, 382
postadjudicatory review, 382
post-juvenile court era, 382–384
preliminary hearings, 378
secure institutions for juveniles, 381
transfer hearings, 379
juvenile petition, 376

K

Kansas City experiment, 108–109
Katrina disaster, 2, 84
Knapp Commission, 160
knowing behavior, 67

L

landmark cases, 118
larceny-theft, 34
latent evidence, 152
law. *See also* criminal law
definition of, 59
nature and purpose of, 59–60
procedural, 61–62
rule of, 60
types of, 60–63
law enforcement. *See* Police
Law Enforcement Assistance Administration (LEAA), 108
Law Enforcement Code of Ethics, 183, 184
Law Enforcement Oath of Honor, 162
lay witness, 217, 229–230
legal aspects of policing, 115–153. *See also* search and seizure
abuse of police power, 116
Bill of Rights, 116–117
Burger Court (1969–1986) and the Rehnquist Court (1986–2005), 122–128
civil liability issues, 172–176
electronic eavesdropping, 148–153
individual rights, 118
Warren Court (1953–1969), 121–122

legal attaché offices (legats), 94
legal cause, 69
legal guilt, 234
legalistic style of policing, 102
legality, principle of, 69
less-lethal weapons, 182–183
line operations, 97
local law enforcement agencies, 95–96
Los Angeles Police Department (LAPD), community mapping project, 177

M

M'Naghten rule, 79, 80
malice aforethought, 71
malware, 52
mandatory release, 292
mandatory sentencing, 263
Mann, Coramae Richey, 42
manslaughter, 71
mediation centers, 199
mens rea (guilty mind), 65, 67–69
mental incompetence, 82–83
mentally ill and mentally deficient inmates, 361
minimization requirement for electronic surveillance, 149
Miranda rights (*Miranda* warnings), 143–146
  inevitable-discovery exception to, 145–146
  public-safety exception to, 146
  waiver of, 145
Miranda triggers, 147
misdemeanors, 63
mistakes, as defense, 77–78
mitigating circumstances, 70, 256–257
mixed sentences, 301
Model Rules of Professional Conduct (ABA), 221, 227
motions, pretrial and post-trial, 241
motive, 68
motor homes, searches of, 136–137
motor vehicle checkpoints, 136
motor vehicle theft, 38
MPC rule, 80
multiculturalism, 15–16
multiculturalism and diversity
  investigating crime in a multicultural setting, 187
  policing a multicultural society, 158
murder, 29–32
  elements of, 70–71

N

National Academy Program, 94
National Center for State Courts (NCSC), 199
National Center for Women and Policing (NCWP), 188
National Commission on Law Observance and Enforcement (Wickersham Commission), 185
National Crime Information Center (NCIC), 265
National Crime Prevention Council (NCPC), 187
National Crime Victimization Survey (NCVS), 21, 40–43
National Criminal Intelligence Sharing Plan (NCISP), 172
National District Attorneys Association (NDAA), 222
National DNA Index System (NDIS), 94
National Incident-Based Reporting System (NIBRS), 23–24
National Institute of Justice (NIJ), 14
National Judicial College (NJC), 219
National Victims' Constitutional Amendment Project (NVCAP), 266
National White Collar Crime Center (NW3C), 48
NCIS: Naval Criminal Investigative Service, 20
necessary attendant circumstances, 70
necessity, defense of, 76
neglected child, 370
neighborhood-oriented policing, 105
Neighborhood Watch programs, 90
new era, 100
1983 lawsuits, 174–176
NLETS (International Justice and Public Safety Information Sharing Network), 172
nolo contendere (no-contest), 212

O

offenses, 65
Office for Domestic Preparedness (ODP), 106
Office of Justice Programs (OJP), 108
Office of Juvenile Justice and Delinquency Prevention (OJJDP), 367
ongoing communications, eavesdropping on, 150
opening statements, 239
Operation Identification, 89
Operation Nest Egg, 52
organized crime, 48–49
original jurisdiction, 197
overcrowding, at prisons, 317

P

Packer's crime-control model, 13
parens patriae, principle of, 368, 371
parole, 13, 291–294
  advantages of, 293–294
  disadvantages of, 294–296
  future of, 304–309
  U.S. Supreme Court decisions of special significance for, 296
parole boards, 291
parole officers, 296–299
parole revocation, 292
Part I offenses, 29–39
Part II offenses, 39–40
patria potestas, principle of, 368
Peace Officer Standards and Training (POST) program, 184
penal code, 59
Pennsylvania Constabulary, 95
peremptory challenges, 237–238
perjury, 242
personality, police, 156–157
petty crimes, 90
phishing, 53
physical abuse, police interrogation and, 140–141
plaintiff, 63
plain-view doctrine, 124, 126
plea bargaining, 213–214
  under the federal sentencing guidelines, 258–259
pleas, 212
police (policing), 88–112
  federal agencies, 91–95
  local agencies, 95–97
  purposes of, 88–91
  state agencies, 95
police administration, 97–100
police-community relations, 102–108
police corruption, 157–163
police discretion, 111–112
Police Executive Research Forum (PERF), 26–27, 170, 178–179, 185
police fraud, 84–85
police interrogation, 140–143
police management, 97
  scientific, 108
police officers, career profile of, 168
police organization and structure, 97–100
police subculture, 156
Police Training Officer (PTO) program, 185
police working personality, 156–157
policing epochs and styles, 100–102
political era, 100
precedent, 63
  problems with, 119–120
predicting crime, 90
preliminary hearings, 12, 212
  of juveniles, 378
presentation of evidence, 239–243
presentence investigation, 264–266
preserving the peace, 90–91
President's Commission on Law Enforcement and Administration of Justice, 14
the press, 232
presumptive sentencing, 256
pretrial activities, 205–214
pretrial release/detention, 205–207, 209–211
pretrial services agencies, 210
preventing crime, 89–90
Principles for Promoting Police Integrity, 162
prison argot, 334, 335
Prison Break (TV show), 333
prisoner reentry, 291
prisoners' rights, 349–359
  grievance procedures, 352, 355–356
prisonization, 334
prison life, 333–364. *See also* prison subcultures
  female inmate's world, 339–344
  homosexuality and sexual victimization, 337–341
  male inmate's world, 334–339
  prisoner lifestyles and inmate types, 336–337
  research on, 333–334
  riots, 347–349
  staff world, 344–347
Prison Litigation Reform Act (PLRA), 358–359
prison rape, 338
Prison Rape Elimination Act (PREA), 338

prison riots, 347–349
prisons, 312–323. *See also* prison life
classification systems and, 321–322
current issues facing, 359–364
federal prison system, 322–323
overcrowding in, 317–319
philosophy of imprisonment and, 315–317
private, 329–331
recent improvements in, 323
security levels at, 319–321
terrorist recruiting in, 364
women's, 339–344
prison subcultures, 334
evolution of, 334–335
functions of, 335–336
privacy, right to, 148
private attorneys, 222
private prisons, 329–331
private protective services, 189–191
probable cause, 123, 205
hearings, 206
probation, 13, 288–291
advantages of, 293–294
disadvantages of, 294–296
future of, 304–309
intensive probation supervision (IPS), 301–302
reinvention of, 308–309
revocation of, 289
U.S. Supreme Court decisions of special significance for, 296
probation officers, 296–299
probative value of an item of evidence, 240
problem police officers, 180
problem-solving courts, 200
problem-solving policing, 104
procedural defenses, 73, 83–85
procedural law, 61–62
professionalism, 183–184
professionalization of corrections officers, 345–348
profiling, racial, 176–178
Prohibition era, 161
property bonds, 209
property crimes, 29
proportionality, 255
prosecutorial discretion, 220–221
prosecutorial misconduct, 84
prosecutors (prosecuting attorneys), 219–222
professional responsibility of, 221–222
PROTECT Act of 2003, 374
protected liberties, 356
Protection of Lawful Commerce in Firearms Act, 49–50
provocation, 78
psychological manipulation, 142
public defenders, 223, 226
Public Safety Partnership and Community Policing Act of 1994, 105
punishment, 61
principle of, 70

Q

qualified immunity, doctrine of, 175
quality-of-life offenses, 90–91

R

race, 16
criminal justice system and, 35, 42
jury selection and, 238
racially-biased policing, 178–179
racial profiling, 176–178
ransomware, 52
rape
forcible, 32–33
in prison, 338
real evidence, 240
Real Justice Conferencing (RJC), 378
reasonable force, 75
reasonable suspicion, 131–133
recidivism, 301
reckless behavior, 67
recruitment and selection, 186–188
redirect examination, 242
reentry policies, 306–308
reform era, 100
regional jails, 328
Regional Terrorism Task Forces (RTTFs), 171
rehabilitation, 252
release
conditional, 209
nonjudicial pretrial, 210
pretrial, 209–211
on recognizance (ROR), 208
under supervision, 209
religion, public safety and, 135
Religious Land Use and Institutionalized Persons Act, 351
remote location monitoring, 302–303
resisting unlawful arrest, 76–77
restitution, 292
restoration, as sentencing goal, 252–253
restorative justice, 253
retentionist position, 280
retribution, as rationale for punishment, 251
revocation hearings, 295
rights, role of the courts in defining, 12–13
riots, prison, 347–349
roadblocks, 136
robbery, 33
Ruby Ridge incident, 176, 181
rule of law, 60
rules of evidence, 234

S

Safe Homes for Women Act, 45
Safe Streets Act, 14
Safe Streets for Women Act, 45
San Diego State University (SDSU), 50–51
scientific jury selection, 237
scientific police management, 108
search and seizure, 118–138. *See also* exclusionary rule
body-cavity searches, 148
emergency searches, 126–127
emergency searches of persons, 133
fruit of the poisonous tree doctrine and, 120–121
high-technology searches, 138
incident to arrest, 121–122, 131–133
plain-view doctrine, 124
roadblocks and motor vehicle checkpoints, 136
"sneak and peek" searches, 151
subway searches, 130
suspicionless searches, 137–138
vehicle searches, 134–136
warrantless searches, 133, 153
watercraft and motor homes, 136–137
search warrants, anticipatory, 127–128
Second Chance Act, 357
security threat groups (STGs), 349
selective incapacitation, 318–319
selective prosecution, 84
self-defense, 74, 75
sentencing, 13, 250–285. *See also* death penalty
current practices, 270–271
determinate, 256
federal sentencing guidelines, 257–259
fines, 271–272
indeterminate, 254–255
innovations in, 264
intermediate sanctions, 299–304
mandatory, 263
mixed sentences, 301
modern sentencing options, 270–272
philosophy and goals of, 250–254
presentence investigation, 264–266
presumptive, 256
rationales for, 270
split, 300
structured, 255–263
three-strikes laws and, 261–262
victims and, 266–270
voluntary/advisory sentencing guidelines, 256
Sentencing Project, 299
Sentencing Reform Act of 1984, 257
September 11, 2001, terrorist attacks, 2–5, 30, 43, 47, 54, 64
sequestered juries, 238
serial murder, 30
Serious Violent Offender Reentry Initiative (SVORI), 306–307
services provided by the police, 91
service style of policing, 102
sex offenders, 305
sex-offender websites, 189
sexual battery, 32
sexual victimization in prison, 337–341
shadow jury, 238
Shari'ah (Islamic law), 73
sheriff's departments, 96, 105
shock incarceration, 300–301
shock probation, 300
signature bonds, 209
Sixth Amendment, 237
"sneak and peek" searches, 151
social control, 13
social debt, 256
social justice, 7
social policy, crime data and, 20–29
Sourcebook of Criminal Justice Statistics, 21
sovereign immunity, doctrine of, 175
spam, 53
span of control, 100
specific deterrence, 252

spectators, courtroom, 232–233
speedy trial, denial of a, 84
Speedy Trial Act, 236–237
split sentencing, 300
spontaneous statements, 243
staff operations, 97
stalking, 43, 45
Standardized Chapel Library Project (SCLP), 357
standing mute, 212
stare decisis, 63
state appellate courts, 198–199
state court administration, 199
state courts (state court system), 195–200
state-created liberty interests, 356
state law enforcement agencies, 95
state trial courts, 198
status offenses, 370
statutory law, 59, 62
strategic policing, 104
stress and fatigue, among police officers, 167–169
strict liability, 66
structured sentencing, 255–263
  legal environment of, 260–261
stun guns, 183
subcultures
  police, 334
  prison, 334–336
subpoenas, 230
substantial-capacity test, 80
substantive criminal law, 61
subway searches, 130
Sudden Fall, 50
superior courts, 198
supremacy of law, 60
Supreme Court, U.S., 203–205
  appeals to, 198–199
  juvenile justice and, 370–371
surveillance cameras, 9
suspect rights, 143–146
suspicionless searches, 137
SVORI (Serious Violent Offender Reentry Initiative), 306–307
systems model of criminal justice, 8

T

Tasers, 183
Tazir crimes, 73
team policing, 103
Technical Working Group for Electronic Crime Scene Investigation (TWGECSI), 152–153
Telecommunications Act of 1996, 150
temporary insanity, defense of, 81
terrorism, 54–56
  community policing and, 106
  correctional agencies and, 362–364
  the FBI and, 94–95
  impact on policing, 169–173
terry-type stops, 131
testimony, 241–243
Texas Rangers, 95
theft
  identity, 34, 36
  motor vehicle, 38
third-party custody, 209
Third Way Culture Program, 27
threatening to act, be as a criminal offense, 66
three-strikes laws, 261–262
tort, 63
total institutions, 333
transfer hearings, 379
transferred intent, doctrine of, 67
transnational organized crime, 48
treason, 65
trial court administrator, 228
trial courts, state, 198
trial *de novo*, 198
trials, criminal, 216, 234–247
truth in sentencing, 257

U

unconsciousness, 78
undisciplined child, 370
Uniform Crime Reporting (UCR)
  comparisons of the NCVS and, 41–43
  development of, 21–23
  historical trends in, 24–27
  Part I offenses, 29–39
  Part II offenses, 39–40
  transitional phase of, 27
Uniform Crime Reporting (UCR) Program (UCR/NIBRS Program), 21–40
unlawful killing, 70
unmanned aerial vehicles (UAVs), 174
unsecured bonds, 209
U.S. Courts of Appeal, 201–203
USA PATRIOT Act, 150–152, 268, 272

V

vagrancy laws, 66
vehicle searches, 134–136
Victim and Witness Protection Act (VWPA), 267
victim-impact statements, 269–270
victimless crimes (social-order offenses), 42, 69
victims, 231–232
  sentencing and, 266–270
victims' assistance programs, 230
Victims of Crime Act (VOCA), 267–268
victims' rights, 266–269
violence
  in the line of duty, 164–165
  in women's prisons, 344
Violence against Women Act (VAWA), 44–45, 268
Violent Crime Control and Law Enforcement Act of 1994, 49, 268, 269
violent crimes (personal crimes), 29
voir dire examination, 237
voluntary/advisory sentencing guidelines, 256

W

warrantless searches, 133, 153
watchman style of policing, 101
watercraft and motor homes, searches of, 136–137
Westfall Act (Federal Employees Liability Reform and Tort Compensation Act), 175
white-collar crime, 4, 47–48
Wickersham Commission (National Commission on Law Observance and Enforcement), 185
witnesses
  children as, 242–243
  expert, 229
  lay, 229–230
  testimony of, 241–243
women
  crimes against, 43–45
  jails and, 325
  prisoners, 339–344
writ of *certiorari*, 120
writs of *habeas corpus*, 273–275, 352

ANNOTATED INSTRUCTOR'S EDITION

Criminal Justice

A Brief Introduction

Ninth Edition

Frank Schmalleger, Ph.D.
Distinguished Professor Emeritus
The University of North Carolina at Pembroke

Prentice Hall
Boston Columbus Indianapolis New York San Francisco Upper Saddle River
Amsterdam Cape Town Dubai London Madrid Milan Munich Paris
Montreal Toronto Delhi Mexico City Sao Paulo Sydney Hong Kong
Seoul Singapore Taipei Tokyo